TOXIC AND ENVIRONMENTAL TORTS
CASES AND MATERIALS

■ ■ ■

By

Robin Kundis Craig
*Attorneys' Title Professor of Law &
Associate Dean for Environmental Programs
Florida State University College of Law*

Michael D. Green
*Williams Professor of Law
Wake Forest University School of Law*

Andrew R. Klein
*Paul E. Beam Professor of Law
Indiana School of Law–Indianapolis*

Joseph Sanders
*A.A. White Professor of Law
University of Houston Law Center*

AMERICAN CASEBOOK SERIES®

A Thomson Reuters business

Mat #40824256

American Casebook Series is a trademark registered in the U.S. Patent and Trademark Office.

© 2011 Thomson Reuters
   610 Opperman Drive
   St. Paul, MN 55123
   1–800–313–9378

Printed in the United States of America

ISBN: 978–0–314–92694–4

R.K.C. to
My husband Don, with gratitude for his love and patience.

and M.D.G. to
The memory of Gino Carignan.

and A.R.K. to
Diane, Tim, and Jason, with love.

and J.S. to
My grandchildren, who keep me young.

PREFACE

This casebook strives to give students an overview of the law of toxic and environmental torts. Which torts are these? This book adopts an expansive definition of these terms. We include coverage of cases in which there is personal injury or property damage suffered because of exposure to toxic substances, including drugs. The personal injury with which we are concerned is almost always a disease, although a wide range of such are included, from cancers to respiratory disfunction to neurotoxicity to birth defects and seizure disorders.

The legal system's response to these substances is both proactive and retroactive. For example, statutes such as the Food, Drug and Cosmetic Act (FDCA) and the Resource Conservation and Recovery Act (RCRA) seek to prevent injury ex ante by assessing a drug's safety before permitting it to be marketed and by regulating the disposal and handling of hazardous waste. Common law tort suits—sounding in negligence, products liability, nuisance, trespass, and strict liability for abnormally dangerous activities—provide potential redress for injuries caused by toxic substances and drugs, as do statutes such as the Comprehensive Environmental Response, Compensation, and Liability Act (CERCLA), which seeks to ensure that sites that have been contaminated are cleaned up to safe standards. This book explores both responses within the context of private tort law and statutes.

The book is designed to meet differing course needs. It is readily adaptable for either a two or three hour course. Depending on the instructor's particular interests, the course can focus on the basic common law responses to toxic injuries, statutory responses, or both. For courses that have the time to explore the topic in greater depth, the book provides individual chapters on the admissibility of expert witnesses, workplace injuries, the science of assessing causation, apportionment of liability, insurance, and procedural issues such as class actions and the Multidistrict Litigation Act. Throughout the book, we strive to combine an historic overview of the field with coverage of the current issues confronting the courts and Congress.

We would like to thank several dedicated people who assisted us in writing this book. They include: Kathy Blanton and Matthew Sidler at Florida State University; Hattie Harman '10 and Mary Deer at Indiana University School of Law—Indianapolis; Rachel Reese '11 and Mary Gilbert '10 at the

University of Houston; and LuAnne Simpson of Wake Forest University. A special thank you to Murphy Horne '12 of Wake Forest University Law School who worked diligently and helped enormously in sheperding a manuscript into this text.

ROBIN KUNDIS CRAIG
MICHAEL D. GREEN
ANDREW R. KLEIN
JOSEPH SANDERS

November 2010

ACKNOWLEDGEMENTS

The authors wish to thank the publishers and authors of the following works for allowing them to include excerpts.

Abraham, Kenneth S., Environmental Liability and the Limits of Insurance, 88 Colum. L. Rev. 942, 942–65, 988 (1988). © 1988 Columbia Law Review. Reprinted with permission.

American Law Institute. Restatement (Second) of Torts. © 1938, 1965, 1977, 1979. Reprinted with the permission of the American Law Institute.

American Law Institute. Restatement (Third) of Torts: Products Liability. © 1998. Reprinted with the permission of the American Law Institute.

American Law Institute. Restatement (Third) of Torts: Apportionment of Liability. © 2000. Reprinted with the permission of the American Law Institute.

American Law Institute. Restatement (Third) of Torts: Liability for Physical and Emotional Harm. © 2010. Reprinted with the permission of the American Law Institute.

American Law Institute. Principles of the Law of Aggregate Litigation. © 2010. Reprinted with the permission of the American Law Institute.

DES Daughters & Breast Cancer, New York Times, June 27, 2010, at 11. Reprinted with permission.

Erichson, Howard M., The Vioxx Settlement. © Howard Erichson. Reprinted with permission.

Faigman, David L., Evidentiary Incommensurability: A Preliminary Exploration of the Problem of Reasoning from General Scientific Data to Individualized Legal Decision–Making, 75 Brooklyn Law Review 1151, 1133–1134 (2010) © 2010, David L. Faigman. Reprinted with permission.

Green, Michael D., The Inability of Offensive Collateral Estoppel to Fulfill Its Promise: An Examination of Estoppel in Asbestos Litigation, 70 Iowa L. Rev. 141 (1984). Reprinted with permission.

Rabin, Robert L., Environmental Liability and the Tort System, 24 Hous .L. Rev. 27, 29–32 (1987) © 1987, Robert L. Rabin. Reprinted with permission.

Sanders, Joseph, Bendectin on Trial: a Study of Mass Tort Litigation pp. 45–61 (1998) © 1998 University of Michigan Press. Reprinted with permission.

Schwartz, Gary, Forward: Understanding Products Liability, 62 Cal. L. Rev. 435, 435–96 (1979) © 1979 California Law Review. Reprinted by permission.

Summary of Contents

TABLE OF CONTENTS

─────────

TABLE OF CASES

The principal cases are in bold type. Cases cited or discussed in the text are in roman type. References are to pages. Cases cited in principal cases and within other quoted materials are not included.

TOXIC AND ENVIRONMENTAL TORTS
CASES AND MATERIALS

CHAPTER I

INTRODUCTION

∎ ∎ ∎

What happens when a person or company releases toxic materials into a workplace, the air, or a water supply, and people are injured as a result? What if injuries do not occur immediately, but instead manifest decades later in the form of cancer? What happens if a drug company markets a drug that turns out to cause other types of disease many years later? In some of these situations, the person or company may be subject to fines for violating state or federal laws—that is, there may be a *public law* component to the defendant's liability. However, statutory schemes do not address every kind of toxic harm, nor do they provide compensation for individuals suffering injury. So, those injured often turn to private law— *the common law tort system*—as well, seeking damages and injunctions. Together, these private and public law mechanisms for redressing toxic exposures are known as toxic and environmental torts.

Toxic and environmental torts are an evolving field of law and draw from several legal fields. As a result, some material in this course may overlap with topics that you have studied in other classes—for example, the basic components of negligence from first-year Torts, the key statutes set out in Environmental Law, or perhaps theories from upper-level electives in Products Liability or Hazardous Waste Regulation. However, toxic and environmental tort law covers a broad range of topics that you are unlikely to encounter elsewhere in the law school curriculum. From a factual perspective, we will study an array of cases involving personal injury, property damage, statutory damages, emotional distress, and even the potential of compensation for harm that has not yet occurred. Regarding the legal system's responses, our coverage will run the gamut from ancient causes of action like trespass to land to modern concepts of strict liability and medical monitoring to regulatory schemes designed to protect the environment.

One aspect of toxic and environmental tort cases that you will notice repeatedly is the critical issue of causation. The requirement of factual causation exists for every tort claim considered in this book—indeed, for all tort claims. Sometimes the link between a plaintiff's toxic exposure and resulting injury is obvious, or at least easy to prove. More typically, however, toxic and environmental tort cases turn on the difficulty that claimants face in establishing a connection between injury and any particular exposure. Perhaps the most well-known example comes from asbestos, a substance now known to cause respiratory illness, lung cancer, and a form of cancer called mesothelioma. As we shall see, the long latency period between exposure and disease presents litigants with difficulties in identifying defendants and proving causation. Latency periods also create problems for the application of statutes of limitations and repose. Moreover, given the length of time involved, claimants can also face challenges in distinguishing a particular toxic substance as the cause of the injury. For example, suppose a worker exposed to asbestos was also a heavy smoker. How can the worker attribute his or her lung cancer to the asbestos and not to the smoking?

Long latency periods also present significant hurdles for legislators and regulators who seek to address the consequences of environmental contamination. Meeting these challenges often requires engagement with technical aspects of scientific disciplines such as toxicology, epidemiology, and even genetics. As a practical matter, moreover, public law strategies for addressing environmental contamination focus on preventing the exposure in the first place rather than redressing harms afterward. This is the strategy of the federal Resource Conservation and Recovery Act (RCRA), the Food, Drug and Cosmetic Act (FDCA), and the Occupational Safety and Health Act (OSHA). (One prominent exception is the federal Comprehensive Environmental Response, Compensation, and Liability Act (CERCLA), which exists to ensure that contaminated sites get cleaned up.) While preventing toxic exposures is unquestionably a worthy enterprise, these public law statutes do leave liability gaps when things go wrong. As a result, the interplay of statutory law and tort law can be critically important.

The fact that today's lawyers use sophisticated tools to address the consequences of toxic exposure, however, does not mean that the factual and legal issues are of recent origin. Courts have been grappling with the same fundamental problems for many years. Consider the following opinion from the New York Court Appeals, decided in the early part of the twentieth century. While the court did not have the benefit of modern science to address the claims at hand, the issues raised by the litigants required the court to confront the same problems that are at play in modern toxic and environmental tort actions.

STUBBS v. CITY OF ROCHESTER

Court of Appeals of New York, 1919.
226 N.Y. 516, 124 N.E. 137.

HOGAN, J.

[Defendant City of Rochester supplied Hemlock system water for drinking and Holly system water for firefighting. The evidence revealed that because of the city's negligence in May, 1910, the systems had become intermingled near the Brown street bridge. Sewage in the Holly water had contaminated the Hemlock water. However, the contamination was not discovered until October. The plaintiff contracted typhoid fever in September and attributed it to the city's negligence. By a 3–2 vote, without opinion, the Appellate Division affirmed a nonsuit granted by the trial judge.]

* * *

The important question in this case is, Did the plaintiff produce evidence from which inference might reasonably be drawn that the cause of his illness was due to the use of contaminated water furnished by defendant. Counsel for respondent argues that even assuming that the city may be held liable to plaintiff for damages caused by its negligence in furnishing contaminated water for drinking purposes, (a) The evidence adduced by plaintiff fails to disclose that he contracted typhoid fever by drinking contaminated water; (b) that it was incumbent upon the plaintiff to establish that his illness was not due to any other cause to which typhoid fever may be attributed for which defendant is not liable. The evidence does disclose several causes of typhoid fever which is a germ disease, the germ being known as the typhoid bacillus, which causes may be classified as follows:

First. Drinking of polluted water. Second. Raw fruits and vegetables in certain named localities where human excrement is used to fertilize the soil are sometimes sources of typhoid infection. Third. The consumption of shell fish, though not a frequent cause. Fourth. The consumption of infected milk and vegetables. Fifth. The house fly in certain localities. Sixth. Personal contact with an infected person by one who has a predilection for typhoid infection and is not objectively sick with the disease. Seventh. Ice, if affected with typhoid bacilli. Eighth. Fruits, vegetables, etc., washed in infected water. Ninth. The medical authorities recognize that there are still other causes and means unknown. This fact was developed on cross-examination of physicians called by plaintiff.

[Counsel argues first] that the evidence fails to disclose that plaintiff contracted typhoid fever by drinking contaminated water. The plaintiff, having been nonsuited at the close of his case, is entitled to the most favorable inference deducible from the evidence. That plaintiff, on or about September 6th, 1910, was taken ill, and very soon thereafter typhoid fever developed, is not disputed. That he was employed in a factory located one block distant from the Brown street bridge in which Hemlock lake water was the only supply of water for potable and other purposes, and that the water drawn from faucets in that neighborhood disclosed that the water was roily and of unusual appearance is not questioned. And no doubt prevails that the Holley system water was confined to the main business part of the city for use for fire purposes and sprinkling streets and is not furnished for domestic or drinking purposes.

The evidence of the superintendent of waterworks of the city is to the effect that Hemlock Lake water is a pure wholesome water free from contamination of any sort at the lake, and examinations of the same are made weekly; that the Holley water is not fit for drinking purposes taken as it is from the Genesee river. Further evidence was offered by plaintiff by several witnesses, residents in the locality of Brown street bridge, who discovered the condition of the water at various times during July, August and September and made complaint to the water department of the condition of the same. Dr. Goler, a physician and health officer of the city, was called by plaintiff and testified that in September, when complaint was made to him by a resident of the district, he went to the locality, visited houses in the immediate neighborhood, found that the water drawn from the faucet of the Hemlock supply looked badly and smelled badly. He took a sample of the water to the laboratory and had it examined by a chemist who found that it contained an increase in solids and very many times, that is, 20 to 30 times as much chlorine or common salt as is found in the domestic water supply—the presence of chlorine in excessive quantities indicates contamination in that quantity, bad contamination and usually sewage contamination. Further examination followed in the district. Water was collected from various houses and a large number of samples, perhaps less than 100, but over 25. * * * About the following day, the source of contamination having been discovered, the doctor made an investigation as to the reported cases of typhoid fever in the city in the months of August, September and October, for the purpose of determining the number of cases, where the cases came from, what gave rise to it, and he stated that in his opinion the outbreak of typhoid was due to polluted water, contaminated as he discovered afterwards by sewage. In answer to a hypothetical question embracing generally the facts asserted by plaintiff the witness testified that he had an opinion as to the cause of the infection of plaintiff and such opinion was that it was due to contaminated water.

Dr. Dodge, of the faculty of the University of Rochester, a professor of biology, also bacteriologist of the city of Rochester, about October [first] made an analysis of samples of water * * *. While his examination did not disclose any colon bacillus, it did disclose some evidence of the same. Dr. Brady, the physician who attended the plaintiff, and Dr. Culkin both testified that in their opinion the plaintiff contracted typhoid fever from drinking polluted water.

Plaintiff called a witness who resided on Brown street about two minutes' walk from the bridge, and proved by her that she drank water from the Hemlock mains in the fall of 1910 and was ill with typhoid fever. Thereupon counsel for defendant stipulated that 57 witnesses which the plaintiff proposed to call will testify that they drank water from the Hemlock taps in the vicinity of the district west of the Genesee river and north of Allen street in the summer and fall of 1910, and during said summer and fall suffered from typhoid fever, that in view of the stipulation such witnesses need not be called by plaintiff, and the stipulation shall have the same force and effect as though the witnesses had been called and testified to the facts.

The plaintiff resided with his wife some three miles distant from the factory where he was employed. The water consumed by him at his house outside the infected district was Hemlock water. The only water in the factory was Hemlock water, and he had there an individual cup from which he drank. He was not outside of the city during the summer of 1910. Therefore, the only water he drank was in the city of Rochester.

A table of statistics as to typhoid fever in the city of Rochester for the years 1901–1910, inclusive, was produced by the health officer and received in evidence. * * * The statistics disclose that the number of typhoid cases in the city in 1910 was 223, an excess of 50 cases of any year of the nine years preceding. Recalling that complaints as to water commenced in the summer of 1910 and as shown by the evidence that typhoid fever does not develop until two or three weeks after the bacilli have been taken into the system, in connection with the fact that the source of contamination was not discovered until October, the statistics disclose that of the 223 cases of typhoid in the city in the year 1910, 180 cases appear during the months of August, September, October, and November as against 43 cases during the remaining eight months, 35 of which were prior to August and 8 in the month of December, two months after the source of contamination of the water was discovered.

The evidence on the trial discloses that at least 58 witnesses, residents of the district, drank the contaminated water and suffered from typhoid fever in addition to plaintiff; thus one-third of the 180 cases during the months stated were shown to exist in that district.

Counsel for respondent asserts that there was a failure of proof on the part of plaintiff in that he did not establish that he contracted disease by drinking contaminated water, and in support of his argument cites a rule of law that when there are several possible causes of injury for one or more of which a defendant is not responsible, plaintiff cannot recover without proving that the injury was sustained wholly or in part by a cause for which defendant was responsible. He submits that it was essential for plaintiff to eliminate all other of seven causes from which the disease might have been contracted. If the argument should prevail and the rule of law stated is not subject to any limitation, the present case illustrates the impossibility of a recovery in any case based upon like facts. One cause of the disease is stated by counsel to be "personal contact with typhoid carriers or other persons suffering with the disease, whereby bacilli are received and accidentally transferred by the hands or some other portion of the person or clothes to the mouth." Concededly a person is affected with typhoid some weeks before the disease develops. The plaintiff here resided three miles distant from his place of employment and traveled to and from his work upon the street car. To prove the time when he was attacked with typhoid, then find every individual who traveled on the same car with him, and establish by each one of them that he or she was free from the disease even to his or her clothing is impossible. Again the evidence disclosed that typhoid fever was caused by sources unknown to medical science. If the word of the rule stated is to prevail plaintiff would be required to eliminate sources which had not yet been determined or ascertained. I do not believe the rule stated to be as inflexible as claimed for. If two or more possible causes exist, for only one of which a defendant may be liable, and a party injured establishes facts from which it can be said with reasonable certainty that the direct cause of the injury was the one for which the defendant was liable, the party has complied with the spirit of the rule.

The plaintiff was employed in the immediate locality where the water was contaminated. He drank the water daily. The consumption of contaminated water is a very frequent cause of typhoid fever. In the locality there were a large number of cases of typhoid fever and near to 60 individuals who drank the water and had suffered from typhoid fever in that neighborhood appeared as witnesses on behalf of plaintiff. The plaintiff gave evidence of his habits, his home surroundings, and his method of living, and the medical testimony indicated that his illness was caused by drinking contaminated water. Without reiteration of the facts disclosed on the trial I do not believe that the case on the part of plaintiff was so lacking in proof as matter of law that his complaint should be dismissed. On the contrary, the most favorable inferences deducible from the plaintiff were such as would justify a submission of the facts to a jury as to the reasonable inferences to be drawn therefrom, and a verdict rendered thereon for either party would rest, not in conjecture but upon reasonable possibilities.

The judgment should be reversed, and a new trial granted, costs to abide the event.

NOTES AND QUESTIONS

1. Although nearly 100 years old, *Stubbs* raised issues that often arise in contemporary toxic tort litigation, and the court's approach to these issues was surprisingly modern. For example, consider the court's discussion of the plaintiff's need to prove sufficient exposure to a substance that could cause disease. The issue of substance exposure remains important today, and we will discuss the topic in Chapter 3 in connection with general principles of causation and in Chapter 6 when we examine toxic exposures in the workplace.

2. As noted in the introductory paragraphs above, one consistently vexing issue in toxic and environmental tort cases is connecting individual harm to a particular exposure. The defendants in *Stubbs* made the most of this problem, pointing out that exposure to any number of substances could have caused the plaintiff's illness. Ultimately, the court did not require the plaintiff to disprove every possible cause other than the contamination of the Hemlock water, but neither did the court relieve the plaintiff of the traditional burden of proving causation by a preponderance of the evidence. What other hurdles did the plaintiff face in proving causation? What facts might have helped overcome these hurdles?

3. Context is often important in causation battles, especially in terms of the state of the relevant science. In the case of typhoid fever, both the state of the science and recent New York history bore on the decision in *Stubbs*. By 1919, the year of the decision, the cause of typhoid fever was known: Georg Theodor August Gaffky established in 1884 that the typhoid bacillus is the causative agent of typhus, although the carrier can vary, as the *Stubbs* court explained. In addition, local events in the decade before this case were also relevant. In summer 1906, Charles Henry Warren took his family on vacation to Long Island, hiring Mary Mallon to be their cook. At the end of August, typhoid fever struck one of the Warren daughters, eventually infecting six of the 11 members of the household. Upon investigation, it turned out that Mary Mallon—known now to history as "Typhoid Mary"—was the carrier of the disease. She was passing the disease to family members without becoming infected herself; no public water system was involved.

Does the Typhoid Mary history provide more factual ammunition for the plaintiff or for the defendant in *Stubbs*?

4. Note the court's use of statistics in addressing the likelihood that contamination of the Hemlock water system led to the plaintiff's typhoid fever. Today, an entire scientific discipline—epidemiology—has developed to study the causes of human disease. The beginnings of modern epidemiology are traced in part to John Snow, a London general practitioner who confronted a situation not too different from that in *Stubbs*. Dr. Snow developed a hypothesis that cholera was spread through contaminated drinking water and conducted a set of tests to verify his theory. One test entailed comparing the incidence of the disease in a community drawing its water from the Thames upstream from London with the incidence in a community drawing its water downstream of the city. He then attempted to control for other variables by looking at a single London region that was supplied drinking water by two different companies, and observed significant differences in the incidence of the disease in sub-districts supplied by each firm. Finally, he conducted what is known today as a case-control study by going to the homes of each cholera fatality, discovering who supplied the drinking water and comparing this to the total number of houses supplied by each company. The results, confirming the connection between the disease and the source of drinking water, were published in 1849.

Understanding epidemiologic principles is important for attorneys working in the toxic substances arena, and epidemiologists often provide expert testimony on issues of causation in modern toxic tort cases. We will study a number of examples in Chapter 3, Chapter 4 on causation in the multi-party context, and Chapter 5 on the admissibility of evidence and the standard of proof on causation. An excellent resource on scientific methods, including epidemiology, which is written for judges and lawyers, is Federal Judicial Center, Reference Manual on Scientific Evidence (2d ed.2000). The third edition of the Reference Manual is to be published shortly after this text went to press.

5. Even if the plaintiff in a case like *Stubbs* uses probabilistic evidence to prove that disease is more likely than not connected with the exposure at issue, there is still a chance that the opposite is true. How should this affect plaintiff's award of damages? Should plaintiff recover the full amount of his loss, or something less? Suppose, for example, that all 58 residents of the district who contracted typhoid fever filed suit. Suppose further that studies from earlier years when there was no intermingling of water supplies suggest that only 10 residents would have contracted typhoid fever from other possible causes. If all 58 residents collected full damages, liability would exceed the city's "true" responsibility, potentially leading to overdeterrence. One solution to this problem is to award plaintiffs "proportional liability," providing each of the 58 victims with 48/58 of his or her damages. Are there problems with this approach? We will address this topic in more detail at several points in the book, including in Chapter 4 and in Chapter 12 on remedies.

   6. Notice that *Stubbs* involved contamination of the public water supply—a perfect situation for the intervention of preventive public law. And public law has so intervened. Two federal statutes (and their state implementation) now address the risks in *Stubbs*. First, the Clean Water Act requires permits and technology-based controls before anyone can discharge pollutants into the waters of the United States. Regulated dischargers include sewage treatment facilities, and the Act requires that sewage be treated with at least secondary treatment, which incorporates both physical settling of the solids and biological treatment of the wastewater. Additionally, beginning in the 1940s and continuing into the adoption of the Clean Water Act, the federal government provided grants to states and communities to facilitate the building of sewage treatment plants. Largely as a result of this funding, according to the EPA, 113.0 million people in the United States were served by advanced wastewater treatment in 2008, compared to only 7.8 million people in 1972, when Congress enacted the Act. Sewage treatment is credited with the prevention of a number of water-borne diseases such as typhoid fever and cholera.

   Second, the Safe Drinking Water Act requires suppliers to treat drinking water before it is delivered to people's homes and other buildings—anywhere you can turn on a tap. Treatment standards under this Act are health-based, meaning that they are designed specifically to ensure that drinking water does not injure people's health.

   As noted, Public law—in the form of federal and state statutes and local ordinances—now plays a significant role in preventing toxic torts. Public laws generally operate to limit or eliminate people's exposures to toxic substances. This is the goal, for example, of not only the Clean Water Act and the Safe Drinking Water Act but also the Occupational Safety and Health Act (OSH Act), the Federal Insecticide, Fungicide, and Rodenticide Act (FIFRA), the Toxic Substances Control Act (TSCA), the Food, Drug, and Cosmetic Act (FDCA), the Resource Conservation and Recovery Act (RCRA), and the Comprehensive Environmental Response, Compensation, and Liability Act (CERCLA). Chapter 6 covers the OSH Act in connection with workplace exposures and work-based toxic torts. Chapter 8 focuses on the two hazardous waste statutes, RCRA and CERCLA, while Chapter 9 covers the products statutes—FIFRA, TSCA, and the FDCA. Because these statutes also interact with common law toxic torts in other ways, briefer discussions of certain aspects of these statutes and their effects on toxic torts—such as the threat of federal preemption and the role of statutes of limitations—appear in other chapters, as well.

It is important to remember, however, that public law statutes can never prevent all harm or even all tortiously-caused harm. Therefore, no matter how many statutes Congress and state legislatures enact, there will always be a role for the tort system to redress accidents, deliberate misconduct, and emerging problems, and injuries that come about as a result of gaps or limits in the regulatory system.

On the other hand, the more specifically that Congress crafts public law responses to environmental and toxic harms, the more likely the provisions of these statutes will come in conflict with individual efforts to seek state common law remedies. We discuss these potential conflicts in Chapter 10.

7. *Stubbs* is an early example of a court grappling with special issues that arise in toxic tort actions. As courts encountered more cases raising these issues, it became possible to identify particular characteristics that help us frame a category of toxic and environmental torts distinct from other causes of action. The following article excerpt written by Professor Robert Rabin provides an excellent starting point in doing so.

ENVIRONMENTAL LIABILITY AND THE TORT SYSTEM

Robert L. Rabin.
24 Hous.L.Rev. 27, 29–32 (1987).

[E]nvironmental liability stands out in bold relief from the generality of everyday risks embraced by tort law because of three critical characteristics that are found, singly or in combination, in every case of harm from toxics or other pollutants. I will refer to these characteristics of environmental liability as problems of *identification*, *boundaries* and *source*.

(1) *Problems of Identification.* Through the centuries of common law development, the identification of a tortious injury has hardly ever been a problem. At earliest common law, it was the unwanted intrusion on the land of another or the physical violation of a right to bodily integrity. Well into the twentieth century, one finds remarkably little change on this score. Auto accidents and overcharged coke bottles are the modern-day counterpart of trespassers and runaway buggies from the pre-industrial era. The focus is consistently on an accidental injury, the relatively sudden event in which the victim's bodily security or property is violated. If problems of causation exist, they are ordinarily of the "whodunit" variety rather than issues of whether the victim actually suffered identifiable harm that can be isolated from the everyday risks of living.

But it is precisely this latter inquiry which characterizes the case of environmental harm. Toxics of all sorts—impure water, hazardous chemicals, defective synthetics—often breed disease rather than cause immediate injury. As a consequence, the tort system is severely tested. Since diseases do not occur instantaneously, there are serious time-lag issues. And because diseases are frequently a product of the background risks of living (or at least intertwined with those risks), technical information is essential to establish attribution. Thus, *identification*, ordinarily a routine issue of cause in fact at common law, is a costly enterprise that relies on types of evidence and probability judgments which can be regarded as ill-suited to traditional resolution through the adversary process.

(2) *Problems of Boundaries.* Let us assume that through epidemiological studies, laboratory tests or rough mortality data it can be established that a particular widespread incidence of disease was "caused" by the release of an identifiable toxic substance. At first blush, environmental liability may then appear to be similar to a classical mass tort episode—akin to a commercial airline disaster or the collapse of a hotel balcony. But appearances are deceiving; once again, the case of environmental harm frequently creates problems that place special stress on the tort system.

The crux of the matter, again, is the accident/disease distinction. The harm suffered in an airplane crash is extensive but it is also bounded. Most of the victims die, and, apart from derivative loss, there are virtually no post-generational consequences. Contrast the toxic tort scenario. In cases like Agent Orange and hazardous waste dump exposure, the claims are potentially unbounded. Victims of exposure not yet ill fear that it is only a matter of time before they show signs of pathology, *in utero* exposure is an overriding concern, and generations not yet conceived may suffer genetic damage.

Moreover, these are only the most peripheral claims. Even with respect to first-generation, identifiable victims, the *ex ante* assessment of limits on liability is often highly open-ended. Unlike an airplane or public facilities disaster, the aggregate exposure can be hard to define in advance. In addition, the extent of harm may be unpredictable because the need for post-exposure treatment is extensive (degeneration rather than instant death is, by and large, far more common in toxic tort episodes than mass accident cases) and the array of disorders is far more wide-ranging.

By *boundaries*, then, I have in mind an *ex ante* assessment of the magnitude of harm. Mass accident torts are rare at common law, and in fact, put the flexibility of the tort system to the test when they occur. But they pose nothing like the challenge of unconfined liability intrinsic to many environmental harms. In common law terms, valuation of damages is the crux of the matter. Asbestos and the emerging toxic tort cases claim victims in the thousands, not the low hundreds. And, the intrinsic vagaries of chemically-induced diseases introduce bizarre pathologies that are costly to treat and raise intergenerational concerns which vex a torts process designed for more modest purposes. In sum, it is both the two-party structure of traditional tort litigation and the underlying premise of sudden accidental injury that are confounded by environmental harm.

(3) *Problems of Source.* A generation ago, tort lawyers viewed the frontiers of causal responsibility as defined by cases like *Summers v. Tice* [199 P.2d 1 (Cal.1948)], the classic accident situation in which the victim could not identify which of his two careless hunting companions fired the shotgun pellet which entered his eye. *Summers* seems almost an ancient artifact bearing witness to the practices of an earlier epoch when compared with the source-related issues presented by toxic tort and pollution

cases. To venture for a moment into the world of conjecture (or, perhaps, nightmare), suppose at some future date uncertainty over the harmful effects of chlorofluorocarbon emissions is resolved through an extraordinarily sharp rise in the incidence of skin cancer. To continue in a speculative vein, assume that the multitude of victims can properly pursue a class action. Would the action be appropriately brought against the thousands of emitters of chlorofluorocarbons including the producers of aerosols, foams, solvents, freezers and insulation materials? Should the multinational chemical companies producing the constituent products be joined? What about the host governments that approve (or, at least, allow) the processes to be undertaken? The prospects stagger the imagination.

But one need not create a parade of future horrors to illustrate the problem. The vast array of asbestos producers and insurers, or the typical participants in the hazardous waste chain of distribution—generators, transporters and operators of sites—are present-day examples of the singular difficulties in dealing with problems of *source* in environmental liability cases.

Here, too, the long-standing premises of tort law are challenged by the rise of toxic and pollutant harms. Because tort law has traditionally been concerned with accidents, the search for a responsible source has never raised overwhelming difficulties. At most, the classic single-party focus of responsibility is extended slightly along a horizontal axis in cases like *Summers v. Tice* or a multi-car collision. Under other circumstances, the single-party focus may be extended slightly along a vertical (production/distribution) axis in cases where a defective product may be the responsibility of an assembler and manufacturers of component parts. But these modest variations on the two-party tort configuration in which some*one* is responsible for the harm clearly are of small consequence to the system.

By contrast, environmental torts evoke an entirely different perspective on liability, one which is virtually unknown at common law. Frequently, environmental harm is a consequence of the aggregate risk created by a considerable number of independently acting enterprises. It may be that the risk generated by any single source is, in fact, inconsequential. Or, it may be that the risk inherent in the product is substantial, but it soon merges into a common pool. Whatever the case, environmental harm is very often *collective* harm.

Acid rain, chlorofluorocarbons, Agent Orange, and asbestos fibers confound the private law perspective in a dual sense. Not only are they potentially the source of widespread harm, but they are frequently produced by a vast number of discrete enterprises, each making independent decisions about the extent to which they will degrade or endanger the commons. Traditional tests of causal responsibility—the but-for principle, substantial factor causation, *pro rata* joint-and-several liability—are operating in foreign territory when they are employed in such cases. They are premised on a wrongful act that in itself triggers accidental harm, an act that can be isolated and pinned down as consequential.

In view of these distinctive characteristics, it is small wonder that environmental liability has achieved special recognition in discourse about standards of liability and the efficacy of the torts process. Automobiles and power lawnmowers may wreak havoc, but their dangers are readily cognizable. We understand how they work and why they go awry. Toxic substances evoke the special apprehensions of unseen risks. They emanate from sources that are hard to identify. They attack us unawares, planting the seeds of future debilitating disease. They run a course that we cannot discern. Translated into legal terms, they pose unique challenges to a tort system premised on adversary treatment of easily identifiable two-party accidents.

* * *

NOTES AND QUESTIONS

1. Many of the topics in this course can be directly linked to the special problems that Professor Rabin describes. For example, *"identification"* will be a key consideration in our material on actual causation in Chapters 3 and 4. *"Boundaries"* will be an important part of our coverage of proximate cause and the scope of liability in Chapter 7. Boundaries also come into play when considering special procedures that courts sometimes use to resolve mass tort claims involving large numbers of potential victims. We will consider these procedural issues in Chapter 14. *"Source"* issues arise in a variety of contexts, including the chapters on causation noted above, as well as in our coverage of workplace exposures in Chapter 6. Finally, a large percentage of toxic and environmental tort cases require litigants to present expert testimony to support their positions. The admissibility of such testimony can make or break a plaintiff's case. We will study this topic in Chapter 5.

2. Professor Rabin's three characteristics also help to identify when and how legislatures will turn to public law, and point to some of the problems that legislatures face. The source problem, for example, presents a clear reason for turning away from the tort system and to a public law regulatory system. As Professor Rabin notes, if several small sources contribute to a large public problem—polluted water, a toxic waste dump, polluted air—the tort system will find it difficult to hold any one source responsible for harm that is caused by the cumulative problem. Statutes and regulations, in contrast, can require each small source to take actions to prevent the cumulative problem in the first place: every person who discharges into waters or emits pollutants into the air must have a permit and must limit how much pollution he or she contributes; people who handle toxic and hazardous waste must ensure its proper treatment and disposal.

Similarly, public law can address some of the identification issues by seeking to be preventive, rather than reactive. However, being preventive still leaves a number of issues for legislatures and regulators. For example, who should have the burden of proof—should the proponent of a product have to prove that the product is safe, or should the government have to prove that it is unsafe? As you will see when you study the federal statutes included in this textbook, Congress has made different decisions about the burden of proof regarding safety in different regulatory regimes.

Allocating the burden of proof is related to two other issues that legislatures and regulators often face: the problem of risk and the problem of uncertainty. The problem of risk arises because regulating to create a perfectly safe world is impossible. We all have to accept a certain amount of risk in our lives whether we are eating breakfast, walking around the block, or driving to work. The question becomes, how much risk is acceptable, and of what kind? Congress and federal agencies, for example, often regulate far more stringently when people face a risk of getting cancer sometime in the future than when people face other kinds of health risks, such as asthma. In turn, regulators tend to regulate health risks more stringently than risks to the environment—unless the risks to the environment could also result in risks to health, such as pollution of a stream that in turn contaminates a drinking water supply.

Risks would exist even if everyone understood everything perfectly. Think about drugs: very few drugs have zero risk of side effects; nevertheless, the potential benefit of a drug may still outweigh the risks of the side effects. Or think about pesticides: pesticides are designed to kill things, and hence almost always come with risks. However, we continue to use pesticides because the benefits of using them outweigh the risks that they pose (at least when used properly). These two examples suggest two important tools of public law decisionmaking: risk-benefit analysis (or risk-risk analysis) and cost-benefit analysis.

Legislatures, regulators, and product manufacturers often do not understand everything perfectly, and hence the problem of uncertainty also complicates public law solutions. In part, assigning the burden of proof is a decision about what to do with uncertainty. Can you see why? Uncertainty can arise at many different levels. For example, there may be basic uncertainty as to whether a product is harmful ever, to anyone. This is the regulatory version of the general causation problem in tort.

Even if a product is known to be harmful at least some of the time, or to some persons or aspects of the environment, it still may be difficult for regulators to discern who or what the product is most likely to harm or, especially, in what dose or exposure. In the face of uncertainty, legislatures and regulators can choose to employ a precautionary approach, prohibiting or limiting use until the product and its possible impacts are well understood. In environmental regulation in particular, however, lack of certainty is often an excuse for taking no action, or for requiring more studies.

3. Think back to the facts of *Stubbs* and consider how the problems of "identification," "boundaries," and "source" played out in that case. In your view, which problem presented the most difficulty for the plaintiff in *Stubbs*? Which might be an easier hurdle to clear today?

4. In discussing the "source" problem, Professor Rabin mentions the famous case of *Summers v. Tice*. In the 1980s and 1990s, several state supreme courts expanded the *Summers* rule in a series of case involving the prescription drug diethylstilbestrol (DES). DES is a synthetic substance that mimics the effects of the female hormone estrogen. During the middle part of the twentieth century, it was widely marketed as a miscarriage preventative. All DES shared the same chemical composition, and hundreds of companies manufactured and sold it. In 1971, two scientific studies linked DES to the development of vaginal and cervical cancer in the daughters of women who used the drug during pregnancy. The cancer manifested itself in these women after a latency period of at least 10 to 12 years. Shortly after publication of the studies linking DES to cancer, the FDA banned the use of DES for miscarriage prevention. By the early 1970s, hundreds of women whose mothers had used DES during pregnancy filed lawsuits against DES manufacturers. Nearly all these plaintiffs, however, faced a hurdle: They could not identify the company that produced the DES used by their mother and, therefore, could not prove that their illness would not have occurred but for the action of any particular manufacturer. Several courts, including the high courts of California and New York, allowed the plaintiffs to overcome this hurdle by developing a doctrine of "market share liability," essentially making each defendant liable based on the proportion of DES it sold in the relevant market, regardless of whether a plaintiff could connect her own disease to DES made by a particular company. The topic of market share liability is covered in Chapter 4.

But vaginal and cervical cancer injury to daughters was not the end of the story with regard to DES. Subsequent to the first wave of DES litigation, the daughters of DES daughters began to claim injuries related to their grandmothers' ingestion of the drug. These actions did not fare well in court. See, e.g., Grover v. Eli Lilly & Co., 591 N.E.2d 696 (Ohio 1992); Enright v. Eli Lilly & Co., 570 N.E.2d 198 (N.Y.1991). Studies also have shown that DES daughters themselves face an increased risk of developing breast cancer after age 40 when compared to the population of women who were not exposed to DES in utero. The following advertisement was recently placed in the New York Times by attorneys interested in representing DES daughters in a new round of litigation.

NOTE

Taking account of the issues raised in this introductory Chapter, what hurdles will the lawyers face if they represent clients seeking damages for breast cancer? How are these issues different than those presented in what Professor Rabin describes as traditional "easily identifiable two-party accident" cases? In thinking about these questions, consider the abstract from the scientific article cited at the bottom of the advertisement. The data developed by the authors will be important to plaintiffs' ability to prove causation, and it is representative of material that we will cover in Chapter 3 on that topic.

It has been hypothesized that breast cancer risk is influenced by prenatal hormone levels. Diethylstilbestrol (DES), a synthetic estrogen, was widely used by pregnant women in the 1950s and 1960s. Women who took the drug have an increased risk of breast cancer, but whether risk is also increased in the daughters who were exposed in utero is less clear. We assessed the relation of prenatal DES exposure to risk of breast cancer in a cohort of DES-exposed and unexposed women followed since the 1970s by mailed questionnaires. Eighty percent of both exposed and unexposed women completed the most recent questionnaire. Self-reports of breast cancer were confirmed by pathology reports. Cox proportional hazards regression was used to compute incidence rate ratios (IRR) for prenatal DES exposure relative to no exposure. During follow-up, 102 incident cases of invasive breast cancer occurred, with 76 among DES-exposed women (98,591 person-years) and 26 among unexposed women (35,046 person-years). The overall age-adjusted IRR was 1.40 [95% confidence interval (95% CI), 0.89–2.22]. For breast cancer occurring at ages ≥ 40 years, the IRR was 1.91 (95% CI, 1.09–3.33) and for cancers occurring at ages ≥ 50 years, it was 3.00 (95% CI, 1.01–8.98). Control for calendar year, parity, age at first birth, and other factors did not alter the results. These results, from the first prospective study on the subject, suggest that women with prenatal exposure to DES have an increased risk of breast cancer after age 40 years. The findings support the hypothesis that prenatal hormone levels influence breast cancer risk.

J.R. Palmer et al., Prenatal Diethylstilbestrol Exposure and Risk of Breast Cancer, 15 Cancer Epidemiol. Biomarkers & Prev. 1509 (2006).

Chapter II

Theories of Liability

■ ■ ■

A. NEGLIGENCE

The word "negligence" has two meanings that are used interchangeably. A plaintiff may be said to bring a "negligence" claim. That claim has five elements: (1) Duty; (2) Breach of Duty; (3) Factual Cause; (4) Proximate Cause (now called scope of liability in the Third Restatement of Torts); and (5) Legally Cognizable Harm. As you may recall from your Torts class, the duty imposed is frequently one of reasonable care.

The failure to exercise reasonable care is often also referred to as negligence. In that sense, negligence is used to mean the behavior of the defendant and the second element of a negligence claim. Negligence is not the only claim that can be made in a toxic tort case, but it is a durable and flexible theory that is almost always asserted along with other theories of liability. Negligence is flexible because plaintiffs' lawyers are free to identify many different ways in which the defendant failed to act reasonably. One frequently sees claims of negligence for failing to warn adequately of the dangers posed by a toxic agent, and failing to do adequate research and testing to determine the safety of an agent, and failing to act reasonably in constructing a product that includes a toxic agent.

Factual cause, proximate cause (scope of liability), and legally cognizable harm are not unique to negligence claims but must be established for any of the theories of liability covered in this Chapter, so we defer discussion of them until later chapters.

CABIROY v. SCIPIONE

Superior Court of Pennsylvania, 2001.
767 A.2d 1078.

Del Sole, J.:

This is an appeal from a trial court order granting Appellee–Plaintiff's request for post-trial relief and awarding a new trial. We affirm.

Appellee commenced this action alleging Appellant committed medical malpractice when he treated Appellee with injections of liquid silicone to cosmetically improve a nasal deformity. It was alleged that the silicone injections caused lumps to form on Appellee's nose, which later had to be shaved off with a scalpel. It was established at trial that the FDA had never approved the use of liquid silicone for injections and that Appellee signed a consent form stating he understood that silicone injections were not FDA approved. At the close of Appellee's case, the trial court granted Appellant's motion for non-suit on the issue of negligence *per se* for violation of FDA statutes and regulations. The court also charged the jury that the FDA had no authority to regulate the practice of medicine by a physician treating a patient. The jury returned a verdict in favor of Appellant, in response to which Appellee filed post-trial motions. Appellee claimed the court erred in granting the non-suit on the issue of negligence *per se* and that the court's charge to the jury on the lack of the FDA's authority to regulate the practice of medicine was in error. The trial court accepted these arguments and ordered a new trial. This appeal followed.

Appellant challenges both grounds on which the court ordered a new trial. Initially Appellant claims that the court erred in ruling that the jury should have been permitted to consider the claim of negligence *per se.*

The concept of negligence *per se* establishes both duty and the required breach of duty where an individual violates an applicable statute, ordinance or regulation designed to prevent a public harm. A plaintiff, however, having proven negligence *per se,* cannot recover unless it can be proven that such negligence was the proximate cause of the injury. A violation of a statute may be negligence *per se* and liability may be grounded on such negligence but the plaintiff cannot recover unless such negligence is the proximate and efficient cause of the injury in question. The doctrine of negligence *per se* does no more than satisfy a plaintiff's burden of establishing a defendant's negligence. It does not end the inquiry. The plaintiff still bears the burden of establishing causation.

At issue in this case are the provisions of the FDA. The passage of the Medical Device Amendments (MDA) to the Food, Drug and Cosmetic Act in 1976 gave the federal Food and Drug Administration comprehensive jurisdiction of all "devices intended for human use." 21 U.S.C.A. § 360c(a)(1). The MDA classifies medical devices, depending upon their potential danger to the public, as Class I, II or III. *Id.* Liquid injectable silicone is classified by the FDA as a Class III device. Class III devices are the most heavily regulated and before they obtain FDA approval they must undergo a detailed premarket approval process or it must be established that they are substantially equivalent to a device already on the market. *Id.,* 21 U.S.C. § 360c(1)(C); 21 U.S.C. § 360e(b)(1)(A). The FDA has never approved liquid silicone injections. The trial court summarized the following evidence obtained at trial regarding liquid silicone injections:

> Dow Corning was the only company that manufactured, distributed or sold liquid silicone in the United States. Liquid silicone was first marketed as an industrial grade in the 1950's. However, early in the 1960's Dow Corning developed "medical Grade 360," a type of liquid

silicone used to coat needles and the inside of glass. Purchasers of medical grade silicone were required to sign affidavits stating that the silicone would not be injected in humans. In July, 1965, Dow Corning filed an Investigational Exemption of a new New Drug application with the FDA, authorizing the investigational use of liquid injectable silicone. The silicone used, marketed under the label MDX 4–4011, was a highly purified, sterilized silicone, without any impurities. This study authorizing physicians to inject silicone into humans, ran from 1965 through 1971. Only eight investigators were authorized to participate in the study.

In 1974, Dow applied to the FDA for permission to market silicone for human injection. Approximately two years later, Dow applied for a new investigational exemption for liquid injectable silicone. Twenty-six investigators, selected and approved by the FDA, were authorized to participate in a three-year treatment program and seven-year follow-up of one hundred twenty-eight patients with severe facial deformities. This study, conducted under strict controls, concluded in 1981.

In 1989, Appellant injected Appellee with liquid silicone after advising him that the FDA had not approved the use of liquid injectable silicone, but that in Appellant's opinion it soon would be approved. Appellant testified that he received his supply of liquid injectable silicone from a Richard Webster, M.D., now deceased. Appellant testified that he believed it to be medical grade silicone which was used for the injection, although it was housed in an eight ounce glass bottle which was not sealed, or sterile, and which did not bear a manufacturer's label. It was also established at trial that neither Appellant nor Dr. Webster was an authorized investigator under the approved FDA study.

Appellee sought to establish at trial that Appellant was negligent *per se* for violating the FDA. Specifically the negligence was based on a violation of 21 U.S.C. § 331. In relevant part it provides:

The following acts and the causing thereof are hereby prohibited:

* * *

(c) The receipt in interstate commerce of any food, drug, device, or cosmetic that is adulterated or misbranded, and the delivery or proffered delivery thereof for pay or otherwise.

The trial court found that Appellant's actions were in direct violation of the statute. Appellant obtained through interstate commerce an unlabeled container of a matter he believed to be injectable liquid silicone, which he knew was not approved for use by the FDA, and he delivered that substance to his patient, Appellee, in the form of an injection.

In analyzing whether a claim based on negligence *per se* for violating this provision exists, Appellee must establish whether the purpose of the statute is to protect the interest of a group of individuals, as opposed to the general public, and whether the statute clearly applies to the conduct of the defendant.

Appellant argues that the trial court only considered whether Appellant violated the statute in question and failed to consider that its provisions are intended for the protection of the public welfare and not to protect a particular group of individuals. In support Appellant cites to this court's decision in *Wagner* [*v. Anzon, Inc.*, 684 A.2d 570 (Pa.Super.1996)]. In *Wagner* the appellant sought to establish that the trial court erred in granting a directed verdict on a negligence *per se* claim based upon the appellee's violations of the Philadelphia Air Management Code of 1969. The court noted that the statute or regulation at issue must be designed to protect a class of persons which includes the one whose interest is invaded. *Id.* It concluded that the purpose of the Philadelphia Air Management Code was to protect the atmosphere over the city of Philadelphia "with a concomitant benefits [sic] to its 'inhabitants'." *Wagner*, 684 A.2d at 574. The court wrote: "[t]here is no indication in these findings that the Code was meant to protect a particular class of individuals, rather it was enacted in 'furtherance of the health and welfare of the City's inhabitants, to the conduct of the normal pursuits of life, recreation, commerce and individual activity, and to sustaining life in an urban area'." *Id.* at 575.

The *Wagner* court contrasted those cases allowing negligence *per se* claims to proceed for violations of the Vehicle Code. The court reasoned: "[a] statute governing traffic has as its primary purpose the safety of those who use the roadways, while a statute governing air quality, by its nature, is directed to the population in general." *Id.* It further noted that the statute in question did not provide for a private cause of action which could act as an indicator that the statute did not contemplate enforcement for individual harms.

We conclude that although no private cause of action is set forth in the Act, it was certainly designed to protect a particular class of individuals–those such as Appellee who may be receiving some type of drug or devices. In *Stanton v. Astra Pharmaceutical Products, Inc.*, 718 F.2d 553 (3d Cir.1983) an action was brought after an eight-month old child suffered a severe adverse reaction, including cardiac and respiratory arrest, to Xylocaine, a local anesthetic. It was alleged that Astra, the manufacturer, had been negligent in failing to file with the FDA certain reports concerning the drug as required by federal statutes and regulations. The court wrote "[u]nder Pennsylvania law, the violation of a governmental safety regulation constitutes negligence per se if the regulation 'was, in part, intended to protect the interest of another as an individual [and] the interest of the plaintiff which was invaded, was one which the act intended to protect.'" *Id.* at 563. The court concluded that the reporting requirements of the FDA were "promulgated to protect individuals such as [the plaintiff] from precisely the type of harm that here occurred–an unexpected adverse reaction to Xylocaine." *Stanton*, 718 F.2d at 564.

In this case, Appellee did not assert that the Act created a private statutory cause of action. Rather, his claim was based on a basic common-law tort action for negligence.[1] In *Green v. Dolsky,* 546 Pa. 400, 685 A.2d 110 (1996) where the plaintiff developed an autoimmune disorder after receiving an injection of Zyderm Collagen Implant, the Court wrote that "there is no private right of action under the MDA, and in the absence of state law claims, a party injured by a medical device would have no cause of action against any person or entity." 685 at 115. The court went on to consider whether the state law claims were preempted by the Act but found that "state claims which allege that FDA requirements have not been met are cognizable." *Id.* at 117.

It must be recalled that Appellee sought only to have the jury consider its negligence *per se* claim. "[T]he doctrine of per se liability does not create an independent basis of tort liability but rather establishes, by reference to a statutory scheme, the standard of care appropriate to the underlying tort." *In re Orthopedic Bone Screw Products Liability Litigation,* 193 F.3d 781, 790 (3d Cir.1999).

In *Shamnoski v. P G Energy,* 2000 PA Super 367, this court found that violations of the Dam Safety and Encroachment Act did constitute negligence *per se* and that the statute was designed to protect the interest of a specific class of individual, those with property downstream from a dam. The court found that the statute applied to the Appellant's conduct as owner and operator of dammed reservoirs and there was a direct connection between the harm meant to be prevented and the injury suffered to downstream residents by flooding.

In this case the statute was designed to protect an individual such as Appellee from being administered a non-labeled, non-sterile unapproved drug to avoid unexpected negative results. Through proof of such violation, Appellee proved as a matter of law the first two elements of his cause of action, the duty and the breach of duty. This coupled with any evidence presented on causation and damages were matters for the jury's consideration. The trial court properly reversed its ruling granting a non-suit on the issue of negligence *per se.*

We turn now to the second issue, which challenges the trial court award of a new trial based on its conclusion that it erred in charging the jury on the FDA's lack of authority to regulate the practice of medicine. The court gave the jury the following instruction: "The United States Food and Drug Administration has no authority to regulate the practice of Medicine by a physician treating a patient." Upon reflection the trial court accepted Appellee's claim that this charge "gave the jury the impression that a physician can use any drug he wants, irrespective of whether it has been approved or disapproved by the FDA." Trial Court Opinion, 6/2/00, at 10. The court noted that the charge given was made

---

    1. The courts of this Commonwealth have noted the differences between a statutory civil cause of action and one arising under common law.

before this court's decision in *Southard v. Temple University Hospital,* 731 A.2d 603 (Pa.Super.1999).

The plaintiff in *Southard* underwent a spinal fusion surgery in which bone screws were implanted at a time when the FDA had not classified the screws as safe and effective for spinal use. The court ruled that the doctors involved had a duty to disclose the FDA classification to the plaintiff. Upon so ruling this court noted that "the FDA generally does not regulate the practice of medicine" and that "a physician, using his best medical judgment for the benefit of his patient, generally is free to use a medical device in a manner different from that for which the FDA has approved the device for commercial sale." In a footnote the court also remarked: "We note, however, that the FDA at least minimally regulates the practice of medicine in several ways. For example, it requires that a medical device be approved for sale for at least one use before a physician may use it for another 'off-label' use."

* * *

Thus we find no error in the trial court's decision to award a new trial in an effort not to mislead the jury regarding a physician's role in providing treatment to the patient.

Order affirmed.

NOTES AND QUESTIONS

1. *The relationship between private rights of action and negligence per se.* In footnote 1, the court observes that Pennsylvania courts have distinguished private rights of action from common law tort claims. What is that distinction? When enacting legislation, legislatures sometimes provide for a private right of action for violation of the statute, such as exists in the federal Civil Rights statutes barring certain kinds of discrimination in the workplace, public accommodations, and schools.

Even in the absence of such an "express" private right of action, courts sometimes find an "implied" private right of action in a statute. However, as a result of several Supreme Court decisions, implied rights of action under federal law are quite restricted. See Alexander v. Sandoval, 532 U.S. 275 (2001). Such actions under the statute are different from common law actions for negligence, in which there exists a right of action based on the common law, independent of the existence of any legislation. How should a decision that no private right of action exists bear on whether the statute can be used for negligence? In Negligence Per Se Theories in Pharmaceutical & Medical Device Litigation, 57 Me.L.Rev. 51 (2005), Professor Andrew E. Costa argues that a legislative decision not to provide a private right of action should bar a negligence per se claim. For the most part, courts, including the *Cabiroy* court, have disagreed. See, e.g., Stanton v. Astra Pharm. Prods., Inc., 718 F.2d 553, 565 (3d Cir.1983). But see, e.g., Rodriguez v. American Cyanamid Co., 858 F.Supp. 127 (D.Ariz.1994). There is, however, no question that Congress has the power to preempt state tort claims. See Chapter 9, § A; cf. Buckman Co. v. Plaintiffs' Legal Comm., 531 U.S. 341 (2001) (holding that state law claims based on committing fraud on the FDA in obtaining approval for a medical device were preempted).

2. *Class protected.* The court required that for negligence per se to apply, the statute must protect a specific group instead of the public generally. This requirement, which is traced to section 288(b) of the Restatement (Second) of Torts, appears to be an ill-stated effort to avoid imposing liability for harms that are not ordinarily protected by tort law. The examples in the Second Restatement are statutes designed to ensure unobstructed passage on the public highway and excessive-noise ordinances. Lending support to this understanding of the Restatement is its observation in the same comment: "Under some circumstances, where an individual has been interfered with in his exercise of such a public right, and as a result has suffered special harm, distinct from that suffered by the rest of the community, he may be entitled to maintain a tort action for the violation." The Third Restatement, in section 14, states only that the plaintiff must be among the class of persons the statute is designed to protect.

The *Cabiroy* court concluded that the statute prohibiting delivery of misbranded or adulterated drugs or devices is designed to protect the specific group of those who may be receiving a drug or device. Isn't it equally plausible that the statute is designed to protect all of us from receiving a misbranded drug or device?

3. The court stated that violation of a statute establishes both duty and breach of the duty. It is plain, however, that the defendant had a duty of reasonable care under the common law of torts. Thus, in most cases, the source of the duty is the existing law of torts, and the statute provides a more specific standard of care than the "usual reasonable care under the circumstances." However, there may be instances in which tort law does not provide a duty—for example in rescue situations. Should a statute that requires action in such situations supply the absent duty as well as the applicable standard? Thus, if a state has a statute requiring the reporting of hazardous waste dumping by another might that statute provide both a duty and negligence per se for its violation? Courts sometimes say yes, but by no means universally. See Restatement (Third) of Torts: Liability for Physical and Emotional Harm § 38 (2010) (stating that in deciding whether a common law duty exists, the existence of a statute should be taken into account).

B. PRODUCTS LIABILITY

1. INTRODUCTION

Toxic substances litigation consists of two classes of cases. The first class is products that are toxic and are sold through existing chains of distribution to consumers or to firms where employees are exposed to the products. These products consist of drugs, some medical devices, chemicals, and similar entities. The second class of toxic cases involves hazardous waste that is disposed of or accidentally leaks from where it is contained, resulting in contamination of ground, water, or air and consequent damage to property or to person. The first class of cases is subject to products liability, while the second class of cases typically invokes nuisance and trespass claims. Negligence claims may be asserted in both classes, although the reasonableness balancing of negligence is already built into nuisance doctrine.

We begin with a recounting of the development of strict product liability, much of which may be familiar to you from your first-year Torts class. We then proceed to consider a critical issue for toxic substances litigation: whether the risks posed by the product must be foreseeable at the time of manufacture and sale. We then examine several issues peculiar to drug litigation, including unavoidably unsafe products and learned intermediaries.

2. THE DEVELOPMENT AND EVOLUTION OF PRODUCTS LIABILITY

FOREWORD: UNDERSTANDING PRODUCTS LIABILITY

Gary T. Schwartz.
67 Cal.L.Rev. 435, 435–96 (1979).

Unquestionably, products liability ranks as one of the most conspicuous legal phenomena of the last twenty years, and the California Supreme Court has played a leading role in the elucidation of products liability doctrine. In *Greenman v. Yuba Power Products, Inc.*, decided in 1963, the court first ruled that manufacturers are subject to strict liability for injuries resulting from defective products. In its *Cronin* decision nine years later, the court reemphasized the "defect" prerequisite for strict liability, but rejected the Restatement's "unreasonably dangerous" gloss on "defect," thereby leaving the defect concept in a rather barren state. In *Barker v. Lull Engineering Co.* decided in January 1978, a unanimous court finally attempted an explication of "defect." The court noted (as have others) that product defects can be classed under three headings: "manufacturing" defects, "design" defects, and defects involving inadequate warnings or instructions accompanying the product. For manufacturing defects, the court specified in dictum the appropriateness of a deviation-from-the-normal-product standard. But it is design defects that have engendered the most serious confusion, both in actual litigation and in the products literature. Noting this confusion, *Barker* established a "two-pronged" test for identifying design defects. First, a product's design is defective if the product "fails to perform as safely as an ordinary consumer would expect when used in an intended or reasonably foreseeable manner." Second, the design is defective if the risks inherent in that design are not justified by the design's intrinsic benefits—whether measured in terms of cost savings, improved performance, or other factors. In endorsing this risk-benefit prong, *Barker* also announced a seemingly dramatic allocation of the burden of proof: once the plaintiff shows that the "product's design proximately caused [the plaintiff's] injury," the design is deemed defective unless the manufacturer can persuade the jury that the design's benefits exceed its associated risks. Moreover, the *Barker* opinion twice indicates that the jury is to render its risk-benefit judgments upon the basis of "hindsight." And in a provocative footnote, the *Barker* opinion raises the possibility of strict liability, without proof of ordinary defect, for injuries caused by products "whose norm is danger."

* * *

I

HISTORY: ONE STATE'S EXPERIENCE

* * *

* * * In 1944, in *Escola v. Coca Cola Bottling Co.*, the court liberalized the use of res ipsa loquitur in products actions brought against manufacturers under a negligence theory, thereby easing the plaintiff's burden of proving negligence in cases concerning manufacturing defects. Justice Traynor, concurring in *Escola*, first articulated the formal strict products liability idea.

* * *

Greenman couched the strict liability test in terms of whether a product contained "a defect in design and manufacture of which the plaintiff was not aware that made [the product] unsafe for its intended use." Stimulated by *Greenman,* the American Law Institute approved a section for its Second Torts Restatement—drafted by its Reporter, Dean Prosser—imposing strict liability on the seller of "any product in a defective condition unreasonably dangerous to the user or consumer." Standing alone, "unreasonably dangerous" is a tort-like phrase that seemingly calls for a comparison of the risks and benefits associated with the alleged product defect. But comment i, appended to section 402A, goes on to explain "unreasonably dangerous" as meaning dangerous "to an extent beyond that which would be contemplated by the ordinary consumer who purchases it, with the ordinary knowledge common to the community as to its characteristics." This provides a contract or warranty-like explanation of defect. * * *

In *Escola* and *Greenman,* Justice Traynor had evidently regarded "defect" as a rather easy concept; hence his belief that strict liability would vastly simplify the issues in products litigation. By the time of an important speech he delivered in 1965, however, then-Chief Justice Traynor was beginning to appreciate various perplexities inhering in "defect." Subsequent to the adoption of the Restatement, the supreme court's opinions shuttled back and forth between the *Greenman* language and the Restatement language. Then, in its 1972 *Cronin* decision, the court * * * held that the basic standard of liability should be "defect" rather than "unreasonably dangerous defect." * * *

The *Cronin* opinion, while stripping "defect" of its "unreasonably dangerous" gloss, explicitly declined to set forth any kind of working "defect" definition. As a result, *Cronin* received a decidedly mixed reception in other jurisdictions and in the law reviews. In California, litigation in post-*Cronin* cases—especially those involving product design—was confused, as lawyers and judges struggled with the one word "defect" standard. A few judges evidently felt the jury should be instructed in the language of "defect" and nothing more. Among law professors, it seems fair to say that the general understanding, even after *Cronin*, was that a design defect plaintiff needed to show the existence of some design alternative that would provide greater safety at acceptable cost. Court of appeal opinions after *Cronin* inclined in this direction, although somewhat inconclusively.

The uncertainties engendered by *Cronin* provide the backdrop for *Barker*. In *Barker,* the plaintiff-employee was seriously injured when he jumped off a high-lift loader which the defendant had manufactured and then leased to the victim's employer. The injured employee was filling in for the loader's regular operator, who was absent from work [perhaps because he understood that the loader was to be used that day on sloping terrain that, given the loader's center of gravity and absence of outriggers, created a risk of tipping]. The employee leaped from the loader after it began to tip over while being operated on a sharply sloping terrain. At trial, the plaintiff launched a barrage of design defect accusations against the manufacturer. Although the trial in *Barker* was subsequent to *Cronin*, a confused trial judge gave the jury an "unreasonably dangerous" defect instruction. The jury then returned a verdict for the defendant-manufacturer. The plaintiff appealed and won a reversal in the court of appeal on the ground that the trial court's instruction had ignored *Cronin*. The manufacturer then secured a hearing in the supreme court arguing that in complicated cases involving product design—and especially when the alleged design defect involves the omission of a safety device—the simple language of "defect" provides inadequate guidance to juries; rather, for these cases the language of "unreasonably dangerous" is sensible after all. The manufacturer thus contended for a selective return to the Restatement view.

Rejecting this contention, the supreme court in its *Barker* opinion reaffirmed that "unreasonably dangerous" is no part of the California "defect" definition. The court agreed, however, with the manufacturer's more general position that the word "defect," in isolation, is inadequate as a strict liability instruction in design cases. For these cases, therefore, the court formulated the new "two-pronged" defect test.

[The *Barker* case adopted, as Professor Schwartz explains later in his Article, a two-prong test for product design defect that permitted a plaintiff to establish the existence of a defect through two alternative methods. First, if the product's design could be improved with a safer alternative design that, on balance, was less costly than the dangers it eliminated, a cost-benefit test similar to the balancing involved in negligence, the product was defectively designed. Moreover, once the plaintiff demonstrated that the design of the product proximately caused the plaintiff's harm, the burden of proof on this first cost-benefit prong was shifted to the defendant. Alternatively, if the plaintiff established that the design of the product resulted in its danger being greater than an ordinary consumer or user would expect, the product was also defective. Query: In light of the second, consumer expectations prong for design defect, how would you expect the plaintiff in *Barker* to fare on the existence of a design defect?]

II

GENUINE STRICT LIABILITY

It is quite possible to conceive of a liability rule in the products setting that is genuinely strict: this would be the rule (noted by Prosser) rendering product manufacturers automatically liable for all accidents caused or occasioned by the use of their products. Thus, a car manufacturer would be liable for all injuries in which its cars are involved, a power mower manufacturer would bear the liability for all power mower accidents, a ladder manufacturer would suffer liability for all ladder falls, and a skateboard manufacturer would be fully liable for all skateboarding injuries. Existing strict products liability falls drastically short of such a genuine strict liability rule, since it grants the victim a recovery only if the victim can demonstrate the existence of a product "defect." By stating that products liability does not cast the manufacturer in the role of an "insurer," opinions like *Barker* and *Cronin* clearly (if somewhat awkwardly) reject the idea that the existing liability rule is in any way equivalent to genuine strict liability. Of course, the res ipsa loquitur doctrine, given its *Escola* breakthrough, is now seen as a way station to the *Greenman* rule of strict "defect" liability. Will today's defect doctrine be understood in the future as a transitional stage in the evolution of a genuine strict liability rule? Possibly, but this seems very doubtful. The *Barker* opinion, specifically adverting to the genuine strict liability idea, regards it as "extreme." And the keen interest in proposals like auto no-fault—placing strong liability on the product user—is out of line with the development of any automatic liability rule operating on product manufacturers.

* * *

* * * In light of the problems that such a liability rule would actually raise, however, it is neither surprising nor obviously inappropriate that the supreme court has chosen to remain with the far more moderate rule of strict liability for product "defects" only. But the *Barker* opinion does leave open—in truth, it deliberately draws attention to—one limited but interesting application of the genuine strict liability idea. According to a *Barker* footnote, strict liability might be recognized, without proof of ordinary defect, for products whose design is such that their "norm is danger." The advisability of strict liability for defect-free "norm-is-danger" products will be assessed in a final section of this Foreword. Also, that section will take advantage of the foregoing analysis of genuine strict liability in evaluating *Barker's* suggestion of a "hindsight" approach to its risk-benefit liability standard.

III

A. *The Tort and Contract Bases for Strict Liability*

By the time *Greenman* introduced strict liability, negligence law already afforded the injured product victim generous compensation rights against a negligent manufacturer, and implied warranty law conferred on the product consumer a strict liability right running against the product retailer, if not the product manufacturer. In his *Escola* concurrence, Justice Traynor relied on both the negligence and the warranty precedents in formulating the strict liability proposal which he later accepted, on behalf of the entire court, in *Greenman*; and the *Greenman* doctrine has itself been explained as an imaginative synthesis of negligence and warranty.

If *Greenman* can be seen as synthesizing negligence and warranty, however, *Barker's* two-pronged design defect test threatens to analyze away this synthesis. As the *Barker* opinion recognizes, its ordinary consumer expectations prong manifests the warranty heritage upon which California products liability doctrine partially rests. Indeed, "consumer expectations" is a plausible restatement of the criterion for liability in a common implied warranty action. Meanwhile, *Barker's* risk-benefit prong reveals the strong indebtedness of strict liability doctrine to tort law's negligence principle, which itself has historically been understood as calling for a risk-benefit balancing. *Barker's* indications of the warranty and negligence bases of strict liability doctrine invite an assessment of the logic underlying the negligence and warranty theories.

Negligence law, in its product applications, seems at first to take no account of the point that the product manufacturer stands in a kind of contractual relationship with the product purchaser; it imposes on the manufacturer the same obligation of reasonable care as it places on defendants in "stranger" cases of the sort typified by *Brown v. Kendall*. This obligation is anchored in a fairness principle (that a potential injurer should not egoistically rank his own welfare above the welfare of others) and an accident prevention principle (that a party should be discouraged from engaging in conduct which entails risks to others that exceed its benefits to the actor). Warranty law, by contrast, is drawn directly from the essentially contractual relationship between the consumer and the manufacturer. Its purpose is to give effect to the reasonable expectations which that relationship engenders in the parties, particularly the consumer; "the assumption [is] that the parties themselves [to a contract of sale], had they thought of it, would specifically have so agreed [to a merchantability guarantee]."

* * *

* * * It is undeniable that the issues in design cases often become extremely difficult, and it is also apparent that when a products case is sent to the jury under amorphous instructions, almost anything can happen. The objections are therefore valuable inasmuch as they suggest important criteria to rely on in evaluating the law's design-defect rules. If product design litigation is to achieve satisfying results, the law is obliged to formulate standards which identify the proper variables, which are capable of being administered in the civil trial context, and which provide the jury with effective, intelligent guidance. These criteria will be returned to repeatedly in the evaluation of *Barker* in Parts III and IV.

* * *

If strict products liability is compared to early or immature systems of warranty and negligence, the importance of the strict liability synthesis may seem immense. The proper comparison, however, is between a mature strict liability system on the one hand and mature warranty and negligence systems on the other–a mature negligence system being one that has dispensed with privity, approved of res ipsa loquitur, extended itself to matters of product design, and acquired a sophisticated plaintiffs' bar. In this comparison, the impact of strict liability is far less dramatic. What is it that the *Greenman* rule really adds?

* * *

* * * The core concept of *Greenman* strict liability is the product's "defect." The core concept of negligence liability is the manufacturer's faulty conduct. The core concept of implied warranty liability is the product's "unmerchantability," its "unfitness for the ordinary purposes for which such goods are used." These concepts obviously overlap and intermingle. The warranty literature specifies that a "defect" most clearly renders a product unmerchantable. In like manner, negligence cases have often indicated that the presence of a "defect" raises the issue of the manufacturer's negligence. And "strict" liability, given its defect requirement, can plausibly be regarded as a "fault" rule after all, one that simply shifts the focus from the "fault" of the manufacturer to the "fault" in the product itself.

The *Barker* opinion professes to highlight the difference between manufacturer negligence and product defect. But if it is true that each involves a kind of fault, one should inquire when, if ever, the theories of negligence liability and defect liability actually lead to divergent results. The two theories can first be tested in their application to manufacturing defects. Typically, such defects are introduced into the product by a mishap somewhere in the manufacturing process. This mishap, in turn, is usually due to either the negligence of an employee of the manufacturer or the negligence of the manufacturer's supplier. Two vicarious liability rules—one quite ancient and the other just emerging—render the manufacturer liable in either event.

Negligence law, however, imposes on the plaintiff-victim the burden of proving his case. Since the circumstances of the particular mishap are commonly unknown even to the manufacturer and hence are quite beyond the plaintiff's ability to discover, the latter has little choice but to fall back upon res ipsa loquitur. In an early article, Dean Prosser claimed that if a victim can demonstrate a manufacturing defect, he can secure a res ipsa negligence verdict from the jury in almost all cases. Prosser subsequently backed away from this strong claim, and contented himself with the softer allegation that a negligence plaintiff who identifies a manufacturing defect will "usually" prevail. Only this latter assessment is faithful to the chanciness of the res ipsa argument. Even when the law allows resort to res ipsa, under California's "conditional" res ipsa standards there is a real risk that the jury will decline to accept the res ipsa invitation. While res ipsa can be perceived as "a simple, understandable rule of circumstantial evidence," lawyers agree that many juries either fail to understand the res ipsa theory or regard it as not entirely fair–perhaps implicitly sympathizing with the claim that "[s]urmise ought not be substituted for strict proof when it is sought to fix a defendant with serious liability."

In manufacturing defect cases, therefore, the basic consequence of the products liability rule is clear enough. The rule recognizes that manufacturers can be held vicariously liable for any negligence in the manufacturing process, that these defects are almost always a result of negligence somewhere within that process, but that res ipsa can be a cumbersome method of proving negligence in the individual case. By imposing automatic liability on the manufacturer, the rule correctly concludes that whatever marginal fine-tuning a mature negligence system makes possible would not justify the corresponding complication of the trial process, a complication that would disserve product victims by delaying. rendering more costly, and sometimes preventing the vindication of their valid negligence claims. Products liability thus serves the highly intelligent function of a "negligence shortcut." In most of these defect cases, however, negligence principles justify liability only insofar as they are extended by certain rules of vicarious liability, and it should not be forgotten that vicarious liability embodies strict liability of a limited but important sort.

* * *

* * * In *design* defect cases, by comparison, it is far from clear that strict liability performs even this limited function. Technically speaking, the issue in a negligence action should be whether the manufacturer's conduct in reaching a design decision was unreasonable. But in practice, even in negligence cases the focus tends to shift from the unreasonableness of the design decision to the unreasonableness of the design itself. And since unreasonableness as a negligence notion is measured in risk-benefit terms, the negligence issue in design cases assumes a form almost identical to the defect issue under strict liability—especially given *Barker*'s risk-benefit defect prong. Moreover, negligence law's willingness to blur the distinction between conduct and product makes sense. Since design decisions are made deliberately by manufacturers' design officials, an unreasonable decision almost necessarily leads to an unreasonable design, and conversely an unreasonable design is almost always the consequence of an unreasonable design decision. Perceiving this, courts in some jurisdictions have found it meaningless to apply strict liability in design cases.

In a limited number of design situations, however, the equivalence of the negligence and strict liability theories can break down. The two theories remain equivalent so long as the relevant risks and benefits either are known by the manufacturer's design officials or could reasonably be known by them. What if those officials are unaware of a relevant risk or benefit at the time they reach their design decision, and if their lack of awareness is reasonable and nonnegligent? To take extreme examples, what if the risk that the product contains is both unknown and unknowable at the time the product is designed and sold? Or what if a safety device capable of eliminating or reducing a product's risk at acceptable cost is not invented until after the time of the product's design and sale? Clearly, negligence principles would not afford a recovery in either of these situations. To the extent that recoveries are authorized by strict liability, that doctrine does make a difference. Unfortunately, however, the results that strict liability actually reaches in cases of this sort remain somewhat uncertain. Since these cases lie on the outskirts of the *Greenman–Barker* doctrine, consideration of them helps clarify that doctrine's boundaries. A discussion of the issues they raise will be presented in the final section of this Foreword.

* * *

2. The Contract–Based Consumer Expectations Prong

[T]he consumer expectations standard attempts both to take advantage of strict liability's legitimate "warranty heritage" and to take account of limited consumer knowledge of particular product hazards.

Examined more closely, the prong is effective in bolstering the support for already recognized products liability principles. But as an independent basis for products liability verdicts, its value is burdened by doubts. These doubts can be explained by considering * * * the nature of the consumer's "ordinary expectations."

* * *

b. What Are "Ordinary Expectations"?

When the victim is the product purchaser or that person's intended beneficiary, the warranty foundation of strict liability gives good reason for attending to the purchaser's product expectations. But the problem remains of ascertaining, in any satisfying way, what those expectations are.

Expectations can be fostered by communications about the product from the manufacturer to the product purchaser. Assume the manufacturer has issued statements or advertisements praising the product. If those statements include claims that meet minimum standards of specificity and materiality, and if the product's failure to comply with these claims results in an injury, the victim has no need to rely on anything in *Barker*; the Restatement doctrine of false product representation and the U.C.C. doctrine of express warranty can be called upon to assure a recovery. A consumer expectations analysis is undeniably helpful in explaining the rationale for those doctrines; yet the doctrines themselves do not justify the *Barker* prong, given their clear recognition in pre-*Barker* law and the advantage of maintaining their doctrinal independence. Now, what if the manufacturer's statements commending its product are either too vague or too trivial to qualify as false representations or express warranties? Insofar as the Restatement and the U.C.C. have good reasons for deliberately declining to take these statements into account, it is very difficult to see how or why they should be ruled relevant to a *Barker* consumer expectations claim.

So much for "affirmative" communications. What about "negative" communications in the form of warnings about the product's dangers? As *Barker* recognizes, when a product's defect is "patent" or obvious, its obviousness usually undermines any claim that the defect contravenes the purchaser's product expectations. Similarly, receipt of a warning lowers the purchaser's reasonable expectations in a way that prevents him from later arguing that his expectations were defeated by the warned-of product hazard.

Of course, given the received "defect" typology, warnings of this sort are hardly at the option of the manufacturer. If a product contains a hazard that is sufficiently substantial and unusual, the law renders the manufacturer liable if it fails to provide the purchaser with a warning of the hazard so that the purchaser may make an "informed choice" as to whether to buy the product in the first place. Any warnings given by the manufacturer under the threat of liability can correct what might otherwise be the consumer's misimpressions. Thus the warning requirement in products liability law, whether it is violated or complied with, deals directly with most of the cases in which *Barker*'s consumer expectations prong has a possible application.

      * * *

In several ways the question of ordinary consumer expectations thus presents itself, and we need to know what those expectations include. Unfortunately, identifying their substance, or even developing a methodology for identifying their substance, proves to be a frustrating task. * * *

      * * *

* * * If, then, in a not-easy case the mere existence of some design danger does not alone supply a basis for the jury's consumer-expectations factfinding, what evidence can the victim present that is both admissible and entitled to substantial weight? The victim's own after-the-fact testimony that the product failed to meet his expectations? The testimony of some man-on-the-street, selected by the victim and designated by the victim as a typical consumer? Of course, under the risk-benefit standard the testimony of expert witnesses is quite appropriate, and there are many experts competent to testify on matters of risk-benefit product design. But one can hardly imagine what credentials a witness must possess before he can be certified as an expert on the issue of ordinary consumer expectations.

In anything resembling a difficult case, therefore, the consumer expectations standard is unable to stand on its own, and raises the prospect of haphazard, impressionistic jury decisionmaking. Especially since a finding of a denial of consumer expectations is dispositive of liability—no presentation of trade-off evidence can counter or rebut it—this prospect is disquieting. There may be a class of "easy" cases, however, in which the standard is in order. In *Hauter v. Zogarts*, a mother bought, as a present for her son, a "Golfing Gizmo"—a device for unskilled golfers to use in improving their games. The Gizmo was so designed, however, that if the player hit underneath the golf ball, the ball was likely to double back and strike the player. Hitting at balls in such a way is exactly the kind of thing that inexperienced golfers—who comprise the Gizmo's intended market—are likely to do. Fred Hauter suffered brain damage when the golf ball struck him on the head. The supreme court granted him a recovery as a matter of law, relying in part on the U.C.C. theory of implied warranty: the product was obviously "not fit for the ordinary purposes for which such goods are used."

The court's later *Barker* opinion, in explaining its consumer expectations prong, relies on Justice Traynor's *Greenman* observation that "implicit in [a product's] presence on the market . . . [is] a representation that it [will] safely do the jobs for which it was built." In *Hauter,* the victim's use of the product was wholly reasonable and as intended by the manufacturer, and there were no external forces, either behavioral or environmental, that contributed to the accident. In cases which comply with these restrictive conditions, it seems meaningful to say, in line with *Greenman,* that what the consumer assumes is that the product is flat-out "safe."

Even here, however, a warning analysis cannot be avoided. If a warning of the product hazard is not given to the Gizmo's purchaser, that failure sustains liability standing, alone. If, on the other hand, a warning has been effectively communicated, the consumer expectations argument is defeated. The warning analysis thus retains a certain ultimate priority.
* * *

IV

BOUNDARIES OF STRICT PRODUCTS LIABILITY

A. *"Hindsight" Evaluation of Risks and Benefits*

The previous discussion of the relationship between negligence and strict defect liability in matters of product design left open what the strict-liability result should be in each of two cases. In Case A, the product contains a hazard which the manufacturer neither knows of nor could reasonably know of at the time of the product's design and sale. With knowledge, the manufacturer could easily have reduced or eliminated the hazard, either by modifying the product or by issuing instructions or a proper warning. In Case B, the product contains a hazard which, though fully known, is nevertheless unpreventable by the manufacturer at the time of the product's sale; the hazard subsequently becomes preventable when new safety technology is developed.

Case A raises the issue of "unknowable" dangers, which a recent federal study, having canvassed the case law nationwide, concludes are beyond the reach even of strict liability. Case B presents the issue of "state of the art" in strict liability—"state of the art" not in the weak sense of industry custom, but in the strong sense of the full range of design options technologically available at the time of the product's sale. These Cases can be placed in context by noting the kinds of products they are likely to involve. Case B has special relevance for "old" products— products sold many years ago but which are still in use and hence still capable of causing injuries. Case A has special relevance for pharmaceutical products. Here, the hazards unknowable at the time of sale may not manifest themselves until many years later; or, unlike Case B products, their hazards can erupt quite promptly after the drug is brought to market.

What results does *Barker* suggest in these Cases? In its opinion, the court twice indicates that the jury's risk-benefit determination should be rendered on the basis of "hindsight," and the opinion makes clear that these determinations can be adverse to the manufacturer even if the manufacturer "took reasonable precautions in an attempt to design a safe product." These "hindsight" references can easily be interpreted as mandating liability in Cases A and B. Other passages in *Barker*, however, cast doubt on the propriety of this interpretation. Thus, the opinion states that the only product "misuses" for which a manufacturer can be held liable are those that are "reasonably foreseeable." And the opinion explicitly reserves for later decision the "state of the art" issue. In all, it seems prudent to regard Cases A and B as presenting open questions. For these questions, there are no easy answers.

* * *

The two Cases can be further considered from the perspective of the accident prevention goal that *Barker*'s risk-benefit prong incorporates. The stipulation that the product satisfied all risk-benefit standards at the time of its sale indicates that the accident prevention principle implicit in negligence law does not call for liability. As noted, however, a genuine strict liability rule could claim the advantage of giving manufacturers strong incentives to accelerate the future of safety developments. A "hindsight" approach would move beyond negligence in the direction of genuine strict liability by strengthening the manufacturer's incentives to engage in safety research prior to the product's sale. After that sale, however, a hindsight rule would contain a limiting condition sharply separating it from genuine strict liability. While in Cases A and B knowledge of the product's "risk" or of the "benefit"-related technology is lacking at the time of the product's sale, the knowledge must become available, or the new technology must be developed, prior to the time of the plaintiff's lawsuit. Otherwise, even with hindsight, no defect can be identified.

The requirement that the knowledge or technology come into being by the time of the lawsuit prevents a hindsight rule from affording, subsequent to the product's sale, the safety incentives associated with genuine strict liability. Worse, the requirement may even suggest that hindsight liability could negatively operate as a depressant upon the safety discovery process. Consider the product manufacturer thinking of expending funds for either testing existing products or conducting research into possible new safety devices. Under a "hindsight" rule, if the manufacturers expenditure is successful the new hazard information it uncovers or the new safety technology it develops can be used as decisive evidence against it in later suits involving products sold at an earlier date. Insofar as the manufacturer is able to predict these liability consequences, it could be dissuaded from undertaking projects in product safety research.

This disincentive would adversely affect the real world, however, only insofar as it is manufacturers who by their affirmative efforts are responsible for society's product safety advances. Manufacturers are clearly in a good position to seek out information about previously unrecognized product hazards (the Case A problem), and activity by manufacturers in this regard is hardly uncommon. To a great extent, however, this information flows in to manufacturers without much of an effort on their part. Also, in some instances the victim himself, by examining the product and reconstructing the accident, can figure out the product's hazard. Furthermore, the federal government has now launched an extensive program of product accident analysis, so as to acquire knowledge of dangers that existing products possess. In Case B, the effective responsibility for researching new safely technology varies from one industrial setting to another. This responsibility often lies with the manufacturers themselves, either individually or at least as an industry. But frequently the research is undertaken by companies who serve (or who would like to serve) as the manufacturers suppliers, or by outside entities like governmental agencies or university research facilities. In both A and B, therefore, while hindsight liability is capable of deflecting proper safety incentives, this would probably happen only in a limited number of cases; given the background circumstances, my estimate is that the result would be less likely in A than in B.

* * *

Additional factors pertinent to evaluating the hindsight issue concern the reliability of manufacturers' claims that particular cases do indeed fall within A or B, and the judicial system's ability to assess, these claims. Manufacturers frequently allege that a product hazard was unknown and not reasonably knowable at the time of the product's sale. But often enough (though not invariably), we eventually learn that the manufacturers did indeed possess knowledge of the hazard, or at least had reason to know of it, from an early date. Moreover, in light of the obligation negligence law imposes on manufacturers to test their products for hidden hazards, in many cases there will be room for a strong suspicion that a reasonable testing effort would have revealed the hazard in a timely fashion. Yet the art form of a lawsuit seems poorly suited to accomplish either the confirmation or the denial of suspicions of this sort, given the lapse of time between the product's sale and the product lawsuit, and given the elusiveness of the "should have known" issue. Taken in combination, these practical observations are sympathetic to liability in Case A: the difference between knowledge-now and knowledge-then may be something that it is intelligent for litigation to ignore.

* * *

In summary, several indicators, including community values, contract reasoning, and the effective capacity of litigation, point toward liability in Case A, while safety incentive reasoning places at most a limited cloud over the liability idea. * * *

B. Products So Designed that Their "Norm is Danger"

Footnote 10 of *Barker* raises the possibility, without deciding the question, of strict liability for products which, while free of defects in the risk-benefit sense, nevertheless "entail a substantial risk of harm ... even if no safer design is feasible." These are products whose "norm is danger."

The ramifications of the idea referred to in footnote 10 can hardly be understated. Assume a product whose design somehow entails a substantial risk. Either there is or is not an appropriate design alternative. If there is, liability is authorized by *Barker*'s risk-benefit prong. If there is not, liability could still be imposed under the auspices of the "norm is danger" theory. If, therefore, the footnote 10 idea is eventually accepted as a supplement to the risk-benefit standard, "substantial risk" products would bear liability quite without regard to the availability of feasible design alternatives. Ironically, then, the "norm is danger" concept, while couched in terms of a risk-benefit analysis, would directly lead to the exclusion of that analysis; all "substantial-risk"products would be subject to what Part II of this Foreword called a rule of genuine strict liability.

It is difficult to believe that the *Barker* court would accept such a rule. That rule would render irrelevant all issues of risk-benefit as well as of consumer expectations—issues which the *Barker* court was at pains to explore. Additionally, the *Barker* opinion at several junctures indicates its wariness about genuine strict liability, a wariness that is not without warrant, as Part II of this Foreword has suggested. Therefore, there is a need to seek a narrow exegesis of the tersely-stated footnote 10 idea. This search can be aided by considering particular products responsible for substantial risks. Of all the products in our society, motor vehicles are involved in the largest number of accidents. On the 1977 list compiled by the National Injury Information Clearing House, bicycles rank first as an accident producer. Stairs hold the number two position, with power mowers ranking sixth and skateboards seventh (up from eighteenth the year before). Even if these products are flawlessly designed, it can be assumed that substantial risks remain.

Most of the accidents which give rise to these substantial risks, however, are immediately caused by human inexperience or carelessness—the carelessness of the victim himself or some third person. Since this carelessness is all too statistically predictable, it constitutes a "reasonably foreseeable" product "misuse" that manufacturers of cars, bikes, ladders, and skateboards are required to cope with for purposes of the risk-benefit design defect standard. But assuming no such defect, and conceding the primacy of victim or third-party carelessness as the accident cause, the fairness and accident prevention considerations noted in the earlier discussion of the genuine strict liability idea do not justify the assignment of significant liability to the manufacturer.

Given this analysis, the most plausible interpretation of the "norm is danger" proposal would stipulate that a product possesses such a norm only if it is responsible for a major risk even when all relevant actors—including the product designer and the product user—exercise eminently reasonable care. * * *

      * * *

CONCLUSION

Strict products liability is a subtle rather than a sensational doctrine, as is often supposed. The law has refused even to consider a rule of genuine strict liability, not implausible though that rule may be. The existing moderate rule of products liability hinges on the requirement of a "defect." Since "defect" means that there is something "wrong" with the product, it is accurate (if ironic) to understand strict liability as involving a "fault" system after all—one concerned with the fault in the manufacturer's product rather than the fault in its conduct. What becomes interesting is the attempt to identify those circumstances in which these two kinds of fault are *not* equivalent.

      * * *

NOTES AND QUESTIONS

1. Professor Schwartz discusses warranty theories that might be asserted in products liability cases and differences that may exist between warranty and strict liability substantive standards for liability, affirmative defenses, and disclaimers. Thus, in Cipollone v. Liggett Group, Inc., 893 F.2d 541 (3d Cir.1990), aff'd and rev'd on other grounds, 505 U.S. 504 (1992), the plaintiff obtained a jury verdict based on a breach of warranty claim on behalf of decedent smoker, but lost on the strict products claim because the jury found the decedent 80% at fault based on her knowingly and voluntarily assuming the risk of smoking.

2. The "Boundaries" section of the excerpt discusses products whose dangers could not reasonably have been known at the time of manufacturer and sale. Which classes of products would you expect are most likely to have "unknowable" dangers? Professor Schwartz suggests drugs are one such example. Why? Are there others? Subsection 2, infra, considers the issue of whether liability should be imposed on products whose dangers were unknown at the time of manufacture and sale.

3. *Categorical liability.* In the second part of the "Boundaries" section, Professor Schwartz expresses skepticism about products being declared defective simply because of excessive danger that exist in them. In one sense, this "categorical liability" is an extreme form of design defect in which the alternative design is no product at all and all of the benefits of a product are compared with all of its risks. Is it beyond the pale to employ such a standard to determine whether strict liability should be applied? Can you think of products that should qualify?

Professor Schwartz's skepticism turned out to be prophetic. Although a handful of courts have dabbled with the idea, a "norm is danger" approach has not taken hold. The high water mark occurred in O'Brien v. Muskin Corp., 463 A.2d 298 (N.J.1983), a case involving an above-ground swimming pool. The plaintiff was hurt when he dove head first into the pool, which was filled with 3½ feet of water. On his design defect claim, the court suggested that even if there was no reasonable alternative:

> The evaluation of the utility of a product also involves the relative need for that product; some products are essentials, while others are luxuries. A product that fills a critical need and can be designed in only one way should be viewed differently from a luxury item. Still other products, including some for which no alternative exists, are so dangerous and of such little use that under the risk-utility analysis, a manufacturer would bear the cost of liability of harm to others. That cost might dissuade a manufacturer from placing the product on the market, even if the product has been made as safely as possible. Indeed, plaintiff contends that above-ground pools with vinyl liners are such products and that manufacturers who market those pools should bear the cost of injuries they cause to foreseeable users.
>
> * * * The trial court should have permitted the jury to consider whether, because of the dimensions of the pool and slipperiness of the bottom, the risks of injury so outweighed the utility of the product as to constitute a defect. * * * Viewing the evidence in the light most favorable to plaintiff, even if there are no alternative methods of making bottoms for above-ground pools, the jury might have found that the risk posed by the pool outweighed its utility.

Id. at 306.

Very few other courts have accepted this idea of "categorical liability." See, e.g., Baughn v. Honda Motor Co., 727 P.2d 655 (Wash.1986) (rejecting the *O'Brien* suggestion that liability could be imposed simply based on excessive danger in a product). In some of the few that have, legislatures have responded restrictively, as the New Jersey Legislature did in response to *O'Brien*. It enacted a statute exempting a manufacturer from liability when there is no feasible alternative design, except for "egregiously unsafe" products of "little or no usefulness" and the risks of which consumers would not "reasonably be expected to have knowledge." N.J.S.A. 2A:58C–3(b). The Third Restatement on Products Liability recognizes a narrow exception for products with an "egregiously unacceptable" capacity to cause harm and uses a prank exploding cigar as an illustration of such a product, while denying its applicability to alcoholic beverages, firearms, and above-ground swimming pools. Restatement (Third) of Torts: Products Liability § 2 cmts. d & e (1998).

4. In Soule v. General Motors Corp., 882 P.2d 298 (Cal.1994), the California Supreme Court further modified its law on design defects. In that case, the plaintiff was injured when the toe pan of her vehicle was crushed back toward her in an accident, after the left front wheel assembly broke free from the frame. She asserted the vehicle was defective in design based on an alternative design that would limit the amount of travel for the wheel assembly and based, alternatively, on consumer expectations. The court sub silentio modified *Barker*. A consumer expectations instruction would only be available in cases in which the product's failure justified an inference that the product failed to meet minimum standards of safety that might be expected. In this case, the question of how safe an automobile should be designed in 30–70 miles per hour closing speed crash was not a matter appropriate for a consumer expectations test given the complicated design issues and the expert testimony presented with regard to those issues. The intermediate appellate courts have wrestled with where the line is that determines when consumers expectations are appropriate and when they are not in the years since *Soule*, but the Supreme Court has, so far, not provided further guidance. Might the idea be that in certain cases the existence of a defect is so evident that there is no need to identify an alternative design? In this regard, consider the discussion of *Hauter v. Zogarts*, in the Schwartz excerpt. See also Restatement (Third) Torts: Products Liability § 3 (1998) (providing for finding of liability when circumstantial evidence permits an inference that a defect was the most likely cause of the harm).

3. WARNINGS AND DESIGN DEFECTS

The Schwartz excerpt skips lightly over warnings as a distinct basis for product liability. In drug, vaccine, and medical device cases, warnings play a primary role. Moreover, design claims for this class of products are treated more cautiously by courts than for other products. We explore those issues further in the next case.

Warnings and instructions serve two primary purposes: (1) risk reduction and (2) informing consumers of risks that cannot be avoided if the benefits of the product are to be obtained. With regard to the former, risks can be reduced by informing users of the product's risks and their nature, methods to avoid or minimize those risks in the way that the product is used, and how to minimize any harm that may occur, such as when a poison is ingested. Informing consumers of risks that cannot be avoided serves a function much like informed consent—enabling the consumer to make a considered choice whether to consume the product and, along with it, to be exposed to those unavoidable risks. Sometimes these two functions for warnings overlap but keep this distinction in mind as you work through this section of the text. Often the issue in a warnings case is not whether warnings had to be provided but whether the warnings that were provided were adequate. With hindsight, plaintiffs can almost always identify some more specific warning that might have been provided.

a. Imputing Knowledge of Risk

In this section, we pursue the idea raised in Professor Schwartz's article and in note 2 on products whose risks are not known (and could not reasonably have been known) at the time of manufacture. Of course, we contemplate that by the time plaintiff is injured and sues that we have better information that reveals those risks. Should a manufacturer be subject to liability in such instances?

VASSALLO v. BAXTER HEALTHCARE CORP.

Supreme Judicial Court of Massachusetts, 1998.
428 Mass. 1, 696 N.E.2d 909.

GREANEY, JUSTICE.

[Plaintiff received a silicone gel breast implant for which defendant was responsible in February, 1977, at the age of 48. In 1993, suffering from chest pain, plaintiff underwent explantation surgery. That surgery revealed that the implant on one side had ruptured, releasing silicone gel into her body. The surgeon noted severe scarring of her chest muscles, and she was diagnosed as suffering from atypical connective tissue disease, an autoimmune disease that her expert witnesses attributed to silicone gel.

Plaintiff sued, alleging negligent design and warnings claims, statutory consumer protection claims, along with breach of the implied warranty of merchantability. A jury found defendant liable on both the negligence and breach of warranty claims and awarded damages. After the trial court entered judgment, defendant appealed.]

* * *

We conclude that the determinations of liability as to the negligence and [consumer protection] claims are correct, and the judgment can be affirmed on this basis. As a result, we need not consider the defendants' arguments concerning the warranty findings.

We conclude, however, that we should change our products liability law to conform to the clear majority rule regarding what has to be shown to recover in a breach of warranty claim for failure to warn of risks associated with a product, and we do so in Part 3 of this opinion.

* * *

Doctor Bruce Freundlich, chief of rheumatology at Graduate Hospital in Philadelphia and an associate professor of medicine at the University of Pennsylvania, indicated that silicone gel breast implants can cause atypical connective tissue disease with a variety of symptoms that can include joint pain, dry eyes and mouth, difficulty sleeping leading to chronic fatigue, breast pain, fever, reduced sensation in the hands and feet, hair loss, itching, problems swallowing, and heartburn. Doctor Freundlich also offered his opinion that Mrs. Vassallo was suffering from atypical autoimmune disease, based on a review of her medical records and a physical examination that revealed [a variety of symptoms, all attributed to her exposure to silicone gel.]

      *   *   *

There was also extensive testimony as to knowledge, attributable to the defendants, of the risks of silicone gel breast implants up to the time of Mrs. Vassallo's implant surgery in 1977. According to Heyer–Schulte's own internal correspondence, the company was aware of a "Talk Paper," issued by the United States Food and Drug Administration in 1976, that documented migration to the brain, lungs, and heart, and death following injections of liquid silicone into the human body. In 1976, Heyer–Schulte received a report of an animal study, partially funded by Heyer–Schulte and conducted using miniature silicone gel implants supplied by Heyer–Schulte, that documented migration of gel from ruptured implants to the surrounding connective tissues and local inflammatory responses with fibroblastic activity and giant cell formation. The authors of the study stated: "The present tendency by manufacturers of breast implants towards ever thinner envelopes and a filler that is getting further away from gel and closer to silicone liquid must be looked at in the light of these experimental findings, and the question must be asked whether the possible advantages of these changes outweigh the disadvantages." Heyer–Schulte was also aware that some of their implants were rupturing, having received 129 complaints of ruptured gel implants in 1976. In fact, the president of Heyer–Schulte had written in 1975 that "[p]resently, mammary implants have been designed to be increasingly fragile in response to plastic surgeons' demand for softness, realistic feel and mobility." As a result, Heyer–Schulte knew that its implants were "not consistent as far as durability or destructibility is concerned." The encapsulation of the implant, and the viscous nature of the silicone gel, made it difficult to detect that a rupture had occurred, allowing the silicone to leak into the body for long periods before explantation. By 1975, Heyer–Schulte also knew that, even without a rupture of the implant shell, the silicone gel could leak (known as "gel bleed") through to the exterior surface of the implant and possibly produce "detrimental effect[s]" in the body.

Despite this knowledge of the possible adverse long-term consequences of leaking silicone in the body, Heyer–Schulte conducted few animal, and no clinical, studies to document the safety and efficacy of its silicone gel implants. When Heyer–Schulte began using silicone gel manufactured by Dow Corning in 1976, they relied primarily on the animal testing conducted by Dow Corning, despite the observations of a Heyer–Schulte scientist that "the data ... [did] not answer questions concerning migration," and "was lacking in quality and left many questions unanswered." Heyer–Schulte did conduct toxicity testing on the Dow Corning gel; the gel passed the seven-day and thirty-day toxicity tests, but failed the ninety-day toxicity test based on the microscopic tissue evaluation that showed considerably greater fibrous tissue reaction and inflammation to the silicone gel than to the control material. There is no indication in the record that Heyer–Schulte ever repeated this ninety-day toxicity test, and the company continued to use the Dow Corning gel in the manufacture of their silicone gel breast implants.

Heyer–Schulte did furnish warnings to physicians concerning their silicone gel implants in a product insert data sheet (PIDS). The 1976 version of the PIDS that accompanied Mrs. Vassallo's implants included warnings that the implant shell could be easily cut or ruptured by excessive stresses, and that Heyer–Schulte could not guarantee gel containment in the case of a rupture. The warnings did not address the issue of gel bleed, the fact that a rupture could result from normal stresses and could persist undetected for a significant time period, or the consequences of gel migration in the body. The PIDS also contained a list of potential complications associated with breast implants, but this list did not address the risks of chronic inflammation, permanent tissue scarring, or possible effects on the immune system. * * *

        * * *

[Defendant challenged the admissibility of all of plaintiff's expert witnesses, in part because there was no epidemiologic study documenting a relationship between silicone gel and autoimmune disease. The trial court overruled the objections, and on appeal the court concluded the testimony was properly admitted. The court explained that the trial judge "appears to have accepted the testimony of an expert epidemiologist that, in the absence of epidemiology, it is 'sound science . . . to rely on case reports, clinical studies, in vivo tests, [and] animal tests.' "[13]]

The evidence warrants the jury's findings (and their verdicts) on the negligence claims, and the defendants' arguments seeking judgment in their favor or a new trial on the negligence claims have been considered and rejected. No issue is raised as to the amount of damages awarded.

Because the plaintiffs' recoveries can be upheld on the jury's findings of negligence, we need not address the defendants' claims of error concerning the breach of warranty count. We take this opportunity, however, to consider the defendants' argument that we should change our products liability law concerning the implied warranty of merchantability from what is stated in *Hayes v. Ariens Co.*, 391 Mass. 407, 413, 462 N.E.2d 273 (1984), and that the law should be reformulated to adopt a "state of the art" standard that conditions a manufacturer's liability on actual or constructive knowledge of the risks.

Our current law, regarding the duty to warn under the implied warranty of merchantability, presumes that a manufacturer was fully informed of all risks associated with the product at issue, regardless of the

---

13. Although epidemiological studies have been conducted to investigate the associations between silicone breast implants and various diseases, none of these studies has addressed the disease at issue in this trial, namely, atypical connective tissue disease.

state of the art at the time of the sale, and amounts to strict liability for failure to warn of these risks. See *Simmons v. Monarch Mach. Tool Co.,* 413 Mass. 205, 207–208 n. 3, 596 N.E.2d 318 (1992); *Hayes, supra.* This rule has been justified by the public policy that a defective product, "unreasonably dangerous due to lack of adequate warning[s], [is] not fit for the ordinary purposes for which [it is] used regardless of the absence of fault on [a defendant's] part." *Id.*

At trial, the defendants requested a jury instruction that a manufacturer need only warn of risks "known or reasonably knowable in light of the generally accepted scientific knowledge available at the time of the manufacture and distribution of the device." The judge declined this request, and instead gave an instruction using language taken almost verbatim from that in *Hayes, supra.* While the judge's instruction was a correct statement of our law, we recognize that we are among a distinct minority of States that applies a hindsight analysis to the duty to warn.[17]

The majority of States, either by case law or by statute, follow the principle expressed in Restatement (Second) of Torts § 402A comment j (1965), which states that "the seller is required to give warning against [a danger], if he has knowledge, or by the application of reasonable, developed human skill and foresight should have knowledge, of the ... danger." See, e.g., Restatement (Third) of Torts: Products Liability, Reporters' Note to comment m, at 104 (1998) ("An overwhelming majority of jurisdictions supports the proposition that a manufacturer has a duty to warn only of risks that were known or should have been known to a reasonable person"). At least three jurisdictions that previously applied strict liability to the duty to warn in a products liability claim have reversed themselves, either by statute or by decision, and now require knowledge, or reasonable knowability as a component of such a claim. The change in the law of New Jersey is particularly relevant, because we relied in part on New Jersey law in formulating the strict liability standard expressed in the *Hayes* decision. See *Hayes, supra* at 413, 462 N.E.2d 273, citing *Beshada v. Johns–Manville Prods. Corp.,* 90 N.J. 191, 202–207, 447 A.2d 539 (1982).

The thin judicial support for a hindsight approach to the duty to warn is easily explained. The goal of the law is to induce conduct that is capable of being performed. This goal is not advanced by imposing liability for failure to warn of risks that were not capable of being known.

The Restatement (Third) of Torts: Products Liability § 2(c) (1998), recently approved by the American Law Institute, reaffirms the principle expressed in Restatement (Second) of Torts, *supra* at § 402A comment j, by stating that a product "is defective because of inadequate instructions or warnings when the foreseeable risks of harm posed by the product could have been reduced or avoided by the provision of reasonable instruc-

---

17. The Reporters' Note to the Restatement (Third) of Torts: Products Liability § 2(c) comment m, at 106 (1998), lists four States taking the position that a manufacturer is charged with a duty to warn of risks without regard to whether the manufacturer knew or reasonably should have known of the risks, including Massachusetts.

tions or warnings … and the omission of the instructions or warnings renders the product not reasonably safe." The rationale behind the principle is explained by stating that "[u]nforeseeable risks arising from foreseeable product use … by definition cannot specifically be warned against." Restatement (Third) of Torts: Products Liability, *supra* at § 2 comment m, at 34. However, comment m also clarifies the manufacturer's duty "to perform reasonable testing prior to marketing a product and to discover risks and risk-avoidance measures that such testing would reveal. A seller is charged with knowledge of what reasonable testing would reveal." *Id.*

We have stated that liability under the implied warranty of merchantability in Massachusetts is "congruent in nearly all respects with the principles expressed in Restatement (Second) of Torts § 402A." The main difference has been our application of a hindsight approach to the duty to warn of (and to provide adequate instructions regarding) risks associated with a product. * * *

In recognition of the clear judicial trend regarding the duty to warn in products liability cases, and the principles stated in Restatement (Third) of Torts: Products Liability, *supra* at § 2(c) and comment m, we hereby revise our law to state that a defendant will not be held liable under an implied warranty of merchantability for failure to warn or provide instructions about risks that were not reasonably foreseeable at the time of sale or could not have been discovered by way of reasonable testing prior to marketing the product. A manufacturer will be held to the standard of knowledge of an expert in the appropriate field, and will remain subject to a continuing duty to warn (at least purchasers) of risks discovered following the sale of the product at issue. * * *[19]

        * * *

The judgments are affirmed.

NOTES AND QUESTIONS

1. Why doesn't the overruled instruction presuming the defendant's knowledge of the risks for warranty claims require reversal of the plaintiff's judgment and a retrial with the correct instructions?

2. In the cited *Beshada* case, which involved several asbestos claimants, the court unanimously decided that the foreseeability of asbestotic disease was irrelevant and that knowledge of the risks would be "imputed" to the defendants based on what was known at the time of trial, regardless of the "state of the art" at the time of manufacture. Even if the dangers were undiscoverable, given the state of scientific knowledge at the time of manufacture, defendants could be found liable for failing to warn of those dangers.

---

19. As previously stated, the jury's verdict on the negligence count precludes the defendants from benefiting from this change in the warranty law. Moreover, the jury appears to have found that the defendants did have actual or constructive knowledge of risks associated with the silicone breast implants that were not contained in any warnings issued with the product.

Two years later, the same court retreated, holding that knowledge of risk must be available at the time of manufacture. Defendants who claimed that the risk was scientifically unknowable were afforded an affirmative defense, thereby imposing the burden of proof on them to show unknowability. The court explained that it was not overruling *Beshada* but limiting it "to the circumstances giving rise to its holding," without explaining what those circumstances were. Feldman v. Lederle Labs., 479 A.2d 374, 388 (N.J.1984). Unlike New Jersey, the Third Restatement on Products Liability leaves the burden of proving foreseeability of risk on plaintiff. How much do you think it matters how the burden of proof is allocated? How are the parties likely to prove either the existence of such knowledge or its absence?

Much of the controversy over this state of the art issue is how specifically the risk should be described or understood. There is widespread agreement that some cases of asbestotic disease, likely non-malignant asbestosis, emerged in the early part of the twentieth century among those who worked with raw asbestos. Defendants, however, claimed that they didn't know of the risks of other diseases—lung cancer and mesothelioma—until later, in part because of the longer latency periods associated with them. Or they contended that while they were aware of disease among those working with raw asbestos, they did not appreciate that there were risks to those who work with finished products that contained asbestos, such as insulation. The difference, of course, is that there is a lower dose of asbestos to which the latter were exposed. Sometimes, the argument is that some forms of asbestos do not cause certain diseases that other asbestos fibres have been shown to cause. This controversy continues to the latter stages of asbestos litigation. For example, the Delaware Supreme Court recently upheld a judgment on behalf of an auto mechanic who was exposed to asbestos in brake pads despite the defendants argument that asbestos incorporated into brakes has its chemistry changed due to heating and therefore does not cause the same diseases as other asbestos does. See General Motors Corp. v. Grenier, 981 A.2d 531 (Del.2009). Plaintiffs have adopted a similar strategy of narrowing the relevant disease for causation purposes. Thus, in *Vassallo*, the plaintiff claimed that she suffered from "atypical autoimmune disease." Epidemiologic studies up to that point had failed to find any causal relation between silicone gel breast implants and classical autoimmune diseases, such as Lupus or Multiple Sclerosis. But no epidemiology had examined the relationship between implants and the autoimmune disease with which the plaintiff claimed she suffered. See Chapter 5, Section 3 for a discussion of "atypical connective tissue disease" and the admissibility of expert testimony in the silicone gel breast implant cases.

3. As *Vassallo* and the Third Restatement document, there is very little imputing of knowledge left in contemporary strict liability doctrine. Is there as little to recommend it as the *Vassallo* court suggested in its brief passage stating that sellers cannot be expected to warn of unknown dangers? In this respect, reconsider the Schwartz excerpt at pp. 24–37.

4. *State of the art.* The *Vassallo* court described the issue it decided as one involving the "state of the art." The term is often used for a different meaning. In design defect cases, the "state of the art" may refer to existing technology that might be employed for an alternative and safer design. Like knowledge of risk, technology improves over time. Indeed, state of the art with regard to alternative designs can have a spectrum of meanings from not yet scientifically recognized or developed to something approaching the custom adopted in the relevant industry in employing safety devices. See Gary C. Robb, Practical Approach to Use of State of the Art Evidence in Strict Products Liability Cases, 77 Nw.U.L.Rev. 1 (1982).

5. After the *Vassallo* court decided that plaintiff must prove that defendant had or should have had knowledge of the risks for a strict liability warnings claim, what is the difference between a strict liability and negligence warnings claim?

6. The defendant claimed that the plaintiff had failed to prove that its breast implants cause autoimmune disease. Of course, the breast implants she received had no warnings about that disease. In these circumstances where the parties dispute whether there is a causal relationship, the issues of inadequate warnings and causation tend to merge together, aside from the state of the art issue.

7. Exactly when, if ever, in light of the chronology set forth by the court, was there sufficient knowledge available that the defendant should have provided a warning about autoimmune disease? Or is that not an accurate statement of the warnings issue?

b. Unavoidably Unsafe Products and Design and Warnings Defects

GRAHAM v. WYETH LABORATORIES

United States District Court for the District of Kansas, 1987.
666 F.Supp. 1483.

PATRICK F. KELLY, DISTRICT JUDGE.

* * * Plaintiffs Charles and Tammy Graham claim their infant daughter, Michelle Graham, sustained severe and irreversible brain damage after being vaccinated against diptheria, pertussis (whooping cough) and tetanus. The DPT vaccine she received was manufactured and distributed by defendant Wyeth Laboratories ("Wyeth").

The plaintiffs, parents and daughter, brought this diversity action asserting claims of strict liability and negligence for design defect and failure to warn, breach of the implied warranties of merchantability and fitness for a particular purpose, and intentional misrepresentation. * * *

Defendant has moved for summary judgment, contending * * * that under Kansas laws as set forth in *Johnson v. American Cyanamid,* 239 Kan. 279, 718 P.2d 1318 (1986), this court must find as a matter of law that DPT vaccine is an "unavoidably unsafe" prescription drug which contains an adequate warning, and enter judgment in defendant's behalf.

After considering all well-pleaded facts in plaintiffs' favor, the court is convinced that defendant is not entitled to summary judgment and this case must proceed to trial. As will be explained herein, the court finds

* * * that *Johnson* is distinguishable from the case at bar and does not require the entry of judgment in defendant's behalf.

* * *

FACTS

Defendant Wyeth manufactures the DPT vaccine which is used to immunize children against the diseases of diptheria, pertussis (whooping cough) and tetanus (lockjaw). [Plaintiff claimed that the pertussis component of Wyeth's vaccine caused her neurological injury. The pertussis portion of the DTP vaccine was of the "whole cell" variety. Whole cell vaccines consist of the entire pertussis organism, which is first "killed," then administered to stimulate the body's immune system to provide protection against the disease. Unlike acellular or fractionated vaccines, which consist of only the portion of the organism that stimulates the immune system, whole cell vaccines "can cause adverse reactions which may be mild (local), or severe. Mild reactions may include swelling, fever, irritability, and crying spells. Severe reactions include encephalopathy, paralysis and death." The incidence of severe reactions is low, perhaps as low as one in 100,000. Pertussis vaccines were of the whole cell variety because of technical difficulties in isolating the portion of the cell that stimulated the immune system to develop antibodies to the disease.]

* * *

* * * The DPT vaccine containing the "whole cell" pertussis vaccine was licensed by the FDA in 1949. Due to the widespread use of the vaccine in this country, pertussis has virtually been eradicated. However, because of the persistent nature of the pertussis bacteria, there is a continuing and substantial risk of epidemics if the use of the vaccine were to decline significantly.

* * *

In recognition of the dangerous propensities of the whole cell vaccine, efforts have been made to develop a fractionated cell pertussis vaccine. During the 1950s, the Eli Lilly Company developed a "split cell" vaccine called Tri–Solgen. Early studies indicated this vaccine was less toxic than the whole cell and it was approved by the FDA in 1967. At that time, Lilly occupied a substantial share of the DPT market. In 1975, Lilly withdrew from the vaccine business and sold its Tri–Solgen vaccine to Wyeth. According to plaintiffs, in an effort to save on cost, Wyeth substituted its own "ingredients" (or "strains") into the Lilly "recipe" for the split cell vaccine. Wyeth then attempted to license this vaccine, but no license was granted by the FDA. Wyeth has made no further attempts to license a fractionated cell vaccine. Moreover, no such vaccine is licensed in this country today.* Of course, a pharmaceutical company is prohibited from marketing a product absent a license—to do so would constitute a criminal offense.

---

* [By the late 1990s that situation had begun to change and beginning around 2000, all pertussis vaccine was of the acellular variety.—Eds.]

On March 17, 1980, plaintiff Michelle Graham, who was only a few months old, was administered defendant's DPT vaccine by a nurse at a county office of the Missouri Department of Health. Shortly thereafter Michelle developed a severe and irreversible neurological condition known as encephalopathy. For the purposes of this motion, the court will assume the plaintiff's condition was caused by the pertussis vaccine.

Wyeth furnished medical practitioners who purchased the vaccine with pamphlets describing contra-indications and possible adverse reactions to the drug's use. The pamphlet in use at the time of Michelle Graham's immunization stated, in pertinent part:

> The below-listed serious, and occasionally fatal, adverse reactions *have been reported* following administration of pertussis-vaccine-containing preparations. The incidence of these reactions is unknown, but they seem to be exceedingly rare . . . :
>
> 1. Severe temperature elevations–105°F or higher.
> 2. Collapse with rapid recovery.
> 3. Collapse followed by prolonged prostration and a shock-like state.
> 4. Screaming episodes characterized by a prolonged period of peculiar crying during which the infant cannot be comforted.
> 5. Isolated convulsion(s) with or without fever.
> 6. Frank encephalopathy with changes in the level of consciousness, focal neurological signs, and convulsions with or without permanent neurological and/or mental deficit.
> 7. Thrombocytopenic purpura.
>
>   The occurrence of sudden-infant-death syndrome (SIDS) *has been reported* following administration of DTP. *The significance of these reports is unclear.* It should be kept in mind that the three primary immunizing doses of DTP are usually administered to infants between the age of 2 and 6 months and that approximately 85 percent of SIDS cases occur in the period 1 through 6 months of age. . . .
>
> . . . .
>
>   Occurrence of any of the following signs, symptoms, or conditions following administration is a contraindication to further use of this product and/or pertussis vaccine as the single antigen: fever over 103°F (39°C); convulsion(s) with or without accompanying fever; alterations of consciousness; focal neurological signs; screaming episodes (also call screaming fits); collapse; thrombocytopenic purpura.
>
>   The presence of an evolving or changing neurologic disorder is a contraindication to use.

(Emphasis added.) The pamphlet also contained a section entitled "Precautions"; Wyeth's precautions did not advise the doctor to determine the child's personal or family history of central nervous system disease or convulsions. Nor was the doctor advised as to treating adverse reactions.

Prior to the administration of the vaccine to Michelle Graham, Mrs. Graham was given some materials to read about the vaccine and was asked to sign a consent form. The information was prepared by the Missouri Department of Health and discussed the possible "side effects" from the vaccine, stating: "Rarely, about once in every 100,000 shots, inflammation of the brain (encephalitis) or brain damage may occur. Death may occur, even more rarely." The form warned that some children should not take the vaccine without consulting a doctor, including "[t]hose who have had convulsions or other problems of the nervous system," and "[t]hose who have had serious reactions to DTP shots before." The form invited the parent to ask questions prior to signing.

Mrs. Graham did have questions about the possibility of side effects. The nurse told her that the figures were "just statistics" and that "[i]t didn't really happen." When Mrs. Graham asked the nurse what would happen if she decided against having Michelle immunized, she was told that the state would have her immunized and would then place her in a foster home. Mrs. Graham agreed to the vaccine because she thought she had no choice.

As a result of Michelle Graham's severe and permanent injuries, plaintiffs filed suit in this court seeking compensation from Wyeth Labs. The thrust of plaintiffs' claims against Wyeth is that Wyeth has the technical know-how to develop (or design) a safer, yet equally efficacious, fractionated cell pertussis vaccine, but has refused to do so due to the increased manufacturing costs. Plaintiffs further assert that Wyeth has the technical ability to quantify the endotoxin level of each "batch" of vaccine produced, but has failed to do so. In this regard, plaintiffs contend the degree of endotoxin varies from vial to vial and lot to lot. Plaintiffs assert that Wyeth knew the reported risk factors of the whole cell vaccine were inaccurate and that the incidence of adverse reactions was actually much greater. Plaintiffs assert defendant had a duty to accurately disclose to the medical practitioner the inherent hazards of DPT, the contraindication to administering the vaccine, the alternatives to the whole cell vaccine, the likely results of refusing the vaccine, the antidotes to and treatment for adverse reactions to the vaccine, and early warning signs of an adverse reaction. Plaintiffs further assert Wyeth should have warned the medical practitioner to take a family history of the patient prior to administering the vaccine. As previously stated, plaintiffs proceed on theories of strict liability and negligence for design defect and failure to warn, breach of implied warranties, and intentional misrepresentation.

In ruling on a motion for summary judgment, the trial court conducts a threshold inquiry of the need for trial and grants summary judgment where no genuine issue of material fact exists and the moving party is entitled to judgment as a matter of law. * * *

     * * *

II. The Application of Kansas Law

Defendant argues that under Kansas law as stated in *Johnson v. American Cyanamid,* 239 Kan. 279, 718 P.2d 1318 (1986), it is entitled to summary judgment as to each of plaintiffs' claims. Defendant argues that in cases involving prescription biologics, which by their nature are "unavoidably unsafe," the public policy of Kansas, as set forth in *Johnson,* requires that such products be immune from challenge in the courts for defects in design. Defendant further argues that, pursuant to *Johnson,* this court must find the warning adequate as a matter of law.

In *Johnson,* the plaintiff contracted polio after his young daughter received her polio vaccine. * * *

* * *

The plaintiff brought an action in state court for design defect and failure to warn. * * * The jury found defendant Lederle liable on all claims * * *.

On appeal, the Kansas Supreme Court, in a 4–3 decision, reversed the verdict in its entirety, finding *no* liability on the part of Lederle. The court first discussed the history of the polio vaccine in some detail. As noted by the court, there are only two types of polio vaccines in existence—the Sabin vaccine and the Salk vaccine. The Sabin vaccine—which uses a live virus—was developed later than the "killed" Salk vaccine, and is the only type used in this country today. The court noted that the Salk vaccine is somewhat less efficacious than the Sabin vaccine, and that "[v]irtually all of the Western world utilizes the Sabin vaccine over the Salk vaccine in its public health programs." Nevertheless, the plaintiff had contended that defendant Lederle was strictly liable for design defect by virtue of using the Sabin-type vaccine rather than the Salk-type vaccine.

In finding the defendant free from *strict liability* on the design defect claim, the Kansas court adopted comment k to Section 402A of the Restatement (Second) of Torts. Comment k provides:

> k. *Unavoidably unsafe products.* There are some products which, in the present state of human knowledge, are quite incapable of being made safe for their intended and ordinary use. These are especially common in the field of drugs. An outstanding example is the vaccine for the Pasteur treatment of rabies, which not uncommonly leads to very serious and damaging consequences when it is injected. Since the disease invariably leads to a dreadful death, both the marketing and the use of the vaccine are fully justified, notwithstanding the unavoidably high degree of risk which they involve. Such a product, properly prepared, and accompanied by proper directions and warning, is not defective, nor is it *unreasonably* dangerous. The same is true of many other drugs, vaccines, and the like, many of which for this very reason cannot legally be sold except to physicians, or under the prescription of a physician. It is also true in particular of many new or experimental drugs as to which, because of the lack of

time and opportunity for sufficient medical experience, there can be no assurance of safety, or perhaps even of purity of ingredients, but such experience as there is justifies the marketing and use of the drug notwithstanding a medically recognizable risk. The seller of such products, again with the qualification that they are properly prepared and marketed, and proper warning is given where the situation calls for it, is not to be held to strict liability for unfortunate consequences attending their use, merely because he has undertaken to supply the public with an apparently useful and desirable product, attended with a known but apparently reasonable risk.

The Kansas Supreme Court found that the Sabin-type polio vaccine is "unavoidably unsafe" and entitled to comment k immunity as a matter of law. The court noted that "[t]he remote risk of contact polio is inherent in the Sabin-type vaccine and cannot be eliminated," but that it is an "apparently useful and desirable product attended with a known but apparently reasonable risk." The court observed that "[t]he trial judge should have heard the evidence on the issue of [comment k's application] outside the presence of the jury and made the determination thereon."

Having concluded that as a matter of law the defendant could not be held strictly liable for a defect in design, the court reasoned "this leaves only the possible liability of the adequacy of the warning provided by the manufacturer." [*Johnson*, 293 Kan. at 286, 718 P.2d 1318.] In this regard, the court first observed the drug manufacturer's duty is "to adequately warn the physician of a known risk." *Id.* Because the test used in determining warning issues is "reasonableness", the court reasoned that the plaintiff must show *negligence* on the part of the manufacturer. The court quoted at length from *Kearl v. Lederle Laboratories,* 172 Cal.App.3d 812, 218 Cal.Rptr. 453 (1985), in support of this proposition. * * *

The *Johnson* court began its analysis of the warning by noting that the plaintiff's doctor had been warned of the precise "adverse reaction" from which plaintiff suffered: "This, then, is not a failure to warn question, but rather a question of the adequacy of the warning." 239 Kan. at 288, 718 P.2d 1318. The court then analyzed and rejected each of plaintiff's arguments for finding the warning inadequate. In effect, the court reweighed the evidence presented at trial. The court found that nothing in the warning was misstated ("plaintiff did not challenge [the risk figures given] directly"), or omitted ("the warning clearly states the scientific fact that some persons in close contact with vaccines may develop a paralytic disease from such contact.... It hardly takes a medical degree to know that a person immune to the virus cannot acquire the disease."). An additional factor which the court noted in finding the warning adequate was that "[t]he warning given ... had been approved by the Federal Drug Administration and was consistent with an overwhelming bulk of the current medical opinion." The court concluded that the warning was adequate as a matter of law, and that the trial court erred by failing to direct a verdict in defendant's behalf.

     * * *

A. Design Defect

The defendant argues that in *Johnson* the Kansas Supreme Court held that *any* prescription biological vaccine is "unavoidably unsafe" as a matter of law, and thus this court must find Wyeth free from liability for design defect. In this court's view, however, the *Johnson* decision is not—nor is it intended to be—so far reaching.

In *Johnson,* the Kansas Supreme Court adopted comment k to Restatement (Second) of Torts § 402A. Section 402A imposes *strict liability* on a product manufacturer "who sells any product in a defective condition unreasonably dangerous to the user...." Strict liability differs from negligence in that it obviates the need to show the manufacturer acted unreasonably, or, in other words, that he knew or should have known of the risk posed by the product. Strict liability in a products case focuses only on whether the product was defective, thereby imputing knowledge of the defect to the manufacturer.

Comment k recognizes that some products, such as certain drugs, are so beneficial and necessary that the manufacturer of these products should not, in all instances, be held strictly liable for unforeseeable harm. "Society wishes to encourage the manufacture of ethical drugs, and the research and development of new drugs. The imposition of strict liability would stifle these goals." Schwartz, *Unavoidably Unsafe Products: Clarifying the Meaning and Policy Behind Comment k,* 42 Wash. & Lee L.Rev. 1139, 1141 (1985). Under comment k, if the drug is shown to be "unavoidably unsafe" (i.e., highly beneficial, yet inherently and unavoidably risky), the manufacturer cannot be held strictly liable for design defect *unless* the vaccine is improperly manufactured or contains an inadequate warning. Neither comment k nor *Johnson* stands for the rule that *all* prescription drugs are unavoidably unsafe as a matter of law. *See Toner v. Lederle Laboratories,* 732 P.2d 297, 308 ("We do not believe comment k was intended to provide nor should it provide all ethical drugs with blanket immunity from design defect claims.... [N]ot all drugs are so perfectly designed that they cannot be made more pure or more safe, or that there are not safer, suitable alternatives."). *Johnson* addressed only the Sabin-type polio vaccine, finding that particular vaccine to be unavoidably unsafe. In doing so, the court considered that while there was evidence of a somewhat safer alternative (the Salk-type vaccine), this alternative was not as efficacious. The court clearly recognized that whether or not the vaccine was "unavoidably unsafe" was an issue needing resolution ("[t]he trial judge should have heard the evidence on this issue outside the presence of the jury and made the determination thereon"), and not simply a tautology. Thus, the court did *not* find that drugs by definition are unavoidably unsafe.

The *Kearl* decision, cited with approval in *Johnson,* suggests the following approach in determining whether a given drug is unavoidably unsafe:

In our view, the decision as to whether a drug, vaccine, or any other product triggers unavoidably dangerous product exemption from strict liability design defect analysis, poses a mixed question of law and fact and can be made only after evidence is first taken, out of the jury's presence, on the relevant factors to be considered. [Citations omitted.] A trial court should take evidence as to: (1) whether, when distributed, [footnote omitted] the product was intended to confer an exceptionally important benefit that made its availability highly desirable; (2) whether the then-existing risk posed by the product both was "substantial" and "unavoidable"; and (3) whether the interest in availability (again measured as of the time of distribution) outweighs the interest in promoting enhanced accountability through strict liability design defect review. In determining the first aspect of the second factor (i.e., whether the risk posed was "substantial") a court should consider whether, at the time of distribution, the risk posed permanent or long-term disability (e.g., loss of body functions, organs, or death) as opposed to mere temporary or insignificant inconvenience (e.g., skin rash, minor allergic reaction, etc.). In determining the second aspect of the second factor (i.e., whether the risk posed was "unavoidable") a court should consider (i) whether the product was designed to minimize—to the extent scientifically knowable at the time it was distributed—the risk inherent in the product, and (ii) the availability—again, at the time of distribution—of any alternative product that would have as effectively accomplished the full intended purpose of the subject product.

218 Cal.Rptr. 453, 464. *See also, Toner v. Lederle Laboratories,* 732 P.2d 297, 305–09 ("Clearly, the comment contemplates a weighing of the benefit of the product against its risk ... the weighing must be done at the time the product is distributed to the plaintiff.... [T]he design must be as safe as the best available testing and research permits.... Knowledge of the product's risks based on reliable and obtainable information is imputed to the seller.").

This court is convinced that such factors *must* be considered before a court can determine whether a given drug falls within comment k's protection. In this case, the issue cannot be resolved as a matter of law at the summary judgment stage. Although defendant contends the whole cell DPT vaccine posed an *unavoidable* risk of severe injury, this is hotly contested by plaintiffs. Plaintiffs have submitted the affidavit of one of their experts, a Dr. Zahalsky, who will testify that Wyeth had the capability to produce a safer vaccine. Plaintiffs claim that Wyeth's own records substantiate this contention. Accordingly, there is an issue of material fact as to whether the "unsafety" of the DPT vaccine manufactured by Wyeth was unavoidable.

Even if this court had concluded—or were eventually to conclude—that the vaccine is "unavoidably unsafe," the plaintiffs could still pursue their design defect claim under a negligence theory. Syllabus ¶ 1 to *Johnson* states:

Although in standard products liability litigation plaintiff may utilize a strict liability design defect theory, such strict liability cause of action must be prohibited for public policy reasons where the product complained of is an unavoidably unsafe product within the purview of comment k to § 402A of Restatement (Second) of Torts (1963). *In such special circumstances, plaintiff may proceed on a design defect theory only on the basis of negligence.*

It is noteworthy that in the body of the opinion, *negligent* design defect is never mentioned or discussed, although this court understands it was a theory pursued at trial level. While the court is aware that Kansas is not a "syllabus state" (i.e., the body of the case, not the syllabus, controls in case of a conflict), the court is also aware that the Kansas Supreme Court justice who authors an opinion also writes its syllabus. Thus, while negligent design defect was not directly addressed in *Johnson,* there is at least limited authority—contained in the syllabus—that finding a drug to be "unavoidably unsafe" does not preclude the jury from considering the manufacturer's reasonableness. * * * The cases which have addressed the issue are in agreement that even though a product is deemed "unavoidably unsafe," the plaintiff may proceed under a negligence cause of action. Accordingly, this court must conclude that comment k's application does *not* shield the seller of a product from negligence claims. Such a result fits within the policy of comment k—i.e., by denying plaintiffs recovery based on finding the manufacturer strictly liable if the drug is dangerous, and requiring the plaintiff to prove *negligence,* the policy of encouraging the production and marketing of safe, useful products is furthered.

Of course, the inquiry into whether a manufacturer acted negligently is, in a general sense, similar to the comment k inquiry of whether a drug is unavoidably unsafe.Thus, in a case such as this where both theories (strict liability and negligence) are asserted, the evidence from which the court must determine if the product is unavoidably unsafe need *not* be heard outside the presence of the jury as it will be the *same* evidence from which the jury will determine negligence.

B. *Adequacy of Warning*

Even if the evidence in this case shows that Wyeth used the best available vaccine and the product was "unavoidably unsafe," it will not be entitled to comment k immunity if it did not provide an adequate warning.[7] The comment thus recognizes that while some products are inherently dangerous, the user has a right to know of these inherent risks so that he can make an informed decision; in the absence of such warning, the product is deemed to be defective.

An adequate warning is one that is reasonable under the circumstances. A warning may be inadequate in factual content, the expression of facts, or in the method by which it is conveyed. [*Wooderson v. Ortho*

---

7. Because Mrs. Graham was warned that brain damage could result from the vaccine, the issue before the court is not failure to warn, but rather, adequacy of the warning.

Pharmaceutical Corp., 235 Kan. 387, 400, 681 P.2d 1038.] In the case of mass innoculations, vaccinees must be informed,[8] in clear and simple terms, by the manufacturer of: (1) the reasonably foreseeable risk inherent in the product; (2) reasonable available alternative products (if any) and the reasonably foreseeable risks posed by such alternatives; and, in appropriate cases, (3) the reasonably foreseeable results of remaining untreated. The manufacturer's duty is to warn of all potential dangers which it knew, or in the exercise of reasonable care should have known, to exist. This duty is a continuous one, requiring the manufacturer to keep abreast of the current state of knowledge.

To impose liability on the defendant for inadequate warning, the plaintiff must show *negligence* on the part of the manufacturer. Accordingly, plaintiffs are precluded from asserting a claim of strict liability for failure to warn and summary judgment will be entered for defendant on that claim.

Defendant argues that the warning given was adequate as a matter of law. In this regard, defendant urges the court to find that *Johnson* is directly on point and *requires* a finding of adequate warning. This court cannot agree.

Johnson must necessarily be limited to its facts on the warning issue. As previously stated, the adequacy of a warning turns on its reasonableness *under the circumstances*. The *Johnson* court found that under the circumstances before it, reasonable minds could not differ on the adequacy of the warning. *Johnson* does nothing to change the factual nature of the inquiry.

It is well established in Kansas that whether a warning is adequate is an issue for the trier of fact. * * *

In this case the plaintiffs will offer evidence that the warning misstated the statistical incidence of severe reactions, failed to adequately identify the level of endotoxin in each vial or lot, and failed to state that persons with a family or personal history of seizures or central nervous system disorders should forego immunization and seek further medical evaluation prior to vaccination. Although defendant adamantly challenges these allegations, these are clearly issues which must be resolved by the trier of fact.

Defendant further argues that the court should find it non-negligent *per se* as the warning given had been approved by the FDA. However, * * * FDA standards are *minimum* standards. While the FDA's approval

---

    8. Generally, in the case of prescription drugs, the manufacturer's duty is to adequately warn the physician of known risks. *Johnson*, 239 Kan. at 286. This is known as the "learned intermediary" rule. However, there is authority that when a vaccine is dispensed at a clinic without close supervision by a physician, the manufacturer's duty to warn extends to the vaccinee. In *Johnson*, the vaccine was administered by a doctor, and the court found that "under such circumstances" the learned intermediary rule applied. In the case at bar, the vaccine was administered by a nurse at a clinic. However, the plaintiffs herein seem to assume the learned intermediary doctrine applies.

    * * *

is a factor to be considered by the jury, it does not establish non-negligence *per se*. The *Johnson* decision is not to the contrary: the FDA's approval of the warning was only one of the several factors it considered in finding the warning adequate as a matter of law.

Finally, the defendant argues that this court must grant summary judgment on the warning claim because the inadequacy of the warning was not the proximate cause of Michelle Graham's injuries. In this regard, defendant asserts that Mrs. Graham based her decision to have her baby immunized *solely* on the nurse's remarks indicating that she had no other choice.

However, the defendant's argument fails to recognize the rule that if a jury finds a warning inadequate, causation is presumed. In other words, it is presumed that an adequate warning would be heeded by the patient. [*Wooderson*, 235 Kan. at 410, 681 P.2d 1038.] Thus, in this case, if an adequate warning had been given (assuming arguendo that the one given was inadequate), it is possible the nurse would have not said the things she did, or perhaps would have suggested alternatives. This, though, is a matter of pure speculation; hence, the presumption.

* * *

III. *Conclusion*

Vaccines such as the DPT vaccine play an important and critical role in this society. Millions of lives are saved. However, some innocent people—such as Michelle Graham—are grievously injured by these vaccines. * * * The fact that the vaccine manufacturer complied with FDA regulations is evidence that should be considered by a jury; however, these regulations set minimum standards. Manufacturers are *not* precluded from taking steps to improve their vaccine, or to better inform as to its dangerous propensities. In this case, the evidence must be heard before it can be determined that the whole cell vaccine was the safest and most efficacious available—in other words, that it was "unavoidably unsafe." And in any case, the adequacy of the warning is an issue for the trier of fact. Thus, this court will not rule that as a matter of law Michelle Graham will be denied any recourse. This case will proceed to trial.

IT IS ACCORDINGLY ORDERED this 21 day of July, 1987, that defendant's motion for summary judgment is granted as to plaintiffs' claim of strict liability for failure to warn, and is denied as to all remaining claims.

* * *

NOTES AND QUESTIONS

1. Later in 1987, after a two month jury trial, the jury found for the plaintiffs and awarded $15 million in compensatory damages. See Graham v. Wyeth Labs., 118 F.R.D. 511 (D.Kan.1988).

Comment k and Design Claims

2. Recall the discussion of categorical liability for a product with no alternative design available in the Schwartz excerpt and note 3 following that excerpt. Does it have any application to drugs, vaccines, and comment k?

3. *Unavoidably unsafe products.* What characteristic makes vaccines and drugs unavoidably unsafe while other consumer products are not? Is the absence of an alternative safer design the difference? If so, then how could Wyeth's vaccine, for which the court suggested there was an alternative design, be found unavoidably unsafe? Or is it whether the product, as formulated, provides more benefit than risk? Isn't that also true of virtually all consumer goods? Is it the rigorous FDA approval process prescription drugs must go through before they are approved for sale? Perhaps this is about whether the product has exceptionally beneficial qualities, as the court suggested. Consider a kidney dialysis machine that, because of the way the electrical system is designed, causes one in 10,000 of those treated to be electrocuted.

With regard to the availability of alternative designs, do you see why prescription drugs, at least single component drugs, are different from the pertussis vaccine involved in this case? Note that while another drug to treat the same condition might be thought of as an alternative, there are two significant advantages in having alternative drugs: (1) Some alternatives may be better for certain subpopulations of those treated, such as a drug that is somewhat less efficacious than other alternatives but gentler for those with compromised livers or a drug for acne that is limited to males and women past child-bearing age because the drug can cause birth defects; (2) There are individual variations that affect the efficacy of a given drug for a particular patient, so that physicians may try a second or third drug to treat a condition when the first one prescribed is not effective. Should medical devices be treated the same as prescription drugs under the comment k, unavoidably-unsafe-product approach?

4. In the cited *Johnson* case, the Kansas Supreme Court found that the Sabin polio vaccine was an unavoidably unsafe product and therefore not subject to a design defect claim. Approximately 10 years after *Johnson*, the Centers for Disease Control changed its recommendation for polio vaccination from use of the live-virus Sabin version to the killed-virus Salk vaccine. This occurred because wild-virus polio had been eradicated in the United States and the only incidence of polio occurring was vaccine induced from the Sabin vaccine. Today, most polio vaccinations employ the Salk vaccine. See Samuel L. Katz, From Culture to Vaccine–Salk and Sabin, 351 New Eng.J.Med. 1485 (2004).

5. The *Graham* court, relying on *Kearl v. Lederle Laboratories,* adopted a case-by-case balancing approach to whether Wyeth's vaccine is deserving of comment k protection. Some courts have provided more protection. Indeed, the *Kearl* case was rejected by the California Supreme Court in Brown v. Superior Court, 751 P.2d 470 (Cal.1988). *Brown* held that all prescription drugs should not be subject to design defect review. The Third Restatement, in section 6(d), adopts a provision that permits a design defect claim for prescription drugs or medical devices but only when the risks are sufficiently greater than the benefits that a reasonable health care provider would not prescribe the drug or device for any class of patients. Is this standard more limited than *Graham*? As limited as *Brown*?

6. *Consumer expectations.* What outcome for plaintiffs' design defect claim under a consumer expectations test? Whose expectations are relevant, the prescribing physician's or the patient's? Doesn't the matter of consumer expectations collapse into the question of whether there was an adequate warning?

7. *The negligent design claim.* The court concluded that, regardless of whether strict liability is available, the plaintiff may pursue a negligent design claim. The court also suggested, relying on the cited *Johnson* case, that the difference between a strict liability and negligence claim is that knowledge of risk is imputed in strict liability, while the plaintiff must prove in a negligence case that the manufacturer knew or should have known of the risk. Recall that in *Vassallo*, the court changed Massachusetts law so that knowledge of risk would no longer be imputed. In a jurisdiction like Massachusetts, what difference is there between a strict liability and negligent design claim? Doesn't that render comment k moot, at least in those jurisdiction that permit a negligent design claim for unavoidably unsafe products? Note that the Third Restatement on Products Liability subsumes both strict liability and negligence claims in the defect standards it provides, including section 6(d).

Warnings

8. In the introduction to the Warnings and Design Defects section of this Chapter, we noted that warnings can serve two functions—risk amelioration and providing informed consent. Which function(s) did the warning in the *Graham* case serve?

9. *Adequacy of the content.* The *Graham* court stated that a warning must be reasonable under the circumstances and provided three considerations that might guide warnings in mass vaccination situations. Another useful statement of the aspects of an adequate warning is contained in Pittman v. Upjohn Co., 890 S.W.2d 425, 429 (Tenn.1994):

> A reasonable warning not only conveys a fair indication of the dangers involved, but also warns with the degree of intensity required by the nature of the risk. Among the criteria for determining the adequacy of a warning are:
>
> 1. the warning must adequately indicate the scope of the danger; 2. the warning must reasonably communicate the extent or seriousness of the harm that could result from misuse of the drug; 3. the physical aspects of the warning must be adequate to alert a reasonably prudent person to the danger; 4. a simple directive warning may be inadequate when it fails to indicate the consequences that might result from failure to follow it and, ... 5. the means to convey the warning must be adequate.

Id. at 429 (citing Serna v. Roche Labs., 101 N.M. 522, 684 P.2d 1187, 1189 (App.1984)).

Can you think of other categories of information that should also be provided? In which respect was the warning provided by Wyeth for its vaccine inadequate according to the plaintiff?

10. *The means of conveyance.* The fifth item in the *Pittman* court's list recognizes that even the best of warnings will not serve their purpose unless they are adequately communicated to the relevant party. While the FDA regulates the method of conveyance for drugs and devices, for other products the method of conveyance is not regulated and left to manufacturer determination.

11. *The consequences of excessive detail.* The costs of providing warnings is quite low—only involving some paper and ink (or space on a website). Thus, the marginal cost of some additional detail appears to quite small, and one can, in hindsight, often identify additional specific details that might have contributed to a better understanding by the consumer. In Cotton v. Buckeye Gas Products Co., 840 F.2d 935, 937–38 (D.C.Cir.1988), the court identified another cost of accumulating warnings:

> Failure-to-warn cases have the curious property that, when the episode is examined in hindsight, it appears as though addition of warnings keyed to a particular accident would be virtually cost free. What could be simpler than for the manufacturer to add the few simple items noted above? The primary cost is, in fact, the increase in time and effort required for the user to grasp the message. The inclusion of each extra item dilutes the punch of every other item. Given short attention spans, items crowd each other out; they get lost in fine print. * * *

> Plaintiff's analysis completely disregards the problem of information costs. He asserts that "it would have been neither difficult nor costly for Buckeye to have purchased or created for attachment to its propane cylinders a clearer, more explicit label, such as the alternatives introduced at trial, warning of propane's dangers and instructing how to avoid them." * * * He [fails to consider] what the cannister warning would have looked like if Buckeye had supplemented it not only with the special items he is personally interested in—in hindsight—but also with all other equally valuable items * * *. If every foreseeable possibility must be covered, "[T]he list of foolish practices warned against would be so long, it would fill a volume."

12. *Learned intermediaries.* As the court stated in footnote 8, the learned intermediary doctrine requires a drug manufacturer only to warn the doctor who prescribes the drug. Note that the learned intermediary doctrine is not that the doctor must *also* be warned; rather it is that *only* the doctor need be warned, and the patient for whom the drug is prescribed does not have to be provided a warning by the drug manufacturer. What reasons might justify this exclusion of patients from receiving risk information? See Lars Noah, The Learned Intermediary Doctrine: A Sensible Duty Limitation or an Anachronism?, 10–Fall Kan.J.L. & Pub.Pol'y 98 (2000), providing three reasons: (1) not intruding on the doctor-patient relationship; (2) superior knowledge of physicians enabling them to tailor information for the needs of individual patients; and (3) lack of means for drug manufacturers to communicate with patients who receive prescription drugs in non-manufacturer-provided containers. Are these reasons persuasive? Has their power diminished in recent times?

The learned intermediary doctrine has not fared well in a few recent cases. In State v. Karl, 647 S.E.2d 899 (W.Va.2007), the court refused to adopt the learned intermediary doctrine. Characterizing it as outdated and not in keeping with modern conditions in the pharmaceutical industry and health care delivery, the court discussed direct to consumer advertising and the growth of the internet as the source of health care information and drug dispensing. Influenced by the West Virginia Supreme Court in *Karl*, Rimbert v. Eli Lilly & Co., 577 F.Supp.2d 1174 (D.N.M.2008), predicted that the New Mexico Supreme Court would also decline to adopt the learned intermediary defense.

As the *Graham* court explained, one exception to the learned-intermediary rule is mass immunization programs in which a doctor is not present and therefore making individualized determinations about the appropriateness of a vaccine. See, e.g., Brazzell v. United States, 788 F.2d 1352 (8th Cir.1986) (first swine-flu vaccination program).

13. *Bulk suppliers and sophisticated users.* Two other related doctrines that limit who must be warned and that are applicable outside the drug context concern bulk suppliers and sophisticated users. The two are often confused and Taylor v. American Chemistry Council, 576 F.3d 16 (1st Cir. 2009), goes a long way toward explaining differences between these two similar doctrines. To take the latter first, when a seller provides a dangerous product to users who are sophisticated and understand the risks involved in the product, no warning duty is imposed. The bulk supplier defense concerns the obligation to provide warnings to "downstream users" when the seller provides the product in bulk to its immediate buyer. This defense involves a balancing between the difficulties of communicating a warning to downstream users when the product is supplied in a bulk container with the foreseeable risks if such a warning is not communicated. Comment n to section 388 of the Restatement (Second) of Torts has been influential in both negligence and strict liability suits:

> [I]f the danger involved in the ignorant use of a particular chattel is very great, it may be that the supplier does not exercise reasonable care in entrusting the communication of the necessary information even to a person whom he has good reason to believe to be careful. Many such articles can be made to carry their own message to the understanding of those who are likely to use them by the form in which they are put out, by the container in which they are supplied, or by a label or other device, indicating with a substantial sufficiency their dangerous character. Where the danger involved in the ignorant use of their true quality is great and such means of disclosure are practicable and not unduly burdensome, it may well be that the supplier should be required to adopt them.

Restatement (Second) of Torts § 388 cmt. n.

In Higgins v. E.I. DuPont de Nemours & Co., 671 F.Supp. 1055 (D.Md. 1987), both the bulk supplier and sophisticated user doctrines were applicable. The plaintiffs (two firefighters whose children died at birth) sued two chemical suppliers and DuPont because paint that DuPont manufactured contained chemicals that posed a risk of causing birth defects. The paint was sold to the Baltimore City Fire Department, which distributed it throughout the fire department for use without any warnings. The court granted summary judgment to the two chemical suppliers on the ground that they had no duty to warn the ultimate purchaser because DuPont was a sophisticated user that understood the risks of the chemicals as well as the chemical suppliers and was in a better position to warn the purchaser than the chemical suppliers. Suppose DuPont had sought summary judgment on similar grounds, alleging that the Fire Department was knowledgeable about the risks and better situated to get information to its employees. The exclusive remedy bar to a tort suit by an employee against an employer for work-related injury, covered in Chapter 7, would not affect a suit on behalf of the deceased children or likely a consortium claim by their parents. See, e.g., Omori v. Jowa Hawaii Co., 981 P.2d 714 (Haw.App.1999).

14. *The causal issue in warnings cases.* The plaintiffs alleged that Wyeth should have provide more risk information about its pertussis vaccine. Even if it had, what difference would that information have made? Recall that Michelle's mother was told that if she refused to have her vaccinated, it would be done anyway (many, but not all, states require pertussis vaccination before a child can be admitted to school). While most warnings cases do not provide such strong evidence suggesting a lack of causation, in many there is considerable doubt about what plaintiff would have done if there had been greater disclosure. Some jurisdictions have adopted a "heeding presumption" that shifts the burden of coming forward with evidence and, in some jurisdictions, the burden of persuasion on causation to the defendant once plaintiff proves that the warning was inadequate, while others have rejected it. Compare Smith v. Brown & Williamson Tobacco Corp., 275 S.W.3d 748 (Mo.App.2008) (heeding presumption applied to smoker's claim of inadequate warnings), with Rivera v. Philip Morris, Inc., 209 P.3d 271 (Nev.2009) (declining to adopt a heeding presumption in a smoking case on the ground that the burden of proof on causation should remain with the plaintiff).

We should note the interaction of proof of causation and the learned intermediary rule. Since the prescribing physician is the relevant decision-maker, the causation issue in a drug-warnings case is whether the physician would have done something differently with regard to the drug prescribed for the plaintiff. If the doctor testifies either that she already knew about omitted information or that her prescribing decision would not have been affected by it, the plaintiff will be unable to prove causation. See Eck v. Parke, Davis & Co., 256 F.3d 1013 (10th Cir.2001) (heeding presumption rebutted by testimony of prescribing physician that even if warning of dangerous drug interaction had been provided, physician would still have prescribed same drug).

C. THEORIES RELATING TO ACTIVITIES ON LAND

Two different tort theories protect interests in land, and it is difficult to discuss them separately. Any discussion of protection of those interests also requires attention to available remedies. Trespass is designed to protect an owner or possessor's interest in exclusive possession and control of land. Nuisance, on the other hand, protects the possessor's "quiet enjoyment" and use of the land. While a technical trespass occurs whenever someone intentionally enters property owned by another without consent of the owner, damages are limited to actual harm caused and "nominal" damages. Nominal damages, usually in the amount of one dollar, recognize the owner's right of exclusive possession and its violation, but do not provide much incentive for modern tort claims. Nuisance claims, by contrast, require real injury in the form of significant diminution of the benefit of using and enjoying one's land. These two tort theories are applicable to environmental contaminants that affect land or its use. They may also support damages for personal injuries caused by those contaminants when the injuries are consequential to the property invasion. They obviously have no role in the consumer and occupational product context that we examined in the previous two sections of this chapter.

Note that trespass is an "intentional" tort. But the intent required is different from that for the traditional intentional torts, such as assault and battery. The intent requirement merely requires an intent to enter the property and thus does not necessarily involve culpable behavior, such as when the trespasser has a genuine belief that the entry is legitimate. In this sense, trespass is also a "strict liability" tort in that it does not require wrongdoing. In addition to intentional trespass, one may be liable for negligence in entering another's property. Finally, one can be liable for engaging in an abnormally dangerous activity that invades another's property (entry can be by a person or an inanimate object).

In recent years, some courts have blurred the line between trespass and nuisance. Trespass traditionally required a "direct" entry of the trespasser or by some tangible property. The direct entry requirement was a product of the common law writ system and has been abandoned today. But consider whether invisible flouride compounds that are the by-product of an aluminum plant that settle on another's property constitute a trespass. Rejecting historical notions of what constitutes trespass, the court in Martin v. Reynolds Metals Co., 342 P.2d 790 (Or.1959), decided that "the object's energy or force rather its size" is the better consideration for determining trespass. Thus, invisible chemical compounds that made the land unusable to raise livestock constituted a trespass. No doubt, the impact of those chemicals was also a nuisance, but because of different statutes of limitations for the two torts, the court was required to determine whether a trespass was also committed. Trespass, as well, may be a preferable theory for a plaintiff because it does not require an unreasonable intrusion, as nuisance does.

Courts that have permitted intangible invasions to constitute a trespass have tended to adopt some limitations from nuisance law. Thus, some courts insist on there being actual damage for trespass to lie, thereby eliminating nominal damages and, even more importantly, injunctive relief requiring the defendant to cease trespassing. Other courts have insisted on actual and substantial damages for a trespass claim arising from an intangible invasion.

A wide variety of operations and conduct with toxic substances may result in a trespass or nuisance action. If hazardous waste is disposed of, chemicals are used, or radioactive material is stored in a way that they may reach or affect another's property, either by leaching through the ground or traveling in a body of water or through the air, these tort claims are implicated. The hazardous waste or chemicals may foul a well, harm landscaping, create unpleasant odors, cause physical injury, harm crops, or cause other related injuries.

1. TRESPASS TO LAND

JOHN LARKIN, INC. v. MARCEAU

Supreme Court of Vermont, 2008.
184 Vt. 207, 959 A.2d 551.

JOHNSON, J.

Real estate developers, who sued a neighboring landowner for trespass based on the neighbor's spraying of pesticides in his apple orchard, appeal the superior court's decision rejecting their trespass theory. Because the developers failed to make a showing sufficient to survive the neighbor's motion for summary judgment, we affirm the court's judgment in favor of the neighbor.

Plaintiffs John Larkin, Inc. and Larkin Family Partnership (Larkin) own undeveloped land adjoining that of defendant J. Edward Marceau, Jr., who operates an apple orchard on his property. Larkin purchased the property from Marceau's former spouse in 2001 for the purpose of building a residential development. To increase the density of the proposed development, Larkin later obtained a transfer of the development rights from Marceau's property and another adjoining parcel of land.

* * *

In March 2005, * * * Larkin filed suit against Marceau, seeking injunctive and compensatory relief based on Marceau's spraying of pesticides in his orchard. The lawsuit sounded in trespass, with Larkin alleging that winds carried detectable levels of pesticides onto its property, thereby damaging the property. In his answer to the complaint, Marceau asserted, among other things, that Larkin had failed to state a claim upon which relief could be granted, that the claims were not ripe, and that the claims were barred by Vermont's right-to-farm law, 12 V.S.A. §§ 5751–5754, which establishes a rebuttable presumption that agricultural activities are not a nuisance. *Id.* § 5753(a)(1). The superior court initially dismissed the trespass claim, but later allowed it to proceed beyond the pleadings stage.

In January 2007, after discovery was closed, Marceau moved for summary judgment, arguing that Larkin was in fact making a nuisance claim but couching the complaint in terms of trespass to circumvent the right-to-farm law. Larkin opposed the motion and filed a cross-motion for summary judgment * * *. Concluding that Larkin's suit actually sounded in nuisance rather than trespass, the superior court stated that it would not endorse the fiction that Marceau's pesticides occupied Larkin's land, which would allow Larkin to evade the Legislature's plain intent to offer heightened protection to agricultural activities with respect to claims of this nature. The court declined to grant either party summary judgment, however, stating that the right-to-farm law did not necessarily preclude Larkin's complaint from surviving a motion for summary judgment insofar as the law established only a rebuttable presumption that no nuisance existed. The parties later stipulated to dismissal of Larkin's claims to the extent that they sounded in nuisance, and the superior court entered a final judgment against Larkin.

On appeal, Larkin argues that: (1) the superior court erred by recharacterizing its trespass action as a nuisance action subject to the right-to-farm law and thus effectively dismissing its trespass claim; (2) the right-to-farm law does not insulate farmers from liability for trespass, regardless of the nature of the trespass; and (3) the right-to-farm law is an unconstitutional taking to the extent that it permits farmers to deposit pesticides on neighbors' lands in a manner that precludes use of those lands. In response, Marceau argues that Larkin's claims are actually nuisance claims subject to the right-to-farm law, and that Larkin cannot avoid that law by alleging trespass. * * * We conclude that Larkin failed to make a showing sufficient to survive summary judgment on its trespass claim, and thus affirm the superior court's judgment in favor of Marceau.

The parties frame the primary issue as whether the deposit of airborne particulates on land may sound in trespass rather than nuisance. They both acknowledge the accepted distinction "that trespass is an invasion of the plaintiff's interest in the exclusive possession of his land, while nuisance is an interference with his use and enjoyment of it." W. Keeton et al., Prosser and Keeton on the Law of Torts § 87, at 622 (5th ed.1984). Compare Restatement (Second) of Torts § 158 cmt. c, at 277 (1965) (describing trespass as an "intrusion" invading "the possessor's interest in the exclusive possession of his land" (internal quotations omitted)) with Restatement (Second) of Torts § 821D cmt. d, at 101 (1979) (defining nuisance as "an interference with the interest in the private use and enjoyment of the land [that] does not require interference with the possession," and distinguishing trespass as "an invasion of the interest in the exclusive possession of land"). Larkin claims that Marceau's application of pesticides that settle onto its property effectively ousted it from the property. Marceau counters that Larkin is actually asserting a loss in the use and enjoyment of its property, which is a claim sounding in nuisance.

Traditionally, courts held that although a personal entry is unnecessary for trespass to take place, a defendant's act "must cause an invasion of the plaintiff's property by some tangible matter." See *Maddy v. Vulcan Materials Co.*, 737 F.Supp. 1528, 1539 (D.Kan.1990) (citing cases); see also

Adams v. Cleveland–Cliffs Iron Co., 237 Mich.App. 51, 602 N.W.2d 215, 219 (Ct.App.1999) (citing cases); D. Dobbs, The Law of Torts § 50, at 96 (2001) ("The law of nuisance deals with indirect or intangible interference with an owner's use and enjoyment of land, while trespass deals with direct and tangible interferences with the right to exclusive possession of land."). Plaintiffs showing a direct and tangible invasion of their property may obtain injunctive relief and at least nominal damages without proof of any other injury. *Adams,* 602 N.W.2d at 219.

On the other hand, plaintiffs claiming a nuisance have to demonstrate actual and substantial injury. *Id.* Under this traditional view, the intrusion of smoke, gas, noise, or other invisible particles onto another's property is not actionable as a trespass, but only as a private nuisance. Keeton, *supra,* § 13, at 71; see Dobbs, *supra,* § 53, at 105 (explaining that courts have been reluctant to allow trespass actions based on the invasion of microscopic or intangible particles because trespass "provided no mechanism for limiting liability to serious or substantial invasions").

Some courts eventually adopted a so-called "modern" theory of trespass that permits actions based on the invasion of intangible airborne particulates. Compare *Maddy,* 737 F.Supp. at 1539–40 (explaining and adopting "modern trend" of trespass) with *Adams,* 602 N.W.2d at 220–21 (explaining and rejecting "modern view" of trespass). Under this modern theory, invasions of intangible matter are actionable in trespass only if they cause substantial damage to the plaintiff's property, sufficient to be considered an infringement on the plaintiff's right to exclusive possession of the property. Hence, the modern view "departs from traditional trespass rules by refusing to infer damages as a matter of law" with respect to intangible invasions of property, as would be the case with direct, tangible invasions of property. *Maddy,* 737 F.Supp. at 1539; *Bradley v. Am. Smelting & Ref. Co.,* 104 Wash.2d 677, 709 P.2d 782, 791 (1985) (en banc) (explaining that trespass from airborne particles cannot occur unless plaintiff has suffered actual and substantial damages).

At least one court has rejected this modern view and held that recovery for trespass is available "only upon proof of an unauthorized direct or immediate intrusion of a physical, tangible object onto land over which the plaintiff has a right of exclusive possession." *Adams,* 602 N.W.2d at 222. In so holding, the Michigan court reasoned that requiring a showing of substantial damage for a trespass of intangible matter would "conflate [ ] nuisance with trespass to the point of rendering it difficult to delineate the difference between the two theories of recovery" and would weaken property owners' automatic right of exclusion in traditional trespass cases involving invasions of tangible objects. *Id.* at 221; see Keeton, *supra,* § 13, at 72 ("The historical requirement of an intrusion by a person or some tangible thing seems the sounder way to go about protecting the exclusive right to the use of property.").

In considering these alternatives, we note that Vermont law is silent on this issue, although we have recently looked to the Restatement of

Torts for guidance on the law of trespass and nuisance. See, e.g., *Harris v. Carbonneau,* 165 Vt. 433, 437, 685 A.2d 296, 299 (1996) (citing Restatement § 158 in defining liability for trespass); *Canton,* 171 Vt. at 552, 762 A.2d at 810 (citing Restatement §§ 158. 821D, and 833 in defining liability for trespass and comparing nuisance). But neither the Restatement provisions nor their accompanying commentaries address the thorny question of whether the dispersion of particulate matter on property may be actionable as a trespass in addition to a nuisance. The Restatement does note, however, that the two actions are not necessarily exclusive and may overlap. Restatement (Second) of Torts § 821D cmt. e, at 102; see *Bradley,* 709 P.2d at 790 (noting that "remedies of trespass and nuisance are not necessarily mutually exclusive") (quotations omitted).

We recognize that the dispersion of airborne particles, whatever their nature, may technically be considered an entry onto land creating liability for trespass irrespective of whether any damage was caused. Because the ambient environment always contains particulate matter from many sources, such a technical reading of trespass would subject countless persons and entities to automatic liability for trespass absent any demonstrated injury. Plainly, that cannot be the law–and, as far as we can tell, no jurisdiction has so held. The question, then, is whether the physical entry onto land of intangible airborne particulates can ever be a trespass, or whether such an invasion may be actionable only as a nuisance. Because Larkin has failed to demonstrate any impact on its property from Marceau's pesticides, we find it unnecessary in this case to adopt a hardline position that the dispersion of airborne particulates on property may never be actionable as a trespass, irrespective of the nature of the invasion or the right invaded. We leave for another day the question of whether the intrusion of airborne particulates may ever be a trespass, and, if so, what impact is required to sustain such an action.

Here, absent a demonstrated physical impact on Larkin's property resulting from the airborne particulates, the superior court did not err in granting summary judgment to Marceau. When particles enter the ambient environment without any demonstrated impact on the land, we fail to see how a trespass has occurred. In such a case, there is no ouster from the land, as Larkin claims here, and no interference with the landowner's right to exclusive possession of the land. Hence, under such circumstances, the landowner has no action in trespass. In a traditional trespass action, the right to exclusive possession of property may not depend on an analysis of the impact on the use of the land, but we cannot presume an intrusion on that right in situations where the plaintiff fails to show that an intangible invasion of airborne particulates had a demonstrated physical impact.

Despite having an opportunity during discovery to make out a case of trespass under the modern view examining the nature of the right invaded, Larkin failed to make any showing whatsoever that the presumed dispersion of detectable levels of pesticides onto its property from Marceau's orchard deprived it of exclusive possession of its property or had any other impact on the property. Larkin makes only a bald assertion that it has been ousted from its property because of the presumed detectable level of pesticides landing on the property, and because Marceau requested, and the Agency of Agriculture recommended, that there be a buffer zone to avoid any potential conflict over use of the adjoining properties. Larkin neither conducted depositions nor offered any expert testimony. Nor did Larkin proffer evidence indicating the extent of the dispersion of pesticides on its property or any potential safety or health concerns related to the pesticide use. * * *

Without question, there are situations in which both trespass and nuisance—two distinct actions that are not mutually exclusive—will be cognizable in the same lawsuit. This is not such a case, however.

Given our affirmance of the trial court's order rejecting Larkin's trespass action, and the parties' stipulation for dismissal of the nuisance action, we need not address Larkin's constitutional arguments.

Affirmed.

NOTES AND QUESTIONS

1. Often whether a claim is one in trespass or nuisance is of little consequence, but because of the right-to-farm law, *Larkin* is a case in which the difference was critical. Statutes of limitations, the availability of injunctive relief, and the threshold of requisite harm also may be different for these two claims.

2. Trespass requires a showing of intent—not to harm—but to enter the property or cause an entry to the property. How could the defendant, who surely would have preferred to keep his pesticides on his property where they would benefit his apple trees, have had an intent that his pesticides enter the plaintiff's land?

Recall that intent can be satisfied either when defendant has a purpose or knowledge to a degree of substantial certainty that the outcome will occur. Here, based on wind and experience, the defendant likely knew, with substantial certainty, that some of his pesticides would migrate onto adjacent land. That knowledge would be sufficient to satisfy the intent requirement, even if the defendant had no purpose in putting his pesticides on the plaintiff's land. In the cited *Bradley* case, which involved the migration of microscopic particles produced by the defendant's copper smelting, the court explained:

> The man who fires a bullet into a dense crowd may fervently pray that he will hit no one, but since he must believe and know that he cannot avoid doing so, he intends it. The practical application of this principle has meant that where a reasonable man in the defendant's position would believe that a particular result was substantially certain to follow, he will be dealt with by the jury, or even by the court, as though he had intended it.

Bradley, 709 P.2d at 786 (citing W. Prosser, Torts § 8, at 31–32).

3. Defendant stored chemicals on his property. During a fire on adjacent property, the water used to fight the fire washed those chemicals onto plaintiffs' adjacent property, allegedly contaminating their water supply, the consumption of which caused them personal injury. Would trespass lie for these damages? What other theories might? In Scottish Guarantee Insurance Co. v. Dwyer, 19 F.3d 307 (7th Cir.1994), the court recognized "negligent trespass," which one might think is an oxymoron because of the intent requirement for trespass, but recognized that classic trespass does not displace suits based on negligence. Negligent trespass, unlike its intentional relative, would not support either nominal damages or injunctive relief. See Restatement (Second) of Torts § 165 (providing for trespass arising from negligence or abnormally dangerous activity but requiring harm to be actionable). Courts that deny the existence of negligent trespass, e.g., Antolovich v. Brown Group Retail, Inc., 183 P.3d 582 (Colo.App.2007) may reflect a rhetorical rather than real difference. The plaintiffs in *Antolovich*, while unsuccessful on their trespass claims, which required intent, nevertheless were successful in their negligence claims.

4. The extreme for recognizing intangible invasions as sufficient for trespass is Public Service Co. of Colorado v. Van Wyk, 27 P.3d 377 (Colo. 2001). There, an upgraded electrical line allegedly caused electromagnetic waves and radiation to enter the plaintiff's property. While chemicals and microscopic particulates may be imperceptible, they have tangible existence. By contrast, the invading substances in *Van Wyk* had no physical mass. As in *Larkin*, the court required a showing of actual damage to the property to sustain a trespass claim. See also San Diego Gas & Elec. Co. v. Superior Court, 920 P.2d 669 (Cal.1996) (trespass unavailable for intangible invasions unless they cause physical damage to the property).

5. *Temporary, continuing, and permanent trespasses.* Trespasses are subcategorized into temporary, continuing, and permanent one. These classifications are important for res judicata and statute of limitations reasons. See Chapter 10, Section B. Categorization depends on the nature of trespass, rather than the defendant's conduct. Thus, a defendant who permits a plume of noxious chemicals to escape its manufacturing plant may create a temporary trespass because the chemicals cause a one-shot harm to agricultural crops on adjacent property. On the other hand, disposal of hazardous waste that seeps into the ground and is dispersed onto others' property is a continuing trespass because it remains on that property causing continuing harm. Hazardous waste disposal may not be permanent because it can be cleaned up, thereby ending the harm. While a person who trespasses on another's land is also engaged in wrongdoing on a continual basis, the relevant matter is the continuing nature of the harm not the defendant's conduct. See Hoery v. United States, 64 P.3d 214 (Colo.2003). In the case of permanent harms, the cause of action accrues when the trespass first occurs and plaintiff must recover for all current and future harm in that suit. By contrast, a continuing trespass permits successive actions for the harm with each limited to harm that has occurred within the applicable statute of limitations. See Capogeannis v. Superior Court, 15 Cal.Rptr.2d 796 (App. 1993).

That an invasion is continuing and defendant has knowledge of the continuing nature of the invasion does not affect whether the intent requirement is satisfied. Thus, in United Proteins, Inc. v. Farmland Industries, Inc., 915 P.2d 80 (Kan.1996), the release of the defendant's chemical was accidental, but remained on the plaintiff's property for some time. The court held that it was the state of mind of the defendant at the time of entry not subsequent knowledge of its existence that was relevant for purposes of satisfying the intent requirement.

6. *The Price–Anderson Act.* Congress enacted the Price–Anderson Act, 42 U.S.C. § 2011 et seq., to encourage investment in nuclear power, which holds the potential for catastrophic losses that challenge the adequacy of private insurance markets. The Act applies to any incident that involves the release of nuclear material and provides thresholds of liability for the nuclear operators with the government indemnifying the operator for any liability above that amount. The significance of the Act for private toxic tort claims is that it provides a federal cause of action, thereby supporting federal court jurisdiction in all such cases. That federal claim, however, derives its substance from applicable state law, so long as the state law is not inconsistent with provisions in the Act that limit liability of a an operator to the liability threshold. See Nieman v. NLO, Inc., 108 F.3d 1546 (6th Cir.1997). Most courts have concluded the Act preempts any state law tort claims.

2. NUISANCE

a. Private Nuisance

Unlike trespass, which protects a property right that we might think of as inviolate, nuisance often involves competing interests of neighbors— one to use his property in a fashion advantageous to the owner and the other to the use and enjoyment of her property without interference. Thus, you should not be surprised to find that nuisance entails more balancing of rights or interests than does trespass.

We begin our treatment with private nuisances. These are interferences with a land possessor's use and enjoyment of private property. By contrast, some nuisances affect the public generally (imagine radioactive fallout that descends on an entire community) and enforcement is limited to public officials or regulatory agencies, unless a private party suffers "special damages," which means harm different from and more severe than that suffered by the public.

Because nuisance entails questions of competing land uses, it overlaps with zoning laws, modern environmental regulation, as well as property law and its provisions for covenants and easements in the use of land owned by another. Thus, proof that a defendant's operations conform with existing zoning laws may be relevant, if not dispositive, in a common law nuisance claim. We focus in this section on private enforcement in tort seeking either damages or injunctive relief as remedies.

PESTEY v. CUSHMAN

Supreme Court of Connecticut, 2002.
259 Conn. 345, 788 A.2d 496.

VERTEFEUILLE, J.

* * *

The plaintiffs, James Pestey and Joan Pestey, brought this action against the defendants, Nathan R. Cushman, Nathan P. Cushman and Cushman Farms Limited Partnership, seeking money damages and injunctive and declaratory relief. After a lengthy trial, the jury returned a partial verdict for the plaintiffs for $100,000 in damages. * * * The trial court denied all of the defendants' posttrial motions, and rendered judgment in accordance with the jury's verdict. The defendants appealed * * *.

The jury reasonably could have found the following facts. The plaintiffs' home is situated on property they own located along the west side of Route 87 in North Franklin. The defendants own and conduct farming operations on a large tract of land on the opposite side of Route 87, approximately one third of one mile north of the plaintiffs' property. In 1990, the defendants constructed a 42,000 square foot free stall barn and milking parlor on their land to house a herd of dairy cows and a pit in which to store the manure generated by the herd.

The plaintiffs first noticed objectionable odors emanating from the defendants' farm in early 1991, after the construction of the new barn. The odors were, at first, nothing more than the typical stercoraceous [the smell of feces] odors generated by a farm containing livestock. Over time, however, the odors became substantially more pungent and their character changed as they took on a sharp, burnt smell. In 1997, the defendants installed an anaerobic digestion system on their farm to process the manure generated by the dairy herd. The system was designed to mimic in a controlled manner the anaerobic process that occurs in nature. Under this process, manure is fed into the digester, which, through the use of high temperature and bacteria, breaks the organic compound into its constituent parts. The end result of a properly functioning anaerobic digestion process is the production of a low odor biosolid and a gaseous mixture that can be used as an energy source to power the digester's generators. Following the installation of the digester, the character of the odors affecting the plaintiffs' property changed again, becoming more acrid and evincing the smells of sulphur and sewage. This change was caused by the digester being either undersized or overloaded, which resulted in partially digested, higher odor manure being released at the end of the anaerobic digestion process. At times, the odors emanating from the defendants' farm were so strong that the smell would awaken the plaintiffs during the night, forcing them to close the windows of their home. Further facts will be set forth where relevant.

The plaintiffs commenced this action in three counts seeking monetary damages and injunctive and declaratory relief. In the first count of the amended complaint, sounding in common-law private nuisance, the plaintiffs alleged that the defendants' farm generated offensive odors that unreasonably interfered with the plaintiffs' use and enjoyment of their property. The plaintiffs further alleged in this count that the defendants' farm operation was not entitled to the protections of General Statutes § 19a–341,[1] which concerns the right to farm and protects farms from nuisance claims, because the odors resulted from the defendants' negligent operation of their farm. Only this first count was ultimately submitted to the jury to decide.[2]

In addition to returning a plaintiffs' verdict, the jury answered interrogatories demonstrating that it specifically found that the offensive odors emanating from the defendants' farm unreasonably interfered with the plaintiffs' enjoyment of their property, that the interference was continuous, and that the odors had a natural tendency to inflict harm by interfering with the plaintiffs' use of their property. The jury further found that the defendants' farm operation was the proximate cause of the plaintiffs' loss of enjoyment of their property and that the defendants' use of their property was either unreasonable or unlawful. Lastly, the jury found that § 19a–341 did not apply because the plaintiffs had proven that the offensive odors produced by the defendants' farm were the result of the defendants' negligence in the operation of their farm. After the trial court rendered judgment in accordance with the jury's verdict, this appeal followed.

The defendants * * * assert that the trial court improperly: (1) instructed the jury with regard to the unreasonableness element of the private nuisance claim * * *.

I

We first address the defendants' claim that the trial court improperly instructed the jury with regard to the unreasonableness element of the

---

1. General Statutes § 19a–341 provides in relevant part: "(a) Notwithstanding any general statute or municipal ordinance or regulation pertaining to nuisances to the contrary, no agricultural or farming operation, place, establishment or facility, or any of its appurtenances, or the operation thereof, shall be deemed to constitute a nuisance, either public or private, due to alleged objectionable (1) odor from livestock, manure, fertilizer or feed ... provided such agricultural or farming operation, place, establishment or facility has been in operation for one year or more and has not been substantially changed, and such operation follows generally accepted agricultural practices. Inspection and approval of the agricultural or farming operation, place, establishment or facility by the Commissioner of Agriculture or his designee shall be prima facie evidence that such operation follows generally accepted agricultural practices....

"(c) The provisions of this section shall not apply whenever a nuisance results from negligence or wilful or reckless misconduct in the operation of any such agricultural or farming operation, place, establishment or facility, or any of its appurtenances."

2. In the second count, seeking equitable relief, the plaintiffs alleged that the offensive odors generated by the defendants' farm violated General Statutes § 22a–16, which prohibits the "unreasonable pollution, impairment or destruction" of the state's air, water or other natural resources. Since neither party requested * * * that the jury determine the factual issues of the equitable claim, the court retained its authority as the fact finder with respect to the second count, which the trial court decided in favor of the defendants. In the third count, the plaintiffs alleged that the odors were the result of the defendants' wilful, reckless and wanton misconduct. At the close of the evidence, the defendants filed a motion for directed verdict as to the third count, which was granted by the trial court. Neither the second nor the third count is the subject of this appeal.

nuisance claim. Specifically, the defendants argue that the trial court's instruction to the jury was improper because it failed to instruct the jury adequately with respect to the balancing of interests that must be performed in deciding whether a use of property is unreasonable. The defendants contend that, although the trial court correctly instructed the jury to consider a multiplicity of factors in determining whether the defendants' use of their property was unreasonable, the court did not adequately instruct the jury to consider the defendants' legitimate interest in using their property. We conclude that the trial court's instruction to the jury on this issue was proper under the law both as expressed in our prior decisions and as clarified herein.

* * *

In order to analyze properly the defendants' claim, we must reexamine and clarify the elements that a plaintiff must prove to prevail on a claim for damages in a common-law private nuisance cause of action. Specifically, we must clarify two sources of confusion. First, we must distinguish the concept of unreasonable *interference* with the use and enjoyment of property from the concept of an unreasonable *use* of property. Second, we must reaffirm the distinction between private and public nuisance actions.

"A private nuisance is a nontrespassory invasion of another's interest in the private use and enjoyment of land." 4 Restatement (Second), Torts § 821D (1979); see also *Herbert v. Smyth,* 155 Conn. 78, 81, 230 A.2d 235 (1967). The law of private nuisance springs from the general principle that "[i]t is the duty of every person to make a reasonable use of his own property so as to occasion no unnecessary damage or annoyance to his neighbor." "The essence of a private nuisance is an interference with the use and enjoyment of land." W. Prosser & W. Keeton, Torts (5th ed.1984) § 87, p. 619.

The defendants' claim is based on the principle of private nuisance law that, in determining unreasonableness, "[c]onsideration must be given not only to the interests of the person harmed but also [to] the interests of the actor and to the interests of the community as a whole." 4 Restatement (Second), supra, § 826, comment (c). "Determining unreasonableness is essentially a weighing process, involving a comparative evaluation of conflicting interests. . . ." 4 Restatement (Second), supra, § 826, comment (c). Unreasonableness cannot be determined in the abstract, but, rather, must be judged under the circumstances of the particular case.

In determining the propriety of the jury instructions regarding the unreasonableness element in this case, we look to our recent decision in *Walsh v. Stonington Water Pollution Control Authority,* supra, 250 Conn. 443, 736 A.2d 811, in which the plaintiff had sought damages in common-law private nuisance for odors and insects emanating from a sewage treatment plant owned by the defendant town. With regard to this element, the trial court in *Walsh* had instructed the jury as follows: "[Y]ou must decide whether the use the town was making of the property was a reasonable use.... Now, that's not to suggest that the mere use of the property for a [sewage] treatment plant is reasonable or unreasonable. Clearly, that's a reasonable use of property and the plaintiffs don't claim otherwise." The trial court further explained: "If you find that the plant is producing odors–or was or is producing odors or insects, that is the use of the property that you will find that is either reasonable or unreasonable. [The] [p]laintiffs must prove that the use of the property as they have proven the property to ... have been used was unreasonable...." On appeal, this court held that the trial court's charge to the jury was proper because the instructions "conveyed to the jury that it was to take into consideration and weigh the conflicting interests involved." *Id.*, at 457, 736 A.2d 811; accord *Maykut v. Plasko,* supra, 170 Conn. at 315, 365 A.2d 1114 (trial court applied proper test where facts described in findings included consideration of interests of both plaintiff and defendants).

In the present case, the trial court instructed the jury with respect to the unreasonableness element of the nuisance claim in the following manner: "You must also ask yourselves whether the defendants' use of their property [was] reasonable. A use which is permitted or even required by law and which does not violate local land use restrictions may nonetheless be unreasonable and create a common-law nuisance. You must ... consider and weigh ... the location of the defendants' dairy farm, the size of the farm, the manner in which they operate the farm, including their handling and maintenance of the manure, the free stall barn, the milking parlors and the anaerobic manure digester and associated equipment and any other circumstance which you find proven which indicates whether the defendants [were] making a reasonable use of their property." The court stated further: "The question is not whether the plaintiffs or the defendants would regard the condition as unreasonable, but whether reasonable persons generally looking at the whole situation impartially and objectively would consider it [to] be reasonable."

As the charge indicates, the trial court instructed the jury to consider a multiplicity of factors in determining the unreasonableness element. The defendants' argument that the instruction did not adequately instruct the jury to consider the defendants' interests assumes that the factors set forth by the trial court only regard the plaintiffs' interests. Such an assumption is unwarranted. The jury, for instance, was instructed to consider the location of the farm in making its finding regarding reasonableness. The location of the farm as a factor inherently includes the interests of both the plaintiffs and the defendants, and the jury was just as entitled to find that the location of the farm tended to show that the defendants' use was reasonable as it was to find that the location tended to show that the defendants' use was unreasonable. In addition, the trial court explicitly instructed the jury to consider any other circumstances that it found proven that would indicate "whether the defendants [were] making a reasonable use of their property." This instruction underscored the trial court's previous instruction that the jury was to consider various factors in reaching its decision, including factors relating to the interests of both the plaintiffs and the defendants. Although the trial court did not instruct the jury that the mere use of the property for a dairy farm was clearly a reasonable use if considered in a vacuum, as had the trial court in *Walsh* with respect to the wastewater treatment plant in that case; see *Walsh v. Stonington Water Pollution Control Authority,* supra, 250 Conn. at 450, 736 A.2d 811; the trial court's charge nonetheless provided the jury with adequate guidance with which to reach its verdict.

Although the trial court's jury charge was proper under *Walsh* and the decisions upon which *Walsh* relied, a thorough review of the law of nuisance reveals that this area of the law has been prone to confusion, and our case law has been no exception. Our nuisance jurisprudence has become muddled and is in need of clarification. Only after we clarify this area of the law can we determine fully whether the jury charge in this case was proper.

"There is perhaps no more impenetrable jungle in the entire law than that which surrounds the word 'nuisance.'" W. Prosser & W. Keeton, supra, § 86, p. 616. This court has stated often that a plaintiff must prove four elements to succeed in a nuisance cause of action: "(1) the condition complained of had a natural tendency to create danger and inflict injury upon person or property; (2) the danger created was a continuing one; (3) the use of the land was unreasonable or unlawful; [and] (4) the existence of the nuisance was the proximate cause of the plaintiffs' injuries and damages." (Internal quotation marks omitted.) *Walsh v. Stonington Water Pollution Control Authority,* supra. These elements developed through a long line of cases that can be described best as public nuisance cases. See, e.g., *DeLahunta v. Waterbury,* 134 Conn. 630, 631, 59 A.2d 800 (1948) (passengers in automobile brought nuisance action for damages against defendant municipality for injuries sustained when car in which they were riding struck concrete traffic stanchion installed by defendant); *Prifty v. Waterbury,* 133 Conn. 654, 655, 54 A.2d 260 (1947) (plaintiffs brought nuisance claim against defendant municipality for injuries sustained by child when ornamental cannon in public park fell); *Hoffman v. Bristol,* 113 Conn. 386, 387, 155 A. 499 (1931) (plaintiff brought nuisance claim against defendant municipality seeking to recover for injuries sustained from jumping off diving board in shallow water at pond owned and maintained by defendant).

Despite its grounding in public nuisance law, this four factor analysis has since been applied without distinction to both public and private nuisance causes of action. See, e.g., *Walsh v. Stonington Water Pollution Control Authority,* supra, 250 Conn. at 449 n. 4, 736 A.2d 811. Although there are some similarities between a public and a private nuisance, the two causes of action are distinct. Indeed, Professors Prosser and Keeton in their treatise on the law of torts have stated: "The two have almost nothing in common, except that each causes inconvenience to someone, and it would have been fortunate if they had been called from the beginning by different names." W. Prosser & W. Keeton, supra, § 86, p. 618. Public nuisance law is concerned with the interference with a public right, and cases in this realm typically involve conduct that allegedly interferes with the public health and safety.

Private nuisance law, on the other hand, is concerned with conduct that interferes with an individual's private right to the use and enjoyment of his or her land. Showing the existence of a condition detrimental to the public safety, or, as the first two elements of the four factor analysis discussed previously require, showing that the condition complained of had a natural tendency to create a continuing danger, is often irrelevant to a private nuisance claim. In light of the fundamental differences between these two distinct causes of action, we conclude that further attempts to employ the four part test discussed previously herein in the assessment of private nuisance causes of action would be imprudent; private nuisance claims simply do not fit comfortably within the same analytical rubric as public nuisance claims. We must restate, therefore, the elements that a plaintiff must prove to prevail on a claim for damages in a common-law private nuisance action.

In prescribing these specific elements, we look to the leading authorities in the field of common-law private nuisance for guidance. According to the Restatement (Second) of Torts, a plaintiff must prove that: (1) there was an invasion of the plaintiff's use and enjoyment of his or her property; (2) the defendant's conduct was the proximate cause of the invasion; and (3) the invasion was either intentional and unreasonable, or unintentional and the defendant's conduct was negligent or reckless. 4 Restatement (Second), supra, § 822. Although the language used in this third element does not make the point clearly, under this test, showing unreasonableness is an essential element of a private nuisance cause of action based on negligence or recklessness. See id., § 822, comment (k). Professors Prosser and Keeton define the plaintiff's burden in a similar manner. According to their view, a plaintiff in a private nuisance action must demonstrate that: (1) the defendant acted with the intent of interfering with the plaintiff's use and enjoyment of his or her property; (2) the interference with the use and enjoyment of the land was of the kind intended; (3) the interference was substantial; and (4) the interference was unreasonable. W. Prosser & W. Keeton, supra, § 87, p. 622–25. In the context of a private nuisance, they define a defendant's intent as meaning merely that "the defendant has created or continued the condition causing the interference with full knowledge that the harm to the plaintiff's interests are occurring or are substantially certain to follow."

This requirement of unreasonableness, a part of the third element in the test set forth in the Restatement (Second) and the fourth element in the test enunciated by Professors Prosser and Keeton, often has been stated, not in terms of whether the *interference* was unreasonable, but, rather, in terms of whether the defendant's *conduct* was unreasonable. See, e.g., *Walsh v. Stonington Water Pollution Control Authority*, supra, 250 Conn. at 446, 736 A.2d 811 (determining whether defendants' operation of wastewater treatment plant was " 'unreasonable use' "). In its charge to the jury, the trial court in the present case framed the inquiry in such a manner.

Although similar, "[t]he two concepts—unreasonable interference and unreasonable conduct—are not at all identical." W. Prosser & W. Keeton, supra, § 87, p. 623. "Confusion has resulted from the fact that the ... interference with the plaintiff's use of his property can be unreasonable even when the defendant's conduct is reasonable.... Courts have often found the existence of a nuisance on the basis of unreasonable use when what was meant is that the interference was unreasonable, i.e., it was unreasonable for the defendant to act as he did without paying for the harm that was knowingly inflicted on the plaintiff. Thus, an industrial enterprise who properly locates a cement plant or a coal-burning electric generator, who exercises utmost care in the utilization of known scientific techniques for minimizing the harm from the emission of noxious smoke, dust and gas and who is serving society well by engaging in the activity may yet be required to pay for the inevitable harm caused to neighbors." *Id.*, § 88, p. 629. As this example amply demonstrates, while an unreasonable use and an unreasonable interference often coexist, the two concepts are not equivalent, and it is possible to prove that a defendant's use of his property, while reasonable, nonetheless constitutes a common-law private nuisance because it unreasonably interferes with the use of property by another person. That was the situation in *Walsh v. Stonington Water Pollution Control Authority,* supra, 250 Conn. 443, 736 A.2d 811.

In *Walsh,* this court rejected the defendants' argument on appeal that their operation of the wastewater treatment plant in question could not constitute a nuisance since the operation of such a plant was clearly a reasonable use of property. This court held that the production of odors by the defendants' plant could constitute a nuisance, notwithstanding the fact that operating a wastewater treatment plant was clearly a reasonable use of the property in question. Although the proposition was not stated expressly in *Walsh,* our holding in that case demonstrates that, while the reasonableness of a defendant's conduct is a factor in determining whether an interference is unreasonable, it is *not* an independent element that must be proven in order to prevail in all private nuisance causes of action. The inquiry is cast more appropriately as whether the defendant's conduct unreasonably interfered with the plaintiff's use and enjoyment of his or her land rather than whether the defendant's conduct was itself unreasonable. *Quinnett v. Newman,* supra, 213 Conn. at 348, 568 A.2d 786 (nuisance refers to condition that exists and not to act that creates it). The proper focus of a private nuisance claim for damages, therefore, is whether a defendant's conduct, i.e., his or her use of his or her property, causes an unreasonable interference with the plaintiff's use and enjoyment of his or her property.

On the basis of our reexamination of our case law and upon our review of private nuisance law as described by the leading authorities, we adopt the basic principles of § 822 of the Restatement (Second) of Torts and conclude that in order to recover damages in a common-law private nuisance cause of action, a plaintiff must show that the defendant's conduct was the proximate cause of an unreasonable interference with the plaintiff's use and enjoyment of his or her property. The interference may be either intentional; or the result of the defendant's negligence. Whether the interference is unreasonable depends upon a balancing of the interests involved under the circumstances of each individual case. In balancing the interests, the fact finder must take into consideration all relevant factors, including the nature of both the interfering use and the use and enjoyment invaded, the nature, extent and duration of the interference, the suitability for the locality of both the interfering conduct and the particular use and enjoyment invaded, whether the defendant is taking all feasible precautions to avoid any unnecessary interference with the plaintiff's use and enjoyment of his or her property, and any other factors that the fact finder deems relevant to the question of whether the interference is unreasonable. No one factor should dominate this balancing of interests; all relevant factors must be considered in determining whether the interference is unreasonable.

The determination of whether the interference is unreasonable should be made in light of the fact that some level of interference is inherent in modern society. There are few, if any, places remaining where an individual may rest assured that he will be able to use and enjoy his property free from all interference. Accordingly, the interference must be substantial to be unreasonable. See 4 Restatement (Second), supra, § 822, comment (g); W. Prosser & W. Keeton, supra, § 88, p. 626.

Ultimately, the question of reasonableness is whether the interference is beyond that which the plaintiff should bear, under all of the circumstances of the particular case, without being compensated. See *Walsh v. Stonington Water Pollution Control Authority,* supra, 250 Conn. at 458–59, 736 A.2d 811; see also 4 Restatement (Second), supra, § 822, comment (g), and § 826, comment (e); W. Prosser & W. Keeton, supra, § 88, p. 629. With these standards in mind, we turn to the present case.

In reaching its verdict, the jury completed a set of interrogatories provided by the trial court. Each interrogatory asked the jury whether the plaintiffs had proven a specific element of the private nuisance claim, and the jury answered each interrogatory affirmatively. The first interrogatory asked: "Did the plaintiffs prove [that] the defendants' dairy farm produced odors which unreasonably interfered with [the] plaintiffs' enjoyment of their property?" This interrogatory correctly captured the crux of a common-law private nuisance cause of action for damages, i.e., whether the defendants' conduct unreasonably interfered with the plaintiffs' use and enjoyment of their property. It correctly stated that the focus in such a cause of action is on the reasonableness of the interference and not on the use that is causing the interference. In light of this conclusion, the fourth interrogatory, which involved the unreasonable use element that is at issue in this case, was superfluous. The fourth interrogatory asked: "Did the plaintiffs prove the defendants' use of their property is either unreasonable or unlawful?" As our previous discussion herein demonstrates, a plaintiff seeking damages in a common-law private nuisance cause of action is not required to prove that the defendant's conduct was unreasonable. Rather, the plaintiff must show that the interference with his or her property was unreasonable. The fourth interrogatory, therefore, in effect, required the plaintiffs to prove an additional, nonessential element to prevail on their claim. We conclude that the jury interrogatories and the jury charge, considered together, properly informed the jury of the necessary elements of a common-law private nuisance cause of action for damages and provided the jury with adequate guidance with which to reach its verdict. Accordingly, the trial court's jury charge was proper under the law as clarified herein.

* * *

[The court concluded that plaintiffs introduced sufficient evidence to support the jury's finding that the defendants' farming operation was the source of the objectionable odors. While there was contrary evidence and other sources that might have been responsible, resolution of this conflict was properly the domain of the jury.[12]]

The judgment is affirmed.

NOTES AND QUESTIONS

1. As *Pestey* reveals, nuisance (and trespass) is different from many other torts in that it is about a specific type of harm rather than about conduct. Thus, the essence of nuisance is harm to one's use or enjoyment of land, and as section 822 of the Second Restatement provides, nuisance may occur either through intentional or negligent conduct and through abnormally dangerous activity, as well. The *Pestey* court decides that private and public nuisance should be separated for clarity of analysis. In keeping with that observation, we defer consideration of public nuisance until after we conclude our consideration of private nuisance. See subsection b infra.

2. Because of the right-to-farm statute, plaintiffs had to establish negligence by the defendants in order to prevail. But consider an intentional nuisance claim. Would plaintiffs have been able to prove an intentional nuisance, putting aside the right-to-farm statute? Surely not, in the sense of the defendants desiring to subject plaintiffs to the stench from the farm operations. But recall that intent can also be satisfied when the defendant knows with substantial certainty that an act will cause harm to another. Section 825 of the Second Restatement of Torts confirms that a person acts intentionally if she "knows . . . or is substantially certain" that her act will invade another's use or enjoyment of property. Do you see why, in any continuing nuisance, such as in *Pestey*, defendants will have acted with intent?

---

12. In its memorandum of decision on the second count of the amended complaint seeking equitable relief, the trial court's factual findings were in contrast with the jury's findings on the nuisance count. Although the trial court was "unwilling to infer that the odors claimed by the plaintiffs and their witnesses emanated from the defendants' farm," the court stated correctly that "[t]here was [however] sufficient evidence for the jury to decide that odors did emanate from the defendants' operation and constitute[d] an unreasonable interference with the plaintiffs' use and enjoyment of their property."

3. Section 822 of the Second Restatement, adopted and quoted by *Pestey*, requires not only that an interference be intentional but that it also be unreasonable. Recall that with intentional torts causing physical harm, such as battery, do not require unreasonableness. If a defendant acts intentionally to cause bodily harm, there is liability, subject only to any applicable defenses. Why should harm to use and enjoyment of land be different from harm to one's bodily integrity? Could acting out of spite to deny a disliked neighbor the use of his property ever be reasonable? Might acting in a way that one knows will cause harm to another's use or enjoyment of property sometimes be reasonable?

4. Recall that negligence requires unreasonably risky conduct by a defendant. Given the reasonableness/balancing already required for negligence, why should negligent nuisance require an independent determination of unreasonableness, as the *Pestey* court did? That is, once the jury found that the defendants acted negligently, shouldn't that have been the end of any reasonableness inquiry? Note that the defendants did not challenge the jury's finding of negligence. Suppose that the defendants were negligent because instead of using the gas by-product of their digestion system as fuel, they simply let those gases drift away in the prevailing winds, and the gases were producing the odors about which the plaintiffs complained. Should the plaintiffs have to demonstrate any more than the unreasonableness of the defendants' conduct in operating their farm? Although the *Pestey* court suggested they do, section 822 does not have such a requirement.

5. While the court required unreasonableness as an element for a nuisance claim, it insisted that it need not be unreasonable conduct by defendant. Even if a defendant acts reasonably in its operations, a nuisance may impose an unreasonable interference on another's use or enjoyment of land. Does that principle have any application in the *Pestey* case? (Recall that the plaintiff's only basis for nuisance was negligent nuisance because of the right-to-farm statute.)

6. One might understand the court's requirement of an unreasonable interference with use or enjoyment of land as requiring a certain threshold of interference, below which nuisance will not be available. As the *Pestey* court explained, the Second Restatement in section 821F does impose a threshold of "significant harm," that would be suffered by "a normal person in the community," but this is independent of any unreasonableness requirement. Suppose a plaintiff has a super-sensitive sense of smell and is offended and nauseated by odors that most in the community would readily tolerate? Can the outcome be squared with the thin-skull plaintiff rule? Can the two rules be reconciled?

The threshold of a "significant harm" recognizes the reality that operations on adjacent land will often have an impact on neighbors and that in the hurly-burly of everyday activities, we all must simply learn to tolerate some low-level of interferences by others.

7. *The adequacy of the unreasonableness instruction.* Don't the defendants have an interest in conducting dairy farm operations on their land? Did the challenged instruction tell the jury that? The court did suggest that the jury was told it could consider any other circumstance in its assessment of reasonableness. Suppose the jury felt that the nasty personality of one of the defendants or the unkempt appearance of another justified a finding of unreasonableness? Since when do we leave to a jury's unfettered discretion the choice of which factors are relevant to a determination requiring balancing? And, since when is a catchall "all other factors" sufficient to inform the jury of those factors that the law has determined are relevant?

8. *Intentional nuisance.* By far the predominant form of private nuisance is intentional. To evaluate when an intentional nuisance is unreasonable, the Second Restatement provides two alternatives in section 826: (1) the gravity of the harm outweighs the utility of the actor's conduct or (2) the harm is serious and defendant can feasibly compensate plaintiff for the harm without affecting the continuation of the defendant's activities. Note that these two alternatives assume that there is no cost-effective way for defendant to either curtail or ameliorate the nuisance, and if there were, defendant would be liable based on negligence. Thus, as the *Pestey* court observed, a nuisance may be unreasonable despite defendant acting entirely reasonably in its operations. See also Martins v. Interstate Power Co., 652 N.W.2d 657 (Iowa 2002):

> Negligence is a type of liability-forming conduct, for example, a failure to act reasonably to prevent harm. In contrast, nuisance is a liability-producing condition. Negligence *may or may not* accompany a nuisance; negligence, however, is not an essential element of nuisance. If the condition constituting the nuisance exists, the person responsible for it is liable for resulting damages to others even though the person acted reasonably to prevent or minimize the deleterious effect of the nuisance.

Bormann, 584 N.W.2d at 315 (emphasis added).

Martins, 652 N.W.2d at 660.

How is the balancing under prong (1) above different from the traditional negligence balancing? Note that with an intentional nuisance, the harm has already occurred, so rather than balancing *risk* we are considering the harm that is caused to plaintiff. Second, rather than considering marginal changes in behavior that may reduce risk, we are concerned with the scope of the defendant's operation and its social utility.

Does this mean that an unusually useful activity is immunized from liability for nuisance? The Wisconsin Supreme Court, in Jost v. Dairyland Power Cooperative, 172 N.W.2d 647 (Wis.1969), rejected an electric utility's argument that the benefits of its production of electricity for the community outweighed the harm suffered by the plaintiff:

> We therefore conclude that the court properly excluded all evidence that tended to show the utility of the Dairyland Cooperative's enterprise. Whether its economic or social importance dwarfed the claim of a small farmer is of no consequence in this lawsuit. It will not be said that, because a great and socially useful enterprise will be liable in damages, an injury small by comparison should go unredressed. We know of no acceptable rule of jurisprudence that permits those who are engaged in important and desirable enterprises to injure with impunity those who

are engaged in enterprises of lesser economic significance. Even the government or other entities, including public utilities, endowed with the power of eminent domain—the power to take private property in order to devote it to a purpose beneficial to the public good—are obliged to pay a fair market value for what is taken or damaged. To contend that a public utility, in the pursuit of its praiseworthy and legitimate enterprise, can, in effect, deprive others of the full use of their property without compensation, poses a theory unknown to the law of Wisconsin, and in our opinion would constitute the taking of property without due process of law.

Id. at 653.

Compare Carpenter v. Double R Cattle Co., 701 P.2d 222 (Idaho 1985). The Idaho Supreme Court refused to adopt the second prong of section 826 in a case involving a cattle feedlot that produced similar unpleasant conditions to those in *Pestey*. The benefits of farming for a rural state like Idaho are too important to permit a nuisance to be found without consideration of the utility of the defendant's conduct, reasoned the court.

   9. *Remedies.* Note that the *Jost* court advocated damages to compensate the plaintiff. But what if the plaintiff sought injunctive relief that would shut down the electrical utility? Both damages and injunctive relief are potential remedies—recall that the plaintiff in *Pestey* sought both damages and injunctive relief, and the court found against the plaintiff on the count seeking an injunction. Should different considerations govern which remedy is available? We address these different remedies below in the remaining two cases in this section.

   10. *Coming to the nuisance.* Suppose that plaintiffs purchased their land in the late 1990s, after the odors from defendants' operation were in full bloom? The inelegant term, "coming to the nuisance," is used to describe this situation. See Erbrich Prods. Co. v. Wills, 509 N.E.2d 850 (Ind.App.1987) (statutory version of coming to the nuisance). One might think that plaintiffs who choose to purchase with full knowledge are not entitled to any relief. Indeed, wouldn't the price that they paid for the property reflect the conditions that existed? While the idea that plaintiff chose to confront conditions that she now claims are a nuisance can play a role in whether there is liability for nuisance, the doctrine has its limits. Change is inevitable, and sometimes the character of an area undergoes change, as occurred in Spur Industries, Inc. v. Del E. Webb Development Co., 494 P.2d 700 (Ariz.1972). Growth of suburban developments in the greater Phoenix area approached a cattle feedlot that produced unpleasant conditions for residents. The feedlot was there first, but because of the need to accommodate growth, a nuisance was found. The developer was required to compensate the feedlot for its costs of relocating.

   Mark v. State ex rel. Department of Fish and Wildlife, 84 P.3d 155 (Or.App.2004) reveals another limitation on the coming to the nuisance doctrine. The plaintiffs purchased a waterfront lot and built a home on it unaware that adjacent state property had long been used as a nude beach. The activity on the beach increased in volume and hundreds of nude bathers descended on the area in warmer months. The plaintiffs were subjected to "explicit sexual conduct on and around their property [that included] adults engaged in sexual intercourse, oral sex, the touching of genitals and breasts, men masturbating individually and in groups, men walking on the beach and on the road with erections, and individuals photographing others' genitals." The court rejected the defendant's coming to the nuisance argument because the plaintiffs neither had actual (they purchased the property while residing in Alaska) nor constructive knowledge of the activities at the beach.

11. Successful plaintiffs may recover damages for any diminution in the market value of their property, physical damage to their property, personal injury consequential to the nuisance, and discomfort of the sort experienced by the plaintiffs in *Pestey*. What about recovery for "stigma" damages when the value of property declines because of an incorrect perception that the property has been contaminated with dangerous substances? In Adkins v. Thomas Solvent Co., 487 N.W.2d 715 (Mich.1992), the property owners who lived near a contaminated site sued for the diminished value of their land. Evidence revealed, however, that the contamination would never migrate onto their land. The court held that unfounded fears that affected property values could not be the basis for a nuisance. Some physical intrusion by the contamination onto the plaintiffs' property was required for recovery of damages.

What about recovery for pure emotional distress? If there is a release of carcinogens that pose a risk of those exposed to contracting cancer, albeit in the future, can the property owners successfully prosecute a nuisance claim? In Chapter 12, we address suits for "cancerphobia," claims for emotional harm when a person has been exposed to an agent that increases their risk of cancer in the absence of some physical injury.

12. Statutes like the right-to-farm statute explained in the *Pestey* court's footnote 1 have been enacted in many states, including even ones like Connecticut, which does not have a large agricultural industry. How effective was this statute in protecting farming interest from liability for nuisance? See generally, Neil D. Hamilton, Right-to-Farm Laws Reconsidered: Ten Reasons Why Legislative Efforts to Resolve Agricultural Nuisances May Be Ineffective, 3 Drake J.Agric.L. 103 (1998).

PENLAND v. REDWOOD SANITARY SEWER SERVICE DISTRICT

Court of Appeals of Oregon, 1998.
156 Or.App. 311, 965 P.2d 433.

HASELTON, JUDGE.

This case is before us on remand from the Supreme Court. In our original opinion, we held that, regardless of whether the defendant District's operation of a composting facility constituted a nuisance, the operation was shielded by "discretionary function" immunity under the Oregon Tort Claims Act (OTCA), and, thus, the trial court had erred in enjoining the facility's operation. The Supreme Court reversed, concluding that discretionary function immunity under the OTCA "confers immunity on public bodies only from liability for damages and does not confer immunity from injunctive actions" including, particularly, an action to enjoin a nuisance.

Thus, on remand, we must address two issues that we initially deferred: First, is the composting operation a nuisance? *Second*, if so, does the balance of equities warrant issuance of permanent injunctive relief? On *de novo* review, we answer both questions in the affirmative and, consequently, affirm.

To "reset the scene," we reproduce the summary of undisputed facts from our first opinion:

> "The District operates sewage-related facilities, including a sewage treatment plant, in rural Josephine County. As part of the sewage treatment process, the District reduces incoming raw sewage to sludge, or biosolids, a bacteria-laden condensed form of sewage, by draining the liquids from the solids. Before 1988, the District trucked the sludge to various sites for land application, which involved spreading the sludge over a large area for agricultural and disposal purposes.

> "In 1988, the District's manager, Weber, who was charged with day-to-day oversight of its operations, instituted a small-scale pilot composting operation at the treatment plant. In July 1990, the District instituted composting on a permanent basis.

> "In the initial stages of the composting process, sludge is solidified by being poured into an outdoor levee, or 'drying ring,' which is exposed to the open air. After about two weeks, the material loses enough moisture to be mixed with organic material for composting. The reduced sludge, or biosolids, is then mixed with organic materials, such as wood, animal bedding, including animal waste, and yard waste, provided by local residents and businesses. The bacteria in the sludge break down the mixture. In order for the bacteria to decompose the sludge, the mixture must be exposed to air. Thus, the mixture is placed in a large pile, approximately nine feet high, 20 feet wide, and 100 hundred feet long, and exposed to the open air. The composted material is first piled over a perforated pipe for aeration. After two to three weeks, the pile is removed from the pipe and is turned every two weeks for aeration. There are normally seven piles at one time, each in a different stage of the composting process. Defendant uses heavy equipment to move the piles as they decompose and to load the finished product.

> "After approximately 90 days, the material becomes finished compost, which defendant sells to the public as mulch or soil amendment. The product, called Jo–Gro, contains no nutrients for fertilizing but is valuable for retaining moisture in soils.

> "If the sludge mixture is not aerated, it becomes anaerobic and, as a result, generates hydrogen sulfide. Hydrogen sulfide can cause headaches, nausea, and throat problems, and its odor is akin to that of rotten eggs. Hydrogen sulfide is generally released whenever a

compost pile or the sludge pool is disturbed, but some level of hydrogen sulfide is always present as a result of the composting operation.

"Plaintiffs are landowners and homeowners who live in rural Josephine County near the plant and composting operation. Many lived in the neighborhood before the District instituted the permanent composting operation. The closest plaintiffs, the Penlands, live about 180 feet from the property where the composting activities take place. Plaintiffs and other neighbors began to notice odor, noise, and dust, which they associated with the composting operation, in October 1991. Beginning in February 1992, plaintiffs and others complained to the District that, because of the odor and noise they ascribed to the plant, they were unable to enjoy outdoor activities, such as gardening, sitting on their porches, and barbequing. In response to those complaints, the District undertook several measures, including placing sound deflection panels on the electric wood grinder. Plaintiffs apparently found those measures to be ineffective and their complaints continued.

* * *

"[In the summer of 1994, after receiving the recommendation of an advisory committee, the District's board of directors voted] to continue the composting operation at the sewage plant while implementing 21 of the *ad hoc* committee's recommended mitigation measures. Those measures included using a quieter loader, constructing vegetation screens, adding sound mufflers to equipment, eliminating construction lumber demolition, applying a commercial deodorizer, mixing the sludge more rapidly and efficiently, using fly bait, and adding dust-reducing spray misters.

"In August 1994, plaintiffs filed this action, seeking to enjoin the continuation of the composting operation. Plaintiffs alleged that that operation created a nuisance in that it created excessive odor, noise, and dust and interfered with the reasonable use of their properties."

In determining whether the composting operation constitutes a nuisance—*i.e.*, whether it substantially and unreasonably interferes with the use and enjoyment of plaintiffs' property—we must assess five factors: (1) the location of the claimed nuisance; (2) the character of the neighborhood; (3) the nature of the thing complained of; (4) the frequency of the intrusion; and (5) the effect upon the plaintiff's enjoyment of life, health and property. *Jewett*, 281 Or. at 473, 575 P.2d 164. Whether a condition constitutes a nuisance depends on its effect on "an ordinarily reasonable [person], a normal person of ordinary habits and sensibilities." *Id.* at 476, 575 P.2d 164.

The trial court, in oral remarks that comported with its ultimate written findings and conclusions, explained its application of those factors:

"I want to start out, first of all, before I go on to the issue of nuisance, I'd just like for the record—I know it's not really evidence, but I was taken on a view of the property and I think it's important that the record reflect, as everyone agrees, that this is a residential area. It fronts the Rogue River. The day we were out there, there were osprey flying over the river. There's fish. It's a beautiful, very much a residential, rural nature, despite the fact that it's been divided into small parcels.

* * *

"I do find that the nature of the defendant's use of its property has substantially changed since most of the plaintiffs purchased their property. It's changed from a use that would have been consistent with just the sewage treatment facility plant, with the rural residential nature of the surrounding properties, to a use that's more akin to, in the words of one of the defendant's witnesses, an industrial site. The changing nature, in this respect, of the defendant's use of the property, I do not believe could have been reasonably foreseen by the plaintiffs.

"I do find specifically that—I find the plaintiffs to be credible in their testimony. With respect to the noise regulations, the defendant's witnesses testified that they are to be enforced at the county level, not by DEQ; that DEQ lacks both the authority and the staff to pursue noise complaints, and that the county has not done any testing as to the noise complaints on this property, nor pursued really any complaint in that respect. The acoustical expert hired by the county, by the sewage district, stated his opinion that the noise level at one point at least did result from the composting operations and that they exceeded established levels.

"Odor is a very subjective type of issue. There is certainly testimony from many of the defendant's witnesses that there's no odor at all. I can't believe that. There is no dispute that hydrogen sulfide is produced by these operations. There's no dispute that hydrogen sulfide can cause the very symptoms that the plaintiffs testified they were experiencing. And in fact there has been no government agency that has tested for hydrogen sulfide levels at this site, so any finding that they're in compliance is not based on any study or any testing that has been done on the site.

"I am completely convinced that the nature of the odor that's produced by the defendant's composting operations does cause some of the plaintiffs to gag, to be nauseated, to have headaches, to be unable to eat, and to be unable to sit in their yards or patios or otherwise utilize their yards. And by doing so, that the odor substantially and unreasonably interferes with the plaintiffs' use and enjoyment of their property. I also am convinced that the nature of the noise and the frequency of the noise at the site caused by the composting operations also substantially and unreasonably interferes with the plaintiffs' use and enjoyment of their property."

Without exhaustively detailing the evidence and our analysis, we agree with the trial court that the composting operation is a nuisance. The District's sewage treatment plant, including the composting operation, is located in an area zoned RR–1 (rural residential one-acre) on the Rogue River. Many, and perhaps all, of the plaintiffs live or own property within one-quarter mile of the facility.

Two dozen witnesses, sixteen of whom reside or own property near the treatment facility, testified that the composting operation frequently created an offensive odor. Those witnesses variously described the odor as: "Stench." "Real offensive." "Sickening, very sickening." "Between a rotten egg and a rotten skunk." "Like a cat litter box." "Never smelled anything like it in my life." "About 500 outhouses all at once." And "I was in World War II, and I smelled some dead bodies and it had a smell something like that." Plaintiffs' witnesses testified that the intensity and frequency of the odor varied but, in general, depending on the location, the odor could be unbearably nauseating as often as several times a week.

The District points to testimony by other witnesses, including scientists and experts in sewage treatment, that the composting operation did not generate an offensive odor—or at least not an odor that could be consistently detected as offensive at plaintiffs' property. In a related sense, the District argues that, given expert meteorological evidence based on evaluation of wind-direction data and the timing of certain plaintiffs' complaints, the source of the odor plaintiffs' witnesses described was a dairy across the river from the treatment plant.

Conversely, many of plaintiffs' witnesses testified that they could distinguish the dairy smell from the compost smell: "It's a characteristic sewage smell. It's completely different from any agricultural or dairy-type smell." "We had cows so we knew what the cows' odor was." "I have never found a dairy odor so offensive that I could not stand it." "I was raised on a cattle ranch, and I know the difference between the odor of human excrement and cattle." "I've got a dairy. I do smell the dairy too, and I know which one is which * * * The dairy can be bad at times, but Jo–Gro's smell is so distinctive. I can't handle that one. I go inside." We note further that many of the plaintiffs who testified, albeit not all, owned their property before the composting facility began full-scale operation.

* * * We * * * affirm the trial court's determination that the composting facility generated offensive odors that were consistently detectable on plaintiffs' property.

We further affirm the trial court's finding that the odor did, in fact, substantially and unreasonably interfere with plaintiffs' use and enjoyment of their property. Plaintiffs testified that the odor made them nauseated and prevented them from sitting on their decks or outside, or even from leaving their windows open at night for a summer breeze. For example, one plaintiff testified that she could not work in her garden when the odor was present and to get relief from the odor, "we have to go in the house or go to town or something." Another testified, "I can sit down and eat on the back porch with the dairy smell, but I can't with the Jo–Gro smell. I get sick." And a third testified, "we like to sleep with the windows open, and it is so offensive that I became sick at my stomach, and we had to close the windows to be able to sleep." Again, the trial court expressly found that testimony to be credible and, giving that assessment due deference, so do we.

The District argues, nevertheless, that, as a matter of law, there can be no nuisance because it has complied with all applicable regulations and permits in operating the composting facility. However, the District's purported regulatory compliance does not preclude a determination that its operation constitutes a nuisance. We categorically rejected an identical argument in *Lunda v. Matthews*, 46 Or.App. 701, 707, 613 P.2d 63 (1980). Thus, in affirming an injunction against a nuisance, we explained:

> "[D]efendants argue that the operation of their plant was reasonable as a matter of law because they had secured an air contaminant discharge permit from the Department of Environmental Quality and they had not been cited for violation of the fallout standards. Conformance with pollution standards does not preclude a suit in private nuisance."

We proceed to the second, and final, issue: Do the equities warrant the issuance of an injunction abating the nuisance? Concerning that issue, the trial court observed:

> "With respect to the balance of the equities in this case, and the remedy, I want to state first of all, I have no intention to enjoin the Board of Directors of the sewage service district. I don't intend to micro-manage the affairs of the sewer service district. So for that reason I can't really get into a situation where I'm setting what needs to be done to remedy the situation. I considered the alternative of damages because of that difficulty, but quite frankly, I don't think I can ascertain the damages because I think what the damages might be today might be different two years from now once the capacity of the plant has doubled. And I don't think that damages, for that reason, are easily ascertained in this situation, nor do I think it would be a final solution. I think you would just be inviting further litigation down the line if I tried to go that route.

> * * *

> "[T]he defendant, since they have been aware of the plaintiffs' complaint, have expanded their operations and further invested in the composting operations on site, after becoming aware and having been notified of the complaints that were being made in this case. And I think that by doing that, quite frankly, it demonstrates some arrogance on the part of the defendant, as well as, doing so, they did it at their own risk. So I'm rejecting any consideration of the cost that has been expended since they've been aware of these complaints in

balancing the equities. I don't think they're entitled to go out and make substantial expenditures when the case is in litigation and to try to use those as some way to avoid responsibility.

* * *

"[A]s I said, balancing the equities in this case is really the most difficult. * * * I don't deny that there are other people who are not in this courtroom—the other patrons of the district who are going to be affected by my decision—and that's been the hardest part probably of making this decision is those considerations. But having considered that and considered the lack of any other remedy that I feel like would fit in the premises, I am going to grant the request for an injunction."

In *York v. Stallings*, 217 Or. 13, 22, 341 P.2d 529 (1959), the Court enunciated the standard for issuance of injunctive relief. Once a nuisance is established,

"it does not follow that an injunction should issue as a matter of course. The court may refuse an injunction in certain cases *where the hardship caused to the defendant by the injunction would greatly outweigh the benefit resulting to the plaintiff.* The injunction does not issue as a matter of absolute or unqualified right but is subject to the sound discretion of the court."

Id. at 22, 341 P.2d 529 (emphasis added). *See also Jewett*, 281 Or. at 478, 575 P.2d 164 (reiterating the "greatly outweighs" standard).

Thus, we must compare the benefit to plaintiffs with the hardship to the District resulting from a permanent injunction. The benefit to plaintiffs is the ability to enjoy their property in a manner consistent with its rural character—to garden, and eat outside, and keep their windows open on summer evenings. For plaintiffs, an injunction would mean being able to use and enjoy their property as they did before the nuisance came to them—to live, and breathe, free from a pervasive, nauseating odor.

The concomitant detriment to the District is essentially, but not completely, economic. If use of the existing composting facility is enjoined, the District has, at least, two arguably feasible alternatives: (1) move the composting activities to another site; or (2) return to its prior practice of trucking the sludge and applying it to acceptable agricultural sites.[5] Either of those options, even if otherwise practicable, would involve substantial additional expense. In addition, a return to the District's prior practice of land application would result in loss of significant environmental benefits.

---

5. Although a third alternative would be for the District to buy out the plaintiffs, there is no evidence of the feasibility or expense of that option. A fourth alternative might be for the District to adopt additional and *effective* mitigation measures while maintaining the operation at its present site. There is, however, no evidence in this record concerning the practical availability and efficacy, much less the cost, of any such measures. *Cf.* G. Calabresi and A.D. Melamed, *Property Rules, Liability Rules, and Inalienability: One View of the Cathedral*, 85 Harv. L.Rev. 1089, 1115–24 (1972) (describing various "rules" or approaches for abating or paying compensation for nuisances, derived from considerations of economic efficiency, "distributional goals" and "other justice reasons").

The District's plant manager, Robert Webber, and Steven Gilbert, an environmental engineer retained by the District, testified persuasively that composting was an environmentally superior alternative to land application of biosolids. Webber explained, in some detail, why returning to its previous practice of land application was no longer a feasible alternative for the District, notwithstanding the fact that many districts and nearby municipalities in southern Oregon, including the City of Grants Pass, continue that practice. The concerns that Webber identified include groundwater contamination monitoring, site constraints, land use restrictions, sludge runoff, and grazing restrictions.

In contrast, the District's objections to relocating the composting operation to an alternative, non-residential site appear to be purely financial. That is, in contrast to land application, there is no evidence that practical or legal impediments, including land use or environmental restrictions, would somehow preclude such relocation. The capital cost of relocating the existing composting operation (as distinct from any expansion of that operation to accommodate projected population growth and demands) would be approximately $1,000,000. The District currently serves approximately 1,800 households. The additional capital costs associated with relocating, amortized over a 20–year period, would result in a $5.00 per month rate increase per household over that period. In addition the District's annual operating costs would increase by approximately $100,000, representing the expense of trucking the present volume of biosolids/sludge from the existing treatment plant to the newly-relocated composting operation.

Assessing those alternatives, we conclude, as did the trial court, that the hardship to the District from the issuance of an injunction does not "greatly outweigh" the benefit to plaintiffs. There is no question that relocating the composting operation will, in fact, be expensive. Nevertheless, two factors especially bear on our assessment of the equities.

First, although a precise apportionment is impossible, the District's relocation expenses have been exacerbated by actions and additional expenditures that the District undertook after becoming aware of the Penlands' initial complaints in 1991 and of other plaintiffs' complaints by late 1992. This was not merely a case of the nuisance coming to the homeowners, but of the District expanding its operations after plaintiffs protested. *See generally Swaggerty v. Petersen*, 280 Or. 739, 748–49, 572 P.2d 1309 (1977) (in action to enjoin violation of restrictive building covenant, "[d]efendant cannot, after suit has been filed [to abate violation] * * * deprive [plaintiffs] of their right to complete relief by increasing his investment, and thus his potential hardship, before the final decision."); *Taylor v. McCollom*, 153 Or.App. 670, 680, 958 P.2d 207 (1998) (where "the defendant has continued to build notwithstanding notification of a clear violation * * * the court may order injunctive relief, even if the balance of hardship cuts against the plaintiff.").

Second, although the additional cost to the District will be substantial, the impact will be ameliorated because it can be spread among the District's rate-payers—over 1,800 households. In that "cost-spreading" respect, *Thornburg v. Port of Portland*, 233 Or. 178, 376 P.2d 100 (1962), which involved an inverse condemnation claim by homeowners whose property lay beneath jet flightpaths of the then-newly expanded Portland Airport, is instructive. In reversing the trial court's limitation of the plaintiff property owners' claims, the court observed:

> "[W]hen the government conducts an activity upon its own land which, after balancing the question of reasonableness, is sufficiently disturbing to the use and enjoyment of neighboring lands to amount to a taking thereof, then the public, and not the subservient landowner, should bear the cost of such public benefit. * * * The real question was * * * one of * * * reasonableness based upon nuisance theories. In effect, the inquiry should have been whether the government had undertaken a course of conduct on its own land which, in simple fairness to its neighbors, required it to obtain more land so that the substantial burdens of the activity would fall upon public land, rather than upon that of involuntary contributors who happen to lie in the path of progress."

Thornburg, 233 Or. At 193–94, 376 P.2d 100 (footnote omitted).

So too here. If the District and those whom it serves are committed to the environmental values and benefits of composting, that may well be laudable. But the cost of that commitment should be commonly borne and not visited solely upon a handful of "involuntary contributors who happen to lie in the path of progress." *Id.* at 194, 376 P.2d 100. We emphasize that this is not a case of simple-minded "NIMBY" ["Not in my backyard"] parochialism–of narrow-minded refusal to assume burdens that are, reasonably and necessarily, part of living as a community. It is, rather, a clear and compelling case of living next to a public nuisance. The equities favor the issuance of an injunction.

Affirmed.

BOOMER v. ATLANTIC CEMENT CO.

Court of Appeals of New York, 1970.
26 N.Y.2d 219, 309 N.Y.S.2d 312, 257 N.E.2d 870.

BERGAN, JUDGE.

Defendant operates a large cement plant near Albany. These are actions for injunction and damages by neighboring land owners alleging injury to property from dirt, smoke and vibration emanating from the plant. A nuisance has been found after trial, temporary damages have been allowed; but an injunction has been denied.

The public concern with air pollution arising from many sources in industry and in transportation is currently accorded ever wider recognition accompanied by a growing sense of responsibility in State and Federal

Governments to control it. Cement plants are obvious sources of air pollution in the neighborhoods where they operate.

But there is now before the court private litigation in which individual property owners have sought specific relief from a single plant operation. The threshold question raised by the division of view on this appeal is whether the court should resolve the litigation between the parties now before it as equitably as seems possible; or whether, seeking promotion of the general public welfare, it should channel private litigation into broad public objectives.

A court performs its essential function when it decides the rights of parties before it. Its decision of private controversies may sometimes greatly affect public issues. Large questions of law are often resolved by the manner in which private litigation is decided. But this is normally an incident to the court's main function to settle controversy. It is a rare exercise of judicial power to use a decision in private litigation as a purposeful mechanism to achieve direct public objectives greatly beyond the rights and interests before the court.

Effective control of air pollution is a problem presently far from solution even with the full public and financial powers of government. In large measure adequate technical procedures are yet to be developed and some that appear possible may be economically impracticable.

It seems apparent that the amelioration of air pollution will depend on technical research in great depth; on a carefully balanced consideration of the economic impact of close regulation; and of the actual effect on public health. It is likely to require massive public expenditure and to demand more than any local community can accomplish and to depend on regional and interstate controls.

A court should not try to do this on its own as a by-product of private litigation and it seems manifest that the judicial establishment is neither equipped in the limited nature of any judgment it can pronounce nor prepared to lay down and implement an effective policy for the elimination of air pollution. This is an area beyond the circumference of one private lawsuit. It is a direct responsibility for government and should not thus be undertaken as an incident to solving a dispute between property owners and a single cement plant—one of many—in the Hudson River valley.

The cement making operations of defendant have been found by the court at Special Term to have damaged the nearby properties of plaintiffs in these two actions. That court, as it has been noted, accordingly found defendant maintained a nuisance and this has been affirmed at the Appellate Division. The total damage to plaintiffs' properties is, however, relatively small in comparison with the value of defendant's operation and with the consequences of the injunction which plaintiffs seek.

The ground for the denial of injunction, notwithstanding the finding both that there is a nuisance and that plaintiffs have been damaged substantially, is the large disparity in economic consequences of the nuisance and of the injunction. This theory cannot, however, be sustained without overruling a doctrine which has been consistently reaffirmed in several leading cases in this court and which has never been disavowed here, namely that where a nuisance has been found and where there has been any substantial damage shown by the party complaining an injunction will be granted.

The rule in New York has been that such a nuisance will be enjoined although marked disparity be shown in economic consequence between the effect of the injunction and the effect of the nuisance.

The problem of disparity in economic consequence was sharply in focus in Whalen v. Union Bag & Paper Co., 208 N.Y. 1, 101 N.E. 805. A pulp mill entailing an investment of more than a million dollars polluted a stream in which plaintiff, who owned a farm, was "a lower riparian owner." The economic loss to plaintiff from this pollution was small. This court, reversing the Appellate Division, reinstated the injunction granted by the Special Term against the argument of the mill owner that in view of "the slight advantage to plaintiff and the great loss that will be inflicted on defendant" an injunction should not be granted. "Such a balancing of injuries cannot be justified by the circumstances of this case," Judge Werner noted. He continued: "Although the damage to the plaintiff may be slight as compared with the defendant's expense of abating the condition, that is not a good reason for refusing an injunction."

Thus the unconditional injunction granted at Special Term was reinstated. The rule laid down in that case, then, is that whenever the damage resulting from a nuisance is found not "unsubstantial," viz., $100 a year, injunction would follow. This states a rule that had been followed in this court with marked consistency.

* * *

Although the court at Special Term and the Appellate Division held that injunction should be denied, it was found that plaintiffs had been damaged in various specific amounts up to the time of the trial and damages to the respective plaintiffs were awarded for those amounts. The effect of this was, injunction having been denied, plaintiffs could maintain successive actions at law for damages thereafter as further damage was incurred.

The court at Special Term also found the amount of permanent damage attributable to each plaintiff, for the guidance of the parties in the event both sides stipulated to the payment and acceptance of such permanent damage as a settlement of all the controversies among the parties. The total of permanent damages to all plaintiffs thus found was $185,000.[†] This basis of adjustment has not resulted in any stipulation by the parties.

This result at Special Term and at the Appellate Division is a departure from a rule that has become settled; but to follow the rule

---

† [Seven residents were joined as plaintiffs in this case and would share the $185,000 permanent damages award.—Eds.]

literally in these cases would be to close down the plant at once. This court is fully agreed to avoid that immediately drastic remedy; the difference in view is how best to avoid it.*

One alternative is to grant the injunction but postpone its effect to a specified future date to give opportunity for technical advances to permit defendant to eliminate the nuisance; another is to grant the injunction conditioned on the payment of permanent damages to plaintiffs which would compensate them for the total economic loss to their property present and future caused by defendant's operations. For reasons which will be developed the court chooses the latter alternative.

If the injunction were to be granted unless within a short period—e.g., 18 months—the nuisance be abated by improved methods, there would be no assurance that any significant technical improvement would occur.

The parties could settle this private litigation at any time if defendant paid enough money and the imminent threat of closing the plant would build up the pressure on defendant. If there were no improved techniques found, there would inevitably be applications to the court at Special Term for extensions of time to perform on showing of good faith efforts to find such techniques.

Moreover, techniques to eliminate dust and other annoying by-products of cement making are unlikely to be developed by any research the defendant can undertake within any short period, but will depend on the total resources of the cement industry nationwide and throughout the world. The problem is universal wherever cement is made.

For obvious reasons the rate of the research is beyond control of defendant. If at the end of 18 months the whole industry has not found a technical solution a court would be hard put to close down this one cement plant if due regard be given to equitable principles.

On the other hand, to grant the injunction unless defendant pays plaintiffs such permanent damages as may be fixed by the court seems to do justice between the contending parties. All of the attributions of economic loss to the properties on which plaintiffs' complaints are based will have been redressed.

The nuisance complained of by these plaintiffs may have other public or private consequences, but these particular parties are the only ones who have sought remedies and the judgment proposed will fully redress them. The limitation of relief granted is a limitation only within the four corners of these actions and does not foreclose public health or other public agencies from seeking proper relief in a proper court.

It seems reasonable to think that the risk of being required to pay permanent damages to injured property owners by cement plant owners

---

* Respondent's investment in the plant is in excess of $45,000,000. There are over 300 people employed there.

would itself be a reasonable effective spur to research for improved techniques to minimize nuisance.

The power of the court to condition on equitable grounds the continuance of an injunction on the payment of permanent damages seems undoubted.

The damage base here suggested is consistent with the general rule in those nuisance cases where damages are allowed. "Where a nuisance is of such a permanent and unabatable character that a single recovery can be had, including the whole damage past and future resulting therefrom, there can be but one recovery." (66 C.J.S. Nuisances § 140, p. 947). It has been said that permanent damages are allowed where the loss recoverable would obviously be small as compared with the cost of removal of the nuisance (Kentucky–Ohio Gas Co. v. Bowling, 264 Ky. 470, 477, 95 S.W.2d 1).

* * *

Thus it seems fair to both sides to grant permanent damages to plaintiffs which will terminate this private litigation. The theory of damage is the "servitude on land" of plaintiffs imposed by defendant's nuisance.

The judgment, by allowance of permanent damages imposing a servitude on land, which is the basis of the actions, would preclude future recovery by plaintiffs or their grantees.

This should be placed beyond debate by a provision of the judgment that the payment by defendant and the acceptance by plaintiffs of permanent damages found by the court shall be in compensation for a servitude on the land.

Although the Trial Term has found permanent damages as a possible basis of settlement of the litigation, on remission the court should be entirely free to re-examine this subject. It may again find the permanent damage already found; or make new findings.

The orders should be reversed, without costs, and the cases remitted to Supreme Court, Albany County to grant an injunction which shall be vacated upon payment by defendant of such amounts of permanent damage to the respective plaintiffs as shall for this purpose be determined by the court.

JASEN, JUDGE (dissenting).

I agree with the majority that a reversal is required here, but I do not subscribe to the newly enunciated doctrine of assessment of permanent damages, in lieu of an injunction, where substantial property rights have been impaired by the creation of a nuisance.

It has long been the rule in this State, as the majority acknowledges, that a nuisance which results in substantial continuing damage to neighbors must be enjoined. (Whalen v. Union Bag & Paper Co., 208 N.Y. 1, 101 N.E. 805) To now change the rule to permit the cement company to continue polluting the air indefinitely upon the payment of permanent damages is, in my opinion, compounding the magnitude of a very serious problem in our State and Nation today.

In recognition of this problem, the Legislature of this State has enacted the Air Pollution Control Act (Public Health Law, Consol.Laws, c. 45, ss 1264 to 1299–m) declaring that it is the State policy to require the use of all available and reasonable methods to prevent and control air pollution.

The harmful nature and widespread occurrence of air pollution have been extensively documented. Congressional hearings have revealed that air pollution causes substantial property damage, as well as being a contributing factor to a rising incidence of lung cancer, emphysema, bronchitis and asthma.

The specific problem faced here is known as particulate contamination because of the fine dust particles emanating from defendant's cement plant. The particular type of nuisance is not new, having appeared in many cases for at least the past 60 years. (See Hulbert v. California Portland Cement Co., 161 Cal. 239, 118 P. 928 (1911).) It is interesting to note that cement production has recently been identified as a significant source of particulate contamination in the Hudson Valley. This type of pollution, wherein very small particles escape and stay in the atmosphere, has been denominated as the type of air pollution which produces the greatest hazard to human health.We have thus a nuisance which not only is damaging to the plaintiffs, but also is decidedly harmful to the general public.

I see grave dangers in overruling our long-established rule of granting an injunction where a nuisance results in substantial continuing damage. In permitting the injunction to become inoperative upon the payment of permanent damages, the majority is, in effect, licensing a continuing wrong. It is the same as saying to the cement company, you may continue to do harm to your neighbors so long as you pay a fee for it. Furthermore, once such permanent damages are assessed and paid, the incentive to alleviate the wrong would be eliminated, thereby continuing air pollution of an area without abatement.

It is true that some courts have sanctioned the remedy here proposed by the majority in a number of cases, but none of the authorities relied upon by the majority are analogous to the situation before us. In those cases, the courts, in denying an injunction and awarding money damages, grounded their decision on a showing that the use to which the property was intended to be put was primarily for the public benefit. Here, on the other hand, it is clearly established that the cement company is creating a continuing air pollution nuisance primarily for its own private interest with no public benefit.

This kind of inverse condemnation (Ferguson v. Village of Hamburg, 272 N.Y. 234, 5 N.E.2d 801) may not be invoked by a private person or corporation for private gain or advantage. Inverse condemnation should only be permitted when the public is primarily served in the taking or impairment of property. The promotion of the interests of the polluting cement company has, in my opinion, no public use or benefit.

Nor is it constitutionally permissible to impose servitude on land, without consent of the owner, by payment of permanent damages where the continuing impairment of the land is for a private use. This is made clear by the State Constitution (art. I, § 7, subd. (a)) which provides that "(p)rivate property shall not be taken for *public use* without just compensation" (emphasis added). It is, of course, significant that the section makes no mention of taking for a *private* use.

In sum, then, by constitutional mandate as well as by judicial pronouncement, the permanent impairment of private property for private purposes is not authorized in the absence of clearly demonstrated public benefit and use.

I would enjoin the defendant cement company from continuing the discharge of dust particles upon its neighbors' properties unless, within 18 months, the cement company abated this nuisance.

It is not my intention to cause the removal of the cement plant from the Albany area, but to recognize the urgency of the problem stemming from this stationary source of air pollution, and to allow the company a specified period of time to develop a means to alleviate this nuisance.

I am aware that the trial court found that the most modern dust control devices available have been installed in defendant's plant, but, I submit, this does not mean that *better* and more effective dust control devices could not be developed within the time allowed to abate the pollution.

Moreover, I believe it is incumbent upon the defendant to develop such devices, since the cement company, at the time the plant commenced production (1962), was well aware of the plaintiffs' presence in the area, as well as the probable consequences of its contemplated operation. Yet, it still chose to build and operate the plant at this site.

In a day when there is a growing concern for clean air, highly developed industry should not expect acquiescence by the courts, but should, instead, plan its operations to eliminate contamination of our air and damage to its neighbors.

Accordingly, the orders of the Appellate Division, insofar as they denied the injunction, should be reversed, and the actions remitted to Supreme Court, Albany County to grant an injunction to take effect 18 months hence, unless the nuisance is abated by improved techniques prior to said date.

NOTES AND QUESTIONS

1. The *Boomer* court concluded that the best way to resolve the tension between the conflicting land uses is to require defendant pay plaintiffs permanent damages. In *Penland*, damages were not an option because of governmental immunities that existed. In the absence of governmental immunity, do you think that *Penland* would have reached the same result as *Boomer* of affording the plaintiffs a remedy of damages rather than injunctive relief? If not, can the cases be reconciled?

2. The trial court in *Penland* rejected damages, concerned that the harm to the plaintiffs might increase in the future. By contrast, permanent damages, which compensated the plaintiffs for all harm, past, current, and future, were awarded in *Boomer*. Just as with trespasses, see note 5 in section C1 supra, nuisances can be temporary, continuing, or permanent. Aside from immunity, could the *Penland* court have treated the nuisance as continuing and award damages for harm to date, permitting the plaintiffs to recover damages for any future harm?

3. The *Boomer* court conditionally granted an injunction against the defendant. The defendant can continue operating and the injunction will be vacated on payment of the amount determined to reflect permanent damages. Why not simply enter a judgment for the plaintiffs in the amount of their permanent damages? Does it make any difference which way the relief is structured?

4. The *Penland* court ruled that an injunction should issue unless the burden on the defendant "greatly outweighs" the harm suffered by the plaintiffs. The Second Restatement reflects this balancing approach as to whether an injunction should issue in section 826, which declares that an intentional nuisance is unreasonable "if the gravity of the harm outweighs the utility of the actor's conduct." Should the utility of the actor's conduct (i.e., defendant's composting site) have to be "greatly outweighed" by the harm for injunctive relief to be provided? Why?

5. In comparing the harm suffered by the plaintiffs with the utility of the defendant's conduct, the *Penland* court observed that while the plaintiffs have suffered quality-of-life harm, defendants will only be burdened with economic loss if required to cease operations. Should the type of harm matter in balancing the plaintiff's harm against the utility of defendant's conduct? Won't nuisance cases frequently involve quality of life balanced against economic consequences?

6. The *Penland* court reasoned that the burden on the defendant of moving its composting operations is ameliorated by the fact that it can be "spread" among the rate-payers who live in the sewer district. Does that reasoning put a finger on the scale against any enterprise or governmental entity while benefitting individual land owners in nuisance cases? Wouldn't the same reasoning be applicable to the Atlantic Cement Co.? Or is it, being in a competitive market, in a different position with regard to its ability to pass along costs to its customers?

7. The *Boomer* court discussed the growth of regulation and governmental enforcement of pollution such as the cement dust involved in that case. That trend has continued in the decades since *Boomer*. The federal government (and often the states with their own analog to federal efforts) regulates environmental harms that occur through air and water pollution, the disposal of hazardous wastes, and toxic substances. The primary federal regulatory efforts are covered in Chapters 8 and 9. How should common law courts confronted with nuisance and trespass claims arising out of environmental contamination view their roles in light of the significant regulatory efforts in place? To put the point slightly differently, with extensive environmental regulation, is there a continuing role for private nuisance claims?

In this regard, consider San Diego Gas & Electric Co. v. Superior Court, 920 P.2d 669 (Cal.1996), in which homeowners alleged that electro-magnetic fields created by an electric utility's power transmission constituted a private nuisance. The state utility commission had addressed and approved the power lines about which the plaintiffs complained. The court held that permitting a private nuisance would impermissibly interfere with the regulatory authority of the state utility commission. Suppose that the electric company were transmitting power in violation of regulations adopted by the state utility commission? See, e.g., Rushing v. Kansas City Southern Ry. Co., 185 F.3d 496 (5th Cir.1999) (plaintiff could maintain a private nuisance so long as the limits on noise and vibration exceeded those adopted in federal regulations). In a similar vein and revealing limits on *Boomer* is Little Joseph Realty, Inc. v. Town of Babylon, 363 N.E.2d 1163 (N.Y.1977). The defendants constructed an asphalt plant that violated existing zoning laws. The intermediate appellate court entered an injunction requiring defendants to install a device that would substantially reduce the emissions from the plant. On appeal, the New York Court of Appeals held that an injunction against any operation of the asphalt plant should have been entered. Regardless of the economic consequences of shutting the plant down, this use was one that had already been deemed improper. The zoning violation thus distinguished *Boomer*.

8. Consider the available remedial options—injunctive relief, continuing damages, and permanent damages—for operations like the defendants in *Penland* and *Boomer*. Which remedy will be most effective in spurring the defendant to take steps to abate the nuisance or to encourage research into methods for ameliorating or abating the nuisance?

9. In an important article cited by the *Penland* court, Property Rules, Liability Rules, and Inalienbility: One View of the Cathedral, 85 Harv.L.Rev. 1089 (1972), Guido Calabresi and Doug Melamed identify four different outcomes available when land uses conflict. The first, an injunction, as was issued in *Penland*, provides plaintiff with a property right. The only way defendant can continue operations is to pay a price agreed to by the homeowners, and they can, if they desire, prevent defendant from continuing its composting activities. The second, a liability rule, provides only damages—an amount determined by the court—that permits continued operations, as occurred in *Boomer*. The third, no liability, is equivalent to providing a property right to the party engaged in the conflicting use. Thus, in *Penland*, if the court had found no nuisance, the sewer district could continue composting unless the homeowners paid a price the sewer district accepted, presumably at least the $1 million it would cost to move the operations. Finally, and most exotically, defendants activity might be protected with a liability rule. Thus, again in *Penland*, the court would set damages to be paid by the homeowners to the sewer district, which would then be required to move. This last alternative was employed in Spur Industries v. Del E. Webb Development Co., discussed in note 10 following *Pestey*. The developer sought an injunction against a feedlot operator, which was granted but on the condition that the developer pay the defendant's costs to relocate. Professor Rabin puts these four outcomes in context in Nuisance Law: Rethinking Fundamental Assumptions, 63 Va.L.Rev. 1299, 1322 (1977):

> Thus, an unconditional injunction is an unalloyed victory for the cinema owner and an unalloyed defeat for the track owner. An award of damages for future annoyances, without any injunction, is a partial victory for the cinema owner and a partial defeat for the track owner. An injunction conditional upon compensation by the cinema owner to the track owner is a partial victory for the track owner and a partial defeat for the cinema owner. Finally, denial of both an injunction and damages is a total victory for the track owner and a total defeat for the cinema owner.

(discussing Amphitheaters, Inc. v. Portland Meadows, 198 P.2d 847 (Or.1948))

10. Suppose that the *Boomer* court had adhered to prior precedent and granted the plaintiffs an injunction requiring the defendant to either shut down or sufficiently ameliorate its dust pollution so that it no longer caused substantial damage. Assuming the court's skepticism about the defendant's ability unilaterally to develop technology to address the dust pollution is well-founded, would you expect the defendant's cement manufacturing plant would simply shut down and lose its $45 million investment? What advice might you give a client facing this situation?

The Coase Theorem

In a seminal article, Ronald Coase, who later won the Nobel Prize in economics, claims that when there are conflicting uses, such as exists in nuisance, from an economic efficiency standpoint it does not matter what liability rule is adopted, so long as transaction costs are zero. Coase's fundamental insight was that regardless of which party the law favored, if the competing use was more valuable economically, the higher-value activity would buy out the rights of the other. Thus, in *Boomer*, if the plaintiffs were provided an injunction, the defendant, rather than closing its cement factory, would pay the plaintiffs to permit continued operations. In *Penland*, by contrast, if the residents valued continued living in the area at more than the costs of moving the composting operation, then they would negotiate with and buy out the sewer district. Of course, even though an efficient result will be reached in either case, how the right is allocated will have *distributional* effects. If defendant is liable in a nuisance case, plaintiff will receive some of the benefit of defendant's operation when the parties agree to continued operation. That benefit will remain with the defendant if the law denies liability.

To illustrate the point with an example, reconsider *Penland* with the following hypothetical facts: the total cost to the defendant to move its operations in current dollars is $2 million. The permanent damages to which the homeowners would be entitled if the composting operations were not moved would be $1 million. If the court held in favor of the homeowners, it appears that society would be worse off by $1 million–incurring the $2 million cost of moving the defendant's operations while avoiding but $1 million in damage to the homeowners. Coase's point is that the sewer district would bargain with the homeowners to buy their right to require the district to move operations. The carrot for the homeowners is that the district would pay them more than the $1 million in damages that they would suffer from the continuing nuisance. The advantage for the district is that by buying out the homeowners for some amount less than $2 million, the district has saved money and benefitted as well. Coase conditions his theory on there being no transaction costs, i.e., impediments to the district and homeowners reaching an agreement.

Of course, inevitably there are transaction costs—the plaintiffs in *Penland* may not have been able to organize to buy out the sewer district because there were holdouts who were convinced they did not have to participate and could ride the coattails of the others. Had the sewer district been trying to buy out the plaintiffs, the last homeowners may have held out for an exorbitant price. Even when just two parties are negotiating, they may not get to an outcome that would make each of them better off because they are competing to obtain the surplus created by the transaction for themselves, rather than sharing it with the other side. The implications, under various assumptions about bargaining, are examined in A. Mitchell Polinsky, Resolving Nuisance Disputes: The Simple Economics of Injunctive and Damage Remedies, 32 Stan.L.Rev. 1075 (1980).

In an illuminating article, Professor Ward Farnsworth examines post-judgment behavior in a number of private nuisance cases. Ward Farnsworth, Do Parties to Nuisance Cases Bargain After Judgment? A Glimpse Inside the Cathedral, 66 U.Chi.L.Rev. 373, 421 (1999). He reports:

> A study of twenty old-fashioned nuisance cases litigated to judgment revealed no bargaining after judgment in any of them. Nor did any of the lawyers contacted believe that bargaining after judgment would have occurred if the loser had won. They attributed the lack of bargaining after judgment to acrimony between the parties and to attitudes the parties held toward their rights that made them reluctant to bargain. The size of the sample considered here is small, so it would not be wise to draw strong conclusions from these results about how nuisance cases ought to be decided. We do not know just how often these sorts of problems—of enmity and of resistance on various grounds to treating certain rights as commodities—are sufficient to foreclose the possibility of bargaining after judgment. But in view of the consistency of the results recounted here, it does seem reasonable to conclude that these problems often can be substantial impediments to bargaining after judgment in nuisance cases. These difficulties generally have been overlooked in the economic literature, which uses models of human behavior that focus instead on the danger that each side will engage in strategic behavior that may derail otherwise promising bargains. If a court deciding a nuisance case were to base its decision on these models of nuisance litigation and its aftermath that have been offered in the economic literature, it thus would be acting hazardously; the models exclude details that can have important practical consequences. Perhaps courts understand this. It is not clear that economic models have had an effect on the way that courts fashion remedies, at least in this area of law. If the models have not had much effect, it may

be because judges can sense in them the absence of details that make a difference.

Id.

Another aspect of Coase's article is his observation that causation is reciprocal in nuisance cases with conflicting uses (maybe in all tort cases). Thus, in *Boomer*, it was the cement company's operations that caused harm to the neighboring landowners. At the same time, it was the presence of those landowners and their use of the land that caused harm to the cement company, in its ability to use its land. A West Virginia case in which reciprocal causation is more intuitive is Hendricks v. Stalnaker, 380 S.E.2d 198 (W.Va. 1989). One neighbor sued an adjacent neighbor who had dug a well on his property claiming it was a nuisance. The plaintiff wanted to build a septic system on his property, but could not obtain a permit because the site for the septic system was too close to the well. The trial court found for the plaintiff and entered an injunction. Who is causing harm to whom? On appeal, the West Virginia Supreme Court reversed, noting that "either use, well or septic system, burdens the adjacent property." Balancing interests, the court thought that the well was not an unreasonable use of land because, unlike the septic system, which risked drainage onto the adjacent land, the well posed no such risk.

b. Public Nuisance

Public nuisance is a very old cause of action. Increasingly, plaintiffs attempt put this tort to work to achieve remedies that for whatever reason are unattainable using other tort causes of action such as negligence or products liability and which, in their opinion, have been inadequately addressed by the legislature. These efforts have met with mixed success. In the following case, the Rhode Island Supreme Court refuses to endorse this remedy to deal with the serious social problem of childhood brain injury due to the ingestion of lead.

STATE v. LEAD INDUSTRIES ASS'N.

Rhode Island Supreme Court, 2008.
951 A.2d 428.

OPINION

Addressing the issues *seriatim* for a unanimous Court, Chief Justice Williams authored Tracks I and II * * *. In this landmark lawsuit, filed in 1999, the then Attorney General, on behalf of the State of Rhode Island (the state), filed suit against various former lead pigment manufacturers and the Lead Industries Association (LIA), a national trade association of lead producers formed in 1928.

* * *

Track I

Liability

* * *

I
Facts and Travel

It is undisputed that lead poisoning constitutes a public health crisis that has plagued and continues to plague this country, particularly its children. The General Assembly has declared that although "[c]hildhood lead poisoning is completely preventable," G.L. 1956 § 23–24.6–2(3), it is "the most severe environmental health problem in Rhode Island." Section 23–24.6–3. Indeed, Providence has received the unfavorable nickname "the lead paint capital" because of its disproportionately large number of children with elevated blood-lead levels.

A
Dangers of Lead Poisoning

Lead is a toxic chemical that contributes to the "most common environmental disease of young children." Office of Lead–Based Paint Abatement and Poisoning Prevention, 61 Fed. Reg. 29170 (June 7, 1996) (quoting Strategic Plan for the Elimination of Lead Poisoning, Centers for Disease Control (CDC), U.S. Department of Health and Human Services, Atlanta, Georgia (1991)). There seems to be little public debate that exposure to lead can have a wide range of effects on a child's development and behavior. Contact with low levels of lead may lead to "permanent learning disabilities, reduced concentration and attentiveness and behavior problems, problems which may persist and adversely affect the child's chances for success in school and life." Section 23–24.6–2(1). The consequences are more injurious when children are exposed to higher lead levels. * * * Children exposed to elevated levels of lead can suffer from comas, convulsions, and even death.

Lead was widely used in residential paints in the United States until the mid–1970s. There is no doubt that lead-based paint is the primary source of childhood lead exposure. In the United States, children most often are lead-poisoned by ingesting lead paint chips from deteriorating walls or inhaling lead-contaminated surface dust.

Children under six years of age are the most susceptible to lead poisoning for two primary reasons. First, children are more likely to encounter lead; young children spend a significant portion of their time on the floor, among the dust and chips of lead paint. Second, because they are young, children's growing bodies have a tendency to absorb more lead, and their brains and nervous systems are more sensitive to the lead.

   * * *

B
Lead Poisoning in Rhode Island

[F]rom January 1993 to December 2004 at least 37,363 children in Rhode Island were poisoned by lead in paint. In 2004, a total of 1,685 children in Rhode Island were affected. * * * Fortunately, the prevalence of lead poisoning in children under the age of six recently has declined. In 2005, RIDOH reported a 76 percent decline in the number of lead-poisoned children—from 20.5 percent in 1995 to 5 percent in 2004. However, despite this significant decrease in childhood lead poisonings, the 5 percent prevalence rate is more than double the national average of 2.2 percent.

C
Legislative Responses

In 1971, Congress recognized the prevalence of childhood lead poisonings and enacted chapter 63 of title 42 of the United States Code, the Lead–Based Paint Poisoning Prevention Act (LPPPA), a law aimed at studying the effects of childhood lead exposure and eliminating lead-based paint from federally owned or federally financed housing. Finally, in 1978, the Consumer Product Safety Commission banned the sale of residential paint containing more than 0.06 percent lead. *See* Ban of Lead–Containing Paint and Certain Consumer Products Bearing Lead–Containing Paints, 16 C.F.R. § 1303.1 (2008); *see also* Office of Lead–Based Paint Abatement and Poisoning Prevention, 61 Fed. Reg. at 29171.

Rhode Island, with a housing stock of older homes, also has recognized the depth of this problem. * * *

[T]he General Assembly enacted the Lead Poisoning Prevention Act (LPPA), chapter 24.6 of title 23, which required RIDOH to implement various programs, including statewide blood-screening programs, lead-poisoning prevention programs, and educational programs. The LPPA's stated purpose was to establish "a comprehensive program to reduce exposure to environmental lead and prevent childhood lead poisoning, the most severe environmental health problem in Rhode Island." Section 22–24.6–3.

To supplement this initiative, in 2002, the General Assembly later enacted the Lead Hazard Mitigation Act (LHMA) (P.L. 2002, ch. 187, § 3), G.L. 1956 chapter 128.1 of title 42, to help identify and correct lead hazards in this state. The LHMA imposed, *inter alia,* several duties on the owners of rental dwellings that were constructed prior to 1978, which included correcting lead hazards on their premises. This Court upheld challenged provisions of the LHMA in 2007.

    * * *

D
Attorney General's Lawsuit

On October 12, 1999, the Attorney General, on behalf of the state filed a ten-count complaint against eight former lead pigment manufacturers, John Doe corporations, and the LIA.[7] * * *

---

7. The Lead Industries Association (LIA) declared bankruptcy before the second trial of this case.

The state alleged that the manufacturers or their predecessors-in-interest had manufactured, promoted, distributed, and sold lead pigment for use in residential paint, despite that they knew or should have known, since the early 1900s, that lead is hazardous to human health. The state also contended that the LIA was, in essence, a coconspirator or aider and abettor of one or more of the manufacturers from at least 1928 to the present. The state asserted that defendants failed to warn Rhode Islanders of the hazardous nature of lead and failed to adequately test lead pigment. In addition, the state maintained that defendants concealed these hazards from the public or misrepresented that they were safe. The state further alleged that defendants' actions caused it to incur substantial damages. As such, the state asserted, defendants were liable for public nuisance, violations of Rhode Island's Unfair Trade Practices and Consumer Protection Act, strict liability, negligence, negligent misrepresentation, fraudulent misrepresentation, civil conspiracy, unjust enrichment, and indemnity. * * * The state sought compensatory and punitive damages, in addition to an order requiring defendants to (1) abate lead pigment in all Rhode Island buildings accessible to children and (2) fund educational and lead-poisoning prevention programs.

 * * *

 * * * Eventually, only the state's public nuisance claim proceeded to trial. After a seven-week trial, however, the jury was deadlocked and the trial justice declared a mistrial.

Before a second trial commenced, the state moved to strike defendants' demand for a jury trial, contending that its public nuisance claim was equitable in nature and that defendants had no right to a jury trial on that issue. At that time, the state voluntarily dismissed with prejudice all other non-equitable claims remaining in the case, including the following counts: strict liability, negligence, negligent misrepresentation, and fraudulent misrepresentation. The trial justice, however, denied the state's motion to strike the jury demand, concluding that the existence of a nuisance was a factual issue to be resolved by a jury and, further, that the state's demand for compensatory and punitive damages entitled defendants to a jury trial.

 * * *

After these and other motions were dealt with, the second trial proceeded, this time against only four manufacturers—Millennium, NL, Sherwin–Williams, and ARCO.

 * * *

The jury * * * found that the "cumulative presence of lead pigment in paints and coatings on buildings throughout the State of Rhode Island" constituted a public nuisance. The jury further found that defendants, Millennium, NL, and Sherwin–Williams, were liable for causing or substantially contributing to the creation of the public nuisance. Lastly, the jury concluded that those three defendants "should be ordered to abate the public nuisance." The jury found that a fourth defendant, ARCO, was not liable.

After the verdict, defendants renewed their motions for judgment as a matter of law pursuant to Rule 50 and moved alternatively for a new trial pursuant to Rule 59 of the Superior Court Rules of Civil Procedure. The trial justice denied both these motions. * * *

On March 16, 2007, the court entered a judgment of abatement in favor of the state against defendants, Millennium, NL, and Sherwin–Williams, from which they appeal.

* * *

II

Analysis

A

Standard of Review

When reviewing a trial justice's decision on a Rule 12(b)(6) motion to dismiss, this Court applies the same standards as the trial justice and, accordingly, "must assume that the allegations contained in the complaint are true, and examine the facts in the light most favorable to the nonmoving party." *A.F. Lusi Construction, Inc. v. Rhode Island Convention Center Authority*, 934 A.2d 791, 795 (R.I.2007). * * *

B

Public Nuisance

* * * The defendants contend that the public nuisance claim should have been dismissed at the outset–or, at the very least, that judgment as a matter of law should have been entered in their favor because suppliers of lead pigment cannot be held liable under a public nuisance theory for harm resulting from lead-based paint in Rhode Island. * * * We agree with defendants that the public nuisance claim should have been dismissed at the outset because the state has not and cannot allege that defendants' conduct interfered with a public right or that defendants were in control of lead pigment at the time it caused harm to children in Rhode Island. * * *

* * *

1

History of Public Nuisance

The definition of public nuisance and the description of the elements comprising this cause of action have been developed and refined by this Court over the years. Mindful of the admonition of United States Supreme Court Justice Oliver Wendell Holmes, Jr. that "[i]n order to know what [the law] is, we must know what it has been, and what it tends to become" as that is "necessary to the knowledge of what the law is," we begin our analysis by retracing the history of public nuisance at common law. Oliver Wendell Holmes, Jr., *The Common Law* 1, 37 (Dover ed., General Publishing Co., Ltd., 1991) (1881).

Today, public nuisance and private nuisance are separate and distinct causes of action, but both torts are inextricably linked by their joint origin as a common writ, dating to twelfth-century English common law. *See* Richard O. Faulk and John S. Gray, *Alchemy in the Courtroom? The Transmutation of Public Nuisance Litigation,* 2007 Mich. St. L. Rev. 941, 951 (2007) (citing C.H.S. Fifoot, *History and Sources of the Common Law: Tort and Contract* 3–5 (1949)); Donald G. Gifford, *Public Nuisance as a Mass Products Liability Tort,* 71 U. Cin. L. Rev. 741, 790–91, 794 (2003)). In its earliest form, nuisance was a criminal writ used to prosecute individuals or require abatement of activities considered to "be *'nocumentum iniuriousum propter communem et publicam utiliatem'*—a nuisance by reason of the common and public welfare." Public nuisance, or common nuisance as it originally was called, was "an infringement of the rights of the Crown." 4 Restatement (Second) Torts § 821B cmt. *a* at 87 (1979). Although the earliest cases involved encroachments on the royal domain, public nuisance law evolved to include "the invasion of the rights of the public."

By the fourteenth century, courts began to apply public nuisance principles to protect rights common to the public, including "roadway safety, air and water pollution, disorderly conduct, and public health * * *." Faulk & Gray, 2007 Mich. St. L. Rev. at 951. Nuisance became a "flexible judicial remedy" that allowed courts to address conflicts between land use and social welfare at a time when government regulations had not yet made their debut. *Id.*

It was not until the sixteenth century that the crime of public nuisance largely was transformed into the tort that is familiar in our courts today. Faulk & Gray, 2007 Mich. St. L. Rev. at 952. However, additional parameters were necessary to limit the reach of the new tort. A private party seeking to bring a public nuisance claim was required to demonstrate that he or she had "suffered a 'particular' or 'special' injury that was not common to the public." *Id.; see also* 4 Restatement (Second) Torts § 821B cmt. *a* at 87–88.

* * *

Public nuisance as it existed in English common law made its way to Colonial America without change. In time, public nuisance became better known as a tort, and its criminal counterpart began to fade away in American jurisprudence. * * *

The criminal origins of public nuisance in Rhode Island still can be found in statutes designating certain criminal activities and the places in which they are conducted as "common nuisances." *See, e.g.,* G.L. 1956 § 11–30–2 (defining the unlicensed manufacture or distribution of intoxicating liquor as a common nuisance).

2
Public Nuisance in Rhode Island

* * * Some of Rhode Island's earliest cases involved activities designated as "common nuisances" by the General Assembly. Those cases recognized that " 'a public nuisance becomes a private one to him who is specially and in some particular way inconvenienced thereby * * *.' " *State v. Keeran,* 5 R.I. 497, 511 (1858).

* * *

* * * Over centuries, this Court has taken careful steps to refine the common law definition of public nuisance to reflect societal changes. We are cognizant of the fact that the common law is a knowable judicial corpus and, as such, serves the important social value of stability; although the common law does evolve, that evolution takes place gradually and incrementally and usually in a direction that can be predicted. * * *

This Court has defined public nuisance as "an unreasonable interference with a right common to the general public." *Citizens for Preservation of Waterman Lake v. Davis,* 420 A.2d 53, 59 (R.I.1980). * * * Put another way, "public nuisance is an act or omission which obstructs or causes inconvenience or damage to the public in the exercise of rights common to all." *Iafrate v. Ramsden,* 96 R.I. 216, 222, 190 A.2d 473, 476 (1963) (citing Prosser, *Torts,* ch. 14, § 71 at 401 (2d ed. 1955)).

Although this Court previously has not had the opportunity to address all the elements of public nuisance, to the extent that we have addressed this common law cause of action, our definition largely is consistent with that of many other jurisdictions, the Restatement (Second) of Torts, and several scholarly commentators.

The Restatement (Second) defines public nuisance, in relevant part, as follows:

> "(1) A public nuisance is an unreasonable interference with a right common to the general public.

> "(2) Circumstances that may sustain a holding that an interference with a public right is unreasonable include the following:

> > "(a) Whether the conduct involves a significant interference with the public health, the public safety, the public peace, the public comfort or the public convenience * * *." 4 Restatement (Second) Torts § 821B at 87.

* * *

This Court recognizes three principal elements that are essential to establish public nuisance: (1) an unreasonable interference; (2) with a right common to the general public; (3) by a person or people with control over the instrumentality alleged to have created the nuisance when the damage occurred. After establishing the presence of the three elements of public nuisance, one must then determine whether the defendant caused the public nuisance. We will address each element in turn.

i

Unreasonable Interference

Whether an interference with a public right is unreasonable will depend upon the activity in question and the magnitude of the interference it creates. Activities carried out in violation of state laws or local ordinances generally have been considered unreasonable if they interfere with a public right. * * * The plaintiff bears the burden of showing that a legal activity is unreasonable.

In public nuisance law, as in other areas of the law, what is reasonable *vel non* is not determined by a simple formula.

ii

Public Right

A respected legal authority has identified "[t]he interference with a public right [as] the *sine qua non* of a cause of action for public nuisance." 58 Am.Jur.2d *Nuisances* § 39 at 598–99 (2002). * * *

The Restatement (Second) provides * * * assistance in defining a public right.

"A public right is *one common to all members of the general public.* It is collective in nature and not like the individual right that everyone has not to be assaulted or defamed or defrauded or negligently injured. Thus the pollution of a stream that merely deprives fifty or a hundred lower riparian owners of the use of the water for purposes connected with their land does not for that reason alone become a public nuisance. If, however, the pollution prevents the use of a public bathing beach or kills the fish in a navigable stream and so deprives all members of the community of the right to fish, it becomes a public nuisance." 4 Restatement (Second) *Torts* § 821B cmt. *g* at 92 (emphasis added).

* * * As the Restatement (Second) makes clear, a public right is more than an aggregate of private rights by a large number of injured people. * * *

Professor Donald G. Gifford of the University of Maryland School of Law explained the essential nature of a public right by contrasting it with a public interest:

"That which might benefit (or harm) 'the public interest' is a far broader category than that which actually violates 'a public right.' For example, while promoting the economy may be in the public interest, there is no public right to a certain standard of living (or even a private right to hold a job). Similarly, while it is in the public interest to promote the health and well-being of citizens generally, there is no common law public right to a certain standard of medical care or housing." Gifford, 71 U. Cin. L. Rev. at 815.

iii

Control

As an additional prerequisite to the imposition of liability for public nuisance, a defendant must have *control* over the instrumentality causing the alleged nuisance *at the time the damage occurs.*

* * *

[C]ontrol at the time the damage occurs is critical in public nuisance cases, especially because the principal remedy for the harm caused by the nuisance is abatement.

* * *

The party in control of the instrumentality causing the alleged nuisance is best positioned to abate it and, therefore, is legally responsible.

Recently, the New Jersey Supreme Court similarly held that control at the time the damage occurs is a time-honored element of public nuisance. *In re Lead Paint Litigation,* 924 A.2d at 499. In ruling that the manufacturers of lead pigment could not be held liable for nuisance under New Jersey law, the high court of that state emphasized that "a public nuisance, by definition, is related to conduct, performed in a location within the actor's control * * *." *Id.*

* * *

Other courts and commentators likewise have emphasized the element of control. A leading treatise concerning products liability law states that "a product which has caused injury cannot be classified as a nuisance to hold liable the manufacturer or seller for the product's injurious effects * * *." 2 *American Law of Products Liability* § 27:6 at 11 (3d 2006). Indeed, "a product manufacturer who builds and sells the product and does not control the enterprise in which the product is used is not in the situation of one who creates a nuisance * * *."

iv

Causation

* * * Causation is a basic requirement in any public nuisance action; such a requirement is consistent with the law of torts generally.

A defendant will be held liable in public nuisance only if the conduct complained of actually *caused* an interference with a public right. * * * Although it is true that public nuisance is characterized by an unreasonable interference with a public right, basic fairness dictates that a defendant must have caused the interference to be held liable for its abatement.

In addition to proving that a defendant is the cause-in-fact of an injury, a plaintiff must demonstrate proximate causation. * * * A leading treatise speaks as follows about proximate cause:

"As a practical matter, legal responsibility must be limited to those causes which are so closely connected with the result and of such significance that the law is justified in imposing liability. Some boundary must be set to liability for the consequences of any act, upon the basis of some social idea of justice or policy." W. Page Keeton et al., *Prosser and Keeton on the Law of Torts* § 41 at 264 (5th ed. 1984).

* * *

v
Another Attribute of Public Nuisance

In concluding this discussion of the elements necessary to establish a public nuisance, we also believe that it is advisable to mention the following.

A common feature of public nuisance is the occurrence of a dangerous condition at a specific location. This Court has recognized that the existence of a nuisance depends in large part on its location, and, to date, the actions for nuisance in this jurisdiction have been related to *land*. * * *

* * * Professor William L. Prosser, the highly respected authority on the law of torts, remarked that "[i]f 'nuisance' is to have any meaning at all, it is necessary to dismiss a considerable number of cases which have applied the term to matters not connected either with land or with any public right, as mere aberration * * *." *Prosser and Keeton on the Law of Torts,* § 86 at 618.

Unlike private nuisance, public nuisance does not necessarily involve an interference with a particular *individual's* use and enjoyment of his or her land. Rather, public nuisance typically arises on a defendant's land and interferes with a public right. For example, a nuisance may originate on a defendant's land as in the case of a mosquito pond, or an activity conducted on a defendant's land may interfere with a right of the general public, as in a stream-polluting business.

3
Whether the Presence of Lead Paint Constitutes a Public Nuisance

After thoroughly reviewing the complaint filed by the state in this case, we are of the opinion that the trial justice erred in denying defendants' motion to dismiss under Rule 12(b)(6) of the Superior Court Rules of Civil Procedure.

As the foregoing analysis demonstrates, under Rhode Island law, a complaint for public nuisance minimally must allege: (1) an unreasonable interference; (2) with a right common to the general public; (3) by a person or people with control over the instrumentality alleged to have created the nuisance when the damage occurred; and (4) causation.

Even considering the allegations of fact as set forth in the complaint, we cannot ascertain allegations in the complaint that support each of these elements. The state's complaint alleges simply that "[d]efendants created an environmental hazard that continues and will continue to unreasonably interfere with the health, safety, peace, comfort or convenience of the residents of the [s]tate, thereby constituting a public nuisance." Absent from the state's complaint is any allegation that defendants have interfered with a public right as that term long has been understood in the law of public nuisance. Equally problematic is the absence of any allegation that defendants had control over the lead pigment at the time it caused harm to children.

* * *

A necessary element of public nuisance is an interference with a public right—those indivisible resources shared by the public at large, such as air, water, or public rights-of-way. The interference must deprive all members of the community of a right to some resource to which they otherwise are entitled. *See* 4 Restatement (Second) Torts § 821B cmt. *g* at 92. The Restatement (Second) provides much guidance in ascertaining the fine distinction between a public right and an aggregation of private rights. "Conduct does not become a public nuisance merely because it interferes with the use and enjoyment of land by a large number of persons." *Id.*

Although the state asserts that the public's right to be free from the hazards of unabated lead had been infringed, this contention falls far short of alleging an interference with a public right as that term traditionally has been understood in the law of public nuisance. The state's allegation that defendants have interfered with the "health, safety, peace, comfort or convenience of the residents of the [s]tate" standing alone does not constitute an allegation of interference with a public right. * * * Expanding the definition of public right based on the allegations in the complaint would be antithetical to the common law and would lead to a widespread expansion of public nuisance law that never was intended * * *.

The right of an individual child not to be poisoned by lead paint is strikingly similar to other examples of nonpublic rights cited by courts, the Restatement (Second), and several leading commentators. *See Beretta U.S.A. Corp.*, 290 Ill.Dec. 525, 821 N.E.2d at 1114 (concluding that there is no public right to be "free from unreasonable jeopardy to health, welfare, and safety, and from unreasonable threats of danger to person and property, caused by the presence of illegal weapons in the city of Chicago"). * * * The enormous leap that the state urges us to take is wholly inconsistent with the widely recognized principle that the evolution of the common law should occur gradually, predictably, and incrementally. Were we to hold otherwise, we would change the meaning of public right to encompass all behavior that causes a widespread interference with the private rights of numerous individuals.

* * *

Like the *Beretta* court, we see no reason to depart from the long-standing principle that a public right is a right of the public to shared resources such as air, water, or public rights of way.

Even had the state adequately alleged an interference with a right common to the general public, which we conclude it did not, the state's complaint also fails to allege any facts that would support a conclusion that defendants were in control of the lead pigment at the time it harmed Rhode Island's children.

* * * For the alleged public nuisance to be actionable, the state would have had to assert that defendants not only manufactured the lead pigment but also controlled that pigment at the time it caused injury to children in Rhode Island—and there is no allegation of such control.

* * *

We conclude, therefore, that there was no set of facts alleged in the state's complaint that, even if proven, could have demonstrated that defendants' conduct, however unreasonable, interfered with a public right or that defendants had control over the product causing the alleged nuisance at the time children were injured. Accordingly, we need not decide whether defendants' conduct was unreasonable or whether defendants caused an injury to children in Rhode Island.

* * *

[O]ur decision that defendants' conduct does not constitute a public nuisance as that term has for centuries been understood in Anglo–American law does not leave Rhode Islanders without a remedy. For example, an injunction requiring abatement may be sought against landlords who allow lead paint on their property to decay. In addition, the LPPA provides for penalties and fines against those property owners who violate its rules or procedures. The LHMA further authorizes a private cause of action to be brought on behalf of households with at-risk occupants to seek injunctive relief to compel property owners to comply with the act. G.L. 1956 § 42–128.1–10.

Apart from these actions, the proper means of commencing a lawsuit against a manufacturer of lead pigments for the sale of an unsafe product is a products liability action. The law of public nuisance never before has been applied to products, however harmful. Courts in other states consistently have rejected product-based public nuisance suits against lead pigment manufacturers, expressing a concern that allowing such a lawsuit would circumvent the basic requirements of products liability law.

* * *

[E]ven if a lawsuit is characterized as a public nuisance cause of action, the suit nonetheless sounds in products liability if it is against a manufacturer based on harm caused by its products. Regardless of the label placed on the cause of action, the elements of products liability still must be met to properly maintain such a product-based proceeding.

* * *

The Rhode Island General Assembly has recognized that lead paint has created a public health hazard and, pursuant to its power to legislate, has adopted several statutory schemes to address this problem. Collectively, the LPPA and the LHMA reflect the General Assembly's chosen means of responding to the state's childhood lead poisoning problem. * * * Quite tellingly, the General Assembly's chosen means of remedying childhood lead poisoning in Rhode Island did not include an authorization of an action for public nuisance against the manufacturers of lead pigments, despite the fact that this action seeking to impose liability on various lead pigment manufacturers was well under way at the time the LHMA was enacted. * * * By focusing on the party in control of the instrumentality at the time the harm occurs, the General Assembly's enactments are wholly consistent with the law of public nuisance in this state and all other jurisdictions.

Conclusion

For the foregoing reasons, we conclude that the trial justice erred in denying defendants' motion to dismiss.

* * *

NOTES AND QUESTIONS

1. Other than the requirement that public nuisance interferes with a public right, how is public nuisance different from private nuisance covered in the previous section? Could you envision a case in which both public and private nuisance claims would be appropriate?

2. For a review of public nuisance claims against lead paint manufacturers in Rhode Island and other states, see Richard O. Faulk & John S. Gray, Alchemy in the Courtroom? The Transmutation of Public Nuisance Litigation, 2007 Mich.St.L.Rev. 941.

3. Efforts to use public nuisance law to control other products have generally been met with limited success. The most noteworthy cases attempted to use public nuisance law as a means of gun control. Most courts that considered public nuisance claims against the gun industry have dismissed the claims, but a substantial minority have not done so. Compare Ileto v. Glock Inc., 349 F.3d 1191, 1211–12 (9th Cir.2003) (upholding the viability of a private action for public nuisance), and City of Cincinnati v. Beretta U.S.A. Corp., 768 N.E.2d 1136, 1143–44 (Ohio 2002) (upholding the viability of public action for public nuisance), with Camden County Bd. of Chosen Freeholders v. Beretta, U.S.A. Corp., 273 F.3d 536, 540 (3d Cir.2001), and City of Philadelphia v. Beretta U.S.A., Corp., 126 F.Supp.2d 882, 909 (E.D.Pa.2000) (dismissing the city's and private organizations' public nuisance claims). For a discussion of these cases, see Eric L. Kinter, Bad Apples and Smoking Barrels: Private Actions for Public Nuisance Against the Gun Industry, 90 Iowa L.Rev.

1163, 1165 (2005). In 2005, Congress barred such suits with the passage of the Protection of Lawful Commerce in Arms Act, 15 U.S.C. §§ 7901–03. The purpose of the act is "to prohibit causes of action against manufacturers, distributors, dealers, and importers of firearms or ammunition products, and their trade associations, for the harm solely caused by the criminal or unlawful misuse of firearm products or ammunition products by others when the product functioned as designed and intended." 15 U.S.C. §§ 7901.

4. In *Lead Industries*, the defendants moved for summary judgment on the basis that the state could not identify any specific defendant whose lead pigment was present in any Rhode Island property. They cited Gorman v. Abbott Laboratories, 599 A.2d 1364, 1364 (R.I.1991) (mem.), in which the Rhode Island Supreme Court rejected the market-share theory of products liability. The trial judge held that product identification is not a necessary element in a public nuisance suit and that the state "need only show that each defendant (or such defendants as it seeks to hold liable for the public nuisance here claimed) has engaged in activities which were a substantial factor in bringing about the alleged public nuisance and the injuries and harm found to have been proximately caused thereby." *Lead Industries*, 951 A.2d at 441. Is this responsive to the defendant's motion? Were the state to prevail, how would a court allocate damages or abatement costs among the defendants? See Lisa A. Perillo, Scraping Beneath the Surface: Finally Holding Lead–Based Paint Manufacturers Liable by Applying Public Nuisance and Market–Share Liability Theories?, 32 Hofstra L.Rev. 1039, 1041 (2004).

5. The line between public and private nuisance is not always bright. A public nuisance must interfere with a "public right" but exactly where is the line between a public right and injury to a large number of people? The Second Restatement of Torts, in comment g of section 821B, draws the following distinction:

> *Interference with public right.* Conduct does not become a public nuisance merely because it interferes with the use and enjoyment of land by a large number of persons. There must be some interference with a public right. A public right is one common to all members of the general public. It is collective in nature and not like the individual right that everyone has not to be assaulted or defamed or defrauded or negligently injured. Thus the pollution of a stream that merely deprives fifty or a hundred lower riparian owners of the use of the water for purposes connected with their land does not for that reason alone become a public nuisance. If, however, the pollution prevents the use of a public bathing beach or kills the fish in a navigable stream and so deprives all members of the community of the right to fish, it becomes a public nuisance.
>
> * * *
>
> It is not, however, necessary that the entire community be affected by a public nuisance, so long as the nuisance will interfere with those who come in contact with it in the exercise of a public right or it otherwise affects the interests of the community at large.

CONNECTICUT v. AMERICAN ELECTRIC POWER CO.

United States Court of Appeals, Second Circuit, 2009.
582 F.3d 309.

PETER W. HALL, CIRCUIT JUDGE:

In 2004, two groups of Plaintiffs, one consisting of eight States and New York City, and the other consisting of three land trusts (collectively "Plaintiffs"), separately sued * * * six electric power corporations that own and operate fossil-fuel-fired power plants in twenty states (collectively "Defendants"), seeking abatement of Defendants' ongoing contributions to the public nuisance of global warming. Plaintiffs claim that global warming, to which Defendants contribute as the "five largest emitters of carbon dioxide in the United States and ... among the largest in the world," *Connecticut v. American Electric Power Co.*, 406 F.Supp.2d 265, 268 (S.D.N.Y.2005), by emitting 650 million tons per year of carbon dioxide, is causing and will continue to cause serious harms affecting human health and natural resources. They explain that carbon dioxide acts as a greenhouse gas that traps heat in the earth's atmosphere, and that as a result of this trapped heat, the earth's temperature has risen over the years and will continue to rise in the future. Pointing to a "clear scientific consensus" that global warming has already begun to alter the natural world, Plaintiffs predict that it "will accelerate over the coming decades unless action is taken to reduce emissions of carbon dioxide."

Plaintiffs brought these actions under the federal common law of nuisance or, in the alternative, state nuisance law, to force Defendants to cap and then reduce their carbon dioxide emissions. Defendants moved to dismiss on a number of grounds. The district court held that Plaintiffs' claims presented a non-justiciable political question and dismissed the complaints.

On appeal, Plaintiffs argue that the political question doctrine does not bar adjudication of their claims; that they have standing to assert their claims; that they have properly stated claims under the federal common law of nuisance; and that their claims are not displaced by federal statutes. Defendants respond that the district court's judgment should be upheld, either because the complaints present non-justiciable political questions or on a number of alternate grounds: lack of standing; failure to state a claim; and displacement of federal common law. * * *

We hold that the district court erred in dismissing the complaints on political question grounds; that all of Plaintiffs have standing; that the federal common law of nuisance governs their claims; that Plaintiffs have stated claims under the federal common law of nuisance; [and] that their claims are not displaced * * *. We therefore vacate the judgment of the district court and remand for further proceedings.

* * *

III. Standing

The district court explicitly declined to address Defendants' standing arguments * * *. Because we hold that the complaints should not have been dismissed on the ground that they presented non-justiciable political questions, we must explore whether Plaintiffs have standing. The parties in this appeal have fully briefed the issue of standing.

* * *

A. *The States' Parens Patriae Standing*

1. *Background*

Parens patriae is an ancient common law prerogative which "is inherent in the supreme power of every state . . . [and is] often necessary to be exercised in the interests of humanity, and for the prevention of injury to those who cannot protect themselves." *Late Corp. of the Church of Jesus Christ of Latter–Day Saints v. United States,* 136 U.S. 1, 57, 10 S.Ct. 792, 34 L.Ed. 478 (1890).

* * *

[*Snapp v. Puerto Rico ex rel. Barez,* 458 U.S. 592, 603, 102 S.Ct. 3260, 73 L.Ed.2d 995 (1982)], the seminal modern-day *parens patriae* standing case, * * * formulated a test for *parens patriae* standing. A state: (1) "must articulate an interest apart from the interests of particular private parties, *i.e.,* the State must be more than a nominal party"; (2) "must express a quasi-sovereign interest"[11]; and (3) must have "alleged injury to a sufficiently substantial segment of its population." *Id.* at 607, 102 S.Ct. 3260. * * *

* * *

4. *States' Allegations Satisfy the Snapp Test*

The States have adequately alleged the requirements for *parens patriae* standing pursuant to the *Snapp* * * * [standard]. They are more than "nominal parties." Their interest in safeguarding the public health and their resources is an interest apart from any interest held by individual private entities. Their quasi-sovereign interests involving their concern for the "health and well-being—both physical and economic—of [their] residents in general," *Snapp,* 458 U.S. at 607, 102 S.Ct. 3260, are classic examples of a state's quasi-sovereign interest. The States have alleged that the injuries resulting from carbon dioxide emissions will affect virtually their entire populations. Moreover, it is doubtful that individual plaintiffs filing a private suit could achieve complete relief.

* * *

B. *The States' and the Trusts' Article III Proprietary Standing*

In [*Lujan v. Defenders of Wildlife,* 504 U.S. 555, 560, 112 S.Ct. 2130, 119 L.Ed.2d 351 (1992)], the Supreme Court explained that standing "is an essential and unchanging part of the case-or-controversy requirement of Article III." * * * [T]he Court set out the well-known three-part test:

---

11. The Court identified two types of quasi-sovereign interests: (1) protecting "the health and well-being . . . of its residents," and (2) "securing observance of the terms under which [the state] participates in the federal system." *Snapp,* 458 U.S. at 607–08, 102 S.Ct. 3260. * * *

First, the plaintiff must have suffered an injury in fact—an invasion of a legally protected interest which is (a) concrete and particularized and (b) actual or imminent, not conjectural or hypothetical. Second, there must be a causal connection between the injury and the conduct complained of—the injury has to be fairly trace[able] to the challenged action of the defendant, and not . . . th[e] result [of] the independent action of some third party not before the court. Third, it must be likely, as opposed to merely speculative, that the injury will be redressed by a favorable decision.

Id. at 560–61, 112 S.Ct. 2130. * * *

* * *

1. *Have Plaintiffs Sufficiently Alleged Injury-in-Fact?*

* * *

b. Future Injury

The bulk of the States' allegations concern future injury. For example, those Plaintiff States with ocean coastlines, including New York City, charge that a rise in sea level induced by global warming will cause more frequent and severe flooding, harm coastal infrastructure including airports, subway stations, tunnels, tunnel vent shafts, storm sewers, wastewater treatment plants, and bridges, and cause hundreds of billions of dollars of damage. * * * Global warming threatens Plaintiff States bordering the Great Lakes with substantial injury by lowering the water levels of the Great Lakes, which would disrupt hydropower production. Warmer temperatures would threaten agriculture in Iowa and Wisconsin and increase the frequency and duration of summer heat waves with concomitant crop risk. Global warming will also disrupt ecosystems by negatively affecting State-owned hardwood forests and fish habitats, and substantially increase the damage in California due to wildfires. Plaintiff States predict these injuries will come to pass in the next 10 to 100 years.

The Trusts' complaint also focuses on future injury. For instance, the Trusts claim that the ecological value of their properties will be diminished or destroyed by the global warming to which Defendants' emissions contribute. They contend that sea level rise caused by global warming will "permanently inundate some low-lying property along coasts and tidal rivers, including property that Plaintiffs own or on which they hold conservation easements" and will salinize marshes on their properties, destroying fish and migratory bird habitats. They assert that global warming "will diminish or destroy the particular ecological and aesthetic values that caused [them] to acquire, and cause them to maintain, the properties they hold in trust," and will undermine their objectives by "interfering with their efforts to preserve ecologically significant and sensitive land for scientific and educational purposes, and for human use and enjoyment." They posit that reducing carbon dioxide emissions will reduce those injuries. * * *

* * *

We find that Plaintiffs have sufficiently alleged * * * injury-in-fact.

2. *Causation*

To satisfy the causation requirement, the alleged injury must be "fairly traceable to the actions of the defendant." *Bennett v. Spear,* 520 U.S. 154, 162, 117 S.Ct. 1154, 137 L.Ed.2d 281 (1997). * * *

* * *

[W]e find that Plaintiffs have sufficiently alleged that their injuries are "fairly traceable" to the actions of Defendants. * * * Defendants' attempts to argue the insufficiency of Plaintiffs' allegations of traceability must be evaluated in accordance with the standard by which a common law public nuisance action imposes liability on contributors to an indivisible harm. *See, e.g.,* Restatement (Second) of Torts § 840E ("[T]he fact that other persons contribute to a nuisance is not a bar to the defendant's liability for his own contribution."); *id.* § 875 ("Each of two or more persons whose tortious conduct is a legal cause of a single and indivisible harm to the injured party is subject to liability to the injured party for the entire harm.").

* * *

Plaintiffs * * * are not required to pinpoint which specific harms of the many injuries they assert are caused by particular Defendants, nor are they required to show that Defendants' emissions alone cause their injuries. It is sufficient that they allege that Defendants' emissions contribute to their injuries.

3. *Redressability*

Finally, a complaint must sufficiently allege "a substantial likelihood that the requested relief will remedy the alleged injury in fact." *Jana–Rock Const., Inc. v. N.Y. State Dep't of Econ. Dev.,* 438 F.3d 195, 204 (2d Cir.2006). * * * A party need only demonstrate that it would receive "at least some" relief to establish redressability.

* * *

Defendants' assertions echo their arguments for nonjusticiability under the political question doctrine: because global warming is a world-wide problem, federal courts are not the proper venue for this action, nor could the courts redress the injuries about which Plaintiffs complain because global warming will continue despite any reduction in Defendants' emissions. *Massachusetts* [*v. EPA,* 549 U.S. 497, 532, 127 S.Ct. 1438, 167 L.Ed.2d 248 (2007)] disposed of this argument. The Court recognized that regulation of motor vehicle emissions would not "by itself *reverse* global warming," but that it was sufficient for the redressability inquiry to show that the requested remedy would "*slow or reduce* it." *Massachusetts,* 549 U.S. at 525, 127 S.Ct. 1438 ("[A] plaintiff satisfies the redressability requirement when he shows that a favorable decision will relieve a discrete injury to himself. He need not show that a favorable decision will relieve his *every* injury."). * * * [T]he Court observed that although EPA regulation of greenhouse gas emissions might not reverse global warming, in light of the fact that China and India were "poised to increase greenhouse gas emissions substantially over the next century," the remedy sought—reduction of domestic emissions—"would slow the pace of global emissions increases, no matter what happens elsewhere." *Massachusetts*, 549 U.S. at 525–26, 127 S.Ct. 1438. * * *

In conclusion, we hold that all Plaintiffs have standing to maintain their actions.

V.   Stating a Claim under the Federal Common Law of Nuisance

A.   *Standard of Review*

Defendants have also argued—here and before the district court—that Plaintiffs have failed to state a claim under the federal common law of nuisance. The district court did not reach this issue, dismissing the cases on the ground that they presented political questions. In the interest of judicial economy, we exercise our discretion to address the question now, which has been fully briefed to this Court.

* * *

United States v. Bushey & Sons, Inc., 363 F.Supp. 110 (D.Vt.1973), *aff'd* 487 F.2d 1393 (2d Cir.1973), was one of the first cases to apply the standards of public nuisance, as defined in Restatement § 821B, to the federal common law of nuisance. * * *

* * * The Restatement definition of public nuisance has since been used in other federal cases involving the federal common law of nuisance and the Restatement principles have served as the backbone of state nuisance law.[28]

* * * We believe the Restatement definition provides a workable standard for assessing whether the parties have stated a claim under the federal common law of nuisance. * * * The Restatement definition of public nuisance set out in § 821B(1) has two elements: an "unreasonable interference" and "a right common to the general public." Section 821B(2) further explains:

> Circumstances that may sustain a holding that an interference with a public right is unreasonable include the following:
>
> (a) Whether the conduct involves a significant interference with the public health, the public safety, the public peace, the public comfort or the public convenience, or
>
> (b) whether the conduct is proscribed by a statute, ordinance or administrative regulation, or
>
> (c) whether the conduct is of a continuing nature or has produced a permanent and long-lasting effect, and, as the actor knows

---

28. A majority of states have adopted the Restatement's definition of public nuisance. *See* David A. Grossman, *Warming Up to a Not–So–Radical Idea: Tort–Based Climate Change Litigation,* 28 Colum. J. Envtl. L. 1, 53 (2003). * * *

or has reason to know, has a significant effect upon the public right.

Restatement § 821B(2).

We examine separately the questions of whether the State Plaintiffs and the non-State Plaintiffs (New York City and the Trusts) have stated a claim under the federal common law of nuisance.

C. Have the States Stated a Claim under the Federal Common Law of Nuisance?

1. Applying the Public Nuisance Definition to the States

The States have sued in both their *parens patriae* and proprietary capacities. As quasi-sovereigns and as property owners, they allege that Defendants' emissions, by contributing to global warming,

> constitute a substantial and unreasonable interference with public rights in the plaintiffs' jurisdictions, including, *inter alia,* the right to public comfort and safety, the right to protection of vital natural resources and public property, and the right to use, enjoy, and preserve the aesthetic and ecological values of the natural world.

These grievances suffice to allege an "unreasonable interference" with "public rights" within the meaning of § 821B(2)(a). The States have additionally asserted that the emissions constitute continuing conduct that may produce a permanent or long lasting effect, and that Defendants know or have reason to know that their emissions have a significant effect upon a public right, satisfying § 821B(2)(c). We hold that the States, in their *parens patriae* and proprietary capacities, have properly alleged public nuisance under Restatement § 821B, and therefore have stated a claim under the federal common law of nuisance as it incorporates the Restatement's definition of public nuisance.

* * *

2. Defendants' Arguments

* * *

[A] limitation that Defendants seek to impose on the federal common law of nuisance is that the nuisance must be "poisonous" or "noxious" in order to be actionable. They insist that because carbon dioxide is neither, Plaintiffs' claim must fail. But none of the federal common law of nuisance cases impose this requirement. * * *

Nor does public nuisance theory require that the harm caused must be immediate, as even threatened harm is actionable under the federal common law of nuisance.* * *

Defendants' assertion that the federal common law of nuisance mandates that the harm be localized is similarly misplaced. The touchstone of a common law public nuisance action is that the harm is widespread, unreasonably interfering with a right common to the general public.

The only qualification that the Supreme Court has placed upon a state bringing a nuisance action against another state was that "the case should be of serious magnitude, clearly and fully proved." * * *

In sum, the States have stated a claim under the federal common law of nuisance.

> D. *May Non–State Parties Sue under the Federal Common Law of Nuisance? Analysis of Federal Common Law of Nuisance Case Law*

* * *

> 2. The Restatement (Second) of Torts's Requirements for Maintaining an Action for Public Nuisance under § 821C

Because we apply the Restatement's definition of public nuisance in federal common law of nuisance suits, we will also look to the Restatement for guidance on whether non-state entities may bring claims for public nuisance. The question of whether such entities may maintain a public nuisance suit under § 821C is a threshold issue that must be addressed before the Court can examine whether the parties have stated a claim for public nuisance under § 821B.

Section 821C, entitled "Who can recover for public nuisance," provides:

> (1) In order to recover damages in an individual action for public nuisance, one must have suffered harm of a kind different from that suffered by other members of the public exercising the right common to the general public that was the subject of the interference.

> (2) In order to maintain a proceeding to enjoin to abate a public nuisance, one must

>> (a) have the right to recover damages, as indicated in Subsection (1), or

>> (b) have the authority as a public official or public agency to represent the state or a political subdivision in the matter, or

>> (c) have standing to sue as a representative of the general public, as a citizen in a citizen's action or as a member of a class in a class action.

Restatement (Second) of Torts § 821B; *see also, e.g., In re Exxon Valdez,* 104 F.3d 1196, 1197 (9th Cir.1997) (applying § 821C to whether individuals could assert a public nuisance claim under Alaska law).

> a. Can New York City Maintain a Public Nuisance Suit under § 821C?

New York City has alleged that it is "responsible for protecting the health and well-being of its citizens and residents and protecting the natural resources of the City." It maintains that unrestrained emissions of greenhouse gases will increase the temperature in the City, which will in turn increase heat-related deaths, damage the coastal infrastructure, and wreak havoc in residents' daily lives. Under these circumstances, the City has sufficiently alleged interference with rights common to the general public. In addition, cities are political subdivisions of states. * * *

b. Can the Trusts Maintain a Public Nuisance Suit under § 821C?

We must conduct a more extensive analysis to determine if the Trusts, as private entities, may maintain an action for public nuisance. The relevant subsection of § 821C(2) asks whether the Trusts would "have the right to recover damages." Restatement § 821C(2)(a). * * *

The * * * question is whether the Trusts may maintain an action for public nuisance because they have suffered harm to that right of a kind different from that suffered by the general public. Section 821C cmt. b, provides some insight into what constitutes harm different in kind and degree:

> The private individual can recover in tort for a public nuisance only if he has suffered harm of a different kind from that suffered by other persons exercising the same public right. It is not enough that he has suffered the same kind of harm or interference but to a greater extent or degree. . . . The explanation of the refusal of the courts to take into account these differences in extent undoubtedly lies in the difficulty or impossibility of drawing any satisfactory line for each public nuisance at some point in the varying gradations of degree, together with the belief that to avoid multiplicity of actions invasions of rights common to all of the public should be left to be remedied by action by public officials.

Restatement § 821C cmt. b. Difference in degree, however, as a measure of a different kind of harm, is not entirely out of the picture. Comment c provides:

> Difference in degree of interference cannot, however, be entirely disregarded in determining whether there has been difference in kind. Normally there may be no difference in the kind of interference with one who travels a road once a week and one who travels it every day. But if the plaintiff traverses the road a dozen times a day he nearly always has some special reason to do so, and that reason will almost invariably be based upon some special interest of his own, not common to the community. Significant interference with that interest may be particular damage, sufficient to support the action in tort. . . . Thus in determining whether there is a difference in the kind of harm, the degree of interference may be a factor of importance that must be considered.

Id. § 821C cmt. c.

Numerous commentators have discussed the problems associated with determining whether a private entity may maintain an action for public nuisance. Despite the still-evolving nature of public nuisance, especially when plaintiffs are seeking equitable remedies, the experts agree that a line must be drawn between the many who suffer from a public nuisance and those who may properly bring an action. That line is especially important in this case, where the harms allegedly inflicted by global warming have an impact on millions of people to greater or lesser degrees. Prosser states that "Defendants are not to be harassed, and the time of the courts taken up, with complaints about public matters from a multitude who claim to have suffered.... This insistence upon the rejection of the trivial has been especially marked in the decisions...." William L. Prosser, *Private Action for Public Nuisance,* 52 Va. L.Rev. 997, 1007 (1966). Twenty-five years later, commentators observed,

> [A] court confronted with a private plaintiff would likely require a stronger showing that the plaintiff indeed represented the larger public interest before a *public* nuisance was found. Logically, a private citizen whose interest in the litigation arises solely from having incurred special—and private—damages should not be regarded as equivalent to the public official who brings an action in public nuisance.

Robert Abrams & Val Washington, *The Misunderstood Law of Public Nuisance: A Comparison with Private Nuisance Twenty Years After Boomer,* 54 Alb. L.Rev. 359, 389 (1990). These views underscore the importance of setting forth how the difference in "kind" must be assessed when private entities seek to maintain an action for public nuisance, particularly when the nuisance concerns carbon dioxide and other greenhouse gas emissions that lead to global warming.

Fortunately, in the case before us, we need not demarcate the outer limits of § 821C(1)'s requirement that the harms be different in kind (sometimes called "special injury"), because the harms asserted by the Trusts qualify. The Trusts are nonprofit land trusts with legally recognized missions to preserve ecologically sensitive land areas, and they own land threatened with significant harm (as a result of global warming). The Trusts have opened that land for public use—an invitation the public has accepted in significant numbers. Put another way, although the Trusts are private entities, they share similar features with public entities due to the fact that their lands are open to the public and they are private property owners "whose charter, purpose and mission is to preserve land for public use, enjoyment, and benefit." These factors lead us to conclude that the Trusts will suffer harms different in kind from the harms suffered by other members of the public, including individual landholders. The magnitude of the Trusts' land ownership also constitutes such a difference in degree as to become a difference in kind, the sort of difference explicated in § 821C cmt. c. Because the Trusts have satisfied the requirements of § 821C(1), they may maintain an action for public nuisance.

We hold that New York City and the Trusts may properly maintain actions under the federal common law of nuisance. We now turn to the question of whether the Trusts and New York City have stated a claim.

> 3. *Have New York City and the Trusts Stated a Claim for Public Nuisance under § 821B?*

We have determined that the City and private entities are not barred by their status from bringing a public nuisance cause of action. We now return to the ultimate question: have the non-State Plaintiffs alleged a public nuisance, *i.e.*, an "unreasonable interference with a right common to the general public," pursuant to the definition found in Restatement § 821B(1)? * * *

* * *

We have found that New York City and the Trusts have alleged interference with rights common to the general public. Their pleadings must also satisfy § 821B(2)'s requirement that the interference be unreasonable. Subsections 821B(2)(a) ("whether the conduct involves a significant interference with the public health, the public safety, the public peace, the public comfort, or the public convenience") and 821B(2)(c) ("whether the conduct is of a continuing nature or has produced a permanent or long-lasting effect, and, as the actor knows or has reason to know, has a significant effect upon the public right") apply here.

New York City, as a public entity, has pleaded an unreasonable interference with public rights. It has alleged significant interference: with public health (where heat-related deaths could double and increased smog will increase residents' respiratory illnesses); with public safety (where increased flooding in its coastal areas will damage to city-owned property, creating hazardous conditions); and with public comfort and convenience (by flooding of airports, subway stations, tunnels, storm sewers and wastewater treatment plants). These allegations constitute significant interference, satisfying § 821B(2)(a). * * *

Similarly, the Trusts have pleaded an unreasonable interference with public rights. The Trusts have asserted that Defendants' carbon dioxide emissions, "by contributing to global warming, constitute a substantial and unreasonable interference with public rights including, *inter alia*, the rights to use, enjoy, and preserve the aesthetic and ecological values of the natural world." This alleged significant interference with the public right to be free from widespread environmental harm caused by the effects of global warming satisfies § 821B(2)(a)'s requirement that Defendants' conduct significantly interferes with the public health, comfort, and convenience. The Trusts have also asserted that "Defendants know or should know that their emissions of carbon dioxide contribute to global warming, to the general public injuries such warming will cause, and to plaintiffs' special injuries," and that "Defendants and their predecessors in interest have emitted large amounts of carbon dioxide from the combustion of fossil fuels for at least many decades." These statements are sufficient to allege that Defendants' conduct was "of a continuing nature," as well as that it has already produced a "permanent or long-lasting effect," and that Defendants "know or have reason to know" that their conduct "has a significant effect on the public right." As such, the allegations establish a claim for public nuisance under § 821B(2)(c).

* * *

In conclusion, we hold that New York City and the Trusts have stated a claim under the federal common law of nuisance.

* * *

VII. State Law Claims

In the alternative, the States and New York City have alleged that "[D]efendants are liable under the statutory and/or common law of public nuisance of each of the States where their fossil-fuel fired electric generating facilities are located." The Trusts have also alleged "[i]n the alternative, if federal common law were not to apply, Defendants are liable to Plaintiffs under the statutory and/or common law of private and public nuisance of each of the states where they own, manage, direct, and/or operate fossil fuel-fired electric generating facilities."

In [*City of Milwaukee v. Illinois,* 451 U.S. 304, 317, 101 S.Ct. 1784, 68 L.Ed.2d 114 (1981)] *Milwaukee II,* the Supreme Court observed that federal and state nuisance law could not both apply to the case. "If state law can be applied, there is no need for federal common law; if federal common law exists, it is because state law cannot be used." *Milwaukee II,* 451 U.S. at 314 n. 7, 101 S.Ct. 1784. Accordingly, since we hold that the federal common law of nuisance applies in this case, we do not address the States' and Trusts' alternative claims based on state public nuisance law.

CONCLUSION

* * *

The judgment of the district court is VACATED, and the cases are REMANDED for further proceedings.

NOTES AND QUESTIONS

1. For another case addressing issues similar to those discussed in *American Electric Power,* see Comer v. Murphy Oil USA, 585 F.3d 855 (5th Cir.2009). In *Comer,* the court held that landowners of property along the Mississippi Gulf coast had standing under state law to bring private nuisance, public nuisance, trespass and negligence claims against oil companies and energy companies alleging their operations caused the emission of greenhouse gases that contributed to global warming which in turn added to the ferocity of Hurricane Katrina, which destroyed their property. However, the court subsequently vacated the judgment and granted an en banc review. Comer v. Murphy Oil USA, 598 F.3d 208 (5th Cir.2010); see also Native Vill. of Kivalina v. ExxonMobil Corp., 663 F.Supp.2d 863 (N.D.Cal.2009). For a discussion of global warming litigation, see David A. Grossman, Warming Up to a Not–So–Radical Idea: Tort–Based Climate Change Litigation, 28 Colum.J.Envtl.L. 1 (2003).

North Carolina ex rel. Cooper v. Tennessee Valley Authority, 593 F.Supp.2d 812 (W.D.N.C.2009), is another recent pollution case. The plaintiff claimed that the emissions from several coal-fired power plants were a public nuisance. The court held that untreated air pollution from coal-fired power plants in Alabama and Tennessee were a public nuisance to the citizens of North Carolina. However, two Kentucky coal-fired plants were too remote to significantly impact air quality in North Carolina. The court issued an injunction, requiring the defendant to install appropriate pollution control technology. Note that this case involves traditional ambient air quality questions, not questions of greenhouse gases and global warming.

2. In Massachusetts v. E.P.A., 549 U.S. 497 (2007), discussed in *American Electric Power*, the Supreme Court allowed states, in their parens patriae capacity, to challenge the EPA's denial of a petition to regulate greenhouse gases ("GHG") from new vehicle emissions on the grounds that the EPA lacked authority under the Clean Air Act. The Court held that they did have standing and determined that the EPA has legal authority under the Act to regulate GHG emissions from motor vehicles. It remanded to the agency to determine whether GHG emissions endanger public health and welfare. As a result, in April 2009 the EPA issued its Proposed Endangerment and Cause or Contribute Findings for Greenhouse Gases Under Section 202(a) of the Clean Air Act ("Proposed Endangerment Finding"). 74 Fed. Reg. 18,886 (Apr. 24, 2009) (to be codified at 40 C.F.R. ch. 1). The EPA concluded that six greenhouse gases—carbon dioxide, methane, nitrous oxide, hydroflourocarbons, perflouro-carbons, and sulfur hexafluoride, are air pollutants that can be anticipated to endanger public health or welfare. It also determined that motor vehicle emissions of these pollutants from motor vehicles can "cause or contribute" to human-induced climate change. The proposed findings became final in late 2009 and the EPA must now establish emission standards for new motor vehicles. See Bradford Mank, Should States Have Greater Standing Rights Than Ordinary Citizens?: *Massachusetts v. EPA's* New Standing Test for States, 49 Wm.& Mary L.Rev. 1701 (2008).

3. A central issue in *American Electric Power* is whether the plaintiffs stated a claim under the federal common law of nuisance. In an omitted section of the opinion, the court recognized that federal common law nuisance causes of action are displaced if Congress has enacted relevant legislation. A cause of action has been displaced when "federal statutory law governs a question previously the subject of federal common law." City of Milwaukee v. Illinois, 451 U.S. 304 (1981) (*Milwaukee II*). "Federal common law is a 'necessary expedient' to which federal courts may turn when compelled to consider federal questions which cannot be answered from federal statutes alone." *American Electric Power*, 582 F.3d at 371.

The specific question to be answered is whether the relevant statute(s) speak to the particular issues raised in the case. In the *Milwaukee* litigation, the state of Illinois sued four Wisconsin municipalities, claiming their pollution of Lake Michigan constituted a public nuisance. At the time of *Milwaukee I*, the Federal Water Pollution Control Act (FWPCA) required the EPA to "prepare or develop *comprehensive* programs for eliminating or reducing the pollution of interstate waters and tributaries thereof and improving the sanitary condition of surface and underground waters." 33 U.S.C. § 1153 (1970). The Supreme Court determined relief was available under federal common law because "[t]he remedy sought by Illinois"—to abate the public nuisance of water pollution—was "not within the precise scope of remedies prescribed by Congress." Illinois v. City of Milwaukee, Wisconsin, 406 U.S. 91 (1972). The Supreme Court noted, however, that in the future new federal regulations may pre-empt this common law claim. The case was then remanded to the district court, which found in favor of the plaintiff. However, in the interim, Congress amended the Water Pollution Control Act. In *Milwaukee II* the Supreme Court considered the effect of this legislation on Illinois' cause of action.

The Court declared that the new legislation occupied the field by establishing a comprehensive regulatory program overseen by an expert administrative agency and that under the revised act, every point source discharge is prohibited unless covered by a permit. Because the issue of effluent limitations was now addressed in the FWPCA administrative regime, the federal courts were precluded from applying federal common law to impose more stringent limitations than those imposed under the act.

In *American Electric Power*, the court rejected the defendant's argument that existing federal statutes, including the Clean Air Act have not lead to the regulation of greenhouse gases in ways that "speak directly" to the "particular issue" raised by the plaintiffs. 582 F.3d at 387. At the time *American Electric Power* was decided, the EPA had issued its proposed findings that greenhouse gases constitute pollution under the Clean Air Act. The court noted that these "proposed" findings did not "speak directly" to plaintiff's problems. As noted above, subsequent to the opinion, the EPA in fact found that greenhouse gases "threaten the public health and welfare of the American people" and that the pollutants—mainly carbon dioxide from burning fossil fuels—may be regulated under the Clean Air Act. See U.S. E.P.A., Endangerment & Cause or Contribute Findings for Greenhouse Gases Under Section 202(a) of the Clean Air Act, available at http://www.epa.gov/climate change/endangerment.html.

Note that the focus in *Massachusetts* is on emissions from mobile sources, not fixed sources such as power plants. However, the EPA is proposing rules governing fixed sources. See Air Pollution Standards for Stationary Sources–Next Moves, 40 Envtl.L.Rep. News & Analysis 10012 (2010). Do you think an EPA finding with respect to stationary sources similar to the finding with respect to mobile sources would be enough to cause the Court to agree that the Clean Air Act displaces a common law nuisance suit or must the EPA actually regulate greenhouse gas emissions from power plants?

4. Unlike a private nuisance, a public nuisance does not necessarily involve interference with use and enjoyment of land. However, when a particular harm consists of interference with the use and enjoyment of land, the public nuisance may also be a private nuisance. Is the lead paint in *Lead Industries Ass'n*, a private nuisance to some individuals? What about the greenhouse gas emissions in *American Electric Power*?

Private Enforcement of Public Nuisance: The Special Injury Rule

5. In part because public nuisances need not involve interference with the use and enjoyment of property, courts have erected barriers to private enforcement of public nuisance. As noted in *American Electric Power*, for private individuals to recover damages for a public nuisance they must have suffered a harm of a kind different from those suffered by members of the general public.

The question of whether a private individual has suffered a special injury sufficient to support a public nuisance claim is tied up with the nature of the alleged harm and the *economic loss rule*. The economic loss rule provides that individuals suffering purely economic losses due to defendant's negligent conduct cannot maintain a tort action unless they also have suffered a physical harm to person or property, physical damage to a proprietary interest, or are entitled to recover under a separate tort such as fraud.

East River Steamship Corp. v. Transamerican Delaval, Inc., 476 U.S. 858 (1986) is a straightforward application of the rule. In *East River*, the court held that a ship charterer suffering economic loss because of defects in turbines manufactured by the defendant could not recover under a products liability theory. Does the same limitations apply to public nuisance claims?

Yes, said the Fifth Circuit in State of Louisiana ex rel Guste v. M/V TESTBANK, 752 F.2d 1019 (5th Cir.1985). *Testbank* involved the collision of two vessels resulting in a chemical spill of twelve tons of pentachloraphenol (PCP), at the mouth of the Mississippi River. The spill caused the Coast Guard to close the channel for over two weeks. In an en banc ruling, the court held that summary judgment was properly granted against shipping interests, marina and boat rental operators, wholesale and retail seafood enterprises not actually engaged in fishing, seafood restaurants, tackle and bait shops, and recreational fishermen.

> The problem in public nuisance theory of determining when private damages are sufficiently distinct from those suffered by the general public so as to justify recovery is as difficult, if not more so, as determining which foreseeable damages are too remote to justify recovery in negligence. In each case it is a matter of degree, and in each case lines must be drawn. With economic losses such as the ones claimed here the problem is to determine who among an entire community that has been commercially affected by an accident has sustained a pecuniary loss so great as to justify distinguishing his losses from similar losses suffered by others. Given the difficulty of this task, we see no jurisprudential advantage in permitting the use of nuisance theory to skirt the [economic loss] rule.

> Were we to allow plaintiffs recovery for their losses under a public nuisance theory we would permit recovery for injury to the type of interest that, as we have already explained, we have consistently declined to protect. Nuisance, as Dean Prosser has explained, is not a separate tort subject to rules of its own but instead is a type of damage. W. Prosser, *Law of Torts* § 87 (4th ed. 1971).

Testbank, 752 F.2d at 1030.

Unlike the accidental spill in *Testbank* the emissions in *American Electric Power* were intentional in the sense that the defendants intended to emit greenhouse gases from their plants. Should this affect the ability of those suffering economic loss to bring a claim?

6. The claims of commercial fishermen who were unable to fish the polluted waters were not before the *Testbank* court. Their injury is also an economic loss, but do they stand in a different position because the source of their livelihood was the thing that was injured? Do they have a proprietary interest in the fishing grounds themselves and, if so, is the physical injury to these waters sufficient to give them standing.?

In Union Oil Co. v. Oppen, 501 F.2d 558 (9th Cir.1974), a case brought on statutory grounds, the court permitted commercial fishermen to pursue a claim to recover for economic loss—their economic loss from their inability to fish—due to the defendant's oil spill in the Santa Barbara Channel. In *Testbank,* the court appeared to support this position.

> A substantial argument can be made that commercial fishermen possess a proprietary interest in fish in waters they normally harvest sufficient to allow recovery for their loss. Whether the claims of commercial fishermen ought to be analyzed in this manner or simply carved from the rule today announced, in the fashion of *Union Oil,* or allowed at all, we leave for later. That is, today's decision does not foreclose free consideration by a court panel of the claims of commercial fishermen.

Testbank, 752 F.2d at 1027 n.10.

However, in a concurring opinion, Judge Williams noted that he had "considerable doubt that commercial fishermen can establish a proprietary interest in the right to fish in their fishing waters. Certainly the common legal synonym for 'proprietary interest' is 'ownership,' as legal lexicons attest." *Testbank*, 752 F.2d at 1034. He preferred a rule based on the foreseeability that fishermen's economic livelihood would be disrupted by the oil spill. This approach parallels the analysis in *Oppen* and the Restatement (section 821C, comment h). However, on this issue the foresight quagmire is every bit as deep as the proprietary interest quagmire. Certainly oil-spill induced injury to other commercial interests, e.g., beachside hotels and other businesses is just as foreseeable as injury to fishermen. Nevertheless, these parties are not permitted to recover damages.

The problem with applying the special injury rule is highlighted in a group of public nuisance claims arising out of the crash of the Exxon Valdez. Following *Oppen* the district court allowed the plaintiffs to proceed with their commercial fishing claims. In re Exxon Valdez, 1994 WL 182856, at *6. However, it rejected a similar claim by sports fishers. In re Exxon Valdez, 1993 WL 735037, at *1, aff'd on other grounds, Alaska Sport Fishing Ass'n v. Exxon Corp., 34 F.3d 769 (9th Cir.1994). And in In re The Exxon Valdez: Alaska Native Class v. Exxon Corp., 104 F.3d 1196 (9th Cir.1997), the appellate court affirmed the district court's summary judgment in favor of the defendant on all noneconomic claims for injury to culture or a subsistence way of life asserted by a class of Alaskan natives. "Admittedly, the oil spill affected the communal life of Alaska Natives, but whatever injury they suffered (other than the harvest loss), though potentially different in degree than that suffered by other Alaskans, was not different in kind." Id. at 1198. See also Lloyd's Leasing Ltd. v. Conoco, 868 F.2d 1447 (5th Cir.1989) (denying recovery to businesses whose livelihood was disrupted by an oil spill that polluted beaches in Galveston, Texas).

The commercial fisherman exception has been recognized in other cases as well. See Burgess v. M/V Tamano, 370 F.Supp. 247 (D.Me.1973), aff'd, 559

F.2d 1200 (1st Cir.1977) (commercial clam diggers and commercial fishermen); Leo v. General Elec. Co., 538 N.Y.S.2d 844 (App.Div.1989) (commercial fishermen). Perhaps the commercial fisherman exception may be best thought of as simply that: the fisherman exception. See George Christie, The Uneasy Place of Principle in Tort Law, 49 SMU L.Rev. 525 (1996); Lloyd's Leasing Ltd. v. Conoco, 868 F.2d 1447 (5th Cir.1989) (oil spill polluted beaches in Galveston, Texas).

If in *American Electric Power* the Second Circuit ultimately adopts the position expressed in the *Exxon Valdez Alaska Native* case, which of the Trust plaintiffs' claims are most likely to be dismissed?

7. The special injury question is much more straightforward when plaintiff has suffered a physical harm to person or property. Courts routinely find that individuals in this situation have suffered an injury different in kind and, therefore, are permitted to bring a public nuisance claim. Quite frequently, these individuals also have a private nuisance claim. See Anderson v. W.R. Grace & Co., 628 F.Supp. 1219 (D.Mass.1986); Burns v. Jaquays Mining Corp., 752 P.2d 28 (Ariz.App.1987); Brown v. County Comm'rs of Scioto County, 622 N.E.2d 1153 (Ohio App.1993); Graham Oil Co. v. BP Oil Co., 885 F.Supp. 716 (W.D.Pa.1994).

Private Plaintiffs and Equitable Remedies

8. Usually, public nuisance suits brought by the state seek equitable remedies, such as injunctions and abatement, while plaintiffs seeking the private enforcement of public nuisances seek damages. What barriers confront a private plaintiff seeking equitable relief for a public nuisance? Recall that section 821C(2) of the Second Restatement of Torts envisions that private individuals can seek equitable remedies in a public nuisance suit. Moreover, the standing requirements are eased to some degree. Section 821C(2) requires either,

> a) that one has a right to recover damages as indicated in subsection (1) or

> b) that one have authority as a public official agency to represent the state or

> c) that one have standing to sue as a representative of the general public, a citizen in a citizen's action or a member of a class in a class action.

Comment j has this to say about the new subsection (2)(c), which did not exist in the first Restatement:

> It has been the traditional rule that if a member of the public has not suffered damages different in kind and cannot maintain a tort action for damages, he also has no standing to maintain an action for an injunction. The reasons for this rule in the damage action are that it is to prevent the bringing of a multiplicity of actions by many members of the public and the bringing of actions for trivial injury. These reasons are much less applicable to a suit to enjoin the public nuisance and there are indications of a possible change. Statutes allowing citizens' actions or authorizing an individual to represent the public, and extensive general developments regarding class actions and standing to sue are all pertinent. Since

standing to sue is primarily a procedural matter, not fully appropriate for a Restatement of the substantive law of Torts, it has been regarded as outside the scope of this Section to set forth the rules for determining when there is standing to sue for abatement or injunction. The purpose of the Subsection is to point out that there may be a distinction between an individual suit for damages and a suit in behalf of the public or a class action. The Subsection is worded so as to leave the courts free to proceed with developments regarding standing to sue without the restrictive effect that would be imposed by a categoric statement of the traditional rule, which is found in a limited number of cases.

Restatement (Second) § 821C cmt. j.

With the exception of state and federal statutes that specifically empower individuals to enjoin public and common nuisances—see e.g. Texas Civil Practice and Remedy Code § 125.002; Clean Air Act, 42 U.S.C. § 7604; Comprehensive Environmental Response, Compensation and Liability Act (CERCLA), 33 U.S.C. § 9659—there is relatively little case law on the question of when private individuals who have suffered no special harm can enjoin a public nuisance. Not long after the adoption of section 821C(2) the Hawai'i Supreme Court permitted individuals with no special injury to bring a class action to enforce a right-of-way along once public trails to a beach that crossed the defendants' property. Akau v. Olohana Corp., 652 P.2d 1130 (Haw.1982); see also Miotke v. City of Spokane, 678 P.2d 803 (Wash.1984); Rowe v. E.I. Dupont De Nemours & Co., 262 F.R.D. 451 (D.N.J.2009).

But see Rhodes v. E.I. du Pont de Nemours and Co., 657 F.Supp.2d 751 (S.D.W.Va.2009), a case involving a class action by residential customers of water district complaining that the defendant's chemicals contaminated their drinking water, the court noted:

> Though the Second Restatement of Torts suggests that a class representative may have standing to bring a public nuisance action even without a special injury, *see* Restatement (Second) of Torts § 821C(2)(c), I am not persuaded that the suggestion applies to the instant matter. The Restatement adopted its new rule based on the development of "[s]tatutes allowing citizens' actions or authorizing an individual to represent the public, and extensive general developments regarding class actions and standing to sue." *Id.* § 821C cmt. j. The Restatement references cases involving state statutes that have expanded the standing rules for public nuisance claims, but it does not identify any cases in which a court has adopted an exception to the public nuisance standing rule for class representatives. Though the Supreme Court of Appeals has followed the Restatement's guidance in developing West Virginia tort law, I can find no authority advocating a class action exception to the special-injury rule absent legislative measures.

Rhodes, 657 F.Supp. 2d at 768 n.14.

Likewise, in Anderson v. W.R. Grace & Co, 628 F.Supp. 1219 (D.Mass. 1986), the case made famous by Jonathan Haar's book, *A Civil Action*, the court permitted the plaintiffs to seek damages but not injunctive relief in their public nuisance suit.

When should courts permit private plaintiffs to seek an equitable remedy? At least four factors seem to come into play. First, statutes may authorize private actions. Note, however, that in the great majority of these situations, the remedy is fixed in the statute itself. A prevailing plaintiff can only compel statutory compliance, not some other remedy.

Second, the role of the state in the litigation may have an influence. In some cases, such as *American Electric Power*, the government is a co-plaintiff. This may influence the court's willingness to permit a private plaintiff to participate in the litigation. In other circumstances, the government may itself be the source of the nuisance, in which case private parties may be the only viable plaintiffs. This was the situation in Miotke v. City of Spokane, 678 P.2d 803 (Wash.1984). The city had discharged raw sewage into the Spokane river. In this context, the plaintiff is acting like a private attorney general.

Third, as noted in comment j, courts must guard against a multitude of similar suits. The courts are more likely to permit a private claim when they are assured the plaintiff represents a larger number of aggrieved parties. This was the case in *Akau* where the court held that a plaintiff would have standing to sue if he could, through the mechanism of a class action or otherwise, alleviate concerns about a multitude of suits.

Finally, there is the nature of the nuisance itself. When abatement involves the total cessation of a nuisance, e.g., providing a traditional access point to a beach or prohibiting the discharge of raw sewage into a river, any plaintiff will afford the court the opportunity to impose a remedy satisfactory to all potential plaintiffs. However, when the remedy involves something other than full cessation, the remedy sought by some plaintiffs may differ from those desired by other potential plaintiffs. In this circumstance, a class action or similar device is all the more important to avoid the possibility of a multiplicity of suits. The situation is further exacerbated if a private plaintiff sues some, but not all of the sources of a public nuisance, as occurred in *American Electric Power*, potentially imposing different abatement plans on similarly situated defendants.

9. On what grounds did the *American Electric Power* court permit the Trust plaintiffs to seek an equitable remedy? Under the court's analysis, could the Trusts bring an action for damages? If so, how would they be measured?

10. When the government sues on a public nuisance theory, can it seek common law damages or is it restricted to seeking equitable remedies, i.e., abatement and injunctions? See In re Lead Paint Litig., 924 A.2d 484, 498 (N.J.2007); Victor E. Schwartz & Phil Goldberg, The Law of Public Nuisance: Maintaining Rational Boundaries on a Rational Tort, 45 Washburn L.J. 541 (2006). Does it matter whether the state is suing in its parens patriae or its proprietary capacity? See In re Lead Paint Litig., 924 A.2d at 502 n.8.

11. For a useful review of public nuisance law up to the turn of the millennium, see Denise E. Antolini, Moderning Public Nuisance: Solving the Paradox of the Special Injury Rule, 28 Ecology L.Q. 755 (2001).

D. STRICT LIABILITY FOR ABNORMALLY DANGEROUS ACTIVITY

STATE DEPARTMENT OF ENVIRONMENTAL PROTECTION v. VENTRON CORP.

Supreme Court of New Jersey, 1983.
94 N.J. 473, 468 A.2d 150.

POLLOCK, J.

This appeal concerns the responsibility of various corporations for the cost of the cleanup and removal of mercury pollution seeping from a forty-acre tract of land into Berry's Creek, a tidal estuary of the Hackensack River that flows through the Meadowlands. The plaintiff is the State of New Jersey, Department of Environmental Protection (DEP); the primary defendants are Velsicol Chemical Corporation (Velsicol), its former subsidiary, Wood Ridge Chemical Corporation (Wood Ridge), and Ventron Corporation (Ventron), into which Wood Ridge was merged. Other defendants are F.W. Berk and Company, Inc. (Berk), which no longer exists, United States Life Insurance Company, which was dismissed by the lower courts in an unappealed judgment, and Robert M. and Rita W. Wolf (the Wolfs), who purchased part of the polluted property from Ventron.

Beneath its surface, the tract is saturated by an estimated 268 tons of toxic waste, primarily mercury. For a stretch of several thousand feet, the concentration of mercury in Berry's Creek is the highest found in fresh water sediments in the world. The waters of the creek are contaminated by the compound methyl mercury, which continues to be released as the mercury interacts with other elements. Due to depleted oxygen levels, fish no longer inhabit Berry's Creek, but are present only when swept in by the tide and, thus, irreversibly toxified.

The contamination at Berry's Creek results from mercury processing operations carried on at the site for almost fifty years. In March, 1976, DEP filed a complaint against Ventron, Wood Ridge, Velsicol, Berk, and the Wolfs, charging them with violating the "New Jersey Water Quality Improvement Act of 1971," *N.J.S.A.* 58:10–23.1 to–23.10, and *N.J.S.A.* 23:5–28, and further, with creating or maintaining a nuisance. * * * Velsicol and Ventron counterclaimed against DEP, which amended its complaint to allege the violation of the "Spill Compensation and Control Act" (Spill Act), *N.J.S.A.* 58:10–23.11 to –23.11z (repealing *N.J.S.A.* 58:10–23.1 to –23.10), enacted in 1977. The Spill Compensation Fund (Fund), created by the Spill Act to provide funds to abate toxic nuisances, *N.J.S.A.* 58:10–23.11i, intervened.

Because of issues related to the liability of the Fund, a number of its contributors (Mobil Oil Corporation; Chevron U.S.A., Inc.; Texaco, Inc.; and Exxon Company, U.S.A.) filed a complaint, later consolidated with the present action, seeking a declaratory judgment that the Spill Act not be retroactively applied to discharges of toxic wastes occurring before the effective date of the act.

After a fifty-five-day trial, the trial court determined that Berk and Wood Ridge were jointly liable for the cleanup and removal of the mercury; that Velsicol and Ventron were severally liable for half of the costs; that the Wolfs were not liable; and that, while the Spill Act liability provisions did not apply retroactively, monies from the Fund should be made available. * * *

The Appellate Division substantially affirmed the judgment, but modified it in several respects, including the imposition of joint and several liability on Ventron and Velsicol for all costs incurred in the cleanup and removal of the mercury pollution in Berry's Creek. Because of an amendment to the Spill Act after the trial, the Appellate Division further modified the judgment by imposing retroactive liability under the act on Wood Ridge, Velsicol, and Ventron. * * *

We granted certification to consider the retroactive application of the Spill Act, [and] the liability of Velsicol for the removal of mercury pollution in Berry's Creek * * *. We modify and affirm the judgment of the Appellate Division.

I

From 1929 to 1960, first as lessee and then as owner of the entire forty-acre tract, Berk operated a mercury processing plant, dumping untreated waste material and allowing mercury-laden effluent to drain on the tract. Berk continued uninterrupted operations until 1960, at which time it sold its assets to Wood Ridge and ceased its corporate existence.

In 1960, Velsicol formed Wood Ridge as a wholly-owned subsidiary for the sole purpose of purchasing Berk's assets and operating the mercury processing plant. In 1967, Wood Ridge subdivided the tract and declared a thirty-three-acre land dividend to Velsicol, which continued to permit Wood Ridge to dump material on the thirty-three acres. As a Velsicol subsidiary, Wood Ridge continued to operate the processing plant on the 7.1–acre tract from 1960 to 1968, when Velsicol sold Wood Ridge to Ventron.

Although Velsicol created Wood Ridge as a separate corporate entity, the trial court found that Velsicol treated it not as an independent subsidiary, but as a division. From the time of Wood Ridge's incorporation until the sale of its capital stock to Ventron, Velsicol owned 100% of the Wood Ridge stock. All directors of Wood Ridge were officers of Velsicol, and the Wood Ridge board of directors met monthly in the Velsicol offices in Chicago. At the meetings, the board not only reviewed financial statements, products development, and public relations, but also the details of the daily operations of Wood Ridge. For example, the Wood Ridge board considered in detail personnel practices, sales efforts, and production. Velsicol arranged for insurance coverage, accounting, and credit approvals for Wood Ridge. Without spelling out all the details, we find that the record amply supports the conclusion of the trial court that "Velsicol personnel, directors, and officers were constantly involved in the day-to-day operations of the business of [Wood Ridge]."

In 1968, Velsicol sold 100% of the Wood Ridge stock to Ventron, which began to consider a course of treatment for plant wastes. Until this time, the waste had been allowed to course over the land through open drainage ditches. In March 1968, Ventron engaged the firm of Metcalf & Eddy to study the effects of mercury on the land, and three months later, Ventron constructed a weir to aid in monitoring the effluent.

Ventron's action was consistent with a heightened sensitivity in the 1960's to pollution problems. Starting in the mid–1960's, DEP began testing effluent on the tract, but did not take any action against Wood Ridge. The trial court found, in fact, that the defendants were not liable under intentional tort or negligence theories.

Nonetheless, in 1970, the contamination at Berry's Creek came to the attention of the United States Environmental Protection Agency (EPA), which conducted a test of Wood Ridge's waste water. The tests indicated that the effluent carried two to four pounds of mercury into Berry's Creek each day. Later that year, Wood Ridge installed a waste treatment system that abated, but did not altogether halt, the flow of mercury into the creek. The operations of the plant continued until 1974, at which time Wood Ridge merged into Ventron. Consistent with *N.J.S.A.* 14A:10–6(e), the certificate of ownership and merger provided that Ventron would assume the liabilities and obligations of Wood Ridge. Ventron terminated the plant operations and sold the movable operating assets to Troy Chemical Company, not a party to these proceedings.

* * *

The trial court concluded that the entire tract and Berry's Creek are polluted and that additional mercury from the tract has reached, and may continue to reach, the creek via ground and surface waters. Every operator of the mercury processing plant contributed to the pollution; while the plant was in operation, the discharge of effluent resulted in a dangerous and hazardous mercurial content in Berry's Creek. The trial court found that from 1960–74 the dangers of mercury were becoming better known and that Berk, Wood Ridge, Velsicol, and Ventron knew of those dangers. Furthermore, the lower courts concluded that Velsicol so dominated Wood Ridge as to justify disregarding the separate entity of that corporation and imposing liability on Velsicol for the acts of Wood Ridge. Those courts also found that Ventron assumed all of Wood Ridge's liabilities in their merger. Based on those findings, the lower courts concluded that Berk, Wood Ridge, Velsicol, and Ventron were liable for damages caused by the creation of a public nuisance and the conduct of an abnormally dangerous activity.

The trial court also determined that the 1977 Spill Act did not impose retroactive liability for discharges of mercury into a waterway of the State. After the entry of the judgment, however, the Legislature amended the act to impose retroactive strict liability on "[a]ny person who has discharged a hazardous substance or is in any way responsible for any hazardous substance" being removed by DEP.

[T]he Appellate Division found "overwhelming evidence of mercury pollution in the sediments and waters of Berry's Creek and its substantial and imminent threat to the environment, to marine life and to human health and safety." Consequently, the Appellate Division held Wood Ridge jointly and severally liable under the 1979 amendment to the Spill Act.

II

The lower courts imposed strict liability on Wood Ridge under common-law principles for causing a public nuisance and for "unleashing a dangerous substance during non-natural use of the land." In imposing strict liability, those courts relied substantially on the early English decision of *Rylands v. Fletcher, L.R. 1 Ex.* 265 (1866), *aff'd, L.R. 3 H.L.* 330 (1868). An early decision of the former Supreme Court, *Marshall v. Welwood,* 38 *N.J.L.* 339 (Sup.Ct.1876), however, rejected *Rylands v. Fletcher. But see City of Bridgeton v. B.P. Oil, Inc.,* 146 *N.J.Super.* 169, 179, 369 *A.2d* 49 (Law Div.1976) (landowner is liable under *Rylands* for an oil spill).

Twenty-one years ago, without referring to either *Marshall v. Welwood* or *Rylands v. Fletcher,* this Court adopted the proposition that "an ultrahazardous activity which introduces an unusual danger into the community . . . should pay its own way in the event it actually causes damage to others." *Berg v. Reaction Motors Div., Thiokol Chem. Corp.,* 37 *N.J.* 396, 410, 181 *A.2d* 487 (1962). Dean Prosser views *Berg* as accepting a statement of principle derived from *Rylands.* W. Prosser, *Law of Torts* § 78 at 509 & n. 7 (4th ed. 1971).

In imposing liability on a landowner for an ultrahazardous activity, *Berg* adopted the test of the *Restatement of the Law of Torts* (1938). See *id.,* §§ 519–20. Since *Berg,* the *Restatement (Second) of the Law of Torts* (1977) has replaced the "ultrahazardous" standard with one predicated on whether the activity is "abnormally dangerous." Imposition of liability on a landowner for "abnormally dangerous" activities incorporates, in effect, the *Rylands* test. *Restatement (Second)* § 520, comments (d) & (e).

We believe it is time to recognize expressly that the law of liability has evolved so that a landowner is strictly liable to others for harm caused by toxic wastes that are stored on his property and flow onto the property of others. Therefore, we overrule *Marshall v. Welwood* and adopt the principle of liability originally declared in *Rylands v. Fletcher.* The net result is that those who use, or permit others to use, land for the conduct of abnormally dangerous activities are strictly liable for resultant damages. Comprehension of the relevant legal principles, however, requires a more complete explanation of their development.

Even in its nascent stages, the English common law recognized the need to provide a system for redressing unlawful interference with a landowner's right to the possession and quiet enjoyment of his land. *See* 2 W. Blackstone, Commentaries *218; 1 F. Harper & F. James, *The Law of Torts,* § 1.23 (1956); 2 F. Pollock and F. Maitland, *The History of English Law* 53 (1895). Trespass and nuisance developed as the causes of action available to a landowner complaining of an unauthorized intrusion on his lands. *See* P. Keeton, "Trespass, Nuisance, and Strict Liability," 59 *Colum.L.Rev.* 457 (1959). In their early forms, predating the development of negligence as a basis for liability, neither trespass nor nuisance required a showing of fault as a prerequisite to liability. *See* Keeton, *supra,* at 462–65. Historically, any actual invasion that was the direct result of the defendant's act and that interfered with the plaintiff's exclusive possession of his land constituted an actionable trespass, even in the absence of fault. Keeton, *supra,* at 464–65. In contrast, nuisance required only an interference with the enjoyment and possession of land caused "by things erected, made, or done, not on the soil possessed by the complainant but on neighboring soil." 2 Pollock & Maitland, *supra,* at 53.The continuing nature of the interference was the essence of the harm, and as with trespass, fault was largely irrelevant.

Such was the state of the common law in England when, in 1868, the English courts decided *Rylands v. Fletcher.* In that case, defendants, mill owners in a coal-mining region, constructed a reservoir on their property. Unknown to them, the land below the reservoir was riddled with the passages and filled shafts of an abandoned coal mine. The waters of the reservoir broke through the old mine shafts and surged through the passages into the working mine of the plaintiff. *Id.* As Dean Prosser explains, the courts were presented with an unusual situation: "[n]o trespass could be found, since the flooding was not direct or immediate; nor any nuisance, as the term was then understood, since there was nothing offensive to the senses and the damage was not continuing or recurring."

The Exchequer Chamber, however, held the mill owners liable, relying on the existing rule of strict liability for damage done by trespassing cattle. The rationale was stated:

> We think that the true rule of law is that the person who for his own purposes brings on his land and collects and keeps there anything likely to do mischief if it escapes, must keep it at his peril, and if he does not do so, is *prima facie* answerable for all damage which is the natural consequence of its escape.

On appeal, the House of Lords limited the applicability of this strict liability rule to "nonnatural" uses of land. Consequently, if an accumulation of water had occurred naturally, or had been created incident to a use of the land for "any purpose for which it might in the ordinary course of enjoyment of land be used," strict liability would not be imposed. *Rylands v. Fletcher, L.R. 3 H.L.* 330, 338–39.

Early decisions of this State recognized the doctrine of nuisance as a basis for imposing liability for damages. *See, e.g., Cuff v. Newark & N.Y.*

R. Co., 35 *N.J.L.* 17, 22 (1870) (when the owner of land undertakes to do work that is, in the ordinary mode of doing it, a nuisance, he is liable for any injuries to third persons, even when an independent contractor is employed to do the work). The former New Jersey Supreme Court, however, became one of the first courts to reject the doctrine of *Rylands v. Fletcher.* See *Marshall v. Welwood,* 38 *N.J.L.* 339 (1876). That Court reached this result by referring to the Exchequer Chamber's broad formulation of the rule, which extended liability to anything on the land "likely to cause mischief," rather than the narrowed version affirmed by the House of Lords, which limited liability to "nonnatural" use of the land. Writing for the Court, Chief Justice Beasley refused to adopt *Rylands* because it did not require the challenged activity to be a nuisance *per se.* Using the example of an alkalai works, however, he distinguished those situations in which the causes of injury partake "largely of the character of nuisances," even when they "had been erected upon the best scientific principles." *Marshall v. Welwood,* 38 *N.J.L.* at 342–43.

The confusion occasioned by the rejection of the *Rylands* principle of liability and the continuing adherence to the imposition of liability for a "nuisance" led to divergent results. *See Majestic Realty Assocs., Inc. v. Toti Contracting Co.,* 30 *N.J.* 425, 433–35, 153 A.2d 321 (1959); *see also McAndrews v. Collerd,* 42 *N.J.L.* 189 (1880) (storing explosives in Jersey City is a nuisance *per se,* and one who stores them is liable for all actual "injuries caused thereby"). In *Majestic Realty,* this Court abandoned the term "nuisance *per se,*" and adopted a rule of liability that distinguished between an "ultrahazardous" activity, for which liability is absolute, and an "inherently dangerous" activity, for which liability depends upon proof of negligence. In making that distinction, the Court implicitly adopted the rule of landowner liability advocated by section 519 of the original *Restatement of Torts, supra.*

This rule, while somewhat reducing the confusion that permeated the law of nuisance, presented the further difficulty of determining whether an activity is "ultrahazardous" or "inherently dangerous." *See, e.g., Adler's Quality Bakery, Inc. v. Gaseteria, Inc.,* 32 *N.J.* 55, 159 A.2d 97 (1960) (discussing in *dicta* whether aviation should be considered an ultrahazardous activity). Subsequently, in *Berg,* this Court confirmed strict liability of landowners by noting that it was "primarily concerned with the underlying considerations of reasonableness, fairness and morality rather than with the formulary labels to be attached to the plaintiffs' causes of action or the legalistic classifications in which they are to be placed." 37 N.J. at 405, 181 A.2d 487.

More recently, the *Restatement (Second) of Torts* reformulated the standard of landowner liability, substituting "abnormally dangerous" for "ultrahazardous" and providing a list of elements to consider in applying the new standard. *Id.,* §§ 519–20. As noted, this standard incorporates the theory developed in *Rylands v. Fletcher.* Under the *Restatement* analysis, whether an activity is abnormally dangerous is to be determined on a case-by-case basis, taking all relevant circumstances into consideration. As set forth in the *Restatement:*

> In determining whether an activity is abnormally dangerous, the following factors are to be considered:
>
> (a) existence of a high degree of risk of some harm to the person, land or chattels of others;
>
> (b) likelihood that the harm that results from it will be great;
>
> (c) inability to eliminate the risk by the exercise of reasonable care;
>
> (d) extent to which the activity is not a matter of common usage;
>
> (e) inappropriateness of the activity to the place where it is carried on; and
>
> (f) extent to which its value to the community is outweighed by its dangerous attributes.

[*Restatement (Second) of Torts* § 520 (1977)].

Pollution from toxic wastes that seeps onto the land of others and into streams necessarily harms the environment. See Special Report to Congress, *Injuries and Damages from Hazardous Wastes–Analysis and Improvement of Legal Remedies in Compliance with section 301(e) of the Comprehensive Environmental Response Compensation and Liability Act of 1980 By the "Superfund Section 301(c) Study Group"* (reprinted as Comm. Print for the Senate Comm. on Envtl. & Pub. Works, Serial No. 97–12, 97th Cong., 2d Sess., 1982) [hereinafter cited as *Special Report*]. Determination of the magnitude of the damage includes recognition that the disposal of toxic waste may cause a variety of harms, including ground water contamination via leachate, surface water contamination via runoff or overflow, and poison via the food chain. The lower courts found that each of those hazards was present as a result of the contamination of the entire tract. Further, as was the case here, the waste dumped may react synergistically with elements in the environment, or other waste elements, to form an even more toxic compound. With respect to the ability to eliminate the risks involved in disposing of hazardous wastes by the exercise of reasonable care, no safe way exists to dispose of mercury by simply dumping it onto land or into water.

The disposal of mercury is particularly inappropriate in the Hackensack Meadowlands, an environmentally sensitive area where the arterial waterways will disperse the pollution through the entire ecosystem. Finally, the dumping of untreated hazardous waste is a critical societal problem in New Jersey, which the Environmental Protection Agency estimates is the source of more hazardous waste than any other state. From the foregoing, we conclude that mercury and other toxic wastes are "abnormally dangerous," and the disposal of them, past or present, is an abnormally dangerous activity. We recognize that one engaged in the disposing of toxic waste may be performing an activity that is of some use to society. Nonetheless, "the unavoidable risk of harm that is inherent in it requires that it be carried on at his peril, rather than at the expense of the innocent person who suffers harm as a result of it." *Restatement (Second), supra,* comment h at 39.

The Spill Act expressly provides that its remedies are in addition to existing common-law or statutory remedies. Our examination leads to the conclusion, consistent with that of the lower courts, that defendants have violated long-standing common-law principles of landowner liability. Wood Ridge and Berk were at all times engaged in an abnormally dangerous activity—dumping toxic mercury. Ventron remains liable because it expressly assumed the liability of Wood Ridge in the merger. After 1967, Velsicol, as an adjacent landowner, permitted Wood Ridge to dump mercury onto its land. That activity has poisoned the land and Berry's Creek. Even if they did not intend to pollute or adhered to the standards of the time, all of these parties remain liable. Those who poison the land must pay for its cure.

We approve the trial court's finding that Berk, Wood Ridge, Velsicol, and Ventron are liable under common-law principles for the abatement of the resulting nuisance and damage. * * *

III

In this case, we need not impose liability solely on common-law principles of nuisance or strict liability. In a 1979 amendment to the Spill Act, the Legislature imposed strict liability on any person "who has discharged a hazardous substance or is in any way responsible for any hazardous substance" removed by DEP. That statute is consistent with the long-standing principle that the Legislature may prohibit activities that constitute a nuisance. At all times pertinent to this decision, New Jersey statutes have regulated or prohibited activities leading to pollution of the State's waters.

[The court traced the history of environmental statutes: the first, enacted in 1899, was designed to ensure potable supplies of drinking water and was strengthened several times throughout the twentieth century. In 1976, the Spill Act addressed the storage, transfer, and disposal of hazardous wastes. By 1979, the statute provided that anyone who discharged a hazardous substance or was otherwise "in any way responsible" for a discharge requiring cleanup and removal was jointly and severally liable with others on a strict liability basis. Moreover, the act was retroactive and applied to discharges that preceded the statute if those discharges posed "a substantial risk of imminent damage" to health, safety, or the environment. The court affirmed the lower court's finding that Berk, Wood Ridge, and Velsicol were liable under the Spill Act.]

The remaining question concerns the propriety of imposing liability under the Spill Act on Ventron and Velsicol for the acts of Wood Ridge. Resolution of this question involves recognition that the limited liability generally inherent in the creation of a corporation presents the potential for avoidance of responsibility for the dumping of toxic wastes by the creation of a wholly-owned subsidiary. Implicit in that consideration is a need to balance the policy in favor of granting limited liability to investors against the policy of imposing liability on polluters for environmental torts. The lower courts struck the balance by piercing Wood Ridge's corporate veil and holding Velsicol liable for the pollution caused by its subsidiary. Although we disagree with the reasoning of those courts, we affirm the finding that Velsicol is responsible for the cleanup of Berry's Creek under the 1979 amendment to the Spill Act.

We begin with the fundamental propositions that a corporation is a separate entity from its shareholders, and that a primary reason for incorporation is the insulation of shareholders from the liabilities of the corporate enterprise. Berle, "The Theory of Enterprise Entity," 47 *Colum.L.Rev.* 343 (1947). Even in the case of a parent corporation and its wholly-owned subsidiary, limited liability normally will not be abrogated.

Except in cases of fraud, injustice, or the like, courts will not pierce a corporate veil. The purpose of the doctrine of piercing the corporate veil is to prevent an independent corporation from being used to defeat the ends of justice, to perpetrate fraud, to accomplish a crime, or otherwise to evade the law.

Under certain circumstances, courts may pierce the corporate veil by finding that a subsidiary was "a mere instrumentality of the parent corporation." Application of this principle depends on a finding that the parent so dominated the subsidiary that it had no separate existence but was merely a conduit for the parent. Even in the presence of corporate dominance, liability generally is imposed only when the parent has abused the privilege of incorporation by using the subsidiary to perpetrate a fraud or injustice, or otherwise to circumvent the law.

In holding that Velsicol is liable for the acts of Wood Ridge, the lower courts found it "immaterial" that Wood Ridge was not undercapitalized and that it did not engage exclusively in business with Velsicol. Those courts found dispositive the facts that Velsicol created Wood Ridge for the sole purpose of acquiring and operating Berk's mercury processing business and that, as the trial court found, "Velsicol personnel, directors, and officers were constantly involved in the day-to-day business" of Wood Ridge. By themselves those conclusions are not sufficient to support the further conclusion that the intrusion of Velsicol into Wood Ridge's affairs reached the point of dominance. Furthermore, it appears that Velsicol incorporated Wood Ridge for a legitimate business purpose. Contrary to the implication of the trial court opinion, it is proper to establish a new corporation for the sole purpose of acquiring the assets of another corporation and continuing its business. We cannot conclude that Velsicol incorporated Wood Ridge for an unlawful purpose.

Although it would be inappropriate to pierce Wood Ridge's corporate veil by applying the traditional common-law doctrine, liability of Velsicol may be predicated upon the 1979 amendment to the Spill Act. As amended, the Spill Act provides: "Any person who has discharged a hazardous substance *or is in any way responsible* for any hazardous substance ... shall be strictly liable, jointly and severally, without regard to fault, for all clean up and removal costs."

The phrase "in any way responsible" is not defined in the statute. As we have noted previously, however, the Legislature intended the Spill Act to be "liberally construed to effect its purposes." The subsequent acquisition of land on which hazardous substances have been dumped may be insufficient to hold the owner responsible. Ownership or control over the property at the time of the discharge, however, will suffice. From 1967 to 1974, and thereafter, Velsicol could have controlled the dumping of mercury onto its own thirty-three-acre tract. By permitting Wood Ridge, even after it became a Ventron subsidiary in 1968, to use that tract as a mercury dump, Velsicol made possible the seepage of hazardous wastes into Berry's Creek. Furthermore, from 1960 to 1968, Velsicol was the sole shareholder of Wood Ridge and all members of the Wood Ridge Board of Directors were Velsicol employees. Velsicol personnel, officers, and directors were involved in the day-to-day operation of Wood Ridge. In addition to constant involvement in Wood Ridge's activities, Velsicol permitted the dumping of waste material on the thirty-three-acre tract. When viewed together, those facts compel a finding that Velsicol was "responsible" within the meaning of the Spill Act for the pollution that occurred from 1960 to 1968.

Given the extended liability of the Spill Act, we conclude that the Legislature intended that the privilege of incorporation should not, under the circumstances that obtain here, become a device for avoiding statutory responsibility. A contrary result would permit corporations, merely by creating wholly-owned subsidiaries, to pollute for profit under circumstances when the Legislature intended liability to be imposed.

The question remains to what extent Velsicol should share with Ventron the costs of containing and cleaning up the contaminated area. Wood Ridge, as a successor landowner that purchased all of the assets and continued the activities of Berk, was liable for the damage caused by its own operations and those of Berk. *See New Jersey Dep't of Transp. v. PSC Resources, Inc.,* 175 *N.J.Super.* 447, 419 A.2d 1151 (Law Div.1980); *State v. Exxon Corp.,* 151 *N.J.Super.* 464, 376 A.2d 1339 (Ch.Div.1977); Note, "Successor Landowner Liability for Environmental Torts: Robbing Peter to Pay Paul?," 13 *Rutgers L.J.* 329, 334–42 (1982). Through the merger of Wood Ridge into Ventron, the latter corporation assumed all of Wood Ridge's liabilities, including those arising out of the pollution of Berry's Creek. Ventron, however, did not assume Velsicol's liability.

Pursuant to the mandate of the Spill Act, *see N.J.S.A.* 58:10–23.11g(c), Berk, Wood Ridge, Velsicol, and Ventron are jointly and severally liable without regard to fault. Only Ventron and Velsicol remain in existence, and we affirm that portion of the Appellate Division judgment that holds them jointly and severally liable for the cleanup and removal of mercury from the Berry's Creek area.

* * *

As modified, the judgment of the Appellate Division is affirmed.

NOTES AND QUESTIONS

1. Note that the plaintiff's common law claim was for nuisance. Was this a private nuisance or public nuisance theory? The trial court exonerated the defendants on negligence and intentional tort theories, leaving only abnormally dangerous activity as the basis for a non-statutory recovery. Why weren't the defendants liable for discharging their hazardous waste based on negligence? Why wasn't an intentional nuisance theory available? What difference, if in this case, the plaintiff omitted the nuisance claim and asserted only a claim based on abnormally dangerous activity?

2. The court stated that Wood Ridge and Berk "were at all times engaged in an abnormally dangerous activity," dating back to 1929. Yet the opinion intimates that it was not until the 1960s that the combination of knowledge of mercury's toxicity and heightened environmental concerns would have raised an alert about the dumping of mercury that was going on. This raises the question of whether foreseeability is required for strict liability—of course, many dangerous activities are known to be so—but what about one that is not? The Restatement (Third) of Torts: Liability for Physical and Emotional Harm addresses this matter in section 20, comment i:

> [I]f a defendant disposes of chemicals under circumstances where the defendant knows or should know of their harmful or toxic quality, a finding that the activity is abnormally dangerous may be appropriate. However, if the defendant engages in conduct with neither actual nor constructive knowledge that the conduct is other than harmless, there is inadequate reason to impose strict liability.

Restatement (Third) of Torts: Liability for Physical & Emotional Harm § 20, cmt. i (2010).

Eight years after failing to confront this issue in *Ventron* (likely because none of the parties raised it), the court confronted it in T & E Industries, Inc. v. Safety Light Corp., 587 A.2d 1249 (N.J.1991), in which the defendant argued that it could not be held strictly liable because the dangers of its processing radium were unknown at the time it began its activity. The court declined to resolve the question because it found that the defendant had constructive knowledge of the general sort of dangers involved in processing radium.

3. *Piercing the corporate veil.* The court concluded that Velsicol could not be liable on a veil-piercing theory; its setting up a subsidiary to operate the mercury processing plant was a legitimate corporate structuring to insulate Velsicol's assets from any liabilities that might arise in its subsidiary's operation. You should be familiar with piercing of the corporate veil from your course on Corporations and we do not pursue it here. What was the basis, though, for holding Velsicol liable for violations of the Spill Act? What was the basis for holding Velsicol liable on the common law nuisance claim? The court also held that Wood Ridge, which did not exist until 1960, could be liable for Berk's mercury disposal going back to 1929 based on successor liability. We elaborate on corporate successor liability at the end of this Chapter.

4. Is it fair to say that *Ventron* held that the disposal of hazardous waste is an abnormally dangerous activity? Daigle v. Shell Oil Co., 972 F.2d 1527 (10th Cir.1992) confronted a hazardous waste site at an army arsenal facility that was rated as one of the two worst Superfund sites and a Colorado state court case (Colorado provided the substantive law in *Daigle* based on *Erie*) that refused to impose strict liability for the disposal of a small quantity of caustic hazardous waste. Observing that that hazardous waste is a broad category and that while some operations may not be abnormally dangerous, others could be, the court concluded that the defendant could be found strictly liable for its activity. The New Jersey Supreme Court concurred in *T & E Industries*, discussed in note 2, observing that the determination of whether an activity is abnormally dangerous must be on a case-by-case basis.

5. In reviewing the historical roots of strict liability, the *Ventron* court relied on the "non-natural use" standard of *Rylands v. Fletcher* as the basis for modern strict liability for abnormally dangerous activity. Is non-natural use equivalent to abnormally dangerous activity? Many commentators, contrary to the *Ventron* opinion, are of the view that the abnormally dangerous activity doctrine that evolved in the United States is considerably more limited than a full-throated *Rylands* theory.

But Great Britain has not allowed *Rylands* to flourish as a basis for strict liability for all activity that causes harm to another's property. The non-natural use requirement has been employed to narrow the scope of *Rylands* to unusual or special uses of land that are out of ordinary and proper use of that land. Rickards v. Lothian, [1913] A.C. 263, 279–80. Subsequently, *Rylands* was narrowed to require conduct that is distinctively dangerous, although the House of Lords denied that it provides the basis for a theory of strict liability for dangerous activity, akin to United States law. Instead, *Rylands* is veiwed as related to nuisance, requiring an escape that interferes with another's enjoyment and use of property. See Transco Plc v. Stockport Metro. Borough Council, [2004] 2 A.C. 1; Cambridge Water Co. v. Eastern Counties Leather Plc, [1994] 2 A.C. 264. Australia, another common law country, has rejected *Rylands*. Burnie Port Auth. v. General Jones Pty Ltd., 120 A.L.R. 42 (1994).

6. The court adopted sections 519 and 520 of the Second Restatement and its factors approach as the basis for determining whether a given activity is abnormally dangerous. The Third Restatement of Torts in section 20 returns to a rule approach that the first Torts Restatement employed. That section requires: (1) "a foreseeable and highly significant risk of physical harm even when reasonable care is exercised by all actors;" and (2) "the activity is not one of common usage." Comment k explains that many of the factors employed in the Second Restatement will be relevant to determining one or the other of the two requirements, but those factors are not independently relevant to the court's determination whether an activity is abnormally dangerous.

The Third Restatement explains that an important article by the late Gerry Boston documents the critical role that the first requirement in section 20—great risk despite reasonable care—played among courts considering whether to impose strict liability. Gerald W. Boston, Strict Liability for Abnormally Dangerous Activity: The Negligence Barrier, 36 San Diego L.Rev. 597 (1999). The Third Restatement also explains the prominence of an absence of common usage in determining whether an activity is abnormally dangerous and, by comparison, the unimportance of location and social value in the same determination. See Restatement (Third) of Torts: Liability for Physical and Emotional Harm § 20, cmt. j & i, rptrs. note (2010).

7. The 1979 amendment to the Spill Act, referred to by the court, parallels the federal Comprehensive Environmental Response, Compensation, and Liability Act (CERCLA), commonly known as Superfund, which was enacted the following year. Many states, like New Jersey, have state statutes that are analogues to the federal environmental statutes. The federal statutes, including CERCLA, are addressed infra in Chapters 8 and 9. For a discussion of the interaction among federal and state environmental statutes and determinations of abnormally dangerous activity for common law purposes, see Alexandra B. Klass, From Reservoirs to Remediation: The Impact of CERCLA on Common Law Strict Liability Environmental Claims, 39 Wake Forest L.Rev. 903 (2004).

E.   SUCCESSOR LIABILITY

The corporate relationships and the corporate successions that took place in *Ventron* included a merger, a dissolved company that no longer existed, a subsidiary corporation formed to purchase business assets, a parent company that dominated its subsidiary, and the sale of all of the stock of a company. These transactions and relationships raise the question of when a company—parent, subsidiary, merged entity, and purchaser—may be liable for the actions of another company. Recall the basic proposition of corporate limited-liability law recited in *Ventron*: the shareholders of a company are not liable for its obligations. Thus, the parent, absent exceptions mentioned by the *Ventron* court, is not liable for the obligations of its subsidiary. At the same time, there was no issue about Ventron assuming the obligations of Wood Ridge, after the latter was merged into Ventron. This section addresses the question of assuming liabilities after a successor corporation purchases the assets of another corporation (the predecessor) and continues to operate the predecessor's business, albeit with different ownership.

LEO v. KERR–MCGEE CHEMICAL CORP.

United States Court of Appeals for the Third Circuit, 1994.
37 F.3d 96.

GREENBERG, CIRCUIT JUDGE.

I. FACTUAL AND PROCEDURAL HISTORY

This matter is before the court following entry of our order on November 30, 1993, granting defendant-appellant Kerr–McGee Chemical Corporation permission to appeal pursuant to 28 U.S.C. § 1292(b). We will reverse the order of the district court denying Kerr–McGee's motion for summary judgment entered on September 8, 1993, and we will remand the matter to the district court for entry of a summary judgment in its favor.

The facts are largely not in dispute, and, in any event, we accept the allegations of the plaintiffs-appellees Elaine Leo and Linda Yoder for purposes of this appeal. From prior to the turn of the 20th century continuing until 1940, the Welsbach Incandescent Light Company maintained and operated a factory in Gloucester City, New Jersey, for manufacturing incandescent gas mantles, a process involving extracting thorium from monazite ores. This process generated toxic wastes consisting of thorium by-products which Welsbach deposited on the factory site, thus contaminating the surrounding land. In 1940, Welsbach's Illinois-based competitor, Lindsay Light and Chemical Company, purchased Welsbach's gas mantle business. In the sale, Lindsay acquired Welsbach's outstanding orders, records, formulas, raw materials, inventory, customer lists, gas mantle production line, and the right to use the "Welsbach" name. However, Lindsay did not acquire the Gloucester City land and factory. Rather, it moved the gas mantle business to its own plant in Illinois.

Following a series of acquisitions, Kerr–McGee acquired Lindsay, and it thus concedes that in this litigation it stands in Lindsay's shoes. Accordingly, we will refer to Lindsay and Kerr–McGee simply as Kerr–McGee. * * * Welsbach was dissolved in 1944.

In 1961, Leo and Yoder, who are sisters, and their parents, Thomas and Catherine Bekes, moved to a home close to the former site of the Welsbach factory in Gloucester City, though Leo and Yoder now live elsewhere. On December 5, 1988, Thomas Bekes died from bladder cancer. In March 1991, the New Jersey Department of Environmental Protection notified Catherine Bekes of the high levels of gamma radiation and thorium on her property and on June 3, 1991, the New Jersey Spill Compensation Fund acquired her residence, forcing her to relocate. Soon thereafter she also died from bladder cancer. Leo and Yoder allege that their parents contracted their bladder cancer from exposure to thorium and other waste substances deposited on the Welsbach land.

On January 29, 1993, Leo and Yoder filed suit, individually, and on behalf of their parents' estates, in the Superior Court of New Jersey against Kerr–McGee and certain other defendants to recover for death, injuries, and the potential risk of cancer arising from their exposure to thorium and other waste substances generated in the Welsbach gas mantle operation and deposited on the Gloucester City property. As germane here, Leo and Yoder seek to impose liability on Kerr–McGee on a theory of strict liability. While Leo and Yoder do not claim that Kerr–McGee itself generated the waste which caused the deaths and injuries, they assert that it is liable by reason of its acquisition of Welsbach's gas mantle business. * * *

Subsequently, Kerr–McGee filed a motion to dismiss under Fed. R.Civ.P. 12(b)(6) on the ground that the complaint did not state a claim on which relief may be granted inasmuch as Kerr–McGee never has owned the Gloucester City land and factory. In its bench opinion the district court treated the motion as a motion for summary judgment because it considered material other than the complaint submitted on the motion. The court then predicted that the New Jersey Supreme Court would extend the product line doctrine of successor corporate liability, as explicated in *Ramirez v. Amsted Indus., Inc.,* 86 N.J. 332, 431 A.2d 811 (1981), to the toxic tort at issue, because the toxic by-products were generated directly from the manufacturing of Welsbach's gas mantles. Thus, the court denied Kerr–McGee's motion by the order of September 8, 1993. Kerr–McGee then moved for an amendment of the order to allow an interlocutory appeal, and the district court granted the amendment by an order entered on November 1, 1993. We then granted Kerr–McGee leave to appeal.

II. DISCUSSION

We exercise plenary review as the appeal presents an issue of law. Furthermore, we will apply New Jersey law as the parties agree that it is applicable. Thus, we undertake to predict how the Supreme Court of New Jersey would resolve the issues in this case.

We start, of course, with *Ramirez,* 431 A.2d 811, in which the Supreme Court of New Jersey held that:

> where one corporation acquires all or substantially all the manufacturing assets of another corporation, even if exclusively for cash, and undertakes essentially the same manufacturing operation as the selling corporation, the purchasing corporation is strictly liable for the injuries caused by defects in the units of the same product line, even if previously manufactured and distributed by the selling corporation or its predecessor.

431 A.2d at 825. As the district court acknowledged, *Ramirez* is distinguishable from this case. Unlike the injuries in *Ramirez,* the injuries of Leo, Yoder, and their parents were not caused by a unit in the product line manufactured first by Welsbach and then by Kerr–McGee. Instead the injuries in this case were caused by conditions created by Welsbach's operations on land which Welsbach retained at the time of the sale of the gas mantle business to Kerr–McGee and on which Kerr–McGee never conducted any manufacturing activities. Therefore, we must determine whether in light of these distinctions from *Ramirez,* the New Jersey Supreme Court nevertheless would apply the result in *Ramirez* to this case.[3]

---

3. A corporate successor can be liable for its predecessor's debts on theories other than that recognized in *Ramirez*. For example, liability can be imposed on the successor if it assumes the

The *Ramirez* court predicated its conclusion that the successor corporation could be liable for injuries caused by its predecessor's defective product on three rationales: (1) the sale of the enterprise virtually destroyed the injured party's remedy against the original manufacturer; (2) the successor has the ability to assume the original manufacturer's risk-spreading role; and (3) it is fair to require the successor to assume a responsibility for defective products as that responsibility was a burden necessarily attached to the original manufacturer's good will being enjoyed by the successor in the continued operation of the business. *Id.* 431 A.2d at 820. Clearly these rationales do not support the extension of successor liability to Kerr–McGee in this case.

The first factor, the destruction of the injured party's remedy is a *necessary* but not a *sufficient* basis on which to place liability on the successor. Accordingly, if the selling corporation remains a viable entity able to respond in damages to the injured party, a successor acquiring a product line will not be liable for injuries caused by the predecessor's product after the product's sale as in that circumstance there would be no reason to impose successor liability. This initial rationale for the product-line doctrine of successor liability merely focuses on the need for imposition of successor liability rather than whether it is fair to impose it. Therefore, we will not hold that proof that Leo and Yoder cannot recover against Welsbach because it has been dissolved is in itself a sufficient basis for the imposition of successor liability on Kerr–McGee.

The second rationale on which the Supreme Court of New Jersey based its result in *Ramirez* was the successor's ability to assume the predecessor corporation's risk-spreading role. We think that the Supreme Court of New Jersey would recognize that Kerr–McGee does not have the capacity to assume Welsbach's risk-spreading role. In this regard, we point out that if successor liability can be imposed for a toxic tort arising from the predecessor's operations at a facility which the successor never acquires or controls, a prudent manufacturer acquiring a product line would make an analysis of environmental risks associated with the seller's facilities similar to that now undertaken by purchasers of real estate. The purchaser then would attempt to acquire insurance for possible liabilities associated with the seller's real estate.

The impediment to commercial transactions from such a process is evident. Indeed, inasmuch as a manufacturer might build a product or its component parts at more than one facility, a purchaser of a product line might face daunting obstacles in attempting to assess its risks of successor toxic tort liability for conditions on property to be retained by the seller of the product line. Furthermore, a product-line purchaser not acquiring its predecessor's manufacturing facility probably would not be able to lessen the risks of toxic tort liability associated with the real estate. It is doubtful

_____

predecessor's liabilities or if the predecessor merges into the successor. *Ramirez*, 431 A.2d at 815. But we confine our opinion to the question of whether Kerr–McGee may be liable based on the product-line doctrine of successor liability as that is the only basis for liability that Leo and Yoder advance against Kerr–McGee.

that such a product-line purchaser would be able to undertake cleanup operations on land it did not own. Moreover, the product-line purchaser might be unwilling to undertake such potentially costly projects.[5] It seems clear, therefore, that if *Ramirez* applies here, a purchaser of a product line will be subject to liabilities for toxic torts of unpredictable scope for an indefinite period. Overall, we cannot conceive that the Supreme Court of New Jersey would believe that the purchaser of a product line not acquiring the real estate at which the product was manufactured reasonably could assume its predecessor's risk spreading role for toxic torts.[6]

In contrast, a successor to a product line may be able to take steps to reduce its risk of liability for injuries caused by the predecessor's products through recall and educational programs which include those products. Furthermore, successor liability for injuries caused by units manufactured by the predecessor, at least when compared to potential toxic tort liability, is a discrete manageable matter. First, the successor may be able reasonably to anticipate the risks associated with a product it is acquiring. Second, product-line successor liability is applied in cases of the production of personal property. Inasmuch as such property is not likely to have an indefinite useful life, passage of time will diminish the chance of liability being imposed on the successor.

This constant diminution of exposure to product liability is enhanced by the rule followed in New Jersey and elsewhere that a manufacturer cannot be strictly liable unless there was a defect in the product when it left the manufacturer's control. It seems apparent that, except perhaps in design defect cases, a defect in a product when the manufacturer distributed the product is likely to manifest itself and cause injury within a reasonable time after the product is manufactured. Accordingly, as a practical matter, successor liability under *Ramirez* is likely to be imposed in most cases, if at all, for a limited period. Furthermore, if there is an injury from a product a long time after it leaves the manufacturer's hands, the injured plaintiff may have difficulty establishing that the defect existed in the product when manufactured and originally distributed. Thus, using the time scenario here, it would be unusual for the successor in a product line case to be defending an action in the 1990's for a product that could have been built at the latest in 1940.

On the other hand toxic tort liability can be imposed for activities in the distant past. *See T & E Indus., Inc. v. Safety Light Corp.,* 123 N.J. 371, 587 A.2d 1249 (1991). This tail on potential toxic tort liability following the disposal of chemical wastes is attributable to the fact that the toxic wastes may remain in the ground for long periods, thus exposing persons and property to injury long after manufacturing has ended.

---

5. In *FMC Corp. v. United States Dep't of Commerce,* 29 F.3d 833, 838–39 (3d Cir.1994) (in banc), the government estimated the cost of environmental cleanup of the facility involved in that litigation at between $26,000,000 and $78,000,000.

6. In *Ramirez* the Supreme Court of New Jersey acknowledged that the negative effect of successor liability in a product liability case on the sale of manufacturing assets was a "legitimate" concern. 431 A.2d at 822. Thus, we think it appropriate for us to consider that effect.

Indeed, this case demonstrates how long the successor can face claims for toxic torts. Furthermore, the difficulty that the purchaser of a product line will have in assessing its risk of liability for toxic torts as compared to its risk of successor product liability is further heightened by the fact that whereas injuries from defective products are likely to be traumatic, and thus be immediately obvious, injury from exposure to toxic wastes may develop over an extended period. We also observe that it would be more likely that the successor could acquire insurance coverage for the discrete risks flowing from injuries caused directly by a predecessor's product than for environmental risks from conditions on real estate.

The third *Ramirez* rationale, that it is fair to require a successor to assume a responsibility for defective products as that responsibility is a burden necessarily attached to the successor's acquisition of the predecessor's good will, has no application in this case. The good will that Kerr–McGee acquired from Welsbach was attached to the product line it acquired, gas mantles, rather than to the site at which Welsbach manufactured the product. Thus, Leo and Yoder do not assert that this is a case in which Welsbach and Kerr–McGee encouraged the purchasers of the gas mantles to associate them with their geographical source, as, *e.g.,* "a genuine widget manufactured in the widget center of the world." Consequently, while Leo and Yoder point out that Kerr–McGee's purchase of the Welsbach gas mantle product line was profitable, and they attribute that profit in part to the good will it acquired from Welsbach, that point is immaterial.

In reaching our result, we quite naturally consider our opinion in *City of Philadelphia v. Lead Indus. Ass'n,* 994 F.2d 112 (3d Cir.1993). There we indicated that while:

> [a] federal court may act as a judicial pioneer when interpreting the United States Constitution and federal law ... [i]n a diversity case, however, federal courts may not engage in judicial activism. Federalism concerns require that we permit state courts to decide whether and to what extent they will expand state common law.... Our role is to apply the current law of the jurisdiction, and leave it undisturbed.

Id. at 123.

We could allow liability to be imposed in this case on Kerr–McGee only if we stretched *Ramirez* far beyond its original scope and, in light of *City of Philadelphia v. Lead Indus. Ass'n, Inc.,* we will not do that. While the district court believed that this case could come within the *Ramirez* holding, in large part it reached that conclusion because of what it thought was "the traditional New Jersey view that if you are injured somebody ought to be liable for it." But we reject that approach. While we might be willing to apply the precedents of the New Jersey Supreme Court in circumstances somewhat beyond the limits of liability that court has recognized in extant cases, we will not apply *Ramirez* in the circumstances here, which are far beyond the limits of that case.

In closing, we note that the parties in their briefs discuss cases involving liability of successors acquiring contaminated property and other cases involving liabilities arising from the ownership of and activities on real estate. *See, e.g., T & E Indus., Inc. v. Safety Light Corp.*, 587 A.2d 1249; *State of New Jersey, Dep't of Envtl. Protection v. Ventron Corp.*, 94 N.J. 473, 468 A.2d 150 (1983). We have examined these cases but do not discuss them, as they have only the most tangential relationship to this case in light of the fact that Kerr–McGee never owned, controlled or engaged in activities on the Gloucester City property.

III. CONCLUSION

We will reverse the order of September 8, 1993, and will remand the matter to the district court for entry of a summary judgment in favor of Kerr–McGee.

ATKINS, SENIOR DISTRICT JUDGE, specially concurring:

While the record does not reflect the fact, this judge takes judicial notice of the procedure, adopted by 44 of the Supreme Courts or comparable final state appellate courts, permitting federal appellate courts to submit questions for resolution by such courts, involving state common law issues that remain "open." Such procedure cries out for decision in the appeal *sub judice*. The issue concerns, as the majority opinion so clearly demonstrates, whether this court should hold an entity liable for environmental degradation of land for commercial engrandizement after it obviously profited from such degradation, even though acquisition of land was not part of the product line purchase. This salutary certification procedure avoids the charge, admittedly valid, that the federal courts should avoid extending, gratuitously, the common law of the states within the ambit of their jurisdiction. *City of Philadelphia v. Lead Industries Ass'n*, 994 F.2d 112 (3d Cir.1993).

Here, we are called upon to decide what, under a new set of facts, the Supreme Court of New Jersey would decide in an issue it has never been called upon to consider. Our problem is complicated by New Jersey's failure to provide a certification procedure permitting it to have a needed and proper voice in the development of the common law of its state.

A. *The Development of New Jersey's "Product Line" Doctrine*

When the district court denied the plaintiffs' Motion for Summary Judgment, it relied on a string of cases defining the present "product line" theory of successor corporation liability for strict liability torts. From the trend formed by these opinions, the district court "predicted" how the New Jersey Supreme Court would rule under the present factual circumstances. The district court held that the product line doctrine of successor liability originally adopted in *Ramirez v. Amsted Industries, Inc.*, 86 N.J. 332, 431 A.2d 811 (1981), should be applied to include circumstances where a predecessor corporation improperly disposed of toxic manufacturing by-products on its factory site and then sold its entire product line patented process, good will, inventory, sales records and trade name, but not the factory site itself, to a successor corporation which continues the same manufacturing process at different site. Upon review of the line of cases dealing with the "product line" theory of successor corporate liability in products liability cases, I believe that the district court was correct in determining that the New Jersey Supreme Court would apply the strict liability doctrine to a strict liability environmental tort under these factual circumstances.

B. *Analysis*

This is not a case where the corporate successor purchases some of the land that the predecessor contaminated and then continued a separate business on that land. Therefore, *State Dept. of Environmental Protection v. Exxon Corp.,* 151 N.J.Super. 464, 376 A.2d 1339 (Ch.Div.1977), is distinguishable. This case is, however, more like *Ramirez, supra,* in that Welsbach's product line could be considered as all or substantially all of the manufacturing assets which were acquired by Kerr–McGee's predecessors. Thus, even if the assets were acquired exclusively for cash, and Kerr–McGee and its predecessors undertook essentially the same manufacturing operation as Welsbach, Kerr–McGee should be strictly liable for injuries caused by defects in units or by *waste from production of those units* of the same *product line,* even if previously manufactured and distributed by Welsbach. *See Ramirez,* 431 A.2d at 825.

The policies in *Ray v. Alad Corp.,* 19 Cal.3d 22, 136 Cal.Rptr. 574, 560 P.2d 3 (1977), and *Ramirez, supra,* apply similarly to the present case. First the plaintiff's potential remedy against Welsbach, the original manufacturer who caused the contamination, was destroyed by the Kerr–McGee's purchase of Welsbach's assets, trade name, good will and Welsbach's resulting dissolution. In other words, Kerr–McGee's acquisition destroyed whatever remedy plaintiff might have had against Welsbach. Second, the imposition of successor corporation liability upon Kerr–McGee is consistent with the public policy of spreading the risk to society at large for the costs of injuries from contamination due to a product line. This is because the successor corporation is in a better position to bear accident-avoidance costs. In this case, Kerr–McGee is in a better position to bear the costs because Welsbach transferred to Kerr–McGee the resource that had previously been available to Welsbach for meeting its responsibilities to persons injured by the product line it operated. Third, the imposition upon Kerr–McGee of responsibility to answer claims of liability for injuries allegedly caused by Welsbach's product line is justified as a burden necessarily attached to its enjoyment of Welsbach's trade name, good will and the continuation of an established manufacturing enterprise. For "[p]ublic policy requires that having received the substantial benefits of the continuing manufacturing enterprise, the successor corporation should also be made to bear the burden of the operating costs that other established business operations must ordinarily bear." *Ramirez,* 431 A.2d at 822. "[I]n light of the social policy underlying the law of products liability, the true worth of a predecessor corporation must reflect the potential liability that the shareholders have escaped through the sale of their corporation." *Id.* To avoid such liability Kerr–McGee could have "obtain[ed] products liability insurance for contingent liability claims, and it [could have entered] into full or partial indemnification or escrow agreements with the selling corporation." *Id.* 431 A.2d at 823.

Kerr–McGee, like Bruno in *Nieves v. Bruno Sherman Corp.*, 86 N.J. 361, 431 A.2d 826 (1981), was able "to gauge the risks of injury from defects in the [Welsbach] product line and to bear the accident-avoidance costs," since Kerr–McGee was intimately familiar with the production of gas mantles and the unavoidable thorium manufacturing waste. *Id.* 431 A.2d at 830. Evidence to support this conclusion is found by Lindsay's acquisition of all the assets and sources of information related to the Welsbach product line. The liability also should apply to Kerr–McGee because Kerr–McGee's "acquisition of the business assets and manufacturing operation of [Welsbach] contributed to the destruction of the plaintiff's remedies against the original manufacturer"—Welsbach. *Id.* 431 A.2d at 831. * * *

The district court in this case "predicted" that the New Jersey Supreme Court would apply the *Ramirez* successor corporation strict liability product line doctrine to strict liability environmental actions. Since this is an issue of first impression in New Jersey, the district court truly was "predicting" the result. Hence, if permitted to prognosticate, I too would hold that the New Jersey Supreme Court would apply the doctrine of strict liability to this environmental case and thus affirm the district court. However, while I believe that the decision to apply the doctrine to environmental cases should be left in the hands or the highest state court, there is no method to certify such a question to the court.

C.   *The Restraint of City of Philadelphia*

Despite my firm conviction that the district court should be affirmed, I am constrained by the philosophical tenet of this court in *City of Philadelphia, supra,* which I respect and adopt. We are not appointed to be activists but to interpret and apply the law as we see it. However, I believe that a dangerous precedent will be set if this court continues down the path which prohibits direct application of state doctrines. Primarily, the removal and jurisdictional statutes will be used as a sword to prevent final resolution of a state claim. For example, where a defendant realizes that the state's highest court has not ruled on their specific factual circumstance, but has developed a doctrine that might be adverse to that defendant, then the defendant will most assuredly remove the case to federal court knowing that, on appeal, the circuit court will grant summary judgment in their favor based on *City of Philadelphia*. The result will create an atmosphere where state rights will never be vindicated and cases will not proceed to their ultimate conclusion.

Accordingly and reluctantly, I join the majority remanding this matter to the district court for entry of a summary judgment in favor of Kerr–McGee.

NOTES AND QUESTIONS

1. *The traditional bases for successor liability.* Under corporate law, as the court stated in note 3, there are a limited number of bases for imposing the liabilities of a predecessor on a successor corporation. In addition to express or implicit assumption of them as part of the contract for sale and mergers, mentioned by the court, the two others include the successor's being a mere continuation of the predecessor and, when the transaction is fraudulent, an effort to avoid the liabilities of the predecessor.

Mergers can occur pursuant to statutory law governing mergers or when a de facto merger occurs. The latter entails a purchase of assets paid for with stock of the successor company. When a stock purchase occurs, the ownership of the successor includes the former owners of the predecessor. Mere continuation is a limited doctrine, requiring that the predecessor be, with regard to employees, ownership, name, location, and management, a continuation of the predecessor. The purchase of a corporation's stock, it should be noted, does not implicate successor liability, as the original company remains unchanged with only different owners—those with claims against the company remain in precisely the same position as before the stock sale.

2. *The expansion of successor liability for strict products liability claimants.* Thus, the successor-liability rubber meets the road when a successor purchases all of the assets of a predecessor for cash, and the predecessor then proceeds to dissolve under state dissolution statutes. The cash assets from the sale are distributed to stockholders after known liabilities are paid. State dissolution laws provide a period, typically of a few years, after which the distributions to shareholders are shielded from any claims that might still exist against the dissolved corporation.

"Long tail" creditors, which include products liability claimants who can be injured many years after a product is manufactured, may have no legal or practical remedy against the predecessor or its shareholders. In response to this situation, some courts, beginning in the heyday of the strict products liability reform, created two additional doctrines that expanded successor liability. One is the product-line doctrine addressed in the *Leo* case, first advanced by the California Supreme Court in *Ray v. Alad*, cited in the concurring opinion, and subsequently adopted by the New Jersey Supreme Court in *Ramirez*.

The second expansionary doctrine is known as continuity of enterprise and is considerably more liberal than its namesake, the mere continuation basis for successor liability. Reasoning that, other than in form, there is little difference between the sale of assets for cash and for stock (mere continuations), the court in Turner v. Bituminous Casualty Co., 244 N.W.2d 873 (Mich.1976), held that if, after a sale of assets, under the "totality of the circumstances" the successor continues the enterprise of its predecessor it can be held liable for the latter's products liabilities.

3. Despite some adoptions of one or the other of these expanded theories of successor liability in the halcyon period for strict products liability, through the 1970s and into the 1980s it never obtained widespread support. Professor Richard Cupp and a co-author identify 12 jurisdictions as having adopted a liberalized version of successor liability. Richard L. Cupp, Jr. & Christopher L. Frost, Successor Liability for Defective Products: A Redesign Ongoing, 72 Brook.L.Rev. 1173 (2007). The sentiment among courts declining to expand successor liability is reflected by the New York Court of Appeals, in Semenetz v. Sherling & Walden, Inc., 851 N.E.2d 1170 (N.Y.2006). The court declined to adopt a product line exception to the traditional successor liability rules based on concern about the impact on small business owners:

> Importantly, the "product line" exception threatens "economic annihilation" for small businesses. Because small businesses have limited assets, they face potential financial destruction if saddled with liability for their predecessors' torts. This threat would deter the purchase of ongoing businesses that manufacture products and, instead, force potential sellers to liquidate their companies. As the Florida Supreme Court has observed, 90% of the nation's manufacturing enterprises are small businesses, and "[i]f small manufacturing corporations liquidate rather than transfer ownership, the chances that the corporations will be replaced by other successful small corporations are decreased."

Id. at 1174.

The Third Restatement on Products Liability concurs, limiting successor liability to the four traditional exceptions. See Restatement (Third) of Torts: Products Liability § 12 (1998).

4. *The impact on asset sales.* The concern expressed by the New York Court of Appeals as well as the *Leo* court—see footnote 6—is a frequent refrain. The concern is that when the products liability burden of a firm exceeds its goodwill, the company will not be marketable. "Goodwill" is a term of art that reflects the additional value of a going concern over and above its value if assets are liquidated. Thus, for a company with negative goodwill (because of its future products liability obligations), the company would maximize its sale price by selling assets piecemeal (for which there will be no successor liability) rather than selling the entire company for a lower price that any buyer would insist on given that the buyer-successor is required to assume the future products-liability burden. In that scenario, society loses the value of going concerns and long-tail products claimants are no better off with expanded successor liability. Do you see why?

5. *The successor as conduit.* The concurrence cited a passage from *Ramirez* that the value of the predecessor should be available to compensate long-tail products claimants. After all, it is the predecessor that manufactured and sold a defective product that injured the claimant and should, therefore, be responsible for compensating the claimant. Thus some courts and commentators have suggested that the proper role of the successor is to channel liability back to the predecessor by discounting the price paid for the predecessor's assets. See Savage Arms, Inc. v. W. Auto Supply Co., 18 P.3d 49 (Alaska 2001). Thus, it is not the successor bearing these costs but the predecessor. Recall that Lindsay purchased the gas mantle business of Welsbach in 1940.

What impediments exist to Lindsay serving as a conduit to channel the future products liability burden to Welsbach in the transaction transferring the gas mantle business?

For proposals to effectuate having successors serve as "conduits" to channel liability to the predecessor by discounting the price paid in an asset sale, see Michael D. Green, Successor Liability: The Superiority of Statutory Reform to Protect Products Liability Claimants, 72 Cornell L.Rev. 17 (1986) (advocating modification of state dissolution statutes to require consideration of long-tail claims before permitting distribution of a dissolved company's assets to its shareholders); Note, Successor Liability, Mass Tort, and Mandatory–Litigation Class Action, 118 Harv.L.Rev. 2357 (2005) (proposing non-opt-out class action consisting of current and future claims that might be made based on predecessor's defective products).

6. Successor liability also arises for environmental liabilities, such as CERCLA cleanup costs. (Comprehensive coverage of CERCLA is in {Chapter 8}). Although governed by federal law, federal courts generally look to state law to inform on the appropriate scope of federal law in this context. A few courts, however, had adopted a broader scope for successor liability under federal common law. See, e.g., B.F. Goodrich v. Betkoski, 99 F.3d 505 (2d Cir.1996). The Supreme Court subsequently decided that CERCLA reveals no intent by Congress "that the entire corpus of state corporation law is to be replaced simply because a plaintiff's cause of action is based upon a federal statute." United States v. Bestfoods, 524 U.S. 51, 63 (1998). Interestingly, some asset purchases that might be the basis for successor liability occurred prior to 1980, when CERCLA was enacted. See, e.g., California Dep't. of Toxic Substances Control v. California–Fresno Inv. Co., 2007 WL 1345580 (E.D.Cal. 2007). How could an acquirer purchasing the assets of a predecessor anticipate such liability and discount the purchase price to reflect it?

7. The *Leo* court expressed concern about the impact of imposing the product-line successor doctrine on a purchaser such as Lindsay for environmental liabilities remaining on the predecessor's real property, arguing the "daunting obstacles" to assessment of such liability. That difficulty might, in turn, impede the free transfer of assets, such as real property. How much more difficult would Lindsay's task be than a subsequent purchaser of the land, who would succeed to liability for CERCLA (see Chapter 8) cleanup costs by virtue of being an owner of the property? The *Leo* court also contrasts the scope of successor liability proposed for environmental liabilities with a similar scope for durable goods, such as automobiles. Is successor liability for toxic products closer to the environmental situation or the durable good context?

8. In his concurring opinion, Judge Atkins quoted the *Ramirez* opinion for the proposition that Kerr–McGee could have obtained products liability insurance for contingent claims such as those arising in *Leo*. In 1940, do you think it would have been possible for Lindsay to purchase insurance for injuries arising out of Welsbach's pollution of its factory site? Would it be possible to purchase such insurance today? See Chapter 11 for a discussion of these questions.

9. *The successor's duty to warn.* Independently of successor liability based on purchasing the assets of a predecessor, some courts have imposed a duty to warn on successors who have a relationship with purchasers of the predecessor's products. The Third Restatement on Products Liability contains a provision providing the contours of this obligation:

§ 13. Liability Of Successor For Harm Caused By Successor's Own Post–Sale Failure To Warn.

(a) A successor corporation or other business entity that acquires assets of a predecessor corporation or other business entity, whether or not liable under the rule stated in § 12, is subject to liability for harm to persons or property caused by the successor's failure to warn of a risk created by a product sold or distributed by the predecessor if:

> (1) the successor undertakes or agrees to provide services for maintenance or repair of the product or enters into a similar relationship with purchasers of the predecessor's products giving rise to actual or potential economic advantage to the successor, and

> (2) a reasonable person in the position of the successor would provide a warning.

(b) A reasonable person in the position of the successor would provide a warning if:

> (1) the successor knows or reasonably should know that the product poses a substantial risk of harm to persons or property; and

> (2) those to whom a warning might be provided can be identified and can reasonably be assumed to be unaware of the risk of harm; and

> (3) a warning can be effectively communicated to and acted on by those to whom a warning might be provided; and

> (4) the risk of harm is sufficiently great to justify the burden of providing a warning.

Restatement (Third) of Torts: Products Liability § 13 (2010).

10. *Bankruptcy law.* One might think that if a corporation is insolvent and its assets sold in bankruptcy that purchasers would obtain those assets free and clear of any successor liability. In the broadest ruling to date, the Seventh Circuit punctured that intuition:

> [The] price received in a bankruptcy sale will be lower if a court is free to disregard a condition in the sale agreement enjoining claims against the purchaser based on the seller's misconduct. If the condition is invalid the purchaser will be buying a pig in a poke, never knowing when its seller's customers may come out of the woodwork and bring suit against it under some theory of successor liability. This possibility will depress the price of the bankrupt's assets, to the prejudice of creditors. All this is true, but proves too much. It implies, what no one believes, that by virtue of the arising-under jurisdiction a bankruptcy court enjoys a blanket power to enjoin all future lawsuits against a buyer at a bankruptcy sale in order to maximize the sale price: more, that the court could in effect immunize such buyers from all state and federal laws that might reduce the value of the assets bought from the bankrupt; in effect, that it could discharge the

debts of nondebtors (like Zerland) as well as of debtors even if the creditors did not consent; that it could allow the parties to bankruptcy sales to extinguish the rights of third parties, here future tort claimants, without notice to them or (as notice might well be infeasible) any consideration of their interests. If the court could do all these nice things the result would indeed be to make the property of bankrupts more valuable than other property—more valuable to the creditors, of course, but also to the debtor's shareholders and managers to the extent that the strategic position of the debtor in possession in a reorganization enables the debtor's owners and managers to benefit from bankruptcy. But the result would not only be harm to third parties, such as the [injured person pursuing successor liability claims], but also a further incentive to enter bankruptcy for reasons that have nothing to do with the purposes of bankruptcy law.

Zerand–Bernal Group, Inc. v. Cox, 23 F.3d 159, 163 (7th Cir.1994).

PROBLEM

Perry Chemical Corporation ("Perry") was the sole manufacturer of Chlorotrast when it was administered to the decedent, David Mogan in 1959. In 1999, Mogan contracted liver cancer and died the next year. His widow brought a wrongful death and survival action against American Cyanotics, on the basis of successor liability. Cyanotics moved to dismiss the complaint.

In 1964, Perry sold all of the assets of its antibiotic division to Cyanotics for approximately $13,700,000. The sale included assets relating to Chlorotrast, which, although not an antibiotic, was manufactured at the same facility where the antibiotics division was located. The antibiotics division constituted less than 20% of Perry's business and the Chlorotrast assets were a very small part of the business. Chlorotrast sales for the first 11 months of 1963 totaled approximately $140,000, while Perry reported net sales of about $23,400,000 for that year. Cyanotics did not assume the contingent tort liabilities of Perry as part of its purchase of the antibiotic division, although it did assume all ongoing liabilities of Perry's business along with all of the physical assets of the antibiotic division. Perry continued to market Chlorotrast to hospitals and it provided consumer support for those hospitals that continued to use it. In 1969, Perry ceased manufacturing Chlortrast, although it remained in business until 1979, when its fortunes declined and it sold off its assets to creditors. Perry was never formally dissolved and no assets were distributed to shareholders.

How should the court rule on Cyanotics' motion to dismiss?

CHAPTER III

CAUSATION

■ ■ ■

A. INTRODUCTION

Causation is the glue that holds a tort case together. It bonds defendant's misconduct to plaintiff's injury. Prior to the rise of toxic torts in the last half of the twentieth century, causal questions were often a minor, fairly uncontroversial part of most tort cases. With the rise of toxic torts, however, proof of causation has become one of the most complex and controversial aspects of tort liability.

It would be a mistake to argue that the causal issues in toxic tort cases are fundamentally different from those presented in all tort cases, but toxic tort cases do differ in degree in several significant ways. First, all too often there is causal ambiguity. This may be the case for a variety of reasons: the level of exposure to a substance or a drug (i.e., the dosage) is uncertain; the evidence of a relationship between the substance and the injury is sketchy; or the timing between exposure and disease is suspect.

Second, there is the fundamental problem of competing causes. Some substances, such as asbestos, produce "signature" diseases uniquely or strongly tied to the substance, namely asbestosis and mesothelioma. However, other substances do not cause unique injuries. Even substances that do cause signature diseases may also cause other diseases. If an individual is exposed to asbestos and develops lung cancer, one cannot be certain whether or not the exposure caused the disease. The cancer could have been caused by something else, such as cigarette smoke.

Third, and related to the problem of competing causes, is the fact that plaintiff may find it difficult to prove that a particular injury was the result of defendant's substance as opposed to some other cause. This problem is exacerbated by the long latency periods that often occur in toxic torts. Frequently, decades may pass between the time an individual is exposed to asbestos and the time that individual develops mesothelioma, a cancer of the pleural lining of the lung.

This Chapter reviews the causal requirement in tort cases with a special focus on the unique problems presented by toxic torts. We begin with a case from the early days of toxic tort litigation.

MILLER v. NATIONAL CABINET CO.

Court of Appeals of New York, 1960.
8 N.Y.2d 277, 204 N.Y.S.2d 129, 168 N.E.2d 811.

VAN VOORHIS, JUDGE.

An award in workmen's compensation has been made to the widow of Jacob Miller, who died on August 10, 1950. He was last employed by a firm known as Krakauer Bros. where he had worked from January 31, 1949 to April 23, 1950, except for an absence of about five months due to a back injury consisting of a fractured vertebra. He received disability payments during this interval based on the certificate of his personal physician, Dr. Louis Granirer, that this injury resulted from moving a piano while at work. After he died, his widow filed a claim against Krakauer Bros. for death benefits based on the theory that his death was caused by this fractured vertebra. Dr. Granirer refused to support that claim, certifying to the Workmen's Compensation Board that in his opinion the industrial accident mentioned did not cause his death. The claim was superseded by another based on the theory "that decedent's death may have resulted from an occupational disease, having been employed as a piano finisher and associated work for many years prior to his death."

This man died from leukemia. He had worked as a piano or cabinet finisher for five different employers since 1928. * * * One of them was appellant National Cabinet Company. The theory of claimant became that the blood disease from which he died was caused by exposure to a chemical known as benzene—whose trade name is benzol—which was contained in varnish removers utilized by each of the employers for whom he worked during this quarter of a century of his career.

The Referee who heard this workmen's compensation proceeding called in an associate industrial hygiene physician of the Division of Industrial Hygiene and Safety Standards, New York State Department of Labor, to whom he issued the following direction: "It may be that substances used in one or more of these employments were injurious and causative factors in the death * * *. Will you please investigate and let me know what substances were used and whether or not you believe such substances were injurious."

After executing this assignment, Dr. McBirney reported: "As this disease is one in which there is no known cause, and there are no substances used in any of these work places which produce symptoms and signs similar to the signs and symptoms of this leukemia—an investigation is not able to disclose any causal relation."

Dr. Granirer, decedent's personal physician for 8 years who attended him at his death, was called as a witness for claimant, but declined to express an opinion that the leukemia resulted from his employment. Dr. Angrist, pathologist at the Queens General Hospital of the Department of

Hospitals of the City of New York, on whose report the diagnosis of leukemia was made, testified that leukemia of this kind varies from a few days to 23 years in producing death, is a cancerous process of the white cells of the blood and that he has no idea what factors prolong or shorten its duration. The Referee disallowed the claim, finding that it had not been established that death was due to the back injury sustained in moving a piano or to exposure to benzene. The Workmen's Compensation Board reversed the Referee, finding: "That decedent developed leukemia as the result of work exposure to benzol during his employment with National Cabinet Company, that this was a slow starting disease within the provisions of Section 40 of the Workmen's Compensation Law and that death resulted therefrom. * * * "

[A] serious defect in claimant's case is that the causes of leukemia or its aggravation are unknown. This clearly appears from the testimony of claimant's witness, Dr. Angrist, of the New York City Department of Hospitals, of Dr. McBirney, of the State Labor Department who was called by the Compensation Referee, and from the eloquent silence of decedent's own physician. Whatever case claimant might have would depend entirely upon the testimony of Dr. Paul Reznikoff, who had no contact with the deceased, and was called as an expert witness to answer hypothetical questions. This witness distinguished, as did all of the other medical witnesses, between leukemia and aplastic anemia, which was the disease involved in our decision in Zaepfel v. du Pont de Nemours & Co., 284 App.Div. 693, 134 N.Y.S.2d 377, affirmed 309 N.Y. 962, 132 N.E.2d 327. Aplastic anemia is the classical case of benzol poisoning * * *. Aplastic anemia is not leukemia. Indeed, there is testimony by Dr. Reznikoff himself that the effect of benzol is to reduce rather than to increase the number of white corpuscles, and that it has sometimes been injected as an antidote to leukemia, which consists of the uncontrolled multiplication of white blood corpuscles.

Dr. Reznikoff was guarded and hesitant about expressing any opinion concerning exposure to benzol as a cause of leukemia. He testified that he believes that a person exposed to benzol may develop this kind of leukemia. He said that nobody knows how much exposure it takes. The award depends entirely upon his statement that the incidence of leukemia "is quite high in patients who have been exposed to benzol," and that "it is possible that this man's leukemia resulted from his alleged exposure to inhalation of benzol or benzene."

* * * Dr. Reznikoff made crystal clear, however, that, when he used the word "possible" in answering the hypothetical question, he meant that and nothing more. He demonstrated this beyond peradventure when he was asked on cross-examination what made him feel that this decedent's disease resulted from the cause mentioned, by replying: "I didn't say that. I was asked whether this could follow benzol. *I didn't say this particular man had it*." (Italics supplied.) Asked whether this particular disease could have had its cause outside of any employment exposure, Dr. Reznikoff replied: "As I answered the previous attorney, most of the

patients that we do see with this disease, we never find out a reason for it with any certainty."

* * *

Nobody contends that there is scientific understanding of the cause of this leukemia. The only possible basis for drawing an inference in favor of claimant from Dr. Reznikoff's evidence, even if he had not cancelled it by saying that he was not speaking of this decedent, would be statistics indicating that in many instances leukemia follows benzol exposure without knowing why. It was along this line that Dr. Reznikoff began to testify that the incidence of leukemia "is quite high" in patients who have been exposed to benzol. This line of testimony might have led to something had not the doctor added "I am sorry I can't give you any statistics, but we don't have them."

Not every supposition of a witness concerning what might be has the force of evidence, even though he has been licensed to practice medicine. If the witness is unfamiliar with any statistical data in the medical literature or in his own practice to give an inkling either to himself or to the court or board of how high the incidence of these cases is in situations of this kind, then the doctor's assumption that it is "quite high" is without significance. The lack of any kind of statistical data, which in the absence of scientific understanding is all that there would be to go on, is the more inexplicable if the claim is well founded in view of the large number of persons who die of leukemia and of workers in industry who are exposed to benzol. If there were any observed correlation between the two, it is certain that a physician of Dr. Reznikoff's standing would be in possession of the information.

* * *

* * * In the training of a scientist anything conceivable is a possibility. That is the first tenet accepted by the scientific mind. Many of the scientific discoveries and applied technologies today would have been thought by the average person to have been impossible of attainment less than a generation ago. No trained scientist, medical or other, would have the effrontery to state today that space travel is impossible, that the discovery of a cure for leukemia or other forms of cancer is impossible, or that any other speculation is dogmatically beyond the realm of knowledge or accomplishment. Still that would not justify a court in assuming that it is presently known or is presently achievable merely for the reason that a trained scientist has said that it is not impossible. * * *

* * *

The courts have been confronted before with cancer cases, and this is not likely to be the last. This is not an isolated situation. * * * Would, for example, evidence that there are 4 to 11 times as many cases of lung cancer among cigarette smokers as among nonsmokers (Journal of National Cancer Institute, April, 1953, pp. 1237–1257) be sufficient to establish a cause of action for breach of warranty in the sale of cigarettes? The

United States District Court in Pittsburgh has apparently held not (Pritchard v. Liggett & Myers Tobacco Co. [Miller, J.], decided May 3, 1960). There appear to be no decisions upholding causation in so complex a variety of the disease as leukemia. The cancer decisions in the courts where recovery has been allowed have dealt almost entirely with trauma, and there only in instances where the trauma occurred in the spot in the body where the pre-existing cancer was and the symptoms of its aggravation were immediately apparent. * * *

* * *

We recognize that the scientific repugnance to the principle of *"post hoc, ergo proper hoc"* cannot fully extend to the law, and that, as in cases of circumstantial evidence, we regard as proof that which would be rejected by the scientist. Nevertheless, there comes a point even in legal thinking where the relationship of cause and effect becomes too attenuated to be regarded. An illustration of the correct legal approach to the problem is found in Stubbs v. City of Rochester, 226 N.Y. 516, 124 N.E. 137, 5 A.L.R. 1396, where the cause of disease was reached by process of elimination of other causes.

In the case at bar, causation has not been established. This is true not only on account of the considerable number of past employers of the decedent, engaged in the same operations where he was exposed to the same hypothetical dangers, without any clear showing that he contracted this disease while at National Cabinet Company but, even more importantly, for the reason that * * * there is * * * an absence of any statistical basis for [an] opinion * * *. The speculative nature of Dr. Reznikoff's conclusions, appearing from his own testimony, and in the face of the testimony of all of the other doctors on both sides of the case, renders the result reached too conjectural for recognition in a court of law. * * * Here, in addition to the other weaknesses in claimant's case, is a long lapse of time before leukemia was discovered after he had ceased to work for appellant employer. In testifying that leukemia can develop over a period of 20 years, Dr. Reznikoff did not recognize that an immediately observable aggravation is the only proof of causation that exists in the legal cases that have been decided.

* * *

[T]he courts will not in all instances demand scientific demonstration of cause and effect relationships but will insist only on practical probability * * *. But * * * a question of fact [does not arise] whenever a medical expert testifies in measured terms that an asserted cause of a disease is possible * * *. Otherwise for so long as the causes of a disease—like cancer—are unknown to science, everyone contracting the disease could secure medical testimony that it is "possible" that the disease is contracted from a wide variety of causes, choosing in each instance the particular possibility having the greatest promise of holding liable some responsible defendant. Any cancer expert could readily state that cancer could be caused by virus infection or by exposure to automobile exhaust fumes, sunlight, radiation, smog, smoking, hormone imbalance or according to any other theory which has been entertained by researchers or specialists as a possibility. * * *

* * *

The order appealed from should be reversed and the claim dismissed.

DYE, JUDGE (dissenting).

The Workmen's Compensation Board has found as a fact, which has been affirmed in the court below, that the decedent in the course of his work as a piano finisher, and as a result of occupational exposure to, contact with and inhalation of benzol, or its preparations and/or compounds, contracted, became disabled from and died of chronic monocytic leukemia * * *.

At the hearing the medical experts gave conflicting opinions respecting the fact of causal relationship of death to the occupational exposure. The board, in the exercise of its authorized discretion, resolved such conflict in favor of claimant which, having been affirmed, we may not disturb (Workmen's Compensation Law, § 20).

The sole question then is whether there is any substantial evidence in support of causal connection. I think there is.

Dr. Reznikoff, an outstanding, nationally known hematologist, gave as his opinion that "a person exposed to benzol may develop leukemia, certainly chronic myelocytic leukemia, probably other types of leukemia, I cannot tell you how much exposure it takes. I don't think anybody knows, but we do know that the incidence of leukemia, especially chronic myelocytic leukemia, is quite high in patients who have been exposed to benzol. The only two causes we know of leukemia, are first, X-ray exposure, and secondly, benzol," and when asked: "you say it is possible that this man's leukemia resulted from his alleged exposure to inhalation of benzol or benzene?" he answered: "That is right."

This is not a bare guess—a mere scintilla of proof—but a carefully considered answer to a comprehensive hypothetical question. It was an honest effort by a well-qualified doctor to give the board the benefit of his experience and observation in diagnosing and treating this baffling disease. He could not rule out benzol as a possible cause. He had observed that many persons suffering from this type of leukemia had a history of benzol exposure, which observation had been noted by other eminent authorities. Three other doctors disagreed with Dr. Reznikoff but that is not to say that he was wrong or that his opinion should be rejected. Probative acceptance does not depend on quantity.

* * *

Here, there is uncontradicted proof of exposure to benzol. Here, as was pointed out in Zaepfel v. du Pont de Nemours & Co. (supra), which we approved, there is enough proof to satisfy the statutory requirements of causal connection.

* * *

NOTES AND QUESTIONS

1. Why did the plaintiff lose in *Miller*? Because she failed to prove that benzene causes leukemia, because she failed to prove that her husband's leukemia was caused by benzene, or both?

2. The *Miller* case presages many of the toxic tort causation issues and problems that have beset the courts in the ensuing half century. They include: the division of the causal question into questions of specific and general causation, the relevance of temporal order on the question of causation, the need for statistical evidence of the relationship between substance and disease in order to prove causation, the existence of multiple defendants exposing plaintiff to the same substance, the long latency period between exposure and disease, the fact that the causes of many diseases are unknown, and the role of probabilistic evidence as proof of causation. Look for the many places where these issues re-emerge in the remainder of this Chapter.

3. The dangers posed by benzene were just being recognized in the 1950s when Miller was exposed. Benzene's primary danger comes from inhalation. Over the ensuing decades, permissible levels of airborne benzene exposures have been adjusted downward several times. During the period Miller was working, the time weighted average (TWA) for an eight-hour workday was 100 parts per million (ppm). Today, OSHA regulations call for a TWA of 1 ppm. See David Allen Galbraith, Stretching the Truth, 48 No. 9 DRI For Def. 56 (2006). Occasionally, the question arises whether failure to meet these standards is sufficient to prove causation in a toxic tort case. In Parker v. Mobil Oil Corp., 857 N.E.2d 1114, 1122 (N.Y.2006), the court, like most courts that have considered the issue, concluded that exposures in excess of protective standards promulgated by regulatory agencies are inadequate to demonstrate legal causation. See also Sutera v. Perrier Group of Am. Inc., 986 F.Supp. 655, 665 (D.Mass.1997) ("In other words, the fact that an agency, ex ante, sets an exposure standard of 5 ppb for drinking water does not compel, or even necessarily support, the ex post conclusion that Sutera's leukemia was caused by [benzene in] Perrier.") Justifying this position, the court in Mitchell v. Gencorp Inc., 165 F.3d 778 (10th Cir.1999) noted:

> The methodology employed by a government agency "results from the preventive perspective that the agencies adopt in order to reduce public exposure to harmful substances. The agencies' threshold of proof is reasonably lower than that appropriate in tort law, which traditionally makes more particularized inquiries into cause and effect and requires a plaintiff to prove that it is more likely than not that another individual has caused him or her harm." [Allen v. Pennsylvania Engineering Corp., 102 F.3d 194, 198 (5th Cir.1996).]

Mitchell, 165 F.3d at 783 n.3.

There is no longer any doubt that benzene causes leukemia. Today, the question presented in most benzene cases is whether the particular type of leukemia from which plaintiff suffers is associated with benzene exposure. See David L. Faigman, Michael J. Saks, Joseph Sanders & Edward K. Cheng, 4 Modern Scientific Evidence, Ch. 29 Benzene (2009–10).

4. The *Miller* court cited *Stubbs v. City of Rochester* which we read in Chapter 1. Recall that the *Stubbs* court held that the plaintiff's evidence that contaminated drinking water was sufficient if he eliminated enough competing causes to make the contaminated water the probable cause of his typhoid fever. Why couldn't the plaintiff in *Miller* have used analogous proof? We return to this topic in section C(3) infra.

5. The *Miller* case firmly resisted relaxing causation standards for toxic torts. The next cases deal with this issue in a contemporary context.

B. *SINE QUA NON* AND SUBSTANTIAL FACTOR TESTS FOR CAUSATION

JUNE v. UNION CARBIDE CORP.

United States Court of Appeals, Tenth Circuit, 2009.
577 F.3d 1234.

HARTZ, CIRCUIT JUDGE.

The lawsuit before us arises out of alleged radiation injuries to residents of Uravan, Colorado, a former uranium and vanadium milling town owned and operated by Defendants Union Carbide Corporation and Umetco Minerals Corporation. Plaintiffs brought an action in the United States District Court for the District of Colorado under the Price–Anderson Act of 1957, Pub.L. No. 86–256, 71 Stat. 576 (codified as amended in scattered sections of 42 U.S.C.). They assert claims for personal injury based on disease or death allegedly caused by radiation and claims for medical monitoring to detect the onset of disease in those Plaintiffs who were asymptomatic. The district court dismissed all the claims on pretrial motions, and Plaintiffs appealed. Exercising jurisdiction under 28 U.S.C. § 1291, we affirm. Plaintiffs' personal-injury claims fail for lack of evidence of factual causation. Their medical-monitoring claims fail for lack of evidence of a "bodily injury" as required by the Price–Anderson Act.

I. BACKGROUND

A. Factual Background

Mining and milling have been conducted in the Uravan area for many years. The Standard Chemical Company was producing radium in the region as early as 1914. In 1928 Defendants purchased Standard Chemical's holdings, and in 1936 began milling vanadium and uranium. To accommodate workers, Defendants founded the community of Uravan, constructing homes and a number of facilities, including a medical clinic, elementary school, community center, tennis courts, and a swimming pool.

Defendants ceased operations in Uravan in 1984, having produced 42 million pounds of uranium oxide. This production did not come without environmental costs. In 1986 the Environmental Protection Agency placed Uravan on the National Priorities List, *see* 51 Fed.Reg. 21054, 21063 (June 10, 1986), which ranks the nation's most environmentally hazardous sites to prioritize remedial action, *see* 42 U.S.C. § 9605(a)(8)(B). About this time, Uravan's remaining residents were evacuated and remedial activities began. The last structures standing in Uravan were razed after this lawsuit was filed.

Plaintiffs either resided in Uravan during some period between 1936 and 1986, or represent decedents who did. (For ease of exposition, we shall use the term *Plaintiffs* to refer to those allegedly injured by Defendants, whether they be the Plaintiffs personally or the Plaintiffs' decedents.) The thrust of their claims is that Defendants' milling operations exposed Uravan residents to various radioactive materials, and that such exposure has caused, or increased the risk of, radiation-related illnesses.

B. Procedural History

Plaintiffs brought this action under the Price–Anderson Act, which grants federal district courts jurisdiction over lawsuits "arising out of or resulting from a nuclear incident." 42 U.S.C. § 2210(n)(2). Unless inconsistent with § 2210 of the Act, state law supplies the substantive law governing claims under the Act. *See id.* § 2014(hh). Plaintiffs also pleaded seven causes of action under Colorado tort law, but the district court ruled that they were preempted by the Price–Anderson Act because they arose from an alleged "nuclear incident," and it converted the claims to federal claims under the Act.

Twenty-seven Plaintiffs are pursuing personal-injury claims and 152 are pursuing only medical-monitoring claims. Of the 27 personal-injury Plaintiffs, 11 have been diagnosed with nonthyroid cancer and 16 have been diagnosed with thyroid disease (including one case of thyroid cancer).

Defendants challenged Plaintiffs' claims with two motions for summary judgment. One motion argued that the personal-injury claimants had failed to show the but-for causation required by Colorado tort law. The other argued that the medical-monitoring claims could not proceed because (1) Colorado does not recognize such a cause of action and (2) the medical-monitoring Plaintiffs had not alleged a "bodily injury," as required by the Price–Anderson Act.

In opposition to the first motion, Plaintiffs argued that causation in Colorado is determined not by a but-for test but by a "substantial factor" test requiring only that the defendant's tortious conduct be "a substantial contributing cause of the injury." Plaintiffs contended that their experts' opinions created a triable issue of fact "as to whether the Defendants' emission of radiation over the course of decades substantially contributed" to the personal-injury Plaintiffs' illnesses. * * *

The district court rejected the substantial-contributing-cause argument in support of Plaintiffs' personal-injury claims. It stated that a tort claimant in Colorado must demonstrate both of two distinct components of causation: (1) that "but for" the defendant's conduct the claimant would not have been injured and (2) that the defendant's conduct was a "substantial factor in bringing about the injury." Because Plaintiffs had submitted no evidence of but-for causation, the court granted summary judgment.

* * *

* * * Plaintiffs then appealed to this court, presenting the following questions: (1) whether Plaintiffs were required to show "but for" causation under Colorado law and (2) whether unmanifested, subclinical injuries resulting from exposure to radiation can support a "bodily injury" claim under the Price–Anderson Act.

II. DISCUSSION

* * *

As previously mentioned, actions brought under the Price–Anderson Act are governed by the "substantive rules for decision" of the state in which the putative nuclear incident occurred. 42 U.S.C. § 2014(hh) * * * and the parties agree that Colorado tort law governs Plaintiffs' claims. * * *

A. Personal–Injury Claims

In Colorado, as elsewhere, a party seeking recovery in tort must demonstrate that the defendant's conduct caused the alleged injury. The general rule for causation is that the plaintiff must prove that the alleged "injury would not have occurred but for the defendant's negligent conduct." *Kaiser Found. Health Plan v. Sharp,* 741 P.2d 714, 719 (Colo.1987). Plaintiffs do not dispute that proposition but argue that when there are "potential multiple or concurring causes" for an injury, Colorado applies a "substantial factor test" for causation, not the more stringent but-for test. Under the substantial-factor test, Plaintiffs contend, an actor's conduct can be deemed causal " 'where it is of sufficient significance in producing the harm as to lead reasonable persons to regard it as a cause and to attach responsibility.' " *Id.* at 52 (quoting *Sharp v. Kaiser Found. Health Plan,* 710 P.2d 1153, 1155 (Colo.Ct.App.1985), *aff'd on other grounds,* 741 P.2d 714 (Colo.1987)).[1] Because the illnesses at issue in this case (cancer and thyroid disease) can have multiple causes, Plaintiffs conclude that this more permissive substantial-factor test applies.

The legal issues regarding causation that arise when a disease has multiple possible causes are subtle. Plaintiffs' statement of the substan-

---

1. The quoted language can ultimately be traced to Restatement (Second) of Torts § 431 cmt. a ("The word 'substantial' is used to denote the fact that the defendant's conduct has such an effect *in producing the harm as to lead reasonable men to regard it as a cause,* using the word in the popular sense, in which there always lurks the idea of *responsibility....*" (emphasis added)), although, as we shall see, the court-of-appeals decision in *Sharp* ignored essential requirements of the substantial-factor test.

tial-factor test reflects the difficulty of the issues; it relies on certain language from the Restatement (Second) of Torts but misstates the law by overlooking other language. To better understand the proper test, it is helpful to review the more precise, and clearer, treatment of multiple possible causes in the Proposed Final Draft of the Restatement (Third) of Torts: Liability for Physical Harm.[2] We then compare that treatment to the treatment in the Restatement (Second) and see that the ultimate legal standards in the two Restatements are essentially identical for our purposes. Roughly speaking (we will become more precise as we discuss the underlying concepts), under the Restatements a Plaintiff could recover from Defendants only if either (1) Uravan radiation was a but-for cause of the Plaintiff's ailments or (2) that radiation (either alone or with other factors) would have caused the ailments. Because Colorado law has been consistent with the treatment of causation in the Restatements, we presume that it, too, would impose this requirement for recovery. We therefore reject Plaintiffs' version of the substantial-factor test.

To explain how we have arrived at this conclusion, we turn to an extended discussion of general principles. Applying those principles to this case, we then affirm the summary judgment.

1. General Principles

The term *substantial factor* appears in the treatment of causation in the Restatement (Second) of Torts (as well as its predecessor, the original Restatement of Torts). It has been abandoned, however, in the Restatement (Third) of Torts because of the misunderstanding that it has engendered. *See id.* § 26 cmt. j.

Causation under the Restatement (Third) has two components. First, the tortious conduct must be the "factual cause" of the physical harm to the plaintiff. *See id.* §§ 26, 27. Ordinarily, a cause is a "factual cause" only if it is a but-for cause, *see id.* § 26, although there is a potential exception, which we will discuss shortly, when there are multiple causes, *see id.* § 27. Second, the harm must be among the "harms that result from the risks that made the actor's conduct tortious." *Id.* § 29. Traditionally, this second component has been referred to as "proximate cause," a term that has baffled law students (to say nothing of jurors, lawyers, and judges) for generations; but the Restatement (Third) has wisely redescribed the subject matter as "scope of liability." *See id.* Ch. 6, Special Note on Proximate Cause; *id.* § 29 cmt. b. We need not dwell on this topic—the focus of our attention is on factual cause—but an illustration in the Restatement (Third) conveys what is necessary to show that an injury factually caused by the defendant is within the scope of liability:

> Richard, a hunter, finishes his day in the field and stops at a friend's house while walking home. His friend's nine-year-old daughter, Kim,

---

2. The proposed final draft has been approved by the American Law Institute, but its publication has been delayed until work on other topics covered in the Restatement is finished. *See* Press Release, American Law Institute, Agenda Set for the American Law Institute's 86th Annual Meeting in Washington, D.C. (April 16, 2009). [The volume containing these sections was published in 2010.–Eds.]

greets Richard, who hands his loaded shotgun to her as he enters the house. Kim drops the shotgun, which lands on her toe, breaking it. Although Richard was negligent for giving Kim his shotgun, the risk that made Richard negligent was that Kim might shoot someone with the gun, not that she would drop it and hurt herself (the gun was neither especially heavy nor unwieldy). Kim's broken toe is outside the scope of Richard's liability, even though Richard's tortious conduct was a factual cause of Kim's harm.

Id. cmt. b, illus. 3.

Returning to the concept of factual cause, § 26 states that "[c]onduct is a factual cause of harm when the harm would not have occurred absent the conduct." As comment b to the section states, this standard "is familiarly referred to as the 'but-for' test." That test "requires a counterfactual inquiry" in which the court considers "what would have occurred if the actor had not engaged in the tortious conduct." *Id.* cmt. e. If the harm complained of would have occurred notwithstanding the actor's conduct, then that conduct is not a but-for cause. *See id.*

Section 27, however, recognizes that it is sometimes appropriate to impose liability even when the harm would have occurred without the defendant's act. This exceptional circumstance is narrowly defined to impose liability only "when a tortfeasor's conduct, while not necessary for the outcome, would have been a factual cause if the other competing cause had not been operating." *Id.* § 27 cmt. a. The black letter of § 27 states: "If multiple acts exist, each of which alone would have been a factual cause under § 26 of the physical harm at the same time, each act is regarded as a factual cause of the harm." Again, an illustration clarifies the concept:

Rosaria and Vincenzo were independently camping in a heavily forested campground. Each one had a campfire, and each negligently failed to ensure that the fire was extinguished upon retiring for the night. Due to unusually dry forest conditions and a stiff wind, both campfires escaped their sites and began a forest fire. The two fires, burning out of control, joined together and engulfed Centurion Company's hunting lodge, destroying it. Either fire alone would have destroyed the lodge. Each of Rosaria's and Vincenzo's negligence is a factual cause of the destruction of Centurion's hunting lodge.

Id. cmt. a, illus. 1.

The formulation of the requirements for causation in the Restatement (Third) employs different nomenclature from that in the Restatement (Second), but it does not impose a stricter requirement for factual causation. We explain.

Section 430 of the Restatement (Second) states that a negligent person is liable for another's harm only if the negligent conduct was a "legal cause" of the harm. Section 431 then introduces the notion of "substantial factor," stating that "negligent conduct is a legal cause of harm to another if . . . his conduct is a substantial factor in bringing about the harm" and no rule of law exempts him from liability. Section 433 sets forth considerations that are "important in determining whether the actor's conduct is a substantial factor in bringing about harm to another." Those considerations are:

> (a) the number of other factors which contribute in producing the harm and the extent of the effect which they have in producing it; (b) whether the actor's conduct has created a force or series of forces which are in continuous and active operation up to the time of the harm, or has created a situation harmless unless acted upon by other forces for which the actor is not responsible; (c) lapse of time.

Restatement (Second) of Torts § 433.

Reading the black letter of §§ 430, 431, and 433, one could easily conclude that courts and juries have substantial leeway to depart from but-for causation in imposing liability. It would appear to be enough if the considerations listed in § 433 suggest that liability is appropriate. This is how Plaintiffs appear to understand the doctrine. But this conclusion cannot stand once one reads § 432, which imposes a requirement for liability that is at least as stringent as the factual-cause requirement in the Restatement (Third). Section 432(1) sets forth the general requirement of but-for causation; and § 432(2) recognizes what has become the exception in Restatement (Third) § 27 for "multiple sufficient causes." Section 432 states:

> (1) Except as stated in Subsection (2), the actor's negligent conduct is not a substantial factor in bringing about harm to another if the harm would have been sustained even if the actor had not been negligent.

> (2) If two forces are actively operating, one because of the actor's negligence, the other not because of any misconduct on his part, and each of itself is sufficient to bring about the harm to another, the actor's negligence may be found to be a substantial factor in bringing it about.

Thus, as we understand the substantial-factor requirement in the Restatement (Second), it adopts essentially the same standard for factual cause as the Restatement (Third). And that standard is different from what Plaintiffs advocate. What Plaintiffs would apparently use to determine whether conduct is a substantial factor–the conditions set forth in § 433–are actually limitations on what conduct can qualify as a substantial factor. Once conduct satisfies one of the alternative requirements in § 432(1) and (2)–which in the Restatement (Third) §§ 26, 27 are the alternative grounds for being a factual cause–it must still qualify under § 433 if it is to be considered a substantial factor. (The counterpart to § 433 in the Restatement (Third) is § 36, which states that "[w]hen an actor's negligent conduct constitutes only a trivial contribution to a causal set that is a factual cause of physical harm under § 27, the harm is not within the scope of liability." An actor's trivial contribution thus would still be a factual cause, but the actor would not be liable because the harm was outside the scope of liability. It should be noted that § 36, unlike Restatement (Second) § 433, applies only to one of multiple sufficient causes, not to a but-for factual cause.)[3]

There are two further nuances regarding factual cause that need to be explained: the notion of causal sets and the meaning of the term *sufficient cause*. The notion of a causal set is a helpful innovation in the Restatement (Third). A number of factors (often innocent) generally must coexist for a tortfeasor's conduct to result in injury to the plaintiff. Even when the defendant drives his car into the plaintiff's car, no injury would have resulted if the plaintiff had not entered her car and driven to the accident site. That there are many factors does not mean that the defendant's conduct was not a cause. As comment c to § 26 of the Restatement (Third) explains:

> A useful model for understanding factual causation is to conceive of a set made up of each of the necessary conditions for plaintiff's harm. Absent any one of the elements of the set, the plaintiff's harm would not have occurred. Thus, there will always be multiple (some say, infinite) factual causes of a harm, although most will not be of significance for tort law and many will be unidentified. That there are a large number of causes of an event does not mean that everything is a cause of an event. The vast majority of acts, omissions, and other factors play no role in causing any discrete event.

> This causal-set model does not imply any chronological relationship among the causal elements involved, although all causes must precede the plaintiff's harm. An actor's tortious conduct may occur well before the other person suffers harm and require a number of subsequent events to produce the harm. Thus, a gas valve negligently constructed may not fail for many years. Toxic substances may be sold without adequate warnings but not produce harm for decades. Conversely, the tortious conduct may occur after a number of other necessary events have already occurred but close in time to the occurrence of harm. Nor does this model imply any relationship among the causal elements; causal elements may operate independently, as when a property owner neglects a patch of ice on a sidewalk and a careless pedestrian fails to notice the condition, producing a fall.

When § 27 of the Restatement (Third) speaks of "multiple sufficient causes," it could more precisely speak of "multiple sufficient causal *sets*." *See id.* § 27 cmt. f. For example, the evidence at trial may show (1) that conditions A, B, C, D, E, and F were present; (2) that if only A, B, and C had been present, the injury would probably have occurred; and (3) that if only D, E, and F had been present, the injury would probably have occurred. If F is the defendant's misconduct, then F was not a but-for cause of the injury; even without F, the injury would have occurred (all it

---

3. Restatement (Third) § 36 comment a implies that § 433 did not apply to but-for causes. But the Reporters for the Restatement now believe that the comment was erroneous in that respect. *See* Joseph Sanders, William C. Powers, Jr. & Michael D. Green, *The Insubstantiality of the "Substantial Factor" Test for Causation*, 73 Mo. L.Rev. 399, 421–22 n. 90 (2008).

took was A, B, and C). But since D, E, and F would also have caused the injury, F is a component of a second causal set. F must, of course, be a *necessary* component of the second causal set to be a factual cause of the injury. *See id.* That is, F would not be a factual cause if D and E alone would have been enough to cause the injury; F must be a "but for" component of at least one causal set for liability to attach.

Moreover, multiple causal sets may share some components. If A, B, and C would probably have caused the injury (with each of A, B, and C being necessary) and so would have A, B, and D, the tortfeasor who committed D would be liable. The Restatement (Third) provides the following example:

> Able, Baker, and Charlie, acting independently but simultaneously, each negligently lean on Paul's car, which is parked at a scenic overlook at the edge of a mountain. Their combined force results in the car rolling over the edge of a diminutive curbstone and plummeting down the mountain to its destruction. The force exerted by each of Able, Baker, and Charlie would have been insufficient to propel Paul's car past the curbstone, but the combined force of any two of them is sufficient. Able, Baker, and Charlie are each a factual cause of the destruction of Paul's car.

Id. § 26 cmt. f, illus. 3.

A real-world example would be a typical asbestosis lawsuit. A person suffering from asbestosis may have been exposed to asbestos from a number of sources (say, four), and the total exposure may have been more than enough to cause asbestosis. It may well be (1) that asbestosis would probably have arisen even without exposure of the victim to Source A, so Source A is not a but-for cause; and (2) that Source A by itself would not have caused asbestosis. But Source A may be a factual cause if it was a necessary component of a causal set that included, say, two of the other sources and the three together would probably have caused asbestosis. *See, e.g., Spaur v. Owens–Corning Fiberglas Corp.,* 510 N.W.2d 854, 858 (Iowa 1994); *Eagle–Picher v. Balbos,* 326 Md. 179, 604 A.2d 445, 459 (1992); Restatement (Third) of Torts § 27 Reporters' Note cmt. g.

Finally, we attempt to dispel some confusion that may arise from use of the word *sufficient* in the provisions of the Restatement (Second) and the Restatement (Third) that provide an alternative to but-for causation in limited circumstances. Restatement (Second) § 432(2) employs the phrase "forces . . . sufficient to bring about harm to another" and Restatement (Third) § 27 is entitled "Multiple Sufficient Causes." The use of the word *sufficient* in both Restatements does not mean that either of them would impose liability for conduct that is not a but-for cause if only the conduct *could* have caused the injury. Rather, it is necessary for the plaintiff to show that the conduct (or the causal set of which it is a necessary part) *would* in fact have caused the injury. As we all know, in the modern world of many hazardous substances, there may be many possible causes of a particular cancer. Each could be said to be *sufficient* to cause a specific person's cancer. But one who suffers that cancer does not have a cause of action based on each such substance to which he was exposed, regardless of how unlikely it is that the cancer resulted from that exposure. Only a substance that would have actually (that is, probably) caused the cancer can be a factual cause without being a but-for cause. This is clear in the black letter of Restatement (Third) § 27, which states: "If multiple acts exist, each of which alone *would have been* a factual cause under § 26 of the physical harm at the same time, each act is regarded as a factual cause of the harm." *Id.* (emphasis added). And the illustrations to the section confirm this reading. We have already quoted the illustrations involving two fires, each of which "alone would have destroyed the lodge," *id.* cmt. a, illus. 1, and involving three persons leaning on a car, "the combined force of any two of [whom] is sufficient [to propel the car]," *id.* cmt. f, illus. 3. We leave to a footnote a third illustration, the one most pertinent to the case before us, which requires proof that a drug "would have caused" the birth defect that could also have been caused by an unrelated genetic condition. *Id.* cmt. e, illus. 2. It is not enough that the drug *could have* caused the defect, as might be inferred from use of the term *sufficient cause*.[5]

The Restatement (Second) is not as clear as the Restatement (Third) in excluding conduct that merely "could have" caused the injury, but the sole illustration to the point in Restatement (Second) § 432 is essentially the same as the concurrent-fires illustration in Restatement (Third) § 27. In any event, the very notion of two (or more) causes (or causal sets), neither of which is a but-for cause, necessarily assumes that each of the causes *would have* caused the injury. Say there are two such causes, A and B. The reason that A is not a but-for cause is that the injury would probably have occurred even if A had not been present. But that is merely another way of saying that even in the absence of A, B probably *would have* caused the injury; it would not be enough (to prevent A from being a but-for cause) that B may have caused the injury on its own but probably would not have.

---

5. Comment e, Illustration 2 states:

Trent is the guardian ad litem and father of Lakeesha, an infant born with a birth defect. Trent sues Pharmco, a pharmaceutical company, alleging both that Pharmco's drug caused Lakeesha's birth defect and that Pharmco was negligent for its failure to warn that its drug was teratogenic. Pharmco makes a third-party claim against Wardman, alleging that it negligently released chemicals that contaminated Trent's ground and drinking water. Trent introduces sufficient evidence for the factfinder to find that Pharmco's failure to warn was negligent, that the drug was a cause of Lakeesha's birth defect, and that an adequate warning would have prevented the birth defect. * * * Pharmco contends that its drug did not cause Lakeesha's birth defect. Rather, Pharmco contends, Lakeesha's birth defect was caused by a genetic condition wholly unrelated to the drug. Pharmco introduces sufficient evidence in support of its claims. The factfinder must determine if the drug, absent Lakeesha's genetic condition, *would have caused* the birth defect. The factfinder must also determine if, absent the drug, Lakeesha's genetic condition *would have caused* the birth defect. If the factfinder determines that either the drug or the genetic condition would have, in the absence of the other, caused Lakeesha's birth defect at the same time then each is a factual cause pursuant to this section. If the factfinder determines that either the drug or genetic condition played no role in the birth defect, then the other's causal status is determined under the but-for standard of § 26.

(Emphases added).

To sum up, as we understand the Restatement (Second) and the Restatement (Third), a defendant cannot be liable to the plaintiff unless its conduct is either (a) a but-for cause of the plaintiff's injury or (b) a necessary component of a causal set that (probably) would have caused the injury in the absence of other causes. In particular, conduct was not a "substantial factor," within the meaning of the term in the Restatement (Second), in bringing about a plaintiff's injury unless it satisfied (a) or (b), and also was a sufficiently significant factor under the considerations set forth in Restatement (Second) § 433. Thus, Plaintiffs' substantial-factor argument misconceives the meaning of substantial factor in the Restatement (Second).

To be sure, it is Colorado law that governs here, not the Restatements. The Colorado Supreme Court may have decided to disagree with the Restatements and adopt a different standard for causation. But we see no evidence of this. We have reviewed the Colorado opinions relied upon by Plaintiffs for their view of the substantial-factor standard. None expressly addresses multiple sufficient causes. All but one are fully consonant with our above analysis. The sole exception is the opinion by the Colorado Court of Appeals in *Sharp*, 710 P.2d at 1155. That decision held that the trial court had erred in requiring evidence of but-for causation because the plaintiff had been required to show only that the misdiagnosis of her heart condition was a "substantial factor" in causing her heart attack. In language ultimately derived from Restatement (Second) § 431 cmt. a, the court said, "A defendant's conduct is a substantial factor where it is of sufficient significance in producing the harm as to lead reasonable persons to regard it as a cause and to attach responsibility." *Sharp*, 710 P.2d at 1155; *see* Restatement (Second) § 431 cmt. a ("The word 'substantial' is used to denote the fact that the defendant's conduct has such an effect *in producing the harm as to lead reasonable men to regard it as a cause,* using the word in the popular sense, in which there always lurks the idea of *responsibility....*" (emphasis added)). But the court apparently ignored Restatement (Second) § 432, discussed above, which states that conduct is not a substantial factor unless it is a but-for cause or one of multiple sufficient causes. In any event, the state Supreme Court took the case and affirmed on a different theory. *See Sharp,* 741 P.2d at 718, 720 (finding sufficient evidence of but-for causation and affirming court of appeals without reaching its " 'substantial factor' analysis").

Our role here is to predict what the Colorado Supreme Court would adopt as the governing law. Predicting another court's decision is necessarily an uncertain proposition. In our view, however, it would be too adventurous on our part to assume that Colorado would depart from the Restatements. We therefore hold that Defendants would be liable only upon proof of one of the following: (1) that exposure of a Plaintiff to Uravan radiation was a but-for cause of the Plaintiff's medical condition or (2) that such exposure to Uravan radiation was a necessary component of a causal set that would have caused the medical condition.

We now examine whether Plaintiffs supplied such evidence.

2. Causation Evidence

Plaintiffs failed to raise in district court a genuine issue of fact regarding factual causation. That is, they failed to present to the court evidence, or even an argument, that Uravan radiation was either a but-for cause of any medical condition suffered by one of the Plaintiffs or that Uravan radiation was a necessary component of a causal set that would probably have caused one of those conditions.

* * * Dr. A. James Ruttenber addressed only general causation, that is, whether radiation at Uravan had the capacity to cause the cancers and thyroid diseases that the Plaintiffs developed. *See Neiberger v. Fed Ex Ground Package Sys., Inc.*, 566 F.3d 1184, 1191 (10th Cir.2009) (discussing general and specific causation); Restatement (Third) of Torts § 28 cmt. c(3), c(4) (same). Dr. F. Owen Hoffman provided the raw data upon which the final two experts relied. He estimated the mean dose of radiation received by each Plaintiff from Uravan operations. * * *

To prove specific causation for each Plaintiff—that is, to prove that the Uravan radiation caused the specific ailment of which the Plaintiff complained—Plaintiffs relied on the remaining two experts: Drs. Inder J. Chopra and Robert Peter Gale. Dr. Chopra addressed the Plaintiffs with thyroid disease (including the one case of thyroid cancer) and Dr. Gale addressed the remaining Plaintiffs, all of whom had suffered cancer.

Dr. Chopra prepared a report that assessed each thyroid Plaintiff and concluded that the Plaintiff's exposure to radiation from Uravan and NTS fallout was a "substantial factor contributing to" the Plaintiff's thyroid disease. *See, e.g., id.,* Vol. IX at 1562. A "substantial factor," he explained, "is intended to mean that the exposures were one of the variables that contributed to the observed health effect (thyroid disease)." *Id.* at 1556. He defined "substantial" as "an amount that is not trivial." * * * Dr. Chopra's report did not, however, state with respect to any Plaintiff that Uravan radiation was a but-for cause of the Plaintiff's thyroid disease or was a necessary component of a causal set that probably would have caused the Plaintiff to suffer the disease.

For the Plaintiffs with cancer (other than thyroid cancer), Dr. Gale's report opined that "to a reasonable medical probability exposure to ionizing radiations was a substantial factor contributing to each plaintiff developing cancer(s)." * * * As was true of Dr. Chopra, however, Dr. Gale did not opine that Uravan radiation was either a but-for cause of any Plaintiff's cancer or was a necessary component of a causal set that would have caused the cancer.

Thus, the evidence relied on by Plaintiffs did not show that Uravan radiation was a factual cause of any of their ailments. In reaching this conclusion we are not being hypertechnical. The problem for Plaintiffs is not that their experts failed to utter some magic words, such as "but for." Nor are we relying on any expertise of this court in analyzing the data and opinions from Plaintiffs' experts. We claim no such expertise. For all we know, the data would support but-for claims of some, or even all, Plaintiffs. The problem for Plaintiffs is that they did not make a timely argument that they had produced evidence of but-for causation, and they have never (not even in this court) contended that they have produced evidence that Uravan radiation was a necessary component of a causal set that probably would have caused the Plaintiffs' ailments.

* * *

Plaintiffs make better but-for arguments on appeal. But they come too late. Based on the evidence and arguments properly before the district court, summary judgment on all personal-injury claims was appropriately granted. *See Hutton Contracting Co. v. City of Coffeyville,* 487 F.3d 772, 782 (10th Cir.2007) ("Absent special circumstances, we will not reverse on a ground not raised below.").

* * *

III. CONCLUSION

The judgment of the district court is AFFIRMED.

NOTES AND QUESTIONS

1. *Substantial factor.* As the *June* court noted, following in the footsteps of the first Restatement, the Second Restatement of Torts made "substantial factor" the key concept for determining cause-in-fact. Most courts still employ this rubric when discussing causation. However, in nearly all cases they mean to use the term as a synonym for but-for causation. The first two Restatements turned to the substantial factor test to resolve the problem of the "two-fire" cases. See, e.g., Kingston v. Chicago & Nw. Ry. Co., 211 N.W. 913 (Wis.1927). As the *June* case demonstrates, however, there was pressure to use the test to permit recovery even in the absence of proof the defendant's tortious conduct was a but-for cause by a preponderance of the evidence. As David Fischer notes, "Over the years, courts used the substantial factor test to do an increasing variety of things it was never intended to do and for which it is not appropriate. As a result, the test now creates unnecessary confusion in the law and has outlived its usefulness." David A. Fischer, Insufficient Causes, 94 Ky.L.J. 277, 277 (2005). The Third Restatement's solution to the two-fire problem is to create a special rule for multiple sufficient causation situations. Restatement (Third) of Torts: Liability for Physical and Emotional Harm § 27 (2010). See the notes following the *Rutherford* case in the next Chapter for a discussion of this rule.

The Second Restatement contemplates a second role for the substantial factor test: to cut off liability where but-for causes are sufficiently trivial that they should be ignored.

In order to be a legal cause of another's harm, it is not enough that the harm would not have occurred had the actor not been negligent. Except as stated in [Section] 432(2), this is necessary, but it is not of itself sufficient. The negligence must also be a substantial factor in bringing about the plaintiff's harm. The word "substantial" is used to denote the fact that the defendant's conduct has such an effect in producing the harm as to lead reasonable men to regard it as a cause, using that word in the popular sense, in which there always lurks the idea of responsibility, rather than in the so-called "philosophic sense," which includes every one of the great number of events without which any happening would not have occurred. Each of these events is a cause in the so-called "philosophic sense," yet the effect of many of them is so insignificant that no ordinary mind would think of them as causes.

Restatement (Second) of Torts § 431 cmt. a.

Comment a makes it clear that this second use of the substantial factor test is not intended to expand causation where the but-for test is unsatisfied. Rather, it is intended to do the opposite—to prevent a determination of causation where the but-for test would otherwise provide it. Its purpose is to excuse defendants whose conduct is a but-for cause of harm when the effect of that conduct "is so insignificant that no ordinary mind would think of [it] as [a] cause[]." As the reporter's note to comment j of section 26 of the Third Restatement suggests, it might be useful to think of this use of the substantial factor test as an aspect of the scope of liability, i.e., a question of proximate cause. We return to the use of the term in this way in Chapter 6, section B.

2. The Ninth Circuit adopted a similar position on but-for causation in In re Hanford Nuclear Reservation Litigation, 534 F.3d 986 (9th Cir.2008).

3. The *June* court noted that answering the but-for question involves a counterfactual inquiry. In a very useful article, Professor Robertson sets forth a four-step framework for answering but-for questions. First, one must identify the injury. Second, one must identify as precisely as possible the exact nature of the defendant's wrongful act.

> The third step is the trickiest. It involves using the imagination to create a counterfactual hypothesis. One creates a mental picture of a situation identical to the actual facts of the case in all respects save one: the defendant's wrongful conduct is now "corrected" to the minimal extent necessary to make it conform to the law's requirements. It is important to stress that the mental operation performed at this third step must be careful, conservative, and modest; the hypothesis must be counterfactual only to the extent necessary to ask the but-for question. Only the defendant's wrongful conduct must be "changed," and that only to the extent necessary to make it conform to the requirements of law.

David W. Robertson, The Common Sense of Cause in Fact, 75 Tex.L.Rev. 1765, 1770 (1997). The fourth step asks whether plaintiff's injuries would probably have occurred had defendant behaved correctly.

4. The issue of whether one may recover for medical monitoring and/or for asymptomatic sub-cellular injuries is discussed in Chapter 12.

5. The *June* court noted that the plaintiffs' state law claims were preempted by the Price Anderson Act. We discuss preemption in Chapter 10, section A. The Price Anderson Act is addressed in Chapter 2, at p. 69.

6. The *June* opinion briefly refers to the concept of proximate cause and notes that it has been renamed "scope of liability" in the Third Restatement. We discuss scope of liability issues in Chapter 6.

7. In both *Miller* and *June* the causal question was discussed in two parts, "general causation" and "specific causation." The next section of this Chapter explores these concepts in greater depth.

C. GENERAL AND SPECIFIC CAUSATION

1. GENERAL CAUSATION

DELUCA v. MERRELL DOW PHARMACEUTICALS, INC.

United States Court of Appeals, Third Circuit, 1990.
911 F.2d 941

STAPLETON, CIRCUIT JUDGE:

This is an appeal in a diversity action brought under New Jersey law by the DeLuca family against Merrell Dow Pharmaceuticals Corporation, the manufacturer of Bendectin. The DeLucas seek damages for severe birth defects suffered by Cindy DeLuca's daughter Amy. * * * The DeLucas allege that these birth defects were caused by Cindy DeLuca's use of Bendectin during the time she was pregnant with Amy.

Merrell Dow filed a motion for summary judgment alleging that the only causation evidence produced by the DeLucas was inadmissible because all relevant epidemiological studies have determined there is no statistically significant link between the use of Bendectin during pregnancy and the type of birth defects suffered by Amy DeLuca and these studies were the only reasonable basis for expert opinions. In response, the DeLucas proffered affidavits and deposition testimony by Dr. Alan Done, an expert in pediatric pharmacology, in which Dr. Done opined that the available epidemiological data does support the conclusion that Bendectin causes limb reduction defects and that he believed, to a reasonable degree of medical certainty, Bendectin caused Amy's defects. The district court held that Dr. Done's testimony would be inadmissible at trial because it was not based on data of a type reasonably relied upon by experts in the pertinent fields in issuing opinions on these subjects, as is required by Federal Rule of Evidence 703. 131 F.R.D. 71. Since Dr. Done's testimony was the sole causation evidence the DeLucas tendered in response to Merrell Dow's motion, the district court entered summary judgment for Merrell Dow. On appeal, the DeLucas argue that the district court misapplied Federal Rule of Evidence 703 in excluding Dr. Done's testimony. We agree and we will reverse and remand for proceedings consistent with the principles articulated herein.

I. THE LEGAL AND SCIENTIFIC SETTING

This is one of the last of over 1,000 suits alleging that birth defects were caused by the drug * * * Bendectin, a prescription drug prescribed for morning sickness in pregnant women. * * *

* * *

In this case, the district court faced one of the difficult questions that has pervaded Bendectin litigation to this point: whether an expert may testify, in light of existing scientific knowledge, that Bendectin is a teratogen, i.e., an agent that causes birth defects. * * *

* * *

B. *The Relevant Scientific Principles and Tendered Evidence*

To competently analyze the legal issues presented by this appeal, an understanding of the relevant scientific principles * * * is essential. Problematic issues of causation arise in Bendectin cases because the etiology of most birth defects is unknown. There is no apparent way to determine from clinical examinations of Amy DeLuca whether her limb defects were the result of her mother's exposure to Bendectin, as opposed to another possible teratogen, or whether her birth defects are simply an inexplicable natural occurrence not induced by her mother's exposure to an outside agent. Rather, the only particularistic evidence the DeLucas can show to strengthen the inference that Amy DeLuca's birth defects were caused by Bendectin is to rule in Bendectin as a possible cause by showing that Amy was exposed to it during the time her limbs were developing, i.e., during organogenesis, and to rule out other possible causes by showing that Amy was not exposed to them during the critical period of organogenesis. * * *

Thus, the DeLucas must rely primarily on inferences drawn from epidemiological data to show causation in Amy's case. Epidemiology, a branch of science and medicine, uses studies to "observe the effect of exposure to a single factor upon the incidence of disease in two otherwise identical populations." Black & Lilienfeld, *Epidemiological Proof In Toxic Tort Litigation,* 52 Fordham L.Rev. 732, 755 (1984). In the Bendectin context, an epidemiological study ideally attempts to determine the incidence of birth defects among the children of two groups of women, identical in all respects except for their use of Bendectin during pregnancy. Epidemiological studies do not provide direct evidence that a particular plaintiff was injured by exposure to a substance. Such studies have the potential, however, of generating circumstantial evidence of cause and effect through a process known as hypothesis testing, a process which "amounts to an attempt to falsify the null hypothesis and by exclusion accept the alternative." K.J. Rothman, Modern Epidemiology 116 (1986) ("Rothman"). The null hypothesis is the hypothesis that there is no association between two studied variables, *id.*; in this case the key null hypothesis would be that there is no association between Bendectin exposure and an increase in limb reduction defects. The important alternative hypothesis in this case is that Bendectin use is associated with an increased incidence of limb reduction defects.

The great weight of scientific opinion * * * sides with the view that Bendectin use does not increase the risk of having a child with birth defects. Sailing against the prevailing scientific breeze is the DeLucas' expert Dr. Alan Done, formerly a Professor of Pharmacology and Pediatrics at Wayne State University School of Medicine, who continues to hold fast to his position that Bendectin is a teratogen. In spite of his impressive curriculum vitae, Dr. Done's opinion on this subject has been rejected as inadmissible by several courts.

Dr. Done's opinion that Bendectin is a teratogen largely rests on inferences he draws from epidemiological data, most of which he contends are the same that was utilized by the experts, including the FDA committee, to whom Merrell Dow cites to bolster its contention that Bendectin does not cause birth defects.[8] * * * The principal difference is that Dr. Done analyzes that data using an approach, advocated by Professor Kenneth Rothman of the University of Massachusetts Medical School, that places diminished weight on so-called "significance testing." *See* K.J. Rothman, Modern Epidemiology (1986) ("Rothman").

Epidemiological studies, of necessity, look to the experience of sample groups as indicative of the experience of a far larger population. Epidemiologists recognize, however, that the experience of the sample groups may vary from that of the larger population by chance. Thus, a showing of increased risk for birth defects among women using Bendectin in a particular study does not automatically prove that Bendectin use creates a higher risk of having a child with birth defects because the discrepancy between the exposed and unexposed groups could be the product of chance resulting from the use of only a small sample of the relevant populations. As a result of the acknowledged risk of this so-called "sampling error," researchers typically have rejected the associations suggested by epidemiological data unless those associations survive the rigors of "significance testing." This practice has also found favor in the legal context. A number of judicial opinions, discussed *infra,* have found Bendectin plaintiffs' causation evidence inadmissible because every published epidemiological study of the relationship of Bendectin exposure to the incidence of birth defects has concluded that there is not a "statistically significant" relationship between these two events.

Significance testing has a "P value" focus; the P value "indicates the probability, assuming the null hypothesis is true, that the observed data will depart from the absence of association to the extent that they actually

---

8. The conclusion Dr. Done draws from these studies is buttressed by inferences he draws from less probative, but nevertheless relevant, sources. These include analogies between the effect substances with a chemical structure similar to Bendectin have on human fetuses and the effect Bendectin may have, and inferences drawn from studies of the incidence of birth defects in the offspring of animals given Bendectin during pregnancy, *in vivo* studies, and the effect Bendectin has on animal fetuses outside an animal host, *in vitro* studies.

* * *

do, or to a greater extent, by actual chance." Rothman, *supra*, at 116. If P is less than .05 (or 5%) a study's finding of a relationship supportive of the alternative hypothesis is considered statistically significant, if P is greater than 5% the relationship is rejected as insignificant. Accordingly, the results of a particular study are reported as simply "significant" or "not significant" or as P<.05 or P>.05.

Use of a .05 P value to determine whether to accept or reject the null hypothesis necessarily enhances one of two types of possible error. Type one error is when the null hypothesis is rejected when it is in fact true. Type two error is when the null hypothesis is in fact false but is not rejected. Rothman notes that at .05, the null hypothesis will "be rejected about 5 percent of the time when it is true," a relatively small risk of type one error. *Id.* at 117. Unfortunately, the relationship between type one error and type two error is not simple * * *.

Rothman contends that there is nothing magical or inherently important about .05 significance; rather this is just a common value on the tables scholars use to calculate significance. Rothman, *supra*, at 117; *see also* Kaye, *Is Proof of Statistical Significance Relevant?*, 61 Wash.L.Rev. 1333, 1343–44 (1986). He stresses that the data in a certain study may indicate a strong relationship between two variables but still not be "statistically significant" and that the level of significance which should be required depends on the type of decision being made and the relative values placed on avoiding the two types of risk.

To convey both the extent to which two variables are associated in the data, and the extent to which this association might be the product of chance, Rothman advocates reporting both a "relative risk" (or point estimate) and "confidence intervals." In the context of an epidemiological study of Bendectin's relationship to birth defects, the relative risk is the ratio of the incidence rate of birth defects in the study group exposed to Bendectin divided by the rate in the control group not exposed to Bendectin. If a study found no difference in the rate of birth defects between the Bendectin exposed group and the control group, it yields a relative risk identical to the null hypothesis that Bendectin exposure is not associated with an increased incidence of birth defects. The relative risk would thus be reported as "1", signifying no difference between the rate of birth defects in each group.

A confidence interval is a way of graphically representing the probability that the relative risk figure or any other relationship between two studied variables is the actual relationship. The interval is a range of sets of possible values for the true parameter that is consistent with the observed data within specified limits. A 95% confidence interval is constructed with enough width so that one can be confident that it is only 5% likely that the relative risk attained would have occurred if the true parameter, i.e., the actual unknown relationship between the two studied variables, were outside the confidence interval. If a 95% confidence interval thus contains "1", or the null hypothesis, then a researcher cannot say that the results are "statistically significant," that is, that the null hypothesis has been disproved at a .05 level of significance. Kaye, *Is Proof of Statistical Significance Relevant?, supra,* at 1348.

The result of a study should be reported, in Rothman's view, by reference to the confidence intervals at various confidence levels, e.g., 90%, 95%, 99%. The inclusion of confidence intervals of a variety of levels reflects Rothman's view that the predominating choice of a 95% confidence level is but an arbitrarily selected convention of his discipline. More importantly, however, Rothman insists that the precise locations of the boundaries of the confidence intervals, the all important focus of "significance testing," are far less important than their size and location. According to Rothman, statistical theory suggests that it is "much more likely that the [true] parameter [i.e. the true relationship between the studied variables] is located centrally within an interval than it is that the parameter is located near the limits of the interval." Rothman, *supra,* at 124. As such, the primary focus should not be on the ends of an interval but rather on the "approximate position of the interval as a whole on its scale of measurement. . . ." *Id.*

Finally, Rothman contends that the use of significance testing is especially unhelpful when a decisionmaker is attempting to draw inferences from more than one study. Different studies may each be rejected as insignificant, yet, when the studies are looked at collectively, a majority of the data may be moderately or strongly contradictory to the null hypothesis. By failing to look at the collective data in the context of confidence intervals and the most likely estimate for the true parameter suggested by that data, researchers focusing solely on significance testing tolerate a high risk of type two error. *Id.* at 117–18.

Rothman suggests a less rigid approach in which researchers look at the confidence intervals produced by various studies. By charting the range of possibilities consistent with the data found in different studies it is possible to evaluate whether the collective data is more supportive of the proposition that the null hypothesis is false than that it is true. *Id.* at 124. At the same time, the use of confidence intervals indicates the risks inherent in generating any estimate of the true parameter from the data, and allows the decisionmaker to adjust the confidence level depending on the context in which a decision is required. *Id.* at 123–25; *see also* Kaye, *Is Proof of Statistical Significance Relevant?, supra,* at 1364.

Dr. Done attached the article and chapter by Rothman to his affidavit on behalf of the DeLucas and expressly indicated that his analysis was predicated on the methodology advocated by Rothman. Dr. Done purports to have analyzed all of the epidemiological data from the published epidemiological studies of the relationship between birth defects and Bendectin, as well the data from several unpublished studies, utilizing the author's confidence interval if calculated, a 95% confidence interval if the author indicated a preference for that figure, or 90% otherwise.

Dr. Done has graphed the relative risks and confidence intervals for each of the separate sets of data together, so that the collective trend may be visualized. He concludes from analysis of these intervals that the "bulk of the available human epidemiological data ... are indicative of Bendectin's human teratogenicity." App. at 345. Dr. Done contends that the effect in the data is strongest for, among other birth defects, limb reduction defects like Amy DeLuca's. Dr. Done did not, however, quantify the increased risk for limb reduction defects he believed was posed by use of Bendectin during pregnancy. Dr. Done's analysis has not been published nor has it been subjected to peer review by experts in the field.

C. *The Bendectin Case Law*

We recognize that the district court's decision to exclude Dr. Done's proposed testimony was heavily influenced by the decisions of other courts that have grappled with the difficult question of whether expert testimony that Bendectin causes birth defects is admissible and/or sufficient to sustain a verdict. * * *

* * *

* * * *Lynch v. Merrell–National Laboratories*, 830 F.2d 1190 (1st Cir.1987), and *Richardson by Richardson v. Richardson–Merrell Inc.*, 857 F.2d 823 (D.C.Cir.1988), *cert. denied,*493 U.S. 882, 110 S.Ct. 218, 107 L.Ed.2d 171 (1989), * * * reviewed appeals from grants of j.n.o.v. in Bendectin limb reduction defect cases. Both held that Dr. Done's opinion that Bendectin is a teratogen is not only insufficient to support a verdict in light of the currently available scientific and medical evidence, but that it is inadmissible under Federal Rule of Evidence 703. Each court held that an opinion that Bendectin is a teratogen would be admissible under Federal Rule of Evidence 703 only if it were based on a new epidemiological study concluding that Bendectin was associated in a statistically significant way with an increase in birth defects.[10]

* * *

[W]e do not view the absence of statistically significant findings or the great weight of contrary opinion as being relevant to the Rule 703 question posed here. Rule 703 is satisfied once there is a showing that an expert's testimony is based on the type of data a reasonable expert in the field would use in rendering an opinion on the subject at issue; it does not address the reliability or general acceptance of an expert's methodology. When a statistician refers to a study as "not statistically significant," he is not making a statement about the reliability of the data used, rather he is

---

10. These courts also rejected Dr. Done's attempt to use structure activity analysis and *in vivo* and *in vitro* studies to support his opinion that Bendectin is a teratogen: "Studies of this kind, singly or in combination, are not capable of proving causation in human beings in the face of the overwhelming body of contradictory epidemiological evidence." *Richardson*, 857 F.2d at 830; *accord Lynch*, 830 F.2d at 1194; *see also In re Agent Orange Product Liability Litigation*, 611 F.Supp. 1223, 1234 (E.D.N.Y.1985) (where a number of sound epidemiological studies had been conducted on the health effects of Agent Orange there was no other reasonable basis for expert testimony on the subject), *aff'd*, 818 F.2d 187 (2d Cir.1987).

making a statement about the propriety of drawing a particular inference from that data.[12]

* * *

Implicit in the district court's decision, and in the decisions in *Richardson* and *Lynch*, is the principle that Rule 703 requires an expert to accept the conclusions reached by the authors of studies if the expert wishes to utilize the data underlying those studies as a basis for testimony. However, the Federal Rules of Evidence contain no requirement that an expert's testimony be based upon reasoning subjected to peer-review and published in the professional literature. * * *

* * *

We stress * * * that the confidence level or "significance" of a statistical analysis is but a part of a meaningful evaluation of its reliability. *See generally,* J. Monahan & L. Walker, *Social Science in Law: Cases and Materials* 33–75 (1990). The results of such a study may fail to correspond to reality for a number of reasons other than "sampling error." Faulty data collection resulting from design or execution flaws, for example, can create a much greater risk of error than the sampling error. Thus, a poorly conceived or conducted study that disproves the null hypothesis at a .01 level of significance may be far less reliable than a well conceived and conducted study that is significant at a .1 level. Kaye, *Is Proof of Statistical Significance Relevant?, supra* at 1362. * * *

By directing such an overall evaluation, however, we do not mean to reject at this point Merrell Dow's contention that a showing of a .05 level of statistical significance should be a threshold requirement for any statistical analysis concluding that Bendectin is a teratogen regardless of the presence of other indicia of reliability. That contention will need to be addressed on remand. The root issue it poses is what risk of what type of error the judicial system is willing to tolerate. This is not an easy issue to resolve and one possible resolution is a conclusion that the system should not tolerate any expert opinion rooted in statistical analysis where the results of the underlying studies are not significant at a .05 level. We believe strongly, however, that this issue should not be resolved in a case where the record contains virtually no relevant help from the parties or from qualified experts. The literature evidences that there are legal scholars and epidemiologists who have given considerable thought to this and related issues[16] and we would hope that this expertise could be made available to the court, on remand, in some acceptable manner.

* * *

---

12. He is making a statement about the degree to which the relationship found in the data may be due to chance, but his decision to use a certain significance level as a check on the permissible inference to be drawn from the data is a methodological value judgment which is separate from the question of whether the data is of the type an expert would rely upon.

16. A sampling of the pertinent law review literature includes Black, *A Unified Theory of Scientific Evidence,* 56 Fordham L.Rev. 595 (1988); Cohen, *Confidence in Probability: Burdens of Persuasion in a World of Imperfect Knowledge,* 60 N.Y.U.L.Rev. 385 (1985); Kaye, *Apples and Oranges: Confidence Coefficients and the Burden of Persuasion,* 73 Cornell L.Rev. 54 (1987);

In considering the question of reliability on remand, the district court is permitted to identify relevant scientific communities and make determinations about the degree of acceptance of Dr. Done's methodology within those communities. Conversely, it may consider the extent to which members of these communities decline to give any weight to inferences not supported by .05 statistical significance. * * * The fact that a scientific community may require a particular level of assurance for its own purposes before it will regard a null hypothesis as disproven does not necessarily mean that expert opinion with somewhat less assurance is not sufficiently reliable to be helpful in the context of civil litigation.

* * *

III. THE SUFFICIENCY OF THE EVIDENCE ISSUE

Since the district court held that the Deluca's sole evidence of causation was inadmissible, it had no difficulty in concluding that they had not met their burden * * * to produce evidence sufficient to raise a genuine issue of material fact as to whether Amy DeLuca's birth defects were caused by Bendectin. If Dr. Done's testimony is ultimately held to be admissible, however, a different issue will be presented. While we express no opinion on that issue, we wish to make clear that nothing in this opinion is intended to suggest that this issue is or is not susceptible of resolution by summary judgment.

As we have earlier noted, a court presented with a motion for summary judgment must ultimately determine whether the admissible evidence tendered by the party having the burden of proof on an issue is sufficient to permit a rational factfinder to find for that party on that issue under the appropriate burden of proof. In the present context, Dr. Done's testimony may be found sufficiently helpful to be admissible and sufficiently probative to support a jury finding that Bendectin *can cause* birth defects or even that Bendectin *not infrequently causes* such defects. However, assuming that New Jersey would apply the traditional "more probable than not" burden of proof standard to the causation issue in this case, this admissible testimony would not alone bar summary judgment for Merrell Dow unless it would support a jury finding that Bendectin *more likely than not caused* the birth defects in *this particular case*.

Hypothetically, Dr. Done may be able to testify, on the basis of adequate data and the application of reasonably reliable methodology, for example, that of women who took Bendectin and had children with birth defects, 25% of the cases of birth defects can be attributed to Bendectin exposure. This testimony would be admissible as it would be a basis from which a jury could rationally find that Bendectin *could have* caused Amy DeLuca's birth defects; however, it would not without more suffice to satisfy the DeLucas' burden on causation under a more likely than not standard since a fact finder could not say on the basis of this evidence

---

Nesson, *Agent Orange Meets the Blue Bus: Factfinding at the Frontier of Knowledge*, 66 B.U.L.Rev. 521 (1986).

alone that Amy DeLuca's birth defects were more likely than not caused by Bendectin.

If New Jersey law requires the DeLucas to show that it is more likely than not that Bendectin caused Amy DeLuca's birth defects, and they are forced to rely solely on Dr. Done's epidemiological analysis in order to avoid summary judgment, the relative risk of limb reduction defects arising from the epidemiological data Done relies upon will, at a minimum, have to exceed "2":

> A relative risk of "2" means that the disease occurs among the population subject to the event under investigation twice as frequently as the disease occurs among the population not subject to the event under investigation. Phrased another way, a relative risk of "2" means that, on the average, there is a fifty per cent likelihood that a particular case of the disease was caused by the event under investigation and a fifty per cent likelihood that the disease was caused by chance alone. *A relative risk greater than "2" means that the disease more likely than not was caused by the event.*

Manko v. United States, 636 F.Supp. 1419, 1434 (W.D.Mo.1986), *aff'd in relevant part,* 830 F.2d 831 (8th Cir.1987).

We express no opinion on whether Dr. Done's epidemiological analysis fails to meet this threshold requirement. While it is not clear to our untrained eyes that it does, without the benefit of an expert affidavit critiquing that analysis we are not sufficiently confident of our own critical capacities to resolve that issue. Nor do we suggest that the DeLucas will be required to rely solely on Dr. Done's epidemiological analysis at trial or in any subsequent summary judgment proceedings. The alternative support that he finds for his conclusion in structural activity analysis, for example, may be entitled to some weight in determining whether they have met their burden of establishing a *prima facie* case. We note only that even if Dr. Done's epidemiological analysis is found to be admissible, the DeLucas are entitled to get to trial only if the district court is satisfied that this analysis together with any other evidence relevant to the causation issue would permit a jury finding that Amy's birth defects were, when measured against the appropriate burden of proof, caused by her mother's exposure to Bendectin.[24]

IV. CONCLUSION

We hold that the present record cannot sustain the exclusion of Dr. Done's testimony. Therefore, we will reverse the grant of summary judgment in Merrell Dow's favor and remand for further proceedings consistent with this opinion.

---

24. Even if Dr. Done's statistical analysis is found to be admissible, its lack of statistical significance at the .05 level may appropriately play some role in deciding this subsequent issue. The relationship between confidence levels and the more likely than not standard of proof is a very complex one, however, and in the absence of more education than can be found in this record, we decline to comment further on it. * * *

NOTES AND QUESTIONS

1. On remand, the district court once again excluded Dr. Done's testimony. This time, however, the exclusion was accompanied by a lengthy opinion pointing out the deficiencies in his analysis. Among other things, it noted that neither the defendant's expert epidemiologists nor another plaintiff expert epidemiologist could replicate Dr. Done's re-analysis of published epidemiologic research. DeLuca v. Merrell Dow Pharms., Inc., 791 F.Supp. 1042 (D.N.J.1992). This time the court of appeals affirmed without an opinion. DeLuca v. Merrell Dow Pharms. Inc., 6 F.3d 778 (3d Cir.1993).

2. *DeLuca* was decided prior to the Supreme Court's *Daubert* opinion. Like many other appellate court admissibility opinions from that era, it based its analysis primarily on Federal Rule of Evidence 703. As we discuss in Chapter 5, *Daubert* focused almost all of its analysis on Federal Rule of Evidence 702. As a result, Rule 703 has slowly faded into the background. For many courts, Rule 703's original mandate that experts may only rely on data of a type that a reasonable expert would rely upon was readily folded into the reliability demands of *Daubert*.

A PRIMER ON THE TYPES OF SCIENTIFIC EVIDENCE IN TOXIC TORT CASES*

Types of Evidence

There are several general categories of scientific evidence concerning Bendectin and similar toxic substances: structure-activity, in vitro, in vivo (animal studies), data on humans, including clinical trials, epidemiology, aggregate time trend data and biological mechanism evidence. The first, structure-activity, is an argument by analogy. Toxicologists attempt to draw inferences about the biological activity of a drug by examining its chemical structure and comparing its structure to that of substances whose biological activity is better understood. As the trial judge in *DeLuca* indicated, the structure-activity analogy by itself is weak evidence as to whether a chemical will be a teratogen. Molecules with minor structural differences can produce very different biological effects.

In vitro studies test teratogenicity by exposing single cells, organs, culture-maintained embryos, or limb buds to a suspect substance and examining the biochemical events. Organ cultures of embryonic limb buds are the most frequent subjects of in vitro studies testing for teratogenicity. At present, however, extrapolation of in vitro results to live animals, not to mention humans, is difficult. Impediments to extrapolation include the following factors: a chemical may not be absorbed by living organisms; the chemical is distributed in a living organism such that more (or less) reaches specific locations than would be predicted based on its absorption; and the chemical is rapidly metabolized into a metabolite that has a different profile of activity than the parent agent.

---

* The following materials are drawn from Joseph Sanders, Benedictin on Trial 45–61 (1998).

In vivo studies examine the effects of a drug on various animal species thought to be similar to humans in their response to certain drugs. The choice of a species for comparison is not an easy one. Ideally, one wants to employ a species that is most like humans with respect to the way it responds to a particular substance. However, cost also plays a role. For example, primate labs are very expensive to operate. Early animal studies failed to detect the teratogenetic effects of thalidomide, in part because they used species unaffected by the drug.[1] As a result of the thalidomide experience, the FDA has developed standardized protocols for animal testing on new drugs.[2] Because species choice is difficult, the protocols call for tests on at least two species at three dose levels. Other regulatory agencies have their own animal testing protocols.[3]

The "gold standard" for trials on human beings are clinical trials that are employed when testing new drugs. Because people are randomly assigned to treatments, i.e., they receive the drug or a placebo, other variables that might influence the outcome are, at least in theory, controlled for. Imagine, for example, that there is some unknown genetic trait that strongly influences how someone responds to a drug. In a randomized trial, those who possess this trait are equally likely to be in the control (placebo) or the experimental (receive the drug) group and, therefore, this trait should not affect the observed relationship between the presence or absence of the drug and the course of the illness it is designed to treat.

In many situations, clinical trials cannot be performed. This is often true for ethical reasons. We cannot ethically expose young children to lead paint to observe its effects on their mental development. In such situations, we must turn to non-experimental or "observational" methods. The most widely used methods are epidemiologic. There are two general types of epidemiologic studies: cohort studies and case-control studies. Cohort studies compare the incidence of injury in groups of persons exposed to the drug to the incidence in groups of persons not exposed. They are sometimes called "prospective studies" because often they look forward from the time some people are exposed and examine whether those who are exposed become ill at the same rate as those who are not exposed. (In point of fact, some cohort studies are done retrospectively. The data is collected after both exposure and injury have occurred.) Case-control studies compare a group of persons who have the injury in question ("cases") with another group that do not have it ("controls"). The two groups then are compared with regard to the frequency of exposure to the drug. Case-control studies are sometimes called "retrospective studies"

---

1. Max Sherman & Steven Strauss, Thalidomide: A Twenty–Five Year Perspective, 41 Food, Drug & Cosmetics L.J. 458, 461 (1986) (Thalidomide is not a teratogen in rats, mice, or hamsters.)

2. See, e.g., FDA, U.S. Dep't of Health & Human Service., Guidance for Industry: Animal Models—Essential Elements to Address Efficacy Under the Animal Rule 5 (2009), available at http://www.fda.gov/downloads/Drugs/GuidanceComplianceRegulatoryInformation/Guidances/UCM 078923.pdf .

3. For a discussion of this topic, see Amanda Hungerford, Back to Basics: Courts' Treatment of Agency Animal Studies After *Daubert*, 110 Colum.L.Rev. 70 (2010).

because we look backward to compare the rate of exposure to the substance in question among those who are ill and those who are not.

Epidemiologic studies typically measure risk by using the concepts of prevalence rate, relative risk, attributable risk, and odds ratio. The prevalence rate is the number of persons with an injury divided by the total number of people in a group. The relative risk is a ratio that divides the prevalence of injury among people exposed to a risk factor by the prevalence of injury among those who were not exposed. For example, imagine that in a certain area there were 5,000 newborns and the mothers of 1,000 of these children took Bendectin during pregnancy. Among the 1,000 children whose mothers took Bendectin, 60 have a birth defect and 940 do not. Among the 4,000 children whose mothers did not take Bendectin we find that 160 have a birth defect and 3,840 do not. The prevalence among the exposed children is $60/(60+940) = .06$. The prevalence among non-exposed children is $160/(160+3840) = .04$. The relative risk is $.06/.04 = 1.5$.[4] The attributable risk is a measure of the difference in the risks between exposed and unexposed groups. In our example, the unexposed risk is .04 and the exposed risk is .06. Thus the risk attributable to Bendectin, *if* Bendectin use were the only difference between exposed and unexposed children, is .02. Sometimes researchers will report an attributable risk ratio, which is the percentage of the risk due to the substance. In the previous example, the attributable risk ratio is $(.02/.06)$ x 100 = 33%.

Relative Risk in a Cohort Study

	Injured	Not Injured	Total
Exposed	a	b	(a + b)
Not Exposed	c	d	(c + d)

$$\textit{Relative Risk} = \frac{a/(a+b)}{c/(c+d)}$$

$$\textit{Relative Risk} = \frac{60/(60+940)}{160/(160+3840)} = \frac{.06}{.04} = 1.5$$

Finally, there is the odds ratio. Because of the way case-control studies are conducted, prevalence rates are not available. Recall that in case-control studies, we compare a group of persons who have the disease

---

4. Unlike birth defects, which occur at a single point in time, other diseases may occur at different times. With them, rather than measuring prevalence, researchers measure *incidence*, which is the prevalence of disease within a specified time period. When calculating a relative risk, the time period that is the denominator for the incidence rate is included for both the exposed and unexposed groups and thus drops out in the calculation of relative risk, which is also sometimes called an incidence rate ratio, as in the study abstracted in Chapter 1.

or defect in question ("cases") with another group that do not have it ("controls"). Typically, case-control studies will attempt to match the cases with an equal number of controls or perhaps twice as many controls as cases. The two groups then are compared by looking back in time to assess what percentage of people in each group were exposed to the substance in question. Using this method, we have no way of knowing the percentage of individuals in the community actually exposed to the substance and, therefore, do not know the value of the two denominators in the relative risk equation.

The odds ratio does not require this information. The odds ratio is the cross product in a 2 by 2 table. In a case-control study comparing a group of cases (people with the injury in question) to a group of controls (people without the injury), the odds ratio is the ratio of the odds that the cases were exposed to the odds that the controls were exposed.

Odds Ratio in a Case–Control Study

	Cases (Injury)	Controls (No Injury)
History of Exposure	a	b
No History of Exposure	c	d

$$Odds\ Ratio\ = \frac{a/b}{c/d} = \frac{a*d}{b*c}$$

For example, using the data from above, the odds ratio would be (60 * 3840) / (940 * 160) = 1.53.

One can compute an odds ratio for cohort studies as well. Note that cohort and case-control studies differ in how they are conducted, but not in how the odds ratio is computed. The odds ratio is a good approximation of the relative risk when the disease or defect is rare in the population.[5]

A final type of evidence is aggregate time trend data. This type of data has been used to trace the spread of epidemics or the cyclical pattern of influenza outbreaks. In the case of Bendectin, researchers compared the annual incidence of birth defects with annual Bendectin sales. They attempted to ascertain whether the rapid increase in Bendectin prescriptions in the 1970s or the precipitous drop in prescriptions in the early 1980s matched similar increases or decreases in birth defects.

Note that this research is not conducted at an individual level. This poses a serious limitation on the value of such evidence. For example, if

---

5. The two values are similar when the injury is rare because then b is a good approximation of a+b and d is a good approximation of c+d. Thus in our example, because the injury is rare, the odds ratio and relative risk are quite close. Consider, however, a situation where the prevalence of injury in the exposed population is 60% and in the unexposed population is 40%. Using the previous example, the relative risk is still 1.5 [600/(600 + 400) / 1600/ (1600 + 2400) = 1.5]. However the odds ratio is (600*2400)/(1600*400) = 2.25.

we do observe an increase in the incidence of some ailment following the introduction of some toxic substance into the population, we cannot be sure it was the toxic substance that caused the increase because we do not know whether the people who are getting sick were in fact exposed to the substance. We also don't know whether some other factor, unrelated to the toxic substance, also changed at the same time and is responsible for the increased incidence.

Mechanistic evidence may also offer insights as to whether a substance causes a given injury. If the way we believe a drug acts on the body is inconsistent with plaintiff's injury, this suggests a lack of causal relationship.[6]

The Causal Question in Toxic Tort Cases

The cause-in-fact issue in most toxic tort cases is usefully thought of as two separate issues: general causation and specific causation. General causation asks whether exposure to a substance causes harm to anyone. Specific causation asks whether exposure to a substance caused a particular plaintiff's injury. As the *DeLuca* court noted, the causation task facing plaintiffs in toxic tort cases is first to "rule in" the agent in question as a possible source of plaintiff's injury, i.e., prove general causation, and then to "rule out" other possible causes of this plaintiff's injury, i.e., prove specific causation.

Comment c of section 28 of the Restatement (Third) of Torts: Liability for Physical and Emotional Harm has the following to say about the role of specific and general causation in toxic tort cases:

> In most traumatic-injury cases, the plaintiff can prove the causal role of the defendant's tortious conduct by observation, based upon reasonable inferences drawn from everyday experience and a close temporal and spatial connection between that conduct and the harm. Often, no other potential causes of injury exist. When a passenger in an automobile collision suffers a broken limb, potential causal explanations other than the collision are easily ruled out; common experience reveals that the forces generated in a serious automobile collision are capable of causing a fracture. By contrast, the causes of some diseases, especially those with significant latency periods, are general-

---

6. See Austin v. Kerr–McGee Refining Corp., 25 S.W.3d 280 (Tex.App.2000). The plaintiff suffered from a specific form of chronic leukemia. Studies demonstrated a causal relationship between benzene and all leukemias, but there was a paucity of evidence on the relationship between benzene and the specific form of leukemia from which the plaintiff suffered. The court required that the plaintiff's expert demonstrate the similarity of the biologic mechanism among leukemias as a condition for the admissibility of his causation testimony, a requirement the court concluded was not satisfied.

More recently, the Court of Appeals for the Federal Circuit affirmed a special master's denial of recovery under the National Childhood Vaccine Act for a young girl who began to suffer seizures shortly after a DTP vaccine inoculation. Moberly v. Secretary of Health & Human Servs., 592 F.3d 1315, 1320 (Fed.Cir.2010). The court was persuaded by the government's expert's opinion that the child's seizure disorder did not reflect a "single pathological process with an underlying clinical or pathological explanation." Rather, her disorder was typical of infants with epilepsy unrelated to immunization.

ly much less well understood. Even known causes for certain diseases may explain only a fraction of the incidence of such diseases, with the remainder due to unknown causes. Causal agents are often identified in group (epidemiologic) studies that reveal an increase in disease incidence among a group exposed to the agent as compared to a group not exposed. Biological mechanisms for disease development—i.e., a series of causally linked physiological changes from exposure to disease development—are frequently complicated and difficult to observe. Science continues to develop a better understanding of the biological steps in the development of diseases, but current knowledge in this respect is considerably more modest than for traumatic injury. As a consequence, courts in toxic-substances cases often must assess various alternative methods proffered with regard to factual causation.

* * *

Most causation issues are resolved under the "but-for" standard for factual cause. See § 26. The plaintiff must prove by a preponderance of the evidence that, but for the defendant's tortious conduct with respect to the toxic substance, the plaintiff would not have suffered harm. When group-based statistical evidence is proffered in a case, this means that the substance must be capable of causing the disease ("general causation") and that the substance must have caused the plaintiff's disease ("specific causation"). In other cases, when group-based evidence is unavailable or inconclusive, and other forms of evidence are used, the general and specific causation issues may merge into a single inquiry. In any case, plaintiff's exposure to the toxic agent must be established.

Thus, courts often address "exposure," "general causation," and "specific causation." Nevertheless, these items are not "elements" of a plaintiff's cause of action, and in some cases may not require separate proof. So long as the plaintiff introduces admissible and sufficient evidence of factual causation, the burden of production is satisfied.

Restatement (Third) of Torts: Liability for Physical and Emotional Harm § 28 cmt. c (2010).

The Restatement is certainly correct when it says that "general causation" and "specific causation" are not "elements" of the plaintiff's cause of action. As a practical matter, however, plaintiffs suffering from many toxic injuries must present evidence on both or face a summary judgment or a directed verdict. An early statement of this requirement is to be found in Cavallo v. Star Enterprise, 892 F.Supp. 756, 771 (E.D.Va. 1995), aff'd in part and rev'd in part, 100 F.3d 1150 (4th Cir.1996):

The process of differential diagnosis is undoubtedly important to the question of "specific causation." If other possible causes of an injury cannot be ruled out, or at least the probability of their contribution to causation minimized, then the "more likely than not" threshold for proving causation may not be met. But, it is also important to recognize that a fundamental assumption underlying this method is that the final, suspected "cause" remaining after this process of elimination must actually be *capable* of causing the injury. That is, the expert must "rule in" the suspected cause as well as "rule out" other possible causes. And, of course, expert opinion on this issue of "general causation" must be derived from a scientifically valid methodology.

One of the fundamental objectives of science is to make causal assertions. Such assertions are typically based on some set of empirical observations. However, these observations may mislead us. The causal conclusions we draw from the observations may be invalid. There are a number of fundamental threats to the validity of causal assertions that must be considered before concluding that a causal relationship does or does not exist.

Cook and Campbell have identified four basic types of validity: statistical conclusion validity, internal validity, construct validity, and external validity.[7] Each may be threatened to various degrees and in a number of ways.

Statistical Conclusion Validity.

When researchers observe a correlation between two variables, they may wish to conclude that the variables are causally related. Statistics help quantify threats to valid conclusions based on quantitative data.

Animal, clinical trial, epidemiologic, and aggregate time trend studies may be thought of as samples from an underlying population. Statistics allow us to quantify the element of random chance involved in making inferences about population parameters from sample data. Typically, statistical analyses of data involve testing the hypothesis that there is no relationship between exposure and birth defects. The hypothesis that there is no relationship is called the null hypothesis (H_0). In epidemiologic studies the null hypothesis is that the relative risk, or odds ratio, is equal to 1. The null hypothesis is tested against an alternative hypothesis (H_1). Typically the alternative hypothesis is simply that there are differences between exposed and unexposed individuals, that is, the relative risk is not equal to 1.

A test statistic can assist the investigator in deciding whether to accept or reject the null hypothesis by quantifying the likelihood that a difference as big or bigger than the one observed between exposed and unexposed samples could have occurred by chance if the null hypothesis is actually the true case.

Given the existence of a null hypothesis and an alternative hypothesis, the investigator may choose whether to accept the null hypothesis or

---

7. Thomas D. Cook & Donald T. Campbell, Quasi–Experimentation: Design and Analysis Issues for Field Testing (1979).

reject it. This choice can be either correct or incorrect. The following figure presents the possible decisions and errors.

	Population Reality	
	H_0 true	H_1 true
D₁: Reject H_0	False Positive Type I Error [α = Probability of Committing Type I Error]	True Positive No Error
D₀: Accept H_0	True Negative No Error	False Negative Type II Error [β = Probability of Committing Type II Error]

Decision based on Sample Data (D₁: Reject H_0 / D₀: Accept H_0)

If one rejects the null hypothesis and in fact there is a relationship between exposure to a substance and an injury then there is no error. This is a true positive. Similarly, if one accepts the null hypothesis and in fact there is no relationship, again there is no error. This is a true negative. There are two threats to statistical conclusions, or two ways for a decision to be in error, called, unimaginatively, Type I and Type II errors.

A Type I Error is the error of concluding that there is a relationship when in fact there is no relationship. Tests of statistical significance guard against making Type I errors. They assist the researcher in distinguishing between results that are likely to be due to chance and, therefore, consistent with the null hypothesis (non-significant results) and results that suggest the null hypothesis is not true (statistically significant results). Scientists, being conservative, generally try to minimize Type I errors; that is, they decline to declare a causal relationship unless it is quite unlikely that the observed results occurred by chance. The Greek letter Alpha (α) is by custom used to designate this criterion. Traditionally and typically, the null hypothesis will not be rejected unless the results of the study would occur less than 1 time in 20 if the true case is that there is no relationship. Alpha must be less than .05.[8] As the *DeLuca* court correctly noted, there is nothing magic about an Alpha of .05. Under varying circumstances an Alpha of .10 is not inappropriate, nor is an Alpha of .01. Importantly, statistical significance tests only assess the probability of a false-positive error, not a false-negative error.

---

8. A test employing a .05 significance level does not mean that when we observe a significant result the null hypothesis has a 95% chance of being false. Rather, it means that if the null hypothesis is correct there was less than a five percent chance of generating this data. As Adelman notes,

Interpreting frequentist significance levels as quantifying the degree of support for a hypothesis is equivalent to concluding that where A implies B it necessarily follows that B implies A. Significance tests quantify how likely a test hypothesis is to predict the observed data; they do not quantify how well the observed data support a test hypothesis.

David E. Adelman, Scientific Activism and Restraint: The Interplay of Statistics, Judgment, and Procedure in Environmental Law, 79 Notre Dame L.Rev. 497, 552 (2004).

A Type II Error is the opposite of a Type I error, concluding there is no relationship when a relationship exists. We would commit a Type II error if we concluded that a substance does not cause a given type of injury when in fact it does. Obviously, we would also like to minimize the probability of this error, which by custom is designated as Beta (β). The probability of rejecting the null hypothesis when some specific alternative hypothesis is true is called the *power* of the test, and is equal to one minus Beta. Power is a function of the study's sample size, the size of the effect one wishes to detect, and the significance level used to guard against Type I error. Because power is a function of, among other things, the Alpha chosen to guard against Type I errors, all things being held equal, minimizing the probability of one type of error can be done only by increasing the probability of making the other. In contingency table analyses typical of epidemiologic research, the power of a study is also a function of the frequency of exposure in the population (e.g., percentage of pregnant women using Bendectin) and the incidence of the effect (e.g., frequency of birth defects). Because the power of any test declines as the incidence of the effect declines, Type II threats to causal conclusions are particularly relevant with respect to rare events such as limb reduction birth defects. See Michael D. Green, Expert Witnesses and Sufficiency of Evidence in Toxic Substances Litigation: The Legacy of Agent Orange and Bendectin Litigation, 86 Nw.U.L.Rev. 643 (1992).

Plaintiffs make a fair criticism of randomized trials or epidemiologic cohort studies when they note that sometimes the studies have insufficient power to detect rare events. Failure to reject the null hypothesis may not be evidence of no association. Rather it may simply be inconclusive because of insufficient statistical power. In this situation, case-control studies are particularly valuable because of their relatively greater power. Another way to increase power is to conduct a meta-analysis, a method of combining a set of studies to reach a more statistically powerful conclusion.[9]

In most toxic tort contexts, defendant would prefer to minimize Type I Error while plaintiff would prefer to minimize Type II Error. Ideally, what we would prefer are studies that minimize the probability of both types of errors.[10] Given the importance of power in assessing epidemiolog-

9. For examples of meta-analyses of the Bendectin epidemiologic studies, see Jon Todd Powell, How to Tell The Truth with Statistics: A New Statistical Approach to Analyzing the Bendectin Epidemiological Data in the Aftermath of *Daubert v. Merrell Dow Pharmaceuticals*, 31 Hous. L.Rev. 1241 (1994); Paul M. McKeigue, Steven H. Lamm, Shai Linn, & Jeffrey S. Kutcher, Bendectin and Birth Defects: I. A Meta–Analysis of the Epidemiologic Studies, 50 Teratology 27 (1994).

10. From a purely legal perspective, we might argue that at least in civil litigation the two types of error should be equalized because these errors roughly conform to the burden of persuasion by a preponderance of the evidence. That is, plaintiff and defendant should run a roughly equal risk that the results of a statistical analysis are incorrect and this may be interpreted to mean that the probability of a Type I error should be similar to the probability of a Type II error. See Michael Green, Expert Witnesses and Sufficiency of Evidence in Toxic Substances Litigation: The Legacy of Agent Orange and Bendectin Litigation, 86 Nw.U.L.Rev. 643, 688–90 (1992). However, as David Kaye notes, we would hardly wish to advise a scientist to equalize Type I and Type II errors if this were done at the expense of substantially increasing the sum of the two types of errors. He argues that the proper understanding of the preponderance

ic evidence, surprisingly few appellate opinions discuss the issue.[11]

One additional threat to statistical conclusion validity deserves special mention. First, there is the error rate problem. Researchers engaged in a fishing expedition, sifting through a large number of correlations in search of significant relationships, will inevitably find some spurious ones. A .05 significance test means that if the null hypothesis of no relationship is true, there is only one chance in 20 that we would get a relationship as strong as or stronger than the relationship found in the study. Thus, 1 time in 20 we should expect to observe a relationship this strong even when the null hypothesis is true. For example, if one made 60 comparisons, we would expect there would be, on average, 3 significant correlations, even if no true causal relationships exist.

Internal Validity.

Statistical conclusion validity presents a special case of internal validity, which Cook and Campbell define as "the approximate validation with which we infer that a relationship between two variables is causal or that the absence of a relationship implies the absence of cause."[12]

The unreliability of measurement techniques pose such a threat. Epidemiologic research depends on determining whether individuals have or have not been exposed to a toxic substance and whether or not they suffer from some adverse effect. Coding errors occur when researchers treat individuals who were not exposed as having been exposed and those exposed as not exposed, or the researchers misdiagnose individuals. Unreliable coding threatens validity by inflating error variance and attenuating true relationships. With respect to the Bendectin research, epidemiologic results are threatened by the inability to pinpoint precisely when an expectant mother took the drug. This is important because many teratogenic injuries occur only during organogenesis, when cells and tissues migrate and associate to form organ rudiments. During this period, the fetus is most vulnerable to structural defects. If women who took Bendectin at some later time in their pregnancy are counted among the "exposed" group, the study may underestimate any effect that might exist.

Most threats to internal validity usually can be thought of as specification errors. Specification errors occur when the researcher fails to consider a factor that mediates the observed effect between two variables, either because it explains changes in both the "cause" and the "effect" or intervenes between the "cause" and the "effect" and acts independently on the "effect."

---

burden of persuasion is as a command to reduce the total error rate, not to equalize error rates. D.H. Kaye, Apples and Oranges: Confidence Coefficients and the Burden of Persuasion, 73 Cornell L.Rev. 54, 72 (1987).

11. See Merrell Dow Pharms. v. Havner, 953 S.W.2d 706, 722–23 (Tex.1997); Miller v. Pfizer, Inc., 2001 WL 1793169 (D.Kan.2001), adopted, 196 F.Supp.2d 1062 (D.Kan.2002), aff'd, 356 F.3d 1326 (10th Cir.2004).

12. Thomas D. Cook & Donald T. Campbell, Quasi–Experimentation: Design and Analysis Issues for Field Testing 37 (1979).

Cook and Campbell discuss a number of threats to internal validity. The most important of these is *selection threat.* A selection threat exists when there is a possibility that the groups being compared are composed of different types of individuals, and, therefore, that observed differences are due to factors other than the treatment or exposure under investigation. For example, in a study of the effect of drinking on heart ailments the results may be threatened by the fact that drinkers are more likely than non-drinkers to also be smokers. Selection effects take many different forms and often interact with other threats to internal validity.

If they are known, selection threats may be controlled for statistically or by the design of a study. For example, epidemiologic case-control studies may match cases and controls in an attempt to control for factors that might affect the outcome. A study on birth defects may match cases and controls on factors such as maternal age or maternal smoking and drinking behavior, all of which are known to be associated with the incidence of some types of birth defects. A basic advantage of clinical trials and other experimental research are their ability to control for many selection effects by randomly assigning individuals to treatments.

Construct Validity.

The third broad type of validity is construct validity. What one investigator may interpret as evidence of a causal relationship between constructs A and B, another investigator may interpret as a relationship between constructs X and B or even X and Y. There are several sources of construct invalidity. One, experimenter expectancy, occurs when the experimenter anticipates a certain outcome. Another, evaluation apprehension, arises when the subject wishes to please the investigator. Hypothesis-guessing may threaten construct validity when the subject attempts to guess the hypothesis being tested and adjust his or her answers accordingly. Drug testing experiments often present construct validity concerns because any observed effect between the drug and a therapeutic effect may not be due to the chemical action of the drug, but rather to the psychological expectation that the drug will have a beneficial effect. In an effort to increase construct validity, scientists have designed methods such as placebo controls and double blind designs. In a double blind design, neither the subject nor the researcher knows who is receiving the treatment and who is receiving the placebo.

Epidemiologic case-control studies are subject to a construct validity threat due to the existence of recall bias. People who have suffered some injury are more likely to recall being exposed to a suspected toxic agent than people who have not suffered the injury. Observed differences in outcome may, therefore, be measuring differential memory rather than the effect of the agent in question, i.e., the effect of X on B, not A on B. The result of recall bias is that the effects are overestimated.

Another source of construct invalidity is the confounding of constructs and levels of constructs. One might conclude that A does not cause B when the test involves very low levels of A. At higher levels of A, however, the researcher might uncover a relationship. The requirement that laboratory animal studies routinely expose animals to suspect agents at more than one dose level is an effort to avoid this construct validity threat.

Assessing construct validity is frequently a question of convergence across measures. One is much more likely to believe that a cause and effect relationship exists when different measurements and methods converge to produce the same result. We are more likely to believe an agent causes injury when both experimental animal studies and epidemiologic research indicate this is the case.

External Validity.

Finally, there is external validity. Just as statistical conclusion validity is a special type of internal validity, construct validity is a type of external validity. External validity involves the ability to generalize conclusions to *particular* persons, settings, and times and to *types* of persons, settings, and times. Cook and Campbell list two basic threats to external validity, each of which can be expressed in terms of an interaction between a treatment and some other factor. First, the potential interaction between selection and treatment poses a threat to external validity. If a study uncovers a cause and effect relationship, the researcher must determine to which categories of individuals the relationship can be generalized. For example, if a study includes only men as subjects, the researcher must determine whether the results can be generalized to women. Other examples involve the ability to generalize across age, race, ethnicity, and class.

External validity threats are particularly significant in non-epidemiologic research. Perhaps the central issue with respect to in vivo teratology studies is the degree to which the results can be extrapolated from animals to humans. Unfortunately, there is no uniformly accepted formula for the extrapolation across species. Two common formulas respectively compare either the body weight or the surface area of the animal with the corresponding human measurement. The use of these different scaling factors can lead to divergent estimates of effects on humans. Compounding this calculation is again the problem of different metabolic processing of a chemical in the animal species and in humans. "Differences among animal species, or even among strains of the same species, in metabolic handling of a chemical, are not uncommon and can account for toxicity differences."[13] The case for a human effect is much stronger if there are significant effects in several animal species and strains of laboratory animals.

The interaction between setting and treatment creates a second external threat to validity. A researcher may not be able to generalize studies done in one setting to other settings. All laboratory studies are vulnerable to this threat. Even well-crafted experiments that do their best

---

13. National Research Council, Committee on Risk Assessment of Hazardous Air Pollutants, Science and Judgment in Risk Assessment 59 (1995).

to increase external validity cannot ensure that their results can be transferred from the laboratory to the world at large. Some laboratory studies suffer from multiple threats to external validity. Laboratory animal studies encounter difficulty in this regard due to dose rate differences. Because many substances produce an adverse effect in only a small percentage of organisms, when ingested at a rate similar to that encountered in the environment or prescribed by a physician, it takes a large number of animal subjects to detect a substance's effects with any reliability. Smaller samples would generate an unacceptably large number of false negatives (failure to detect an effect when it exists), a threat to internal validity. Thus, animals are generally administered high doses of the substance in question in hopes of maximizing the incidence of effects. If there is a positive result, toxicologists must then extrapolate a predicted incidence at a more realistic lower rate. Unfortunately, there are a number of ways in which high-dose toxicity testing differs from lower-dose effects: there may be limits to the solubility of the compound; enzymes may become saturated at high doses, limiting absorption; detoxification mechanisms in the liver and elsewhere may be saturated; and metabolites may cause toxicity that would not occur with lower doses. All of these factors produce non-linear effects. Because of these differences, there is no single agreed upon extrapolation model for dose-rate effects, and competing models generate different predictions at low-dose rates. See Bernard Goldstein, Toxic Torts: The Devil is in the Dose, 16 J.L. & Pol'y 551 (2008).

Summary.

This brief review of validity's different facets indicates some of the ways in which conclusions about causation may be in error. Statistical conclusion validity and other types of internal validity concentrate on the danger of Type I or Type II errors, drawing false positive or false negative conclusions about causation. Statistical conclusion validity deals with threats to internal validity caused by random error, the possibility that an observed relationship could be due to chance. Other threats to internal validity are due to the possible existence of bias through factors that systematically affect the value of the means of variables. Construct validity and other types of external validity address the dangers of generalization. The principal threat stems from the possible existence of an undetected interaction. With respect to construct validity, the danger is that an effect can be obtained using one measure, such as individual recall of drug ingestion, followed by a different effect using a different measure, such as hospital prescription records. The risk of undetected interaction effects is even easier to see with respect to other threats to external validity, such as the interaction between selection and treatment. In each case, a relationship observed in one circumstance may not apply in a different circumstance.

Because careful research designs may minimize, but cannot eliminate all threats to validity, researchers have developed a number of criteria that should be used in assessing whether a relationship is causal. One of the most well known is a set of nine criteria originally developed by Sir Austin Bradford Hill.[14]

1. Is the temporal relationship correct? Does the "effect" follow the "cause"?

2. Is there evidence from true experiments in humans? Because experiments randomly assign people to treatments, they control for many unknown systematic threats to validity. Ceteris paribus ("all else being equal"), experimental data is more persuasive than other types of data.

3. Is the association a strong one? The stronger the association (usually measured by relative risk or the odds ratio) and the greater the level of statistical significance (usually measured by a chi square test) the more likely the relationship is causal. Both the level of statistical significance and the strength of the relationship are important. With very large samples, a relationship may be statistically significant but not very strong. A relative risk of 1.2 is not significant with an N of 200, but highly significant with an N of 20,000. On the other hand, with small samples, a relationship may be strong but not statistically significant.

4. Is the association consistent from study to study? If one study reveals a statistically significant relationship, can the result be replicated in a later study? If so, the argument for a causal relationship is greatly strengthened.

5. Is there a dose-response gradient? The causal argument is strengthened if higher doses of a substance produce more injury.

6. Is the association specific? For example, exposure to asbestos produces the specific disease asbestosis. Most researchers believe that human teratogens produce a specific pattern of injuries. The existence of such a pattern strengthens the causal argument.

7. Does the association make biological sense? For example, if a drug such as Bendectin is to be found to be a cause of harm to the fetus it must be shown that it can cross the placental barrier, which in fact it can.

8. What is the effect of ceasing exposure? If an agent is a cause of a disease one would expect that cessation of exposure to that agent ordinarily would reduce the risk of the disease. sometimes, however, evidence is unavailable regarding the possible effects of ending the exposure.

9. Is there appropriate analogy to other known causal relationships? For example, the antihistamine component of Bendectin is more suspect because some other antihistamines are known teratogens.

---

14. A.B. Hill, A Short Textbook of Medical Statistics 285–296 (1977); Andrew C. Harper & Laurie J. Lambert, The Health of Populations: An Introduction. 92–95 (1994).

When confronted with complex scientific questions, many courts have come to rely on the Reference Manual on Scientific Evidence published by the Federal Judicial Center. The second edition was published in 2000 and a third edition is scheduled to be published in 2011, as a joint venture of the Federal Judicial Center and the National Academy of Sciences.

2. SPECIFIC CAUSATION

Even when we conclude that exposure to an agent causes injury to some individuals, this alone may not lead to the conclusion that the injury suffered by any given plaintiff was caused by the agent. This is the case whenever there are multiple possible causes of the same ailment. As the *DeLuca* court noted, in New Jersey as in most jurisdictions, unless plaintiff can show that it is more likely than not that her injury was caused by the agent, she has not carried the burden of proof on the causal question.

Section III of the *DeLuca* opinion noted that in those situations where we have a substantial body of epidemiologic research, the results may help us resolve both general and specific causation. Theoretically, a plaintiff can prove specific causation by a preponderance of the evidence by providing epidemiologic evidence that finds a causal relationship with a relative risk greater than 2.0; that is, people exposed to the substance suffer injuries at least more than twice as frequently as those not exposed. Plaintiff can then argue that it is more likely than not that the substance caused this particular injury. For example, if the background risk of a certain type of cancer is 1 in 1000, and the risk among those exposed to some product is 3 in 1000, plaintiffs exposed to the substance who have this type of cancer can argue that more likely than not—two chances out of three—their cancer was caused by the product. That is, the attributable risk ratio is 67%.

Whether a plaintiff should ever be able to prevail with a relative risk less than 2.0 is controversial. The *DeLuca* court suggested, but did not decide, that the DeLucas could not prevail under these circumstances. Other Bendectin and toxic tort cases adopted a similar position. When *Daubert v. Merrell Dow Pharmaceuticals* was remanded to the Ninth Circuit, that court held that the plaintiffs' expert scientific testimony was not admissible to prove that Bendectin caused the plaintiffs' birth defects. On the relationship between relative risk and specific causation, Judge Kozinski had this to say:

> None of plaintiffs' epidemiological experts claims that ingestion of Bendectin during pregnancy more than doubles the risk of birth defects. * * * For an epidemiological study to show causation under a preponderance standard, "the relative risk of limb reduction defects arising from the epidemiological data ... will, at a minimum, have to exceed '2'." *DeLuca*, 911 F.2d at 958. * * * A relative risk of less than two may suggest teratogenicity, but it actually tends to *dis*prove legal

causation, as it shows that Bendectin does not double the likelihood of birth defects.[15]

Merrell Dow Pharmaceuticals v. Havner is still another Bendectin case that is often cited for the proposition that plaintiff must be able to demonstrate a doubling of the risk to prevail.[16] As the Second Circuit noted in *In re Joint Eastern & Southern District Asbestos Litigation*,[17] the argument that epidemiologic studies must show a relative risk greater than 2.0 is a sufficiency argument, not an admissibility argument and in *Deluca, Daubert,* and *Havner* the courts were making a sufficiency point.

However, even in these opinions the court noted that plaintiff may be able to present other evidence to overcome the implications of the epidemiologic findings. For example, in *Daubert* the court stated in a footnote:

> A statistical study showing a relative risk of less than two could be combined with other evidence to show it is more likely than not that the accused cause is responsible for a particular plaintiff's injury. For example, a statistical study may show that a particular type of birth defect is associated with some unknown causes, as well as two known potential causes—e.g., smoking and drinking. If a study shows that the relative risk of injury for those who smoke is 1.5 as compared to the general population, while it is 1.8 for those who drink, a plaintiff who does not drink might be able to reanalyze the data to show that the study of smoking did not account for the effect of drinking on the incidence of birth defects in the general population. By making the appropriate comparison—between non-drinkers who smoke and non-drinkers who do not smoke—the teetotaller plaintiff might be able to show that the relative risk of smoking for her is greater than two. Here, however, plaintiffs' experts did not seek to differentiate these plaintiffs from the subjects of the statistical studies. The studies must therefore stand or fall on their own.[18]

Comment c of section 28 of the Third Restatement of Torts: Liability for Physical and Emotional Harm takes the position that "any judicial requirement that plaintiffs must show a threshold increase in risk or a doubling in incidence in a group study in order to satisfy the burden of proof of specific causation is usually inappropriate."

In the great majority of cases, there is either no epidemiologic evidence or epidemiologic evidence of such limited quality and/or quantity that it cannot be used to determine specific causation. In these cases, the primary way in which plaintiff proceeds is through the use of an expert who offers "differential diagnosis" testimony. The following case deals with this topic.

---

15. Daubert v. Merrell Dow Pharms., Inc., 43 F.3d 1311, 1320–21 (9th Cir.1995).

16. 953 S.W.2d 706 (Tex.1997).

17. 52 F.3d 1124, 1134 (2d Cir.1995).

18. Daubert v. Merrell Dow Pharms., Inc., 43 F.3d 1311, 1321 n.16 (9th Cir.1995). This position is echoed in other cases as well. See Landrigan v. Celotex Corp., 605 A.2d 1079 (N.J.1992).

BEST v. LOWE'S HOME CENTERS, INC.

United States Court of Appeals, Sixth Circuit, 2009.
563 F.3d 171.

RONALD LEE GILMAN, CIRCUIT JUDGE.

David L. Best claims to suffer from permanent anosmia—the loss of his sense of smell—as a result of a pool chemical spilling onto his face and clothing at a Lowe's Home Center store. After filing suit against Lowe's, Best planned to introduce the expert testimony of Dr. Francisco Moreno, a board-certified otolaryngologist (an ear, nose, and throat doctor) and a former chemical engineer, in order to establish the causal link between the chemical spill and his injuries. The district court excluded Dr. Moreno's testimony, holding that the method employed by the doctor in drawing his conclusions regarding causation was "unscientific speculation." This resulted in summary judgment being granted in favor of Lowe's. For the reasons set forth below, we **REVERSE** the judgment of the district court and **REMAND** the case for further proceedings consistent with this opinion.

I. BACKGROUND

A. Factual background

Best visited a Lowe's store in Knoxville, Tennessee in June 2003. Intending to purchase chemicals for his swimming pool, he located a product called Aqua EZ Super Clear Clarifier (Aqua EZ). When Best lifted the plastic container from the shelf, an unknown quantity of the contents splashed onto his face and clothing. The container had allegedly been accidentally punctured with a knife by the Lowe's employee who had opened the shipping box. Best went to the emergency room of a hospital for treatment on the day that the spill occurred. Four months later, Best sought care and treatment from Dr. Moreno for the injuries associated with the incident. Dr. Moreno has practiced medicine as an otolaryngologist since 1982. Before attending medical school, Dr. Moreno earned a Bachelor of Science degree in chemical engineering. He was employed as a chemical engineer from 1968 until 1972.

At the time of his initial visit to Dr. Moreno, Best described the incident at Lowe's. He said that the spilled product had a strong odor, and that immediately thereafter he had suffered from irritation and burning of his skin, irritation to his nasal passages and mouth, dizziness, and shortness of breath. Best also reported that he experienced clear drainage from his nose following the spill and that he eventually lost his sense of smell completely. Dr. Moreno was unable to inspect Best's mucous membranes for physical damage because they are located too far inside the nasal passages to permit visual examination.

Best was seen for a second time by Dr. Moreno in January 2007. Dr. Moreno took a new medical history and again performed a physical examination to the extent possible in light of the position of the mucous membranes in the nose. At that time, Best was experiencing rhinitis–otherwise known as a runny or stuffy nose–with swelling and decreased airflow. Best reported that, during the three-and-a-half year period since the spill incident, he had struggled with rhinitis, anosmia, and dizzy spells.

In April 2008, Dr. Moreno administered to Best the University of Pennsylvania Smell Identification Test (UPSIT), a standardized test of olfactory function. The test involves various sample chemicals, requiring the test subject to choose one of four descriptions of each sample's scent. Best scored a six on the test, a score consistent with complete anosmia.

Dr. Moreno testified in his deposition that "[l]oss of smell is caused by either a virus, an accident, tumors to the brain, surgery into the brain, or exposure to chemicals." He also conceded that sometimes anosmia is idiopathic, meaning that it occurs for unknown reasons, and that some medications can cause a loss of the sense of smell. Dr. Moreno proceeded to list the following medications that Best reported taking at the time of his chemical exposure: aspirin, Atenolol, Effexor, hydrochlorithiazide, Lescol, Letensin, moxamorphin, OxyContin, Protonix, and Remeron. Dr. Moreno stated that Atenolol and Lotensin are for blood pressure; aspirin, moxamorphin, and OxyContin are for pain; Effexor is for depression; hydrochlorothiazide is a fluid pill; and Protonex is for the stomach. He was unfamiliar with the drug Lescol. Referring to all of the medications, he stated that "[i]n my practice, with the patients that I have seen ... over the years ..., I have never seen an anosmia caused from the use of these medications." He also said that he had looked up all of the medications except Lescol in the course of his practice. Dr. Moreno was unable to list the general types of medications that can cause a loss of the sense of smell.

Lowe's provided Best's attorney with a one-page document identifying the pool chemical as Aqua EZ. * * * After receiving this document, Best's attorney obtained a Material Safety Data Sheet (MSDS) prepared by Ciba Specialty Chemicals Corporation, the supplier of the active ingredient in Aqua EZ. Dr. Moreno reviewed the MSDS, which describes the characteristics of the active ingredient.

The relevant ingredient is an organic cationic polyelectrolyte. Specifically, the compound is a homopolymer with the name 2-Propen-1-aminium, N, N-dimethyl-N-2-propenyl-chloride. The MSDS identifies the chemical as "hazardous" and states that "[p]rolonged or repeated contact may cause eye and skin irritation." Primary routes of entry for the compound are listed as "Ingestion, Skin, Inhalation, Eyes." According to the MSDS, if the chemical is inhaled, the person should be "[r]emove[d] to fresh air, if not breathing give artificial respiration. If breathing is difficult, give oxygen and get immediate medical attention." The Handling Instructions state: "Do not inhale.... Use only with adequate ventilation." Under the heading "Engineering Controls," the MSDS instructs: "Work in well ventilated areas. Do not breathe vapors or mist." The MSDS also notes that "Acute Inhalation Toxicity" for the compound has not been determined. Dr. Moreno later reviewed a second MSDS, published by Sigma–Aldrich, another supplier of the relevant compound. That MSDS confirmed that the compound is "irritating to the mucous membrane and upper respiratory tract" and that it "[m]ay be harmful if inhaled."

Dr. Moreno concluded, based on the MSDS information, that the inhalation of Aqua EZ has the potential to cause damage to the nasal and sinus mucosa and the nerve endings of the olfactory bulb. According to Dr. Moreno, the culprit components of the polymer in question include a chlorine derivative and an ammonium derivative. He offered his opinion that "a chemical burn can cause a loss of smell on a time basis" due to "scarring of the tissue," and reported that he has treated other chemical exposures with anosmic side effects following exposure to chlorine derivatives. But Dr. Moreno did not know the precise amount of the offending chemical that Best had been exposed to, nor was he able to determine the threshold level of exposure that could cause harm. Dr. Moreno summarized his diagnosis regarding causation this way:

> The patient had an accident, chemical was spilled, the patient cannot smell. If we have any trust in the patient at all, all I can say is he cannot smell. I did test him, his test was positive in the fact that he was anosmic. All I can tell you is that exposure to the—the only exposure that he had at the time that I talked to him was exposure to this chemical. There was nothing else in his history that dictated the fact that he was anosmic otherwise.

In short, because of the temporal relationship between Best's exposure to the chemical and the onset of his symptoms, in conjunction with a principled effort to eliminate other possible causes of anosmia, Dr. Moreno formed the opinion that the inhalation of Aqua EZ caused Best to lose his sense of smell.

　　　* * *

D. Differential diagnosis

Dr. Moreno employed a methodology known as "differential diagnosis" in forming his opinion. Differential diagnosis is "[t]he method by which a physician determines what disease process caused a patient's symptoms. The physician considers all relevant potential causes of the symptoms and then eliminates alternative causes based on a physical examination, clinical tests, and a thorough case history." *Hardyman v. Norfolk & W. Ry. Co.*, 243 F.3d 255, 260 (6th Cir.2001) (quoting Federal Judicial Center, Reference Manual on Scientific Evidence 214 (1994)).

As described above, Dr. Moreno formed his opinion regarding Best's alleged loss of his sense of smell by considering a list of the possible causes of such an injury—"a virus, an accident, tumors to the brain, surgery into the brain, or exposure to chemicals"—as well as Best's use of medications and the possibility of another, unknown (idiopathic) cause. He took note of the temporal proximity between Best's exposure to Aqua EZ and discovered that the pool clarifier contained a chemical that, according to the MSDS, is "irritating to the mucous membrane and upper respiratory tract" and "[m]ay be harmful if inhaled." Although Dr. Moreno was unable to quantify the level of Best's exposure, he noted that the chemical was quite concentrated—a "little bottle" is poured into a "whole swimming pool"—and relied on Best's report that the material splashed onto his face and clothing. Dr. Moreno ruled out medications as the cause, based on his knowledge of the side effects of nine out of Best's ten medications (he had no information about the tenth), and also because he had never known of a patient who had used any of the medications and developed anosmia. Finally, Dr. Moreno ruled out idiopathic anosmia because of the remote likelihood that some unknown cause would bring about anosmia "all of a sudden" around the same time as an exposure to a chemical that is known to irritate the nasal mucous membranes.

This court recognizes differential diagnosis as "an appropriate method for making a determination of causation for an individual instance of disease." *Hardyman*, 243 F.3d at 260. An "overwhelming majority of the courts of appeals" agree, and have held "that a medical opinion on causation based upon a reliable differential diagnosis is sufficiently valid to satisfy the first prong [reliability] of the Rule 702 inquiry." *Westberry v. Gislaved Gummi AB*, 178 F.3d 257, 263 (4th Cir.1999) (collecting cases from the First, Second, Third, Ninth, and D.C. Circuits). Differential diagnosis is considered to be "a standard scientific technique of identifying the cause of a medical problem by eliminating the likely causes until the most probable one is isolated." *Hardyman*, 243 F.3d at 260 (quoting *Westberry*, 178 F.3d at 262).

* * *

* * * The problem is that no case in this circuit has previously provided detailed guidance for the district courts in separating reliable differential diagnoses from unreliable ones. We find the Third Circuit's opinion in the case of *In re Paoli Railroad Yard PCB Litigation*, 35 F.3d 717 (3d Cir.1994), instructive in this regard.

In *Paoli Railroad Yard*, the court evaluated the differential-diagnosis-based causation testimony of two physicians regarding the various ailments of a large number of plaintiffs who lived near a facility where polychlorinated biphenyls (PCBs) were used for an extended period of time. The Third Circuit * * * stated that, "to the extent that a doctor utilizes standard diagnostic techniques in gathering ... information," a finding that "the doctor's methodology is reliable" is "more likely." *Id.* [at 758]. * * * [T]he * * * "performance of physical examinations, taking of medical histories, and employment of reliable laboratory tests all provide significant evidence of a reliable differential diagnosis," and * * * "their absence makes it much less likely that a differential diagnosis is reliable." *Id.* "The core of differential diagnosis is a requirement that experts at least consider alternative causes." *Id.* at 759.

We hereby adopt the following differential-diagnosis test, adapted from the Third Circuit's well-reasoned opinion: A medical-causation opinion in the form of a doctor's differential diagnosis is reliable and admissible where the doctor (1) objectively ascertains, to the extent possible, the nature of the patient's injury, *see id.* at 762 ("A physician who evaluates a patient in preparation for litigation should seek more than a patient's self-report of symptoms or illness and ... should ... determine that a patient is ill and what illness the patient has contracted."), (2) "rules in" one or more causes of the injury using a valid methodology, and (3) engages in "standard diagnostic techniques by which doctors normally rule out alternative causes" to reach a conclusion as to which cause is most likely. *Id.* at 760.

In connection with the third "rules out" prong, if the doctor "engage[s] in very few standard diagnostic techniques by which doctors normally rule out alternative causes," the doctor must offer a "good explanation as to why his or her conclusion remain[s] reliable." *Id.* Similarly, the doctor must provide a reasonable explanation as to why "he or she has concluded that [any alternative cause suggested by the defense] was not the sole cause." *Id.* at 758 n. 27.

Our approach is similar to those employed in other circuits that recognize differential diagnosis as a valid basis for medical-causation opinions. *See, e.g., Ruggiero v. Warner–Lambert Co.*, 424 F.3d 249, 254 (2d Cir.2005) ("Where an expert employs differential diagnosis to 'rule out' other potential causes for the injury at issue, he must also 'rule in' the suspected cause, and do so using scientifically valid methodology." (internal quotation marks omitted)); *Glastetter v. Novartis Pharm. Corp.*, 252 F.3d 986, 989 (8th Cir.2001) ("In performing a differential diagnosis, a physician begins by 'ruling in' all scientifically plausible causes of the plaintiff's injury. The physician then 'rules out' the least plausible causes of injury until the most likely cause remains.").

E. Dr. Moreno's opinion was sufficiently reliable to warrant admissibility

Applying our newly formulated test to Dr. Moreno's opinion, we conclude that his methodology meets the minimum threshold for admissibility. We consider each element of the differential-diagnosis test in turn.

1. Dr. Moreno ascertained, to the extent possible, that Best is anosmic

Dr. Moreno employed a well-recognized test—the UPSIT—to confirm Best's complaint that he could not smell. Based on the research that Dr. Moreno had done regarding tests for anosmia, he concluded that the UPSIT is "as objective as you're ever going to get." Lowe's has made no attempt to discredit that test.

Instead, Lowe's argues that Dr. Moreno had never before administered the UPSIT and that Best's score was only one point outside the range for malingering, suggesting that Best purposely manipulated the result. Lowe's also points out that when Best took the UPSIT, Dr. Moreno possessed conflicting information about Best's smoking habits—a factor that the doctor knew could affect the test results. In addition, Lowe's complains that Dr. Moreno did not examine the record of Best's visit to the hospital's emergency room, during which Best allegedly stated that he did not inhale the Aqua EZ. But Best also reported at that time that the chemical spilled on his face and clothing, and he described its strong odor. Dr. Moreno accordingly observed that he "would have to assume that regardless of the statements made that [Best] had to have had some exposure."

All of Lowe's attacks on Dr. Moreno's efforts to ascertain whether Best is anosmic amount to factual disputes suitable for cross-examination. * * *

2. Dr. Moreno employed a valid methodology to "rule in" Aqua EZ as a potential cause

* * * Lowe's strongest argument is that no published material confirms that inhalation of the chemical in Aqua EZ can cause anosmia. But "there is no requirement that a medical expert must always cite published studies on general causation in order to reliably conclude that a particular object caused a particular illness." *Kudabeck v. Kroger Co.*, 338 F.3d 856, 862 (8th Cir.2003) (internal quotation marks omitted). Dr. Moreno did not arbitrarily "rule in" Aqua EZ as a potential cause, but instead concluded from the MSDS sheet and his own knowledge of medicine and chemistry that the chemical it contains can cause damage to the nasal and sinus mucosa upon inhalation.

In addition, Dr. Moreno has treated other patients who developed anosmic symptoms after inhaling chlorine derivatives. The opinion presented by Dr. Moreno thus differs markedly from those in cases like *Ruggiero v. Warner–Lambert Co.*, 424 F.3d 249, 254 (2d Cir.2005), where the Second Circuit excluded a doctor's opinion that a particular diabetes medication could cause liver cirrhosis and death because the expert could not point to *anything* suggesting such a possibility.

Another Second Circuit case, *McCullock v. H.B. Fuller Co.*, 61 F.3d 1038 (2d Cir.1995), comes much closer to the circumstances in the present case. In *McCullock*, the plaintiff developed throat polyps after being exposed to hot-glue fumes. Her treating physician, "an experienced medical doctor ... certified by the American Board of Otolaryngology," opined that the plaintiff's polyps resulted from "inhalation of the fumes from the hot-glue pot." *Id.* at 1042–43. The MSDS sheet for the hot glue at issue in *McCullock* contained similar warnings to those in this case, including: "Avoid breathing vapors/fumes," and "Vapors and fumes may cause irritation of the nose, throat and respiratory tract." *Id.* at 1040. Despite the defendant's insistence that the expert "could not point to a single piece of medical literature that says glue fumes cause throat polyps," *id.* at 1043, the court admitted the doctor's testimony, citing in support the doctor's "review of [the] MSDS" and his "training and experience," among other things. *Id.* at 1044. Dr. Moreno's testimony should likewise be admitted here.

3. Dr. Moreno engaged in standard techniques to "rule out" alternate causes

Having no evidence that virus, accident, brain tumor, or brain surgery were applicable in Best's case, Dr. Moreno focused on chemicals, medications, or ideopathic causes. Dr. Moreno concluded, based on his own experience, that an ideopathic anosmia would not appear over such a short period of time. He also eliminated nine of Best's ten medications as potential causes of anosmia.

Lowe's makes much of Dr. Moreno's failure to eliminate Lescol* as a possible cause. But doctors need not rule out every conceivable cause in order for their differential-diagnosis-based opinions to be admissible. *E.g., Westberry v. Gislaved Gummi AB*, 178 F.3d 257, 266 (4th Cir.1999) (citing *In re Paoli R.R. Yard PCB Litig.*, 35 F.3d 717, 764–65 (3d Cir.1994)). Lowe's presented no evidence that Lescol might cause anosmia. If such evidence exists, or if Dr. Moreno failed to consider some other likely cause, Lowe's is free to attack Dr. Moreno's opinion on that basis at trial.

Admissibility under Rule 702 does not require perfect methodology. Rather, the expert must "employ[ ] in the courtroom the same level of intellectual rigor that characterizes the practice of an expert in the relevant field." *Kumho Tire Co. v. Carmichael*, 526 U.S. 137, 152, 119 S.Ct. 1167, 143 L.Ed.2d 238 (1999). Dr. Moreno's diagnosis might not stand up to exacting scrutiny if he were testifying as a research scientist or a chemist, but he is neither of those. He performed as a competent, intellectually rigorous treating physician in identifying the most likely cause of Best's injury. Any weaknesses in his methodology will affect the weight that his opinion is given at trial, but not its threshold admissibility.

F. Dr. Moreno's opinion is distinguishable from differential-diagnosis opinions that have been excluded in other cases

A review of several cases in which differential-diagnosis testimony has been excluded further solidifies our conclusion that Dr. Moreno's opinion falls on the admissible side of the elusive line separating reliable opinions from "junk science." * * *

* * *

Dr. Moreno's testimony here * * * materially contrasts with that of experts whose differential-diagnosis testimony has been excluded in earlier Sixth Circuit cases. In *Conde v. Velsicol Chemical Corp.*, 24 F.3d 809 (6th Cir.1994), for example, Dr. James Conde was a general practitioner and the lead plaintiff in the case. He testified that chlordane, a termiticide that was applied to the basement of his home, caused various ailments in himself and his family members. Dr. Conde's opinion was discredited because "[n]ineteen epidemiologic studies in humans ha[d] found little

---

* [Lescol is a cholesterol lowering agent.–Eds.]

evidence of longterm adverse health effects from chlordane doses hundreds of times higher than those the Condes were subjected to under a worst-case scenario." *Id.* at 813–14.

The three remaining causation experts offered by the plaintiffs in *Conde* were "non-medical doctors unqualified to render differential diagnoses of medical conditions." *Id.* at 813. Their opinions were not admitted because they were "unable to exclude other potential causes for [the plaintiffs'] symptoms, and their theories [were] inconsistent with the negative chlordane test results on the Condes' tissue and the vast majority of the relevant, peer-reviewed scientific literature." *Id.* at 814. Although Dr. Moreno did not provide any study concluding that Aqua EZ can cause anosmia, he did discover that it could damage nasal and sinus mucosa. The record reveals no studies comparable to those in *Conde* that discredit Dr. Moreno's reasonable conclusion that a chemical insult to the sinuses can lead to anosmia.

Two unpublished Sixth Circuit cases that excluded medical-causation testimony founded upon differential diagnoses are also distinguishable. * * *

Kolesar v. United Agriproducts, Inc., 246 Fed. Appx. 977 (6th Cir. 2007), is the other unpublished case involving a differential-diagnosis opinion that fell short of the one developed by Dr. Moreno. In that case, the testifying physician opined that a chemical spill caused the plaintiff's Reactive Airways Dysfunction Syndrome (RADS). But the plaintiff suffered from asthma and a serious preexisting "smoker's cough"—possible causes of RADS that the doctor did not consider. No such unconsidered alternative causes of Best's alleged anosmia have been identified in the case before us.

* * *

G. Need for medical expert testimony

We further note that, even without Dr. Moreno's expert testimony, summary judgment might be inappropriate in this case in light of this court's recent decision in *Gass v. Marriott Hotel Services*, 558 F.3d 419, 434 (6th Cir.2009) (holding that expert testimony was not required to prove the causation element of a negligence case where the plaintiffs were allegedly exposed to pesticides and immediately developed respiratory injuries). Because we conclude that Dr. Moreno's opinion is admissible, however, we have no need to decide whether the holding in *Gass* is applicable to the present case.

III. CONCLUSION

For all of the reasons set forth above, we **REVERSE** the judgment of the district court and **REMAND** the case for further proceedings consistent with this opinion.

NOTES AND QUESTIONS

1. *Causal sufficiency and admissibility.* Specific causation is a crucial issue in many toxic tort cases. Plaintiff must present sufficient evidence to persuade the factfinder that more likely than not the substance under consideration caused her injury. As the *Best* case demonstrates, however, this issue is very frequently resolved within the context of an expert witness admissibility ruling. In *Best* and many similar cases, questions of sufficiency (the domain of tort law) and admissibility (the domain of evidence law) are intertwined. Indeed the two issues overlap in so many ways that disentangling them is impossible. First, modern evidence rules surrounding the admissibility of expert testimony are, to a large extent, creatures of toxic tort and drug cases. Second, a clear majority of all reported tort cases that discuss specific causation involve questions of admissibility. Third, these opinions do not restrict themselves to narrow issues of admissibility. Many of the substantive legal discussions of the causal proof needed to prevail in a toxic tort cases are to be found in opinions whose primary purpose is to resolve admissibility controversies. See In re Breast Implant Litig., 11 F.Supp.2d 1217, 1224 (D.Colo.1998). Finally, in many of these cases the admissibility decision is outcome dispositive. The trial court assesses plaintiff's causal proof in terms of both general and specific causation; it excludes the testimony on one or both of these causal grounds, and finally it enters a summary judgment for the defense because plaintiff no longer has any admissible evidence on the causal question. See, e.g., Turner v. Iowa Fire Equip. Co., 229 F.3d 1202 (8th Cir.2000). Whenever this occurs, the line between the evidentiary question of admissibility and the tort question of the sufficiency is at best blurred. See Joseph Sanders, The Controversial Comment *c*: Factual Causation in Toxic–Substance and Disease Cases, 44 Wake Forest L.Rev. 1029 (2009).

Because today it is difficult to define the separate emulsified domains of evidence law and tort law, admissibility rulings are often the best examples of how courts deal with causal questions that arise in toxic tort cases. However, we defer a full discussion of admissibility rules per se to Chapter 5, where we discuss the *"Daubert* revolution" and its impact on toxic torts.

2. *Best* is a close case and might well have gone either way. Can you think of modest changes in the evidence that would have tipped the scales for or against one side? For example, would it have mattered if the proportion of anosmia due to unknown causes had been provided? If so, which side would it have favored? For a discussion of idiopathic causes, see note 5, below.

3. *Differential diagnosis.* In Cavallo v. Star Enterprise, 892 F.Supp. 756, 771 (E.D.Va.1995), differential diagnosis is defined as "a process whereby medical doctors experienced in diagnostic techniques provide testimony countering other possible causes . . . of the injuries at issue." Unfortunately, the term is not used this way in medical discourse. Medical dictionaries define differential diagnosis as the "determination of which one of two or more diseases with similar symptoms is the one from which the patient is suffering." American Heritage Stedman's Medical Dictionary (2002). The confusion is reflected in the *Best* opinion where the court defined differential diagnosis as "[t]he method by which a physician determines what disease process caused a patient's symptoms. The physician considers all relevant potential causes of the symptoms and then eliminates alternative causes based on a physical examination, clinical tests, and a thorough case history." Note that the court's definition commingles the two usages of the term.

Some courts do recognize that legal usage is contrary to medical usage and employ the more appropriate term "differential etiology" (the study of the causes of disease). At one level, the confusion in terminology is only semantic. However, at another level, the confusion can mislead. It is often said that physicians are well trained in the process of differential diagnosis and that they devote considerable attention in medical school to learning clinical reasoning. But training in the process of deducing disease based on a set of symptoms and laboratory tests and deducing the cause of an ailment are not the same thing. Many physicians may have far less training in the latter task. As the district court in Wynacht v. Beckman Instruments, Inc., 113 F.Supp.2d 1205 (E.D.Tenn.2000) noted:

> [T]here is a fundamental distinction between Dr. Ziem's ability to render a medical diagnosis based on clinical experience and her ability to render an opinion on causation of Wynacht's injuries. Beckman apparently does not dispute, and the Court does not question, that Dr. Ziem is an experienced physician, qualified to diagnose medical conditions and treat patients. The ability to diagnose medical conditions is not remotely the same, however, as the ability to deduce, delineate, and describe, in a scientifically reliable manner, the causes of these medical conditions.

Id. at 1209.

The frequency with which physicians are called on to do a differential etiology varies from field to field. Allergists routinely engage in the process of differential etiology in the process of determining what environmental agent is causing the patient's allergic reaction. On the other hand, oncologists may have far fewer occasions to ascertain the cause of a given cancer. As the court in Bowers v. Norfolk Southern Corp., 537 F.Supp.2d 1343 (M.D.Ga.2007) noted, for physicians such as oncologists, much more rides on their differential diagnosis than on their differential etiology.

> When a doctor develops his *differential diagnosis* in treating a patient, two factors strongly insure that the doctor will follow a reliable methodology to diagnose the patient's condition. First, if he misdiagnoses the patient's condition, the patient may die. And second, if he misdiagnoses the patient's condition and the patient dies, then the patient's family will sue the doctor for medical malpractice.

> By contrast, when an expert witness uses the *differential etiology* approach to testify in court to support a litigant's case, he has very little at stake. He renders his opinion, and then gets paid, often quite handsomely. The plaintiff is at no risk of harm, and the expert will not get sued for malpractice.

> The differential diagnosis method has an inherent reliability; the differential etiology method does not. This conclusion does not suggest that the differential etiology approach has no merit. It simply means that courts, when dealing with matters of reliability, should consider opinions

based on the differential etiology method with more caution. It also means that courts should not conflate the two definitions.

Id. at 1360–61.

4. *Temporal order.* A recurring issue in specific causation is whether temporal order alone is sufficient to rule out other causes of a plaintiff's injury. The answer to this question turns in part on the nature of the temporal order. Judge Becker provided the following examples in Heller v. Shaw Industries, Inc., 167 F.3d 146 (3d Cir.1999):

> [I]f there was a minor oil spill on the Hudson River on the same day that Heller began experiencing her symptoms in West Chester, Pennsylvania, and she recovered around the time the oil was cleaned up, a proper differential diagnosis and temporal analysis by a well-qualified physician * * * could not possibly lead to the conclusion that the oil spill caused Heller's illness. Conversely, "if a person were doused with chemical X and immediately thereafter developed symptom Y, the need for published literature showing a correlation between the two may be lessened."

Id. at 154.

Where on this continuum does the *Best* case fall? Note that Best visited Dr. Moreno soon after he was injured in 2003 but Dr. Moreno did not test him for loss of olfactory function until 2007. What outcome if Best visited Dr. Moreno for the first time in 2007 and at that time Best told him that he had been experiencing loss of smell since the time of the spill? Under similar circumstances, the court in Viterbo v. Dow Chemical, Co., 826 F.2d 420 (5th Cir.1987) had this to say:

> Here, however, Dr. Johnson has admitted that Viterbo's symptoms could have numerous causes and, without support save Viterbo's oral history, simply picks the cause that is most advantageous to Viterbo's claim. Indeed, Dr. Johnson's testimony is no more than Viterbo's testimony dressed up and sanctified as the opinion of an expert. Without more than credentials and a subjective opinion, an expert's testimony that "it is so" is not admissible.

Id. at 424.

Many courts note that simply observing that an adverse event occurs shortly after exposure to a suspect agent is not sufficient to prove causation. In McClain v. Metabolife International Inc., 401 F.3d 1233 (11th Cir.2005), users of herbal weight-loss supplement containing ephedrine and caffeine sued the supplement manufacturer alleging that the over-the-counter diet drug caused their ischemic strokes. Reversing a jury verdict in favor of the plaintiff, the court noted:

> [P]roving a *temporal* relationship between taking Metabolife and the onset of symptoms does not establish a *causal* relationship. In other words, simply because a person takes drugs and then suffers an injury does not show causation. Drawing such a conclusion from temporal relationships leads to the blunder of the *post hoc ergo propter hoc* fallacy.

The *post hoc ergo propter hoc* fallacy assumes causality from temporal sequence. It literally means "after this, because of this." BLACK'S LAW DICTIONARY 1186 (7th ed.1999).

McClain v. Metabolife, 401 F.3d at 1243. Assuming the plaintiffs in *McClain* suffered their strokes very shortly after taking Metabolife, how is this different from the *Best* situation?

Occasionally, courts are asked to consider the methodological adequacy of what is commonly called "dechallenge-rechallenge" evidence. Typically, the patient(s) are exposed to a substance, then the substance is removed and later the substance is reintroduced. The investigator is interested in whether the patients' symptoms disappear and reappear when exposure is withdrawn and then reintroduced. Depending on how it is done, this type of "dechallenge-rechallenge" testimony is much stronger evidence of causation than the mere existence of a temporal order. In *Westberry v. Gislaved Gummi, AB*, cited in the *Best* opinion, the Fourth Circuit affirmed the trial judge's decision to permit an expert to testify that exposure to airborne talc caused the aggravation of the plaintiff's preexisting sinus condition. The court admitted the evidence partly because the expert testified that when the plaintiff stayed home from work his sinus condition improved and when he returned to work it worsened. Dechallenge-rechallenge evidence is only practical with acute-response diseases; the method could not be used for long latency period diseases.

5. *Idiopathic causes.* Should courts permit experts to present differential diagnosis testimony when the clear weight of scientific evidence points to the fact that the substantial majority of a certain type of injury is from unknown causes? This problem existed in the Bendectin cases where experts agree that the cause of most limb-reduction birth defects is unknown. Even if an expert were able to use differential etiology to eliminate other known causes of an injury, it would remain far more likely that an unknown cause is the source of the individual's injury. For example, if with respect to some injury we know that five percent of the cases are caused by an exposure to a drug, five percent are caused by another known cause, and 90% have no known cause, a differential diagnosis that clearly excludes the other known cause still leaves it much more likely than not that the cause in any particular case is not the drug. Most courts, like *Best*, ignore or do not seriously confront this issue.

Perry v. Novartis Pharmaceuticals Corp., 564 F.Supp.2d 452 (E.D.Pa. 2008) wrestled with this issue. The plaintiffs claimed their child's T-cell lymphoblastic lymphoma (T-LBL) (a type of non-Hodgkin's lymphoma) was caused by her use of Elidel, a prescription cream used to treat eczema.

The court gave a useful discussion of what an expert must do in the circumstance where most occurrences of a particular disease are from unknown causes, as is case with T–LBL. Pimecrolimus is the active ingredient in Elidel and is one of a class of drugs known as calcineurin inhibitors. Calcineurin inhibitors are known to inhibit immune system function. Other calcineurin inhibitors are used in immunosuppressive therapy to prevent rejection after organ transplants and have been associated with increased incidence of post-transplant lymphoproliferative disorder, an illness similar to non-Hodgkin's lymphoma.

When the plaintiffs' experts were questioned about how they excluded "no known cause" in the child's illness, they simply repeated the existence of a known risk factor, primecrolimus. The court responded, "Standing alone, the presence of a known risk factor is not a sufficient basis for ruling out idiopathic origin in a particular case, particularly where most cases of the disease have no known cause." Id. at 470. However, the trial judge did not leave the matter here. Rather he went on to make the following comment:

> This is not to say that where most diagnoses of a disease are idiopathic it is impossible to prove specific causation. But in those cases, analysis beyond a differential diagnosis will likely be required. Here, for example, because lymphoma caused by immunosuppressant drugs is well-understood, Drs. Smith and Kolb could have compared the presentation of Andreas Perry's symptoms with those common in post-transplant lymphoma cases. Doing so, however, would not have served plaintiffs' purposes.

Id.

The court explained this last sentence by noting that the post-transplant cancers have a history consistent with B-cell origin, whereas the child's lymphoma had a T-cell origin. This fact made the district court's task somewhat easier. But there may be other situations where there is no known distinction between forms of a disease, and a court would have to decide if the simple failure to exclude idiopathic causes is reason for exclusion when in fact there is no way to exclude (or include) them. See also Henricksen v. Conoco-Phillips Co., 605 F.Supp.2d 1142, 1162 (E.D.Wash.2009)("Here, Gardner (and all of Plaintiffs experts, for that matter) fail to exclude—much less address in their reports—the likelihood that Henricksen's AML had no known cause. * * * This is not to say that where most diagnoses of a disease are idiopathic it is impossible to prove specific causation. But in those cases, analysis beyond a differential diagnosis is required.").

6. *Ruling in and dosage.* The *Best* court quoted *Glastetter v. Novartis Pharmaceuticals Corp.*, for the proposition that in performing a differential diagnosis an expert first "rules in" all scientifically plausible causes and then "rules out" some of these causes until the most likely cause remains. Many differential diagnoses have been excluded because the expert failed to rule in the suspect cause before ruling out other possibilities.

The "rule in" requirement sometimes is presented as a question of dosage: assuming that some dose of the substance in question might cause harm, does the expert have adequate grounds for asserting that the dosage to which plaintiff was exposed could cause anyone harm? In Mancuso v. Consolidated Edison Co. of New York, Inc. 56 F.Supp.2d 391 (S.D.N.Y.1999), vacated on other grounds, 216 F.3d 1072 (2d Cir.2000), the plaintiffs' expert apparently found that the concentration of PCBs at the plaintiffs' marina was four parts in 10 billion, less than one ten thousandth as high as the level which the EPA has found to be acceptable. The court responded with the following passage:

> A fundamental tenet of toxicology is that the "dose makes the poison" and that all chemical agents, including water, are harmful if consumed in large quantities, while even the most toxic substances are

harmless in minute quantities. Therefore, in determining whether plaintiffs' exposure to PCBs could have caused any illnesses that they have, it is necessary to establish the dose/response relationship between PCBs and those particular illnesses.

Id. at 403. For a useful discussion of dosage issues see Bernard Goldstein, Toxic Torts: The Devil is in the Dose, 16 J.L.& Pol'y 551 (2008).

7. *Is differential diagnosis reliable?* The *Best* court quoted *Westberry* for the proposition that differential diagnosis is "a standard scientific technique of identifying the cause of a medical problem." In what sense is this technique scientific? One must be careful in addressing this question. There is no "scientific method" in the sense that we can point to a scientific way of knowing that is different from other ways of knowing things. As Susan Haack notes,

> What is distinctive about natural-scientific inquiry isn't that it uses a peculiar mode or modes of inference, but the vast range of helps to inquiry scientists have developed, many of them—specific instruments, specific kinds of precaution against experimental error, specific models and metaphors—local to this or that field or sub-discipline.

Susan Haack, Defending Science Within Reason: Between Scientism and Cynicism 167 (2003). It is these methods that provide some assurance that expert causal opinions are reliable.

In many areas of inquiry, scientific research has developed well defined methodologies for assessing the effects of purported causes. It does not provide such clear procedures for establishing the causes of effects. With respect to this second undertaking, David Faigman makes the following comment:

> The specific application of general propositions that are themselves supported by adequate research—requires two abilities, neither of which are clearly within most scientists' skill sets. The first, and perhaps less problematic, is that of forensic investigator. Almost no matter what the empirical relationship, whether medical or psychological, exposure or dosage levels will be relevant to the diagnosis. The first principle of toxicology is that "the dose is the poison," since any substance in sufficient quantities could injure or kill someone. * * * The expert testifying to specific causation must determine exposure and dosage levels for the suspected cause (i.e., the source suspected by the client) as well as for all other known or possible causes. This task is difficult enough alone, but is enormously complicated by the significant potential for recall bias, given that the litigation will be profoundly affected by what is recalled.

> The second skill set that is needed has not yet been invented or even described with precision. Somehow, the diagnostician must combine the surfeit of information concerning the multitude of factors that make up the general model, combine it with the case history information known or suspected about the individual, and offer an opinion with some level of confidence that substance or experience X was the likely cause of condition Y. In practice, this opinion is usually stated as follows: "within a reasonable degree of medical/psychological certainty, it is my opinion that

X caused [a particular case of] Y." This expression has no empirical meaning and is simply a mantra repeated by experts for purposes of legal decision makers who similarly have no idea what it means ... Experts' case-specific conclusions appear largely to be based on an admixture of an unknown combination of knowledge of the subject, experience over the years, commitment to the client or cause, intuition, and blind-faith. Science it is not.

David L. Faigman, Evidentiary Incommensurability: A Preliminary Exploration of the Problem of Reasoning from General Scientific Data to Individualized Legal Decision Making, 75 Brooklyn L.Rev. 1137, 1155–57 (2010). Given this reality, perhaps it is not surprising that the *Best* court noted that: "Dr. Moreno's diagnosis might not stand up to exacting scrutiny if he were testifying as a research scientist or a chemist, but he is neither of those. He performed as a competent, intellectually rigorous treating physician in identifying the most likely cause of Best's injury." For the proposition that differential diagnosis testimony is judged by a lower methodological standard than evidence of general causation, see Joseph Sanders, Applying *Daubert* Inconsistently?: Proof of Individual Causation in Toxic Tort and Forensic Cases, 75 Brooklyn L. Rev. 1367 (2010). Unfortunately, because there are no generally accepted methodological aids to assessing the causes of effects, it is often difficult to assess the reliability of differential diagnosis testimony. Comment e of section 28 of the Third Restatement of Torts: Liability for Physical and Emotional Harm agrees with Professor Faigman that resolving this difficult issue is not assisted by requiring experts to repeat the "reasonable degree of medical certainty" mantra.

8. Some scholars have proposed eliminating the preponderance of the evidence requirement for specific causation in toxic torts. Under some schemes, if a plaintiff could prove, for example, that her risk increased 25% because of her exposure to substance X she could recover 25% of her damages from the maker of X. As Ken Abraham notes, however, these alternatives require a body of epidemiologic evidence sufficient to provide reliable "probabilistic measures of causation." Kenneth Abraham, Individual Action and Collective Responsibility: The Dilemma of Mass Tort Reform, 73 Va.L.Rev. 845 (1987). In many situations, this body of evidence simply does not exist. Michael Green has argued that even if a body of epidemiologic evidence existed that suggested increased risks of that magnitude, these findings are as likely to be the result of noise as of a true causal effect. Michael D. Green, The Future of Proportional Liability: The Lessons of Toxic Substance Litigation, in Exploring Tort Law 352 (M. Stuart Madden, ed. 2005). Thus far, most courts have refused to adopt proportional liability.

For discussions of various ways in which courts might alter causal proofs in mass exposure cases, see Steve Gold, Causation in Toxic Torts: Burdens of Proof, Standards of Persuasion, and Statistical Evidence, 96 Yale L.J. 376 (1986); David Rosenberg, Individual Justice and Collectivizing Risk–Based Claims in Mass Exposure Cases, 71 N.Y.U. L.Rev. 211 (1996); Margaret Berger, Eliminating General Causation: Notes Towards a New Theory of Justice and Toxic Torts, 97 Colum.L.Rev. 2117 (1997); Margaret Berger & Aaron Twerski, Uncertainty and Informed Choice: Unmasking *Daubert*, 104 Mich.L.Rev. 257 (2005). But see David Bernstein, Learning the Wrong Lessons From "An American Tragedy": A Critique of the Berger–Twerski Informed Choice Proposal, 104 Mich.L.Rev. 1961 (2006).

D. THE FUTURE: GENETICS, GENOMICS AND THE DEFINITION OF INJURY

As the preceding discussion indicates, proof of causation in toxic tort cases nearly always requires proof of general causation and this proof often turns on epidemiologic evidence and/or laboratory animal studies. Without proof of general causation, the courts in many jurisdictions will not permit the plaintiff to attempt to prove specific causation.

Even when there is evidence of general causation, plaintiff must still produce evidence of specific causation. As we have seen in the *Best* case, usually plaintiff calls upon an expert to provide a "differential diagnosis." Unfortunately, often this process does not involve much more than guesswork. Traditionally, unless a disease is a "signature disease," i.e., a disease known to be caused almost exclusively by exposure to a particular substance, there has been no way to distinguish between the causes of an ailment based on the ailment itself. When a smoker who has been exposed to asbestos develops lung cancer, we cannot perform a test that will reveal that this particular lung cancer is caused by asbestos exposure.

The emerging field of genomics offers hope that this state of affairs may change in the future. Steve Gold notes that the ambitious goal, "is to develop a giant matrix with human genotypes on one axis of the array, diseases on the other, and at each intersection, a value for the risk of that disease associated with that genotype." Steve C. Gold, The More We Know, the Less Intelligent We Are? How Genomic Information Should, and Should Not, Change Toxic Tort Causation Doctrine, 34 Harv. Env't.L.Rev. 369, 386 (2010). Gold notes that one research approach is to expose genetic material to a toxin and determine if genetic variation is associated with variation in the probability the substance will have a toxic effect. If so, the investigation yields a biomarker of susceptibility. That is, the presence of the biomarker increases or decreases the probability that exposure will result in harm. A second approach is to examine exposed and non-exposed biological material for differences in gene mutations or other biochemical indicators.

Scientists are not only discovering biomarkers associated with disease, they are also uncovering the specific genetic sources of ailments. How will these new understandings affect toxic tort cases? The following case is, perhaps, a precursor of many cases to come.

BOWEN v. E.I. DU PONT DE NEMOURS & CO., INC.

Superior Court of Delaware, 2005.
2005 WL 1952859, aff'd, 906 A.2d 787.

TOLIVER, J.

STATEMENT OF FACTS AND NATURE OF THE PROCEEDINGS

Factual Background

[T]he plaintiffs are eight minor children and their parents who have alleged that the children suffered injuries manifested at birth as a result of the exposure of the children's mothers to an agricultural product sold under the trade name of Benlate. Benlate was manufactured by the defendant, the DuPont Company. More specifically, the plaintiffs contend that the mothers of the children were dermally exposed to Benlate during the early stages of their pregnancies. Once deposited, the Benlate was alleged to have passed thru the skin to the developing fetus via the placenta where it acted to retard fetal growth and cell development. The product, which the plaintiffs allege is a human teratogen,[1] was being used as directed at the time of the exposure.

The exposure and births in question are alleged to have taken place between 1984 and 1995. * * * The injuries the children suffered which the plaintiffs attribute to Benlate include anophthalmia and microphthalmia[4] as well as other forms of arrested development, physical, emotional and intellectual.

* * *

The defendant denies that Benlate is a human teratogen or that it otherwise was responsible for the problems experienced by the plaintiffs. Those problems, the defendant contends, were caused by factors independent of the defendant and Benlate. * * *

Benlate is described as a fungicide developed by the defendant primarily for commercial agricultural use and is designed to prevent and cure fungal infections in plants and crops. The defendant first placed the product on the market for sale in 1970. Although it was only sold commercially in the United States, the product was available for purchase for home use outside the United States, and in particular, in the United Kingdom and New Zealand where the exposures complained about herein took place. The sale of Benlate was halted and it was withdrawn from all markets in 1995.

* * *

* * * On April 27, 2004, this Court * * * ordered the cases grouped in pairs, resulting in four trials. The claims made by and on behalf of Emily Bowen and Darren Griffin were to be tried first * * *.

B.　Motion to Exclude Plaintiffs' Expert Witnesses Based Upon DRE 702

As was to be expected, both sides retained numerous experts to provide assistance in preparing the case for trial generally as well as for purposes of testifying at trial concerning general and specific causation.

---

1. A teratogen is defined as "a drug or other agent that causes abnormal prenatal development." *PDR Medical Dictionary*, at 1796 (Lippencott, Williams and Wilkins, 2nd Ed. 2000).

4. Children afflicted with anophthalmia are born with no eyes and those suffering from microphthalmia are born with very small eyes.

* * * The plaintiffs engaged * * * experts in the fields of genetics, teratology, toxicology, dermal exposure and dermal absorption * * *. They are Dr. Charles V. Howard, Dr. David L. MacIntosh, [and] Dr. Michael A. Patton * * *.

* * *

The defendant has contended from the start of this litigation that Emily Bowen's injuries and condition constitute CHARGE Syndrome, which is generally thought to be genetic, as opposed to environmental, in origin.[9] The plaintiffs disputed this contention and initially offered the testimony and opinions of Dr. Patton. Dr. Patton's qualifications as an expert in the field of genetics in this case are not questioned by the defense.

Based upon his initial examinations and review of her medical records and related information, Dr. Patton concluded in 2002 and in 2003 that Emily Bowen's features did not constitute CHARGE Syndrome. Dr. Patton agreed with two other physicians that had seen her during this period of time, that Emily Bowen did not meet enough of the criteria that would make such a diagnosis appropriate. As a result and given the state of the science at that time, he concluded that her problems did not have any recognizable root in genetics. However, he acknowledged that if his findings relative to her physical condition or the state of the science changed, his opinion could change.

As his curriculum vitae reveals, Dr. Howard is a medical doctor and lecturer at the University of Liverpool in Liverpool, England, where he received his medical training from 1965 to 1970. He began at that institution in 1971 and assumed his current position as a senior lecturer in 1991 in the Department of Human Anatomy and Cell Biology. * * * Dr. Howard belongs to several professional organizations, including the British Society of Toxicological Pathologists and the Society for Developmental Pathology. He considers himself a toxicologist and a fetal pathologist, and is not, by his own admission, an expert in genetics.

Dr. Howard, relying on the initial opinions of Dr. Patton, i.e., that Emily Bowen's birth defects did not constitute the "CHARGE Syndrome", ruled out genetics as a cause. Given that conclusion and Dr. McIntosh's findings relative to the amount of Benlate that was dermally absorbed, Dr. Howard, based upon his education, training, research and experience regarding Benlate, concluded that Benlate was a human teratogen to which Emily Bowen was exposed while being carried in her mother's

---

9. "CHARGE" is an acronym which stands for Coloboma (absence of or defect in ocular tissue), heart defect, atresia of choanae (blockage between back of nose and mouth), retarded growth and development, genital hypoplasia (arrested development) and ear anomalies. Lalani SR, Safiullah AM, Molinari LM, Fernbach SD, Martin DM, Belmont JW. *SEMA3E Mutation in a Patient with CHARGE Syndrome.* J.Med.Genet. 41:99, 2004. According to Dr. Patton's declaration, CHARGE is defined as an association of features or pattern of malformations which occur together more commonly than by happenstance. Dr. Patton also stated that the principal debate seems to have been whether there is a common underlying cause or causes.

uterus. It was that exposure, he opined, that proximately caused the birth defects experienced by Emily Bowen.

* * *

The defendant, based upon DRE 702 in light of *Daubert v. Merrell Dow Pharmaceuticals, Inc.*, and its Delaware progeny, moved, on March 23, 2003, to exclude the testimony of Drs. Howard [and] MacIntosh * * *. The motions were taken under advisement.

C.   Further Genetic Testing

* * *

[B]ased upon newly developed genetic testing methodologies and the results of related testing in the six remanded cases, the defendant moved, on July 12, 2004, to subject Emily Bowen and Darren Griffin to testing for gene mutations that had been cast as causes of conditions similar to those suffered by the instant plaintiffs. That motion was initially denied and the defendant, after supplementing the record, moved the Court to reconsider. Over the plaintiffs' objections, the Court, on October 15, 2004, ordered that the testing take place * * *.

In January 2005, the parties became aware of the results of the additional testing. The tests revealed that Emily Bowen's genetic profile contained a gene, CHD7, which had mutated. The geneticists who discovered that mutation as well as those who confirmed its existence, now believe it is the cause of CHARGE Syndrome. While not all individuals with CHARGE Syndrome tested up to that point in time had the aforementioned mutation, it appears that each individual with the CHD7 mutation was diagnosed with CHARGE Syndrome.[19] The defense contends as a result that Emily Bowen not only has CHARGE Syndrome, but that it was caused by the CHD7 mutation which is genetic in origin only. Stated differently, there were no environmental or external causes.[20]

Two of the plaintiffs' experts, Dr. Howard and Dr. Patton, have responded to the additional test results with conclusions that are different than those originally offered.

Dr. Patton, notwithstanding his previous conclusion that Emily Bowen did not exhibit CHARGE Syndrome and that he could rule out genetics as a cause of her afflictions, now believes that the CHARGE Syndrome diagnosis is correct. He further opines that the mutated CHD7 gene played a substantial role in bringing about that condition. However, he could not rule out a teratogenic cause in general or Benlate specifically, because as he conceded, he is not qualified to do so in that he is not a teratologist, a toxicologist or an expert in either field.

---

19.   The study first identifying the CHD7 mutation as a cause of CHARGE Syndrome, was presented in the medical journal "Nature Genetics" in its August 2004 edition (hereinafter the "Vissers Study"). Vissers, L., Brunner, H., et. al., *Mutations in a New Member of the Chromodomain Gene Family Cause CHARGE Syndrome,* Nature Genetics 36(9): 955, 2004.

20.   The results of the testing were negative as to Darren Griffin.

By contrast, Dr. Howard, continues to argue that Benlate is somehow the cause of Emily Bowen's problems and now believes that the CHD7 acted together with Benlate to bring about those injuries. In spite of that position, he does concede that it is very likely that Emily Bowen has CHARGE Syndrome. That concession is based upon Dr. Patton's supplemental findings upon which Dr. Howard relied since he has no expertise in the field of genetics. He further acknowledged that Benlate is not responsible for the mutation in question and that he knows nothing about the CHD7 gene other than what he read in one article on the subject, i.e., the Vissers Study.

Although he is able to maintain his view of Benlate as a human teratogen, Dr. Howard is not able to state how or in what percentage or proportion Benlate and the CHD7 mutation act together to produce CHARGE Syndrome in Emily Bowen. Nor is he aware of any testing or studies which confirm or support his theory regarding the interaction between Benlate and the CHD7 mutation.

D.   Supplemental and Renewed DRE 702 Motions

On April 11, 2005, the defendant filed several supplemental motions based upon the recent genetic test results and the expert opinions filed in response by the plaintiffs' expert witnesses. * * *

Argument was held on April 27 and 28, 2005. At the conclusion of that presentation, the Court granted the defendant's motions as to Dr. Patton, Dr. McIntosh and Dr. Howard. Given those findings, the defendant's motion for summary judgment was also granted as to both plaintiffs. This Court reasoned that without the testimony of those witnesses the plaintiffs could not establish that Benlate was a human teratogen or that it was the specific cause of the injuries being complained of by either plaintiff.

The motion as to Dr. Patton was granted limiting his testimony as requested on grounds of relevance and competency based upon his admitted lack of expertise in teratology and toxicology. * * *

> * * *

* * * Dr. Howard was excluded as an expert witness in Emily Bowen's case based upon Dr. Patton's amended opinion that Emily Bowen's injuries could be deemed genetic in origin and Dr. Howard's reliance on Dr. Patton as an expert in that area. Since he could not, given his lack of expertise and/or qualification as a geneticist, provide an opinion resting in genetics or otherwise supporting his post-CHD7 discovery theory that the CHD7 mutation and Benlate acted together, Dr. Howard could not testify as a expert witness as to Emily Bowen via DRE 702.

> * * *

Dr. Howard's Testimony Regarding Emily Bowen

In order to establish the cause of a condition, an expert must not only be able to state the cause of a condition, the witness, or the party offering the testimony, must also be able to exclude other possible/putative causes. In scientific circles, this is known as performing a differential diagnosis. It is a commonly accepted method of addressing the issue of the origin or cause of a medical condition. As the Fourth Circuit Court of Appeals stated in *Westberry,* such a diagnosis:

> is a standard scientific technique of identifying the cause of a medical problem by eliminating the likely causes until the most probable one is isolated. A reliable differential diagnosis typically, though not invariably, is performed after "physical examinations, the taking of medical histories, and the review of clinical tests, including laboratory tests," and generally is accomplished by determining the possible causes for the patient's symptom and then eliminating each of these potential causes until reaching one that cannot be ruled out or determining which of those that cannot be excluded is the most likely.... (Citations omitted.) [Westberry v. Gislaved Gummi AB, 178 F.3d 257, 262–63 (4th Cir.1999).]

In the instant case, both sides have referenced this method of addressing the question of causation. The defense argues that the plaintiffs must not only be able to attribute responsibility for Emily Bowen's injuries to Benlate, they must also be able to exclude the most likely cause of Emily Bowen's problems, genetics and CHARGE Syndrome. The plaintiffs state that they did perform a differential diagnosis via the testimony of Dr. Patton and Dr. Howard and were able to establish Benlate as the cause of her problems. That conclusion was based upon the negative results of prior chromosomal based genetic testing. Two years later, as indicated above, dramatic advances had been made thus allowing the more precise testing of Emily Bowen and Darren Griffin ordered here.

When Dr. Patton changed his diagnosis following the CHD7 test results, Dr. Howard could no longer exclude genetics as, in the words of Dr. Patton, a "substantial cause" of the injuries in question. Dr. Howard then amended his opinion that Benlate was the sole cause of Emily Bowen's injuries to conclude that Benlate interacted with the CHD7 mutation to proximately bring about the problems visited upon her. Dr. Howard did so without any expertise in genetics, having very little knowledge about CHD7 or how, when, and to what degree it combined with Benlate to cause the injuries complained about. Moreover, he admitted that his theory has never been tested, peer reviewed or otherwise subjected to professional scrutiny.

The Court's decision to exclude Dr. Howard as a witness in Emily Bowen's case was based in the first instance on DRE 702's requirement that the witness be "qualified." * * * Given the fact that Dr. Howard admits that he is not a geneticist and has no training, education or experience generally, or specifically, as to CHD7, he is not qualified via DRE 702 to opine relative to any interaction between CHD7 mutation and Benlate. Nor can he perform a valid differential diagnosis excluding CHD7 or genetics as a cause of the injuries visited upon Emily Bowen under the circumstances.[50]

Dr. Howard's amended opinion and proposed testimony was further excluded because it was not reliable and therefore runs afoul of DRE 402 and 702. His theory regarding the interaction between the CHD7 mutation and Benlate as the cause of Emily Bowen's injuries has not been validated by any scientific discipline, study or entity. It has not been the subject of any peer review nor has it been accepted by any relevant scientific community. There was no testing or publication of this theory prior to the discovery of the CHD7 mutation and its link to CHARGE Syndrome. It is readily apparent as a result, that the theory did not arise out of research or testing but was a product of the instant litigation, a factor which supports its rejection.

Lastly, there is no evidence of any cause other than the CHD7 mutation. Dr. Howard is unable to explain how, why, or where the CHD7/Benlate combination works. Nor have the plaintiffs been able to otherwise produce any testimony, at least from those qualified to provide it, that there exists a disease or disability producing gene, in this case CHD7, which requires the presence of an environmental agent to manifest itself. The position advocated by the defense is clear–the mutated CHD7 gene was the sole and proximate cause of Emily Bowen's CHARGE Syndrome. That theory has substantial support in the record in that it has been tested, peer reviewed and published, apparently without consequential dissent.

The Court must further conclude that Dr. Howard's revised opinion is not sufficiently tied to the facts of the case so as to assist the jury in resolving any of the issues involved in this case. It is not the product of reliable scientific principles and methods. In short, while it does relate to causation, the proposed testimony is nothing more than an unsupported theory, or "ipse dixit."

[The court also concluded that Dr. McIntosh was not qualified to provide expert testimony in the field of dermal absorption. "Most telling is his own admission regarding his alleged expertise. According to Dr. McIntosh, while he might be an expert in dermal exposure, dermal absorption is a specialized area in which he was not an expert but had only a working knowledge of the subject. Unfortunately for the plaintiffs, there is no authority in support of the proposition that a 'working knowledge' is the equivalent of 'expertise' for purposes of DRE 702, at least not in these circumstances." Moreover, his testimony was not reliable, "i.e., it was not based upon a relevant methodology. It had not been tested, subjected to peer reviewed publication or been accepted within any recognized scientific community relating to dermal absorption

---

50. In espousing his amended or supplemental theory, Dr. Howard has apparently forgotten his deposition testimony where he stated that if Dr. Patton's opinion relative to CHARGE and genetics as the source of Emily Bowen's problems changed, his view concerning causation would be similarly affected.

prior to its use here." [Chapter 5, is devoted to the admissibility of expert witnesses.]

CONCLUSION

For the foregoing reasons, the Court entered the orders relative to Drs. Patton, Howard and McIntosh on May 9, 2005. It was based upon the May 9 orders that the defendant's motion for summary judgment was granted on that same date. There was no need as a result to proceed to a trial on the merits.

NOTES AND QUESTIONS

1. The Delaware Supreme Court affirmed the Superior Court summary judgment. Bowen v. E.I. DuPont de Nemours & Co., Inc., 906 A.2d 787 (Del.2006). However, it focused on the testimony of Dr. MacIntosh. It agreed with the trial court that his method of calculating dermal absorption did not meet Delaware's admissibility standard and, therefore, the plaintiffs did not have any admissible evidence that the dosage to which their mothers were exposed was sufficient to cause their injuries. Given this ruling, it did not need to decide whether Dr. Howard's testimony was admissible.

What should be the outcome if Dr. McIntosh's testimony were admissible? With respect to Emily Bowen? With respect to Darren Griffin?

2. Other cases where the plaintiffs have attempted (unsuccessfully) to use biomarker information include Young v. Burton, 567 F.Supp.2d 121 (D.D.C.2008); City of San Antonio v. Pollock, 284 S.W.3d 809 (Tex.2009); Snyder v. Sec'y of Dept. of HHS, 2009 WL 332044 (Fed.Cl.2009).

3. For other discussions of this emerging field see, Andrew R. Klein, Causation and Uncertainty: Making Connections in a Time of Change, 49 Jurimetrics J. 5 (2008); Jamie A. Grodsky, Genomics and Toxic Torts: Dismantling the Risk–Injury Divide, 59 Stan.L.Rev. 1671, 1672 (2007); Gary E. Marchant, Genetic Data in Toxic Tort Litigation, 14 J.L.& Pol'y 7 (2006); Gary E. Marchant, Genetics and Toxic Torts, 31 Seton Hall L.Rev. 949 (2001); Gary E. Marchant, Genetic Susceptibility and Biomarkers in Toxic Injury Litigation, 41 Jurimetrics J. 67 (2000).

4. Advances in genetics and genomics increase the possibility that we can detect the effects of a toxic exposure well before they manifest themselves in a noticeable physical or mental impairment. This may increase pressure on courts to allow individuals to bring claims based on sub-cellular harm, fear of an illness based on evidence of such harm, or medical monitoring designed to detect when an exposure manifests itself in a disease. We defer discussion of these various remedies to Chapter 12.

5. *Privacy.* Genetic information is a powerful tool, both in and out of the courtroom. Congress recognized the power of this information in the *Genetic Information Non–Discrimination Act* ("GINA") of 2008, which prohibits discrimination by insurance companies and employers, based on genetic information, and limits the ability of these entities to require a person to undergo genetic testing. 42 U.S.C. § 2000ff, Pub. L. No. 110–233, 122 Stat. 881.

Privacy concerns are also raised when plaintiff's genetic make-up becomes an issue in litigation There are three types of privacy that become an issue when a plaintiff is compelled to undergo genetic testing: (1) physical privacy, (2) informational privacy, and (3) decisional privacy. Mark A. Rothstein, Preventing the Discovery of Plaintiff Genetic Profiles By Defendants Seeking to Limit Damages in Personal Injury Litigation, 71 Ind.L.J. 877, 894 (1996).

Physical privacy is the freedom from contact. This is really a more extreme version of a problem currently faced by plaintiffs in toxic tort litigation. Do plaintiffs, by putting their health in issue, waive objection to any medical tests defendant may wish to force upon them during discovery? Courts have generally answered the question in the affirmative, citing plaintiff's affirmative act in bringing the case as a waiver of their privacy rights and defendant's need for the information to effectively put on their case. See Il Grande v. DiBenedetto, 841 A.2d 974, 982–83 (N.J.App.2004) (discussing the need to balance the potential harm to the objecting party against the need of the party requesting the medical exam); Coates v. Whittington, 758 S.W.2d 749, 753 (Tex.1988) (balancing the plaintiff's right to privacy against the defendant's right to a fair trial). It should be noted that this decision is usually discretionary. Most state courts use some form of a balancing test and/or track the decisions of federal courts, which are governed by Federal Rule of Civil Procedure 35. This Rule gives the court the right to order a mental or physical examination of a party when it is "in controversy" and defendant can show "good cause" for the examination.

Informational privacy is the freedom from personal information being accessible by others. Having one's genes mapped reveals many things about a person, not just the matter at issue in litigation. Plaintiff's susceptibility to other diseases, chromosomal anomalies, and perhaps latent diseases that have not yet manifested themselves, would all be discoverable by defendant. These matters, if relevant to the case, might be brought up in open court and become public record, accessible by anyone, from family members to insurance carriers.

Decisional privacy is the freedom to make personal choices in our own lives. This freedom would be invaded by a defendant forcing information on plaintiffs about their genetic make-up, separate from the genes at issue, that perhaps they did not want to know. A powerful example is Huntington's disease. Huntington's disease is a genetic disease that does not present symptoms until late in life. P. Michael Conneally, Huntington Disease: Genetics and Epidemiology, 36 Am.J.Hum.Genet. 506 (1984). After presenting, the disease destroys cells in the brain, affecting a person's ability to move and think. There is currently no cure for Huntington's disease, and unlike some genetic diseases, a positive test means the person has the disease and will most certainly present symptoms later in life. A positive test would undoubtedly affect a person's life. The decision whether or not to have this information is a very personal and private choice.

In the present context, the information sought by defendant goes to the question of causation. However, defendant might also be interested in discovering information about plaintiff's genetic makeup with respect to damages.

In personal injury cases, the life expectancy of the plaintiff is taken into account when calculating future damages. Thus, if defendant could show, through a genetic test, that plaintiff has a shorter life expectancy, it can reduce the amount of damages for which it will be liable.

Balancing these various privacy interests will remain a challenge. Courts will increasingly be asked to issue protective orders regarding the information gathered from a genetic test that could potentially limit the scope of the information gleaned and those who would be privy to it. There is also always the option of federal or state legislation on the matter.

E. LATENCY

The time between exposure to a harmful event and an ensuing injury is always an important component of any causal analysis. However, in many non-toxic tort situations the effect almost immediately follows the cause. Indeed, if the effect does not follow in short order, we begin to lose confidence that it was actually produced by the purported cause. In the toxic tort arena, some plaintiffs have been denied recovery because their injury occurred too long after their exposure. This occurred in litigation surrounding the question of whether a swine flu inoculation caused the plaintiff's Guillain–Barré syndrome. For example, in Heyman v. United States, 506 F.Supp. 1145 (S.D.Fla.1981), the court concluded that the time lapse between vaccination and illness (16 weeks) was too long to attribute the ailment to this cause.

Sometimes the problem may be in the opposite direction. Plaintiff is sick "too soon." See Burleson v. Glass, 268 F.Supp.2d 699, 707 (W.D.Tex. 2003). There, the court granted the defendant's motion to exclude plaintiff's expert testimony in part because the two-year latency period from alleged exposure to onset of cancer was unusually short given the scientific literature indicating typical latency of 10 to 15 years for the tumor type. See Association of British Insurers, Guidelines for Apportioning and Handling Employers' Liability Mesothelioma Claims 9 (2003)(excluding exposures within 10 years of diagnosis of mesothelioma as contributing to its risk, presumably on the ground that those exposures could not have caused a disease whose minimum latency period is considerably greater than 10 years). Note that in both of the above instances, the ability to rule out a suspect cause depended on knowledge of the latency period for the disease.

Even when the time between exposure and plaintiff's injury falls within the latency window, long latency periods pose multiple causal problems for plaintiffs. Latency periods are the primary reason specific causation and temporal order problems loom so large in many toxic tort cases, especially those cases where plaintiff is suffering from an ailment that is not uniquely caused by the substance in question. Moreover, the passage of time between exposure and illness erodes plaintiff's ability to prove who exposed her to a substance and the dose to which she was exposed. Some latency periods are stunningly long. The average latency period for mesothelioma is 30 years after asbestos exposure. David L. Eaton, Scientific Judgment and Toxic Torts—A Primer in Toxicology for Judges and Lawyers, 12 J.L.& Pol'y 5, 32 (2003). Even when plaintiff can point to a source of her exposure, the mere lapse of time may mean defendant is no longer in business or is in some other way judgment proof. With respect to some exposures, most notably the DES cases, plaintiffs cannot identify which of a large number of potential defendants exposed them to the allegedly harmful substance, forcing courts to create special causation rules to deal with these cases. See Sindell v. Abbott Labs., 607 P.2d 924 (Cal.1980). The *Sindell* case is found at p. 261 infra.

Long latency periods present a problem not only because of their average length, but also because of their variance. For example, if we knew precisely how long it took for exposure to asbestos to produce mesothelioma we might well be able to pinpoint causation to a particular defendant. Unfortunately, this is not possible. The latency period for many toxic torts varies widely from individual to individual. Some have estimated that one might contract mesothelioma as early as six years after exposure to asbestos or as late as 45 years after exposure. See A. Chovil & C. Stewart, Latency Period for Mesothelioma, 314 Lancet 853 (1979). When plaintiff has been serially exposed to the products of multiple defendants, this indetermincy produces a special set of causation problems. Note that foreseeable advances in genomics will not resolve this problem. The problem is made even more difficult when plaintiff's own negligent conduct may be a competing potential cause of her harm.

The next Chapter explores the special causal problems that emerge when there are multiple defendants and when plaintiff cannot point to any specific defendant as the entity that caused his injury.

CHAPTER **IV**

CAUSATION IN A MULTI-PARTY CONTEXT

■ ■ ■

As we noted at the end of Chapter 3, many toxic tort suits involve multiple parties. When this is the case, a set of additional causal problems confront the courts. In this Chapter, we address these problems that began to emerge at the very beginning of the toxic tort era.

A. CAUSAL APPORTIONMENT AMONG DEFENDANTS FOR DIVISIBLE AND INDIVISIBLE INJURIES

Although there had been a few congregations of toxic tort cases before asbestos, none played such an important role in the emergence of this class of cases. Over the latter part of the twentieth century, asbestos was the largest class of toxic tort litigation and dwarfed virtually every other mass toxic tort. By the early 2000s, approximately 700,000 plaintiffs who allegedly suffered from asbestotic injury had sued thousands of defendants. The expansion of the number of defendants was driven by the primary asbestos products defendants, such as Johns Manville, Celotex, and more than 70 others, declaring bankruptcy in order to restructure and remove asbestos liabilities from their day-to-day operations.

Asbestos has many of the characteristics of toxic torts that distinguish them from other personal injury litigation: (1) plaintiffs suffer from disease rather than traumatic injury; (2) they are exposed to varying doses of asbestos that are hard to ascertain in retrospect; (3) the diseases from which plaintiffs suffer have long latencies—the time from first exposure until the disease manifests itself—ranging from 20 to 50 years; (4) some of the diseases, such as lung cancer, have causes other than exposure to asbestos, although some are "signature diseases"; and (5) plaintiffs are exposed to multiple defendants' asbestos products. It is this last characteristic that creates an additional set of causal issues in toxic tort cases. In this Chapter, we address these issues, issues that began to emerge with the first appellate case to affirm a judgment for an asbestos plaintiff.

BOREL v. FIBREBOARD PAPER PRODUCTS CORP.

United States Court of Appeals, Fifth Circuit, 1973.
493 F.2d 1076.

WISDOM, CIRCUIT JUDGE:

This product liability case involves the scope of an asbestos manufacturer's duty to warn industrial insulation workers of dangers associated with the use of asbestos.

Clarence Borel, an industrial insulation worker, sued certain manufacturers of insulation materials containing asbestos to recover damages for injuries caused by the defendants' alleged breach of duty in failing to warn of the dangers involved in handling asbestos. Borel alleged that he had contracted the diseases of asbestosis and mesothelioma as a result of his exposure to the defendants' products over a thirty-three year [period] beginning in 1936 and ending in 1969. The jury returned a verdict in favor of Borel on the basis of strict liability. We affirm.

I.

Clarence Borel began working as an industrial insulation worker in 1936. During his career, he was employed at numerous places, usually in Texas, until disabled by the disease of asbestosis in 1969. Borel's employment necessarily exposed him to heavy concentrations of asbestos dust generated by insulation materials. In his pre-trial deposition, Borel testified that at the end of a day working with insulation material containing asbestos his clothes were usually so dusty he could "just barely pick them up without shaking them." Borel stated: "You just move them just a little and there is going to be dust, and I blowed this dust out of my nostrils by handfuls at the end of the day, trying to use water too, I even used Mentholatum in my nostrils to keep some of the dust from going down in my throat, but it is impossible to get rid of all of it. Even your clothes just stay dusty continually unless you blow it off with an air hose."

Borel said that he had known for years that inhaling asbestos dust "was bad for me" and that it was vexatious and bothersome, but that he never realized that it could cause any serious or terminal illness. * * *

When asked about the use of respirators, Borel replied that they were not furnished during his early work years. Although respirators were later made available on some jobs, insulation workers usually were not required to wear them and had to make a special request if they wanted one. Borel stated that he and other insulation workers found that the respirators furnished [to] them were uncomfortable, could not be worn in hot weather, and—"you can't breathe with the respirator." Borel further noted that no respirator in use during his lifetime could prevent the inhalation of asbestos dust. * * *

* * *

On January 19, 1969, Borel was hospitalized and a lung biopsy performed. Borel's condition was diagnosed as pulmonary asbestosis. Since the disease was considered irreversible, Borel was sent home. Borel testified in his deposition that this was the first time he knew that he had asbestosis.

Borel's condition gradually worsened during the remainder of 1969. On February 11, 1970, Borel underwent surgery for the removal of his right lung. The examining doctors determined that Borel had a form of [cancer] known as mesothelioma, which had been caused by asbestosis. As a result of these diseases, Borel later died before the district case reached the trial stage.

The medical testimony adduced at trial indicates that inhaling asbestos dust in industrial conditions, even with relatively light exposure, can produce the disease of asbestosis. The disease is difficult to diagnose in its early stages because there is a long latent period between initial exposure and apparent effect. This latent period may vary according to individual idiosyncrasy, duration and intensity of exposure, and the type of asbestos used. In some cases, the disease may manifest itself in less than ten years after initial exposure. In general, however, it does not manifest itself until ten to twenty-five or more years after initial exposure. This latent period is explained by the fact that asbestos fibers, once inhaled, remain in place in the lung, causing a tissue reaction that is slowly progressive and apparently irreversible. Even if no additional asbestos fibers are inhaled, tissue changes may continue undetected for decades. By the time the disease is diagnosable, a considerable period of time has elapsed since the date of the injurious exposure. Furthermore, the effect of the disease may be cumulative since each exposure to asbestos dust can result in additional tissue changes. A worker's present condition is the biological product of many years of exposure to asbestos dust, with both past and recent exposures contributing to the overall effect. All of these factors combine to make it impossible, as a practical matter, to determine which exposure or exposures to asbestos dust caused the disease.

A second disease, mesothelioma, is a form of [cancer] caused by exposure to asbestos. It affects the pleural and peritoneal cavities, and there is a similarly long period between initial contact and apparent effect. As with asbestosis, it is difficult to determine which exposure to asbestos dust is responsible for the disease.

At issue in this case is the extent of the defendants' knowledge of the dangers associated with insulation products containing asbestos. We pause, therefore, to summarize the evidence relevant to this question.

Asbestosis has been recognized as a disease for well over fifty years.[3] The first reported cases of asbestosis were among asbestos textile workers. In 1924, Cooke in England discovered a case of asbestosis in a person who

---

3. Asbestos has been known to man since ancient times. As a generic term, it applies to a number of inorganic, fibrous, silicate minerals that possess a crystalline structure. * * * Asbestos insulation material has been commercially produced since at least 1874.

had spent twenty years weaving asbestos textile products. In the next decade, numerous similar cases were observed and discussed in medical journals. An investigation of the problem among textile factory workers was undertaken in Great Britain in 1928 and 1929. In the United States, the first official claim for compensation associated with asbestos was in 1927. By the mid–1930's, the hazard of asbestosis as a pneumoconiotic dust was universally accepted. Cases of asbestosis in insulation workers were reported in this country as early as 1934. The U.S. Public Health Service fully documented the significant risk involved in asbestos textile factories in a report by Dreesen et al., in 1938. The authors urged elimination of hazardous exposures.

The first large-scale survey of asbestos insulation workers was undertaken in the United States by Fleischer–Drinker et al., in 1945. The authors examined insulation workers in eastern Navy shipyards and found only three cases of asbestosis. They concluded that "asbestos covering of naval vessels is a relatively safe operation." Significantly, ninety-five percent of those examined had worked at the trade for less than ten years. Since asbestosis is usually not diagnosable until ten to twenty years after initial exposure, the authors' conclusion has been criticized as misleading. Perhaps recognizing this possibility, the authors cautioned that the study did not "give a composite picture of the asbestos dust that a worker may breathe over a period of years," and that "if pipe coverers had worked steadily [under conditions] where the amount of asbestos dust in the air was consistently high, the incidence of asbestosis among these workers would have been considerable greater." The authors stated that "the suggestions relative to exhaust ventilation and respiratory protection are therefore of value in maintaining this low incidence of asbestosis."

In 1947, the American Conference of Governmental Industrial Hygienists, a quasi-official body responsible for making recommendations concerning industrial hygiene, issued guidelines suggesting threshold limit values for exposure to asbestos dust. In its first report, the ACGIH recommended that there should be no more than five million parts per cubic foot of air. It later determined in 1968 that the threshold limit value should be reduced to two million.

Throughout the 1950's and 1960's, further studies and medical reports on asbestosis were published. In 1965, I.J. Selikoff and his colleagues published a study entitled "The Occurrence of Asbestosis Among Insulation Workers in the United States." The authors examined 1,522 members of an insulation workers union in the New York–New Jersey metropolitan area. Evidence of pulmonary asbestosis was found in almost half the men examined. Among those with more than forty years experience, abnormalities were found in over ninety percent. The authors concluded that "asbestosis and its complications are significant hazards among insulation workers." Other studies have since confirmed these findings.

The plaintiff introduced evidence tending to establish that the defendant manufacturers either were, or should have been, fully aware of the many articles and studies on asbestosis. The evidence also indicated, however, that during Borel's working career no manufacturer ever warned contractors or insulation workers, including Borel, of the dangers associated with inhaling asbestos dust or informed them of the ACGIH's threshold limit values for exposure to asbestos dust. Furthermore, no manufacturer ever tested the effect of their products on the workers using them or attempted to discover whether the exposure of insulation workers to asbestos dust exceeded the suggested threshold limits.

On October 20, 1969, Borel initiated the present diversity action in the United States District Court for the Eastern District of Texas. Borel named as defendants eleven manufacturers of asbestos insulation materials used by him during his working career. He settled with four defendants before trial. The trial court instructed a verdict as to a fifth. * * * Borel died before trial * * *.

The plaintiff sought to hold the defendants liable for negligence, gross negligence, and breach of warranty or strict liability. The negligent acts alleged in the complaint were: (1) failure to take reasonable precautions or to exercise reasonable care to warn Borel of the danger to which he was exposed as a worker when using the defendant's asbestos insulation products; (2) failure to inform Borel as to what would be safe and sufficient wearing apparel and proper protective equipment and appliances or method of handling and using the various products; (3) failure to test the asbestos products in order to ascertain the dangers involved in their use; and (4) failure to remove the products from the market upon ascertaining that such products would cause asbestosis. The plaintiff also alleged that the defendants should be strictly liable in warranty and tort. The plaintiff contended that the defendants' products were unreasonably dangerous because of the failure to provide adequate warnings of the foreseeable dangers associated with them.

The defendants denied the allegations in the plaintiff's complaint and interposed the defenses of contributory negligence and assumption of risk.

The trial court submitted the case to the jury on general verdicts accompanied by a special interrogatory as to Borel's contributory negligence. As to the negligence count, the jury found that all the defendants, except Pittsburgh and Armstrong, were negligent but that none of the defendants had been grossly negligent. It found also, however, that Borel had been contributorily negligent.

As to the strict liability count, the jury found that all the defendants were liable and determined that the total damages were $79,436.24. Since four defendants originally named in the complaint had previously settled, paying a total of $20,902.20, the trial court gave full credit for the sums paid in settlement and held the remaining six defendants jointly and severally liable for the balance of $58,534.04. The defendants appealed.

II.

At the outset, we meet the question whether the trial court properly instructed the jury on strict liability. Since federal jurisdiction is based on diversity of citizenship, the substantive law of the forum state, Texas, controls. Erie R.R. Co. v. Tompkins, 1938, 304 U.S. 64, 58 S.Ct. 817, 82 L.Ed. 1188.

Under Texas law, a manufacturer of a defective product may be liable to a user or consumer in either warranty or tort. With respect to personal injuries caused by a defective product, the Texas Supreme Court has adopted the theory of strict liability in tort as expressed in section 402A of the Restatement (Second) of Torts (1964). * * *

* * *

Here, the plaintiff alleged that the defendants' product was unreasonably dangerous because of the failure to give adequate warnings of the known or knowable dangers involved. As explained in comment j to section 402A, a seller has a responsibility to inform users and consumers of dangers which the seller either knows or should know at the time the product is sold. The requirement that the danger be reasonably foreseeable, or scientifically discoverable, is an important limitation of the seller's liability.[22] In general, "[t]he rule of strict liability subjects the seller to liability to the user or consumer even though he has exercised all possible care in the preparation and sale of the product." Section 402A, Comment a. This is not the case where the product is alleged to be unreasonably dangerous because of a failure to give adequate warnings. Rather, a seller is under a duty to warn of only those dangers that are reasonably foreseeable. The requirement of foreseeability coincides with the standard of due care in negligence cases in that a seller must exercise reasonable care and foresight to discover a danger in his product *and to warn users and consumers of that danger.*

* * *

* * * The utility of an insulation product containing asbestos may outweigh the known or foreseeable risk to the insulation workers and thus justify its marketing. The product could still be unreasonably dangerous, however, if unaccompanied by adequate warnings. An insulation worker, no less than any other product user, has a right to decide whether to expose himself to the risk.

Furthermore, in cases such as the instant case, the manufacturer is held to the knowledge and skill of an expert. This is relevant in determining (1) whether the manufacturer knew or should have known the danger, and (2) whether the manufacturer was negligent in failing to communicate this superior knowledge to the user or consumer of its product. Wright v. Carter Products, Inc., 2 Cir. 1957, 244 F.2d 53. The manufacturer's status as expert means that at a minimum he must keep abreast of scientific knowledge, discoveries, and advances and is presumed to know what is

---

22. Several commentators, including Dean Keeton, have argued that the seller should be strictly liable if the sale of the product is under circumstances that would subject someone to an unreasonable risk in fact. Under this standard, the fact that the maker was excusably unaware of the extent of the danger would be irrelevant. *See* Keeton, P., Inadequacy of Information, 48 Tex.L.Rev. 398, 404, 409 (1970).

imparted thereby. But even more importantly, a manufacturer has a duty to test and inspect his product. The extent of research and experiment must be commensurate with the dangers involved. A product must not be made available to the public without disclosure of those dangers that the application of reasonable foresight would reveal. Nor may a manufacturer rely unquestioningly on others to sound the hue and cry concerning a danger in its product. Rather, each manufacturer must bear the burden of showing that its own conduct was proportionate to the scope of its duty.

* * *

III.

We now turn to the question whether the trial court erred in denying the defendants' motions for a directed verdict and for judgment notwithstanding the verdict. In diversity cases, a federal rather than a state test is applied to determine whether there was sufficient evidence to create a jury question. * * *

* * *

A. First, we approach the question whether the danger to Borel and other insulation workers was foreseeable at the time the products causing Borel's injury were sold. The defendants' position is that they did not breach their duty to warn because the danger from inhaling asbestos was not foreseeable until about 1968 and that, in view of the long latent period of the disease, Borel must have contracted asbestosis well before that date.

To begin, we note that the disease of asbestosis is cumulative. Thus, both Borel's earliest exposure to asbestos dust, occurring in the late 1930's, and his most recent exposure, occurring in 1968, could have contributed to his overall condition. The defendants' failure to warn of the dangers of the exposures occurring in 1968 may have resulted in an actionable injury to Borel. But even if it is assumed that Borel's condition was attributable principally to his earlier exposures, the defendants argument still fails since there is ample evidence in the record that the danger of inhaling asbestos, including the disease of asbestosis, was widely recognized at least as early as the 1930's. An expert witness, Dr. Hans Weill, testified that prior to 1935 there were literally "dozens and dozens" of articles on asbestos and its effect on man. Dr. Clark Cooper, an expert witness for the defendants, stated that it was known in the 1930's that inhaling asbestos dust caused asbestosis and that the danger could be controlled by maintaining a modest level of exposure. Dr. Cooper testified as follows:

"Q. The state of knowledge in the 1930's, let's say, in your opinion was asbestosis as a disease known about and recognized as a danger caused by inhaling asbestos dust?

"A. Yes.

"Q. And would you say that would have been rather common knowledge known in the 1930's?

"A.   Yes, I would say that. The answer to the would be yes."

As stated in our recital of the facts, several studies published during the 1930's and 1940's reported the danger to asbestos plant workers and others exposed to asbestos dust and urged precautionary measures to eliminate hazardous concentrations. The American Conference of Governmental Industrial Hygienists, beginning in 1947, issued guidelines suggesting threshold limit values for exposure to asbestos dust. Even the Fleischer–Drinker report in 1945, relied on by the defendants, cautioned that exposure to high concentrations of asbestos dust could cause asbestosis and recommended the use of ventilation and respiratory protection devices.

The evidence also tended to establish that none of the defendants ever tested its product to determine its effect on industrial insulation workers. Nor did any defendant ever attempt to determine whether the exposure of insulation workers or others to asbestos dust exceeded the A.C.G.I.H.'s recommended threshold limit values, or indeed, whether those standards were accurate or reliable.

As previously mentioned, the foreseeability of the danger must be measured in light of the manufacturer's status as an expert and the manufacturer's duty to test its product. In these circumstances, we think the jury was entitled to find that the danger to Borel and other insulation workers from inhaling asbestos dust was foreseeable to the defendants at the time the products causing Borel's injuries were sold.

* * *

The jury found that the unreasonably dangerous condition of the defendants' product was the proximate cause of Borel's injury. This necessarily included a finding that, had adequate warnings been provided, Borel would have chosen to avoid the danger.

* * *

C.   We next consider whether there was substantial evidence to support the jury's finding that each defendant was the cause in fact of injury to Borel. The traditional rule is that a defendant's conduct is the cause of the event if it was a substantial factor in bringing it about. Second Restatement of Torts, §§ 431, 433. Whether the defendant's conduct was a substantial factor is a question for the jury, unless the court determines that reasonable men could not differ.

In the instant case, it is impossible, as a practical matter, to determine with absolute certainty which particular exposure to asbestos dust resulted in injury to Borel. It is undisputed, however, that Borel contracted asbestosis from inhaling asbestos dust and that he was exposed to the products of all the defendants on many occasions. It was also established that the effect of exposure to asbestos dust is cumulative, that is, each exposure may result in an additional and separate injury. We think, therefore, that on the basis of strong circumstantial evidence the jury could find that each defendant was the cause in fact of some injury to Borel.

Relying on expert testimony that asbestosis does not usually manifest itself until fifteen, twenty, or even twenty-five years after initial exposure, Pittsburgh Corning Company and Armstrong Cork Company contend that they cannot be liable because Borel was not exposed to their products until after 1962 and 1966 respectively. As we have pointed out, however, the length of this latent period varies according to individual idiosyncracy, duration and intensity of exposure, and the type of asbestos used; in some cases the effect of the exposure may manifest itself in less than five or ten years. Thus, even the most recent exposures could have added to or accelerated Borel's overall condition.

IV.

Having concluded that each defendant was the cause in fact of some injury to Borel, we now come to the question of apportionment of damages. In general, a defendant is liable only for that portion of the harm which he in fact caused. A problem arises, however, where, as here, several causes combine to produce an injury that is not reasonably capable of being divided. In the instant case, the trial court resolved this issue by holding the defendants jointly and severally liable for the entire harm. Asserting error, the defendants argue that if the injury cannot be reasonably apportioned, the plaintiff must bear the entire loss unless it can be shown that the tortfeasors acted in concert or with unity of design.

The defendants' argument is best illustrated by Sun Oil v. Robicheaux, Tex.Com.App.1930, 23 S.W.2d 713, a case in which several defendants, acting independently, were polluting a bayou from which the plaintiff was taking water for irrigation. The court held that an action at law for damages could not be maintained jointly against the defendants and that each was liable only for the part of the injury which he caused. The court stated:

> Under such circumstances each tortfeasor is liable only for the part of the injury of damages caused by his own wrong; that is, where a person contributes to an injury along with others, he must respond in damages, but if he acts independently, and not in concert of action with other persons in causing such injury, he is liable only for the damages which directly and proximately result from his own act, and the fact that it may be difficult to define the damages caused by the wrongful act of each person who independently contributed to the final result does not affect the rule.

23 S.W.2d at 715.

The effect of the *Robicheaux* rule was to make it impossible to join several wrongdoers whose independent acts caused an injury which, although theoretically divisible, was indivisible as a practical matter. The burden was placed on the plaintiff to prove with reasonable certainty what portion of the total damage was attributable to each defendant. Failing that, recovery would be denied even though it was undisputed that each defendant caused some harm.

In 1952, the *Robicheaux* case was expressly overruled by the Texas Supreme Court in Landers v. East Texas Salt Water Disposal Co., 151 Tex. 251, 248 S.W.2d 731. In that case, an oil company and a salt water disposal company each owned pipe lines running near the plaintiff's land. At about the same time, each pipe line broke, pouring oil and salt water onto the plaintiff's land and into his lake. The plaintiff sought to hold the defendants liable for the entire harm. In upholding the joinder of the two defendants, the court noted that prior cases "seem to have embraced the philosophy ... that it is better that the injured party lose all of his damages than that any of the several wrongdoers pay more of the damages than he individually and separately caused. If such has been the law, then from the standpoint of justice it should not have been; if it is now, it will not be hereafter." 248 S.W.2d at 734. The court then announced the new rule:

> Where the tortious acts of two or more wrongdoers join to produce an indivisible injury, that is, an injury which from its nature cannot be apportioned with reasonable certainty to the individual wrongdoers, all of the wrongdoers will be held jointly and severally liable for the entire damages and the injured party may proceed to judgment against any one separately or against all in one suit. *Id.*

The effect of the *Landers* case may be stated as follows: Where several defendants are shown to have each caused some harm, the burden of proof (or burden of going forward) shifts to each defendant to show what portion of the harm he caused. If the defendants are unable to show any reasonable basis for division, they are jointly and severally liable for the total damages.

* * *

Applying these principles to the present case, we conclude that the defendants may be held jointly and severally liable for the total damages.

* * *

[The court proceeded to address and reject a laundry list of other claims of error by the defendants relating to affirmative defenses, including the availability of contributory negligence as a defense to a strict liability claim, assumption of risk by the decedent, the existence of a statute of limitations bar to plaintiff's claim, and as the appropriate amount to credit the judgment defendants for the payments made by settling defendants. We address the affirmative defense matters in Chapter 10 and settlement credits in Chapter 7, section C.]

For the reasons stated, the decision of the district court is

Affirmed.

NOTES AND QUESTIONS

1. The extraordinary demands of the asbestos litigation led to many efforts to find legislative solutions and procedural mechanisms to ease the burden on courts. A number of judges have asked Congress to devise a remedy similar to the plan crafted for coal miners suffering from black lung disease. Black Lung Benefits Act, 26 U.S.C. § 9501. The most prominent of these pleas came from the Chief Justice in a concurring opinion in Ortiz v. Fibreboard Corp., 527 U.S. 815 (1999), where he called upon Congress to devise a legislative solution to the "elephantine mass of asbestos cases." Justice Rehnquist's request was not the first. Judge Garza made an earlier plea in the long-running *Cimino* litigation for Congress to fashion an administrative remedy. Cimino v. Raymark Indus., Inc., 151 F.3d 297, 335 (5th Cir.1998). Academics have also called for legislative solutions. See Paul Carrington, Asbestos Lessons: The Consequences of Asbestos Litigation, 26 Rev.Litig. 583, 605 (2007). For reviews of proposed legislative solutions see Francis Mc-Govern, Asbestos Legislation II: Section 524(G) Without Bankruptcy, 31 Pepp.L.Rev. 233 (2003); Patrick Hanlon, An Elegy for the FAIR Act, 12 Conn.Ins.L.J. 517 (2006).

In the absence of a legislative remedy, judges have searched for procedural mechanisms to ease the burden imposed on courts. Suspended dockets for plaintiffs who had not yet suffered any clinical symptoms, mass settlements, industry-wide settlement facilities, mandatory and option class actions, extrapolations of damages determined in trials of a sample of plaintiffs to a larger class of victims, multidistrict litigation, consolidation of multiple cases (and plaintiffs) for trial, and collateral estoppel were all tried, most unsuccessfully, leaving asbestos litigation to grind on (and increasing numbers of defendants to seek protection in bankruptcy court).

2. Ward Stephenson, a workers' compensation lawyer, represented Clarence Borel. Borel was Stephenson's second asbestos client. Stephenson's efforts on behalf of Borel that resulted in the first asbestos verdict and appeal that set the stage for the subsequent asbestos litigation are colorfully recounted in Paul Brodeur, Outrageous Misconduct (1985).

3. Clarence Borel was exposed to asbestos insulation from 1936 through 1968. Based on the chronology of recognition of the dangers for asbestos, when was the risk of asbestosis reasonably foreseeable to insulation manufacturers? Recall that the court concluded that for both the plaintiff's negligence and strict liability failure to warn claims, he must prove the risk was foreseeable. In a consolidated trial of five different plaintiffs' claims, in which a separate jury was empaneled for each plaintiff, but each jury heard the same evidence, the juries' answers to this question ranged from 1935 to 1965. See Chapter 14, pp. 787–792.

If the danger of asbestosis was reasonably foreseeable, should that suffice for other diseases, such as the mesothelioma that Borel also contracted? The *Borel* court did not address that question, ignoring the chronology of recognition of the risk of mesothelioma from asbestos exposure, which was considerably later than asbestosis because of its longer latency period and the failure of doctors and medical examiners in the mid-twentieth century to recognize it as a disease distinct from other more common cancers.

4. Under Texas law, both the negligence claim—failure to warn—and the strict liability claim require that the danger be foreseeable. Note, however, they differed in the way they treated the plaintiff's contributory negligence. Borel's negligence claim was barred because of his contributory negligence. He was successful only because contributory negligence had no effect on his strict liability claims. Those outcomes would be substantially different today, after the advent of comparative fault and responsibility, which we address in Chapter 10.

5. *Casual issues: signature diseases.* In one important sense the causal issues in *Borel* were easy because both asbestosis and mesothelioma are "signature diseases." The plaintiff did not have to prove that some substance other than asbestos did not cause his disease. So, what are the causal issues in asbestos? How many different sub-issues can you identify that exist in resolving the question of whether defendant's tortious conduct caused plaintiff's harm?

6. *Divisible and indivisible injuries.* You will recall from your first-year Torts class that damages are thought to be divisible or indivisible. In *Borel*, the defendants argued that there was insufficient evidence that each was a cause of Borel's harm. The court employed the "substantial factor" test from the Second Restatement and concluded that because asbestosis is a cumulative disease—"that is, each exposure may result in an additional and separate injury"—the jury could find that exposure to each defendant's asbestos made some contribution to the severity of Borel's asbestosis. However, later in the opinion the court described asbestosis as an "indivisible injury." Can asbestosis be both? In what sense is asbestosis an indivisible injury? In what sense is it a divisible injury?

Section 26 of the Third Restatement of Torts: Apportionment of Liability provides the following guidance in determining whether or not an injury is divisible:

> § 26. Apportionment Of Liability When Damages Can Be Divided By Causation
>
> (a) When damages for an injury can be divided by causation, the factfinder first divides them into their indivisible component parts and separately apportions liability for each indivisible component part under Topics 1 through 4.
>
> (b) Damages can be divided by causation when the evidence provides a reasonable basis for the factfinder to determine:
>
>> (1) that any legally culpable conduct of a party or other relevant person to whom the factfinder assigns a percentage of responsibility was a legal cause of less than the entire damages for which the plaintiff seeks recovery and
>>
>> (2) the amount of damages separately caused by that conduct.
>
> Otherwise, the damages are indivisible and thus the injury is indivisible.

Restatement (Third) of Torts: Apportionment of Liability § 26 (2002). Section 26 replaced section 433A of the Second Restatement of Torts, which called for damages to be apportioned among two or more causes where there are distinct harms or there is a reasonable basis for determining the contribution of each cause to a single harm. How would the Second and Third Restatements apportion liability among defendants for plaintiff's asbestosis? By what reasoning did the court arrive at the conclusion that each defendant was jointly and severally liable for the entirety of Borel's asbestosis-related harm?

7. Borel suffered two separate injuries due to his asbestos exposure: asbestosis and mesothelioma. The court devoted almost all of its discussion to the former disease, which is a bit surprising given that it is the latter disease that killed Borel. The few references to mesothelioma seem to assume that for legal purposes the diseases are interchangeable. However, unlike asbestosis, mesothelioma and other cancers are not diseases whose severity is dependent on dose. Although the biology of cancer is not fully understood, many scientists subscribe to the "one hit" theory for cancer. That theory specifies that it is a single hit of an agent on a cell that transforms it into a cancer cell, which then multiplies and develops into the cancer. Should this difference matter in how we analyze causation? The next case deals with this issue.

RUTHERFORD v. OWENS–ILLINOIS, INC.

Supreme Court of California, 1997.
16 Cal.4th 953, 941 P.2d 1203, 67 Cal.Rptr.2d 16.

BAXTER, JUSTICE.

I. Introduction.

In this consolidated action for asbestos-related personal injuries and wrongful death brought and tried in Solano County, defendant Owens–Illinois, Inc. (Owens–Illinois) contends the trial court erred in instructing the liability phase jury pursuant to Solano County Complex Asbestos Litigation General Order No. 21.00. This instruction shifts the burden of proof to defendants in asbestos cases tried on a products liability theory to prove that their products were *not* a legal cause of the plaintiff's injuries, provided the plaintiff first establishes certain predicate facts, chief among them that the defendant manufactured or sold defective asbestos-containing products to which plaintiff was exposed, and that plaintiff's exposure to asbestos fibers generally was a legal cause of plaintiff's injury. The Court of Appeal concluded the trial court erred in giving the burden-shifting instruction.

* * *

We conclude the Court of Appeal correctly determined that the burden-shifting instruction should not have been given in this case. For reasons to be explained, we hold that in cases of asbestos-related cancer, a jury instruction shifting the burden of proof to asbestos defendants on the element of causation is generally unnecessary and incorrect under settled statewide principles of tort law. Proof of causation in such cases will always present inherent practical difficulties, given the long latency period of asbestos-related disease, and the occupational settings that commonly exposed the worker to multiple forms and brands of asbestos products with varying degrees of toxicity. In general, however, no insuperable barriers prevent an asbestos-related cancer plaintiff from demonstrating that exposure to the defendant's asbestos products was, in reasonable medical probability, a substantial factor in causing or contributing to his risk of developing cancer. We conclude that plaintiffs are required to prove no more than this. In particular, they need *not* prove with medical exactitude that fibers from a particular defendant's asbestos-containing products were those, or among those, that actually began the cellular process of malignancy. Instruction on the limits of the plaintiff's burden of proof of causation, together with the standardized instructions defining cause-in-fact causation under the substantial factor test (BAJI No. 3.76) and the doctrine of concurrent proximate legal causation (BAJI No. 3.77) will adequately apprise the jury of the elements required to establish causation. No burden-shifting instruction is necessary on the matter of proof of causation, and in the absence of such necessity, there is no justification or basis for shifting part of the plaintiff's burden of proof to the defendant to prove that it was not a legal cause of plaintiff's asbestos-related disease or injuries. (See *Summers v. Tice* (1948) 33 Cal.2d 80, 86, 199 P.2d 1 (*Summers*) [burden shift justified because without it all tortfeasors might escape liability and the injured plaintiff be left "remediless."].) However, as will be explained, the giving of the burden-shifting instruction in this case was harmless.

Ultimately, the sufficiency of the evidence of causation will depend on the factual circumstances of each case. Although the plaintiff must, in accordance with traditional tort principles, demonstrate to a reasonable medical probability that a product or products supplied by the defendant, to which he became exposed, were a substantial factor in causing his disease or risk of injuries, he is free to further establish that his particular asbestos disease is cumulative in nature, with many separate exposures each having constituted a "substantial factor" (BAJI No. 3.76) that contributed to his risk of injury. And although a defendant cannot escape *liability* simply because it cannot be determined with medical exactitude the precise contribution that exposure to fibers from defendant's products made to plaintiff's ultimate contraction of asbestos-related disease, all joint tortfeasors found liable as named defendants will remain entitled to limit *damages* ultimately assessed against them in accordance with established comparative fault and apportionment principles.

II. Factual and Procedural Background.

Charles Rutherford (Rutherford) was in the Air Force from 1935 to 1940, after which he became an apprentice sheet metal worker at the Mare Island Naval Shipyard (Mare Island). He worked in the sheet metal shop for several years, and then became an engineering technician working with ventilation before retiring from Mare Island after 40 years. * * *

In January 1988, three months before his death, Rutherford filed an asbestos-related personal injury action in Solano County Superior Court naming as defendants nineteen manufacturers and/or distributors of asbestos products, including the sole defendant in this appeal, Owens–Illinois. The original complaint alleged Rutherford had contracted lung cancer as a result of his exposure to defendants' asbestos products while on the job at Mare Island, and alleged causes of action for products liability, negligent and intentional infliction of emotional distress, and loss of consortium. After Rutherford died of lung cancer in April 1988, the complaint was amended to allege a wrongful death action * * *.

Plaintiffs' case was consolidated for trial with four other actions presenting the similar claims of various other plaintiffs * * *.

Under procedures adopted by the Solano County Superior Court for general use in complex asbestos litigation within that county, trial of these consolidated cases was bifurcated into "damages" and "liability" phases (heard by separate juries). In the first damages phase of trial, the jury was to determine, as to each plaintiff, whether exposure to asbestos was a proximate cause of injury (i.e., whether plaintiff was suffering from asbestos-related disease or, as here, plaintiffs' decedent had died from asbestos-related disease) and, if so, the total amount of resulting damages.

Plaintiffs presented medical evidence that Rutherford had died of asbestos-related lung cancer. He had worked aboard ships around asbestos insulators at Mare Island starting in 1940. Although Rutherford's answers to interrogatories reflected he had never himself worked as an installer of asbestos insulation, he nevertheless had been exposed to respirable asbestos dust on a daily basis during periods of his employment at Mare Island. * * * Evidence was also presented that Rutherford had smoked approximately a pack of cigarettes a day over a period of 30 or more years until he quit smoking in 1977. As will be explained, this evidence took on heightened relevance at the second "liability" phase of trial.

At the end of the first phase of trial, the jury answered the question, "Did the decedent, Charles Rutherford, have lung cancer legally caused by his inhalation of asbestos fibers?" in the affirmative. The jury returned a verdict finding that a total of $278,510 in economic damages had been incurred by plaintiffs, and $280,000 in noneconomic damages suffered by plaintiffs as a result of decedent's death. Owens–Illinois has not challenged the damages phase jury's verdict finding Rutherford's injuries and death were proximately caused by his exposure to asbestos, nor has it challenged the plaintiffs' total award of economic and noneconomic damages.

Between the first and second phases of trial, nearly all the defendants except Owens–Illinois settled with plaintiffs.[3] The second liability phase

---

3. The record reflects that before his death, Rutherford identified three additional asbestos manufacturers to whose products he believed he had been exposed: Johns–Manville, Unarco and Amatex. The parties suggest those manufacturers were not named as defendants because they were bankrupt. Owens–Illinois further states in its brief that of the 19 named defendants in the

thus involved only issues of Owens–Illinois's percentage of fault and apportionment of damages. At this phase of trial, the Rutherford plaintiffs elected to proceed under the burden-shifting instruction authorized, once again, under the procedures adopted by the Solano County Superior Court for general use in complex asbestos litigation within that county. * * * Briefly, the instruction, available in asbestos personal injury actions tried on a products liability theory, provides that if the plaintiff has proved that a particular asbestos supplier's product was "defective," that the plaintiff's injuries or death were legally caused by asbestos exposure *generally,* and that he was exposed to asbestos fibers from the defendant's product, the burden then shifts to the defendant to prove, if it can, that its product was not a legal cause of the plaintiff's injuries or death.

* * *

Medical testimony was also presented to establish that the plaintiffs' asbestos-related disease was "dose-related"—i.e., that the risk of developing asbestos-related cancer increased as the total occupational dose of inhaled asbestos fibers increased. Dr. Allan Smith, a professor of epidemiology, testified that asbestos-related lung cancers are dose-related diseases, and that all occupational exposures through the latency period can contribute to the risk of contracting the diseases. Owens–Illinois's own medical expert, Dr. Elliot Hinckes, testified that asbestos-related cancers are dose responsive, and that if a worker had occupational exposure to many different asbestos-containing products, each such exposure would contribute to the degree of risk of contracting asbestos-related lung cancer, although he testified further that a very light or brief exposure could be considered "insignificant or at least nearly so" in the "context" of other, very heavy exposures. There was no evidence in this case that Rutherford had been exposed predominantly to any one kind or brand of asbestos product. All of the evidence regarding Rutherford's asbestos exposure was specifically related to industrial-occupational exposure, i.e., exposure to asbestos products while they were being installed or removed at Mare Island.

Owens–Illinois was allowed to establish that other asbestos manufacturers, and the plaintiffs' various employers, shared comparative fault for the plaintiffs' long-term exposure to asbestos. Owens–Illinois was also permitted to present evidence that smoking was a "negligent" contributing factor to each plaintiff's condition. Undisputed evidence indicated that smoking sharply increases the risk of lung disease, including lung cancer, and works "synergistically" with asbestos exposure to enhance the severity of resulting damage to the lungs. The trial court's instructions made clear that each plaintiff's entire recovery must be reduced to the extent of his own comparative "negligence" contributing to his condition, because each had continued to smoke tobacco long after he had notice that

---

Rutherford action, "[o]nly one of these entities—Owens–Illinois—remained through trial, because the rest of them settled with, or were dismissed by plaintiffs. Thus . . . it was a case in which almost every defendant implicitly acknowledged its potential for liability."

smoking was hazardous to health, and that the long-term consumption of tobacco products could be a contributing cause of lung disease.

* * *

The liability phase jury was instructed to assign percentages of fault for each injury, adding up to a total of 100 percent, among (1) the plaintiff himself (here, plaintiffs' decedent); (2) Owens–Illinois; (3) other manufacturers of asbestos to which the plaintiff or decedent was exposed; and (4) each employer that contributed to the exposure. In Rutherford's case, the jury apportioned fault as follows: 1.2 percent to Owens–Illinois, 2.5 percent to Rutherford himself, and 96.3 percent to the remaining entities to which the jury was allowed to assign fault. After further adjustment for pretrial settlements, the Rutherford plaintiffs recovered a net judgment of $177,047 in economic damages and $2,160 in noneconomic damages against defendant Owens–Illinois.*

Owens–Illinois appealed. In its Court of Appeal briefs, Owens–Illinois asserted as trial error * * * the giving of the burden-shifting instruction, and several other unrelated evidentiary issues of no direct concern to us on review. * * *

* * *

[The Court of Appeal resolved that the burden-shifting instruction was erroneous.]

* * * We conclude the Court of Appeal correctly determined plaintiffs should not have been permitted to elect to proceed under the * * * burden-shifting instruction. We also find, however, that defendant has not demonstrated prejudice from the instructional error. Accordingly, we shall reverse the judgment of the Court of Appeal * * *.

III. Discussion.

1. *Preliminary Considerations; Solano County Superior Court's Local Rulemaking Authority in Complex Asbestos Litigation.*

Owens–Illinois urged the Court of Appeal to reverse the liability (second phase of trial) verdicts on the ground that the trial court improperly shifted the burden to defendant to prove that its products were not a legal cause of Rutherford's injuries and death. * * *

Upon plaintiffs' election, the trial court instructed the jury at the second liability phase of trial * * *. [A]t the commencement of the liability phase of an asbestos products liability action (tried under either the consumer expectation or risk/benefit theories of product liability), the plaintiff "shall elect whether to request that all defendants carry the burden of proof regarding the legal cause of the plaintiff's or plaintiff's

---

* [Proposition 51, adopted by the voters in 1968, provides that in a tort action governed by principles of comparative fault, a defendant shall not be jointly liable for the plaintiff's *noneconomic* damages, but shall only be severally liable for such damages "in direct proportion to the defendant's percentage of fault." (Civ. Code, § 1431.2, subd. (a).)—Eds.]

decedent's injury as to each said defendant. [¶] The plaintiff so requesting [the burden-shifting instruction] must, as to each defendant, prove by a preponderance of the evidence each of the following: [¶] a) That the asbestos product manufactured or distributed by said defendant was defective; [¶] b) That plaintiff's or plaintiff's decedent's injury was legally caused by his exposure to or contact with asbestos fibers, or products containing asbestos, and [¶] c) That plaintiff's exposure to or contact with asbestos fibers, or products containing asbestos, included exposure to or contact with such fibers or products manufactured or distributed by said defendant. [¶] The burden shall then shift to each defendant to prove by a preponderance of the evidence that this product was not a legal cause of the plaintiff's or plaintiff's decedent's injury. * * * "

     * * *

2. *Alternative Liability and Burden Shifting.*

We are in basic agreement with Owens–Illinois and those courts that have concluded asbestos plaintiffs can meet their burden of proving legal causation under traditional tort principles, without the need for an "alternative liability" burden-shifting instruction. Indeed, the burden-shifting instruction offered * * * appears in conflict with certain aspects of these basic tort principles, and with standardized instructions on which the liability phase jury in this case was also instructed.

Generally, the burden falls on the plaintiff to establish causation. (*Sindell v. Abbott Laboratories* (1980) 26 Cal.3d 588, 597, 163 Cal.Rptr. 132, 607 P.2d 924 (*Sindell*).) Most asbestos personal injury actions are tried on a products liability theory. In the context of products liability actions, the plaintiff must prove that the defective products supplied by the defendant were a substantial factor in bringing about his or her injury. (*Cronin v. J.B.E. Olson Corp.* (1972) 8 Cal.3d 121, 127, 104 Cal.Rptr. 433, 501 P.2d 1153).

California has definitively adopted the substantial factor test of the Restatement Second of Torts for cause-in-fact determinations. (*Mitchell v. Gonzales* (1991) 54 Cal.3d 1041, 1044, fn. 2, 1052, fn. 7, 1 Cal.Rptr.2d 913, 819 P.2d 872.) Under that standard, a cause in fact is something that is a substantial factor in bringing about the injury. (Rest. 2d Torts, § 431, subd. (a), p. 428; BAJI No. 3.76 (8th ed.1994).) The substantial factor standard generally produces the same results as does the "but for" rule of causation which states that a defendant's conduct is a cause of the injury if the injury would not have occurred "but for" that conduct. (Prosser & Keeton on Torts (5th ed.1984) § 41, p. 266.) The substantial factor standard, however, has been embraced as a clearer rule of causation—one which subsumes the "but for" test while reaching beyond it to satisfactorily address other situations, such as those involving independent or concurrent causes in fact.

The term "substantial factor" has not been judicially defined with specificity, and indeed it has been observed that it is "neither possible nor desirable to reduce it to any lower terms." (Prosser & Keeton on Torts, *supra*, § 41, p. 267.) This court has suggested that a force which plays only an "infinitesimal" or "theoretical" part in bringing about injury, damage, or loss is not a substantial factor. Undue emphasis should not be placed on the term "substantial." For example, the substantial factor standard, formulated to aid plaintiffs as a broader rule of causality than the "but for" test, has been invoked by defendants whose conduct is clearly a "but for" cause of plaintiff's injury but is nevertheless urged as an insubstantial contribution to the injury. (Prosser & Keeton on Torts (5th ed., 1988 supp.) § 41, pp. 43–44.) Misused in this way, the substantial factor test "undermines the principles of comparative negligence, under which a party is responsible for his or her share of negligence and the harm caused thereby." (*Mitchell v. Gonzales, supra,* 54 Cal.3d at p. 1053, 1 Cal.Rptr.2d 913, 819 P.2d 872.)

An instruction shifting the burden of proof on causation constitutes a fundamental departure from these principles, and can only be justified on a showing of necessity for application of the specific theory of causation— alternative liability—first approved by this court in the celebrated case of *Summers, supra,* 33 Cal. 2d 80, 199 P.2d 1. * * *

Summers involved a hunting accident in which two quail hunters negligently fired their shotguns in the direction of the plaintiff at about the same time. A single birdshot pellet struck plaintiff in the eye, causing serious injury. It was impossible to determine which of the negligent hunters had fired the single pellet, but it was clear only one of them had to have directly caused the injury. This court concluded both hunters could be found jointly and severally liable for plaintiff's injuries. We observed that each defendant was a wrongdoer who had acted negligently toward an innocent plaintiff, and that together the two had brought about a situation in which the negligence of one of them had injured the plaintiff. Under the then applicable traditional proximate cause standards, the plaintiff would have been unable to establish which defendant had caused his eye injury. To remedy this problem, the lower court shifted to each defendant the burden of proving, if he could, that he was *not* the cause of plaintiff's injury. We approved of the procedure.

A number of important factors present in *Summers* thus combined to lead this court to conclude that it would be fair and just to apply the theory of alternative liability and its concomitant burden-shifting rule. First, all the tortfeasors were named as defendants and before the court— the two hunters. In certainty one of them had caused the plaintiff's eye injury; there were no other potential tortfeasors. Second, it was established in *Summers* that each hunter was a wrongdoer who had acted negligently in firing his shotgun in the direction of the plaintiff at about the same time. Nor were there any facts to distinguish the nature or extent of the negligent conduct of each defendant; they were coequals from the standpoint of fault. Third, the plaintiff's injury was instantaneous and indivisible (as opposed to a latent, progressively deteriorating injury). Fourth, there was no contributing or concurrent causation—one of the hunters was the cause-in-fact of the entirety of plaintiff's injury resulting from a single shotgun pellet lodging in his eye. There was no factual basis on which to *apportion* "fault" or liability for the injury. Finally, given the nature of the injury, the plaintiff in *Summers* was without any evidentiary means whatsoever to prove from which hunter's shotgun the injurious single pellet had been fired. In short, given the facts of *Summers,* without the burden-shifting instruction the tortfeasors would have escaped liability, leaving the injured plaintiff without the legal means to seek redress for his negligently inflicted injuries.

The *Summers* alternative liability theory was incorporated in the Restatement Second of Torts, section 433B, subdivision (3) pages 441–44 (Section 433B(3)), which provides: "Where the conduct of two or more actors is tortious, and it is proved that harm has been caused to plaintiff by only one of them, but there is uncertainty as to which one has caused it, the burden is upon each actor to prove that he has not caused the harm."

The express language of Section 433B(3) therefore envisions the theory of alternative liability to be applicable as between two or more defendants only where all have been shown to be tortfeasors in the first instance, and where the conduct of only one of them caused the harm. The comments to Section 433B(3) are in accord. Comment g to Section 433B(3), at page 446, states that the burden shifts to the defendant only if the plaintiff can demonstrate that all defendants "acted tortiously and that the harm resulted from the conduct of . . . one of them." And comment h indicates that the theory of alternative liability is generally limited to cases where the defendants' conduct creates a substantially similar risk of harm ("The cases thus far decided in which the rule stated in Subsection (3) has been applied have all been cases in which all of the actors involved have been joined as defendants. All of these cases have involved conduct simultaneous in time, or substantially so, and all of them have involved conduct of substantially the same character, creating substantially the same risk of harm, on the part of each actor. . . ."). (*Ibid.*)

The majority of courts have refused to extend the doctrine of alternative liability and its burden-shifting rule to asbestos-related latent personal injury actions brought against multiple suppliers of asbestos products. These cases have found the factors which support application of *Summers* alternative liability and burden shifting readily distinguishable from the facts typically involved in complex asbestos litigation.

For example, in *Goldman v. Johns–Manville Sales Corp.* (Ohio 1987) 33 Ohio St.3d 40, 514 N.E.2d 691 (*Goldman*), the Supreme Court of Ohio rejected application of *Summers* alternative liability/burden shifting to asbestos personal injury actions, concluding that given the nature of such litigation, it is often the case that the culpable party or parties will not be before the court, making a *Summers*-type burden shift unfair to the named defendants standing trial. The *Goldman* court observed that "[i]n asbestos litigation, it is often uncertain that the culpable party is before the court * * *."

The *Goldman* court also observed that the wide variation in form and toxicity of asbestos products further distinguishes asbestos cases from the facts of *Summers,* making the burden-shifting rule inappropriate in such cases. "Asbestos-containing products do not create similar risks of harm because there are several varieties of asbestos fibers, and they are used in various quantities, even in the same class of product." (*Goldman, supra,* 514 N.E.2d at p. 697.)

* * *

In *Sindell, supra,* 26 Cal.3d 588, 163 Cal.Rptr. 132, 607 P.2d 924, this court too *rejected* application of a pure *Summers* alternative liability theory—in the case that went on to establish an important variation of that doctrine, "market share liability"—under circumstances where all potential tortfeasors that may have actually caused plaintiff's injuries were not before the court as named defendants in the lawsuit.

* * *

Although many of the above cited cases focus on the fact that not all potential tortfeasors may be before the court to ensure that the *actual* tortfeasor will be held liable if it cannot disprove its role in causing plaintiff's injuries, or that different toxicities and brands of asbestos products and their differing effects on different asbestos-related diseases make it inappropriate to apply a *Summers* alternative liability/burden-shifting rule to asbestos cases, we believe the most fundamental reason why a burden-shifting instruction is unnecessary to proving an asbestos-related cancer latent injury case becomes clear when the limits on the plaintiff's burden of proof on causation are properly understood. A fuller analysis of the medical problems and uncertainties accompanying factual proof of causation in an asbestos cancer case will serve to illustrate the point.

At the most fundamental level, there is scientific uncertainty regarding the biological mechanisms by which inhalation of certain microscopic fibers of asbestos leads to lung cancer and mesothelioma. Although in some cases medical experts have testified that asbestos-related cancer is the final result of the fibrosis (scarring) process (see *Armstrong World Industries, Inc. v. Aetna Casualty & Surety Co.* (1996) 45 Cal.App.4th 1, 37–39, 52 Cal.Rptr.2d 690), a general reference on the subject describes the link between fibrosis and carcinogenesis as "a debated issue for which further extensive analysis is needed." (1 Encyclopedia of Human Biology (1991) Asbestos, p. 423.) An answer to this biological question would be legally relevant, because if each episode of scarring contributes cumulatively to the formation of a tumor or the conditions allowing such formation, each significant exposure by the plaintiff to asbestos fibers would be deemed a cause of the plaintiff's cancer; if, on the other hand, only one fiber or group of fibers actually causes the formation of a tumor, the others would not be legal causes of the plaintiff's injuries.

If, moreover, the question were answered in favor of the latter (single cause) theory, another question—apparently unanswerable—would arise:

which particular fiber or fibers actually caused the cancer to begin forming. Because of the irreducible uncertainty of the answer, asbestos-related cancer would, under the single-fiber theory of carcinogenesis, be an example of alternative causation, i.e., a result produced by a single but indeterminable member of a group of possible causes. The disease would thus be analogous to the facts of the hunting accident in *Summers, supra,* 33 Cal.2d 80, 199 P.2d 1.

Apart from the uncertainty of the causation, at a much more concrete level uncertainty frequently exists whether the plaintiff was even exposed to dangerous fibers from a product produced, distributed or installed by a particular defendant. The long latency periods of asbestos-related cancers mean that memories are often dim and records missing or incomplete regarding the use and distribution of specific products. In some industries, many different asbestos-containing products have been used, often including several similar products at the same time periods and worksites. Not uncommonly, plaintiffs have been unable to prove direct exposure to a given defendant's product.

Finally, at a level of abstraction somewhere between the historical question of exposure and the unknown biology of carcinogenesis, the question arises whether the risk of cancer created by a plaintiff's exposure to a particular asbestos-containing product was significant enough to be considered a legal cause of the disease. Taking into account the length, frequency, proximity and intensity of exposure, the peculiar properties of the individual product, any other potential causes to which the disease could be attributed (e.g., other asbestos products, cigarette smoking), and perhaps other factors affecting the assessment of comparative risk, should inhalation of fibers from the particular product be deemed a "substantial factor" in causing the cancer?

The burden of proof as to exposure is not disputed in this case. Even with the jury instruction at issue, plaintiffs bore the burden of proof on the issue of exposure to the defendant's product; plaintiffs do not complain of that burden, which is properly theirs under California law. Only in one circumstance have we relieved toxic tort plaintiffs of the burden of showing exposure to the defendant's product: where hundreds of producers had made the same drug from an identical formula, practically precluding patients from identifying the makers of the drugs they took. (*Sindell, supra,* 26 Cal.3d at pp. 610–613, 163 Cal.Rptr. 132, 607 P.2d 924.) Plaintiffs do not here argue that a comparable situation exists with asbestos makers justifying adoption of a market-share liability theory.

Nor is the burden of proof as to the mechanism of carcinogenesis disputed here; defendant *concedes* that plaintiff does not bear such a burden to "connect the manufacturer and the fibers." Asbestos plaintiffs, Owens–Illinois acknowledges, "are *not* required to identify the manufacturer of specific fibers" that caused the cancer. We agree: Plaintiffs cannot be expected to prove the scientifically unknown details of carcinogenesis, or trace the unknowable path of a given asbestos fiber. But the impossibility of such proof does not dictate use of a burden shift. Instead, we can bridge this gap in the humanly knowable by holding that plaintiffs may prove causation in asbestos-related cancer cases by demonstrating that the plaintiff's exposure to defendant's asbestos-containing product in reasonable medical probability was a substantial factor in contributing to the aggregate *dose* of asbestos the plaintiff or decedent inhaled or ingested, and hence to the *risk* of developing asbestos-related cancer, without the need to demonstrate that fibers from the defendant's particular product were the ones, or among the ones, that *actually* produced the malignant growth.

In refining the concept of legal cause we must also ensure that the triers of fact in asbestos-related cancer cases know the precise contours of the plaintiff's burden. The generally applicable standard instructions on causation are insufficient for this purpose. Those instructions tell the jury that every "substantial factor in bringing about an injury" is a legal cause (BAJI No. 3.76), even when more than one such factor "contributes concurrently as a cause of the injury" (BAJI No. 3.77). They say nothing, however, to inform the jury that, in asbestos-related cancer cases, a particular asbestos-containing product is deemed to be a substantial factor in bringing about the injury if its contribution to the plaintiff or decedent's *risk* or *probability* of developing cancer was substantial.

Without such guidance, a juror might well conclude that the plaintiff needed to prove that fibers from the defendant's product were a substantial factor *actually contributing* to the development of the plaintiff's or decedent's cancer. In many cases, such a burden will be medically impossible to sustain, even with the greatest possible effort by the plaintiff, because of irreducible uncertainty regarding the cellular formation of an asbestos-related cancer. We therefore hold that, in the trial of an asbestos-related cancer case, although no instruction "shifting the burden of proof as to causation" to defendant is warranted, the jury should be told that the plaintiff's or decedent's exposure to a particular product was a substantial factor in causing or bringing about the disease if in reasonable medical probability it was a substantial factor contributing to plaintiff's or decedent's *risk* of developing cancer.

We turn, finally, to the aspect of uncertainty about causation that *is* directly disputed by the parties here—the question of which exposures to asbestos-containing products contributed significantly enough to the total occupational dose to be considered "substantial factors" in causing the disease. Who should bear the burden of proof, including the risk of nonpersuasion, on that question? On this point, we agree with defendant: in the absence of a compelling need for shifting the burden, it should remain with the plaintiff. The fundamental justification for a *Summers*-type shift of the burden is that without it all defendants might escape liability and the plaintiff be left "remediless." (*Summers*, *supra*, 33 Cal.2d at p. 86, 199 P.2d 1.) On the issue of which exposures to asbestos were substantial factors increasing the risk of cancer, the difficulties of proof do not in general appear so severe as to justify a shift in the burden of proof.

The substantial factor standard is a relatively broad one, requiring only that the contribution of the individual cause be more than negligible or theoretical. A standard instruction (BAJI No. 3.77) tells juries that each of several actors or forces acting concurrently to cause an injury is a legal cause of the injury "regardless of the extent to which each contributes to the injury." A plaintiff who suffers from an asbestos-related cancer and has proven exposure to inhalable asbestos fibers from several products will not, generally speaking, face insuperable difficulties in convincing a jury that a particular one of these product exposures, or several of them, were substantial factors in creating the risk of asbestos disease or latent injury. No burden-shifting instruction is therefore necessary on this question, and in the absence of necessity the justification for shifting part of the plaintiff's ordinary burden of proof onto a defendant also disappears.

While the above analysis provides fully adequate grounds for rejecting use of a burden-shifting instruction in the asbestos-related cancer context, we also note that, in other respects as well, asbestos-related cancer cases do not fit easily into the alternative liability model represented by *Summers*. As courts in California and other jurisdictions have observed, unlike the situation in *Summers,* asbestos cases often have less than the complete set of possible tortfeasors before the court, and do not display the same symmetry of "comparative fault" or "indivisible injury" as was the factual case in *Summers.*

    * * *

In conclusion, our general holding is as follows. In the context of a cause of action for asbestos-related latent injuries, the plaintiff must first establish some threshold *exposure* to the defendant's defective asbestos-containing products, *and* must further establish in reasonable medical probability that a particular exposure or series of exposures was a "legal cause" of his injury, i.e., a *substantial factor* in bringing about the injury. In an asbestos-related cancer case, the plaintiff need *not* prove that fibers from the defendant's product were the ones, or among the ones, that actually began the process of malignant cellular growth. Instead, the plaintiff may meet the burden of proving that exposure to defendant's product was a substantial factor causing the illness by showing that in reasonable medical probability it was a substantial factor contributing to the plaintiff's or decedent's *risk* of developing cancer. The jury should be so instructed. * * *

    * * *

3. *Prejudice.*

Lastly, we face the question of prejudice from the giving of the erroneous burden-shifting instruction in this case. Owens–Illinois asserts that the instruction deprived it of its jury trial right on causation and "[t]he verdict must be reversed on this basis alone." We have, however, recently considered and rejected precisely this theory of inherent prejudice from instructional error in civil cases. (*Soule v. General Motors Corp.* (1994) 8 Cal.4th 548, 573–580, 34 Cal.Rptr.2d 607, 882 P.2d 298.) Instead, we held, instructional error requires reversal only " 'where it seems probable' that the error 'prejudicially affected the verdict' " (*Id.* at p. 580, 34 Cal.Rptr.2d 607, 882 P.2d 298.) The reviewing court should consider not only the nature of the error, "including its natural and probable effect on a party's ability to place his full case before the jury," but the likelihood of actual prejudice as reflected in the individual trial record, taking into account "(1) the state of the evidence, (2) the effect of other instructions, (3) the effect of counsel's arguments, and (4) any indications by the jury itself that it was misled." (*Id.* at pp. 580–581, 34 Cal.Rptr.2d 607, 882 P.2d 298.) Applying this analysis, we conclude defendant has failed to demonstrate a miscarriage of justice arose from the erroneous instruction.

* * *

Finally, the record does not contain any indications the jury was actually misled. To the contrary, the jury's verdict suggests that, regardless of the burden shift, it accepted much of the defense's *factual* theory, concluding that exposure to Kaylo contributed a relatively small amount to decedent's cancer risk, but rejected defendant's argument that such a small contribution should be considered insubstantial. Thus the jury found inhalation of fibers from Kaylo was a substantial causative factor, but allocated only 1.2 percent of the total legal cause to defendant's comparative fault. (2.5 percent of the total cause was allocated to the decedent's own fault, 25 percent to that of decedent's employer, and the remainder, divided by type of product, to makers of other asbestos-containing products used at the shipyard.) From the jury's low estimate of defendant's share of causation, it appears they resolved most of the factual uncertainty in defendant's favor despite the burden-shifting instruction. In the absence of any instruction or evidence that a small amount was necessarily insubstantial, and guided by BAJI No. 3.77's command that every contributing cause was a legal cause regardless of the degree of its contribution, the jury concluded even 1.2 percent of the cause was, on the facts of this case, substantial. A different result seems unlikely to have ensued had they been correctly instructed plaintiffs bore the burden of showing exposure to Kaylo was a substantial factor increasing the decedent's risk of developing lung cancer.

We are, for these reasons, unconvinced the instructional error was prejudicial.

IV. Conclusion.

Although the Court of Appeal correctly determined Solano County General Order No. 21.00 should not have been given in this case, no miscarriage of justice has been shown to have resulted from the trial court's error in giving the burden-shifting instruction. * * *

NOTES AND QUESTIONS

1. In a dissenting opinion, Justice Mosk argued that:

Without a burden-shifting instruction, if each defendant argues that its product was only a small part of a plaintiff's total exposure, and that it therefore could not have been a substantial factor in causing his injury, there is a risk that a jury might find that *no* one manufacturer was responsible for the injury, even though all of the manufacturers together caused the harm. This is particularly true in light of the exceptionally long latency periods from initial exposure to the onset of asbestos-related disease and the nature of the typical industrial environment, involving multiple exposures to various asbestos products over a period of time.

Without the burden-shifting instruction, it would appear that many innocent plaintiffs who were unknowingly exposed to products such as Kaylo in the workplace would face serious, even insurmountable, difficulties in establishing that exposure to a specific defendant's defective product was a substantial cause of injury.

Rutherford, 941 P.2d. at 1226–1227 (Mosk, J., dissenting). Do you think this is a realistic concern?

2. As noted in Chapter 3, the Restatement (Third) of Torts: Liability for Physical and Emotional Harm, in section 26, rejects the substantial factor test in favor of a "but for" test. "Conduct is a factual cause of harm when the harm would not have occurred absent the conduct." Restatement (Third) of Torts: Liability for Physical and Emotional Harm § 26 (2010). As comment e notes, a hallmark of the but-for test is the need for a counterfactual inquiry. "One must ask what would have occurred if the actor had not engaged in the tortious conduct." Id. § 26 cmt. e.

3. If one is to reject the substantial factor test, how is one to deal with cases such as *Rutherford*? Section 27 of the Third Restatement states an exception to the "but for" test adopted in section 26:

If multiple acts exist, each of which alone would have been a factual cause under § 26 of the physical harm at the same time, each act is regarded as a factual cause of the harm.

Id. § 27. Comments f and g address fact patterns such as that arising in *Rutherford*:

f.   Multiple sufficient causal sets. In some cases, tortious conduct by one actor is insufficient, even with other background causes, to cause the plaintiff's harm. Nevertheless, when combined with conduct by other persons, the conduct overdetermines the harm, i.e., is more than sufficient to cause the harm. This circumstance thus creates the multiple sufficient causal set situation addressed in this Comment. The fact that an actor's conduct requires other conduct to be sufficient to cause another's harm does not obviate the applicability of this Section. Moreover, the fact that the other person's conduct is sufficient to cause the harm does not prevent the actor's conduct from being a factual cause of harm pursuant to this Section, if the actor's conduct is necessary to at least one causal set. For example, one actor's contribution may be sufficient to bring about the harm while another actor's contribution is only sufficient when combined with some portion of the first actor's contribution. Whether the second actor's contribution can be so combined into a sufficient causal set is a matter on which this Restatement takes no position and leaves to future development in the courts. See Comment *i*.

     * * *

     g. Toxic substances and disease. Since the publication of the Restatement Second of Torts, the situation addressed in Comment *f* has occurred most frequently in cases in which persons have been exposed to multiple doses of a toxic agent. When a person contracts a disease such as cancer, and sues multiple actors claiming that each provided some dose of a toxic substance that caused the disease, the question of the causal role of each defendant's toxic substance arises. Assuming that there is some threshold dose sufficient to cause the disease, the person may have been exposed to doses in excess of the threshold before contracting the disease. Thus, some of the person's exposures may not have been a but-for cause of the disease. Nevertheless, each of the exposures prior to the person contracting the disease (or the time at which the person's contracting the disease was determined, see § 26, Comment *k*) is a factual cause of the person's disease under the rule in this Section. Whether there are some exposures that are sufficiently de minimis that the actor should not be held liable is a matter not of factual causation, but rather of policy, and is addressed in § 36.

Id. § 27 cmts. f & g. The relevant portion of comment i referred to in comment f states:

Comment *f* addresses cases in which three candidates for cause combine to bring about a result, and any two would have been sufficient. In this situation, no candidate is a but-for cause, and none is a sufficient cause. Nevertheless, Comment *f* provides that each is a factual cause under the rule stated in this Section. Comment *g* addresses this issue in the context of combined doses of toxic substances. The situation is more complicated, however, if two of the three candidates for cause—or doses in a toxic-substances case—come from the same defendant or source. In that case, one of the defendants' conduct or toxic substance would have been sufficient, whereas the other defendant's conduct or toxic substance would not. Intuition might suggest that the latter is not a cause, especially if the latter is small in comparison to the former. This intuition may simply be an example of a de minimis contribution, already discussed and addressed in § 36, Comment *b*, but it may also be based on other factors, including notions of preemption. Moreover, and significantly, it may not be widely shared. In a case addressed by Comment *f*, in which three actors each provide one-half of a sufficient toxic dose, why should the result change if one actor provides two doses and another actor provides one? And should it matter if the two doses come combined from the source or in two discrete contributions? * * *

Id. § 27 cmt. i. The black letter of section 36 states:

     When an actor's negligent conduct constitutes only a trivial contribution to a causal set that is a factual cause of physical harm under § 27, the harm is not within the scope of the actor's liability.

Id. § 36. Other than rejecting use of the "substantial factor" test and replacing it with section 27, how is the Third Restatement's approach different from *Rutherford*? At the end of the day, do you believe the Third Restatement provides a more coherent way of dealing with cases like *Rutherford* than the Second Restatement's reliance on a substantial factor test of causation?

4. The causal difficulties posed by toxic exposures are not unique to the United States, nor are judicial attempts to respond to them. In Fairchild v. Glenhaven Funeral Servs. Ltd., [2003] 1 A.C. 32, the House of Lords dealt with the case of individuals who contracted mesothelioma after being exposed to asbestos produced by a number of defendants. The following are excerpts from Lord Bingham of Cornhill's opinion:

> **2** The essential question underlying the appeals may be accurately expressed in this way. If (1) C was employed at different times and for differing periods by both A and B, and (2) A and B were both subject to a duty to take reasonable care or to take all practicable measures to prevent C inhaling asbestos dust because of the known risk that asbestos dust (if inhaled) might cause a mesothelioma, and (3) both A and B were in breach of that duty in relation to C during the periods of C's employment by each of them with the result that during both periods C inhaled excessive quantities of asbestos dust, and (4) C is found to be suffering from a mesothelioma, and (5) any cause of C's mesothelioma other than the inhalation of asbestos dust at work can be effectively discounted, but (6) C cannot (because of the current limits of human science) prove, on the balance of probabilities, that his mesothelioma was the result of his inhaling asbestos dust during his employment by A or during his employment by B or during his employment by A and B taken together, is C entitled to recover damages against either A or B or against both A and B? To this question (not formulated in these terms) the Court of Appeal (Brooke, Latham and Kay LJJ), in a reserved judgment of the court reported at [2002] 1 WLR 1052, gave a negative answer. It did so because, applying the conventional "but for" test of tortious liability, it could not be held that C had proved against A that his mesothelioma would probably not have occurred but for the breach of duty by A, nor against B that his mesothelioma would probably not have occurred but for the breach of duty by B, nor against A and B that his mesothelioma would probably not have occurred but for the breach of duty by both A and B together. So C failed against both A and B. The crucial issue on appeal is whether, in the special circumstances of such a case, principle, authority or policy requires or justifies a modified approach to proof of causation.

* * *

> **7** From about the 1960s, it became widely known that exposure to asbestos dust and fibres could give rise not only to asbestosis and other pulmonary diseases, but also to the risk of developing a mesothelioma. This is a malignant tumour, usually of the pleura, sometimes of the peritoneum. In the absence of occupational exposure to asbestos dust it is a very rare tumour indeed, afflicting no more than about one person in a

million per year. But the incidence of the tumour among those occupationally exposed to asbestos dust is about 1,000 times greater than in the general population, and there are some 1,500 cases reported annually. It is a condition which may be latent for many years, usually for 30–40 years or more; development of the condition may take as short a period as ten years, but it is thought that that is the period which elapses between the mutation of the first cell and the manifestation of symptoms of the condition. It is invariably fatal, and death usually occurs within one to two years of the condition being diagnosed. The mechanism by which a normal mesothelial cell is transformed into a mesothelioma cell is not known. It is believed by the best medical opinion to involve a multi-stage process, in which six or seven genetic changes occur in a normal cell to render it malignant. Asbestos acts in at least one of those stages and may (but this is uncertain) act in more than one. It is not known what level of exposure to asbestos dust and fibre can be tolerated without significant risk of developing a mesothelioma, but it is known that those living in urban environments (although without occupational exposure) inhale large numbers of asbestos fibres without developing a mesothelioma. It is accepted that the risk of developing a mesothelioma increases in proportion to the quantity of asbestos dust and fibres inhaled: the greater the quantity of dust and fibre inhaled, the greater the risk. But the condition may be caused by a single fibre, or a few fibres, or many fibres: medical opinion holds none of these possibilities to be more probable than any other, and the condition once caused is not aggravated by further exposure. So if C is employed successively by A and B and is exposed to asbestos dust and fibres during each employment and develops a mesothelioma, the very strong probability is that this will have been caused by inhalation of asbestos dust containing fibres. But C could have inhaled a single fibre giving rise to his condition during employment by A, in which case his exposure by B will have had no effect on his condition; or he could have inhaled a single fibre giving rise to his condition during his employment by B, in which case his exposure by A will have had no effect on his condition; or he could have inhaled fibres during his employment by A and B which together gave rise to his condition; but medical science cannot support the suggestion that any of these possibilities is to be regarded as more probable than any other. There is no way of identifying, even on a balance of probabilities, the source of the fibre or fibres which initiated the genetic process which culminated in the malignant tumour. It is on this rock of uncertainty, reflecting the point to which medical science has so far advanced, that the three claims were rejected by the Court of Appeal and by two of the three trial judges.

* * *

9 The issue in these appeals does not concern the general validity and applicability of [the but for] requirement, which is not in question, but is whether in special circumstances such as those in these cases there should be any variation or relaxation of it. The overall object of tort law is to define cases in which the law may justly hold one party liable to compensate another. Are these such cases? * * *

* * *

Conclusion

34 To the question posed in paragraph 2 of this opinion I would answer that where conditions (1)–(6) are satisfied C is entitled to recover against both A and B. That conclusion is in my opinion consistent with principle, and also with authority (properly understood). Where those conditions are satisfied, it seems to me just and in accordance with common sense to treat the conduct of A and B in exposing C to a risk to which he should not have been exposed as making a material contribution to the contracting by C of a condition against which it was the duty of A and B to protect him. I consider that this conclusion is fortified by the wider jurisprudence reviewed above. Policy considerations weigh in favour of such a conclusion. It is a conclusion which follows even if either A or B is not before the court. It was not suggested in argument that C's entitlement against either A or B should be for any sum less than the full compensation to which C is entitled, although A and B could of course seek contribution against each other or any other employer liable in respect of the same damage in the ordinary way. No argument on apportionment was addressed to the House. I would in conclusion emphasise that my opinion is directed to cases in which each of the conditions specified in (1)–(6) of paragraph 2 above is satisfied and to no other case. It would be unrealistic to suppose that the principle here affirmed will not over time be the subject of incremental and analogical development. Cases seeking to develop the principle must be decided when and as they arise. For the present, I think it unwise to decide more than is necessary to resolve these three appeals which, for all the foregoing reasons, I concluded should be allowed.

Id.

5. The *Fairchild* opinion has a useful discussion of how a number of European and Commonwealth countries approach the problem presented in the case. In Germany, this type of case is covered by the second sentence of BGB § 830(1) which provides:

> If several persons have caused damage by an unlawful act committed in common each is responsible for the damage. The same rule applies if it cannot be discovered which of several participants has caused the damage by his act.

Bürgerliches Gesetzbuch [BGB] [Civil Code] § 830(1).

Article 926 of the Greek Civil Code, entitled "Damage caused by several persons" provides:

> If damage has occurred as a result of the joint action of several persons, or if several persons are concurrently responsible for the same damage, they are all jointly and severally implicated. The same applies if several persons have acted simultaneously or in succession and it is not possible to determine which person's act caused the damage.

Astikos Kodikas [A.K.] [Civil Code] 926 (Greece).

A similar provision exists in the Austrian Civil Code:

1302. In such a case, if the injury is inadvertent, and it is possible to determine the portions thereof, each person is responsible only for the injuries caused by his mistake. If, however, the injury was intentional, or if the portions of the individuals in the injury cannot be determined, all are liable for one and one for all; however, the individual who has paid damages is granted the right to claim reimbursement from the others.

Allgemeines Bürgerliches Gesetzbuch [ABGB] [Civil Code] § 1302 (Austria).

6. Does the House of Lord's approach depend on a certain theory of how asbestos exposure causes mesothelioma? Does the *Rutherford* approach depend on a certain theory of how asbestos exposure causes lung cancer? Would either court adopt a different approach if it were known that there was or was not a strong dose-response relationship between exposure and the likelihood of developing the disease? If in fact we do not know whether the relationship between exposure and development of a given disease follows a single hit or a cumulative dose model, should the law adopt a default model for purposes of litigation? If your answer is yes, which model is preferable? If scientists eventually conclude that the one-hit model is correct, can this be squared with the toxicological law that "the dose makes the poison?"

7. In a part of the *Rutherford* opinion not reproduced above, the court refused to permit the defendants to join the tobacco companies who sold cigarettes to the plaintiffs. What are the arguments for and against this position? See Owens Corning v. R.J. Reynolds Tobacco Co., 868 So.2d 331 (Miss.2004).

8. Both the *Mulcahy* and the *Rutherford* opinions discuss *Summers v. Tice* and its burden-shifting, alternative liability approach to indeterminate defendant problems. The *Summers* rule is reflected in the Third Restatement of Torts: Liability for Physical and Emotional Harm:

§ 28. Burden of Proof

(a) Subject to Subsection (b), the plaintiff has the burden to prove that the defendant's tortious conduct was a factual cause of the plaintiff's physical harm.

(b) When the plaintiff sues all of multiple actors and proves that each engaged in tortious conduct that exposed the plaintiff to a risk of physical harm and that the tortious conduct of one or more of them caused the plaintiff's harm but the plaintiff cannot reasonably be expected to prove which actor caused the harm, the burden of proof, including both production and persuasion, on factual causation is shifted to the defendants.

Id. § 28. The Restatement's requirement that plaintiff sue *all* the entities whose tortious acts exposed plaintiff to a risk of harm reflects the position of the great majority of courts that have adopted this approach. See § 28 cmt. g.

9. Both *Rutherford* and *Fairchild* eased the plaintiff's causal burden by permitting him to prove each defendant's product increased the *risk* of injury rather than proving that each defendant's product was the but-for *cause* of his injury. How, if at all, does this differ from the *Summers v. Tice* approach? How does it differ from the market share liability approach discussed in the next case? If we accept that a "risk" approach is appropriate in asbestos cases, should it be generally available in all toxic tort cases where causal mechanisms are poorly understood? Why or why not? See Joseph Sanders, Risky Business: Causation in Asbestos Cancer Cases (and Beyond?), in Perspectives on Causation (Richard Goldberg, ed. forthcoming 2010).

B.   DEFENDANT INDETERMINACY

Summers v. Tice, 199 P.2d 1 (Cal.1948) stands out as the first American case to directly confront the causation problem created by an indeterminate defendant. The court's solution came to be known as "alternative liability" and found its way into both the Second and Third Restatements. As we saw in the *Rutherford* opinion, the *Summers* burden-shifting solution is one that the courts have employed sparingly. For many years following *Summers*, there was little pressure to do so because the types of situations that would give rise to the need for shifting the causal burden were few and far between. With the rise of toxic injuries and their very long latency periods, however, the situation changed dramatically. During the 1980s, several state supreme courts extended the reach of the *Summers* rule in a series of cases involving the drug diethylstilbestrol (DES), a synthetic substance that mimics the effects of the female hormone estrogen. DES was at one time widely prescribed to prevent miscarriages. Scientific studies, however, subsequently linked the drug to a particular form of cancer in the daughters of women who used it during pregnancy. Hundreds of these daughters subsequently filed lawsuits against DES manufacturers. Nearly all, however, faced a virtually insurmountable hurdle: they could not identify the manufacturer that produced the DES used by their mothers, and therefore could not satisfy the traditional causation element of their claims. The next case addressed that problem.

SINDELL v. ABBOTT LABORATORIES

Supreme Court of California, 1980.
26 Cal.3d 588, 607 P.2d 924, 163 Cal.Rptr. 132.

MOSK, JUSTICE.

This case involves a complex problem both timely and significant: may a plaintiff, injured as the result of a drug administered to her mother during pregnancy, who knows the type of drug involved but cannot identify the manufacturer of the precise product, hold liable for her injuries a maker of a drug produced from an identical formula?

Plaintiff Judith Sindell brought an action against eleven drug companies and Does 1 through 100, on behalf of herself and other women similarly situated. The complaint alleges as follows:

Between 1941 and 1971, defendants were engaged in the business of manufacturing, promoting, and marketing diethylstilbesterol (DES), a drug which is a synthetic compound of the female hormone estrogen. The drug was administered to plaintiff's mother and the mothers of the class she represents, for the purpose of preventing miscarriage. In 1947, the Food and Drug Administration authorized the marketing of DES as a miscarriage preventative, but only on an experimental basis, with a requirement that the drug contain a warning label to that effect.

DES may cause cancerous vaginal and cervical growths in the daughters exposed to it before birth, because their mothers took the drug during pregnancy. The form of cancer from which these daughters suffer is known as adenocarcinoma, and it manifests itself after a minimum latent period of 10 or 12 years. It is a fast-spreading and deadly disease, and radical surgery is required to prevent it from spreading. DES also causes adenosis, precancerous vaginal and cervical growths which may spread to other areas of the body. * * *

In 1971, the Food and Drug Administration ordered defendants to cease marketing and promoting DES for the purpose of preventing miscarriages, and to warn physicians and the public that the drug should not be used by pregnant women because of the danger to their unborn children.

During the period defendants marketed DES, they knew or should have known that it was a carcinogenic substance, that there was a grave danger after varying periods of latency it would cause cancerous and precancerous growths in the daughters of the mothers who took it, and that it was ineffective to prevent miscarriage. Nevertheless, defendants continued to advertise and market the drug as a miscarriage preventative. They failed to test DES for efficacy and safety; the tests performed by others, upon which they relied, indicated that it was not safe or effective. In violation of the authorization of the Food and Drug Administration, defendants marketed DES on an unlimited basis rather than as an experimental drug, and they failed to warn of its potential danger.

Because of defendants' advertised assurances that DES was safe and effective to prevent miscarriage, plaintiff was exposed to the drug prior to her birth. She became aware of the danger from such exposure within one year of the time she filed her complaint. As a result of the DES ingested by her mother, plaintiff developed a malignant bladder tumor which was removed by surgery. She suffers from adenosis and must constantly be monitored by biopsy or colposcopy to insure early warning of further malignancy.

The first cause of action alleges that defendants were jointly and individually negligent in that they manufactured, marketed and promoted DES as a safe and efficacious drug to prevent miscarriage, without adequate testing or warning, and without monitoring or reporting its effects.

A separate cause of action alleges that defendants are jointly liable regardless of which particular brand of DES was ingested by plaintiff's mother because defendants collaborated in marketing, promoting and testing the drug, relied upon each other's tests, and adhered to an industry-wide safety standard. DES was produced from a common and mutually agreed upon formula as a fungible drug interchangeable with other brands of the same product; defendants knew or should have known that it was customary for doctors to prescribe the drug by its generic rather than its brand name and that pharmacists filled prescriptions from whatever brand of the drug happened to be in stock.

* * *

Defendants demurred to the complaint. While the complaint did not expressly allege that plaintiff could not identify the manufacturer of the precise drug ingested by her mother, she stated in her points and authorities in opposition to the demurrers filed by some of the defendants that she was unable to make the identification, and the trial court sustained the demurrers of these defendants without leave to amend on the ground that plaintiff did not and stated she could not identify which defendant had manufactured the drug responsible for her injuries. Thereupon, the court dismissed the action. This appeal involves only five of ten defendants named in the complaint.

* * *

This case is but one of a number filed throughout the country seeking to hold drug manufacturers liable for injuries allegedly resulting from DES prescribed to the plaintiffs' mothers since 1947. According to a note in the Fordham Law Review, estimates of the number of women who took the drug during pregnancy range from 1 1/2 million to 3 million. Hundreds, perhaps thousands, of the daughters of these women suffer from adenocarcinoma, and the incidence of vaginal adenosis among them is 30 to 90 percent. (Comment, *DES and a Proposed Theory of Enterprise Liability* (1978) 46 Fordham L.Rev. 963, 964–967 [hereafter Fordham Comment].) * * *

We begin with the proposition that, as a general rule, the imposition of liability depends upon a showing by the plaintiff that his or her injuries were caused by the act of the defendant or by an instrumentality under the defendant's control. The rule applies whether the injury resulted from an accidental event or from the use of a defective product.

There are, however, exceptions to this rule. Plaintiff's complaint suggests several bases upon which defendants may be held liable for her injuries even though she cannot demonstrate the name of the manufacturer which produced the DES actually taken by her mother. The first of these theories, classically illustrated by *Summers v. Tice* (1948) 33 Cal.2d 80, 199 P.2d 1, places the burden of proof of causation upon tortious defendants in certain circumstances. The second basis of liability emerging from the complaint is that defendants acted in concert to cause injury to plaintiff. There is a third and novel approach to the problem, sometimes called the theory of "enterprise liability," but which we prefer to designate by the more accurate term of "industry-wide" liability, which might obviate the necessity for identifying the manufacturer of the injury-causing drug. We shall conclude that these doctrines, as previously interpreted, may not be applied to hold defendants liable under the allegations of this complaint. However, we shall propose and adopt a fourth basis for permitting the action to be tried, grounded upon an extension of the *Summers* doctrine.

I

Plaintiff places primary reliance upon cases which hold that if a party cannot identify which of two or more defendants caused an injury, the burden of proof may shift to the defendants to show that they were not responsible for the harm. This principle is sometimes referred to as the "alternative liability" theory.

The celebrated case of *Summers v. Tice, supra,* 33 Cal.2d 80, 199 P.2d 1, a unanimous opinion of this court, best exemplifies the rule. In *Summers,* the plaintiff was injured when two hunters negligently shot in his direction. It could not be determined which of them had fired the shot which actually caused the injury to the plaintiff's eye, but both defendants were nevertheless held jointly and severally liable for the whole of the damages. We reasoned that both were wrongdoers, both were negligent toward the plaintiff, and that it would be unfair to require plaintiff to isolate the defendant responsible, because if the one pointed out were to escape liability, the other might also, and the plaintiff-victim would be shorn of any remedy. In these circumstances, we held, the burden of proof shifted to the defendants, "each to absolve himself if he can." (*Id.,* p. 86, 199 P.2d p. 4.) We stated that under these or similar circumstances a defendant is ordinarily in a "far better position" to offer evidence to determine whether he or another defendant caused the injury.

In *Summers,* we relied upon *Ybarra v. Spangard* (1944) 25 Cal.2d 486, 154 P.2d 687. There, the plaintiff was injured while he was unconscious during the course of surgery. He sought damages against several doctors and a nurse who attended him while he was unconscious. We held that it would be unreasonable to require him to identify the particular defendant who had performed the alleged negligent act because he was unconscious at the time of the injury and the defendants exercised control over the instrumentalities which caused the harm. Therefore, under the doctrine of res ipsa loquitur, an inference of negligence arose that defendants were required to meet by explaining their conduct.

* * *

Defendants assert that these principles are inapplicable here. First, they insist that a predicate to shifting the burden of proof under *Summers–Ybarra* is that the defendants must have greater access to information regarding the cause of the injuries than the plaintiff, whereas in the present case the reverse appears.

Plaintiff does not claim that defendants are in a better position than she to identify the manufacturer of the drug taken by her mother or, indeed, that they have the ability to do so at all, but argues, rather, that *Summers* does not impose such a requirement as a condition to the shifting of the burden of proof. In this respect we believe plaintiff is correct.

In *Summers*, the circumstances of the accident themselves precluded an explanation of its cause. To be sure, *Summers* states that defendants are "[o]rdinarily . . . in a far better position to offer evidence to determine which one caused the injury" than a plaintiff (33 Cal.2d 80, at p. 86, 199 P.2d 1 at p. 4), but the decision does not determine that this "ordinary" situation was present. Neither the facts nor the language of the opinion indicate that the two defendants, simultaneously shooting in the same direction, were in a better position than the plaintiff to ascertain whose shot caused the injury. As the opinion acknowledges, it was impossible for the trial court to determine whether the shot which entered the plaintiff's eye came from the gun of one defendant or the other. Nevertheless, burden of proof was shifted to the defendants.

      * * *

Thus we conclude that the fact defendants do not have greater access to information which might establish the identity of the manufacturer of the DES which injured plaintiff does not per se prevent application of the *Summers* rule.

Nevertheless, plaintiff may not prevail in her claim that the *Summers* rationale should be employed to fix the whole liability for her injuries upon defendants, at least as those principles have previously been applied. There is an important difference between the situation involved in *Summers* and the present case. There, all the parties who were or could have been responsible for the harm to the plaintiff were joined as defendants. Here, by contrast, there are approximately 200 drug companies which made DES, any of which might have manufactured the injury-producing drug.

Defendants maintain that, while in *Summers* there was a 50 percent chance that one of the two defendants was responsible for the plaintiff's injuries, here since any one of 200 companies which manufactured DES might have made the product which harmed plaintiff, there is no rational basis upon which to infer that any defendant in this action caused plaintiff's injuries, nor even a reasonable possibility that they were responsible.

These arguments are persuasive if we measure the chance that any one of the defendants supplied the injury-causing drug by the number of possible tortfeasors. In such a context, the possibility that any of the five defendants supplied the DES to plaintiff's mother is so remote that it would be unfair to require each defendant to exonerate itself. There may be a substantial likelihood that none of the five defendants joined in the action made the DES which caused the injury, and that the offending producer not named would escape liability altogether. While we propose, *infra*, an adaptation of the rule in *Summers* which will substantially overcome these difficulties, defendants appear to be correct that the rule, as previously applied, cannot relieve plaintiff of the burden of proving the identity of the manufacturer which made the drug causing her injuries.

II

The second principle upon which plaintiff relies is the so-called "concert of action" theory. * * *

* * *

* * * The elements of this doctrine are prescribed in section 876 of the Restatement of Torts. The section provides, "For harm resulting to a third person from the tortious conduct of another, one is subject to liability if he (a) does a tortious act in concert with the other or pursuant to a common design with him, or (b) knows that the other's conduct constitutes a breach of duty and gives substantial assistance or encouragement to the other so to conduct himself, or (c) gives substantial assistance to the other in accomplishing a tortious result and his own conduct, separately considered, constitutes a breach of duty to the third person." With respect to this doctrine, Prosser states that "those who, in pursuance of a common plan or design to commit a tortious act, actively take part in it, or further it by cooperation or request, or who lend aid or encouragement to the wrongdoer, or ratify and adopt his acts done for their benefit, are equally liable with him. * * * Express agreement is not necessary, and all that is required is that there be a tacit understanding...." (Prosser, Law of Torts (4th ed. 1971), sec. 46, p. 292.)

Plaintiff contends that her complaint states a cause of action under these principles. She alleges that defendants' wrongful conduct "is the result of planned and concerted action, express and implied agreements, collaboration in, reliance upon, acquiescence in and ratification, exploitation and adoption of each other's testing, marketing methods, lack of warnings ... and other acts or omissions ..." and that "acting individually and in concert, [defendants] promoted, approved, authorized, acquiesced in, and reaped profits from sales" of DES. These allegations, plaintiff claims, state a "tacit understanding" among defendants to commit a tortious act against her.

In our view, this litany of charges is insufficient to allege a cause of action under the rules stated above. The gravamen of the charge of concert is that defendants failed to adequately test the drug or to give sufficient warning of its dangers and that they relied upon the tests performed by one another and took advantage of each others' promotional and marketing techniques. These allegations do not amount to a charge that there was a tacit understanding or a common plan among defendants to fail to conduct adequate tests or give sufficient warnings, and that they substantially aided and encouraged one another in these omissions.

* * *

III

A third theory upon which plaintiff relies is the concept of industry-wide liability, or according to the terminology of the parties, "enterprise liability." This theory was suggested in *Hall v. E. I. Du Pont de Nemours & Co., Inc.* (E.D.N.Y.1972) 345 F.Supp. 353. In that case, plaintiffs were 13 children injured by the explosion of blasting caps in 12 separate incidents which occurred in 10 different states between 1955 and 1959. The defendants were six blasting cap manufacturers, comprising virtually the entire blasting cap industry in the United States, and their trade association. There were, however, a number of Canadian blasting cap manufacturers which could have supplied the caps. The gravamen of the complaint was that the practice of the industry of omitting a warning on individual blasting caps and of failing to take other safety measures created an unreasonable risk of harm, resulting in the plaintiffs' injuries. The complaint did not identify a particular manufacturer of a cap which caused a particular injury.

The court reasoned as follows: there was evidence that defendants, acting independently, had adhered to an industry-wide standard with regard to the safety features of blasting caps, that they had in effect delegated some functions of safety investigation and design, such as labeling, to their trade association, and that there was industry-wide cooperation in the manufacture and design of blasting caps. In these circumstances, the evidence supported a conclusion that all the defendants jointly controlled the risk. Thus, if plaintiffs could establish by a preponderance of the evidence that the caps were manufactured by one of the defendants, the burden of proof as to causation would shift to all the defendants. The court noted that this theory of liability applied to industries composed of a small number of units, and that what would be fair and reasonable with regard to an industry of five or ten producers might be manifestly unreasonable if applied to a decentralized industry composed of countless small producers.

Plaintiff attempts to state a cause of action under the rationale of *Hall*. She alleges joint enterprise and collaboration among defendants in the production, marketing, promotion and testing of DES, and "concerted promulgation and adherence to industry-wide testing, safety, warning and efficacy standards" for the drug. We have concluded above that allegations that defendants relied upon one another's testing and promotion methods do not state a cause of action for concerted conduct to commit a tortious act. Under the theory of industry-wide liability, however, each manufacturer could be liable for all injuries caused by DES by virtue of adherence to an industry-wide standard of safety.

    * * *

We decline to apply this theory in the present case. At least 200 manufacturers produced DES; *Hall*, which involved 6 manufacturers representing the entire blasting cap industry in the United States, cautioned against application of the doctrine espoused therein to a large number of producers. (345 F.Supp. at p. 378.) Moreover, in *Hall*, the conclusion that the defendants jointly controlled the risk was based upon allegations that they had delegated some functions relating to safety to a trade association. There are no such allegations here, and we have concluded above that plaintiff has failed to allege liability on a concert of action theory.

Equally important, the drug industry is closely regulated by the Food and Drug Administration, which actively controls the testing and manufacture of drugs and the method by which they are marketed, including the contents of warning labels. To a considerable degree, therefore, the standards followed by drug manufacturers are suggested or compelled by the government. Adherence to those standards cannot, of course, absolve a manufacturer of liability to which it would otherwise be subject. But since the government plays such a pervasive role in formulating the criteria for the testing and marketing of drugs, it would be unfair to impose upon a manufacturer liability for injuries resulting from the use of a drug which it did not supply simply because it followed the standards of the industry.

IV

If we were confined to the theories of *Summers* and *Hall*, we would be constrained to hold that the judgment must be sustained. Should we require that plaintiff identify the manufacturer which supplied the DES used by her mother or that all DES manufacturers be joined in the action, she would effectively be precluded from any recovery. As defendants candidly admit, there is little likelihood that all the manufacturers who made DES at the time in question are still in business or that they are subject to the jurisdiction of the California courts. There are, however, forceful arguments in favor of holding that plaintiff has a cause of action.

In our contemporary complex industrialized society, advances in science and technology create fungible goods which may harm consumers and which cannot be traced to any specific producer. The response of the courts can be either to adhere rigidly to prior doctrine, denying recovery to those injured by such products, or to fashion remedies to meet these changing needs. Just as Justice Traynor in his landmark concurring opinion in *Escola v. Coca Cola Bottling Company* (1944) 24 Cal.2d 453, 467–468, 150 P.2d 436, recognized that in an era of mass production and complex marketing methods the traditional standard of negligence was insufficient to govern the obligations of manufacturer to consumer, so should we acknowledge that some adaptation of the rules of causation and liability may be appropriate in these recurring circumstances. The Restatement comments that modification of the *Summers* rule may be necessary in a situation like that before us.

The most persuasive reason for finding plaintiff states a cause of action is that advanced in *Summers*: as between an innocent plaintiff and negligent defendants, the latter should bear the cost of the injury. Here, as in *Summers*, plaintiff is not at fault in failing to provide evidence of causation, and although the absence of such evidence is not attributable to the defendants either, their conduct in marketing a drug the effects of which are delayed for many years played a significant role in creating the unavailability of proof.

From a broader policy standpoint, defendants are better able to bear the cost of injury resulting from the manufacture of a defective product. As was said by Justice Traynor in *Escola*, "[t]he cost of an injury and the loss of time or health may be an overwhelming misfortune to the person injured, and a needless one, for the risk of injury can be insured by the manufacturer and distributed among the public as a cost of doing business." (24 Cal.2d p. 462, 150 P.2d p. 441; see also Rest.2d Torts, § 402A, com. c, pp. 349–350.) The manufacturer is in the best position to discover and guard against defects in its products and to warn of harmful effects; thus, holding it liable for defects and failure to warn of harmful effects will provide an incentive to product safety. These considerations are particularly significant where medication is involved, for the consumer is virtually helpless to protect himself from serious, sometimes permanent, sometimes fatal, injuries caused by deleterious drugs.

Where, as here, all defendants produced a drug from an identical formula and the manufacturer of the DES which caused plaintiff's injuries cannot be identified through no fault of plaintiff, a modification of the rule of *Summers* is warranted. As we have seen, an undiluted *Summers* rationale is inappropriate to shift the burden of proof of causation to defendants because if we measure the chance that any particular manufacturer supplied the injury-causing product by the number of producers of DES, there is a possibility that none of the five defendants in this case produced the offending substance and that the responsible manufacturer, not named in the action, will escape liability.

But we approach the issue of causation from a different perspective: we hold it to be reasonable in the present context to measure the likelihood that any of the defendants supplied the product which allegedly injured plaintiff by the percentage which the DES sold by each of them for the purpose of preventing miscarriage bears to the entire production of the drug sold by all for that purpose. * * *

If plaintiff joins in the action the manufacturers of a substantial share of the DES which her mother might have taken, the injustice of shifting the burden of proof to defendants to demonstrate that they could not have made the substance which injured plaintiff is significantly diminished. * * *

The presence in the action of a substantial share of the appropriate market also provides a ready means to apportion damages among the defendants. Each defendant will be held liable for the proportion of the judgment represented by its share of that market unless it demonstrates that it could not have made the product which caused plaintiff's injuries. In the present case, as we have see, one DES manufacturer was dismissed from the action upon filing a declaration that it had not manufactured DES until after plaintiff was born. Once plaintiff has met her burden of joining the required defendants, they in turn may cross-complaint against other DES manufacturers, not joined in the action, which they can allege might have supplied the injury-causing product.

Under this approach, each manufacturer's liability would approximate its responsibility for the injuries caused by its own products. * * *

We are not unmindful of the practical problems involved in defining the market and determining market share, but these are largely matters of proof which properly cannot be determined at the pleading stage of these proceedings. Defendants urge that it would be both unfair and contrary to public policy to hold them liable for plaintiff's injuries in the absence of proof that one of them supplied the drug responsible for the damage. Most of their arguments, however, are based upon the assumption that one manufacturer would be held responsible for the products of another or for those of all other manufacturers if plaintiff ultimately prevails. But under the rule we adopt, each manufacturer's liability for an injury would be approximately equivalent to the damages caused by the DES it manufactured.

The judgments are reversed.

NOTES AND QUESTIONS

1. How is the *Sindell* situation different from that presented in *Borel*? How is it different from the situation presented in *Rutherford*? How are the situations similar?

2. One issue left open in *Sindell* was how to handle a situation where the market share of the defendants in a case totaled less than 100%. Should all defendants' liability be inflated to achieve full compensation? Or should an individual defendant's liability be several only, limited based on its percentage of the market? In Brown v. Superior Court, 751 P.2d 470, 485–87 (Cal.1988), the California Supreme Court opted for the latter approach:

The question of joint liability was not considered in *Sindell*, and this omission should not be read as an implied holding in favor of such a rule.

* * *

In creating the market share doctrine, this court attempted to fashion a remedy for persons injured by a drug taken by their mothers a generation ago, making identification of the manufacturer impossible in many cases. We realized that in order to provide relief to an injured DES daughter faced with this dilemma, we would have to allow recovery of damages against some defendants which may not have manufactured the drug that caused the damage. To protect such defendants against excessive liability, we considered and rejected three separate theories of liability suggested by the plaintiff, and formulated, instead, the market share concept.

We explained the basis of the doctrine as follows: In order to decrease the likelihood that a manufacturer of DES would be held liable for injuries caused by products not of its making, and to achieve a reasonable approximation of its responsibility for injuries caused by the DES it produced, the plaintiff should be required to join in the action the manufacturers of a substantial share of the relevant DES market. If this were done, the injustice of shifting the burden of proof to defendants to exonerate themselves of responsibility for the plaintiff's injuries would be diminished. Each defendant would be held liable for the proportion of the judgment represented by its market share, and its overall liability for injuries caused by DES would approximate the injuries caused by the DES it manufactured. A DES manufacturer found liable under this approach would not be held responsible for injuries caused by another producer of the drug. The opinion acknowledged that only an approximation of a manufacturer's liability could be achieved by this procedure, but underlying our holding was a recognition that such a result was preferable to denying recovery altogether to plaintiffs injured by DES.

* * * In short, the imposition of joint liability among defendant manufacturers in a market share action would frustrate *Sindell*'s goal of achieving a balance between the interests of DES plaintiffs and manufacturers of the drug.

Id. *Brown*, however, still begged an important question. What is the "relevant DES market" for purposes of calculating market share? Other jurisdictions that considered this question have looked to the narrowest possible construction of the term. See Conley v. Boyle Drug Co., 570 So.2d 275, 284 (Fla.1990); George v. Parke–Davis, 733 P.2d 507, 512 (Wash.1987). Such a determination provided the most accurate assessment of the likelihood that any defendant caused plaintiff's harm.

3. In the decade following *Sindell*, a number of other jurisdictions considered whether to adopt market share liability in DES cases. Some jurisdictions refused, viewing the theory as an inappropriate expansion of the traditional rule requiring plaintiff to prove causation in tort law. See, e.g., Sutowski v. Eli Lilly & Co., 696 N.E.2d 187 (Ohio 1998); Gorman v. Abbott Labs., 599 A.2d 1364 (R.I.1991); Smith v. Eli Lilly & Co., 560 N.E.2d 324 (Ill.1990); Mulcahy v. Eli Lilly & Co., 386 N.W.2d 67, 76 (Iowa 1986); Zafft v. Eli Lilly & Co., 676 S.W.2d 241, 246 (Mo.1984). Other jurisdictions, however, not only adopted market share liability, but expanded upon it. The Washington Supreme Court was the first to do so in Martin v. Abbott Laboratories, 102 Wash.2d 581, 689 P.2d 368 (1984). Most notably, the *Martin* court eliminated the requirement from *Sindell* that a plaintiff sue a "substantial share" of those companies in the market producing DES. Instead, the *Martin* court held that a plaintiff could go forward by suing as few as one DES manufacture that produced the product in the relevant market at the relevant time:

We reject the *Sindell* requirement of joinder of a "substantial share" of the market because it does not alter the probability under [market share liability] that a particular defendant caused the injury. [Rather], a particular defendant's potential liability is proportional to the probability that it caused plaintiff's injury.

Individual defendants [however] are entitled to exculpate themselves from liability by establishing, by a preponderance of the evidence, that they did not produce or market the particular type DES taken by the plaintiff's mother [or] that they did not market the DES in the geographic market area of plaintiff mother's obtaining the drug.

Id. at 382. Five years later, the New York Court of Appeals went further in *Hymowitz v. Eli Lilly & Co.*, 539 N.E.2d 1069 (N.Y.1989), ruling that a DES manufacturer could be liable for its share of the *national* DES market—even if that defendant could prove that it did not produce the pill that caused the plaintiff's harm:

> [B]ecause liability here is based on the over-all risk produced, and not causation in a single case, there should be no exculpation of a defendant who, although a member of the market producing DES for pregnancy use, appears not to have caused a particular plaintiff's injury.

Id. at 1078. What do you think of the *Hymowitz* approach? Does it effectively eradicate the need to prove actual causation? What about its use of a national market, rather than the local market preferred in *Conley* and *George*? The *Hymowitz* court explained its choice of a national market, expressing concern that ascertaining accurate market share data for any smaller market would not be practicable. Id. at 1077.

4. One state that has been unusually active in applying market share liability is Wisconsin. The Wisconsin Supreme Court first applied the theory in a DES case in Collins v. Eli Lilly Co., 342 N.W.2d 37 (Wis.1984). Like the Washington Supreme Court in *Martin*, the *Collins* court stated that it would allow a claim to go forward against as few as one manufacturer of DES. The *Collins* version of market share differed from others, however, in conceptualizing the theory on the basis of risk contribution beyond the simple accounting of how much DES the manufacturer sold. See *Collins*, 342 N.W.2d at 49. More recently, the Wisconsin Supreme Court applied its risk-contribution theory against several manufacturers of white lead carbonate pigment contained in paint. The manufacturers were sued by a boy who claimed that his cognitive abilities were diminished by lead poisoning caused by the ingestion of paint chips containing lead carbonate pigment. The boy, however, could not connect his harm to any the pigment of any particular manufacturer. The defendants argued that market share liability should not apply in any form, as their products were not chemically identical, like DES. The court, however, disagreed, and found it sufficient that the manufacturers' pigments were fungible in the sense that they were "functionally interchangeable." Thomas ex rel. Gramling v. Mallett, 701 N.W.2d 523, 561 (Wis.2005). See Allen Rostron, Beyond Market Share Liability: A Theory of Proportional Liability for Nonfungible Products, 52 UCLA L.Rev. 151, 163–64 (2004). The Wisconsin Supreme Court, however, subsequently limited the scope of its holding in *Thomas*, ruling that the risk contribution theory would not apply in a case brought against manufacturers of residential paint, as residential paints are not fungible in the same way as white lead carbonate paint. See Godoy ex rel. Gramling v. E.I. du Pont de Nemours & Co., 768 N.W.2d 674, 683 (Wis.2009).

5. Beyond the Wisconsin cases cited in the previous note, courts have rejected market share liability in virtually every setting that has not involved DES. See, e.g., Hamilton v. Beretta U.S.A. Corp., 750 N.E.2d 1055 (N.Y.2001) (rejecting market share liability in a case involving marketing of handguns); Kinnett v. Mass Gas & Elec. Supply Co., 716 F.Supp. 695, 697 (D.N.H.1989) (electrical heat tape); York v. Lunkes, 545 N.E.2d 478, 480–81 (Ill.1989) (automobile batteries); Griffin v. Tenneco Resins, Inc., 648 F.Supp. 964, 967

(W.D.N.C.1986) (benzidine congener dyes); Mason v. Spiegel, Inc., 610 F.Supp. 401, 406 n.7 (D.Minn.1985) (flammable cotton tennis dress); Bradley v. Firestone Tire & Rubber Co., 590 F.Supp. 1177, 1181 (D.S.D.1984) (multi-piece truck wheel); see also Leng v. Celotex Corp., 554 N.E.2d 468, 470 (Ill.1990) (rejecting market share liability in asbestos case, and listing numerous citations to opinions consistent with decision). But see Smith v. Cutter Biological, Inc., 823 P.2d 717 (Haw.1991) (adopting market share liability in case involving contaminated blood products); In re Methyl Tertiary Butyl Ether (MTBE) Prods. Liab. Litig., 643 F.Supp.2d 461 (S.D.N.Y.2009) (adopting a "commingled product" theory). The following case provides an example of why so many courts are hesitant to expand market share liability beyond DES.

SHACKIL v. LEDERLE LABORATORIES

Supreme Court of New Jersey, 1989.
116 N.J. 155, 561 A.2d 511.

CLIFFORD, JUSTICE.

This is a medical-malpractice and products-liability action arising out of the 1972 inoculation of the infant plaintiff with a combined diphtheria-pertussis-tetanus vaccine, commonly known as DPT vaccine. Despite extensive discovery, plaintiffs were unable to identify the manufacturer of the DPT vaccine administered to the infant plaintiff. The issue is whether, in the context of childhood vaccinations, New Jersey should substitute for the element of causation-in-fact a theory of "market share" liability, thereby shifting to defendant manufacturers the burden of proof on the issue of causation.

We conclude that the imposition of a theory of collective liability in this case would frustrate overarching public-policy and public-health considerations by threatening the continued availability of needed drugs and impairing the prospects of the development of safer vaccines. Moreover, we are satisfied that an alternative compensation scheme established by Congress, entitled the National Childhood Vaccine Injury Act of 1986, 42 *U.S.C.A.* §§ 300aa–1 to–34 (West Supp.1988), will fulfill in large measure the goal of providing compensatory relief to vaccine-injured plaintiffs.

We therefore reverse the judgment of the Appellate Division and reinstate summary judgment in favor of defendant manufacturers.

I

Underlying this appeal is a profound human tragedy. On October 24, 1972, two days before her second birthday, plaintiff Deanna Marrero was given a final "booster" shot of a DPT vaccine by Dr. Feld, defendant pediatrician. Plaintiff Clara Morgan Shackil, the child's mother, noticed that within twenty-four hours of the inoculation Deanna displayed symptoms of extreme pain. The rapid deterioration of her condition resulted in the loss of her then-acquired verbal, motor, and mental capacities. Deanna, now eighteen years of age, has been diagnosed as having chronic encephalopathy and severe retardation. She is institutionalized and requires constant care.

In April 1985, thirteen years after the inoculation that allegedly caused plaintiff's condition, Deanna Marrero and her parents brought suit against Dr. Feld and Lederle Laboratories, one of the manufacturers of DPT during 1971–72. The complaint asserted theories of negligence, breach of warranty, misrepresentation, and strict liability based on design defect. Plaintiffs' delay in filing suit was occasioned by the fact that it was not until 1984 that Mrs. Shackil became aware of the linkage between brain damage and the pertussis portion of the DPT vaccine.

Largely because of the extensive time that had elapsed between the inoculation and the lawsuit, plaintiffs were unable to establish that Lederle Laboratories in fact manufactured the vaccine that caused Deanna's injuries. The pediatrician, Dr. Feld, retained no records that would have revealed the brand name of the vaccine administered, and his pharmacist is no longer alive. In his deposition, Dr. Feld testified that he had used Lederle's vaccine "for the most part"; however, he also indicated that on occasion he had used DPT vaccines manufactured by Eli Lilly, Wyeth Laboratories, Parke–Davis, and Pitman–Moore. Dr. Feld did not mention the name of National Drug Company, the only remaining manufacturer of DPT at the time of Deanna's inoculation.

Plaintiffs amended their complaint to include the additional manufacturers referred to in Dr. Feld's deposition but not National Drug Company. After several months of discovery, however, plaintiffs were still unable to identify the manufacturer of the vaccine administered to Deanna. Consequently, defendants Lederle, Eli Lilly, Wyeth, and Parke–Davis moved for summary judgment based on plaintiffs' failure to satisfy an essential element of a *prima facie* case—the identity of the manufacturer and distributor of the DPT dosage.

[T]he trial court granted defendant manufacturers' motions for summary judgment and entered orders dismissing the complaints as to those defendants. The Appellate Division granted leave to appeal and reversed.

  * * *

II

At the center of this appeal is the traditional element of causation-in-fact, "that reasonable connection between the act or omission of the defendant and the damages which plaintiff has suffered." W. Keeton, D. Dobbs, R. Keeton & D. Owen, *Prosser & Keeton on the Law of Torts* § 41 at 263 (5th ed. 1984) [hereinafter *Prosser & Keeton*]. The purpose of the causation-in-fact requirement, besides assigning blameworthiness to culpable parties, is to limit the scope of potential liability and thereby encourage useful activity that would otherwise be deterred if there were excessive exposure to liability. Although proof of causation-in-fact is ordinarily an indispensable ingredient of a *prima facie* case, exceptions have nevertheless arisen that have allowed plaintiffs to shift to defendant or a group of defendants the burden of proof on the causation issue. Those exceptions include * * * alternative liability * * * and market-share liability. In fact, the theory that we are urged to adopt in this case, modified market-share liability, is essentially an extension of the alternative-liability theory. * * *

* * *

The market-share theory announced in *Sindell* was subsequently adopted, with modifications, by three states' highest courts. *See Hymowitz v. Eli Lilly & Co., supra*, 73 *N.Y.*2d 487, 541 *N.Y.S.*2d 941, 539 *N.E.*2d 1069 (N.Y.1989) (adopting market-share theory of liability in which DES defendants are liable in proportion to their share in national market irrespective of proof that they did not cause the injury); *Martin v. Abbott Laboratories, supra*, 102 *Wash.*2d 581, 689 *P.*2d 368 (adopting "modified market share" liability, in which plaintiff must join only one defendant who produced or marketed injury-causing product; burden is then shifted to defendant to prove its percentage share of market and thereby lower presumptive equal share of market); *Collins v. Eli Lilly & Co.*, 116 *Wis.*2d 166, 342 *N.W.*2d 37 (adopting modified market-share theory of liability in which each DES defendant is liable in proportion to its "respective contribution" to the result, as measured by various factors), *cert.* den., 469 *U.S.* 826, 105 *S.Ct.* 107, 83 *L.Ed.*2d 51 (1984) * * *.

* * *

III

[W]e proceed to the question of whether New Jersey should expand current principles of tort law to adopt risk-modified market-share liability in the DPT context. * * * [T]he central consideration on which our decision is essentially premised is whether as a matter of sound public policy this Court should modify traditional tort theory to allow plaintiffs' design-defect claims to proceed. * * *

* * *

IV

This Court has adopted the basic tenet that "[t]he torts process, like the law itself, is a human institution designed to accomplish certain social objectives." *People Express Airlines, Inc. v. Consolidated Rail Corp.*, 100 *N.J.* 246, 254, 495 *A.*2d 107 (1985). One of the primary objectives is to ensure "that innocent victims have avenues of legal redress, absent a contrary, overriding public policy." *Id.* at 254–55, 495 *A.*2d 107. Thus, implicit in any decision to broaden liability in order to provide compensation is a judgment that the goals of public policy will likewise be served. In this case, however, we are presented with a difficult circumstance in which societal goals, in encouraging the use and development of needed drugs, would be thwarted by the imposition of unlimited liability on manufacturers in order to provide compensation to those injured by their products.

We deem it a matter of paramount importance that this case involves a vaccine—a product regarded as essential to the public welfare. Before the vaccine's appearance, the disease pertussis claimed the lives of thousands of children in the United States each year and left many others with severe injuries, including spastic paralysis, mental retardation, and other neurological disorders. In one epidemic alone, pertussis was responsible for as many as 7,518 deaths, afflicting a total of 265,269 children. As a result of national immunization efforts sponsored by the federal government and begun in the early 1950s after the development of the vaccine, the country showed a ninety-nine percent reduction in the number of reported cases per 100,000 population during the years 1943 to 1976, and an even more dramatic reduction in the number of deaths. * * *

Those efforts notwithstanding, pertussis, not having been entirely eradicated, continues to pose a threat to the health of this country's children. Where there has been a reduced level of pertussis immunization, such as in Great Britain and Japan, major epidemics of the disease have recurred. Hence, the federal government continues actively to finance and monitor immunization efforts through the National Institutes of Health, the Food and Drug Administration, and the Center for Disease Control. New Jersey has assisted in this effort, as have the majority of states, by mandating that all school children be immunized before beginning their elementary-school education. Nevertheless, a recent study from the Children's Defense Fund indicates that DPT immunization rates have fallen sharply since 1980 * * *.

Recent trends in the production and distribution of DPT have threatened the supply of the vaccine, with a predictable effect on the nation's immunization efforts.

These trends include rapidly increasing prices for vaccines, a decline in the number of organizations involved in the production and distribution of vaccines which in turn may lead to interruptions in the supply of vaccines, and an increasing number of product liability lawsuits against vaccine manufacturers which allege injuries due to vaccines. [*Staff of the House Subcomm. on Health and the Environment of the House Comm. on Energy and Commerce, 99th Cong., 2d Sess., Report on Childhood Immunizations* 59.]

There are now only two commercial entities willing to produce the DPT vaccine as contrasted with five in 1984. The overwhelming reason for the decrease in the number of manufacturers is the "extreme liability exposure, [the] cost of litigation and the difficulty of continuing to obtain adequate insurance." *Vaccine Injury Compensation: Hearing Before Subcomm. on Health and the Environment of the House Comm. on Energy and Commerce*, 98th Cong., 2d Sess. 295 (Sept. 10 1984) (Statement of Daniel Shaw, Jr., Vice–President for Medical Affairs, Wyeth Laboratories). * * * The market's fragility has been reflected in the exorbitant increase in price of the DPT vaccine from eleven cents a dose in 1984 to $11.40 a dose in 1986 (eight dollars of which goes to insurance costs).

In addition to the policy of ensuring the continued use of this essential drug is the more immediate need to develop a safer alternative vaccine. The creation of an alternative-vaccine design is a slow and complex process that demands the consolidated efforts of scientists, researchers, government agencies, and manufacturers. More importantly, it involves significant expense, shouldered almost entirely by vaccine manufacturers. * * *

It is against this backdrop that we are asked to expand the scope of liability to which vaccine manufacturers may be held, irrespective of whether they actually produced the injury-causing product. We are told that this expansion represents the "trend" in modern tort law—an assertion that fails to take into account that "[i]t is not, however, the trend, but the social policy underlying it, that should guide the development of the common law." *Frame v. Kothari*, 115 *N.J.* 638, 653, 560 *A*.2d 675, 683 (1989) (Wilentz, C.J., and Garibaldi, J., concurring) (citing B. Cardozo, *The Paradoxes of Legal Science (1928), reprinted in Selected Writings of Benjamin Nathan Cardozo* 251, 284 (M. Hall ed. 1947). It is apparent that DPT manufacturers would have difficulty sustaining the increased cost attendant on the imposition of market-share liability while simultaneously covering ascending research costs in order to halt the unfortunate sequence of events that spawned this appeal, as well as continuing to meet current production needs. * * * Of broader concern is the effect of market-share liability on the development of other experimental drugs, such as a vaccine against the spread of acquired-immune-deficiency syndrome (AIDS)).

The overriding public policy of encouraging the development of necessary drugs is not unfamiliar to products-liability law. It is encompassed within comment k of the *Restatement (Second) of Torts* 402A, which provides that the producers of unavoidably unsafe products (products, including vaccines, that in the current state of human knowledge are incapable of being made safe for their intended and ordinary use) are not strictly liable for the unfortunate consequences attending their use. To merit that protection the product must be properly prepared and accompanied by proper directions and warnings. The exemption is premised on the ground that it would be "against the public interest" to apply strict liability to unavoidably dangerous products because of "the very serious tendency to stifle medical research and testing." *White v. Wyeth Laboratories*, 40 Ohio St.3d 390, 533 *N.E.*2d 748 (1988). * * *

Mindful of the desirability of providing compensatory relief to vaccine-injured persons, we look to the recent comprehensive efforts of Congress. After extensive research and hearings on the subject of the unique problems presented by childhood vaccine injuries, Congress devised a no-fault compensation scheme, entitled the National Childhood Vaccine Injury Act of 1986, 42 *U.S.C.A.* §§ 300aa–1 to –34, "under which awards can be made to vaccine-injured persons quickly, easily, and with certainty and generosity." H. Rep. No. 908, 99th Cong., 2d Sess., at 3 (1986), *reprinted in* "1986 U.S.Code Cong. & Admin.News" 6344 [hereinafter *House Report*].

The Act provides that a person who has suffered illness, injury, or death need only submit a petition to the United States Claims Court alleging that the injury is vaccine-related. A presumption of vaccine-relatedness arises when the injury suffered is listed in the Vaccine Injury Table, contained in 42 *U.S.C.A.* § 300aa–14, and when the first symptoms of the injury occurred within the time period set forth in the Table. A special master then reviews the claim and the evidence, and prepares findings of fact and conclusions of law on whether compensation is appropriate, and, if so, the amount of the award.

For those injured by a vaccine administered before October 1, 1988, the award is to represent "actual unreimbursable expenses" incurred from the date of the judgment awarding such expenses, and "reasonable projected unreimbursable expenses" including rehabilitation costs and costs incurred for custodial care. The only significant limitation is that the amount for pain and suffering, lost earnings, and attorneys fees may not exceed $30,000. If the petitioner filed a civil action before the effective date of the compensation program and chose to withdraw from the action in order to file a petition, however, the Court of Claims may award costs and expenses incurred in the civil action, including the reasonable value of the attorney's time if suit was filed under a contingent-fee arrangement.

The Act is funded by a "Manufacturers Excise Tax on Childhood Vaccines." The tax is "set to generate sufficient annual income for the [National Vaccine Injury Compensation Trust] Fund to cover all costs of compensation...." [House Report at 6375]. To assure funding during the nascent stages of the Act, Congress has authorized and appropriated advances to the Fund. Specifically, for payments of claims associated with post-Act administrations of vaccines, Congress has appropriated, for fiscal year 1989 alone, "such sums as may be necessary"; for those claims associated with pre-Act administrations, Congress has appropriated "such sums as may be necessary, not to exceed eighty million dollars." *Ibid.* Therefore, as we understand it, Congress has appropriated, for pre-Act vaccine injuries, up to eighty million dollars for fiscal year 1989 as an advance or "front" money to the Fund, so that there will be funds on hand immediately for the payment of claims. Those dollars came from general revenues. The scheme contemplates that once the excise tax gets up to speed and generates enough money to keep the Act funded, the Fund will pay back, with interest, the amount it "borrowed" from the general revenues. We are therefore satisfied that the Act currently enjoys sufficient funding; moreover, it is clear that Congress has exercised the foresight to maintain that status in the future.

The goal of Congress was to afford a remedy for plaintiffs who would otherwise engage in protracted litigation against a vaccine manufacturer with the consequent risk of being denied recovery because of failure to prove the *prima facie* elements of a tort-law cause of action. The compensation scheme contained in the Act therefore does away with the traditional tort-law requirements of proof with respect to causation, injury, negligence, and defect. * * * Thus * * * [i]t could even be argued that in one sense the Act embodies a theory of collective liability, inasmuch as it does not require identification of a manufacturer; moreover, it allocates the cost of vaccine-related accidents among all manufacturers by imposing a tax on each dose of vaccine produced.

In addition to serving the goal of compensation, the Act was also intended to protect the unstable vaccine market by maintaining an adequate number of vaccine manufacturers. * * *

* * *

Instead of pursuing that remedy under the Act, however, plaintiffs have chosen the more hazardous and cumbersome route of attempting to reshape tort-law theory to encompass their claim. They remind us that if we affirm the order of summary judgment, and thereby disallow collective liability in this instance, they will then be precluded from filing a claim under the Act. But that predicament, admittedly harsh, was a risk of which they were well aware and one that they willingly encountered. It therefore cannot form the basis of a determination by this Court to allow market-share liability or any modification thereof. The aim of the Act has always been to make vaccine liability more predictable by attracting claimants like these plaintiffs, whose legal position is tenuous, *before* they received a final determination by a court of law. No statutory purpose would be served if all potential claimants were permitted to cast the die first in a lawsuit and then turn to the Act in the event they were denied relief.

In sum, the existence of the Act is critical in this case for several reasons. First, it illustrates the complex nature of the problem underlying this appeal, which cannot be resolved simply by expanding tort-law theory. Second, it made available a means of compensatory relief for this plaintiff, which, although potentially smaller than a jury award might have been, was nonetheless certain. Finally, it satisfies the tort goal of encouraging safer products, inasmuch as the Act establishes a national program for the research and development of safer vaccines.

* * *

IV

Rather than approach our decision from the perspective of an analytical criticism of the market-share approach, we have chosen to posit today's ruling on the regressive effect that collective liability would have on the social policy of encouraging vaccine production and research. * * *

* * *

Although we agree * * * that New Jersey's approach to tort law "has been flexible to adapt traditional limitations on causation and recovery to the evolving needs of a complex society," a more significant countervailing consideration informs today's decision: the imposition of market-share liability in this case would cut against the societal goals of maintaining an adequate supply of life-saving vaccines and of developing safer alternatives to current methods of vaccinations. Our aim is not to insulate vaccine manufacturers from liability, but to acknowledge a painful reality—that the excessive exposure to liability that imposition of this novel theory would produce would inevitably discourage highly useful activity.

V

The foregoing discussion should make clear that our opinion is confined solely to the context of vaccines. It should not be read as forecasting an inhospitable response to the theory of market-share liability in an appropriate context, perhaps one in which its application would be consistent with public policy and where no other remedy would be available. This case, the Court's first exposure to market-share liability, may therefore come to represent the exception rather than the rule.

Reversed. The judgment for defendant manufacturers is reinstated. No costs.

NOTES AND QUESTIONS

1. The *Shackil* court rested its decision, in large part, on the existence of the National Childhood Vaccine Injury Act (NCVIA). Congress enacted the NCVIA in 1986, when many people felt that the cost of vaccine-related tort litigation was leading to a decline in the number of vaccine manufacturers and a consequent fear of vaccine shortages. The NCVIA is a no-fault compensation fund for persons injured through use of childhood vaccines. It limits the level of compensation for a claimant and precludes punitive damage awards. To receive compensation under the NCVIA, a petitioner must waive potential tort claims against vaccine manufacturers. However, a petitioner may subsequently reject an award and file suit directly against a vaccine manufacturer. Under the NCVIA, awards for injuries caused by pre–1988 vaccinations are paid through congressional appropriations. Awards for injuries caused by post–1988 vaccinations are funded through money derived from a vaccine excise tax. More recently, the NCVIA has been in the news regarding the question of the extent to which it preempts state law design defect claims. See Bruesewitz v. Wyeth, Inc., 561 F.3d 233 (3d Cir.2009), cert. granted, ___ U.S. ___, 130 S.Ct. 1734 (2010).

2. Setting aside the NCVIA, plaintiffs had a very difficult time prevailing in products liability actions against vaccine manufacturers. Some of the difficulties were noted in Chapter 2, section B.3.b. Proving both general and specific causation also proved to be a challenge, along with the indeterminate defendant problems noted in this Chapter.

3. The NCVIA is not the only time that Congress has stepped in to create a compensation program where indeterminacy or other problems make the tort system problematic as a means of compensating those injured by toxic exposures. See, e.g., Ricky Ray Hemophilia Relief Fund Act of 1998, 42 U.S.C. § 300c–22 (providing compensation to victims of contaminated blood products); Lung Benefits Act, 30 U.S.C. §§ 901–44 (providing compensation to coal miners who suffer from occupational respiratory illnesses); National Swine Flu Immunization Program of 1976, 42 U.S.C. § 247(b) (providing compensation to victims of flu vaccine side effects).

4. Given the outcome in *Shakil* and other, non-DES indeterminate defendant cases, is market share liability largely a thing of the past? Why are courts so uneasy with this mechanism?

C. CAUSAL APPORTIONMENT BETWEEN THE PLAINTIFF AND DEFENDANT(S)

DAFLER v. RAYMARK INDUSTRIES, INC.

Superior Court of New Jersey, Appellate Division, 1992.
259 N.J.Super. 17, 611 A.2d 136.

KING, P.J.A.D.

I

This appeal and cross-appeal are taken from a verdict in plaintiff's favor and a jury's apportionment of responsibility between plaintiff and defendant in an asbestos product liability case. The case presents a question of first impression in this State concerning apportionment of damages for lung cancer between an asbestos producer and a cigarette smoker. The jury found that plaintiff contributed 70% to his lung cancer by cigarette smoking and that defendant Keene Corporation (Keene) contributed 30% to plaintiff's lung cancer by its asbestos products used in shipbuilding. The damage verdict for lung cancer was molded to reflect this apportionment. We conclude that both the apportionment by the jury and the general verdict in plaintiff's favor find reasonable factual support in the record and we affirm.

II

This is the procedural background. On October 10, 1986 plaintiff sued 11 defendants, all manufacturers or distributors of asbestos products. At the jury trial in May 1991 the only remaining defendant was Keene * * *. Plaintiff claimed that he developed asbestosis and lung cancer as a result of occupational exposure to asbestos during his six-year employment at the New York Shipyard in Camden, from 1939 to 1945.

On May 21, 1991 the jury returned liability and damage verdicts in plaintiff's favor. The jury found unanimously that "asbestos exposure was a substantial contributing cause of Mr. Dafler's lung cancer." The jury found Keene, through its predecessors, a substantial contributing cause and 95% responsible. The jury found Garlock, Inc., a defendant who had settled for $2,500 before trial, 5% responsible. The monetary awards were: for asbestosis, $60,000; for lung cancer, $140,000—an aggregate of $200,000. * * *

As a result of these findings, the overall verdict of $200,000 was reduced by 5% to $190,000 because of the liability attributed to Garlock, Inc. The lung cancer verdicts alone were subjected to the 30/70% apportionment ratio between plaintiff and defendant Keene arrived at by the jury. The residual asbestosis injury award, of course, was not subject to apportionment since it was all attributable to defendant Keene. The net aggregate award to plaintiff, after these adjustments for the settlement with Garlock, Inc. and the plaintiff's own contribution to his lung cancer by smoking, was $96,900.

* * *

Both plaintiff and Keene appeal. In this appeal plaintiff raises these claims of error: (1) there was insufficient evidence to allow the jury to apportion damages for plaintiff's lung cancer; (2) the judge improperly influenced the jury's apportionment decision * * *.

III

These are the facts presented at trial. Plaintiff, Frank Dafler, age 70, worked as a shipfitter at the New York Shipyard in Camden from 1939 to 1945. During the World War II era New York Shipyard was one of the world's busiest ship building facilities, employing 36,000 men. During this period plaintiff worked on 12 to 13 ships. He could not recall the dates, but he remembered the names of the ships. He worked on the battleship, South Dakota; the light cruisers: Alaska, Cleveland, Guam, Hawaii and Montpelier; the carriers: Belleauwood, Cowpens, Cabot, Princeton, Independence, and Monterey; and a tender, Vulcan.

Dafler spent all of his time at the Shipyard working on board these ships. He spent about 70% of his time working in engine rooms and boiler rooms in very close proximity to the pipefitters who used asbestos and asbestos-containing products to cover the numerous pipes housed in those areas. Dafler himself did not work with asbestos, but he said it was all around him. The pipefitters and pipe coverers worked continuously, cutting and cementing pipes. * * * He saw no health warning signs anywhere. No masks were used or provided. He did recall that the pipefitters' use of asbestos made the air very dusty. There was no ventilation in the boiler or engine rooms during construction. He described the asbestos, held in 80 to 100–pound bags, as "very, very dusty" and likened it to pulverized lime. He had no further exposure to asbestos after leaving the Shipyard.

* * *

The plaintiff began experiencing shortness of breath in the 1970s. In 1984 he went to the hospital for breathing problems. The diagnosis in 1984 was asbestosis. He then decreased the time that he worked between 1984 and 1989 because of his breathing problem. In 1984 he began seeing Dr. Agia, a pulmonary specialist, twice a year for x-rays and pulmonary function tests. In 1989 the doctors found a cancerous tumor in plaintiff's lung and surgery ensued. Since his surgery plaintiff has had limited mobility and physical capacity. Plaintiff said that he smoked cigarettes for almost 45 years, since age 18. He had a pack-a-day habit until his diagnosis of asbestosis in 1984 when he quit.

The plaintiff presented two medical experts: Dr. Guidice, a pulmonary specialist, and Dr. Stone, a pathologist. Dr. Guidice explained that the cause of plaintiff's asbestosis and later bronchogenic carcinoma, or lung cancer, was his occupational exposure to asbestos at the Shipyard. His opinion, and Dr. Stone's, on causation amply created a jury question on the claimed work-connected genesis of the lung cancer, a causation which defendant's expert, Dr. DeMopolous, a pathologist, denied completely. He thought that cigarettes alone caused the plaintiff's lung cancer.

The experts also testified on the epidemiological aspects of [lung cancer] and cigarette smoking. Dr. Guidice explained that there is a "base line" relative risk of 11 cases of lung cancer per 100,000 persons in the general population per year. This "base line" is for people in the general population who do not smoke and are not exposed to asbestos. The relative risk of lung cancer with industrial exposure to asbestos, like plaintiff's occupational exposure, increases five-fold (5:1), or to 55 cases per 100,000 of population per year. The relative risk with cigarette smoking increases ten-fold (10:1), or to 110 cases per 100,000 of population per year. The relative risk of exposure to asbestos *plus* cigarette smoking is not additive, *i.e.*, 10 + 5 or 15–fold, but becomes what Dr. Guidice described as "multiplicative or synergistic," or 50 times (50:1) the "base line," *i.e.*, 550 cases per 100,000 of population per year.

Dr. Guidice could not apportion the causation of plaintiff's lung cancer between his asbestosis and his long-term cigarette smoking. He said when asked about apportionment: "No, and I don't know anybody that's able to do that. That's not possible. This relationship is synergistic and multiplicative between those two cancer causing agents. It's not possible to distinguish which contribution is caused by asbestos and which is caused by cigarette smoking." He conceded that the major cause of lung cancer in the United States is cigarette smoking.

Dr. Stone essentially agreed with Dr. Guidice on the epidemiological data. He thought the relative risk for cigarette smoking alone was about 10 to 12:1 above the "base line," the relative risk for asbestosis alone was about 6 to 7:1 above the "base line." He said that "the lung cancer was caused by the synergistic interaction of his cigarette smoking and asbestos exposure." He also agreed that cigarette smoking was by far the greatest cause of all lung cancers in the United States. He did not attempt to apportion responsibility, saying that "both were significant contributory causes." Both doctors agreed that the relative risk of smoking was twice as great as the relative risk for asbestos with respect to cancer.

As noted, the defendant's expert, Dr. DeMopolous, completely discounted any role for asbestos in causing the plaintiff's lung cancer. * * * Dr. DeMopolous did not speak to apportionment.

The jury seemed to have apportioned the damages for plaintiff's lung cancer according to the relative risk factors for asbestos (5:1 or 30%) and cigarette smoking (10:1 or 70%), roughly one-third to two-thirds. The judge molded the jury's monetary verdict on the lung cancer aspect, $140,000, accordingly.

IV

Plaintiff's principal claim on this appeal is that the judge erred in submitting the issue of apportionment to the jury in the first place. Plaintiff contends that there was insufficient evidence in the record to provide any basis for apportionment. Judge Weinberg thought this case presented enough evidence to justify allowing the issue to go to the jury. He said:

> The case before us involves an exposure to asbestos of approximately five years. It involves cigarette smoking for almost half a century. I have never—or I have not in the past apportioned this. I did not have a case before me in the past that I felt there was sufficient facts and sufficient expert testimony that would permit the jury to do anything other that [sic] utter speculation.
>
> I think this is a case that permits the jury to consider the facts regarding exposure to asbestos and the extent and the amount and the time of cigarette smoking in conjunction with the expert evidence, if the jury accepts the same, and the jury can make a determination regarding a percentage of causation as to the lung cancer.
>
> I am not suggesting that every case where cigarette smoking happens to be involved is an appropriate case for the apportionment being made. I am making a determination that in this particular case with the facts in this case and the testimony in this case, that I believe that it is a proper item for jury consideration and I intend to submit it to them for that purpose. They will provide us a verdict as to the apportionment.

Although the issue is novel in this jurisdiction, we agree with the trial judge and affirm on this point.

Plaintiff asserts that the lung cancer was an indivisible harm with indivisible damages, that the defendant failed to meet its burden of showing that there was a reasonable basis for apportionment, and that the percentages found by the jury, 30%–70%, were against the weight of the evidence. Defendant Keene contends that the use of apportionment in this case was consistent with the evidence and the development of the law in this State.

Apportionment of damages among multiple causes is a well-recognized tort principle. The *Restatement (Second) of Torts* § 433A, at 434 (1965), regarding apportionment of harm to causes, states:

> (1) Damages for harm are to be apportioned among two or more causes where

(a) there are distinct harms, or

(b) there is a reasonable basis for determining the contribution of each cause to a single harm.

(2) Damages for any other harm cannot be apportioned among two or more causes.

Comment (a) to the *Restatement* indicates that "[t]he rules stated apply also where one of the causes in question is the conduct of the plaintiff himself, whether it be negligent or innocent." *Restatement (Second) of Torts* § 433A, Comment (a), at 435. * * *

The *Restatement* * * * recognizes that the concern in apportioning responsibility is more practical than theoretical: is there "a reasonable basis for determining the contribution of each cause to a single harm?" *Restatement, supra,* § 433A(1)(b) at 434. Here the single harm to the plaintiff was his lung cancer. The two causes were his six-year occupational exposure to asbestos and his 45–year cigarette smoking habit. The trial judge had to determine, as a matter of law in the first instance, whether the harm was capable of apportionment. *See Martin v. Owens–Corning Fiberglas Corp.,* 515 *Pa.* 377, 528 *A.2d* 947, 949 (1987). The burden of proving that the harm is capable of apportionment is on the party seeking it, here defendant Keene. *Restatement, supra,* § 433B(2), at 441.

Several state and federal courts have considered the apportionment issue in similar occupational asbestos-smoking cases. The Pennsylvania Supreme Court addressed the apportionment issue in *Martin v. Owens–Corning Fiberglas Corp., supra.* The plaintiff, a former insulation worker, brought suit against various asbestos manufacturers seeking damages for asbestosis and lung impairment. Plaintiff worked with asbestos for about 39 years, and smoked for about 37 years. At trial, plaintiff's experts testified that his lung impairment was due to the combined effect of emphysema, caused by cigarette smoking, and asbestosis, from occupational asbestos exposure. They said that it was impossible to apportion the lung impairment between the two causes. 515 *Pa.* at 383, 528 *A.2d* at 950. Defendant's expert testified that the lung impairment was caused solely by plaintiff's cigarette smoking. The question presented on appeal was whether the trial judge erred in instructing the jury that it could apportion damages between the asbestos exposure and smoking. *Id.* at 379, 528 A.2d at 948. There were no epidemiological data or relative risk factors before the jury in *Martin.*

A plurality of the Pennsylvania Supreme Court applied § 433A of the *Restatement* and held that it was error for the trial judge to instruct the jury on apportionment since the evidence failed to establish a reasonable basis on which to apportion. * * *

        * * *

Some other jurisdictions have permitted apportionment in these cases. In *Brisboy v. Fibreboard Corp.,* 429 *Mich.* 540, 418 *N.W.2d* 650 (1988), the Supreme Court of Michigan upheld a jury finding that plaintiff's smoking contributed 55% to his lung cancer while 45% was attributable to his asbestos exposure, apparently without the benefit of epidemiological testimony. *See Jenkins v. Halstead Indus.,* 17 *Ark.App.* 197, 706 *S.W.*2d 191 (1986) (92% of worker's chronic obstructive pulmonary disease apportioned to life-long cigarette smoking in workers' compensation case). *Champagne v. Raybestos–Manhattan, Inc.,* 212 *Conn.* 509, 562 *A.*2d 1100, 1118 (1989) (plaintiff's smoking found 75% contributory to his lung cancer, citing Michigan's *Brisboy v. Fibreboard Corp., supra*).

No New Jersey cases have specifically addressed the issue of apportionment of civil law damages in an asbestos-exposure cigarette smoking context. * * * However, the concept of apportionment of damages is not alien to this jurisdiction. The theory of § 433A of the *Restatement (Second) of Torts* has been applied in varied circumstances. *See Scafidi v. Seiler,* 119 *N.J.* 93, 574 *A.*2d 398 (1990) ("increased risk" and "lost chance" concepts in medical malpractice); *Waterson v. General Motors Corp.,* 111 *N.J.* 238, 270, 544 *A.*2d 357 (1988) (automobile "crashworthiness" case). These cases involve pre-existing or concurrent injuries; apportionment was limited to instances of distinct injuries or to circumstances when a reasonable basis existed to determine the contribution of each cause. The burden with respect to proof of apportionment rested, of course, with the party seeking it.

* * *

As we well know, apportionment is also consistent with the principles of the Comparative Negligence Act, *N.J.S.A.* 2A:15–5.1 to–5.3, and the Contribution Among Tortfeasors Act, *N.J.S.A.* 2A:53A–1 to–5.

We conclude that there was ample basis in the record of this trial to submit the issue of apportionment to the jury. The extant legal precedent supports rational efforts to apportion responsibility in such circumstances rather than require one party to absorb the entire burden. The jury obviously accepted the epidemiological testimony based on relative risk factors, the smoking history over 45 years, and the substantial occupational exposure over six years. The synergistically resultant disease, lung cancer, was produced by a relative risk factor of 10:1 contributed by plaintiff and 5:1 contributed by defendant. The jury probably shaded the apportionment slightly in defendant's favor, 70% instead of two-thirds, because of the strong emphasis on cigarette smoking as the greatly predominant overall cause of lung cancer in this country.

The result was rational and fair. We can ask no more. This is fairer than requiring defendant to shoulder the entire causative burden where its contribution in fact was not likely even close to 100%. Or fairer, for certain, than no recovery at all for plaintiff who, while a victim of the disease of asbestosis which probably led in part to the lung cancer, confronts a reluctant jury which might not want to saddle a defendant with a 100% verdict in the circumstances of a particular case.

We conclude that our Supreme Court's recent decision in *Landrigan v. Celotex Corp.,* 127 *N.J.* 404, 415–416, 605 *A.*2d 1079 (1992), a colon cancer asbestos claim, supports the result we reach in relying on the epidemiological data for apportionment. This discipline of epidemiology "studies the relationship between a disease and a factor suspected of causing the disease, using statistical methods. . . ." *Id.* at 415. The Supreme Court recognized that "proof of causation in toxic-tort cases depends largely on inferences derived from statistics about groups," *id.* at 422; and conceded that plaintiffs in toxic-tort cases "may be compelled to resort to more general evidence, such as that provided by epidemiological studies." *Id.* at 415.

V

* * * Plaintiff alleges that the judge improperly influenced the jury on the issue of apportionment during his charge. * * *

* * *

Regarding the issue of apportionment, the judge correctly instructed the jury on Keene's burden to prove that cigarette smoking was a substantial contributing factor to plaintiff's condition, as well as on its burden to prove that responsibility *should* and *could* be apportioned. * * *

* * *

Affirmed.

NOTES AND QUESTIONS

1. Recall that the black letter of section 433A of the Second Restatement of Torts provides two circumstances where damages may be apportioned based on causation:

(1) Damages for harm are to be apportioned among two or more causes where

(a) there are distinct harms, or

(b) there is a reasonable basis for determining the contribution of each cause to a single harm.

Restatement (Second) of Torts § 433A. Comment d offers the following example of the application of alternative (b):

There are other types of harm which, while not so clearly marked out as severable into distinct parts, are still capable of division upon a reasonable and rational basis, and of fair apportionment among the causes responsible. Thus, where the cattle of two or more owners trespass upon the plaintiff's land and destroy his crop, the aggregate harm is a lost crop, but it may nevertheless be apportioned among the owners of the cattle, on the basis of the number owned by each, and the reasonable assumption that the respective harm done is proportionate to that number. Where such apportionment can be made without injustice to any of the parties, the court may require it to be made.

Id. § 433A cmt. d. Which alternative did the court use to assign liability for Dafler's asbestosis injury? For his lung cancer injury? In what sense are these two "causes" of Mr. Dafler's lung cancer like the trespassing cattle in comment d? How are they different?

2. In note 6 following the *Borel* case, p. 241 we noted that section 433A of the Second Restatement was replaced by Restatement (Third) of Torts: Apportionment of Liability, section 26. There we set forth the black letter of section 26. Here, once again, is part (b) of that section.

(b) Damages can be divided by causation when the evidence provides a reasonable basis for the factfinder to determine:

(1) that any legally culpable conduct of a party or other relevant person to whom the factfinder assigns a percentage of responsibility was a legal cause of less than the entire damages for which the plaintiff seeks recovery and

(2) the amount of damages separately caused by that conduct.

Otherwise, the damages are indivisible and thus the injury is indivisible.

Restatement (Third) of Torts: Apportionment § 26 (2002). Does section 26 support the type of apportionment done in *Dafler*?

3. At the time section 433A was adopted in 1965, almost all American jurisdictions still operated under a contributory negligence regime. Negligent plaintiffs were barred from any recovery. Fortunately for Dafler, New Jersey adopted comparative responsibility in 1973. N.J.S.A. 2A:15–5.1. Did the apportionment to Dafler involve his comparative negligence?

4. Typically in a tort case, there are multiple causes (in a but-for sense) of plaintiff's harm. Plaintiff had to have chosen to walk across a busy city street at the time that defendant went through a red light and the din of the intersection had to have existed so that plaintiff didn't hear the approaching defendant. We don't apportion liability to those other causes because they do not implicate tortious conduct. As the Third Restatement on Apportionment puts it in section 26, comment m, "Apportionment of liability depends on findings that each person was legally culpable * * *." Restatement (Third) of Torts: Apportionment of Liability § 26 cmt. m (2002). For that reason, most courts do not permit apportionment in the *Dafler* context without a finding of tortious conduct relating to the contribution from smoking. See, e.g., Richards v. Owens–Illinois, Inc., 928 P.2d 1181 (Cal.1997) (statutory immunity of tobacco suppliers prevented apportionment of comparative responsibility to them); Champagne v. Raybestos–Manhattan, Inc., 562 A.2d 1100, 1118 (Conn. 1989) (permitting plaintiff's smoking to be the basis for comparative-responsibility apportionment); In re Asbestos Litig. Pusey Trial Group, 669 A.2d 108, 111–13 (Del.1995) (trial court erred in permitting apportionment without instructing on and requiring jury to find that plaintiff's smoking constituted comparative fault).

5. In the *Martin* case, discussed in *Dafler*, the Pennsylvania Supreme Court refused to apportion the plaintiff's emphysema injuries between asbestos exposure and tobacco use. Can the outcome in these two cases be reconciled? If the *Dafler* court had determined that causal apportionment was inappropriate, how should responsibility be allocated? What allocation would you argue for if you were on the *Dafler* jury?

6. Recall that in the *Rutherford* case the jury assigned 1.2 percent of the liability to the defendant and 2.5 percent to the plaintiff, presumably due to his use of tobacco.

7. *The causal question in failure to warn cases. Borel, Rutherford, Sindell, Shakil* and *Dafler* are all products liability failure to warn cases. Plaintiff must prove both that defendant had a duty to warn and that the failure to fulfill this duty was the cause of plaintiff's injury. In some situations the duty and causation issues are intertwined. This is the case with respect to obvious dangers and dangers of which plaintiff is already aware. Judge Calabresi makes a useful distinction between these two situations in Burke v. Spartanics, Ltd., 252 F.3d 131 (2d Cir.2001). Defendants have no duty to warn of "obvious dangers." While the boundary between obvious and non-obvious dangers is sometimes vague, clearly some dangers are so obvious there is no duty to warn. There is no duty to warn that a knife may cut someone. See Restatement (Third) of Torts: Products Liability § 2 cmt. j (1998). Even when a danger is not obvious, however, defendant may not be liable for failing to warn an injured individual if that person already knew of the danger in question. The reason this is the case touches on the central causal question in failure to warn cases. In most situations plaintiff has the burden of proving that he would have acted differently if an adequate warning had been provided. If a plaintiff already understands the danger and proceeds anyway, a further warning presumably would not have changed his behavior. See Chapter 2, pp. 39–40, supra for a discussion of duty to warn in products liability cases.

With respect to prescription drugs, the duty to warn is governed by the learned intermediary rule. The manufacturer must warn the doctor or other medical professional who is then obligated to explain the risks and benefits to the patient. In this context, plaintiffs' claims sometimes fail because the physician testifies that even had she been warned more thoroughly she would have nevertheless prescribed the drug to plaintiff. See Ackermann v. Wyeth Pharms., 526 F.3d 203 (5th Cir.2008).

What of situations where there was no warning but it is almost certain that even if plaintiff had read an adequate warning, the warning would not have altered her behavior? For example, a vaccine may have a rare side effect but failure to be vaccinated may expose one to a greater risk of serious illness. Should one be entitled to a warning based on the idea that individuals should be provided the opportunity to make their own autonomous risk decisions in every instance? What problem does this rationale pose for the assessment of damages?

PROBLEM

Jack Jones worked for many years at the Williamson Valve Corporation. Over a period of 20 years, he installed asbestos insulation in pipe valves designed to be used to carry high pressure steam in power plants. Recently, he was diagnosed with lung cancer. Mr. Jones did the exact same job over his entire 20 year work career. A lengthy discovery process revealed that four different manufacturers supplied asbestos products to Williamson during the time Mr. Jones was employed there. All of the manufacturers supplied asbestos products over the entire period. Assume that all of the defendants knew about the dangers of asbestos but failed to warn Mr. Jones. Also assume that Mr. Jones never smoked and he has no other known risk factors, such as family genetic predisposition to lung cancer. The relative percentage of asbestos supplied by each manufacturer is as follows: Acme Corp.—20%, Beacon Corp.—20%, Corning Corp.—10%, Drako Corp.—50%.

1. If the state in which Mr. Jones brings his action follows the Restatement's position on divisible and indivisible injuries, how should the court instruct the jury as to how they should apportion liability?

2. Now assume that Mr. Jones smoked a pack of cigarettes a day over this 20 year period. Recall from the discussion in *Dafler* that epidemiologic studies reveal a strong relationship between lung cancer and both asbestos exposure and smoking. On average, the relative risk between significant asbestos exposure and the disease is approximately 5, while the relative risk between smoking and lung cancer is closer to 10. (With respect to both asbestos and tobacco use the relationship is dose related. For example, in one study the relative risk of lung cancer for those smoking one to 10 cigarettes daily was 5.5 compared to nonsmokers, while for those smoking more than 31 cigarettes a day the relative risk was 22.0. The same dose-response relationship exists with respect to asbestos exposure. For the purposes of the problem, however, assume that Mr. Jones' risk factors are 5.0 and 10.0.).

Asbestos exposure and tobacco use have a synergistic effect, sometimes called a multiplicative effect, on the likelihood of developing lung cancer. Although the mean relative risk of developing lung cancer from tobacco use is approximately 10 and the mean relative risk of developing lung cancer from asbestos exposure is approximately 5, the mean relative risk for someone who is exposed to asbestos and uses tobacco as compared to someone who has neither risk factor is on the order of 50.

Given these facts, what causal allocation might Mr. Jones' attorney propose? What allocation might the defendants propose? How do they compare to the allocation the jury made in *Dafler?* Is the causal analysis now so complex that the court should abandon any effort along these lines and simply treat this as an indivisible injury? Would your answer be different if comparative responsibility were available as an alternative means to apportion liability?

3. How, if at all, would your analysis change if Mr. Jones were suffering from asbestosis? How would it change if he were suffering from mesothelioma?

For two approaches to this problem, see Michael D. Green, A Future for Asbestos Apportionment, 12 Conn.Ins.L.J. 315 (2005–2006); Michael D. Green, Second Thoughts About Apportionment in Asbestos Litigation, 37 Sw.U.L.Rev. 531 (2008).

CHAPTER V

ADMISSIBILITY OF EVIDENCE

■ ■ ■

A. THE *DAUBERT* STANDARD

As the preceding Chapter makes clear, toxic tort cases often turn on complicated testimony from expert witnesses. It is no surprise, therefore, that lawyers often expend significant resources litigating the admissibility of such testimony in the first place.

Until the 1990s, an overwhelming number of courts—both state and federal—applied an admissibility standard from the famous case of Frye v. United States, 293 F. 1013 (D.C.Cir.1923). *Frye* was a criminal case in which the defendant sought to introduce testimony supporting his truthfulness based on a systolic blood pressure test, a precursor to the modern polygraph. The trial court excluded the evidence, and the D.C. Court of Appeals affirmed. In a short opinion, the court based its decision on the defendant's failure to demonstrate that the test had gained "general acceptance" in the fields of psychology and physiology.

[The defendant claims, on this novel question, the following principle:]

> "The rule is that the opinions of experts or skilled witnesses are admissible in evidence in those cases in which the matter of inquiry is such that inexperienced persons are unlikely to prove capable of forming a correct judgment upon it, for the reason that the subject-matter so far partakes of a science, art, or trade as to require a previous habit or experience or study in it, in order to acquire a knowledge of it. When the question involved does not lie within the range of common experience or common knowledge, but requires special experience or special knowledge, then the opinions of witnesses skilled in that particular science, art, or trade to which the question relates are admissible in evidence."

* * * Just when a scientific principle or discovery crosses the line between the experimental and demonstrable stages is difficult to define. Somewhere in this twilight zone the evidential force of the principle must be recognized, and while courts will go a long way in admitting expert testimony deduced from a well-recognized scientific

principle or discovery, the thing from which the deduction is made must be sufficiently established to have gained general acceptance in the particular field in which it belongs.

> We think the systolic blood pressure deception test has not yet gained such standing and scientific recognition among physiological and psychological authorities as would justify the courts in admitting expert testimony deduced from the discovery, development, and experiments thus far made.

Id. at 1014.

Although *Frye* itself set forth little in the way of rationale behind its decision, later courts supported the standard as necessary protection against the risk that jurors would overestimate the probative value of expert scientific testimony. At the same time, *Frye* had its critics, many of whom viewed the general acceptance standard as both too broad and too vague, leaving the question of admissibility to the counting of noses, rather than by considering the validity of experts' opinions.

Nonetheless, by the 1970s, every federal circuit and some 45 states adhered to the *Frye* standard. In 1975, however, the Supreme Court promulgated the Federal Rules of Evidence, including Rule 702, which spoke to the admissibility of expert testimony. Rule 702 provides:

> If scientific, technical, or other specialized knowledge will assist the trier of fact to understand the evidence or to determine a fact in issue, a witness qualified as an expert by knowledge, skill, experience, training, or education, may testify thereto in the form of an opinion or otherwise.

Fed.R.Evid. 702. As Rule 702 did not speak to general acceptance, an obvious issue arose as to whether the Rule superseded *Frye* and provided a substantially different standard. Federal circuit courts split on the issue, but it was not until 1993 that the U.S. Supreme Court resolved the matter in the case of *Daubert v. Merrell Dow Pharamaceuticals, Inc.*

DAUBERT v. MERRELL DOW PHARMACEUTICALS, INC.

United States Supreme Court, 1993.
509 U.S. 579, 113 S.Ct. 2786, 125 L.Ed.2d 469.

Blackmun, Justice.

In this case we are called upon to determine the standard for admitting expert scientific testimony in a federal trial.

I

Petitioners Jason Daubert and Eric Schuller are minor children born with serious birth defects. They and their parents sued respondent in California state court, alleging that the birth defects had been caused by the mothers' ingestion of Bendectin, a prescription antinausea drug marketed by respondent. Respondent removed the suits to federal court on diversity grounds.

After extensive discovery, respondent moved for summary judgment, contending that Bendectin does not cause birth defects in humans and that petitioners would be unable to come forward with any admissible evidence that it does. In support of its motion, respondent submitted an affidavit of Steven H. Lamm, physician and epidemiologist, who is a well-credentialed expert on the risks from exposure to various chemical substances. Doctor Lamm stated that he had reviewed all the literature on Bendectin and human birth defects—more than 30 published studies involving over 130,000 patients. No study had found Bendectin to be a human teratogen (*i.e.*, a substance capable of causing malformations in fetuses). On the basis of this review, Doctor Lamm concluded that maternal use of Bendectin during the first trimester of pregnancy has not been shown to be a risk factor for human birth defects.

Petitioners did not (and do not) contest this characterization of the published record regarding Bendectin. Instead, they responded to respondent's motion with the testimony of eight experts of their own, each of whom also possessed impressive credentials. These experts had concluded that Bendectin can cause birth defects. Their conclusions were based upon "in vitro" (test tube) and "in vivo" (live) animal studies that found a link between Bendectin and malformations; pharmacological studies of the chemical structure of Bendectin that purported to show similarities between the structure of the drug and that of other substances known to cause birth defects; and the "reanalysis" of previously published epidemiological (human statistical) studies.

The District Court granted respondent's motion for summary judgment. The court stated that scientific evidence is admissible only if the principle upon which it is based is " 'sufficiently established to have general acceptance in the field to which it belongs.' " The court concluded that petitioners' evidence did not meet this standard. Given the vast body of epidemiological data concerning Bendectin, the court held, expert opinion which is not based on epidemiological evidence is not admissible to establish causation. Thus, the animal-cell studies, live-animal studies, and chemical-structure analyses on which petitioners had relied could not raise by themselves a reasonably disputable jury issue regarding causation. Petitioners' epidemiological analyses, based as they were on recalculations of data in previously published studies that had found no causal link between the drug and birth defects, were ruled to be inadmissible because they had not been published or subjected to peer review.

The United States Court of Appeals for the Ninth Circuit affirmed. Citing *Frye v. United States*, the court stated that expert opinion based on a scientific technique is inadmissible unless the technique is "generally accepted" as reliable in the relevant scientific community. The court declared that expert opinion based on a methodology that diverges "significantly from the procedures accepted by recognized authorities in the field ... cannot be shown to be 'generally accepted as a reliable technique.' "

The court emphasized that other Courts of Appeals considering the risks of Bendectin had refused to admit reanalyses of epidemiological studies that had been neither published nor subjected to peer review. Those courts had found unpublished reanalyses "particularly problematic in light of the massive weight of the original published studies supporting [respondent's] position, all of which had undergone full scrutiny from the scientific community." Contending that reanalysis is generally accepted by the scientific community only when it is subjected to verification and scrutiny by others in the field, the Court of Appeals rejected petitioners' reanalyses as "unpublished, not subjected to the normal peer review process and generated solely for use in litigation." The court concluded that petitioners' evidence provided an insufficient foundation to allow admission of expert testimony that Bendectin caused their injuries and, accordingly, that petitioners could not satisfy their burden of proving causation at trial.

We granted certiorari in light of sharp divisions among the courts regarding the proper standard for the admission of expert testimony.

II

A

In the 70 years since its formulation in the *Frye* case, the "general acceptance" test has been the dominant standard for determining the admissibility of scientific evidence at trial. Although under increasing attack of late, the rule continues to be followed by a majority of courts, including the Ninth Circuit.

The *Frye* test has its origin in a short and citation-free 1923 decision concerning the admissibility of evidence derived from a systolic blood pressure deception test, a crude precursor to the polygraph machine. In what has become a famous (perhaps infamous) passage, the then Court of Appeals for the District of Columbia described the device and its operation and declared:

> "Just when a scientific principle or discovery crosses the line between the experimental and demonstrable stages is difficult to define. Somewhere in this twilight zone the evidential force of the principle must be recognized, and while courts will go a long way in admitting expert testimony deduced from a well-recognized scientific principle or discovery, *the thing from which the deduction is made must be sufficiently established to have gained general acceptance in the particular field in which it belongs*." Frye, 293 F., at 1014 (emphasis added).

Because the deception test had "not yet gained such standing and scientific recognition among physiological and psychological authorities as would justify the courts in admitting expert testimony deduced from the discovery, development, and experiments thus far made," evidence of its results was ruled inadmissible. *Ibid.*

The merits of the *Frye* test have been much debated, and scholarship on its proper scope and application is legion. Petitioners' primary attack, however, is not on the content but on the continuing authority of the rule. They contend that the *Frye* test was superseded by the adoption of the Federal Rules of Evidence. We agree.

* * *

Here there is a specific Rule that speaks to the contested issue. Rule 702, governing expert testimony, provides:

> "If scientific, technical, or other specialized knowledge will assist the trier of fact to understand the evidence or to determine a fact in issue, a witness qualified as an expert by knowledge, skill, experience, training, or education, may testify thereto in the form of an opinion or otherwise."

Nothing in the text of this Rule establishes "general acceptance" as an absolute prerequisite to admissibility. Nor does respondent present any clear indication that Rule 702 or the Rules as a whole were intended to incorporate a "general acceptance" standard. The drafting history makes no mention of *Frye*, and a rigid "general acceptance" requirement would be at odds with the "liberal thrust" of the Federal Rules and their "general approach of relaxing the traditional barriers to 'opinion' testimony." Given the Rules' permissive backdrop and their inclusion of a specific rule on expert testimony that does not mention " 'general acceptance,' " the assertion that the Rules somehow assimilated *Frye* is unconvincing. *Frye* made "general acceptance" the exclusive test for admitting expert scientific testimony. That austere standard, absent from, and incompatible with, the Federal Rules of Evidence, should not be applied in federal trials.

B

That the *Frye* test was displaced by the Rules of Evidence does not mean, however, that the Rules themselves place no limits on the admissibility of purportedly scientific evidence. Nor is the trial judge disabled from screening such evidence. To the contrary, under the Rules the trial judge must ensure that any and all scientific testimony or evidence admitted is not only relevant, but reliable.

The primary locus of this obligation is Rule 702, which clearly contemplates some degree of regulation of the subjects and theories about which an expert may testify. "*If scientific,* technical, or other specialized *knowledge will assist the trier of fact* to understand the evidence or to determine a fact in issue" an expert "may testify *thereto.*" (emphasis added). The subject of an expert's testimony must be "scientific . . . knowledge." The adjective "scientific" implies a grounding in the methods and procedures of science. Similarly, the word "knowledge" connotes more than subjective belief or unsupported speculation. The term "applies to any body of known facts or to any body of ideas inferred from such facts or accepted as truths on good grounds." Of course, it would be unreasonable to conclude that the subject of scientific testimony must be "known" to a certainty; arguably, there are no certainties in science. But, in order to qualify as "scientific knowledge," an inference or assertion must be derived by the scientific method. Proposed testimony must be supported by appropriate validation—*i.e.*, "good grounds," based on what is known. In short, the requirement that an expert's testimony pertain to "scientific knowledge" establishes a standard of evidentiary reliability.

Rule 702 further requires that the evidence or testimony "assist the trier of fact to understand the evidence or to determine a fact in issue." This condition goes primarily to relevance. "Expert testimony which does not relate to any issue in the case is not relevant and, ergo, non-helpful." ("An additional consideration under Rule 702—and another aspect of relevancy—is whether expert testimony proffered in the case is sufficiently tied to the facts of the case that it will aid the jury in resolving a factual dispute"). The consideration has been aptly described by Judge Becker as one of "fit." "Fit" is not always obvious, and scientific validity for one purpose is not necessarily scientific validity for other, unrelated purposes. The study of the phases of the moon, for example, may provide valid scientific "knowledge" about whether a certain night was dark, and if darkness is a fact in issue, the knowledge will assist the trier of fact. However (absent creditable grounds supporting such a link), evidence that the moon was full on a certain night will not assist the trier of fact in determining whether an individual was unusually likely to have behaved irrationally on that night. Rule 702's "helpfulness" standard requires a valid scientific connection to the pertinent inquiry as a precondition to admissibility.

        * * *

C

Faced with a proffer of expert scientific testimony, then, the trial judge must determine at the outset * * * whether the expert is proposing to testify to (1) scientific knowledge that (2) will assist the trier of fact to understand or determine a fact in issue. This entails a preliminary assessment of whether the reasoning or methodology underlying the testimony is scientifically valid and of whether that reasoning or methodology properly can be applied to the facts in issue. We are confident that federal judges possess the capacity to undertake this review. Many factors will bear on the inquiry, and we do not presume to set out a definitive checklist or test. But some general observations are appropriate.

Ordinarily, a key question to be answered in determining whether a theory or technique is scientific knowledge that will assist the trier of fact will be whether it can be (and has been) tested. "Scientific methodology today is based on generating hypotheses and testing them to see if they can be falsified; indeed, this methodology is what distinguishes science from other fields of human inquiry."

Another pertinent consideration is whether the theory or technique has been subjected to peer review and publication. Publication (which is but one element of peer review) is not a *sine qua non* of admissibility; it does not necessarily correlate with reliability, and in some instances well-grounded but innovative theories will not have been published. Some propositions, moreover, are too particular, too new, or of too limited interest to be published. But submission to the scrutiny of the scientific community is a component of "good science," in part because it increases the likelihood that substantive flaws in methodology will be detected. The fact of publication (or lack thereof) in a peer reviewed journal thus will be a relevant, though not dispositive, consideration in assessing the scientific validity of a particular technique or methodology on which an opinion is premised.

Additionally, in the case of a particular scientific technique, the court ordinarily should consider the known or potential rate of error, and the existence and maintenance of standards controlling the technique's operation.

Finally, "general acceptance" can yet have a bearing on the inquiry. A "reliability assessment does not require, although it does permit, explicit identification of a relevant scientific community and an express determination of a particular degree of acceptance within that community." *United States v. Downing*, 753 F.2d, at 1238. Widespread acceptance can be an important factor in ruling particular evidence admissible, and "a known technique which has been able to attract only minimal support within the community," *Downing*, 753 F.2d, at 1238, may properly be viewed with skepticism.

The inquiry envisioned by Rule 702 is, we emphasize, a flexible one. Its overarching subject is the scientific validity—and thus the evidentiary relevance and reliability—of the principles that underlie a proposed submission. The focus, of course, must be solely on principles and methodology, not on the conclusions that they generate.

* * *

III

We conclude by briefly addressing what appear to be two underlying concerns of the parties and *amici* in this case. Respondent expresses apprehension that abandonment of "general acceptance" as the exclusive requirement for admission will result in a "free-for-all" in which befuddled juries are confounded by absurd and irrational pseudoscientific assertions. In this regard respondent seems to us to be overly pessimistic about the capabilities of the jury and of the adversary system generally. Vigorous cross-examination, presentation of contrary evidence, and careful instruction on the burden of proof are the traditional and appropriate means of attacking shaky but admissible evidence. Additionally, in the event the trial court concludes that the scintilla of evidence presented supporting a position is insufficient to allow a reasonable juror to conclude that the position more likely than not is true, the court remains free to direct a judgment, and likewise to grant summary judgment. These conventional devices, rather than wholesale exclusion under an uncompromising "general acceptance" test, are the appropriate safeguards where the basis of scientific testimony meets the standards of Rule 702.

Petitioners and, to a greater extent, their *amici* exhibit a different concern. They suggest that recognition of a screening role for the judge that allows for the exclusion of "invalid" evidence will sanction a stifling and repressive scientific orthodoxy and will be inimical to the search for truth. It is true that open debate is an essential part of both legal and scientific analyses. Yet there are important differences between the quest for truth in the courtroom and the quest for truth in the laboratory. Scientific conclusions are subject to perpetual revision. Law, on the other hand, must resolve disputes finally and quickly. The scientific project is advanced by broad and wide-ranging consideration of a multitude of hypotheses, for those that are incorrect will eventually be shown to be so, and that in itself is an advance. Conjectures that are probably wrong are of little use, however, in the project of reaching a quick, final, and binding legal judgment—often of great consequence—about a particular set of events in the past. We recognize that, in practice, a gatekeeping role for the judge, no matter how flexible, inevitably on occasion will prevent the jury from learning of authentic insights and innovations. That, nevertheless, is the balance that is struck by Rules of Evidence designed not for the exhaustive search for cosmic understanding but for the particularized resolution of legal disputes.

IV

To summarize: "General acceptance" is not a necessary precondition to the admissibility of scientific evidence under the Federal Rules of Evidence, but the Rules of Evidence—especially Rule 702—do assign to the trial judge the task of ensuring that an expert's testimony both rests on a reliable foundation and is relevant to the task at hand. Pertinent evidence based on scientifically valid principles will satisfy those demands.

The inquiries of the District Court and the Court of Appeals focused almost exclusively on "general acceptance," as gauged by publication and the decisions of other courts. Accordingly, the judgment of the Court of Appeals is vacated, and the case is remanded for further proceedings consistent with this opinion.

It is so ordered.

Notes and Questions

1. The subsequent history of *Daubert* is interesting. On remand, the plaintiffs argued that the Ninth Circuit should send the case back to the district court for a determination of admissibility under the new standard. The Ninth Circuit, however, rejected the argument and took on the task itself: "In the peculiar circumstances of this case * * * we have determined that the interests of justice and judicial economy will best be served by deciding those issues that are properly before us and, in the process, offering guidance on the application of the *Daubert* standard in this circuit." Daubert v. Merrell Dow Pharms., Inc., 43 F.3d 1311, 1315 (9th Cir.1995). In offering this guidance, the court re-affirmed exclusion of the testimony because the testimony lacked "fit" with the issue of whether Bendectin actually caused the plaintiffs' birth defects. The court explained:

> Plaintiffs do not quantify this possibility, or otherwise indicate how their conclusions about causation should be weighted, even though the substantive legal standard has always required proof of causation by a preponderance of the evidence. Unlike these experts' explanation of their methodology, this is not a shortcoming that could be corrected on remand; plaintiffs' experts could augment their affidavits with independent proof that their methods were sound, but to augment the substantive testimony as to causation would require the experts to change their conclusions altogether. Any such tailoring of the experts' conclusions would, at this stage of the proceedings, fatally undermine any attempt to show that these findings were "derived by the scientific method." Plaintiffs' experts must, therefore, stand by the conclusions they originally proffered, rendering their testimony inadmissible under the second prong of Fed.R.Evid. 702.

Id. at 1322.

What do you think of the Ninth Circuit's decision? Should it have sent the case back to the district court for an evaluation of whether the expert's testimony satisfied Rule 702 under the Supreme Court's new standard before affirming the grant of summary judgment? Or was the problem with "fit" on the issue of causation sufficient to affirm without a remand?

2. Before ruling on fit, the Ninth Circuit evaluated the reliability of the expert testimony using the factors set out by the Supreme Court. Noting that these factors were not intended as a "definitive checklist," the court also considered whether the experts had developed opinions specifically for the purpose of testifying in litigation. The court allowed that paid testimony is not inherently unreliable, but appeared skeptical of the fact that none of the plaintiffs' experts studied the teratogenic impact of Bendectin before being hired to testify in litigation. Id. at 1317. Does the fact that an opinion is developed for the purposes of litigation make it less reliable?

3. *Daubert* provides district court judges with a great deal of latitude to act as "gatekeepers" of expert testimony. But does this role suggest that judges should send more cases to the jury than under *Frye*? The Supreme Court's precise language in *Daubert* suggests a more liberal standard ("a rigid 'general acceptance' requirement would be at odds with the 'liberal thrust' of the Federal Rules and their 'general approach of relaxing the traditional barriers to "opinion" testimony,' " *Daubert*, 509 U.S. at 588). Subsequent studies, however, reveal that *Daubert* has had an opposite effect, making judges more likely to exclude expert testimony after pre-trial scrutiny. Professor Margaret Berger argues that this affects plaintiffs in toxic tort litigation more than defendants because of plaintiffs' burden of proof. Professor Berger explains: "[T]here is little point in plaintiffs going to the expense of [challenging defendants' experts] until they know if their case will proceed. So if more experts are now being excluded, then *Daubert* has undoubtedly shifted the balance between plaintiffs and" defendants and made it more difficult for plaintiffs to litigate successfully. Margaret A. Berger, What Has a Decade of *Daubert* Wrought?, 95 Am.J.Pub.Health S59, S64 & n.27 (2005). Do you agree with Professor Berger's view? Or is *Daubert* simply compelling plaintiffs to come forward with stronger evidence to support their claims? If so, is the same true in criminal cases? Consider one scholar's conclusion: "The questionable sciences of criminal cases, often among the weakest of the scientific evidence that comes to court, are by one device or another usually admitted...." Kelly M. Pyrek, Forensic Science Under Siege: The Challenges of Forensic Laboratories and the Medico–Legal Investigation System 358 (2007) (quoting David L. Faigman, David H. Kaye, Michael J. Saks, & Joseph Sanders, 1 Modern Scientific Evidence: The Law and Science of Expert Testimony 105–30 (2005)).

4. The Advisory Committee's notes to Federal Rule of Evidence 702 state that rejection of expert testimony is still "the exception rather than the rule." See Fed.R.Evid. 702 advisory committee's notes. Many of these are criminal cases. In civil cases, including toxic tort cases before the 1970s, the reality was that very few courts looked beyond expert qualifications in making admissibility determinations. Thus, the *Frye* standard was limited to criminal cases. Courts often took the "willing testifier" approach, reasoning that "if experts are willing to testify that [a causal] link exists, it is for the jury to decide whether to credit such testimony." See Michael D. Green, The Road Less Well Traveled (and Seen): Contemporary Lawmaking in Products Liability, 49 DePaul L.Rev. 377, 387 (1999) (quoting Oxendine v. Merrell Dow Pharmaceuticals, Inc., 506 A.2d 1100, 1104 (D.C.1986)). Professor Green's article traced the evolution of courts as gatekeepers and the practical effect of that evolution on outcomes in toxic tort litigation. Does this movement toward judicial gatekeeping essentially turn a question of fact into a question of law?

5. The *Daubert* Court suggested flexibility in conducting the reliability inquiry, yet the four factors it supplied have been widely employed to determine the admissibility of a variety of scientific testimony. Sometimes these factors are stretched by courts beyond reasonable bounds, as they simply are inapplicable to the state of testimony provided. Thus, no scientific study would be performed, published, or peer reviewed regarding whether a known carcinogen, say tobacco smoke, caused an individual plaintiff's lung cancer. Similarly, general acceptance for such an issue would not exist. Nor can a rate of error be determined for the sorts of epidemiologic or toxicologic studies that were involved in *Daubert*. No one knows, overall, how often the conclusions worked—and often they are indeterminate, calling for further research. Yet courts seem to have manipulated these factors to assess how well justified an expert's testimony is based on the scientific evidence proffered by that expert claimed to support the opinion.

6. The Court in *Daubert* alluded to the issue of whether the standard for admissibility on expert testimony might affect substantive rights: "Because we hold that *Frye* has been superseded and base the discussion that follows on the content of the congressionally enacted Federal Rules of Evidence, we do not address petitioners' argument that application of the *Frye* rule in this diversity case, as the application of a judge-made rule affecting substantive rights, would violate the doctrine of Erie R. Co. v. Tompkins, 304 U.S. 64, 58 S.Ct. 817, 82 L.Ed. 1188 (1938)." *Daubert*, 509 U.S. at 589 & n.6. Commentators and courts have subsequently concluded that Rule 702 and its application through *Daubert* can be applied in conjunction with state substantive requirements on issues such as causation. See Robin Kundis Craig, When *Daubert* Gets *Erie*: Medical Certainty and Medical Expert Testimony in Federal Court, 77 Denv.U.L.Rev. 69 (1999); Legg v. Chopra, 286 F.3d 286 (6th Cir.2002).

B. THE *DAUBERT* TRILOGY

As the preceding notes suggest, *Daubert* left open a host of questions as to its reach. Broadly speaking, the greatest uncertainty surrounded the scope of the power that district court judges have to serve as gatekeepers of expert testimony under Federal Rule of Evidence 702. Subsequently, the Supreme Court decided two important cases that confirmed a strong role for district court judges in assessing the reliability of expert testimony for admissibility purposes. Along with *Daubert* itself, the cases have come to be known as the *Daubert* trilogy.

GENERAL ELECTRIC CO. v. JOINER

United States Supreme Court, 1997.
522 U.S. 136, 118 S.Ct. 512, 139 L.Ed.2d 508.

CHIEF JUSTICE REHNQUIST delivered the opinion of the Court.

We granted certiorari in this case to determine what standard an appellate court should apply in reviewing a trial court's decision to admit or exclude expert testimony under *Daubert v. Merrell Dow Pharmaceuticals, Inc.*, 509 U.S. 579, 113 S.Ct. 2786, 125 L.Ed.2d 469 (1993). We hold that abuse of discretion is the appropriate standard. We apply this standard and conclude that the District Court in this case did not abuse its discretion when it excluded certain proffered expert testimony.

I

Respondent Robert Joiner began work as an electrician in the Water & Light Department of Thomasville, Georgia (City), in 1973. This job required him to work with and around the City's electrical transformers, which used a mineral-oil-based dielectric fluid as a coolant. Joiner often had to stick his hands and arms into the fluid to make repairs. The fluid would sometimes splash onto him, occasionally getting into his eyes and mouth. In 1983 the City discovered that the fluid in some of the transformers was contaminated with polychlorinated biphenyls (PCB's). PCB's are widely considered to be hazardous to human health. Congress, with limited exceptions, banned the production and sale of PCB's in 1978.

Joiner was diagnosed with small-cell lung cancer in 1991. * * * In his complaint Joiner linked his development of cancer to his exposure to PCB's and their derivatives, polychlorinated dibenzofurans (furans) and polychlorinated dibenzodioxins (dioxins). Joiner had been a smoker for approximately eight years, his parents had both been smokers, and there was a history of lung cancer in his family. He was thus perhaps already at a heightened risk of developing lung cancer eventually. The suit alleged that his exposure to PCB's "promoted" his cancer; had it not been for his exposure to these substances, his cancer would not have developed for many years, if at all.

Petitioners removed the case to federal court. Once there, they moved for summary judgment. They contended that (1) there was no evidence that Joiner suffered significant exposure to PCB's, furans, or dioxins, and (2) there was no admissible scientific evidence that PCB's promoted Joiner's cancer. Joiner responded that there were numerous disputed factual issues that required resolution by a jury. He relied largely on the testimony of expert witnesses. In depositions, his experts had testified that PCB's alone can promote cancer and that furans and dioxins can also promote cancer. They opined that since Joiner had been exposed to PCB's, furans, and dioxins, such exposure was likely responsible for Joiner's cancer.

The District Court ruled that there was a genuine issue of material fact as to whether Joiner had been exposed to PCB's. But it nevertheless granted summary judgment for petitioners because (1) there was no genuine issue as to whether Joiner had been exposed to furans and dioxins, and (2) the testimony of Joiner's experts had failed to show that there was a link between exposure to PCB's and small-cell lung cancer. The court believed that the testimony of respondent's experts to the contrary did not rise above "subjective belief or unsupported speculation." Their testimony was therefore inadmissible.

The Court of Appeals for the Eleventh Circuit reversed. It held that "[b]ecause the Federal Rules of Evidence governing expert testimony display a preference for admissibility, we apply a particularly stringent standard of review to the trial judge's exclusion of expert testimony." Applying that standard, the Court of Appeals held that the District Court had erred in excluding the testimony of Joiner's expert witnesses. The District Court had made two fundamental errors. First, it excluded the experts' testimony because it "drew different conclusions from the research than did each of the experts." The Court of Appeals opined that a district court should limit its role to determining the "legal reliability of proffered expert testimony, leaving the jury to decide the correctness of competing expert opinions." Second, the District Court had held that there was no genuine issue of material fact as to whether Joiner had been exposed to furans and dioxins. This was also incorrect, said the Court of Appeals, because testimony in the record supported the proposition that there had been such exposure.

We granted petitioners' petition for a writ of certiorari, and we now reverse.

II

Petitioners challenge the standard applied by the Court of Appeals in reviewing the District Court's decision to exclude respondent's experts' proffered testimony. They argue that that court should have applied the traditional "abuse-of-discretion" review. Respondent agrees that abuse of discretion is the correct standard of review. He contends, however, that the Court of Appeals applied an abuse-of-discretion standard in this case. As he reads it, the phrase "particularly stringent" announced no new standard of review. It was simply an acknowledgment that an appellate court can and will devote more resources to analyzing district court decisions that are dispositive of the entire litigation. All evidentiary decisions are reviewed under an abuse-of-discretion standard. He argues, however, that it is perfectly reasonable for appellate courts to give particular attention to those decisions that are outcome determinative.

We have held that abuse of discretion is the proper standard of review of a district court's evidentiary rulings. * * * The Court of Appeals suggested that *Daubert* somehow altered this general rule in the context of a district court's decision to exclude scientific evidence. But *Daubert* did not address the standard of appellate review for evidentiary rulings at all. It did hold that the "austere" *Frye* standard of "general acceptance" had not been carried over into the Federal Rules of Evidence. But the opinion also said:

> "That the *Frye* test was displaced by the Rules of Evidence does not mean, however, that the Rules themselves place no limits on the admissibility of purportedly scientific evidence. Nor is the trial judge disabled from screening such evidence. To the contrary, under the Rules the trial judge must ensure that any and all scientific testimony or evidence admitted is not only relevant, but reliable." 509 U.S., at 589, 113 S.Ct., at 2794–2795.

Thus, while the Federal Rules of Evidence allow district courts to admit a somewhat broader range of scientific testimony than would have been admissible under *Frye*, they leave in place the "gatekeeper" role of the trial judge in screening such evidence. A court of appeals applying "abuse-of-discretion" review to such rulings may not categorically distinguish between rulings allowing expert testimony and rulings disallowing it. We likewise reject respondent's argument that because the granting of summary judgment in this case was "outcome determinative," it should have been subjected to a more searching standard of review. On a motion for summary judgment, disputed issues of fact are resolved against the moving party—here, petitioners. But the question of admissibility of expert testimony is not such an issue of fact, and is reviewable under the abuse-of-discretion standard.

We hold that the Court of Appeals erred in its review of the exclusion of Joiner's experts' testimony. In applying an overly "stringent" review to that ruling, it failed to give the trial court the deference that is the hallmark of abuse-of-discretion review.

III

We believe that a proper application of the correct standard of review here indicates that the District Court did not abuse its discretion. Joiner's theory of liability was that his exposure to PCB's and their derivatives "promoted" his development of small-cell lung cancer. In support of that theory he proffered the deposition testimony of expert witnesses. Dr. Arnold Schecter testified that he believed it "more likely than not that Mr. Joiner's lung cancer was causally linked to cigarette smoking and PCB exposure." Dr. Daniel Teitelbaum testified that Joiner's "lung cancer was caused by or contributed to in a significant degree by the materials with which he worked."

Petitioners contended that the statements of Joiner's experts regarding causation were nothing more than speculation. Petitioners criticized the testimony of the experts in that it was "not supported by epidemiological studies . . . [and was] based exclusively on isolated studies of laboratory animals." Joiner responded by claiming that his experts had identified "relevant animal studies which support their opinions." He also directed the court's attention to four epidemiological studies on which his experts had relied.

The District Court agreed with petitioners that the animal studies on which respondent's experts relied did not support his contention that exposure to PCB's had contributed to his cancer. The studies involved infant mice that had developed cancer after being exposed to PCB's. The infant mice in the studies had had massive doses of PCB's injected directly into their peritoneums or stomachs. Joiner was an adult human being whose alleged exposure to PCB's was far less than the exposure in the animal studies. The PCB's were injected into the mice in a highly concentrated form. The fluid with which Joiner had come into contact generally had a much smaller PCB concentration of between 0–to–500 parts per million. The cancer that these mice developed was alveologenic adenomas; Joiner had developed small-cell carcinomas. No study demonstrated that adult mice developed cancer after being exposed to PCB's. One of the experts admitted that no study had demonstrated that PCB's lead to cancer in any other species.

Respondent failed to reply to this criticism. Rather than explaining how and why the experts could have extrapolated their opinions from these seemingly far-removed animal studies, respondent chose "to proceed as if the only issue [was] whether animal studies can ever be a proper foundation for an expert's opinion." Of course, whether animal studies can ever be a proper foundation for an expert's opinion was not the issue. The issue was whether *these* experts' opinions were sufficiently supported by the animal studies on which they purported to rely. The studies were so dissimilar to the facts presented in this litigation that it was not an abuse of discretion for the District Court to have rejected the experts' reliance on them.

The District Court also concluded that the four epidemiological studies on which respondent relied were not a sufficient basis for the experts' opinions. The first such study involved workers at an Italian capacitor plant who had been exposed to PCBs. The authors noted that lung cancer deaths among ex-employees at the plant were higher than might have been expected, but concluded that "there were apparently no grounds for associating lung cancer deaths (although increased above expectations) and exposure in the plant." Given that [the study's authors] were unwilling to say that PCB exposure had caused cancer among the workers they examined, their study did not support the experts' conclusion that Joiner's exposure to PCB's caused his cancer.

The second study followed employees who had worked at Monsanto's PCB production plant. The authors of this study found that the incidence of lung cancer deaths among these workers was somewhat higher than would ordinarily be expected. The increase, however, was not statistically significant and the authors of the study did not suggest a link between the increase in lung cancer deaths and the exposure to PCB's.

The third and fourth studies were likewise of no help. The third involved workers at a Norwegian cable manufacturing company who had been exposed to mineral oil. A statistically significant increase in lung cancer deaths had been observed in these workers. The study, however, (1) made no mention of PCB's and (2) was expressly limited to the type of mineral oil involved in that study, and thus did not support these experts' opinions. The fourth and final study involved a PCB-exposed group in Japan that had seen a statistically significant increase in lung cancer deaths. The subjects of this study, however, had been exposed to numerous potential carcinogens, including toxic rice oil that they had ingested.

Respondent points to *Daubert's* language that the "focus, of course, must be solely on principles and methodology, not on the conclusions that they generate." 509 U.S., at 595, 113 S.Ct., at 2797. He claims that because the District Court's disagreement was with the conclusion that the experts drew from the studies, the District Court committed legal error and was properly reversed by the Court of Appeals. But conclusions and methodology are not entirely distinct from one another. Trained experts commonly extrapolate from existing data. But nothing in either *Daubert*, or the Federal Rules of Evidence requires a district court to admit opinion evidence that is connected to existing data only by the *ipse dixit* of the expert. A court may conclude that there is simply too great an analytical gap between the data and the opinion proffered. That is what the District Court did here, and we hold that it did not abuse its discretion in so doing.

We hold, therefore, that abuse of discretion is the proper standard by which to review a district court's decision to admit or exclude scientific evidence. We further hold that, because it was within the District Court's discretion to conclude that the studies upon which the experts relied were not sufficient, whether individually or in combination, to support their conclusions that Joiner's exposure to PCB's contributed to his cancer, the District Court did not abuse its discretion in excluding their testimony.

* * * We accordingly reverse the judgment of the Court of Appeals and remand this case for proceedings not inconsistent with this opinion.

It is so ordered.

NOTES AND QUESTIONS

1. In holding that appellate courts should review admissibility determinations of expert testimony for an abuse of discretion, *Joiner* stated a rule consistent with the deferential standard applied to most evidentiary rulings. *Joiner*, however, marked a departure from the approach of most state courts in treating the admissibility of scientific evidence as a question of law to be reviewed by appellate courts de novo. Prior to *Daubert,* of course, most state courts determined admissibility based on *Frye*'s general acceptance rule. Does *Daubert*'s rejection of *Frye* necessitate a different standard of review? Regardless, does the deferential abuse of discretion standard of review make good sense? One potential problem with the abuse of discretion standard arises in cases where expert testimony has implications for issues that might arise in multiple cases—for example, the question of general causation relating to a particular toxic substance. Suppose, for example, that an appellate court concludes that an expert may not testify that a toxin is capable of causing a certain disease. Should the same issue be reconsidered by trial courts in subsequent cases? See David L. Faigman, David H. Kaye, Michael J. Saks, & Joseph Sanders, 1 Modern Scientific Evidence: The Law and Science of Expert Testimony § 1:34 (2009–10). Should such a ruling be reconsidered in every new case, or only under certain circumstances, such as when there has been a scientific advance permitting a more thorough analysis? Do you read *Joiner* broadly enough to permit this?

2. Is it necessary for appellate courts to use the same standard of review for all decisions that a trial court judge makes regarding the admissibility of expert testimony? Or could courts limit application of the abuse of discretion standard to case-specific admissibility issues, while continuing to use a less deferential standard in reviewing decisions about the soundness of scientific methodology and theories? Consider Vargas v. Lee, 317 F.3d 498 (5th Cir. 2003), in which a trial court judge permitted the introduction of expert testimony connecting the plaintiff's fibromyalgia syndrome with impact from a motor vehicle accident involving the defendant. An earlier Fifth Circuit case had found similar testimony on the issue to be unreliable. The *Vargas* court reversed the trial court's decision, finding admission of the testimony an abuse of discretion:

> Because nothing in the record alters the outcome reached [in the earlier Fifth Circuit decision], we conclude that the admission of [the expert's] testimony was an abuse of discretion. We do not, however, purport to hold that trauma does not cause fibromyalgia syndrome or that admission of expert testimony on that subject is permanently foreclosed. Medical science may someday determine with sufficient reliability that such a causal relationship exists. As the Supreme Court recognized

in *Daubert*: "[I]n practice, a gatekeeping role for the judge, no matter how flexible, inevitably on occasion will prevent the jury from learning of authentic insights and innovations."

Vargas, 317 F.3d at 502–03. How deferential was the Fifth Circuit to the trial court's decision about the reliability of the expert's testimony? Was this a de novo review under an abuse of discretion label?

3. What if a trial court fails adequately to exercise its obligation to operate as a gatekeeper for determining the admission of expert testimony? Expert witnesses, unlike other witnesses, may offer testimony with no basis in firsthand knowledge. Further, the underlying facts and data on which experts base their opinions need not be admissible in evidence. See Fed.R.Evid. 703. It is for precisely this reason that experts must be vetted by the trial court before being permitted to testify before the factfinder. As the *Daubert* court noted, the relaxation of typical evidentiary requirements "is premised on the assumption that the expert's opinion will have a reliable basis in the knowledge and experience of the discipline." *Daubert*, 509 U.S. at 592. One appellate court concluded that it need not defer to the trial court's approach. See Chapman v. Maytag Corp., 297 F.3d 682, 687 (7th Cir.2002) (deciding de novo that "the district court failed to properly assess whether [the expert's] theory [was] scientifically valid").

4. Beyond resolving the standard of review issue, *Joiner* is important for making "it clear that courts could scrutinize the reliability of an expert's reasoning process as well as the expert's general methodology" and that "nothing in *Daubert* or the Federal Rules of Evidence requires a district court to admit opinion evidence that is connected to existing data only by the *ipse dixit* of the expert." See David E. Bernstein & Jeffrey D. Jackson, The *Daubert* Trilogy in the States, 44 Jurimetrics J. 351, 354 (2004) (quoting *Joiner*, 522 U.S. at 146). This is no minor matter, as before *Joiner*, some courts and commentators took the position that *Daubert* compelled only an evaluation of methodology, and not the conclusion that an expert derived from any data produced. See Robert J. Goodwin, Fifty Years of *Frye* in Alabama: The Continuing Debate Over Adopting the Test Established in *Daubert v. Merrell Dow Pharmaceuticals, Inc.*, 35 Cumb.L.Rev. 231, 272 (2005). Is this scrutiny consistent with the original spirit of *Daubert*? Consider the final case in the "trilogy" as you think about the expanding role of the trial court judge as a gatekeeper.

KUMHO TIRE CO. v. CARMICHAEL

United States Supreme Court, 1999.
526 U.S. 137, 119 S.Ct. 1167, 143 L.Ed.2d 238.

BREYER, J., delivered the opinion of the Court.

In *Daubert v. Merrell Dow Pharmaceuticals, Inc.*, this Court focused upon the admissibility of scientific expert testimony. It pointed out that such testimony is admissible only if it is both relevant and reliable. And it held that the Federal Rules of Evidence "assign to the trial judge the task of ensuring that an expert's testimony both rests on a reliable foundation and is relevant to the task at hand." *Id.*, at 597, 113 S.Ct. 2786. The Court also discussed certain more specific factors, such as testing, peer review, error rates, and "acceptability" in the relevant scientific community, some or all of which might prove helpful in determining the reliability of a particular scientific "theory or technique." *Id.*, at 593–594, 113 S.Ct. 2786.

This case requires us to decide how *Daubert* applies to the testimony of engineers and other experts who are not scientists. We conclude that *Daubert*'s general holding—setting forth the trial judge's general "gatekeeping" obligation—applies not only to testimony based on "scientific" knowledge, but also to testimony based on "technical" and "other specialized" knowledge. See Fed. Rule Evid. 702. We also conclude that a trial court *may* consider one or more of the more specific factors that *Daubert* mentioned when doing so will help determine that testimony's reliability. But, as the Court stated in *Daubert*, the test of reliability is "flexible," and *Daubert*'s list of specific factors neither necessarily nor exclusively applies to all experts or in every case. Rather, the law grants a district court the same broad latitude when it decides *how* to determine reliability as it enjoys in respect to its ultimate reliability determination. *See General Electric Co. v. Joiner*, 522 U.S. 136, 143, 118 S.Ct. 512, 139 L.Ed.2d 508 (1997) (courts of appeals are to apply "abuse of discretion" standard when reviewing district court's reliability determination). Applying these standards, we determine that the District Court's decision in this case—not to admit certain expert testimony—was within its discretion and therefore lawful.

I

On July 6, 1993, the right rear tire of a minivan driven by Patrick Carmichael blew out. In the accident that followed, one of the passengers died, and others were severely injured. In October 1993, the Carmichaels brought this diversity suit against the tire's maker and its distributor, whom we refer to collectively as Kumho Tire, claiming that the tire was defective. The plaintiffs rested their case in significant part upon deposition testimony provided by an expert in tire failure analysis, Dennis Carlson, Jr., who intended to testify in support of their conclusion.

Carlson's depositions relied upon certain features of tire technology that are not in dispute. A steel-belted radial tire like the Carmichaels' is made up of a "carcass" containing many layers of flexible cords, called "plies," along which (between the cords and the outer tread) are laid steel strips called "belts." Steel wire loops, called "beads," hold the cords together at the plies' bottom edges. An outer layer, called the "tread," encases the carcass, and the entire tire is bound together in rubber, through the application of heat and various chemicals. See generally, *e.g.*, J. Dixon, Tires, Suspension and Handling 68–72 (2d ed.1996). The bead of the tire sits upon a "bead seat," which is part of the wheel assembly. That assembly contains a "rim flange," which extends over the bead and rests against the side of the tire. See M. Mavrigian, Performance Wheels & Tires 81, 83 (1998).

Carlson's testimony also accepted certain background facts about the tire in question. He assumed that before the blowout the tire had traveled far. (The tire was made in 1988 and had been installed some time before the Carmichaels bought the used minivan in March 1993; the Carmichaels had driven the van approximately 7,000 additional miles in the two months they had owned it.) Carlson noted that the tire's tread depth, which was 11/32 of an inch when new, had been worn down to depths that ranged from 3/32 of an inch along some parts of the tire, to nothing at all along others. He conceded that the tire tread had at least two punctures which had been inadequately repaired.

Despite the tire's age and history, Carlson concluded that a defect in its manufacture or design caused the blowout. He rested this conclusion in part upon three premises which, for present purposes, we must assume are not in dispute: First, a tire's carcass should stay bound to the inner side of the tread for a significant period of time after its tread depth has worn away. Second, the tread of the tire at issue had separated from its inner steel-belted carcass prior to the accident. Third, this "separation" caused the blowout.

Carlson's conclusion that a defect caused the separation, however, rested upon certain other propositions, several of which the defendants strongly dispute. First, Carlson said that if a separation is *not* caused by a certain kind of tire misuse called "overdeflection" (which consists of underinflating the tire or causing it to carry too much weight, thereby generating heat that can undo the chemical tread/carcass bond), then, ordinarily, its cause is a tire defect. Second, he said that if a tire has been subject to sufficient overdeflection to cause a separation, it should reveal certain physical symptoms. These symptoms include (a) tread wear on the tire's shoulder that is greater than the tread wear along the tire's center; (b) signs of a "bead groove," where the beads have been pushed too hard against the bead seat on the inside of the tire's rim; (c) sidewalls of the tire with physical signs of deterioration, such as discoloration; and/or (d) marks on the tire's rim flange. Third, Carlson said that where he does not find *at least two* of the four physical signs just mentioned (and presumably where there is no reason to suspect a less common cause of separation), he concludes that a manufacturing or design defect caused the separation.

Carlson added that he had inspected the tire in question. He conceded that the tire to a limited degree showed greater wear on the shoulder than in the center, some signs of "bead groove," some discoloration, a few marks on the rim flange, and inadequately filled puncture holes (which can also cause heat that might lead to separation). But, in each instance, he testified that the symptoms were not significant, and he explained why he believed that they did not reveal overdeflection. For example, the extra shoulder wear, he said, appeared primarily on one shoulder, whereas an overdeflected tire would reveal equally abnormal wear on both shoulders. Carlson concluded that the tire did not bear at least two of the four overdeflection symptoms, nor was there any less obvious cause of separation; and since neither overdeflection nor the punctures caused the blowout, a defect must have done so.

Kumho Tire moved the District Court to exclude Carlson's testimony on the ground that his methodology failed Rule 702's reliability requirement. The court agreed with Kumho that it should act as a *Daubert*-type reliability "gatekeeper," even though one might consider Carlson's testimony as "technical," rather than "scientific." The court then examined Carlson's methodology in light of the reliability-related factors that *Daubert* mentioned, such as a theory's testability, whether it "has been a subject of peer review or publication," the "known or potential rate of error," and the "degree of acceptance ... within the relevant scientific community." The District Court found that all those factors argued against the reliability of Carlson's methods, and it granted the motion to exclude the testimony (as well as the defendants' accompanying motion for summary judgment).

The plaintiffs, arguing that the court's application of the *Daubert* factors was too "inflexible," asked for reconsideration. And the court granted that motion. After reconsidering the matter, the court agreed with the plaintiffs that *Daubert* should be applied flexibly, that its four factors were simply illustrative, and that other factors could argue in favor of admissibility. It conceded that there may be widespread acceptance of a "visual-inspection method" for some relevant purposes. But the court found insufficient indications of the reliability of

> "the component of Carlson's tire failure analysis which most concerned the Court, namely, the methodology employed by the expert in analyzing the data obtained in the visual inspection, and the scientific basis, if any, for such an analysis."

It consequently affirmed its earlier order declaring Carlson's testimony inadmissible and granting the defendants' motion for summary judgment.

The Eleventh Circuit reversed. It "review[ed] ... *de novo*" the "district court's legal decision to apply *Daubert*." It noted that "the Supreme Court in *Daubert* explicitly limited its holding to cover only the 'scientific context,'" adding that "a *Daubert* analysis" applies only where an expert relies "on the application of scientific principles," rather than "on skill- or experience-based observation." It concluded that Carlson's testimony, which it viewed as relying on experience, "falls outside the scope of *Daubert*," that "the district court erred as a matter of law by applying *Daubert* in this case," and that the case must be remanded for further (non-*Daubert*-type) consideration under Rule 702.

Kumho Tire petitioned for certiorari, asking us to determine whether a trial court "may" consider *Daubert's* specific "factors" when determining the "admissibility of an engineering expert's testimony." We granted certiorari in light of uncertainty among the lower courts about whether, or how, *Daubert* applies to expert testimony that might be characterized as based not upon "scientific" knowledge, but rather upon "technical" or "other specialized" knowledge.

II

A

In *Daubert*, this Court held that Federal Rule of Evidence 702 imposes a special obligation upon a trial judge to "ensure that any and all scientific testimony ... is not only relevant, but reliable." 509 U.S., at 589, 113 S.Ct. 2786. The initial question before us is whether this basic gatekeeping obligation applies only to "scientific" testimony or to all expert testimony. We, like the parties, believe that it applies to all expert testimony.

For one thing, Rule 702 itself says:

"If scientific, technical, or other specialized knowledge will assist the trier of fact to understand the evidence or to determine a fact in issue, a witness qualified as an expert by knowledge, skill, experience, training, or education, may testify thereto in the form of an opinion or otherwise."

[As in *Daubert*, t]his language makes no relevant distinction between "scientific" knowledge and "technical" or "other specialized" knowledge. It makes clear that any such knowledge might become the subject of expert testimony. In *Daubert*, the Court specified that it is the Rule's word "knowledge," not the words (like "scientific") that modify that word, that "establishes a standard of evidentiary reliability." 509 U.S., at 589–590, 113 S.Ct. 2786. Hence, as a matter of language, the Rule applies its reliability standard to all "scientific," "technical," or "other specialized" matters within its scope. We concede that the Court in *Daubert* referred only to "scientific" knowledge. But as the Court there said, it referred to "scientific" testimony "because that [wa]s the nature of the expertise" at issue. *Id.*, at 590, n.8, 113 S.Ct. 2786.

Neither is the evidentiary rationale that underlay the Court's basic *Daubert* "gatekeeping" determination limited to "scientific" knowledge. *Daubert* pointed out that Federal Rules 702 and 703 grant expert witnesses testimonial latitude unavailable to other witnesses on the "assumption that the expert's opinion will have a reliable basis in the knowledge and experience of his discipline." 509 U.S., at 592, 113 S.Ct. 2786 (pointing out that experts may testify to opinions, including those that are not based on firsthand knowledge or observation). The Rules grant that latitude to all experts, not just to "scientific" ones.

Finally, it would prove difficult, if not impossible, for judges to administer evidentiary rules under which a gatekeeping obligation depended upon a distinction between "scientific" knowledge and "technical" or "other specialized" knowledge. There is no clear line that divides the one from the others. Disciplines such as engineering rest upon scientific knowledge. Pure scientific theory itself may depend for its development upon observation and properly engineered machinery. And conceptual efforts to distinguish the two are unlikely to produce clear legal lines capable of application in particular cases.

Neither is there a convincing need to make such distinctions. Experts of all kinds tie observations to conclusions through the use of what Judge Learned Hand called "general truths derived from ... specialized experience." And whether the specific expert testimony focuses upon specialized observations, the specialized translation of those observations into theory, a specialized theory itself, or the application of such a theory in a particular case, the expert's testimony often will rest "upon an experience confessedly foreign in kind to [the jury's] own." The trial judge's effort to assure that the specialized testimony is reliable and relevant can help the jury evaluate that foreign experience, whether the testimony reflects scientific, technical, or other specialized knowledge.

We conclude that *Daubert*'s general principles apply to the expert matters described in Rule 702. The Rule, in respect to all such matters, "establishes a standard of evidentiary reliability." 509 U.S., at 590, 113 S.Ct. 2786. It "requires a valid ... connection to the pertinent inquiry as a precondition to admissibility." *Id.*, at 592, 113 S.Ct. 2786. And where such testimony's factual basis, data, principles, methods, or their application are called sufficiently into question, see Part III, *infra*, the trial judge must determine whether the testimony has "a reliable basis in the knowledge and experience of [the relevant] discipline." 509 U.S., at 592, 113 S.Ct. 2786.

B

Petitioners ask more specifically whether a trial judge determining the "admissibility of an engineering expert's testimony" *may* consider several more specific factors that *Daubert* said might "bear on" a judge's gatekeeping determination. These factors include:

—Whether a "theory or technique ... can be (and has been) tested";

—Whether it "has been subjected to peer review and publication";

—Whether, in respect to a particular technique, there is a high "known or potential rate of error" and whether there are "standards controlling the technique's operation"; and

—Whether the theory or technique enjoys " 'general acceptance' " within a " 'relevant scientific community.' "

Emphasizing the word "may" in the question, we answer that question yes.

Engineering testimony rests upon scientific foundations, the reliability of which will be at issue in some cases. In other cases, the relevant reliability concerns may focus upon personal knowledge or experience. As the Solicitor General points out, there are many different kinds of experts, and many different kinds of expertise. Our emphasis on the word "may" thus reflects *Daubert*'s description of the Rule 702 inquiry as "a flexible one." 509 U.S., at 594, 113 S.Ct. 2786. *Daubert* makes clear that the factors it mentions do *not* constitute a "definitive checklist or test." *Id.*, at 593, 113 S.Ct. 2786. And *Daubert* adds that the gatekeeping inquiry must be " 'tied to the facts' " of a particular "case." *Id.*, at 591, 113 S.Ct. 2786 (quoting *United States v. Downing*, 753 F.2d 1224, 1242 (C.A.3 1985)). We agree with the Solicitor General that "[t]he factors identified in *Daubert* may or may not be pertinent in assessing reliability, depending on the nature of the issue, the expert's particular expertise, and the subject of his testimony." Brief for United States as *Amicus Curiae* 19. The conclusion, in our view, is that we can neither rule out, nor rule in, for all cases and for all time the applicability of the factors mentioned in *Daubert*, nor can we now do so for subsets of cases categorized by category of expert or by kind of evidence. Too much depends upon the particular circumstances of the particular case at issue.

Daubert itself is not to the contrary. It made clear that its list of factors was meant to be helpful, not definitive. Indeed, those factors do not all necessarily apply even in every instance in which the reliability of scientific testimony is challenged. It might not be surprising in a particular case, for example, that a claim made by a scientific witness has never been the subject of peer review, for the particular application at issue may never previously have interested any scientist. Nor, on the other hand, does the presence of *Daubert*'s general acceptance factor help show that an expert's testimony is reliable where the discipline itself lacks reliability, as, for example, do theories grounded in any so-called generally accepted principles of astrology or necromancy.

At the same time, and contrary to the Court of Appeals' view, some of *Daubert*'s questions can help to evaluate the reliability even of experience-based testimony. In certain cases, it will be appropriate for the trial judge to ask, for example, how often an engineering expert's experience-based methodology has produced erroneous results, or whether such a method is generally accepted in the relevant engineering community. Likewise, it will at times be useful to ask even of a witness whose expertise is based purely on experience, say, a perfume tester able to distinguish among 140 odors at a sniff, whether his preparation is of a kind that others in the field would recognize as acceptable.

We must therefore disagree with the Eleventh Circuit's holding that a trial judge may ask questions of the sort *Daubert* mentioned only where an expert "relies on the application of scientific principles," but not where an expert relies "on skill- or experience-based observation." We do not believe that Rule 702 creates a schematism that segregates expertise by type while mapping certain kinds of questions to certain kinds of experts. Life and the legal cases that it generates are too complex to warrant so definitive a match.

     * * *

C

The trial court must have the same kind of latitude in deciding *how* to test an expert's reliability, and to decide whether or when special briefing or other proceedings are needed to investigate reliability, as it enjoys when it decides *whether or not* that expert's relevant testimony is reliable. Our opinion in *Joiner* makes clear that a court of appeals is to apply an abuse-of-discretion standard when it "review[s] a trial court's decision to admit or exclude expert testimony." 522 U.S., at 138–139, 118 S.Ct. 512. That standard applies as much to the trial court's decisions about how to determine reliability as to its ultimate conclusion. Otherwise, the trial judge would lack the discretionary authority needed both to avoid unnecessary "reliability" proceedings in ordinary cases where the reliability of an expert's methods is properly taken for granted, and to require appropriate proceedings in the less usual or more complex cases where cause for questioning the expert's reliability arises. Indeed, the Rules seek to avoid "unjustifiable expense and delay" as part of their search for "truth" and the "jus[t] determin[ation]" of proceedings. Fed. Rule Evid. 102. Thus, whether *Daubert*'s specific factors are, or are not, reasonable measures of reliability in a particular case is a matter that the law grants the trial judge broad latitude to determine. And the Eleventh Circuit erred insofar as it held to the contrary.

III

We further explain the way in which a trial judge "may" consider *Daubert*'s factors by applying these considerations to the case at hand, a matter that has been briefed exhaustively by the parties and their 19 *amici*. The District Court did not doubt Carlson's qualifications, which included a masters degree in mechanical engineering, 10 years' work at Michelin America, Inc., and testimony as a tire failure consultant in other tort cases. Rather, it excluded the testimony because, despite those qualifications, it initially doubted, and then found unreliable, "the methodology employed by the expert in analyzing the data obtained in the visual inspection, and the scientific basis, if any, for such an analysis." After examining the transcript in "some detail," and after considering respondents' defense of Carlson's methodology, the District Court determined that Carlson's testimony was not reliable. It fell outside the range where experts might reasonably differ, and where the jury must decide among the conflicting views of different experts, even though the evidence is "shaky." *Daubert*, 509 U.S., at 596, 113 S.Ct. 2786. In our view, the doubts that triggered the District Court's initial inquiry here were reasonable, as was the court's ultimate conclusion.

For one thing, and contrary to respondents' suggestion, the specific issue before the court was not the reasonableness *in general* of a tire expert's use of a visual and tactile inspection to determine whether overdeflection had caused the tire's tread to separate from its steel-belted carcass. Rather, it was the reasonableness of using such an approach, along with Carlson's particular method of analyzing the data thereby obtained, to draw a conclusion regarding *the particular matter to which the expert testimony was directly relevant*. That matter concerned the likelihood that a defect in the tire at issue caused its tread to separate from its carcass. The tire in question, the expert conceded, had traveled far enough so that some of the tread had been worn bald; it should have been taken out of service; it had been repaired (inadequately) for punctures; and it bore some of the very marks that the expert said indicated, not a defect, but abuse through overdeflection. The relevant issue was whether the expert could reliably determine the cause of *this* tire's separation.

Nor was the basis for Carlson's conclusion simply the general theory that, in the absence of evidence of abuse, a defect will normally have caused a tire's separation. Rather, the expert employed a more specific theory to establish the existence (or absence) of such abuse. Carlson testified precisely that in the absence of *at least two* of four signs of abuse (proportionately greater tread wear on the shoulder; signs of grooves caused by the beads; discolored sidewalls; marks on the rim flange), he concludes that a defect caused the separation. And his analysis depended upon acceptance of a further implicit proposition, namely, that his visual and tactile inspection could determine that the tire before him had not been abused despite some evidence of the presence of the very signs for which he looked (and two punctures).

For another thing, the transcripts of Carlson's depositions support both the trial court's initial uncertainty and its final conclusion. Those transcripts cast considerable doubt upon the reliability of both the explicit theory (about the need for two signs of abuse) and the implicit proposition (about the significance of visual inspection in this case). Among other things, the expert could not say whether the tire had traveled more than 10, or 20, or 30, or 40, or 50 thousand miles, adding that 6,000 miles was "about how far" he could "say with any certainty." The court could reasonably have wondered about the reliability of a method of visual and tactile inspection sufficiently precise to ascertain with some certainty the abuse-related significance of minute shoulder/center relative tread wear differences, but insufficiently precise to tell "with any certainty" from the tread wear whether a tire had traveled less than 10,000 or more than 50,000 miles. And these concerns might have been augmented by Carlson's repeated reliance on the "subjective[ness]" of his mode of analysis in response to questions seeking specific information regarding how he could differentiate between a tire that actually had been overdeflected and a tire that merely looked as though it had been. They would have been further augmented by the fact that Carlson said he had inspected the tire itself for the first time the morning of his first deposition, and then only for a few hours. (His initial conclusions were based on photographs.)

Moreover, prior to his first deposition, Carlson had issued a signed report in which he concluded that the tire had "not been ... overloaded or underinflated," not because of the absence of "two of four" signs of abuse, but simply because "the rim flange impressions ... were normal." That report also said that the "tread depth remaining was 3/32 inch," though the opposing expert's (apparently undisputed) measurements indicate that the tread depth taken at various positions around the tire actually ranged from .5/32 of an inch to 4/32 of an inch, with the tire apparently showing greater wear along *both* shoulders than along the center.

Further, in respect to one sign of abuse, bead grooving, the expert seemed to deny the sufficiency of his own simple visual-inspection methodology. He testified that most tires have some bead groove pattern, that where there is reason to suspect an abnormal bead groove he would ideally "look at a lot of [similar] tires" to know the grooving's significance, and that he had not looked at many tires similar to the one at issue.

Finally, the court, after looking for a defense of Carlson's methodology as applied in these circumstances, found no convincing defense. Rather, it found (1) that "none" of the *Daubert* factors, including that of "general acceptance" in the relevant expert community, indicated that Carlson's testimony was reliable; (2) that its own analysis "revealed no countervailing factors operating in favor of admissibility which could outweigh those identified in *Daubert*,"; and (3) that the "parties identified no such factors in their briefs." For these three reasons *taken together*, it concluded that Carlson's testimony was unreliable.

* * *

The particular issue in this case concerned the use of Carlson's two-factor test and his related use of visual/tactile inspection to draw conclusions on the basis of what seemed small observational differences. We have found no indication in the record that other experts in the industry use Carlson's two-factor test or that tire experts such as Carlson normally make the very fine distinctions about, say, the symmetry of comparatively greater shoulder tread wear that were necessary, on Carlson's own theory, to support his conclusions. Nor, despite the prevalence of tire testing, does anyone refer to any articles or papers that validate Carlson's approach. Cf. Bobo, Tire Flaws and Separations, in Mechanics of Pneumatic Tires 636–637 (S. Clark ed.1981); C. Schnuth, R. Fuller, G. Follen, G. Gold, & J. Smith, Compression Grooving and Rim Flange Abrasion as Indicators of Over–Deflected Operating Conditions in Tires, presented to Rubber Division of the American Chemical Society, Oct. 21–24, 1997; J. Walter & R. Kiminecz, Bead Contact Pressure Measurements at the Tire–Rim Interface, presented to the Society of Automotive Engineers, Inc., Feb. 24–28, 1975. Indeed, no one has argued that Carlson himself, were he still working for Michelin, would have concluded in a report to his employer that a similar tire was similarly defective on grounds identical to those upon which he rested his conclusion here. Of course, Carlson himself claimed that his method was accurate, but, as we pointed out in *Joiner*, "nothing in either *Daubert* or the Federal Rules of Evidence requires a district court to admit opinion evidence that is connected to existing data only by the *ipse dixit* of the expert." 522 U.S., at 146, 118 S.Ct. 512.

* * *

In sum, Rule 702 grants the district judge the discretionary authority, reviewable for its abuse, to determine reliability in light of the particular facts and circumstances of the particular case. The District Court did not abuse its discretionary authority in this case. Hence, the judgment of the Court of Appeals is

Reversed.

NOTES AND QUESTIONS

1. *Kumho Tire* emphasizes that the *Daubert* factors are not a definitive checklist. How much latitude should a trial court have in determining what factors to consider? Should such decisions be given the same deferential appellate review as suggested by the Court in *Joiner*? Consider the concern raised by several scholars in thinking about the issue:

> [A]ppellate deference to the factors used to assess the different categories of expertise is a possible Achilles' heel in [the *Kumho Tire* court's] otherwise well reasoned opinion. If taken literally, it would allow different judges in the same district to apply different factors to similar kinds of expert testimony. It might allow the same judge to apply different factors to similar kinds of experts.

David L. Faigman, David H. Kaye, Michael J. Saks, & Joseph Sanders, 1 Modern Scientific Evidence: The Law and Science of Expert Testimony § 1:25, at pp. 68–69 (2009–2010). What do you think of this concern? Is it likely to present a major problem among trial courts in a district? Among different districts? See id.

2. The *Kumho Tire* court also made clear that the factors identified in *Daubert* itself need not be considered in every case. But should a court be compelled to take those factors into account when it is possible to do so? Consider the factor of whether a method can or has been tested. Should a court require that testing be done where it is feasible? Or can a court still admit the testimony of an expert who has failed to test his theories, despite the capability to do so? Compare Bitler v. A.O. Smith Corp., 391 F.3d 1114, 1123 (10th Cir.2004) ("testing is not necessary in all instances to establish reliability under *Daubert*"), with Zenith Elecs. Corp. v. WH–TV Broadcast. Corp., 395 F.3d 416, 419 (7th Cir.2005) (finding expert testimony unreliable where the expert "preferred intuition to the empirical toolkit of the social sciences"). See Faigman et al., 1 Modern Scientific Evidence, supra, at § 1:16.

3. Federal Rule of Evidence 702 was amended in 2002 to account for the *Daubert* trilogy. The revised rule reads as follows:

> If scientific, technical, or other specialized knowledge will assist the trier of fact to understand the evidence or to determine a fact in issue, a witness qualified as an expert by knowledge, skill, experience, training, or education, may testify thereto in the form of an opinion or otherwise, *if (1) the testimony is based upon sufficient facts or data, (2) the testimony is the product of reliable principles and methods, and (3) the witness has applied the principles and methods reliably to the facts of the case.*

Fed.R.Evid. 702 (emphasis indicates new language). The Advisory Committee's note to the 2000 amendment of Rule 702 discusses *Daubert* and its progeny at length. An excerpt follows.

Rule 702 has been amended in response to *Daubert v. Merrell Dow Pharmaceuticals, Inc.*, 509 U.S. 579 (1993), and to the many cases applying *Daubert*, including *Kumho Tire Co. v. Carmichael*, 119 S.Ct. 1167 (1999). In *Daubert* the Court charged trial judges with the responsibility of acting as gatekeepers to exclude unreliable expert testimony, and the Court in *Kumho* clarified that this gatekeeper function applies to all expert testimony, not just testimony based in science. *See also Kumho*, 119 S.Ct. at 1178 (citing the Committee Note to the proposed amendment to Rule 702, which had been released for public comment before the date of the *Kumho* decision). The amendment affirms the trial court's role as gatekeeper and provides some general standards that the trial court must use to assess the reliability and helpfulness of proffered expert testimony. Consistently with *Kumho*, the Rule as amended provides that all types of expert testimony present questions of admissibility for the trial court in deciding whether the evidence is reliable and helpful. Consequently, the admissibility of all expert testimony is governed by the principles of Rule 104(a). Under that Rule, the proponent has the burden of establishing that the pertinent admissibility requirements are met by a preponderance of the evidence. See *Bourjaily v. United States*, 483 U.S. 171 (1987).

* * *

No attempt has been made to "codify" these specific factors [from *Daubert*]. *Daubert* itself emphasized that the factors were neither exclusive nor dispositive. Other cases have recognized that not all of the specific *Daubert* factors can apply to every type of expert testimony. * * * The standards set forth in the amendment are broad enough to require consideration of any or all of the specific *Daubert* factors where appropriate.

* * *

When a trial court, applying this amendment, rules that an expert's testimony is reliable, this does not necessarily mean that contradictory expert testimony is unreliable. The amendment is broad enough to permit testimony that is the product of competing principles or methods in the same field of expertise. As the court stated in *In re Paoli R.R. Yard PCB Litigation*, 35 F.3d 717, 744 (3d Cir. 1994), proponents "do not have to demonstrate to the judge by a preponderance of the evidence that the assessments of their experts are correct, they only have to demonstrate by a preponderance of evidence that their opinions are reliable.... The evidentiary requirement of reliability is lower than the merits standard of correctness."

The Court in *Daubert* declared that the "focus, of course, must be solely on principles and methodology, not on the conclusions they generate." 509 U.S. at 595. Yet as the Court later recognized, "conclusions and methodology are not entirely distinct from one another." *General Elec. Co. v. Joiner*, 522 U.S. 136, 146 (1997). Under the amendment, as under *Daubert*, when an expert purports to apply principles and methods in accordance with professional standards, and yet reaches a conclusion that other experts in the field would not reach, the trial court may fairly suspect that the principles and methods have not been faithfully applied.

The amendment specifically provides that the trial court must scrutinize not only the principles and methods used by the expert, but also whether those principles and methods have been properly applied to the facts of the case. As the court noted in *In re Paoli R.R. Yard PCB Litig.*, 35 F.3d 717, 745 (3d Cir. 1994), "*any* step that renders the analysis unreliable . . . renders the expert's testimony inadmissible. *This is true whether the step completely changes a reliable methodology or merely misapplies that methodology.*"

* * *

If the witness is relying solely or primarily on experience, then the witness must explain how that experience leads to the conclusion reached, why that experience is a sufficient basis for the opinion, and how that experience is reliably applied to the facts. The trial court's gatekeeping function requires more than simply "taking the expert's word for it." *See Daubert v. Merrell Dow Pharmaceuticals, Inc.*, 43 F.3d 1311, 1319 (9th Cir. 1995) ("We've been presented with only the experts' qualifications, their conclusions and their assurances of reliability. Under *Daubert*, that's not enough."). The more subjective and controversial the expert's inquiry, the more likely the testimony should be excluded as unreliable.

Fed.R.Evid. 702 advisory committee's note.

C.   LOSING A CASE ON ADMISSIBILITY: THE SILICONE GEL BREAST IMPLANT

Silicone gel breast implants are essentially breast-shaped sacks made of silicone rubber, filled with a silicone gel. They have long been used both in breast reconstruction (for example, after a woman has a mastectomy to get rid of breast cancer) and in breast enhancement, despite the availability of alternatives, such as saline-filled breast implants.

Moreover, silicone gel breast implants have spawned various kinds of tort litigation. Until the 1990s, however, most such litigation involved two types of factual situations. The first general category of silicone gel breast implant claims involved rather routine assertions of medical malpractice—surgically inserting the implants when the patient had told the doctor not to; using silicone gel breast implants instead of saline breast implants when the patient had instructed the doctor to use saline; failure to warn the patient that severe scarring was possible; and so on. The second general category of cases involved implants that ruptured after being implanted, prompting defective manufacture claims against the companies that produced the implants and medical malpractice/negligence claims against the doctors who implanted them.

In the 1990s, however, women plaintiffs with silicone gel breast implants brought multiple toxic tort claims against the implants' manufacturers in both state and federal courts, claiming that the long-term presence of the implants in their bodies had caused a number of diseases and symptoms, generally neurological ("skin crawling") and/or immunological (autoimmune diseases and symptoms). At the time these claims were brought, the scientific studies regarding the long-term effects of these implants on women were limited.

In the federal courts, therefore, these claims required *Daubert* screenings of plaintiffs' and defendants' expert witnesses. One of the earlier evidentiary decisions in this case was *Hall v. Baxter Healthcare Corp.*, presented below. As you read this case, consider what the plaintiffs' claims required the district judge to wrestle with in his *Daubert* gate-keeping role and the effect that *Daubert* had on the Oregon federal litigation of these claims.

HALL v. BAXTER HEALTHCARE CORP.

United States District Court for the District of Oregon, 1996.
947 F.Supp. 1387.

ROBERT E. JONES, DISTRICT JUDGE.

I. INTRODUCTION

Currently pending in this court are a number of silicone breast implant cases brought by or on behalf of the plaintiffs against various breast implant manufacturers. Plaintiffs seek damages for injuries they claim to have suffered as a result of implantation with silicone gel breast implants.

Among other things, the plaintiffs assert that silicone from the implants has migrated and degraded in their bodies and has caused a systemic syndrome or illness, which they generally refer to as "atypical connective tissue disease" (ACTD). In essence, plaintiffs claim a "unique constellation of symptoms" consisting of hundreds of symptoms commonly experienced by the general population.

This opinion addresses the defendants' motions in limine to exclude testimony by plaintiffs' experts concerning any causal link between silicone breast implants and the alleged systemic disease or syndrome. To resolve these motions, the court, in its role as "gatekeeper" (*see Daubert v. Merrell Dow Pharmaceuticals, Inc.*, 509 U.S. 579 (1993) (hereinafter *Daubert I*)), initiated proceedings under Federal Rule of Evidence 104.
* * *

II. FACTS AND PROCEDURAL BACKGROUND

The breast implant cases at issue here were either filed initially in this court or removed from state court. The cases were then transferred to the Judicial Panel for Multidistrict Litigation, *In re Silicone Gel Breast Implant Products Liability Litigation*, MDL No. 926, where they have been managed expeditiously under the watchful eye of the transferee judge, Chief Judge Sam C. Pointer, Jr. In 1995 and 1996, Judge Pointer remanded a number of cases to Oregon for trial.

All breast implant cases remanded to Oregon federal district court have been assigned to this judge. * * * [The court grouped similar cases together for trial.]

After initial trial dates were set, the court instructed counsel for Groups 1 and 2 to provide a list of all lay and expert witnesses to be called at trial, together with a narrative statement of each witness' proposed testimony. * * *

Once the witness materials were duly filed, in July 1996, defendants jointly filed a series of motions in limine to exclude plaintiffs' experts' testimony concerning causation. To address these motions, I scheduled an integrated hearing under Rule 104(a) on the admissibility of the scientific evidence. * * *

In view of the complicated scientific and medical issues involved and in an effort to effectively discharge my role as "gatekeeper" under *Daubert I*, I invoked my inherent authority as a federal district court judge to appoint independent advisors to the court. * * * Dr. Richard Jones, M.D., Ph.D., assisted the court by screening dozens of potential appointees and ultimately selecting four totally unbiased and uncommitted experts in the necessary fields, which the court approved and appointed. The technical advisors and their fields of expertise are: Merwyn R. Greenlick, Ph.D. (epidemiology); Robert F. Wilkens, M.D. (rheumatology); Mary Stenzel–Poore, Ph.D. (immunology/toxicology); and Ronald McClard, Ph.D. (polymer chemistry).

* * *

At the hearing, which spanned four intense days (August 5–8, 1996), experts on both sides were questioned by counsel, the court, and the technical advisors. The parties then submitted videotaped summations, which the court and all technical advisors reviewed. The court also asked the parties to submit proposed questions to guide the technical advisors in evaluating the testimony and preparing their reports. After considering the parties' proposed questions, the court prepared and submitted * * * questions to the advisors * * *.

* * *

The technical advisors submitted their reports to the court in September 1996, and on September 13, 1996, the court gave counsel on both sides an opportunity to question them. * * *

Having fully reviewed the entire record and the reports of the advisors, I am now prepared to rule on the pending rule 104 hearing motions in limine. For the reasons explained below, the defendants' motions in limine to exclude plaintiffs' expert testimony concerning causation of any systemic disease or syndrome are GRANTED.

I note, however, that while this court was in the midst of the Rule 104 proceedings, Judge Pointer appointed a national panel of experts pursuant to FRE 706 to assist in a similar evaluation of the scientific evidence in the MDL. * * *

* * *

In view of the ongoing national proceedings and the potential for further scientific developments during their pendency, the court will defer the effective date of this opinion until the findings of the national Rule 706 panel are available. Depending on the court's evaluation of those findings, plaintiffs in these cases may seek reconsideration, if appropriate, of this decision. * * *

III. *ADMISSIBILITY STANDARDS*

A. Rule 702 and Rule 104(a)

The Federal Rules of Evidence [generally] govern in diversity cases * * *. With respect to the issues presently before the court, no state evidence rule supplants the federal rules.

Rule 702 is the starting point for any evaluation of the admissibility of expert testimony. * * *

The assessment of whether proffered expert testimony is admissible under Rule 702 is a preliminary question for the court under Rule 104(a). * * *

The Ninth Circuit recently emphasized that the proponent of the expert testimony bears the burden of proving admissibility under Rule 104. *Lust v. Merrell Dow Pharmaceuticals, Inc.*, 89 F.3d 594, 598 (9th Cir.1996); *see also Daubert v. Merrell Dow Pharmaceuticals, Inc.*, 43 F.3d 1311, 1316 (9th Cir. 1995) (hereinafter *Daubert II*). In this case, the plaintiffs, as proponents of the evidence, have the burden of establishing admissibility by a preponderance of the evidence.

In determining whether the plaintiffs have met their burden of establishing the admissibility of their expert evidence, the court is guided by Rule 702 and the recent Supreme Court and Ninth Circuit decisions interpreting it, particularly *Daubert I* and *Daubert II*. [U]nder *Daubert I*, which focused closely on the language of Rule 702, expert scientific opinion is admissible if it qualifies as "scientific knowledge" and is therefore sufficiently "reliable." *Daubert I*, 509 U.S. at 589–90.

According to *Daubert I*, "the adjective 'scientific' implies a grounding in the methods and procedures of science," and "the word 'knowledge' connotes more than subjective belief or unsupported speculation." 509 U.S. at 590. * * * The requirement that an expert's testimony pertain to "scientific knowledge" "establishes a standard of evidentiary reliability," *i.e.*, trustworthiness. 509 U.S. at 590 and n.9.

The Supreme Court charged district courts with the duty to act as "gatekeepers," to ensure that any and all scientific testimony or evidence admitted is not only relevant, but reliable. Thus, the court must determine at the outset, pursuant to Rule 104(a), "whether the expert is proposing to testify to (1) scientific knowledge that (2) will assist the trier of fact to understand or determine a fact in issue." *Id.* at 592–93. This determination "entails a preliminary assessment of whether the reasoning or methodology underlying the testimony is scientifically valid and of whether that reasoning or methodology properly can be applied to the facts in issue." *Id*.

The task before this court, then, is two-pronged. First, the court must determine whether plaintiffs' experts' testimony reflects "scientific knowledge," constitutes "good science," and was "derived by the scientific method." *Daubert II*, 43 F.3d at 1316. Second, the court must ensure that the proposed testimony "fits," that is, that the testimony is " 'relevant to the task at hand' " in that it "logically advances a material aspect of the proposing party's case." *Id*. at 1315 (quoting *Daubert I*, 509 U.S. at 597).

1. Reliability.

Daubert I and *Daubert II* list several factors to guide federal courts in deciding the first prong, whether the expert testimony is scientifically valid and therefore reliable. These factors, which may or may not apply in a particular case, include:

1. Whether the theory or technique employed by the expert is generally accepted in the scientific community;

2. Whether the theory has been subjected to peer review and publication;

3. Whether the theory can be and has been tested;

4. Whether the known or potential rate of error is acceptable; and

5. Whether the experts are proposing to testify about matters growing naturally or directly out of research, or whether they have developed their opinions expressly for purposes of testifying.

Daubert I, 509 U.S. at 593–94 (first four factors); *Daubert II*, 43 F.3d at 1316–17 (adding fifth factor). The list is illustrative, not exhaustive. *Daubert II*, 43 F.3d at 1317.

* * *

2. Fit.

Even if the proponents meet their burden of establishing that an expert's testimony qualifies as scientific knowledge, the court must still exclude the evidence if it does not "fit" the matters at issue in the case. *Daubert I*, 509 U.S. at 591. As the Ninth Circuit in *Daubert II*, explained, to "fit," testimony must "logically advance a material aspect of the proposing party's case." *Daubert II*, 43 F.3d at 1315. * * *

As the defendants correctly point out in their proposed findings and conclusions, the issue before the court, as in the Bendectin litigation considered in *Daubert II*, is causation. In *Daubert II*, the Ninth Circuit concluded that the plaintiffs in that case failed to make any objective showing of admissibility under the first prong of Rule 702. * * * In doing so, the court explained that in assessing whether proffered expert testimony "will assist the trier of fact" in resolving the causation issue, the court must look to the substantive standard—in that case, California tort law. The court commented:

California tort law requires plaintiffs to show not merely that Bendectin increased the likelihood of injury, but that it more likely than not caused their injuries. * * * In terms of statistical proof, this means that plaintiffs must establish not just that their mothers' ingestion of Bendectin increased somewhat the likelihood of birth defects, but that it more than doubled it—only then can it be said that Bendectin is more likely than not the source of their injury. * * *

Id. at 1320 (citation omitted).

The substantive standard under Oregon tort law is quite similar to the California standard. Under Oregon law, the plaintiffs in this litigation must prove not merely the possibility of a causal connection between breast implants and the alleged systemic disease, but the medical probability of a causal connection. * * *

Under this substantive standard, if an expert cannot state the causal connection in terms of probability or certainty, the expert's testimony must be excluded under the second prong of Rule 702. * * *

3. Methodology v. Conclusions.

The plaintiffs insist that this court must focus solely on the expert's methodology and may not consider the experts' conclusions in any respect. Certain language in *Daubert I* can be read, superficially, to support plaintiffs' position. * * *

Since *Daubert I* was decided, however, courts and commentators have wrestled with the methodology/conclusion distinction, concluding that the distinction is of limited practical import. * * *

> * * *

There appears to be no clear demarcation between scientific methodology and the conclusions it generates. *Daubert I* acknowledged this much, recognizing that science is a process, not "an encyclopedic body of knowledge." 509 U.S. at 590 (citation omitted). This court need not and should not ignore any step in that process, but must ensure that in each step, from initial premise to ultimate conclusion, the expert faithfully followed valid scientific methodology. In other words, this court need not accept, as scientifically reliable, any conclusion that good science does not permit to be drawn from the underlying data but which, instead, constitutes "unsupported speculation," or, in the words of Dr. Stenzel–Poore, a "leap of faith." The Ninth Circuit requires no less.

> * * *

IV. *FINDINGS AND CONCLUSIONS*

Physicians have used silicone products in the human body for various purposes since the 1950s. * * * The silicone gel breast implants involved in this litigation consist of 80 to 90 percent liquid silicone combined with 10 to 20 percent silicone gel, contained in a silicone rubber shell.

Plaintiffs' theory of causation—or, as they refer to it, bioplausibility—begins with the premise that silicone from breast implants is released into a woman's body, either through implant rupture or through "gel bleed," the slow but continuous release of very small droplets ("microdroplets") of silicone gel through the silicone rubber implant cover. Once released into the body, plaintiffs assert, silicone migrates throughout the body, either by diffusing through cell membranes or by being carried by macrophages, the cells in a person's body that devour and eliminate invading foreign bodies and wastes. In the process, the silicone degrades, or is chemically converted, into more reactive molecules such as silanols. The released silicone and the reactive products of silicone degradation purportedly elicit an autoimmune response from the woman's immune system, essentially turning her immune system against her. The result, plaintiffs conclude, is general, systemic disease and particular signs and symptoms such as muscle and joint pain, headaches, rashes, and an inability to concentrate.

Plaintiffs' theory of causation thus brings four general areas of science into play: epidemiology; rheumatology; immunology/toxicology; and polymer chemistry. * * *

A. Atypical Connective Tissue Disease

Plaintiffs premise many of their claims on the existence of a variously-titled atypical connective tissue disease (ACTD). This "disease" allegedly manifests itself through a constellation of various symptoms and is allegedly caused by an autoimmune response to silicone from breast implants. Plaintiffs have offered Dr. Eric Gershwin and Dr. Kip Kemple as experts in rheumatology to testify that silicone exposure is the probable cause of plaintiffs' atypical constellation of symptoms.

By definition, ACTD is not one of the classical autoimmune diseases, such as lupus, scleroderma, or rheumatoid arthritis. In addition, plaintiffs' expert Dr. Goldsmith testified that ACTD does not exist even as a hypothesis yet. * * * A silicone research group has proposed criteria for this alleged disease, but these criteria have not yet been tested, nor does the rheumatology community generally accept the existence of ACTD. * * * Finally, women who allegedly have ACTD do not uniformly exhibit the same signs and symptoms, and there is no "signature" disorder to suggest either that the cause is silicone exposure or that the cause is the same for all women showing this constellation of symptoms. Instead, the asserted constellation of symptoms comprising ACTD overlaps significantly with those comprising chronic fatigue syndrome and fibromyalgia.

Because ACTD is at best an untested hypothesis, there is no scientific basis for any expert testimony as to its causes and presence in plaintiffs. Therefore, defendants' motions are GRANTED as regards any expert testimony relating to the existence and causation of any atypical, silicone-caused, autoimmune disorder.

* * *

B. Epidemiology

Plaintiffs offer Dr. David Goldsmith as an expert to testify that there is epidemiological and other scientific data showing that women with silicone breast implants have significantly elevated probability of suffering from classical diseases when compared to women without breast implants. In contrast, plaintiffs offer Dr. Shanna Swan, through transcripts of her previous testimony in other cases, to testify that no valid epidemiological studies regarding the relationship of silicone breast implants and disease have been completed as of August 1996.

Epidemiology is the medical science devoted to determining the causes of disease in human beings. Epidemiologists compare control groups of unexposed individuals to groups of individuals exposed to a hypothetical cause of the disease being studied to determine whether exposed individuals have a greater risk of manifesting that disease. In epidemiological terms, any difference in risk of getting the disease between the two groups is the exposed individuals' relative risk. The existence or nonexistence of relevant epidemiology can be a significant factor in proving general causation in toxic tort cases.

To support admissible expert opinions, epidemiological evidence must fit the legal as well as the substantive issues of the case. Because this is a diversity action, Oregon substantive standards of law must apply. * * * This burden requires plaintiffs to demonstrate that exposure to breast implants more than doubled the risk of their alleged injuries.

In epidemiological terms, Oregon's standard of proof means that plaintiffs must be able to show a relative risk of greater than 2.0 * * *. The Ninth Circuit has reached a similar conclusion under California's standard of proof, which is very similar to Oregon's, holding that "[f]or an epidemiological study to show causation under a preponderance standard, 'the relative risk of [the condition at issue] arising from the epidemiological data ... will, at minimum, have to exceed "2".' " *Daubert II*, 43 F.3d at 1321 (quoting *DeLuca v. Merrell Dow Pharmaceuticals*, 911 F.2d 941, 958 (3d Cir.1990)). * * *

Plaintiffs' experts base their proffered expert opinions on the sixteen epidemiological studies assessing the relationship of silicone breast implants to classical connective tissue disease. In addition, plaintiffs have called this court's attention to the 1996 Liang–Schottenfeld abstract recently presented at a meeting of the American College of Rheumatology that reports a relative risk of 2.27 for Undifferentiated Connective Tissue Diseases (UCTD).

Dr. Goldsmith testified in the proceedings before this court that he was not willing to testify, based on the 16 then-available studies, that silicone more likely than not could cause disease in women. * * *

With the release of the Liang–Schottenfeld abstract, Dr. Goldsmith now indicates a willingness to testify that such causation is "more likely than not." This court cannot accept his proffered change in testimony because it finds the methodology supporting this changed testimony unreliable under *Daubert I* and *Daubert II*. First, none of the 16 epidemiological studies found that women with silicone breast implants faced a relative risk of classical diseases or disease signs and symptoms of anywhere near 2.0. Indeed, only one study—the Hennekens study—found any statistical relationship between the presence of silicone breast implants and disease, and there the relative risk was only 1.24. Therefore, these studies cannot support expert testimony that silicone "more likely than not" causes disease or signs and symptoms of disease in women.

Second, the Liang–Schottenfeld abstract cannot in itself support Dr. Goldsmith's change in testimony. The abstract is not yet published, nor is a full write-up of the study, including the supporting data, yet available. Indeed, Dr. Goldsmith admitted in his New York testimony that his only knowledge of the details of the study came from a telephone inquiry. According to the abstract, moreover, the study included only three women with breast implants, calling its epidemiological significance severely into question. In addition, the abstract explicitly concludes that "silicone breast implants were not significantly associated with UCTD," suggesting that silicone gel breast implants are *not* associated with disease. In contrast, the abstract concludes overall that, "[a]mong all types of implanted devices, including breast implants, both those containing silicone * * * and those that did not contain silicone * * * were significantly associated with UCTD." This apparent internal contradiction within the abstract's conclusions calls the value of this study further into question. In light of these shortcomings and in the face of the other 16 studies, which Dr. Goldsmith has already admitted do not support expert testimony that silicone "more likely than not" causes disease in women, this court GRANTS defendant's motion to exclude Dr. Goldsmith's epidemiological testimony.

As for defendants' motion to exclude Dr. Swan's proffered testimony, the motion must be GRANTED because Dr. Swan's testimony is unreliable and no longer "fits" plaintiffs' theory of the case. I first note that several courts have rejected Dr. Swan's testimony and her "reanalysis" approach as unreliable. Dr. Swan's reanalysis of the silicone epidemiology has never been subjected to peer review. Moreover, her theory has not been espoused by any other scientist whose work has been subjected to the peer review process. Peer review and publication weigh heavily in the calculus of the reliability of expert testimony because such peer review "increases the likelihood that substantive flaws in methodology will be detected." *Daubert I*, 509 U.S. at 594. Thus, the lack of peer review for Dr. Swan's theories weighs heavily against the admissibility of Dr. Swan's testimony.

In addition, Dr. Swan's testimony involves only her opinions and criticisms of others' work; as such, it is not based on any technique that can be scientifically tested. Moreover, her criticisms of the existing epidemiology for silicone gel breast implants have not been generally accepted. In fact, they have not been accepted at all. In contrast, Dr. Swan admits that no studies have established a causal link of any scientific significance between silicone breast implants and disease, and this is the recognized consensus of the relevant scientific community.

* * *

In addition, Dr. Swan's testimony has no "fit." As discussed above, even if the proponents of expert testimony establish that that testimony is reliable scientific knowledge, the court must still exclude the evidence if it does not fit the issues to be decided in the case. In the Ninth Circuit, testimony only "fits" a case if it logically advances a material aspect of the proponent party's case. Here, Dr. Swan seeks to testify that current epidemiology regarding the relationship of silicone breast implants and classical disease is invalid. However, this court has already determined that the proffered testimony based on that epidemiology is inadmissible, and it will determine, see discussion below, that plaintiffs cannot base their entire case on differential diagnosis. In addition, to the extent that plaintiffs intended to use Dr. Swan's testimony to support their argument that silicone breast implants can cause ACTD, I have already ruled that no testimony regarding ACTD will be permitted. Therefore, Dr. Swan's testimony is now a stepping stone that leads nowhere; it no longer "fits" plaintiffs' case.

* * * Therefore, for all of the above reasons, I GRANT defendants' motions to exclude Dr. Swan's testimony.

C. Immunology and Toxicology

Plaintiffs have offered Dr. Eric Gershwin as an expert in immunology to testify that silicone is capable of causing plaintiffs' constellation of symptoms because (1) silicone in contact with human tissue results in chronic inflammation through immune activation and cellular reactions; (2) silicone is an immune adjuvant and thus can produce enhanced immune responses when in the presence of a triggering condition and exacerbate existing immune-mediated conditions; and (3) the surface of silicone changes or degrades *in vivo* into silanol groups and/or silica. He relies on the epidemiological studies discussed above, his own clinical experience, biomarker, immune activation, and toxicological studies, and the work of the Harvard NMR Center on the degradation of silicone as the bases of his proffered opinion.

Plaintiffs also offer Dr. Kip Kemple to testify that silicone can produce an immunological response in women. Dr. Kemple relies on immunological studies showing that autoantibodies are elevated in women with breast implants and his own study of antiganglioside antibodies in women with breast implants.

The court submitted immunological/toxicological issues to its expert, Dr. Mary Stenzel–Poore, who specifically looked at the adjuvant potential of silicone gel implants, the potential for immune stimulation of T cells by silicone gel implants, altered natural killer cell activity, and immune system cancer formation in rodents. She opined that * * * "[d]irect attempts to demonstrate that immunization with these agents emulsified with 'auto-antigens' or given in the absence of antigens failed to show evidence of autoimmune disease despite obvious disease induction by Freund's adjuvant," except in a genetic strain of rat developed to have a high susceptibility of developing arthritis. Thus, *in rodents only*, "enhanced immune responses are not found if the antigen is not emulsified with the silicone agents * * *."

Dr. Stenzel–Poore further stated that "[f]orming the conclusion that elicitation of autoimmune and/or inflammatory disease occurs in women with SBI based on the evidence that silicone gel acts as an adjuvant *when emulsified with antigen* is **unsupported by the data** since peer-reviewed studies failed to show evidence of any autoimmune-mediated disease." * * *

With regard to T-cell stimulation, Dr. Stenzel–Poore opined that "[t]he view that SBIs stimulate antigen-specific T cell mediated responses in vivo is not well substantiated by the experimental studies reported in the literature." Moreover, although "[s]everal studies have been performed attempting to establish a link between silicone breast implantation in women and silicone-specific T-cell responses," "these studies have a number of methodological shortcomings and thus should not form the basis of an opinion." * * *

Dr. Stenzel–Poore also examined the literature regarding changes in natural killer cell function. She noted that "[c]hanges in natural killer (NK) cell function have been reported to be associated with silicone gel exposure in rodents and humans." * * * [However, she also concluded:] "It is invalid to conclude that silicone-gel breast implants in women lead to a depressed NK cell activity that is reversible with explanation."

Finally, in evaluating the studies evaluating the development of immune system cancer in response to silicone, Dr. Stenzel–Poore stated that "Dr. Gershwin's opinions regarding the development of immune system cancers in women with silicone breast implants is unwarranted" from the current studies, which are all animal studies. "There is no conclusive evidence to date that this model of tumor formation in mice has any human correlate."

I agree with and accept Dr. Stenzel–Poore's assessments of Dr. Gershwin's scientific methodology in light of legal standards for *Daubert* hearings. As a preliminary matter, I note that most if not all of the studies that Dr. Gershwin and Dr. Kemple rely upon are animal studies (generally involving rodents), case reports or collections of case reports, and/or studies involving crystalline silica. Extrapolations of animal studies to human beings are generally not considered reliable in the absence of a scientific explanation of why such extrapolation is warranted. Plaintiffs offer no explanation of why extrapolations from the rodent studies their experts rely upon to humans are warranted here.

Similarly, case reports and case studies are universally regarded as an insufficient scientific basis for a conclusion regarding causation because case reports lack controls. Therefore, these cannot be the basis of an opinion based on scientific knowledge under *Daubert*.

Third, as will be discussed below, studies based on crystalline silica cannot support the testimony of plaintiffs' experts because plaintiffs make no showing that silicone breast implants are associated with the presence of crystalline silica in women. In other words, the purported disease-causing agent in the silica studies has not been show to be scientifically relevant regarding the purported disease-causing agent—namely, silicone gel—in these cases.

Finally, *Daubert*'s establishment of the court as gatekeeper requires that proffered scientific expert opinions that make too great a leap of faith from the scientific knowledge currently available be excluded. * * * In other words, those conclusions are themselves not the result of the faithful application of valid scientific methodology. Therefore, defendants' motions to exclude Dr. Gershwin's and Dr. Kemple's testimony on these issues is GRANTED.

D. Chemistry

Plaintiffs offer Dr. Christopher Batich as an expert in chemistry to testify that: (1) silicone migrates out of breast implant capsules; (2) there is an increase in surface area of silicone from gel breast implants to which the body reacts over time; (3) silicone changes in the body and forms bioreactive silanol groups on its surface; (4) silicone degrades into silica in the body; and (5) there is similar surface chemistry in all siloxics (silicones, silicates, and silicas) that make the siloxics reactive in humans. In addition, plaintiffs offer Dr. Harold Alexander, a biomaterials engineer, to testify that: (1) silicone microdroplets and/or particles are released from breast implants through gel bleed or rupture and have a high potential to cause inflammatory reactions in body tissues, and (2) the small size of silicone microdroplets and/or particles allows them to migrate through the body via microphages and other migrating cells, and their low molecular weight allows them to diffuse through tissue.

The court's technical advisor for polymer chemistry, Dr. Ronald McClard, carefully reviewed the question of whether the scientific evidence supports Dr. Batich's and Dr. Alexander's proffered testimony that silicone degrades to silica *in vivo*. In reviewing the plaintiffs' main scientific support for silica-induced biological reactions, a paper published by B. Razzaboni and P. Bolsaitis in *Environmental Health Perspectives*, Dr. McClard stated that:

> The Razzaboni article * * * clearly attempts to offer a biochemical explanation for the silica-caused hemolytic process. This article seems scientifically sound. If silicones are converted to silica then this article seems relevant to the issue at hand. *I am unaware that any of the papers that I reviewed clearly demonstrated the conversion of silicone to silica (most likely amorphous forms thereof)*, though the process

seems possible given the known chemistry of silicon. *The link between silicones and the Razzaboni article is a prospective one.*

* * * As with the immunological/toxicological conclusions discussed above, plaintiffs' experts again make too great a leap of faith in their proffered testimony that silicone gel from breast implants degrades to silica. This is especially true for any testimony that silicone gel degrades *in vivo* to crystalline, as opposed to amorphous, silica. Therefore, I hereby GRANT defendants' motions as pertains to such testimony.

In addition, because there is no scientifically valid evidence to support the conclusion that silicone gel degrades to silica in the human body, any other immunological or toxicological studies involving the inhalation, ingestion, or absorption of crystalline silica cannot "fit" the issue of whether silicone breast implants can cause signs or symptoms of disease in women. Therefore, as discussed above, I must also exclude testimony based on this evidence under the "fit" prong of *Daubert I* and *Daubert II*.

* * *

* * * Therefore, I hereby GRANT defendants' motions to exclude the testimony of Dr. Batich and Dr. Alexander.

E. Differential Diagnosis

Plaintiffs have offered Dr. Robert Bennett, M.D., both to testify that silicone gel breast implants can cause disease in women and to testify as a case-specific expert in *LeaAnn Hall v. Baxter Healthcare*. Dr. Bennett is plaintiff Hall's treating physician and is prepared to testify, on the basis of differential diagnosis, that plaintiff Hall suffers from systemic sclerosis sine scleroderma, manifested by her pulmonary fibrosis, as a result of having silicone gel breast implants.

As has been noted, the issue before me in this *Daubert* hearing is silicone gel's ability to cause disease in women with breast implants. Courts, however, have recognized two levels of causation: general causation (*i.e.*, whether silicone gel can cause disease in anyone) and specific causation (*i.e.*, whether silicone gel breast implants caused disease in this plaintiff).

Differential diagnosis is a patient-specific process of elimination that medical practitioners use to identify the "most likely" cause of a set of signs and symptoms from a list of possible causes. However, differential diagnosis does not by itself *prove* the cause, even for the particular patient. Nor can the technique speak to the issue of general causation. Indeed, differential diagnosis *assumes* that general causation has been proven for the list of possible causes it eliminates * * *.

* * *

* * * Therefore, I must exclude Dr. Bennett's testimony for all cases to the extent that plaintiffs proffer it to prove general causation.

Nor is Dr. Bennett's testimony admissible to prove specific causation in LeaAnn Hall's case, and for two reasons. General causation issues aside, an expert must rule out other potential causes of the patient's condition in order for differential diagnosis testimony to be admissible. Here, Dr. Bennett has not testified as to how he eliminated other potential causes of Ms. Hall's disease. Moreover, his conclusion is inconsistent with the epidemiology for classical diseases. Therefore, his testimony is unreliable and exclusion of it is warranted on that basis.

In addition, in the absence of proof of general causation, Dr. Bennett's testimony regarding his differential diagnosis does not "fit" LeaAnn Hall's case because there will be no evidence that silicone gel breast implants are a legitimate possible cause of Ms. Hall's disease. Therefore, for all of the above reasons, I hereby GRANT defendants' motions to exclude the testimony of Dr. Bennett.

V. CONCLUSION

For the reasons stated above, those portions of defendants' motions in limine * * * that seek exclusion of any expert testimony concerning a general causal link between silicone gel breast implants and ACTD or any systemic illness or syndrome are GRANTED. The remaining portions of the above-listed motions are MOOT, with leave to refile as necessary in further pretrial proceedings.

* * *

[However], as stated earlier, I will defer the effective date of this decision pending the reports of the national Rule 706 panel, and likewise will defer plaintiffs' motion to incorporate the panel members as witnesses. Nonetheless, I wish to make it abundantly clear that while I will evaluate the Rule 706 panel reports before finalizing my decision, I am unlikely to amend these findings and conclusions absent substantial and compelling developments in the scientific arena.

I am mindful that this opinion goes farther in evaluating and in eliminating plaintiffs' claims than any other opinion in breast implant litigation pending in this country. However, litigation over the ability of silicone gel breast implants to cause disease in women has been chaotic in its results, in part because, as *Hopkins* demonstrates, the interjection of the *Daubert* standards into the screening process for proposed scientific evidence has substantially heightened the scrutiny through which such evidence must pass. In my opinion, *Daubert I* and *Daubert II* and their progeny command this disposition.

NOTES AND QUESTIONS

1. *Applying* Daubert: *court-appointed experts.* What do you make of the federal district courts' willingness to use court-appointed experts to help them evaluate the reliability and fitness of the parties' experts' testimony under *Daubert*? Did the Supreme Court essentially necessitate this development for federal toxic tort cases when complex causation issues arise, given that most federal judges do not possess the relevant scientific expertise? Notably, Judge

Jones, the judge in *Hall*, appointed the court's experts after an early hearing in which the parties were encouraged to explain the science at issue in the case to the court.

The "battle of the experts" in toxic torts cases often raises the specter that expert witnesses on each side are biased—for example, because companies in the litigation financed the expert's research or because the expert makes a living testifying for plaintiffs or defendants. Judge Jones' use of court-appointed experts can be one technique for avoiding biased experts. Indeed, Judge Jones described the four experts that he appointed as "totally unbiased."

Do you think that is true? Is any expert witness unbiased? Even if appointed expert witnesses are biased, are there still advantages to using court-appointed experts? Several commentators certainly think so, including Justice Breyer, concurring, in *Joiner*. See Howard M. Erichson, Mass Tort Litigation and Inquisitorial Justice, 87 Geo.L.J. 1983, 1986–95 (1999); Joe S. Cecil & Thomes E. Willging, Accepting *Daubert*'s Invitation: Defining the Role of Court–Appointed Experts in Assessing Scientific Validity, 43 Emory L.J. 995 (1994). For a more focused discussion on the use of court-appointed experts in the *Hall* case and how Judge Jones' procedure differed from the appointment of experts through the process established in Federal Rule of Evidence 706, see Joseph Sanders & D.H. Kaye, Expert Advice on Silicone Implants*: Hall v. Baxter Healthcare Corp.*, 37 Jurimetrics J. 113 (1997).

Despite the favorable commentary, court-appointed experts are rarely employed, even in toxic tort cases. What conditions are most favorable for their use? The Federal Judicial Center studied the use of court-appointed experts in the federal courts by surveying federal judges. It found four significant reasons why federal judges rarely employ court-appointed experts. First, court-appointed experts are generally not required in a case that does not pose difficult and contested scientific issues. Second, the use of court-appointed experts is perceived as being inconsistent with the adversarial system. Third, court-appointed experts cost money, and judges report awkwardness in requiring the parties to pay those costs. Finally, there can be difficulties in identifying expert witnesses who both have the relevant expertise and who are uninvolved in and unbiased with respect to the litigation. Federal Judicial Center, Court–Appointed Experts: Defining the Role of Experts Appointed Under Federal Rule of Evidence 706 (1993).

Court-appointed experts potentially raise other issues, as well. For example, is there a risk that federal judges in these situations might substitute the court expert's scientific judgment for the trial judge's legal judgment? Consider Judge Jones's use of Dr. Stenzel–Poore. Can the argument be made that the judge simply found Dr. Stenzel–Poore more credible than the proffered witnesses whose testimony she was evaluating? Why or why not? How did Judge Jones seek to guard against that possibility? Can you articulate important distinctions between the scientific evaluations involved in a *Daubert* hearings and the ultimate legal conclusions regarding the admissibility of the expert testimony?

2. *The* Daubert *inquiry and epidemiologic evidence.* In Chapter 3, we saw that some courts have imposed a requirement that, before an epidemiologic study can support a finding of specific causation, that study must find a causal association (relative risk) of at least 2.0. Following the U.S. Court of Appeals for the Ninth Circuit's decision in *Daubert II*, the *Hall* court expressly used this standard. Did the *Hall* court (or the Ninth Circuit in *Daubert II*) confuse general and specific causation—i.e., did it apply the 2.0 relative risk requirement to a general causation issue? Why or why not? Should such a relative risk threshold be relevant to establishing general causation? Why or why not?

Consider, too, the U.S. District Court for the District of Colorado's discussion of epidemiology in a silicone gel breast implant case decided two years after *Hall*:

> The diseases and symptoms allegedly associated with breast implants occur in non-implanted women as well as implanted women. Many of the conditions that Plaintiffs attribute to breast implants appear in the general population. Without a controlled study, there is no way to determine if these symptoms are more common in women with silicone breast implants than women without implants. "The most important evidence relied upon by scientists to determine whether an agent (such as breast implants) cause disease is controlled epidemiologic studies. Epidemiology can be viewed as the study of the causes of diseases in humans." Therefore, epidemiological studies are necessary to determine the cause and effect between breast implants and allegedly associated diseases. A valid epidemiologic study requires that study subjects, cases, and controls are chosen by an unbiased sampling method from a definable population. Epidemiology is the best evidence of causation in the mass torts context.

In re Breast Implant Litig., 11 F.Supp.2d 1217, 1224 (D.Colo.1998) (quoting Ory Affidavit, Exhibit A p. 7 to Defendants' June 2, 1997 Science Brief). Colorado is in the Tenth Circuit; therefore, the Colorado District Court was not bound by the Ninth Circuit's post-*Daubert I* decisions. Nevertheless, it repeatedly cited *Hall* with approval. Is the Colorado District Court's view of the role of epidemiology the same as the Oregon District Court's? Why or why not? Would the Oregon District Court have let the plaintiffs try their claims without epidemiologic studies? Why or why not?

Finally, consider some of the ethical constraints that could limit the availability of epidemiologic studies of the kind the Colorado District Court demanded, as was discussed in Chapter 3. Are such epidemiologic studies likely after a substance has been identified as an actual or potential toxin? Why or why not?

3. *Non-epidemiologic evidence in federal court.* In addition to epidemiologic experts who testified based on statistical studies that had been performed, the plaintiffs also offered the testimony of immunologists and a chemist. These experts' testimony was quite different from that of the epidemiologists because these experts offered *mechanism evidence*—that is, evidence to establish the mechanisms through which silicone gel might cause immunological disease in women. Mechanism evidence can be quite strong evidence of causation—consider our understanding of the mechanism by which a car crashing into a tree produces a broken limb. However, it can also amount to speculation, which is where the *Daubert* admissibility analysis becomes relevant. Why did Judge Jones in *Hall* exclude the experts who employed mechanism evidence? How well do you think judges can judge the reliability of mechanism evidence in cases like *Hall*?

4. *Toxic torts,* Daubert*, and federal procedure.* As the *Hall* case makes clear, toxic tort litigation in the federal courts can prompt extraordinary use of federal case management procedures. For example, in *Hall*, Judge Jones noted that the Oregon cases proceeding to trial had been remanded to the Oregon District Court from the Northern District of Alabama Multidistrict Litigation. On June 25, 1992, in response to motions involving 78 silicone gel breast implant cases in 33 different federal district courts, the federal Judicial Panel on Multidistrict Litigation consolidated those cases into the Northern District of Alabama, under Judge Pointer, for pretrial management. In re Silicone Gel Breast Implants Prods. Liab. Litig., 793 F.Supp. 1098, 1098, 1099–1100 (Jud.Pan.Mult.Lit.1992). At the time, the judicial panel noted that approximately 200 other similar cases had been filed in various courts and that six additional cases were unsuitable for multidistrict litigation for a variety of reasons—some were being remanded to state court, some had already been tried, and so on. Id. at 1098 n.1, 1099 n.2. Within a year, over 1700 silicone gel breast implant cases had been consolidated into Judge Pointer's court. In re Silicone Gel Breast Implants Products Liability Litigation, 1993 WL 223106, at *1 (Jud.Pan.Mult.Lit. June 3, 1993). We address multidistrict litigation more thoroughly in Chapter 14.

Settlement procedures were also complex for the silicone gel breast implant cases. For example, some of the cases involved in the multidistrict litigation consolidation settled in 1994, while still under Judge Pointer's direction. In re Silicone Gel Breast Implant Prods. Liab. Litig., 1994 WL 114580 (N.D.Ala.1994); 1994 WL 578353 (N.D.Ala.1994). However, a class action settlement fell apart. Compensation for the class action was contingent in part on how many plaintiffs made claims. As the number of plaintiffs exploded, the amount of the award to each plaintiff decreased. For this and other reasons, the plaintiffs began to opt out of the class and settlement. However, when it became clear that many of the plaintiffs would opt out, the defendants pulled out of the settlement pursuant to a clause in the settlement agreement that allowed them to withdraw if too many plaintiffs opted out. After the panel report was issued (see note 5), however, the remaining defendants made a unilateral offer to settle the cases based on a typical mass-tort grid. Of course, the payments were much lower than the earlier offers, but apparently the great majority of plaintiffs went ahead and accepted them because they could see the handwriting on the wall regarding their chances of recovery in litigation. Dow Corning, the largest defendant, had filed for Chapter 11 bankruptcy at this point and hence did not participate in the settlement offer. However, when it emerged from bankruptcy in 2004, it set aside $2.35 billion to settle the claims against it.

The remanded cases prompted much innovation in case management, even beyond the use of court-appointed experts. For example, in New York, the judges trying the silicone gel breast implant cases in the Southern District of New York (Judge Baer), the Eastern District of New York (Judge Weinstein, who also presided over the Agent Orange litigation), and the New York state court all collaborated to appoint court experts and to hear the evidentiary claims, and the two federal judges issued a joint ruling. In re Breast Implant Cases, 942 F.Supp. 958, 960–61 (S.D. & E.D.N.Y.1996) (for both federal courts, denying summary judgment to the defendants despite the apparent deficiencies in the plaintiffs' evidence in order to wait for the National Science Panel report); Matter of New York State Silicone Breast Implant Litig., 656 N.Y.S.2d 97, 98–99, 100 (N.Y.Sup.Ct.1997) (describing how the state judge had worked with the two federal judges and also staying the litigation until the National Science Panel report).

5. *The life cycle of mass torts.* The silicone breast implant litigation is a casebook example of how courts alter their responses to expert testimony as scientific evidence accumulates. In the earliest years of the litigation, before much scientific evidence had accumulated, courts generally admitted plaintiffs' expert testimony. This occurred in Hopkins v. Dow Corning Corp., 33 F.3d 1116 (9th Cir.1994) where the Ninth Circuit wrote that "[t]he record reflects that Hopkins experts based their opinions on the types of scientific data and utilized the types of scientific techniques relied upon by medical experts in making determination regarding toxic causation where there is no solid body of epidemiological data to review." Id. at 1124. Plainly, *Hopkins* rejected the view that one needs a solid body of human epidemiologic studies to reach an admissible conclusion concerning causation.

By the late 1990s results were more mixed. There was more epidemiologic data pointing in the direction of no causal relationship between implants and traditional auto-immune disease. In the New York courts, for example, Judges Baer and Weinstein expressed skepticism that plaintiff experts could withstand a *Daubert* challenge but as in *Hall* refused to make a final ruling prior to the National Science Panel Report. In re Breast Implant Cases, 942 F.Supp. 958 (S.D. & E.D.N.Y.1996). Plaintiff experts were simply excluded in another federal case from this period. See In re Breast Implant Litig., 11 F.Supp.2d 1217 (D.Colo.1998).

On the other hand, during this period several state court opinions admitted plaintiff expert testimony—but not necessarily under the same standards as *Daubert* imposes. For example, in Dow Chemical Co. v. Mahlum, 970 P.2d 98 (Nev.1998), the Nevada Supreme Court expressly refused to adopt the *Daubert* test and noted that once a trial court "certifies an expert as qualified, the expert may testify on all matters within the expert's experience and training." Id. at 108 & n.21. Not only did the court reject the *Daubert* test, it also apparently rejected the *Frye* test. It noted that the plaintiff "did not need to wait until the scientific community developed a consensus that breast implants caused their diseases." Id. at 109.

Experts were also admitted in Vassallo v. Baxter Healthcare Corp., 696 N.E.2d 909 (Mass.1998) and Jennings v. Baxter Healthcare Corp., 14 P.3d 596 (Or.2000). In *Jennings*, the plaintiff's expert reviewed animal studies conducted by Dow Corning. In addition, the expert testified as to the results of neurological tests he had performed on approximately 50 patients with multiple silicone breast implants. He found that 95% of these women had two symptoms in common: inner ear dysfunction and loss of sensation in their extremities. He also conducted an unspecified differential diagnosis to rule out other causes of the plaintiff's injury. On these bases, he was prepared to testify that, to a reasonable degree of scientific probability, silicone-related neurological conditions exist in patients who exhibit the kinds of symptoms that the plaintiff displayed. The trial court excluded the expert on general causation grounds. However, the Oregon Court of Appeals reversed. As to the argument that a conclusion based upon differential diagnosis is inadmissible in the absence of proof of general causation, the court said, "[a]lthough a differential diagnosis under these facts assumes that silicone is a possible cause, that assumption is logically supported by the unique symptoms and neurological patterns displayed by the women that were examined." Jennings v. Baxter Healthcare Corp., 954 P.2d 829, 834 (Or.App.1998), 14 P.3d 596 (Or.2000). In affirming, the Oregon Supreme Court concluded that the plaintiff's experts' methodology, which relied on clinical case studies, "was scientifically valid." Id. at 606. Moreover, it emphasized that epidemiology is not the only legitimate way of proving causation. Id. at 606–08.

What do you think of the appellate court's analysis? Did the plaintiff's expert use a reliable method to determine general causation? Why or why not? Would the expert's opinion be admissible under a *Frye* test? In answering these questions you may wish to glance at the findings of the National Science Panel and the Institute of Medicine summarized below.

These cases drew the ire of parts of the scientific community. See Marcia Angell, Science on Trial: The Clash of Medical Evidence and the Law in the Breast Implant Case (1996). At the time she wrote her book, Dr. Angell was the executive editor of the *New England Journal of Medicine.*

In December 1998, the National Science Panel published its report, and in 2000 the Institute of Medicine released its report. As the *Hall* case intimates, the findings parroted those of its court-appointed experts. The U.S. District Court for the District of Arizona summarized the National Science Panel findings as follows:

> One of the two main reports presented and reviewed by this Court arose of out the Multi district Breast Implant Litigation 926. Those cases were assigned to transferee Chief Judge Sam C. Pointer, from the northern district of Alabama, to handle pretrial discovery and simplify issues for trial. Judge Pointer appointed a national committee of experts under Federal Rule of Evidence 706, deemed the National Science Panel (NSP), to consider evidence on whether silicone breast implants cause systemic disease and to assist Judge Pointer in making evidentiary rulings concerning whether there was a causal link between breast implants and any of the individual connective tissue diseases, all definitive connective tissues diseases combined, or other autoimmune/rheumatic conditions.

> Four experts were appointed to the NSP: an epidemiologist (Dr. Barbara Hulka), an immunologist and rheumatologist (Dr. Betty Diamond); a rheumatologist and epedimiologist (Dr. Peter Tugwell), and a toxicologist (Dr. Nancy Kerkvliet). For over two years, the NSP considered the alleged causal relationship between disease and silicone breast implants with plaintiffs and defendants each providing the top forty articles in each field supporting their position. In November 1998, the Panel issued its report entitled "Silicone Breast Implants in Relation to Connective Tissue Diseases and Immunologic Dysfunction." The execu-

tive summary of that Panel reported their conclusion that "[n]o association was evident between breast implants and any of the individual connective tissue diseases, all definite connective tissue diseases combined, or the other autoimmune/rheumatic conditions." The Panel also found no association between breast implants and atypical connective tissue diseases or any distinctive constellation of symptoms observed in women with breast implants. Panelists noted that their findings and conclusions were unanimous, and that "a large majority of scientists in our respective disciplines would find merit on our reviews and analysis."

Grant v. Bristol–Myers Squibb, 97 F.Supp.2d 986, 989–90 (D.Ariz.2000).

Even more influential than the National Science Panel report was the subsequent Institute of Medicine (IOM) report. The IOM is the medical arm of the National Academy of Sciences. It undertook a study of the safety of implants at the express request of Congress and the U.S. Department of Health and Human Services. In its Executive Summary, the IOM discussed the safety of silicone gel breast implants as follows:

> The committee has reached three major conclusions regarding local and preoperative complications. First, reoperations and local and preoperative complications are frequent enough to be a cause for concern and to justify the conclusion that they are the primary safety issue with silicone breast implants. Complications may have risks themselves, such as pain, disfigurement and serious infection and they may lead to medical and surgical interventions, such as reoperations, that have risks. Second, risks accumulate over the lifetime of the implant, but quantitative data on this point are lacking for modern implants and deficient historically. Third, information concerning the nature and the relatively high frequency of local complications and reoperations is an essential element of adequate informed consent for women undergoing breast implantation.

> The committee has also come to the following conclusions:

> • Studies addressing the immunology of silicones are limited and technical problems substantial, providing the committee with no support for immunologic role of silicone.

> • A novel syndrome or disease associated with silicone breast implants has been proposed by a small group of physicians. Evidence for this proposed disease rests on case reports and is insufficient and flawed. The disease definition includes, as a precondition, the presence of silicone gel breast implants, so it cannot be studied as an independent health problem. The committee finds that the diagnosis of this condition could depend on the presence of a number of symptoms that a nonspecific and common in the general population. Thus, there does not appear to be even suggestive evidence of a novel syndrome in women with breast implants. In fact, epidemiological evidence suggests that there is no novel syndrome.

> • There is no increase in primary or recurrent breast cancer in implanted women.

> • In an overall consideration of the epidemiological evidence, the committee noted that because there are more than 1.5 million adult

women of all ages in the United States with silicone breast implants, some of these women would be expected to develop connective tissue diseases, cancer, neurological diseases or other systematic complaints or conditions. Evidence suggests that such diseases or conditions are no more common in women with breast implants than in women without implants.

• The committee finds no evidence of elevated silicone in breast milk or any other substances that would be deleterious to infants; the committee strongly concludes that all mothers with implants should attempt breast feeding.

Institute of Medicine, Safety of Silicone Breast Implants 10–11 (Stuart Bondurant et al. eds., 2000). A condensed version of the IOM report, authored by Stuart Bondurant and Roger Herdman, may be found in Faigman et al., 3 Modern Scientific Evidence, supra, at §§ 28:16–:30.

The result of these two reports were what one would expect. Plaintiffs' experts were routinely excluded and as a result silicone breast implant cases dealing with autoimmune and connective tissue diseases—but not cases dealing with localized injury—soon became a thing of the past. See Allison v. McGhan Med. Corp., 184 F.3d 1300 (11th Cir.1999); Grant v. Bristol–Myers Squibb, 97 F.Supp.2d 986 (D.Ariz.2000); Norris v. Baxter Healthcare Corp., 397 F.3d 878 (10th Cir.2005). The *Grant* opinion is typical of post-panel cases:

As a whole, the Court finds that the evidence regarding systemic disease as proposed by Plaintiffs' experts is not scientifically valid and therefore will not assist the trier of fact. As for the atypical syndrome that is suggested, where experts propose that breast implants cause a disease but cannot specify the criteria for diagnosing the disease, it is incapable of epidemiological testing. This renders the experts' methods insufficiently reliable to help the jury.

* * *

This Court finds that Plaintiffs' experts conclusions about systemic disease have not gained acceptance in the relevant scientific community and none of the proffered experts demonstrated that scientific methods practiced by a recognized minority in the field were followed. There is no explanation of why these opinions should outweigh the over twenty epidemiological studies finding no valid risk of autoimmune disease resulting from breast implants in humans. The Court will not allow the jury to speculate based on any experts' opinion based only on clinical experience in the absence of evidence showing consistent, statistically significant association between breast implants and systemic disease.

Grant v. Bristol–Myers Squibb, 97 F.Supp.2d at 992.

This conclusion is a far cry from the *Hopkins* opinion but it would be a mistake to say that one is right and the other wrong. Courts are sensitive to the quality and quantity of available evidence when they make admissibility rulings. This is especially true in those situations where scientists amass a large body of epidemiologic evidence. Once this occurs, courts are quite reluctant to permit an expert to base an opinion on non-epidemiological evidence.

The court in Richardson v. Richardson–Merrell, Inc., 857 F.2d 823 (D.C.Cir.1988), a Bendectin case, summarized this point nicely in comparing its decision with that in Ferebee v. Chevron Chemical Co., 736 F.2d 1529 (D.C.Cir.1984). In *Ferebee*, the question was whether exposure to the herbicide Paraquat could cause pulmonary fibrosis. The court admitted the testimony of the plaintiff's experts even though they had no epidemiologic or in vivo data. It concluded, "Thus, a cause-effect relationship need not be clearly established by animal or epidemiological studies before a doctor can testify that, in his opinion, such a relationship exists." Id. at 1535. When the *Richardson* court was asked by plaintiffs to follow the *Ferebee* example, it responded:

> The case before us, however, is not like *Ferebee*. Indeed, we are at the other end of the spectrum, a great distance from the "frontier of current medical and epidemiological inquiry." And far from a paucity of scientific information on the oft-asserted claim of causal relationship of Bendectin and birth defects, the drug has been extensively studied and a wealth of published epidemiological data has been amassed, none of which has concluded that the drug is teratogenic. Uniquely to this case, the law now has the benefit of twenty years of scientific study, and the published results must be given their just due.

Richardson v. Richardson–Merrell, Inc., 857 F.2d at 832. For discussions of how the quality of evidence needed to pass through the *Daubert* gate varies depending on the quality of the available science, see David L. Faigman et al., How Good is Good Enough? Expert Evidence Under *Daubert* and *Kumho*, 50 Case W.Res.L.Rev. 645 (2000); Joseph Sanders, Applying *Daubert* Inconsistently? Proof of Individual Causation in Toxic Tort and Forensic Cases, __Brooklyn L.Rev. __ (2010). For discussions of the life cycle of mass tort congregations, see Francis McGovern, Toward a Functional Approach for Managing Complex Litigation, 53 U.Chi.L.Rev. 440, 488 (1986); Joseph Sanders, The Bendectin Litigation: A Case Study in the Life Cycle of Mass Torts, 43 Hastings L.J. 301 (1992).

    6. *Science and the rule of law.* The silicone gel breast implant litigation demonstrates later scientific studies might prove the federal courts "right"— or "wrong." Do the National Science Panel and Institute of Medicine reports mean that the *Hall* court was "right" in its *Daubert* evidentiary decisions? What if these reports had reached the opposite conclusions? Consider that *Daubert* hearings can result in federal courts dismissing plaintiffs' toxic torts claims—perhaps forever—even though the science is not yet fully developed. What procedural safeguard did the *Hall* opinion create to avoid that potentially unjust possibility?

    7. Daubert, *expert admissibility, and the outcomes of cases.* Because there were thousands of cases in both state and federal courts, the silicone gel breast implant litigation provides a window into the effect that *Daubert* can have on toxic tort litigation. As note 5 indicates, the differences in admissibility decisions could be quite stark, especially before the two scientific reports were issued, between the federal courts bound to follow *Daubert* and state courts following *Frye* or some other standard of admissibility.

Ironically, one of the clearest distinctions between state and federal evaluations of silicone gel breast implant expert evidence came in Oregon when the Oregon Supreme Court reversed the Oregon trial court in excluding the plaintiff's evidence of causation. Judge Jones mentioned in footnote 21 of *Hall* that, while he was a Justice on the Oregon Supreme Court, he had authored Oregon's leading opinion on the admissibility of scientific evidence, State v. Brown, 687 P.2d 751 (Or.1984). Like *Daubert*, *Brown* rejected the *Frye* general acceptance test in favor of a factor-based analysis. Id. at 759 & n.5. As footnote 21 of *Hall* made clear, Judge Jones considered the *Daubert* and *Brown* analyses to be functionally equivalent.

Nevertheless, the Oregon Supreme Court reached a different decision from the Oregon District Court in the state silicone gel breast implant cases, concluding that the plaintiff's experts should not have been excluded. Jennings v. Baxter Healthcare Corp., 14 P.3d 596, 604–05 (Or.2000). The Oregon Supreme Court concluded that the plaintiff's experts' methodology, which relied on clinical case studies, "was scientifically valid." Id. at 606. Moreover, it emphasized that epidemiology is not the only legitimate way of proving causation. Id. at 606–08.

8. *The rest of the story on silicone gel breast implants: toxic tort litigation and regulation.* As Chapters 8 and 9 make clear, toxic tort litigation interacts in numerous ways with regulatory schemes, both state (workers' compensation, for example) and federal. Moreover, the paths of litigation and regulation do not always align perfectly. In response to the growth in litigation over silicone gel breast implants, in 1992, the federal Food and Drug Administration (FDA) banned the use of silicone gel breast implants in the United States except for research purposes. The FDA relied on its authority under the federal Food, Drug, and Cosmetic Act, which we examine more closely in Chapter 9.

Notably, silicone gel breast implants first went on the market in 1962, before the FDA had regulatory authority to require pre-market approval of medical devices. As a result, the explosion of litigation prompted serious concerns that the implants posed real medical risks to patients. Despite the National Science Panel and IOM reports in 1998 and 2000, respectively, the FDA did not re-approve silicone gel breast implants for use in the United States until November 2006, ending the 14–year ban well after the toxic tort litigation was essentially over. Before re-approving these devices, the FDA required Mentor and Allergan, two major manufacturers of silicone gel breast implants, to conduct 10–year studies of the effects of such implants on over 40,000 women.

In light of the results of those and other studies, including the IOM report, the FDA approved use of silicone gel breast implants for any purpose in women 22 years of age or older or for breast reconstruction surgery for any age patient. However, the FDA warned that most women would need to replace their implants at some point: As the 2000 IOM report found, implant rupture rates are as high as 77%. This high rate of rupture has prompted commentators to continue to view silicone gel breast implants as the most defective medical devices that the FDA has ever approved, and products liability actions based on ruptures remain an active part of the legal issues surrounding these implants.

D. STATE VARIATIONS ON ADMISSIBILITY

Daubert and its progeny are binding only in federal court, as the decisions interpret the Federal Rules of Evidence. State court approaches to expert testimony vary widely, even among those jurisdictions that have adopted rules similar to Rule 702. Indeed, even broadly categorizing a jurisdiction as a *"Frye* state" or a *"Daubert* state" can be difficult. Consider the following opinion and think about how you would describe the court's approach.

CASTILLO v. E.I. DU PONT DE NEMOURS & CO.

Supreme Court of Florida, 2003.
854 So.2d 1264.

QUINCE, J.

* * *

Procedural History

This case involves a products liability and negligence claim against E.I. Du Pont de Nemours & Co., Inc. (DuPont), the manufacturer of Benlate, and Pine Island Farms, Inc. (Pine Island), the owners of a "u-pick" farm which used Benlate and operated in the petitioners' neighborhood. Donna and John Castillo (the Castillos) allege that when Mrs. Castillo was seven weeks pregnant, she was exposed to Benlate, an agricultural fungicide used by Pine Island. They further allege that benomyl, the active ingredient in Benlate, entered her bloodstream and caused microphthalmia, a rare birth defect involving severely underdeveloped eyes, in her unborn son John.

The complaint against DuPont and Pine Island was filed after the Castillos were contacted by British reporter John Ashton, who was conducting an investigation into the relationship between Benlate and children born with microphthalmia in Great Britain. He asked Mrs. Castillo if she lived on or near a farm. She told him she lived near the "u-pick" farm. Ashton then contacted Lynn Chaffin, the manager of Pine Island, and asked him if Pine Island had sprayed Benlate on the "u-pick" field in November 1989. Chaffin told him that Pine Island had sprayed Benlate in November of 1989. Although at trial Chaffin testified that he did not remember such a conversation, telephone records confirm an eight-minute phone conversation originating in London, England.

The Third District's opinion below recites the following facts:

According to Donna Castillo's trial testimony, she passed by the "u-pick" farm in question on either November 1st or 2nd, 1989, as she walked with her young daughter, Adriana, while pregnant with John.

As she walked, she observed a tractor that she described as "bucking and jerking" and spraying "tons" of mist into the air. As the mist drifted over her (she indicated that it was a windy day), it completely drenched her. She returned to her home and did not shower that night. She was in her seventh week of pregnancy at the time. * * *

The Castillos' expert, Dr. Charles Vyvyan Howard, testified in pretrial depositions that he believed that fetal exposure to benomyl at the concentration of 20 parts per billion (ppb) in the maternal bloodstream would cause microphthalmia in humans based on his conclusions from (1) rat gavage studies; (2) lab experiments on human and rat cells; and (3) the results of dermal exposure testing done by DuPont's own scientist. He testified that he considered epidemiological studies but that those studies were flawed and offered little information.

At the *Frye* hearing, DuPont and Pine Island moved to exclude Dr. Howard's testimony, arguing that his methodology for determining whether and at what level Benlate could cause birth defects in humans was not generally accepted in the scientific community and thus was inadmissible. The trial court denied DuPont and Pine Island's motion and the expert testimony was admitted.

At the close of evidence at trial, DuPont moved for a directed verdict arguing that the Castillos failed to prove that Benlate is defective and that any such defect proximately caused the microphthalmia. The jury returned a verdict for the child, John Castillo, holding DuPont strictly liable and holding both DuPont and Pine Island negligent. The total award was $4 million, allocating 99.5% against DuPont and .5% against Pine Island.

On appeal, Pine Island raised two issues: (1) that there was no evidence that Benlate was used on the farm in November 1989; and (2) that the Castillos' scientific evidence should not have been admitted into evidence. As to the first issue, the Third District found Chaffin's "admission" that Benlate was used in November 1989 compelling evidence against Pine Island and affirmed the trial court's judgment. As to the second issue, involving the admissibility of the expert scientific testimony, the Third District reversed the jury verdict and determined that the testimony did not meet the test set out in *Frye*.

DuPont raised [two issues that the court of appeals found persuasive]: (1) that the Castillos failed to prove that Mrs. Castillo was exposed to Benlate in their case against DuPont, since Chaffin's admission was not admissible hearsay against DuPont; and (2) the scientific evidence should not have been admitted into evidence under *Frye*.

* * *

For the reasons discussed below, we quash the Third District's decision and hold that the trial court properly admitted the Castillos' experts' testimony under *Frye v. United States,* 293 F. 1013 (D.C.Cir. 1923). * * *

Expert Testimony Under Frye

To determine whether expert testimony is admissible under section 90.702, Florida Statutes (2001), Florida courts follow the test set out in [*Frye*]:

> Just when a scientific principle or discovery crosses the line between the experimental and demonstrable states is difficult to define. Somewhere in this twilight zone the evidential force of the principle must be recognized, and while courts will go a long way in admitting expert testimony deduced from a well-recognized scientific principle or discovery, *the thing from which the deduction is made must be sufficiently established to have gained general acceptance in the particular field in which it belongs.*

Id., at 1014 (emphasis added). "This test requires that the scientific principles undergirding this evidence be found by the trial court to be generally accepted by the relevant members of its particular field." *Hadden v. State*, 690 So.2d 573, 576 (Fla. 1997).

The proponent of the evidence bears the burden of establishing by a preponderance of the evidence the general acceptance of the underlying scientific principles and methodology. The standard of review of a *Frye* issue is de novo. * * * "Our *de novo* review of the *Frye* issue in these cases includes an examination of three methods of proof: (1) expert testimony, (2) scientific and legal writings, and (3) judicial opinions." 709 So.2d, at 557 (citing *Flanagan v. State*, 586 So.2d 1085, 1112 (Fla. 1st DCA 1991), *approved*, 625 So.2d 827 (Fla.1993)). Furthermore, the issue of general acceptance is to be made at the time of appeal, rather than at the time of trial.

The Castillos' experts testified: (1) that benomyl is a teratogen; and (2) as to the dosage level at which it becomes a teratogen. We must consider whether the scientific principles upon which the Castillos' experts based their opinions are generally accepted in the scientific community.

The Castillos' expert's methodology for reaching his opinion that benomyl is a human teratogen at 20 ppb, involved the following considerations:

(1) animal studies, including DuPont's own rat studies, which showed that Benlate is teratogenic and that it specifically causes microphthalmia and anophthalmia;

(2) in vitro tests performed by DuPont, Dr. Van Velzen, and Dr. Howard, which showed the levels at which Benlate can impair neurite growth and functioning and induce cell death—either of which could impair or prevent development of the eyes;

(3) clinical epidemiological studies are not available because Benlate is a toxic chemical and thus not suitable for human experiment;

(4) geneticists had conducted every conceivable genetic test and could find no known genetic cause of John Castillo's microphthalmia; and

(5) there was no evidence of any other environmental cause.

DuPont and Pine Island attack the Castillos' expert alleging that (1) he failed to use epidemiological studies, (2) he erroneously relied upon differential diagnosis, (3) he failed to consider the fact that John Castillo did not have multiple malformations, (4) the in-vitro testing and rat gavage* studies were inappropriate methods to determine the dosage at which benomyl becomes a human teratogen, and (5) the extrapolation of data was not an accepted scientific method. We will address each of these allegations.

Epidemiological Studies

* * *

The Castillos assert that there are no valid epidemiological studies that exist as to the teratogenicity of benomyl * * *.

* * *

While epidemiology is considered generally accepted in the scientific community as a way of studying causal links between disease and chemicals, these types of studies are not necessarily required for a party to meet its burden of showing the causal link by a preponderance of the evidence. * * *

It is clear that the Castillos do not need to present epidemiological studies to meet their burden. It is also clear that there were at least three studies at the time of the *Frye* hearing that the Castillos' experts considered and then deemed inconclusive to establish a causal link between benomyl exposure and microphthalmia, or lack thereof. DuPont and Pine Island's objections are to the conclusions the Castillos' experts reached, not the methodology itself. The Castillos' experts did indeed consider epidemiological studies, and the consideration of the studies in light of the parties' assertions as to their effect was properly put to the jury.

Differential Diagnosis

Differential diagnosis is "a term used 'to describe a process whereby medical doctors experienced in diagnostic techniques provide testimony countering other possible causes ... of the injuries at issue.'" *Berry v. CSX Transportation, Inc.*, 709 So.2d 552, 562 n. 9 (Fla. 1st DCA 1998) (quoting *Hines v. Consolidated Rail Corp.*, 926 F.2d 262, 270 n. 6 (3d Cir.1991)). "It is well-settled that an expert's use of differential diagnosis to arrive at a specific causation opinion is a methodology that is generally accepted in the relevant scientific community." *United States Sugar Corp. v. Henson*, 787 So.2d 3, 19 (Fla. 1st DCA 2001) (citing *Berry*, 709 So.2d at 571).

---

* [Administration through a feeding tube into the stomach.—Eds.]

DuPont's expert, Dr. Robert L. Brent, stated in his affidavit presented at the *Frye* hearing, "One should eliminate the more likely causes of a birth defect before determining that another cause is probable. This is the generally accepted method. . . . Dr. Howard cannot and does not exclude the most likely cause of John Castillo's microphthalmia, which is genetic."
* * *

* * * The Castillos argue that all the experts who testified for all the parties in this case agree that the Castillo family was subjected to a full battery of all available genetic testing, and the tests showed that there was no known genetic cause for the malformation. Amici admit that Dr. Howard, the Castillos' expert, employed differential diagnosis, which is a generally accepted methodology, stating in their brief that, "[w]hile Dr. Howard employed a generally accepted methodology for addressing specific medical causation (differential diagnosis), he did not use a generally accepted methodology for determining whether a substance is a human teratogen." Clearly, the Castillos' experts did utilize differential diagnosis, and as amici admit, this was a generally accepted method for addressing specific medical causation.

Multiple Malformations

DuPont and Pine Island assert that when embryonic cells are exposed to toxic substances, the cells of the embryo produce multiple malformations, not an isolated malformation as in John Castillo's case. The Castillos counter that in the rat studies, the pregnant rats exposed to benomyl whose offspring had microphthalmia did not have multiple malformations.
* * *

The multiple malformation issue does not involve the *methodology* the Castillos' experts used. While this may be an appropriate issue to explore during trial, it is irrelevant to the reliability of the underlying methodology used by the Castillos' experts.

The Castillos' experts did consider multiple malformation and determined that a single malformation was consistent with their assessment of the scientific evidence. The method used in reaching this conclusion is not being attacked; the conclusion itself is. This is a proper issue for the trier of fact.

In–Vitro Testing

DuPont and Pine Island challenge whether Dr. Howard's in-vitro testing of sample tissues from human lungs and rats is generally accepted in the scientific community for the purpose of determining the *dose* at which benomyl becomes a teratogen.

DuPont and Pine Island assert that this is the only testing the Castillos' experts relied upon to make the determination that benomyl is a human teratogen at 20 ppb, and that as a sole means of determining toxicity, it is scientifically rejected. The Castillos assert that in-vitro testing is wholly appropriate and scientifically accepted, and in fact necessary. Most importantly, the Castillos argue, their experts did not rely solely on in-vitro testing, but as one source of data in conjunction with various other sources of reliable scientific data to calculate their conclusion that benomyl is a human teratogen at 20 ppb.

Throughout his testimony at the *Frye* hearing, Dr. Van Velzen agreed with DuPont and Pine Island's position that in-vitro testing alone cannot establish a low effect level for benomyl, or any other toxic substance, in human beings. Dr. Van Velzen repeatedly stated that he did not solely rely upon the in-vitro testing in coming to the conclusion that the low effect level in humans is 20 ppb. He repeatedly asserted that he used the in-vitro testing as one source of data, in conjunction with other reliable data, to reach the conclusion. He testified that the consideration of all the data together is a commonly accepted scientific practice.

DuPont, Pine Island, and amici continually refer to Dr. Van Velzen's in-vitro testing as a pioneering effort and repeatedly argue that in-vitro, in and of itself, is not scientifically accepted as a method of determining the dose at which benomyl becomes toxic in humans. Dr. Van Velzen concedes that the use of in vitro testing in the particular manner in which he used it is new. DuPont and Pine Island argue that it is therefore not scientifically accepted.

DuPont and Pine Island's position that Dr. Van Velzen's technique fails the *Frye* standard solely because it is a new technique is contrary to *Frye*. The whole purpose of *Frye* is to weed out "junk science" from valid science and is only used when new scientific methodology is being presented. Clearly "new" scientific methodology can be admissible when it is shown that it is not "junk science." If we accepted DuPont and Pine Island's position, every new scientific method would be denied. "This Court, as most other courts, will accept new scientific methods of establishing evidentiary facts only after a proper predicate has first established the reliability of the new scientific method." *Ramirez v. State*, 542 So.2d 352, 355 (Fla.1989). * * * It is clear that in-vitro studies are commonly accepted scientific studies. In this case, the data from the in-vitro studies was used in conjunction with certain other reliable data to reach a conclusion. DuPont and Pine Island disagree with the conclusion, and the disagreement between the parties was properly put before the jury to resolve.

Rat Gavage Studies

DuPont and Pine Island argue the Castillos' expert exposed rats to benomyl through the gavage method, not dermal exposure, that rats were exposed to far greater quantities than the 20 ppb which Dr. Howard concludes is the low effect level for benomyl to become a human teratogen, and rats are different species than humans so there can be no analogy from the rat gavage data to humans.

* * *

DuPont and Pine Island's dispute is not that rat gavage studies are inappropriate scientific studies per se, but that the dosages given to the rats were far greater than any amount a human would be exposed to, and thus the study in this case was invalid. The underlying scientific methodology in general is undisputedly accepted in the scientific community. DuPont and Pine Island do not argue that rat gavage studies are per se junk science. What DuPont and Pine Island dispute is the result that the Castillos' experts reached. That is not what *Frye* considers, and DuPont and Pine Island had the opportunity to attack the findings and conclusions at trial.

Extrapolation

DuPont and Pine Island argue that the Castillos' experts improperly extrapolated the dosage level of 20 ppb, which the Castillos' experts say is the low effect level, or the level at which cells exposed to benomyl are damaged. They argue that, "in vitro animal test data are not relied upon by experts in the field of teratology for extrapolating the results found directly to the human experience." *Wade–Greaux v. Whitehall Laboratories, Inc.*, 874 F.Supp. 1441, 1484 (D.V.I.1994), *aff'd*, 46 F.3d 1120 (3d Cir.1994). They further argue that direct extrapolation of data from tissue soaked in benomyl in a petri dish to the human body makes no sense, and that scientists do not generally accept this extrapolation.

The Castillos respond that the petri dish studies are common. It does not matter that the tissue samples are soaked for a 24–hour period of time because the cell only divides once. The study examines the dosage at which the cell's division is affected. The information provides indicia for the substance's potential for toxicity but still requires further testing to determine whether the metabolic processes of a living organism will increase, decrease, or have no effect on the toxicity of the substance. Because scientists cannot ethically administer benomyl to humans, they use animal testing, which is the reason for the rat gavage study. Dr. Howard used DuPont's own studies which indicate that benomyl has a half life of 45 minutes, and that it would make one full pass through the mother's circulatory system in approximately 60 to 90 seconds, with the full dose in the mother's system passing through the placenta and to the fetus. According to the Castillos' expert, the fetus cannot rid itself of the toxin, so it soaks in it until the next pass through the mother's circulatory system, when it is slightly diluted. DuPont's data also suggests that in a dermal exposure incident, approximately 15% of the chemical penetrates the skin. Dr. Howard considered what clothes Donna Castillo was wearing when she was exposed, and her height and weight to determine the amount of skin exposed, and used DuPont's data to calculate the amount of benomyl that would have been absorbed and passed though her system to the fetus.

The Castillos also respond that extrapolation is common in the scientific community * * *.

The issue is not whether the in-vitro tests or the DuPont tests or the fact that the Castillos' experts relied upon professional experience are scientifically accepted methodologies. The issue is whether the use or extrapolation of the data from all of these sources to reach a conclusion is in itself generally accepted. The underlying methodology is not so much the testing as it is the use of the test results from the methodology to bridge the gap from raw data to a conclusion.

* * *

Neither party here cites any case for the proposition that the way the Castillos' experts extrapolated from the data to reach their conclusions is or is not generally accepted. * * * In this case, the Castillos' experts asserted they were not only using in-vitro data, they were using that in addition to other data, including data generated directly by DuPont's own scientists. The Castillos' experts relied upon commonly accepted scientific methodology and used the data generated from that methodology in a new or novel way. * * * The trial court in this case was correct in admitting the experts' testimony for consideration of the jury. * * *

Daubert and Frye

In 1993 the United States Supreme Court decided *Daubert v. Merrell Dow Pharmaceuticals, Inc.*, which created a new test for the admissibility of experts' testimony. *Daubert* is not binding on the states, however, because it interpreted a federal statute, Federal Rule of Evidence 702, as opposed to the Constitution.

Daubert involved Bendectin, an antinausea medication given to pregnant women. The Court said that where novel scientific evidence is concerned, Federal Rule of Evidence 702 essentially requires a two-part assessment of (1) the validity of the scientific knowledge in question, and (2) the "fit" between the proffered scientific evidence and the circumstances of the plaintiff's case.

The first prong of *Daubert* is the *Frye* test, which is the test followed in Florida. The second prong requires the court to consider everything from the methodology to the extrapolation of data, all the way to the ultimate conclusion. The Third Circuit explained that a challenge to the second prong of *Daubert* "is very close to a challenge to the expert's ultimate conclusion about the particular case." *In re Paoli Railroad Yard PCB Litigation*, 35 F.3d 717, 746 (3d Cir.1994). In this case, the Third District reviewed the experts' method of extrapolating the data to the final conclusion, stating:

> We do, however, conclude that where, as here, plaintiffs wish to establish a substance's teratogenicity in human beings based on animal and in vitro studies, the methodology used in the studies, including the method of extrapolating from the achieved results, must be generally accepted in the relevant scientific community.

By considering the extrapolation of the data from the admittedly acceptable experiments, the Third District went beyond the requirements of *Frye*, which assesses only the validity of the underlying science. *Frye* does not require the court to assess the application of the expert's raw data in reaching his or her conclusion. We therefore conclude that the Third District erroneously assessed the Castillos' expert testimony under *Frye* by considering not just the underlying science, but the application of the data generated from that science in reaching the expert's ultimate conclusion. At least one commentator has pointed this out, calling the Third District's analysis "essentially a Daubert analysis" because it focused on the expert's methodology and reasoning.

* * *

For reasons expressed above, we quash the Third District's decision.

It is so ordered.

NOTES AND QUESTIONS

1. The *Castillo* court stated that the *Frye* test is the test followed in Florida. Is that correct? Or was the court trying to articulate a combined approach to the admissibility issue? How would you characterize Florida? As a "*Frye* jurisdiction," a "*Daubert* jurisdiction," or something else?

2. Consider the court's treatment of the rat gavage studies. It rejected the defendants' challenge to their admissibility based on the validity of the inferences drawn by the plaintiffs' experts, on the grounds that rat gavage studies are an accepted methodology.

DuPont and Pine Island did not argue that rat gavage studies are per se junk science. What DuPont and Pine Island dispute is the result that the Castillos' experts reached. That is not what *Frye* considers, and DuPont and Pine Island had the opportunity to attack the findings and conclusions at trial.

Suppose the plaintiffs' experts performed an epidemiologic study and based on that study testified that general causation existed. Would it matter that the study found a relative risk of one, indicating no association between exposure and disease?

3. A significant number of state courts continue to adhere to the tests they used before *Daubert*—either the *Frye* general acceptance test or some other standard. However, even among states that claim to be *Frye* jurisdictions, there is substantial variation and many "*Frye* jurisdictions" incorporate at least some aspects of the *Daubert* test. For example, a pure *Frye* jurisdiction would, one presumes, simply count expert noses to determine whether an expert's theory or technique was generally acceptable. Note, however, that the *Castillo* court did something else entirely. It reviewed the animal and in vitro research and discussed why there could be no significant epidemiologic data in accidental chemical exposure cases where the injury is rare in the population. All of this is the sort of thing a *Daubert* court would do under the first of the *Daubert* factors. In addition, the *Castillo* court rejected the idea that even valid new techniques must achieve general acceptance before they are admissible. Nevertheless, the court continued to insist that Florida is a *Frye* state. One way to summarize the Florida version of *Frye* is that it rejects that part of *Daubert* (and *Kumho Tire*) that is commonly called a "fit" analysis. As its handling of the rat gavage studies and the plaintiff's expert's differential diagnosis indicated, the court was not willing to exclude evidence because the data upon which the expert relied did not support the expert's conclusion. On the other hand, Florida courts are willing to assess the reliability of a body of research in assessing admissibility.

4. New York also remains a *Frye* state but has adopted a course that is in some ways the opposite of Florida. As is the case with many *Frye* jurisdictions, New York applies the admissibility test only to novel methodologies and techniques. And when applying their version of *Frye*, New York courts focus more exclusively than Florida courts on whether a method or technique is generally accepted. However, in Parker v. Mobil Oil Corp., 857 N.E.2d 1114 (N.Y.2006), the New York Court of Appeals clarified how that state's version of the *Frye* test applied to toxic injuries and in the process adopted an approach similar to a "fit" analysis. In *Parker*, a gas station attendant sued gasoline producers, alleging that he contracted acute myelogenous leukemia (AML) as result of his occupational exposure to gasoline containing benzene. The trial court refused to exclude the plaintiff's experts. The Supreme Court, Appellate Division reversed and held that the trial court should have granted the defendants a summary judgment. The Court of Appeals affirmed, holding there was no evidence that exposure to benzene as a component of gasoline caused the plaintiff to contract AML. With respect to the present case, the Court of Appeals said:

> Here, there is a question as to whether the methodologies employed by Parker's experts lead to a reliable result—specifically, whether they provided a reliable causation opinion without using a dose-response relationship and without quantifying Parker's exposure. There is no particular novel methodology at issue for which the Court needs to determine whether there is general acceptance. Thus, the inquiry here is more akin to whether there is an appropriate foundation for the experts' opinions, rather than whether the opinions are admissible under *Frye*.

Id. at 1120. A pair of California cases reached a similar outcome by sidestepping the *Frye* question and concluding that since the plaintiffs' experts could not prove a significant exposure their conclusion ran afoul of California Rule of Evidence 801. Geffcken v. D'Andrea, 41 Cal.Rptr.3d 80 (Cal.App.2006); Dee v. PCS Prop. Mgmt., Inc., 94 Cal.Rptr.3d 456 (Cal.App.2009) Ultimately, the outcome of these decisions turned on dosage and, therefore, on the ability of the substance to cause the plaintiffs' injuries in this particular situation. Florida, however, remains committed to a version of *Frye* that does not look beyond general principles to the application of those principles to case-specific facts. See Marsh v. Valyou, 977 So.2d 543 (Fla.2007).

5. For a thorough discussion of how state courts have approached the problem, see David E. Bernstein & Jeffrey D. Jackson, The *Daubert* Trilogy in the States, 44 Jurimetrics J. 351 (2004).

CHAPTER VI

SCOPE OF LIABILITY (PROXIMATE CAUSE)

■ ■ ■

Few law students have fond memories of their first-year encounter with the concept of proximate cause. From In re Polemis, 3 K.B. 560 (1921), to Palsgraf v. Long Island Railroad, 248 N.Y. 339, 162 N.E. 99 (1928), to Overseas Tankship (U.K.) Ltd. v. Mort's Dock & Engineering Co. (The Wagon Mound), [1961] A.C. 388, to In re Kinsman Transit Co., 338 F.2d 708 (2d Cir.1964), the cases present Rube Goldberg-like fact patterns combined with legal analyses that seem to be designed to confuse. Part of the problem is the terminology itself. As the Third Restatement of Torts: Liability for Physical and Emotional Harm notes in the introduction to the Scope of Liability Chapter, "Although the term 'proximate cause' has been in widespread use in judicial opinions, treatises, casebooks, and scholarship, the term is not generally employed in this Chapter because it is an especially poor one to describe the idea to which it is connected." Restatement (Third) of Torts: Liability for Physical and Emotional Harm, ch. 6 (2010). What is the idea? At bottom it is rather simple. There must be some limits on the scope of liability for tortious conduct that causes harm.

Limits on liability can be imposed in two doctrinal ways. One is scope of liability, as explained above. The other is through no-duty rulings. Recall that *Palsgraf* decided that the Long Island Railroad was not liable to Mrs. Palsgraf because it owed her no duty, rather than on proximate cause grounds (to be sure, Judge Andrews, in his dissent, employed proximate cause). In general, we think limitations of liability based on categories of cases is the bailiwick of duty, while limitations specific to the facts of the case at hand are best decided as a matter of scope of liability. Thus, in deciding whether social hosts can be held liable to their guests who are injured as a result of becoming intoxicated at the host's home, duty would be the rubric employed. By contrast, if in a given case an intoxicated guest was injured by a tree that fell on his car, we might consider whether the defendant should be liable on scope of liability grounds. This division comports with the way in which these two elements are allocated between judge and jury: duty is a matter of law for the court, while scope of liability is for the jury. As you read the next two cases, are they more appropriately duty or scope of liability cases?

In this Chapter, we do not intend to reprise all of proximate cause or duty. Our goal is more limited: to point out those areas in toxic tort where scope of liability or duty limitations are most frequently employed.

A. DUTY, FORESEEABILITY, AND REMOTENESS

GROVER v. ELI LILLY & CO.

Supreme Court of Ohio, 1992.
63 Ohio St.3d 756, 591 N.E.2d 696.

WRIGHT, JUSTICE.

The United States District Court for the Northern District of Ohio has certified the following question to us:

> "Does Ohio recognize a cause of action on behalf of a child born prematurely, and with severe birth defects, if it can be established that such injuries were proximately caused by defects in the child's mother's reproductive system, those defects in turn being proximately caused by the child's grandmother ingesting a defective drug (DES) during her pregnancy with the child's mother?"

For purposes of this question, we are required to assume that Charles Grover can prove that his injuries were proximately caused by his mother's exposure to DES. We are not evaluating the facts of this case, but determining, as a matter of law, whether Charles Grover has a legally cognizable cause of action.

DES was prescribed to pregnant women during the 1940s, 1950s and 1960s to prevent miscarriage. The FDA banned its use by pregnant women in 1971 after medical studies discovered that female children exposed to the drug *in utero* had a high incidence of a rare type of vaginal cancer. See 36 Fed.Reg. 21,537 (1971). Candy Grover was exposed to DES as a fetus. Her son, Charles Grover, claims that his mother's DES-induced injuries were the cause of his premature birth and resulting injuries.

Because the mother and the child whose injury results from her injury are uniquely interrelated, and because it is possible that the mother may not discover the extent of her own injury until she experiences difficulties during pregnancy, the facts of this case pose a novel issue. Courts and commentators refer to the child's potential cause of action in such cases as a "preconception tort." See, *e.g.,* Note, Preconception Torts: Foreseeing the Unconceived (1977), 48 U.Colo.L.Rev. 621. The terminology stems from the fact that a child is pursuing liability against a party for a second injury that flows from an initial injury to the mother that occurred before the child was conceived.

Only a handful of courts have addressed whether a child has a cause of action for a preconception tort. One recurring issue is whether a child has a cause of action if a physician negligently performs a surgical procedure on the mother, such as an abortion or a Caesarean section, and the negligently performed procedure causes complications during child-birth several years later that injure the infant. See *Albala v. New York* (1981), 54 N.Y.2d 269, 445 N.Y.S.2d 108, 429 N.E.2d 786 (child has no cause of action for doctor's negligence during abortion performed four years prior to his conception); *Bergstreser v. Mitchell* (C.A.8, 1978), 577 F.2d 22 (construing Missouri law) (child has a cause of action against a doctor based on the doctor's negligence during a Caesarean section performed two years prior to the child's conception). In another malpractice suit, the Illinois Supreme Court recognized that a child had a cause of action against a hospital that negligently transfused her mother with Rh-positive blood eight years prior to the child's conception. *Renslow v. Mennonite Hospital* (1977), 67 Ill.2d 348, 10 Ill.Dec. 484, 367 N.E.2d 1250. As a result, the mother's body produced antibodies to the Rh-positive blood that later injured her fetus during pregnancy.

In *McAuley v. Wills* (1983), 251 Ga. 3, 303 S.E.2d 258, the Supreme Court of Georgia evaluated a wrongful death action brought on behalf of an infant who died during childbirth due to the mother's paralysis. The suit was brought against the driver who had originally caused the mother's paralysis in an automobile accident. The court held that a person may owe a duty of care to a child conceived in the future, but also held that the injury in that case was too remote as a matter of law to support recovery. *Id.* at 6–7, 303 S.E.2d at 260–261. The driver could not reasonably foresee, *as a matter of law,* that his lack of care in driving a motor vehicle would result in complications during the delivery of a child who was not yet conceived at the time of the accident. *Id.*[1]

The facts of these cases are significantly different from those of the case before us. The cause of action certified to us involves the scope of liability for the manufacture of a prescription drug that allegedly had devastating side effects on the original patient's female fetus. However, this case is not about the devastating side effects of DES on the women who were exposed to it * * *. This case is concerned with the rippling effects of that exposure on yet another generation, when that female child reaches sexual maturity and bears a child. Because a plaintiff in Charles Grover's position cannot be injured until the original patient's child bears children, the second injury will typically have occurred more than sixteen years after the ingestion of the drug.

Several courts have addressed a fact pattern virtually identical to the facts of the case currently before this court. The New York Court of Appeals held that a child does not have a cause of action, in negligence or strict liability, against a prescription drug company based on the manufacture of DES if the child was never exposed to the drug *in utero. Enright v.*

---

1. The Supreme Court of Georgia limited its holding to the facts of the case before it. The Court of Appeals for New York has taken the opposite approach and held that a plaintiff does not have a cause of action for *any* preconception tort, regardless of the facts alleged. See *Albala v. New York* (1981), 54 N.Y.2d 269, 445 N.Y.S.2d 108, 429 N.E.2d 786. * * *

This court declines to adopt an absolute rule at this time, but addresses an alleged cause of action that is far more tenuous than that raised in *Albala v. New York.* * * *

Eli Lilly & Co. (1991), 77 N.Y.2d 377, 568 N.Y.S.2d 550, 570 N.E.2d 198, certiorari denied (1991), 502 U.S. 868, 112 S.Ct. 197, 116 L.Ed.2d 157. The court relied in part on its earlier opinion in *Albala v. New York, supra.* In both cases, the court was concerned with the "staggering implications of any proposition which would honor claims assuming the breach of an identifiable duty for less than a perfect birth and by what standard and the difficulty in establishing a standard or definition of perfection. * * * " 570 N.E.2d at 201. The court was troubled by the possibility that doctors would forgo certain treatments of great benefit to persons already in existence out of fear of possible effects on future children. In *Enright,* the court noted that "the cause of action plaintiffs ask us to recognize here could not be confined without the drawing of artificial and arbitrary boundaries. For all we know, the rippling effects of DES exposure may extend for generations. It is our duty to confine liability within manageable limits * * *. Limiting liability to those who ingested the drug or were exposed to it in utero serves this purpose." 570 N.E.2d at 203.

One court has held that a plaintiff situated similarly to Charles Grover has a cause of action. The United States Court of Appeals for the Seventh Circuit reversed a lower court's directed verdict on the issue of a pharmaceutical company's liability to a child for injuries caused by a premature birth. *McMahon v. Eli Lilly & Co.* (C.A.7, 1985), 774 F.2d 830. The court concluded that under Illinois law the company could be liable for failing to warn of the dangerous propensities of the drug, and need not have anticipated a particular side effect.

We find the reasoning applied by the New York Court of Appeals persuasive on the issue currently before us. * * *

* * * The Seventh Circuit held that knowledge of the general dangerous propensities of the drug was sufficient to subject the company to liability for failure to warn. This court has stated that "[i]n a products liability case where a claimant seeks recovery for failure to warn or warn adequately, it must be proven that the manufacturer knew, or should have known, in the exercise of ordinary care, of the risk or hazard about which it failed to warn." (Footnote omitted.) *Crislip v. TCH Liquidating Co., supra,* 52 Ohio St.3d at 257, 556 N.E.2d at 1182–1183. Even if knowledge of the drug's "dangerous propensities" is sufficient to create liability to the women exposed to the drug *in utero,* this same knowledge does not automatically justify the extension of liability to those women's children. It is one thing to say that knowledge of a propensity to harm the reproductive organs is sufficient to impose liability for a variety of different injuries to the reproductive organs. It is yet another thing to say that this generalized knowledge is sufficient to impose liability for injuries to a third party that occur twenty-eight years later.[2]

2. It is on this same point of law that the dissent confuses the issue by characterizing the question as whether the pharmaceutical companies should have known that DES could cause reproductive abnormalities in a developing fetus. The issue is not whether the pharmaceutical companies knew of some dangers from the use of this drug. To the contrary, the question is whether the drug companies should have known, at the time that it was prescribed, that DES

Knowledge of a risk to one class of plaintiffs does not necessarily extend an actor's liability to every potential plaintiff. While we must assume that DES was the proximate cause of Charles Grover's injuries, an actor is not liable for every harm that may result from his actions. " * * * The plaintiff sues in her own right for a wrong personal to her, and not as the vicarious beneficiary of a breach of duty to another." *Palsgraf v. Long Island RR. Co.* (1928), 248 N.Y. 339, 342, 162 N.E. 99, 100. An actor does not have a duty to a particular plaintiff unless the risk to that plaintiff is within the actor's "range of apprehension." *Id.* at 344, 162 N.E. at 100. " * * * If the actor's conduct creates such a recognizable risk of harm only to a particular class of persons, the fact that it in fact causes harm to a person of a different class, to whom the actor could not reasonably have anticipated injury, does not make the actor liable to the persons so injured." 2 Restatement of the Law 2d, Torts (1965), Section 281, Comment c. The existence of a legal duty is a question for the court, unless alternate inferences are feasible based on the facts. *Palsgraf, supra,* 248 N.Y. at 345, 162 N.E. at 101.

When a pharmaceutical company prescribes drugs to a woman, the company, under ordinary circumstances, does not have a duty to her daughter's infant who will be conceived twenty-eight years later. Charles Grover's injuries are not the result of his own exposure to the drug, but are allegedly caused by his mother's injuries from her *in utero* exposure to the drug. Because of the remoteness in time and causation, we hold that Charles Grover does not have an independent cause of action, and answer the district court's question in the negative. A pharmaceutical company's liability for the distribution or manufacture of a defective prescription drug does not extend to persons who were never exposed to the drug, either directly or *in utero.*

Judgment accordingly.

ALICE ROBIE RESNICK, JUSTICE, dissenting.

I dissent from the result reached in this case, but more importantly from the superficial treatment of the issue which was certified to this court, in light of its complexity.

* * *

In the present case, June Rose ingested DES during her pregnancy in 1952 and 1953. June gave birth to Candace Grover on March 30, 1953. Petitioners maintain that as a result of her mother's ingestion of DES, Candace was born with an incompetent cervix. Candace gave birth, prematurely, to Charles Grover, who was born with cerebral palsy. Petitioners assert Charles' disabilities are directly and proximately attributable to his premature birth, which in turn was caused by his mother's DES-induced incompetent cervix.

---

could cause a birth defect that would result in the delivery of a premature child twenty or thirty years later. Modern studies may provide us with twenty-twenty hindsight, but the only medical studies relevant to this issue are those that occurred before DES was banned in 1971.

The majority is persuaded by the rationale of the New York Court of Appeals' decision in *Enright, supra*. Although the basis of the holding is not entirely clear, the majority essentially holds that for public policy reasons there is no legal duty owed to a person who was not *in utero* at the time of injury.[4] As does the court in *Enright*, the majority relies upon the DES manufacturers' age-old public policy arguments that the imposition of liability would invoke "staggering implications" and "rippling effects," or would require doctors to forgo certain treatments of great benefit to persons already in existence. But as the dissent in *Enright* cogently points out, " * * * this sort of 'floodgates of litigation' [alarm] seems singularly unpersuasive in view of our Court's repeated admonitions that it is not 'a ground for denying a cause of action that there will be a proliferation of claims' and ' * * * if a cognizable wrong has been committed, that there must be a remedy, whatever the burden of the courts.' * * * Beyond that, however, when defendants' arguments are applied here to urge that although the claims of DES daughters should be allowed the claims of the granddaughters should not be, their forebodings strike a particularly ironic note: i.e., the very fact of the 'insidious nature' of DES which may make the defendants liable for injuries to a future generation is advanced as the reason why they should not be liable for injuries to that generation." *Enright, supra,* 77 N.Y.2d at 393, 568 N.Y.S.2d at 559, 570 N.E.2d at 207 (Hancock, J., dissenting).

I discern no sound basis, in law or public policy, for holding that there is no duty owed to persons in Charles Grover's position. * * * Petitioners aver that, despite warnings from independent researchers dating back to the 1930s that DES caused reproductive tract abnormalities and cancer in exposed animal offspring, that drug companies, including Eli Lilly, performed no tests as to the effects of DES on the developing fetus, either in animals or humans. Petitioners also assert that by 1947 there were twenty-one studies which supported these findings; that recent medical studies have established a significant link between DES exposure and various uterine and cervical abnormalities in DES daughters; and that these studies have demonstrated that mature DES daughters have a significantly higher risk of miscarriage, infertility and premature deliveries.

In light of the foregoing there can be no question that pharmaceutical companies should have known the dangers of this drug. If in the 1930s and 1940s the manufacturers of DES knew or should have known of the reproductive system defects in the animal fetus exposed to DES, how then is it not foreseeable that this might mean abnormalities in the human fetus' reproductive system? In other words, it would appear that DES manufacturers knew or should have known that the human fetus exposed *in utero* might have a defect in the female reproductive system. Addition-

---

4. The reason the majority's holding is not clear is because in one breath it correctly states that "we are required to assume that Charles Grover can prove that his injuries were *proximately caused* by his mother's exposure to DES," but then ultimately concludes that "[b]ecause of the remoteness in time and *causation*, we hold that Charles Grover does not have an independent cause of action." (Emphasis added.)

ally, is it not then foreseeable that that female fetus would at some point seek to employ the defective reproductive system? The answer must be a resounding "yes." Hence, there can be no logic to the holding of the majority that "[b]ecause of the remoteness in time and causation, * * * Charles Grover does not have an independent cause of action." What could have a more direct causal connection than a premature birth by a woman who was known to have an incompetent cervix? From this it becomes readily apparent that DES grandchildren were a foreseeable group of plaintiffs. It can hardly be argued that there is no duty owed to a *foreseeable* plaintiff. In the landmark case of *Palsgraf v. Long Island RR. Co.* (1928), 248 N.Y. 339, 162 N.E. 99, the court held that an actor has a duty to all plaintiffs within the actor's "range of apprehension." *Id.* at 344, 162 N.E. at 100. * * *

      * * *

Conclusion

* * * To hold under these circumstances that Charles Grover's injuries were not foreseeable is to ignore an entire body of scientific information which was available or could have easily become available with a measure of care concerning the effects of DES on subsequent generations.

* * * I would conclude that individuals such as Charles Grover properly have a cause of action for their injuries. This in no way opens the floodgates because litigation can easily be concluded with Charles Grover's generation. Moreover, the majority completely disregards the fact that the petitioners still bear the burden of proving proximate cause. I strenuously dissent.

NOTES AND QUESTIONS

1. Both the majority and the dissent cited *Palsgraf* as authority for their positions. Recall that in *Palsgraf*, railroad employees negligently assisted a passenger onto a train leaving the station. In the process, they knocked an innocuous package from the passenger's hands and it apparently fell onto the tracks. The package contained fireworks, which then exploded. The explosion caused a scale to fall upon Mrs. Palsgraf, who was standing some distance away. Judge Cardozo held for the majority that she could not recover, because the defendant owed her no duty. That is, he saw the question as one of duty, not proximate cause. And why did the defendant owe no duty to Mrs. Palsgraf? Because "[t]he risk reasonably to be perceived defines the duty to be obeyed, and risk imports relation; it is risk to another or to others within the range of apprehension." *Palsgraf*, 162 N.E. at 100. That is, defendant must foresee a risk of harm to the class of persons to which plaintiff belongs.

Do you think the majority and the dissent disagree about the meaning of *Palsgraf* or about the application of *Palsgraf* to the facts of the case?

2. Recall that in the *Wagon Mound*, the Privy Council overruled *In re Polemis* and in the process made it clear that legal limits on liability would be measured by foresight rather than by the directness or remoteness of the causal chain of events between the defendant's conduct and the plaintiff's harm. Although the majority and the dissent in *Grover* argued over whether the plaintiff's injuries were foreseeable at the time his grandmother took DES, was the case really about remoteness? Do you think remoteness by itself is a reason to limit liability? If remoteness is not a reason, can the dissent offer any principled reason to cut off liability after only three generations?

3. The *Grover* case is a poster child for the confusion created by the use of the term "proximate cause." Both the federal district court that certified the question to the Ohio Supreme Court and the majority opinion in *Grover* used the term to refer to cause-in-fact, not legal limitations on the scope of liability, even when defendant's behavior is the cause-in-fact of plaintiff's injury. The dissent, perhaps disingenuously, picked up on this point in footnote 4. Do you think the majority was confused on this point?

4. The difficulty in applying proximate cause limitations also arises from the many ways courts have chosen to define the limits. Even if we agree that the test should incorporate a foresight test, the question arises: foresight of what? As we have already noted, one approach, associated with *Palsgraf*, is to require that defendant foresee a risk of harm to the class of persons to which plaintiff belongs. Another common answer is that defendant must foresee the *type* of harm. This is one way to understand *Wagon Mound*. Pollution damages from the oil spill in Sydney Harbor were foreseeable, but not fire damages. Courts frequently say that the manner in which a harm occurs is not relevant. However, in many products liability cases, when the manner of harm has to do with how an individual used a product, then "unforeseeable misuse" may cut off liability.

Section 29 of the Third Restatement of Torts: Liability for Physical and Emotional Harm adopts the following limitation on liability for tortious conduct:

> An actor's liability is limited to those harms that result from the risks that made the actor's conduct tortious.

Restatement (Third) of Torts: Liability for Physical and Emotional Harm § 29 (2010). Following this rule, what outcome in *Grover*? Does the answer to this question turn on how one describes the risk in that case? How did the majority and the dissent describe the risk in *Grover*? With respect to this issue, comment i of section 29 offers limited help: "No rule can be provided about the appropriate level of generality or specificity to employ in characterizing the type of harm for purposes of this Section." Id. § 29 cmt. i.

5. *Grover* was decided on a certified question from the federal district court. The *Grover* court explained that it was deciding a pure question of law, accepting the allegations of the complaint. But isn't the matter of the foreseeability of third generation victims from DES a question that requires factual consideration? How can the court determine whether Eli Lilly had sufficient information about the risk of harm to third generations to require a warning without consideration of the facts? Or is foreseeability not the basis of the court's determination there should be no liability? See Restatement (Third) of Torts: Liability for Physical and Emotional Harm § 29 cmt. j (2010) (use of foreseeability for duty purposes obscures principle or policy at work).

IN RE CERTIFIED QUESTION FROM THE FOURTEENTH DISTRICT COURT OF APPEALS OF TEXAS

Supreme Court of Michigan, 2007.
479 Mich. 498, 740 N.W.2d 206.

MARKMAN, J.

Plaintiffs filed suit in Texas against defendant, alleging that the decedent contracted mesothelioma from washing the work clothes of her stepfather, who worked for independent contractors hired by defendant to reline the interiors of blast furnaces with materials that contained asbestos. * * * Pursuant to MCR 7.305(B), the Fourteenth District Court of Appeals of Texas certified the following question to this Court:

> Whether, under Michigan law, Ford, as owner of the property on which asbestos-containing products were located, owed to Carolyn Miller, who was never on or near that property, a legal duty specified in the jury charge submitted by the trial court, to protect her from exposure to any asbestos fibers carried home on the clothing of a member of Carolyn Miller's household who was working on that property as the employee of an independent contractor.

* * *

I. FACTS AND PROCEDURAL HISTORY

Plaintiffs allege that the decedent, Carolyn Miller, died from mesothelioma, an incurable and fatal form of * * * cancer, that she contracted from washing the work clothes of her stepfather, Cleveland "John" Roland. From 1954 through 1965, Roland worked for independent contractors who were hired on various occasions by defendant to reline the interiors of blast furnaces used to melt iron ore at the Ford Rouge plant in Dearborn, Michigan. Plaintiffs allege that the materials used to reline the interiors of the blast furnaces contained asbestos. There is no dispute that Miller was never on or near defendant's premises. Miller was diagnosed with mesothelioma in 1999 and died in 2000. After the Texas trial court denied defendant's motion for a directed verdict, a Texas jury awarded plaintiffs $9.5 million for Carolyn Miller's death on the basis of a theory of negligence. After the trial court denied defendant's motion for judgment notwithstanding the verdict, defendant filed an appeal in the Fourteenth District Court of Appeals of Texas. At defendant's request and over plaintiffs' objections, the Fourteenth District Court of Appeals of Texas certified the above-quoted question to this Court. We granted the request to answer the question and heard oral argument.

II. STANDARD OF REVIEW

Whether a defendant owes a duty to a plaintiff to avoid negligent conduct is a question of law that is reviewed de novo. *Dyer v. Trachtman,* 470 Mich. 45, 49, 679 N.W.2d 311 (2004).

III. ANALYSIS

A. LEGAL DUTY IN GENERAL

There is no dispute among the parties that the substantive law of Michigan governs plaintiffs' claims. In Michigan, "the question whether the defendant owes an actionable legal duty to the plaintiff is one of law which the court decides after assessing the competing policy considerations for and against recognizing the asserted duty." *Friedman v. Dozorc,* 412 Mich. 1, 22, 312 N.W.2d 585 (1981). * * * Thus, the ultimate inquiry in determining whether a legal duty should be imposed is whether the social benefits of imposing a duty outweigh the social costs of imposing a duty. The inquiry involves considering, among any other relevant considerations, "the relationship of the parties, the foreseeability of the harm, the burden on the defendant, and the nature of the risk presented.' " *Dyer, supra* at 49, 679 N.W.2d 311

The most important factor to be considered is the relationship of the parties. "[A] duty arises out of the existence of a relationship 'between the parties of such a character that social policy justifies' its imposition." *Dyer, supra* at 49, 679 N.W.2d 311, quoting Prosser & Keeton, Torts (5th ed.), § 56, p. 374. * * *

In *Dyer,* this Court focused exclusively on the relationship between the parties to determine whether the defendant owed the plaintiff a legal duty. * * * Because we found that only a limited relationship existed, we did not even address the other factors, i.e., the foreseeability of the harm, the burden on the defendant, or the nature of the risk presented. Consideration of the other factors was unnecessary because when there is only a limited relationship between the parties, only a limited duty can be imposed.

    * * *

On the other hand, even when there is a relationship between the parties, a legal duty does not necessarily exist. In order to determine whether a duty exists, the other enumerated factors must also be considered. The foreseeability of the harm is one of these. Just as the existence of a relationship between the parties is not dispositive, that the harm was foreseeable is also not dispositive. A defendant does not have a duty to protect everybody from all foreseeable harms. * * * When the harm is not foreseeable, no duty can be imposed on the defendant. But when the harm is foreseeable, a duty still does not necessarily exist.

    * * *

B. DUTY WITH REGARD TO ASBESTOS LIABILITY

Because this Court has never addressed whether property owners owe a duty to protect people who have never been on or near their property from exposure to asbestos carried home on a household member's clothing, it is helpful to review the decisions of other courts that have addressed this issue.

In *CSX Transportation, Inc. v. Williams,* 278 Ga. 888, 891, 608 S.E.2d 208 (2005), the Supreme Court of Georgia, answering a certified question from the United States Court of Appeals for the Eleventh Circuit, held that "an employer does not owe a duty of care to a third-party, non-employee, who comes into contact with its employee's asbestos-tainted work clothing at locations away from the workplace." That court explained:

> " '[I]n fixing the bounds of duty, not only logic and science, but policy play an important role.' However, it must also be recognized that there is a responsibility to consider the larger social consequences of the notion of duty and to correspondingly tailor that notion so that the illegal consequences of wrongs are limited to a controllable degree. The recognition of a common-law cause of action under the circumstances of this case would, in our opinion, expand traditional tort concepts beyond manageable bounds and create an almost infinite universe of potential plaintiffs. Accordingly, we decline to promulgate a policy which would extend the common law so as to bring the ... plaintiff[s] within a class of people whose interests are entitled to protection from the defendant's conduct." [*Id.* at 890, 608 S.E.2d 208.][11]

In *In re New York City Asbestos Litigation,* 5 N.Y.3d 486, 840 N.E.2d 115, 806 N.Y.S.2d 146 (2005), New York's highest court held that the defendant owed no duty to the defendant's employee's wife, who was allegedly injured from exposure to asbestos the employee introduced into the family home on soiled work clothes that the plaintiff wife laundered. * * * The court was concerned about "limitless liability" and questioned why, if a duty was owed to an employee's spouse, a duty would not also be owed to the employee's babysitter or an employee of a neighborhood laundry. * * * The court held that because there was no relationship between the defendant and the defendant's employee's wife, no duty could be imposed.

In *Adams v. Owens–Illinois, Inc.,* 119 Md.App. 395, 705 A.2d 58 (1998), the Maryland Court of Special Appeals held that the defendant did not owe a duty to the defendant's employee's wife who was allegedly exposed to asbestos from her husband's clothes. The court explained:

> If liability for exposure to asbestos could be premised on Mary Wild's handling of her husband's clothing, presumably Bethlehem would owe a duty to others who came in close contact with Edwin Wild, including other family members, automobile passengers, and co-workers. Bethlehem owed no duty to strangers based upon providing a safe workplace for employees. [*Id.* at 411, 705 A.2d 58.]

In *Zimko v. American Cyanamid,* 905 So.2d 465, 482 (La.App., 2005), the Louisiana Court of Appeals, "recogniz[ing] the novelty of the duty," held that the defendant owed a duty to the defendant's employee's son

---

11. As in Michigan, "mere foreseeability was rejected by [the Georgia Supreme] Court as a basis for extending a duty of care...." *CSX Transportation, supra* at 890, 608 S.E.2d 208.

who was allegedly exposed to asbestos from his father's work clothes that he brought home. * * *

[T]he Louisiana Court of Appeals reaffirmed its decision in *Zimko*. *Chaisson v. Avondale Industries, Inc.*, 947 So.2d 171 (La.App., 2006). * * * Unlike Louisiana, Michigan relies more on the relationship between the parties than foreseeability in determining whether a duty exists.

In addition, in Louisiana, unlike in Michigan, "a 'no duty' defense in a negligence case is seldom appropriate," *Zimko, supra* at 482 * * *. For these reasons, we do not find *Chaisson* persuasive.

In *Olivo v. Owens–Illinois, Inc.*, 186 N.J. 394, 895 A.2d 1143 (2006), the New Jersey Supreme Court held that if the defendant owed a duty to the worker, the defendant owed a duty to the wife of the worker who was exposed to asbestos when she washed the clothes of her husband, who was hired by an independent contractor to perform work at the defendant's premises.[12] * * * In *Olivo, supra* at 402, 895 A.2d 1143, the New Jersey Supreme Court described "foreseeability of harm" as "a crucial element in determining whether imposition of a duty on an alleged tortfeasor is appropriate." * * * However, as explained above, Michigan, like New York, relies more on the relationship between the parties than foreseeability of harm when determining whether a duty exists. For this reason, we do not find *Olivo* persuasive.[14]

C. APPLICATION TO THIS CASE

* * *

In the instant case, the relationship between Miller and defendant was highly tenuous—defendant hired an independent contractor who hired Roland who lived in a house with Miller, his stepdaughter, who sometimes washed his clothes. Miller had never been on or near defendant's property and had no further relationship with defendant. Therefore, the "relationship between the parties" prong of the duty test, which is the most important prong in this state, strongly suggests that no duty should be imposed.

The "burden [that would be imposed] on the defendant" prong also suggests that no duty should be imposed because protecting every person with whom a business's employees and the employees of its independent

12. It is important to note that the court did not hold that the defendant owed the worker's wife a duty. In fact, it held that if the defendant owed no duty to the worker, the defendant necessarily owed no duty to the worker's wife. The court remanded the case because a question of fact existed regarding whether the defendant owed the worker a duty because the worker was an employee of an independent contractor.

14. For the same reason, the California Court of Appeals decision in *Condon v. Union Oil Company of California*, 2004 WL 1932847, 2004 Cal. App. Unpub. LEXIS 7975 (Cal.App., 2004), is not persuasive. The court in that case relied exclusively on the foreseeability factor. * * * In addition, *Satterfield v. Breeding Insulation Co., Inc.*, 2007 WL 1159416, *8, 2007 Tenn. App. LEXIS 230, *25 (Tenn.App., 2007), which held that the defendant employer could be liable for the plaintiff's injuries caused by asbestos being taken home on her father's clothes, is not persuasive because "[i]n Tennessee, [unlike in Michigan,] 'the foreseeability prong [of the balancing test] is paramount because foreseeability is the test of negligence.'" [The court of appeals opinion was affirmed in *Satterfield v. Breeding Insulation Co.*, 266 S.W.3d 347 (Tenn. 2008).—Eds.]

contractors come into contact, or even with whom their clothes come into contact, would impose an extraordinarily onerous and unworkable burden.

Given what we know about asbestos today, i.e., that there is a causal relationship between exposure to asbestos and mesothelioma, and assuming that defendant directed the independent contractor to work with asbestos-containing materials, the "nature of the risk" was serious. Therefore, the "nature of the risk" prong suggests that a duty should be imposed.

However, the "foreseeability of the harm" prong suggests that no duty should be imposed. From 1954 to 1965, the period during which Roland worked at defendant's plant, we did not know what we know today about the hazards of asbestos. * * *

Because the ultimate inquiry in determining whether a duty should be imposed involves balancing the social benefits of imposing a duty with the social costs of imposing a duty, we cannot decide whether a duty should be imposed without "assessing the competing policy considerations...." *Friedman, supra* at 22, 312 N.W.2d 585. * * *

As the United States Supreme Court has recognized, this country is experiencing an "asbestos-litigation crisis" as a result of the " 'elephantine mass of asbestos cases' lodged in state and federal courts...." *Norfolk & W. R. Co. v. Ayers,* 538 U.S. 135, 166, 123 S.Ct. 1210, 155 L.Ed.2d 261 (2003) (citation omitted). Asbestos claims have given rise to one of the most costly products-liability crises ever within our nation's legal system. "Asbestos claims continue to pour in at an extraordinary rate [and] scores of employers have been forced into bankruptcy." Behrens & Cruz–Alvarez, *A potential new frontier in asbestos litigation: Premises owner liability for "take home" exposure claims,* 21 Mealey's Litig. Rep. Abs. 1, 4 (2006). Some commentators have said that "[b]efore it ends, the litigation may cost up to $195 billion—on top of the $70 billion spent through 2002." *Id.* These same commentators have explained:

> [A]doption of a new duty rule for employers could bring about a perverse result: nonemployees with secondary exposures could have greater rights to sue and potentially reap far greater recoveries than employees. Namely, secondarily exposed nonemployees could obtain noneconomic damages, such as pain and suffering, and possibly even punitive damages; these awards are not generally available to injured employees under workers' compensation. [*Id.* at 5.]

* * *

Plaintiffs have asked us to recognize a cause of action that departs drastically from our traditional notions of a valid negligence claim. Beyond this enormous shift in our tort jurisprudence, judicial recognition of plaintiffs' claim may also have undesirable effects that neither we nor the parties can satisfactorily predict. * * *

* * *

IV.   CONCLUSION

In Michigan, "the question whether the defendant owes an actionable legal duty to the plaintiff is one of law which the court decides after assessing the competing policy considerations for and against recognizing the asserted duty." *Friedman, supra* at 22, 312 N.W.2d 585. * * * [T]he most important factor pertains to the relationship between the parties. Because any relationship between Miller and defendant was highly tenuous, the harm was, in all likelihood, not foreseeable, the burden on defendant would be onerous and unworkable, and the imposition of a duty, under these circumstances, would " 'expand traditional tort concepts beyond manageable bounds and create an almost infinite universe of potential plaintiffs,' " *CSX Transportation, supra* at 890, 608 S.E.2d 208 (citation omitted), we conclude that a legal duty should not be imposed. For these reasons, we answer the certified question in the negative. That is, we hold that, under Michigan law, defendant, as owner of the property on which asbestos-containing products were located, did not owe to the deceased, who was never on or near that property, a legal duty to protect her from exposure to any asbestos fibers carried home on the clothing of a member of her household who was working on that property as the employee of independent contractors, where there was no further relationship between defendant and the deceased. Having answered the certified question, we now return the matter to the Fourteenth District Court of Appeals of Texas for such further proceedings as that court deems appropriate.

MICHAEL F. CAVANAGH, J. (*dissenting*).

* * *

I * * * disagree that Michigan law compels the result the majority reaches. Contrary to the majority's conclusion, defendant could be found to owe a duty to Carolyn Miller with respect to asbestos contamination through take-home exposure. * * *

* * *

[A]lthough the majority spends considerable time opining that, in a duty analysis, "[t]he most important factor to be considered is the relationship of the parties," *ante* at 211, this is not a bright-line rule in this state, and it is not true in every factual situation.* * * The fact that the relationship between the parties is a component of a duty analysis and may, at times, be given more weight than another of the components certainly does not mean that the relationship is the most important inquiry. How heavily to weigh each of the several factors depends on the precise situation at hand.

Many variables are considered in a duty analysis. * * * Each of these factors is significant, and the majority incorrectly represents the law in this state by asserting that the relationship between the parties is the most important. Only by subordinating these factors to that of relationship is the majority able to discount every opinion of another state in which a duty was found with respect to take-home exposure.

With respect to relationship, the majority states that because Carolyn Miller was never "on or near defendant's property," the relationship prong "strongly suggests that no duty should be imposed." *Ante* at 216. But the majority's severely curtailed view of "relationship" seems to be based on its view of premises liability law rather than on the principles of ordinary negligence. Under the latter (and the former as well, although that is not at issue here), a harmed person need not visit the property of the injuring party. This case involves an employer who exposed a worker to asbestos, knowing that the asbestos fibers were toxic and could be carried home, thus exposing the worker's family to asbestos. Under these circumstances, I have no difficulty concluding that the relationship—that a jury found defendant had to Cleveland "John" Roland—extended to Carolyn Miller. To conclude otherwise, as does the majority, ignores basic negligence principles and gives employers carte blanche to expose workers to communicable toxic substances without taking any measure whatsoever to prevent those substances from harming others. This I cannot do. * * *

Moreover, I disagree that the burden defendant would bear by shouldering a duty with respect to Carolyn Miller is so great that innocent people must suffer without recourse. * * *

The majority * * * seriously overstates what the consequences of imposing a burden on defendant would truly be by asserting that, if a duty were imposed, businesses would have to "protect[ ] every person with whom a business's employees and the employees of its independent contractors come into contact, or even with whom their clothes come into contact...." *Ante* at 217. That is incorrect. The certified question is specific to this case in that it asks whether this defendant should be found to have a duty owed to Carolyn Miller. Thus, the potential burden must be examined in this limited context, not extrapolated to all other imaginable potential litigants. * * * I would not conclude that the burden of imposing a duty on defendant, whose actions led to Carolyn Miller's exposure to a toxic substance, would be too large to bear.

I further take issue with the majority's conclusion regarding foreseeability. * * *

* * *

[A] finding regarding foreseeability must be based on the evidence specific to a particular case. And here, plaintiffs presented evidence, which the jury clearly believed, that this defendant knew of the hazards of asbestos at the relevant times. * * *

* * *

Moving on, I differ greatly with the majority regarding the outcome of what it deems the "ultimate inquiry": "whether the social benefits of imposing a duty outweigh the social costs of imposing that duty." *Ante* at 218. * * * Quite simply, there has been no showing in this case that were defendant found to have a duty, "a potentially limitless pool of plaintiffs" or " 'an almost infinite universe of potential plaintiffs' " would be created. *Ante* at 219–20 (citation omitted). In fact, one of the very commentators the majority quotes recently wrote that "after years of downward spiral, the asbestos litigation tide finally may be turning." Behrens & Goldberg, *The asbestos litigation crisis: The tide appears to be turning,* 12 Conn. Ins. L. J. 477, 478 (2006).

* * *

But even so, the majority's conclusion that the social costs of imposing a duty outweigh the social benefits requires elevating corporate vitality over the health and well-being of humanity. The majority's statements regarding the social burden abound with tales of corporate bankruptcy, litigation crises, and the costs in dollars that have stemmed *from exposing workers to asbestos.* But the majority is strangely silent with respect to the toll that asbestos exposure has taken on human life. By focusing solely on the losses suffered by businesses, the majority fails to account for the social benefits that would ensue from ensuring that people who are exposed to detrimental substances and who, consequently, suffer ruined health, life-altering and life-ending diseases, and the loss of family members, are compensated. When workers are protected from deadly substances, society benefits. When corporations are held accountable for the consequences their processes have on those who toil to make the corporations viable, society benefits. When our justice system fairly places the burden of responsibility for dangerous products on the offending party, rather than the one who suffers, society benefits.

Unlike the majority, I would find a tremendous social benefit in imposing corporate accountability, and I would conclude that the social benefits of corporate responsibility and a valued, healthy society easily outweigh the burden of imposing a duty on corporations to mitigate the risk of take-home exposure * * *.

* * *

Further, in a duty analysis, the extremely toxic nature of asbestos and the fact that the risk of injury can be reduced must be given proper weight because duty is a function of the level of risk. * * *

* * *

It is a sad day for our citizens indeed when, confronted with a substance that is so dangerous that compensating victims for their losses has had such hefty financial consequences, this Court tilts the scales of justice to *lessen* liability. The analysis should be the opposite. The more dangerous the product, the more critical it is to impose a duty of protection. If protection and accountability increase, litigation eventually decreases because, obviously, the protections reduce injury.

I am persuaded by the reasoning from courts in our sister states that have held that imposing a duty on an employer to mitigate the risk of take-home exposure is reasonable. Like the court in *Zimko v. American*

Cyanamid, 905 So.2d 465 (La.App., 2005), I would conclude that, assuming defendant knew or should have known of the dangers of take-home exposure, " 'it is hardly a quantum leap to extend the duty of care owed to employees to members of the employee's household who predictably come into routine contact with the employee's clothing. Such persons would certainly fall within the 'range of reasonable apprehension' created by defendant's alleged negligence.' " *Id.* at 483. * * *

Fortunately, the majority does not foreclose the possibility of finding a duty with respect to take-home exposure under different circumstances. But I would hold that, under close examination of the circumstances of this case, and accepting the jury's finding that defendant knew or should have known of the risk of take-home exposure, imposing a duty on defendant would be, without doubt, fair and just. Accordingly, I dissent.

NOTES AND QUESTIONS

1. Remember that, in this case, a Texas jury had found the defendant liable. The court concluded that the risk of harm to the decedent was unforeseeable during the period that her husband was employed at the Ford plant. Who properly should be deciding foreseeability in this case, the court or the jury? As with *Grover*, is this case about foreseeability at all?

2. The Michigan Supreme Court is not alone in noting that the conflict among the states in the asbestos family member cases is largely explained by whether the jurisdiction adopts a "duty" approach or a "forseeability" approach. As note 1 following the *Grover* case indicates, the duty approach traces its roots to Judge Cardozo's opinion in *Palsgraf*. The foresight approach traces some of its roots to *Wagon Mound* and some of its roots to Judge Andrews' dissent in *Palsgraf*. What, exactly, is at stake in the choice between these approaches? Does the duty approach allow courts to avoid any of the difficult issues involved in traditional proximate cause analyses? Does the Third Restatement adopt either of these approaches or does it try to forge a different path? How would a court decide this case if it were to adopt the Third Restatement approach, set forth in note 4 following the *Grover* case?

3. Do you think the majority would have resolved the case in the same way if the plaintiff had been the wife of a Ford employee? Would it reach the same outcome if the plaintiff were a consultant to Ford who spent one day a week on the premises, but whose only exposure to asbestos was at home? Why or why not?

4. Suppose that a toxic byproduct of the furnace relining work escaped from the Ford plant where the plaintiff worked and flowed from there to the home of the plaintiff and his decedent, where it caused the latter to contract a fatal form of cancer. Would a suit against Ford for her death be any different from the instant case? Why or why not? Section 54 of the Third Restatement of Torts imposes a duty of reasonable care on land possessors for conduct on the land that poses a risk of harm to those not on the land.

5. The third-party asbestos exposure cases are collected at Marjorie A. Shields, Liability of Property Owners to Persons Who Have Never Been on or

Near Their Property for Exposure to Asbestos Carried Home on Household Member's Clothing, 33 A.L.R.6th 325.

6. The "elephantine mass" of asbestos cases does appear to be abating. As noted in the dissent, the decline in filings is due primarily to the decline in claims by people who do not currently have any physical impairment. Mark Behrens, What's New In Asbestos Litigation?, 28 Rev.Litig. 501, 510 (2009). This decline is the result of steps in many states to defer the claims of those without current physical impairment. See Joseph Sanders, Medical Criteria Acts: State Statutory Attempts to Control the Asbestos Litigation, 37 Sw. U.L.Rev. 671 (2008); Philip Zimmerly, The Answer is Blowing in Procedure: States Turn to Medical Criteria and Inactive Dockets to Better Facilitate Asbestos Litigation, 59 Ala.L.Rev. 771 (2008). Nevertheless, the dissent cites studies indicating that take-home exposure cases represented about six percent of total asbestos cases in the early 2000s. Ironically, the take-home cases disproportionately involve those with the most serious disease, mesothelioma, which is almost invariably fatal. Recall from earlier cases that this disease can be caused by a relatively low level of exposure.

We discuss the issue of whether courts should recognize a cause of action based solely on exposure without a requirement of a present injury in Chapter 11.

7. The majority and the dissent disagreed as to whether the court should consider other potential litigants when deciding the duty question. In an omitted footnote, the majority argued that, "One cannot assess 'social benefits' and 'social costs' by considering only a 'particular' case or without considering other 'potential litigants.' Unlike Justice Cavanagh, we refuse to consider whether to impose a new legal duty without regard to the consequences of such a decision for future cases." *In re Certified Question*, 740 N.W.2d at 217 n.17. Do you agree? If the court did agree to extend the defendant's duty to the plaintiff, how might it limit this obligation with respect to people such as the maid who washed the worker's clothes, or should it simply extend the duty to all foreseeable plaintiffs?

8. Scope of liability issues arose in a number of suits brought by both individuals and municipalities against manufacturers of firearms. We discuss some of these cases in note 3, p. 113 supra. These suits advanced a number of different legal claims, including negligence, product liability, and public and private nuisance. In nearly all of the cases, the defendants argued that proximate cause considerations barred the claims. Some jurisdictions rejected this argument, at least at the pleading stage. See City of Cincinnati v. Beretta U.S.A. Corp., 768 N.E.2d 1136 (Ohio 2002); Ileto v. Glock Inc., 349 F.3d 1191 (9th Cir.2003)(permitting a claim that a faulty distribution system led foreseeably to providing guns to felons); City of Gary ex rel. King v. Smith & Wesson Corp., 801 N.E.2d 1222 (Ind.2003)(denying defendant's motion at pleading stage, but noting the many proximate cause barriers to recovery for any particular claim). Other courts ruled in the defendant's favor. Young v. Bryco Arms, 821 N.E.2d 1078 (Ill.2004)(gun manufacturers' and dealers' business practices were not the proximate cause of injuries to individuals shot and killed by third parties.); People v. Sturm, Ruger & Co., 761 N.Y.S.2d 192

(App.Div.2003). Some courts cited section 448 of the Second Restatement of Torts. Here is the text of that section:

> § 448. Intentionally Tortious Or Criminal Acts Done Under Opportunity Afforded By Actor's Negligence
>
> The act of a third person in committing an intentional tort or crime is a superseding cause of harm to another resulting therefrom, although the actor's negligent conduct created a situation which afforded an opportunity to the third person to commit such a tort or crime, unless the actor at the time of his negligent conduct realized or should have realized the likelihood that such a situation might be created, and that a third person might avail himself of the opportunity to commit such a tort or crime.

Restatement (Second) of Torts § 448. Which side in these cases, plaintiffs or defendants, is most benefitted by this section? Why?

9. Another group of cases presenting scope of liability issues was brought by entities such as Blue Cross and Labor Unions who were seeking to recoup medical expenses caused by cigarette related disease. More often than not, the tobacco industry has succeed in its efforts to have these cases dismissed. For example, in Blue Cross & Blue Shield of New Jersey, Inc. v. Philip Morris, Inc., 178 F.Supp.2d 198 (E.D.N.Y.2001), the trial produced a jury verdict of $17 million in a suit claiming the defendants' misrepresentation of smoking risks violated New York's consumer protection statute. On appeal, the Second Circuit certified to the New York Court of Appeals the question of whether "claims by a third party payer of health care costs seeking to recover costs of services provided to subscribers as a result of those subscribers being harmed by a defendant's or defendants' violation of N.Y. Gen. Bus. Law § 349 is too remote to permit suit under that statute?" Blue Cross & Blue Shield of New Jersey, Inc. v. Philip Morris USA, Inc., 344 F.3d 211, 229 (2d Cir.2003). The Court of Appeals answered in the affirmative. Blue Cross & Blue Shield of New Jersey, Inc. v. Philip Morris, Inc., 818 N.E.2d 1140 (N.Y.2004). Consequently, the Second Circuit reversed the trial court and ordered it to enter a judgment with prejudice on all of the plaintiff's claims. Empire Healthchoice, Inc. v. Philip Morris USA, Inc., 393 F.3d 312 (2d Cir.2004).

B. SUBSTANTIAL FACTOR

In Chapter 3, we noted that the first and Second Restatements of Torts defined causation in terms of a "substantial factor" test. The test was designed primarily to resolve the causal problem presented by the "two-fire" cases, that is cases where there are, in the language of the Third Restatement, multiple sufficient causal sets. However, the substantial factor test played another role in the earlier Restatements. It could be used to dismiss cases in which the causal contribution of defendant's tortious actions to plaintiff's injury was de minimis. The following case involves this use of the term in this way.

BYERS v. LINCOLN ELECTRIC CO.

United States District Court, N.D. Ohio, 2009.
607 F.Supp.2d 840.

MEMORANDUM & ORDER

KATHLEEN MCDONALD O'MALLEY, DISTRICT JUDGE.

This case is one of the approximately 2,600 pending cases that are a part of the Multi–District Litigation known as *In re Welding Fume Products Liability Litigation,* MDL No. 1535. As with all of the *Welding Fume* cases, the plaintiff in this case, Eddie Byers, is a welder who claims: (1) he inhaled fumes given off by welding rods; (2) these fumes contained manganese; (3) this manganese caused him permanent neurological injury and other harm; and (4) the defendants knew or should have known that the use of welding rods would cause these damages. * * *

* * *

I. Facts.

Plaintiff Eddie Byers, who is 48 years old, was raised in Texas. Byers' father was a welder and taught Byers to weld when he was a young boy. As Byers grew older, he helped his father on welding jobs during the summer, and Byers eventually became a welder himself in 1978, when he was 17 years old. Byers worked as a welder for various employers while living in Texas until 1997. He then moved to Alabama and continued to work as a welder until 2003. Byers then quit welding because he could no longer perform the physical requirements, due to hand tremor and other symptoms of what his doctor diagnosed as a neurological disease known as Manganese–Induced Parkinsonism.

During the time he lived in Texas, almost all of Byers' welding jobs were also in Texas, although he also had occasional welding jobs out of state, such as in Mississippi, Louisiana, Arkansas, Utah, and California. Similarly, during the time he lived in Alabama, most of Byers' welding jobs were in Alabama, although he also worked welding jobs in other states, ranging from Florida to Minnesota. Discovery produced by Byers lists over 100 different job sites in 15 different states.

During his lifetime, Byers used welding consumables produced by a variety of manufacturers. It is unsurprising that Byers does not have a precise recollection of which manufacturers' welding rods he used at each job location, given the length of his career, the number of his job sites, and the number of different welding rod products he used. Nonetheless, the chart below fairly summarizes his use of different manufacturers' welding consumables in the two states where he lived—Texas and Alabama.

Welding Rod Manufacturer	Byers' Use of Manufacturer's Welding Rod Products
Lincoln Electric Co.	Regular and consistent use in both TX and AL.
Hobart Brothers Company	Regular and consistent use in both TX and AL.
ESAB Group	Regular and consistent use in both TX and AL.
BOC Group	Used in TX during one job in 1981, and also possibly as a child. BOC stopped manufacturing welding rods in 1986, so he could not have used their products in AL.
TDY Industries	Possibly used their products but recalls no details regarding when or where. TDY stopped manufacturing welding rods in 1992, so he could not have used their products in AL, except possibly during a short job in 1991.
Union Carbide Corporation ("UCC")	Used their products but recalls no details regarding when or where. UCC stopped manufacturing welding rods in 1985, so he could not have used their products in AL.
Eutectic Corporation	Used in TX as a child.
Sandvik, Inc.	Used their stainless steel TIG products during various jobs between 1981–97 while living and working primarily in TX.
Westinghouse Electric Corp. ("WEC")	Used in TX as a child. WEC stopped manufacturing welding rods in 1983, so he could not have used their products in AL.

The evidence was undisputed that the first three manufacturers listed above (Lincoln, Hobart, and ESAB) supplied the overwhelming majority of the welding rod products that Byers used during his career.[4] As to the last six manufacturers, it is undisputed that Byers either did not use their welding rod products in Alabama, or at least has no evidence he ever used their welding rod products anywhere besides Texas.

II. Choice of Law.

Conceivably, the laws of Texas (where Byers did most of his welding), Alabama (where Byers welded and now lives), or Ohio (where Byers filed his lawsuit, where this MDL Court is located, and where two of the largest defendants are headquartered) might apply to Byers' claims. It is clear, however, that the applicable laws of these states are in actual conflict. For example, Ohio and Texas recognize comparative negligence and do not bar recovery where the plaintiff's fault is no greater than the combined fault of all defendants; in contrast, Alabama follows the doctrine of contributory negligence, so that a plaintiff's own negligence is a complete defense. Also, each of the three states has a different statutory cap on punitive damages.

---

4. At trial, for example, Byers testified that he used products supplied by these three manufacturers for 90–95% of the welding he performed during his career; and that, as between the three, his use could be broken down roughly as follows: Lincoln 40%, Hobart 35%, and ESAB 25%.

Accordingly, before addressing defendants' summary judgment motions, the Court must determine which state's law applies.

* * *

[D]efendants argue that Texas law applies, while Byers argues that Ohio law applies. An examination of the relevant factors reveals that defendants' position is correct.

* * *

III. Specific Causation.

In their motion for summary judgment, defendants argue Byers cannot prevail at trial because he has insufficient evidence regarding: "(1) what level of exposure to welding fumes—if any—causes neurological injury; and (2) whether [he] was exposed to fumes from each individual defendant's products at that level." Defendants cite * * * *Borg–Warner*[51] * * * to support their argument. Before assessing Byers' evidence, the Court examines the holding * * *.

A. Texas Law on Specific Causation.

In *Borg–Warner,* the Texas Supreme Court "continue[d] [its] struggle with the appropriate parameters for lawsuits alleging asbestos-related injuries." Specifically, the court "had the occasion to decide whether [evidence of exposure to] 'some' respirable fibers is sufficient to show that a product containing asbestos was a substantial factor in causing asbestosis."[52] The court concluded that a plaintiff's showing of exposure only to "some fibers" was insufficient to support a verdict—more precision was required.

The facts of *Borg–Warner* were as follows. The plaintiff, Arturo Flores, worked as a brake mechanic for about 35 years. Part of his job involved applying a grinder to new break pads, so they would not squeal when installed. This grinding process created visible clouds of dust. Flores worked in a relatively small room and routinely inhaled this dust. The brake pads that Flores worked on were manufactured by half a dozen companies, one of which was Borg–Warner. More specifically, the evidence showed that Flores worked with Borg–Warner brake pads during a three-year period early in his career (1972–75), and about one quarter to one third of the brake pads Flores worked with during that period were Borg–Warner products.

Some of the brake pads Flores worked on contained asbestos, including the Borg–Warner products, which were comprised of up to 28% asbestos by weight. At trial, Flores presented an expert toxicologist who engaged in a medico-scientific literature review and testified that: (1) most of the asbestos contained in brake pads is destroyed by the heat of friction, and therefore is not released into the air; but (2) nonetheless, the dust produced during brake pad grinding still contains "some" respirable asbestos fibers. Flores also presented an expert pulmonologist, who testified that: (1) the obstructive lung disease revealed by Flores's pulmonary function tests was unrelated to asbestos exposure; but (2) the interstitial

---

51. *Borg–Warner Corp. v. Flores,* 232 S.W.3d 765 (Tex.2007).

52. *Id.* at 766.

lung disease revealed by Flores's x-rays was asbestosis. The manufacturing defendants, in contrast, presented an expert pulmonologist who testified that Flores's x-rays did not show he had any asbestos-related disease. Flores also presented his medical records, including: (1) the opinion of a NIOSH-certified B-reader physician that the changes in Flores's lung tissue were "consistent with asbestosis;" and (2) a report from his cardiologist that Flores had admitted to smoking more than a pack of cigarettes a day since age 25.

The jury concluded that Flores had sustained an asbestos-related injury proximately caused by Borg–Warner and three other defendants, and that Borg–Warner was responsible for 37% of $112,000 in compensatory damages. Borg–Warner appealed, arguing that, among other things, Flores had not proved liability because he had not adduced sufficient evidence of exposure to injurious levels of asbestos from Borg–Warner products.

The *Borg-Warner* court began its analysis by quoting "the most widely cited standard for proving causation in asbestos cases," known as the "*Lohrmann* 'frequency, regularity, and proximity' test."[56] Under the *Lohrmann* test, "[t]o support a reasonable inference of substantial causation from circumstantial evidence, there must be evidence of [1] exposure to a specific product [2] on a regular basis [3] over some extended period of time [4] in proximity to where the plaintiff actually worked."[57] The *Lohrmann* test is explicitly more strict than the standard "that if the plaintiff can present *any* evidence that a company's asbestos-containing product was at the workplace while the plaintiff was at the workplace, a jury question has been established as to whether that product proximately caused the plaintiff's disease."[58]

The *Borg-Warner* court agreed with the *Lohrmann* court "that a 'frequency, regularity, and proximity test' is appropriate." But the *Borg-Warner* court added that "those terms do not, in themselves, capture the emphasis [that Texas] jurisprudence has placed on causation as an essential predicate to liability." *Id.* Rather, under Texas law, there must *also* be evidence allowing the fact-finder to "determine whether the asbestos in the defendant's product was a substantial factor in bringing about the plaintiff's injuries." And, more specifically, this means the plaintiff must present "quantitative information" regarding his "dose."

The *Borg-Warner* court observed that: (1) "[a]sbestosis appears to be dose-related, so that the more one is exposed, the more likely the disease is to occur, and the higher the exposure the more severe the disease is likely to be;" (2) "asbestos is 'plentiful' in the ambient air and ... 'everyone' is exposed to it[;] * * * therefore, some exposure 'threshold' must be demonstrated before a claimant can prove his asbestosis was caused by a particular product;" and (3) "[t]here is general agreement

---

56. *Id.* at 769 (citing *Lohrmann v. Pittsburgh Corning Corp.*, 782 F.2d 1156 (4th Cir.1986).)

57. *Id.* (quoting *Lohrmann*, 782 F.2d at 1162–63).

58. *Id.* (emphasis added) (quoting *Lohrmann*, 782 F.2d at 1163).

from epidemiologic studies that the development of asbestosis requires heavy exposure to asbestos ... in the range of 25 to 100 fibers per cubic centimeter-year."[63] Given these parameters, the *Borg–Warner* court concluded, simple proof of "some exposure" to asbestos—even proof that the plaintiff worked in close proximity to a specific asbestos product on a fairly regular basis over an extended period of time—was "necessary but not sufficient."[64] This is because evidence regarding "frequency, regularity, and proximity" to a particular defendant's asbestos product, without any evidence of dose, did not prove that the product was a substantial factor in causing asbestosis. The *Borg–Warner* court explained its ruling in the context of Flores's circumstances:

> [The record in this case] reveals nothing about how much asbestos Flores might have inhaled. He performed about fifteen to twenty brake jobs a week for over thirty years, and was therefore exposed to "some asbestos" on a fairly regular basis for an extended period of time. Nevertheless, absent any evidence of dose, the jury could not evaluate the quantity of respirable asbestos to which Flores might have been exposed or whether those amounts were sufficient to cause asbestosis. Nor did Flores introduce evidence regarding what percentage of that indeterminate amount may have originated in Borg–Warner products. * * * Thus, while some respirable fibers may be released upon grinding some brake pads, the sparse record here contains no evidence of the approximate quantum of Borg–Warner fibers to which Flores was exposed, and whether this sufficiently contributed to the aggregate dose of asbestos Flores inhaled, such that it could be considered a substantial factor in causing his asbestosis. * * *

> * * * In a case like this, proof of mere frequency, regularity, and proximity is necessary but not sufficient, as it provides none of the quantitative information necessary to support causation under Texas law.[65]

Notably, the *Borg–Warner* court added that the Texas law requirement of "quantitative information" regarding dose, "which separates the speculative from the probable, need not be reduced to mathematical precision." Rather, "[d]efendant-specific evidence relating to the approximate dose to which the plaintiff was exposed, coupled with evidence that the dose was a substantial factor in causing the asbestos-related disease, will suffice." Put differently, a plaintiff "cannot be expected to ... trace the unknowable path of a given asbestos fiber," but "there must be reasonable evidence that the exposure was of sufficient magnitude to exceed the threshold before a likelihood of 'causation' can be inferred."[68]

---

63. *Id.* at 771, 773.

64. *Id.* at 772.

65. *Id.* at 771–72 (citations and footnotes omitted).

68. *Id.* at 772–73 (quoting *Rutherford v. Owens–Illinois, Inc.,* 16 Cal.4th 953, 67 Cal.Rptr.2d 16, 941 P.2d 1203, 1219 (1997)). The *Borg–Warner* court also cited the following language from *Rutherford* with approval: "plaintiffs may prove causation in asbestos-related cancer cases by

Ultimately, then, the Texas Supreme Court held that a plaintiff can "prove that the defendant's product was a substantial factor in causing the alleged harm" only by adducing quantitative evidence of (1) how much asbestos exposure is usually required before harm will result; and (2) how much asbestos exposure the plaintiff actually suffered from the defendant's products.

* * *

Having examined Texas law as set forth in *Borg–Warner* * * *, the Court now applies [this ruling] to the instant case.

B. Byers' Quantitative Evidence.

In this case, each defendant argues that the evidence Byers developed regarding his exposure to their particular products does not meet the *Borg–Warner* test, as a matter of law. Turning to the easiest questions first, the Court quickly concludes that six defendants—BOC, TDY, Union Carbide, Eutectic, Sandvik, and Westinghous—are correct, and so are entitled to summary judgment under Texas law.

As *Borg–Warner* makes clear, to find against a defendant in this case, the jury must be presented with "evidence of the approximate quantum of [manganese in welding fume] to which [Byers] was exposed, and whether this sufficiently contributed to the aggregate dose of [manganese fume that Byers] inhaled, such that it could be considered a substantial factor in causing his [neurological injury]."[89] In this case, there is no material question of fact as to whether the quantum of welding fumes given off by the products manufactured by each of these six defendants could be considered a substantial factor in causing Byers' alleged injury—it could not.[90]

For example, Byers used defendant BOC's welding rods during only one job in 1981, and also possibly as a child while welding with his father. There is no evidence that the BOC welding rods Byers used during this 1981 job emitted fumes that were especially copious, or had an unusually high manganese content; nor is there any evidence that he was exposed to

demonstrating that the plaintiff's exposure to defendant's asbestos-containing product in reasonable medical probability was a substantial factor in contributing to the aggregate *dose* of asbestos the plaintiff or decedent inhaled or ingested, and hence to the *risk* of developing asbestos-related cancer, without the need to demonstrate that fibers from the defendant's particular product were the ones, or among the ones, that *actually* produced the malignant growth." *Id.* (emphasis in original). The *Borg–Warner* court also suggested that, in some cases, the plaintiff's exposure to toxic levels of a product may be so clearly established that this quantitative analysis becomes unnecessary, such as when "workers were so covered with asbestos as to be dubbed 'the snowmen of Grand Central.'" *Id.* at 774 (quoting *Temple–Inland Forest Prods. Corp. v. Carter*, 993 S.W.2d 88, 95 (Tex.1999)) (some internal quotation marks omitted).

89. *Borg–Warner,* 232 S.W.3d at 772.

90. As the Court stated in its oral ruling from the bench before trial: "The Court also concludes that the Defendants' motion for summary judgment as to those Defendants is well taken. The Court finds—actually believes it would be well taken under Alabama or Texas law or, frankly, the laws of most of the other states that the Court has considered to date. The product I.D. and exposure evidence as it relates to those Defendants is insufficient to rise to the level of allowing any reasonable juror to conclude that exposure to the products of those Defendants could be a substantial factor, and cause harm or injury to Mr. Byers. So the Court finds that the defendant's motion for summary judgment is well taken as to all of those six Defendants."

these fumes while in a confined space with no ventilation, so that his exposure to BOC welding fumes was especially injurious. Indeed, Byers essentially conceded during oral argument that, given the evidence he had discovered and adduced, his exposure to BOC welding fumes was fairly characterized as "de minimis." Thus, it is clear that the "dose" of BOC manganese fumes to which Byers was exposed did not contribute to his "aggregate dose" such that it could be considered a substantial factor in causing his alleged injury.

Similarly, while Byers used Sandvik welding consumables sporadically between 1981 and 1997, the evidence is undisputed that: (1) the only Sandvik products he used were stainless steel TIG products, which are low-fume, low-manganese products; and (2) he did TIG welding for only a small percentage of his welding, and used Sandvik products for only a small percentage of that. Thus, it is again undisputed that the "dose" of Sandvik manganese fumes to which Byers was exposed did not contribute to his "aggregate dose" such that Sandvik products could be considered a substantial factor in causing his alleged injury.

The same analysis applies to defendants TDY, Union Carbide, Eutectic, and Westinghouse. Under the *Lohrmann* "frequency, regularity, and proximity" test, "there must be evidence of [1] exposure to a specific product [2] on a regular basis [3] over some extended period of time [4] in proximity to where the plaintiff actually worked" to support a jury determination that the product was a substantial factor in causing injury. There is no evidence of record in this case of any regular or extended use by Byers of welding rods manufactured by any of these other four defendants. Accordingly, defendants' motion for summary judgment must be granted as to BOC, TDY, Union Carbide, Eutectic, Sandvik, and Westinghouse.

The analysis is different and more complicated with respect to defendants Lincoln, Hobart, and ESAB. In contrast to the sporadic and infrequent use of welding rods manufactured by the six other defendants, Byers used welding rods manufactured by Lincoln, Hobart, and ESAB regularly and often throughout all of his 25–year career. With respect to each of these defendants, Byers adduced sufficient evidence at the summary judgment stage to submit to the jury the *Lohrmann* "frequency, regularity, and proximity" test, unmodified by *Borg–Warner*. That is, there is no question but that Byers was prepared to present evidence at trial that he commonly and ordinarily used the welding rods manufactured by each of these three defendants, and he did so for many years. As such, there existed evidence upon which a reasonable jury could conclude that each of these three defendants' products contributed substantially to the aggregate dose of manganese fume that Byers inhaled.

Borg–Warner, however, mandates that Byers provide more than just the information required by *Lohrmann*—he must also provide evidence related to the "quantitative information [of his exposure] necessary to support causation under Texas law.''[96] While this quantitative information need not be mathematically precise, it must be sufficiently finespun to allow a jury to determine: (1) the quantity of manganese fume to which Byers might have been exposed, (2) whether that amount was sufficient to cause neurological injury, and (3) whether the amount of exposure attributable to each defendant was a substantial cause of that alleged injury. A comparison of the quantitative evidence offered in *Borg–Warner* * * * on the one hand, and in Byers' case, on the other hand, convinces the Court that Byers *has* adduced sufficient quantitative evidence to create a jury question on specific causation for each of the remaining three defendants.

    * * *

As this Court has explained in detail in other written opinions, several governmental and professional entities have established various measures to define safe exposure limits to manganese in welding fumes. These limits include: (1) the Threshold Limit Value ("TLV"), promulgated by the American Conference of Governmental Industrial Hygienists ("ACGIH"), which is the maximum *average* amount to which, it is believed, a person may be safely exposed over an 8–hour time period;[97] and (2) Permissible Exposure Limits ("PELs"), promulgated by the Occupational Safety and Health Agency ("OSHA"), which is the maximum *ceiling* amount to which a person may be safely exposed at any moment in time.

* * * Thus, there is in this case evidence of a quantitative threshold against which a jury can measure Byers' exposure, together with evidence that exposure above this threshold is sufficient to cause what defendants' own warnings and MSDSs describe as progressive neurological changes— which can include languor, sleepiness, muscular weakness, emotional disturbances, poor coordination, difficulty in speaking, spastic gait, tremor of arms and legs, and irreversible damage to the central nervous system, including the brain. In sum, Byers has adduced sufficient evidence regarding "toxic threshold" to allow a jury to determine whether a given exposure level to manganese fumes is sufficient to cause the kinds of neurological injury Byers claims to have suffered.

The next question is whether Byers has adduced sufficient quantitative evidence to allow a jury to determine whether, more probably than not, the amount of manganese fume from each defendant's products to which *he* was actually exposed exceeded this threshold. * * * The very best evidence Byers could present on this issue would be air sampling data that showed, at any point during his career, the actual concentrations of manganese fume in his breathing space. Byers does not point to any air sampling data at all, however, in support of his assertion that his exposures exceeded the threshold level necessary to cause harm.[101] The next

---

96. *Borg–Warner*, 232 S.W.3d at 772.

97. The current TLV for manganese fume is an 8–hour time-weighted average of 0.2 mg/mm3.
* * *

101. Of course, virtually no welder could ever provide this evidence, which is why the law does not require mathematical precision to show toxic exposure. As stated by the *Reference Manual on Scientific Evidence,* "[o]nly rarely are humans exposed to chemicals in a manner that permits a

best evidence Byers could present on this issue would be expert testimony detailing a quantitative dose reconstruction, premised upon supportable data and reasonable assumptions. Again, however, Byers does not point to this type of evidence.[102] Rather, Byers points to three types of circumstantial evidence suggesting that his actual exposure levels exceeded the critical threshold: (1) defendants' own documents; (2) an OSHA database; and (3) anecdotal descriptions regarding the type and number of his exposures.

* * *

There is one thing that the sum of this evidence offered by Byers clearly is *not:* an approximate, stand-alone, quantitative measure of the total amount of manganese in welding fume he inhaled during his career. For example, Byers is not offering evidence from which a jury could conclude that he was exposed to manganese fume above 0.2 mg/mm³ during (say) 10% of his working hours; or that he suffered exposure to manganese fume above 1.0 mg/mm³ 50 discrete times in his career. But, as earlier discussed, Texas law does not require Byers to offer evidence this specific. The critical passage from *Borg–Warner* is that "there must be reasonable evidence that *the exposure was of sufficient magnitude to exceed the threshold* before a likelihood of 'causation' can be inferred."[109] In other words, it is sufficient under Texas law for a plaintiff to adduce evidence that: (1) as a general matter, exposure to a toxin at more than a certain, threshold level substantially increases the likelihood of toxin-related injury; and (2) as a specific matter, more probably than not, he was exposed to more than this threshold level of the toxin, and this exposure can be attributed in substantial part to the particular defendant's products. While it is a close call on the second prong, the Court concludes Byers has offered sufficient evidence addressing both prongs of this test, so he avoids summary judgment.

* * *

* * * Ultimately, * * * Byers does far more than simply assert he was exposed to "some" manganese fume, and it was this approach that the Texas Supreme Court rejected. Byers offers quantitative evidence that he was, more likely than not, repeatedly exposed to manganese in welding fumes above the TLV during the course of his long career. This satisfies the *Borg–Warner* requirement that a plaintiff provide enough specific

---

quantitative determination of adverse outcomes.... Human exposure occurs most frequently in occupational settings where workers are exposed to industrial chemicals like lead or asbestos; however, even under these circumstances, it is usually difficult, if not impossible, to quantify the amount of exposure." Federal Judicial Center, *Reference Manual on Scientific Evidence* 405 (2nd ed. 2000). * * * The Court rejects defendants' arguments in this case suggesting that *Borg–Warner* * * * [requires] a level of evidentiary precision that the *Reference Manual on Scientific Evidence* calls "difficult, if not impossible," to achieve.

102. Evidence of quantitative dose reconstruction is also elusive, at best. * * *

109. *Borg–Warner*, 232 S.W.3d at 773 (quoting David L. Eaton, *Scientific Judgment and Toxic Torts—A Primer in Toxicology for Judges and Lawyers,* 12 J. Law & Policy 5, 39 (2003)) (emphasis added).

information to allow a jury to determine whether, more probably than not, his exposure was sufficient to cause neurological injury.

This leaves the third type of quantitative evidence required by *Borg–Warner*—evidence that allows a jury to determine whether the amount of exposure *attributable to each defendant* was a substantial cause of the alleged injury. In *Borg–Warner,* the plaintiff did not "introduce evidence regarding [the] percentage of [the asbestos to which he was exposed that] may have originated in Borg–Warner products."[114] * * * Here, in contrast, Byers has evidence quantifying the number of jobs where he used the products made by remaining defendants Lincoln, Hobart, and ESAB, as well as the relative overall percentages attributable to each defendant. * * * The Court concludes that Byers has adduced sufficient defendant-specific evidence to allow a reasonable jury to determine whether each defendant was responsible for a substantial amount of Byers' total exposure to manganese fume.

IV. Conclusion.

As an initial matter, the Court concludes that this case is governed by Texas law. Under Texas law, the motion by defendants BOC, TDY, Union Carbide, Eutectic, Sandvik, and Westinghouse for summary judgment, based on lack of evidence of specific causation, is **granted;** however, the same motion by defendants Lincoln, Hobart, and ESAB is **denied.**

IT IS SO ORDERED.

NOTES AND QUESTIONS

1. Judge O'Malley originally ruled on the defendants' summary judgement motions without a written opinion. At the time, the court promised the parties a written opinion explaining its oral ruling. This opinion was written after the conclusion of the trial in which the jury returned a verdict in favor of the defendants.

2. The *Byers* court said with respect to one of the "minor" defendants:

> Byers used defendant BOC's welding rods during only one job in 1981, and also possibly as a child while welding with his father. * * * Byers essentially conceded during oral argument that * * * his exposure to BOC welding fumes was fairly characterized as "de minimis." Thus, it is clear that the "dose" of BOC manganese fumes to which Byers was exposed did not contribute to his "aggregate dose" such that it could be considered a substantial factor in causing his alleged injury.

Byers, 607 F.Supp.2d at 860.

This passage reveals the ambiguity surrounding the term "substantial factor." Was the court arguing that the BOC fumes may have contributed to Byers' condition, but because their contribution was de minimis, they were not a legal cause of his injury? Or was it arguing that they were not a cause-

---

114. *Borg–Warner,* 232 S.W.3d at 772.

in-fact of his injury? This ambiguity infests other cases that have employed the substantial factor rubric to exonerate defendants. For example, in Gregg v. V–J Auto Parts, Co., 943 A.2d 216 (Pa.2007), the court held that a trial court could use a substantial factor analysis to determine whether exposure to the defendant's product was sufficient to allow the plaintiff to get to the jury. However, when the case was remanded, the appellate court affirmed a grant of a defense summary judgment primarily on the grounds that "There is no evidence at all to support the conclusion that the decedent had definite contact with Appellant's products, which contained asbestos." Id. at 1178.

3. *Byers'* discussion of whether the plaintiff may pursue his claim against the "major" suppliers of welding rods—Lincoln Electric, Hobart Brothers, and ESAB—clearly is not about de minimis use of the rods. Rather, it is about proof of dose rate and the sort of evidence, e.g., quantitative versus qualitative, a plaintiff must present to prove dosage. The *Lohrmann* frequency, regularity and proximity test is one indirect and qualitative way to establish a minimal dosage. Why did the Texas Supreme Court conclude that meeting the *Lohrmann* test was a necessary but not a sufficient proof of causation? Is this a cause-in-fact question or a scope of liability question?

4. When applying the substantial factor test, should courts be sensitive to the specific relationship between a substance and a disease? In *Borg–Warner* the court noted that the relationship between asbestos and asbestosis is dose related in the sense that the total lifetime exposure affects the severity of the disease. The greater the exposure, the greater the impairment. In the *Gregg* case, cited in note 2 above, the plaintiff suffered from mesothelioma, also an asbestos related disease. There is a dose-response relationship between asbestos exposure and mesothelioma, as the greater the exposure the more likely one will contract the disease. However, some individuals have contracted the disease after relatively low levels of exposure and, once contracted, the severity of the disease is unrelated to the level of exposure. Less is known about the dose-response relationship between manganese and neurological injuries. See National Institute for Occupational Safety and Health, Welding and Manganese: Potential Neurological Effects, available at http://www.cdc.gov/niosh/topics/welding/. For example, it is not entirely clear whether long-term, very low-dose exposures have adverse effects. And of course there are other possible causes of similar neurological injuries. Should any of this affect a court's judgment about the minimal exposure necessary for an exposure to rise to the level of a "substantial factor"?

5. Should the level of exposure needed to meet a substantial factor test be judged in absolute terms or in relation to other known exposures? For example, suppose there were 10,000 welding rod suppliers who each provided the same amount of product as TDY, with none providing any more. Is your answer to this question affected by the nature of the relationships discussed in note 4 above?

6. In the *Gregg* case, the plaintiff originally alleged that Gregg, now deceased, was exposed to asbestos throughout a 40-year history of employment with telecommunications companies as a cable splicer and line man; over a four-year period in which he worked as a gas station attendant; and during a three-year period while serving in the United States Navy. The complaint also alleged that Gregg occasionally installed and removed brake linings and clutches on cars and trucks, albeit this was never his occupation. Ultimately, the plaintiff was unable to offer any evidence of his occupational exposure and brought suit against only one defendant, an auto parts store that allegedly sold Gregg brake products containing asbestos. The Pennsylvania Supreme Court noted that if every exposure to asbestos, no matter how minimal in relation to other exposures, implicates a fact issue concerning substantial-factor causation in every case, the result "is to subject defendants to full joint-and-several liability for injuries and fatalities in the absence of any reasonably developed scientific reasoning that would support the conclusion that the product sold by the defendant was a substantial factor in causing the harm." *Gregg*, 943 A.2d at 227.

As this passage indicates, in Pennsylvania each defendant was jointly and severally liable for the full damages awarded to the defendant. Should this affect the level of exposure needed to meet the substantial factor test? What if a state only imposes several liability? Isn't the real issue in many of these cases the allocation of damages among defendants, settlers, and plaintiffs? For a discussion of the issues discussed in notes 4, 5, and 6, see Joseph Sanders, Michael D. Green & William C. Powers Jr., The Insubstantiality of the "Substantial Factor" Test for Causation, 73 Mo.L.Rev. 399 (2008).

7. A good deal of the *Byers* opinion deals with choice of law issues. Choice of law is often problematic in toxic tort cases because plaintiffs have been exposed to substances in multiple jurisdictions. On the crucial issue of the liability of the "minor" welding rod providers, the *Byers* court was able to resolve the issue in favor of Texas law, because the plaintiff used these rods only in Texas while he was living in Texas. However, other fact patterns may lead to more problematic outcomes. The court offered the following hypothetical to indicate the nature of these complexities.

> Imagine that: (1) Welder used only Defendant A's product for 10 years while living in Ohio, and Defendant A is headquartered in Ohio; (2) Welder moved to Michigan, used only Defendant B's product for 10 years while living in Michigan, and Defendant B is headquartered in Michigan; and (3) Welder then retired to Florida, and brought suit in Florida for injuries caused by welding fume exposure. Given that Welder suffered no exposure to Defendant A's products anywhere except Ohio, there is virtually no basis for applying anything but Ohio law to Welder's claims against Defendant A. This is true even though Welder alleges he suffered a single, indivisible injury caused by both Defendants' products. Similarly, given that Welder suffered no exposure to Defendant B's products anywhere except Michigan, there is no basis for applying anything but Michigan law to Welder's claims against Defendant B. While it might be easier or more convenient for the Florida court to apply, say, only Ohio law to all of Welder's claims, there is no nexus between Ohio and Defendant B that would allow this to occur. Indeed, to apply Ohio law to Welder's claims against Defendant B would likely be unconstitutional.[15]

Byers, 607 F.Supp.2d at 845–46.

---

15. *See Phillips Petroleum Co. v. Shutts,* 472 U.S. 797, 821–22, 105 S.Ct. 2965, 86 L.Ed.2d 628 (1985)(holding that "application of Kansas law to every claim in this case is sufficiently arbitrary and unfair as to exceed constitutional limits," because Kansas did not have a "significant contact or significant aggregation of contacts" to some of plaintiffs' claims).

CHAPTER VII

TOXIC EXPOSURE IN THE WORKPLACE

■ ■ ■

A. INTRODUCTION

The workplace is a significant source of injury and disease to those employed. The U.S. Bureau of Labor Statistics reports that there are almost 4 million occupational injuries and illnesses on an annual basis. While the majority of these harms are of the traumatic, accidental type, approximately five percent comprise illness due to disease. This Chapter addresses those episodes.

Toxic exposures and diseases in the workplace are different from those arising elsewhere for a number of reasons that are developed in this Chapter.

First, workers' compensation provides an alternative compensation system to tort law. Second, because only employers are subject to liability for worker's compensation, tort law also operates in the workplace with claims against "third parties," such as the manufacturer of a toxic agent used there. While workers' compensation is the "exclusive remedy" against employers, employees are generally free to sue third parties in tort for the same injury or disease. Employees often seek out third parties to sue because recoveries under workers' compensation regimes are generally much less than tort recoveries for the same injury. The special problems of determining eligibility for workers' compensation for occupational diseases is addressed in the next section of this Chapter. Tort claims against third parties are covered in section C, which also addresses the difficulties of coordination when both systems are operating for the same employee's disease.

Third, proof of causation is often more complicated in the workplace. Employees are often exposed to "cocktails" of toxic chemicals, unlike, for example, a patient who takes a prescription drug. Even when there is a single identifiable agent, as with occupational asbestos, there may be many suppliers of that asbestos, as we saw in Chapter 4. Finally, determining the dose to which employees were exposed is frequently difficult or impossible, especially retrospectively over the lengthy latency period exhibited by many toxic substances.

As with so many other risks that are the subject of this book, a regulatory regime exists to control occupational hazards. The scope of other regulatory regimes of interest (covered in Chapters 8 and 9) is based on the type of toxic agent or product. Unlike those regulatory schemes, the *Occupational Safety and Health Act* focuses on the workplace and its risks, imposing on employers, rather than manufacturers and others, obligations to control the toxic (and other) risks that exist for their employees in the workplace. That statute is the subject of section D of this Chapter.

B. WORKERS' COMPENSATION

Workers' compensation plans began in Germany in the late 1800s, as the toll of occupational injuries grew with the fundamental changes wrought by the Industrial Revolution. This idea later spread to the United States, where there was widespread dissatisfaction with the way in which injured employees were treated by the tort system. The first state plans were adopted early in the twentieth century and by mid-century had been adopted in every state.

Workers' compensation statutes were grounded in a fundamental compromise. Employers would pay all injured workers regardless of fault on the part of the employer, the worker, or fellow workers. In exchange, employees gave up their right to sue in tort, and compensation was rigidly fixed in the statute at a considerable discount to the full damages provided in tort, thus providing employers with a calculable, insurable cost of doing business. Workers' compensation became a cause-based compensation program. See Lawrence M. Friedman & Jack Ladinsky, Social Change and the Law of Industrial Accidents, 67 Colum.L.Rev. 50 (1967).

As initially conceived, workers' compensation covered workplace "accidents," sudden unexpected events that caused traumatic injury. Determining whether an injury "arose out of employment" and therefore was covered by workers' compensation was not ordinarily difficult. Workers' compensation was initially expanded to occupational diseases through scheduled lists of diseases that qualified for compensation. Later, those statutes were expanded to cover all diseases that resulted from employment.

Thus, since fault plays no role in workers' compensation cases, the "trigger" for compensation is whether an individual's injury is sufficiently work-related to entitle her to recover under the relevant act. When the disease has non-occupational sources as well, the issue becomes whether the cause was occupational or from those other sources. The following case deals with this sometimes thorny question.

LINDQUIST v. CITY OF JERSEY
CITY FIRE DEPARTMENT

New Jersey Supreme Court, 2003.
175 N.J. 244, 814 A.2d 1069.

COLEMAN, J.

The issue raised in this appeal is whether petitioner's employment as a fireman for approximately twenty-three years caused or contributed to his development of pulmonary emphysema within the meaning of the occupational disease provisions of the Workers' Compensation Act. Resolution of that issue requires us to decide how much workplace contribution is enough to trigger employer responsibility. The Judge of Compensation found that petitioner's occupational exposure materially contributed to the development of emphysema. The Appellate Division reversed, finding that the evidence was insufficient to establish medical causation between the employment and the emphysema. We disagree and reverse.

I.

Petitioner Richard Lindquist was employed as a full-time paid fireman with the City of Jersey City Fire Department from July 1972 until his retirement in January 1995. He was promoted to the rank of captain in 1979. Petitioner testified that during the first ten years of his employment, he responded to "30 to 60 large fires per year," "small one-room" fires, car fires, and "dump" fires. When he began his job in 1972, each firefighter was given a self-contained breathing apparatus, "but it was just very new and people didn't seem to use it until 1982." Although petitioner was exposed to "heavy smoke" for up to forty-five minutes to an hour and a half during larger fires, he frequently did not use the apparatus. * * * Some of the fires involved burning chemicals, plastics, household cleaners, and propane.

* * *

From 1986 to 1992, petitioner was assigned to supervise the Hazardous Materials Unit of the fire department. During that time, petitioner responded to both residential and industrial fires. The burning items consisted of plastics and chemicals, causing "much more toxic smoke than the '70s and '60s." After 1992, petitioner returned to his position as captain.

* * *

Petitioner retired in 1995 at the age of forty-seven, due in part to an early buyout offer and in part to health considerations. At the time of his retirement, petitioner was less able to perform his responsibilities as a firefighter, and in particular as captain, because his energy and normal breathing capacity gradually had diminished. * * * He also suffers from dry eyes and shortness of breath and is no longer able to play basketball with his son or take long walks with his wife. He is able to walk only one quarter to one half of a mile "before [he begins] breathing heavily." He cannot perform yard work or house work, such as "building sheds, [and] putting [together] decks," without some difficulty. * * *

Petitioner smoked approximately three-fourths of a pack of cigarettes per day for twenty-two years, stopping in 1992 or 1994. * * *

Dr. Bernard Eisenstein testified on petitioner's behalf. Dr. Eisenstein specializes in heart and lung medicine and is Board Certified in internal medicine. He performed a complete examination of petitioner on January 16, 1995, to evaluate his pulmonary disability. In addition to the physical examination, Dr. Eisenstein performed a chest x-ray, and pulmonary function studies. * * *

Based on those tests, Dr. Eisenstein concluded that petitioner suffered from "chronic obstructive pulmonary disease in the form of emphysema." He attributed petitioner's condition primarily to occupational exposure as a firefighter to fire, smoke, hazardous waste, combustion, and secondarily to cigarette smoking. However, he was unable to allocate an exact percentage to each cause. * * * The doctor concluded that, "based upon a reasonable degree of medical probability," petitioner suffered "30 percent of partial total" permanent disability. On cross-examination, Dr. Eisenstein admitted that he could not cite any studies in which non-smoking firefighters developed emphysema.

In response to Dr. Eisenstein's testimony, respondent presented the testimony of Dr. Douglas Hutt. Dr. Hutt is Board Certified in internal, pulmonary, and critical care medicine. During his examination of petitioner on December 19, 1996, petitioner informed Dr. Hutt that his primary symptom was a post-nasal drip that began one year after he retired from the fire department. * * * [Dr. Hutt] noted that petitioner "did not remember any long term symptoms that he had after any of the . . . exposures to any of [the] bad fires." * * * He * * * told Dr. Hutt that * * * his grandfather died from emphysema.

* * *

Based on the physical examination and the diagnostic testing, Dr. Hutt concluded that petitioner suffers from emphysema caused by petitioner's cigarette smoking. According to the doctor, "even though only [20%] of people that smoke cigarettes actually get emphysema, that number is [between 70 and 80%] higher if you have relatives that smoke cigarettes and get emphysema which is true in this patient's family in his grandfather." He concluded that petitioner suffered "approximately [30%] pulmonary impairment."

* * * According to the doctor, out of approximately "a hundred" studies concerning firefighters and lung disease in general, none address emphysema but rather deal with air flow obstruction, chronic bronchitis, and other "more serious diseases." He stated that he had not "seen

[studies] that specifically mention emphysema as an increased risk when you factor out cigarette smoking in firefighters." * * *

* * *

The Judge of Compensation concluded that "petitioner's occupa-tion[al] disease is due in a material degree to the occupational exposures described" during the trial. The judge also determined that petitioner had suffered an "appreciable impairment of [his] ability to carry on the ordinary pursuits of his retirement lifestyle." The judge awarded petition-er a disability of thirty percent for emphysema.

On appeal, the Appellate Division reversed in an unpublished opinion, concluding that "the evidence of the causal connection between petition-er's employment and his emphysema is insufficient to sustain the award." The court noted that the primary requirement of *N.J.S.A.* 34:15–31 is that "petitioner's disease be caused, to a material degree, by conditions in the workplace." The second requirement of the statute, according to the panel, was "that the conditions contributing to the compensable disease must be characteristic of or peculiar to a particular trade." The court concluded that the testimony of Dr. Eisenstein that " 'exposure to hazard-ous wastes played a significant role in causing [petitioner's] emphysema, and the cigarettes ... played a less dominant role,'" and his inability to assign a percentage to each cause, was "insufficient to show that petition-er's work exposure *exceeded the exposure caused by his smoking ciga-rettes*." (Emphasis added). The court also observed that Dr. Eisenstein relied "solely on petitioner's general characterizations of his work expo-sures over the years and not on any existing medical, epidemiological or scientific studies establishing causation."

* * *

We granted petitioner's petition for certification and now reverse.

II.

Petitioner argues that the Appellate Division exceeded the scope of its appellate review and ignored testimony in the record that provided an evidentiary basis to support medical causation. He also contends that * * * the higher standard adopted in *Fiore v. Consolidated Freightways,* 140 *N.J.* 452, 659 *A.*2d 436 (1995), with respect to dual causation should be limited to cardiovascular injuries and was applied improperly by the Appellate Division.

III.

* * * When our Workers' Compensation Act (Act), *N.J.S.A.* 34:15–1 to–128, originally was enacted in 1911, *L.* 1911 *c.* 95, it provided no coverage for occupational diseases. The Act was amended thirteen years later to include occupational diseases. *L.* 1924, *c.* 124. Even then, only nine specifically enumerated diseases were covered: "anthrax, lead poison-ing, mercury poisoning, arsenic poisoning, phosphorus poisoning, poison-ing from all homologues and derivatives of benzine, wood alcohol poison-

ing, chrome poisoning, and caisson disease." Eventually, the Act was amended to "replace[ ] its limited list of specific-named occupational diseases with a definitional phrase, 'compensable occupational disease.'" * * * [Currently section N.J.S.A. 34:15–31(a)] * * * defines "compensable occupational disease[s]" as those diseases established by a preponderance of the credible evidence to have arisen "out of and in the course of employment, which are due in a *material degree* to causes and conditions which are or were characteristic of or peculiar to a particular trade, occupation, process or place of employment." "Material degree" means "a degree [substantially] greater than *de minimis*." N.J.S.A. 34:15–7.2.

* * *

[T]he Act "involved a historic trade-off whereby employees relinquished their rights to pursue common-law remedies in exchange for automatic entitlement to certain, but reduced, benefits whenever they suffered injuries by [compensable] accident." *See generally* Richard A. Epstein, *The Historical Origins and Economic Structure of Workers' Compensation Law,* 16 *Ga. L.Rev.* 775 (1982). * * * That concept is sometimes referred to as the social compromise theory because of both the gain and the loss experienced by employees and employers alike. Ellen R. Peirce and Terry Morehead Dworkin, *Workers' Compensation and Occupational Disease: A Return to Original Intent,* 67 *Or. L.Rev.* 649, 653 (1988).

Consequently, when the Division of Workers' Compensation and appellate courts are called upon to decide whether a particular occupational disease is causally related to a particular employment, they should utilize the original bargain rationale for workers' compensation * * * to assist with the determination. * * *

Still another well-established principle is "the social policy of liberally construing the Act," which is social legislation designed "to implement the legislative policy of affording coverage to as many workers as possible." *Brower v. ICT Group,* 164 N.J. 367, 373, 753 A.2d 1045 (2000). * * *

[A] successful petitioner in workers' compensation generally must prove * * * causation.

It is sufficient in New Jersey to prove that the exposure to a risk or danger in the workplace was in fact a contributing cause of the injury. That means proof that the work related activities probably caused or contributed to the employee's disabling injury as a matter of medical fact. Direct causation is not required; proof establishing that the exposure caused the activation, acceleration or exacerbation of disabling symptoms is sufficient. As one commentator has observed, "[t]he legal question is how much workplace contribution will be enough to trigger the employer's liability under workers' compensation." Jordan Yospe, Note and Comment, *U.S. Industries v. Director: "Claim" Versus "Condition" in the Analysis of Workers' Compensation Cases,* 12 *Am. J.L. & Med.* 273, 275 (1986).

* * *

The petitioner has the burden to demonstrate by a preponderance of the evidence that his or her environmental exposure while fighting fires was a substantial contributing cause of his or her occupational disease. Such a petitioner is not required to "prove that the nexus between the disease and the place of employment is certain."

IV.

First, we address whether the standard articulated in *Fiore* for deciding occupational heart-attack cases applies to this case. We agree with petitioner that the discussion in *Fiore* with respect to dual causes of cardiovascular injuries requiring a petitioner to prove that his or her work exposure exceeded the exposure caused by personal factors such as cigarette smoking does not apply to non-heart cases such as this pulmonary case. * * * A higher standard was adopted for occupational heart cases because *N.J.S.A.* 34:15–7.2 was enacted to increase a petitioner's burden beyond that previously required * * *. Under [the earlier rule] there was an "assumption that employers take their employees as they find them" and that " 'ordinary work effort or strain' " was sufficient to satisfy the material-degree contribution requirement. *Fiore, supra,* 140 N.J. at 466–67, 659 A.2d 436. To make certain that the higher standard required by *N.J.S.A.* 34:15–7.2 was limited to cardiovascular and cerebrovascular cases, we stated that "a petitioner asserting an *occupational heart-disease claim* must show that the work exposure exceeds the exposure caused by the petitioner's personal-risk factors." *Fiore, supra,* 140 *N.J.* at 473, 659 A.2d 436 (emphasis added). Because *Fiore* does not apply to pulmonary cases, the Appellate Division should not have applied its holding here.

The controlling test to be applied in this case is whether the work exposure substantially contributed to the development or aggravation of emphysema. Petitioner had the burden to demonstrate by a preponderance of the evidence that his environmental exposure while fighting fires was a substantial contributing cause or aggravation of his emphysema. To satisfy that obligation, he was not required to prove that his work exposure exceeded the exposure caused by smoking cigarettes. * * *

In a case such as this one in which petitioner concedes that his personal risk factor played a significant role in developing emphysema, the Legislature has provided some relief to employers. When there are dual causes of an injury or disease, such as cigarette smoking and employment exposure, a 1979 amendment to the Act, *L.* 1979, *c.* 283, effective January 10, 1980, codified as *N.J.S.A.* 34:15–12(d), requires a credit to "be given [to] the employer or the employer's insurance carrier for the previous loss of function and the burden of proof in such matter shall rest on the employer." *Ibid.* The purpose of that amendment was to ameliorate the effect of prior law that an employer takes an employee as he finds the employee. Although that theory still pertains, the amendment permits a credit, regardless of whether or not the previous loss was work-related, "to encourage [the] hiring [of] workers with pre-existing disabilities."

* * *

VI.

A.

We now consider whether petitioner's emphysema is medically related to his work exposure. * * * Emphysema is a "[c]hronic obstructive pulmonary disease (COPD), also called chronic obstructive lung disease[. It] is a term that is used for two closely related diseases of the respiratory system: chronic bronchitis and emphysema. In many patients these diseases occur together...." Div. of Lung Diseases & Office of Prevention, Educ. & Control, Nat'l Insts. of Health, Pub. No. 95–2020, *Chronic Obstructive Pulmonary Disease* 1 (3d prtg.1995).

> * * * In the general population, emphysema usually develops in older individuals with a long smoking history. However, there is also a form of emphysema that runs in families. People with familial emphysema have a hereditary deficiency of a blood component, alpha–1–protease inhibitor, also called alpha–1–antitrypsin (AAT). The number of Americans with this genetic deficiency is quite small, probably no more than 70,000. It is estimated that 1 in 3,000 newborns have a genetic deficiency of AAT, and 1 to 3 percent of all cases of emphysema are due to AAT deficiency.

[*Id.* at 2–4 (emphasis omitted).]

Although "[c]igarette smoking is the most important risk factor for COPD ... [o]ther risk factors include age, heredity, *exposure to air pollution at work* and in the environment...." [Div. of Lung Diseases & Office of Prevention, Educ. & Control, Nat'l Insts. of Health, Pub. No. 95–2020, *Chronic Obstructive Pulmonary Disease* 1 (3d prtg.1995).] That means the National Institutes of Health has recognized that exposure to air pollutants at work can cause both chronic bronchitis and emphysema. Furthermore, "[s]cientists believe that, in addition to smoke-related processes, there must be other factors that cause emphysema in the general population since only 15 to 20 percent of smokers develop emphysema." *Id.* at 4.

* * *

B.

Predictably, the expert witnesses who testified for the parties disagreed over whether petitioner's occupational exposure contributed to his emphysema. * * *

Dr. Eisenstein agreed that emphysema can be caused exclusively by smoking cigarettes, from fighting fires and inhaling the smoke, fumes, gases, and heat alone or a combination of smoking cigarettes and occupational exposure. * * * Based on his experience in examining firefighters, Dr. Eisenstein concluded that petitioner's

emphysema is due to his work plus his smoking. * * *

* * * He stated that he could point to no study done on firefighters who are non-smokers and who had emphysema.

In contrast, Dr. Hutt testified that the emphysema was caused by petitioner's cigarette smoking and family history that revealed that his grandfather died of emphysema. * * *

Dr. Hutt also testified that although he has read many unspecified studies on lung diseases that included firefighters, none dealt with firefighting and emphysema. * * * He was unaware of any studies linking emphysema to any smoke except cigarette smoke.

* * *

C.

When, as in this case, studies of firefighters and other groups have been utilized to assist experts with the medical causation issue * * *, consideration of some or all of those studies would be useful to a reviewing court. Although the numerous studies Dr. Hutt stated that he utilized in arriving at his opinion in this matter were never identified in the record and have not been made part of the appellate record before us, our independent research has uncovered many studies in this field. We have examined some of the articles presumably reviewed by Dr. Hutt. In any event, we take judicial notice of the studies uncovered in our research. * * *

* * *

* * * The "healthy worker effect," whereby sick workers leave employment and are not included in studies, complicates most studies of disease in firefighters. To reduce that effect, two studies were performed comparing mortality in firefighters and police officers. Because the socio-economic background, smoking habits, and health requirements of these groups are similar, any increase in lung disease among firefighters is likely to have been caused by their employment. Paul A. Demers et al., *Mortality Among Firefighters From Three Northwestern United States Cities,* 49 *British J. Indus. Med.* 664, 668–69 (1992). * * * Linda Rosenstock et al., *Respiratory Mortality Among Firefighters,* 47 *British J. Indus. Med.* 462, 464 (1990).

The Demers study is a follow-up of the Rosenstock study, published two years later. It found a smaller increase in the risk of non-malignant respiratory disease for firefighters than previously thought, but nonetheless concluded that "a raised risk of emphysema was found among firefighters compared with both United States white men and police." Demers, *supra,* at 668–69. Those studies contain a predictable list of limitations, such as small sample size, difficulty in tracking subjects after retirement, vague death certificates, and inability to determine the amount and chemical content of smoke exposure. * * * Those studies comparing populations of healthy workers, similar in all relevant respects except fire smoke exposure, present the strongest scientific support for the proposition that firefighting is a significant cause of lung disease. Additional studies support that conclusion.

* * *

D.

* * *

This Court has recognized for many years that the Act is "humane social legislation designed to place the cost of work-connected injury upon the employer who may readily provide for it as an operating expense." *Tocci v. Tessler & Weiss, Inc.,* 28 N.J. 582, 586, 147 A.2d 783 (1959). * * * Similarly, this Court should be solicitous of firefighters who have demonstrated a substantial likelihood that their fire suppression duties have contributed to the development of emphysema.

* * *

When the possibility of causal connection is accepted, we cannot deny relief in all cases simply because science is unable decisively to dissipate the blur between possibility and probability. In such circumstances judges must do the best they can, with the hope their decisions square with the truth, and with a willingness to consider in succeeding cases whatever contribution scientific advances may offer.

[*Dwyer, supra,* 36 *N.J.* at 516, 178 *A.*2d 161 (Weintraub, C.J., concurring).]

More than a possibility of causal connection exists in this case. Although we do not relax the requirement that petitioner must prove his case by a preponderance of the evidence, and that his evidence must be scientifically reliable, we must examine the evidence in light of science's inability to provide conclusive answers to every question of causation. * * *

In this case, it is true that petitioner's expert did not cite any scientific studies to support his conclusion. Respondent's expert, Dr. Hutt, testified that he had read about one hundred unspecified studies concerning firefighters and lung disease, none of which established a causal link between firefighting and emphysema. However, our independent review of articles addressing firefighting and lung disease confirmed that some evidence to the contrary exists.

* * *

Dr. Hutt suggested that petitioner's family history could account for his emphysema, and studies do indicate that "familial factors" can increase the risk. * * * Alpha–1–antitrypsin deficiency is detectible by a blood test that apparently was not performed on petitioner. We therefore do not know the extent to which petitioner's family history contributed to his emphysema.

We find that enough scientific data exists in support of petitioner's case to allow a Judge of Compensation to find in petitioner's favor. * * * That conclusion is compelled by the principles that the Act represents social legislation, and is to be interpreted to expand rather than limit coverage, and that under the social compromise theory it is intended that a petitioner's burden of proof be lighter than in a common-law tort action.

The conclusion is further compelled by the fact that the studies reveal that although smoking is the most significant risk factor, some other causal factors must exist because no more than twenty percent of smokers contract emphysema. Nat'l Insts. of Health, *supra,* at 4. Both experts testified that industrial exposure can cause emphysema and that the signs and symptoms have the same manifestation regardless of whether they are caused by cigarette smoking, industrial exposure, or a combination of exposures. We reemphasize that it is not necessary for petitioner to prove that firefighting was the most significant cause of his disease. Rather, he need only show that his employment exposure contributed in a material degree to the development of his emphysema. We hold that there is sufficient scientific evidence to support the Judge of Compensation's conclusion that petitioner sustained his burden of proof. * * *

VII.

The judgment of the Appellate Division is reversed, and the judgment of the Division of Workers' Compensation is reinstated.

NOTES AND QUESTIONS

1. How is the causal question in *Lindquist* different from the causal question in the cases in Chapter 3?

2. In an omitted part of the *Lindquist* opinion, the court discussed New Jersey statutory presumption that "any condition or impairment of health of a member of a volunteer fire department caused by any disease of the respiratory system shall be held and presumed to be an occupational disease unless contrary be made to appear in rebuttal by satisfactory proof," N.J.S.A. 34: 15–43, 2, applies to members of professional fire departments. In an appendix, the court listed states with these and similar presumptions.

3. In *Lindquist,* the court had to sidestep a statute making it more difficult for those suffering from a cardiovascular injury to recover workers' compensation benefits. N.J.S.A. 34: 15–7.2. The statute was passed in response to Dwyer v. Ford Motor Co., 178 A.2d 161 (N.J.1962), in which the court awarded benefits to an individual who died on the job from a heart attack. The claimant had the burden of showing by preponderance of evidence that the ordinary work effort or strain in reasonable probability contributed in "some material degree" to the precipitation, aggravation, or acceleration of his existing heart disease and death, but did not have to show that some specific, excessive, work-related event precipitated the attack. "It is enough that a usual strain associated with the work was of itself too much at that time because of the condition of the heart, or that such routine effort in combination with the diseased condition of the heart produced the collapse." Id. at 163. The statute requires that the claimant prove by a preponderance of the evidence that "the injury or death was produced by the work effort or strain involving a substantial condition, event or happening in excess of the wear and tear of the claimant's daily living." In *Fiore,* cited in *Lindquist,* the court interpreted the statute to mean that "a petitioner asserting an *occupational heart-disease claim* must show that the work exposure exceeds the exposure caused by the petitioner's personal-risk factors." *Fiore*, 659 A.2d at 446 (emphasis added). Were this standard applied to *Lindquist*, could he recover? Do you think the claimant in *Lindquist* demonstrated that smoke encountered in his fire fighting activities contributed in a "material degree" to his emphysema? What would your answer be if a blood test indicated that he suffered from an Alpha–1–antitrypsin (AAT) deficiency? Recall that the statute defines "material degree" as "an appreciable degree or a degree substantially greater than de minimis."

4. Several times in the opinion, the court referred to the fact that only 20% of smokers develop emphysema. With respect to this fact, the court made the following statement: "The conclusion [that smoke encountered as a firefighter contributed to the claimant's emphysema] is further compelled by the fact that the studies reveal that although smoking is the most significant risk factor, some other causal factors must exist because no more than twenty percent of smokers contract emphysema." *Lindquist*, 814 A.2d at 1092. Is there a logical fallacy in this argument?

5. *Intentional torts.* Recall that workers' compensation is limited to "accidents," which means that the injuries are unintended. Thus, if an employee suffers harm as the result of an intentional tort, workers' compensation is inapplicable and the employee may bring a tort suit against the employer. Employees sometimes think that the tort system, with its more generous damages, is more attractive than workers' compensation and so they bring tort suits against their employers asserting that workers' compensation does not bar their claims. Employers rarely act with a purpose to visit harm on their employees, but recall the dual elements of intent and the alternative that intent exists, even in the absence of purpose, when the actor is substantially certain that harm will occur. Courts, thus, have been called upon to decide how significant and known the risks from toxic substances in the workplace must be to satisfy this threshold. In Helf v. Chevron U.S.A., Inc., 203 P.3d 962 (Utah 2009), the employer required the plaintiff and others to clean toxic sludge with different and cheaper methods than was standard. The employer knew its alternative method released toxic and noxious gases and, indeed, had observed a purple cloud of noxious gases arise after its first attempt at this new method. Yet the plaintiff was directed to employ the same method, without modification, on the very next shift, and she was injured. The court acknowledged that the employer was not trying to harm the employee. Nevertheless, intent could be satisfied under the substantially-certain standard. This only requires an expectation that injury would occur, in contrast with knowledge that injury is "virtually certain" to occur, according to the court. Accidents are unexpected, so if the harm is expected, the court reasoned, it is not accident and therefore outside the scope of workers' compensation. The court found its test satisfied on the facts of the case.

Suppose that an employer intentionally removes the guards from an industrial machine and the operator is injured as a result. Would the injured employee be limited to workers' compensation or would she be able to bring a tort suit under the intentional tort exception to the exclusive remedy bar? See Reed Tool Co. v. Copelin, 689 S.W.2d 404 (Tex.1985) (intentional acts that create risk do not satisfy the intent requirement; employer must intend harm).

Suppose that, in order to increase production, an employer alters its safety procedure so as to make an accident more likely. Over time, it is now substantially certain that two out of a thousand workers will be hurt, whereas under the old procedure only one out of a thousand would be hurt. Does this meet the intent requirement? See Restatement (Third) of Torts: Liability for Physical and Emotional Harm § 1 cmt. e (2010).

6. Some other harms that arise in the workplace may not be covered by workers' compensation and hence provide the employee an opportunity to bring a tort suit. Thus, in McCarthy v. Department of Social and Health Services, 759 P.2d 351 (Wash.1988), the plaintiff was disabled due to exposure to passive cigarette smoke that caused pulmonary disease. Her workers' compensation claim was denied on the grounds that her disease was neither "the result of an industrial injury, nor did it constitute an occupational disease." She then filed sued in tort, which the court held was not barred by the exclusive-remedy provision of the state's act. Some, but by no means all, states permit victims of workplace sexual harassment to pursue remedies available outside workers' compensation. See, e.g., Anderson v. Save–A–Lot, Ltd., 989 S.W.2d 277 (Tenn.1999).

7. As we have seen, employees ultimately won the expansion of workers' compensation to "disease" cases. In more recent years, a new fight has emerged as to whether workers' compensation statutes cover emotional harms unaccompanied by physical injury. See Fenwick v. Oklahoma State Penitentiary, 792 P.2d 60 (Okla.1990); Caron v. Maine Sch. Admin. Dist. No. 27, 594 A.2d 560 (Me.1991). What problems do you foresee with this expansion of coverage?

8. What do you think of the court's *ex parte* research on the causes of emphysema among firefighters? Should courts routinely engage in such activity? For a valuable discussion, see Edward K. Cheng, Independent Judicial Research in the *Daubert* Age, 56 Duke L.J. 1263 (2007).

C. COMMON LAW TORT CLAIMS

As we explained at the beginning of this Chapter, toxic exposures in the workplace present different and often more complicated causal issues. While the applicable scientific methods remain the same, often researchers are interested in different questions from the ones in which tort law is interested. As you read the next case, you will see evidence and expert testimony similar to that in Chapter 3. At the same time, ask yourself the ways in which the issues are different from those in Chapter 3.

WATTS v. RADIATOR SPECIALTY CO.

Supreme Court of Mississippi, 2008.
990 So.2d 143.

LAMAR, JUSTICE, for the Court.

¶ 1. This case comes before the Court on appeal from the Circuit Court of Smith County. Following a trial in which the jury returned a verdict for the plaintiff, Circuit Judge Robert G. Evans granted the defendants' motion for judgment notwithstanding the verdict (JNOV) after finding that the testimony of the plaintiff's expert on the issue of causation should have been excluded as scientifically unreliable. The trial court entered an order dismissing the plaintiff's case with prejudice, and the plaintiff appeals.

FACTS

¶ 2.   Plaintiff Milton C. Watts was diagnosed with small-cell lymphocytic lymphoma, a subtype of non-Hodgkin's lymphoma in 1999.[1] At the time of trial, Watts was 72 years old. Beginning in 1947, and throughout much of his career, Watts used a product called Liquid Wrench which was manufactured by Defendant Radiator Specialty Company. [footnote omitted] Liquid Wrench was made with a solvent called raffinate which contained benzene. The benzene-containing raffinate used by Radiator Specialty to manufacture Liquid Wrench was produced by Defendant U.S. Steel Corporation.[3]

¶ 3.   Watts first used Liquid Wrench while in vocational school in 1947. Watts testified that between 1953 and 1961, that he used Liquid Wrench one to five times per day while working odd jobs as a mechanic. There were times, Watts testified, where he would have to clean parts for hours at a time in a room with no ventilation. Watts began working on locomotives for a company called Masonite in 1970, and he continued to work there until his retirement in 1996. He used Liquid Wrench consistently while working on the locomotives.

¶ 4.   It is Watts's contention that his lymphoma was caused by his exposure to the benzene-containing raffinate in Liquid Wrench. It is undisputed that benzene can cause serious health problems in individuals who are exposed to it. However, the defendants contend that there is no evidence of a link between benzene exposure and small-cell lymphocytic lymphoma. * * *

COURSE OF PROCEEDINGS

        * * *

¶ 6.   The trial began on November 8, 2004, and the jury returned a verdict for Watts in the amount of $2 million.[4] Following entry of the judgement on March 9, 2005, defendants made a motion for JNOV (or, in the alternative, a new trial) claiming, *inter alia*, that the trial court had

---

1. According to testimony, there are at least twenty-five different types of non-Hodgkin's lymphoma.

3. It is undisputed that Liquid Wrench contained raffinate produced by U.S. Steel from 1960 through 1978. Plaintiff alleges that Radiator Specialty used U.S. Steel raffinate as early as 1941. However, it is Defendants' contention that U.S. Steel's raffinate was sold to Radiator Specialty only from 1960 through 1978. It is the further contention of Radiator Specialty that no one knows the formula used to produce Liquid Wrench in the 1940s and 1950s, nor is it known whether that formula included a benzene-containing agent. The period from 1960–1978 is the only time when it is undisputed that Liquid Wrench did contain benzene.

4. The jury found that Radiator Specialty was forty percent at fault and U.S. Steel was forty-five percent at fault, with the remaining fifteen percent of fault attributed to Watts's former employers.

erred in admitting the testimony of Dr. Levy as to causation. After briefing and argument on the motion, the trial court agreed that Dr. Levy's causation testimony was scientifically unreliable. In particular, the trial court found that "neither the cohort studies nor the case control studies relied upon by Dr. Levy at trial supported his opinion that a causal connection exists between benzene exposure and non-Hodgkin's lymphoma." The court entered an order granting the defendants' motion for JNOV and conditionally granting the defendants a new trial should this Court reverse the grant of JNOV. The trial court entered a judgment of dismissal with prejudice, and this appeal followed.

ANALYSIS

I. The trial court's exclusion of Dr. Levy's testimony

¶ 7. "When reviewing a trial court's decision to allow or disallow evidence, including expert testimony, we apply an abuse of discretion standard." *Canadian Nat'l/Ill. Cent. R.R. v. Hall,* 953 So.2d 1084, 1094 (Miss.2007). * * * Under Mississippi Rule of Evidence 702, trial courts are charged with being gatekeepers in evaluating the admissibility of expert testimony. *Id.* "We are confident that our learned trial judges can and will properly assume the role as gatekeeper on questions of admissibility of expert testimony." *Miss. Transp. Comm'n v. McLemore,* 863 So.2d 31, 40 (Miss.2003). * * * This rule [Mississippi's version of F.R.E. 702] makes it necessary for a trial court to apply a two-pronged inquiry when evaluating the admissibility of expert testimony: (1) is the witness qualified, and (2) is the testimony relevant and reliable? *McLemore,* 863 So.2d at 35.[5] There is no dispute that Dr. Levy was properly qualified as an expert in epidemiology and occupational medicine. Thus, the admissibility of Dr. Levy's causation testimony turns on its reliability and its relevance.

¶ 8. Dr. Levy testified as to general causation (that benzene causes non-Hodgkin's lymphoma) and specific causation (that benzene-containing Liquid Wrench caused Mr. Watts's non-Hodgkin's lymphoma). The methodology used in forming his opinion as to general causation was the review of eighteen case studies done by different researchers between 1979 and 2004. While the defendants do not challenge this methodology, they do challenge the reliability and relevance of the case studies Dr. Levy relied upon.

¶ 9. While case-study review is certainly an accepted methodology, trial courts still must be certain that the content of those case studies is relevant to the facts at hand. A review of the case studies supports the trial court's finding that Dr. Levy's testimony as to the content of the studies and their relevance to the facts of this case could easily have misled the jury. This Court recently spoke to the danger of unreliable

---

5. In *McLemore,* this Court adopted the standard prescribed by the U.S. Supreme Court in *Daubert v. Merrell Dow Pharmaceuticals Inc.,* 509 U.S. 579, 113 S.Ct. 2786, 125 L.Ed.2d 469 (1993).

expert testimony and the effect that it can have on the decision-making process of a juror.

> Juries are often in awe of expert witnesses because, when the expert witness is qualified by the court, they hear impressive lists of honors, education and experience. An expert witness has more experience and knowledge in a certain area than the average person. Therefore, juries usually place greater weight on the testimony of an expert witness than that of a lay witness.

Edmonds v. State, 955 So.2d 787, 792 (Miss.2007). Being no exception, Dr. Levy's testimony about his education and experience covered five pages of transcript. This included his testimony that he attended Tufts College in Boston and Cornell Medical School in New York, and that he obtained a master's degree in public health from the Harvard School of Public Health. Because of the weight that is given to expert testimony, it is imperative that trial judges remain steadfast in their role as gatekeepers under the *Daubert* standard.

¶ 10. In striking Dr. Levy's causation testimony, the trial court specifically cited Radiator Specialty's brief supporting the motion for JNOV. In that brief, Radiator Specialty reviewed each of the eighteen case studies and criticized Dr. Levy's reliance upon them. Of the eighteen studies Dr. Levy cited, he testified that only half showed a statistically significant increase in risk due to benzene exposure. None of the studies specifically looked at the possible risks associated with use of Liquid Wrench. None specifically studied the risks of development of non-Hodgkin's lymphoma in mechanics, Watts's profession.[8] One of the studies suggested that the reported increase in risk of non-Hodgkin's lymphoma was not occupationally related. Another of the studies, which included a review of other studies, reported no significant increase in risk of non-Hodgkin's lymphoma due to benzene exposure. Several of the studies did not provide a dose-response ratio.[9] Finally, not one study concluded that there is a causal link between benzene exposure and non-Hodgkin's lymphoma. In fact, one of the authors of a study relied upon by Dr. Levy testified that there was no legitimate basis to conclude that there is a link between benzene exposure, much less Liquid Wrench, and non-Hodgkin's lymphomas.[10]

¶ 11. These facts call into question the reliability and relevance of the studies upon which Dr. Levy based his conclusion that Liquid Wrench caused Watts's small-cell lymphocytic lymphoma. None of these studies provide a basis for the conclusion that there is a causal connection between benzene exposure and non-Hodgkin's lymphoma, much less

---

8. The studied occupations included oil refinery workers, gas station attendants, general chemical workers, and seamen on tankers.

9. A dose-response ratio is needed to indicate the level of exposure to benzene of the subjects of the study. This information is crucial under the case-study methodology to show specific causation so that Watts's level of exposure could be specifically compared to subjects with similar exposure.

10. Dr. Philip Cole, co-author of the Delzell study, testified as the defendants' expert witness.

small-cell lymphocytic lymphoma, the particular type from which Watts suffers.

¶ 12. Relevance, as defined by our standard for admitting expert testimony, depends upon whether the reasoning or methodology employed by the expert witness may be properly applied to the facts at hand. *Daubert,* 509 U.S. at 593, 113 S.Ct. 2786. Dr. Levy's testimony gave very little detail, if any, as to the specific findings of each case study and glossed over many of the findings. All that was provided to the jury were two pages which listed the author of each study, the year of the study, a one-or-two word description of the test subjects, and a number signifying the increased risk due to exposure. Based on this evidence and Dr. Levy's testimony, we cannot say that the trial court abused its discretion in excluding Dr. Levy's testimony.

¶ 13. The dissent disagrees with this conclusion, arguing that the trial court abused its discretion in excluding Dr. Levy's testimony. Specifically, the dissent takes issue with our pointing out that none of the studies concludes that there is a link between benzene exposure and non-Hodgkin's lymphoma. In support of its argument, the dissent cites *Knight v. Kirby Inland Marine Inc.,* which stated, "in epidemiology hardly any study is ever conclusive, and we do not suggest that an expert must back his or her opinion with published studies that unequivocally support his or her conclusions." At no point do we suggest that experts must rely on studies that explicitly support their testimony. The fact that not one of the studies relied upon by Dr. Levy finds a conclusive link between benzene exposure and non-Hodgkin's lymphoma is just one of the many problems with the studies cited by the trial court.

¶ 14. For example, the dissent specifically points readers to the Hayes study and its assertion that benzene-exposed workers are four times more likely to develop non-Hodgkin's lymphoma. The Hayes study itself points out that its findings with regard to non-Hodgkin's lymphoma are not statistically significant. Richard B. Hayes, et al., *Benzene and the Dose–Related Incidence of Hematologic Neoplasms in China,* J. Nat'l Cancer Inst., July 16, 1997, 1065–1071. Further, the article admits that the notably higher risk of non-Hodgkin's lymphoma was found among chemical workers who were exposed to a number of chemicals other than benzene and that the "observed risks could be due to some other exposures." *Id.* at 1070.

¶ 15. Curiously, the dissent points to this quote from the Hayes study, which makes our point even clearer:

> As in most industrial settings, the workers in this investigation were likely exposed to a number of chemicals other than benzene and the observed risks could be due to some other exposures. However, the subjects in this study were employed in a variety of occupations, and excesses of hematologic disease were not restricted to a particular subset of benzene-related occupations, with the possible exception of the notably higher risks for NHL among chemical workers. This

observation suggests that *the effects are more likely due to the common exposure to benzene than due to other exposures.*

(Emphasis added by dissent). In this passage, the authors of the study are simply pointing out that the increased risk for non-Hodgkin's lymphoma was found among general chemical workers while the other hematologic diseases analyzed in the study were not restricted to any particular occupation. The observation that the *other* blood disorders were not restricted to any particular occupation suggests that the common exposure to benzene was the cause. The quote specifically excludes non-Hodgkin's lymphoma from this finding. This is a common theme among the eighteen studies involved here. While the dissent claims that "all eighteen of the studies found some correlation between benzene exposure and non-Hodgkin's lymphoma," it must be noted that these studies involve exposures to solvents or chemicals other than just benzene. In fact, the Massoudi study analyzes "chemical exposure" in general, and never even refers to benzene exposure. Barbara L. Massoudi, et al., *A Case–Control Study of Hematopoietic and Lymphoid Neoplasms: The Role of Work in the Chemical Industry,* Am. J. Indus. Med., 1997, 31:21–27.

* * *

¶ 19.   There can be no doubt that there does exist in this instance a gap such as the one of which the Supreme Court spoke in *Joiner.* On one side of that gap is a collection of studies which is, in the dissent's own words, "to be sure, not particularly strong." On the other side is Dr. Levy's assertion that "to a reasonable degree of medical certainty" Watts's non-Hodgkin's lymphoma was caused by his exposure to Liquid Wrench. The leap across the chasm from the data in the studies to Dr. Levy's proffered opinion was more than the trial court could allow, and this Court cannot say that the ruling amounted to an abuse of discretion.

* * *

II.   The trial court's grant of JNOV

* * *

¶ 23.   We have held that it was not an abuse of discretion for the trial court to strike Dr. Levy's testimony. As that testimony was the only evidence Watts presented as to causation, the trial court's grant of JNOV was proper.

* * *

¶ 25.   **AFFIRMED.**

Diaz, Presiding Justice, Dissenting.

¶ 26.   I find that Dr. Levy's testimony is clearly admissible under Mississippi Rule of Evidence 702 and thus that the trial court abused its discretion in striking his testimony. Based on that finding, I conclude that the trial court erred in granting the defendants' motion for judgment notwithstanding the verdict. Accordingly, I cannot join the majority opinion.

¶ 27. Regarding the admissibility of Dr. Levy's testimony about general causation, the sole issue is whether his testimony is reliable. "Reliability ... is part of an inquiry under Rule 702, which is unquestionably flexible." *Poole ex rel. Poole v. Avara*, 908 So.2d 716, 723 (Miss.2005) (citing *Daubert v. Merrell Dow Pharmaceuticals, Inc.,* 509 U.S. 579, 594, 113 S.Ct. 2786, 2797, 125 L.Ed.2d 469 (1993)). " '[T]he requirement that an expert's testimony pertain to "scientific knowledge" establishes a standard of evidentiary reliability.' " *Howard v. State,* 853 So.2d 781, 804 (Miss.2003) (quoting *Daubert,* 509 U.S. at 590, 113 S.Ct. at 2795). "Scientific 'implies a grounding in the methods and procedures of science.' " *Id.* "Knowledge 'connotes more than subjective belief or unsupported speculation.' " *Id.* " 'Proposed testimony must be supported by appropriate validation—i.e., "good grounds," based on what is known.' " *Id.* In other words, in order to be admissible, Dr. Levy's testimony about general causation must be "based on sufficient facts or data...." M.R.E. 702. Accordingly, the question before this Court is whether the trial court abused its discretion by ruling that the eighteen epidemiological case studies reviewed by Dr. Levy did not provide adequate support for his opinion that there is a causal connection between exposure to benzene and the development of non-Hodgkin's lymphoma.

¶ 28. Of the eighteen epidemiological studies upon which Dr. Levy relied, nine concluded that exposure to benzene was more likely than not the cause of the type of non-Hodgkin's lymphoma developed by the individuals studied. One of these nine studies, the Hayes study, was conducted by the National Cancer Institute, which is part of the National Institutes of Health. The Hayes study (a cohort study conducted in China) involved almost 75,000 workers in many different occupations who had been exposed to benzene and a control group of more than 30,000 people who had not been exposed to benzene. The study found that workers who had been exposed to benzene for more than ten years were four times as likely to be afflicted with some form of non-Hodgkin's lymphoma than people who had not been exposed to benzene. The majority correctly notes that the authors of the Hayes study acknowledged that the findings with respect to non-Hodgkin's lymphoma were not "statistically significant." But the majority does not explain the meaning of "statistically significant." A result is considered to be statistically significant when there is only a five percent probability or less that it is attributable to mere chance. *E.g. Ottaviani v. State Univ. of N.Y.,* 875 F.2d 365, 371 (2nd Cir.1989) ("A finding of two standard deviations corresponds approximately to a one in twenty, or five percent, chance that a disparity is merely a random deviation from the norm, and most social scientists accept two standard deviations as a threshold level of statistical significance.") (internal quotation marks and citations omitted). I do not see how one can conclude that the Hayes study provides no support for Dr. Levy's testimony on the basis that its authors were not ninety-five percent confident that the increased incidence of non-Hodgkin's lymphoma among workers exposed to benzene was not "a random deviation from the norm." The majority also argues that the Hayes study does not support Dr. Levy's testimony regarding general causation because the workers studied were exposed to chemicals other than benzene. However, the majority fails to point out that, after noting this problem, the authors of the study concluded that the exposure to benzene was the most likely cause of the diseases developed by the subjects of the study:

> As in most industrial settings, the workers in this investigation were likely exposed to a number of chemicals other than benzene and the observed risks could be due to some other exposures. However, the subjects in this study were employed in a variety of occupations, and excesses of hematologic disease were not restricted to a particular subset of benzene-related occupations, with the possible exception of the notably higher risks for NHL among chemical workers. This observation suggests that *the effects are more likely due to the common exposure to benzene than due to other exposures.*

Richard B. Hayes, et al., *Benzene and the Dose–Related Incidence of Hematologic Neoplasms in China*, J. Nat'l Cancer Inst., July 16, 1997, 1065–1071, p. 1070 (emphasis added).[17]

¶ 29.   The majority misleadingly states that "not one study concluded that there is a causal link between benzene exposure and non-Hodgkin's lymphoma." While it is true that none of the studies found a *direct* causal connection between benzene exposure and non-Hodgkin's lymphoma, it is undisputed that all eighteen of the studies found some correlation between benzene exposure and non-Hodgkin's lymphoma. That none of the studies relied upon by Dr. Levy concluded that benzene exposure was *the* cause of the type of non-Hodgkin's lymphoma developed by the subjects of the study does not render Levy's testimony unreliable. *See Poole,* 908 So.2d at 723–24 ("Requiring that the subject of expert testimony be known to a certainty is not necessary either, however, because, as the *Daubert* Court pointed out, 'there are no certainties in science.'") (quoting *Daubert,* 509 U.S. at 590, 113 S.Ct. at 2795); *Knight v. Kirby Inland Marine, Inc.,* 482 F.3d 347, 351(5th Cir.2007) ("[I]n epidemiology hardly any study is ever conclusive, and we do not suggest that an expert must back his or her opinion with published studies that unequivocally support his or her conclusions.") (citations omitted); *Bonner v. ISP Technologies, Inc.,* 259 F.3d 924, 929 (8th Cir.2001) ("[T]here is no requirement that published epidemiological studies supporting an expert's opinion exist in order for the opinion to be admissible.") (citation omitted). Moreover, Dr. Levy's testimony cannot be deemed unreliable based on the fact that none of the studies upon which he relied looked at the risk of developing non-Hodgkin's lymphoma associated with the use of Liquid Wrench or the

---

17.   The majority's assertion that this "quote specifically excludes non-Hodgkin's lymphoma from this finding" is incorrect. It excludes chemical workers who developed non-Hodgkin's lymphoma, but not workers in other fields who also developed non-Hodgkin's lymphoma. The study found an increased risk for non-Hodgkin's lymphoma "among several occupational groups," not just chemical workers.

prevalence of non-Hodgkin's lymphoma among mechanics—no such studies have been conducted.

¶ 30.   Accordingly, I conclude that the studies clearly provide "good grounds" for Dr. Levy's opinion and thus that the trial court abused its discretion by ruling that his testimony regarding general causation is unreliable. *See, e.g., In re Paoli R.R. Yard PCB Litig.,* 35 F.3d 717, 746 (3rd. Cir.1994) (holding that "[t]he judge should only exclude the evidence if the flaw is large enough that the expert lacks good grounds for his or her conclusions") (internal quotation marks and citations omitted). The support provided by these studies is, to be sure, not particularly strong; however, the strength of that support goes to the weight, not the admissibility, of Dr. Levy's testimony. The defendants were given an opportunity to cross-examine Dr. Levy on the scientific basis for his opinion that exposure to benzene can cause non-Hodgkin's lymphoma; they were, moreover, allowed to call their own expert to rebut Dr. Levy's testimony. The question of whether the epidemiological studies relied upon by Dr. Levy established a connection between exposure to benzene and non-Hodgkin's lymphoma was for the jury to answer. Therefore, I find that the trial court abused its discretion by striking Dr. Levy's testimony regarding general causation.

* * *

¶ 35.   For these reasons, I would reverse and render. I dissent.

NOTES AND QUESTIONS

1.   *Special problems with toxic torts in the workplace.* As is true in many toxic tort cases, the primary legal focus of *Watts* is the admissibility of expert testimony on causation. However, *Watts* also demonstrates some of the many special problems that arise when a worker claims that workplace exposure to a specific toxic agent—here, Liquid Wrench—later caused a specific disease. Consider the reasons that the court provided for dismissing the studies relied on by Dr. Levy. What complications emerge from the rejection of these studies for determining causation in an occupational setting? Of what relevance are the facts mentioned by the court that none of the studies examined Legal Wrench and none examined non-Hodgkins Lymphoma among mechanics, Watts' occupation?

2.   In footnote 3, the court explained a dispute about when raffinate was first a component of Liquid Wrench. Why does that matter? Occupational exposure cases are frequently bedeviled by dose uncertainty. Thus, in LeBlanc v. Chevron USA, Inc., 513 F.Supp.2d 641 (E.D.La.2007), aff'd, 2010 WL 3824509 (5th Cir. 2010), the range of estimates from the low end of the defendant's expert's assessment to the high end of the plaintiffs' expert's estimate was 400%. Frequently, dose is even more difficult to determine in occupational exposure cases. See also Mitchell v. Gencorp Inc., 165 F.3d 778 (10th Cir.1999); Marsch v. Exxon Mobil Corp., 2005 WL 2246006 (E.D.Mo. 2005).

3.   Would it fair to conclude from the two opinions in *Watts* that the relevant issue, when there is a *Daubert* challenge to the admissibility of an expert's testimony on causation, is whether the scientific evidence provided by the expert is sufficient to support an inference of causation? If so, how is that inquiry on admissibility different from challenges to the sufficiency of the evidence presented by a party bearing the burden of proof?

4. *A note on terminology.* Both opinions refer to the scientific evidence relied on by Dr. Levy as "case studies." That terminology is non-standard and suggests case reports. Case reports are write-ups of individual cases of a single instance of disease, lack controls, and are almost never sufficient evidence to justify an inference of causation. Yet it is clear that Dr. Levy relied on epidemiology studies of groups of individuals that included controls. One type of study is a case-control study, explained in Chapter 3. The studies relied on by Dr. Levy were both case-control and cohort studies.

5. *Statistical significance.* The dissent stated that failure to obtain a statistically significant result means that "there is only a five percent probability or less that it is attributable to mere chance." What is wrong with that explanation of statistical significance?

6. The court vacillated between describing the plaintiff's disease as non-Hodgkins Lymphoma and small-cell lymphocytic lymphoma. Note that the more specific the relevant disease, the less likely there will be studies addressing that disease. Note also that if benzene only causes one or a few of the subtypes of non-Hodgkins Lymphoma, any study of non-Hodgkins will understate that relationship. How should a court in this situation determine the relevant disease for purposes of assessing the reliability of an expert's opinion?

7. Is the majority or the dissent more persuasive on the proper interpretation of the Hayes' study? Why?

8. The majority expressed concern that the plaintiff's expert, with his impressive credentials, would overwhelm the jury, which would be unable to critically assess his testimony. Why wouldn't any such "dazzle effect" be neutralized by the defendant's expert? The defendant's expert, Dr. Philip Cole, graduated from Yale and has an M.D. and Ph.D. degree from Johns Hopkins University where he is a Professor and Director of the Department of Pharmacology and Molecular Sciences.

In fact, several studies have found that juries are not overwhelmed by experts simply because of their credentials. Rather, juries are far more skeptical in their assessments and frequently dismiss some experts simply as "hired guns." A review of some of the research can be found in Joseph Sanders, The Merits of the Paternalistic Justification for Restrictions on the Admissibility of Expert Evidence, 33 Seton Hall L.Rev. 881, 907–08 (2003).

9. *Meshing workers' compensation and tort law.* The damages available under workers' compensation are not as generous as tort law provides—typically workers' compensation provides compensation around 1/3 of what tort law does, although there is significant variation. Thus, as in *Watts*, even if workers' compensation is available, injured employees sue third parties, such as Radiator Specialty and U.S. Steel, the manufacturers of Liquid Wrench and raffinate. Others—distributors, sellers, and other suppliers of the toxic agent—may also be sued in occupational exposure cases. Meshing workers' compensation and the tort system when an employee is successful in both depends significantly on whether joint and several liability exists and, if not, what other form of multi-defendant liability is in place.

If a jurisdiction has retained joint and several liability, the third party is liable for all of the employee's damages due to the occupational injury. Thus, in *Watts* (if joint and several liability applied—it didn't, as Mississippi has pure several liability—more on this below), Radiator Specialty and U.S. Steel would be jointly and severally liability for the full $2 million in damages found by the jury, even though the former employers were found 15% responsible. In most jurisdictions, the employer has a subrogation lien against any tort recovery by the worker for the amount of workers' compensation benefits paid, less the costs, such as attorney's fees, of obtaining the tort recovery. Thus, the employee must pay back to the employer the workers' compensation benefits previously provided. This is true regardless of the culpability of the employer and the role its conduct played in causing the employee's harm. Assuming Watts received $700,000 in workers' compensation, he would have to pay that amount, less the costs of obtaining it, to his former employers. This would leave—costs aside—the employers bearing none of the loss, the plaintiff recovering the full amount of his tort damages, and the third-party defendants paying for all of the damages.

In most joint and several jurisdictions, third-party defendants are not permitted to assert a contribution claim against the employer—against any immune party, which is what employers are because of the exclusive remedy provision of workers' compensation. Indeed, in those jurisdictions, the employer may not be joined in the suit and may not have a percentage of comparative responsibility assigned to it, unlike what occurred in *Watts*. In a few states, a third party may obtain some contribution from the employer, often limited to the amount of workers' compensation the employer paid the employee. See Lambertson v. Cincinnati Welding Corp., 257 N.W.2d 679 (Minn.1977). New York is perhaps the only state that permits full contribution from responsible employers, although this is available only when the employee has suffered a "grave injury."

The modification of joint and several liability in a number of jurisdictions changes the apportionment calculus and explains why the jury was permitted to apportion comparative responsibility to the former employers in *Watts*. In many jurisdictions with several liability, non-parties, including the employer, may be apportioned comparative responsibility in order to determine the share of each defendant. (Recall, the central idea behind several liability is that a defendant's "share" of the liability is limited to the damages discounted by the defendant's comparative share of responsibility.) Thus, even if contribution claims are barred against employers (and with several liability, contribution claims largely disappear), comparative responsibility can be assigned to non-party employers. Consider how this affects the apportionment of liability for workplace injuries: given the jury's finding that Watts suffered $2 million in damages, what would be the liability of U.S. Steel and Radiator Specialty? Is this apportionment preferable to that in joint and several liability jurisdictions? Is it preferable to the allocation that occurs in Minnesota or New York? In jurisdictions that have adopted several liability, should the employer have any subrogation rights against employee recoveries from third parties? Should it matter, based on how much comparative responsibility is assigned to the employer? To make this concrete, take the apportionment of responsibility found in *Watts* and assume that the employer claims it should recover from Watts $500,000, representing the net recovery in his tort suit reflecting the workers' compensation he had previously received. For proposals as to how to handle these problems, see Andrew R. Klein, Apportionment of Liability in Workplace Injury Cases, 26 Berkeley J.Emp. & Lab.L. 65 (2005); Jeffrey O'Connell, Bargaining for Waivers of Third–Party Tort Claims: An Answer to Products Liability Woes for Employers and Their Employees and Suppliers, 1976 U.Ill.L.F. 435 (1976).

D. THE OSH ACT AND OSHA

Like the states, Congress has recognized that workplace hazards can be a significant problem. It enacted the *Occupational Safety and Health Act of 1970* (OSH Act), 29 U.S.C. §§ 650 et seq., to help protect employees from dangerous conditions in their workplaces. Specifically, Congress found "that personal injuries and illnesses arising out of work situations impose a substantial burden upon, and are a hindrance to, interstate commerce in terms of lost production, wage loss, medical expenses, and disability compensation payments." 29 U.S.C. § 651(a).

The OSH Act creates the Occupational Safety and Health Administration, or OSHA, as part of the Department of Labor. Importantly, the OSH Act and OSHA address a wide variety of occupational hazards, not just toxic exposures. For example, OSHA offers advice and establishes requirements for employees working during hot weather, see OSHA, OSHA Offers Tips on Working Safely in Hot Weather, available at http://www. osha.gov/pls/oshaweb/owadisp.show_document?p_table=NEWS_RELEASES&p_id=18131, and many of its regulations cover basic workplace safety, such as how to operate farm equipment. 29 C.F.R. § 1928.57.

Nevertheless, the OSH Act also empowers OSHA to promulgate regulations governing worker exposure to toxic chemicals. The following decision by the U.S. Supreme Court, which is about OSHA's regulation of benzene, discusses many of the issues that can arise when OSHA seeks to protect workers from such occupational toxic exposures. As you read this case, see if you can discern the variety of approaches to worker safety that might be possible in OSHA toxic substances regulation. What does the OSH Act require with respect to toxic substances in the workplace? What was OSHA trying to accomplish in its benzene regulation with respect to avoiding risks to workers? What did it consider an acceptable risk? In contrast, how did the Supreme Court characterize acceptable risks? What roles do OSHA and the Supreme Court think that costs should play in workplace regulation of toxic substances?

INDUSTRIAL UNION DEPARTMENT, AFL–CIO
v. AMERICAN PETROLEUM INSTITUTE

United States Supreme Court, 1980.
448 U.S. 607, 100 S.Ct. 2844, 65 L.Ed.2d 1010.

MR. JUSTICE STEVENS announced the judgment of the Court and delivered an opinion, in which THE CHIEF JUSTICE and MR. JUSTICE STEWART joined and in Parts I, II, III–A, III–B, III–C and III–E of which MR. JUSTICE POWELL joined.

The Occupational Safety and Health Act of 1970 (Act), 29 U.S.C. § 651 *et seq.*, was enacted for the purpose of ensuring safe and healthful working conditions for every working man and woman in the Nation. This litigation concerns a standard promulgated by the Secretary of Labor to regulate occupational exposure to benzene, a substance which has been shown to cause cancer at high exposure levels. The principal question is whether such a showing is a sufficient basis for a standard that places the most stringent limitation on exposure to benzene that is technologically and economically possible.

The Act delegates broad authority to the Secretary to promulgate different kinds of standards. The basic definition of an "occupational safety and health standard" is found in § 3(8), which provides:

> "The term 'occupational safety and health standard' means a standard which requires conditions, or the adoption or use of one or more practices, means, methods, operations, or processes, reasonably necessary or appropriate to provide safe or healthful employment and places of employment." 29 U.S.C. § 652(8).

Where toxic materials or harmful physical agents are concerned, a standard must also comply with § 6(b)(5), which provides:

> "The Secretary, in promulgating standards dealing with toxic materials or harmful physical agents under this subsection, shall set the standard which most adequately assures, to the extent feasible, on the basis of the best available evidence, that no employee will suffer material impairment of health or functional capacity even if such employee has regular exposure to the hazard dealt with by such standard for the period of his working life. Development of standards under this subsection shall be based upon research, demonstrations, experiments, and such other information as may be appropriate. In addition to the attainment of the highest degree of health and safety protection for the employee, other considerations shall be the latest available scientific data in the field, the feasibility of the standards, and experience gained under this and other health and safety laws." 29 U.S.C. § 655(b)(5).

Wherever the toxic material to be regulated is a carcinogen, the Secretary has taken the position that no safe exposure level can be determined and that § 6(b)(5) requires him to set an exposure limit at the lowest technologically feasible level that will not impair the viability of the industries regulated. In this case, after having determined that there is a causal connection between benzene and leukemia (a cancer of the white blood cells), the Secretary set an exposure limit on airborne concentrations of benzene of one part benzene per million parts of air (1 ppm), regulated dermal and eye contact with solutions containing benzene, and imposed complex monitoring and medical testing requirements on employers whose workplaces contain 0.5 ppm or more of benzene. 29 CFR §§ 1910.1028(c), (e) (1979).

On pre-enforcement review pursuant to 29 U.S.C. § 655(f), the United States Court of Appeals for the Fifth Circuit held the regulation invalid. The court concluded that the Occupational Safety and Health Administration (OSHA) had exceeded its standard-setting authority because it had not shown that the new benzene exposure limit was "reasonably necessary or appropriate to provide safe or healthful employment" as required by § 3(8), and because § 6(b)(5) does "not give OSHA the unbridled discretion to adopt standards designed to create absolutely risk-free workplaces regardless of costs." Reaching the two provisions together, the Fifth Circuit held that the Secretary was under a duty to determine whether the benefits expected from the new standard bore a reasonable relationship to the costs that it imposed. The court noted that OSHA had made an estimate of the costs of compliance, but that the record lacked substantial evidence of any discernible benefits.

We agree with the Fifth Circuit's holding that § 3(8) requires the Secretary to find, as a threshold matter, that the toxic substance in question poses a significant health risk in the workplace and that a new, lower standard is therefore "reasonably necessary or appropriate to provide safe or healthful employment and places of employment." Unless and until such a finding is made, it is not necessary to address the further question whether the Court of Appeals correctly held that there must be a reasonable correlation between costs and benefits, or whether, as the federal parties argue, the Secretary is then required by § 6(b)(5) to promulgate a standard that goes as far as technologically and economically possible to eliminate the risk.

* * *

I

Benzene is a familiar and important commodity. It is a colorless, aromatic liquid that evaporates rapidly under ordinary atmospheric conditions. Approximately 11 billion pounds of benzene were produced in the United States in 1976. Ninety-four percent of that total was produced by the petroleum and petrochemical industries, with the remainder produced by the steel industry as a byproduct of coking operations. Benzene is used in manufacturing a variety of products including motor fuels (which may contain as much as 2% benzene), solvents, detergents, pesticides, and other organic chemicals.

The entire population of the United States is exposed to small quantities of benzene, ranging from a few parts per billion to 0.5 ppm, in the ambient air. Over one million workers are subject to additional low-level exposures as a consequence of their employment. The majority of these employees work in gasoline service stations, benzene production (petroleum refineries and coking operations), chemical processing, benzene transportation, rubber manufacturing, and laboratory operations.

Benzene is a toxic substance. Although it could conceivably cause harm to a person who swallowed or touched it, the principal risk of harm comes from inhalation of benzene vapors. When these vapors are inhaled, the benzene diffuses through the lungs and is quickly absorbed into the blood. Exposure to high concentrations produces an almost immediate effect on the central nervous system. Inhalation of concentrations of 20,000 ppm can be fatal within minutes; exposures in the range of 250 to 500 ppm can cause vertigo, nausea, and other symptoms of mild poisoning. Persistent exposures at levels above 25–40 ppm may lead to blood deficiencies and diseases of the blood-forming organs, including aplastic anemia, which is generally fatal.

Industrial health experts have long been aware that exposure to benzene may lead to various types of nonmalignant diseases. * * *

As early as 1928, some health experts theorized that there might also be a connection between benzene in the workplace and leukemia. In the late 1960's and early 1970's a number of epidemiological studies were published indicating that workers exposed to high concentrations of benzene were subject to significantly increased risk of leukemia. In a 1974 report recommending a permanent standard for benzene, the National Institute for Occupational Safety and Health NIOSH), OSHA's research arm, noted that these studies raised the "distinct possibility" that benzene caused leukemia. But, in light of the fact that all known cases had occurred at very high exposure levels, NIOSH declined to recommend a change in the 10 ppm standard, which it considered sufficient to protect against nonmalignant diseases. NIOSH suggested that further studies were necessary to determine conclusively whether there was a link between benzene and leukemia and, if so, what exposure levels were dangerous.

Between 1974 and 1976 additional studies were published which tended to confirm the view that benzene can cause leukemia, at least when exposure levels are high. In an August 1976 revision of its earlier recommendation, NIOSH stated that these studies provided "conclusive" proof of a causal connection between benzene and leukemia. Although it acknowledged that none of the intervening studies had provided the dose-response data it had found lacking two years earlier, NIOSH nevertheless recommended that the exposure limit be set low as possible. * * *

In October 1976, NIOSH sent another memorandum to OSHA, seeking acceleration of the rulemaking process and "strongly" recommending the issuance of an emergency temporary standard pursuant to § 6(c) of the Act, 29 U.S.C. § 655(c), for benzene and two other chemicals believed to be carcinogens. NIOSH recommended that a 1 ppm exposure limit be imposed for benzene. Apparently because of the NIOSH recommendation, OSHA asked its consultant to determine the cost of complying with a 1 ppm standard instead of with the "minimum feasible" standard. It also issued voluntary guidelines for benzene, recommending that exposure levels be limited to 1 ppm on an 8–hour time-weighted average basis wherever possible.

In the spring of 1976, NIOSH had selected two Pliofilm plants in St. Marys and Akron, Ohio, for an epidemiological study of the link between leukemia and benzene exposure. In April 1977, NIOSH forwarded an interim report to OSHA indicating at least a fivefold increase in the expected incidence of leukemia for workers who had been exposed to benzene at the two plants from 1940 to 1949. The report submitted to OSHA erroneously suggested that exposures in the two plants had generally been between zero and 15 ppm during the period in question. As a result of this new evidence and the continued prodding of NIOSH, OSHA did issue an emergency standard effective May 21, 1977, reducing the benzene exposure limit from 10 ppm to 1 ppm, the ceiling for exposures of up to 10 minutes from 25 ppm to 5 ppm, and eliminating the authority for peak concentrations of 50 ppm. In its explanation accompanying the emergency standard, OSHA stated that benzene had been shown to cause leukemia at exposures below 25 ppm and that, in light of its consultant's report, it was feasible to reduce the exposure limit to 1 ppm.

On May 19, 1977, the Court of Appeals for the Fifth Circuit entered a temporary restraining order preventing the emergency standard from taking effect. Thereafter, OSHA abandoned its efforts to make the emergency standard effective and instead issued a proposal for a permanent standard patterned almost entirely after the aborted emergency standard.

In its published statement giving notice of the proposed permanent standard, OSHA did not ask for comments as to whether or not benzene presented a significant health risk at exposures of 10 ppm or less. Rather, it asked for comments as to whether 1 ppm was the minimum feasible exposure limit. As OSHA's Deputy Director of Health Standards, Grover Wrenn, testified at the hearing, this formulation of the issue to be considered by the Agency was consistent with OSHA's general policy with respect to carcinogens. Whenever a carcinogen is involved, OSHA will presume that no safe level of exposure exists in the absence of clear proof establishing such a level and will accordingly set the exposure limit at the lowest level feasible. The proposed 1 ppm exposure limit in this case thus was established not on the basis of a proven hazard at 10 ppm, but rather on the basis of "OSHA's best judgment at the time of the proposal of the feasibility of compliance with the proposed standard by the [a]ffected industries." Given OSHA's cancer policy, it was in fact irrelevant whether there was any evidence at all of a leukemia risk at 10 ppm. The important point was that there was no evidence that there was *not* some risk, however small, at that level. * * *

     * * *

As presently formulated, the benzene standard is an expensive way of providing some additional protection for a relatively small number of employees. According to OSHA's figures, the standard will require capital investments in engineering controls of approximately $266 million, first-year operating costs (for monitoring, medical testing, employee training, and respirators) of $187 million to $205 million and recurring annual costs of approximately $34 million. The figures outlined in OSHA's explanation of the costs of compliance to various industries indicate that only 35,000 employees would gain any benefit from the regulation in terms of a reduction in their exposure to benzene. Over two-thirds of these workers (24,450) are employed in the rubber-manufacturing industry. Compliance costs in that industry are estimated to be rather low, with no capital costs and initial operating expenses estimated at only $34 million ($1,390 per employee); recurring annual costs would also be rather low, totaling less than $1 million. By contrast, the segment of the petroleum refining industry that produces benzene would be required to incur $24 million in capital costs and $600,000 in first-year operating expenses to provide additional protection for 300 workers ($82,000 per employee), while the petrochemical industry would be required to incur $20.9 million in capital costs and $1 million in initial operating expenses for the benefit of 552 employees ($39,675 per employee).

Although OSHA did not quantify the benefits to each category of worker in terms of decreased exposure to benzene, it appears from the economic impact study done at OSHA's direction that those benefits may be relatively small. Thus, although the current exposure limit is 10 ppm, the actual exposures outlined in that study are often considerably lower. For example, for the period 1970–1975 the petrochemical industry reported that, out of a total of 496 employees exposed to benzene, only 53 were exposed to levels between 1 and 5 ppm and only 7 (all at the same plant) were exposed to between 5 and 10 ppm.

II

The critical issue at this point in the litigation is whether the Court of Appeals was correct in refusing to enforce the 1 ppm exposure limit on the ground that it was not supported by appropriate findings.

Any discussion of the 1 ppm exposure limit must, of course, begin with the Agency's rationale for imposing that limit. The written explanation of the standard fills 184 pages of the printed appendix. Much of it is devoted to a discussion of the voluminous evidence of the adverse effects of exposure to benzene at levels of concentration well above 10 ppm. This discussion demonstrates that there is ample justification for regulating occupational exposure to benzene and that the prior limit of 10 ppm, with a ceiling of 25 ppm (or a peak of 50 ppm) was reasonable. It does not, however, provide direct support for the Agency's conclusion that the limit should be reduced from 10 ppm to 1 ppm.

The evidence in the administrative record of adverse effects of benzene exposure at 10 ppm is sketchy at best. OSHA noted that there was "no dispute" that certain nonmalignant blood disorders, evidenced by a reduction in the level of red or white cells or platelets in the blood, could result from exposures of 25–40 ppm. It then stated that several studies had indicated that relatively slight changes in normal blood values could result from exposures below 25 ppm and perhaps below 10 ppm. OSHA did not attempt to make any estimate based on these studies of how significant the risk of nonmalignant disease would be at exposures of 10 ppm or less. Rather, it stated that because of the lack of data concerning the linkage between low-level exposures and blood abnormalities, it was impossible to construct a dose-response curve at this time. OSHA did conclude, however, that the studies demonstrated that the current 10 ppm exposure limit was inadequate to ensure that no single worker would suffer a nonmalignant blood disorder as a result of benzene exposure. Noting that it is "customary" to set a permissible exposure limit by applying a safety factor of 10–100 to the lowest level at which adverse effects had been observed, the Agency stated that the evidence supported the conclusion that the limit should be set at a point "substantially less than 10 ppm" even if benzene's leukemic effects were not considered. OSHA did not state, however, that the nonmalignant effects of benzene exposure justified a reduction in the permissible exposure limit to 1 ppm.

OSHA also noted some studies indicating an increase in chromosomal aberrations in workers chronically exposed to concentrations of benzene "probably less than 25 ppm." However, the Agency took no definitive position as to what these aberrations meant in terms of demonstrable health effects and stated that no quantitative dose-response relationship had yet been established. * * *

With respect to leukemia, evidence of an increased risk (*i.e.*, a risk greater than that borne by the general population) due to benzene exposures at or below 10 ppm was even sketchier. Once OSHA acknowledged that the NIOSH study it had relied upon in promulgating the emergency standard did not support its earlier view that benzene had been shown to cause leukemia at concentrations below 25 ppm, there was only one study that provided any evidence of such an increased risk. That study, conducted by the Dow Chemical Co., uncovered three leukemia deaths, versus 0.2 expected deaths, out of a population of 594 workers; it appeared that the three workers had never been exposed to more than 2 to 9 ppm of benzene. * * * The Agency made no finding that the Dow study, any other empirical evidence, or any opinion testimony demonstrated that exposure to benzene at or below the 10 ppm level had ever in fact caused leukemia. * * *

In the end OSHA's rationale for lowering the permissible exposure limit to 1 ppm was based, not on any finding that leukemia has ever been caused by exposure to 10 ppm of benzene and that it will *not* be caused by exposure to 1 ppm, but rather on a series of assumptions indicating that some leukemias might result from exposure to 10 ppm and that the number of cases might be reduced by reducing the exposure level to 1 ppm. In reaching that result, the Agency first unequivocally concluded that benzene is a human carcinogen. Second, it concluded that industry had failed to prove that there is a safe threshold level of exposure to benzene below which no excess leukemia cases would occur. In reaching this conclusion OSHA rejected industry contentions that certain epidemiological studies indicating no excess risk of leukemia among workers exposed at levels below 10 ppm were sufficient to establish that the threshold level of safe exposure was at or above 10 ppm. It also rejected an industry witness' testimony that a dose-response curve could be constructed on the basis of the reported epidemiological studies and that this curve indicated that reducing the permissible exposure limit from 10 to 1 ppm would prevent at most one leukemia and one other cancer death every six years.

Third, the Agency applied its standard policy with respect to carcinogens, concluding that, in the absence of definitive proof of a safe level, it must be assumed that *any* level above zero presents *some* increased risk of cancer. As the federal parties point out in their brief, there are a number of scientists and public health specialists who subscribe to this view, theorizing that a susceptible person may contract cancer from the absorption of even one molecule of a carcinogen like benzene.

Fourth, the Agency reiterated its view of the Act, stating that it was required by § 6(b)(5) to set the standard either at the level that has been demonstrated to be safe or at the lowest level feasible, whichever is higher. If no safe level is established, as in this case, the Secretary's interpretation of the statute automatically leads to the selection of an exposure limit that is the lowest feasible. Because of benzene's importance to the economy, no one has ever suggested that it would be feasible to eliminate its use entirely, or to try to limit exposures to the small amounts that are omnipresent. Rather, the Agency selected 1 ppm as a workable exposure level, and then determined that compliance with that level was technologically feasible and that "the economic impact of . . . [compliance] will not be such as to threaten the financial welfare of the affected firms or the general economy." It therefore held that 1 ppm was the minimum feasible exposure level within the meaning of § 6(b)(5) of the Act.

Finally, although the Agency did not refer in its discussion of the pertinent legal authority to any duty to identify the anticipated benefits of the new standard, it did conclude that some benefits were likely to result from reducing the exposure limit from 10 ppm to 1 ppm. This conclusion was based, again, not on evidence, but rather on the assumption that the risk of leukemia will decrease as exposure levels decrease. * * *

It is noteworthy that at no point in its lengthy explanation did the Agency quote or even cite § 3(8) of the Act. It made no finding that any of the provisions of the new standard were "reasonably necessary or appropriate to provide safe or healthful employment and places of employment." Nor did it allude to the possibility that any such finding might have been appropriate.

III

Our resolution of the issues in these cases turns, to a large extent, on the meaning of and the relationship between § 3(8), which defines a health and safety standard as a standard that is "reasonably necessary and appropriate to provide safe or healthful employment," and § 6(b)(5), which directs the Secretary in promulgating a health and safety standard for toxic materials to "set the standard which most adequately assures, to the extent feasible, on the basis of the best available evidence, that no employee will suffer material impairment of health or functional capacity...."

     * * *

[W]e think it is clear that § 3(8) does apply to all permanent standards promulgated under the Act and that it requires the Secretary, before issuing any standard, to determine that it is reasonably necessary and appropriate to remedy a significant risk of material health impairment. Only after the Secretary has made the threshold determination that such a risk exists with respect to a toxic substance, would it be necessary to decide whether § 6(b)(5) requires him to select the most protective standard he can consistent with economic and technological feasibility, or whether, as respondents argue, the benefits of the regulation must be commensurate with the costs of its implementation. Because the Secretary did not make the required threshold finding in these cases, we have no occasion to determine whether costs must be weighed against benefits in an appropriate case.

     * * *

D

Given the conclusion that the Act empowers the Secretary to promulgate health and safety standards only where a significant risk of harm exists, the critical issue becomes how to define and allocate the burden of proving the significance of the risk in a case such as this, where scientific knowledge is imperfect and the precise quantification of risks is therefore impossible. The Agency's position is that there is substantial evidence in the record to support its conclusion that there is no absolutely safe level for a carcinogen and that, therefore, the burden is properly on industry to prove, apparently beyond a shadow of a doubt, that there *is* a safe level for benzene exposure. The Agency argues that, because of the uncertainties in this area, any other approach would render it helpless, forcing it to wait for the leukemia deaths that it believes are likely to occur before taking any regulatory action.

We disagree. As we read the statute, the burden was on the Agency to show, on the basis of substantial evidence, that it is at least more likely than not that long-term exposure to 10 ppm of benzene presents a significant risk of material health impairment. Ordinarily, it is the proponent of a rule or order who has the burden of proof in administrative proceedings. In some cases involving toxic substances, Congress has shifted the burden of proving that a particular substance is safe onto the party opposing the proposed rule. The fact that Congress did not follow this course in enacting the Occupational Safety and Health Act indicates that it intended the Agency to bear the normal burden of establishing the need for a proposed standard.

In this case OSHA did not even attempt to carry its burden of proof. The closest it came to making a finding that benzene presented a significant risk of harm in the workplace was its statement that the benefits to be derived from lowering the permissible exposure level from 10 to 1 ppm were "likely" to be "appreciable." * * *

* * *

Contrary to the Government's contentions, imposing a burden on the Agency of demonstrating a significant risk of harm will not strip it of its ability to regulate carcinogens, nor will it require the Agency to wait for deaths to occur before taking any action. First, the requirement that a "significant" risk be identified is not a mathematical straitjacket. It is the Agency's responsibility to determine, in the first instance, what it considers to be a "significant" risk. Some risks are plainly acceptable and others are plainly unacceptable. If, for example, the odds are one in a billion that a person will die from cancer by taking a drink of chlorinated water, the risk clearly could not be considered significant. On the other hand, if the odds are one in a thousand that regular inhalation of gasoline vapors that are 2% benzene will be fatal, a reasonable person might well consider the risk significant and take appropriate steps to decrease or eliminate it. Although the Agency has no duty to calculate the exact probability of harm, it does have an obligation to find that a significant risk is present before it can characterize a place of employment as "unsafe."

Second, OSHA is not required to support its finding that a significant risk exists with anything approaching scientific certainty. Although the Agency's findings must be supported by substantial evidence, 29 U.S.C. § 655(f), § 6(b)(5) specifically allows the Secretary to regulate on the basis of the "best available evidence." As several Courts of Appeals have held, this provision requires a reviewing court to give OSHA some leeway where its findings must be made on the frontiers of scientific knowledge. Thus, so long as they are supported by a body of reputable scientific thought, the Agency is free to use conservative assumptions in interpreting the data with respect to carcinogens, risking error on the side of overprotection rather than underprotection.

Finally, the record in this case and OSHA's own rulings on other carcinogens indicate that there are a number of ways in which the Agency can make a rational judgment about the relative significance of the risks associated with exposure to a particular carcinogen.

It should also be noted that, in setting a permissible exposure level in reliance on less-than-perfect methods, OSHA would have the benefit of a backstop in the form of monitoring and medical testing. Thus, if OSHA properly determined that the permissible exposure limit should be set at 5 ppm, it could still require monitoring and medical testing for employees exposed to lower levels. By doing so, it could keep a constant check on the validity of the assumptions made in developing the permissible exposure limit, giving it a sound evidentiary basis for decreasing the limit if it was initially set too high. Moreover, in this way it could ensure that workers who were unusually susceptible to benzene could be removed from exposure before they had suffered any permanent damage.

* * *

In this case the record makes it perfectly clear that the Secretary relied squarely on a special policy for carcinogens that imposed the burden on industry of proving the existence of a safe level of exposure, thereby avoiding the Secretary's threshold responsibility of establishing the need for more stringent standards. In so interpreting his statutory authority, the Secretary exceeded his power.

* * *

The judgment of the Court of Appeals remanding the petition for review to the Secretary for further proceedings is affirmed.

It is so ordered.

NOTES AND QUESTIONS

1. *The rest of the story.* On June 19, 1981, OSHA withdrew the benzene regulations at issue in this case. 46 Fed. Reg. 32,021. This withdrawal had the effect of reinstating the prior benzene regulations for workplaces, which imposed an 8–hour average exposure limit to airborne benzene of 10 parts per million (ppm), with a ceiling of 25 ppm and a maximum peak exposure of 50 ppm in any 10–minute period.

On April 14, 1983, several workers' unions petitioned OSHA to issue an Emergency Temporary Standard to reduce workplace exposures to benzene. The petitioners included the Oil, Chemical, and Atomic Workers Union; the Industrial Union Department, AFL–CIO; the AFL–CIO; the International Union of Allied Industrial Workers; the International Chemical Workers Union; the United Rubber, Cork, Linoleum and Plastic Workers of America; the United Steel Workers of America; the Public Citizen Health Research Group; and the American Public Health Association. What does this collection of petitioners suggest about the perception of benzene in the workplace?

In July 1983, OSHA published a notice in the Federal Register that it was soliciting information from industry and health entities to inform a new benzene rulemaking. 48 Fed. Reg. 31,412. OSHA announced that it was considering 8–hour exposure limits of 5, 1, and 0.55 ppm, on average. At the time, OSHA expected to complete the new benzene rulemaking by June 1984.

That didn't happen. In fact, the delays were so long that the petitioners filed a lawsuit in federal court seeking a mandamus order to force OSHA to complete the benzene rulemaking. As the U.S. Court of Appeals for the D.C. Circuit explained, OSHA finally issued its Notice of Proposed Rulemaking for benzene "virtually on the eve of oral argument." United Steelworkers of America, AFL–CIO v. Rubber Manufacturers Ass'n, 783 F.2d 1117, 1119 (D.C.Cir.1986). The court refused to issue the mandamus order, concluding that OSHA was not being clearly unreasonable in its delays, given the "host of complex scientific and technical issues" involved in the benzene rulemaking. Id. at 1120. In an estimated timetable produced for the court, OSHA estimated that its final rule would appear by February 1987.

OSHA issued its proposed benzene rule in December 1985 and scheduled four public hearings to occur around the country, lasting through April 1986. 50 Fed. Reg. 50,512. The proposed rule would establish an 8–hour average exposure limit to airborne benzene of 1 ppm. OSHA finally published its final benzene rule in September 1987, which finalized the 8–hour 1 ppm exposure limit, plus added a short-term exposure limit of 5 ppm over any 10–minute period. 52 Fed. Reg. 34,460.

The current (2009) OSH Act benzene regulations largely retain the 1987 benzene exposure standards. Thus, "[t]he employer shall assure that no employee is exposed to an airborne concentration of benzene in excess of one part of benzene per million parts of air (1 ppm) as an 8–hour time weighted average." 29 C.F.R. § 1910.1028(c)(1). However, the short-term exposure limit is now 5 ppm over any 15–minute period. Id. § 1910.1028(c)(2).

Why would the re-issuance of the benzene regulations take so long? What did the U.S. Supreme Court require that OSHA be able to prove before it could issue the regulations? What kind of evidence was OSHA going to need to meet that standard? What other evidence might it further need for the regulation to hold up legally?

2. *OSHA's justification for the 1 ppm standard.* One aspect of the 1987 re-issued benzene standard is the development of the relevant science between 1978, when OSHA proposed the regulation at issue in the principal case, and 1987, when it issued the final standard. As OSHA explained in its Federal Register notice:

> Since the issuance of the 1978 standard and 1980 Supreme Court decision, there have been a number of major scientific developments. The two major epidemiologic studies available at the time have been upgraded and extended. (Infante/Rinsky and Ott/Bond). Several additional major epidemiologic studies have been completed (Wong, Decoufle et al.). These continue to demonstrate that benzene exposure causes increased risk of leukemia and other blood disorders. Several recent studies have demonstrated that benzene causes multiple-site specific cancers in animals. Other studies, which took substantially longer and proved to be more complex than predicted, have definitively demonstrated that benzene is absorbed through the skin. In addition, a number of risk assessments have been performed.

A series of studies (Infante 1977, Rinsky 1981, Rinsky 1986), analyzing the mortality of workers exposed to benzene at two rubber hydrochloride manufacturing locations, demonstrated excess risk of leukemia. The most recent demonstrated a Standardized Mortality Ratio (SMR) of 337 leukemia and 409 for multiple myeloma (an SMR of 100 is the normal value if an excess is not observed. An SMR of 200 represents a 100% excess risk over normal). The Rinsky 1986 study has excellent follow-up, 98.6% of the employees were traced to determine whether they were dead or alive and if dead, the cause of death. The study also carefully analyzed extensive past exposure data and was able to assign doses to individuals exposed 10 to 40 years in the past.

The Rinsky 1986 study also demonstrates a dose-response relationship. Workers who had lower exposure to benzene had a smaller excess risk (SMR=105). Medium exposure workers experienced medium excess risks (SMR=322 & 1186) and high exposure workers, very high excess risk (SMR=6637). The dose-response relationship increases the confidence in the results, provides a stronger basis for risk assessment and provides measured as opposed to extrapolated evidence that lowering exposure substantially reduces risk.

The Ott 1978 study and the Bond 1986 follow-up study demonstrate myelogenous leukemia risks about 4 times greater for benzene-exposed workers than for the general population. Because these studies were of small numbers of employees, the confidence intervals of the relative risks are large. However, the workers were exposed to low levels of benzene with average exposure being about 5 ppm of benzene.

The Chemical Manufacturers Association sponsored a study, Wong, 1983, of workers in chemical plants. The mortalities of the benzene-exposed workers at the plant were compared to the mortalities or workers at the plants who were not exposed to benzene and to the general population. A statistically demonstrable dose response relationship between benzene exposure and leukemia was observed. The workers exposed to benzene had an excess risk of leukemia and all lymphatic and hematopoietic cancer (which includes leukemia) as compared to the workers who were not exposed to benzene. The low exposure group (180 ppm months, or 15 ppm-years of exposure; the equivalent of 5 ppm exposure for 3 years) demonstrated a relative risk of 2.10; the medium exposure group (15–60 ppm-years), a relative risk of 2.95; and the higher exposure workers (more than 60 ppm-years), a relative risk of 3.93. (Relative risk (RR) is a concept similar to SMR; 3.93 RR can be considered equivalent to a 393 SMR).

OSHA believes these studies clearly demonstrate an association between benzene exposure and increased risk of leukemia. The Agency does not believe this conclusion is now seriously challenged.

Since the 1978 standard, three animal studies have demonstrated that benzene is carcinogenic in animals. For example, the National Toxicology Program study demonstrated excess risk of several types of cancers in both sexes of rats and mice. There was clear dose response for many sites of cancer. For example, among the male rats for oral squamous cell carcinoma (cancer of the oral cavity), there were no cancers in the controls, 6 percent in the low exposure group, 10 percent in the medium exposure group and 14 percent in the high exposure group. There was excess cancer incidence down to an equivalent of 20 ppm inhalation, the lowest exposure level tested.

Benzene has also been associated with several other diseases and various toxic effects in both human beings and animals. This includes multiple myeloma, aplastic anemia, an often fatal blood disease and various other sometimes reversible blood disorders, such as leukopenia and thrombocytopenia. Benzene also has been shown to cause damage to the genetic material in both human and animal cells resulting in chromosomal aberrations.

Both the human and animal studies furnish excellent bases for risk assessment, providing far more high quality data than would be necessary for a reasonable assessment. In addition to providing better human exposure data than is normally available, the studies show clear, measured dose-response and demonstrate increased leukemia risk as a result of exposures not much above the existing levels. Moreover, the estimates of excess cancer risk from different studies are similar.

Risk assessment on benzene have been performed by a number of authoritative organizations and distinguished scientists. For example, the Environmental Protection Agency–Carcinogen Assessment Group (EPA–CAG) estimate, adjusted to occupational exposures, shows that benzene presents a risk of 34 excess leukemia deaths per 1000 workers exposed at 10 ppm and 3.4 per 1000 at 1 ppm. The International Agency for Research on Cancer's assessment, based on the Rinsky 1981 study, converted to an occupational setting, shows an excess risk of 14–140 at 10 ppm and 1.4–14 at 1 ppm. The White et al. risk assessment estimated excess leukemia risks of 44–156 at 10 ppm and 5–16 at 1 ppm.

Crump and Allen performed risk assessments using data from the three major epidemiologic studies that evaluated benzene and leukemia. Among various analyses, they use data from the Rinsky and Ott studies and a weighted cumulative dose and relative risk model. They also combined data from the Ott, Wong and Rinsky studies, and used a cumulative dose and relative risk model. This analysis utilized the most detailed exposure data available for the Rinsky study. That assessment indicated an excess risk per 1000 exposed workers of 95 leukemia deaths at 10 ppm and 10 at 1 ppm. The confidence intervals were also computed and are quite narrow. There is 95% confidence that for 1000 benzene-employees the risk is between 37 and 186 at 10 ppm and between 4 and 22 at 1 ppm.

NIOSH (Rinsky 1986) and the American Petroleum Institute (API) presented assessments utilizing a conditional logistic regression analysis. This type of analysis is more commonly used for differentiating between influencing variables than for risk assessment. It has an exponential term resulting in very large changes in risk over small changes in exposure. The NIOSH estimate of risk converted to the method of presentation used here is 634 per 1000 at 10 ppm and 5 at 1 ppm.

The API presented an assessment by Chinchilli as analyzed by Rodricks and Brett. Their preferred estimate, based on the Rinsky study, utilizing a conditional logistic regression analysis, the initial Crump exposure assessment and various adjustments, is 8 excess leukemia deaths per 1000 at 10 ppm and 0.6 at 1 ppm. However, they argued the risk will probably be lower because they believe past exposures might have been higher.

Several risk assessments based on animal data have been performed. EPA–CAG estimated 30 excess human deaths per 1000 exposed workers at 10 ppm and 3 at 1 ppm based on Zymbal gland carcinoma in female rats. This estimate is virtually identical to the risk CAG projected based upon epidemiologic data. Crump, estimated 20 and 2 excess deaths based on all squamous cell carcinomas in male mice.

52 Fed. Reg. 34,460, 34,662–63. The agency concluded that "OSHA's best estimate of risk is that 95 excess leukemia deaths per 1000 workers are associated with an average of 10 ppm for 45 years (occupational lifetime) and 10 excess leukemia deaths per 1000 workers are associated with exposure to 1 ppm benzene. These estimates are based on high quality epidemiologic studies, and represents the mid-range of estimates presented to the Agency. They are also based on a risk assessment model that is well supported for cancer risk assessment." Id. at 34,490. Responding directly to the Supreme Court's decision in the principal case, OSHA concluded

that significant risk exists at the 10 ppm level. Based on the best supported estimates of 95 excess deaths per 1000, the risk is clearly greater than the risks in riskiest occupations or the risk of one in 1000 the Supreme Court found a reasonable person might find significant.

The lowest estimate presented was 8 per 1000 at 10 ppm. That is greater than the risks of average occupations and greater than the risk the Supreme Court indicates a reasonable person might choose to reduce. Therefore even based on this estimate, OSHA would, as it also stated in its proposal, determine that the risk was significant. No major party challenged OSHA's decision to reduce exposures from 10 ppm.

Id. at 34,508.

Did OSHA in 1978 "jump the gun" on the science? How do all of these additional scientific studies help the agency to justify the 1 ppm standard?

With regard to costs, OSHA estimated that the new standard would cost over $8.8 million to implement, in 1983 dollars (not accounting for the passing through of costs to consumers). 52 Fed. Reg. at 34,516. As for benefits, OSHA estimated that "[t]he new standard will result in a reduction of at least 85 excess leukemia deaths per 1000 employees exposed at the current 10 ppm level, a 90 percent reduction," id. at 34,510, or about 230 leukemia deaths prevented in seven industries over 45 years. Id. at 34,511. In addition, there would be numerous other health benefits, such as reduction of aplastic anemia. Id. at 34,510–11.

3. *The OSH Act's regulatory requirements.* What two requirements does the OSH Act provide to govern OSHA's implementation of standards for toxic substances in the workplace? How do those two standards interact, according to the Supreme Court? When can OSHA actually issue standards to govern toxic substance exposures in the workplace? Why had OSHA failed to meet these statutory requirements in its benzene regulation?

Consider OSHA's burden of proof in light of other burdens of proof in toxic tort litigation. For example, how does OSHA's burden of proof for the benzene regulation compare to the admissibility standards under *Daubert* in a toxic tort case in federal court? (In this respect, you might note that several studies quoted in note 2 estimated a relative risk of leukemia from benzene exposure of more than 2.0. Did that help OSHA's case for the new standard?) How does OSHA's burden of proof compare to the ultimate burden of proof in toxic tort litigation? If you think the standards are ultimately different, why might Congress want different standards in a regulatory context than exist in a litigation context?

4. *Risk, cancer, toxics regulation, and the OSH Act.* As the Supreme Court made clear, the OSH Act demands that OSHA and the courts think about risk. What was OSHA's "cancer rule," and how did that rule affect OSHA's view of risked-based regulation of carcinogens? In particular, how did that rule affect its regulation of benzene exposure in the workplace? Why would OSHA have a special rule for cancer-causing substances? How did OSHA's risk tolerance under the cancer rule differ from OSHA's normal (non-carcinogen) view of risk-based regulation? What was the Supreme Court's view of acceptable and unacceptable risks? Do you agree?

Note that the Supreme Court emphasized that Congress has, in other statutory contexts, *required* "zero tolerance" of cancer-causing substances. The most famous of these provisions is the Delaney Clause. The Delaney Clause was a provision in the 1958 Food Additives Amendment to the Food, Drug and Cosmetics Act of 1938. It provided that "[t]he Secretary of the Food and Drug Administration shall not approve for use in food any chemical additive found to induce cancer in man, or, after tests, found to induce cancer in animals."

Can you see any problems with a "zero tolerance" standard for cancer-causing compounds in the workplace? Consider that even in the foods context, Congress eventually clarified that the Delaney Clause does not apply to pesticide residues found in processed foods. Food Quality Protection Act of 1996, Pub. L. No. 104–170, § 404.

5. *Worker safety, uncertainty, and the costs of regulation.* Both the Fifth Circuit and the Supreme Court seemed fairly concerned about the costs of OSHA's benzene standard, especially compared to the apparently limited benefits that it would provide. Should such cost-benefit analyses be a part of workplace safety? If so, how much is a saved life worth? When should regulators go ahead and "let people die" because the costs to industry are too expensive? Or is that even a fair question?

The use of cost-benefit analysis in the safety and environmental regulation has been highly controversial for decades, *especially* in the context of saving human lives. Many people object to putting any dollar value on a human life. For example, the George W. Bush Administration faced a near public relations disaster when it suggested that the elderly are worth less than the young—specifically, that people over 70 were worth 63% ($2.3

million) of those under 70 ($3.7 million). OMB Watch, Administration Devalues the Elderly, available at http://www.ombwatch.org/node/1268.

Nevertheless, the issues in cost-benefit analyses are more complex than they might appear. As a practical matter, some kind of rationing of costs is often necessary. For example, under the OSH Act, OSHA must pick standards that are not so prohibitively expensive that they put the relevant industries out of business.

Even so, the use of "statistical lives" and cost rationing remain controversial, as can often be seen in debates about health care reform and regulation. For example, in 2008 in the health care/Medicare context, economists at Stanford University determined that a human life was worth about $129,000. Kathleen Kingsbury, "The Value of a Human Life: $129,000," Time.com, available at http://www.time.com/time/health/article/0,8599, 1808049,00.html.

Uncertainty often complicates the use of cost-benefit analysis. What uncertainties surrounded OSHA's benzene regulation in 1978? How did OSHA try to deal with those uncertainties? Was it pursuing a precautionary approach to toxic substances regulation? Why or why not? Did the new scientific studies discussed in note 2 reduce those uncertainties? Why or why not? Interestingly, OSHA's 1987 regulation apparently went unchallenged in the courts.

6. *OSH Act standards and toxic tort litigation.* The OSH Act expressly preserves standard tort and workers' compensation remedies available to injured workers. 29 U.S.C. § 653(b)(4). That does not mean, however, that the existence of OSHA standards is or should be irrelevant in a toxic tort case. Consider the following possibilities:

- If an employer is violating the relevant OSHA standards, such as for benzene, should that qualify as negligence *per se* if the exclusive-remedy bar is inapplicable?

- Even if a relevant OSHA standard does not define negligence per se, should the standard be relevant as evidence of the employer's breach of the duty of care? Of a third-party's breach?

- Conversely, what if the employer is complying with the relevant OSHA standard, such as the benzene standard. Should that compliance be a complete defense to the employer's or a third party's toxic tort liability?

- If compliance does not provide a complete defense, should compliance with a relevant OSHA standard nevertheless be evidence that is relevant to the existence of negligence?

7. *State regulation of worker safety and health.* Section 18 of the OSH Act explicitly allows states to regulate worker safety and health, so long as OSHA has not already set a federal standard. 29 U.S.C. § 667(a). Moreover, even if OSHA has established federal standards for certain industries and/or safety issues, states can take over the administration of those standards if they submit implementation and enforcement plans to OSHA and receive OSHA's approval. Id. § 667(b), (c). Twenty-six states and territories have approved plans, although Connecticut's, New Jersey's, New York's, and the Virgin Islands' plans apply only to the states' public sectors (state and local government). OSHA, State Occupational Safety and Health Plans, available at http://www.osha.gov/dcsp/osp/index.html.

Without an approved state plan, the OSH Act and OSHA's regulations preempt related state law—regardless of whether the state requirements actually conflict with the OSHA standards or not. See Gade v. Nat'l Solid Wastes Mgmt. Ass'n, 505 U.S. 88, 98–104, 112 S.Ct. 2374, 120 L.Ed.2d 73 (1992) (holding that OSHA standards for hazardous waste workers preempted state requirements governing the training, testing, and licensing of hazardous waste site workers).

OSHA's standards and pronouncements on toxics and safe employee exposures can lead to other legal issues in the workplace, as well. You may have read the following case in an Employment Law or Employment Discrimination course. If so, reconsider it now as a toxic tort case. How should the OSH Act's goal of protecting employees from toxic substance exposures in the workplace dovetail with other federal employment law policies, such as the elimination of discrimination based on gender or sex? How should the law balance openness of and access to employment with the employer's potential tort liability for toxic substance exposures?

INTERNATIONAL UNION, UNITED AUTOMOBILE, AEROSPACE AND AGRICULTURAL IMPLEMENT WORKERS OF AMERICA, UAW v. JOHNSON CONTROLS, INC.

United States Supreme Court, 1991.
499 U.S. 187, 111 S.Ct. 1196, 113 L.Ed.2d 158.

JUSTICE BLACKMUN delivered the opinion of the Court.

In this case we are concerned with an employer's gender-based fetal-protection policy. May an employer exclude a fertile female employee from certain jobs because of its concern for the health of the fetus the woman might conceive?

I

Respondent Johnson Controls, Inc., manufactures batteries. In the manufacturing process, the element lead is a primary ingredient. Occupational exposure to lead entails health risks, including the risk of harm to any fetus carried by a female employee.

Before the Civil Rights Act of 1964 became law, Johnson Controls did not employ any woman in a battery-manufacturing job. In June 1977, however, it announced its first official policy concerning its employment of women in lead-exposure work:

> "[P]rotection of the health of the unborn child is the immediate and direct responsibility of the prospective parents. While the medical profession and the company can support them in the exercise of this responsibility, it cannot assume it for them without simultaneously infringing their rights as persons.

".... Since not all women who can become mothers wish to become mothers (or will become mothers), it would appear to be illegal discrimination to treat all who are capable of pregnancy as though they will become pregnant."

Consistent with that view, Johnson Controls "stopped short of excluding women capable of bearing children from lead exposure," but emphasized that a woman who expected to have a child should not choose a job in which she would have such exposure. The company also required a woman who wished to be considered for employment to sign a statement that she had been advised of the risk of having a child while she was exposed to lead. The statement informed the woman that although there was evidence "that women exposed to lead have a higher rate of abortion," this evidence was "not as clear ... as the relationship between cigarette smoking and cancer," but that it was, "medically speaking, just good sense not to run that risk if you want children and do not want to expose the unborn child to risk, however small...."

Five years later, in 1982, Johnson Controls shifted from a policy of warning to a policy of exclusion. Between 1979 and 1983, eight employees became pregnant while maintaining blood lead levels in excess of 30 micrograms per deciliter. This appeared to be the critical level noted by the Occupational Safety and Health Administration (OSHA) for a worker who was planning to have a family. See 29 CFR § 1910.1025 (1990). The company responded by announcing a broad exclusion of women from jobs that exposed them to lead:

"... [I]t is [Johnson Controls'] policy that women who are pregnant or who are capable of bearing children will not be placed into jobs involving lead exposure or which could expose them to lead through the exercise of job bidding, bumping, transfer or promotion rights."

The policy defined "women ... capable of bearing children" as "[a]ll women except those whose inability to bear children is medically documented." It further stated that an unacceptable work station was one where, "over the past year," an employee had recorded a blood lead level of more than 30 micrograms per deciliter or the work site had yielded an air sample containing a lead level in excess of 30 micrograms per cubic meter.

II

In April 1984, petitioners filed in the United States District Court for the Eastern District of Wisconsin a class action challenging Johnson Controls' fetal-protection policy as sex discrimination that violated Title VII of the Civil Rights Act of 1964, as amended, 42 U.S.C. § 2000e *et seq.* * * *

The District Court granted summary judgment for defendant-respondent Johnson Controls. Applying a three-part business necessity defense derived from fetal-protection cases in the Courts of Appeals for the Fourth and Eleventh Circuits, the District Court concluded that while "there is a disagreement among the experts regarding the effect of lead on the fetus," the hazard to the fetus through exposure to lead was established by "a considerable body of opinion"; that although "[e]xpert opinion has been provided which holds that lead also affects the reproductive abilities of men and women . . . [and] that these effects are as great as the effects of exposure of the fetus . . . a great body of experts are of the opinion that the fetus is more vulnerable to levels of lead that would not affect adults"; and that petitioners had "failed to establish that there is an acceptable alternative policy which would protect the fetus." The court stated that, in view of this disposition of the business necessity defense, it did not "have to undertake a bona fide occupational qualification's [sic] (BFOQ) analysis."

The Court of Appeals for the Seventh Circuit, sitting en banc, affirmed the summary judgment by a 7–to–4 vote. The majority held that the proper standard for evaluating the fetal-protection policy was the defense of business necessity; that Johnson Controls was entitled to summary judgment under that defense; and that even if the proper standard was a BFOQ, Johnson Controls still was entitled to summary judgment.

* * *

With its ruling, the Seventh Circuit became the first Court of Appeals to hold that a fetal-protection policy directed exclusively at women could qualify as a BFOQ. We granted certiorari to resolve the obvious conflict between the Fourth, Seventh, and Eleventh Circuits on this issue, and to address the important and difficult question whether an employer, seeking to protect potential fetuses, may discriminate against women just because of their ability to become pregnant.

III

The bias in Johnson Controls' policy is obvious. Fertile men, but not fertile women, are given a choice as to whether they wish to risk their reproductive health for a particular job. Section 703(a) of the Civil Rights Act of 1964, 42 U.S.C. § 2000e–2(a), prohibits sex-based classifications in terms and conditions of employment, in hiring and discharging decisions, and in other employment decisions that adversely affect an employee's status. Respondent's fetal-protection policy explicitly discriminates against women on the basis of their sex. The policy excludes women with childbearing capacity from lead-exposed jobs and so creates a facial classification based on gender. Respondent assumes as much in its brief before this Court.

Nevertheless, the Court of Appeals assumed, as did the two appellate courts that already had confronted the issue, that sex-specific fetal-protection policies do not involve facial discrimination. These courts analyzed the policies as though they were facially neutral, and had only a discriminatory effect upon the employment opportunities of women. Consequently, the courts looked to see if each employer in question had established that its policy was justified as a business necessity. The business necessity standard is more lenient for the employer than the statutory BFOQ defense. The Court of Appeals here went one step further and invoked the burden-shifting framework set forth in *Wards Cove Packing Co. v. Atonio,* 490 U.S. 642 (1989), thus requiring petitioners to bear the burden of persuasion on all questions. The court assumed that because the asserted reason for the sex-based exclusion (protecting women's unconceived offspring) was ostensibly benign, the policy was not sex-based discrimination. That assumption, however, was incorrect.

First, Johnson Controls' policy classifies on the basis of gender and childbearing capacity, rather than fertility alone. Respondent does not seek to protect the unconceived children of all its employees. Despite evidence in the record about the debilitating effect of lead exposure on the male reproductive system, Johnson Controls is concerned only with the harms that may befall the unborn offspring of its female employees. * * * Johnson Controls' policy is facially discriminatory because it requires only a female employee to produce proof that she is not capable of reproducing.

* * *

* * * Johnson Controls' policy is not neutral because it does not apply to the reproductive capacity of the company's male employees in the same way as it applies to that of the females. Moreover, the absence of a malevolent motive does not convert a facially discriminatory policy into a neutral policy with a discriminatory effect. Whether an employment practice involves disparate treatment through explicit facial discrimination does not depend on why the employer discriminates but rather on the explicit terms of the discrimination. * * * The beneficence of an employer's purpose does not undermine the conclusion that an explicit gender-based policy is sex discrimination under § 703(a) and thus may be defended only as a BFOQ.

* * *

* * * We hold that Johnson Controls' fetal-protection policy is sex discrimination forbidden under Title VII unless respondent can establish that sex is a "bona fide occupational qualification."

IV

Under § 703(e)(1) of Title VII, an employer may discriminate on the basis of "religion, sex, or national origin in those certain instances where religion, sex, or national origin is a bona fide occupational qualification reasonably necessary to the normal operation of that particular business or enterprise." 42 U.S.C. § 2000e–2(e)(1). We therefore turn to the question whether Johnson Controls' fetal-protection policy is one of those "certain instances" that come within the BFOQ exception.

* * *

Johnson Controls argues that its fetal-protection policy falls within the so-called safety exception to the BFOQ. Our cases have stressed that discrimination on the basis of sex because of safety concerns is allowed only in narrow circumstances. * * *

* * *

Our case law, therefore, makes clear that the safety exception is limited to instances in which sex or pregnancy actually interferes with the employee's ability to perform the job. This approach is consistent with the language of the BFOQ provision itself, for it suggests that permissible distinctions based on sex must relate to ability to perform the duties of the job. Johnson Controls suggests, however, that we expand the exception to allow fetal-protection policies that mandate particular standards for pregnant or fertile women. We decline to do so. * * *

* * *

V

We have no difficulty concluding that Johnson Controls cannot establish a BFOQ. Fertile women, as far as appears in the record, participate in the manufacture of batteries as efficiently as anyone else. Johnson Controls' professed moral and ethical concerns about the welfare of the next generation do not suffice to establish a BFOQ of female sterility. Decisions about the welfare of future children must be left to the parents who conceive, bear, support, and raise them rather than to the employers who hire those parents. Congress has mandated this choice through Title VII, as amended by the [Pregnancy Discrimination Act]. Johnson Controls has attempted to exclude women because of their reproductive capacity. Title VII and the PDA simply do not allow a woman's dismissal because of her failure to submit to sterilization.

Nor can concerns about the welfare of the next generation be considered a part of the "essence" of Johnson Controls' business. * * *

Johnson Controls argues that it must exclude all fertile women because it is impossible to tell which women will become pregnant while working with lead. This argument is somewhat academic in light of our conclusion that the company may not exclude fertile women at all; it perhaps is worth noting, however, that Johnson Controls has shown no "factual basis for believing that all or substantially all women would be unable to perform safely and efficiently the duties of the job involved." *Weeks v. Southern Bell Tel. & Tel. Co.*, 408 F.2d 228, 235 (CA5 1969), quoted with approval in *Dothard*, 433 U.S., at 333. Even on this sparse record, it is apparent that Johnson Controls is concerned about only a small minority of women. Of the eight pregnancies reported among the female employees, it has not been shown that any of the babies have birth defects or other abnormalities. The record does not reveal the birth rate for Johnson Controls' female workers, but national statistics show that approximately nine percent of all fertile women become pregnant each year. The birthrate drops to two percent for blue collar workers over age 30. Johnson Controls' fear of prenatal injury, no matter how sincere, does not begin to show that substantially all of its fertile women employees are incapable of doing their jobs.

VI

A word about tort liability and the increased cost of fertile women in the workplace is perhaps necessary. * * *

More than 40 States currently recognize a right to recover for a prenatal injury based either on negligence or on wrongful death. According to Johnson Controls, however, the company complies with the lead standard developed by OSHA and warns its female employees about the damaging effects of lead. It is worth noting that OSHA gave the problem of lead lengthy consideration and concluded that "there is no basis whatsoever for the claim that women of childbearing age should be excluded from the workplace in order to protect the fetus or the course of pregnancy." 43 Fed. Reg. 52952, 52966 (1978). Instead, OSHA established a series of mandatory protections which, taken together, "should effectively minimize any risk to the fetus and newborn child." *Id.*, at 52966. See 29 CFR § 1910.1025(k)(ii) (1990). Without negligence, it would be difficult for a court to find liability on the part of the employer. If, under general tort principles, Title VII bans sex-specific fetal-protection policies, the employer fully informs the woman of the risk, and the employer has not acted negligently, the basis for holding an employer liable seems remote at best.

Although the issue is not before us, Justice WHITE observes that "it is far from clear that compliance with Title VII will pre-empt state tort liability." * * * [T]he tort liability that Justice WHITE fears will punish employers for *complying* with Title VII's clear command. When it is impossible for an employer to comply with both state and federal requirements, this Court has ruled that federal law pre-empts that of the States.

      * * *

If state tort law furthers discrimination in the workplace and prevents employers from hiring women who are capable of manufacturing the product as efficiently as men, then it will impede the accomplishment of Congress' goals in enacting Title VII. Because Johnson Controls has not argued that it faces any costs from tort liability, not to mention crippling ones, the pre-emption question is not before us. * * *

The tort-liability argument reduces to two equally unpersuasive propositions. First, Johnson Controls attempts to solve the problem of reproductive health hazards by resorting to an exclusionary policy. Title VII plainly forbids illegal sex discrimination as a method of diverting attention from an employer's obligation to police the workplace. Second, the specter of an award of damages reflects a fear that hiring fertile women will cost more. The extra cost of employing members of one sex, however, does not provide an affirmative Title VII defense for a discriminatory refusal to hire members of that gender. * * *

We, of course, are not presented with, nor do we decide, a case in which costs would be so prohibitive as to threaten the survival of the employer's business. We merely reiterate our prior holdings that the incremental cost of hiring women cannot justify discriminating against them.

VII

Our holding today that Title VII, as so amended, forbids sex-specific fetal-protection policies is neither remarkable nor unprecedented. Concern for a woman's existing or potential offspring historically has been the excuse for denying women equal employment opportunities. Congress in the PDA prohibited discrimination on the basis of a woman's ability to become pregnant. We do no more than hold that the PDA means what it says.

It is no more appropriate for the courts than it is for individual employers to decide whether a woman's reproductive role is more important to herself and her family than her economic role. Congress has left this choice to the woman as hers to make.

The judgment of the Court of Appeals is reversed, and the case is remanded for further proceedings consistent with this opinion.

It is so ordered.

NOTES AND QUESTIONS

1. *The OSHA standard in the background.* What OSHA standard—and for what toxic substance—informed the background of this case? How did the employer, Johnson Controls, react to OSHA's pronouncement? Why?

2. *Employment discrimination.* What other federal statutes were relevant in this case besides the OSH Act? Why? How did the U.S. Supreme Court reconcile those policies with the potential risk to fetuses from lead exposure?

3. *Lead exposures in the workplace.* How had OSHA characterized the risks from lead at the time of this case? Is that characterization relevant in any way to the Supreme Court's decision? How did the Court seem to view the risks from lead exposure? In this case, who got to decide about worker exposure to lead—OSHA, the employer, or the employee? Why did the Court reach that conclusion?

Under the current OSHA standards for lead, "[t]he employer shall assure that no employee is exposed to lead at concentrations greater than fifty micrograms per cubic meter of air (50 μg/m^3) averaged over an 8–hour period." 29 C.F.R. § 1910.1025(c)(1). As OSHA notes in its Appendix to this standard, however, daily exposures to airborne concentrations of lead are not nearly as important as a person's overall blood-lead levels:

> Chronic overexposure to lead impairs the reproductive systems of both men and women. Overexposure to lead may result in decreased sex drive, impotence and sterility in men. *Lead can alter the structure of sperm cells raising the risk of birth defects.* There is evidence of miscarriage and

stillbirth in women whose husbands were exposed to lead or who were exposed to lead themselves. Lead exposure also may result in decreased fertility, and abnormal menstrual cycles in women. The course of pregnancy may be adversely affected by exposure to lead since lead crosses the placental barrier and poses risks to developing fetuses. *Children born of parents either one of whom were exposed to excess lead levels are more likely to have birth defects, mental retardation, behavioral disorders or die during the first year of childhood.*

* * * Prevention of adverse health effects for most workers from exposure to lead throughout a working lifetime requires that worker blood lead (PbB) levels be maintained at or below forty micrograms per one hundred grams of whole blood (40 μg/100g). *The blood lead levels of workers (both male and female workers) who intend to have children should be maintained below 30 μg/100g to minimize adverse reproductive health effects to the parents and to the developing fetus.*

The measurement of your blood lead level is the most useful indicator of the amount of lead being absorbed by your body. Blood lead levels (PbB) are most often reported in units of milligrams (mg) or micrograms of lead (1 mg=1000 mug) per 100 grams (100g), 100 milliliters (100 ml) or deciliter (dl) of blood. These three units are essentially the same. Sometime PbB's are expressed in the form of mg% or mug%. This is a shorthand notation for 100g, 100 ml, or dl.

PbB measurements show the amount of lead circulating in your blood stream, but do not give any information about the amount of lead stored in your various tissues. PbB measurements merely show current absorption of lead, not the effect that lead is having on your body or the effects that past lead exposure may have already caused. Past research into lead-related diseases, however, has focused heavily on associations between PbBs and various diseases. As a result, your PbB is an important indicator of the likelihood that you will gradually acquire a lead-related health impairment or disease.

29 C.F.R. § 1910.1025, App. A (emphasis added). Does this information support Johnson Controls' attempted rules, or does it support the U.S. Supreme Court's conclusion? Why?

Complicating the regulation of workplace exposures to airborne lead is the fact that the human body can, left to its own devices, clear lead out of the bloodstream. This is one reason why *chronic* exposures are the most important in regulating lead exposures. In contrast, in regulating benzene, OSHA was concerned about both *chronic* and *acute* exposures to benzene. Why?

4. *OSHA regulation and toxic tort lawsuits.* Johnson Controls was clearly worried about its tort liability if lead exposures in the workplace caused birth defects, as was Justice White. How did the Supreme Court handle the tort liability issue in this case? Which federal law—the OSH Act or something else—would insulate Johnson Controls from liability, according to the Court? How?

5. *Toxic exposures in the workplace, toxic torts, and assumption of risk.* Assumption of risk is a classic defense in torts lawsuits: defendant will not be liable if plaintiff knowingly assumed the risks of a particular activity or situation. Thus, for example, professional boxers and football players cannot sue each other for the standard injuries that occur during a boxing match or football game.

Assumption of risk can also be important in the workplace. Think about the women plaintiffs in this case. They *want* to work in jobs where they might be exposed to lead, which in turn might lead to birth defects in their children. Have they assumed the risks from such lead exposure, at least so far as birth defects are concerned? Compare, e.g., Del Raso v. Elgin, J. & E. Ry. Co., 228 N.E.2d 470, 482–83 (Ill.App.1967) (holding that employees continuing to strip gondola cars with knowledge that smoke from the burning lead-based paint was making them sick constituted assumption of risk, not contributory negligence, which did not bar their recovery under the Federal Employers' Liability Act), and Foreman v. Dorsey Trailers, 54 So.2d 499, 503–04 (Ala. 1951) (holding that employees' continuing exposure to lead-based paint did not constitute assumption of risk in light of the employers' overriding duty under state law to provide a safe workplace), with Grover v. Aaron Ferer & Sons, 241 N.W. 539, 541 (Neb.1932) (holding that the judge properly instructed the jury on assumption of risk when the plaintiff suffering from lead poisoning knew that he worked in a foundry where lead was used), and Whitehead v. St. Joe Lead Co., 729 F.2d 238, 251–52 (3rd Cir.1984) (holding that material questions of fact remained regarding the assumption of risk defense when an employee who spooled lead solder suffered from lead poisoning as a result of airborne lead particles coming from elsewhere in the factory).

Closely related to an employee's assumption of risk is the employer's duty to warn, because an employee cannot knowingly assume an unknown (or not reasonably suspected) risk. For example, OSHA's regulation on lead provides that:

(1) *General*.

    (i) The employer may use signs required by other statutes, regulations or ordinances in addition to, or in combination with, signs required by this paragraph.

    (ii) The employer shall assure that no statement appears on or near any sign required by this paragraph which contradicts or detracts from the meaning of the required sign.

(2) *Signs*.

    (i) The employer shall post the following warning signs in each work area where the PEL is exceeded:

WARNING

LEAD WORK AREA

POISON

NO SMOKING OR EATING

    (ii) The employer shall assure that signs required by this paragraph are illuminated and cleaned as necessary so that the legend is readily visible.

29 C.F.R. § 1910.1025(m). The regulation also requires employers to provide employees with information about potential lead exposure and training in workplace safety. Id. § 1910.1025(l).

Chapter VIII

Federal Law Regulation
of Hazardous Waste

■ ■ ■

A. INTRODUCTION

As Chapter 7 noted in connection with the Occupational Safety and Health Act (OSH Act), the federal government has taken an active role in regulating toxic substances in a variety of situations. There are now dozens of federal statutes that can be relevant to the handling, sale, and disposal of toxic and hazardous materials. The OSH Act, as you saw, seeks to protect employees from toxic exposures in the workplace and hence to prevent the occurrence of workplace toxic harms.

Disposal of hazardous wastes—both proper and improper—is a source of potential toxic torts. For example, if you have read the book or seen the movie *A Civil Action*, or if you have seen the movie *Erin Brockovich*, then you should recall that improper disposal of hazardous waste was the source of the communities' toxic exposure to a variety of hazardous substances. Moreover, in both stories, one prominent route of exposure to the toxic substances was through contaminated ground- and drinking-water. Land-based contamination of groundwater, leading to contaminated drinking water, is unfortunately both common and difficult to remedy.

This Chapter examines the two major federal statutes that govern the handling and cleanup of hazardous wastes. The Resource Conservation and Recovery Act (RCRA) seeks to control the handling of hazardous waste from its creation through its ultimate disposal in order to prevent new contamination of land and groundwater. Its companion statute, the Comprehensive Environmental Response, Compensation, and Liability Act (CERCLA), seeks to ensure that sites that have been or may become contaminated are cleaned up to safe standards.

B. RCRA: CRADLE-TO-GRAVE REGULATION OF HAZARDOUS WASTES

1. OVERVIEW OF RCRA

Congress originally enacted the *Solid Waste Disposal Act* (SWDA), 42 U.S.C. §§ 6901–6992k, in 1976, but it was the 1980 amendments to this statute in the *Resource Conservation and Recovery Act* (RCRA) that gave the statute its more common name. In the SWDA and RCRA, Congress sought to address the problem of solid and hazardous waste.

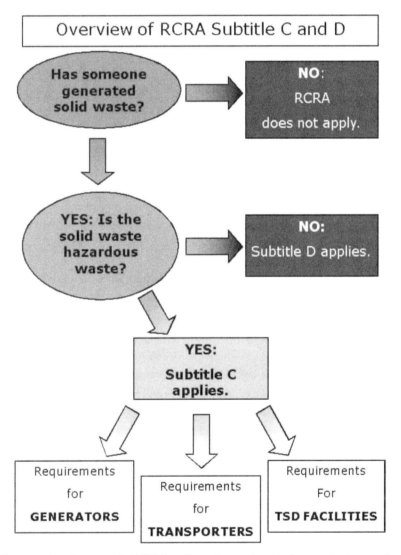

The main focus of RCRA, therefore, is to keep toxic and other hazardous materials from contaminating and polluting *land*–and, related-ly, groundwater. RCRA § 1002(b)(1), (2), 42 U.S.C. § 6901(b)(1) & (2).

However, RCRA is only a *waste disposal statute*. Specifically, RCRA is triggered by the creation of *solid waste*. Thus, RCRA does not regulate toxic and hazardous materials being used in ongoing manufacturing, production, and other forms of commercial use. Instead, other federal statutes regulate the production and use of toxic and hazardous materials, including the Occupational Safety and Health Act (OSH Act) discussed in Chapter 7 and several statutes discussed in Chapter 9—the Toxic Substances Control Act (TSCA), the Federal Insecticide, Fungicide, and Rodenticide Act (FIFRA), and the Food, Drug, and Cosmetic Act (FDCA).

Once solid waste is created, the second question for purposes of RCRA regulation is whether that solid waste is also *hazardous waste*. RCRA hazardous waste includes toxic waste.

Under RCRA, pursuant to Subtitle C, the federal Environmental Protection Agency (EPA) has primary authority for regulating hazardous waste. Subtitle C seeks to regulate and control hazardous waste from "cradle to grave"—that is, from the creation of hazardous waste by RCRA generators through its transportation by RCRA transporters to its ultimate treatment, storage, and disposal at RCRA treatment, storage, and disposal (TSD) facilities. TSD facilities are subject to the most stringent regulations under RCRA, to ensure that contamination by hazardous waste is minimized.

If solid waste is *not* hazardous, the less stringent requirements in RCRA Subtitle D apply. States have the primary authority to regulate non-hazardous solid waste under RCRA. Subtitle D seeks primarily to eliminate open dumps, to require all landfills to be sanitary landfills, and to prevent groundwater contamination from the disposal of non-hazardous waste.

In Subtitle I, RCRA regulates underground storage tanks (USTs), such as those used to store gasoline at service stations. (Subtitle I does not apply to sewage systems or to USTs that individuals use to store heating oil for personal use.) Congress sought to ensure early detection of leaks from these tanks in order to minimize contamination by the generally hazardous substances those tanks contain.

2. DEFINING "SOLID WASTE"

As noted, RCRA applies to "solid waste," which the statute defines as:

any garbage, refuse, sludge from a waste treatment plant, water supply treatment plant, or air pollution control facility and other discarded material, including solid, liquid, semisolid, or contained gaseous material resulting from industrial, commercial, mining, and agricultural operations, and from community activities, but does not include solid or dissolved material in domestic sewage, or solid or dissolved materials in irrigation return flows or industrial sources which are point sources subject to permits under section 1342 of Title 33 [the Clean Water Act], or source, special nuclear, or byproduct material as defined by the Atomic Energy Act of 1954, as amended.

RCRA § 1004(27), 42 U.S.C. § 6903(27). Several aspects of this definition are noteworthy. First, solid waste does not have to be solid—liquids, semisolids, and even some gaseous materials qualify. Second, solid waste *does* have to be waste—that is, *discarded material.* Finally, Congress expressly exempted from RCRA wastes that other federal statutes like the Atomic Energy Act already regulated.

The EPA has further defined "solid waste" in its RCRA regulations. As is generally the case for RCRA, the regulatory definitions are far more complex than the statutory definitions. However, the EPA, like Congress, has emphasized that "solid waste" is "discarded material," and that material can be discarded by being abandoned, recycled, "considered inherently waste-like," or a military munition as defined in 40 C.F.R. § 266.202. 40 C.F.R. § 261.2(a).

Abandonment is a very old concept from property law that RCRA borrows. In the following case, consider the role of abandonment in determining whether solid wastes existed.

NO SPRAY COALITION, INC. v. CITY OF NEW YORK

United States Court of Appeals for the Second Circuit, 2001.
252 F.3d 148.

Per Curiam:

In an effort to control West Nile Virus—a fatal, mosquito-borne disease—the City of New York last summer undertook an insecticide spraying program, and may renew that program in the summer of 2001. Plaintiffs appeal an order of the United States District Court for the Southern District of New York (Martin, J.), denying, inter alia, a preliminary injunction against the renewed spraying and dismissing their claim under the citizen suit provision of the Resource Conservation Recovery Act ("RCRA"), 42 U.S.C. §§ 6972(a)(1)(A) and (B). * * *

I.

The RCRA provides for an injunction where:

the past or present handling, storage, treatment, transportation, or *disposal* of *any solid* or hazardous *waste* [] may present an *imminent and substantial endangerment* to health or the environment....

Id. § 6972(a) (emphasis added). The term "solid waste"

means any garbage, refuse, sludge, from a waste treatment plant, water supply treatment plant, or air pollution control facility and *other discarded material*....

Id. § 6903(27) (emphasis added).

Plaintiffs claim, in essence, that (i) the spraying of the pesticides constitutes the "disposal" of a "solid waste" in a manner that renders it "discarded material" causing "imminent and substantial endangerment" to people, and (ii) the spraying into the air of densely populated areas is in violation of the label instructions and this improper use constitutes disposal of a hazardous solid waste without a permit, in violation of 42 U.S.C. § 6925(a).

II.

* * *

The district court did not abuse its discretion in denying injunctive relief. Plaintiffs argue that "[o]nce pesticides are sprayed onto or into the air, land, and waters of New York City, they become discarded solid wastes within the meaning of RCRA § 1004(27)." But we have indicated that material is not discarded until after it has served its intended purpose. *Cf. Connecticut Coastal Fishermen's Assoc. v. Remington Arms Co.*, 989 F.2d 1305, 1316 (2d Cir.1993). We therefore agree with the district court that the pesticides are not being "discarded" when sprayed into the air with the design of effecting their intended purpose: reaching and killing mosquitoes and their larvae.

* * *

NOTES AND QUESTIONS

1. *The definition of "disposed of."* When is a substance "disposed of" for purposes of triggering RCRA, according to the Second Circuit? Why didn't the sprayed pesticides qualify as "discarded materials"?

2. *The timing of RCRA disposal.* In Connecticut Coastal Fishermen's Ass'n v. Remington Arms Co., 989 F.2d 1305 (2d Cir.1993), cited in *No Spray Coalition*, the Second Circuit addressed a similar issue to the one in *No Spray Coalition* but reached the opposite conclusion. The case involved a skeet and trap shooting club that had been operating on Long Island Sound since 1945. As club members pursued their shooting activities, clay targets and lead shot fell into the Sound, accumulating there for over 55 years. The plaintiff argued that the club owners had violated RCRA because they had disposed of the targets and shot without proper permits. The Second Circuit agreed that the citizens had a claim under RCRA that the club "[had] created an 'imminent and substantial endangerment' to human health and the environment under § 6972(a)(1)(B)." Id. at 1316. Relying heavily on the EPA's amicus brief, the Second Circuit concluded that "the EPA states that the materials are discarded because they have been 'left to accumulate long after they have served their intended purpose.' Without deciding how long materials must accumulate before they become discarded—that is, when the shot is fired or at some later time—we agree that the lead shot and clay targets in Long Island Sound have accumulated long enough to be considered solid waste." Id. How can you explain the differences in outcome between *No Spray Coalition* and *Connecticut Coastal Fishermen's Ass'n?*

3. *RCRA and pesticides.* No Spray Coalition involved the intersection of RCRA and pesticides. As we shall see later in Chapter 9, the EPA also regulates pesticide manufacture and use pursuant to its authority under FIFRA, and New York's mosquito spraying program to eliminate the West

Nile virus also prompted challenges under FIFRA. See, e.g., Fox v. Cheminova, Inc., 387 F.Supp.2d 160, 168–69 (E.D.N.Y.2005). Nevertheless, *No Spray Coalition* remains one of very few cases, state or federal, examining the intersection of RCRA and FIFRA. After you have studied FIFRA, think about why that might be so—how do RCRA and FIFRA differ in their approaches to regulating toxic and hazardous substances?

4. *Recycling and* RCRA. Like products that are still serving their useful life after being released into the environment, industrial *recycling* can raise many issues regarding the existence of "solid waste" and hence the applicability of RCRA. The issue of recycling is one of the most complex regarding RCRA solid wastes, even though EPA's regulations presume, as a general matter, that recycled materials *qualify* as solid waste. 40 C.F.R. § 261.2(a).

In a seminal case, American Mining Congress v. United States Environmental Protection Agency, 824 F.2d 1177 (D.C.Cir.1987) (*"AMC I"*), the U.S. Court of Appeals for the D.C. Circuit concluded that RCRA did not extend to reuse of materials in an ongoing manufacturing process. The case invalidated the EPA's attempt to regulate mining and petroleum refining processes that require repeated processing of ore or crude oil, respectively. Even though this reprocessing is a form of recycling, the D.C. Circuit concluded that Congress had not intended for RCRA to reach that kind of recycling:

> RCRA was enacted, as the Congressional objectives and findings make clear, in an effort to help States deal with the ever-increasing problem of solid waste *disposal* by encouraging the search for and use of alternatives to existing methods of disposal (including recycling) and protecting health and the environment by regulating hazardous wastes. To fulfill these purposes, it seems clear that EPA need not regulate "spent" materials that are recycled and reused in an *ongoing* manufacturing or industrial process. These materials have not yet become part of the waste disposal problem; rather, *they are destined for beneficial reuse or recycling in a continuous process by the generating industry itself.*

Id. at 1185–86.

In 1990, the D.C. Circuit refined its view of "solid wastes" in American Mining Congress v. United States Environmental Protection Agency, 907 F.2d 1179 (D.C.Cir.1990) (*"AMC II"*), in which the industry petitioners challenged the EPA's regulation of six kinds of mining wastes, including wastewater sludges. According to AMC, under *AMC I* "sludges from wastewater that are stored in surface impoundments and that *may* at some time in the future be reclaimed are not 'discarded.'" Id. at 1186. The D.C. Circuit, however, disagreed:

> Petitioners read *AMC* too broadly. *AMC's* holding concerned only materials that are "destined for *immediate reuse* in another phase of the industry's ongoing production process," and that "have not yet become part of the waste disposal problem[.]" Nothing in *AMC* prevents the agency from treating as "discarded" the wastes at issue in this case, which are managed in land disposal units that *are* part of wastewater treatment systems, which *have* therefore become "part of the waste disposal problem," and which are *not* part of ongoing industrial processes.

Id. Are *AMC I* and *AMC II* reconcilable? Why or why not? How does *AMC II* refine the recycling problem for RCRA "solid wastes"?

5. *Speculatively accumulated materials.* As the *AMC II* case suggests, used or byproduct materials (*secondary materials*) that a company accumulates because there is a *possibility* that the company will reuse those materials in the future are still considered "discarded materials" for RCRA purposes. See 40 C.F.R. § 261.2(c)(4). The closed-loop recycling exemption generally applies *only* if the company *immediately* reuses the materials in an on-going manufacturing process. More specifically, the EPA will consider used materials to be speculatively accumulated, and hence subject to RCRA regulation, if: (1) there is no viable market for those materials; or (2) the regulated entity has not used 75% of the accumulated materials within a calendar year. Office of Solid Waste, U.S. E.P.A., RCRA Orientation Manual 111–7, available at http://www.epa.gov/osw/inforesources/pubs/orientat/rom31.pdf.

6. *Sham recycling.* Because RCRA's regulatory requirements can be burdensome and expensive, especially for hazardous wastes, potentially regulated entities might seek to "hide" their discarded secondary materials by injecting them back, uselessly, into ongoing manufacturing processes. The EPA considers such tactics *sham recycling*, and it will continue to regard any of the discarded materials involved as RCRA "solid wastes." In determining whether claimed recycling is legitimate recycling or sham recycling, the EPA considers a number of factors, "includ[ing] whether the secondary material is effective for the claimed use, if secondary material is used in excess of the amount necessary, and whether or not the facility has maintained records of the recycling transactions." Office of Solid Waste, U.S. E.P.A., RCRA Orientation Manual 111–9, available at, http://www.epa.gov/osw/inforesources/pubs/orientat/rom31.pdf.

7. *New "solid waste" regulations.* On October 30, 2008, the EPA issued new RCRA regulations clarifying the definition of "solid waste" in the recycling context. U.S. EPA, Revisions to the Definition of Solid Waste, 73 Fed. Reg. 64,668 (2008). The new regulations exclude several categories of recycling/reclamation from RCRA regulation. For example, the new regulations "exclude certain hazardous secondary materials (i.e., listed sludges, listed by-products, and spent materials) that are generated and legitimately reclaimed within the United States or its territories under the control of the generator, when such materials are handled only in non-land-based units (e.g., tanks, containers, or containment buildings)." Id. at 64,669 (describing the new 40 C.F.R. § 261.2(a)(2)(ii)). Most controversially, the regulations create a new (and conditional) "transfer-based exclusion" that "applies to hazardous secondary materials (i.e., spent materials, listed sludges, and listed by-products) that are generated and subsequently transferred to a different person or company for the purpose of reclamation." Id. at 64,670 (describing new 40 C.F.R. § 261.4(a)(24)).

8. *Requirements for the handling of non-hazardous solid waste: Subtitle D.* Congress included Subtitle D in RCRA in recognition of the growing non-hazardous waste disposal problem. Much of this waste is *municipal solid waste*—that is, waste collected and disposed of by local governments. In 2000, the United States generated 232 tons of municipal solid waste, 15% of which was disposed of through combustion and 30% of which was disposed of through recycling. Office of Solid Waste, U.S. E.P.A., RCRA Orientation Manual 11–4, fig. 11–3, available at http://www.epa.gov/osw/inforesources/ pubs/orientat/rom2. The remaining municipal solid waste—55% of the total generated—was disposed of on land, generally in *landfills*. Id.

States received the primary authority under RCRA to regulate non-hazardous solid waste. First, states had to enact *state solid waste management plans*. RCRA § 4003, 42 U.S.C. § 6943. To induce states to do that, Congress provided *federal financial assistance* to states that submitted qualifying plans on time. RCRA § 4007(b), 42 U.S.C. § 6947(b). In order to receive federal approval, these state plans had to meet six statutory requirements. Most importantly, states had to forbid new open dumps within their borders and provide for the closing or upgrading of all existing open dumps. RCRA § 4003(a)(2), (3), 42 U.S.C. § 6943(a)(2), (3). As part of these controls, states implement permit programs for *solid waste management facilities* to control their intake of hazardous waste. RCRA § 4005(c)(1), 42 U.S.C. § 6945(c)(1). In addition, new disposal could only occur at *sanitary landfills*. RCRA § 4004(b), 42 U.S.C. § 6944(b).

Congress also imposed new requirements for sanitary landfills. All new, replacement, and expanded landfills had to be built with at least two liners and leachate collection systems and had to provide for groundwater monitoring. RCRA § 3004(*o*), 42 U.S.C. § 6924(*o*). These requirements reflect Congress's recognition that one of the biggest problems from open dumps and nonsanitary landfills is contamination of groundwater

3. DEFINING "HAZARDOUS WASTE"

RCRA's most stringent regulatory provisions apply to *hazardous wastes*. RCRA hazardous wastes are a *subset* of RCRA solid wastes. In other words, in order to qualify as a "hazardous waste," materials must first qualify as "solid wastes," as shown in Figure VIII–1.

Like "solid waste," "hazardous waste" is defined by the statute itself. A "hazardous waste" is

> a solid waste, or combination of solid wastes, which because of its quantity, concentration, or physical, chemical, or infectious characteristics may—
>
> (A) cause, or significantly contribute to an increase in mortality or an increase in serious irreversible, or incapacitating reversible, illness; or
>
> (B) pose a substantial present or potential hazard to human health or the environment when improperly treated, stored, transported, or disposed of, or otherwise managed.

RCRA § 1004(5), 42 U.S.C. § 6903(5).

Under RCRA, the EPA has the responsibility to "develop and promulgate criteria for identifying the characteristics of hazardous waste, and for listing hazardous waste" and to actually list hazardous wastes subject to

RCRA's Subtitle C requirements, "taking into account toxicity, persistence, and degradability in nature, potential for accumulation in tissue, and other related factors such as flammability, corrosiveness, and other hazardous characteristics." RCRA § 3001(a), (b)(1), 42 U.S.C. § 6921(a), (b)(1). In addition, State Governors can petition the EPA to add particular materials to the hazardous waste lists. RCRA § 3001(c), 42 U.S.C. § 6921(c).

As a result of the EPA's rulemaking, there are two basic ways that a solid waste qualifies as a hazardous waste: (1) the solid waste may be a *characteristic hazardous waste* because it exhibits one of four regulatory characteristics; or (2) the solid waste may be a *listed hazardous waste* because the EPA specifically listed that waste as hazardous in the EPA's regulations. 40 C.F.R. § 261.3(a). A solid waste qualifies as a *characteristic hazardous waste* if it exhibits any one of four regulatory characteristics: *ignitability*; *corrosivity*; *reactivity*; or *toxicity*.

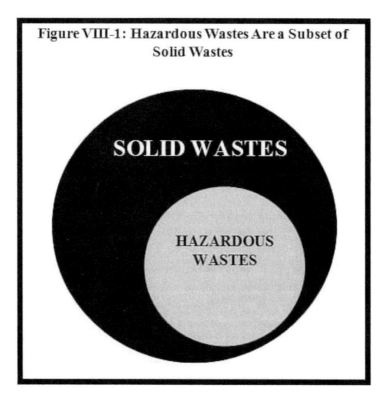

Figure VIII-1: Hazardous Wastes Are a Subset of Solid Wastes

The EPA's regulations classify a solid waste as an *ignitable hazardous waste* if: (1) the waste is a liquid with a flash point of less than 140°F; (2) the waste is a non-liquid that can catch fire at normal temperatures and pressures; (3) the waste is an ignitable condensed gas; *or* (4) the waste is an oxidizer. 40 C.F.R. § 261.21(a). A solid waste is a *corrosive hazardous waste* if: (1) it has a pH of 2 or less or a pH of 12.5 or greater (i.e., it is either a strong acid or a strong base); or (2) it corrodes steel at a rate faster than 6.35 millimeters per year at 130°F. 40 C.F.R. § 261.22. *Reactive hazardous wastes* are solid wastes that are "normally unstable" and that undergo "violent change" or react "violently with water," that generate toxic gases when mixed with water, or that can detonate or explode. Id. § 261.23.

Finally, solid wastes qualify as characteristic *toxic hazardous wastes* through *Toxicity Characteristic Leachate Procedure* (TCLP). Id. § 261.24. Under this procedure, water is run through the waste to generate a *leachate*, which is then tested for 39 chemicals. The waste is considered a characteristic hazardous waste if its leachate contains any of the chemicals listed in Figure VIII–2 in concentrations equal to or greater than the thresholds indicated.

Figure VIII-2: Toxicity Characteristic Constituents and Regulatory Levels, in Milligrams per Liter (mg/l)

EPA chart.

Waste Code	Contaminants	Concentration
D004	Arsenic	5.0
D005	Barium	100.0
D018	Benzene	0.5
D006	Cadmium	1.0
D019	Carbon tetrachloride	0.5
D020	Chlordane	0.03
D021	Chlorobenzene	100.0
D022	Chloroform	6.0
D007	Chromium	5.0
D023	o-Cresol*	200.0
D024	m-Cresol*	200.0
D025	p-Cresol*	200.0
D026	Total Cresols*	200.0
D016	2,4-D	10.0
D027	1,4-Dichlorobenzene	7.5
D028	1,2-Dichloroethane	0.5
D029	1,1-Dichloroethylene	0.7
D030	2,4-Dinitrotoluene	0.13
D012	Endrin	0.02
D031	Heptachlor (and its epoxide)	0.008
D032	Hexachlorobenzene	0.13
D033	Hexachlorobutadiene	0.5
D034	Hexachloroethane	3.0
D008	Lead	5.0
D013	Lindane	0.4
D009	Mercury	0.2
D014	Methoxychlor	10.0
D035	Methyl ethyl ketone	200.0
D036	Nitrobenzene	2.0
D037	Pentachlorophenol	100.0
D038	Pyridine	5.0
D010	Selenium	1.0
D011	Silver	5.0
D039	Tetrachloroethylene	0.7
D015	Toxaphene	0.5
D040	Trichloroethylene	0.5
D041	2,4,5-Trichlorophenol	400.0
D042	2,4,6-Trichlorophenol	2.0
D017	2,4,5-TP (Silvex)	1.0
D043	Vinyl chloride	0.2

The EPA has designated *listed hazardous wastes* in three regulations and four lists. The *F list* designates general hazardous wastes that can derive from a variety of sources, like F001, spent halogenated solvents. Id. § 261.31. The *K list,* in contrast, specifies hazardous wastes that derive from very specific sources. Id. § 261.32. K175, for example, identifies "wastewater treatment sludges from the production of vinyl chloride monomer using mercuric chloride catalyst in an acetylene-based process." Id. *P list* and *U list* hazardous wastes designate discarded commercial chemical products, such as arsenic oxide (P012), barium cyanide (P013), calcium chromate (U032), or vinyl chloride (U043). Id. § 261.33.

Characteristic and listed hazardous wastes differ in how long they are potentially subject to regulation under RCRA Subtitle C. In general, characteristic hazardous wastes, especially ignitable, corrosive, and reactive wastes, are subject to RCRA Subtitle C only so long as they exhibit the characteristic(s) that made them hazardous. For example, concentrated hydrochloric acid and concentrated sodium hydroxide both qualify as corrosive hazardous wastes. Thus, if you have a gallon of discarded concentrated hydrochloric acid and a gallon of discarded concentrated sodium hydroxide, stored separately, you have two gallons of hazardous waste. If you mix them together (carefully!), you'll end up with two gallons of salt water—and no RCRA hazardous wastes.

In contrast, listed hazardous wastes tend to remain hazardous wastes forever because of two special EPA rules. Under the EPA's *mixture rule*, when a listed hazardous waste is mixed with other materials, even non-hazardous materials, the entire resulting mixture is a listed hazardous waste. Id. § 261.3(a)(2)(iv), (b)(2). Moreover, under the *derived from rule*, any material derived from a listed hazardous waste is also a listed hazardous waste. Id. § 261.3(c)(1)(i). Thus, once a facility generates a listed hazardous waste, it is unlikely that the facility will be able to change the classification of that material. The EPA *has* created a *treatment exemption* for listed hazardous wastes that are listed because the wastes are ignitable, reactive, or corrosive (*ICR wastes*). Id. § 261.3(g)(1), (2). However, that exemption has limited application because the EPA lists most listed hazardous wastes on the basis of their *toxicity*.

4. SUBTITLE C REQUIREMENTS FOR GENERATORS

As noted, in Subtitle C, Congress aimed to address the country's hazardous waste problem through a *cradle-to-grave* regulatory and tracking program. As a result, Subtitle C regulates hazardous waste *generators*, hazardous waste *transporters*, and hazardous waste *treatment, storage, and disposal* (TSD) *facilities*.

According to RCRA, hazardous waste *generation* is "the act or process of producing hazardous waste." RCRA § 1004(6), 42 U.S.C. § 6903(6). RCRA requires the EPA to regulate hazardous waste generators "to protect human health and the environment." RCRA § 3002(a), 42 U.S.C. § 6922(a). Specifically, hazardous waste generators must:

- *keep records* that accurately identify the hazardous wastes generated;

- *properly label* containers of hazardous waste for transportation, storage, treatment, or disposal;

- *use appropriate containers* to store the hazardous waste;

- *furnish information* about the hazardous waste's chemical composition;

- *begin the manifest system* to track the hazardous waste from generation through transport to a TSD facility; and

- *file reports* with the EPA.

Id.

5. SUBTITLE C REQUIREMENTS FOR TRANSPORTERS

RCRA does not define "transporter" or "transportation." Under the EPA's RCRA regulations, however, *transportation* "means the movement of hazardous waste by air, rail, highway, or water." 40 C.F.R. § 260.11. *Transporter*, in turn, "means a person engaged in the offsite transportation of hazardous waste by air, rail, highway, or water." Id.

As was true with generators, the EPA regulates hazardous waste transporters "to protect human health and the environment." RCRA § 3003(a), 42 U.S.C. § 6923(a). Transporters must:

- *keep records* about the hazardous waste they transport, including the source and point of delivery;

- *refuse to transport* improperly labeled hazardous waste;

- *continue the manifest system* started by the generators; and

- transport hazardous waste *only to a permitted TSD facility* designated on the manifest.

Id.

6. SUBTITLE C REQUIREMENTS FOR TSD FACILITIES

Subtitle C's most onerous requirements apply to *treatment, storage, and disposal* (TSD) *facilities*. According to the statute, hazardous waste *treatment* is:

> any method, technique, or process, including neutralization, designed to change the physical, chemical, or biological character or composition of any hazardous waste so as to neutralize such waste or so as to render such waste nonhazardous, safer for transport, amenable for recovery, amenable for storage, or reduced in volume.

RCRA § 1004(34), 42 U.S.C. § 6903(34). *Storage*, in turn, is "the containment of hazardous waste, either on a temporary basis or for a period of years, in such a manner as not to constitute disposal of such hazardous waste." RCRA § 1004(33), 42 U.S.C. § 6903(33). Finally, *disposal* is:

the discharge, deposit, injection, dumping, spilling, leaking, or placing or any solid waste or hazardous waste into or on any land or water so that such solid waste or hazardous waste or any constituent thereof may enter the environment or be emitted into the air or discharged into any waters, including ground waters.

RCRA § 1004(3), 42 U.S.C. § 6903(3).

Any facility that treats, stores, or disposes of hazardous waste is subject to RCRA Subtitle C's provisions for TSD facilities. TSD facilities must:

- *maintain records* of all hazardous wastes that they treat, store, and/or dispose of, including the manner in which those wastes were treated, stored, or disposed of;

- comply with *reporting, monitoring, and inspection requirements*;

- *complete the manifest* started by the generator;

- treat, store, and/or dispose of hazardous waste *in accordance with EPA's regulations*;

- comply with EPA's requirements regarding the *location, design, and construction of the facility;*

- generate *contingency* plans in case of emergencies;

- comply with *financial responsibility requirements*; and

- get a RCRA *permit*.

RCRA § 3004(a), 42 U.S.C. § 6924(a).

The permitting process for RCRA TSD facilities is complex, long, and expensive. For facilities that intend to become TSD facilities, being properly permitted as a RCRA TSD facility can result in a profitable business of treating and disposing hazardous wastes. However, for facilities that do *not* intend to become TSD facilities but who accidentally trigger the "treatment," "storage," and/or "disposal" categories, RCRA liability can be quite onerous.

In addition to having to complete this lengthy permitting process, TSD facilities become liable for *corrective actions*—that is, for cleanups at the TSD facility and beyond the TSD facility if hazardous wastes escape from the TSD facility. RCRA § 3004(v), 42 U.S.C. § 6924(v). Corrective actions are intended to prevent problems at TSD facilities from becoming significantly contaminated sites requiring clean-up under the Comprehensive Environmental Response, Compensation, and Liability Act (CERCLA).

Consider the various TSD facility issues raised in the following EPA enforcement action.

UNITED STATES v. POWER ENGINEERING CO.

United States Court of Appeals for the Tenth Circuit, 1999.
191 F.3d 1224.

EBEL, CIRCUIT JUDGE.

Plaintiff–Appellee United States, acting on behalf of the Environmental Protection Agency ("EPA"), sought a mandatory preliminary injunction directing Defendant–Appellants Power Engineering Company ("PEC"), Redoubt, Ltd., and Richard J. Lilienthal (collectively, "Defendants"), to comply with the financial assurance regulations adopted by the Colorado Department of Public Health and Environment ("CDPHE") under authority delegated to Colorado by the EPA pursuant to the Resource Conservation and Recovery Act of 1976 ("RCRA"). The district court granted the mandatory preliminary injunction, requiring Defendants to provide financial assurances in the amount of $3,500,000 to ensure remediation of ground and water contamination caused by chromium and other by-products of PEC's metal refinishing business. Defendants appeal the grant of the preliminary injunction. We affirm.

I. BACKGROUND

Statutory and Regulatory Background

In 1976, Congress enacted RCRA, a comprehensive statutory scheme providing cradle-to-grave oversight of solid and hazardous waste. RCRA's Subtitle C, 42 U.S.C. §§ 6921–39, governs the generation, transportation, storage, disposal, and treatment of hazardous wastes to minimize present and future threats to human health and the environment. To that end, section 3004 of RCRA, 42 U.S.C. § 6924, directs the EPA to promulgate regulations establishing standards for owners and operators of hazardous waste facilities, such as standards for "financial responsibility (including financial responsibility for corrective action) as may be necessary or desirable." 42 U.S.C. § 6924(a)(6). Section 3004 also permits the EPA to promulgate regulations establishing standards for compliance with section 3005 of RCRA. *See* 42 U.S.C. § 6924(a)(7). Section 3005 of RCRA, 42 U.S.C. § 6925, prohibits any person from treating, storing, or disposing of hazardous waste or constructing any hazardous waste facility for such treatment, storage, or disposal without (1) a permit issued pursuant to Section 3005; or (2) designation of "interim status," obtained by notifying the EPA of the person's hazardous waste activities and submitting an application for a permit. 42 U.S.C. § 6925(a) & (e).

If authorized by the EPA, a state may "carry out [its own hazardous waste] program in lieu of the Federal program" under Subtitle C and "issue and enforce permits for the storage, treatment, or disposal of hazardous waste." 42 U.S.C. § 6926(b). Action taken by a state pursuant to its federally authorized program has "the same force and effect as action taken by the [EPA]." 42 U.S.C. § 6926(d).

Pursuant to EPA authorization, Colorado implemented its own hazardous waste program, and promulgated regulations governing generators of hazardous waste and the operation and maintenance of hazardous waste treatment, storage, and disposal facilities. Colorado's regulations are substantially identical to the EPA's regulations, such that analysis of the federal scheme can "overlay[ ] and define[ ] that of Colorado." *See Sierra Club v. United States Dept. of Energy,* 734 F. Supp. 946, 947 (D.Colo.1990). Among the state's regulations are the so-called financial assurance requirements, * * * which require owners and operators of all hazardous waste facilities to document that they have secured the financial resources required for closure and, if necessary, post-closure of their facilities in an appropriate and safe manner, and to pay third-party claims that may arise from their operations. * * *

  * * *

Parties

The United States is the plaintiff acting on behalf of the EPA. PEC is a Colorado corporation located in Denver. From approximately 1968, PEC has operated a business of refinishing metal crankshafts, connecting rods, and rod journals for large diesel engines used in heavy equipment. Redoubt owns the land and buildings leased to PEC, and thus is the owner of PEC's facility under Colorado regulations. Lilienthal is the president of PEC and owns 51% of the outstanding stock of both PEC and Redoubt. For purposes of the preliminary injunction motion, Lilienthal agreed that he is an "owner" and "operator" of PEC and as such subject to any order entered by the district court directing Defendants to secure financial assurances.

Nature of the Case

PEC's refurbishing operations produce more than 1,000 kilograms of hazardous waste per month, and the facility stores more than 6,000 kilograms per month. The facility generates approximately thirteen different waste streams, including arsenic, lead, mercury, and hexavalent chromium contaminated media. In 1992, Denver Health and Hospitals ("DHH") contacted the CDPHE concerning a discharge into the Platte River of high levels of hexavalent chromium. After investigation, DHH determined that PEC was the likely sources of the discharge. The CDPHE then conducted compliance review inspections at PEC in August and September of 1992, and reported numerous violations of federal and state regulations governing the treatment, storage, and disposal of hazardous waste, which the district court set out at length. In addition, PEC never applied for a permit or obtained interim status.

Although PEC notified the CDPHE in 1986 that it was a generator of certain hazardous waste, PEC failed to assess adequately its generation, treatment, storage, and disposal of hazardous waste, and the CDPHE did not know the severity and extent of PEC's noncompliance with the state hazardous waste program until the August 1992 inspection. As a result of

PEC's illegal storage and disposal of hazardous waste, groundwater at and under the facility, as well as groundwater under areas outside the facility, is contaminated with levels of hexavalent chromium greatly exceeding established toxicity levels. A plume of chrome contamination extends from the facility approximately 3,310 feet into the South Platte Valley Fill Aquifer, which is connected to the South Platte River.

After inspecting PEC's facility again in 1993 and 1994, the CDPHE issued an Initial Compliance Order on June 28, 1994. That order was stayed at PEC's request, while PEC and the CDPHE held conferences between 1994 and 1996. The CDPHE then issued a Final Administrative Compliance Order on June 13, 1996 ("Order"). While complying with certain requirements of the Order, PEC failed to meet others. Accordingly, on December 26, 1996, the CDPHE issued an Administrative Penalty Order assessing civil penalties of approximately $1,875,000. Defendants did not appeal the penalty, but neither have they paid any portion of it.

The EPA was displeased with the manner in which the CDPHE sought to enforce the RCRA regulations. At the EPA's request, the United States exercised its authority to seek Defendant's compliance with the state regulations. As part of its suit, the United States sought a mandatory preliminary injunction directing Defendants to comply with the regulations for financial assurances. After a hearing, the district court granted the preliminary injunction pursuant to § 3008(a) of RCRA, 42 U.S.C. § 6928(a), and Fed. R. Civ. P. 65. Defendants now appeal.

II. DISCUSSION

Standard of Review

We review the grant of a preliminary injunction for abuse of discretion. Granting a preliminary injunction is proper where the moving party shows: (1) a substantial likelihood of success on the merits; (2) irreparable harm in the absence of an injunction; (3) the threatened harm outweighs injury which the injunction may cause the opposing party; and (4) the injunction will not be adverse to the public interest. * * * We review the underlying issues of law decided by the district court de novo.

The district court found all four factors supporting a preliminary injunction. As the government notes, Defendants on appeal do not appear to challenge the finding of the latter three factors. Rather, Defendants challenge the applicability of RCRA and state implementing regulations, an attack that goes to the government's likelihood of success on the merits. Additionally, Defendants raise questions about the appropriateness of a preliminary injunction ordering financial assurances. We address Defendants' arguments in turn.

A.

Defendants challenge the district court's holding that PEC currently disposes of hazardous waste, an activity which would subject it to Colorado's regulations for facilities treating, storing, or disposing of hazardous waste ("TSD facilities"). We agree with the district court.

Colorado regulations define a TSD facility as "a location at which hazardous waste is subjected to treatment, storage, or disposal and may include a facility where hazardous waste is generated." C.C.R. § 260.10. Under the regulations, "[a] generator [of hazardous waste] who treats, stores, or disposes of hazardous waste on-site must comply with the applicable standards and permit requirements set forth in Parts 264, 265, 266, and Part 100 of these regulations." C.C.R. § 262.10 n. 2. C.C.R. § 266 further provides that its financial assurance requirements "apply to owners and operators of all hazardous waste facilities." C.C.R. § 266.10(a). RCRA and the state regulations define "disposal" as

> the discharge, deposit, injection, dumping, spilling, leaking, or placing of any solid or hazardous waste into or on any land or water so that such solid waste or hazardous waste or any constituent thereof may enter the environment or be emitted into the air or discharged into any waters, including ground waters.

42 U.S.C. § 6903(3); C.C.R. § 260.10.

For substantially the same reasons discussed thoroughly in the district court's opinion, we find that Defendants currently are disposing of hazardous wastes illegally in three ways:

> (1) the Facility's air scrubbers dispose a mist of hexavalent chromium onto Facility soil; (2) the Facility failed to remediate the soil contaminated by a yellow/orange liquid that leaked from air scrubbers down the west side of the Facility's main building; and (3) the Facility failed to remediate the three open waste piles of contaminated soil excavated from beneath the chrome-plating tanks and the remaining contaminated soil located beneath the chrome-plating tanks.

PEC, 10 F.Supp.2d at 1157, 1157–60.

Furthermore, we conclude that PEC is subject to Colorado's financial assurance requirements. By stipulation before the district court for purposes of the preliminary injunction motion, the parties agreed that PEC "is and was a 'generator' " of hazardous waste as defined by RCRA and Colorado regulations. Thus, PEC "must comply with the applicable standards and permit requirements" of the Colorado regulations for generators of hazardous waste who are TSD facilities, including the financial assurance requirements of § 266. C.C.R. § 262.10 n. 2. Additionally, those financial assurance requirements "apply to" Redoubt and Lilienthal as "owners and operators of [a] hazardous waste facilit[y]." C.C.R. § 266.10(a).

We do not find Defendants' argument to the contrary persuasive. Defendants contend that, even if they are disposers of hazardous waste, they are not a disposal facility and therefore not a TSD facility. Defendants rely on C.C.R. § 260.10, which defines a "disposal facility" as a facility "at which hazardous waste is *intentionally* placed into or on any land or water, *and at which waste will remain after closure.*" Defendants argue that because they intend "to remedy the contamination of the site while PEC is still a going concern," no waste will remain after closure, thereby precluding them from being a disposal facility by definition.

We find no merit to this argument. Defendants essentially contend that any generator currently disposing of hazardous waste on their facility does not have to comply with regulations for TSD facilities so long as they intend to clean up the waste before closure. There is no basis in the provision cited for such a sweeping subjective loophole. As an initial matter, the intent element in the definition of "disposal facility" pertains to whether hazardous waste was "intentionally placed" on land or water, not whether the polluter intends the hazardous waste to remain. As the EPA has indicated, the purpose of the intent element in the definition of "disposal facility" is "to indicate the [EPA's] intent that the term does not apply to activities involving truly accidental discharge of hazardous waste," because the EPA posits that "permits logically can only be required for intentional disposal of hazardous waste." 45 Fed. Reg. 33066, 33068 (1980).

Moreover, we need not decide whether PEC is a "disposal facility." Unlike "disposal facility," the definition of "disposal" does not limit its reference only to those facilities at which hazardous waste will remain after closure. Rather, as noted, "disposal" encompasses "the discharge, deposit, injection, dumping, spilling, leaking, or placing of any solid or hazardous waste into or on any land or water so that such solid waste or hazardous waste or any constituent thereof may enter the environment or be emitted into the air or discharged into any waters." C.C.R. § 260.10. As a generator of hazardous waste that engages in its disposal, PEC is a TSD facility. *See* C.C.R. § 260.10. Furthermore, as a TSD facility, PEC must comply with the requirements of C.C.R. §§ 264, 265, 266, and 100; and as PEC's owner and operator, Redoubt and Lilienthal must meet the financial assurance requirements of C.C.R. § 266. The definition of "disposal facility" on its face does not negate these regulatory mandates, and Defendants' argument does not convince us otherwise.

B.

Defendants argue that "financial assurances are part and parcel of an integrated regulatory scheme governing pre-operational permitting of a TSD [facility] which cannot be severed and applied separately from the balance of the regulatory scheme." Since the amount of financial assurances depends on the cost estimates of closure and post-closure of the TSD facility, and since closure and post-closure plans are required for a person to obtain a permit, Defendants argue that the financial assurance requirements come into play only at the tail end of the regulatory scheme for permitting. Thus, Defendants assert that the district court at most could only require Defendants to (1) secure a permit covering treatment, storage, or disposal of hazardous waste; or (2) cease its illegal activities.

Defendants conclude that the district court therefore erred in enjoining compliance with the financial assurance provisions.

We find Defendants' argument unsupportable. As an initial matter, § 3008 of RCRA, 42 U.S.C. § 6928, authorizes the EPA to commence an action "for appropriate relief, including a temporary or permanent injunction," for "any requirement" of Subtitle C, and to do so in states that have authorized hazardous waste programs as long as the EPA gives prior notice to the state. *See* 42 U.S.C. § 6928(a)(1)–(2). [T]he district court stated, and neither party challenges, that the EPA may bring an overfile action under RCRA to enforce state implementing regulations. Thus, we turn to whether the EPA may require Defendants to comply only with Colorado's financial assurance requirements independent of requiring compliance with the entire permitting scheme.

Colorado's financial assurance requirements "apply to owners and operators of *all* hazardous waste facilities," and *inter alia* require "[a]n owner or operator of *each* facility ... [to] establish financial assurances for closure, and if applicable, post-closure of the facility." C.C.R. §§ 266.10(a) & 266.14 (emphasis added). By their terms, these regulations apply to all owners and operators of hazardous waste facilities; they are not limited to permit holders or applicants. In light of these clear provisions, we do not believe that the mere fact that the permit application requires a showing of compliance with the financial assurance provisions somehow renders these provisions applicable only in the context of permitting. *See* C.C.R. § 100.41. Based on the plain language of the Colorado financial assurance requirements, we conclude that the EPA's power to enforce Colorado's regulations includes the power to enforce the financial assurance requirements independent of requiring a permit.

Defendants' remaining arguments on this issue do not dissuade us from our conclusion. Defendants attempt to buttress their position by arguing that the CDPHE shares their view that the financial assurance requirements cannot be enforced separately from the entire permitting scheme. As support, Defendants state that the "CDPHE has never required a generator of hazardous waste, such as PEC, who is illegally treating, storing or disposing of hazardous waste to provide financial assurances." In a related point, Defendants contend that the CDPHE has only considered PEC to be a generator of hazardous waste, and has never considered it also to be a TSD facility "subject to the permit regulations, including the financial assurance requirements."

The record belies Defendants' argument, because PEC's own environmental manager testified that the CDPHE told PEC that it was a storage and disposal facility that needed to obtain a permit pursuant to state regulations. Additionally, while the CDPHE did not choose to require Defendants to comply with the financial assurance requirements in its Final Compliance Order, it believed it "[had] that option."

Rejecting Defendants' arguments, we hold that the EPA can enforce the state financial assurance requirements independent of requiring compliance with permitting.

C.

Defendants assert that the district court's grant of a preliminary injunction directing them to provide financial assurances in the amount of $3,500,000 was "not directed towards requiring Defendants to obtain financial assurances for the operation of a TSD [facility], but was a thinly disguised attempt to obtain prejudgment security to enforce any future judgment of the District Court." * * * Additionally, Defendants contend that the district court erred in granting the preliminary injunction because "RCRA does not have a provision providing prejudgment remedies to secure a future judgment in an enforcement action under § 3008."

We reject Defendants' arguments at the outset, because we do not interpret the district court's preliminary injunction for financial assurances to be an order for prejudgment security for pre-closure remediation. We recognize that the district court ordered financial assurances based upon the costs of remediating the present contamination around the PEC facility. However, we believe the district court associated these remediation costs with closure and post-closure of the facility. * * * [Specifically,] given Defendants' history of unwillingness to comply with RCRA and state implementing regulations, we believe that the district court properly considered remediation costs for the present contamination in calculating costs associated with financial assurances necessary for the facility's closure or post-closure. Accordingly, we hold that the district court properly ordered financial assurances for closure and post-closure of the facility.

D.

Finally, Defendants contend that the district court's calculation of the $3,500,000 figure for financial assurances was based on "nothing more than gross and speculative approximation." Because Defendants never have complied with applicable RCRA regulations by providing closure and post-closure plans, Defendants contend that the absence of those plans "is fatal to the United States' request for financial assurances," as such financial assurances "cannot be calculated without the detailed closure cost estimates required by the regulations."

We disagree with Defendants' argument. Even though PEC does not have closure and post-closure plans pursuant to C.C.R. § 265, the district court properly based its estimate of financial assurances on the costs of remediating present contamination at the site, under the assumption that the contamination will remain at closure. Furthermore, the district court based its figure on estimates from the CDPHE and PEC itself. The CDPHE estimated the cost to remediate the contaminated soil and groundwater at between $3,000,000 and $6,000,000. PEC's counsel estimated that remediation of the site for contaminated soil would cost $2,300,000, and PEC's hydrologist estimated that remediation of the groundwater would cost $1,200,000. From these figures, the district court concluded that the government's request for financial assurances in the amount $3,500,000 was a "fair estimate of the costs of remediation," and ordered financial assurances in that amount. *PEC*, 10 F.Supp.2d at 1154.

We believe the district court's figure was supported by the evidence, given that the amount of financial assurances equaled the sum of PEC's own remediation estimates ($2,300,000 for site remediation and $1,200,000 for groundwater remediation), and was within the remediation estimated provided by the CDPHE ($3,000,000 to $6,000,000). While Defendants and the government both admit that the estimates were rough rather than exacting, Defendants in large part were responsible for the inexact nature of the estimates because of their failure to develop closure and post-closure cost estimates pursuant to state regulations. The district court did its best to estimate fairly closure costs under non-ideal circumstances of Defendants' creation, and we find the evidence supported the estimate.

CONCLUSION

The district court did not abuse its discretion in issuing the mandatory preliminary injunction ordering Defendants to provide financial assurances in the amount of $3,500,000 pursuant to C.C.R. § 266. The district court's order is AFFIRMED.

NOTES AND QUESTIONS

1. *The dangers of being an "accidental" TSD facility.* Were the defendants in this case intending to operate a TSD facility? How did they nevertheless manage to qualify as one? Did their lack of a permit matter regarding their status? Why not? What larger policies does this approach to RCRA liability serve?

2. *The presence of hazardous waste.* Notice that the defendants in this case stipulated that PEC was handling hazardous wastes, rather than contesting that they had triggered RCRA Subtitle C—or, more precisely, Colorado's EPA-approved implementation of RCRA Subtitle C, which the court said is virtually identical to the federal requirements. Why, do you suppose? What were the hazardous wastes at issue in this case? Why do you suppose these substances were deemed "hazardous" under RCRA?

3. *RCRA and toxic torts.* Notice that one of the more important problems PEC created in this case was contaminating groundwater with hexavalent chromium. Similar groundwater contamination by hexavalent chromium in California gave rise to the massive toxic tort litigation that was the subject of the 2000 movie *Erin Brockovich*, starring Julia Roberts. How does RCRA seek to both prevent and remedy that kind of toxic tort lawsuit? Do corrective actions under RCRA provide comprehensive remedies for actual contamination? Why or why not?

4. *States and the EPA under Subtitle C.* As discussed, Congress gave the EPA the primary authority for implementing Subtitle C of RCRA. As this case demonstrates, however, the states can apply to the EPA to implement their own RCRA hazardous waste programs. RCRA § 3006, 42 U.S.C. § 6926(b). The state program must be equivalent to the federal program, 42 U.S.C. § 6926(b), and "[a]ny action taken by a State under a hazardous waste program authorized under this section shall have the same force and effect as action taken by the Administrator" of the EPA. Id. § 6926(d).

5. *Financial responsibility and corrective actions for underground storage facilities.* Under Subtitle I of RCRA, underground storage tanks (USTs) are subject to the same kinds of financial responsibility and corrective action requirements as TSD facilities, along with leak detection, recordkeeping, and reporting requirements. RCRA § 9003(c), 42 U.S.C. § 6991b(c). Consider that some of the most common USTs are used to store gasoline at service stations. Why would Congress want to ensure that such USTs were covered by financial responsibility and corrective action requirements?

6. *The RCRA land ban.* Another issue for TSD facilities, particularly those facilities that *dispose* of hazardous wastes, is the RCRA *land ban*. Congress enacted the so-called "land ban"—severe restrictions on disposal of hazardous wastes into landfills—in the 1984 amendments to RCRA. Under these amendments, "after November 8, 1984 * * * the land disposal of the hazardous wastes * * * is prohibited unless the Administrator determines the prohibition on one or more methods of land disposal of such waste is not required in order to protect human health and the environment for as long as the waste remains hazardous * * *." RCRA § 3004(d)(2), 42 U.S.C. § 6924(d)(1).

Congress required the EPA to enact regulations regarding land disposal of all of the listed hazardous wastes by May 8, 1990. RCRA § 3004(g)(5), (6)(C), 42 U.S.C. § 6924(g)(5), (6)(C). Congress also stated that if the EPA failed to meet the final deadline, "such hazardous waste shall be prohibited from land disposal." RCRA § 3004(g)(6)(C), 42 U.S.C. § 6924(g)(6)(C). This last provision is known as the land ban *hammer provision*, which Congress used to induce the EPA to promulgate the regulations expeditiously. The EPA finished the land disposal regulations on time. See 55 Fed. Reg. 22,520–720 (1990).

In order to allow land disposal of hazardous wastes, the EPA had to ensure that the waste would be treated to minimize the short-term and long-term threats to human health and the environment posed by toxic and hazardous constituents. RCRA § 3004(m), 42 U.S.C. § 6924(m). Alternatively, land disposal of hazardous wastes could be allowed if the EPA could find that no migration of hazardous constituents from the facility would occur after disposal. Id. § 3004(g)(5), 42 U.S.C. § 6924(g)(5).

7. ENFORCEMENT BY THE EPA AND STATES

United States v. Power Engineering Co. is an example of government enforcement under RCRA. RCRA expressly gives the EPA authority to take enforcement actions against people who violate Subtitle C's requirements for hazardous waste. RCRA §§ 3008, 7003, 42 U.S.C. §§ 6928, 6973. Civilly, whenever on the basis of any information the Administrator determines that any person has violated or is in violation of any requirement of this subchapter, the Administrator may issue an order assessing a civil penalty for any past or current violation, requiring compliance immediately or within a specified time period, or both, or the Administrator may commence a civil action in the United States district court in the district in which the violation occurred for appropriate relief, including a temporary or permanent injunction.

RCRA § 3008(a)(1), 42 U.S.C. § 3008(a)(1).

Look again at *Power Engineering*. How did the EPA use its RCRA enforcement authority in that case? As discussed in *Power Engineering*, the EPA can both incorporate approved state RCRA requirements into its own enforcement actions and *overfile* state enforcement actions that it believes to be inadequate.

Civil liability under RCRA is *strict liability*—and, as *Power Engineering* makes clear, it can subject violators to substantial penalties. According to RCRA itself, civil penalties can be up to $25,000 per day of violation. Id. § 3008(c), 42 U.S.C. § 6928(c). However, in 1996, in the Debt Collection Improvement Act of 1996, 28 U.S.C. § 2461, Congress allowed the EPA to increase RCRA civil penalties. The EPA exercised this authority in May 1997, raising the maximum level for civil penalties under RCRA (and most other pollution control statutes) to $27,500. The EPA has continued to increase civil penalty maximums to account for inflation. Through January 12, 2009, maximum penalties for most statutes were increased to $32,500. After January 12, 2009, those maximums increased to $37,500. Environmental Protection Agency, Civil Monetary Penalty Inflation Adjustment Rule, 74 Fed. Reg. 626, 627–28 (Jan. 7, 2009).

The EPA may also seek injunctive relief against people and businesses who are creating imminent hazards to health and the environment through their handling of solid and hazardous waste. Specifically,

upon receipt of evidence that the past or present handling, storage, treatment, transportation or disposal of any solid waste or hazardous waste may present an imminent and substantial endangerment to health or the environment, the Administrator may bring suit on behalf of the United States in the appropriate district court against any person (including any past or present generator, past or present transporter, or past or present owner or operator of a treatment, storage, or disposal facility) who has contributed or who is contributing to such handling, storage, treatment, transportation or disposal to restrain such person from such handling, storage, treatment, transportation, or disposal, to order such person to take such other action as may be necessary, or both.

RCRA § 7003(a), 42 U.S.C. § 6973(a). Persons who violate the Administrator's orders are subject to fines. RCRA § 7003(b), 42 U.S.C. § 6973(b).

RCRA also subjects violators to criminal liability for several kinds of *"knowing"* violations of its provisions, such as when a person "knowingly transports or causes to be transported any hazardous waste * * * to a facility that does not have a permit," "knowingly treats, stores, or disposes of any hazardous waste" without a RCRA permit or in knowing violation of a permit, or knowingly transports hazardous wastes without a manifest. RCRA § 3008(d)(1), (2), (5), 42 U.S.C. § 6928(d)(1), (2), (5). In addition, section 3008 recognizes the crime of *knowing endangerment*, creating criminal liability for "[a]ny person who knowingly transports, treats, stores, disposes of, or exports any hazardous waste * * * who knows at the time that he thereby places another person in imminent danger of death or serious bodily injury * * *." RCRA § 3008(e), 42 U.S.C. § 6928(e).

According to section 3008,

[a] person's state of mind is knowing with respect to—

(A) his conduct, if he is aware of the nature of his conduct;

(B) an existing circumstance, if he is aware or believes that the circumstance exists; or

(C) a result of his conduct, if he is aware or believes that his conduct is substantially certain to cause danger or death or serious bodily injury.

RCRA § 3008(f)(1), 42 U.S.C. § 6928(f)(1). Persons convicted of knowing endangerment can be fined up to $250,000 or imprisoned or both. RCRA § 3008(e), 42 U.S.C. § 6928(e).

8. ENFORCEMENT BY CITIZENS

As it did with most federal environmental statutes, Congress included within RCRA a *citizen-suit provision*. Environmental citizen-suit provisions allow private individuals and private organizations to sue people and entities—including the EPA itself—who violate RCRA's requirements. More specifically, RCRA's citizen-suit provision states that:

[A]ny person may commence a civil action on his own behalf—

(1)(A) against any person (including (a) the United States, and (b) any other governmental instrumentality or agency, to the extent permitted by the eleventh amendment to the Constitution) who is alleged to be in violation of any permit, standard, regulation, condition, requirement, prohibition, or order which has become effective pursuant to this chapter, or

(B) against any person, including the United States and any other governmental instrumentality or agency, to the extent permitted by the eleventh amendment to the Constitution, and including any past or present generator, past or present transporter, or past or present owner or operator of a treatment, storage, or disposal facility, who has contributed or who is contributing to the past or present handling, storage, treatment, transportation, or disposal of any solid or hazardous waste which may present an imminent and substantial endangerment to health or the environment; or

> (2) against the Administrator [of the EPA] where there is alleged a failure of the Administrator to perform any act or duty under this chapter which is not discretionary with the Administrator.

42 U.S.C. § 6972(a).

The *No Spray Coalition* case, presented at the beginning of this Chapter and discussing the status of in-use pesticides as solid wastes, was a RCRA citizen suit. Go back and review that case. What part of RCRA's citizen-suit provision were the plaintiffs attempting to use? How do you know?

9. RCRA AND STATE–LAW TOXIC TORT CLAIMS

RCRA explicitly preserves state-law causes of action for toxic tort claims arising out of the generation, transportation, storage, treatment, and disposal of hazardous wastes. Specifically, RCRA's citizen-suit provision states that nothing in that provision

> shall restrict any right which any person (or class of persons) may have under any statute or common law to seek enforcement of any standard or requirement relating to the management of solid waste or hazardous waste, or to seek any other relief (including relief against the Administrator [of the EPA] or a State agency).

RCRA § 7002(f), 42 U.S.C. § 6972(f). In addition, nothing in RCRA "shall * * * preempt any State or local law." RCRA § 11007, 42 U.S.C. § 6992f(b).

Beyond merely co-existing, however, RCRA violations can reinforce and support state-law toxic tort claims, as the following recent case makes clear.

LOZAR v. BIRDS EYE FOODS, INC.

United States District Court for the Western District of Michigan, 2009.
678 F.Supp.2d 589.

PAUL L. MALONEY, CHIEF JUDGE.

* * *

Randall and Heather Lozar and thirty-three other plaintiffs (collectively "the Lozars") reside or own property near a fruit-processing plant owned and operated by defendant Bird's Eye Foods, Inc. ("BEF") in Fennville, Michigan. BEF has not denied that it meets any pertinent federal or state statutory definitions of owner/operator of the Fennville facility.

BEF's operations at the Fennville facility creates wastewater which contains organic matter from the fruit, such as dissolved sugar and suspended solids, and it disposes of this wastewater by spraying it onto its fields ("spray irrigation"), which are east of the facility and south of the road called M–89. The Lozars allege that since the BEF facility opened, its spray irrigation has caused elevated levels of "contaminants" in the soil and "groundwater" on and around the facility premises. * * *

In addition to the spray irrigation, the Lozars also allege that there are at least two other potential sources of contaminants emanating from the BEF facility, including iron, manganese, arsenic, chloride, and sodium: at least one allegedly unpermitted and undocumented landfill on BEF's property, created and used by BEF; and cans, fruit-pit waste, and other debris that BEF has buried in the soil of the facility.

The Lozars allege that the spray irrigation at the facility has caused a phenomenon known as "groundwater mounding," which they describe as "an outward and upward expansion of the free water table caused by shallow reinjection which can alter flow rates and direction." The groundwater mounding has allegedly caused the contaminants to spread in directions different than they would have spread otherwise. As a result of the spray irrigation and other causes of contaminant emission and migration, the Lozars allege, residential wells belonging to plaintiffs and others "down-gradient" from the BEF facility do not meet accepted residential water-quality criteria, and the water has also developed odors, coloration, and fixture staining which would not have occurred otherwise.

By letters dated between May 8, 2008 and July 24, 2008, BEF notified plaintiffs and other Fennville residents that water had migrated from their facility off their premises, and in some cases plaintiffs received MDEQ letters stating that their drinking water is contaminated.

The Lozars acknowledge that there may be a layer of "glacial till"— poorly sorted sand, silt, and clay of glacial origin—which may act as a confining layer between the upper and lower aquifers, thereby ruling out BEF as the source of some of the contaminants, but they point out that environmental investigation of the affected land is ongoing. After sampling both groundwater and the drinking water of plaintiffs and other Fennville residents, BEF notified them (on unspecified dates) that groundwater sampling has revealed elevated levels of arsenic and manganese which exceed the State of Michigan's drinking standards.

The Lozars allege that their water emits a foul odor and causes rust stains to accumulate on everything it touches, while the Cortezes allege that their drinking water smells like rotten eggs and is very discolored and dirty-looking, and the Martinezes likewise allege that their drinking water is yellow, cloudy and smells like rotten eggs, and they had to replace their water heater, plumbing and water lines due to the contaminated water. The Rodriguezes allege that their water has a high iron content and stains everything that it touches, while DeLucas alleges that his water "has a strange color and flavor" and cannot be used for drinking or any other purpose.

As for symptoms allegedly related to groundwater contamination, Mr. Lozar complains that he developed chest pains while living at his home near the BEF facility and that the pains stopped after he stopped drinking the water from his well. Plaintiff Erica Cortez alleges that she suffered clotting in her ovaries and an inflamed liver and pancreas and that her physician was unable to identify the cause of these conditions, and that the Cortezes' dog developed a massive lump in his neck after drinking their water. Plaintiff Juanita Rodriguez has recurring joint problems, has lost a significant amount of weight, and developed very dry skins and "large bumps" shortly after moving in; her husband Juan has developed a severe rash on his hands and all over his body; her daughter Jsenia lost large amounts of hair while living at the residence; her granddaughter M.V. has developed skin blemishes which her physician has been unable to diagnose and treat; and several of their pets who drank their water became sick and died. About seven or eight years before this complaint was filed, plaintiff Nyoka Martinez developed clogged arteries and both of her legs had to be amputated, but her physicians were unable to determine the cause of her medical conditions. Plaintiff Felipa Diaz alleges that she has suffered heart disease, thyroid problems, heartburn, a swollen liver, and hair loss; her relative Martha has suffered heartburn and high cholesterol; and Juvencio has suffered twenty years of hair loss, as well as dementia symptoms which she believes may be Alzheimer's. Finally, the Rodriguezes have suffered hair loss, heartburn, and heart disease.

For more than 18 months prior to the filing of the second amended complaint, BEF provided bottled drinking water to plaintiffs and other Fennville residents.

All the plaintiffs allege that the groundwater contamination and resultant health risks and expense have rendered their houses unmarketable despite the efforts of many plaintiffs to sell. Plaintiff Zuidema, who has owned a 20–acre farm in Fennville for 13 years and used to rent the house for rental income, alleges that groundwater contamination has prevented him from renting it for at least a year and a half.

Finally, many of the plaintiffs allege that an unusual number of their household pets died, suffered severe medical maladies, or gave birth to deformed offspring, while living in their Fennville homes and after drinking the water from their wells.

BEF denies responsibility for any groundwater contamination.

The Lozars bring this diversity environmental-protection action asserting a state common-law claim for negligence (count one), a claim for recovery of response/remediation costs under federal and state environmental statutes (count two), and another state common-law claim (count three) which is not the subject of the instant opinion. Pursuant to Fed. R. Civ. P. 12(b)(6), BEF moves to dismiss *part* of count one of the second amended complaint, which asserts a claim for negligence, including negligence *per se* based on BEF's alleged violation of * * * the federal Resource Conservation and Recovery Act, 42 U.S.C. § 6901 *et seq.* ("RCRA"); * * *

and Michigan's Natural Resources Environmental Protection Act, MICH. COMP. LAWS § 324.101 *et seq.* ("NREPA").

* * *

DISCUSSION:

Count 1, Claim for Michigan Common–Law Negligence

Under Michigan common law, a plaintiff seeking to recover for ordinary negligence must establish four elements: (1) a duty owed by the defendant to the plaintiff, (2) a breach of that duty, (3) causation, and (4) damages.

The Michigan Court of Appeals has held that " '[i]f no duty is owed by the defendant to the plaintiff, an ordinance [or statutory] violation committed by the defendant is not actionable as negligence.' " *Sidhu v. Hansen,* 2009 WL 3683315, *3 (Mich.App. Nov. 5, 2009).

"In other words, 'violation of an ordinance, without more, will not serve as the basis for imposing a legal duty cognizable in negligence theory.' " *Sidhu v. Hansen,* 2009 WL 3683315, *3 (Mich.App. Nov. 5, 2009).

However, once the plaintiff establishes that the defendant owed him a duty of care, evidence that the defendant violated a relevant statute or ordinance may constitute *prima facie* evidence that the defendant breached that duty.

Whether a violation of a statute constitutes evidence of negligence depends on the statute's purpose and the class of persons it was designed to protect. Specifically, under Michigan law, proof that a defendant violated a statute sets up a rebuttable presumption of negligence if (1) "the purpose of the [statute] was to prevent the type of injury and harm actually suffered" and (2) the plaintiff was "within the class of persons which [sic] the [statute] was designed to protect." *Cipri,* 596 N.W.2d at 628, 235 Mich.App. at 16. In *Cipri,* for example, a lake-owner sued various companies for negligence and other causes of action against companies which were allegedly responsible for leachate from fermenting cornhusks flowing into his lake and killing all aquatic life. The Michigan Court of Appeals held that the defendants' violations of the former Michigan Environmental Protection Act ("MEPA") and the former Michigan Environmental Response Act ("MERA") (both repealed and replaced by the current MEPA in 1995) were properly considered as establishing that they had, and had violated, a duty of care to the lake-owner:

> [T]he purpose of the statutes is to prevent environmental contamination and to promote compensation for remediation, and that liability flows from anyone fitting the definition of a responsible party [to] any member of the public who incurs response costs or whose natural resources are injured by such contamination. We therefore conclude that the statutes were intended to prevent precisely this type of injury

and that plaintiff was within the class of persons intended to be protected by the statutes.

* * *

Finally, we believe that the burdens and consequences of imposing a duty on [the corporate defendant] are no harsher than the liability already imposed on it by the MERA and the MEPA. Thus, we conclude that the trial court did not err in finding that [corporate defendant] had a duty of care toward plaintiff.

Cipri, 596 N.W.2d at 628–29 and 629, 235 Mich.App. at 16–17 and 18.

If the plaintiff satisfies these two criteria and establishes the rebuttable presumption of negligence due to violation of a statute, the defendant must proffer a legal excuse for violating the statute. "Absent a legally sufficient excuse, a jury may infer negligence on the basis of the violation and, if the violation of the statute was a proximate cause of the injury, may return a verdict for the plaintiff." *Sanford St. Local Dev. Corp. v. Textron, Inc.*, 768 F.Supp. 1218, 1224 (W.D.Mich. 1991)(Gibson, C.J.).

BEF does not seek to dismiss the Lozars' negligence claim in its entirety, nor even its use of the negligence *per se* theory in its entirety. Rather, BEF seeks to dismiss the negligence claim only to the extent that it relies on a negligence *per se* theory predicated on violations of * * * RCRA * * *. BEF's instant motion does not seek to dismiss the negligence count to the extent that it claims negligence *per se* based on an alleged violation of Michigan statutes or ordinances.

* * *

Unlike CERCLA, the "RCRA is not principally designed to effectuate the cleanup of toxic waste sites or to compensate those who have attended to the remediation of environmental hazards." *Meghrig v. KFC Western*, 516 U.S. 479, 483 (1996) (O'Connor, J., for unanimous Court). Rather, RCRA's primary purpose is to "reduce the generation of hazardous waste" in the first instance, "and to ensure the proper treatment, storage, and disposal of" whatever waste is nonetheless generated " 'so as to minimize the present and future threat to human health and the environment.' " *Meghrig*, 516 U.S. at 483 (quoting 42 U.S.C. § 6902(b)).

RCRA defines hazardous waste as

a solid waste, or combination of solid wastes, which because of its quantity, concentration, or physical, chemical, or infectious characteristics may

(A) cause, or significantly contribute to an increase in mortality or an increase in serious irreversible, or incapacitating reversible, illness; or

(B) pose a substantial present or potential hazard to human health or the environment when improperly treated, stored, transported, or disposed of, or otherwise managed.

42 U.S.C. § 6903(5). In turn, RCRA defines solid waste as

any garbage, refuse, sludge from a wastewater treatment plant, water supply treatment plant, or air pollution control facility or other discarded material, including solid, liquid, semisolid or contained gaseous material resulting from industrial, commercial, mining, and agricultural operations, and from community activities, *but does not include* solid or dissolved material in domestic sewage, or solid or dissolved materials in irrigation return flows or industrial discharges which are point sources subject to permits under section 1342 of title 33, or source, special nuclear, or byproduct material as defined by the Atomic Energy Act of 1954, as amended (68 Stat. 923) [42 U.S.C. § 2011 *et seq.*].

42 U.S.C. § 6903(27) (emphasis added, paragraph break added).

To the extent that the negligence claim is based on negligence *per se* from a violation of the federal RCRA, BEF notes that the second amended complaint cites only two provisions of RCRA: 42 U.S.C. § 6924(d)(1) and § 6924(d)(2)(B)(i), which prohibit the disposal of hazardous wastes "containing" arsenic at levels greater than 500 milligrams per liter. BEF asserts that

> [n]owhere do the allegations of the second amended complaint indicate that the organic wastewater that Birds Eye sprays on its fields 'contains' *any* arsenic, let alone in quantities [sic, concentrations] that exceed 500 mg/l. Moreover, Plaintiffs fail to identity any testing that could support a finding that Birds Eye disposed of arsenic on land in concentrations above 500 mg/l. Instead, they allege that certain metals are present in soil or groundwater in the area, or that those metals are associated, directly or indirectly, with Birds Eye's irrigation. These minimal allegations are insufficient to implicate any provision of RCRA and cannot serve to ground a negligence claim on [a violation of] this federal environmental statute.

BEF's argument on this score is unavailing, because this is a motion merely testing whether the second amended complaint states a claim for RCRA violation, not a summary-judgment motion testing the sufficiency of the plaintiffs' evidence to permit a factfinder to find a violation. With much discovery ahead, it is eminently reasonable for the plaintiffs to provide the data and inferences that are currently available to them, as to apparent arsenic levels and the source of any unsafe arsenic concentrations in their soil and groundwater. If, after the completion of discovery, BEF believes that the plaintiffs are unable to present evidence supporting a finding that it caused concentrations of arsenic or other substances to exceed legally permitted levels on plaintiffs' property or in plaintiffs' water, BEF can test that position by moving for summary judgment. At this early stage of the case, the second amended complaint puts BEF adequately on notice of the existence and fundamental nature of the RCRA claim against it. Specifically, it is obvious from the second amended complaint that the plaintiffs are alleging that BEF violated RCRA by improperly treating, storing and/or disposing of several substances—including arsenic and manganese—which arguably qualify as hazardous wastes, at least in certain concentrations, as defined by 42 U.S.C. § 6903(5) (defining "hazardous waste" as a solid waste or wastes with certain characteristics or effects) and 42 U.S.C. § 6903 (defining "solid waste").

NOTES AND QUESTIONS

1. *RCRA and negligence.* How were the plaintiffs in *Lozar* attempting to use RCRA to support their negligence claim? Does that use of RCRA seem appropriate? Why or why not?

2. *The blending of RCRA, CERCLA, and the common law.* As this case makes clear, the lines between regulation under RCRA and the operation of common law toxic tort claims can blur. Similarly, in anticipation of the next section, it is worth noting that RCRA and CERCLA can blend into one another, especially when a generator of hazardous waste for RCRA purposes allows that hazardous waste to be released into the environment, causing contamination. In a part of *Lozar* not reproduced above, the court addressed the defendant's potential CERCLA liability. Moreover, it held, as it had for RCRA, that CERCLA could define the scope of the defendant's duty for purposes of the plaintiffs' negligence claim. *Lozar*, 678 F.Supp.2d at 601–02.

C. THE COMPREHENSIVE ENVIRONMENTAL RESPONSE, COMPENSATION, AND LIABILITY ACT (CERCLA)

1. TRIGGERING CERCLA LIABILITY

As was true with RCRA, Congress enacted the *Comprehensive Environmental Response, Compensation, and Liability Act of 1980* (CERCLA), 42 U.S.C. §§ 9601–9675, to deal with hazardous waste contamination through statutory requirements, deeming the common law inadequate to meet that challenge. However, whereas RCRA is *proactive*—as you have seen, Congress designed RCRA to prevent hazardous wastes from escaping into the environment by regulating such wastes from their generation to their disposal—CERCLA is *reactive*, designed to deal with the many hazardous waste disposal sites (and other hazardous substance problems) created before RCRA took effect in 1976. The problems with these pre-RCRA sites became very clear to Congress and the public in 1978, when hazardous waste contamination forced the evacuation of Love Canal, New York.

At Love Canal, over 21,000 tons of chemical wastes were deposited in a landfill. The landfill closed in 1952, and was then covered over the next year. Over time, a community grew around the abandoned landfill. Under the old scenario of "out of sight—out of mind," that should have been the end of the story.

However, more than two decades later, increasing numbers of Love Canal residents began complaining of health problems, including chronic headaches, respiratory discomforts, and skin ailments. Residents also noticed high incidents of cancer and deafness. The State of New York investigated and found high levels of chemical contaminants in the soil and air—with a high incidence of birth defects and miscarriages in the immediate area around the Love Canal landfill. President Jimmy Carter declared a State of Emergency in 1978, and Federal funds were used to permanently relocate 239 families in the first two rows of houses that encircled the landfill area.

But the tragedy did not end. A New York State investigation found "extensive migration of potentially toxic materials outside the immediate canal area." In 1979, 300 additional families in a 10–block area around the site were relocated because of health problems from chemical exposures. In 1980, the EPA announced the results of blood tests that showed chromosome damage in Love Canal residents. Residents were told that this could mean an increased risk of cancer, reproductive problems, and genetic damage. Later that year, President Carter issued a second State of Emergency—providing funding for the permanent relocation of all 900 residents of the Love Canal area. U.S. E.P.A., Superfund: 20 Years of Protecting Human Health and the Environment 1–4, available at http://www.epa.gov/superfund/20years/index.htm.

CERCLA is triggered any time that there is a *release of a hazardous substance from a facility*. The Act defines *"release"* broadly to be:

> any spilling, leaking, pumping, pouring, emitting, emptying, discharging, injecting, escaping, leaching, dumping, or disposing into the environment (including the abandonment or discarding of barrels, containers, and other closed receptacles containing any hazardous substance or pollutant or contaminants) * * *.

CERCLA § 101(22), 42 U.S.C. § 9601(22).

One other thing that is important to remember about CERCLA is that Congress enacted it *after* most of the other major federal environmental statutes. As a result, CERCLA both defers to and relies upon those other statutory regimes. For example, CERCLA's definition of "release" explicitly excludes releases that are regulated under other environmental statutes—workplace releases covered by the Occupational Safety and Health Act (OSH Act; see Chapter 7); engine emissions from cars, trucks, airplanes, and pipeline pumping station engines, which are regulated through a variety of federal statutes, especially the Clean Air Act; and releases of nuclear and radioactive materials covered by the Atomic Energy Act of 1954. Id. In addition, people cannot be liable *under CERCLA* for releases of pesticides regulated by the Federal Insecticide, Fungicide, and Rodenticide Act (FIFRA), 7 U.S.C. §§ 136 et seq. (discussed later in Chapter 9), or for releases of materials already permitted under other federal statutes, such as through Clean Water Act permits. CERCLA § 107(i), (j), 42 U.S.C. § 9607(i), (j).

Similarly, CERCLA defines *"hazardous substance"* largely through reference to other federal statutes. CERCLA § 101(14), 42 U.S.C. § 9601(14). Thus, hazardous substances include:

- oil and associated pollutants regulated under the Clean Water Act;
- hazardous wastes regulated under RCRA;
- toxic pollutants regulated under the Clean Water Act;
- hazardous air pollutants regulated under the Clean Air Act; and
- imminently hazardous chemicals regulated under the Toxic Substances Control Act (TSCA) (discussed later in Chapter 9).

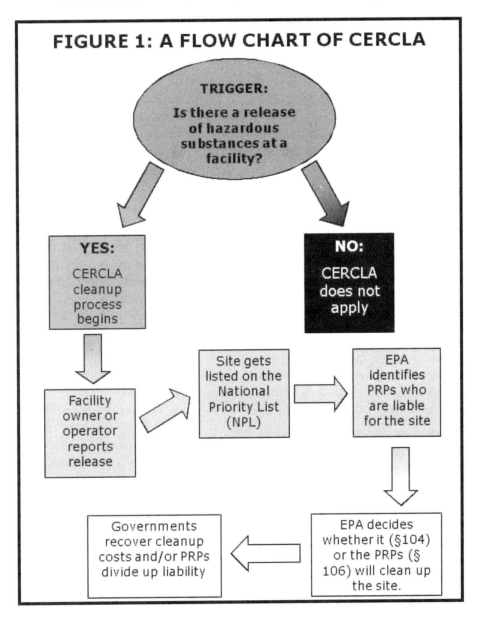

FIGURE 1: A FLOW CHART OF CERCLA

Id. Nevertheless, pursuant to CERCLA itself, the EPA also can designate additional substances as "hazardous substances." CERCLA § 101(14), 42 U.S.C. § 9601(14).

CERCLA contains two major exemptions from the list of hazardous substances. First, "petroleum, including crude oil or any fraction thereof which is not otherwise specifically listed or designated as a hazardous substance," is not a "hazardous substance." Id. Similarly, "natural gas, natural gas liquids, liquified natural gas, or synthetic gas usable for fuel (or mixtures of natural gas and such synthetic gas" are explicitly excluded from CERCLA's list. CERCLA § 101(14), 42 U.S.C. § 9601(14)

Finally, CERCLA defines *"facility"* very broadly, to include:

(A) any building, structure, installation, equipment, pipe or pipeline (including any pipe into a sewer or publicly owned treatment works), well, pit, pond, lagoon, impoundment, ditch, landfill, storage container, motor vehicle, rolling stock, or aircraft, or (B) any site or area where a hazardous substance has been deposited, stored, disposed of, or placed, or otherwise come to be located; but does not include any consumer product in consumer use or any vessel.

CERCLA § 101(9), 42 U.S.C. § 9601(9).

2. PRPS AND CERCLA LIABILITY

a. Overview of PRPs and CERCLA Liability

As many courts have noted, CERCLA is a *remedial statute*, designed to correct an existing and recognized problem. As a result, courts interpret the statute broadly. Moreover, CERCLA imposes *strict liability* on those who are deemed responsible for the release of hazardous substances. These people are known as *potentially responsible parties*, or *PRPs*, and they generally are *jointly and severally liable* for the entire costs of cleaning up the release.

Section 107 of CERCLA establishes four categories of PRPs:

(1) the owner or operator of a vessel or a facility,

(2) any person who at the time of disposal of any hazardous substance owned or operated any facility at which such hazardous substances were disposed of,

(3) any person who by contract, agreement, or otherwise arranged for disposal or treatment, or arranged with a transporter for transport for disposal or treatment, of hazardous substances owned or possessed by such person, by any other party or entity, at a facility or incineration vessel owned or operated by another party or entity and containing such hazardous substances, and

(4) any person who accepts or accepted any hazardous substances for transport to disposal or treatment facilities, incineration vessels or

sites selected by such person, from which there is a release, or a threatened release which causes the incurrence of response costs, of a hazardous substance * * *.

CERCLA § 107(a), 42 U.S.C. § 9607(a). Moreover, section 107 creates only three general defenses to CERCLA liability:

(1) an act of God;

(2) an act of war; or

(3) an act or omission of a third party other than an employee or agent of the defendant, or than one whose act or omission occurs in connection with a contractual relationship, existing directly or indirectly, with the defendant (except where the sole contractual relationship arises from a published tariff and acceptance for carriage by a common carrier by rail) if the defendant establishes by a preponderance of the evidence that (a) he exercised due care with respect to the hazardous substance concerned, taking into consideration the characteristics of such hazardous substance, in light of all relevant facts and circumstances, and (b) he took precautions against foreseeable acts or omissions of any such third party and the consequences that could foreseeably result from such acts or omissions * * *.

CERCLA § 107(b), 42 U.S.C. § 9607(b).

Notably, most arguments by PRPs that they did not actually cause the release, or that they contributed very little hazardous material to it, have failed. Such failure generally results from the fact that CERCLA effectively shifts the burden of proof on causation from plaintiffs—generally, the EPA or a state—to defendant PRPs. As a result, all PRPs are presumed liable—and jointly and severally liable, at that—unless they can prove otherwise. As the Supreme Court recently summarized, relying on the Restatement (Second) of Torts:

the courts of appeals have acknowledged that "[t]he universal starting point for divisibility of harm analyses in CERCLA cases" is § 433A of the Restatement (Second) of Torts. Under the Restatement,

when two or more persons acting independently caus[e] a distinct or single harm for which there is a reasonable basis for division according to the contribution of each, each is subject to liability only for the portion of the total harm that he has himself caused. Restatement (Second) of Torts, §§ 433A, 881 (1976); Prosser, Law of Torts, pp. 313–314 (4th ed. 1971).... But where two or more persons cause a single and indivisible harm, each is subject to liability for the entire harm. Restatement (Second) of Torts, § 875.

In other words, apportionment is proper when "there is a reasonable basis for determining the contribution of each cause to a single harm." Restatement (Second) of Torts § 433A(1)(b), p. 434 (1963–1964).

Not all harms are capable of apportionment, however, and CERC-LA defendants seeking to avoid joint and several liability bear the burden of proving that a reasonable basis for apportionment exists. When two or more causes produce a single, indivisible harm, "courts have refused to make an arbitrary apportionment for its own sake, and each of the causes is charged with responsibility for the entire harm." Restatement (Second) of Torts § 433A, Comment *i*, p. 440 (1963–1964).

Burlington Northern & Santa Fe Railway Co. v. United States, ___ U.S. ___, 129 S.Ct. 1870, 1881 (2009).

Given CERCLA's goals and policies, why would Congress enact a regime that essentially presumes that, when multiple parties contribute to a contaminated site: (1) harm results; and (2) that harm is indivisible unless the *PRPs* prove otherwise?

b. Current Owner or Operator Liability

Under section 107(a)(1) of CERCLA, the *current* owner or operator of the site is liable for any release of hazardous substances on the premises, regardless of the time the release occurred or the current owner or operator's fault in causing the release. CERCLA § 107(a)(1), 42 U.S.C. § 9607(a)(1). CERCLA's definitions of *"owner"* and *"operator"* are not very helpful—the owner is the person who owns a facility or vessel, while the operator is the person who operates the facility or vessel. CERCLA § 101(20)(A), 42 U.S.C. § 9601(20)(A). Nevertheless, owners and operators are generally fairly easy to identify.

Certain kinds of property relationships, however, can create ambiguities regarding who counts as the current "owner" and "operator" of a CERCLA site. For example, state and local governments can acquire contaminated properties involuntarily through operation of law, such as abandonment or tax delinquency. Are they then CERCLA owners, subject to CERCLA liability? Similarly, banks often take mortgages on properties as security for loans, never intending to own or operate the property in the usual sense, although the bank may acquire a deed to the property as part of the mortgage process. Is the bank then an owner or operator of the property? What happens if the bank has to foreclose in order to protect its interests regarding a defaulted loan?

In 1996, Congress amended CERCLA's definition of "owner or operator" to deal with many of these problems. For governments, "[t]he term 'owner or operator' does not include a unit of State or local government which acquired ownership or control involuntarily through bankruptcy, tax delinquency, abandonment, or other circumstances in which the government involuntarily acquires title by virtue of its function as sovereign." CERCLA § 101(20)(D), 42 U.S.C. § 9601(20)(D). Instead, in such cases, "any person who owned, operated, or otherwise controlled activities at such facility immediately 'beforehand' is deemed the owner or operator." CERCLA § 101(20)(A), 42 U.S.C. § 9601(20)(A). This exclusion does *not* apply if the state or local government caused or contributed to the release or threatened release of hazardous substances, in which case the government is liable like any other PRP. CERCLA § 101(20)(D), 42 U.S.C. § 9601(20)(D).

As for banks and other creditors, "owner or operator" "does not include a person who, without participating in the management of a vessel or facility, holds indicia of ownership primarily to protect his security interest in the vessel or facility." CERCLA § 101(20)(A), (E)(i), 42 U.S.C. § 9601(20)(A), (E)(i). The definition of "owner or operator" contains an extended definition of "participation in management," which essentially imposes an *actual participation*—as opposed to *capacity to control*—test on the security holder's activities. CERCLA § 101(20)(F), 42 U.S.C. § 9601(20)(F). Congress specified the test in order to resolve a split among the federal courts of appeals that had confronted this issue. Moreover, the person holding the security interest can foreclose on the property without becoming an owner or operator for CERCLA liability purposes, so long as "the person seeks to sell, re-lease (in the case of a lease finance transaction), or otherwise divest the person of the vessel or facility at the earliest practicable, commercially reasonable time, on commercially reasonable terms, taking into account market conditions and legal and regulatory requirements." CERCLA § 101(20)(E)(ii), 42 U.S.C. § 9601(20)(E)(ii).

One problem that CERCLA still does not directly address is the issue of current "owners" and "operators" among parent and subsidiary corporations. In particular, can a parent corporation be deemed to "own" or "operate" a CERCLA facility simply because it owns a subsidiary corporation that owns and/or operates the facility?

In 1998, the Supreme Court answered that question "no." United States v. Bestfoods, 524 U.S. 51, 61–62 (1998). In this case, the federal government was going to spend tens of millions of dollars to clean up a CERCLA site where the Ott Chemical Company had been dumping hazardous substances since 1957, polluting the surrounding soil and ground water. By the time the EPA sued, however, Ott Chemical was defunct. As a result, the EPA sought clean-up funds from the two parent corporations—CPC International and Aeroject—that had owned Ott Chemical and its successors.

The Supreme Court first concluded that CERCLA incorporated basic principles of corporation law, including the corporate shield:

> It is a general principle of corporate law deeply "ingrained in our economic and legal systems" that a parent corporation (so-called because of control through ownership of another corporation's stock) is not liable for the acts of its subsidiaries. * * * Although this respect for corporate distinctions when the subsidiary is a polluter has been severely criticized in the literature, nothing in CERCLA purports to reject this bedrock principle, and against this venerable common-law backdrop, the congressional silence is audible. The Government has indeed made no claim that a corporate parent is liable as

an owner or an operator under § 107 simply because its subsidiary is subject to liability for owning or operating a polluting facility.

Bestfoods, 524 U.S. at 61–62. However, the Court further concluded that this principle extended to rules governing a corporation's *derivative liability* for the actions of its subsidiaries:

> But there is an equally fundamental principle of corporate law, applicable to the parent-subsidiary relationship as well as generally, that the corporate veil may be pierced and the shareholder held liable for the corporation's conduct when, *inter alia,* the corporate form would otherwise be misused to accomplish certain wrongful purposes, most notably fraud, on the shareholder's behalf. Nothing in CERCLA purports to rewrite this well-settled rule, either.

Id. at 62–63. Thus, parent corporations can be held derivatively liable for their subsidiary's contaminated sites under CERCLA if and only if the relevant state's law would allow the corporate veil to be pierced. Id. at 63–64.

Otherwise, the parent corporation must either directly own or directly operate the CERCLA "facility." Ownership is fairly straightforward. As for whether the parent corporation was "operating" the facility, the Court concluded that,

> under CERCLA, an operator is simply someone who directs the workings of, manages, or conducts the affairs of a facility. To sharpen the definition for purposes of CERCLA's concern with environmental contamination, an operator must manage, direct, or conduct operations specifically related to pollution, that is, operations having to do with the leakage or disposal of hazardous waste, or decisions about compliance with environmental regulations.

Id. at 66–67.

CERCLA's extension of cleanup liability to current owners and operators is a disincentive to purchasers wishing to redevelop property known or expected to be contaminated. As a result, such developers often sought out "green" sites for new projects, contributing to urban sprawl and leaving many industrialized areas abandoned and unwanted. To address these perverse incentives, in 2002, Congress enacted the Small Business Liability Relief and Brownfields Revitalization Act ("the Brownfields Act"), Pub. L. No. 107–118, 115 Stat. 2356 (Jan. 11, 2002), which amended CERCLA § 107(a)(1) owner or operator liability to encourage people to purchase lightly contaminated commercial properties, known as *brownfields*, and to redevelop them for commercial use. A *"brownfield,"* under these amendments, is "real property, the expansion, redevelopment, or reuse of which may be complicated by the presence or potential presence of a hazardous substance, pollutant, or contaminant." CERCLA § 101(39)(A), 42 U.S.C. § 9601(39)(A).

Congress sought to encourage purchases and redevelopments of brownfields by exempting *bona fide prospective purchasers* from normal

CERCLA "owner or operator" liability. Thus, section 107 now specifies that "[n]otwithstanding subsection (a)(1) of this section, a bona fide prospective purchaser whose potential liability for a release or threatened release is based solely on the purchaser's being considered to be an owner or operator of the facility shall not be liable as long as the bona fide prospective purchaser does not impede the performance of a response action or natural resource restoration." CERCLA § 107(r)(1), 42 U.S.C. § 9607(r)(1). To qualify as a *bona fide prospective purchaser*, the buyer must establish eight conditions by a preponderance of the evidence, including the facts that "[a]ll disposal of hazardous substances at the facility occurred before the person acquired the facility," "[t]he person made all appropriate inquiries into the previous ownership and uses of the facility," "[t]he person exercises appropriate care with respect to the hazardous substances found at the facility," and the person cooperates with all cleanup actions. CERCLA § 101(40), 42 U.S.C. § 9601(40). In addition, if the United States does not recover all of its response costs from cleaning up the brownfield property, it can put a lien on the property up to the amount of those unrecovered response costs, to the extent that the cleanup increased the value of the former brownfields property. CERCLA § 107(r)(2)–(4), 42 U.S.C. § 9607(r)(2)–(4).

c. The Liability of Past Owners and Operators

In addition to designating current owners and operators as PRPs, CERCLA also establishes that "any person who at the time of disposal of any hazardous substance owned or operated any facility at which such hazardous substances were disposed of" is also a PRP. CERCLA § 107(a)(2), 42 U.S.C. § 9607(a)(2). Thus, past owners and operators are liable if they owned or operated the facility at the time when a release occurred. CERCLA's imposition of liability on past owners and operators raises two main issues: (1) the issue of *retroactive application* of the statute—that is, the later imposition of liability for conduct that was perfectly legal at the time it occurred; and (2) what it means for an past owner to have been the owner "at the time of disposal."

Most courts have concluded that CERCLA cleanup liability is indeed retroactive. See, e.g., United States v. Olin Corp., 107 F.3d 1506, 1511–15 (11th Cir.1997); Velsicol Chem. Corp. v. Enenco, Inc., 9 F.3d 524, 528–30 (6th Cir.1993). Courts reach this conclusion not only because section 107 extends liability to past owners and operators but also because CERCLA's natural resource damages provision states that there "shall be no recovery [of natural resource damages] where such damages and the release of a hazardous substance from which such damages resulted have occurred wholly before December 11, 1980" (CERCLA's effective date). CERCLA § 107(f)(1), 42 U.S.C. § 9607(f)(1).

In contrast, courts do *not* agree on how to decide whether a person owned or operated a facility "at the time of disposal." CERCLA defines "disposal" by referencing the definition of "disposal" in RCRA, see 42 U.S.C. § 9601(29), which in turn states that:

The term "disposal" means the discharge, deposit, injection, dumping, spilling, leaking, or placing of any solid waste or hazardous waste into or on any land or water so that such solid waste or hazardous waste or any constituent thereof may enter the environment or be emitted into the air or discharged into any waters, including ground waters.

42 U.S.C. § 6903(3). The issue that arises under CERCLA is whether a past owner or operator of a facility becomes a CERCLA PRP merely because previously-released hazardous substances continue to spread on the property during the past owner's or operator's tenure.

The federal courts of appeals have approached this so-called *"passive migration" problem* in a variety of ways, and the Supreme Court has not yet resolved the issue. The U.S. Court of Appeals for the Fourth Circuit determined "that § 9607(a)(2) imposes liability not only for active involvement in the 'dumping' or 'placing' of hazardous waste at the facility, but for ownership of the facility at a time that hazardous waste was 'spilling' or 'leaking.' " Nurad, Inc. v. William E. Hooper & Sons Co., 966 F.2d 837, 846 (4th Cir.1992); accord Crofton Ventures Ltd. Partnership v. G & H Partnership, 258 F.3d 292, 300 (4th Cir.2001). Thus, in the Fourth Circuit, if a person owned or operated a facility while, for example, buried drums of hazardous substances continued to leak into the ground, that person would be deemed a PRP.

The Third Circuit reached a more modest conclusion. United States v. CDMG Realty Co., 96 F.3d 706, 710 (3d Cir.1996). It held that "the passive migration of contamination dumped in the land prior to [the past owner's] ownership does not constitute disposal." Id. at 711. However, the Third Circuit explicitly did not address "the question whether the movement of contaminants unaided by human conduct can ever constitute 'disposal,' " id., concluding that "[w]hile 'leaking' and 'spilling' may not require affirmative human conduct, neither word denotes the gradual spreading of contamination alleged here." Id. at 714. Thus, if buried drums were still leaking during the person's past ownership or operation of the facility, it is unclear in the Third Circuit whether that person is a PRP.

A similar ambiguity exists in the Second Circuit, where the court followed the Third Circuit's reasoning. ABB Industrial Systems, Inc. v. Prime Tech., Inc., 120 F.3d 351, 353–59 (2d Cir.1997). Thus, according to the Second Circuit, "prior owners and operators of a site are not liable under CERCLA for mere passive migration." Id. at 359. However, like the Third Circuit, the court "express[ed] no opinion" as to whether "prior owners are liable if they acquired a site with leaking barrels [and] the prior owner's actions are purely passive." Id. at 358 n. 3.

The Sixth Circuit, in contrast, has expressly eliminated passive migration as a basis of CERCLA liability for past owners and operators, even if leaking or spilling continues during their ownership or operation. United States v. 150 Acres of Land, 204 F.3d 698, 706 (6th Cir.2000). According to the Sixth Circuit, there is no disposal "[i]n the absence of any evidence that there was human activity involved in whatever movement of hazardous substances occurred on the property since [the current owners] have owned it." Id.; see also Bob's Beverage, Inc. v. Acme, Inc., 264 F.3d 692, 697–98 (6th Cir.2001).

The Ninth Circuit has constructed the most fluid resolution to the passive migration problem. Focusing on the words that define disposal, it noted that "one can find both 'active' *and* 'passive' definitions for nearly all of these terms in any standard dictionary. We therefore reject the absolute binary 'active/passive' distinction used by some courts." Carson Harbor Village, Ltd. v. Unocal Corp., 270 F.3d 863, 878–79 (9th Cir.2001). Thus "[i]nstead of focusing solely on whether the terms are 'active' or 'passive,' we must examine each of the terms in relation to the facts of the case and determine whether the movement of contaminants is, under the plain meaning of the terms, a 'disposal.' Put otherwise, do any of the terms fit the hazardous substance contamination at issue?" Id. at 879. The Ninth Circuit concluded that the gradual passive migration of tar and slag materials across a property "was not a 'discharge, deposit, injection, dumping, spilling, leaking, or placing' and, therefore, was not a 'disposal' within the meaning of § 9607(a)(2)." Id.

d. Arranger Liability

The third category of CERCLA PRPs includes "any person who by contract, agreement, or otherwise arranged for disposal or treatment, or arranged with a transporter for transport for disposal or treatment, of hazardous substances owned or possessed by such person, by any other party or entity, at a facility or incineration vessel owner or operated by another party or entity and containing such hazardous substances * * *." CERCLA § 107(a)(3), 42 U.S.C. § 9607(a)(3). This so-called "arranger" liability is the most complex of the PRP provisions.

In 2009, for example, the Supreme Court considered whether Shell Oil Co. could be considered a CERCLA "arranger" because it supplied pesticides and other chemical products to Brown & Bryant Co. In part because of Brown & Bryant's sloppy handling of these chemicals (and despite Shell's instructions on safe handling), Brown & Bryant's property became contaminated and subject to cleanup under CERCLA. The United States and the state sought to hold Shell liable as an arranger, but the Supreme Court ultimately rejected their arguments. According to the Court:

> It is plain from the language of the statute that CERCLA liability would attach under § 9607(a)(3) if an entity were to enter into a transaction for the sole purpose of discarding a used and no longer useful hazardous substance. It is similarly clear that an entity could not be held liable as an arranger merely for selling a new and useful product if the purchaser of that product later, and unbeknownst to the seller, disposed of the product in a way that led to contamination.

Burlington Northern & Santa Fe Railway Co. v. United States, ___ U.S. ___, 129 S.Ct. 1870, 1878 (2009). Moreover, beyond those two ends of the spectrum, according to the Court, "under the plain language of the statute, an entity may qualify as an arranger under § 9607(a)(3) when it takes intentional steps to dispose of a hazardous substance." Id. at 1879. Because Shell was selling products to Brown & Bryant rather than in any way arranging for the disposal of them, it could not be deemed an "arranger" under CERCLA even if it knew that Brown & Bryant was mishandling the chemicals. Id. at 1879–80.

e. Transporter Liability

CERCLA's fourth category of PRPs creates liability for "any person who accepts or accepted any hazardous substances for transport to disposal or treatment facilities, incineration vessels or sites *selected by such person*, from which there is a release, or threatened release * * *." CERCLA § 107(a)(4), 42 U.S.C. § 9607(a)(4) (emphasis added). The italicized phrase indicates that transporters must have some involvement in selecting the disposal site or treatment facility for the hazardous substances they are transporting before they become liable under CERCLA. However, it is generally enough to make a transporter a PRP if the transporter helps the shipper decide on a destination. Tippins Inc. v. USX Corp., 37 F.3d 87, 95–96 (3d Cir.1994). Moreover, persons sending hazardous waste off for treatment or disposal—say, RCRA generators—often rely on the professional transporters for recommendations and advice, so many transporters do remain on the CERCLA hook.

3. THE CERCLA CLEANUP PROCESS

Cleaning up a site contaminated with hazardous substances is a long, multi-step process. It begins with discovery of the contaminated site and the reporting of that discovery to the EPA. The EPA then lists the site in the Comprehensive Environmental Response Compensation and Liability Information System (CERCLIS), which provides a centralized repository of information about the site and its release(s) for use by state, local, and federal officials. The EPA then assesses the site's hazards, relying on a *Preliminary Assessment* to determine whether immediate emergency containment and clean-up measures are required; a *Site Inspection* to determine the true extent of the release and the potential dangers it poses; and the *Hazard Ranking System* to determine how hazardous the site is compared to other contaminated sites. If the situation demands, during these assessments—or at any time during the cleanup process—the EPA or the state can order or take *removal actions*, which are immediate, short-term actions to contain and address obvious problems to public health and safety. For example, if a tanker crashes on a freeway and spills toxic materials, officials would immediately undertake removal actions to contain the spill, keep the public out of harm's way, protect any nearby waterways and wildlife, and to clean up the substance.

If the discovered site poses a large enough hazard, the EPA will add it to the *National Priority List* (NPL) of sites to be cleaned up under CERCLA. Most sites on the NPL are abandoned or sites of uncontrolled releases that will require a long time to clean up or remediate. In addition to listing the site on the NPL, the EPA also searches for PRPs to participate in cleanup and/or to help pay for the cleanup. To design a cleanup plan, the EPA, the state, or the PRPs conduct a *Remedial Investigation and Feasibility Study* (RI/FS) to determine what can and should be done to clean up the site. The RI/FS includes risk assessments of the various cleanup options. For example, if the site contains contaminated soil, the RI/FS will consider whether it is better to burn the soil on site or to remove it and send it to be treated elsewhere. When the RI/FS is complete, the EPA or the state decides on a cleanup plan in a *Record of Decision*, and the plan is then finalized in a *Remedial Design*, the technical plans and specifications for completing the cleanup plan. Whoever is cleaning up the site—the EPA, the state, or the PRPs—then follows the plan to complete the *Remedial Action*—that is, the final and permanent cleanup of the site.

Completion of the cleanup activities is followed by an operation and maintenance period to ensure that the cleanup is working as it should. When the EPA certifies that the site is fully remediated, it deletes the site from the NPL.

How clean is clean enough? The EPA sets the clean up standards for the remedial action on the basis of *applicable or relevant and appropriate requirements* (ARARs). CERCLA § 121(d)(2)(A), 42 U.S.C. § 9621(d)(2)(A)(ii). ARARs can come from other federal environmental statutes such as the Clean Water Act, the Safe Drinking Water Act, or the Toxic Substances Control Act, or from state environmental law requirements. CERCLA § 121(d)(2)(A), 42 U.S.C. § 9621(d)(2)(A)(ii). For example, when PRPs had contaminated groundwater under the Rose Site in Michigan with polychlorinated biphenyls (PCBs), lead, arsenic, and other toxic materials, the Sixth Circuit upheld the imposition of the State of Michigan's water-quality related antidegradation laws as ARARs for the site. United States v. Akzo Coatings of America, Inc., 949 F.2d 1409, 1421 n.9, 1442–48 (6th Cir.1991).

4. THE FOUR CATEGORIES OF CERCLA DAMAGES

Pursuant to section 107(a), CERCLA PRPs are liable for four kinds of damages:

(A) all costs of removal or remedial action incurred by the United States Government or a State or Indian Tribe not inconsistent with the national contingency plan;

(B) any other necessary costs or response incurred by any other person consistent with the national contingency plan;

(C) damages for injury to, destruction of, or loss of natural resources, including the reasonable costs of assessing such injury, destruction, or loss resulting from such release; and

(D) the costs of any health assessment or health effects study carried out under section 9604(i) of this title.

CERCLA § 107(a)(1), 42 U.S.C. § 9607(a)(4).

In order for *response costs* to be recoverable, they must be consistent with the *National Contingency Plan* (NCP). However, as quoted above, CERCLA distinguishes between costs recoverable by governments—the United States, States, and Tribes—and costs recoverable by private PRPs. Governments can recover remedial and removal costs that are "not inconsistent" with the NCP, while private PRPs can only recover necessary response costs that are "consistent" with the NCP.

CERCLA specifies a statute of limitations for actions under section 107 to recover response costs. Actions to recover removal costs "must be commenced * * * within 3 years after the completion of the removal action," unless there is a waiver or unless "the remedial action is initiated within 3 years after the completion of the removal action * * *." CERCLA § 113(g)(2), 42 U.S.C. § 9613(g)(2). In other words, if the immediate removal action proceeds relatively quickly (governed by a three-year statute of limitations) then turns into the longer-term permanent clean-up—the remedial action—the statute of limitations for the initial removal costs is effectively extended. In turn, an action for remedial costs "must be commenced * * * within 6 years after initiation of physical on-site construction of the remedial action * * *." CERCLA § 113(g)(2)(B), 42 U.S.C. § 9613(g)(2)(B).

In addition to allowing non-liable persons (generally governments) who pay for CERCLA cleanups to recover all response costs from liable PRPs, CERCLA also allows any PRP who paid all or the majority of the response costs at a CERCLA site—as in tort law, more than its fair share—to recover *contribution* from other non-settling PRPs. CERCLA § 113(f)(1), 42 U.S.C. § 9613(f)(1). PRPs must bring contribution actions within three years of the date of the cost recovery judgment or the date of an administrative or judicial settlement order. CERCLA § 113(g)(3), 42 U.S.C. § 9613(g)(3).

Under CERCLA's *natural resources damages* provisions, PRPs are liable for "damages for injury to, destruction of, or loss of natural resources, including the reasonable costs of assessing such injury, destruction, or loss resulting from such a release * * *." CERCLA § 107(a)(C), 42 U.S.C. § 9607(a)(C). "Natural resources" are "land, fish, wildlife, biota, air, water, ground water, drinking water supplies, and other such resources belonging to, managed by, held in trust by, appertaining to, or otherwise controlled by the United States * * *, any State or local government, any foreign government, any Indian tribe, or, if such resources are subject to a trust restriction on alienation, any member of an Indian tribe." CERCLA § 101(16), 42 U.S.C. § 9601(16). Thus, CERCLA requires PRPs to pay for injury to *public* natural resources, but not for injury to private property and private natural resources. As a result, only government or tribal trustees can sue to recover *natural resources damages* (NRDs). CERCLA § 107(f)(1), (2), 42 U.S.C. § 9607(f)(1), (2).

Public trustees must sue for NRDs within three years of "[t]he date of the discovery of the loss and its connection to the release in question" or the date on which the EPA promulgates NRD regulations, whichever is *later*. CERCLA § 113(g)(1), 42 U.S.C. § 9613(g)(1). Congress structured the NRD statute of limitations this way because the EPA took a very long time to promulgate the CERCLA NRD regulations, not issuing the first set until 1986, and Congress did not want PRPs to escape liability for NRDs that they caused between 1980 and the time the regulations were promulgated.

The fourth, rather limited category of CERCLA liability states that PRPs are liable for "the costs of any *health assessment or health effects study* carried out under section 9604(i) of this title." CERCLA § 107(a)(D), 42 U.S.C. § 9607(a)(D). The referenced section created the *Agency for Toxic Substances and Disease Registry* (ATSDR) within the U.S. Public Health Service. CERCLA § 104(i)(1), 42 U.S.C. § 9604(i)(1). The Administrator of the ATSDR must complete a *health assessment* for every site on the National Priority List (NPL) within a year of the site being listed. CERCLA § 104(i)(6)(A), 42 U.S.C. § 9604(i)(6)(A). This health assessment

> shall include preliminary assessments of the potential risk to human health posed by individual sites and facilities, based on such factors as the nature and extent of contamination, the existence of potential pathways of human exposure (including ground or surface water contamination, air emissions, and food chain contamination), the size and potential susceptibility of the community within the likely pathways of exposure, the comparison of expected human exposure levels to the short-term and long-term health effects associated with identified hazardous substances and any available recommended exposure or tolerance limits for such hazardous substances, and the comparison of existing morbidity and mortality data on diseases that may be associated with the observed levels of exposure.

CERCLA § 104(i)(6)(F), 42 U.S.C. § 9604(i)(6)(F). The Administrator of the ATSDR is also supposed to finish the assessment "promptly, and, to the maximum extent practicable, before the completion of the remedial investigation and feasibility study at the facility concerned." CERCLA § 104(i)(6)(D), 42 U.S.C. § 9604(i)(6)(D). In other words, the health assessment is supposed to inform the EPA's decision regarding the remedial action taken at the site.

The Administrator of the ATSDR can also, "on the basis of the results of a health assessment, * * * conduct a pilot *study of health effects* for selected groups of exposed individuals in order to determine the desirability of conducting full scale epidemiological or other health studies of the entire exposed population." CERCLA § 104(i)(7)(A), 42 U.S.C. § 9604(i)(7)(A). If the pilot studies indicate that full-scale studies are warranted, "the Administrator shall conduct such full scale epidemiological or other health studies as may be necessary to determine the health effects on the population exposed to hazardous substances from a release or threatened release." CERCLA § 104(i)(7)(B), 42 U.S.C. § 9604(i)(7)(B). If these studies reveal "a significant increased risk of adverse health effects in humans from exposure to hazardous substances," the ATSDR must initiate a *health surveillance program* for the exposed population, including periodic medical testing and a referral system for treatment. CERCLA § 104(i)(9), 42 U.S.C. § 9604(i)(9).

5. CERCLA, TOXIC TORTS, AND PRIVATE DAMAGES

a. CERCLA and State–Law Toxic Tort Claims

PRPs are *not* liable under CERCLA for any private damages, such as damage to private property or the actual costs of medical treatment. Does that mean that PRPs are off the hook for these damages—i.e., that CERCLA eliminated tort liability, including toxic tort liability? No.

In general, CERCLA specifies that "[t]his chapter does not affect or otherwise impair the rights of any person under Federal, State, or common law * * *." CERCLA § 310(h), 42 U.S.C. § 9659(h). In other words, CERCLA explicitly *preserves* common law tort claims. Moreover, on occasion, a determination of CERCLA liability—or at least the establishment of the facts that establish CERCLA liability—can aid plaintiffs bringing common law toxic tort claims. Consider the interaction of CERCLA and land-based toxic tort claims in the following case.

SCRIBNER v. SUMMERS

United States Court of Appeals for the Second Circuit, 1996.
84 F.3d 554.

McLaughlin, Circuit Judge:

Douglas and Laurie Scribner appeal from a decision and order of the United States District Court for the Western District of New York (David G. Larimer, *Judge*), entered after a bench trial. The district court found that the Scribners had not proven common law causes of action, under New York law, for strict liability, trespass, or private nuisance.

BACKGROUND

K. Douglas Scribner and Laurie B. Scribner own property located in the Town of Perinton, Monroe County, New York. Their property consists of about 0.8 acres, is zoned industrial, and includes a 9,500 square-foot single-story building. The Scribners use the property both for their family business and to rent to tenants.

Jasco Sun–Steel Treating, Inc., John Summers, and Stephen Summers (together, "Jasco") own and operate a steel-treating business on property bordering the Scribners' property to the north and east. A drainage "swale," basically a drainage ditch, runs downhill from Jasco's property to an area adjacent to the Scribners' property line.

Jasco is in the business of heat-treating metal objects and ball bearings to harden them for military and industrial uses. In its treatment process, Jasco uses several large concrete furnaces that leave a sludge residue containing high levels of barium chloride. From time to time, those furnaces needed to be cleaned and/or replaced. As part of that process, Jasco took the old furnaces outside the building and washed them down with water, in close proximity to the Scribners' property. In addition, from 1979 until 1990, Jasco used jackhammers to break up these old furnaces outside the building so that they could be more easily transported off site for disposal. A drain, which empties into the swale, is located on the concrete pad where the furnaces were cleaned and demolished.

In 1986, the New York State Department of Environmental Conservation ("NYDEC") designated barium as a hazardous waste. Several years later, the NYDEC began investigating both Jasco's facility and its other waste disposal practices. After this investigation, Jasco was indicted in New York state court for violations of the Environmental Conservation Law, and the NYDEC registered Jasco's facility as an inactive hazardous waste site. In 1994, Jasco and one of its officers were convicted and were substantially fined.

In late 1991, the Scribners decided to sell their property. In 1992, an offer was made on the property, and the Scribners began negotiations with the potential buyer. The Scribners offered to sell the property for $375,000, and the buyer countered with $335,000. Eventually, the Scribners reduced their sale price to $350,000. The buyer, however, withdrew his offer. According to the Scribners' real estate broker, the offer was withdrawn because of published reports that Jasco "had been indicted on charges of improperly disposing hazardous material." The Scribners have been unable to sell the property since that time.

The Scribners sued Jasco in the United States District Court for the Western District of New York, claiming that their property had been contaminated by Jasco's waste disposal practices. In particular, the Scribners asserted claims under the Comprehensive Environmental Response Compensation and Liability Act of 1980 ("CERCLA"), 42 U.S.C. § 9601 *et seq.*, as well as strict liability, trespass, and private nuisance claims under New York common law.

A bench trial was held before Judge David G. Larimer. After resolving a boundary dispute in the Scribners' favor, the court concluded that the Scribners' "property is contaminated because of the high levels of barium," and—most significantly—"that that chemical substance originated on [Jasco's] property."

Having found that Jasco contaminated the Scribners' property, the court granted the Scribners their response costs, pursuant to CERCLA § 107(a), 42 U.S.C. § 9607(a), as well as a declaratory judgment that Jasco is responsible for the Scribners' future response costs. It then held, however, that the Scribners had failed to prove any of their asserted common law tort causes of action.

The Scribners now appeal, arguing that the district court erred by holding that Jasco was not liable under strict liability, trespass, or private nuisance. Jasco does not appeal the district court's finding of liability under CERCLA.

We reverse and remand.

DISCUSSION

The notion that each must use his property so as not to injure his neighbor—*sic utere tuo ut alienum non laedas*—may be traced at least to the Digest of Justinian. * * * Although a New York court has found it "utterly useless as a legal maxim," its core value continues to permeate modern property law.

The Scribners contend that the district court erred by holding that Jasco was not liable under the tort-law theories of trespass, private nuisance, or strict liability. We agree with the Scribners as to trespass and nuisance, but take no position on the strict liability theory.

* * *

II. *Trespass*

The Scribners maintain that Jasco trespassed on their property because of the migration or leaching of barium particles across Jasco's property onto the Scribners' property. We agree.

Under New York law, trespass is the intentional invasion of another's property. To be liable, the trespasser "need not intend or expect the damaging consequences of his intrusion[;]" rather, he need only "intend the act which amounts to or produces the unlawful invasion." *Phillips* [v. *Sun Oil Co.*], 307 N.Y. [328,] 331, 121 N.E.2d 249 [(1954)]. The intrusion itself "must at least be the immediate or inevitable consequence of what [the trespasser] willfully does, or which he does so negligently as to amount to willfulness." *Phillips*, 307 N.Y. at 331.

There is a body of law on trespass claims arising from the movement of noxious liquids from one property to another. The New York Court of Appeals has held that:

> even when the polluting material has been deliberately put onto, or into, defendant's land, he is not liable for his neighbor's damage therefrom, unless *he (defendant) had good reason to know or expect* that subterranean and other conditions were such that there would be passage from defendant's to plaintiff's land.

Phillips, 307 N.Y. at 331 (emphasis added).

Although the district court cited the *Phillips* case as the appropriate standard for a cause of action in trespass, it held that the Scribners had failed to prove the requisite intent on the part of Jasco:

Although officers of defendants were aware that barium chloride was created by its manufacturing process, barium was not put on the state's hazardous waste list until 1986. This barium material was apparently generated from operation on defendants' site, most likely in connection with the cleaning and destruction of old furnaces and equipment used in the business. *There is no evidence, however, that defendants intended the water used in that cleaning process to enter plaintiffs' land.* In fact, there was no proof that anyone ever observed water running off of defendants' property onto plaintiffs' property. If water that had been contaminated seeped into the soil on defendants' property and thereafter migrated through the soil onto plaintiffs' property, there is no proof that defendants intended that to occur or that defendants' acts were so reckless that they should be charged with that consequence.

We find this holding erroneous. In determining whether Jasco had the requisite intent for trespass under New York law, the issue is not, as the district court held, whether "defendants intended the [contaminated] water used in [its] cleaning process to enter plaintiffs' land." Rather, under *Phillips*, the appropriate standard is whether Jasco: (i) "intend[ed] the *act* which amounts to or produces the unlawful invasion," and (ii) "had good reason *to know or expect* that subterranean and other conditions were such that there would be passage [of the contaminated water] from defendant's to plaintiff's land." *Phillips*, 307 N.Y. at 331 (emphasis added).

Applying this standard, we conclude that Jasco is liable to the Scribners in trespass. In 1986, the NYDEC listed barium as a hazardous waste. Nonetheless, from 1986 until 1990, Jasco continued to take its barium-tainted furnaces outside its building and demolish them on site using jackhammers. Moreover, it was Jasco's practice to "wash [the furnaces] down with water on site in close proximity to [the Scribners'] property." As Jasco concedes, "in the process of removing and breaking up the worn out furnaces, small amounts of barium salts escaped onto the pavement. These barium particles were carried by moving water into a swale on Jasco's land, but near the boundary with plaintiffs." Further, the parties agree that the Scribners' property was located downhill from Jasco's property. While the swale appears to run parallel to the Scribners' property, the briefs are fuzzy on this important issue. Nevertheless, one conclusion is inescapable: the barium in the Scribners' soil came from the Jasco site. The district court so found.

The district court cited several New York cases to support a finding that the Scribners had not proven their trespass claim. In the cases cited, however—unlike our case—the release of toxic substances into the environment was inadvertent (*i.e.,* nonwillful) and/or defendants did not have "good reason to know or expect" that the invasion of plaintiff's property would occur. The cases are simply inapposite.

Under *Phillips,* Jasco intended the acts which caused the invasion of the Scribners' property. And, on these facts, we find that Jasco "had good reason to know or expect," *see Phillips,* 307 N.Y. at 331, that barium particles would pass from the pavement where the furnaces were washed and demolished, into the swale, and onto the Scribners' property, which was located at a lower elevation level. We therefore conclude that Jasco is liable in trespass for the damage caused to the Scribners' property.

III. *Private Nuisance*

The Scribners also contend that Jasco's conduct was sufficient to create a private nuisance. Again, we agree.

"A private nuisance threatens one person or a relatively few, an essential feature being an interference with the use or enjoyment of land. It is actionable by the individual person or persons whose rights have been disturbed." *Copart Indus. v. Consolidated Edison Co.,* 41 N.Y.2d 564, 568 (1977) (citations omitted). In order to establish liability under a private nuisance theory, plaintiff must show that defendant's conduct:

> is a legal cause of the invasion of the interest in the private use and enjoyment of land and such invasion is (1) intentional and unreasonable, (2) negligent or reckless, *or* (3) actionable under the rules governing liability for abnormally dangerous conditions or activities.

Copart, 41 N.Y.2d at 569 (emphasis added).

The elements of a private nuisance cause of action, premised on an intentional and unreasonable invasion, are: "(1) an interference substantial in nature, (2) intentional in origin, (3) unreasonable in character, (4) with a person's property right to use and enjoy land, (5) caused by another's conduct in acting or failure to act." *Id.* at 570. In particular, an invasion of another's interest in the use and enjoyment of land is "intentional in origin" " 'when the actor (a) acts for the purpose of causing it; or (b) knows that it is resulting or is substantially certain to result from his conduct.' " *Id.* at 571 (citations omitted).

We conclude that Jasco's conduct constituted a private nuisance, based on intentional and unreasonable conduct. Specifically, under *Copart,* we find that: (1) there were "high levels of barium" contamination on the Scribner's property; (2) Jasco knew that contamination was "substantially certain to result" from its conduct, *see Copart,* 41 N.Y.2d at 571 * * *, based on its demolition and cleansing practices, as well as the "mov[ement of] water into a swale on Jasco's land, but near the boundary with plaintiffs," which was located downhill from Jasco's property; (3) Jasco's on-site disposal and cleansing practices from 1986 to 1990—coupled with its knowledge that barium is a hazardous waste—were unreasonable; (4) the contamination interfered with the Scribners' use and enjoyment of their land, at the very least because the Scribners are faced with the inconvenience of having the hazardous waste removed from their property; and (5) Jasco's conduct caused the invasion. We therefore hold that Jasco is liable under a theory of private nuisance.

IV. *Strict Liability*

The Scribners also argue that Jasco's method of disposal was an ultrahazardous activity that proximately caused the contamination of their property, and thus Jasco is strictly liable for the damage. Because we reverse on the trespass and nuisance claims, however, we decline to reach the issue of strict liability, and take no position that issue.

V. *Damages*

Although the Scribners ask us to determine damages, we decline the invitation. This task is better left to the district court in the first instance. Thus, we remand this case to the district court, solely on the issue of damages. We note, however, that although we find that Jasco is liable in both trespass and private nuisance, the Scribners are obviously entitled to recover only once for the damage sustained to their property.

CONCLUSION

Robert Frost counseled that "good fences make good neighbors." Robert Frost, "Mending Wall," in *The Poetry of Robert Frost* 33–34 (Edward Latham ed., 1969). Alas, if only Mr. Frost had fashioned a solution to migrating barium. The decision of the district court is REVERSED and REMANDED for a determination of damages.

b. The Potential Effect of CERCLA Cleanups on Other Claims

While CERCLA generally preserves other claims, including toxic tort claims, arising from the release of hazardous substances, it does not do so without limitation. For example, CERCLA specifies that "[t]his chapter does not affect or otherwise impair the rights of any person under Federal, State, or common law, *except with respect to the timing of review as provided in section [113(h),] 9613(h) of this title * * *.*" CERCLA § 310(h), 42 U.S.C. § 9659(h) (emphasis added). The referenced section 113(h) limits the availability of judicial review until after the site is cleaned up, stating that "[n]o Federal court shall have jurisdiction under Federal law * * * to review any challenges to removal or remedial action selected under section 9604 of this title, or to review any order issued under section 9606(a) of this title * * *." CERCLA § 113(h), 42 U.S.C. § 9613(h). Thus, the existence of CERCLA cleanup decisions can affect the availability of certain kinds of tort claims, as the following case demonstrates.

NEW MEXICO v. GENERAL ELECTRIC CO.

United States Court of Appeals for the Tenth Circuit, 2006.
467 F.3d 1223.

BALDOCK, CIRCUIT JUDGE.

This is a case in which the Attorney General for the State of New Mexico (AG) seeks unrestricted money damages exclusively under state law for groundwater contamination in Albuquerque's South Valley. The district court granted summary judgment to Defendants General Electric (GE) and ACF Industries (ACF) because the AG "failed to raise genuine issues of material fact on the essential elements of injury and damages." We exercise jurisdiction under 28 U.S.C. § 1291, and affirm in part and dismiss in part.

I.

Because federal law, namely CERCLA, impacts the AG's damage claim in a myriad of ways, we first trace the course of federally-mandated remedial efforts over the past two decades to clean up the contamination. The South Valley is located in a largely industrial area east of the Rio Grande River and west of the Albuquerque International Sunport, near the intersection of Broadway and Woodward Avenues. The contaminated site encompasses approximately one square mile. A residential area with around 600 residents lies just north of the site. The contamination affects the city's San Jose well field, one of twenty-five well fields serving the city. The property from which the chemical contamination involved in this case originated is located on the western portion of the site. In 1951, the Atomic Energy Commission procured the property, and, through Defendant ACF, engaged in production activities related to the manufacture of nuclear weapons components. In 1967, the United States Air Force (USAF) converted the facility into an aircraft engine parts manufacturing plant. For the next sixteen years, Defendant GE operated Plant 83, as it is commonly known, under a series of contracts with the USAF. In 1983, GE purchased Plant 83 and operates it still today.

A.

The city first suspected groundwater contamination in the South Valley in 1978 when irregular tastes and odors appeared in water from private wells near the area's industrial facilities. Subsequent sampling revealed certain volatile organic compounds (VOCs) harmful to health and the environment in the area's municipal wells, including the San Jose No. 6 (SJ–6). In 1981, after further sampling, the Environmental Improvement Division of the New Mexico Health and Environment Department (NMEID) decommissioned SJ–6. Shutting down SJ–6 significantly impacted the San Jose well field's production. SJ–6 had been a productive and economical source of potable water for thousands of Albuquerque residents and played a key role in providing sufficient fire protection to the South Valley. As a result of SJ–6's pivotal role in providing water to the city, NMEID named the South Valley site as the State's top priority for environmental cleanup.

The State, pursuant to CERCLA, requested the United States Environmental Protection Agency (EPA) to place the site on the "National Priorities List" (NPL). See 42 U.S.C. § 9605(a)(8)(B). The EPA placed the

South Valley site on the NPL in 1983 and, at the State's request, began the remedial investigation and feasibility study the same year. The EPA's first task was to determine if initial remedial measures were necessary to mitigate potential threats to human health and/or the environment connected with the shutdown of SJ–6. In its March 1985 Record of Decision (ROD), the EPA noted certain contaminants detected during 1984 well sampling were suspected carcinogens with recommended maximum contaminant levels of zero in drinking water. Consequently, the EPA concluded the water quality of SJ–6 was unfit for human consumption. The EPA further concluded the lack of available water at the tap from SJ–6 adversely impacted available fire protection in the South Valley. Initial remedial measures, also termed "removal" measures, were therefore necessary to limit exposure to both health and environmental hazards in the South Valley.

The EPA selected as an initial remedy the installation of a new well, the Burton No. 4 (B–4), to replace the capacity of the contaminated SJ–6. * * * The EPA labeled the work surrounding the replacement of SJ–6 with B–4 as Operable Unit (OU)1. In its 1985 ROD on OU1, the EPA reported: "The State of New Mexico requested this measure and has been consulted and agrees with the approved remedy."

B.

The city placed B–4 into service in July 1988. Meanwhile, work continued on the remedial investigation and feasibility study at the South Valley site. The investigation surrounding SJ–6, *i.e.*, OU2, first sought to identify the source and extent of contaminants in the groundwater that supplied the well. In September 1988, the EPA delivered an ROD which identified six industrial facilities in the South Valley as the likely sources of SJ–6's contamination. Potentially responsible parties (PRPs) included the USAF, GE, Chevron, Texaco, Whitfield Tank Lines, Univar Corporation, and Duke City Distributing. * * *

Based on extended testing post 1984, the ROD noted "chlorinated solvents detected in SJ–6 most likely do not represent groundwater contamination, but contamination of sediments at the base of the well." Because of source control and remediation of contaminated plumes through other operable units in the South Valley, the EPA concluded "these [SJ–6] contaminants do not appear to pose a significant health threat." Because B–4 had replaced SJ–6's water supply, the EPA chose to clean and seal SJ–6 (along with at least one other municipal well and numerous private wells in the area), monitor the groundwater in the vicinity of SJ–6 for at least thirty years, and place access restrictions on new well construction in the vicinity of SJ–6. According to the ROD, the selected remedy would prevent SJ–6 from serving as a conduit for contaminant migration into the deep aquifers responsible for supplying municipal water.

To assure the permanence and effectiveness of the selected remedy, the EPA provided for a review of environmental conditions surrounding

SJ–6 after five years. The EPA also created a "Design Review Committee" consisting of representatives from the EPA, NMEID, the City of Albuquerque, and PRPs. Still today, the committee's responsibility is to coordinate the various remedial actions implemented at the South Valley Superfund site to ensure site cleanup. In a letter to the EPA, NMEID concurred in the proposed remedy for SJ–6 "conditional on the timely implementation of the remedy selected in the GE/USAF [Plant 83] Record of Decision." * * *

Together with its ROD on OU2, the EPA delivered its ROD on GE's Plant 83, *i.e.*, OU5 and OU6, in September 1988. OU5 and OU6 respectively address remediation of the shallow and deeper zone groundwater aquifers underlying Plant 83. PRPs identified in the Plant 83 ROD included, among others, Defendants ACF and GE, the USAF, and the United States Department of Energy (USDOE). The USAF conducted a first round of investigation at Plant 83 in 1984 and 1985 and a second round of investigation in 1987 and 1988, each under a Memorandum of Understanding with the EPA. Based on the USAF's investigation, the EPA concluded VOCs present in the groundwater posed an unacceptable health risk, "requiring remediation to depths of up to 160 feet." * * * The EPA reached its conclusion based on "Applicable or Relevant and Appropriate Requirements" (ARARs) as set forth in the Federal Safe Drinking Water Act, 42 U.S.C. §§ 300f thru 300j–26, the New Mexico Water Quality Act, N.M. Stat. Ann § 74–6–1 thru 74–6–17, and accompanying regulations. * * *

To rectify the groundwater contamination emanating from Plant 83, the EPA elected to extract the contaminated groundwater through extraction wells and treat it with carbon adsorption, and in the case of the deeper zone, air stripping before reinjecting it into the aquifer. * * * The selected remedy also included groundwater monitoring both during and after completion of remediation to ensure the remedy's effectiveness. Finally, the EPA scheduled five-year reviews as required by CERCLA to assure the remedy remained protective of human health and the environment. NMEID agreed with the selected remedy in a letter to the EPA * * *.

C.

The remedial design and action phase of the cleanup followed. In June 1989, the EPA issued a Unilateral Administrative Order (UAO) to GE to perform the necessary work on OU2. In September 1994, GE completed work on OU2 pursuant to that order. SJ–6, as well as one other less significant municipal well, SJ–3, and several private wells, were successfully plugged and abandoned. GE also established a groundwater monitoring program as required by the ROD. Both the EPA's 2000 and 2005 memoranda approving the five-year reviews for OU2 concluded "the analysis of the data shows that the plugging and abandonment program was effective.... [T]he remedy for OU2 has been, and is expected to continue to be, protective of human health and the environment."

At the same time, the EPA issued a second UAO to GE to cleanup the contamination associated with Plant 83 in a manner consistent with the ROD on OU5 and OU6. GE agreed and, following additional investigation at the site, began design of shallow and deeper zone remediation systems in 1991. The shallow and deeper zone systems became operable in May 1994 and April 1996, respectively. Today, the shallow zone system includes thirty monitoring wells, eight extraction wells, an injection well, and a groundwater treatment system. The extracted groundwater is conveyed through a dual-contained pipe to the treatment system where it is treated using liquid-phase granulated activated carbon to adsorb the VOCs. Following treatment, the water is reinjected into the shallow aquifer. * * * As reported in the 2000 and 2005 five-year review reports, approved by both EPA and NMED, VOC concentrations in the groundwater from the shallow extraction and monitoring wells have been steadily decreasing. The extent of the contaminant plume is decreasing as well. Both reports concluded: "[T]he Shallow Zone Groundwater Remediation System is working as designed and reducing the VOC concentrations in the Shallow Zone groundwater."

GE initially installed numerous wells to identify the boundaries of Plant 83's deeper zone plume. The design objectives of the deeper zone remediation system (addressing the intermediate and deep zones as described in the ROD) included hydraulic control of the deeper zone plume and flushing the VOCs from the aquifer to meet ARARs. The design established a hydraulic barrier between the contaminant plume and the nearest city water supply well three-quarters mile to the east. Today, the system consists of seventy-nine monitoring wells, four high volume extraction wells, twelve injection wells, and a groundwater treatment system. The system operates by extracting groundwater and conveying it via dual-contained pipe to the treatment center. The water is then pumped through two air-stripping towers on its way to two granulated active carbon vessels. Once in a holding tank, the water is piped through a filter system to remove particles. Finally, the water travels to twelve injection wells where it is returned to the deeper zone aquifer. Monitoring wells monitor the progress of the remediation both horizontally and vertically inside and outside the plume boundaries. According to the 2005 five-year review report: "[T]he Deep Zone Ground Water Remediation System is an effective hydraulic control, and operates as designed to maintain capture of impacted groundwater in the Deep Zone plume."

Since startup, the deeper zone treatment system has operated 24 hours a day except for routine maintenance and unplanned stoppages due to, among other things, ice formation, lightning, and high winds. As stated in the 2000 five-year review report and reiterated in the 2005 report: "[T]he VOC plume has been captured by the Deep Zone Remediation System." "The aerial extent of the Deep Zone Plume is shrinking, and concentrations of VOCs have reduced significantly since the Deep Zone Plant became operational[.]" "The treatment system has been effective in removing constituents to concentrations below the ARARs, and water injected back into the Deep Zone Aquifer is in compliance with the applicable discharge requirements." "VOCs above ARARs have not been detected in any monitoring or water supply wells downgradient of the remediation system." Both reports concluded the shallow and deeper zone remediation systems "are protective of human health and the environment."

D.

Recently, the EPA and NMED approved the 2005 five-year review report for the South Valley site. Although remediation continues at OU5 and OU6 due to hazardous wastes in the subsurface above contaminant levels allowing for unlimited use and unrestricted exposure, the overall remedy remains protective of human health and the environment. The EPA's approval memorandum, dated September 2005, indicates that "[f]rom system startup through July 2005, approximately 900,000 gallons of groundwater have been extracted and treated from the shallow zone aquifer [OU5]." "The shallow zone groundwater remediation system has mitigated the migration of VOCs in the saturated portion of the shallow zone aquifer and the size of the contaminant plume is decreasing." * * *

The 2005 memo's comment on the deeper zone remediation system was similarly favorable. From system startup through July 2005, "over 3.7 billion gallons of groundwater were extracted, treated, and returned to the subsurface at an average flow rate of over 900 gallons per minute.... Approximately 1,400 pounds of VOC mass have been removed." Regarding the deep plume, the EPA's memo reported: "The deep groundwater remediation system has been effective in capturing the groundwater contaminant plume associated with OU #6." * * *

As the foregoing history illustrates, the State of New Mexico, through NMED and its predecessor NMEID, from the outset has played a meaningful role in the CERCLA-mandated removal and response plan for the South Valley Superfund site—a plan which to date appears to be achieving its aim of restoring the groundwater in the South Valley to below ARARs. Notably, we find nothing in the record which indicates NMED currently opposes any aspect of the ongoing cleanup which is scheduled to conclude around 2016. Rather, the EPA has worked with and addressed the concerns of NMED at every stage of the cleanup. * * *

II.

In addition to affording the State of New Mexico an opportunity to avail itself of a federally-mandated cleanup response in the South Valley, a form of mandatory injunctive relief, CERCLA empowered the State to bring an action against GE, ACF, and other PRPs for natural resource damages (NRDs) to the public's groundwater. * * *

CERCLA directs New Mexico's Governor to appoint a NRT to act on behalf of the public. *Id.* § 9607(f)(2)(B). Consistent with CERCLA, the New Mexico Legislature enacted the "Natural Resources Trustee Act"

(NRTA) in 1993. *See* N.M. Stat. Ann. §§ 75–7–1 thru 75–7–5. The NRTA created the "Office of Natural Resources Trustee" (ONRT) within NMED. *Id.* § 75–7–2.B. The NRT serves at the pleasure of the Governor. *Id.* §§ 75–7–2.A. Among the NRT's express duties are the assessment and collection of "damages for injury to, destruction of, or loss of natural resources, including bringing legal actions[.]" *Id.* § 75–7–3.A.(5). An award of NRDs in New Mexico "shall consist of those amounts calculated in accordance with federal law, including ... the cost of restoration, replacement or acquisition of equivalent resources, plus compensation for the loss of use or enjoyment of the natural resources...." *Id.* § 75–7–4.A.

Consistent with his duties under CERCLA and the NRTA, in 1999 New Mexico's NRT entered into tolling agreements with several PRPs, including GE, the USAF, and USDOE, to delay a CERCLA-based NRD lawsuit while he attempted to negotiate a settlement of the State's NRD claims. The NRT believed tolling agreements were necessary due to CERCLA's three-year statute of limitations on NRD claims. *See* 42 U.S.C. § 9613(g). At the same time, the NRT was seeking funding from the New Mexico Legislature for a NRD assessment. The NRT apparently believed a NRD assessment pursuant to federal regulations was necessary to the success of the State's NRD claims because such assessments "have the force and effect of a rebuttable presumption on behalf of the trustee in any administrative or judicial proceeding" under CERCLA. *See* 42 U.S.C. § 9607(f)(2)(C).

The regulations, promulgated by the Department of Interior, "provide[ ] a procedure by which a [NRT] can determine compensation for injuries to natural resources that have not been nor are expected to be addressed by response actions conducted pursuant to [CERCLA regulations]." 43 C.F.R. § 11.10. While the assessment procedures set out in Part 11 are not mandatory, a State NRT must use them to obtain the rebuttable presumption contained in § 9607(f)(2)(C). *Id.* Apparently, neither the New Mexico legislature nor the newly-elected AG saw need for such an assessment. Asserting her role as the State of New Mexico's chief law enforcement officer, the AG filed suit against the PRPs on October 1, 1999, absent any NRD assessment.

A.

The AG retained independent counsel to file two separate NRD lawsuits relating to the South Valley Superfund site. The first, filed in federal district court, alleged claims for money damages under CERCLA § 9607(f)(1). Among a host of other business and government entities, the complaint named GE, ACF, the USAF, and USDOE as defendants. The complaint alleged harm arising "from the presence, migration, and threat of further migration of hazardous chemical wastes and other substances from the operable units which comprise the South Valley Superfund Site[.]" The suit named New Mexico's NRT as an "involuntary plaintiff pursuant to Fed. R. Civ. P. 19." The complaint indicated the AG would "provide legal counsel and representation to the ONRT pursuant to the provisions of [the NRTA]." *See* N.M. Stat. Ann. § 75–7–3.C.

The second suit, filed in state district court, alleged various state statutory and common law claims for NRDs, including trespass, public nuisance, and negligence. The complaint omitted the federal entities, but otherwise named the same defendants, including GE and ACF, as the federal suit. The state court complaint summarized the harm giving rise to the AG's case against the PRPs in the exact manner as the federal court complaint. GE and ACF promptly removed the AG's state action to federal court, where the district court, on its own motion, consolidated it with the AG's federal action. * * *

* * *

B.

Over the remaining course of the litigation, the district court issued a trilogy of opinions before ultimately granting summary judgment to GE and ACF. The first opinion, issued in April 2004 and comprising 145 pages, sought to define the scope of triable issues arising from the AG's remaining state law claims, namely, (1) common law trespass, (2) common law public nuisance, (3) statutory public nuisance, and (4) common law negligence. By this time, the AG's NRD demand had fallen from over $4 billion to over $1.2 billion—cash compensation earmarked for the State's general treasury fund.

Distinguishing between private property rights and public trust interests, the court first held the AG could not maintain a trespass action under New Mexico law against GE or ACF. * * * Next, the court held the AG could pursue claims of common law and statutory public nuisance "to remedy the alleged injury to the public's groundwater and to vindicate the State's interest in making that groundwater available for public use." * * * Finally, the court held New Mexico law entitled the AG to maintain a negligence action against GE and ACF for money damages "limited to reasonable compensation for the actual and unavoidable consequences of an injury-in-fact to the State's interests, further limited by the degree of fault, if any, properly attributable to the wrongful conduct [of non-parties]."

* * *

C.

The district court delivered its second opinion in May 2004. That opinion addressed the proposed testimony of numerous expert witnesses, including the testimony of the AG's three principal experts, David Brookshire, Stephen Johnson, and Dennis Williams. Pursuant to GE and ACF's motion, the court excluded large portions of the experts' testimony as irrelevant to the issues of injury and damage. * * *

* * *

D.

With the State's case significantly diminished, the district court delivered its third and final opinion in June 2004. By this time, the AG had narrowed her claim for damages to those "not recoverable under CERCLA for groundwater contamination 'outside' the 'box that GE and the EPA are willing to remediate'—that is, the 'box' defined by the intended scope of the existing EPA-ordered remediation." Thus the "core of the controversy" between the parties became the intended scope of CERCLA-mandated remedial efforts in the South Valley, efforts the AG after a decade described as "woefully inadequate." The AG rested her latest theory of recovery on the presence of a "deep, deep" contaminant plume beneath the South Valley Site, "hundreds of feet below the reach of the existing remediation system," and outside the scope of the ongoing remediation. Once again, the court found the AG's proof "woefully inadequate."

* * *

The district court * * * concluded the AG failed to raise any genuine issue of material fact regarding her "narrower, static view" of the intended scope of the CERCLA-mandated remediation. * * * The record, according to the court, "indicates that the EPA's selected remedy ... is intended to address *all* contamination at or emanating from the Plant 83 site."

More importantly, the AG had failed to establish the presence of any contamination in the South Valley beyond the reach of CERCLA and the EPA's remedial plan, thus leaving the AG without a case * * *.

III.

Throughout the course of this chronicle, the State of New Mexico has availed itself of federal legislative and executive authority to compel the PRPs, including Defendants GE and ACF, to clean up their mess in the South Valley. During such course, New Mexico's NRT, backed by and consistent with his duties under both federal and state law, began his pursuit of NRDs against the PRPs. In mid course, the State AG decided she had a better plan to benefit the public treasury, and, at least in the opinion of some, usurped the authority of the State's NRT and jumped ship. Without any CERCLA-based NRD assessment to rely on, the State undertook the arduous task of proving as an initial matter natural resources injury outside the intended scope of a comprehensive, CERCLA-mandated remediation. The State also confronted the problem of restrictions which both CERCLA and the NRTA impose upon the measure of damages even supposing some redressable injury remains. These are the overlying concerns which lead us, like the district court, to conclude the State, at least for now, is entitled to no relief on its NRD claim arising out of groundwater contamination in the South Valley. We begin by defining the scope of the State's NRD claim.

A.

No one doubts the State of New Mexico manages the public waters within its borders as trustee for the people and is authorized to institute suit to protect those waters on the latter's behalf. * * * Similarly, no one doubts the duty of the State AG generally to prosecute a state law civil action in which the State is a party. In view of the foregoing, neither GE nor ACF challenges the State's Article III standing to pursue this state law action for harm to the public interest in its capacity as trustee of the State's groundwaters.

Armed with standing, the State throughout this litigation has asserted an unrestricted right to pursue against GE and ACF any and all claims, remedies, and damage theories available under state law. The State supports its assertion by referencing two of CERCLA's saving clauses. The first, 42 U.S.C. § 9614(a), provides: "Nothing in this chapter shall be construed or interpreted as preempting any State from imposing any additional liability or requirements with respect to the release of hazardous substances within such State." The second, 42 U.S.C. § 9652(d), provides: "Nothing in this chapter shall affect or modify in any way the obligations or liabilities of any person under other Federal or State law, including common law, with respect to releases of hazardous substances or other pollutants or contaminants." Given these saving clauses, as well as the spirit of cooperative federalism running throughout CERCLA and its regulations, we may safely say Congress did not intend CERCLA to completely preempt state laws related to hazardous waste contamination.

At most then, this is a case of conflict preemption—an affirmative defense available to GE and ACF notwithstanding the presence of the saving clauses. To ascertain CERCLA's preemptive effect in this case and thus define the scope of the State's NRD claim, we ask whether that claim, or any portion thereof, stands as an obstacle to the accomplishment of congressional objectives as encompassed in CERCLA.

1.

CERCLA is best known as setting forth a comprehensive mechanism to cleanup hazardous waste sites under a restoration-based approach. * * * Less well known but increasingly important is CERCLA's comprehensive damage scheme which addresses damage assessment for natural resource injury, damage recovery for such injury, and use of such recovery. As we have seen, CERCLA, at the behest of federal and state NRTs, imposes liability upon PRPs not only for cleanup costs, but also for "damages for injury to, destruction of, or loss of natural resources," including the reasonable costs of assessing such damages. 42 U.S.C. § 9607(a)(4)(c). While damages recovered under CERCLA are "available for use only to restore, replace, or acquire the equivalent of such natural resources by the State," damages are not limited, "by the sums which can be used to restore or replace such resource." *Id.* § 9607(f)(1).

The legislative history of CERCLA's 1986 amendments makes the meaning of § 9607(f)(1) abundantly clear. The *measure* and *use* of damages arising from the release of hazardous waste is restricted to accomplishing CERCLA's essential goals of restoration or replacement, while also allowing for damages due to interim loss of use * * *.

CERCLA's saving clauses (as well as other CERCLA provisions) undoubtedly preserve a quantum of state legislative and common law actions and remedies related to the release and cleanup of hazardous waste. The saving clause found at 42 U.S.C. § 9614(a) ensures that states may enact laws "to supplement federal measures related to the cleanup of hazardous wastes." *Manor Care,* 950 F.2d at 126 (Alito, J.). CERCLA sets a floor, not a ceiling. Section 9614(a) preserves state environmental regulations which in some instances set more stringent cleanup standards. Section 9614(a) reinforces a state's right to demand hazardous waste cleanup apart from CERCLA: "CERCLA [§ 9614(a)] preserves the right of a state or other party to proceed under applicable state law to conduct a cleanup of a site affected by hazardous substances." *Colorado v. Idarado Mining Co.,* 916 F.2d 1486, 1488 (10th Cir.1990).

Meanwhile, the principle [*sic*] purpose of the saving clause located at 42 U.S.C. § 9652(d) "is to preserve to victims of toxic waste the other remedies they may have under federal or state law." *PMC, Inc. v. Sherwin–Williams Co.,* 151 F.3d 610, 617 (7th Cir. 1998) (Posner, J.). "Congress, in enacting CERCLA, intended to provide a vehicle for cleaning up and preserving the environment from the evils of improperly disposed of hazardous substances rather than a new font of law on which private parties could base claims for personal and property injuries." *Artesian Water Co. v. Government of New Castle County,* 659 F.Supp. 1269, 1286 (D.Del.1987) (internal quotations omitted), *aff'd,* 851 F.2d 643 (3d Cir.1988). In *PMC,* 151 F.3d at 618, the Seventh Circuit explained that while "federal environmental laws [were] not intended to wipe out the common law of nuisance[,]" § 9652(d) "must not be used to gut provisions of CERCLA[:]"

> The purpose of a saving clause is merely to nix an inference that the statute in which it appears is intended to be the exclusive remedy for harms caused by the violation of the statute. The legislature doesn't want to wipe out people's rights inadvertently, with the possible consequence of making the intended beneficiaries of the legislation worse off than before it was enacted.

2.

Sound public policy, as reflected in CERCLA (and New Mexico's NRTA), demands that "environmental protection and preservation be the primary, if not the sole, objective of natural resource damage valuation." Frank B. Cross, *Natural Resource Damage Valuation,* 42 Vand.L Rev. 269, 327 (1989). The notion that NRDs should be used to restore or replace the injured natural resource predates CERCLA. * * *

[A]n unrestricted award of money damages does not restore or replace contaminated natural resources. When trust resources, in this case groundwater, are contaminated, however, the trustee as fiduciary should restore or replace the corpus of the trust. Such was the obvious objective of Congress in enacting 42 U.S.C. § 9607(f)(1). Consistent with this objective, we hold CERCLA's comprehensive NRD scheme preempts any state remedy designed to achieve something other than the restoration, replacement, or acquisition of the equivalent of a contaminated natural resource. We reach this conclusion notwithstanding CERCLA's saving clauses because we do not believe Congress intended to undermine CERC-LA's carefully crafted NRD scheme through these saving clauses. The restrictions on the use of NRDs in § 9607(f)(1) represent Congress' considered judgment as to the best method of serving the public interest in addressing the cleanup of hazardous waste. We cannot endorse any state law suit that seeks to undermine that judgment.

This is not to say the State's public nuisance and negligence theories of recovery are completely preempted in view of the ongoing remediation in the South Valley. We need not go that far. Rather the remedy the State seeks to obtain through such causes of action—an unrestricted award of money damages—cannot withstand CERCLA's comprehensive NRD scheme. An interpretation of the saving clauses that preserved the State's NRD claim for money damages in its original form would seriously disrupt CERCLA's principle aim of cleaning up hazardous waste.

Under the logic of the State's approach, hazardous waste sites need never be cleaned up as long as PRPs are willing or required to tender money damages to a state as trustee. Similarly, PRPs conceivably might be liable for double recovery where a state's successful state law claim for money damages precedes an EPA-ordered cleanup. Finally, in a case where an NRD claim is premised upon both CERCLA and state law, a portion of the recovery if earmarked for the state law claims could be used for something other (for example, attorney fees) than to restore or replace the injured resource. The remainder of the NRD recovery, earmarked for the CERCLA claim, would then be insufficient to restore or replace such resource. Clearly, permitting the State to use an NRD recovery, which it would hold in trust, for some purpose other than to "restore, replace, or acquire the equivalent of" the injured groundwater would undercut Congress's policy objectives in enacting 42 U.S.C. § 9607(f)(1).

B.

Having thus defined and narrowed the scope of the State's NRD claim against Defendants GE and ACF, we turn to the underlying merits of the State's arguments in support of NRDs as a result of groundwater contamination in the South Valley. The State essentially seeks to hold GE and ACF liable for both replacement and loss of use costs. According to the State, the CERCLA-mandated remediation process is both underinclusive and inadequate in that (1) a portion of the contaminated groundwater lies outside the parameters of the remediation and (2) the remainder of the contaminated groundwater cannot be restored to below the State's maximum contaminant levels, *i.e.*, appropriate water quality standards. The State further argues it has lost the interim right to appropriate the South Valley's contaminated groundwater for beneficial use. We address these arguments in turn, dismissing the former and rejecting the latter.

1.

Despite the State's contrary assertion, its expert-intense argument that the remedial phase of the cleanup does not address the entirety of the contamination and will not restore the groundwater to beneficial use as drinking water is, in all respects, a challenge to an EPA-ordered remediation. In its opening brief, the State repeatedly takes aim at the ongoing remediation. The State argues the EPA is not applying the "proper remediation standard[s]." The State complains the EPA "abandon[ed] the ROD and require[d] remediation of only the shallowest portion of the total plume." The State attacks the remediation as "limited in scope" and argues the remediation "leaves a substantial portion of contaminated water untreated." The State's assertions are contrary to both the EPA's and NMED's view that the remediation system, which we have described extensively, (a) has fully captured the contaminant plume in the South Valley, (b) is successfully restoring the groundwater to drinking water standards, and (c) will continue to operate until restoration is complete.

Of course, any challenge to the remediation in the South Valley must wait because CERCLA "protects the execution of a CERCLA plan *during its pendency* from lawsuits that might interfere with the expeditious cleanup effort." *McClellan Ecological Seepage Situation v. Perry,* 47 F.3d 325, 329 (9th Cir.1995). Absent certain exceptions inapplicable to this case (including most notably an NRT's NRD lawsuit under § 9607), CERCLA § 9613(h), entitled "Timing of review," provides: "No Federal Court shall have jurisdiction ... under State law ... to review any challenges to removal or remedial action selected...." 42 U.S.C. § 9613(h). Commenting on said section, we have explained: "To the extent a state seeks to challenge a CERCLA response action, the plain language of § 9613(h) would limit a federal court's jurisdiction to review such a challenge." *Colorado,* 990 F.2d at 1576. In other words, "[t]he obvious meaning of [§ 9613(h)] is that when a remedy has been selected, no challenge to the cleanup may occur prior to completion of the remedy." *Schalk v. Reilly,* 900 F.2d 1091, 1095 (7th Cir.1990). Because the State's lawsuit calls into question the EPA's remedial response plan, it is related to the goals of the cleanup, and thus constitutes a "challenge" to the cleanup under § 9613(h).

The State's argument that it is not seeking to alter or expand the EPA's response plan but rather only to acquire money damages falls on deaf ears. Any relief provided the State would substitute a federal court's judgment for the authorized judgment of both the EPA and NMED (lest we forget an arm of the State) that the cleanup is not only comprehensive but flexible and dynamic, readily adjusting as new data is received.

Accepting the State's argument might place GE and ACF in the unenviable position of being held liable for monetary damages because they are complying with an EPA-ordered remedy which GE and ACF have no power to alter without prior EPA approval. No one doubts that § 9613(h) would prohibit us from entertaining a state law action requesting mandatory injunctive relief to alter or expand the ongoing response plan in the South Valley. We will not permit the State to achieve indirectly through the threat of monetary damages, which would be available only to restore or replace the injured natural resource, what it cannot obtain directly through mandatory injunctive relief incompatible with the ongoing CERCLA-mandated remediation.

The State's argument that remediation in the South Valley is not working as the EPA and NMED claim constitutes a dispute over environmental cleanup methods and standards. So viewed, § 9613(h) reflects Congress's judgment that residual injury, if any, to the South Valley's groundwater be addressed at the conclusion of the EPA-ordered remediation. Only then will we know the effectiveness of the cleanup and the precise extent of residual damage. Our view is entirely consistent with the State's most recent characterization of its NRD claim in its reply brief as "residual to a CERCLA remedy." Accordingly, we will dismiss for want of jurisdiction under § 9613(h) the State's claim for monetary damages arising from the alleged inadequacy of the EPA's selected remedy in the South Valley. Because under the common law the State is not subject to a statute of limitations, it may renew its common law claims for residual damages under state law if and when necessary.

2.

Lastly, we address the State's loss-of-use damage theory, namely, the State's argument the contamination in the South Valley has deprived it of the right to appropriate groundwater for beneficial use in that area. As we have seen, the State's groundwaters are public waters subject to appropriation for beneficial use. *See* N.M. Stat. Ann. § 72–12–1. State law vests the State Engineer with oversight of those groundwaters. *See id.* § 72–2–1. In a declared underground basin such as that underlying the South Valley, would-be appropriators must apply to the State Engineer for a water rights permit. *See id.* § 72–12–3.A. The State Engineer may issue a permit *only* if he or she finds unappropriated waters are available and existing water rights would remain unimpaired. *See id.* § 72–12–3.E. The State's position, accepted by neither the State Engineer nor NMED, is that absent the contamination, additional groundwater would be available for appropriation in the South Valley notwithstanding the replacement of SJ–6 with B–4. We conclude, however, the district court was quite correct in concluding the State failed to present any evidence on which a reasonable jury could find such availability and thus loss-of-use damages.

The Rio Grande Compact equitably apportions waters of the Rio Grande River among New Mexico, Texas, and Colorado. The surface waters of the Rio Grande have long been fully appropriated. As part of the

Middle Rio Grande Underground Water Basin, the groundwaters underneath the South Valley are located less than a mile from the river and "contribute substantially to the flow of the Rio Grande, thus constituting a part of the source of the stream flow." Because appropriation of groundwaters from the basin affect the surface flow of the Rio Grande, the State Engineer has the authority to require that previously appropriated water rights affecting such flow be retired as a condition to new appropriations of underground water from the basin.

According to the State Engineer's "Guidelines for Review of Water Rights Applications" in the "Middle Rio Grande Administrative Area" (MRGAA), a region which includes the South Valley: "Since the declaration of the Rio Grande Underground Water Basin, . . . groundwater permittees have been required to obtain valid water rights in an amount sufficient to offset the effects of their diversions on the surface flows of the Rio Grande stream system." "The public welfare is best served by limiting actual groundwater diversions within the MRGAA to the amount of valid surface water rights transferred or otherwise held by the permittees, plus the amount of water the permittee returns directly to the river." In other words, new appropriations of groundwater in the South Valley are unavailable absent an offset of existing water rights. Thus, additional groundwater in the South Valley, *for reasons unrelated to the contamination,* is not as readily available for appropriation as the State would have us believe.

Because B–4 provided a point of groundwater diversion outside the parameters of the contamination surrounding SJ–6, we presume all existing water rights in the South Valley are being and have been satisfied. The State has proffered little except bald assertions to suggest otherwise. At oral argument, the court asked the State whether since the startup of B–4 any water rights holders in the South Valley had complained about impairment of those rights or the lack of available water. The court further inquired whether any potential appropriators had been denied permits *due to* the contamination. In neither instance could the State point to an example. Notably, the groundwater contamination in the South Valley apparently has not prevented the City of Albuquerque, the principle holder of appropriated water rights in the South Valley from extracting and using the water to which it is entitled. That's because B–4 "replaced" SJ–6. Viewed alternatively, when B–4 was placed in operation, the State "acquired the equivalent" of the resources it lost when SJ–6 was decommissioned. *See* 42 U.S.C. § 9607(f)(1). As we have seen, this is precisely the principle measure of damages to which the State is entitled. If a contaminated natural resource such as groundwater can be replaced in a timely manner pending restoration, we have difficulty envisioning any significant loss-of-use damage. Thus, the district court properly entered summary judgment in favor of GE and ACF on the State's loss-of-use damage theory.

IV.

Consistent with the foregoing, the State's NRD claim for injury residual to the outcome of the EPA-ordered remediation in the South Valley, based on state law theories of nuisance and negligence, is dismissed for want of jurisdiction. 42 U.S.C. § 9613(h). Although our analysis is largely but not entirely in accord with the district courts', the court's entry of summary judgment in favor of Defendants GE and ACF is nonetheless in all other respects affirmed.

NOTES AND QUESTIONS

1. *Tort actions in federal court and the CERCLA delay in challenging cleanups.* How was the existence of a CERCLA cleanup plan relevant in *New Mexico v. Gen. Elec. Co.?* Why did the court conclude that the state was challenging the approved cleanup plan? Why was that relevant?

Suppose that the State of New Mexico brought a public nuisance claim against GE based on noxious odors released during the cleanup, seeking an injunction. Would section 113(h) affect *that* lawsuit? Why or why not? What if the state sought a determinate amount of damages instead?

What if the State of New Mexico discovered that GE was contaminating completely different water supplies 100 miles away from this cleanup? Would section 113(h) have any relevance then?

Why did Congress include section 113(h) in CERCLA, do you suppose? What was Congress trying to prevent?

2. *CERCLA natural resources damages and New Mexico's lawsuit.* As the court made clear in *New Mexico v. GE,* CERCLA does not prohibit additional lawsuits, but double recovery is still prohibited. How did the State of New Mexico's tort lawsuit run afoul of the "no double recovery" rule? Why, and to what extent, did CERCLA preempt those tort claims?

3. *The federal jurisdiction limitation.* It is important to remember that section 113(h) of CERCLA limits the jurisdiction only of the federal courts. Thus, strictly speaking, section 113(h) does not prohibit plaintiffs from bringing claims in state courts that effectively challenge CERCLA clean-up plans. However, if the state court's decision would conflict with the CERCLA cleanup, then principles of federal preemption would limit the availability of certain kinds of relief. We will discuss federal preemption in depth in Chapter 10.

4. *CERCLA and the commencement date for state statutes of limitation.* The second way that CERCLA affects common law tort claims is through the imposition of a federally required discovery rule for the commencement of statutes of limitation related to the release of hazardous substances. This requirement is a form of federal preemption, and we will discuss it in Chapter 10.

CHAPTER IX

FEDERAL REGULATION OF POTENTIALLY TOXIC PRODUCTS

■ ■ ■

A. INTRODUCTION

So, you have now already seen two forms of congressional intervention into the regulation of toxic exposures: the Occupational Safety and Health Act (OSH Act), which focuses on safety in the workplace; and the federal government's handling of hazardous wastes, through the Resource Conservation and Recovery Act (RCRA) and the Comprehensive Environmental Response, Compensation, and Liability Act (CERCLA). Congress has also addressed a whole range of products that are or could be toxic in a wide variety of federal statutes.

This Chapter examines three of the most widely applicable of those statutes. The *Federal Insecticide, Fungicide, and Rodenticide Act* (FIFRA) regulates pesticides–substances that are commercially important, but that exist to kill things. More generally, the *Toxic Substances Control Act* (TSCA, pronounced TAH-skuh) seeks to ensure that the myriad of chemical products manufactured and sold in the United States does not pose an unreasonable risk of harm to human health or the environment. Finally, pursuant to the *Food, Drug, and Cosmetic Act* (FDCA), the Food and Drug Administration (FDA) regulates a range of products, including foods, food additives, drugs, medical devices, and cosmetics.

As you have learned from earlier chapters, tort law includes a fairly substantial subset known as products liability law. Moreover, plaintiffs have successfully used products liability causes of action to obtain compensation for toxic exposures and the resulting injuries along with other damages. So why would Congress go ahead and regulate so many toxic products?

Statutory regulation can overcome many of the inherent limitations of the use of tort law as a source of public policy governing toxic and hazardous substances. For example, tort law is inherently reactive–it seeks to redress harms that have already occurred. Indeed, injury or damages is an essential element of most tort causes of action. This structure is necessary in the context of traditional sources of tort claims, such as accidents, which by definition are difficult to predict. However, when people and companies are consciously and deliberately handling toxic and hazardous substances, everyone is better off if the law tries to *prevent* the problems that lead to toxic tort claims. From an environmental point of view, it is almost always cheaper and better for the environment to prevent toxic pollution from occurring, rather than trying to clean it up after toxins have contaminated the soil, water, and food chain. More obviously, most people would prefer not to be exposed at all to toxic and hazardous substances that can cause them harm—or at least not at "unacceptably" unsafe levels—rather than sue someone in tort for the resulting cancer or other health impairment.

Nevertheless, while the general policy objectives—preventing toxic impairment of human and environmental health—may seem obvious and unobjectionable, the devil, as always, is in the details. Regulation of toxic substances is essentially about regulating *risk*: How much risk are we willing to tolerate, how much are we willing to pay to reduce risks from toxic substances, and what are we willing to live without? Think about two obvious examples. First, consider the example of drugs. Many drugs pose risks of side effects, yet doctors prescribe them—and more importantly, patients take them—despite those risks. Why? Sometimes, it may be because the risk of side effects is very small. Other times, it may be because the risk from the untreated disease is very large.

Second, consider the example of pesticides. Pesticides are inherently toxic: their function is to kill things (weeds, insect pests, rodents, etc.). Nevertheless, Americans tolerate the use of many pesticides for a variety of purposes, ranging from termite, ant, and cockroach control in a private home to commercial crop pesticides to pesticides to control disease-bearing mosquitoes. How do we balance the risks and benefits of pesticide use in these varying circumstances? Would we actually be safer to eliminate *all* pesticides?

These examples also show that risk analysis comes in many flavors. One way to analyze risk, for example, is a *risk-benefit* approach: Given that a certain product poses a certain amount of a certain kind of risk, are the expected benefits worth taking the risk? To give one exaggerated example, suppose that a new weight loss drug would let you lose five pounds overnight, but if you took the pill there would be a 90% chance that it would kill you. Most people would conclude without much hesitation that the risks outweigh the benefits. Unfortunately, few risk-benefit analyses in real life are so clear-cut, both because of *scientific uncertainty* and because individuals' *tolerances for risk* (and for different kinds of risk) vary. Therefore, regulating risk always involves policy choices.

Neither Congress nor the regulating agencies take the same approach to regulating risk in all contexts. As you read about the three statutory schemes discussed in this Chapter, try to discern the different kinds of decisions that Congress and the agencies have made about how to approach risk regulation in different circumstances. Here are some questions to guide you:

- What problem or risk is Congress or the agency trying to address? Why does Congress or the agency believe that the problem is worth regulating?

- Who has the burden of proof before action can be taken? Has Congress placed the burden of proof on the regulated entities? If so, why? In contrast, if the agency has the burden of proof, why would Congress take that approach?

- What must be proven before action can be taken? Must a product be absolutely safe? Reasonably safe? Safe under prescribed conditions? If so, safe to what–humans, the environment, or both?

- How do costs and liability fit into the regulatory scheme?

- How does the regulatory scheme handle risk?

B. THE FEDERAL INSECTICIDE, FUNGICIDE, AND RODENTICIDE ACT (FIFRA)

As noted, pesticides present the law with a different kind of problem than most toxic substances: the whole point of a pesticide is to kill something. In other words, the very purpose of a pesticide is to be toxic. Consequently, the law has to balance the societal need for these toxic products to protect crops, protect buildings, eliminate hazards, and eliminate disease-carrying insects with the fact that pesticides can be toxic to humans and other non-target species as well as to their intended targets.

Congress sought to balance these two aspects of pesticides in the Federal Insecticide, Fungicide, and Rodenticide Act (FIFRA), 7 U.S.C. §§ 136–136y. FIFRA relies on a registration process through which the federal Environmental Protection Agency (EPA) approves and dictates labels for various pesticides, generally restricting the manner in which particular pesticides may be used. The Act also makes it illegal for people to use unregistered pesticides or to use registered pesticides in violation of the label.

Under FIFRA, a "pesticide" is:

(1) any substance or mixture of substances intended for preventing, destroying, repelling, or mitigating any pest, (2) any substance or mixture of substances intended for use as a plant regulator, defoliant, or dessicant, and (3) any nitrogen stabilizer * * *.

Id. § 136(u). However, pesticides do not include new animal drugs, animal feed, or liquid sterilizers used in human medicine, which are regulated under the Food, Drug, and Cosmetic Act. Id.

FIFRA requires "any person" to register a pesticide with the EPA before that pesticide can be sold or distributed in the United States. Id. § 136a(a). To register a pesticide, the relevant person (usually the manufacturer or distributor) must apply to the EPA and present the EPA with the pesticide's formula and testing data. Id. § 136a(c)(1). (To gather the test data, a person can apply for an Experimental Use Permit, id. § 136c, which allows for limited application of the pesticide.) The EPA Administrator will then register the pesticide if:

(A) its composition is such as to warrant the proposed claims for it;

(B) its labeling and other material required to be submitted comply with the requirements of [FIFRA];

(C) it will perform its intended function *without unreasonable adverse effects on the environment*; and

(D) when used in accordance with widespread and commonly recognized practice *it will not generally cause unreasonable adverse effects on the environment.*

Id. § 136a(c)(5) (emphasis added). If any of these requirements are not met, the EPA can deny the registration application. Id. § 136a(c)(6).

As noted, pesticide registrations seek to avoid unreasonable adverse effects on the environment. FIFRA defines "unreasonable adverse effects on the environment" to be:

(1) any unreasonable risk to man or the environment, taking into account the economic, social, and environmental costs and benefits of the use of any pesticide, or (2) a human dietary risk from residues that result from a use of a pesticide in or on any food inconsistent with the standard under section 346a of Title 21 [the Food, Drug, and Cosmetic Act]. The Administrator shall consider the risks and benefits of public health pesticides separate from the risks and benefits of other pesticides. In weighing any regulatory action concerning a public health pesticide under this subchapter, the Administrator shall weigh any risks of the pesticide against the health risks such as the diseases transmitted by the vector to be controlled by the pesticide.

Id. § 136(bb). Thus, FIFRA's unreasonable risk analysis incorporates both a risk-benefit analysis—not *all* potential risks of a pesticide are unreasonable—and, for public health pesticides (think about spraying to control disease-bearing mosquitoes), a risk-risk analysis–that is, a comparison of the risks that the pesticide poses and the risks that the disease poses.

If the EPA decides to register a pesticide, it can register the pesticide as a *general use pesticide*, a *restricted use pesticide*, or both (for different uses). A pesticide can be registered as a general use pesticide if the EPA "determines that the pesticide, which applied in accordance with its directions for use, warnings and cautions and for the uses for which it is registered, or for one or more of such uses, or in accordance with a widespread and commonly used practice, will not generally cause unreasonable adverse effects on the environment * * *." Id. § 136a(d)(1)(B). In contrast, if the pesticide might generally cause such adverse effects, "including injury to the applicator," "without additional regulatory restrictions," the EPA will classify the pesticide as a restricted use pesticide and regulate its use more stringently. Id. § 136a(d)(1)(C). These additional restrictions, for example, can include a requirement that only trained and certified applicators apply the pesticide.

To enforce these requirements, FIFRA makes a number of actions illegal, including: selling or distributing an unregistered pesticide; selling or distributing a registered pesticide with claims or for uses other than those approved by the EPA; selling or distributing a registered pesticide with a different formula than that approved by the EPA; selling or distributing a misbranded or adulterated pesticide; detaching, altering, defacing, or destroying required labels; distributing or selling restricted use pesticides for other uses; and using a registered pesticide in a manner inconsistent with its labeling. Id. § 136j(a)(1). Persons who violate the Act can be punished with both civil and criminal penalties. Id. § 136l.

1. IMPLEMENTING FIFRA: AVOIDING UNREASONABLE ADVERSE EFFECTS

FIFRA also allows the EPA to de-register a pesticide in light of emerging information about the pesticide's effects. As the following case demonstrates, the standards for de-registration are similar to those for refusing to register a pesticide in the first place. How does FIFRA deal with the risks from pesticides, according to the U.S. Court of Appeals for the Fifth Circuit?

CIBA–GEIGY CORP. v. UNITED STATES ENVIRONMENTAL PROTECTION AGENCY

United States Court of Appeals for the Fifth Circuit, 1989.
874 F.2d 277.

ALVIN B. RUBIN, CIRCUIT JUDGE:

The issue is whether the Administrator of the United States Environmental Protection Agency (EPA) misapplied § 6(b) of the Federal Insecticide, Fungicide and Rodenticide Act (FIFRA), 7 U.S.C. § 136d(b), in cancelling the registration of the pesticide diazinon for use on golf courses and sod farms on the ground that it "generally causes unreasonable adverse effects on the environment." Ciba–Geigy Corporation, a manufacturer of diazinon, seeks to have this court set aside the Administrator's order, contending that the Administrator failed to give effect to the statutory term "generally". Because FIFRA defines "adverse effects on the environment" to include not merely actual harmful consequences but "any unreasonable risk," we hold that the statute does not require the Administrator to find that diazinon kills birds more often than not in order to ban its use. Because, however, the Administrator improperly gave no effect to the word "generally," we grant Ciba–Geigy's petition in part and remand this case to the Administrator for application of the correct legal standard.

I.

The EPA issued a Notice of Intent to cancel the registrations of pesticide products containing diazinon for use on golf courses and sod farms because of concern about the effects of diazinon on birds. After extensive public hearings, the EPA's Chief Administrative Law Judge concluded that diazinon should be classified for "restricted use" by licensed applicators only and that its label should be amended, but that its registration for use on golf courses and sod farms should not be cancelled. The EPA staff appealed to the Administrator, who, after a careful analysis of the record, ordered diazinon banned from use on golf courses and sod farms. The Administrator accepted many of the Administrative Law Judge's findings and conclusions, but rejected his balancing of the risks and benefits of diazinon use. The Administrator also specifically rejected Ciba–Geigy's argument, made before the Administrative Law Judge but abandoned on appeal, that because FIFRA § 6(b) authorizes cancellation of the registration of products that "generally cause [] unreasonable adverse effects on the environment,"[1] cancellation is justified only if a product causes unreasonable adverse effects most of the time it is used. The Administrator stated:

> FIFRA § 6(b) requires compliance with all other provisions of the statute, including FIFRA § 3(c)(5)(C) which prohibits unreasonable adverse effects on the environment without regard to whether such effects are caused "generally." Moreover, Ciba–Geigy's reading of the word "generally" as meaning "most of the time" is unnatural. In light of the basic statutory standard in FIFRA § 2(bb), which requires consideration of a broad range of factors, "generally" is more appropriately read as meaning "with regard to an overall picture".... It is simply untenable to suggest that FIFRA requires continued registration where a pesticide causes unreasonable adverse effects in less than 51 percent of the cases in which it is used.

In the Administrator's view, FIFRA authorizes him to cancel registration of a pesticide whenever he finds that it causes any unreasonable risk, irrespective of the frequency with which that risk occurs.

Urging that FIFRA requires the EPA to conclude that diazinon "generally" causes unreasonable adverse effects to birds before it can cancel its registration, Ciba–Geigy petitions this court to set aside the Administrator's order.

II.

The Administrative Law Judge concluded that bird kills due to diazinon may be an "unusual occurrence." Ciba–Geigy asserts, therefore,

---

1.   7 U.S.C. § 136d(b).

that even if diazinon sometimes causes adverse environmental effects, it does not do so "generally" as the statute requires.

Ciba–Geigy's argument focuses on a single word in the statutory phrase, ignoring the meaning of the phrase as a whole. FIFRA provides that the Administrator may cancel the registration of a pesticide if it appears to him that, "when used in accordance with widespread and commonly recognized practice, [it] generally causes unreasonable adverse effects on the environment."[2] The statute defines "unreasonable adverse effects on the environment" to mean "any unreasonable risk to man or the environment, taking into account the ... costs and benefits."[3]

Neither the statute nor its legislative history explains the word "generally," but, as the numerous dictionary definitions that the parties have quoted to us make clear, it means "usually," "commonly," or "with considerable frequency," though not necessarily "more likely than not." Interpreting the statutory standard as a whole, therefore, the Administrator may cancel a registration if it appears to him that the pesticide commonly causes unreasonable risks.

Because FIFRA defines "adverse effects" as "unreasonable risks," the Administrator need not find that use of a pesticide commonly causes undesirable consequences, but only that it commonly creates a significant probability that such consequences may occur. FIFRA therefore does not oblige the Administrator to maintain the registration of a pesticide that might not generally have adverse effects but, say, killed children on 30% of the occasions on which it was used. A 30% risk that children might be killed is plainly an "unreasonable risk" more than sufficient to justify cancellation of the noxious pesticide. Similarly, a significant risk of bird kills, even if birds are actually killed infrequently, may justify the Administrator's decision to ban or restrict diazinon use.

Nevertheless, the Administrator improperly read the word "generally" out of FIFRA § 6(b). The word is not superfluous: it requires the Administrator to determine that the use of a pesticide in a particular application creates unreasonable risks, though not necessarily actual adverse consequences, with considerable frequency, and thus requires the Administrator to consider whether he has defined the application he intends to prohibit sufficiently narrowly. If the use of diazinon creates an unreasonable risk of killing birds on only 10% of the golf courses on which it is used, for example, the Administrator should define the class of golf courses on which its use is to be prohibited more narrowly. Without attempting to interpret the vast administrative record ourselves, therefore, we grant Ciba–Geigy's petition to the extent of remanding this case to the Administrator for application of the correct legal standard.

III.

Ciba–Geigy raises two further objections. First, it asserts that substantial evidence does not support the Administrator's conclusions that

2. 7 U.S.C. § 136d(b).

3. 7 U.S.C. § 136(bb).

diazinon has insignificant benefits or substantial environmental costs, or that its costs outweigh its benefits. Because we remand this case to the Administrator, we need not determine whether Ciba–Geigy's objection is valid. Second, Ciba–Geigy asserts that the Administrator cannot find that the risk of adverse effects of diazinon on birds is unreasonable unless use of the chemical not only kills birds but also endangers their overall population. "[S]cientists within government and in academia are in agreement," Ciba–Geigy asserts, "that an effect on wildlife is ecologically significant only if it endangers the ability of a species' population to maintain itself." This argument must be rejected for two reasons. FIFRA gives the Administrator sufficient discretion to determine that recurring bird kills, even if they do not significantly reduce bird population, are themselves an unreasonable environmental effect. Also, even if the Administrator were required to consider the effects of diazinon on bird population alone, he would be required to find only a risk to that population, not an actual reduction in it.

IV.

For the foregoing reasons, the order cancelling the registration of diazinon for use on golf courses and sod farms is set aside, and the case is REMANDED to the Administrator for further proceedings consistent with this opinion.

NOTES AND QUESTIONS

1. *Assessing unreasonable risks.* So, what is an unreasonable risk under FIFRA, according to the Fifth Circuit? Why had the EPA failed to show that that standard was met?

2. *Balancing the need for pesticides and the risks of harm.* How does the "unreasonable risk" standard strike a balance between the societal need for pesticides and the real risks that they pose to humans and to the environment? Have Congress and the Fifth Circuit struck the right balance? Why or why not?

2. FIFRA AND TOXIC TORTS

FIFRA raises preemption issues with respect to toxic tort claims, which we will discuss in Chapter 10. However, FIFRA regulations—like RCRA and CERCLA—can also directly support toxic tort claims by helping to define defendant's duty of care, as the following case shows.

BRADLEY v. BROWN & THE KILL CO.

United States District Court for the Northern District of Indiana, 1994.
852 F.Supp. 690.

MOODY, DISTRICT JUDGE.

From November 29, 1993 to December 1, 1993 the court conducted a bench trial in this case. Based on the following findings of fact and conclusions of law, the court now rules in favor of Cherrye Bradley, Frances Roy, and MaryAnn Welch and **ORDERS** the clerk to enter judgment against Pickens Brown and The Kill Company, jointly and severally, in the amounts stated in the conclusion of this decision. * * *

I.   *Findings of facts.*

    A.   *Undisputed facts.*

There are few facts undisputed in this controversy. The parties do, however, agree to the following:

At all times relevant to this action, Pickens Brown was the owner and sole operator of The Kill Company. In this capacity, Brown did contract extermination work for U.S. Steel Corporation ["USX"] at its Gary Works plant in Gary, Indiana. Responding to repeated employee complaints about insect bites in the file room of the Accounts Payable Building at the Gary Works plant, Brown applied pesticides to the file room on April 20, 1983. Brown conducted the application in the file room between 6:00 a.m. and 6:30 a.m.

Prior to applying the pesticides, Brown sealed the room. The room itself has three entrances: two have doors, the third does not. Brown taped plastic garbage bags over the entrance without the door. When Brown finished the pesticide application, which included fogging the room, he left the Gary Works facility. An air circulation system was then activated. That system recirculated the air within the building, rather than moving the air outside.

Within an hour after the application was completed, employees who had begun arriving to work at the building became nauseous and displayed other symptoms of pesticide exposure. In all, 33 employees, including Roy, Bradley, and Welch had to be treated at the U.S. Steel dispensary. All were given blood serum cholinesterase and other tests to determine what was causing their symptoms. All 33 employees were released later the same day.

    B.   *The court's findings of fact.*

The court makes the following findings of fact based on its determination of the various witnesses' credibility and on other evidence, as noted:
    * * *

The plaintiffs maintain that Brown fogged with Diazinon. The [court finds] that Brown did, in fact, fog the file room with Pyrtox, in a kerosene base * * *.
    * * *

The directions for Pyrtox state that the applicator should

[c]lose windows and doors and shut off ventilating systems. . . . Keep the area closed for at least 15 minutes. Vacate the treated area and ventilate before reoccupying.

It is undisputed that the file room was sealed and no ventilation was operating during the fogging. Brown testified that McFatridge told him that the building could be ventilated after the procedure. Brown testified that there was another man, a USX employee, present in the building and that he assumed that this man would turn the ventilation on when he left. Brown testified that he did not know whether the ventilation fans were on when he left at around 6:30 a.m. . . . He testified that he relied on USX to assure the building would be properly ventilated. The court accepts this testimony as credible.

It is, as noted, undisputed that the purported ventilation system in fact recirculated the air in the Accounts Payable Building. This spread the Pyrtox fog about the building rather than removing it. Consequently, when employees arrived at the building sometime after 7:00 a.m. they were exposed to airborne Pyrtox in a kerosene base.

* * *

Roy arrived first among these. Notwithstanding the fact that she noticed an odiferous mist in the air inside the building, she sat at her desk and poured and drank a cup of coffee. She then began to feel nauseous. Her chest was hot. Her eyes watered. She went outside to get some air, but then returned again to the building. She soon left the building again, and this time she "blacked out." When Larsen arrived, Roy was standing in the building's foyer. Larsen thought Roy "looked bad": Roy was pale and gasping.

Larsen entered the building. There was a haze inside and her eyes stung. She was nauseous and, after entering and leaving the building several times, she vomited.

Bradley arrived at the Accounts Payable Building around 8:00 a.m. There was a group of employees gathered outside. She saw Roy passed out. She saw Welch pacing back and forth outside the building. Bradley nonetheless entered the building at the direction of a union "grievance person." She testified that a mist still hung in the air, but that fans were now on. People were standing around the room, but no one was working. Bradley, who was pregnant, sat at her desk. Eventually, the "grievance person" directed her to leave the building and she was taken by ambulance to the dispensary. She felt nauseous and vomited both in the ambulance and at the dispensary.

Welch had the least reaction to the exposure among the plaintiffs. She worked in the building for two-and-a-half hours on April 20, 1983. She did go outside to get air periodically, and she did go to the dispensary because she was not feeling well around 10:00 a.m.

With regard to harm suffered, the court finds that all three plaintiffs suffered nausea and severe discomfort on the day of the incident. All three joined the other Accounts Payable Building employees at the dispensary and they each visited Dr. Pamela Carter to follow up on that visit. There is no evidence that the visit to Dr. Carter cost the plaintiffs money. All three missed work, but there was no evidence that they lost wages in the days immediately following the incident. Roy and Bradley presented additional evidence of substantial medical and missed-work expenses. These expenses relate to their claim of having contracted a disorder known as multiple chemical sensitivity as a result of the April 20, 1983 exposure.

II. *Conclusions of law.*

* * * Indiana's law-of-negligence requires that a plaintiff establish, by a preponderance of the evidence, that: (1) the defendant owed them a duty, (2) that the defendant failed to conform his or her conduct to a standard consistent with that duty, (3) that such failure (a) proximately caused (b) the plaintiffs' compensable injuries. The plaintiffs here have succeeded in establishing these elements with regard to some, but not all, of their claimed injuries.

A. *Duty.*

Whether Brown owed plaintiffs a duty of care is a question of law in Indiana. Duty exists "where reasonable persons would recognize it and agree that it exists." *Stump v. Commercial Union,* 601 N.E.2d 327, 332 (Ind. 1992). Reasonable persons recognize a duty to conform their actions to avoid the risk of injury to others. This idea is incorporated into the Indiana Supreme Court's formulation of the inquiry into duty in terms of: (1) the relationship between the parties, (2) the reasonable foreseeability of harm, and (3) public policy. *See id.*

Where, as here, the parties do not argue, and the court does not detect, any special relationship between the parties that would give rise to a duty of care, the court's focus is "on whether the type of harm actually inflicted was reasonably foreseeable." *See Webb,* 575 N.E.2d at 997. Based on the undisputed toxicity of both Pyrtox and Diazinon, the court concludes that it is foreseeable that misapplication of those pesticides would result in injury to employees who would be arriving in the Accounts Receivable Building less than an hour later. It is all but self-evident that Indiana public policy would mandate that Brown conform his conduct to avoid that injury. Accordingly, the court concludes that Brown did have a duty to conform his application to a standard that would avoid injury to the U.S. Steel workers employed in the Accounts Receivable Building.

B. *Breach of duty.*

Having concluded that Brown owed a duty of reasonable care to the U.S. Steel employees in the Accounts Payable Building on April 20, 1983, the court also concludes that Brown breached that duty. Put another way, the court concludes that Brown was negligent.

Brown did not conform his conduct to minimize risk to the workers in the Accounts Payable Building. The court concludes that it was unreasonable to fog in the morning prior to the arrival of the workers. Brown's own testimony—that he warned McFatridge of the dangers of fogging on a day when employees would be arriving in the building shortly afterwards—

bolsters this conclusion. Moreover, Brown's reliance on McFatridge's word that the building would be ventilated, his failure to investigate whether the building could be ventilated, and his leaving the building without assuring himself that the building was ventilated all constitute negligent conduct. It was Brown, as the pesticide applicator, who owed the primary duty to the workers not to apply the pesticides in a manner that put the workers in danger. He failed in this regard.

This conclusion is compelled, at any rate, because Brown was negligent *per se* in this regard. Pyrtox's label calls for ventilation subsequent to fogging. Brown did not see to it that the Accounts Payable Building was ventilated. This was a violation of both the United States and Indiana codes, which proscribe the use of any registered pesticide in a manner inconsistent with its labelling. 7 U.S.C. § 136j(a)(2)(G) *and* IND. CODE § 15–3–3.6–14(b). Brown does not contest that Pyrtox is a registered pesticide to which these sections are applicable. Non-excused or non-justified violation of a statutory duty is negligence *per se* where: (1) the purpose of the statute was to protect the persons injured, (2) from the injuries in fact suffered. Sections 136j(a)(2)(G) and 15–3–3.6–14(b) are designed to protect persons in areas in which pesticides are applied from injuries that result from applications that do not comply with the safety warnings on the labels. Accordingly, Brown's non-excused and non-justified failure to comply with the label's strictures constitutes negligence *per se*.

C. *Proximate causation and harm.*

Indiana cases discuss the third element of an Indiana negligence claim, as "an injury to the plaintiff proximately caused by the [defendant's] breach [of duty]." *See Webb,* 575 N.E.2d at 995. This formulation in fact contains two elements of the traditional conception of negligence: (a) proximate cause, and, (b) actual loss or damages. * * *

1. *Proximate cause.*

As used in negligence law, causation "is the requirement for a reasonable connection between a defendant's conduct and the damages which [ ] plaintiff[s] ha[ve] suffered." *Cowe,* 575 N.E.2d at 635. The plaintiffs must draw this connection by showing that their injuries were the "natural and probable consequence" of Brown's negligence "which should have been foreseen." *Watson,* 532 N.E.2d at 1194.

Drawing this connection is particularly difficult in the growing field of hazardous-substance litigation, where the causal relationship between exposure to a hazardous substance and subsequent symptoms may be hypothesized, but not yet tested and proven to the legally required degree of certitude. In such technical cases, "[w]hen the issue of proximate cause is not within the understanding of lay persons, testimony of an expert witness on the issue is necessary." *Watson,* 532 N.E.2d at 1194.

* * *

With regard to the multiple chemical sensitivities ["MCS"] that Bradley and Roy claim they suffer from, the * * * etiology of MCS, to the extent it is understood at all, must turn upon complex medical interactions beyond the ken of a lay person, or for that matter the court. Accordingly, * * * plaintiffs may not make out causation *vis-a-vis* MCS merely by reliance upon the temporal congruity of the events of April 20, 1983 and the onset of their symptoms. * * * Scientific expert testimony is required.

To this end, plaintiffs attempted at trial to have admitted into evidence the depositions of Drs. William J. Rea and Alfred R. Johnson on the subject of MCS. [The court excluded this evidence pursuant to *Daubert*, concluding that "Drs. Rea and Johnson's opinions regarding whether the plaintiffs' exposure caused their symptoms would be entirely too subjective and speculative."]

   * * *

Thus, plaintiffs' own evidence clearly establishes that the "science" of MCS's etiology has not progressed from the plausible, that is, the hypothetical, to knowledge capable of assisting a fact-finder, jury or judge. * * *

b. *Causation.*

   * * *

The exclusion of expert testimony concerning Roy and Bradley's alleged MCS leads the court to conclude that Roy and Bradley have failed to make out their cases in regards to that ailment. Plaintiffs have, however, shown a reasonable connection between Brown's negligence and their becoming ill on April 20, 1983.

Brown's fogging and the air re-circulation system activated on April 20, 1983 resulted in a Pyrtox and kerosene mist pervading the Accounts Payable Building when plaintiffs arrived at work. Drs. Cardiff, Lipsey and Novak testified that the headaches, breathing difficulties, dizziness, and nausea that the plaintiffs experienced were consistent with their exposure to Pyrtox in a kerosene base. The existence of these symptoms in both plaintiffs and the other USX employees exposed to the mist supports the conclusion that all were exposed to Pyrtox and kerosene. A person of Brown's experience applying pesticides should reasonably have foreseen that failure to ventilate the Accounts Payable Building shortly after fogging there would lead to persons being exposed in this way. His failure to assure that the building would, or even could, be ventilated proximately caused plaintiffs' harms.

2. *Actual loss or damages.*

The harms that plaintiffs foreseeably would, and in fact did, suffer as a result of Brown's negligence were nausea and severe discomfort. Because their damages arguments were primarily directed to their MCS claims, plaintiffs did not present much evidence on these more modest injuries. At any rate, the court concludes that only minimal damages are appropriate for the discomfort attributable to the April 20, 1983 exposure. To the extent that Roy and Bradley suffered, or suffer, from more serious disorders, the science is simply too nascent to assign a cause to these.

The evidence did show that Roy and Bradley suffered from more discomfort from the exposure than did Welch. Accordingly, the court hereby **ORDERS** that the clerk enter a final judgment in favor of each of the plaintiffs as follows:

For MaryAnn Welch: "Judgment is hereby entered in favor of Mary-Ann Welch against Pickens Brown and The Kill Company, jointly and severally, in the amount of $500.00."

For Cherrye Bradley: "Judgment is hereby entered in favor of Cherrye Bradley against Pickens Brown and The Kill Company, jointly and severally, in the amount of $1000.00."

For Frances Roy: "Judgment is hereby entered in favor of Frances Roy against Pickens Brown and The Kill Company, jointly and severally, in the amount of $1000.00."

SO ORDERED.

NOTES AND QUESTIONS

1. *FIFRA and common law toxic torts.* How was FIFRA relevant to this negligence case? What was the FIFRA violation? Did that violation guarantee success in the toxic tort lawsuit? Why or why not? Did that violation help the plaintiffs' lawsuit? Why or why not?

2. *Punishing the FIFRA violation.* Review the discussion of FIFRA prohibitions above. Could the EPA enforce against the FIFRA violation at issue in this case? What is the advantage of a FIFRA liability scheme that operates independently of the tort system? Consider, for example: Why might the EPA want to enjoin and punish people who violate FIFRA even if no harm (no toxic tort) arises as a result?

3. *FIFRA and the human factor.* As this case makes clear, for registered pesticides, the primary importance of FIFRA is the label that the EPA approves. This label delineates the conditions under which a pesticide may be used, locations where it may be used, and requirements to ensure the safety of the applicator, bystanders, and the environment. However, as a precautionary measure, labeling is ultimately only as good as the people handling the pesticide allow it to be. Indeed, human error remains a significant factor in the risks associated with pesticides, especially human errors in the application of pesticides. For further discussion of this topic, see Tybe A. Brett & Jane E.R. Potter, Risks to Human Health Associated with Exposure to Pesticides at the Time of Application and the Role of the Courts, 1 Vill.Envtl.L.J. 355 (1990).

C. THE TOXIC SUBSTANCES CONTROL ACT (TSCA)

1. OVERVIEW OF TSCA: RISK, ECONOMICS, AND THE LEAST BURDENSOME REGULATION

When Congress enacted the Toxic Substances Control Act (TSCA), 15 U.S.C. §§ 2601–2695d, in 1976, it recognized that "adequate authority should exist to regulate chemical substances and mixtures which present an unreasonable risk of injury to health or the environment, and to take action with respect to chemical substances and mixtures which are imminent hazards." 15 U.S.C. § 2601(b)(2). However, it also emphasized that:

> authority over chemical substances and mixtures should be exercised in such a manner as not to impede unduly or create unnecessary economic barriers to technological innovation while fulfilling the primary purpose of this chapter to assure that such innovation and commerce in such chemical substances and mixtures do not present an unreasonable risk of injury to health or the environment.

Id. § 2601(b)(3). Thus, TSCA, like FIFRA, seeks to balance protection of human health and the environment with economic realities and needs in society for toxic chemicals and products. Indeed, Congress directed that the EPA Administrator must "consider the environmental, economic, and social impact of any action the Administrator takes or proposes to take under" the Act. Id. § 2601(c).

Most of TSCA's requirements apply to *chemical substances* and *mixtures*. The Act defines "chemical substance" to be:

> any organic or inorganic substance of a particular molecular identity, including—
>
> (i) any combination of such substances occurring in whole or in part as a result of a chemical reaction or occurring in nature and
>
> (ii) any element or uncombined radical.

15 U.S.C. § 2602(2)(A). However, TSCA then immediately exempts a number of substances from this definition, including pesticides regulated under FIFRA, tobacco and tobacco products, nuclear materials regulated under the Atomic Energy Act, and food, food additives, drugs, and cosmetics regulated under the Food, Drug, and Cosmetic Act. Id. § 2602(2)(B).

A "mixture," in turn, is:

> [A]ny combination of two or more chemical substances if the combination does not occur in nature and is not, in whole or in part, the result of a chemical reaction; except that such term does include any combination which occurs, in whole or in part, as a result of a chemical reaction if none of the chemical substances comprising the combination is a new chemical substance and if the combination could have been manufactured for commercial purposes without a chemical

reaction at the time the chemical substances comprising the combination were combined.

Id. § 2602(8).

The EPA implements TSCA. Under the operative provisions of TSCA for chemical substances and mixtures,

If the [EPA] Administrator finds that there is a reasonable basis to conclude that the manufacture, processing, distribution in commerce, use, or disposal of a chemical substance or mixture, or that any combination of such activities, presents or will present an *unreasonable risk of injury to health or the environment*, the Administrator shall by rule apply one or more of the following requirements to such substance or mixture *to the extent necessary to protect adequately against such risk using the least burdensome requirements*:

(1) A requirement (A) prohibiting the manufacturing, processing, or distribution in commerce of such substance or mixture, or (B) limiting the amount of such substance or mixture which may be manufactured, processed, or distributed in commerce.

(2) A requirement—

(A) prohibiting the manufacture, processing, or distribution in commerce of such substance or mixture for (i) a particular use or (ii) a particular use in a concentration in excess of a level specified by the Administrator in the rule imposing the requirement, or

(B) limiting the amount of such substance or mixture which may be manufactured, processed, or distributed in commerce for (i) a particular use or (ii) a particular use in a concentration in excess of a level specified by the Administrator in the rule imposing the requirement.

(3) A requirement that such substance or mixture or any article containing such substance or mixture be marked with or accompanied by clear and adequate warnings and instructions with respect to its use, distribution in commerce, or disposal or with respect to any combination of such activities. The form and content of such warnings and instructions shall be prescribed by the Administrator.

(4) A requirement that manufacturers and processors of such substance or mixture make and retain records of the processes used to manufacture or process such substance or mixture and monitor or conduct tests which are reasonable and necessary to assure compliance with the requirements of any rule applicable under this subsection.

(5) A requirement prohibiting or otherwise regulating any manner or method of commercial use of such substance or mixture.

(6)(A) A requirement prohibiting or otherwise regulating any manner or method of disposal of such substance or mixture, or of any article containing such substance or mixture, by its manufacturer or processor or by any other person who uses, or disposes of, it for commercial purposes.

(B) A requirement under subparagraph (A) may not require any person to take any action which would be in violation of any law or requirement of, or in effect for, a State or political subdivision, and shall require each person subject to it to notify each State and political subdivision in which a required disposal may occur of such disposal.

(7) A requirement directing manufacturers or processors of such substance or mixture (A) to give notice of such unreasonable risk of injury to distributors in commerce of such substance or mixture and, to the extent reasonably ascertainable, to other persons in possession of such substance or mixture or exposed to such substance or mixture, (B) to give public notice of such risk of injury, and (C) to replace or repurchase such substance or mixture as elected by the person to which the requirement is directed.

Any requirement (or combination of requirements) imposed under this subsection may be limited in application to specified geographic areas.

Id. § 2605(a) (emphasis added).

Thus, regulation under TSCA requires the EPA to figure out multiple pieces of information: (1) whether a chemical substance or mixture poses an unreasonable risk of harm to human health or the environment; (2) what the economic impacts of regulating the substance or mixture would be; (3) what the social impacts of regulating a chemical substance or mixture would be; and (4) what the least burdensome method of regulating to eliminate or reduce the unreasonable risks is. Consider all those factors as you read the following case, which reviews the EPA's attempt to ban most asbestos products.

CORROSION PROOF FITTINGS v. ENVIRONMENTAL PROTECTION AGENCY

United States Court of Appeals for the Fifth Circuit, 1991.
947 F.2d 1201.

JERRY E. SMITH, CIRCUIT JUDGE:

The Environmental Protection Agency (EPA) issued a final rule under section 6 of the Toxic Substances Control Act (TSCA) to prohibit the future manufacture, importation, processing, and distribution of asbestos in almost all products. * * * Because the EPA failed to muster substantial evidence to support its rule, we remand this matter to the EPA for further consideration in light of this opinion.

I.

Facts and Procedural History.

Asbestos is a naturally occurring fibrous material that resists fire and most solvents. Its major uses include heat-resistant insulators, cements, building materials, fireproof gloves and clothing, and motor vehicle brake linings. Asbestos is a toxic material, and occupational exposure to asbestos dust can result in mesothelioma, asbestosis, and lung cancer.

* * *

In 1989, the EPA issued a final rule prohibiting the manufacture, importation, processing, and distribution in commerce of most asbestos-containing products. Finding that asbestos constituted an unreasonable risk to health and the environment, the EPA promulgated a staged ban of most commercial uses of asbestos. The EPA estimates that this rule will save either 202 or 148 lives, depending upon whether the benefits are discounted, at a cost of approximately $450–800 million, depending upon the price of substitutes.

* * *

Section 19(a) of TSCA, 15 U.S.C. § 2618(a), grants interested parties the right to appeal a final rule promulgated under section 6(a) directly to this or any other regional circuit court of appeals. Pursuant to this section, petitioners challenge the EPA's final rule * * *.

* * *

IV.

The Language of TSCA.

A.

Standard of Review.

Our inquiry into the legitimacy of the EPA rulemaking begins with a discussion of the standard of review governing this case. EPA's phase-out ban of most commercial uses of asbestos is a TSCA § 6(a) rulemaking. TSCA provides that a reviewing court "shall hold unlawful and set aside" a final rule promulgated under § 6(a) "if the court finds that the rule is not supported by substantial evidence in the rulemaking record ... taken as a whole." 15 U.S.C. § 2618(c)(1)(B)(i).

* * *

We note that in undertaking our review, we give all agency rules a presumption of validity, and it is up to the challenger to any rule to show that the agency action is invalid. The burden remains on the EPA, however, to justify that the products it bans presents an unreasonable risk, no matter how regulated. Finally, as we discuss in detail *infra*, because TSCA instructs the EPA to undertake the least burdensome regulation sufficient to regulate the substance at issue, the agency bears a heavier burden when it seeks a partial or total ban of a substance than when it merely seeks to regulate that product. *See* 15 U.S.C. § 2605(a).

B.

The EPA's Burden Under TSCA.

TSCA provides, in pertinent part, as follows:

(a) Scope of regulation.—If the Administrator finds that there is a *reasonable basis* to conclude that the manufacture, processing, distribution in commerce, use, or disposal of a chemical substance or mixture, or that any combination of such activities, presents or will present an *unreasonable risk of injury* to health or the environment, the Administrator shall by rule apply one or more of the following requirements to such substance or mixture to the extent necessary *to protect adequately* against such risk using the *least burdensome* requirements.

Id. (emphasis added). As the highlighted language shows, Congress did not enact TSCA as a zero-risk statute. The EPA, rather, was required to consider both alternatives to a ban and the costs of any proposed actions and to "carry out this chapter in a reasonable and prudent manner [after considering] the environmental, economic, and social impact of any action." 15 U.S.C. § 2601(c).

We conclude that the EPA has presented insufficient evidence to justify its asbestos ban. * * *

1.

Least Burdensome and Reasonable.

TSCA requires that the EPA use the least burdensome regulation to achieve its goal of minimum reasonable risk. This statutory requirement can create problems in evaluating just what is a "reasonable risk." Congress's rejection of a no-risk policy, however, also means that in certain cases, the least burdensome yet still adequate solution may entail somewhat more risk than would other, known regulations that are far more burdensome on the industry and the economy. The very language of TSCA requires that the EPA, once it has determined what an acceptable level of non-zero risk is, choose the least burdensome method of reaching that level.

In this case, the EPA banned, for all practical purposes, all present and future uses of asbestos—a position the petitioners characterize as the "death penalty alternative," as this is the *most* burdensome of all possible alternatives listed as open to the EPA under TSCA. TSCA not only provides the EPA with a list of alternative actions, but also provides those alternatives in order of how burdensome they are. The regulations thus provide for EPA regulation ranging from labeling the least toxic chemicals to limiting the total amount of chemicals an industry may use. Total bans head the list as the most burdensome regulatory option.

By choosing the harshest remedy given to it under TSCA, the EPA assigned to itself the toughest burden in satisfying TSCA's requirement that its alternative be the least burdensome of all those offered to it. Since, both by definition and by the terms of TSCA, the complete ban of manufacturing is the most burdensome alternative—for even stringent regulation at least allows a manufacturer the chance to invest and meet the new, higher standard—the EPA's regulation cannot stand if there is any other regulation that would achieve an acceptable level of risk as mandated by TSCA.

* * *

The EPA considered, and rejected, such options as labeling asbestos products, thereby warning users and workers involved in the manufacture of asbestos-containing products of the chemical's dangers, and stricter workplace rules. EPA also rejected controlled use of asbestos in the workplace and deferral to other government agencies charged with worker and consumer exposure to industrial and product hazards, such as OSHA * * *. The EPA determined that deferral to these other agencies was inappropriate because no one other authority could address all the risks posed "throughout the life cycle" by asbestos, and any action by one or more of the other agencies still would leave an unacceptable residual risk.

Much of the EPA's analysis is correct, and the EPA's basic decision to use TSCA as a comprehensive statute designed to fight a multi-industry problem was a proper one that we uphold today on review. What concerns us, however, is the manner in which the EPA conducted some of its analysis. * * *

The EPA presented two comparisons in the record: a world with no further regulation under TSCA, and a world in which no manufacture of asbestos takes place. The EPA rejected calculating how many lives a less burdensome regulation would save, and at what cost. Furthermore the EPA, when calculating the benefits of its ban, explicitly refused to compare it to an improved workplace in which currently available control technology is utilized. This decision artificially inflated the purported benefits of the rule by using a baseline comparison substantially lower than what currently available technology could yield.

* * *

This comparison of two static worlds is insufficient to satisfy the dictates of TSCA. While the EPA may have shown that a world with a complete ban of asbestos might be preferable to one in which there is only the current amount of regulation, the EPA has failed to show that there is not some intermediate state of regulation that would be superior to both the currently-regulated and the completely-banned world. Without showing that asbestos regulation would be ineffective, the EPA cannot discharge its TSCA burden of showing that its regulation is the least burdensome available to it.

* * *

2.

The EPA's Calculations.

Furthermore, we are concerned about some of the methodology employed by the EPA in making various of the calculations that it did perform. In order to aid the EPA's reconsideration of this and other cases, we present our concerns here.

First, we note that there was some dispute in the record regarding the appropriateness of discounting the perceived benefits of the EPA's rule. * * *

Although various commentators dispute whether it ever is appropriate to discount benefits when they are measured in human lives, we note that it would skew the results to discount only costs without according similar treatment to the benefits side of the equation. Adopting the position of the commentators who advocate not discounting benefits would force the EPA similarly not to calculate costs in present discounted real terms, making comparisons difficult. Furthermore, in evaluating situations in which different options incur costs at varying time intervals, the EPA would not be able to take into account that soon-to-be-incurred costs are more harmful than postponable costs. Because the EPA must discount costs to perform its evaluations properly, the EPA also should discount benefits to preserve an apples-to-apples comparison, even if this entails discounting benefits of a non-monetary nature.

When the EPA does discount costs or benefits, however, it cannot choose an unreasonable time upon which to base its discount calculation. Instead of using the time of injury as the appropriate time from which to discount, as one might expect, the EPA instead used the time of exposure.

The difficulties inherent in the EPA's approach can be illustrated by an example. Suppose two workers will be exposed to asbestos in 1995, with worker X subjected to a tiny amount of asbestos that will have no adverse health effects, and worker Y exposed to massive amounts of asbestos that quickly will lead to an asbestos-related disease. Under the EPA's approach, which takes into account only the time of exposure rather than the time at which any injury manifests itself, both examples would be treated the same. The EPA's approach implicitly assumes that the day on which the risk of injury occurs is the same day the injury actually occurs. Such an approach might be proper when the exposure and injury are one and the same, such as when a person is exposed to an immediately fatal poison, but is inappropriate for discounting toxins in which exposure often is followed by a substantial lag time before manifestation of injuries.

Of more concern to us is the failure of the EPA to compute the costs and benefits of its proposed rule past the year 2000, and its double-counting of the costs of asbestos use. In performing its calculus, the EPA only included the number of lives saved over the next thirteen years, and counted any additional lives saved as simply "unquantified benefits." 54 Fed. Reg. at 29,486. The EPA and intervenors now seek to use these unquantified lives saved to justify calculations as to which of the benefits seem far outweighed by the astronomical costs. For example, the EPA plans to save about three lives with its ban of asbestos pipe, at a cost of $128–227 million (*i.e.,* approximately $43–76 million per life saved). Although the EPA admits that the price tag is high, it claims that the lives saved past the year 2000 justify the price.

Such calculations not only lessen the value of the EPA's cost analysis, but also make any meaningful judicial review impossible. While TSCA contemplates a useful place for unquantified benefits beyond the EPA's calculation, unquantified benefits never were intended as a trump card allowing the EPA to justify any cost calculus, no matter how high.

The concept of unquantified benefits, rather, is intended to allow the EPA to provide a rightful place for any remaining benefits that are impossible to quantify after the EPA's best attempt, but which still are of some concern. But the allowance for unquantified costs is not intended to allow the EPA to perform its calculations over an arbitrarily short period so as to preserve a large unquantified portion.

Unquantified benefits can, at times, permissibly tip the balance in close cases. They cannot, however, be used to effect a wholesale shift on the balance beam. Such a use makes a mockery of the requirements of TSCA that the EPA weigh the costs of its actions before it chooses the least burdensome alternative.

We do not today determine what an appropriate period for the EPA's calculations would be, as this is a matter better left for agency discretion. We do note, however, that the choice of a thirteen-year period is so short as to make the unquantified period so unreasonably large that any EPA reliance upon it must be displaced.

   * * *

We also note that the EPA appears to place too great a reliance upon the concept of population exposure. While a high population exposure certainly is a factor that the EPA must consider in making its calculations, the agency cannot count such problems more than once. For example, in the case of asbestos brake products, the EPA used factors such as risk and exposure to calculate the probable harm of the brakes, and then used, as an *additional* reason to ban the products, the fact that the exposure levels were high. Considering that calculations of the probable harm level, when reduced to basics, simply are a calculation of population risk multiplied by population exposure, the EPA's redundant use of population exposure to justify its actions cannot stand.

3.

Reasonable Basis.

In addition to showing that its regulation is the least burdensome one necessary to protect the environment adequately, the EPA also must show that it has a reasonable basis for the regulation. 15 U.S.C. § 2605(a). To some extent, our inquiry in this area mirrors that used above, for many of the methodological problems we have noted also indicate that the EPA did not have a reasonable basis. We here take the opportunity to highlight some areas of additional concern.

Most problematical to us is the EPA's ban of products for which no substitutes presently are available. In these cases, the EPA bears a tough burden indeed to show that under TSCA a ban is the least burdensome alternative, as TSCA explicitly instructs the EPA to consider "the benefits of such substance or mixture for various uses and the availability of substitutes for such uses." *Id.* § 2605(c)(1)(C). These words are particularly appropriate where the EPA actually has decided to ban a product, rather than simply restrict its use, for it is in these cases that the lack of an adequate substitute is most troubling under TSCA.

As the EPA itself states, "[w]hen no information is available for a product indicating that cost-effective substitutes exist, the estimated cost of a product ban is very high." 54 Fed. Reg. at 29,468. Because of this, the EPA did not ban certain uses of asbestos, such as its use in rocket engines and battery separators. The EPA, however, in several other instances, ignores its own arguments and attempts to justify its ban by stating that the ban itself will cause the development of low-cost, adequate substitute products.

As a general matter, we agree with the EPA that a product ban can lead to great innovation * * *. As even the EPA acknowledges, however, when no adequate substitutes currently exist, the EPA cannot fail to consider this lack when formulating its own guidelines. Under TSCA, therefore, the EPA must present a stronger case to justify the ban, as opposed to regulation, of products with no substitutes.

　　　* * *

We also are concerned with the EPA's evaluation of substitutes even in those instances in which the record shows that they are available. The EPA explicitly rejects considering the harm that may flow from the increased use of products designed to substitute for asbestos, even where the probable substitutes themselves are known carcinogens. * * *

This presents two problems. First, TSCA instructs the EPA to consider the relative merits of its ban, as compared to the economic effects of its actions. The EPA cannot make this calculation if it fails to consider the effects that alternate substitutes will pose after a ban.

Second, the EPA cannot say with any assurance that its regulation will increase workplace safety when it refuses to evaluate the harm that will result from the increased use of substitute products. While the EPA may be correct in its conclusion that the alternate materials pose less risk than asbestos, we cannot say with any more assurance than that flowing from an educated guess that this conclusion is true.

　　　* * *

In short, a death is a death, whether occasioned by asbestos or by a toxic substitute product, and the EPA's decision not to evaluate the toxicity of known carcinogenic substitutes is not a reasonable action under TSCA. Once an interested party brings forth credible evidence suggesting the toxicity of the probable or only alternatives to a substance, the EPA must consider the comparative toxic costs of each. Its failure to do so in this case thus deprived its regulation of a reasonable basis, at least in regard to those products as to which petitioners introduced credible evidence of the dangers of the likely substitutes.

4.

Unreasonable Risk of Injury.

The final requirement the EPA must satisfy before engaging in any TSCA rulemaking is that it only take steps designed to prevent "unreasonable" risks. In evaluating what is "unreasonable," the EPA is required to consider the costs of any proposed actions and to "carry out this chapter in a reasonable and prudent manner [after considering] the environmental, economic, and social impact of any action." 15 U.S.C. § 2601(c).

As the District of Columbia Circuit stated when evaluating similar language governing the Federal Hazardous Substances Act, "[t]he requirement that the risk be 'unreasonable' necessarily involves a balancing test like that familiar in tort law: The regulation may issue if the severity of the injury that may result from the product, factored by the likelihood of the injury, offsets the harm the regulation itself imposes upon manufacturers and consumers." *Forester v. CPSC,* 559 F.2d 774, 789 (D.C. Cir. 1977). * * *

That the EPA must balance the costs of its regulations against their benefits further is reinforced by the requirement that it seek the least burdensome regulation. While Congress did not dictate that the EPA engage in an exhaustive, full-scale cost-benefit analysis, it did require the EPA to consider both sides of the regulatory equation, and it rejected the notion that the EPA should pursue the reduction of workplace risk at any cost. * * *

Even taking all of the EPA's figures as true, and evaluating them in the light most favorable to the agency's decision (non-discounted benefits, discounted costs, analogous exposure estimates included), the agency's analysis results in figures as high as $74 million per life saved. * * *

While we do not sit as a regulatory agency that must make the difficult decision as to what an appropriate expenditure is to prevent someone from incurring the risk of an asbestos-related death, we do note that the EPA, in its zeal to ban any and all asbestos products, basically ignored the cost side of the TSCA equation. The EPA would have this court believe that Congress, when it enacted its requirement that the EPA consider the economic impacts of its regulations, thought that spending

$200–300 million to save approximately seven lives (approximately $30–40 million per life) over thirteen years is reasonable.

* * *

The EPA's willingness to argue that spending $23.7 million to save less than one-third of a life reveals that its economic review of its regulations, as required by TSCA, was meaningless. As the petitioners' brief and our review of EPA caselaw reveals, such high costs are rarely, if ever, used to support a safety regulation. If we were to allow such cavalier treatment of the EPA's duty to consider the economic effects of its decisions, we would have to excise entire sections and phrases from the language of TSCA. Because we are judges, not surgeons, we decline to do so.

V.

Substantial Evidence Regarding Least Burdensome, Adequate Regulation.

TSCA provides that a reviewing court "shall hold unlawful and set aside" a final rule promulgated under section 6(a) "if the court finds that the rule is not supported by substantial evidence in the rulemaking record ... taken as a whole." 15 U.S.C. § 2618(c)(1)(B)(i). * * *

We have declared that the EPA must articulate an "understandable basis" to support its TSCA action with respect to each substance or application of the substance banned. To make a finding of unreasonable risk based upon this assessment, the "EPA must balance the probability that harm will occur from the activities against the effects of the proposed regulatory action on the availability to society of the benefits of asbestos." 54 Fed. Reg. at 29,467. With these edicts in mind, we now examine each product against the TSCA criteria.

A.

Friction Products.

We begin our analysis with the EPA's ban of friction products, which constitutes the lion's share of the proposed benefits of the asbestos regulation–nearly three-fourths of the anticipated asbestos deaths. The friction products in question, although primarily made up of drum and disk brakes, also include brake blocks and other friction products.

Workers are exposed to asbestos during the manufacture, use, repair, and disposal of these products. The EPA banned most of these products with a stage 2 ban, which would require companies to cease manufacturing or importing the products by August 25, 1993, with distribution to end one year later. The final stage 3 ban would ban any remaining friction products on August 26, 1996, with distribution again ceasing one year later.

We note that of all the asbestos bans, the EPA did the most impressive job in this area, both in conducting its studies and in supporting its contention that banning asbestos products would save over 102 discounted lives. Furthermore, the EPA demonstrates that the population exposure to asbestos in this area is great, while the estimated cost of the measure is low, at least in comparison to the cost-per-life of its other bans. Were the petitioners only questioning the EPA's decision to ban friction products based upon disputing these figures, we would be tempted to uphold the EPA, even in the face of petitioners' arguments that workplace exposure to friction product asbestos could be decreased by as much as ninety percent using stricter workplace controls and in light of studies supporting the conclusion that some forms of asbestos present less danger. Decisions such as these are better left to the agency's expertise.

Such expertise, however, is not a universal talisman affording the EPA unbridled latitude to act as it chooses under TSCA. What we cannot ignore is that the EPA failed to study the effect of non-asbestos brakes on automotive safety, despite credible evidence that non-asbestos brakes could increase significantly the number of highway fatalities, and that the EPA failed to evaluate the toxicity of likely brake substitutes. As we already mentioned, the EPA, in its zeal to ban asbestos, cannot overlook, with only cursory study, credible contentions that substitute products actually might increase fatalities.

* * *

In short, while it is apparent that non-asbestos brake products either are available or soon will be available on new vehicles, there is no evidence indicating that forcing consumers to replace their asbestos brakes with new non-asbestos brakes as they wear out on their present vehicles will decrease fatalities or that such a ban will produce other benefits that outweigh its costs. Furthermore, many of the EPA's own witnesses conceded on cross-examination that the non-asbestos fibrous substitutes also pose a cancer risk upon inhalation, yet the EPA failed to examine in more than a cursory fashion the toxicity of these alternatives. Under these circumstances, the EPA has failed to support its ban with the substantial evidence needed to provide it with a reasonable basis.

* * *

B.

Asbestos–Cement Pipe Products.

The EPA's analysis supporting its ban of asbestos-cement (A/C'') pipe is more troublesome than its action in regard to friction products. Asbestos pipe primarily is used to convey water in mains, sewage under pressure, and materials in various industrial process lines. Unlike most uses of asbestos, asbestos pipe is valued primarily for its strength and resistance to corrosion, rather than for its heat-resistant qualities. The EPA imposed a stage 3 ban on asbestos pipe. 54 Fed. Reg. at 29,462.

Petitioners question EPA's cost/benefit balancing, noting that by the EPA's own predictions, the ban of asbestos pipe will save only 3–4 discounted lives, at a cost ranging from $128–227 million ($43–76 million per life saved), depending upon the price of substitutes. Furthermore, much of EPA's data regarding this product and others depends upon data received from exposures observed during activities similar to the ones to be regulated–the "analogous exposure" analysis that the EPA adopted subsequent to the public comment period, which thus was not subjected to cross-examination or other critical testing. Finally, the petitioners protest that the EPA acted unreasonably because the most likely substitutes for the asbestos pipe, PVC and ductile iron pipe, also contain known carcinogens.

Once again we are troubled by the EPA's methodology and its evaluation of the substitute products. * * *

As with friction products, the EPA refused to assess the risks of substitutes to asbestos pipe. Unlike non-asbestos brakes, which the EPA contends are safe, the EPA here admits that vinyl chloride, used in PVC, is a human carcinogen that is especially potent during the manufacture of PVC pipe. As for the EPA's defense of the ductile iron pipe substitute, the EPA also acknowledges evidence that it will cause cancer deaths but rejects these deaths as overestimated, even though it can present no more support for this assumption than its own *ipse dixit.*

> * * *

The EPA * * * has estimated the cancer risk from PVC plants to be as high as twenty deaths *per year,* a death rate that stringent controls might be able to reduce to one *per year, far in excess of the fractions of a life that the asbestos pipe ban may save each year, by the EPA's own calculations.* Considering that the EPA concedes that there is no evidence showing that *ingested,* as opposed to *inhaled,* asbestos is a health risk, while the EPA's own studies show that ingested vinyl chloride is a significant cancer risk that could cause up to 260 cancer deaths over the next thirteen years, the EPA's failure to consider the risks of substitute products in the asbestos pipe area is particularly troublesome. The agency cannot simply choose to note the similar cancer risks of asbestos and iron pipe and then reject the data underpinning the iron and PVC pipe without more than its own conclusory statements.

> * * *

Finally, we once again note that the EPA failed to discharge its TSCA-mandated burden that it consider and reject less burdensome alternatives before it impose a more burdensome alternative such as a complete ban. The EPA instead jumped immediately to the ban provision, without calculating whether a less burdensome alternative might accomplish TSCA's goals. We therefore conclude that the EPA failed to present substantial evidence to support its ban of asbestos pipe.

C.

Gaskets, Roofing, Shingles, and Paper Products.

We here deal with the remaining products affected by the EPA ban. Petitioners challenge the basis for the EPA's finding that beater-add and sheet gaskets, primarily used in automotive parts, should be banned. The agency estimated its ban would save thirty-two lives over a thirteen-year time span, at an overall cost of $207–263 million ($6–8 million per life saved).

We have little to add in this area, beyond our general discussion and comments on other products, apart from a brief highlight of the EPA's use of analogous exposure data to support its gasket ban. For these products, the analogous exposure estimate constituted almost eighty percent of the anticipated total benefits–a proportion so large that the EPA's duty to give interested parties notice that it intended to use analogous exposure estimates was particularly acute. Considering some of the EPA's support for its analogous exposure estimates–such as its assumption that *none* of the same workers who install beater-add and sheet gaskets *ever* is involved in repairing or disposing of them, and the unexplained discrepancy between its present conclusion that over 50,000 workers are involved in this area and its 1984 estimate that only 768 workers are involved in "gasket removal and installation," *see* 51 Fed. Reg. 22,612, 22,665 (1986)–the petitioners' complaint that they never were afforded the opportunity to comment publicly upon these figures, or to cross-examine any EPA witnesses regarding them, is particularly telling.

The EPA also banned roof coatings, roof shingles, non-roof coatings, and asbestos paper products. Again, we have little to add beyond our discussions already concluded, especially regarding TSCA's requirement that the EPA always choose the least burdensome alternative, whether it be workplace regulation, labeling, or only a partial ban. We note, however, that in those cases in which a complete ban would save less than one statistical life, such as those affecting asbestos paper products and certain roofing materials, the EPA has a particular need to examine the less burdensome alternatives to a complete ban.

D.

Ban of Products Not Being Produced in the United States.

Petitioners also contend that the EPA overstepped TSCA's bounds by seeking to ban products that once were, but no longer are, being produced in the United States. We find little merit to this claim, considering that sections 5 and 6 of TSCA allow the EPA to ban a product "that presents *or will present*" a significant risk. (Emphasis added.)

Although petitioners correctly point out that the value of a product not being produced is not zero, as it may find some future use, and that the EPA here has banned items where the estimated risk is zero, this was not error on the part of the EPA. The numbers appear to favor petitioners only because even products with known high risks temporarily show no risk because they are not part of this country's present stream of commerce. This would soon change if the product returned, which is precisely what the EPA is trying to avoid.

Should some unlikely future use arise for these products, the manufacturers and importers have access to the waiver provision established by the EPA for just these contingencies. Under such circumstances, we will not disturb the agency's decision to ban products that no longer are being produced in or imported into the United States.

Similarly, we also decide that the EPA properly can attempt to promulgate a "clean up" ban under TSCA, providing it takes the proper steps in doing so. A clean-up ban, like the asbestos ban in this case, seeks to ban all uses of a certain toxic substance, including unknown, future uses of the substance. Although there is some merit to petitioners' argument that the EPA cannot possibly evaluate the costs and benefits of banning unknown, uninvented products, we hold that the nebulousness of these future products, combined with TSCA's language authorizing the EPA to ban products that "will" create a public risk, allows the EPA to ban future uses of asbestos even in products not yet on the market.

* * *

VI.

Conclusion.

In summary, of most concern to us is that the EPA has failed to implement the dictates of TSCA and the prior decisions of this and other courts that, before it imposes a ban on a product, it first evaluates and then rejects the less burdensome alternatives laid out for it by Congress. While the EPA spent much time and care crafting its asbestos regulation, its explicit failure to consider the alternatives required of it by Congress deprived its final rule of the reasonable basis it needed to survive judicial scrutiny.

* * *

Finally, the EPA failed to provide a reasonable basis for the purported benefits of its proposed rule by refusing to evaluate the toxicity of likely substitute products that will be used to replace asbestos goods. While the EPA does not have the duty under TSCA of affirmatively seeking out and testing all possible substitutes, when an interested party comes forward with credible evidence that the planned substitutes present a significant, or even greater, toxic risk than the substance in question, the agency must make a formal finding on the record that its proposed action still is both reasonable and warranted under TSCA.

We regret that this matter must continue to take up the valuable time of the agency, parties and, undoubtedly, future courts. The requirements of TSCA, however, are plain, and the EPA cannot deviate from them to reach its desired result. We therefore GRANT the petition for review, VACATE the EPA's proposed regulation, and REMAND to the EPA for further proceedings in light of this opinion.

NOTES AND QUESTIONS

1. *How protective is TSCA?* Given this case, how protective does TSCA appear to be? What is the practical effect, for example, of requiring the EPA to use the "least burdensome" method of regulation? How does the "least burdensome" requirement affect TSCA regulation, compared to regulation under FIFRA? Consider the Government Accountability Office's February 2009 assessment of TSCA:

> TSCA generally places the burden of obtaining data on existing chemicals on EPA, rather than on the companies that produce the chemicals. For example, the act requires EPA to demonstrate certain health or environmental risks before it can require companies to further test their chemicals. As a result, EPA does not routinely assess the risks of the roughly 80,000 industrial chemicals in use. Moreover, TSCA does not require chemical companies to test the approximately 700 new chemicals introduced into commerce annually for their toxicity, and companies generally do not voluntarily perform such testing. Further, the procedures EPA must follow in obtaining test data from companies can take years to complete. In contrast, the European Union's chemical control legislation generally places the burden on companies to provide health effects data on the chemicals they produce. Giving EPA more authority to obtain data from the companies producing chemicals, as GAO has in the past recommended that Congress consider, remains a viable option for improving the effectiveness of TSCA.

> While TSCA authorizes EPA to issue regulations that may, among other things, ban existing toxic chemicals or place limits on their production or use, the statutory requirements EPA must meet present a legal threshold that has proven difficult for EPA and discourages the agency from using these authorities. For example, EPA must demonstrate "unreasonable risk," which EPA believes requires it to conduct extensive cost-benefit analyses to ban or limit chemical production. *Since 1976, EPA has issued regulations to control only five existing chemicals determined to present an unreasonable risk.*

Government Accountability Office, Chemical Regulation: Options for Enhancing the Effectiveness of the Toxic Substances Control Act: Summary, available at http://www.gao.gov/products/GAO–09–428T (emphasis added).

2. *The economics of human lives.* As this case shows, because TSCA requires the EPA to engage in a cost-benefit analysis, it raises the issue of how much we as a society are willing to pay to save lives. How much is a human life worth? This issue has recurred throughout environmental and public health law. According to the Fifth Circuit, how much cost was the EPA willing to incur to prevent one death as a result of asbestos exposure? How did the court react to that figure? Do you agree?

For regulatory purposes, the EPA generally estimates the value of a human life saved as being somewhere between $6.9 million and $8.7 million. How do you suppose that the EPA derived those figures? See National Center for Environmental Economics, U.S. EPA, Frequently Asked Questions on

Mortality Risk Valuation, available at http://yosemite.epa.gov/ee/epa/eed.nsf/pages/MortalityRiskValuation.html.

3. *The discounting problem.* In conducting a cost-benefit analysis, analysts generally *discount* future benefits and future costs to a present value so that they may be more easily compared. For example, suppose a certain regulation will result in a cost of $100.00 today but a benefit of $300.00 10 years from now. Is that later benefit worth the current cost? Discounting allows you to compare the two.

Discounting reflects the time value of money. For example, if you have $1,000 today and can invest it at a 5% rate of return, you will have $1,050 in a year. Conversely, if you need to have $1,050 a year from now and interest rates are 5%, you only need $1,000 today to achieve that future amount.

So, to return to our example: Assuming simple interest of 5% over 10 years, $300.00 10 years from now is worth a little less than $185.00 today. So, that benefit is worth the $100.00 cost today. However, interest rates matter! If the interest rates over the 10 years are 10%, that $300.00 benefit in the future is worth only about $116.00 today. It still exceeds the costs, but not by as much.

Why did the Fifth Circuit question the EPA's discounting in its asbestos rule? Was the problem the choice of interest rate, or something else?

4. *Risk-risk analysis.* The Fifth Circuit's discussions of substitute products in this case also makes it clear that TSCA requires the EPA to engage in a *risk-risk analysis*—that is, to actively compare the risks that arise from use of asbestos with the risks that would arise from the products that would substitute for asbestos. Why did the EPA's bans of specific asbestos products fail this risk-risk analysis requirement? What risks would the asbestos product substitutes pose, according to the Fifth Circuit? In particular, why was the court concerned about the risk-risk analysis regarding the EPA's proposal to replace asbestos water pipes with PVC water pipes?

5. *TSCA's more specific regulatory provisions.* TSCA contains several sets of more specific provisions governing toxic substances. For example, in 1986, Congress added the Asbestos Hazard Emergency Response provisions to TSCA. 15 U.S.C. §§ 2641–2656. Through these provisions, Congress sought:

(1) to provide for the establishment of Federal regulations which require inspection for asbestos-containing material and implementation of appropriate response actions with respect to asbestos-containing material in the Nation's schools in a safe and complete manner;

(2) to mandate safe and complete periodic reinspection of school buildings following response actions, where appropriate; and

(3) to require the Administrator to conduct a study to find out the extent of the danger to human health posed by asbestos in public and commercial buildings and the means to respond to any such danger.

Id. § 2641(b). The amendments authorized the EPA to promulgate regulations to govern asbestos inspections and response actions. Id. § 2643.

TSCA's third subchapter addresses indoor radon abatement, 15 U.S.C. §§ 2661–2671, while Subchapter IV addresses lead exposure reduction. Id.

§§ 2681–2692. Some of the most litigated provisions in TSCA involve polychlorinated biphenyls, or PCBs. In section 6 of TSCA, 15 U.S.C. § 2605, Congress specifically provided that:

> (1) Within six months after January 1, 1977, the Administrator shall promulgate rules to—
>
>> (A) prescribe methods for the disposal of polychlorinated biphenyls, and
>>
>> (B) require polychlorinated biphenyls to be marked with clear and adequate warnings, and instructions with respect to their processing, distribution in commerce, use, or disposal or with respect to any combination of such activities.
>
> Requirements prescribed by rules under this paragraph shall be consistent with the requirements of paragraphs (2) and (3).
>
> (2) (A) Except as provided under subparagraph (B), effective one year after January 1, 1977, no person may manufacture, process, or distribute in commerce or use any polychlorinated biphenyl in any manner other than in a totally enclosed manner.
>
>> (B) The Administrator may by rule authorize the manufacture, processing, distribution in commerce or use (or any combination of such activities) of any polychlorinated biphenyl in a manner other than in a totally enclosed manner if the Administrator finds that such manufacture, processing, distribution in commerce, or use (or combination of such activities) will not present an unreasonable risk of injury to health or the environment.
>
>> (C) For the purposes of this paragraph, the term "totally enclosed manner" means any manner which will ensure that any exposure of human beings or the environment to a polychlorinated biphenyl will be insignificant as determined by the Administrator by rule.

Id. § 2605(e). Congress did, however, permit the EPA to grant numerous exemptions from the general prohibition. Id. § 2605(e)(3). The EPA first promulgated regulations governing the disposal of PCBs in 1978, 43 Fed. Reg. 7, 156, and first promulgated regulations governing the manufacture, processing, distribution, and use of PCBs in 1979. 44 Fed. Reg. 31, 542. The EPA's TSCA regulations for PCBs have been codified at 40 C.F.R., Part 761.

6. *The EPA's asbestos regulations.* The EPA has promulgated asbestos regulations, which are found in 40 C.F.R., Part 763. The regulations that govern the prohibitions on asbestos and labeling requirements are found at 40 C.F.R. §§ 763.160–763.179. They do *not* completely ban asbestos.

2. TSCA REFORM

Given the constraints that TSCA imposes on EPA regulation, the number of chemical products in the United States, and the fact that the EPA has been able to regulate so few of these products (only five!) since Congress enacted TSCA in 1976, reform of TSCA is warranted. Moreover, increasing calls to reform TSCA have been heard since the Obama

Administration took office in January 2009. See, e.g., Richard A. Denison, Ten Essential Elements in TSCA Reform, 39 Envtl.L.Rep., News & Analysis 10020 (Jan.2009); Mark A. Greenwood, TSCA Reform: Building a Program that Can Work, 39 Envtl.L.Rep., News & Analysis 10034 (Jan. 2009).

In February 2009, for example, the Director of the Government Accountability Office's ("GAO") Natural Resources and Environment Section testified to Congress regarding TSCA reform. John Stephenson, U.S. GAO, Options for Enhancing the Effectiveness of the Toxic Substances Control Act, available at http://www.gao.gov/new.items/d09428t. pdf. He emphasized the informational and procedural shortcomings of TSCA. Thus:

> EPA lacks adequate scientific information on the toxicity of many chemicals in the environment. TSCA generally places the burden of obtaining data on chemicals on EPA, rather than on the companies that produce the chemicals. This approach requires that EPA demonstrate certain health or environmental risks before it can require companies to further test their chemicals. As a result, EPA has only limited information on the health and environmental risks posed by these chemicals.

Id. at 2. In addition, "[w]hile TSCA authorizes EPA to review existing chemicals, it generally provides no specific requirement, time frame, or methodology for doing so." Id. at 4.

Several commentators, including the GAO, have pointed to the European Union's June 2007 legislation to regulate chemicals, Registration, Evaluation, and Authorization of Chemicals (REACH), as one model for TSCA reform. As the GAO emphasized, "a key aspect of REACH is that it places the burden on manufacturers, importers, and downstream users to ensure that they manufacture, place on the market, or use such substances that do not adversely affect human health or the environment." Id. at 4. See also John S. Applegate, Synthesizing TSCA and REACH: Practical Principles for Chemical Regulation Reform, 35 Ecology L.Q. 721 (2008).

The Obama Administration has endorsed TSCA reform. In late September 2009, Lisa Jackson, the Administrator of the EPA, announced that the EPA would ask Congress to "overhaul" TSCA and outlined principles for that reform. The EPA's six principles for TSCA reform, as updated in April 2010, are:

Principle No. 1: Chemicals Should be Reviewed Against Safety Standards that are Based on Sound Science and Reflect Risk-based Criteria Protective of Human Health and the Environment.

EPA should have clear authority to establish safety standards that are based on scientific risk assessments. Sound science should be the basis for the assessment of chemical risks, while recognizing the need to assess and manage risk in the face of uncertainty.

Principle No. 2: Manufacturers Should Provide EPA with the Necessary Information to Conclude That New and Existing Chemicals are Safe and Do Not Endanger Public Health or the Environment.

Manufacturers should be required to provide sufficient hazard, exposure, and use data for a chemical to support a determination by the Agency that the chemical meets the safety standard. Exposure and hazard assessments from manufacturers should be required to include a thorough review of the chemical's risks to sensitive subpopulations.

Where manufacturers do not submit sufficient information, EPA should have the necessary authority and tools, such as data call in, to quickly and efficiently require testing or obtain other information from manufacturers that is relevant to determining the safety of chemicals. EPA should also be provided the necessary authority to efficiently follow up on chemicals which have been previously assessed (e.g., requiring additional data or testing, or taking action to reduce risk) if there is a change which may affect safety, such as increased production volume, new uses or new information on potential hazards or exposures. EPA's authority to require submission of use and exposure information should extend to downstream processors and users of chemicals.

Principle No. 3: Risk Management Decisions Should Take into Account Sensitive Subpopulations, Cost, Availability of Substitutes and Other Relevant Considerations.

EPA should have clear authority to take risk management actions when chemicals do not meet the safety standard, with flexibility to take into account a range of considerations, including children's health, economic costs, social benefits, and equity concerns.

Principle No. 4: Manufacturers and EPA Should Assess and Act on Priority Chemicals, Both Existing and New, in a Timely Manner.

EPA should have authority to set priorities for conducting safety reviews on existing chemicals based on relevant risk and exposure considerations. Clear, enforceable and practicable deadlines applicable to the Agency and industry should be set for completion of chemical reviews, in particular those that might impact sensitive sub-populations.

Principle No. 5: Green Chemistry Should Be Encouraged and Provisions Assuring Transparency and Public Access to Information Should Be Strengthened.

The design of safer and more sustainable chemicals, processes, and products should be encouraged and supported through research, education, recognition, and other means. The goal of these efforts should be to increase the design, manufacture, and use of lower risk, more energy efficient and sustainable chemical products and processes.

TSCA reform should include stricter requirements for a manufacturer's claim of Confidential Business Information (CBI). Manufacturers should be required to substantiate their claims of confidentiality. Data relevant to health and safety should not be claimed or otherwise treated as CBI. EPA should be able to negotiate with other governments (local, state, and foreign) on appropriate sharing of CBI with the necessary protections, when necessary to protect public health and safety.

Principle No. 6: EPA Should Be Given a Sustained Source of Funding for Implementation.

Implementation of the law should be adequately and consistently funded, in order to meet the goal of assuring the safety of chemicals, and to maintain public confidence that EPA is meeting that goal. To that end, manufacturers of chemicals should support the costs of Agency implementation, including the review of information provided by manufacturers.

U.S. EPA, Existing Chemicals: Essential Principles for Reform of Chemicals Management Legislation, available at http://www.epa.gov/oppt/existingchemicals/pubs/principles.html; see also Charles M. Auer, Lynn L. Bergeson, & James V. Aidala, EPA's Action Plans Signal a New Chapter for TSCA While Informing the Future Legislative Debate on Chemicals, 40 Envtl.L.Rep., News & Analysis 10243 (March 2010); Brett H. Oberst, Lynn N. Hang, & Lindsay K. Larris, Obama and EPA Take on TSCA Reform, 40 Envtl.L.Rep., News & Analysis 10123 (Feb.2010).

In the spring and summer of 2010, legislation was introduced in both the House and Senate to enact comprehensive reform of TSCA. Reform of TSCA is an EPA priority.

3. ENFORCEMENT OF TSCA AND TOXIC TORTS

Even without reform, however, TSCA is not completely ineffective. Notably, TSCA contains several provisions related to enforcement. First, the Act allows the EPA to conduct inspections. 15 U.S.C. § 2610. Second, the Act allows the Customs Office in the Department of the Treasury to control importation of chemical substances and mixtures regulated under TSCA. Id. § 2612. Third, TSCA makes it illegal for anyone to violate the EPA's regulations; to use a chemical substance or mixture for commercial purposes if the user knew or had reason to know that it was manufactured, processed or distributed in violation of the EPA's TSCA regulations; to fail to keep required records; and to fail to allow inspections. Id. § 2614. Such violations are subject to civil penalties and criminal prosecutions. Id. § 2615. In addition, the EPA and the courts can seize illegal chemical substances and mixtures. Id. § 2616. Finally, like many environmental laws, TSCA allows citizens to bring suit to enforce its provisions. Specifically,

Except as provided in subsection (b) of this section, any person may commence a civil action—

(1) against any person (including (A) the United States, and (B) any other governmental instrumentality or agency to the extent permitted by the eleventh amendment to the Constitution) who is alleged to be in violation of this chapter or any rule promulgated under section 2603, 2604, or 2605 of this title, or subchapter II or IV of this chapter, or order issued under section 2604 of this title or subchapter II or IV of this chapter to restrain such violation, or

(2) against the Administrator to compel the Administrator to perform any act or duty under this chapter which is not discretionary.

Id. § 2619(a). Moreover, TSCA generally does not preempt state law, id. § 2617(a)(1), or eliminate "any other remedies provided by law." Id. § 2618(e). As a result, as was true for RCRA, CERCLA, and FIFRA, regulation under TSCA and toxic tort actions could overlap.

Consider the role of TSCA in the following action. Did the U.S. District Court for the Western District of Virginia apply TSCA's citizen-suit provision correctly?

GIBSON v. WAL–MART STORES, INC.

United States District Court for the Western District of Virginia, 2002.
189 F.Supp.2d 443.

GLEN M. WILLIAMS, SENIOR DISTRICT JUDGE.

This case, involving allegations of negligent product design, manufacture, and marketing in violation of the Federal Hazardous Substances Act, the Poison Prevention Packaging Act, and the Toxic Substance Control Act, as well as negligent product placement and negligent treatment of a business invitee, comes before the court on Defendants' Motion for Summary Judgment. For the reasons contained in this Memorandum Opinion, Defendants' motion is hereby **GRANTED** as to all counts.

I. Factual Background

The essential facts of the case, either undisputed or where disputed, recited in the light most favorable to the nonmovant on the summary judgment record, are as follows.

Plaintiff Sally V. Gibson (Mrs. Gibson) and her husband Silas Gibson (Mr. Gibson) went to the Wal–Mart Store (Wal Mart) in Norton, Virginia, on August 29, 1998 with the intent of purchasing a charcoal grill, charcoal, and charcoal lighter fluid. Mrs. Gibson, at the time of the incident giving rise to this suit, was a five-foot, three-inch tall, 62–year-old woman. Mr. and Mrs. Gibson proceeded to the Lawn and Garden department to gather the items they wished to purchase. After getting a charcoal grill and a bag of charcoal, Mrs. Gibson went to retrieve the lighter fluid.

The lighter fluid was located above Mrs. Gibson's head, but still within her reach. She reached above her head, grasped the center of the container, and tipped it sideways such that the top of the container was lower than the bottom. At that point, lighter fluid spilled from the can onto Mrs. Gibson's clothing and into her mouth. Mrs. Gibson swallowed some of the lighter fluid. Her husband, Mr. Gibson, was present when the incident occurred.

Mrs. Gibson was rendered unable to speak. Mr. Gibson immediately sought help following the incident. A Wal Mart associate brought a chair for Mrs. Gibson. Margaret Lewis (Lewis), a Support Team Manager at the time of the incident, responded to a call over the public announcement system for assistance. Upon learning that Mrs. Gibson had potentially ingested some of the lighter fluid, Lewis contacted St. Mary's Hospital and was directed to call the Poison Control Center. The Poison Control Center directed Lewis to give Mrs. Gibson water to drink, which she did. Lewis then asked Mrs. Gibson if she could fill out an incident report. Mrs. Gibson filled out the incident report at that time.

According to Mr. Gibson, he requested that Lewis contact emergency medical services and arrange for an ambulance transport to the hospital. However, Lewis refused to do so. Lewis states that Mr. Gibson did not request an ambulance at any time. Rather, he asked if he could transport his wife to the hospital after she had filled out the incident report. Lewis further states that she informed Mr. Gibson "that he was free to do whatever he wanted." Thereafter, Mr. Gibson drove Mrs. Gibson to Norton Community Hospital.

Mrs. Gibson filed this cause of action on August 28, 2000, alleging negligent product design, manufacture, and marketing against R.W. Packaging (R.W.), the maker of Easy Start Charcoal Starter, and, in the alternative, against Wal Mart. Mrs. Gibson further alleges violations of the Federal Hazardous Substances Act (FHSA), 15 U.S.C. § 1261 *et seq.*, the Poison Prevention Packaging Act (PPPA), 15 U.S.C. § 1471 *et seq.*, and the Toxic Substances Control Act (TSCA), 15 U.S.C. § 2601 *et seq.* Finally, Mrs. Gibson alleges that Wal Mart negligently breached its duty of care to her after the accident occurred.

This case is now before the court on Defendants' Motion for Summary Judgment. All parties have submitted briefs and been heard at oral argument. The case is therefore ripe for judgment.

II. Analysis

* * *

B. *Product Liability Claim*

Mrs. Gibson has alleged both negligence and breach of express and implied warranties. In order to prevail "[u]nder either the warranty theory or the negligence theory the plaintiff must show, (1) that the goods were unreasonably dangerous either for the use to which they would ordinarily be put or for some other reasonably foreseeable purpose, and (2) that the unreasonably dangerous condition existed when the goods left the defendant's hands." *Logan v. Montgomery Ward & Co.,* 216 Va. 425, 219 S.E.2d 685, 687 (1975). Further, "[i]n determining what constitutes an unreasonably dangerous defect, a court will consider safety standards promulgated by the government or the relevant industry, as well as the reasonable expectations of consumers." *Alevromagiros v. Hechinger Co.,* 993 F.2d 417, 420 (4th Cir.1993). Reasonable consumer expectations can be established through "evidence of actual industry practices, knowledge at the time of other injuries, knowledge of dangers, published literature, and . . . direct evidence of what reasonable purchasers consider defective." *Lemons v. Ryder Truck Rental,* 906 F. Supp. 328, 332–33 (W.D. Va. 1995) (citations omitted).

Mrs. Gibson has failed to show either that the charcoal lighter fluid was unreasonably dangerous or that the condition existed when it left the defendants' hands. Mrs. Gibson has presented evidence of government standards governing the packaging of charcoal lighter fluid, specifically, 16 C.F.R. §§ 1700.14 & 1700.15. However, nothing in the evidence indicates that the packaging used by R.W. violates these standards.

Mrs. Gibson also alleges that the product falls below reasonable consumer expectations. She does so by stating in her affidavit that Easy Start Charcoal Starter did not meet *her* expectations, supported by her husband reiterating the same sentiment. This court is not surprised that a plaintiff against a manufacturer would assert as much. However, more is required than a plaintiff's personal opinion of a product that allegedly injured her. This court has previously required a factual examination of what society expects or demands from a product. Mrs. Gibson's conclusory statement regarding the lighter fluid is insufficient as a matter of law to meet this standard.

The defendants' contend that Mrs. Gibson lacks the requisite expert to prove causation. Mrs. Gibson responds that she in fact does have an expert, Dr. Robinette. Mrs. Gibson further asserts that this expert establishes causation. Reviewing Dr. Robinette's affidavit, the court fails to see how he establishes a defect in the lighter fluid that caused Mrs. Gibson's injuries. Dr. Robinette's affidavit states that plaintiff's ingestion of lighter fluid caused her various injuries, including oral blisters and burning of her upper airway and acute chemical injury to her lungs. However, this testimony fails to show that these injuries were the result of any defect in the product. In fact, the product label itself warns of such dangers.

Finally, Mrs. Gibson fails to prove that the accident was due to an unreasonably dangerous condition that existed when the product left the defendants' hands. Mrs. Gibson does not know how long the container of lighter fluid was on the shelf prior to her incident, nor does she know how the container came to be in the state in which she discovered it. The law of Virginia does not allow recovery when the plaintiff's theory is conjectural. Rather, the plaintiff must affirmatively prove her case, if only by excluding all other explanations. This Mrs. Gibson fails to do.

In sum, Mrs. Gibson fails to prove that the lighter fluid is an unreasonably dangerous product, or that her injuries were due to an unreasonably dangerous condition created by one or both of the defendants. Therefore, summary judgment for the defendants on the issue of product liability is granted.

C. *Federal Statutory Claims*

Mrs. Gibson has also alleged that the defendants violated several federal statutes governing the production and packaging of charcoal lighter fluid. Specifically, Mrs. Gibson alleges violations of the Federal Hazardous Substances Act, 15 U.S.C. § 1261 *et seq.,* the Poison Prevention Packaging Act, 15 U.S.C. § 1471 *et seq.,* and the Toxic Substances Control Act, 15 U.S.C. § 2601 *et seq.* R.W. and Wal Mart contend that these statutes do not grant a private right of action, and therefore Mrs. Gibson's claims under them should be dismissed for failure to state a claim.

The Fourth Circuit has yet to determine the issue of whether the FHSA and PPPA grant private rights of action. However, this has been addressed by the Second Circuit in *Riegel Textile Corp. v. Celanese Corp.,* 649 F.2d 894 (2nd Cir. 1981). * * *

The *Riegel* court concluded, after an extensive analysis, that the FHSA did not grant a private right of action. * * *

* * * This court finds the reasoning of the Second Circuit persuasive and hereby adopts the holdings of that court. The FHSA provides for no private right of action, and, by extension, neither does the PPPA. Enforcement of these Acts has been given to the Consumer Product Safety Commission (CPSC) in order to prevent injury. State tort law provides adequate redress of violations without the creation of an additional federal statutory cause of action. For these reasons, Mrs. Gibson's FHSA and PPPA claims are dismissed.

As earlier mentioned, Mrs. Gibson has also alleged violations of the Toxic Substances Control Act. The defense replies that the TSCA was enacted "to address the manufacture, processing, disposal, distribution and treatment of PCB's (poly-chlorinated biphenyls)." This is only partially true. The TSCA addresses the manufacture, use, and disposal of several toxic substances, PCB's included among them, but also asbestos and others. The TSCA is primarily oriented to environmental protection with the Environmental Protection Agency (EPA) vested with the responsibility of enacting and enforcing regulatory provisions related to the Act. Given the nature of the TSCA, this court fails to see where this Act applies under the facts of this case. No environmental threat has been identified, and no environmental threat regarding the manufacture or disposal of the lighter fluid has been named. Therefore, any claim under the TSCA is dismissed.

D. *Premises Liability Claim*

Mrs. Gibson further alleges that Wal Mart was negligent in its duty to her by failing to ensure her safety while in the store. Further, Mrs. Gibson alleges Wal Mart was negligent in its treatment of her following the accident.

Rules related to premises liability are well settled in Virginia. A store-owner owes an invitee of the business the duty to exercise ordinary care. This requires a store-owner to maintain his facility in a reasonably safe condition, with warnings to the invitee of any unsafe conditions known to the store-owner, or which, in the exercise of reasonable care, should be known to the store owner. Further, "constructive knowledge or notice of a defective condition of a premise or a fixture may be shown by evidence that the defect was noticeable and had existed for a sufficient length of time to charge its possessor with notice of its defective condition." *Grim v. Rahe, Inc.,* 246 Va. 239, 434 S.E.2d 888, 890 (1993).

In the case at bar, Mrs. Gibson has been unable to show that Wal Mart had any notice of any defective condition that existed with the container of charcoal lighter fluid. In fact, Mrs. Gibson admits she does not know how long the lighter fluid was on the shelf. The merchandise was placed in the store to be readily accessible to customers. It is therefore unknown who opened or damaged the can of lighter fluid. Therefore, Mrs. Gibson's claim must fail.

Mrs. Gibson has also alleged that Wal Mart breached its duty to her after the accident occurred. Mrs. Gibson contended at oral argument that when Wal Mart began to administer some medical treatment, it assumed a continuing duty to provide medical treatment, and that this duty was breached by not arranging transport for Mrs. Gibson to the hospital. She has further argued on brief for the extension of the rescue and emergency doctrine to cover situations such as this. Mrs. Gibson has not offered any case law to support such an extension in either argument.

Wal Mart has argued that its duty to provide medical assistance, if any, ended when Mrs. Gibson's husband arrived, as she was in the care of a competent adult. * * * Virginia has not expanded to store-owners any duty to provide medical treatment to those injured on their premises. This court, as a federal court, is loathe to extend state tort law into areas unaddressed by the Virginia Supreme Court, and therefore declines so to do.

Further, the duty of any person is to act reasonably under the circumstances. Lewis, the management member present at the scene, contacted the Poison Control Center and followed their instructions. This court is unable to determine that these actions were in any way unreasonable. Further, Mrs. Gibson was in the presence and care of her husband. Both Mrs. and Mr. Gibson admit in depositions that they were not prevented from leaving at any time. Under these circumstances, Wal Mart conducted itself in a reasonable manner. Therefore, summary judgment as to any premises liability claims is granted.

III. Conclusion

For the foregoing reasons, Defendant's Motion for Summary Judgment is hereby **GRANTED**.

Notes and Questions

1. *The relationship of federal statutes to this toxic tort.* As you have seen in your studies of RCRA, CERCLA, and FIFRA, federal statutes related to hazardous and toxic substances can have many interactions with more standard toxic tort lawsuits. That relationship also becomes important in the context of preemption, which is discussed in Chapter 10.

What were the relationships between each of the three federal statutes invoked in this case to the underlying toxic tort lawsuit? What did you think of the court's analysis of TSCA, in particular?

2. *Other federal statutes governing hazardous and toxic substances.* As this case makes clear, there are numerous other federal statutes besides those included in this Chapter that deal with toxic and hazardous substances. For example, the *Federal Hazardous Substances Act* (FHSA), 15 U.S.C. §§ 1261–1272, mentioned in the principal case, allows the Consumer Product Safety Commission to regulate products if those products meet the Act's definition of "hazardous substance." Id. § 1262(a). The Act defines "hazardous substance" to be:

> (1) (A) Any substance or mixture of substances which (i) is toxic, (ii) is corrosive, (iii) is an irritant, (iv) is a strong sensitizer, (v) is flammable or combustible, or (vi) generates pressure through decomposition, heat, or other means, if such substances or mixture of substances may cause substantial personal injury or substantial illness during or as a proximate result of any customary or reasonably foreseeable handling or use, including reasonably foreseeable ingestion by children.
>
> (B) Any substances which the Commission by regulation finds, pursuant to the provisions of section 1262(a) of this title, meet the requirements of subparagraph (1)(A) of this paragraph.
>
> (C) Any radioactive substance, if, with respect to such substance as used in a particular class of article or as packaged, the Commission determines by regulation that the substance is sufficiently hazardous to require labeling in accordance with this chapter in order to protect the public health.
>
> (D) Any toy or other article intended for use by children which the Commission by regulation determines, in accordance with section 1262(e) of this title, presents an electrical, mechanical, or thermal hazard.
>
> (E) Any solder which has a lead content in excess of 0.2 percent.

Id. § 1261(f)(1). As the above list suggests, the FHSA has a special emphasis on protecting children from hazardous toys and other products that children use. Id. § 1262(e). The FHSA prohibits commercial activities in violation of the Commission's regulations and labeling requirements, id. § 1263, and violations of the Act are punishable through civil penalties and criminal fines. Id. § 1264.

The principal case also involves the federal *Poison Prevention Packaging Act of 1970* (PPPA), 15 U.S.C. §§ 1471–77. The Consumer Product Safety Commission also administers this statute, which aims to increase the safety— particularly with respect to children—of poisonous household products. Pursuant to the PPPA,

> The Commission may establish in accordance with the provisions of this Act, by regulation, standards for the special packaging of any household substance if it finds that—
>
> (1) the degree or nature of the hazard to children in the availability of such substance, by reason of its packaging, is such that special packaging is required to protect children from serious personal injury or serious illness resulting from handling, using, or ingesting such substance; and
>
> (2) the special packaging to be required by such standard is technically feasible, practicable, and appropriate for such substance.

15 U.S.C. § 1472(a). The Commission's packaging requirements generally preempt state laws regarding product packaging, id. § 1476, but state attorneys general may enforce the PPPA's requirements. Id. § 1477.

3. *Private rights of action under federal statutes.* As noted, TSCA contains a citizen-suit provision, clearly allowing private citizens to sue for violations of its provisions. As the U.S. District Court for the Western District of Virginia notes, however, neither the FHSA nor the PPPA contain such citizen-suit provisions. It borrowed the U.S. Court of Appeals for the Second Circuit's application of the *Cort v. Ash* test—which you may have studied in your Civil Procedure or Federal Courts class—to determine whether a private right of action should be allowed. In particular, the Second Circuit and the Western District of Virginia emphasized that the FHSA and the PPPA seek to prevent harm rather than to redress harm. Why should that factor matter to the existence of a private cause of action under each statute? How did the Western District of Virginia view the role of traditional tort law in this context?

Conversely, why do you think that Congress included citizen-suit provisions in TSCA, RCRA, CERCLA, and most of the other environmental and natural resources statutes? Doesn't TSCA also seek to prevent harm?

FIFRA does *not* include a citizen-suit provision. Moreover, the federal courts of appeals have been unwilling to imply a private right of action into FIFRA or to otherwise allow private individuals to sue regarding violations of the Act. No Spray Coal., Inc. v. City of New York, 351 F.3d 602, 605 (2d Cir.2003) (noting FIFRA's lack of a citizen-suit provision and indicating that only governments can enforce its provisions); Almond Hill Sch. v. United States Dep't of Agriculture, 768 F.2d 1030, 1035–38 (9th Cir.1985) (concluding that citizens could not use 42 U.S.C. § 1983 to enforce FIFRA's requirements). Does this distinction between FIFRA and TSCA make sense to you? Why or why not?

D. THE FEDERAL FOOD, DRUG, AND COSMETIC ACT

1. OVERVIEW OF THE FOOD, DRUG, AND COSMETIC ACT: ADULTERATION AND MISBRANDING LIABILITY

As its title implies, the federal Food, Drug, and Cosmetic Act (FDCA), 21 U.S.C. §§ 301–399a, governs a number of products. First enacted in 1938, the Act now covers foods, food additives, drugs, medical devices, and cosmetics.

The FDCA is, as a result, a long and detailed statute that creates specific regulatory regimes for each of these products. Nevertheless, the Act also has an overarching focus on protecting consumers from *misbranded* or *adulterated* products. For example, the Act makes illegal all aspects of commerce in adulterated or misbranded foods, drugs, and cosmetics, including:

(a) The introduction or delivery for introduction into interstate commerce of any food, drug, device, tobacco product, or cosmetic that is adulterated or misbranded.

(b) The adulteration or misbranding of any food, drug, device, tobacco product, or cosmetic in interstate commerce.

(c) The receipt in interstate commerce of any food, drug, device, tobacco product, or cosmetic that is adulterated or misbranded, and the delivery or proffered delivery thereof for pay or otherwise.

21 U.S.C. § 331(a)–(c). Violations of these prohibitions are punishable by imprisonment and fines. Id. § 333(a). Moreover, federal authorities can seize misbranded and adulterated goods. Id. § 334.

In general, "adulteration" refers to the quality and purity of a food, drug, or cosmetic, while "misbranding" refers to the labeling, packaging, information provided about, and claims made for those products. Nevertheless, what exactly qualifies as "adulterated" or "misbranded" varies from item to item. A food, for example, is deemed "adulterated" if, among other things: it contains poisonous or unsanitary ingredients; valuable constituents of the food have been removed; it contains unsafe color additives; or the shipper failed to comply with the Act's shipping requirements. Id. § 342. A food is considered "misbranded" if, among other things: its label is false or misleading; the product advertisements are false or misleading; it is sold under the name of another food; it is an imitation and is not clearly labeled as such; its container is misleading; it is not packaged according to the Act's requirements; it does not include or correctly display nutrition information required under the Act on its label; or the manufacturer makes claims of quality that are not true or in accordance with the FDA's regulations. Id. § 343.

A drug is considered "adulterated" if, among other things: it contains a poisonous or unsanitary ingredient; its strength, quality, or purity is other than what the FDA has approved; its strength is misrepresented; or it is mixed with another substance. Id. § 351. A drug or medical device is deemed "misbranded" if: it has a false or misleading label; it fails to comply with the Act's packaging requirements; it fails to comply with the Act's labeling requirements; it is labeled with the wrong name; or it fails to provide adequate instructions and warnings. Id. § 352.

Finally:

A cosmetic shall be deemed to be adulterated—

(a) If it bears or contains any poisonous or deleterious substance which may render it injurious to users under the conditions of use prescribed in the labeling thereof, or under such conditions of use as are customary or usual, except that this provision shall not apply to coal-tar hair dye, the label of which bears the following legend conspicuously displayed thereon: "Caution–This product contains ingredients which may cause skin irritation on certain individuals and a preliminary test according to accompanying directions should first be made. This product must not be used for dyeing the eyelashes or eyebrows; to do so may cause blindness.", and the labeling of which bears adequate directions for such preliminary testing. For the purposes of this paragraph and paragraph (e) the term "hair dye" shall not include eyelash dyes or eyebrow dyes.

(b) If it consists in whole or in part of any filthy, putrid, or decomposed substance.

(c) If it has been prepared, packed, or held under insanitary conditions whereby it may have become contaminated with filth, or whereby it may have been rendered injurious to health.

(d) If its container is composed, in whole or in part, of any poisonous or deleterious substance which may render the contents injurious to health.

(e) If it is not a hair dye and it is, or it bears or contains, a color additive which is unsafe * * *.

Id. § 361. A cosmetic is deemed "misbranded" if: its label is false or misleading; its label does not comply with the Act or FDA regulations; its packaging does not comply with the Act's or FDA's requirements; its container is misleading; or it does not comply with the requirements for color additives. Id. § 362.

The FDCA has included adulteration and misbranding provisions since its original enactment. What was Congress trying to accomplish through this focus on adulteration and misbranding? How do such requirements contribute to public health and safety? What kinds of regulatory tools are these provisions, compared to the regulatory schemes in FIFRA and TSCA?

2. REGULATION OF FOODS AND FOOD ADDITIVES

The FDCA most lightly regulates foods. However, it makes an important distinction between foods and food additives. The following case provides an excellent overview of the Act's treatment of these two categories of regulated substances.

UNITED STATES v. 29 CARTONS OF * * * AN ARTICLE OF FOOD

United States Court of Appeals for the First Circuit, 1993.
987 F.2d 33.

SELYA, CIRCUIT JUDGE.

The government seized, and seeks to condemn, twenty-nine cartons of undiluted black currant oil (BCO), in capsule form, owned by claimant-appellee Oakmont Investment Co. (Oakmont), alleging that BCO is a food additive of questionable safety. Because we believe that encapsulated BCO, intended to be ingested as purchased, cannot properly be termed a food additive as defined in the Federal Food, Drug, and Cosmetic Act (the Act), *as amended,* 21 U.S.C. §§ 301 *et seq.* (1988), we affirm the district court's dismissal of the government's *in rem* complaint.

I. BACKGROUND

On October 11, 1988, the United States Food and Drug Administration (FDA) seized 200 bottles of encapsulated BCO, packed in twenty-nine cartons, and brought an *in rem* action contending that, under 21 U.S.C. § 342(a)(2)(C), the capsules should be condemned as "adulterated" food because they contain a "food additive," the BCO, that Oakmont had not proven to be safe.

At the ensuing bench trial, certain facts were uncontradicted. BCO is a liquid obtained by squeezing black currant berry seeds. It is composed of polyunsaturated fatty acids. In its pure liquid form, it can be ingested by the spoonful as a dietary supplement. However, Oakmont markets BCO in capsules which are to be swallowed whole. The capsules contain pure BCO—nothing more. They are made from gelatin and glycerin (or an equivalent plasticizer) and have no independent nutritional value. Rather, a capsule serves a dual purpose as a container (enabling consumers to ingest predetermined quantities of BCO in solid form) and as a prophylactic (protecting the BCO from rancidity).

On these and other facts, the district court dismissed the government's complaint and ordered the capsules released. The court reasoned that when, as in this case, BCO comprises the only active ingredient within a gelatin capsule, it can properly be classified as a "food," but not as a "food additive." Accordingly, the FDA erred in seizing the bottles on the ground that they "allegedly contain[ ] an unsafe food additive."

When the FDA appealed, the district court stayed its release order.

II. THE REGULATORY LANDSCAPE

To put this case into workable perspective, we first review the relevant statutory provisions. The Act defines "food" as:

(1) articles used for food or drink for man or other animals, (2) chewing gum, and (3) articles used for components of any such article.

21 U.S.C. § 321(f). The FDA concedes that pure BCO (sold, say, as a bottled liquid) falls within section 321(f)(1) and is, therefore, "food." Substances classified as "food" are presumed safe. Thus, the FDA can prevent sale of bottled BCO or any other "food" only if it proves by a preponderance of the evidence that the food is "injurious to health." 21 U.S.C. § 342(a)(1). Although the FDA suspects that BCO may be unhealthful, it is unable at the present time to translate this suspicion into legally competent proof.

In addition to regulating the sale of food *per se,* the Act contains provisions [regarding] food additives. These provisions are designed to protect consumers against the introduction of untested and potentially unsafe substances, such as flavor, texture, or preservative agents, into food. A gloss was added to the treatment of food additives in 1958. Unlike section 342(a)(1), which places the burden of proving injuriousness upon the government in respect to foods, the food additives amendment allocates the burden quite differently: the FDA can prevent the sale of products containing a food additive unless and until the processor shows that the substance, when added to food, is generally recognized as safe (in the vernacular, "GRAS"). Thus, in contrast to the Act's treatment of "food," any substance that meets the Act's definition of a "food additive" is presumed to be "unsafe" under 21 U.S.C. § 348 until the FDA, or more particularly, the Commissioner of Food and Drugs, has promulgated a regulation prescribing conditions assuring safe use. *See* 21 U.S.C. § 348(a)(2); 21 C.F.R. § 5.10(a)(1) (1992).

The 1958 amendment defines a food additive in pertinent part as:

any substance the intended use of which results or may reasonably be expected to result, directly or indirectly, in its becoming a component or otherwise affecting the characteristics of any food (including any substance intended for use in producing, manufacturing, packing, processing, preparing, treating, packaging, transporting, or holding food; and including any source of radiation intended for any such use), if such substance is not generally recognized, among experts qualified by scientific training and experience to evaluate its safety, as having been adequately shown through scientific procedures ... to be safe under the conditions of its intended use....

21 U.S.C. § 321(s). To be labeled a food additive, then, a substance must (1) be intended, or reasonably expected, to become a component of food or to otherwise affect the characteristics of food, and (2) not be GRAS.

The Act thus creates a distinction between foods and food additives which has meaningful consequences for purveyors and for the public. The distinction also significantly affects the ease with which the FDA may regulate a substance's sale.

III. THE ISSUE

This appeal revolves around the question of whether the FDA or Oakmont must carry out the research necessary to show that BCO is, or is not, GRAS. The issue reduces to whether pure BCO, when sold in encapsulated form, must be regulated as a "food" within the meaning of section 321(f) or as a "food additive" within the meaning of section 321(s).

The meat of the parties' disagreement lies in their differing interpretations of that portion of the Act which states that a substance can be a food additive if its intended use results, or may be expected to result, "in its becoming a component or otherwise affecting the characteristics of any food." 21 U.S.C. § 321(s). The FDA reads the quoted language as creating two independent and disjunctive standards: to satisfy the first prong of the food additive definition, a substance must either (1) be a component of food, or (2) otherwise affect the characteristics of food. Because each constituent part or element of a food (that is, each "component") necessarily affects the food's characteristics, the FDA considers every component, at least potentially, to be a food additive. Drawing on this interpretation, the FDA asserts that the seized capsules are composed of three consumable components—BCO, gelatin, and glycerin—and that, therefore, each of these three ingredients is subject to potential regulation as a food additive.

As Oakmont parses the statute, it creates only a single, unitary food additive standard. The phrase "or otherwise affecting the characteristics of any food" signals that a component is potentially a food additive only if it affects the characteristics of some food to which it is added. Unlike the FDA's interpretation, Oakmont's interpretation attaches no significance to a substance's mere presence as a component of a whole. It focuses instead on the substance's affirmative use in a way that affects food.

Applying its interpretation of the statute to the facts at bar, Oakmont argued below, as it does here, that the BCO contained in the seized capsules is itself a food and not a component of some other food, that it is intended so to serve, and that its sale in a convenient carrier medium does not transmogrify it into a food additive. In holding that food is defined "by its 'use[] for food,' " *29 Cartons,* 792 F.Supp. at 141 (quoting 21 U.S.C. § 321(f)), whereas a food additive is defined by its effect on another substance, *see id.,* the district court substantially adopted Oakmont's reading of the law and its focus on a substance's intended function.

In specific terms, then, we must determine whether, as the FDA would have it, *any* element of *any* substance that has more than one component may be branded a food additive, or, rather, whether, as Oakmont urges and the court below believed, such treatment should be reserved for elements which, when so added, effect a change (or, at least, could be expected to effect a change) in some other active ingredient.

IV. FOOD FOR THOUGHT

The Seventh Circuit has recently grappled with a factually similar case presenting this very issue. *See United States v. Two Plastic Drums, Etc.*, 984 F.2d 814 (7th Cir. 1993). Employing a perspicacious analysis of the Act's text and legislative history, the court rejected the FDA's notion that *all* components of a substance are necessarily food additives. The court observed that the " 'or otherwise' " phrase contained in the statutory definition of a food additive targets only those components that "have the purpose or effect of altering a food's characteristics." *Id.* at 818. The subsequent enumeration of sample food additives, describing each substance by its "function or by [its] effect on food," makes it clear that an additive must stimulate some change in a food to which it is added. *Id.* at 818. Turning to the legislative history, the court observed that the FDA's broad definition of a food additive, which would apply to all components, even a substance which comprises the only active ingredient of the whole, subverts congressional purpose. Blurring the distinction between food additives and food in this way would permit the agency to tilt a delicately balanced statutory scheme that allocates the burden of proving an additive's safety to the processors while leaving the burden of establishing a food's safety with the FDA. *See id.* at 819.

The Seventh Circuit also recognized the incongruity of categorizing a food's single active component as an additive. Because "that single component does not affect the characteristics of the food in question—rather, it constitutes the food," *id.* at 818, it has no place within "the common understanding of an additive, defined by Webster as 'a substance added to another . . . to impart or improve desirable properties or suppress undesirable properties.' " *Id.* at 818 n. 3 (citation omitted). Thus, in order to qualify as a food additive, a component must be added to a food in order to change that food's properties. *See id.* at 819. On that basis, pure BCO, in capsule form, is not a food additive. *See id.* at 820.

Judges should hesitate to write lengthy opinions merely for the sake of committing their own prose to posterity. Given the existence of a cogent, well-reasoned, eminently correct opinion closely on point, we embrace it. We will, therefore, affirm the judgment below for substantially the reasons elucidated in *Two Plastic Drums.* We pause, nevertheless, to essay a few additional observations.

First: We are reluctant to believe that Congress traffics in absurdities. Since it defies common sense to say that a substance can be a "food additive" when there is no (other) food to which it is added, we think that the FDA's reading of the Act is nonsensical, and, hence, must be incorrect. Moreover, classifying BCO as a "component" merely because it is combined with two totally inert substances serving collectively as a carrier medium would itself create a bizarre paradox: as the Seventh Circuit noted, "to hold that BCO is a component of the dietary supplement would be to find that BCO is a component of itself." *Two Plastic Drums,* 984 F.2d at 817.

Second: In the FDA's estimation, a processor's "subjective intent" that only one of a product's components constitutes the food is irrelevant because "it is the *objective* intended use, *i.e.,* the intent to combine two or more components, that counts." But, this harangue misses the mark. We fully agree that a processor's subjective determination of what constitutes a food is not determinative in cases of this stripe—but neither is the naked fact that more than one component has been combined. In the final analysis, what counts is the use of an ingredient for its effect on food. Here, from an objective standpoint, BCO is not being used for its effect on gelatin and glycerine. Thus, contrary to the FDA's loudly expressed fears, eschewing its rendition of the statutory text will not supplant objectivity with subjectivity.

Third: The FDA also maintains that because "the ingredients of multi-ingredient food products, such as cake mixes," indisputably fall within the food additive definition, the statute could not possibly contain a "requirement that a substance must be added to a *preexisting* food, which it must be shown actually to affect." We disagree. Cake mixes are foods composed of many interacting food additives, each with its particular effect on the whole. Absent any one ingredient, the concoction remains a cake mix, albeit one that may be short on sweetness or lumpy in texture. In that sense, cake mixes and products of that ilk are a far cry from a dietary supplement composed of a single active ingredient. What differentiates this case is that, if the BCO is removed, one is left with nothing but an empty capsule.

Fourth: We think it advisable to mention the FDA's insistence, citing *Chevron U.S.A. Inc. v. NRDC, Inc.,* 467 U.S. 837, 843 (1984), that we must obey its interpretation of the Act. In our estimation, the purely legal question facing us in this case presents no occasion for deference. In this realm of judicial expertise, the courts, not the agency, have the last word.

* * *

V. CONCLUSION

We need go no further. The proposition that placing a single-ingredient food product into an inert capsule as a convenient method of ingestion converts that food into a food additive perverts the statutory text, undermines legislative intent, and defenestrates common sense. We cannot accept such anfractuous reasoning.

Affirmed.

NOTES AND QUESTIONS

1. *FDCA definitions of "food" and "food additive."* How does the FDCA define "food"? How does it define "food additive"? Why would Congress make this distinction? Why are these definitions potentially problematic with respect to dietary supplements, which is what this case involved?

2. *Foods, food additives, GRAS, and burdens of proof.* How does the FDCA treat regulation of foods? Who has the burden of proving what before the Food and Drug Administration (FDA) can regulate? Why would Congress create this regulatory standard for foods? How is the FDCA's treatment of food additives different? Who has the burden of proving what with respect to food additives? Why would Congress create this regulatory standard for food additives? What is the GRAS standard, and how does it apply in each case?

3. *The special problem of dietary supplements.* Given the legal differences between foods and food additives, why would the FDA prefer to treat dietary supplements as food additives rather than foods? Consider ephedra, which in 2004 became the first dietary supplement that the FDA had ever banned. Ephedra is an herbal supplement that was routinely added to over-the-counter weight loss aids and energy supplements and drinks. However, ephedra can also cause heart palpitations, tremors, and insomnia, and it was linked to several deaths, including that of Baltimore Orioles pitcher Steve Bechler.

Currently, the Act explicitly deems dietary supplements to be foods. 21 U.S.C. § 321(ff). As you continue reading about the FDCA's treatment of drugs, however, consider whether dietary supplements such as ephedra should continue to be treated as "foods," or whether some other classification under the Act would be more appropriate.

4. *The FDA's other authorities regarding foods and food additives.* Building on the FDA's general authority over food additives, the FDCA requires the agency to set tolerances for poisonous and deleterious substances in foods for contaminants that cannot otherwise be avoided. Id. § 346. Similarly, the FDA must establish standards for pesticide residues in foods, coordinating those regulations with the EPA's requirements under FIFRA. Id. § 346a. Finally, the FDA must set particular requirements for bottled water, id. § 349; vitamins and minerals, id. § 350; and infant formulas. Id. § 350a.

5. *Foods as drugs.* Although foods enjoy the presumption of being GRAS, food manufacturers can get themselves in trouble under the FDCA if they start making drug-like claims. For example, one advertising campaign for the cereal Cheerios claimed that eating Cheerios could lower the consumer's cholesterol levels by four percent in six weeks. This is a drug claim, and in March 2009 the FDA concluded that General Mills, Cheerios' manufacturer, was violating the FDCA.

3. DRUGS

The FDCA's most stringent regulatory provisions apply to drugs. Under the Act, "drugs" include:

(A) articles recognized in the official United States Pharmacopoeia, official Homeopathic Pharmacopoeia of the United States, or official National Formulary, or any supplement to any of them; and (B) articles intended for use in the diagnosis, cure, mitigation, treatment, or prevention of disease in man or other animals; and (C) articles (other than food) intended to affect the structure or any function of the body of man or other animals; and (D) articles intended for use as a component of any article specified in clause (A), (B), or (C).

21 U.S.C. § 321(g)(1).

Historically the Act has been mostly concerned with regulating "new drugs," which it defines as:

> (1) Any drug (except a new animal drug or an animal feed bearing or containing a new animal drug) the composition of which is such that such drug is not generally recognized, among experts qualified by scientific training and experience to evaluate the safety and effectiveness of drugs, as safe and effective for use under the conditions prescribed, recommended, or suggested in the labeling thereof, except that such a drug not so recognized shall not be deemed to be a "new drug" if at any time prior to June 25, 1938, it was subject to the Food and Drugs Act of June 30, 1906, as amended, and if at such time its labeling contained the same representations concerning the conditions of its use; or

> (2) Any drug (except a new animal drug or an animal feed bearing or containing a new animal drug) the composition of which is such that such drug, as a result of investigations to determine its safety and effectiveness for use under such conditions, has become so recognized, but which has not, otherwise than in such investigations, been used to a material extent or for a material time under such conditions.

Id. § 321(p).

After 1962, the FDCA prohibited the introduction into interstate commerce of any new drug without the FDA's approval. Id. § 355(a). The applicant must provide the FDA with evidence sufficient to show that the drug is both safe and effective, id. § 355(b), and the FDA can refuse to approve the drug if this information is insufficient or if it indicates that the drug is unsafe, ineffective for its intended purpose, or both. Id. § 355(d). The FDA can also withdraw approval of a drug if later evidence shows that the drug is unsafe or ineffective. Id. § 355(e). Exemptions are available for drugs being used in research. Id. § 355(i). The FDA must also approve the public disclosure information about the drug, including its label. Id. § 355(l).

One issue regarding the FDA's approval of new drugs involves the common practice of compounding drugs. As you read the following case, consider why the FDA and Congress wanted to subject compounded drugs—at least in some cases—to the FDCA's new drug approval process and decide whether you think they struck the right balance in terms of the risks posed.

MEDICAL CENTER PHARMACY v. MUKASEY

United States Court of Appeals for the Fifth Circuit, 2008.
536 F.3d 383.

JERRY E. SMITH, CIRCUIT JUDGE:

In this appeal we clarify the extent to which the Federal Food Drug and Cosmetic Act of 1938 (the "FDCA" or the "Act"), 21 U.S.C. §§ 301–397, permits the Food and Drug Administration ("FDA") to regulate a common practice of pharmacies known as "compounding." Ten pharmacies specializing in compounding prescription drugs for human and animal use (the "Pharmacies") sued various federal agencies (collectively, the "FDA") for declaratory and injunctive relief permitting them to continue compounding drugs without obtaining the FDA approval required for "new drugs" under the Act, 21 U.S.C. § 321(p) and (v). Concluding that the FDCA, as amended, permits compounded drugs to avoid the new drug approval process but that the exception applies only in certain statutorily-delimited circumstances, we vacate and remand.

I.

A.

Drug compounding is the process by which a pharmacist combines or alters drug ingredients according to a doctor's prescription to create a medication to meet the unique needs of an individual human or animal patient. Compounding is "typically used to prepare medications that are not commercially available, such as medication for a patient who is allergic to an ingredient in a mass-produced product." [*Thompson v. Western States Medical Center*, 535 U.S. 357, 360–61 (2002)] According to the American Pharmacists Association, as *amici*, pharmacists compound patient-specific medication for a variety of medical purposes, including cancer treatment, where dosages must be calibrated to a "patient's body size, the type of cancer, the size and type of tumor, and the clinical condition of the patient;" pediatric treatment, where available drug dosages must be modified and diluted for use in children; elderly hospice care, where patients who no longer benefit from curative treatment use compounded dosages therapeutically to "establish optimal pain and symptom control;" and hospital stays, where "intravenous admixtures" must be highly individualized to allow administration of drugs "not suitable for other routes of administration."

Compounding has deep roots; it "is a traditional component of the practice of pharmacy and is taught as part of the standard curriculum at most pharmacy schools." *Id.* Since 1820, pharmacists have relied on compounding instructions contained in the *U.S. Pharmacopeia,* an independent compendium of drug standards whose authority is recognized by reference in federal law. "Many States specifically regulate compounding practices as part of their regulation of pharmacies. Some require all licensed pharmacies to offer compounding services." *Id.*

In 1938, Congress enacted the FDCA to regulate drug manufacturing, marketing, and distribution. The Act empowers the FDA to require approval of any "new drug," which the Act defines as "[a]ny drug (except a new animal drug . . .) the composition of which is such that such drug is not generally recognized . . . as safe and effective for use under the conditions prescribed, recommended, or suggested in the labeling thereof." The Act likewise requires approval of "new animal drugs" and defines "new animal drug" in similar terms.

To be deemed "safe and effective" and thereby obtain FDA approval, a new drug must undergo an extensive application and approval process. Under the FDCA, an FDA finding of "safe and effective" must be based on "substantial evidence" of expert consensus. The "test is rigorous," requiring expensive and time-consuming clinical trials estimated by some to cost more than $800 million per drug.

A question emerged from Congress's enactment of the FDCA: When a pharmacist creates a compounded medication to suit an individual patient, does the resulting creation constitute a "new drug" requiring FDA approval? If each individualized drug product produced through compounding required FDA approval, few would undergo the costly and arduous approval process. And the lack of approval would in turn make nearly all compounding unlawful under the FDCA. * * *

For roughly fifty years following the FDCA's enactment, the compounding question lay dormant, without dispute and without answer. The FDA did not seek to enforce "new drug" approval requirements against compounding pharmacists but instead left regulation of compounding to the states, and pharmacists continued to compound drugs without seeking FDA approval. In the early 1990's, however, the FDA became concerned that some pharmacies were purchasing bulk quantities of drug products, "compounding" them into specific drug products before receiving individual prescriptions, and marketing those drugs to doctors and patients. Although the agency had long refrained from regulating pharmacist compounding, it believed that pharmacies engaging in large-scale bulk compounding were effectively manufacturing drugs under the guise of compounding them—using the FDA's traditional lenience toward compounding as an end-run around the new drug approval, adulteration, and misbranding provisions of the FDCA.

Ostensibly to prevent this end-run around its regulation of drug manufacturing, the FDA in 1992 promulgated Compliance Policy Guide No. 7132.16 (Mar.1992) ("CPG 7132.16"), deemed by this circuit to be a valid agency rule under the Administrative Procedures Act. The Guide explained that "while retail pharmacies . . . are exempted from certain requirements of the [FDCA], they are not the subject of any general exemption from the new drug, adulteration, or misbranding provisions." CPG 7132.16, at 1.

Although asserting its expansive authority under the FDCA to require formal approval of all compounded drugs, the FDA declared its intention "generally [to] continue to defer to state and local officials regulation of the day-to-day practice of retail pharmacy and related activities." *Id.* at 4. Nevertheless, the FDA warned that it "may, in the exercise of its enforcement discretion, initiate federal enforcement actions against entities and responsible persons when the scope and nature of a pharmacy's activity raises the kind of concerns normally associated with a manufacturer." *Id.* The FDA went on to list nine non-exhaustive factors it would consider in exercising its enforcement discretion against certain kinds of manufacturing-as-compounding considered to be hazardous to public health.

A few years later, in a move the Pharmacies call a reaction to the FDA's 1992 policy and the FDA characterizes as a confirmation of it, Congress amended the FDCA by enacting the Food and Drug Modernization Act of 1997 ("FDAMA"), Pub. L. No. 105–115, 111 Stat. 2296 (codified as amended at 21 U.S.C. § 353a (2000)). Explicitly addressing "pharmacy compounding," FDAMA sought to permit pharmacy compounding by exempting compounded drugs from the FDCA's new drug approval, adulteration, and misbranding provisions, but FDAMA simultaneously conditioned the exemption on compliance with a number of restrictions on compounding practices and pharmacy advertising. Much like the FDA's 1992 policy, FDAMA created a safe harbor from the FDCA's new drug approval requirements so long as a compounding pharmacist observed a number of requirements designed to ensure the pharmacist was engaged in traditional compounding rather than disguised manufacturing.

Although FDAMA did not cover animal drugs, Congress also amended the FDCA by enacting the Animal Medicinal Drug Use Clarification Act of 1994 ("AMDUCA"), Pub. L. No. 103–396, 108 Stat. 4153 (codified as amended at § 360b(a)(4), (5)). In a similar manner as FDAMA, the AMDUCA amended the FDCA by exempting some extra-label uses of animal drugs from the new drug approval process while restricting this exemption to certain narrow circumstances.

Shortly after passage of FDAMA, however, trouble arose. In 2002, the [Supreme] Court invalidated the advertising-related provisions of FDAMA, affirming the Ninth Circuit's holding that those portions were unconstitutional restrictions on commercial speech. Although the Ninth Circuit had deemed FDAMA non-severable and therefore had invalidated FDAMA in its entirety, the Supreme Court declined to address the validity of the remaining non-advertising portions of FDAMA, because the parties had not appealed the severability issue. * * *

After the Court invalidated the advertising-related portions of FDA-MA, the FDA issued revised Compliance Policy Guides addressing the compounding of human and animal drugs. * * * [T]he agency took the position that "all of [FDAMA] is now invalid." CPG 460.200, at 2. Like their 1992 forebearer, the new Guides assert that compounded human and animal drugs are not exempt from the FDCA's new drug approval, adulteration, or misbranding provisions. But the Guides again assure pharmacists that the FDA will use its enforcement discretion against compounding only where a pharmacy's activities raise the kinds of concerns normally associated with manufacturing. And again, the Guides list factors the FDA will use in determining whether to bring enforcement actions.

B.

The Pharmacies sued for declaratory and injunctive relief, challenging the authority of the FDA to regulate compounded drugs under the FDCA. They sought four principal declaratory judgments: first, that compounded drugs are not "new drugs" or "new animal drugs" under § 321(p)(1) and (v)(1), and on this basis, that they are not subject to the requirements and prohibitions imposed by the FDCA on such drugs; second, that the FDCA permits pharmacists to compound drugs from bulk ingredients for non-food animals; third, that the Pharmacies' compliance with 21 U.S.C. § 374(a)(2)(A) makes them exempt from the heightened "records inspection" authorized by § 374(a)(1); and fourth, that CPG 608.400 violates the Administrative Procedures Act.

* * *

III.

Agreeing with the Pharmacies, the district court held that compounded drugs are not "new drugs" within the meaning of § 321(p)(1) of the FDCA, and on that basis, the court held that compounded drugs are uniformly exempt from the FDCA's new drug approval requirements. The FDA argues that compounded drugs *are* "new drugs" and consequently must satisfy the new drug approval requirements. We disagree with the district court and agree with the FDA as to whether compounded drugs are "new drugs." We disagree with both sides, however, regarding the implications of that conclusion.

Though compounded drugs are "new drugs," they are neither *uniformly* exempt from the new drug approval requirements nor *uniformly* subject to them. Properly construed, the statutory scheme as amended by FDAMA creates a *limited* exemption from the new drug approval requirements for compounded drugs that comply with conditions explicitly delineated in FDAMA.

A.

* * *

The FDCA defines "new drug" in § 321(p) as follows:

The term "new drug" means

(1) *Any drug* (except a new animal drug or an animal feed bearing or containing a new animal drug) the *composition of which* is such that such drug is *not generally recognized,* among experts qualified by scientific training and experience to evaluate the safety and effective-

ness of drugs, *as safe and effective for use under the conditions prescribed, recommended, or suggested in the labeling thereof....*

§ 321(p)(1) (emphasis added). The latter portion of this definition—"not generally recognized ... as safe and effective"—invokes the statutory standard a drug must meet to gain FDA approval. *See* § 355(d). Hence, "any drug ... the composition of which" has not already been approved by the FDA constitutes a "new drug" within the meaning of the statute. And the FDCA makes it unlawful to dispense a "new drug" without establishing the safeness and effectiveness of the new drug through the FDA approval process:

> No person shall introduce or deliver for introduction into interstate commerce any *new drug,* unless an approval of an application filed pursuant to subsection (b) or (j) of this section is effective with respect to such drug.

§ 355(a) (emphasis added). In other words, if a drug has not already been approved, it is a "new drug" that must first be approved before it can be dispensed. The term "drug" is also given a broad definition, which includes "articles intended for use in the diagnosis, cure, mitigation, treatment, or prevention of disease in man or other animals." § 321(g)(1)(B).

The FDA argues that the language of the FDCA's "new drug" definition is both plain and expansive. A "new drug" is *"any* drug" the "composition of which" has not already been approved for use in accordance with its labeling. Compounded drugs are, after all, drugs. If a compounder changes the composition of an approved drug—by mixing or combining an approved drug with something else to create a different substance or by creating special dosage or delivery forms of an approved drug inconsistent with a drug's labeling—the composition of the individualized concoction created by a compounding pharmacist will not have been previously approved for use. The resulting substance is therefore a "new drug."

Belying the Pharmacies' argument that compounded drugs are not "new drugs" by virtue of their creation by licensed pharmacists, the definition of "new drug" focuses on the drug's composition and use rather than on the process by which it was created. Under the plain language of § 321(p)(1), it does not matter that the substance has been created through compounding rather than manufacturing—whether it be through rigorous research and development by a pharmaceutical company, through individualized compounding by a pharmacist or through cut-rate production by a rogue manufacturer. Regardless of how and by whom it was created, "any" such substance constitutes a "new drug" within the meaning of § 321(p)(1).

Moreover, the FDCA carves out specific exceptions to the sweeping "new drug" definition for some "grandfathered" old drugs, *see* § 321(p)(1), and for drugs intended only for investigational use, *see* § 355(i). Where Congress creates specific exceptions to a broadly applicable provision, the "proper inference ... is that Congress considered the issue of exceptions and, in the end, limited the statute to the ones set forth." *United States v. Johnson,* 529 U.S. 53, 58 (2000). The "new drug" definition contains no general exception for drugs created by compounding.

* * *

B.

Although the plain language of § 321(p) does not seem ambiguous as applied to compounding, the district court and the Pharmacies rely on their view of the FDCA's purpose as a trump against the statute's text. * * *

* * *

The Pharmacies argue, in essence, that * * * including compounded drugs under the FDCA's "new drug" definition would effectively outlaw the common practice of compounding and that the "new drug" definition is too broad and indefinite to indicate congressional intent for such result. * * *

The Pharmacies reason that Congress never intended to regulate traditional pharmacy compounding and that the FDCA's "new drug" provision was intended only to cover drugs produced through large-scale manufacturing. The Pharmacies contend that at the time of the FDCA's enactment, compounding was adequately regulated by the states, and the FDCA was passed in response to a perceived lack of oversight of drug manufacturing, not compounding. To apply the provision to compounded drugs, the Pharmacies argue, would cause an extraordinary expansion of the FDA's regulatory authority.

To support their view of congressional intent, the Pharmacies quote two statements from the FDCA's legislative history. The President of the American Pharmaceutical Association told a subcommittee of the Senate Committee on Commerce the following:

> Regulations governing ... the practice of pharmacy by pharmacists are very strict, but the privileges of unlicensed persons operating outside of pharmacies are so extensive that the public enjoys little protection in the matter of sales of packaged medicines.

In a similar vein, Representative Coffee made remarks to the House, approvingly quoting the Secretary of Agriculture:

> Pharmacists are licensed to compound and dispense drugs. Electricians, plumbers, and steam engineers pursue their respective trades under license. But there is no such control to prevent incompetent drug manufacturers from marketing any kind of lethal poison.

"Floor statements from two Senators cannot amend the clear and unambiguous language of a statute." *Barnhart*, 534 U.S. at 457, 122 S.Ct. 941. * * * The same, or less, might be said for subcommittee testimony by an industry spokesman and a statement by a Representative.

These bits of legislative history, moreover, establish only that their speakers were concerned about regulating drug manufacturing; they do not express any plain intent to refrain from further regulating the drugs created through pharmacy compounding. * * *

Given the apparent ubiquity of pharmacy compounding at the time Congress passed the FDCA, it would have been unprecedented for the FDCA to regulate compounded drugs. But the same can be said for drugs produced through manufacturing, which had also not previously been regulated by the federal government. The mere prevalence of a practice hardly establishes the obvious intent not to regulate it. Nevertheless, it seems unlikely that Congress intended to force compounded drugs to undergo the new drug approval process, a requirement that would have made compounding nearly impossible and thus nonexistent. Construing the "new drug" definition in a way that makes compounding effectively unlawful appears inconsistent with the likely expectation that compounding would and should persist and with other provisions of the FDCA that expressly acknowledge the existence of compounding.

But this does not quite amount to the *reductio ad absurdum* it might at first seem to be. There are two reasons, one small and one large, why the universally-appreciated practice of compounding would not be extinguished by including compounded drugs within the "new drug" definition. First, if one considers "compounding" to include creating specialized dosage forms consistent with the instructions on a drug's label, that would be a kind of compounding that would not result in a "new drug" under the FDCA's definition. That sort of on-label compounding would be perfectly permissible even without exempting compounded drugs from the "new drug" definition.

Second, and more significantly, even if compounded drugs are effectively made unlawful by the "new drug" definition and approval requirements, pharmacists still could continue compounding to the extent allowed by the FDA's enforcement discretion. The FDA did not enforce the "new drug" requirement against traditional compounding for decades, and the agency's Compliance Policy Guide declared only a limited intention to conduct future enforcement in cases in which compounding looks more like disguised manufacturing. The FDCA explicitly permits the FDA to decline enforcement of "minor violations." 21 U.S.C. § 336, and this court has affirmed such discretion in an analogous context * * *.

Indeed, the Supreme Court has suggested that we should not infer an absurd result from a maximalist interpretation of the FDA's authority where such authority is tempered by enforcement discretion. When it comes to the slippery task of distinguishing true compounding from disguised manufacturing, we should question our own capacity, as a court, to make that distinction in future cases. In exercising its discretion, the FDA relies on numerous factors and considerations to determine whether a pharmacist is engaged in compounding as distinguished from manufacturing. With no guidance from the statutory text, we doubt we could do any better, and we are wary of trading the FDA's discretion for our own.

The Pharmacies may quite understandably find cold comfort in the FDA's promised self-restraint. In light, however, of the agency's statutorily-authorized enforcement discretion and demonstrated willingness to accommodate traditional compounding's continued existence, there is reason to think pharmacies would continue to compound even if compounded drugs were deemed "new drugs." Construing the FDCA to give the FDA authority over compounding would thus not necessarily "lead to a result so bizarre that Congress could not have intended it." *Johnson*, 120 F.3d at 1319.

Nonetheless, it remains at least questionable that Congress would have intended such a large expansion of the FDA's regulatory authority. And it remains no small burden for compounding pharmacists, as they put it, to "live in sin"—their livelihood having no greater assurance than the FDA's good graces.

C.

* * *

In 1997, Congress enacted FDAMA as an amendment to the FDCA. That amendment provides considerable evidence that Congress sought to address pharmacy compounding directly and that it did so with the assumption that the "new drug" provision applies to drugs created through pharmacy compounding. Moreover, FDAMA alters the FDCA in such a way that reading an implicit compounding exemption into the "new drug" definition would render other crucial parts of the statute superfluous. If we read the FDCA in light of its amendment in FDAMA, Congress's intent to include compounded drugs within the FDCA's "new drug" definition becomes obvious: That intent becomes a necessary component of the amended statutory scheme; and the feared chilling effect on the common practice of compounding becomes a much diminished concern. Whatever might have been Congress's intent regarding compounding when it drafted the FDCA, FDAMA substantially clarifies it.

There is potential trouble in relying on FDAMA, however, because the validity of that amendment remains uncertain. * * *

* * *

* * * Accordingly, to rely on FDAMA in construing the "new drug" definition, we first must address FDAMA's validity. After doing so, we consider precisely how FDAMA affects interpretation of the "new drug" definition.

1.

In the supplemental briefing, the FDA argues against severability, and the Pharmacies argue in favor of it. The Ninth Circuit held that FDAMA is not severable. Agreeing with the Pharmacies and differing with the FDA and the Ninth Circuit, we conclude that the invalidated portion of FDAMA is severable and that its surviving portions therefore remain in effect.

* * *

One crucial clue to [Congress's intent regarding severability] is Congress's decision to include an express severability provision in the statute. FDAMA amended Section 353 of Title 21 of the United States Code, which codifies the FDCA. Although FDAMA contains no severability clause, Section 391 provides as follows:

> If any provision of this chapter is declared unconstitutional, or the applicability thereof to any person or circumstances is held invalid, the constitutionality of the remainder of the chapter and the applicability thereof to other persons and circumstances shall not be affected thereby.

21 U.S.C. § 391.

* * *

FDAMA carves out an exception to the new drug approval process for compounding pharmacists who comply with a number of specific, mandatory requirements. One of those requirements, which permitted pharmacists to advertise compounding *services* but barred them from advertising specific compounded *drugs,* was the portion of FDAMA the Court invalidated * * *. FDAMA contained numerous other requirements, however, which the Court enumerated and summarized as follows:

> First, [the compounded drugs] must be compounded by a licensed pharmacist or physician in response to a valid prescription for an identified individual patient, or, if prepared before the receipt of such a prescription, they must be made only in "limited quantities" and in response to a history of the licensed pharmacist's or physician's receipt of valid prescription orders for that drug product within an established relationship between the pharmacist, the patient, and the prescriber. 21 U.S.C. § 353a(a).

> Second, the compounded drug must be made from approved ingredients that meet certain manufacturing and safety standards, §§ 353a(b)(1)(A)–(B), and the compounded drug may not appear on an FDA list of drug products that have been withdrawn or removed from the market because they were found to be unsafe or ineffective, § 353a(b)(1)(C).

> Third, the pharmacist or physician compounding the drug may not "compound regularly or in inordinate amounts (as defined by the Secretary) any drug products that are essentially copies of a commercially available drug product." § 353a(b)(1)(D).

> Fourth, the drug product must not be identified by the FDA as a drug product that presents demonstrable difficulties for compounding in terms of safety or effectiveness. § 353a(b)(3)(A).

Fifth, in States that have not entered into a "memorandum of understanding" with the FDA addressing the distribution of "inordinate amounts" of compounded drugs in interstate commerce, the pharmacy, pharmacist, or physician compounding the drug may not distribute compounded drugs out of state in quantities exceeding five percent of that entity's total prescription orders. § 353a(b)(3)(B).

Finally, and most relevant for this litigation, the prescription must be "unsolicited," § 353a(a), and the pharmacy, licensed pharmacist, or licensed physician compounding the drug may "not advertise or promote the compounding of any particular drug, class of drug, or type of drug," § 353a(c). The pharmacy, licensed pharmacist, or licensed physician may, however, "advertise and promote the compounding service." *Ibid.*

[*Western*] *States*, 535 U.S. at 364–65 * * * (paragraph breaks added).

* * * [W]e do not see the advertising provision as so central to the purpose of FDAMA that Congress would not have passed the statute without it. The advertising requirement indeed helped further Congress's intended balance, but so did FDAMA's five other requirements mentioned above. Much like the advertising provision, those other requirements function to create permissible space for compounding pharmacists while limiting pharmacists' ability to engage in large-scale manufacturing.

Severing the advertising requirement would leave those other considerable requirements intact, and they would continue to effect Congress's purpose. Where a statute's invalidated provision is one of a series of conditions, each of which is designed to promote a common goal, courts have deemed such a statute severable. In light of the five other requirements in FDAMA, excising the advertising provision would not render FDAMA "incapable of functioning independently."

* * *

2.

Because FDAMA remains valid, we must construe the FDCA's "new drug" definition in light of it. FDAMA distinguishes between compounding and manufacturing in much the same way as the Pharmacies urge us to narrow the "new drug" definition. It does so, however, not by changing the definition of "new drug" but instead by explicitly "exempt[ing] compounded drugs from the FDCA's 'new drug' requirements and from other requirements provided the drugs satisfy a number of restrictions." *W. States*, 535 U.S. at 364. Accordingly, compounded drugs are not exempt from the FDCA's "new drug" *definition*, § 321(p), nor are they uniformly exempt from the FDCA's "new drug" *requirements*, §§ 351(a)(2)(B), 352(f)(1), 355. Rather, compounded drugs are in fact "new drugs" as defined by § 321(p) but are exempt from the requirements of §§ 351(a)(2)(B), 352(f)(1), and 355 if and only if they comply with the conditions set forth in § 353a.

FDAMA's conditional exemption reads in part as follows:

Sec. 353a. Pharmacy compounding

(a) In general

Sections 351(a)(2)(B) [adulteration provision], 352(f)(1) [misbranding provision], and 355 [new drug approval provision] of this title *shall not apply* to a drug product *if the drug product is compounded* for an identified individual patient based on the unsolicited receipt of a valid prescription order or a notation, approved by the prescribing practitioner, on the prescription order that a compounded product is necessary for the identified patient, *if the drug product meets the requirements of this section,* and if the compounding [is done by a licensed pharmacist or physician].

§ 353a(a) (emphasis added). FDAMA thus creates a safe harbor for compounding but does so in a particularly significant way within the context of the statute. It does not outlaw all compounding or create a general limitation on the FDA's authority over traditional compounding. Instead, it starts from the default premise that the FDCA's adulteration, misbranding, and new drug approval provisions apply to—and thereby restrict—all drugs created by any means.

Against that statutory background, FDAMA instructs that the adulteration, misbranding, and "new drug" approval provisions "shall not apply ... *if* the drug product is compounded" and "*if* the drug product meets the requirements" of FDAMA. The requirements themselves are thus not freestanding but instead serve to trigger an exemption from the adulteration, misbranding, and new drug approval provisions. If the requirements are not met, the exemption does not apply.

* * *

In summary, 321(p)'s definition of "new drug" applies to drugs created by compounding. Because compounded drugs are "new drugs," the restrictions on "new drugs" set forth in §§ 351(a)(2)(B), 352(f)(1), and 355 generally apply to compounded drugs. Against that backdrop, however, § 353a carves out explicit, conditional exceptions for compounded drugs that comply with its enumerated conditions. If and only if the compounded drugs satisfy § 353a's conditions, those drugs are exempt from the requirements of §§ 351(a)(2)(B), 352(f)(1), and 355.

* * *

V.

In summary, compounded drugs are not subject to a general exemption from the definitions of "new drug" and "new animal drug" contained in § 321(p)(1) and (v)(1). But because the severed portions of FDAMA are valid and in force, new human drugs that result from compounding are exempt from the adulteration, misbranding, and new drug approval provisions of §§ 351(a)(2)(B), 352(f)(1), and 355 if they comply with the conditions in § 353a. Likewise, new animal drugs that result from compounding are exempt from the unsafe, adulteration, and misbranding provisions of §§ 360b(a)(1), 351(a)(5), and 352(f) if they comply with the conditions in § 360b(a).

The judgment is VACATED and REMANDED for further proceedings as appropriate in accordance with this opinion.

NOTES AND QUESTIONS

1. The FDCA has been amended repeatedly over the last 70 years. What amendments were at issue in the principal case, and what new issues was Congress trying to address? How did those amendments affect the scope of the FDCA's "new drug" coverage?

2. *The evolution of FDA risk regulation.* The FDCA is, if nothing else, a historical record of Americans' evolving concerns about the substances that they put into and on their bodies. One of the historical circumstances that drove the original enactment of the FDCA, for example, was the increased availability of commercial canned and packaged foods in supermarkets right before and after World War II. Americans were initially highly suspicious of these new foods, and often with reason: basic ingredients could be suspect, and the packaging process itself could be unreliable, leading to spoiled goods or contamination like botulism. For an excellent history of Americans' changing attitudes toward foods, see Ann Vileisis, Kitchen Literacy: How We Lost Knowledge of Where Food Comes from and Why We Need to Get It Back (2008).

3. *The 1962 Kefauver–Harris Amendments.* Although the FDCA has been amended over 100 times since its inception in 1938, only a few times has Congress made fundamental changes. The 1962 amendments were one such change. These amendments were occasioned to a large extent by the Thalidomide crisis. Thalidomide was a sleeping aid that caused devastating limb reduction defects in many fetuses of women who took the drug. The Wm. S. Merrell Company, the firm that later marketed Bendectin, wanted to distribute the product in the United States, and filed an NDA with the FDA to do so. Dr. Frances Kelsey, the examiner reviewing the submission, refused to permit the marketing of the drug because its manufacturer had failed to provide sufficient evidence of the product's safety. Her decision delayed the introduction of the drug into the American market long enough to avoid a disaster similar to what occurred in Europe. This near miss highlighted the limited ability of the FDA to control the introduction of new drugs.

Prior to the 1962 amendments, a manufacturer could sell its drug 180 days after submitting the product's new drug application unless the FDA raised an objection. The 1962 amendments transformed the pre-market notification system into a pre-market approval system. The manufacturer could no longer sell a drug until the FDA affirmed the product's safety.

Senator Kefauver had long sought to require manufacturers to demonstrate a drug's efficacy as well as its safety. Thus the 1962 amendments also required a manufacturer to demonstrate effectiveness before the FDA would approve its sale. The statute also gave the FDA the authority to withdraw the approval of a new drug if new evidence indicated the drug was not safe or effective.

Clinical trials became the centerpiece of this new regime. Clinical trials are designed to ascertain the optimal dosage, to assess efficacy and safety, and to measure the likelihood and severity of risks associated with taking the drug. Only when a drug successfully passes through this process may the manufacturer submit a new drug application. At this point the FDA must determine whether to approve the new drug by balancing its risks and benefits.

4. *Evaluating the risks and benefits of drugs: risk evaluations and mitigation strategies.* Cost-benefit, risk-benefit, and risk-risk analyses are common in the federal statutes regulating hazardous and toxic substances. The 1962 amendments permit the FDA to engage in a risk-benefit analysis when approving new drugs. Under the FDCA, if the FDA

> determines that a risk evaluation and mitigation strategy is necessary to ensure that the benefits of the drug outweigh the risks of the drug, and informs the person who submits such application of such determination, then such person shall submit to the [FDA] as part of such application a proposed risk evaluation and mitigation strategy. In making such a determination, the Secretary shall consider the following factors:
>
> (A) The estimated size of the population likely to use the drug involved.
>
> (B) The seriousness of the disease or condition that is to be treated with the drug.
>
> (C) The expected benefit of the drug with respect to such disease or condition.
>
> (D) The expected or actual duration of treatment with the drug.
>
> (E) The seriousness of any known or potential adverse events that may be related to the drug and the background incidence of such events in the population likely to use the drug.
>
> (F) Whether the drug is a new molecular entity.

21 U.S.C. § 355–1(a)(1). As a result of the risk investigation, the FDA and its associated agencies might require that a medication guide or patient package insert be distributed to patients with the drug and/or that the applicant create a communication plan for health care providers. Id. § 355–1(e). How does this risk investigation differ from the analyses under FIFRA and TSCA? How is it similar? Why might risk investigations for new drugs result in drugs being approved for some uses but not for others?

5. *Fast-track drug approvals.* Largely because of the 1962 amendments, the costs to develop a new drug rose dramatically. In 2007, the Institute of Medicine reported various estimates of the cost of developing one new drug. They ranged from $500 million to $2 billion. Committee on the Assessment of the U.S. Drug Safety System, Institute of Medicine, The Future of Drug Safety 32 (Alina Baciu et al., eds., 2007). Moreover, the requirements substantially increased the time it took for drugs to reach the marketplace. The average time prior to the amendments was two-and-a-half years, but by 1980 the lag between creation and FDA approval had stretched to between seven and thirteen years. In the late 1980s and early 1990s the Congress authorized "fast track" drug approval processes if the drug "is intended for the treatment of a serious or life-threatening condition and it demonstrates the potential to address unmet medical needs for such a condition." 21 U.S.C. § 356(a)(1). Why would Congress include this provision in the Act? How does this provision fit in with the Act's risk-benefit balancing and its goal of ensuring that all drugs are both safe and effective? See Lynne Kessler Lechter, Regulatory Overkill and the AIDS Patient, 1 Alb.L.J.Sci.&Tech. 131, 145–46 (1991).

Pressure also mounted to provide patients with access to drugs that were still in the clinical trial process. If an otherwise terminally-ill patient is informed by a treating physician that a new drug under investigation and in clinical trials might be of benefit, do they have a right to the drug outside existing trials? If individuals did have this right, what affect would it have on the existing drug approval process? On our ability to determine whether a drug is safe and effective? See Abigail Alliance v. von Eschenbach, 495 F.3d 695 (D.C.Cir.2007) (Abigail II); Elizabeth Weeks Leonard, The Public's Right to Health: When Patient Rights Threaten the Commons, 86 Wash.U.L.Rev. 1335 (2009).

6. *The limits of clinical trials and the Food and Drug Administration Amendments Act (FDAAA) of 2007.* It is not surprising that clinical trials became the centerpiece of the 1962 amendments. Double-blind randomized clinical trials (RCT) are sometimes called the "gold standard" of research designs. However, they have serious limitations. First, much of the information gained from clinical trials concerns efficacy, not safety. Studies are rarely designed to test a specific safety hypothesis and in many cases it would be impossible to do so, since a drug may produce many types of adverse events, some of which are unforeseeable. For example, Dexfenfluramine, part of the "fen-phen" combination of drugs used to treat obesity, was eventually withdrawn when heart-valve abnormalities were reported within a year of its approval by the FDA. Premarket trials failed to detect the unanticipated problem, because, reasonably, the trials did not include echocardiography that might have detected heart-valve impacts.

Even when a RCT is designed to detect a safety concern, quite often its ability to detect adverse effects is limited by sample size and by the duration of the study. In Chapter 3 we discussed the "power" of research studies to detect effects. As we noted there, RCTs often do not have a sufficiently large sample size to detect relatively rare events. If one to two thousand subjects participate in a clinical trial and a serious drug-related event occurs in one out of every 10,000 people who use the drug, the clinical trial may not observe any of these adverse events. Even if it does, the study is likely to be too small to observe a statistically significant relationship between the drug and the adverse outcome. It will, in the language of our discussion in Chapter 3, make a Type II error.

Moreover, clinical trials cannot last forever. As we discussed in the previous note, there is often considerable pressure to bring a promising drug to market. However, many drugs, including an increasing percentage of all prescription drugs, are designed to treat chronic conditions such as diabetes, depression, high cholesterol, osteoporosis, and arthritis. Even trials that last three or four years may not detect adverse effects that arise from long-term usage of a decade or more.

The 2000s saw a series of drugs that were revealed to pose serious risks after they had been approved by the FDA. They include Rezulin (a diabetes drug), SSRIs (anti-depressant drugs), Baycol (a drug to control high cholesterol), and, perhaps most well known, Vioxx (an arthritis drug). In response to these failures, Congress passed the FDAAA. PL 110–85,121 Stat 823 (2007) (codified in scattered sections of 21 U.S.C.).

Prior to the passage of this statute, the FDA employed a weak form of post-market observational study. It relied on a largely voluntary mechanism for reporting safety problems. 21 C.F.R. § 314.80–81 (2009). This system did not detect many adverse effects and it usually took a considerable period of time before sufficient adverse information emerged to cause the FDA to react. Vioxx was on the market for five years before its adverse effects were sufficiently clear to cause the drug to be removed from the market. Thus, a primary goal of the act is to create large-scale observational study databases. FDAAA § 905. The databases are to be populated with individual medicare, military, and private insurance claims data as well as health records and pharmaceutical purchase data. The goal is to have 100 million people in the databases by 2012. Barbara Evans, Seven Pillars of a New Evidentiary Paradigm: The Food, Drug, and Cosmetic Act Enters the Genomic Era, 85 Notre Dame L.Rev. 419, 480–81 (2010).

The FDAAA gives the FDA authority to condition the sale of drugs on specific risk management measures. FDAAA § 901(b). These are called Risk Evaluation and Mitigation Strategies (REMS). A REMS may be required either at the time a drug is initially or subsequently approved if new evidence emerges concerning a drug's safety or efficacy. A REMS may include things such as warning letters to healthcare providers, patient package inserts, altered warnings, etc. All REMS must include a program for ongoing evaluation of risk including the possibility of new clinical trials.

In Wyeth v. Levine, ___ U.S. ___, 129 S.Ct. 1187, 173 L.Ed.2d 51 (2009)—one of the main cases in Chapter 10, see p. 594—the Supreme Court concluded that the pre-FDAAA Act did not preempt state suits based on failure to warn claims. The Court viewed the existing FDA approval and labeling decisions as a set of minimal regulations that could coexist with state products liability law. As Evans notes, "These decisions did not amount to optimal regulation in which a regulator makes delicate risk-benefit tradeoffs that might be disrupted if states established higher de facto requirements through their tort damage awards." Evans, supra, 85 Notre Dame L.Rev. 419, 516.

7. *Drugs and genetics.* Historically, a drug would be approved if *on average* its benefits outweighed its risk. With the rise of genomic medicine, however, we will have better and better indicators of exactly who a drug may help and who it may harm. Under the REMS procedure, the FDA can condition the sale of a drug on specific restrictions, known as "elements to ensure safe use." Among these elements, the statute includes a requirement that patients have complied with safe-use conditions, including testing prior to administration of the drug. Such tests might include biomarker screening and pharmacogenetic tests. The results of such tests might prohibit prescribing drugs to some set of individuals but might also permit the administration of an otherwise banned drug to individuals not susceptible to its adverse effects. How does this new source of information alter the risk-benefit equation in approving new drugs? How does it support or undermine the traditional RCT process for new drug approval?

4. MEDICAL DEVICES

The FDCA regulates medical devices differently from drugs. According to the Act, a "device" is

> an instrument, apparatus, implement, machine, contrivance, implant, in vitro reagent, or other similar or related article, including any component, part, or accessory, which is—
>
> (1) recognized in the official National Formulary, or the United States Pharmacopeia, or any supplement to them,
>
> (2) intended for use in the diagnosis of disease or other conditions, or in the cure, mitigation, treatment, or prevention of disease, in man or other animals, or
>
> (3) intended to affect the structure or any function of the body of man or other animals, and
>
> which does not achieve its primary intended purposes through chemical action within or on the body of man or other animals and which is not dependent upon being metabolized for the achievement of its primary intended purposes.

21 U.S.C. § 321(h).

The FDCA classifies medical devices as either Class I, Class II, or Class III devices. Id. § 360c(a)(1). Class I devices are safe and effective with only general controls. Id. These general controls are found in Sections 350, 351, and 360k. Class II devices require special controls to ensure their safety and effectiveness. Id. These special controls come in the form of performance standards. Id. § 360d(a). Performance standards include:

> (i) provisions respecting the construction, components, ingredients, and properties of the device and its compatibility with power systems and connections to such systems,
>
> (ii) provisions for the testing (on a sample basis or, if necessary, on an individual basis) of the device or, if it is determined that no other more practicable means are available to the Secretary to assure the conformity of the device to the standard, provisions for the testing (on a sample basis or, if necessary, on an individual basis) by the Secretary or by another person at the direction of the Secretary,
>
> (iii) provisions for the measurement of the performance characteristics of the device,

(iv) provisions requiring that the results of each or of certain of the tests of the device required to be made under clause (ii) show that the device is in conformity with the portions of the standard for which the test or tests were required, and

(v) a provision requiring that the sale and distribution of the device be restricted but only to the extent that the sale and distribution of a device may be restricted under a regulation.

Id. § 360d(a)(2)(B).

Class III devices require premarket approval from the FDA. For a device to be categorized as Class III, there must be insufficient information available to ensure the safety and effectiveness of the device with the application of either general or specific controls, *and* the device must either be "for a use in supporting or sustaining human life or for a use which is of substantial importance in preventing impairment of human health" or must "present[] a potential unreasonable risk of illness or injury." Id. § 360c(a)(1).

For all three classes,

the safety and effectiveness of a device are to be determined—

(A) with respect to the persons for whose use the device is represented or intended,

(B) with respect to the conditions of use prescribed, recommended, or suggested in the labeling of the device, and

(C) weighing any probable benefit to health from the use of the device against any probable risk of injury or illness from such use.

Id. § 360c(a)(2)(B). The FDA can also ban any device if that evidence shows that:

(1) a device intended for human use presents substantial deception or an unreasonable and substantial risk of illness or injury; and

(2) in the case of substantial deception or an unreasonable and substantial risk of illness or injury which the Secretary determined could be corrected or eliminated by labeling or change in labeling and with respect to which the Secretary provided written notice to the manufacturer specifying the deception or risk of illness or injury, the labeling or change in labeling to correct the deception or eliminate or reduce such risk, and the period within which such labeling or change in labeling was to be done, such labeling or change in labeling was not done within such period * * *.

Id. § 360f(a).

The FDCA also requires that manufacturers and distributors of medical devices keep records and file reports. Id. § 360j. The import of these requirements is discussed in the following case.

TMJ IMPLANTS, INC. v. UNITED STATES DEPARTMENT OF HEALTH AND HUMAN SERVICES

United States Court of Appeals for the Tenth Circuit, 2009.
584 F.3d 1290.

TACHA, CIRCUIT JUDGE.

TMJ Implants, Inc. ("TMJI") manufactures and distributes temporo-mandibular joint ("TMJ") implants. Dr. Robert W. Christensen is TMJI's founder and president. In July 2005, the Food and Drug Administration ("FDA") filed a complaint for money penalties ("CMP") against TMJI and Dr. Christensen (collectively, "petitioners") after concluding that they had knowingly failed to submit seventeen medical device reports ("MDRs") relating to TMJI's implants. That action culminated administratively in a Final Decision by the Departmental Appeals Board ("DAB") within FDA's parent agency, the Department of Health and Human Services. The Final Decision affirmed determinations by an administrative law judge ("ALJ") that petitioners had knowingly failed to submit each of the seventeen MDRs and that petitioners were each liable for penalties of $170,000 ($10,000 per violation).

TMJI and Dr. Christensen now petition this court for judicial review of the DAB's Final Decision. *See* 21 U.S.C. § 333(f)(6) (allowing appeals of the assessment of civil penalties directly to circuit courts). They contend that: (1) the CMP was premature; (2) they were not required to submit MDRs because Dr. Christensen reasonably concluded that the devices did not cause or contribute to a serious injury; (3) if petitioners were required to submit any MDRs, their failure to do so was not knowing; (4) monetary penalties cannot be assessed against Dr. Christensen because he is an individual, not the manufacturer of the implants; and (5) the amount of the monetary penalties is unwarranted. We AFFIRM.

I. BACKGROUND

The TMJs are located slightly in front of the ears and form the interface between the lower jaw and the bottom of the skull. They are critical to several functions of daily life, such as speaking, eating, swallowing, and breathing. When the TMJs do not function properly, a variety of conditions or symptoms may develop. Common symptoms of TMJ disfunction include reduced ability or inability to open or close the jaw, pain, swelling, ankylosis (fusion of the joint bones), infections, chronic sinus pain, hearing loss, and chronic ear pain. When necessary, a medical provider may surgically remove one or both of the TMJs and replace them with prosthetic joint implants such as those manufactured and marketed by TMJI.

A. *The Statutory and Regulatory System for Medical Device Reporting*

TMJ implants are medical devices within the meaning of 21 U.S.C. § 321(h). Through the Federal Food, Drug and Cosmetic Act, Congress empowered FDA to require every manufacturer of a medical device to "establish and maintain such records, make such reports, and provide such information as the Secretary may by regulation reasonably require to assure that such device is not adulterated or misbranded and to otherwise assure its safety and effectiveness." 21 U.S.C. § 360i(a). Pursuant to this broad delegation of authority, Congress created an expansive reporting system under which FDA must require that every "device manufacturer ... [file an MDR] whenever the manufacturer ... receives or otherwise becomes aware of information that reasonably suggests that one of its marketed devices may have caused or contributed to a death or serious injury." *Id.* § 360i(a)(1)(A). Congress clarified what types of events must be reported to FDA by defining a "serious injury" as one that "is life threatening, results in permanent impairment of a body function or permanent damage to a body structure, or necessitates medical or surgical intervention to preclude permanent impairment of a body function or permanent damage to a body structure." *Id.* § 360i(a)(2)(A)–(C).

FDA has explained the purpose of the reporting requirement and its broad scope:

> To carry out its responsibilities, the agency needs to be informed whenever a manufacturer or importer receives or otherwise becomes aware of information about device problems. Only if FDA is provided with such information will it be able to evaluate the risk, if any, associated with a device and take whatever action is necessary to reduce or eliminate the public's exposure to this risk.

49 Fed. Reg. 36,326, 36,326 (Aug. 27, 1984). In response to public comments expressing concern that broad reporting requirements may impose unduly onerous burdens on medical device manufacturers, FDA reiterated the need for an expansive reporting system and adopted regulations that require manufacturers to file an MDR if they become aware of information suggesting that a device *may have* caused or contributed to a death or serious injury rather than the more limited language proposed that would have required manufacturers to file an MDR only in cases where they receive information suggesting that a device *has* caused or contributed to a death or serious injury. *Id.* at 36,331. FDA explained that the broader language was necessary "because the agency needs to learn of instances in which there may be an association, as well as a causal connection, between the use of a device and a death or serious injury." *Id.*

The implementing regulations to § 360i adopt the statutory definition of "serious injury" and define its crucial term "permanent" as "irreversible impairment or damage to a body structure or function, excluding trivial impairment or damage." 21 C.F.R. § 803.3. The implementing regulations also define the phrase "caused or contributed":

> Caused or contributed means that a ... serious injury was or may have been attributed to a medical device, or that a medical device was or may have been a factor in a ... serious injury, including events occurring as a result of:

(1) Failure;

(2) Malfunction;

(3) Improper or inadequate design;

(4) Manufacture;

(5) Labeling; or

(6) User error.

[User] means a hospital, ambulatory surgical facility, nursing home, outpatient diagnostic facility, or outpatient treatment facility....

Id.

Thus, focusing on the terms most relevant to this case, FDA mandates the filing of an MDR whenever the manufacturer of a medical device is aware of information that reasonably suggests its device (or an error on the part of the practitioner who or facility that implants or services the device) may have been a factor in the need to medically or surgically intervene in a particular individual's case, so long as the intervention is necessary to prevent irreversible, nontrivial impairment of a body function or irreversible, nontrivial damage to a body structure.

The implementing regulations also describe when a manufacturer is *not* obligated to submit an MDR: when the manufacturer "ha[s] information that would lead a person who is qualified to make a medical judgment reasonably to conclude that a device did not cause or contribute to a ... serious injury." 21 C.F.R. § 803.20(c)(2). Put another way, if a qualified person rules out the device (or an error on the part of the practitioner who implants the device) as a factor in the need for medical or surgical intervention to prevent permanent harm to the body, and this conclusion is reasonable, then the manufacturer need not file an MDR. Particularly relevant to this case, however, is FDA's explanation that "[n]owhere in ... the act or its legislative history is FDA's authority limited to requiring only information about reportable events that have been confirmed by the manufacturer or importer of the device." 49 Fed. Reg. at 36,338.

The submission of an MDR is not an admission that the device caused or contributed to the serious injury and a manufacturer may deny that its device caused the injury in their MDR. 21 C.F.R. § 803.16. Indeed, the standard form for the submission of an MDR includes a disclaimer to that effect.

As part of this expansive reporting system, device manufacturers commonly receive information about their devices through FDA's Med-Watch program. Under that program, any person may voluntarily report to FDA an adverse event or problem with a medical device. The voluntary MedWatch report form asks for the patient's name, a description of the event or problem, the name and manufacturer of the suspect device, and the name of the reporter. After FDA receives the report, the agency forwards it to the manufacturer identified on the report. If the reporter requests anonymity, however, regulations require FDA to redact any identifying information of the reporter before forwarding the report to the manufacturer.

A manufacturer is responsible for investigating events described in MedWatch forms to evaluate the cause of the event and whether to submit an MDR for it. A manufacturer is not absolved of this duty when a MedWatch report contains incomplete or redacted information; in those circumstances, the manufacturer is required to file an incomplete report explaining why the report is incomplete and what steps the manufacturer has taken to obtain the relevant information. Ultimately, the manufacturer is responsible for obtaining the relevant information to aid in its investigation and is required to supplement its report once it obtains such information. Manufacturers must also maintain MDR event files that contain information regarding adverse events purportedly associated with their devices, including all documentation of the manufacturer's decision-making process used to determine whether the particular event is reportable. Finally, manufacturers must permit FDA to access, copy, and verify its MDR files.

Under 21 U.S.C. § 333(f)(1)(A), "any person who violates [the MDR reporting requirements] shall be liable to the United States for a civil penalty." The penalty may not exceed $16,500 for each violation. 21 C.F.R. § 17.2. Liability for civil penalties requires proof that the violation was either a significant or knowing departure from the law, or that the violation posed a risk to public health. 21 U.S.C. § 333(f)(1)(B)(i).

B. *The Events Giving Rise to the Imposition of Money Penalties Against Petitioners*

FDA employees conducted an inspection of TMJI's facility and MDR files from July 29, 2003 to August 11, 2003. As a result of that inspection, FDA determined that TMJI should have submitted MDRs for twenty-two events, each of which involved either a device explant (the device was surgically removed) or antibiotic treatment. According to information received by petitioners, these surgical and medical interventions were performed due to, among other things, apparent infections, loose screws, swelling, pain, bone growth, decreased mobility of the jaw, headaches, seizures, inflamed tissue, vertigo, and foreign body reaction occurring after a TMJ had been implanted in the patient. FDA informed petitioners in a February 24, 2004 Warning Letter to Dr. Christensen that written MDRs must be submitted for the twenty-two events within fifteen days. The Warning Letter further notified petitioners that "[y]ou should take prompt action to correct these deviations. Failure to promptly correct these deviations may result in regulatory action without further notice. These actions include, but are not limited to seizure, injunction, and/or civil penalties."

Petitioners did not submit MDRs for these events. Instead, on March 4, Dr. Christensen wrote to FDA to express petitioners' "substantial disagreement with the FDA's position." Christensen requested a meeting with FDA personnel "to arrive at a proper decision with respect to what, if any, actions are required of the company in this matter." Dr. Christensen further expressed his view that FDA may be using Warning Letters to retaliate against TMJI.

Dr. Christensen and three colleagues met with FDA representatives at FDA's District Office in Lakewood, Colorado on March 10, 2004. The meeting can be summarized as follows: Dr. Christensen contended that in each of the disputed events TMJI's devices were not explanted because of any inherent problem with the device itself; rather, natural progression of the TMJ disease necessitated removal of the device. * * *

FDA personnel disagreed with petitioners' position. The agency explained that the definition of serious injury is one that requires medical intervention to prevent a permanent impairment. Thus, while pain and loose screws may not be serious injuries in and of themselves, the failure to medically intervene to treat those conditions could lead to permanent impairment of the TMJ or jaw function. According to FDA, the relevant regulations require TMJI to report all explants and medical interventions when TMJI's devices *may have* been a contributing factor in the need for such interventions, and that if TMJI did not have sufficient information to rule out its device as a potential cause of the interventions then it must report them. FDA made clear that submitting an MDR did not constitute an admission from TMJI that its devices contributed to any injury, and the agency suggested that TMJI articulate a response to the warning letter that addressed each one of the events and why petitioners did not consider them to be reportable.

* * *

Petitioners did not submit the twenty-two MDRs. Instead, they continued to send letters to FDA, pressing for a more comprehensive definition of "serious injury" and noting that petitioners were undertaking another review of the twenty-two events identified in the Warning Letter. Petitioners also continued to request another meeting with FDA to further discuss their concerns. On August 12, petitioners determined that user error was involved in five of the twenty-two events and filed MDRs for those five events.

* * *

On November 16, petitioners refused FDA's offer to consider their explanations as MDRs and requested internal agency review under 21 C.F.R. § 10.75. On July 14, 2005, CDRH filed a CMP against petitioners based on their failure to submit MDRs for the remaining seventeen events identified in the February 2004 Warning Letter. One week later, FDA denied petitioners' request for agency review under 21 C.F.R. § 10.75. The agency reasoned that because the issues were now the subject of a CMP and would be fully developed and determined by a neutral ALJ, it would be inefficient and duplicative for FDA simultaneously to review the matter at that point.

Petitioners and FDA conducted extensive discovery and submitted comprehensive briefs in the CMP action. The ALJ held an evidentiary hearing and ultimately issued an Initial Decision against petitioners on July 6, 2007. In its Final Order of September 25, 2007, the ALJ imposed sanctions in the amount of $170,000 on both TMJI and Dr. Christensen individually. Petitioners appealed to the DAB, *see* 21 C.F.R. § 17.47, which affirmed the ALJ's decision and order against them. Petitioners now petition for judicial review in this court.

II. ANALYSIS

* * *

C. *The DAB Did Not Err in Determining that TMJI Must Submit MDRs for the Seventeen Events Identified in the CMP.*

Petitioners contend that the events at issue do not represent serious injuries under 21 U.S.C. § 360i(a)(1)(A). They argue that the physical conditions preceding the device explant or medical treatment–such as pain, swelling, bone growth, and infection–are relatively trivial and are to be expected following the surgical implant of any medical device.

Again, the DAB's contrary interpretation of the applicable law was reasonable. Indeed, petitioners misread the applicable regulation, which does not define "serious injury" in terms of physical significance. Instead, a "serious injury" is a condition that "necessitates medical or surgical intervention to preclude permanent impairment of a body function or permanent damage to a body structure." 21 C.F.R. § 803.3. In each of the seventeen events at issue, a physician surgically explanted the device or otherwise medically treated the patient as a result of the aforementioned physical conditions–conditions which, if left untreated, could permanently impair the TMJ function. Accordingly, the DAB's decision in accordance with FDA's position that "[a]lthough some of these consequences may be deemed clinically insignificant, they are considered to be serious injuries when coupled with the interventions, e.g., administration of antibiotics or other medications, explant, reconstruction, debridement, or revision surgery" was reasonable.

The DAB's expansive construction of the causation element is also reasonable. 21 C.F.R. § 803.3 states: "Caused or contributed means that a death or serious injury was or may have been attributed to a medical device, or that a medical device was or may have been a factor in a death or serious injury." As the DAB explained: "FDA set out a reasonable explanation ... for reading the statute as justifying broad collection of information about adverse events associated with medical devices in order to discern patterns and surface possible concerns not only with design and manufacture of devices but also with their use and performance in practice and under various circumstances."

Moreover, the DAB's determination that MDRs were required for the seventeen events at issue is supported by the evidence in the record. This evidence includes: (1) MedWatch reports describing the device and the patients' symptoms following the implantation of the device; (2) information received from petitioners' investigations; and (3) testimony from two FDA expert witnesses stating that the physical conditions constitute serious injuries to which TMJI devices may have caused or contributed. The same evidence amply supports the DAB's rejection of petitioners' claim that Dr. Christensen reasonably concluded that TMJI's devices did not cause or contribute to serious injuries.

Finally, the DAB properly rejected petitioners' claim that they should not be required to submit MDRs for events reported on voluntary MedWatch forms because they could not conclusively determine whether their devices were involved in those events. Petitioners contend that redacting the name of the patient, the name of the reporter, the date of the implant, and the date of the event makes it impossible to conduct an investigation about the event. As noted, neither the statute nor its implementing regulations limit FDA's authority to require MDRs to events that are confirmed by the manufacturer. To the contrary, FDA regulations require a manufacturer to file an MDR when it has information "from any source[ ] that reasonably suggests" its device caused or contributed to a serious injury. 21 C.F.R. § 803.50(a)(1). The voluntary MedWatch reports at issue identify TMJI as the device manufacturer. Thus, TMJI had information reasonably suggesting its devices caused or contributed to a serious injury and should have filed MDRs for those events. To the extent petitioners did not subjectively believe that their devices were actually involved and sought to insulate themselves from civil liability based in part on the MDRs, they are permitted to "deny that the report or information submitted under this part constitutes an admission that the device [or petitioners] caused or contributed to a reportable event." 21 C.F.R. § 803.16. They are not permitted, however, to ignore the broad reporting requirements of the statute and its implementing regulations simply because they do not feel that they have all of the information they need to confirm that their device caused a serious injury.

D.   *The DAB Did Not Err in Concluding that Petitioners' Violations Were Knowing*

Liability for a money penalty lies only when the violation constitutes a knowing or significant departure from the § 360i requirements or when the violation poses a risk to public health. 21 U.S.C. § 333(f)(1)(B)(i). The regulations define a "knowing departure" as "a departure from a requirement taken: (a) With actual knowledge that the action is such a departure, or (b) in deliberate ignorance of a requirement, or (c) in reckless disregard of a requirement." 21 C.F.R. § 17.3(a)(2).

The DAB properly determined that petitioners' violations were knowing. From February to November 2004, FDA repeatedly and consistently informed petitioners of FDA's position that they needed to submit MDRs for the events at issue. This position, as explained above, is entirely reasonable given the clear and broad language of § 360i. Petitioners' failure to file those MDRs was thus done either in deliberate ignorance of the § 360i requirements or in reckless disregard of them.

Petitioners contend that they could not have knowingly violated § 360i at the time the CMP was served because the Commissioner had not yet responded to their appeal request. In their view, a knowing violation could have occurred in this case only if petitioners had refused to comply with the Commissioner's ultimate determination that MDRs were required. This argument is belied by the applicable regulation, which requires only deliberate indifference to or reckless disregard of the reporting requirements. Those requirements are clearly and broadly articulated in the statute and its implementing regulations, and petitioners did not require the FDA Commissioner's final decision regarding their review request to be fairly apprised of them. Therefore, the DAB did not err in concluding that petitioners' violations were knowing.

E. *The DAB Reasonably Affirmed the Money Penalties Assessed Against Dr. Christensen*

Dr. Christensen argues that only the manufacturer of the devices, not an individual, may be subject to money penalties under 21 U.S.C. § 333(f). This contention is not supported by the clear language of the governing statutes. Section 333(f) states that "any person who violates a requirement of this chapter which relates to devices shall be liable to the United States for a civil penalty." Section 321(e) defines "person" to include an "individual, partnership, corporation, and association." Moreover, in analogous circumstances, the Supreme Court has explicitly held that corporate officers may be liable for violations of the Food, Drug, and Cosmetic Act. * * *

We also reject Dr. Christensen's argument that § 333(f) should be interpreted to exclude individuals with extensive medical backgrounds who act as a manufacturer's expert under 21 C.F.R. § 803.20(c)(2). Such an interpretation is not founded in the letter or purpose of § 333(f). Therefore, the DAB reasonably affirmed the assessment of monetary penalties against Dr. Christensen.

F. *The DAB Reasonably Affirmed the Amount of the Money Penalties*

Under § 333(f)(1)(A) and the implementing regulations, a civil penalty may not exceed $16,500 for each violation. 21 U.S.C. § 333(f)(1)(A); 21 C.F.R. § 17.2. The appropriate amount of a money penalty is determined by considering mitigating and aggravating factors. 21 C.F.R. § 17.45(b)(3).

FDA sought penalties of $10,000 for each violation from each petitioner, which the ALJ imposed and which the DAB ultimately affirmed. In their petition before this Court, petitioners contend their financial condition was "ignored" in assessing the penalty amount and that several mitigating factors justify a lower penalty. Petitioners' first argument is unfounded. The DAB meticulously explained why petitioners' financial disclosures were inadequate to give a reliable picture of petitioners' ability to pay a $170,000 penalty. TMJI, for example, refused to submit complete tax returns. Dr. Christensen refused to disclose money or property transfers. Neither petitioner explained a significant drop in profitability from 2004 to 2005 ($624,690 in ordinary business income on approximately $2.7 million in net sales in 2004 versus $203,108 in ordinary business income on the same amount of net sales in 2005) combined with a 52% increase in salaries during the same time period. Far from "ignoring" petitioners' financial condition, the DAB justifiably concluded that "the ALJ's findings that TMJI and Dr. Christensen failed to make full financial disclosures are supported by substantial evidence in the record [as] a whole. His inference that a full disclosure would not have supported their assertions of an inability to pay is reasonable."

The DAB also properly evaluated all factors petitioners characterize as mitigating. First, petitioners contend that they never refused to file the seventeen MDRs but only sought a dialogue with FDA to discuss their disagreement regarding whether MDRs were required before they filed them. As the DAB explained, however, the law does not require an explicit "refusal" to file; rather, the failure to file an MDR when the statute and regulations require it constitutes a violation of § 360i. Furthermore, petitioners do not have the authority to make the ultimate determinations of whether and when an MDR must be filed. That authority lies with Congress and FDA, which have clearly articulated their determinations in the statutes and implementing regulations. Accordingly, petitioners' failure to file MDRs and their recalcitrant responses to the repeated FDA warnings can reasonably be interpreted as explicit refusals to file.

Second, the DAB reasonably rejected petitioners' contention that their failure to file MDRs after being informed that they were required to do so was in good faith. This finding is supported by substantial evidence in the administrative record, and petitioners' statement that TMJI's devices are not a threat to the public health is simply petitioners' own opinion. The DAB did not err in failing to accord significant weight to this self-serving assertion.

Third, petitioners' offer to file the required MDRs if FDA promised to drop the CMP is also not a mitigating factor, and FDA's rejection of that offer does not violate the Small Business and Regulatory Enforcement Fairness Act. Indeed, petitioners only made the offer to file MDRs after the ALJ had held them liable and after the DAB had affirmed that decision. Offering to abide by the law only after being punished for not doing so does not mitigate the culpability of the initial unlawful conduct and the DAB's similar conclusion was not error.

Finally, to the extent petitioners contend that other mitigating factors exist, we have carefully reviewed the extensive record in this case and conclude that the DAB's decision is legally tenable and supported by substantial evidence.

III. CONCLUSION

The DAB's Final Decision is AFFIRMED.

NOTES AND QUESTIONS

1. *MDR basics.* What is medical device reporting (MDR)? When is it required, according to the FDA? How does MDR further the purposes and goals of the FDCA?

2. *Interpreting the MDR requirement.* What was the issue regarding the MDR requirements in this case? How did TMJI interpret those requirements? How did the FDA interpret those requirements? What did the Departmental Appeals Board (DAB) determine during the administrative appeal? What did the U.S. Court of Appeals for the Tenth Circuit decide about the MDR requirements, and why?

3. *Information (and litigation?) as a regulatory tool.* Both the drug and medical device provisions of the FDCA incorporate reporting and information-gathering as tools for continuing regulatory oversight. Why and how are consumer complaints important components of drug and medical device regulation? Could toxic tort litigation feed into this information process?

Consider the case of Vioxx. Vioxx is a drug to alleviate arthritis and pain that came out in 1999, but it became associated with a higher rate of heart attacks and strokes than other painkillers. In April 2000, the FDA required the manufacturer, Merck, to add information on the drug's label warning of this risk. Even so, Vioxx has been connected to 27,000 instances of heart attacks and sudden cardiac deaths between 1999 and 2003, and Merck voluntarily pulled it from the market in September 2004. At that time, about two million people still had a Vioxx prescription. Most of the litigation arose *after* Merck pulled Vioxx off the market. Was this litigation serving an informational function at that point? Would you expect this to be a common pattern with prescription drugs? Why or why not? Does this *have* to be the pattern? Why or why not?

5. COSMETICS

After food, cosmetics receive the least regulatory scrutiny under the FDCA. The Act defines "cosmetics" to be: "(1) articles intended to be rubbed, poured, sprinkled, or sprayed on, introduced into, or otherwise applied to the human body or any part thereof for cleansing, beautifying, promoting attractiveness, or altering the appearance, and (2) articles intended for use as a component of any such articles; except that such term shall not include soap." 21 U.S.C. § 321(i). Cosmetics generally include products such as skin moisturizers, hair dyes, fingernail polish, toothpastes, and shampoos. The Act is explicit that the requirements for drugs and devices do not apply to cosmetics, "unless such cosmetic is also a drug or device or component thereof." Id. § 359.

Cosmetics are regulated almost entirely through the FDCA's prohibitions on misbranding and adulteration. Thus, the bulk of cosmetics regulation focuses on keeping harmful ingredients out of cosmetics; there is no general premarket approval process for cosmetics.

An important exception, however, is for color additives. Under the FDCA, color additives, except for coal tar hair dyes, are subject to FDA approval before they may be used in food, drugs, cosmetics, or in medical devices. Id. § 721. The FDA maintains a web site detailing the color additives allowed in cosmetics. FDA, Color Additives in Cosmetics, available at http://www.fda.gov/ForIndustry/ColorAdditives/ColorAdditivesin SpecificProducts/InCosmetics/default.htm.

Otherwise, one of the most important issues in the regulation of cosmetics is whether the product really is a cosmetic. For example, as quoted above, soap is not a cosmetic. More important for many products, however, is the distinction between "cosmetics" and "drugs." Consider a few examples.

- Is sunscreen a cosmetic or a drug? Are you sure?

- How about anti-aging creams?

- How about anti-dandruff shampoos?

- What about fluoridated toothpastes?

Perhaps counterintuitively, the FDA considers all of these products to be drugs or dual-use products subject to the FDCA's new drug provisions. The FDA uses an *"intended use" test* to distinguish cosmetics from drugs: If the product is intended to be used to cleanse or beautify, it is a cosmetic, but if it is intended to diagnose, cure, treat, mitigate, or prevent a disease, or to alter the structure or function of the body, the product is a drug.

There have been suggestions that the FDCA may need a new category—"cosmeceuticals"—to address the special issues that arise in connection with products like anti-aging creams that raise some of the same concerns as drugs, but not to the same degree as prescription drugs. Thus, these "cosmeceuticals," like food supplements, suggest that new categories of risk regulation may be appropriate.

CHAPTER X

DEFENSES

■ ■ ■

A. FEDERAL PREEMPTION

1. INTRODUCTION: THE SUPREMACY CLAUSE AND FEDERAL PREEMPTION

As you have probably already studied in Constitutional Law, the Supremacy Clause of the U.S. Constitution allows federal law to supersede, or preempt, state law. That Clause states that "[the] Constitution and the Laws of the United State which shall be made in Pursuance thereof * * * shall be the supreme Law of the Land; * * * any Thing in the Constitution or Laws of any State to the Contrary notwithstanding." U.S. Const. art. VI, cl. 2.

Obviously, federal preemption of state law can have broad application. In the field of toxic torts, however, most federal preemption issues raise the question of whether a specific federal statute that in some way regulates harmful materials or products preempts state common law tort claims. As you have already seen, a number of federal statutes regulate the handling, marketing, use and disposal of toxic substances and harmful products, including the Resource Conservation and Recovery Act (RCRA), the Comprehensive Environmental Response, Compensation, and Liability Act (CERCLA), the Food, Drug, and Cosmetic Act (FDCA), the Federal Insecticide, Fungicide, and Rodenticide Act (FIFRA), and the Toxic Substances Control Act (TSCA). What is the effect of these statutes on state tort claims for harms from toxic exposures to regulated hazardous wastes, hazardous substances, drugs and medical devices, pesticides, or other regulated toxic substances?

Federal law can preempt state law in a number of ways. Most classically, federal law will preempt state law when state law actually conflicts with federal law. Conflict preemption is the irreducible minimum of the Supremacy Clause: states cannot impose requirements or allow claims that contradict what federal law requires or allows. One way (but not the only way) of assessing whether a conflict exists is to ask whether it is possible to comply with both the federal and state laws. If not, a conflict exists.

Even without a conflict, Congress can *expressly preempt* state law by including a statutory provision that prohibits states from regulating in a certain area. For example, under FIFRA, "A State may regulate the sale or use of any federally registered pesticide or device in the State, but only if and to the extent the regulation does not permit any sale or use prohibited by this subchapter." 7 U.S.C. § 136v(a). Thus, state regulation of pesticide sales and use is preempted to the extent that a state would permit what the EPA prohibits. More clearly, Congress also stated that a "State shall not impose or continue in effect any requirements for labeling or packaging in addition to or different from those required under" FIFRA. 7 U.S.C. § 136v(b). Additional labeling requirements don't necessarily conflict with federal law, but Congress preempted the states' abilities to add new labeling requirements anyway.

Congress explicitly provided for "one-way preemption" in RCRA. Under that statute, "no State or political subdivision may impose any requirements less stringent than those authorized under" RCRA. 42 U.S.C. § 6929. Thus, RCRA explicitly preempts state requirements that are *less* protective than RCRA requires. However, "[n]othing in [RCRA] shall be construed to prohibit any State or political subdivision thereof from imposing any requirements, including those for site selection, which are more stringent than those imposed by" RCRA. Id. Thus, states are free to be *more* protective of human health and the environment than RCRA requires.

The most difficult area of federal preemption law is *implied preemption*. In implied preemption, courts look at the relevant statutory scheme to decide whether Congress intended to preempt certain kinds of state law, even though Congress did not explicitly so state and even though the state law does not absolutely conflict with federal requirements. For example, courts can conclude that Congress intended to "occupy the field" in a particular area of law—that is, that "[t]he scheme of federal regulation [is] so pervasive as to make reasonable the inference that Congress left no room for the states to supplement it." Rice v. Santa Fe Elevator Corp., 331 U.S. 218, 230 (1947) (citations omitted). Thus, for example, because the Natural Gas Act of 1938, 15 U.S.C. §§ 717–717w, gives the Federal Energy Regulatory Commission "exclusive" jurisdiction over the transportation and sale of natural gas in interstate commerce, the Supreme Court concluded that Congress intended to "occupy the field" of natural gas regulation. Schneidewind v. ANR Pipeline Co., 485 U.S. 293, 300–04 (1988).

In addition, the courts will also imply preemption of state law if "the Act of Congress * * * touch[es] a field in which the federal interest is so dominant that the federal system will be assumed to preclude enforcement of state laws on the same subject." *Rice*, 331 U.S. at 230. For example, the Medical Device Amendments to the FDCA prohibit medical device manufacturers from perpetrating fraud on the Food and Drug Administration. The Supreme Court held that the federal interest in fraud on a federal agency was so strong that these provisions of the FDCA preempted state-law fraud-on-the-FDA claims. Buckman Co. v. Plaintiffs' Legal Committee, 531 U.S. 341, 347–48 (2001).

Keep in mind, however, that the Supreme Court has also stated that there is a presumption *against* finding that federal law preempts state law. According to the Court, constitutional principles of federalism dictate "that when a State's exercise of its police power is challenged under the Supremacy Clause, 'we start with the assumption that the historic police powers of the States were not to be superseded by the Federal Act unless that was the clear and manifest purpose of Congress.' " Ray v. Atlantic Richfield Co., 435 U.S. 151, 157 (1978) (quoting Rice v. Santa Fe Elevator Corp., 331 U.S. 218, 230 (1947)). As we shall see in the next section, Congress itself has often explicitly stated that federal statutes governing toxic substances and products do *not* preempt state tort law.

Moreover, even where Congress's intent to preempt is clear, there can still be difficult questions regarding the *scope* of the federal preemption. Given the presumption against federal preemption, courts will often construe preemption provisions narrowly, giving state law as much room as possible in which to operate.

2.   EXPLICIT NON–PREEMPTION: SAVINGS CLAUSES IN FEDERAL STATUTES

Statutory *savings clauses* are the exact opposite of explicit preemption. In a savings clause, Congress specifically *preserves* state law causes of action, disclaiming all intent to preempt state law. For example, in RCRA's citizen-suit provision, Congress stated that "[n]othing in this section shall restrict any right which any person (or class of persons) may have under any statute or common law to seek enforcement of any standard or requirement relating to the management of solid waste or hazardous waste, or to seek any other relief * * *." 42 U.S.C. § 6972(f). CERCLA contains a similar provision. 42 U.S.C. § 9652(d).

Why would Congress include savings provisions in federal statutes? How can the preservation of state law—including state toxic tort law— promote the purposes and goals of these statutes? What remedies might tort law provide that federal statutes do not? Consider the following case as you ponder these questions.

MSOF CORP. v. EXXON CORP.

United States Court of Appeals for the Fifth Circuit, 2002.
295 F.3d 485.

GARWOOD, CIRCUIT JUDGE:

* * *

The plaintiffs own land in the Devil's Swamp area in the Parish of East Baton Rouge, Louisiana. On July 5, 1994, the plaintiffs filed suit against the defendants in Louisiana state court on behalf of themselves and all other similarly situated landowners, alleging that the defendants were responsible for contaminating their land with toxic chemicals. The defendants removed the case to the United States District Court for the Middle District of Louisiana. The plaintiffs filed a motion to remand, asserting that the district court did not have subject matter jurisdiction. [The trial court denied the motion to remand, finding, inter alia, that jurisdiction existed because plaintiffs asserted a claim under CERCLA and therefore federal jurisdiction existed under 28 U.S.C. § 1331.]

PPI, a Louisiana corporation, was the owner and operator of two hazardous waste disposal facilities in the Devil's Swamp region, the Brooklawn Site and the Scenic Highway site. With the exception of NPC, the other corporate defendants were industrial generators of hazardous waste that made use of the PPI disposal facilities. NPC, a Louisiana corporation, was formed by the industrial generator defendants in 1984 to clean up or remediate the PPI sites in accordance with a federal consent decree. * * *

PPI operated its waste disposal facility, just north of Devil's Swamp, during the 1960's and 1970's. Plaintiffs' property is located approximately three miles south of the PPI facility. In 1980, the United States Department of Justice, on behalf of the Environmental Protection Agency, sued PPI and several of the industrial generators in the United States District Court for the Middle District of Louisiana under the Comprehensive Environmental Response, Compensation, and Liability Act (CERCLA), 42 U.S.C. § 9601 *et seq.* The State of Louisiana, the City of Baton Rouge, and the Parish of East Baton Rouge intervened in that suit. On February 16, 1984, a consent decree was entered in that case by the United States District Court for the Middle District of Louisiana under which certain companies, including the industrial generator defendants in the present action, agreed to investigate and clean up contamination from the former PPI facility. The consent decree ordered, *inter alia*, that these sites be monitored for thirty years after the completion of remediation under the continuing supervision and jurisdiction of the district court. On August 28, 1989, the district court ordered that the consent decree be supplemented with a Supplemental Remedial Action Plan prepared by the defendants. In 1984, the industrial generator defendants contracted with NPC to perform the remediation work, which has been underway since 1984 under the supervision of Judge Polozola. None of the plaintiffs in this case was ever a party to the consent decree or the case in which it was entered.

The plaintiffs' state court complaint alleged that toxic chemicals emanating from the PPI facility had contaminated their land in the southern half of Devil's Swamp. * * *

* * * The plaintiffs' complaint alleges negligent and strict liability torts under Louisiana law. Its only reference to federal law is an allegation that the PPI facility was maintained in violation of federal regulations *as well* as in violation of state and local regulations. That, however, does not suffice to render the action one arising under federal law. The defendants

argue that the plaintiffs' complaint, though purporting to seek relief under Louisiana law, actually seeks relief under CERCLA. The defendants note that the plaintiffs' petition demanded compensatory damages in an amount commensurate with the cost of restoring and remediating the plaintiffs' property and that CERCLA creates a cause of action for such costs. *See* 42 U.S.C. § 9607(a). However, Louisiana law also provides a cause of action under which these plaintiffs can attempt to prove that these defendants tortiously caused damage to the plaintiffs' land and can demand the very relief they seek. In enacting CERCLA, Congress expressly disclaimed an intent to preempt state tort liability for the release of hazardous substances. CERCLA contains a general saving clause and several section-specific saving clauses. The general saving clause, 42 U.S.C. § 9652(d), provides:

> "Nothing in this chapter shall affect or modify in any way the obligations or liabilities of any person under other Federal or State law, including common law, with respect to releases of hazardous substances or other pollutants or contaminants. The provisions of this chapter shall not be considered, interpreted, or construed in any way as reflecting a determination, in part or whole, of policy regarding the inapplicability of strict liability, or strict liability doctrines, to activities relating to hazardous substances, pollutants, or contaminants or other such activities."

42 U.S.C. § 9607(j), in the section of the Act that creates liability for response costs, provides, in pertinent part:

> "Recovery by any person ... or response costs or damages resulting from a federally permitted release shall be pursuant to existing law in lieu of this section. Nothing in this paragraph shall affect or modify in any way the obligations or liability of any person under any other provision of State or Federal law, including common law, for damages, injury, or loss resulting from a release of any hazardous substance or for removal or remedial action or the costs of removal or remedial action of such hazardous substance."

This court and other courts have construed the CERCLA saving clauses in accordance with their plain meanings and have held that they preserve parties' rights arising under state law. CERCLA does not completely preempt the plaintiffs' claims under Louisiana state law[, and, as a result, the plaintiffs' complaint did not state a federal cause of action, requiring the court to remand to state court].

NOTES AND QUESTIONS

1. *Federal environmental statutes and tort claims.* As you may remember from Chapters 8 and 9, very few of the federal environmental statutes include standard tort damages—compensatory damages for injury to persons or property—as remedies. Instead, violations of the statute are punished through administrative penalties, civil penalties, criminal penalties, or jail sentences, depending on the severity of the violation. These penalties are all paid to the federal government—even if the court assesses civil penalties in a citizen suit.

Does the lack of private remedies for injuries arising from violations of these statutes help to explain why Congress included savings clauses that preserve state tort remedies? How could toxic tort litigation further the policies and goals of these federal statutes? Professor Robin Craig argues, for example, that federal statutes like RCRA seek to prevent harms at the population level, protecting the general public interest, while tort law seeks to redress actual private injuries. Robin Kundis Craig, Removing "The Cloak of a Standing Inquiry": Pollution Regulation, Public Health, and Private Risk in the Injury-in-Fact Analysis, 29 Cardozo L.Rev. 149, 183–87 (2007).

2. *Use of federal statutes in state-law toxic tort litigation.* As you may also recall from Chapters 8 and 9, the existence of federal statutes also raises the issue of how those statutes should interact with toxic tort claims. For example, if an activity both violates federal law and causes harm that results in state toxic tort litigation, how should courts treat the violation of federal law? Should it be treated as negligence per se? As evidence of negligence? Or should federal regulatory requirements be considered completely irrelevant to state-law toxic tort claims? Compare King v. Danek Med., Inc., 37 S.W.3d 429, 454–57 (Tenn.App.2000) (denying a negligence per se claim based on violations of the FDCA's administrative requirements because those requirements did not establish a standard of care); Osburn v. Danek Med., Inc., 520 S.E.2d 88, 94 (N.C.App.1999) (denying a negligence per se claim based on violations of the FDCA when the plaintiff failed to show a causal connection between the statutory violation and the plaintiff's injury); and Ward v. Ne. Texas Farmers Co-op. Elevator, 909 S.W.2d 143, 149 (Tex.App.1995) (concluding that there could be no negligence per se claim based on a violation of FIFRA sales requirements when there was no allegation that the violating pesticide had actually been used), with McClanahan v. California Spray–Chem. Corp., 75 S.E.2d 712, 723–25 (Va.1953) (upholding a negligence per se claim based on violation of a duty to warn created by FIFRA).

3. EXPRESS PREEMPTION OF STATE TORTS AND THE LIMITS OF EXPRESS PREEMPTION PROVISIONS

As noted, the federal statutes you have studied do contain some express preemption provisions. In light of the presumption against preemption of state law, however, the federal courts tend to construe express preemption provisions narrowly to limit the scope of federal preemption. Consider the Supreme Court's treatment of FIFRA in the following case.

BATES v. DOW AGROSCIENCES LLC

United States Supreme Court, 2005.
544 U.S. 431, 125 S.Ct. 1788, 161 L.Ed.2d 687.

JUSTICE STEVENS delivered the opinion of the Court.

Petitioners are 29 Texas peanut farmers who allege that in the 2000 growing season their crops were severely damaged by the application of respondent's newly marketed pesticide named "Strongarm." The question presented is whether the Federal Insecticide, Fungicide, and Rodenticide Act (FIFRA), 7 U.S.C. § 136 *et seq.* (2000 ed. and Supp. II), pre-empts their state-law claims for damages.

I

Pursuant to its authority under FIFRA, the Environmental Protection Agency (EPA) conditionally registered Strongarm on March 8, 2000, thereby granting respondent (Dow) permission to sell this pesticide—a weed killer—in the United States. Dow obtained this registration in time to market Strongarm to Texas farmers, who normally plant their peanut crops around May 1. According to petitioners—whose version of the facts we assume to be true at this stage—Dow knew, or should have known, that Strongarm would stunt the growth of peanuts in soils with pH levels of 7.0 or greater. Nevertheless, Strongarm's label stated, "Use of Strongarm is recommended in all areas where peanuts are grown," and Dow's agents made equivalent representations in their sales pitches to petitioners. When petitioners applied Strongarm on their farms—whose soils have pH levels of 7.2 or higher, as is typical in western Texas—the pesticide severely damaged their peanut crops while failing to control the growth of weeds. The farmers reported these problems to Dow, which sent its experts to inspect the crops.

* * *

After unsuccessful negotiations with Dow, petitioners gave Dow notice of their intent to bring suit as required by the Texas Deceptive Trade Practices–Consumer Protection Act (hereinafter Texas DTPA). In response, Dow filed a declaratory judgment action in Federal District Court, asserting that petitioners' claims were expressly or impliedly pre-empted by FIFRA. * * * The District Court granted Dow's motion for summary judgment, rejecting one claim on state-law grounds and dismissing the remainder as expressly pre-empted by 7 U.S.C. § 136v(b), which provides that States "shall not impose or continue in effect any requirements for labeling or packaging in addition to or different from those required under this subchapter."

The Court of Appeals affirmed. It read § 136v(b) to pre-empt any state-law claim in which "a judgment against Dow would induce it to alter its product label." The court held that because petitioners' fraud, warranty, and deceptive trade practices claims focused on oral statements by

Dow's agents that did not differ from statements made on the product's label, success on those claims would give Dow a "strong incentive" to change its label. Those claims were thus pre-empted. The court also found that petitioners' strict liability claim alleging defective design was essentially a "disguised" failure-to-warn claim and therefore pre-empted. It reasoned: "One cannot escape the heart of the farmers' grievance: Strongarm is dangerous to peanut crops in soil with a pH level over 7.0, and that was not disclosed to them.... It is inescapable that success on this claim would again necessarily induce Dow to alter the Strongarm label." The court employed similar reasoning to find the negligent testing and negligent manufacture claims pre-empted as well.

This decision was consistent with those of a majority of the Courts of Appeals, as well of several state high courts, but conflicted with the decisions of other courts and with the views of EPA set forth in an *amicus curiae* brief filed with the California Supreme Court in 2000. We granted certiorari to resolve this conflict.

II

Prior to 1910 the States provided the primary and possibly the exclusive source of regulatory control over the distribution of poisonous substances. Both the Federal Government's first effort at regulation in this area, the Insecticide Act of 1910, and FIFRA as originally enacted in 1947 primarily dealt with licensing and labeling. Under the original version of FIFRA, all pesticides sold in interstate commerce had to be registered with the Secretary of Agriculture. The Secretary would register a pesticide if it complied with the statute's labeling standards and was determined to be efficacious and safe. In 1970, EPA assumed responsibility for this registration process.

In 1972, spurred by growing environmental and safety concerns, Congress adopted the extensive amendments that "transformed FIFRA from a labeling law into a comprehensive regulatory statute." *Ruckelshaus v. Monsanto Co.*, 467 U.S. 986, 991 (1984). "As amended, FIFRA regulated the use, as well as the sale and labeling, of pesticides; regulated pesticides produced and sold in both intrastate and interstate commerce; provided for review, cancellation, and suspension of registration; and gave EPA greater enforcement authority." *Id.*, at 991–992. The 1972 amendments also imposed a new criterion for registration–environmental safety. *Id.*, at 992.

Under FIFRA as it currently stands, a manufacturer seeking to register a pesticide must submit a proposed label to EPA as well as certain supporting data. 7 U.S.C. §§ 136a(c)(1)(C), (F). The agency will register the pesticide if it determines that the pesticide is efficacious (with the caveat discussed below), § 136a(c)(5)(A); that it will not cause unreasonable adverse effects on humans and the environment, §§ 136a(c)(5)(C), (D); § 136(bb); and that its label complies with the statute's prohibition on misbranding, § 136a(c)(5)(B); 40 CFR § 152.112(f) (2004). A pesticide is "misbranded" if its label contains a statement that is "false or misleading in any particular," including a false or misleading statement concerning the efficacy of the pesticide. 7 U.S.C. § 136(q)(1)(A); 40 CFR § 156.10(a)(5)(ii). A pesticide is also misbranded if its label does not contain adequate instructions for use, or if its label omits necessary warnings or cautionary statements. 7 U.S.C. §§ 136(q)(1)(F), (G).

Because it is unlawful under the statute to sell a pesticide that is registered but nevertheless misbranded, manufacturers have a continuing obligation to adhere to FIFRA's labeling requirements. Additionally, manufacturers have a duty to report incidents involving a pesticide's toxic effects that may not be adequately reflected in its label's warnings, 40 CFR §§ 159.184(a), (b) (2004), and EPA may institute cancellation proceedings, 7 U.S.C. § 136d(b), and take other enforcement action if it determines that a registered pesticide is misbranded.

Section 136v, which was added in the 1972 amendments, addresses the States' continuing role in pesticide regulation. As currently codified, § 136v provides:

"(a) In general

"A State may regulate the sale or use of any federally registered pesticide or device in the State, but only if and to the extent the regulation does not permit any sale or use prohibited by this subchapter.

"(b) Uniformity

"Such State shall not impose or continue in effect any requirements for labeling or packaging in addition to or different from those required under this subchapter.

"(c) Additional uses

"(1) A State may provide registration for additional uses of federally registered pesticides formulated for distribution and use within that State to meet special local needs in accord with the purposes of this subchapter and if registration for such use has not previously been denied, disapproved, or canceled by the Administrator. Such registration shall be deemed registration under section 136a of this title for all purposes of this subchapter, but shall authorize distribution and use only within such State...."

In 1978, Congress once again amended FIFRA, this time in response to EPA's concern that its evaluation of pesticide efficacy during the registration process diverted too many resources from its task of assessing the environmental and health dangers posed by pesticides. Congress addressed this problem by authorizing EPA to waive data requirements pertaining to efficacy, thus permitting the agency to register a pesticide without confirming the efficacy claims made on its label. § 136a(c)(5). In 1979, EPA invoked this grant of permission and issued a general waiver of efficacy review, with only limited qualifications not applicable here. In a notice published years later in 1996, EPA confirmed that it had "stopped evaluating pesticide efficacy for routine label approvals almost two decades ago," and clarified that "EPA's approval of a pesticide label does not reflect any determination on the part of EPA that the pesticide will be efficacious or will not damage crops or cause other property damage." The notice also referred to an earlier statement in which EPA observed that " 'pesticide producers are aware that they are potentially subject to damage suits by the user community if their products prove ineffective in actual use.' " This general waiver was in place at the time of Strongarm's registration; thus, EPA never passed on the accuracy of the statement in Strongarm's original label recommending the product's use "in all areas where peanuts are grown."

Although the modern version of FIFRA was enacted over three decades ago, this Court has never addressed whether that statute pre-empts tort and other common-law claims arising under state law. Courts entertained tort litigation against pesticide manufacturers since well before the passage of FIFRA in 1947, and such litigation was a common feature of the legal landscape at the time of the 1972 amendments. Indeed, for at least a decade after those amendments, arguments that such tort suits were pre-empted by § 136v(b) either were not advanced or were unsuccessful. It was only after 1992 when we held in *Cipollone v. Liggett Group, Inc.,* 505 U.S. 504, that the term "requirement or prohibition" in the Public Health Cigarette Smoking Act of 1969 included common-law duties, and therefore pre-empted certain tort claims against cigarette companies, that a groundswell of federal and state decisions emerged holding that § 136v(b) pre-empted claims like those advanced in this litigation.

This Court has addressed FIFRA pre-emption in a different context. In *Wisconsin Public Intervenor v. Mortier,* 501 U.S. 597 (1991), we considered a claim that § 136v(b) pre-empted a small town's ordinance requiring a special permit for the aerial application of pesticides. Although the ordinance imposed restrictions not required by FIFRA or any EPA regulation, we unanimously rejected the pre-emption claim. In our opinion we noted that FIFRA was not "a sufficiently comprehensive statute to justify an inference that Congress had occupied the field to the exclusion of the States." *Id.,* at 607. "To the contrary, the statute leaves ample room for States and localities to supplement federal efforts even absent the express regulatory authorization of § 136v(a)." *Id.,* at 613.

As a part of their supplementary role, States have ample authority to review pesticide labels to ensure that they comply with both federal and state labeling requirements. Nothing in the text of FIFRA would prevent a State from making the violation of a federal labeling or packaging require-ment a state offense, thereby imposing its own sanctions on pesticide manufacturers who violate federal law. The imposition of state sanctions for violating state rules that merely duplicate federal requirements is equally consistent with the text of § 136v.

III

Against this background, we consider whether petitioners' claims are pre-empted by § 136v(b), which, again, reads as follows: "Such State shall not impose or continue in effect any requirements for labeling or packaging in addition to or different from those required under this subchapter."

    * * *

The prohibitions in § 136v(b) apply only to "requirements." An occurrence that merely motivates an optional decision does not qualify as a requirement. The Court of Appeals was therefore quite wrong when it assumed that any event, such as a jury verdict, that might "induce" a pesticide manufacturer to change its label should be viewed as a requirement. The Court of Appeals did, however, correctly hold that the term "requirements" in § 136v(b) reaches beyond positive enactments, such as statutes and regulations, to embrace common-law duties. Our decision in *Cipollone* supports this conclusion. While the use of "requirements" in a pre-emption clause may not invariably carry this meaning, we think this is the best reading of § 136v(b).

That § 136v(b) may pre-empt judge-made rules, as well as statutes and regulations, says nothing about the *scope* of that pre-emption. For a particular state rule to be pre-empted, it must satisfy two conditions. First, it must be a requirement *"for labeling or packaging"*; rules governing the design of a product, for example, are not pre-empted. Second, it must impose a labeling or packaging requirement that is *"in addition to or different from* those required under this subchapter." A state regulation requiring the word "poison" to appear in red letters, for instance, would not be pre-empted if an EPA regulation imposed the same requirement.

It is perfectly clear that many of the common-law rules upon which petitioners rely do not satisfy the first condition. Rules that require manufacturers to design reasonably safe products, to use due care in conducting appropriate testing of their products, to market products free of manufacturing defects, and to honor their express warranties or other contractual commitments plainly do not qualify as requirements for "labeling or packaging." None of these common-law rules requires that manufacturers label or package their products in any particular way. Thus, petitioners' claims for defective design, defective manufacture, negligent testing, and breach of express warranty are not pre-empted.

    * * *

Unlike their other claims, petitioners' fraud and negligent-failure-to-warn claims are premised on common-law rules that qualify as "requirements for labeling or packaging." These rules set a standard for a product's labeling that the Strongarm label is alleged to have violated by containing false statements and inadequate warnings. * * *

[Nevertheless,] [u]nlike the pre-emption clause at issue in *Cipollone*, § 136v(b) prohibits only state-law labeling and packaging requirements that are *"in addition to or different from"* the labeling and packaging requirements under FIFRA. Thus, a state-law labeling requirement is not pre-empted by § 136v(b) if it is equivalent to, and fully consistent with, FIFRA's misbranding provisions. * * *

The "parallel requirements" reading of § 136v(b) that we adopt today finds strong support in *Medtronic, Inc. v. Lohr*, 518 U.S. 470 (1996). In addressing a similarly worded pre-emption provision in a statute regulating medical devices, we found that "[n]othing in [21 U.S.C.] § 360k denies Florida the right to provide a traditional damages remedy for violations of common-law duties when those duties parallel federal requirements." *Id.*, at 495. As Justice O'CONNOR explained in her separate opinion, a state cause of action that seeks to enforce a federal requirement "does not impose a requirement that is 'different from, or in addition to,' requirements under federal law. To be sure, the threat of a damages remedy will give manufacturers an additional cause to comply, but the requirements imposed on them under state and federal law do not differ. Section 360k does not preclude States from imposing different or additional *remedies*, but only different or additional *requirements*." *Id.*, at 513 (opinion concurring in part and dissenting in part). Accordingly, although FIFRA does not provide a federal remedy to farmers and others who are injured as a result of a manufacturer's violation of FIFRA's labeling requirements, nothing in § 136v(b) precludes States from providing such a remedy.

* * *

The long history of tort litigation against manufacturers of poisonous substances adds force to the basic presumption against pre-emption. If Congress had intended to deprive injured parties of a long available form of compensation, it surely would have expressed that intent more clearly. Moreover, this history emphasizes the importance of providing an incentive to manufacturers to use the utmost care in the business of distributing inherently dangerous items. Particularly given that Congress amended FIFRA to allow EPA to waive efficacy review of newly registered pesticides (and in the course of those amendments made technical changes to § 136v(b)), it seems unlikely that Congress considered a relatively obscure provision like § 136v(b) to give pesticide manufacturers virtual immunity from certain forms of tort liability. Overenforcement of FIFRA's misbranding prohibition creates a risk of imposing unnecessary financial burdens on manufacturers; under-enforcement creates not only financial risks for consumers, but risks that affect their safety and the environment as well.

* * *

Private remedies that enforce federal misbranding requirements would seem to aid, rather than hinder, the functioning of FIFRA. Unlike the cigarette labeling law at issue in *Cipollone,* which prescribed certain immutable warning statements, FIFRA contemplates that pesticide labels will evolve over time, as manufacturers gain more information about their products' performance in diverse settings. As one court explained, tort suits can serve as a catalyst in this process:

"By encouraging plaintiffs to bring suit for injuries not previously recognized as traceable to pesticides such as [the pesticide there at issue], a state tort action of the kind under review may aid in the exposure of new dangers associated with pesticides. Successful actions of this sort may lead manufacturers to petition EPA to allow more detailed labelling of their products; alternatively, EPA itself may decide that revised labels are required in light of the new information that has been brought to its attention through common law suits. In addition, the specter of damage actions may provide manufacturers with added dynamic incentives to continue to keep abreast of all possible injuries stemming from use of their product so as to forestall such actions through product improvement." *Ferebee,* 736 F.2d, at 1541–1542.

Dow and the United States exaggerate the disruptive effects of using common-law suits to enforce the prohibition on misbranding. FIFRA has prohibited inaccurate representations and inadequate warnings since its enactment in 1947, while tort suits alleging failure-to-warn claims were common well before that date and continued beyond the 1972 amendments. We have been pointed to no evidence that such tort suits led to a "crazy-quilt" of FIFRA standards or otherwise created any real hardship for manufacturers or for EPA. Indeed, for much of this period EPA appears to have welcomed these tort suits. * * *

In sum, under our interpretation, § 136v(b) retains a narrow, but still important, role. In the main, it pre-empts competing state labeling standards—imagine 50 different labeling regimes prescribing the color, font size, and wording of warnings—that would create significant inefficiencies for manufacturers. The provision also pre-empts any statutory or common-law rule that would impose a labeling requirement that diverges from those set out in FIFRA and its implementing regulations. It does not, however, pre-empt any state rules that are fully consistent with federal requirements.

Having settled on our interpretation of § 136v(b), it still remains to be decided whether that provision pre-empts petitioners' fraud and failure-to-warn claims. Because we have not received sufficient briefing on this issue, which involves questions of Texas law, we remand it to the Court of Appeals. We emphasize that a state-law labeling requirement must in fact be equivalent to a requirement under FIFRA in order to survive pre-emption. For example, were the Court of Appeals to determine that the element of falsity in Texas' common-law definition of fraud imposed a broader obligation than FIFRA's requirement that labels not contain "false or misleading statements," that state-law cause of action would be pre-empted by § 136v(b) to the extent of that difference. State-law requirements must also be measured against any relevant EPA regulations that give content to FIFRA's misbranding standards. For example, a failure-to-warn claim alleging that a given pesticide's label should have stated "DANGER" instead of the more subdued "CAUTION" would be pre-empted because it is inconsistent with 40 CFR § 156.64 (2004), which specifically assigns these warnings to particular classes of pesticides based on their toxicity.

  * * *

The judgment of the Court of Appeals is vacated, and the case is remanded for further proceedings consistent with this opinion.

It is so ordered.

JUSTICE THOMAS, with whom JUSTICE SCALIA joins, concurring in the judgment in part and dissenting in part.

I agree with the Court that the term "requirements" in § 24(b) of the Federal Insecticide, Fungicide, and Rodenticide Act (FIFRA), 7 U.S.C. § 136v(b), includes common-law duties for labeling or packaging. I also agree that state-law damages claims may not impose requirements "in addition to or different from" FIFRA's. While States are free to impose liability predicated on a violation of the federal standards set forth in FIFRA and in any accompanying regulations promulgated by the Environmental Protection Agency, they may not impose liability for labeling requirements predicated on distinct state standards of care. Section 136v(b) permits States to add remedies—not to alter or augment the substantive rules governing liability for labeling. Because the parties have not argued that Dow violated FIFRA's labeling standards, the majority properly remands for the District Court to consider whether Texas law mirrors the federal standards.

However, the majority omits a step in its reasoning that should be made explicit: A state-law cause of action, even if not specific to labeling, nevertheless imposes a labeling requirement "in addition to or different from" FIFRA's when it attaches liability to statements on the label that do not produce liability under FIFRA. The state-law cause of action then adds some supplemental requirement of truthfulness to FIFRA's requirement that labeling statements not be "false or misleading." 7 U.S.C. § 136(q)(1)(A). That is why the fraud claims here are properly remanded to determine whether the state and federal standards for liability-incurring statements are, in their application to this case, the same.

Under that reasoning, the majority mistreats two sets of petitioners' claims. First, petitioners' breach-of-warranty claims should be remanded for pre-emption analysis, contrary to the majority's disposition. To the extent that Texas' law of warranty imposes liability for statements on the label where FIFRA would not, Texas' law is pre-empted. Second, the majority holds that petitioners' claim under the Texas Deceptive Trade Practices–Consumer Protection Act (DTPA) is not pre-empted to the extent it is a breach-of-warranty claim. However, the DTPA claim is also (and, in fact, perhaps exclusively) a claim for false or misleading representations on the label. Therefore, all aspects of the DTPA claim should be remanded. The DTPA claim, like petitioners' fraud claims, should be pre-empted insofar as it imposes liability for label content where FIFRA would not. * * *

NOTES AND QUESTIONS

1. *Triggering express preemption provisions.* How can state tort law potentially trigger the express preemption provisions of federal regulatory regimes, according to the Supreme Court? State toxic tort law, after all, rarely addresses labeling and packaging requirements directly. How can toxic tort liability nevertheless create "requirements" that federal law might preempt?

2. *FIFRA's preemption of state tort law.* When will FIFRA actually preempt state tort law? From where did the Supreme Court derive this test? Why did the Court rather quickly conclude that FIFRA did *not* preempt the plaintiffs' claims for defective design, defective manufacture, negligent testing, and breach of express warranty? Why did the Court remand the fraud and failure to warn claims? Why is it more likely that FIFRA preempts those two state-law claims?

3. *The* Bates *dissent.* Why did Justices Thomas and Scalia dissent in part from the majority's opinion? Under their view, is FIFRA's preemptive scope broader or narrower than the majority allowed? Why?

4. *Does FIFRA "occupy the field"?* Review the preemption provisions in FIFRA that were at issue in this case. Could the defendant have argued that Congress intended to "occupy the field" of pesticide regulation through FIFRA? Why or why not?

5. *The role of state tort law in pesticide regulation.* What did the Court say about the role and value of state tort liability in the regulation of pesticides? Does that view accord with Congress's use of savings clauses in RCRA and CERCLA? Why or why not?

6. Suppose that Dow changed the warning on Strongarm to reflect the fact that it should not be used in high PH soils. The EPA subsequently approved the new label. A farmer sues in state court on a products liability failure to warn claim, arguing that the new warning was not sufficiently precise to inform him of the risks of using the product. Dow raises a preemption defense. What result? Why?

7. *The* Cipollone *decision.* In *Bates*, the Supreme Court relies heavily on its prior decision in Cipollone v. Liggett Group, Inc., 505 U.S. 504 (1992). As the case was originally filed, Rose Cipollone brought various tort claims against cigarette manufacturers, claiming that cigarettes had caused her lung cancer. After her death, first her husband and then her son continued the litigation through the Supreme Court. The issue before the Supreme Court was whether the federal statutes governing the warning labels on cigarettes— the Federal Cigarette Labeling and Advertising Act (1965) and its successor, the Public Health Cigarette Smoking Act of 1969—preempted the Cipollones' toxic tort claims.

Section 5 of the 1965 Act stated that:

(a) No statement relating to smoking and health, other than the statement required by section 4 of this Act, shall be required on any cigarette package.

(b) No statement relating to smoking and health shall be required in the advertising of any cigarettes the packages of which are labeled in conformity with the provisions of this Act.

In the 1969 Act, Congress amended Section 5(b) to read: "No requirement or prohibition based on smoking and health shall be imposed under State law with respect to the advertising or promotion of any cigarettes the packages of which are labeled in conformity with the provisions of this Act." 15 U.S.C. § 1334(b). Section 5(a) was unchanged.

The Supreme Court first decided that these provisions governed the scope of the Acts' preemptive force. *Cipollone*, 505 U.S. at 517. With regard to the 1965 Act, it noted that, "on their face, these provisions merely prohibited state and federal rulemaking bodies from mandating particular cautionary statements on cigarette labels (§ 5(a)) or in cigarette advertisements (§ 5(b))." Id. at 518. However, the 1969 Act's preemption scope was much broader:

> Compared to its predecessor in the 1965 Act, the plain language of the pre-emption provision in the 1969 Act is much broader. First, the later Act bars not simply "statement[s]" but rather "requirement[s] or prohibition[s] * * * imposed under State law." Second, the later Act reaches beyond statements "in the advertising" to obligations "with respect to the advertising or promotion" of cigarettes.

Id. at 520.

For toxic torts purposes, the most important part of the decision was the Supreme Court's discussion of the relationship between common law torts and federal preemption, particularly in terms of "requirements." The plaintiffs argued that the two federal statutes could not preempt state common law tort claims because tort liability does not create "requirements." The Supreme Court disagreed:

> The phrase "[n]o requirement or prohibition" sweeps broadly and suggests no distinction between positive enactments and common law; to the contrary, those words easily encompass obligations that take the form of common-law rules. As we noted in another context, "[state] regulation can be as effectively exerted through an award of damages as through some form of preventive relief. The obligation to pay compensation can be, indeed is designed to be, a potent method of governing conduct and controlling policy." *San Diego Building Trades Council v. Garmon*, 359 U.S. 236, 247 (1959).

> Although portions of the legislative history of the 1969 Act suggest that Congress was primarily concerned with positive enactments by States and localities, see S.Rep. No. 91–566, p. 12, the language of the Act plainly reaches beyond such enactments. "We must give effect to this plain language unless there is good reason to believe Congress intended the language to have some more restrictive meaning." *Shaw v. Delta Air Lines, Inc.*, 463 U.S. 85, 97 (1983). In this case there is no "good reason to believe" that Congress meant less than what it said; indeed, in light of the narrowness of the 1965 Act, there is "good reason to believe" that Congress meant precisely what it said in amending that Act.

Moreover, common-law damages actions of the sort raised by petitioner are premised on the existence of a legal duty, and it is difficult to say that such actions do not impose "requirements or prohibitions." See W. Prosser, Law of Torts 4 (4th ed. 1971); Black's Law Dictionary 1489 (6th ed. 1990) (defining "tort" as "always [involving] a violation of some duty owing to plaintiff"). It is in this way that the 1969 version of § 5(b) differs from its predecessor: Whereas the common law would not normally require a vendor to use any specific *statement* on its packages or in its advertisements, it is the essence of the common law to enforce duties that are either affirmative *requirements* or negative *prohibitions*. We therefore reject petitioner's argument that the phrase "requirement or prohibition" limits the 1969 Act's pre-emptive scope to positive enactments by legislatures and agencies.

Id. at 521–22.

Nevertheless, the Court still allowed many state-law claims. Specifically, it concluded that:

[t]he 1965 Act did not pre-empt state law damages actions; the 1969 Act pre-empts petitioner's claims based on a failure to warn and the neutralization of federally mandated warnings to the extent that those claims rely on omissions or inclusions in respondents' advertising or promotions; the 1969 Act does not pre-empt petitioner's claims based on express warranty, intentional fraud and misrepresentation, or conspiracy.

Id. at 530–31. The Court did not address whether the 1969 Act preempted a claim that the warnings (mandated by Congress) on cigarette *packages* were inadequate. Does it? See Michael D. Green, *Cipollone* Revisited: A Not So Little Secret About the Scope of Cigarette Preemption, 82 Iowa L.Rev. 1257 (1998), which argues that such claims are not preempted.

How did the *Cipollone* decision inform the Supreme Court's analysis in *Bates*? In particular, what is the role of state common law tort "requirements" in the context of FIFRA?

4. IMPLIED AND CONFLICT PREEMPTION OF STATE TORTS

Finally, implied and conflict preemption principles remain important in toxic tort litigation, as the following recent case from the Supreme Court makes clear.

WYETH v. LEVINE

United States Supreme Court, 2009.
—— U.S. ——, 129 S.Ct. 1187, 173 L.Ed.2d 51.

JUSTICE STEVENS delivered the opinion of the Court.

Directly injecting the drug Phenergan into a patient's vein creates a significant risk of catastrophic consequences. A Vermont jury found that petitioner Wyeth, the manufacturer of the drug, had failed to provide an adequate warning of that risk and awarded damages to respondent Diana

Levine to compensate her for the amputation of her arm. The warnings on Phenergan's label had been deemed sufficient by the federal Food and Drug Administration (FDA) when it approved Wyeth's new drug application in 1955 and when it later approved changes in the drug's labeling. The question we must decide is whether the FDA's approvals provide Wyeth with a complete defense to Levine's tort claims. We conclude that they do not.

I

Phenergan is Wyeth's brand name for promethazine hydrochloride, an antihistamine used to treat nausea. The injectable form of Phenergan can be administered intramuscularly or intravenously, and it can be administered intravenously through either the "IV-push" method, whereby the drug is injected directly into a patient's vein, or the "IV-drip" method, whereby the drug is introduced into a saline solution in a hanging intravenous bag and slowly descends through a catheter inserted in a patient's vein. The drug is corrosive and causes irreversible gangrene if it enters a patient's artery.

Levine's injury resulted from an IV-push injection of Phenergan. On April 7, 2000, as on previous visits to her local clinic for treatment of a migraine headache, she received an intramuscular injection of Demerol for her headache and Phenergan for her nausea. Because the combination did not provide relief, she returned later that day and received a second injection of both drugs. This time, the physician assistant administered the drugs by the IV-push method, and Phenergan entered Levine's artery, either because the needle penetrated an artery directly or because the drug escaped from the vein into surrounding tissue (a phenomenon called "perivascular extravasation") where it came in contact with arterial blood. As a result, Levine developed gangrene, and doctors amputated first her right hand and then her entire forearm. In addition to her pain and suffering, Levine incurred substantial medical expenses and the loss of her livelihood as a professional musician.

After settling claims against the health center and clinician, Levine brought an action for damages against Wyeth, relying on common-law negligence and strict-liability theories. Although Phenergan's labeling warned of the danger of gangrene and amputation following inadvertent intra-arterial injection, Levine alleged that the labeling was defective because it failed to instruct clinicians to use the IV-drip method of intravenous administration instead of the higher risk IV-push method. More broadly, she alleged that Phenergan is not reasonably safe for intravenous administration because the foreseeable risks of gangrene and loss of limb are great in relation to the drug's therapeutic benefits.

* * *

The evidence presented during the 5–day jury trial showed that the risk of intra-arterial injection or perivascular extravasation can be almost entirely eliminated through the use of IV-drip, rather than IV-push, administration. An IV drip is started with saline, which will not flow properly if the catheter is not in the vein and fluid is entering an artery or surrounding tissue. By contrast, even a careful and experienced clinician using the IV-push method will occasionally expose an artery to Phenergan. While Phenergan's labeling warned against intra-arterial injection and perivascular extravasation and advised that "[w]hen administering any irritant drug intravenously it is usually preferable to inject it through the tubing of an intravenous infusion set that is known to be functioning satisfactorily," the labeling did not contain a specific warning about the risks of IV-push administration.

The trial record also contains correspondence between Wyeth and the FDA discussing Phenergan's label. The FDA first approved injectable Phenergan in 1955. In 1973 and 1976, Wyeth submitted supplemental new drug applications, which the agency approved after proposing labeling changes. Wyeth submitted a third supplemental application in 1981 in response to a new FDA rule governing drug labels. Over the next 17 years, Wyeth and the FDA intermittently corresponded about Phenergan's label. The most notable activity occurred in 1987, when the FDA suggested different warnings about the risk of arterial exposure, and in 1988, when Wyeth submitted revised labeling incorporating the proposed changes. The FDA did not respond. Instead, in 1996, it requested from Wyeth the labeling then in use and, without addressing Wyeth's 1988 submission, instructed it to "[r]etain verbiage in current label" regarding intra-arterial injection. After a few further changes to the labeling not related to intra-arterial injection, the FDA approved Wyeth's 1981 application in 1998, instructing that Phenergan's final printed label "must be identical" to the approved package insert.

* * *

On August 3, 2004, the trial court filed a comprehensive opinion denying Wyeth's motion for judgment as a matter of law. After making findings of fact based on the trial record (supplemented by one letter that Wyeth found after the trial), the court rejected Wyeth's pre-emption arguments. It determined that there was no direct conflict between FDA regulations and Levine's state-law claims because those regulations permit strengthened warnings without FDA approval on an interim basis and the record contained evidence of at least 20 reports of amputations similar to Levine's since the 1960's. The court also found that state tort liability in this case would not obstruct the FDA's work because the agency had paid no more than passing attention to the question whether to warn against IV-push administration of Phenergan. In addition, the court noted that state law serves a compensatory function distinct from federal regulation.

The Vermont Supreme Court affirmed. * * *

The importance of the pre-emption issue, coupled with the fact that the FDA has changed its position on state tort law * * *, persuaded us to grant Wyeth's petition for certiorari. The question presented by the petition is whether the FDA's drug labeling judgments "preempt state law product liability claims premised on the theory that different labeling judgments were necessary to make drugs reasonably safe for use."

II

Wyeth makes two separate pre-emption arguments: first, that it would have been impossible for it to comply with the state-law duty to modify Phenergan's labeling without violating federal law, see *Fidelity Fed. Sav. & Loan Assn. v. de la Cuesta,* 458 U.S. 141, 153 (1982), and second, that recognition of Levine's state tort action creates an unacceptable "obstacle to the accomplishment and execution of the full purposes and objectives of Congress," *Hines v. Davidowitz,* 312 U.S. 52, 67 (1941), because it substitutes a lay jury's decision about drug labeling for the expert judgment of the FDA. * * *

    * * *

* * * The narrower question presented is whether federal law pre-empts Levine's claim that Phenergan's label did not contain an adequate warning about using the IV-push method of administration.

Our answer to that question must be guided by two cornerstones of our pre-emption jurisprudence. First, "the purpose of Congress is the ultimate touchstone in every pre-emption case." *Medtronic, Inc. v. Lohr,* 518 U.S. 470, 485 (1996) (internal quotation marks omitted); see *Retail Clerks v. Schermerhorn,* 375 U.S. 96, 103 (1963). Second, "[i]n all pre-emption cases, and particularly in those in which Congress has 'legislated . . . in a field which the States have traditionally occupied,' . . . we 'start with the assumption that the historic police powers of the States were not to be superseded by the Federal Act unless that was the clear and manifest purpose of Congress.'" *Lohr,* 518 U.S., at 485 (quoting *Rice v. Santa Fe Elevator Corp.,* 331 U.S. 218, 230 (1947)).

In order to identify the "purpose of Congress," it is appropriate to briefly review the history of federal regulation of drugs and drug labeling. In 1906, Congress enacted its first significant public health law, the Federal Food and Drugs Act. The Act, which prohibited the manufacture or interstate shipment of adulterated or misbranded drugs, supplemented the protection for consumers already provided by state regulation and common-law liability. In the 1930's, Congress became increasingly concerned about unsafe drugs and fraudulent marketing, and it enacted the Federal Food, Drug, and Cosmetic Act (FDCA), as amended, 21 U.S.C. § 301 *et seq.* The Act's most substantial innovation was its provision for premarket approval of new drugs. It required every manufacturer to submit a new drug application, including reports of investigations and specimens of proposed labeling, to the FDA for review. Until its application became effective, a manufacturer was prohibited from distributing a drug. The FDA could reject an application if it determined that the drug was not safe for use as labeled, though if the agency failed to act, an application became effective 60 days after the filing. FDCA, § 505(c), 52 Stat. 1052.

In 1962, Congress amended the FDCA and shifted the burden of proof from the FDA to the manufacturer. Before 1962, the agency had to prove harm to keep a drug out of the market, but the amendments required the manufacturer to demonstrate that its drug was "safe for use under the conditions prescribed, recommended, or suggested in the proposed labeling" before it could distribute the drug. §§ 102(d), 104(b), 76 Stat. 781, 784. In addition, the amendments required the manufacturer to prove the drug's effectiveness by introducing "substantial evidence that the drug will have the effect it purports or is represented to have under the conditions of use prescribed, recommended, or suggested in the proposed labeling." § 102(d), *id.*, at 781.

As it enlarged the FDA's powers to "protect the public health" and "assure the safety, effectiveness, and reliability of drugs," *id.*, at 780, Congress took care to preserve state law. The 1962 amendments added a saving clause, indicating that a provision of state law would only be invalidated upon a "direct and positive conflict" with the FDCA. § 202, *id.*, at 793. Consistent with that provision, state common-law suits "continued unabated despite ... FDA regulation." *Riegel v. Medtronic, Inc.*, 552 U.S. 312, 340, 128 S.Ct. 999, 1017 (2008) (GINSBURG, J., dissenting). And when Congress enacted an express pre-emption provision for medical devices in 1976, it declined to enact such a provision for prescription drugs.

In 2007, after Levine's injury and lawsuit, Congress again amended the FDCA. For the first time, it granted the FDA statutory authority to require a manufacturer to change its drug label based on safety information that becomes available after a drug's initial approval. In doing so, however, Congress did not enact a provision in the Senate bill that would have required the FDA to preapprove all changes to drug labels. Instead, it adopted a rule of construction to make it clear that manufacturers remain responsible for updating their labels.

III

Wyeth first argues that Levine's state-law claims are pre-empted because it is impossible for it to comply with both the state-law duties underlying those claims and its federal labeling duties. The FDA's pre-market approval of a new drug application includes the approval of the exact text in the proposed label. See 21 U.S.C. § 355; 21 CFR § 314.105(b) (2008). Generally speaking, a manufacturer may only change a drug label after the FDA approves a supplemental application. There is, however, an FDA regulation that permits a manufacturer to make certain changes to its label before receiving the agency's approval. Among other things, this "changes being effected" (CBE) regulation provides that if a manufacturer is changing a label to "add or strengthen a contraindication, warning, precaution, or adverse reaction" or to "add or strengthen an instruction about dosage and administration that is intended to increase the safe use of the drug product," it may make the labeling change upon filing its supplemental application with the FDA; it need not wait for FDA approval. §§ 314.70(c)(6)(iii)(A), (C).

* * *

We need not decide whether the 2008 CBE regulation is consistent with the FDCA and the previous version of the regulation, as Wyeth and the United States urge, because Wyeth could have revised Phenergan's label even in accordance with the amended regulation. As the FDA explained in its notice of the final rule, " 'newly acquired information' " is not limited to new data, but also encompasses "new analyses of previously submitted data." *Id.*, at 49604. The rule accounts for the fact that risk information accumulates over time and that the same data may take on a different meaning in light of subsequent developments: "[I]f the sponsor submits adverse event information to FDA, and then later conducts a new analysis of data showing risks of a different type or of greater severity or frequency than did reports previously submitted to FDA, the sponsor meets the requirement for 'newly acquired information.' " *Id.*, at 49607; see also *id.*, at 49606.

The record is limited concerning what newly acquired information Wyeth had or should have had about the risks of IV-push administration of Phenergan because Wyeth did not argue before the trial court that such information was required for a CBE labeling change. Levine did, however, present evidence of at least 20 incidents prior to her injury in which a Phenergan injection resulted in gangrene and an amputation. After the first such incident came to Wyeth's attention in 1967, it notified the FDA and worked with the agency to change Phenergan's label. In later years, as amputations continued to occur, Wyeth could have analyzed the accumulating data and added a stronger warning about IV-push administration of the drug.

* * *

Of course, the FDA retains authority to reject labeling changes made pursuant to the CBE regulation in its review of the manufacturer's supplemental application, just as it retains such authority in reviewing all supplemental applications. But absent clear evidence that the FDA would not have approved a change to Phenergan's label, we will not conclude that it was impossible for Wyeth to comply with both federal and state requirements.

* * *

Impossibility pre-emption is a demanding defense. On the record before us, Wyeth has failed to demonstrate that it was impossible for it to comply with both federal and state requirements. The CBE regulation permitted Wyeth to unilaterally strengthen its warning, and the mere fact that the FDA approved Phenergan's label does not establish that it would have prohibited such a change.

IV

Wyeth also argues that requiring it to comply with a state-law duty to provide a stronger warning about IV-push administration would obstruct the purposes and objectives of federal drug labeling regulation. Levine's tort claims, it maintains, are pre-empted because they interfere with "Congress's purpose to entrust an expert agency to make drug labeling decisions that strike a balance between competing objectives." We find no merit in this argument, which relies on an untenable interpretation of congressional intent and an overbroad view of an agency's power to pre-empt state law.

Wyeth contends that the FDCA establishes both a floor and a ceiling for drug regulation: Once the FDA has approved a drug's label, a state-law verdict may not deem the label inadequate, regardless of whether there is any evidence that the FDA has considered the stronger warning at issue. The most glaring problem with this argument is that all evidence of Congress' purposes is to the contrary. Building on its 1906 Act, Congress enacted the FDCA to bolster consumer protection against harmful products. Congress did not provide a federal remedy for consumers harmed by unsafe or ineffective drugs in the 1938 statute or in any subsequent amendment. Evidently, it determined that widely available state rights of action provided appropriate relief for injured consumers. It may also have recognized that state-law remedies further consumer protection by motivating manufacturers to produce safe and effective drugs and to give adequate warnings.

If Congress thought state-law suits posed an obstacle to its objectives, it surely would have enacted an express pre-emption provision at some point during the FDCA's 70–year history. But despite its 1976 enactment of an express pre-emption provision for medical devices, Congress has not enacted such a provision for prescription drugs. Its silence on the issue, coupled with its certain awareness of the prevalence of state tort litigation, is powerful evidence that Congress did not intend FDA oversight to be the exclusive means of ensuring drug safety and effectiveness. * * *

Despite this evidence that Congress did not regard state tort litigation as an obstacle to achieving its purposes, Wyeth nonetheless maintains that, because the FDCA requires the FDA to determine that a drug is safe and effective under the conditions set forth in its labeling, the agency must be presumed to have performed a precise balancing of risks and benefits and to have established a specific labeling standard that leaves no room for different state-law judgments. In advancing this argument, Wyeth relies not on any statement by Congress, but instead on the preamble to a 2006 FDA regulation governing the content and format of prescription drug labels. In that preamble, the FDA declared that the FDCA establishes "both a 'floor' and a 'ceiling,'" so that "FDA approval of labeling ... preempts conflicting or contrary State law." It further stated that certain state-law actions, such as those involving failure-to-warn claims, "threaten FDA's statutorily prescribed role as the expert Federal agency responsible for evaluating and regulating drugs."

This Court has recognized that an agency regulation with the force of law can pre-empt conflicting state requirements. In such cases, the Court has performed its own conflict determination, relying on the substance of state and federal law and not on agency proclamations of pre-emption. We are faced with no such regulation in this case, but rather with an agency's mere assertion that state law is an obstacle to achieving its statutory objectives. Because Congress has not authorized the FDA to pre-empt state law directly, cf. 21 U.S.C. § 360k (authorizing the FDA to determine the scope of the Medical Devices Amendments' pre-emption clause), the question is what weight we should accord the FDA's opinion.

* * *

* * * [T]he FDA's 2006 preamble does not merit deference. When the FDA issued its notice of proposed rulemaking in December 2000, it explained that the rule would "not contain policies that have federalism implications or that preempt State law." 65 Fed.Reg. 81103. In 2006, the agency finalized the rule and, without offering States or other interested parties notice or opportunity for comment, articulated a sweeping position on the FDCA's pre-emptive effect in the regulatory preamble. The agency's views on state law are inherently suspect in light of this procedural failure.

Further, the preamble is at odds with what evidence we have of Congress' purposes, and it reverses the FDA's own longstanding position without providing a reasoned explanation, including any discussion of how state law has interfered with the FDA's regulation of drug labeling during decades of coexistence. The FDA's 2006 position plainly does not reflect the agency's own view at all times relevant to this litigation. Not once prior to Levine's injury did the FDA suggest that state tort law stood as an obstacle to its statutory mission. To the contrary, it cast federal labeling standards as a floor upon which States could build and repeatedly disclaimed any attempt to pre-empt failure-to-warn claims. For instance, in 1998, the FDA stated that it did "not believe that the evolution of state tort law [would] cause the development of standards that would be at odds with the agency's regulations." It further noted that, in establishing "minimal standards" for drug labels, it did not intend "to preclude the states from imposing additional labeling requirements."

In keeping with Congress' decision not to pre-empt common-law tort suits, it appears that the FDA traditionally regarded state law as a complementary form of drug regulation. The FDA has limited resources to monitor the 11,000 drugs on the market, and manufacturers have superior access to information about their drugs, especially in the postmarketing phase as new risks emerge. State tort suits uncover unknown drug hazards and provide incentives for drug manufacturers to disclose safety risks promptly. They also serve a distinct compensatory function that may motivate injured persons to come forward with information. Failure-to-warn actions, in particular, lend force to the FDCA's premise that manu-facturers, not the FDA, bear primary responsibility for their drug labeling at all times. Thus, the FDA long maintained that state law offers an additional, and important, layer of consumer protection that complements FDA regulation. The agency's 2006 preamble represents a dramatic change in position.

* * *

In short, Wyeth has not persuaded us that failure-to-warn claims like Levine's obstruct the federal regulation of drug labeling. Congress has repeatedly declined to pre-empt state law, and the FDA's recently adopted position that state tort suits interfere with its statutory mandate is entitled to no weight. Although we recognize that some state-law claims might well frustrate the achievement of congressional objectives, this is not such a case.

V

We conclude that it is not impossible for Wyeth to comply with its state and federal law obligations and that Levine's common-law claims do not stand as an obstacle to the accomplishment of Congress' purposes in the FDCA. Accordingly, the judgment of the Vermont Supreme Court is affirmed.

It is so ordered.

JUSTICE ALITO, with whom THE CHIEF JUSTICE and JUSTICE SCALIA join, dissenting.

This case illustrates that tragic facts make bad law. The Court holds that a state tort jury, rather than the Food and Drug Administration (FDA), is ultimately responsible for regulating warning labels for prescrip-tion drugs. That result cannot be reconciled with *Geier v. American Honda Motor Co.*, 529 U.S. 861 (2000), or general principles of conflict pre-emption. I respectfully dissent.

I

The Court frames the question presented as a "narro[w]" one–namely, whether Wyeth has a duty to provide "an adequate warning about using the IV-push method" to administer Phenergan. But that ignores the antecedent question of who–the FDA or a jury in Vermont–has the authority and responsibility for determining the "adequacy" of Phener-gan's warnings. Moreover, it is unclear how a "stronger" warning could have helped respondent; after all, the physician's assistant who treated her disregarded at least six separate warnings that are already on Phener-gan's labeling, so respondent would be hard pressed to prove that a seventh would have made a difference.

More to the point, the question presented by this case is not a "narrow" one, and it does not concern whether Phenergan's label should bear a "stronger" warning. Rather, the real issue is whether a state tort jury can countermand the FDA's considered judgment that Phenergan's

FDA-mandated warning label renders its intravenous (IV) use "safe." * * *

Federal law, however, *does* rely on the FDA to make safety determinations like the one it made here. The FDA has long known about the risks associated with IV push in general and its use to administer Phenergan in particular. Whether wisely or not, the FDA has concluded–over the course of extensive, 54–year-long regulatory proceedings–that the drug is "safe" and "effective" when used in accordance with its FDA-mandated labeling. The unfortunate fact that respondent's healthcare providers ignored Phenergan's labeling may make this an ideal medical-malpractice case. But turning a common-law tort suit into a "frontal assault" on the FDA's regulatory regime for drug labeling upsets the well-settled meaning of the Supremacy Clause and our conflict pre-emption jurisprudence.

* * *

To be sure, state tort suits can peacefully coexist with the FDA's labeling regime, and they have done so for decades. But this case is far from peaceful coexistence. The FDA told Wyeth that Phenergan's label renders its use "safe." But the State of Vermont, through its tort law, said: "Not so."

The state-law rule at issue here is squarely pre-empted. Therefore, I would reverse the judgment of the Supreme Court of Vermont.

NOTES AND QUESTIONS

1. *The role of conflict preemption.* How did Wyeth argue for conflict preemption in this case? Why did the majority disagree with Wyeth? Did the dissenters agree with Wyeth? Why or why not?

2. *The role of implied preemption.* How did Wyeth argue for implied preemption in this case? Why did the majority disagree with Wyeth? Did the dissenters agree with Wyeth? Why or why not?

In Chapter 9, pp. 563–64 we discuss the Food and Drug Administration Amendments Act (FDAAA). Once this new statute is fully implemented, will it affect the rule adopted in *Wyeth v. Levine*? Why?

3. *The causation issue.* The dissenters raised another important toxic tort issue: causation. What, specifically, was the causation issue that they raised? Should that issue have made preemption irrelevant? Why or why not?

In a part of the opinion not reproduced above, the Supreme Court noted that the jury in the Vermont trial court had filled out a special verdict form as part of its finding that Wyeth was negligent. On that form, the jury specifically determined that "no intervening cause had broken the causal connection between the product defects and the plaintiff's injury." The Vermont Supreme Court, as the U.S. Supreme Court noted, affirmed the jury verdict and the trial court's decision on preemption. Does the jury's special verdict preclude the causation argument that the dissenters at the U.S. Supreme Court raised? Why or why not? Should the dissenters have even been considering causation at the Supreme Court? Why or why not?

B. STATUTES OF LIMITATION AND REPOSE

1. COMMON LAW CAUSES OF ACTION

JOHN'S HEATING SERVICE v. LAMB

Supreme Court of Alaska, 2002.
46 P.3d 1024.

CARPENETI, JUSTICE.

I. INTRODUCTION

Michael and Cynthia Lamb sued John's Heating Service claiming that John's Heating negligently failed to repair their furnace or to warn the Lambs of its dangerous condition. John's Heating raised a statute of limitations defense that the trial court precluded in a summary judgment order. The trial court also rejected John's Heating's pretrial challenge to the admissibility of the testimony of several of the Lambs' medical experts. After trial, the jury returned a verdict against John's Heating, reduced by the comparative negligence of the Lambs. John's Heating appeals the grant of summary judgment on its statute of limitations defense * * *. Because a disputed issue of fact exists as to when the statute of limitations began to run, we reverse the grant of summary judgment and remand that issue to the superior court for further proceedings. * * *

II. FACTS AND PROCEEDINGS

A. Facts

In August 1991 Michael and Cynthia Lamb bought and moved into a problem-plagued house in Kodiak. On October 15 they called John's Heating to check on their furnace. John's Heating sent an employee, Tim Galloway, to investigate the problem.

The Lambs alleged that they told Galloway that their furnace was not functioning properly, that the furnace seemed to be circulating soot throughout their home, and that they were concerned by the persistent smell of fuel in the house. As evidence of the problem, Cynthia showed Galloway "Bounce" fabric softener sheets that she had been inserting in the floor vents to filter out soot and grime that she suspected the furnace was circulating throughout the house. The Lambs claimed that Galloway did not think the soot-filtering Bounce sheets were a sign of furnace trouble and that he told Cynthia she needed to do a better job of cleaning the house.

John's Heating disputed the Lambs' version of the facts. John's Heating claimed that the Lambs informed neither Galloway nor the employee that answered the Lambs' telephonic request for service that they suspected the furnace was circulating flue gases or other combustion byproducts into the living space. Neither of the business records relating to the Lambs' service call showed that John's Heating was informed of, or suspected, a more serious furnace problem.

Both parties agreed that all Galloway did was level the fuel tank and relight the furnace.

The Lambs began to suffer physical effects from what they later alleged was carbon monoxide poisoning caused by their furnace. Both said that they started to feel tired and confused, and that they lacked concentration and memory.

The Lambs continued to live in the house and to use the furnace until January 31, 1993. At that time, they called Jerry Cloudy at Chase Plumbing, another furnace repair and heating business in Kodiak, to inspect their furnace. Cloudy informed the Lambs that their furnace was probably circulating carbon monoxide and other flue gases throughout their home and advised them not to use it while they were home until they could get it replaced. The Lambs had the furnace replaced six days later. However, they continued to suffer residual physical and neurological problems that they attributed to long-term, low-level carbon monoxide exposure ["chronic exposure"] from their malfunctioning furnace.

B. Proceedings

The Lambs filed suit against a number of defendants, including John's Heating, on December 23, 1993. John's Heating asserted the statute of limitations as an affirmative defense. John's Heating also moved for summary judgment on the statute of limitations issue, claiming that its only contact with the Lambs was on October 15, 1991, and that the Lambs did not file suit until December 23, 1993, more than two years later. The trial court denied John's Heating's motion for summary judgment and granted the Lambs' cross-motion for summary judgment without explanation, precluding John's Heating from asserting a statute of limitations defense at trial.

* * *

After a week-long trial in July 1998, the jury rendered a verdict for the Lambs. The jury awarded $810,000 in damages for Michael Lamb and $815,000 in damages for Cynthia Lamb. Each award was composed of both past and future damages. However, the jury also reduced the awards because it found that both Lambs were comparatively negligent in continuing to operate the furnace even though they knew or should have known that it was dangerous and that it was injuring them. The jury found Michael forty-five percent at fault for his injuries and found Cynthia forty percent at fault for her injuries. The verdict was accordingly reduced by those percentages.

* * *

John's Heating appeals on six issues: (1) whether the superior court erred in granting summary judgment in favor of the Lambs on the statute of limitations issue; * * *.

* * *

IV. DISCUSSION

A. Summary Judgment Was Not Appropriate Because the Date that the Lambs Reasonably Should Have Discovered that They Were Being Exposed to Carbon Monoxide Due to John's Heating Negligence Is a Disputed Factual Issue.

John's Heating argues that summary judgment was improperly granted on the statute of limitations issue. John's Heating notes that whether the Lambs had sufficient information to prompt reasonable people to conduct an inquiry to protect their rights was in dispute when the trial court granted summary judgment. The Lambs counter by arguing that as a matter of law the statute of limitations did not begin to run "until the Lambs had reason to believe not only that the furnace was operating poorly but also to suspect that they were injured and that it had injured them." The Lambs conclude that the date on which their cause of action accrued was therefore January 31, 1993, when Jerry Cloudy of Chase Plumbing told them the furnace was probably malfunctioning. The superior court apparently agreed with the Lambs since it granted summary judgment in their favor on this issue.

Alaska Statute 09.10.070(a) states that "[e]xcept as otherwise provided by law, a person may not bring an action . . . for personal injury or death . . . unless the action is commenced within two years of the accrual of the cause of action."

The date on which the statute of limitations begins to run is a factual question. Because the question is fact dependent, summary judgment ordinarily should not be used to resolve when a statute of limitations commences. Only in the unusual circumstance in which "there exist uncontroverted facts that determine when a reasonable person should have been on inquiry notice" can a court properly resolve the question as a matter of law. Accordingly, we must determine whether the superior court had before it uncontroverted facts sufficient to support its entry of summary judgment.

1. The discovery rule provides the legal test as to when the statute of limitations began to run on the Lambs' negligence claim.

Where an element of a cause of action is not immediately apparent[14], the discovery rule provides the test for the date on which the statute of limitations begins to run. As we have explained,

> the statute of limitations does not begin to run until the claimant
> discovers, or reasonably should have discovered, the existence of all

---

14. The date on which the statute of limitations begins to run is usually the "date on which the plaintiff incurs injury." *Russell*, 743 P.2d at 375 (quoting *Gudenau*, 736 P.2d at 766–67). Injury often occurs simultaneously with the corresponding act of negligence that causes it. However, when the injury is not apparent at the time of the negligent act, the discovery rule applies. *Pedersen v. Zielski*, 822 P.2d 903, 906–07 (Alaska 1991).

elements essential to the cause of action. Thus we have said the relevant inquiry is the date when the claimant reasonably should have known of the facts supporting her cause of action. We look to the date when a reasonable person has enough information to alert that person that he or she has a potential cause of action or should begin an inquiry to protect his or her rights.

Thus, under the discovery rule there are two possible dates on which the statute of limitations can begin to run and, in some cases, "a third part to our discovery rule," which we discuss below. The first potential date is "the date when [the] plaintiff reasonably should have discovered the existence of all essential elements of the cause of action." The second potential accrual date is "the date when the plaintiff has information which is sufficient to alert a reasonable person to begin an inquiry to protect his rights." As we explained in *Cameron v. State*, "[t]he dates are different, since the point when the elements of a cause of action are discovered may come after and as a result of a reasonable inquiry."[21] As we further explained in *Cameron*, the third part of the discovery rule comes into play "where a person makes a reasonable inquiry which does not reveal the elements of the cause of action within the statutory period at a point where there remains a reasonable time within which to file suit." In those circumstances, "the limitations period is tolled until a reasonable person discovers actual knowledge of, or would again be prompted to inquire into, the cause of action."

The Lambs' argument that their cause of action did not accrue until January 1993, when they were informed that they had probably been exposed to carbon monoxide by their furnace, addresses the first potential date provided by the discovery rule. That is, the Lambs argue that their cause of action did not accrue until they had actual knowledge of the source of their injuries.[24] John's Heating argues that the Lambs had information "sufficient to alert a reasonable person to begin an inquiry" before December 22, 1991, or more than two years before the Lambs had filed suit. John's Heating's argument addresses the second accrual date possible under the discovery rule. Accordingly, we must decide whether the trial court erred by granting summary judgment when John's Heating produced evidence supporting the contention that the Lambs had sufficient information to prompt reasonable people to begin an investigation.

---

21. *Cameron*, 822 P.2d at 1366. The earliest possible inquiry-notice date of accrual was October 15, 1991–the date of the allegedly negligent act of Galloway. The latest possible actual-notice date was January 31, 1993–the date Cloudy informed the Lambs that their furnace was probably malfunctioning in a dangerous fashion.

24. We note that this case presents a new variation on the application of the discovery rule, in that here the plaintiffs were arguably aware of the negligent act and its possible consequences and were therefore required to inquire in a timely manner into whether they were being injured. Previously, we have addressed situations in which either the injury and its cause were unknown, or the injury was known, but its cause was not. *Pedersen v. Zielski*, 822 P.2d 903, 907 (Alaska 1991). But in *Pedersen* we made clear that the discovery rule "is broad enough to cover other undiscovered and reasonably undiscoverable elements" of the cause of action. *Id.*

2. John's Heating presented sufficient evidence to create a genuine issue of material fact as to the inquiry-notice date on which the statute of limitations began to run.

Following the inquiry-notice approach under the discovery rule, John's Heating suggests that it provided sufficient information for a jury to find that the Lambs knew or should have known that they were being exposed to carbon monoxide as early as October 15, 1991. In the material supporting its summary judgment motion on this issue, John's Heating presented evidence to support its theory that the Lambs should have known that they were being exposed to combustion byproducts but took no action to protect themselves. John's Heating provided evidence that even under the Lambs' version of the facts they knew: (1) that an apparently malfunctioning furnace was causing them headaches, prompting them to call for a repair of the furnace; (2) that Galloway did not correct the furnace problem because it continued to blow soot into the house; (3) that during the October 15 visit, Cynthia showed Galloway corrosion holes in the furnace cabinet, but Galloway did nothing, noting that he might have to "tear the furnace apart" to figure out what was wrong with it; (4) that Cynthia admitted she knew there was still a problem with the furnace after the Galloway service call; (5) that although Cynthia cleaned out the vents and ducts on a fairly regular basis, the soot problem persisted; (6) that the Lambs switched from the Bounce sheets to cut-up furnace filters because they thought furnace filters would do a better job; and (7) that the fuel smell persisted.

* * *

The facts put forth by John's Heating, and the supporting deposition testimony of the Lambs, created a genuine issue of material fact as to whether the Lambs had sufficient information to constitute inquiry notice under the discovery rule. Accordingly, the trial court improperly granted summary judgment to the Lambs on the statute of limitations issue.

We remand the statute of limitations issue to the superior court for determination as a preliminary question of fact.[28] Because the superior court granted summary judgment on the issue, John's Heating may have additional evidence that it would have presented at trial. In that situation, the superior court has discretion to hear more evidence on the issue.

On remand, the superior court must first determine whether the Lambs had sufficient information to alert a reasonable person to begin an

---

28. *See Pedersen v. Zielski,* 822 P.2d 903, 907 n. 4 & 908 (Alaska 1991) (Questions concerning the application of the discovery rule that "are genuine issues of material fact ... must be resolved at an evidentiary hearing.") * * * *See also Decker v. Fink,* 47 Md.App. 202, 422 A.2d 389, 394 (1980) ("[T]he judge becomes the factfinder for purposes of determining the applicability of the statute of limitations...."); *Shillady v. Elliot Community Hosp.,* 114 N.H. 321, 320 A.2d 637, 639 (1974) ("The discovery rule ... [is] based on certain equitable considerations[, which] ... require that the interests of the opposing parties be identified, evaluated and weighed in arriving at a proper application of the statute. The interpretation and application of a statute of limitations is traditionally within the province of the court.... This determination by the court should be made ordinarily at a preliminary hearing in advance of trial...."); *Lopez v. Swyer,* 62 N.J. 267, 300 A.2d 563, 567 (1973).

inquiry before December 22, 1991. If the superior court finds that the Lambs were on inquiry notice before December 22, 1991, the superior court must also determine whether the third part of the discovery rule applies. If the superior court finds that the Lambs were on inquiry notice and the third part does not apply to toll the statute of limitations, the Lambs' claim would be barred by the statute of limitations, and the jury verdict against John's Heating must be vacated. However, if the superior court finds otherwise, the jury verdict and award should stand subject to our rulings on the remaining issues of this appeal.

* * *

NOTES AND QUESTIONS

1. What must a plaintiff have notice of for the claim to accrue for statute of limitations purposes, according to the *Lamb* court? You should appreciate that a plaintiff in a toxic substances case may not know for some period of time of: (1) the existence of her disease; (2) defendant's tortious conduct; or (3) the causal connection between the tortious conduct and the disease. Alaska's discovery rule is among the most lenient in setting the time for accrual. Some states only require knowledge of the harm for the statute of limitations to begin running and others only the existence of the harm and its causal connection to the toxic substance responsible. See, e.g., Berardi v. Johns–Manville Corp., 482 A.2d 1067, 1070–71 (Pa.Super.1984) (plaintiff must know of disease and cause but need not know of the existence of a valid cause of action). Knowledge is usually judged by an objective standard: what a reasonable person in plaintiff's position would have known.

2. The final section of this Chapter includes O'Connor v. Boeing North American, Inc., 311 F.3d 1139 (9th Cir.2002), In that case, the court distinguished California's tolling rule and that in CERCLA. It said that the two rules are different because in California one has "discovered" an injury when one "suspects that her injury was caused by wrongdoing." According to the court, the CERCLA rule requires "constructive knowledge of the cause of an injury." What is the rule in Alaska?

3. In most traumatic injury cases plaintiff is aware of her injury at the time it occurs, and the statute of limitations begins running then. That is so regardless of whether plaintiff knows of defendant and defendant's negligence. Why should a plaintiff, reasonably unaware of her injury or its causal connection to defendant, such as the plaintiffs in *Lamb*, have accrual of their claims delayed until they are aware of defendant's negligence?

4. In Giordano v. Market America, Inc., 599 F.3d 87 (2d Cir.2010), the plaintiff suffered a stroke while taking "ThermoChrome 5000," a dietary supplement containing ephedra. The injury occurred in 1999. Nearly four years later, in February 2003, Giordano became aware of news reports that the sudden death of major-league baseball player Steve Bechler might have been linked to his use of an ephedra-based dietary supplement. According to Giordano's affidavit, these news reports were his first indication that Thermo-Chrome 5000 may have been a cause of his stroke. Later that year, he brought a claim. The district court granted the defendant summary judgment based on

New York's three-year statute of limitation. Plaintiff appealed. The New York statute of limitations contains the following provision:

2. [T]he three year period within which an action to recover damages for personal injury or injury to property caused by the latent effects of exposure to any substance or combination of substances, in any form, upon or within the body or upon or within property must be commenced shall be computed from the date of discovery of the injury by the plaintiff or from the date when through the exercise of reasonable diligence such injury should have been discovered by the plaintiff, whichever is earlier.

3. * * * [A] claim or action for personal injury or injury to property caused by the latent effects of exposure to any substance or combination of substances, in any form, upon or within the body or upon or within property shall be deemed to have accrued on the date of discovery of the injury by the plaintiff or on the date when through the exercise of reasonable diligence the injury should have been discovered, whichever is earlier.

4. Notwithstanding the provisions of subdivisions two and three of this section, where the discovery of the cause of the injury is alleged to have occurred less than five years after discovery of the injury or when with reasonable diligence such injury should have been discovered, whichever is earlier, an action may be commenced or a claim filed within one year of such discovery of the cause of the injury; provided, however, if any such action is commenced or claim filed after the period in which it would otherwise have been authorized pursuant to subdivision two or three of this section the plaintiff or claimant shall be required to allege and prove that technical, scientific or medical knowledge and information sufficient to ascertain the cause of his injury had not been discovered, identified or determined prior to the expiration of the period within which the action or claim would have been authorized and that he has otherwise satisfied the requirements of subdivisions two and three of this section.

N.Y. C.P.L.R. § 214–c(2–4).

The Second Circuit noted that no New York cases had addressed the application of this provision to injuries such as those suffered by the plaintiff. It posed three separate questions about this provision:

1. Is section 214–c(4) is limited to injuries that are "latent?"

2. Provided that the answer to that question is in the affirmative, are ephedra injuries, which typically are experienced within twenty-four hours of its ingestion, "latent" for section 214–c(4) purposes?

3. If so, does a genuine issue of material fact exists for the trier of fact as to whether technical, medical, or scientific knowledge sufficient to ascertain the cause of Giordano's injury had been discovered, identified, or determined during the otherwise-applicable three-year period? Some studies suggesting a possible connection between ephedra and injuries similar to Giordano's were published in reputable scientific journals that were publicly available during the three-year period after discovery of Giordano's injury, but that there was a lack of awareness of the risks by even the most interested members of the public during that time. The court noted that

these facts reveal two ambiguities regarding the standard that should be used. First, it is unclear what level of certainty is required for knowledge to be "sufficient to ascertain" the cause of an injury. Second, it is unclear what relevant group must possess this knowledge, i.e., the plaintiff and his or her lawyers, or the scientific, technical, or medical community.

Rather than trying to answer this question for itself, the court certified these questions to the New York Court of Appeals. How would you answer the questions if you sat on that court? If you answer "no" to the first question, does that mean that in all cases in New York the statute of limitations may be tolled indefinitely, awaiting future research on dangers posed by a substance?

5. Whatever plaintiff must know, how sure must she be about it? Suppose a plaintiff takes five drugs during her pregnancy and bears a child with birth defects. Upon inquiry to her physician about what might have been responsible, the physician responds that, "one of the drugs might have been the cause, but none has been tested for teratogenicity in humans." Suppose that there are a couple of case reports of women who took one of the drugs during pregnancy and bore children with birth defects? Suppose the National Enquirer runs an expose of one of the drugs, claiming that it is a teratogen and only through a cover-up by the FDA and the manufacturer has this information been suppressed? Cf. Urland v. Merrell–Dow Pharms., Inc., 822 F.2d 1268 (3d Cir.1987) (the plaintiff barred by statute of limitations; discovery by the plaintiff established in part by interview with reporter for the National Enquirer, which published a sensationalized article about drug and its teratogenicity).

Recall the heightened scrutiny of expert witnesses testifying to causation addressed in Chapter 5. Does it make any sense to set the standard for knowledge of causation for accrual purposes differently from the standard for admissible testimony for an expert? On the other hand, doesn't delaying accrual until there is a adequate evidence of causation provide no statute of limitations protection to manufacturers?

6. In a wrongful death claim based on products liability, should the statute of limitations begin to run when the decedent knew or should have known of the underlying products liability claim, or should it begin to run only when the decedent dies? In Cowgill v. Raymark Industries, Inc., 780 F.2d 324 (3d Cir.1985), the court held that because a wrongful death claim is derivative of the decedent's underlying claim, the statute of limitations for the wrongful death claim begins to run at the time of accrual of the decedent's underlying claim, not at the time of the decedent's death. This is the majority rule. Contra White v. Johns–Manville Corp., 693 P.2d 687 (Wash.1985).

In *Cowgill,* the plaintiff was the decedent's wife. Suppose she tried to get her husband to sue before his death, but was not successful? Should her rights be cut off by her husband's refusal to sue? Should the result be the same if plaintiff was the decedent's minor child for whom the statute of limitations would normally be tolled until majority?

In most jurisdictions there is a separate statute of limitations for wrongful death claims. If a person has a claim when she dies, her beneficiaries have an additional period of time, often two years, to bring their wrongful death claim. Sometimes, this has the effect of lengthening the total time a defendant may be exposed to the possibility of a lawsuit.

7. Suppose that evidence of the causal relationship between plaintiff's disease and the defendant's toxic agent does not exist for decades after plaintiff develops her disease. Would (and should) the statute of limitations not begin to run until that scientific evidence existed? Would that be such a bad thing? See Michael D. Green, The Paradox of Statutes of Limitations in Insidious Disease Litigation, 76 Cal.L.Rev. 965 (1989) (arguing that in toxic substances cases there is good reason to toll the statute of limitations because evidence improves with the passage of time, rather than deteriorating).

8. *Trespass and nuisance.* When the statute of limitations accrues for trespass and nuisance claims depends on whether they are continuing or permanent. See Chapter 2 p. 68. The statute of limitations for a permanent trespass or nuisance accrues when harm begins (or, if a discovery rule is available, upon discovery). Plaintiffs may bring only one action for a permanent trespass or nuisance and all relief must be obtained in that suit. By contrast, a continuing trespass or nuisance (meaning that the harm could be remediated) is treated as providing a new cause of action so long as there is harm. Thus, a plaintiff who files suit after the applicable statute of limitations would have run based on the initiation of the trespass or nuisance may nevertheless sue for harm that has occurred in the past. Damages, however, would be limited to the period prior to suit corresponding to the time provided in the statute of limitations.

9. *The single action rule.* Even when the statute of limitations is tolled by a discovery rule, a plaintiff may face a dilemma. Under the "single action rule" a plaintiff is not permitted to divide a claim resulting from a single underlying event into multiple components and bring separate suits with respect to each component. How does this rule apply to latent toxic tort injuries? Does the statute begin to run when plaintiff first discovers some substance-related injury? This has occurred most frequently with respect to those injured by asbestos. Injuries may include pleural plaques with no accompanying physical impairment, asbestosis with varying degrees of impairment, lung cancer, and mesothelioma. If a plaintiff discovers that she is suffering from one disease, i.e., asbestosis, must she bring suit for all of her injuries or can she wait and file a separate suit if and when she contracts another asbestos related disease? See Andrew R. Klein, Fear of Disease and the Puzzle of Futures Cases in Tort, 35 U.C.Davis. L.Rev. 965, 993–99 (2002) (supporting use ofsingle action rule in cases brought by asymptomatic plaintiffs, so long as statutes of limitations are not interpreted to bar claims until injury manifests)

10. The Uniform Commercial Code also contains a statute of limitations. With respect to toxic injuries, this provision becomes relevant when plaintiffs sue on a breach of implied or express warranty theory. The relevant provision, contained in U.C.C. § 2–725(1), states: "An action for breach of any contract for sale must be commenced within four years after the cause of action has accrued." When does a cause of action "accrue?" Section 2–725(2) states that in most situations: "A cause of action accrues when the breach

occurs, regardless of the aggrieved party's lack of knowledge of the breach. A breach of warranty occurs when tender of delivery is made * * *." This limitation is not subject to any discovery rule. As a result, the statute of limitations in the U.C.C. operates like a statute of repose. Suits must be brought within a specified period—four years from the time of delivery of the product to the consumer first occurred—or they are barred.

Many states now have statutes of repose that apply to various tort claims. The next case addresses one such statute.

MONTGOMERY v. WYETH

United States Court of Appeals, Sixth Circuit, 2009.
580 F.3d 455.

SUHRHEINRICH, CIRCUIT JUDGE.

Plaintiff Angela Montgomery sued Defendants Wyeth, Wyeth Pharmaceuticals, Inc., a wholly owned subsidiary of Wyeth, and AHP Subsidiary Holding Corporation, also a subsidiary of Wyeth, after she developed primary pulmonary hypertension ("PPH"), a serious, debilitating, and usually fatal disease, from ingesting "Fenphen," a combination diet drug therapy that included Defendant Wyeth's diet drug, Pondimin.[1] The district court held that Montgomery's claim was barred by Tennessee's statute of repose, which requires that an action "be brought within one (1) year after the expiration of the anticipated life of the product." Tenn.Code Ann. § 29–28–103(a) ("TSOR").[2] Montgomery appeals.

---

1. Pondimin was Wyeth's trade name for fenfluramine. As explained by the district court in the multidistrict litigation:

Fenfluramine is an appetite suppressant that affects blood levels of the neurotransmitter, serotonin. Dexfenfluramine, the "d-isomer" of fenfluramine, is chemically related to fenfluramine and acts as an appetite suppressant by stimulating the release of serotonin from nerve cells in the brain and by reducing the reuptake of the released serotonin. * * *

* * *

In 1992, a series of articles by Michael Weintraub, M.D., were published in the Journal of Clinical Pharmacology and Therapy, in which Dr. Weintraub advocated the use of fenfluramine together with the drug phentermine for weight loss management without the adverse side effects associated with the use of fenfluramine alone. This regimen popularly became known as "Fen–Phen." . . .

Dexfenfluramine, the chemical cousin of Pondimin, was developed by Les Laboratories Servier S.A. ("LLS") in France. The drug afforded the same anorexic effects as Pondimin without the need to add phentermine to ameliorate adverse side effects. Before 1994, the Lederle Division of American Cyanamid Company had the right, together with Interneuron Pharmaceuticals, Inc., to develop and promote dexfenfluramine in the United States under the trade name "Redux." In 1994, AHP acquired American Cyanamid. Following that acquisition, responsibility for the development and promotion of Redux in the United States in conjunction with Interneuron was assumed by AHP. Interneuron received approval to market Redux in the United States in mid–1996.

2. The products liability statute of repose provides as follows:

Any action against a manufacturer or seller of a product for injury to person or property caused by its defective or unreasonably dangerous condition must be brought within the period fixed by §§ 28–3–104, 28–3–105, 28–3–202 and 47–2–725, but notwithstanding any exceptions to these provisions it must be brought within six years of the date of injury, in any event, the action must be brought within ten (10) years from the date on which the product was first purchased for use or consumption, *or within one (1) year after the expiration of the anticipated life of the product, whichever is the shorter,* except in the case of injury to minors whose action

I. Background

The FDA approved the sale of the Pondimin brand of fenfluramine 20 mg tablets as a prescription weight loss medication in 1973. Pondimin 20 mg tablets were manufactured in Richmond, Virginia, and distributed by Wyeth to pharmacies and wholesalers in 100–count and 500–count stock bottles. The expiration date for Pondimin 20 mg tablets was three years from the month of manufacture of each lot. The expiration date was printed on a label affixed to each stock bottle. Wyeth did not sell Pondimin 20 mg tablets directly to consumers. Instead the tablets were packaged by third parties. The product was withdrawn from the market in September 1997.

Montgomery began taking Pondimin in 1997. A Tennessee resident, Montgomery traveled to the Med–X Clinic in Fort Oglethorpe, Georgia, to receive treatment and prescriptions of Pondimin, which was not available in Tennessee at that time. Montgomery received her first treatment in January 1997 and went to Georgia at least eight times during 1997. Each time, she was evaluated by a Georgia physician. She was prescribed, and purchased, Pondimin on seven of those visits. Montgomery saw three doctors: Dr. Merton Sure, who has since died; Dr. David Hargett, who lost his medical license in January 2001; and Dr. Joyce Gray.

Pondimin became available in Tennessee as of March 26, 1997. Wyeth voluntarily withdrew Pondimin from the market on September 15, 1997, and did not manufacture, package, or distribute it after that time. Montgomery stopped using Pondimin in August 1997.

In December 1997, the Judicial Panel on Multidistrict Litigation established MDL No. 1203 in the Eastern District of Pennsylvania for consolidated proceedings relating to a wave of litigation involving Pondimin, Redux, and phentermine. On October 7, 1999, the numerous parties to the action reached an understanding of the principal terms of the settlement in a Memorandum of Understanding ("MOU"). On October 12, 1999, a class action styled *Brown v. Wyeth* was filed on behalf of all users of Pondimin and Redux, in the Eastern District of Pennsylvania and became part of MDL 1203. Montgomery is a member of the *Brown* class. On November 18, 1999, the parties executed a Nationwide Class Action Settlement Agreement ("Settlement Agreement"), which included the *Brown* class members. On August 28, 2000, the district court entered PTO 1415, which certified the class and approved the Settlement Agreement.

Montgomery was not diagnosed with PPH until April 2005. She filed the present action in Tennessee state court in October 2005, within six months after being diagnosed. The case was removed to the United States District Court for the Eastern District of Tennessee, transferred to the MDL for pretrial proceedings in February 2006, and then remanded to the district court in July 2007. Defendants moved for summary judgment,

---

must be brought within a period of one (1) year after attaining the age of majority, whichever occurs sooner.

Tenn.Code Ann. § 29–28–103(a) (West 2008) (emphasis added).

alleging that Montgomery's claim was barred by the TSOR because it had not been brought within one year of the expiration date of the product. The district court reluctantly agreed and granted summary judgment to Defendants on March 19, 2008. Specifically, the court concluded that the TSOR applied to Montgomery's claim under Tennessee's conflict-of-laws rules, the Settlement Agreement did not preserve her right to sue for PPH, Tennessee law rather than Georgia law applied, and Wyeth did not waive its statute of repose defense. *See Montgomery v. Wyeth,* 540 F.Supp.2d 933 (E.D.Tenn.2008). The court also denied Montgomery's Rule 59 motion to alter or amend judgment. This appeal followed.

II. Analysis

* * *

A. Choice of Law

Montgomery argues that the district court erred in applying Tennessee law because the relevant choice-of-law principles dictate that Georgia law should govern. As noted, the district court held that the TSOR barred Montgomery's claim. There is a conflict because Georgia's statute of repose, which limits claims only after ten years, would not bar her claim. *See* Ga.Code Ann. § 51–1–11 (West 2008) (stating that "[n]o action shall be commenced pursuant to this subsection with respect to an injury after ten years from the date of the first sale for use or consumption of the personal property causing or otherwise bringing about the injury").

Because this is a diversity action, the law of the forum state, including the choice-of-law rules, apply. Tennessee follows the "most significant relationship" approach of the Restatement (Second) of Conflict of Laws to choice-of-law questions. * * *

Contacts to be considered in determining which state has the most significant relationship include (1) the place where the injury occurred, (2) the place where the conduct causing the injury occurred, (3) the domicile, residence, nationality, place of incorporation and place of business of the parties, and (4) the place where the relationship, if any, between the parties is centered.

* * *

Weighing these factors, the district court concluded that Tennessee had the most significant relationship because Tennessee was where Montgomery consumed the Pondimin and suffered her injury. By contrast, the only contact she had with Georgia was that she purchased the product from a third party there.

* * *

Although Montgomery obtained Pondimin in Georgia, she received Pondimin from a third party. She took at most a few tablets there, and she does not claim to have suffered any symptoms in Georgia. None of the parties are current or former residents of Georgia. Montgomery alleges that her prescribing physicians received inadequate warnings from Wyeth in Georgia. However, there is no support in the record that her prescribing doctors reviewed Wyeth's inadequate warnings, relied on any other statements made by Wyeth, or were uninformed about the risks of Pondimin when they prescribed it to Montgomery in 1997. Thus, Montgomery's relationship with Wyeth is more significant in Tennessee, the state where she actually used the manufacturer's product and suffered the resulting injury, rather than Georgia, the state where she obtained the product through a third party.

* * *

Montgomery claims that the district court failed to consider whether the TSOR, as applied to *this case*, outweighed "relevant policies of other states and the relative interests of those states in the determination of the particular issue." Restatement (Second) of Conflict of Laws §§ 6(b) and (c). She also asserts that Tennessee has no interest in a claim that is barred by Tennessee law. Thus, Montgomery contends that, as applied to this case, the TSOR does not advance Tennessee's interest in controlling insurance rates. Further, she notes that numerous authorities have noted that statutes like the TSOR do not actually lower insurance premiums, including this Court in *Kochins v. Linden–Alimak, Inc.*, 799 F.2d 1128, 1140 (6th Cir.1986) (acknowledging that the legislative goals of the TSOR are not likely to be accomplished by the means selected based on the views of various authorities).

The primary flaw in Montgomery's argument is that it focuses on the outcome of applying Tennessee's statute of repose rather than on the significance of Tennessee's relationship to the parties and the place of injury * * *. Tennessee's choice-of-law analysis does not turn on whether a plaintiff has a viable claim in one state but not another. *See* Restatement (Second) of Conflict of Laws § 145, cmt. c ("A rule which exempts the actor from liability for harmful conduct is entitled to the same consideration in the choice-of-law process as a rule which imposes liability").

As the Tennessee Supreme Court has recognized, the Tennessee products liability statute of repose "was enacted as an important and specific measure to address products liability actions." *Penley v. Honda Motor Co.*, 31 S.W.3d 181, 187 (Tenn.2000). The preamble to Tennessee Products Liability Act ("TPLA") states:

> WHEREAS, The General Assembly finds and declares that the number of product liability suits and claims for damages and the amount of judgments, settlements and the expense of defending such suits have increased greatly in recent years, and because of these increases[,] the cost of product liability insurance was substantially increased.

Penley, 31 S.W.3d at 187 (quoting preamble). * * *

> [T]he General Assembly perceived that uncertainty as to future liability increased the premiums for product liability insurance, which

in turn increased the costs of production and ultimately consumer prices. The legislature considered the limitation of future liability to a reasonable and specific period to be one of the most important keys in solving the perceived products liability crisis.

Penley, 31 S.W.3d at 187.

We are not in a position to alter this policy decision of the state legislature. Indeed, this Court and the Tennessee Supreme Court have repeatedly upheld the constitutionality of the TSOR. *See Mathis v. Eli Lilly & Co.*, 719 F.2d 134 (6th Cir.1983); *Jones v. Five Star Eng'g, Inc.*, 717 S.W.2d 882 (Tenn.1986). * * * Montgomery's claim that liability is more likely to be determined on a national basis ignores the fact that assessing liability based on the laws of each state would obviously be part of that calculation. In short, as the district court held, Tennessee has a strong interest is applying its statute of repose in products liability actions, even when that forecloses a claim by a Tennessee plaintiff.

In sum, although Georgia has an interest because Montgomery was prescribed Pondimin there, we agree with the district court's conclusion that Tennessee has the stronger interest for the purpose of the choice-of-law analysis.

* * *

C. Expiration Date

Montgomery also claims that the district court misapplied the TSOR because there were no expiration dates on the product dispensed to her. Defendants acknowledge that Montgomery did not get the pills in their original packaging because they were repackaged by the distributor who bought them from Wyeth and sold them to Montgomery.

The "anticipated life of the product" is the "expiration date placed on the product by the manufacturer when required by law but shall not commence until the date the product was first purchased for use or consumption." Tenn.Code Ann. § 29–28–102. As the district court observed, Wyeth stopped manufacturing Pondimin on September 2, 1997. Wyeth offered uncontested evidence that packaging for Pondimin contained the expiration dates as required by law, and those expiration dates were three years from the date of manufacture. Thus, the expirations were at the latest September 2000. Montgomery filed this case in October 2005. Because the undisputed evidence establishes that all Pondimin tablets had an expiration date of five or more years before Montgomery brought this suit, there is no genuine issue of material fact as to the expiration date for purposes of applying the TSOR.

Contrary to Montgomery's assertion, the TSOR does not require that the purchaser have knowledge of the expiration date, but conditions the anticipated life of the product on the expiration date imposed by the manufacturer. This reading of the statute is consistent with the legislative intent. As this Court has noted, the statute of repose operates when "parties may be ignorant about the particular time limitations involved.

Thus, a delay, even without knowledge of the hazard involved in the delay, may preclude the bringing of an otherwise meritorious claim." *Mathis*, 719 F.2d at 140 (holding that the application of ten-year limitation in TSOR does not violate a party's due process rights). However harsh the result, this is a decision of the Tennessee legislature. "Statutes of limitation find their justification in necessity and convenience rather than logic.... They represent a *public policy* about the privilege to litigate." *Id.* (quoting *Chase Sec. Corp. v. Donaldson*, 325 U.S. 304, 314, 65 S.Ct. 1137, 89 L.Ed. 1628 (1945)).

Our decision in *Spence v. Miles Lab.*, 37 F.3d 1185 (6th Cir.1994), is virtually identical. There we held the product liability claim was barred by the statute of repose because the expiration date on a package of blood (which was infected with AIDS and was transferred to the plaintiff) was June 5, 1987, and the plaintiff had filed his product liability claim more than one year after that date, despite the fact that he filed his action less than one year after discovering he had AIDS. *Id.* at 1188, 1190. As the district court held, *Spence* controls the result in this case.

* * *

III. Conclusion

For the foregoing reasons, as well as those in the district court's thorough and thoughtful opinion, the judgment of the district court is **AFFIRMED.**

NOTES AND QUESTIONS

1. For another case that turns on conflicting statutes of repose, see McCann v. Foster Wheeler LLC, 225 P.3d 516 (Cal.2010). There, the plaintiff contracted mesothelioma from asbestos exposure. One of his exposures occurred when, as an Oklahoma resident, he helped install the defendant's boiler in an Oklahoma refinery. Oklahoma has a statute of repose that requires any cause of action against a designer or constructor of an improvement to real property to be filed within 10 years of the substantial completion of the improvement. Applying a choice of law analysis similar to that applied by the Sixth Circuit, the court concluded that Oklahoma law applied to bar the plaintiff's recovery against Foster Wheeler. Of course in this case the plaintiff had many other defendants against whom he could pursue a claim under California's *Rutherford* risk rule. See Chapter 4, pp. 242–61.

2. Statutes of repose come in a number of different forms. Most prevalent are statutes such as the one in *Montgomery* that concern products. Most such statutes of repose are "time certain" statutes. They establish a fixed period of time, beginning when the manufacturer first sold the product, after which a plaintiff's right to sue for an injury caused by the product is terminated. See Ind. Code Ann. § 34–20–3–1(b)(2). Other statutes, commonly called "useful life" statutes, bar plaintiffs' claims after the expiration of the product's useful-life. See Minn. Stat. Ann. § 604.03. Some states adopt a blend of the two types of statutes. See Tenn. Code Ann. § 29–28–103(a). How would you categorize the statute in *Montgomery*?

Many states have also adopted realty improvement statutes of repose. These statutes are generally time-certain statutes that shield builders from suits arising out of injuries caused builder negligence or defects in products that the builder installs as part of the real property improvement. In some states, these statutes are interpreted to shield product manufacturers as well when the product is found to be part of the improvement. These statutes and the products liability statutes of repose often exclude certain products such as asbestos.

Finally, as we saw in Chapter 2, states have enacted statutes of repose that cut off liability against dissolved corporations. See Godbout v. WLB Holding, Inc., 997 A.2d 92 (Me.2010). For a useful discussion of types of statutes of repose, see David G. Owen, Special Defenses in Modern Products Liability Law, 70 Mo.L.Rev. 1 (2005).

3. Some jurisdictions have declared that when applied to latent injuries, statutes of repose are unconstitutional, usually because they violate the state constitution's open courts provision. See Kenyon v. Hammer, 688 P.2d 961 (Ariz.1984) (interpreting the accrual language in its statute of repose as the date of injury, rather than the date of the negligent act, because a contrary interpretation would force the court to "declare the statute unconstitutional" as it would bar causes of action before they accrue); Diamond v. E. R. Squibb & Sons, Inc., 397 So.2d 671 (Fla.1981). In the *Diamond* case, the plaintiff was a DES daughter who did not suffer any injury until after the repose period (12 years) had lapsed. But see Tomlinson v. Celotex Corp., 770 P.2d 825 (Kan. 1989); Aicher ex rel. LaBarge v. Wisconsin Patients Comp. Fund, 613 N.W.2d 849 (Wis.2000); Farber v. Lok–N–Logs, Inc., 701 N.W.2d 368 (Neb.2005) In *Farber*, the plaintiff was exposed to logs treated with Pentachlorophenol (penta), a wood preservative. He suffered injuries many years after his exposure but the court refused to graft a discovery rule for latent medical conditions onto the state's product liability 10–year statute of repose.

C. FEDERAL CAUSES OF ACTION

The federal statutes governing various aspects of toxic substances provide an almost bewildering array of statutes of limitations. It therefore helps to think about these statutes of limitations in categories.

First, most of the federal statutes dealing with toxic substances provide at least one statute of limitations (and sometimes more) that govern lawsuits against the relevant federal agency to challenge that agency's specific implementations of the statute, such as when the agency issues regulations. These statutes of limitations tend to be very short. For example, the Resource Conservation and Recovery Act (RCRA) gives challengers only 90 days to file a lawsuit to review the Environmental Protection Agency's (EPA's) actions under that statute. 42 U.S.C. § 6976(a)(1); see also West Virginia Highlands Conservancy v. Johnson, 540 F.Supp.2d 125, 134–37 (D.D.C.2008) (strictly applying this statute of limitation). The Comprehensive Environmental Response, Compensation, and Liability Act (CERCLA) similarly gives would-be plaintiffs only 90 days to file a lawsuit to challenge the EPA's regulations under the Act. 42 U.S.C. § 9613(a). The Federal Insecticide, Fungicide, and Rodenticide Act (FIFRA) allows even less time for challenges to the EPA's pesticide registration decisions—only 60 days. 7 U.S.C. § 136n(b); see also Selco Supply Co. v. United States EPA, 632 F.2d 863, 865 (10th Cir. 1980) (explaining that this provision is a statute of limitation).

Second, the federal statutes sometimes provide statutes of limitations for the government's enforcement actions against violators. Thus, for example, the Occupational Safety and Health Act (OSH Act) requires the Occupational Safety and Health Administration (OSHA) to issue citations against an employer within six months of the employer's violation of safety standards. 29 U.S.C. § 658(c). The federal courts have indicated that this statute of limitations acts to protect employers. Todd Shipyards Corp. v. Sec'y of Labor, 566 F.2d 1327, 1330 (9th Cir.1977).

Third, the federal statutes sometimes provide statutes of limitations for specific kinds of lawsuits that private parties can bring against each other under the relevant statute. For example, the OSH Act prohibits employers from retaliating against employees who complain about unsafe conditions in the workplace, and an employee has 30 days to file a complaint challenging an employer's alleged retaliatory or discriminatory firing. 29 U.S.C. § 660(c)(2). The courts are in agreement that this is a true statute of limitations and hence subject to equitable tolling. Donovan v. Hahner, Foreman & Harness, Inc., 736 F.2d 1421, 1423 (10th Cir.1984); Chao v. Xanadu Boutique, Inc., 380 F.Supp.2d 134, 135–36 (E.D.N.Y. 2005).

CERCLA has one of the most comprehensive statutes of limitations among these federal acts for the various types of lawsuits possible under its provisions. Specifically, Section 309(g) states that:

(1) Actions for natural resource damages

Except as provided in paragraphs (3) and (4), no action may be commenced for [natural resource] damages * * * under this chapter, *unless that action is commenced within 3 years after the later of the following*:

(A) The date of the discovery of the loss and its connection with the release in question.

(B) The date on which regulations are promulgated under section 9651(c) of this title.

* * *

(2) Actions for recovery of costs

An initial action for recovery of the costs referred to in section 9607 of this title must be commenced–

(A) *for a removal action, within 3 years after completion of the removal action*, except that such cost recovery action must be brought within 6 years after a determination to grant a waiver under section 9604(c)(1)(C) of this title for continued response action; and

(B) *for a remedial action, within 6 years after initiation of physical on-site construction of the remedial action*, except that, if the remedial action is initiated within 3 years after the completion of the removal action, costs incurred in the removal action may be recovered in the cost recovery action brought under this subparagraph.

* * *

(3) Contribution

No action for contribution for any response costs or damages may be commenced more than 3 years after—

(A) the date of judgment in any action under this chapter for recovery of such costs or damages, or

(B) the date of an administrative order under section 9622(g) of this title (relating to de minimis settlements) or 9622(h) of this title (relating to cost recovery settlements) or entry of a judicially approved settlement with respect to such costs or damages.

(4) Subrogation

No action based on rights subrogated pursuant to this section by reason of payment of a claim may be commenced under this subchapter *more than 3 years after the date of payment of such claim.*

(5) Actions to recover indemnification payments

Notwithstanding any other provision of this subsection, where a payment pursuant to an indemnification agreement with a response action contractor is made under section 9619 of this title, an action under section 9607 of this title for recovery of such indemnification payment from a potentially responsible party *may be brought at any time before the expiration of 3 years from the date on which such payment is made.* * * *

42 U.S.C. § 9613(a), (g) (emphasis added). Thus, CERCLA lawsuits are generally subject to three-year statutes of limitations—running from various accrual dates—except for cost recovery actions for remedial actions, which have a six-year statute of limitations.

As a practical matter, therefore, any lawyer needs to read these provisions very carefully to ensure that the lawyer has found the correct statute of limitations. But what if there isn't one? Paradoxically, perhaps, given the level of detail these statutes provide in other contexts, many of them do *not* specify statutes of limitations for various kinds of lawsuits and enforcement actions.

The Toxic Substances Control Act (TSCA), for example, does not provide a statute of limitations for the EPA when the EPA brings administrative enforcement actions. Does that mean that the EPA can assess penalties against a past violator no matter how long it's been since the violation occurred? That's the argument that the U.S. Court of Appeals for the D.C. Circuit had to address in the following case.

3M CO. (MINNESOTA MINING & MANUFACTURING) v. BROWNER

United States Court of Appeals for the District of Columbia Circuit, 1994.
17 F.3d 1453.

RANDOLPH, CIRCUIT JUDGE:

This petition for review of the Environmental Protection Agency's assessment of civil penalties turns on the meaning of 28 U.S.C. § 2462, the direct descendant of a statute of limitations enacted more than a century and a half ago. * * *

I

Between August 1980 and July 1986, 3M unwittingly committed several violations of the Toxic Substances Control Act (TSCA), 15 U.S.C. §§ 2601–2629. On July 28, 1986, after the company became aware of its transgressions, it notified EPA's compliance office. The company had learned that one of its chemicals, Chemical A, was not on an EPA inventory of existing chemicals. * * *

At least ninety days before a new chemical may be imported, TSCA requires the importer to provide EPA with a Premanufacture Notice. 15 U.S.C. § 2604(a)(1). Because Chemical A was both new and imported, 3M's importation of Chemical A without the requisite notice violated this provision. In addition, 3M's brokers wrongly certified to Customs officials that TSCA's requirements had been met.

The mishap with Chemical A spurred 3M to review its other imported chemicals. Thus, it discovered a problem with Chemical B. * * * When 3M imported Chemical B on various occasions between July 15, 1983, and August 4, 1986, it assumed Chemical B was not new and did not require a Premanufacture Notice. * * * As with Chemical A, a Premanufacture Notice had been required but not submitted, and the Customs certifications regarding compliance with TSCA were incorrect. On September 16, 1986, 3M notified EPA of the violations concerning Chemical B.

Two years later, on September 2, 1988, EPA filed an administrative complaint against 3M seeking $1.3 million in civil penalties under § 16(a)(2)(A) of TSCA for 3M's failure to file Premanufacture Notices and for 3M's submitting inaccurate Customs certifications with respect to Chemicals A and B. * * *

In its answer to the complaint, 3M interposed a statute of limitations—28 U.S.C. § 2462—claiming that the statute barred proceedings to impose penalties for 3M's importation of the chemicals without the requisite notices five years prior to EPA's complaint, that is, before

September 1983. An EPA Administrative Law Judge ruled that no statute of limitations applied to § 16(a)(2)(A) proceedings. The ALJ found 28 U.S.C. § 2462 inapplicable on the grounds that it applied only to judicial proceedings; and that, in any event, civil penalty cases under § 16 of TSCA were not the sort of enforcement proceedings covered by § 2462. After the ALJ assessed a civil penalty of $104,720, 3M filed an administrative appeal with the EPA Chief Judicial Officer, who acts as the Administrator's delegate in these cases. The Chief Judicial Officer, "adopt[ing] and incorporat[ing]" the "applicable portions" of the ALJ's opinion, also ruled that § 2462 did not apply. He then assessed a penalty against 3M of $130,650. This petition followed.

II

Any person who violates § 15 of TSCA, 15 U.S.C. § 2614, "shall be liable to the United States for a civil penalty in an amount not to exceed $25,000 for each such violation." 15 U.S.C. § 2615(a)(1). * * *

While TSCA * * * sets a deadline on the alleged violator's petition for judicial review, TSCA contains no provision limiting the time within which the EPA Administrator must initiate the administrative action. If there is such a time limit, it must be derived from the five-year statute of limitations, 28 U.S.C. § 2462, generally applicable to civil fines and penalties, which reads:

> Except as otherwise provided by Act of Congress, an action, suit or proceeding for the enforcement of any civil fine, penalty, or forfeiture, pecuniary or otherwise, shall not be entertained unless commenced within five years from the date when the claim first accrued if, within the same period, the offender or the property is found within the United States in order that proper service may be made thereon.

A

The most fundamental question raised by 3M's invocation of § 2462 is whether the statute applies to civil penalty cases brought before agencies. * * *

It is easy to see why § 2462's application to administrative cases would be taken for granted. What cannot be "entertained" after § 2462's limitation period has expired is "an action, suit or proceeding." An agency's adjudication of a civil penalty case readily fits this description. In this case, EPA's regulations describe the agency's process for assessing civil penalties as a "proceeding." The Administrative Procedure Act, 5 U.S.C. § 554(b), which generally governs agency adjudications of civil penalties and which § 16(b) of TSCA expressly incorporates, calls agency adjudications "proceedings." So does the Judicial Code, *see, e.g.*, 28 U.S.C. §§ 2344(1), 2347. *See also* 31 U.S.C. § 3730(e)(3), referring to an "administrative civil money penalty proceeding."

The ALJ nevertheless ruled that § 2462 related only to *judicial* "actions, suits or proceedings." * * * Much of the ALJ's reasoning rested on the fact that § 2462's predecessor spoke of "suit or prosecution," and that the 1948 revision of the Judicial Code (of which more hereafter) replacing these words with "action, suit or proceeding" intended no change in substance. The ALJ therefore believed that regardless whether EPA's assessment of a civil penalty was a "proceeding," it could not be considered a "suit or prosecution."

We wonder why not. According to the Administrative Procedure Act, agency attorneys who bring administrative complaints, including complaints for civil penalties, are performing "prosecuting functions." 5 U.S.C. § 554(d). * * * The Supreme Court perceives no substantial distinction between the function performed by agency attorneys "presenting evidence in an agency hearing and the function of a prosecutor who brings evidence before a court." *Butz v. Economou*, 438 U.S. 478, 516 (1978). Civil penalty proceedings under TSCA emulate judicial proceedings: a complaint is brought, the defendant answers, motions and affidavits are filed, depositions are taken, other discovery pursued, a hearing is held, evidence is introduced, findings are rendered and an order assessing a civil penalty is issued. 40 C.F.R. §§ 22.13–26. When that sequence of events takes place in a court, we have no trouble calling it a "prosecution," although the modern trend is to reserve the description for criminal cases. When the same sequence of events plays out before an administrative agency, it too may be–and has been–designated a "prosecution."

Given the reasons why we have statutes of limitations, there is no discernible rationale for applying § 2462 when the penalty action or proceeding is brought in a court, but not when it is brought in an administrative agency. The concern that after the passage of time "evidence has been lost, memories have faded, and witnesses have disappeared" pertains equally to factfinding by a court and factfinding by an agency. Statutes of limitations also reflect the judgment that there comes a time when the potential defendant "ought to be secure in his reasonable expectation that the slate has been wiped clean of ancient obligations," Note, *Developments in the Law—Statutes of Limitations*, 63 Harv. L. Rev. 1177, 1185 (1950). Here again it is of no moment whether the proceeding leading to the imposition of a penalty is a proceeding started in a court or in an agency. From the potential defendant's point of view, lengthy delays upset "settled expectations" to the same extent in either case.

The ALJ also supported his ruling that no limitations period applied by invoking a maxim: statutes of limitations ought to be strictly construed in favor of the government. While this accurately recites the Supreme Court's general pronouncements, there is another Supreme Court maxim, older still, a maxim specifically relating to actions for penalties and one pointing in quite the opposite direction: "In a country where not even treason can be prosecuted, after a lapse of three years, it could scarcely be supposed, that an individual would remain for ever liable to a pecuniary forfeiture." *Adams v. Woods*, 6 U.S. (2 Cranch) 336, 341 (1805) (Marshall, C.J.). Justice Story, sitting as a circuit justice in a civil penalty case, made the same point as Chief Justice Marshall: "it would be utterly repugnant to the genius of our laws, to allow such prosecutions a perpetuity of existence." *United States v. Mayo*, 26 F.Cas. 1230, 1231 (C.C.D. Mass. 1813) (No. 15,754).

We therefore reject this aspect of the ALJ's construction of § 2462. * * * And so we move on.

B

If, as we have held, an administrative proceeding under § 16(a)(2) of TSCA is an "action, suit or proceeding," the question remains whether it is—in the language of § 2462—one "for the enforcement of" a civil penalty. EPA thinks not, because "enforcement" connotes an action to collect a penalty already imposed, whereas a proceeding under § 16(a)(2) merely assesses or imposes the penalty. EPA's distinction relies on § 16(a)(4), which authorizes the Attorney General to bring an action against the violator in federal district court to recover the amount, plus interest, of any civil penalty remaining unpaid after final judgment. That, EPA, says is the action for "enforcement," to which § 2462's five-year limitation applies.

* * *

* * * History holds the key. For more than a century, § 2462's predecessors simply provided that "[n]o suit or prosecution for any penalty or forfeiture, pecuniary or otherwise, accruing under the laws of the United States, shall be maintained" unless it is brought within five years "from the time when the penalty accrued." The word "enforcement" did not appear in the statute until the comprehensive revision of the Judicial Code, completed in 1948. The Reviser's Notes on the rewriting of § 2462's predecessor report: "Changes were made in phraseology." H.R.REP. No. 308, 80th Cong., 1st Sess. A191 (1947).

A long line of Supreme Court decisions compels the conclusion that the rewording did not render the new statute different in substance from the old. When the Reviser's Notes describe the alterations as changes in phraseology, the well-established canon of construction is that the revised statute means only what it meant before 1948.

EPA's reading of § 2462 therefore must be rejected. To adopt it would be to treat the Reviser's rewriting of § 2462 as a modification of the statute's substance. * * *

* * *

III

The remaining issue concerns the meaning of § 2462's phrase "unless commenced within five years from the date when the claim first accrued." On the assumption that § 2462 applies, EPA contends, and the ALJ held, that its claim for penalties "first accrued" when it discovered 3M's violations, not beforehand when the company committed those violations.

A claim normally accrues when the factual and legal prerequisites for filing suit are in place. * * * [However, i]f the period always ran from the date of the wrong, actions by workers previously exposed to dangerous chemicals, for example, might be time-barred when brought years later after the workers' injuries manifested themselves. For cases involving such latent injuries or injuries difficult to detect, courts have developed the "discovery rule." * * * The "discovery rule" rests on the idea that plaintiffs cannot have a tenable claim for the recovery of damages unless and until they have been harmed. Damage claims in cases involving hidden injuries or illnesses therefore are viewed as not accruing until the harm becomes apparent. * * * Although use of the rule has not been restricted to personal injury actions, the rule has only been applied to remedial, civil claims.

The rule EPA sponsors is of an entirely different sort. It is a "discovery of violation" rule having nothing whatever to do with the problem of latent injuries. The rationale underlying the discovery of injury rule—that a claim cannot realistically be said to accrue until the claimant has suffered harm—is completely inapposite. The statute of limitations on which EPA would engraft its rule is aimed exclusively at restricting the time within which actions may be brought to recover fines, penalties and forfeitures. Fines, penalties and forfeitures, whether civil or criminal, may be considered a form of punishment. In an action for a civil penalty, the government's burden is to prove the violation; injuries or damages resulting from the violation are not part of the cause of action; the suit may be maintained regardless of damage. Immediately upon the violation, EPA may institute the proceeding to have the penalty imposed. The penalty provision of TSCA, § 16(a)(1), says just that: "Any person who violates a provision of section 2614 or 2689 of this title shall be liable to the United States for a civil penalty in an amount not to exceed $25,000 for each such violation." Because liability for the penalty attaches at the moment of the violation, one would expect this to be the time when the claim for the penalty "first accrued."

* * *

When we return to the statutory language and ask what Congress meant when it required actions to be brought within five years from the date when a claim for a penalty "accrued," the answer readily presents itself. The meaning of this portion of § 2462 has been settled for more than a century. The word "accrued" first appeared in the 1839 version of the statute: the suit for a penalty had to be "commenced within five years from the time when the penalty or forfeiture accrued," Act of Feb. 28, 1839, ch. 36, § 4, 5 Stat. 321, 322. * * *

In 1839, when Congress used the word "accrued," it could not possibly have intended the word to incorporate any discovery of violation rule. Only nine years earlier, the Supreme Court had rejected a discovery rule and held that a claim accrues at the moment a violation occurs. Other Supreme Court opinions of the era consistently used the phrase "claim accrued" to mean the time at which a cause of action first existed, not the time when the violation was first discovered. * * *

In light of the legal meaning of the word "accrued" in 1839, the retention of the word in the 1874 version of § 2462, and its appearance in the current statute, we hold that an action, suit or proceeding to assess or impose a civil penalty must be commenced within five years of the date of the violation giving rise to the penalty. We reject the discovery of violation rule EPA advocates as unworkable; outside the language of the statute; inconsistent with judicial interpretations of § 2462; unsupported by the discovery of injury rule adopted in non-enforcement, remedial cases; and incompatible with the functions served by a statute of limitations in penalty cases.

IV

EPA may not assess civil penalties against 3M for any violations of § 15 of TSCA allegedly committed by the company more than five years before EPA commenced its proceeding under 15 U.S.C. § 2615. The petition for review is granted, and the case is remanded for further proceedings consistent with this opinion.

So Ordered.

NOTES AND QUESTIONS

1. *The source of TSCA's statute of limitations for EPA administrative actions.* As noted, TSCA does not specify a statute of limitations for administrative enforcement. Why did the D.C. Circuit not accept the EPA's argument that there simply is no statute of limitations for a TSCA administrative enforcement action, and that the EPA can bring such an enforcement action whenever it wants? What general policies regarding statutes of limitations did the court consider relevant here?

Deciding that there needs to be a statute of limitations, however, is not the same thing as deciding how long it should be. What is the statute of limitations for a TSCA administrative enforcement action? Where did that statute of limitations come from? Why is it applicable to the EPA's administrative enforcement actions under TSCA?

Another issue, of course, is the accrual date. When does the TSCA statute of limitations start to run, according to the D.C. Circuit? Why? Why doesn't the EPA get the benefit of a discovery rule? As a policy matter, why are the EPA's enforcement actions different from a personal injury action?

The discovery rule is relevant to litigation over toxic substances, of course—even among the federal statutes. As Chapter 8 and the discussion of federal preemption above both noted, the federal statutes generally leave state-law toxic tort remedies in place, so if a state uses the discovery rule for toxic torts, a state-law toxic tort lawsuit based on a violation of a relevant federal statute might well involve application of the discovery rule. Moreover, as will be discussed, CERCLA actively preempts state tort law specifically to impose a discovery rule in CERCLA-related state-law toxic tort cases.

2. *Other uses of 28 U.S.C. § 2462 in lawsuits brought pursuant to the federal toxic substances statutes.* Fairly consistently, Congress has failed to provide a statute of limitations for citizen suits pursuant to the federal statutes related to toxic substances. Most federal environmental statutes have citizen-suit provisions, which allow interested citizens to sue people who violate the relevant statute. Usually, citizen plaintiffs can ask for civil penalties (which are payable to the U.S. Treasury), a declaratory judgment, and/or injunctive relief. While neither the OSH Act nor FIFRA contains a citizen-suit provision or otherwise creates a private right of action, RCRA, CERCLA, and TSCA all have citizen-suit provisions. 42 U.S.C. § 6972 (RCRA); 42 U.S.C. § 9659 (CERCLA); 15 U.S.C. § 2619 (TSCA).

When citizens suing under these citizen-suit provisions are seeking civil penalties, the federal courts generally apply the five-year statute of limitations from 28 U.S.C. § 2462. See, e.g., Pub. Interest Research Group of N.J., Inc. v. Powell Duffryn Terminals Inc., 913 F.2d 64, 73–75 (3rd Cir.1990) (concluding that the five-year statute of limitations in 28 U.S.C. § 2462 applies to Clean Water Act citizen suits); Sierra Club v. Chevron USA, Inc., 834 F.2d 1517, 1522 (9th Cir.1987) (concluding that the five-year statute of limitations in 28 U.S.C. § 2462 applies to Clean Water Act citizen suits); Trawinski v. United Techs. Carrier Corp., 201 F.Supp.2d 1168, 1179–71 (N.D.Ala. 2002) (concluding that the five-year statute of limitations in 28 U.S.C. § 2462 applies to lawsuits brought pursuant to the Energy Policy and Conservation Act).

3. *The statute of limitations in a RCRA injunctive action.* The general federal statute of limitations, 28 U.S.C. § 2462, works fairly well for enforcement actions—whether by the EPA or by private citizens—that seek civil penalties. However, by its terms, this statute does not apply to lawsuits seeking purely injunctive relief, as can often be the case in RCRA citizen suits.

These kinds of RCRA citizen suits have actually generated a fair amount of statute of limitations consternation in the federal courts. As the U.S. District Court for the District of Maine discussed in 1998:

> In Count I, Plaintiff asserts a claim for injunctive relief pursuant to the citizen suit provision of RCRA, 42 U.S.C. § 6972(a)(1)(B). Under this provision, a private plaintiff may bring a civil claim against "any past or present generator, past or present transporter, or past or present owner or operator of a treatment, storage, or disposal facility, who has contributed or who is contributing to the past or present handling, storage, treatment, transportation, or disposal of any solid or hazardous waste *which may present an imminent and substantial endangerment to health or the environment*." 42 U.S.C. § 6972(a)(1)(B) (emphasis added). Defendant contends that it is entitled to summary judgment on this claim because Plaintiff's claim is barred by the statute of limitations and because Plaintiff has failed to establish that the Site may present "an imminent and substantial endangerment to health or the environment." Plaintiff moves for summary judgment on this claim on the basis that the Site currently presents an imminent and substantial endangerment. The Court is persuaded that neither party is entitled to summary judgment on this Count.

> * * *

RCRA itself does not contain a statute of limitations for citizen suits. Generally, where a federal statute provides no statute of limitations courts apply the "most closely analogous" state statute of limitations unless it would "frustrate or interfere with the implementation of federal policies," in which case courts apply a relevant federal limitations period. Defendant contends that either the federal five-year statute of limitations set forth in 28 U.S.C. § 2462, or Maine's six-year limitations period for civil actions set forth in 14 M.R.S.A. § 752 applies to this claim. Under either of these two periods, Defendant argues, Plaintiff's claim is barred. Plaintiff, relying on the Supreme Court's reasoning in *Meghrig v. KFC Western, Inc.,* 516 U.S. 479 (1996), responds that there is no applicable limitations period for a citizen suit under RCRA.

The Court finds Plaintiff's response persuasive. In *Meghrig,* the Supreme Court held that the citizen suit provision of RCRA does not provide a cause of action to recover the prior cost of cleaning up hazardous waste, when that waste does not pose an endangerment to health or the environment at the time the suit is brought. 516 U.S. at 481. The Court reasoned that RCRA's citizen suit provision "was designed to provide a remedy that ameliorates present or obviates the risk of future 'imminent' harms, not a remedy that compensates for past cleanup efforts." *Id.* at 486. The Court bolstered its holding by noting the differences between the enforcement provisions of RCRA and the cost recovery provisions of CERCLA, one difference being that "unlike CERCLA, RCRA contains no statute of limitations." *Id.*

While the *Meghrig* Court's observation that RCRA contains no statute of limitations was dicta, several district courts have relied on the Court's reasoning in concluding that there is no statute of limitations applicable to a RCRA cause of action. These courts have found the federal five-year limitations period set forth in 28 U.S.C. § 2462 inapplicable to a RCRA case such as this one which does not seek civil penalties, because section 2462 creates a limitations period "for the enforcement of any civil fine, penalty, or forfeiture," and a RCRA action "only seeking an order to compel other parties to help with clean-up is not akin to an action seeking a civil fine or penalty." *Nixon–Egli,* 949 F.Supp. at 1440; *see also A–C Reorganization Trust,* 968 F.Supp. at 427–28 (RCRA suits are primarily suits in equity). The Court is persuaded by the reasoning of these decisions, and finds that the timing of Plaintiff's RCRA action is controlled only by the requirement that the hazardous waste present "an imminent and substantial endangerment to the health or the environment."

Lefebvre v. Central Maine Power Co., 7 F.Supp.2d 64, 67–68 (D.Me.1998). How does this resolution strike you as a statute of limitations? In effect, this "statute of limitations" requires the federal courts to examine the merits of the RCRA lawsuit in order to figure out whether the plaintiff filed the case on time.

D. PREEMPTION AND STATUTES OF LIMITATIONS COMBINED: CERCLA'S FEDERALLY REQUIRED DISCOVERY DATE

Private lawsuits related to CERCLA cleanups are also subject to section 309 of CERCLA. CERCLA § 310(h), 42 U.S.C. § 9659(h). Section 309 changes the commencement date for any state statute of limitations for "any action brought under State law for personal injury, or property damages, which are caused or contributed to by exposure to any hazardous substance" to the federal discovery rule. CERCLA § 309(a)(1), (b)(4), 42 U.S.C.§ 9658(a)(1), (b)(4). Specifically, "if the applicable limitations period for such action [under state law] * * * provides a commencement date which is earlier than the federally required commencement date, such period shall commence at the federally required commencement date in lieu of the date specified in such State statute." Id. § 309(a)(1), 42 U.S.C. § 9658(a)(1).

In other words, Congress *preempted* the commencement rules in state statutes of limitations for state-law causes of action brought in connection with CERCLA releases of hazardous substances. The "federally required commencement date" is "the date the plaintiff knew (or reasonably should have known) that the personal injury or property damages * * * were caused or contributed to by the hazardous substance or pollutant or contaminant concerned." Id. § 309(b)(4), 42 U.S.C. § 9658(b)(4). Nevertheless, once the "federally required commencement date" is established, state law still dictates both the length of the limitations period and the causes of action that may be available to plaintiff. See, e.g., Freier v. Westinghouse Elec. Corp., 303 F.3d 176 (2d Cir. 2002) (discussing the availability of wrongful death, survival, and loss of consortium claims under New York law in connection with exposure to hazardous substances deposited in a landfill).

Consider the role of these CERCLA provisions as you read the following toxic tort case.

O'CONNOR v. BOEING NORTH AMERICAN, INC.

United States Court of Appeals for the Ninth Circuit, 2002.
311 F.3d 1139.

PAEZ, CIRCUIT JUDGE.

In 1997, Plaintiffs filed this action against Boeing North America, Inc. and Rockwell International Corporation ("Defendants"), alleging that hazardous radioactive and non-radioactive substances released from four nuclear and rocket testing facilities (the "Rocketdyne facilities") caused their latent illnesses. The district court granted summary judgment against Plaintiffs, ruling as a matter of law that California's one-year statute of limitations barred their state law tort claims. Plaintiffs appeal, asking us to determine when California's statute of limitations began to run on their claims.

Under the California statute of limitations, a plaintiff has one year from the date of injury to bring a personal injury or wrongful death claim. All of the Plaintiffs learned of their diagnoses more than one year before they filed suit. Unless Plaintiffs can show that delayed discovery of their claims warrants tolling of the statute of limitations, the one-year limit bars their claims.

To answer this question, we must decide whether the district court erred in declining to apply the delayed discovery rule of the Comprehensive Environmental Response, Compensation, and Liability Act of 1980 ("CERCLA") to Plaintiffs' claims that the release of hazardous substances caused their injuries. See 42 U.S.C. § 9658. CERCLA does not create a federal statute of limitations. Rather, it retains the state statute of limitations, and establishes a federal standard that governs when delayed discovery of a plaintiff's claims will toll the statute of limitations. This federal standard trumps a less generous state rule that would start the limitations period earlier. Thus, whether CERCLA applies here turns on whether CERCLA's federal standard is more generous than California law in tolling California's one-year statute of limitations.

* * *

BACKGROUND

A. The Parties

Plaintiffs are fifty-two persons who reside or in the past resided in the San Fernando Valley and Simi Valley regions (hereinafter "San Fernando Valley") of southern California. They have been diagnosed with a variety of cancers and other illnesses. These illnesses include cancers of the thyroid, brain, cervix, breast, lung, ovaries, bladder, prostate, pancreas, and stomach; leukemia; lymphoma; hypothyroidism; infertility; and multiple chemical sensitivity sensory neuropathy.

Defendants own or have operated the Rocketdyne facilities, located in Los Angeles and Ventura Counties. The Rocketdyne facilities have been in operation for more than fifty years. The federal government and private entities have used the facilities to conduct testing of rocket and energy technologies, including nuclear technologies. Plaintiffs alleged that testing at the facilities has involved various radioactive contaminants and non radioactive hazardous chemicals. Some Plaintiffs resided in close proximity to the Rocketdyne facilities; others lived miles away.

B. Proceedings Before the District Court

* * * On behalf of the personal injury and wrongful death plaintiffs, the Complaint alleges state tort claims of negligence, negligence per se, and strict liability for ultrahazardous activities. It also asserts a claim under the Price–Anderson Act, 42 U.S.C. § 2210, alleging injury from past nuclear accidents at the Rocketdyne facilities.

* * * All Plaintiffs alleged that they discovered their claims on September 11, 1997, when UCLA released the results of an epidemiological study concluding that employees at one of the four Rocketdyne facilities, the Santa Susana Field Laboratory ("SSFL"), were at an increased risk of contracting cancer.

On December 27, 1999, Defendants filed a motion for summary judgment on the ground that the statute of limitations barred all of Plaintiffs' claims. Plaintiffs countered that the one-year limitations period did not begin until September 1997 when news of the UCLA study alerted them to the connection between the Rocketdyne facilities and their illnesses, and that they filed their action within the year.

The district court granted Defendants' motion. It ruled that, as a matter of law, past publicity about releases of potentially hazardous substances from the Rocketdyne facilities should have led forty-eight of the fifty-two Plaintiffs to suspect prior to the release of the UCLA study that Defendants caused their injuries. * * *

DISCUSSION

The primary focus of this appeal concerns the district court's ruling that the statute of limitations barred Plaintiffs' claims because Plaintiffs filed their claims more than one year after discovering them. We review *de novo* the district court's summary judgment. We hold that the district court erred in concluding that the standard for discovery of claims under California law is the same as the federal standard under CERCLA. Because the California standard results in an earlier commencement date for the statute of limitations, the district court should have applied the federal standard.

Applying the federal standard, we reverse the district court's ruling that as a matter of law publicity about the Rocketdyne facilities was sufficient for a reasonable plaintiff to know that Defendants' actions were the cause of his or her injury. We conclude that there are genuine issues of material fact that a jury must resolve as to whether Plaintiffs should have known of their claims under the federal discovery standard. Finally, we affirm the summary judgment against thirty-four Plaintiffs because they failed to offer evidence sufficient to raise a triable issue of fact regarding how and when they discovered their claims.

I.

The district court's error here was twofold. First, the district court erred in concluding that the federal discovery rule under CERCLA governing commencement of limitations periods was equivalent to California's discovery rule, and in applying the California rule. Second, under CERCLA's discovery rule, summary judgment was improper because factual disputes remain over whether Plaintiffs knew or should have known of their claims more than a year before they filed them.

A. *CERCLA's Federal Commencement Rule Applies to Plaintiffs' State Tort Claims*

1. *The federally required commencement date preempts California's discovery rule*

The district court concluded that, in this case, the federal standard for discovery of claims was the same as the state standard, and under either standard, the limitations period would bar Plaintiffs' claims as a matter of law. "[B]ecause the accrual date would be the same under either rule," it reasoned, the "CERCLA discovery rule does not preempt the California discovery rule." We disagree. We hold that CERCLA preempts California's discovery rule and that the California limitations period did not commence until Plaintiffs knew or should have known of their claim.

2. *42 U.S.C. § 9658*

Section 9658 provides:

§ 9658. Actions under State law for damages from exposure to hazardous substances

(a) State statutes of limitations for hazardous substance cases

(1) Exception to State statutes

In the case of any action brought under State law for personal injury . . . which [is] caused or contributed to by exposure to any hazardous substance, or pollutant or contaminant, released into the environment from a facility, if the applicable limitations period for such action (as specified in the State statute of limitations or under common law) provides a commencement date which is earlier than the federally required commencement date, such period shall commence at the federally required commencement date in lieu of the date specified in such State statute.

The effect of this provision is to ensure that if a state statute of limitations provides a commencement date for claims of personal injury resulting from release of contaminants that is earlier than the commencement date defined in § 9658, then plaintiffs benefit from the more generous commencement date. Section 9658 defines the "federally required commencement date" for state limitations periods as "the date the plaintiff knew (or reasonably should have known) that the personal injury . . . w[as] caused or contributed to by the hazardous substance or pollutant or contaminant concerned." 42 U.S.C. § 9658(b)(4)(A).

Thus, § 9658 preempts California's commencement date if that date is earlier than the federally required commencement date. We must therefore determine whether the limitations period for Plaintiffs' claims would commence earlier under state law than under § 9658. If so, then we apply federal law. On the other hand, if the commencement date is later under state law than under federal law, or they are the same, we apply the state law standard. Here, because the federal standard under CERCLA is more generous than California law in tolling the statute of limitations when a plaintiff's discovery of her claims is delayed, the federal commencement date preempts California's discovery rule.

3. The discovery rule: Federal versus California standards

Because "it is inequitable to bar someone who has no idea he has been harmed from seeking redress, the statute of limitations has generally been tolled by the 'discovery rule.' " *Bibeau v. Pac. N.W. Research Found. Inc.*, 188 F.3d 1105, 1108 (9th Cir. 1999), amended by 208 F.3d 831 (9th Cir. 2000). Under both federal and California law, the discovery rule provides that a limitations period does not commence until a plaintiff discovers, or reasonably could have discovered, his claim. Because "[t]he plaintiff must be diligent in discovering the critical facts" a plaintiff who did not actually know of his claim will be barred "if he should have known [of it] in the exercise of due diligence." *Bibeau*, 188 F.3d at 1108. A plaintiff is "held to her actual knowledge as well as knowledge that could reasonably be discovered through investigation of sources open to her." *Jolly*, 245 Cal.Rptr. 658, 751 P.2d at 927. The concept of constructive notice is captured by the maxim that "the means of knowledge are the same thing in effect as knowledge itself." *Wood v. Carpenter*, 101 U.S. 135, 143 (1879).

In requiring actual or constructive knowledge of the cause of an injury before Plaintiffs can be deemed to be on notice of their claims, § 9658 invokes a formulation of the discovery rule that has been commonly applied in the federal courts. A plaintiff knows or reasonably should know of a claim when he or she knows "both the existence and the cause of his injury."

California courts have formulated the standard for determining when a plaintiff is on inquiry notice in a way that is fundamentally distinct from the federal standard set forth in § 9658. Under California law, a plaintiff discovers a claim when the plaintiff "suspects or should suspect that her injury was caused by wrongdoing." By its terms, § 9658 sets a later date for commencement of the limitations period, tolling the start of the period for filing claims beyond the date that a plaintiff suspects the cause of injury until the time that he or she knows or reasonably should have known of that cause.

Several federal courts have distinguished the federal knowledge standard from a standard that commences a limitations period when a plaintiff merely suspects the cause of injury, reasoning that the federal standard requires more than suspicion alone.

Conversely, under the California discovery rule, "the plaintiff discovers the cause of action when he at least suspects a factual basis, as opposed to a legal theory, for its elements, even if he lacks knowledge thereof." *Norgart*, 87 Cal.Rptr.2d 453, 981 P.2d at 88. The California Supreme Court disapproved an interpretation of the discovery rule that "require[s] that a plaintiff must do more than suspect a factual basis for

the elements of a cause of action in order to discover the cause of action."
Id. at 97 n. 8.

In sum, we reject an interpretation of the federal discovery rule that
would commence limitations periods upon mere suspicion of the elements
of a claim. Under the circumstances presented here, such a standard
would result in "the filing of preventative and often unnecessary claims,
lodged simply to forestall the running of the statute of limitations." We
seek to forestall such a "legal cascade." Because application of California's
suspicion standard would result in an earlier commencement date for the
one-year limitations period than the federal commencement date, we hold
that the federal discovery rule under § 9658 preempts the California rule.

> 4. *The absence of an underlying CERCLA claim does not preclude
>   application of the federal discovery rule*

Defendants contend that the federal standard for discovery of claims
does not apply to Plaintiffs' state tort claims because Plaintiffs, as
individuals, have not alleged an underlying CERCLA claim. We disagree.
Section 9658 applies to actions that assert state law claims without an
accompanying CERCLA claim.

Defendants' argument overlooks the plain language of § 9658. CERC-
LA's rule for commencement of state limitations periods applies to this
action because Plaintiffs allege claims "under State law" for personal
injury relating to environmental contaminants. Consistent with the explicit terms of § 9658(a), Plaintiffs have brought an "action ... for personal
injury ... which [is] caused or contributed to by exposure to any hazardous substance, or pollutant or contaminant, released into the environment
from a facility."

A "pollutant or contaminant" includes substances that "after release
into the environment and upon exposure ... may reasonably be anticipated to cause death, disease, ... [or] cancer." 42 U.S.C. § 9601(33). Many of
the substances that Plaintiffs allege were released from the Rocketdyne
facilities qualify as "pollutants" or "contaminants" and are likely "hazardous substances" as well. The allegations of the Complaint attribute
Plaintiffs' injuries to the "release" of such substances from "facilities,"
within CERCLA's definitions of those terms. Thus, by its terms, § 9658
applies to Plaintiffs' state law claims.

The legislative history of the Superfund Amendments and Reauthori-
zation Act of 1986 confirms this result. It indicates that, after receiving
recommendations concerning the inadequacy of state laws, Congress fully
intended § 9658 to alter the statute of limitations rules applicable to state
law claims, regardless of whether plaintiffs also asserted CERCLA claims.

> B. *Summary Judgment Was Improper Under the Federal "Knew (or
>   Reasonably Should Have Known)"*

Summary judgment is proper only if there are no genuine issues of
material fact in dispute and Defendants are entitled to judgment as a
matter of law. Fed. R. Civ. P. 56(c). * * *

Because Plaintiffs have the burden of proof at trial to establish that they are entitled to the benefit of the discovery rule, to defeat summary judgment they were required to come forward with evidence establishing a triable issue of fact with regard to whether the discovery rule applies. Summary judgment was improper here unless the only reasonable inference that can be drawn is that Plaintiffs knew or should have known more than one year before filing their claims that the Rocketdyne contamination was the cause of their diseases.

Review of the record does not lead inexorably to a single inference that Plaintiffs knew or suspected the cause of their injuries more than one year before filing their claims. Courts routinely recognize the "fact-intensive nature" of the determination of when a plaintiff is on notice of a claim. Critical factual disputes that govern when Plaintiffs knew or should have known of their claims preclude summary judgment here.

A two-part analysis determines whether Plaintiffs reasonably should have known of their claim. The goal of this analysis is to evaluate when a reasonable person would have connected his or her symptoms to their alleged cause. First, we consider whether a reasonable person in Plaintiffs' situation would have been expected to inquire about the cause of his or her injury. [*Bibeau*, 188 F.3d at 1109.] Second, if the plaintiff was on inquiry notice, "we must next determine whether [an inquiry] would have disclosed the nature and cause of plaintiff's injury so as to put him on notice of his claim." *Id.* The plaintiff will be charged with knowledge of facts that he would have discovered through inquiry.

1. *Inquiry notice*

The initial step focuses on whether a plaintiff could reasonably have been expected to make an inquiry in the first place. Particularly when a plaintiff has cancer, the answer to this question may depend on whether there are a number of potential causes. * * *

* * *

Thus, whether Plaintiffs knew or should have known that the contamination from the Rocketdyne facilities caused their injuries depends on whether a reasonable person would have inquired about the cause of his injury in light of public knowledge about the causes of cancer and other latent diseases, including publicity about the release of hazardous substance from the Rocketdyne facilities as well as other potential causes. We conclude that summary judgment was improper because the evidence was susceptible to more than one inference regarding whether Plaintiffs were aware of more than one potential cause of their illnesses. Factual disputes remain regarding whether Plaintiffs should have inquired about whether the contamination from the Rocketdyne facilities, rather than any other source, was connected to their illnesses.

More than one inference can be drawn whether, prior to the UCLA study, Plaintiffs should have inquired about a causal link between their illnesses and the Rocketdyne contamination. The medical advice that

Plaintiffs received from their doctors and publicity about potential causes of cancer reasonably could have led Plaintiffs to suspect that their illnesses resulted from causes unrelated to the Rocketdyne contamination. * * *

Moreover, to substantiate Plaintiffs' contention that a genuine issue of material fact exists whether they were on inquiry notice that the Rocketdyne facilities were the cause of their illnesses, Plaintiffs introduced evidence of extensive publicity between 1989 and 1996 warning that a variety of products–from tobacco, pesticides and diesel fuel to peanut butter, nail polish, cellular telephones and radar guns–were potential causes of cancer. They also presented a profusion of public notices from local businesses disclosing the use of a variety of carcinogens.

* * *

In support of summary judgment and to counter Plaintiffs' statements that they had limited knowledge of publicity about possible contamination from the Rocketdyne facilities, Defendants introduced numerous news articles and publicly available documents that demonstrate that there has been unease about the Rocketdyne facilities for decades. Defendants documented the level of community concern from reports of releases of potentially hazardous substances at the Rocketdyne facilities.

The district court committed two errors in concluding that publicity about the Rocketdyne facilities put Plaintiffs on notice of a connection between their illnesses and releases from Defendants' facilities. First, it improperly made a factual finding that publicity about the Rocketdyne facilities was sufficiently notorious to impute Plaintiffs with knowledge of it. Second, it erroneously concluded that the only reasonable inference to be drawn from that publicity was that Plaintiffs should have suspected a connection to the Rocketdyne contamination.

a. Notoriety of news reports about the contamination

The district court erred in concluding as a matter of law that newspaper reports concerning the Defendants' facilities were sufficiently "numerous and notorious" to impute knowledge of them to Plaintiffs. The district court held that a "reasonable, prudent subscriber" of newspapers in the area, and a "reasonably diligent person living in the area for a substantial period of time between" 1989 and 1991 would have become aware of the release of contaminants from SSFL.

This evaluation of the awareness in Plaintiffs' various communities of a specific fact or event was uniquely an issue for the jury to resolve. * * *

b. Reasonable inferences regarding causation from publicity about Rocketdyne

Even if Plaintiffs should have been aware of publicity about the Rocketdyne facilities, reasonable inferences conflict about whether that publicity would have put Plaintiffs on inquiry notice more than one year before filing their claims that contamination from the Rocketdyne facilities caused their illnesses. Plaintiffs contend, in effect, that it is unreasonable to infer on summary judgment that they should have inquired about whether the contamination caused their diseases until the results of the UCLA study became public. We agree.

To reach the conclusion that Plaintiffs had discovered their claims prior to the limitations period, the district court imputed to Plaintiffs knowledge of media coverage of contamination in the vicinity of the Rocketdyne facilities. The district court's ruling emphasizes that, particularly in the early 1980s and from the late 1980s to the early 1990s, two periods in which public scrutiny seems to have been most intense, there were a number of reports of "contamination" from the Rocketdyne Facilities and the "issue of contamination" was discussed in articles and public meetings. The district court also relied on news reports of various studies undertaken to shed light on the health effects, if any, of the releases from the Rocketdyne facilities. The court imputed to some Plaintiffs knowledge of a 1989 Department of Energy ("DOE") report concluding that "there were contamination problems at SSFL," and to others knowledge of a 1990 California Department of Health Services ("DHS") report "suggesting a possible connection between Rocketdyne facilities and increased cancer in the surrounding communities."

The reports of contamination and Defendants' potential wrongdoing were insufficient to place Plaintiffs on inquiry notice of their claims. Whether Plaintiffs would have suspected on the basis of these media reports that Defendants' contamination caused their injuries, in light of the evidence that the parties presented, is fundamentally a question of fact.

The studies that the district court relied on in granting summary judgment illustrate the fact-intensive nature of the causation question. The 1989 DOE report summarized its findings:

> The Survey found no environmental problems at SSFL that represent an immediate threat to human life. The preliminary findings identified by the Survey do indicate that a few areas are actual or potential sources of soil and/or groundwater contamination and that inadequacies in the ground-water monitoring system make it difficult to characterize the nature and extent of contamination.

> The environmental problems described in this report vary in terms of their magnitude and risk. *A complete understanding of the significance of some of the environmental problems identified requires a level of study and characterization that is beyond the scope of the Survey.*

(emphasis added). Moreover, the DOE team did not purport to study health problems in surrounding communities. The 1990 DHS study similarly reported that the observed cancer incidence rates may have resulted from factors not related to exposure to the waste site and acknowledged that those factors could not be evaluated with the data then available.

A 1999 "Preliminary Site Evaluation" of the SSFL by the Agency for Toxic Substances and Disease Registry (hereinafter, *1999 ATSDR Study*) emphasized that identifying evidence of "contamination" by substances that have potential health effects is only a preliminary step in assessing actual health effects. * * *

* * *

The evidence of publicity that the district court relied on did not connect these dots. None of the publicity from this period suggested that available evidence established contamination from the Rocketdyne facilities as the likely cause, among many possible causes, of public health problems. The media reports and expressions of community concern about the contamination were, at best, equivocal about such a link.

Two aspects of the publicity stand out. First, numerous documents identify as the primary basis of community concern the *lack* of public knowledge about the activities at the Rocketdyne facilities, about the level of contamination from the facilities, and about community health consequences. Second, to the extent that the documents draw conclusions–other than conclusions about the subjective fear caused by the Rocketdyne facilities–it is that further study was needed to draw any responsible conclusions.

Articles about the early studies of the health effects of the contamination sent mixed messages. The media reported that the 1989 DOE study had found no evidence of an immediate health threat and emphasized that further tests were needed. A news report on the 1990 DHS study stated that there was "no evidence of a health threat to workers or the public." In contrast, the 1997 UCLA study sought to resolve these questions with respect to the health of Rocketdyne employees. DHS commissioned the study to determine whether workers at SSFL experienced excessive mortality from cancer as a result of work-related exposures to radiation. For the first time, the study reported an "observed positive relationship between external radiation and lung cancer mortality," as well as increasing trends in mortality rates for other categories of cancers.

Assuming Plaintiffs had seen the media reports, one reasonable inference is that, until learning of UCLA's findings, Plaintiffs relied on the public statements that there was no immediate health threat to the community. Moreover, the evidence Plaintiffs submitted of publicity surrounding numerous suspected causes of cancer not related to the Rocketdyne facilities permits the inference that a reasonable plaintiff would have imputed the cause of his or her illness to commonly-known sources other than the Rocketdyne facilities.

Thus, the record supports conflicting inferences about whether Plaintiffs were on inquiry notice that the contamination caused their diseases. It does not establish that Plaintiffs were aware that releases from the Rocketdyne facilities were the likely cause, among other causes, of their injuries. These issues of fact are the province of the jury.

2. *Whether a reasonable inquiry would have put Plaintiffs on notice of their claim*

The second prong of the test for application of the discovery rule is whether a reasonable inquiry would have put Plaintiffs on notice of their claim. This second step focuses on whether, if the Plaintiffs had inquired about the cause of their illnesses, the result of that inquiry would have provided Plaintiffs with knowledge of the connection between the injury and its cause. Here, too, a plaintiff who has cancer may not have the means to test which, if any, of the possible causes have a substantive basis so as to put the plaintiff on notice of the claim * * *.

Even if Plaintiffs were on inquiry notice of the cause of their illnesses, genuine issues of material fact preclude summary judgment on this second prong. The evidence conflicts as to when Plaintiffs had the means to test the potential causes of their diseases in a way that would "disclose[] the nature and cause" of their injuries so as to put them on notice of their claims. The parties dispute whether Plaintiffs had the means to discover, prior to the UCLA study, that contamination at the Rocketdyne facilities caused their illnesses.

If Plaintiffs could not have discovered that Defendants caused their injuries prior to the study's release despite duly inquiring, then they timely filed their claims. * * * Under these circumstances, involving latent diseases allegedly resulting from exposure to toxins, if Plaintiffs could not discern which among many possible suspected causes was the likely cause of their illnesses, the statute of limitations is tolled. An average plaintiff alleging a connection between latent disease and exposure to hazardous substances does not have the means to conduct the type of comprehensive epidemiological study necessary to bridge the causation gap. * * * Because material issues of fact exist regarding when, under the federal discovery rule, Plaintiffs knew or should have known that Defendants' contamination caused their injuries, the district court erred in concluding that Plaintiffs had discovered all of the essential facts constituting their cause of action prior to release of the 1997 UCLA study. Plaintiffs are therefore entitled to a jury's determination of the factual issues underlying the application of the discovery rule. A jury must decide (1) whether to impute knowledge of the contamination to Plaintiffs, (2) whether the Plaintiffs were on inquiry notice that the Rocketdyne facilities were the likely cause of Plaintiffs' illnesses, and (3) when Plaintiffs had the means to discover the facts to support their claim.

      * * *

CONCLUSION

The district court's summary judgment against those Plaintiffs who filed their claims after the release of the 1997 UCLA Study is REVERSED and REMANDED for further proceedings consistent with this opinion.
* * *

      * * *

NOTES AND QUESTIONS

1. *California's statute of limitations and CERCLA.* As the Ninth Circuit noted, California purportedly uses a discovery rule in its statute of limitations. Why did CERCLA's discovery rule still preempt California's discovery rule? Which was more advantageous to the plaintiffs, and why?

2. *CERCLA preemption in the absence of a CERCLA claim.* The defendants in *O'Connor* argued that CERCLA's discovery rule should not apply in a case that did not include a CERCLA claim. Why did the Ninth Circuit decide otherwise? Do you agree with its reading of CERCLA? Why or why not?

3. A defendant releases a hazardous substance into the air, but does not contaminate the property where the release occurs. If an individual is harmed by the release, would this court permit him to rely on section 9658 to defeat a less generous state discovery rule? Are there any limits to the applicability of this section as long as plaintiff is injured by a hazardous substance? See Barnes ex rel. Estate of Barnes v. Koppers, Inc., 534 F.3d 357 (5th Cir.2008).

4. *The statute of limitations and causation.* As you have learned from other parts of this casebook, proving causation in a toxic tort lawsuit can be quite difficult. How did the causation problem become relevant in *O'Connor*, even in the statute of limitations context?

5. *Other intersections of CERCLA and toxic torts.* Adjudication of CERCLA liability can often help plaintiffs bringing pendant state-law causes of action, especially if those state-law actions are also strict liability offenses. For example, in Scribner v. Summers, 84 F.3d 554 (2d Cir.1996), the defendant's previously-determined liability under CERCLA for releases of barium chloride supported the plaintiff's claims for property damages based on trespass and private nuisance.

6. Suppose an individual suffering from cancer sees the UCLA study but waits more than a year to bring a claim against defendants. What result if the defendants once again raise a statute of limitations defense? Does it matter what type of cancer the individual suffers from?

7. Does section 9658 have any effect on the application of a state statute of repose? See Clark County v. Sioux Equip. Corp. 753 N.W.2d 406 (S.D.2008) (holding that the answer is no).

CHAPTER XI

APPORTIONMENT AMONG
MULTIPLE PARTIES

■ ■ ■

You may recall from your first-year Torts course that under the old contributory negligence regime that existed in most American states until the 1970s, plaintiffs who were in any way negligent were barred from recovery. Moreover, when a case did involve multiple defendants, they were nearly always jointly and severally liable for all of plaintiff's damages. As we saw in the *Dafler* case in Chapter 4, p. 281, courts sometimes causally apportioned liability among defendants or between defendants and plaintiff. If, however, a court determined that an injury was indivisible and could not be apportioned along the lines set forth in section 433A in the Second Restatement of Torts, see pp. 287–88 supra, and if the jurisdiction permitted any allocation among defendants, then apportionment among defendants was on a pro rata basis. If there were two defendants, each was assigned 50% of the liability. If there were three, each was assigned 33% of the liability. There really wasn't any other choice. There was no mechanism in place for juries to apportion liability based on culpability or responsibility.[1] Note that in nearly all situations, defendants were jointly and severally liable to the non-negligent plaintiff. Thus the apportionment issue was solely a question of contribution among defendants. Joseph W. Glannon, Liability of Multiple Tortfeasors in Massachusetts: The Related Doctrines of Joint and Several Liability, Comparative Negligence and Contribution, 85 Mass.L.Rev. 50 (2000). In many jurisdictions, even this was not permitted. See Gus M. Hodges, Contribution and Indemnity among Tortfeasors, 26 Tex.L.Rev. 150 (1947).

The movement to comparative responsibility changed all of this. Juries were now asked to allocate responsibility among defendants, plaintiffs, and often settling parties and others as well.[2] The result was that

---

1. The courts did have at their disposal a few devices, such as the concepts of primary and secondary negligence, that they could employ to deal with some of the potential inequities produced by this system.

2. See, e.g., Vernon Texas Civil Practice and Remedy Code § 33.003.

Determination of Percentage of Responsibility.

courts now had two separate ways of allocating liability: causation and comparative responsibility. The Third Restatement of Torts: Apportionment of Liability has the following to say about the relationship between comparative causation and comparative responsibility:

> No party should be liable for harm it did not cause, and an injury caused by two or more persons should be apportioned according to their respective shares of comparative responsibility. Sometimes these policies converge, but sometimes they conflict. They must be tempered with two additional considerations. A working system must be capable of being understood and applied by courts and juries in a reasonably efficient manner, and available evidence sometimes leaves uncertainty that the legal regime must accommodate.

Restatement (Third) of Torts: Apportionment of Liability § 26 cmt. a (2000).

In Chapter 4, we addressed situations in which courts chose to apportion liability based on causation. In this Chapter, we address apportionment based on responsibility. The cases that follow reflect the Third Restatement's observation that methods of apportionment sometimes converge and at other times conflict.

A. PLAINTIFF CONDUCT

OWENS CORNING FIBERGLAS CORP. v. PARRISH

Supreme Court of Kentucky, 2001.
58 S.W.3d 467.

KELLER, JUSTICE.

I. ISSUES

These asbestos product liability cases, which the circuit court consolidated for trial, present two issues for our consideration.

Parrish and Coyle sought damages from asbestos-manufacturer Owens Corning Fiberglas Corporation ("Owens Corning"), after they allegedly contracted asbestosis, a respiratory disease caused by the inhalation of asbestos fibers. But, while Appellees sought recovery only for their alleged asbestosis, the trial court allowed the jury to consider Appellees' smoking histories in determining their comparative fault. The jury consequently

---

(a) The trier of fact, as to each cause of action asserted, shall determine the percentage of responsibility, stated in whole numbers, for the following persons with respect to each person's causing or contributing to cause in any way the harm for which recovery of damages is sought, whether by negligent act or omission, by any defective or unreasonably dangerous product, by other conduct or activity that violates an applicable legal standard, or by any combination of these:

    (1) each claimant;

    (2) each defendant;

    (3) each settling person; and

    (4) each responsible third party who has been designated under Section 33.004.

allocated fifty (50%) percent of the total fault to each Appellee. Since smoking was a separate cause of harm to Appellees, were these comparative fault instructions appropriate? Because the evidence showed that Appellees' inhalation of asbestos fibers and their smoking combined to produce a single indivisible harm—lung impairment and shortness of breath—we hold that the trial court properly allowed the jury to determine Appellees' comparative fault.

Before trial, Parrish settled an asbestos-based worker's compensation claim with his employer, Louisville Water Company ("LWC"). While LWC never became a party to Parrish's lawsuit, the trial court included LWC within its comparative fault instructions and the jury found LWC responsible for ten percent (10%) of Parrish's damages. Should the trial court have allowed apportionment against LWC? Because the settlement of this asbestos-related worker's compensation claim was tantamount to a settlement with a nonparty against whom a claim has been asserted, we hold that the trial court properly allowed the jury to apportion fault against LWC.

II. FACTS

Parrish and Coyle filed separate actions against asbestos manufacturer Owens Corning and numerous other defendants seeking compensatory and punitive damages for injuries that they claimed to have suffered from repeated workplace exposure to asbestos. Each Appellee sought damages for asbestosis and its resulting shortness of breath and for their increased future risk of developing cancer. Before trial, all defendants except Owens Corning either settled or were dismissed as parties. The trial court then, appropriately, consolidated the cases for trial.

The medical evidence at trial established that the lung disease asbestosis is caused solely by exposure to asbestos, is characterized by the primary symptom of shortness of breath, and, as a progressive disease, may eventually result in death by suffocation. Even though the disease asbestosis itself cannot cause cancer, inhalation of asbestos fibers may increase the risk of lung cancer in other ways, especially when combined with the synergistic effect of smoking. The evidence further established that both Parrish and Coyle had regularly smoked tobacco products and that their past smoking also may have caused harm to their lungs, resulting in shortness of breath, and placed them at an increased risk for cancer.

Other evidence showed that Parrish, while employed with LWC and working with asbestos, did not consistently wear a protective mask. In his defense, Parrish testified that his employer did not offer him a mask until late in his career and that even then he could not wear a mask for long before the mask's filters would become clogged with dust and he would have to remove it.

* * *

At the end of a several-day trial, the jury returned verdicts:

- finding that both Parrish and Coyle "were exposed to asbestos-containing products manufactured" by Appellant Owens Corning and were "thereby caus[ed] ... to contract an asbestos-related disease;"

- awarding Parrish and Coyle damages of $55,000.00 each;[4]

- finding that Parrish and Coyle each violated his general duty "to exercise that degree of care for his own health and safety as expected of a reasonably prudent person;" and

- allocating fault for the damages awarded Parrish and Coyle as follows:[5]

AS TO COYLE:	
Coyle	50%
Owens–Illinois, Inc.	25%
Owens Corning	25%
AS TO PARRISH:	
Parrish	50%
Owens–Illinois, Inc	20%
Owens Corning	20%
Louisville Water Co.	10%

* * *

Parrish and Coyle appealed these judgments to the Court of Appeals and contested the jury's finding that they shared the fault for their conditions. They argued that the trial court improperly allowed the jury to allocate fault to them on the basis of their smoking histories and, in Parrish's case, because of his failure to wear a mask when working with

---

4. The jury awarded Coyle and Parrish $50,000 each for future pain and suffering and, as a separate element of damages, $5,000 each for an "increased likelihood of contracting cancer." The trial court should not have instructed the jury regarding this increased risk of future harm as a separate element of damages, and should have allowed the jury to consider this increased risk only in assessing damages for future pain and suffering. *Capital Holding Corp. v. Bailey,* Ky., 873 S.W.2d 187, 195 (1994) ("A recovery for an increased risk of future harm, when such risk is established as a reasonable likelihood, is not a new element of damages but proof that the jury should consider in compensating for future physical pain and mental suffering, for future impairment or destruction of earning power, and, if there is evidence to support it, for future medical expenses." *Id.*). The parties do not raise this improper, separate damage award for the increase of future harm as an issue in this appeal.

5. In addition to the fault of Owens Corning and LWC and the comparative fault of either Parrish or Coyle, the trial court's comparative fault instructions also allowed the jury to allocate fault among all dismissed parties, nonparties that had settled with either Parrish or Coyle and even one party who had never been named a party to the lawsuit and had not settled with either Coyle or Parrish. The jury apportioned fault against one of these parties, Owens–Illinois, Inc. We first note that the instructions should not have permitted the jury to allocate fault to a nonsettling nonparty. KRS 411.182; *Baker v. Webb,* Ky. App., 883 S.W.2d 898 (1994). Next, we note that the instructions did not require the jury to find *any* fault on the part of the dismissed parties or settling nonparties before it allocated a percentage of the total fault to them. Fault may not be properly allocated to a party, a dismissed party or settling nonparty unless the court or the jury first finds that the party was at fault; otherwise, the party has no fault to allocate. KRS 411.182. The mere fact that a party has been sued or has settled does not permit the factfinder to allocate part of the total fault to that party. As the instructions required no finding of fault on the part of the dismissed parties and settling nonparties included in the apportionment instructions, they were incorrect.

asbestos. Parrish also contested the jury's apportionment of fault to his employer and argued that fault may be apportioned only against an employer who is a party to the action.

The Court of Appeals held that, with respect to Appellees' asbestosis claims, the trial court erred when it allowed the jury to consider either Appellee's smoking or Parrish's failure to wear a mask as comparative fault. The Court of Appeals also found reversible error in the trial court's instructions allowing the jury to apportion fault to Parrish's employer. Accordingly, the Court of Appeals reversed the judgments of the Jefferson Circuit Court and remanded the cases for retrial. We find no error by the trial court with respect to either issue before this Court and reverse the decision of the Court of Appeals.

III. COMPARATIVE FAULT INSTRUCTIONS

* * *

When this Court first established comparative fault as part of the common law, the statutory contributory negligence provisions of Kentucky's Product Liability Act barred a plaintiff from recovery when that plaintiff was negligent in his or her use of the product. But the legislature * * * removed this vestige of contributory fault when it codified comparative fault:

(1) In all tort actions, *including products liability actions*, involving fault of more than one party to the action, including third-party defendants and persons who have been released under subsection (4) of this section, the court, unless otherwise agreed by all parties, shall instruct the jury to answer interrogatories or, if there is no jury, shall make findings indicating:

(a) The amount of damages each claimant would be entitled to recover if contributory fault is disregarded; and

(b) The percentage of the total fault of all the parties to each claim that is allocated to each claimant, defendant, third-party defendant, and person who has been released from liability under subsection (4) of this section.

(2) In determining the percentages of fault, the trier of fact shall consider both the nature of the conduct of each party at fault and the extent of the causal relation between the conduct and the damages claimed.

(3) The court shall determine the award of damages to each claimant in accordance with the findings, subject to any reduction under subsection (4) of this section, and shall determine and state in the judgment each party's equitable share of the obligation to each claimant in accordance with the respective percentages of fault.

(4) A release, covenant not to sue, or similar agreement entered into by a claimant and a person liable, shall discharge that person from all liability for contribution, but it shall not be considered to discharge

any other persons liable upon the same claim unless it so provides. However, the claim of the releasing person against other persons shall be reduced by the amount of the released persons' equitable share of the obligation, determined in accordance with the provisions of this section. * * *

* * *

Appellees correctly submit that the undisputed medical evidence established that exposure to asbestos fibers is the sole cause of asbestosis and that smoking alone can never result in asbestosis. They further observe correctly that, because Appellees' complaints sought damages only for their exposure to "asbestos-containing products," the trial court's instructions limited any award of damages accordingly. Therefore, they posit that the trial court's instructions should not have permitted the jury to apportion fault to them for conduct which caused other, distinct injuries. We disagree with this conclusion.

While asbestosis is a restrictive disease of the lungs, and smoking causes distinct obstruction pulmonary diseases, e.g., emphysema or bronchitis, the trial evidence established that Appellees' exposure to asbestos and their smoking combined to produce a single result or harm, i.e., decreased lung function manifesting itself in shortness of breath. Appellees did not introduce sufficient evidence in this case[27] to allow the factfinder a logical and reasonable basis to apportion this single harm—shortness of breath—between those separate causes. In fact, the medical experts made no attempt to do so.[29] Thus, while Appellees' exposure to asbestos and their smoking are distinct causes, they did not produce either distinct harms or a single harm capable of apportionment between the distinct causes. The trial evidence did not permit the jury to determine the proportion of lung impairment caused exclusively by Appellees' asbestos exposure or exclusively by Appellees' smoking and, consequently, the jury had no basis to apportion Appellee's lung impairment damages between the two causes.[30] An apportionment of damages in this case between the

---

27. One court, however, has suggested that there may be a basis for an apportionment of damages between asbestosis and smoking caused diseases. *Rothermel v. Owen Illinois, Inc.*, 24 Phila. 332, 16 Pa. D. & C.4th 20 (Common Pleas Ct. of Philadelphia Co., 1992) ("Although they have an additive effect, asbestos exposure causes asbestosis, which is a restrictive disease; and cigarette smoking, causes emphysema or bronchitis, which are obstructive diseases. They are separate diseases and can be measured separately." *Id.* at 336.). The evidence in this case, however, provided no basis, scientific or inferential, for separate measurements.

29. The parties presented diametrically opposed medical testimony as to the cause of Appellees' shortness of breath. Appellees' experts testified that the shortness of breath resulted from asbestosis while Owens Corning's experts testified that Appellants did not suffer from asbestosis and that the symptoms stemmed solely from their obesity and smoking habits.

30. * * * *Kalland v. North American Van Lines*, 716 F.2d 570 (9th Cir.1983) ("When it is practically impossible to decide which tortfeasors caused the determinate injuries, an injury must be treated as indivisible even if we know that different tortfeasors probably caused different parts of it." *Id.* at 573.); *Ingram v. ACandS, Inc.*, 977 F.2d 1332 (9th Cir.1992) (holding that it was proper to submit the issue of the plaintiff's comparative fault to the jury, where the plaintiff sought damages only for asbestosis since "[t]he damages for Ingram's lung impairment could not be apportioned between his cigarette smoking and his exposure to asbestos." *Id.* at 1342).

separate causes would have constituted little more than improper jury speculation or conjecture.

Because no apportionment between the separate causes of this shortness of breath, i.e., asbestosis exposure and smoking, was possible, the trial court acted within its discretion when it allowed the jury to consider Appellees' smoking as comparative fault.

To summarize, if distinct causes produce distinct harms, or if distinct causes produce a single harm and the evidence presented at trial provides a reasonable basis for determining the contribution of each cause to the single harm, a trial court should instruct the jury to apportion the damages to the distinct causes without resorting to comparative fault. If, however, as is the case here, the evidence does not permit apportionment of the damage between separate causes, then comparative fault principles apply, and the trial court should instruct the jury to apportion damages according to the proportionate fault of the parties. Accordingly, we hold that the trial judge properly submitted comparative fault instructions and thereby allowed the jury to assign fault to Appellees based upon their smoking histories.

We also agree with Owens Corning's contention that the evidence concerning Parrish's failure to wear a safety mask provided by his employer sufficiently warranted the trial court's comparative fault instruction. Undisputed evidence proved that only the inhalation of asbestos fibers can cause asbestosis. Thus, simple logic permits the inference that Parrish's failure to utilize the safety mask and prevent further inhalation of asbestos fibers may have contributed to his asbestosis. While Parrish's testimony offered several reasons for his failure or refusal to wear a safety mask, the trial court appropriately allowed the jury to evaluate this testimony when determining the reasonableness of Parrish's failure or refusal to wear the safety mask.

IV. APPORTIONMENT OF FAULT TO LOUISVILLE WATER COMPANY

Owens Corning asserts that, based on the evidence, the jury's apportionment of ten (10%) percent of the fault for Parrish's damages to LWC was proper pursuant to the Comparative Fault Statute. Parrish responds that, since LWC never became a party to Parrish's lawsuit, the trial court improperly allowed the jury to apportion fault to LWC. We disagree with Parrish's position.

Kentucky's Comparative Fault Statute expressly provides for apportionment against a person settling with a claimant * * *.

* * *

Thus, if supported by the evidence, proper instructions may allow the jury to apportion fault against a settling nonparty, and a settlement, between an employer and employee, of a claim under the Workers' Compensation Act constitutes a settlement under KRS 411.182(4). We therefore hold that the trial court appropriately submitted a comparative fault instruction as to LWC.

For the reasons outlined above, we reverse the decision of the Court of Appeals and reinstate the judgments of the Jefferson Circuit Court.

NOTES AND QUESTIONS

1. Why did the *Parrish* court eschew the alternative of distributing liability based on causation? Recall that in *Dafler v. Ramark Industries*, p. 281 supra, the court did call upon the jury to allocate liability based on causation. How do the facts in *Parrish* differ from the facts in *Dafler*?

2. Kentucky's comparative fault statute closely parallels the Uniform Comparative Fault Act. In one important respect, however, it adopts a different course. The Act provides for joint and several liability for all parties found to be responsible for an indivisible injury. Uniform Comparative Fault Act § 2. The Kentucky statute has, by and large, abolished joint and several liability. With the abolition of joint and several liability, what practical differences exist between apportionment on the basis of causation and apportionment under KRS 411.182?

3. Kentucky adopts a minority position with respect to whether plaintiff's employer may be assigned a percentage of liability in a common law tort suit. See the notes following *Lindquist v. City of Jersey City Fire Department*, p. 393 supra; Andrew R. Klein, Apportionment of Liability in Workplace Injury Cases, 26 Berkeley J.Emp. & Lab.L. 65 (2005).

B. APPORTIONMENT AMONG DEFENDANTS

1. COMPARATIVE RESPONSIBILITY

In hindsight, the movement from contributory negligence to comparative fault in the 1970s was one of the most fundamental tort law developments in the twentieth century. The primary impetus for the change was the perceived harshness of the contributory negligence rule, but the effects reached much further. Suddenly, juries were asked to make fault allocations among multiple parties, including entities such as settling parties that were not in the courtroom at the time of the trial. The wave of change unmoored many other seemingly secure tort rules, including joint and several liability, the last clear chance doctrine, assumption of the risk, and the collateral source rule. Moreover, most of these changes were accomplished through legislation, which had the effect of codifying substantial swaths of tort law that had up until then been part of the common law. The result is that there is no longer a single approach to apportionment. One must look to the statute in each state to know how liability will be apportioned. Among the many state-to-state differences, three stand out: whether the state adopts modified or pure comparative responsibility; the state's approach to joint and several liability; and the state's definition of what it is to be comparatively responsible.

a. Pure or Modified Comparative Responsibility

Most state statutes adopt a "modified comparative responsibility" regime. Plaintiff is permitted to recover until her share of assigned responsibility rises above some threshold. Once the threshold is exceeded, plaintiff is barred from recovery. The most popular threshold is the so-called Wisconsin formula. Plaintiff can recover part of her damages as long as her percentage of responsibility is not greater than 50%. See Iowa Code Ann. § 668.3. Some states bar recovery if plaintiff's liability is 50% or greater. See Colo. Rev. Stat. 13–21–111(1).

A minority of states have a "pure comparative responsibility" regime. Plaintiff may recover some damages as long as he is not assigned all the responsibility for an accident. Arguments for and against each approach may be found in state supreme court opinions that have adopted each alternative. See Hoffman v. Jones, 280 So.2d 431 (Fla.1973)(justifying pure comparative responsibility); Bradley v. Appalachian Power Co., 163 W.Va. 332, 256 S.E.2d 879 (1979)(justifying modified comparative responsibility).

b. Joint and Several Liability

Prior to the move to comparative responsibility, joint and several liability for each defendant was the norm. Plaintiffs could recover all their damages from any defendant. In a contributory negligence world, the moral justification for this rule is easy to see. Any plaintiff who could recover anything was by definition not negligent. Thus it seemed logical that plaintiff should be able to receive full compensation from any defendant and leave the question of contribution, if any, to be thrashed out among defendants. However, with the advent of comparative responsibility, many prevailing plaintiffs were not without fault themselves. Moreover, even when this was not the case, to some it seemed unfair that a defendant who was found to be marginally responsible for an injury should be burdened with joint and several liability and the attendant possibility that some other defendants might be judgement-proof and, therefore, unable to contribute their fair share to plaintiff's damages.

As noted in the Third Restatement of Torts: Apportionment of Liability, states have adopted five broad approaches to deal with the liability of independent tortious conduct of two or more entities that are the legal cause of an indivisible injury:

A.   Full joint and several liability against those defendants for whom the jury has assessed some responsibility. Plaintiff may recover his entire damages from any defendant who must then seek contribution from other defendants.

B.   Several liability only for all defendants. Plaintiff may recover from each defendant only that percentage of his damages assigned to that defendant by the fact finder.

C.   Joint and several liability with reallocation. Independent tortfeasors are jointly and severally liable. However, if one of the tortfeasors is insolvent and, therefore, unable to contribute her share, the short-fall is reallocated to all responsible parties in proportion to their relative share of responsibility. For example, assume a jury assigns 1/3 of the responsibility for an accident to plaintiff and 1/3 to each of two defendants. If one of defendants is judgment-proof, the court would reallocate this share among the remaining parties, in this case between plaintiff and the remaining defendant. Because, as between the two of them, they are equally responsible, the reallocation would require that the remaining defendant make up half of the shortfall and plaintiff would go uncompensated for the other half. The Restatement expresses support for this alternative, but it has not been widely adopted.

D.   Joint and several liability is imposed on independent tortfeasors whose percentage of comparative responsibility exceeds a specified threshold. Tortfeasors assigned a percentage of comparative responsibility below the threshold are severally liable, while those at or above the threshold are jointly and severally liable. This is perhaps the plurality position in the states. The most common threshold is 50%. A few states have set the bar even higher. See New Jersey Stat. 2A:15–5.3(c)(60%). The result is that when there are multiple tortfeasors it is likely that no defendant will be assigned a percentage of responsibility sufficient to trigger joint and several liability. And, of course, when there is a single defendant, joint and several liability is irrelevant.

A variation on alternative D provides for joint and several liability when defendants share of responsibility is greater than plaintiff but only several liability when a defendant's share is less than that of plaintiff.

E.   A final alternative makes the application of joint and several liability turn on the type of harm suffered by plaintiff. Independent tortfeasors are jointly and severally liable for damages for "economic" or "pecuniary" harms but are severally liable for "noneconomic" or "nonpecuniary" harm, i.e., pain and suffering damages.

Restatement (Third) of Torts: Apportionment of Liability §§ A18–E18 (2000).

c.   Defining Comparative Responsibility

At the beginning of the comparative responsibility movement, most statutes and most cases were only concerned with comparative negligence. The focus was largely on comparing the fault of plaintiff and defendants. Thus, plaintiffs in products liability actions—at least when strict liability governed—were not subject to a contributory or comparative negligence defense, although other defenses often overlapped. Recall that in *Borel v. Fibreboard Paper Products Corp.*, p. 231 suprra, the plaintiff was successful in the strict products liability claim but lost on negligence because of Borel's contributory negligence. In time, however, comparative responsibility was extended to many situations where the conduct of one or more parties was not measured by a negligence standard. Most noteworthy in this regard was the expansion of comparative liability to the area of products liability, an area where liability is minted in the coin of strict liability and defect, not negligence. This development led to semantic, as well as practical problems. In a well-known concurring and dissenting opinion in the California case that expanded comparative concepts to products liability, Justice Jefferson had this to say:

> I consider the majority conclusion a case of wishful thinking and an application of an impractical, ivory-tower approach. The majority's assumption that a jury is capable of making a fair apportionment between a plaintiff's negligent conduct and a defendant's defective product is no more logical or convincing than if a jury were to be instructed that it should add a quart of milk (representing plaintiff's negligence) and a metal bar three feet in length (representing defendant's strict liability for a defective product), and that the two added together equal 100 percent—the total fault for plaintiff's injuries; that plaintiff's quart of milk is then to be assigned its percentage of the 100 percent total and defendant's metal bar is to be assigned the remaining percentage of the total.

Daly v. General Motors Corp., 575 P.2d 1162, 1178 (Cal.1978). Despite the theoretical disconnect, juries have been apportioning liability in cases like *Daly* for 30 years without observable problems.

Justice Jefferson's passage does make clear that comparative fault may not be the best terminology to describe what courts and juries are asked to do. The Texas Supreme Court recognized this problem in a case that extended comparative principles to products liability:

> Many courts and commentators have labeled this type of loss allocation system comparative *fault*. We choose comparative *causation* instead because it is conceptually accurate in cases based on strict liability and breach of warranty theories in which the defendant's "fault," in the traditional sense of culpability, is not at issue. The trier of fact is to compare the harm caused by the defective product with the harm caused by the negligence of the other defendants, any settling tortfeasors and the plaintiff.

Duncan v. Cessna Aircraft Co., 665 S.W.2d 414, 427 (Tex.1984). When multiple parties and a product defect are each the cause of plaintiff's harm, how can liability be apportioned on the basis of causation?

Notwithstanding *Duncan*, most states and the Third Restatement of Torts: Apportionment of Liability eschewed this approach in favor of the concept of comparative responsibility. This leads to a central question. How does comparative responsibility differ from comparative causation? The answer turns in part on how responsibility is defined. In the Third Restatement and other model statutes, responsibility is defined in such a way that it incorporates comparative fault *and* comparative causation.

The Third Restatement of Torts: Apportionment of Liability suggests the fact finder should consider the following factors when apportioning responsibility: (a) the nature of the person's risk-creating conduct, including any awareness or indifference with respect to the risks created by the conduct and any intent with respect to the harm created by the conduct; and (b) the strength of the causal connection between the person's risk-creating conduct and the harm. Restatement (Third) of Torts: Apportionment of Liability § 8 (2000). Likewise, The Uniform Model Product Liability Act § 111(B)(3) provides: "In determining the percentages of responsibility, the trier of fact shall consider, on a comparative basis, both the nature of the conduct of each person or entity responsible and the extent of the proximate causal relation between the conduct and the damages claimed." The Uniform Comparative Fault Act § 2(b) states: "In determining the percentages of fault, the trier of fact shall consider both the nature of the conduct of each party at fault and the extent of the causal relation between the conduct and the damages claimed." In what sense can a "causal relation" be a matter of degree?

Similar language can be found in some state statutes. For example, the Iowa comparative fault statute, which is based on the Uniform Comparative Fault Act, similarly states that, "In determining the percentages of fault, the trier of fact shall consider both the nature of the conduct of each party and the extent of the causal relation between the conduct and the damages claimed." Iowa Code Ann. § 668.39(3).

Not every statute contains such language. Some focus their attention entirely on fault. For example, the Arkansas comparative fault statute contains the following language:

(a) In all actions for damages for personal injuries or wrongful death or injury to property in which recovery is predicated upon fault, liability shall be determined by comparing the fault chargeable to a claiming party with the fault chargeable to the party or parties from whom the claiming party seeks to recover damages.

* * *

(c) The word "fault" as used in this section includes any act, omission, conduct, risk assumed, breach of warranty, or breach of any legal duty which is a proximate cause of any damages sustained by any party.

Ark. Code Ann. § 16–64–122.

Other states prefer "comparative causation." Following *Duncan*, the Texas legislature passed a proportionate responsibility statute that calls on the factfinder to "determine the percentage of responsibility, stated in whole numbers * * * with respect to each person's causing or contributing to cause in any way the harm for which recovery of damages is sought." Vernon's Tex. Civil Practice & Remedy Code § 33.003.

What is not well understood is whether these verbal differences actually shape jury outcomes or even how juries trade off the idea of fault and causation in arriving at proportionate responsibility allocations. The following problem offers you the opportunity to try your hand at this allocation task.

PROBLEM

Abrasive blasting, often less accurately called sandblasting, is accomplished by spraying particles of flint at high pressure against an object one wishes to scour clean. In its natural state the flint, composed mostly of crystalline silica, is not at all dangerous. But when the flint particles are blasted against metal at high pressure, they shatter into an airborne dust of smaller particles. Some particles are as small as 5 microns in diameter (1/20th the diameter of a human hair). Inhaled over months or years they cause silicosis, a progressive, incurable lung disease that can eventually lead to disability and death. Inhalation of free silica particles cannot be prevented by ordinary, disposable paper masks. People working around silica dust must wear air-fed hoods or respirators covering their face. The health risk from inhaling silica dust have been well known for a very long time.

Raymond Gold contracted silicosis while working around abrasive blasting for 5 1/2 years, from 1982–1987, at the Spincote Company. This was the only time in his life that Gold worked in a silica dust environment. Spincote used abrasive blasting to clean oilfield tubing. Gold sued the three companies that supplied flint to Spincote during the years Gold worked there for failure to warn of the health risks associated with sandblasting and the precautions one should take to minimize these risks. The three defendants were: Humble Sand and Gravel, Southern Sandblasting Supply, and Porter Flint. They, in turn, joined Spincote as a "responsible third party" under the state's comparative responsibility statute. The following facts came out during the trial.

All of the defendants supplied flint to Spincote in 100 pound bags.

Humble Sand and Gravel, a small, family-owned business with five employees, began selling flint in 1982. The owner, Pleasant Smith Humble, knew he should include some type of warning on his bags. He made inquiries to OSHA that yielded no useful information and he decided to copy a label used by a competitor that had been in business for 50 years. The label read:

WARNING!
MAY BE INJURIOUS TO HEALTH IF PROPER PROTECTIVE EQUIPMENT IS NOT USED.

Porter Flint was another small business with seven employees. The owner also knew of the dangers of airborne silica, but did not place any warning at all on its bags.

Southern Sandblasting Supply, a much larger company, included the following warning on its bags:

**WARNING: CONTAINS FREE SILICA.
DO NOT BREATHE DUST. MAY CAUSE DELAYED
LUNG INJURY, (SILICOSIS). FOLLOW OSHA SAFETY AND
HEALTH STANDARDS FOR CRYSTALLINE SILICA.**

All parties agree that during the time Gold worked at Spincote, 50% of the flint came from Southern, 35% from Porter, and 15% from Humble.

Eldon Workman, the plant manager during the time of Gold's employment, said that Spincote was aware of the dangers of blasting and that the sand blasters themselves were required to wear air-fed hoods, were reprimanded if they failed to do so, and were fired after three such safety violations. However, other employees such as Gold who worked around the dust created by the blasting were not required to wear hoods. Although employees were warned in general terms of the dangers of inhaling silica dust, Workman could not say whether they were ever warned that doing so could be fatal.

Gold, who had only a ninth grade education, testified that he did see these warnings on the bags but that he did not know what silicosis was nor did he know that inhaling free silica particles could lead to disability or death. He testified that had he known how dangerous silica dust was, he never would have taken or kept a job working around it.

During the time Gold worked at Spincote, another flint manufacturer that did *not* supply the company with flint used the following warning on its bags:

**WARNING.
BREATHING DUST OF THIS PRODUCT CAUSES SILICOSIS,
A SERIOUSLY DISABLING AND FATAL LUNG DISEASE.
AN APPROVED AND WELL–MAINTAINED AIR–SUPPLIED
ABRASIVE BLASTING HOOD MUST BE WORN AT ALL TIMES
WHILE HANDLING AND USING THIS PRODUCT.
FOLLOW ALL APPLICABLE OSHA STANDARDS.**

Under applicable state law, the factfinder is asked to allocate responsibility as follows:

Plaintiff (Gold)	_____
Defendant 1 (Southern)	_____
Defendant 2 (Porter)	_____
Defendant 3 (Humble)	_____
Responsible Third Party (Spincote)	_____
Total	100%

A. How would you allocate responsibility for this accident if the relevant standard for assigning comparative responsibility was that of the Third Restatement? How might your allocation change if you applied the Arkansas standard? If you applied the Texas statutory standard?

B. Disregarding the responsibility of the plaintiff and his employer, how would you allocate liability among the three defendants using the Third

Restatement standard? How might your answer differ using the Arkansas and Texas standards? Do your answers turn on how willing you are to turn to ideas like market share and risk contribution as surrogates for causation?

2. APPORTIONMENT UNDER ENVIRONMENTAL STATUTES

FARMLAND INDUSTRIES, INC. v. COLORADO & EASTERN RAILROAD CO.

United States District Court for the District of Colorado, 1996.
944 F.Supp. 1492.

Babcock, District Judge.

A one-day trial to the court was held on October 28, 1996. Having heard testimony and reviewed the exhibits and the memoranda of law submitted by the parties, I make the following findings of facts and conclusions of law and order the entry of judgment.

FINDINGS OF FACT

A.

A pesticide formulation plant, originally owned by Woodbury Chemical Company, was operated in Commerce City, Colorado, from the late 1950s until mid–1971. In 1965, a fire destroyed the main building of the Woodbury Chemical Company. Pesticide-ridden rubble from the fire contaminated the property. In 1966, a new building was constructed at the same location. A former subsidiary of Farmland Industries, Inc. (Farmland), Missouri Chemical Company, acquired the plant and the property in 1968. In August 1971, Missouri Chemical Company sold the property to McKesson Corporation (McKesson). Herein, the building constructed on the property will be called the "McKesson Building."

In September 1983, the United States Environmental Protection Agency (EPA) determined that ongoing releases of hazardous substances were occurring and placed a 2.2 acre parcel adjacent to and east of the McKesson Building on the National Priorities List as the Woodbury Chemical Superfund Site (the "Woodbury Site" or "Site"). That parcel is about 600 feet east to west by 175 feet north to south. The EPA designated it Operable Unit 1. At that time, the 2.2 acre parcel was owned by Chicago, Rock Island and Pacific Railroad Company (CRIP).

On December 19, 1984, Colorado Eastern Railroad Company (CERC) purchased the CRIP 2.2 acres and another CRIP parcel of land adjacent to the listed Site on the west side (about 1,000 feet east to west; approximately 8–10 acres) (the CERC Parcels), and a shortline railroad track that runs along the northern edge of the Site (the CERC Railroad Tracks). A railroad spur ran from the CERC Railroad Tracks to provide rail service to the McKesson Building. From December 19, 1984, until August 1, 1989, CERC operated the CERC Railroad Tracks.

On August 26, 1985, the EPA notified Gary W. Flanders (Flanders) of CERC's potential liability for releases and threatened releases from the Woodbury Site. On September 22, 1986, the Site was expanded to include the westerly CERC Parcel and the McKesson Property. The EPA designated those parcels Operable Unit 2.

In October 1989, the United States filed suit against all known "PRPs,"* including Farmland, McKesson and CERC. Farmland cross-claimed against CERC, Great Northern Transportation Company (GNTC), and Gary W. Flanders (collectively, the CERC Parties).

On September 4, 1990, the United States, Farmland and McKesson entered into a Partial Consent Decree, pursuant to which Farmland and McKesson Corporation were required to undertake remedial activities at the Woodbury Site and to reimburse the government $700,000 for response costs. By June 1992, Farmland and McKesson had completed all remediation at a cost in excess of $15 million, including $1,439,330.00 to remove certain soil and debris from the CERC Parcels. Farmland paid 51% of those costs.

A consent decree between the United States and CERC was entered by the Court on April 20, 1992. CERC agreed to pay $100,000.00 to the EPA. This payment has not yet been made.

Judge Carrigan granted Farmland's Motion for Partial Summary Judgment on the issue of the amount and reasonableness of the "additional" cleanup costs of $734,058.30 (.51 x $1,439,330.00) incurred by Farmland. *United States v. Colorado & Eastern R.R.,* 832 F.Supp. 304, 306 (D.Colo.1993). In June 1993, after a two day trial, Judge Carrigan held that Farmland, as a matter of law, could recover its response costs against the CERC Parties, jointly and severally, under § 107(a), and entered judgment for Farmland and against the CERC Parties for $734,058.30 (which was later amended to include prejudgment interest of $27,060.00).

The CERC Parties appealed. Upon rehearing, the Tenth Circuit held, *inter alia,* that: (1) PRPs must proceed under § 113(f) (contribution), rather than § 107(a) (strict liability), against other PRPs for the recovery of response costs; and (2) the "matter addressed" in the CERC–EPA consent decree is the government's past response costs, and such consent decree does not bar Farmland's contribution claim against CERC. *United States v. Colorado & Eastern R.R. Co.,* 50 F.3d 1530, 1539 (10th Cir.1995). The Tenth Circuit remanded the case to this court "to consider Farmland's contribution claim under § 113(f) and to apply any equitable factors it determines appropriate." *Id.* at 1539.

I granted in part, and denied in part, Farmland's Motion for Partial Summary Judgment, holding that the CERC Parties are liable parties under CERCLA § 113(f), and, holding that the CERC Parties "were a cause of Farmland's incurrence of increased response costs, the degree of which shall be determined at trial." *Farmland Industries, Inc. v. Colorado*

---

* [PRP's are "potentially responsible parties."—Eds.]

& *Eastern R.R. Co.*, 922 F.Supp. 437, 442 (D.Colo.1996). Thus, the only issue remaining for trial is the allocation of the additional response costs.

B.

Flanders was the sole shareholder of CERC from March 8, 1983, until May 29, 1987. On May 29, 1987, Mr. Flanders exchanged his shares of CERC for common stock of GNTC, thereby causing GNTC to become the 100% owner of CERC. Flanders was the sole shareholder of GNTC from July 2, 1986, until September 30, 1991. Evelyn J. Flanders, Flanders' wife, is the current sole shareholder of GNTC. Evelyn J. Flanders is an officer and director of both GNTC and CERC.

Flanders has been an officer, director and shareholder of both CERC and GNTC. Flanders held the position of officer and director of both companies simultaneously at relevant times in the past. Flanders resigned as an officer and director of CERC and GNTC effective December 30, 1991. Flanders, GNTC and CERC (collectively, the "CERC Parties") are owners and operators within the meaning of 42 U.S.C. § 9607.

Initially, I find Flanders' testimony at trial incredible, especially in the area of his personal finances. Farmland presented evidence showing that Flanders and/or his wife received payments or loans from CERC in amounts ranging from $400,000 to $1,000,000. Pltf. Ex. 11–13, 21. The payments were made from 1986 to 1989, after Flanders had been notified by the EPA of CERC's status as a PRP. Somehow, Flanders, when cross-examined regarding these transactions, could not recall whether they had ever occurred, let alone the reasons for them. Farmland offered into evidence a report of an accountant detailing how Flanders stripped CERC of its assets after he was notified of CERC's PRP status. I am persuaded that Flanders did exactly that, despite Flanders' denial of such intent during his testimony. Given this backdrop, I turn to Farmland's substantive contentions.

Farmland alleges that it incurred additional cleanup costs due to two separate problems on the CERC property. First, a berm that was part of a drainage ditch for the Site was damaged and broke, causing contaminated soil to be washed down onto previously clean areas. Farmland * * * alleges that the CERC parties * * * made the damage worse by refusing to allow Farmland timely access to remediate. Second, Farmland contends that the CERC parties failed to act reasonably to prevent public dumping of trash onto the Site. Trash dumped on the Site by third parties became contaminated and had to be disposed of by Farmland. Farmland alleges that the CERC Parties neither erected a fence to stop the dumping as they were requested to do nor allowed Farmland timely access to erect the fence. I first address the berm issue.

A drainage ditch runs through the CERC properties, roughly from East to West. At the time of the washout in May 1989, a large berm supported the drainage ditch on the north side. The berm ran past the northern edge of the McKesson building and south of the CERC Railroad

Tracks. In late-May 1989, the berm gave way and water was diverted out of the ditch. The water carried contamination from other parts of the property, and it washed contaminated sand and soil onto the CERC Railroad Tracks and other areas of the property.

* * *

* * * Neither Farmland nor the CERC Parties can be held directly responsible for the initial breach of the drainage ditch. It was, as best I can ascertain, an act of God.

CERC's reactions to the initial washout, however, were acts all their own. CERC did not notify either Farmland or the EPA of the problem. Rather, Suzanne Wohlgemuth discovered the breach upon inspecting the property days later. CERC also did not attempt to fix the berm. Flanders testified that he was afraid of incurring liability for incorrectly fixing the berm and that the EPA advised him to do nothing. The evidence, however, fails to bear out Flanders' version of the events.

The initial breach of the drainage ditch occurred in May 1989. CERC apparently did nothing in response except clear the tracks after each heavy rain caused further washout. The breach to the ditch continued to worsen with each washout. Farmland began negotiating with CERC for access to the Site to perform remediation in July 1989. On August 24, 1989, CERC sent EPA a "proposal" to improve drainage conditions on the Site by moving the ditch to a different portion of the property. The proposal was the idea of Jay Turner, CERC property manager. Turner is not an engineer, and no engineer was consulted regarding the proposal.

On October 3, 1989, the EPA notified CERC that it could not comment on the proposal because it involved lands outside of the EPA's jurisdiction. The EPA did state that "[w]ith regard to the suggested repair work for the gap in the existing berm which is on the CERC property . . . again, you may proceed with necessary repairs on your property." The EPA warned, however, that "the burden is on CERC to ensure that the work does not exacerbate the contamination at the site."

Flanders insisted that those warnings from the EPA kept him from repairing the berm. I find Flanders' contention incredible. The EPA's caveat was boilerplate. It is axiomatic that anyone working on a Superfund Site must be careful not to exacerbate the contamination. That does not mean, however, that the CERC Parties were precluded from obtaining the adequate expertise to remedy the situation.

In addition, the CERC parties failed to grant Farmland timely access to the site so that Farmland could prevent further contamination. Despite multiple requests, CERC continued to deny access for remediation. Flanders testified that CERC had certain concerns regarding access that were not being met. I find Flanders' testimony again unbelievable. Even if Flanders' concerns were valid and not met, it need not have taken nearly two years to remedy the situation. The CERC Parties did not consent to access until the EPA threatened to obtain an administrative order for access on February 1, 1991, more than twenty months after the original washout.

The CERC parties acted unreasonably in response to the berm washout. They could have fixed the berm immediately, but did not. They could have granted Farmland and the EPA access to remediate immediately, but they did not. Instead, it took a letter threatening an administrative action to prompt the CERC Parties to allow access to the Site.

* * *

> Farmland and McKesson's cost of remediating the Woodbury Site as outlined above was increased as a result of the activities of [the CERC Parties] and/or its agents including ... the movement of soil which had washed down onto the railroad tracks owned by CERC. Such activities spread the contaminated soil at the Site which had to removed at Farmland and McKesson's expense.

Farmland's expert testified that the total additional cleanup cost due to the breach in the berm was $715,220. Although some of these costs are attributable to the initial washout, a large portion was made necessary by subsequent washouts that occurred when the berm was not repaired in a timely manner.

I turn next to the issue of fencing on the CERC properties. As President of CERC, Flanders had authority to order the installation of a fence around the CERC Parcels and/or consent to access to the Site by the EPA and Farmland for the purpose of fencing the CERC Parcels. Instead, Flanders and CERC consistently avoided their responsibilities, thereby necessitating increased response costs. In the interim, third parties indiscriminately dumped everything from rubber tires to dead dogs in piles on the property.

CERC and/or Mr. Flanders received warnings from the EPA and the Colorado Department of Health of the need to install a fence to prevent the accumulation of debris on the Site. * * * On August 27, 1989, the EPA informed CERC that the fence needed "to go up immediately." Pltf. Ex. 27. CERC, however, refused to erect the fence or grant access to Farmland for that purpose. Among other concessions, CERC sought rental payments of nearly $85,000 per year for the use of the land to put up a fence.

CERC even went so far as to write the Department of Justice in November 1990, requesting it to become involved in the negotiations. In its letter, CERC stated: "From the beginning these negotiations have been conducted under the cloud of threats.... We will not succumb to threats from Farmland, EPA or anyone else in a power position—this is still America." It is not clear to what "threats" CERC refers. In any event, CERC does not present any credible reason why it consistently delayed in erecting the fence or granting fence access.

[I]t was only after the EPA issued a letter dated December 19, 1990, threatening to issue an Administrative Order for Access that Flanders executed an access agreement for fencing on behalf of CERC.

Although some debris was already present on the Site in March 1989, fencing delay led to the accumulation of a vast amount of additional debris that had to be removed from the Site in accordance with the Site Work Plan, the EPA's Record of Decision on the Site and the Farmland and McKesson Consent Decree entered with the United States. Access for purposes of installing a fence was eventually granted by an agreement dated December 21, 1990. Farmland's expert testified that the total cost to Farmland and McKesson for the trash removal was $724,110.

Thus, the total cost incurred in responding to the activities of the CERC Parties was $1,439,330 ($715,220 + $724,110). Farmland paid 51% of those costs, or $734,058.30.

The CERC Parties have stipulated that the value of the CERC Parcels increased from zero dollars to between $615,000.00 and $630,000.00 following the completion of the remedial activities and the delisting of the Woodbury Site from the National Priorities List. The parties have also stipulated that prejudgment interest is to be calculated at 6.5% per annum, beginning from the date of the written demand (November 6, 1992).

CONCLUSIONS OF LAW

The CERC Parties are liable parties under CERCLA Section 113(f)(2). They are also owners and operators within the meaning of 42 U.S.C. § 9607.

The consent decree entered between the CERC Parties and the United States is not a bar to Farmland's claim for contribution under CERCLA § 113(f), 42 U.S.C.A. § 9613(f). The additional remediation costs incurred by Farmland are reasonable, necessary and consistent with the National Contingency Plan and are recoverable under CERCLA Section 113(f), 42 U.S.C.A. § 9613(f). Also, the additional remediation costs incurred by Farmland as a result of actions of the CERC Parties are separable and quantifiable.

Once liability is established, a party's share of liability is apportioned according to those equitable factors the court finds appropriate. 42 U.S.C. § 9613(f). Section 113 does not require me to consider a particular list of factors. Rather, I have broad discretion in allocating response costs among responsible parties. A court should use its moral, as well as its legal sense, in framing an equitable decree.

I may consider many factors, a few factors, or I may find one factor determinative. Among the factors many courts consider are the six "Gore Factors." *See, e.g., Kerr–McGee Chemical Corp. v. Lefton Iron & Metal Co.*, 14 F.3d 321, 326 (7th Cir.1994). The six Gore Factors are:

(i) the ability of the parties to demonstrate that their contribution to a discharge, release, or disposal of a hazardous waste can be distinguished; (ii) the amount of the hazardous waste involved; (iii) the degree of toxicity of the hazardous waste involved; (iv) the degree of involvement by the parties in the generation, transportation, treatment, storage, or disposal of the hazardous waste; (v) the degree of care exercised by the parties with respect to the hazardous waste concerned, taking into account the characteristics of such hazardous waste; and (vi) the degree of cooperation by the parties with the Federal, State or local officials to prevent any harm to the public health or environment.

[*United States v. Colorado & Eastern R.R. Co.*, 50 F.3d at 1536 n. 5.] The Gore factors are neither exhaustive, nor exclusive.

Federal courts have found several other factors to be appropriate for consideration under § 113(f) claims, for example: the state of mind of the parties; the financial resources of the parties; the benefits received by the parties from contaminating activities and the knowledge and/or acquiescence of the parties in the contaminating activities; and the relative fault of the parties. * * *

I previously determined that proof of causation of the particular remediation costs is not necessary to Farmland's contribution claim. However, causation may be an important factor in my decision. I now reaffirm that the CERC Parties caused Farmland to incur additional remediation costs.

The degree of care exercised by a party in managing a Superfund site is another relevant equitable factor. *Hatco Corp. v. W.R. Grace & Co.*, 836 F.Supp. 1049, 1079, 1091 (D.N.J.1993). In *Hatco*, the court considered that Hatco continued to make use of contaminated areas of the site long after it was aware that such use could worsen contamination or complicate future remedial efforts, and the court allocated any additional expenditures required to remediate those areas to Hatco.

In addition, under common law theories of nuisance and trespass, a property owner has a duty to exercise reasonable care to prevent activities and conditions on its property that might injure others. *State of N.Y. v. Shore Realty Corp.*, 759 F.2d 1032 (2d Cir.1985)(stating that landowner is responsible for maintenance of contaminated property, even though another party placed chemicals on property); *see Sterling v. Velsicol Chemical Corp.*, 647 F.Supp. 303, 317 (W.D.Tenn.1986), *aff'd in part, rev'd in part*, 855 F.2d 1188 (6th Cir.1988) (stating that owner of property who contains hazardous waste thereon is answerable for the natural consequences of its escape).

In *Shore Realty Corp.*, the Second Circuit stated that common law doctrines of nuisance are applicable to a CERCLA site. 759 F.2d at 1051. The court applied the Restatement (Second) of Torts § 839 cmt. d (1979) and held that a landowner was liable for maintaining a public nuisance (i.e. a contaminated site) regardless of the fact that other parties placed the chemicals on the site. *Id.* The Restatement (Second) of Torts § 839 cmt. d provides:

> Liability [of a possessor of land] is not based upon responsibility for the creation of the harmful condition, but upon the fact that he has exclusive control over the land and the things done upon it and should have the responsibility of taking reasonable measures to remedy conditions on it that are a source of harm to others.

The CERC Parties' ownership and control of the CERC Parcels obligated the CERC Parties to exercise care and maintain the property to prevent injury to others. I will consider that obligation and the CERC Parties' actions under it when I weigh the equitable factors.

ANALYSIS

I will consider the following equitable factors in allocating remedial costs here: (1) the relative fault of the parties (including causation); (2) the duties of the CERC parties as land owners; (3) the fourth through sixth Gore factors; (4) the state of mind of the parties; and (5) the benefits received by the parties as a result of the cleanup.

1. *Relative Fault*

I have already found that neither party caused the initial breach in the berm. However, this does not mean that the CERC Parties are without fault for the increased costs of remediation incurred by Farmland. The CERC Parties failed to fix the berm or give timely access to Farmland or the EPA to do so, thereby necessitating additional cleanup. In addition, Farmland is utterly without fault for either the original breach of the berm or the need for additional cleanup caused by the lengthy delay in fixing the berm. Farmland diligently attempted to clean up the entire Site and was hindered only by the CERC Parties' failure to cooperate.

Additionally, the CERC Parties failed to fence the CERC Parcels and refused to allow Farmland timely access to the CERC Parcels for the purpose of installing a fence to prevent the accumulation of debris on the Site. CERC and Mr. Flanders received warnings from the EPA and the Colorado Department of Health of the need to install a fence. Despite such warnings, CERC and Mr. Flanders denied timely access to the CERC property at the Site by, among other things, delaying the execution of an access agreement for 21 months. This delay led to the accumulation of a vast amount of additional debris that had to be removed from the Site in accordance with the Site Work Plan, the EPA's Record of Decision on the Site and the Farmland and McKesson Consent Decree entered with the United States.

2. *The CERC Parties' duties as property owner*

The degree of care exercised by a party in managing a Superfund site is an equitable factor that weighs against the CERC Parties. In addition, under common law theories of nuisance and trespass, a property owner has a duty to exercise reasonable care to prevent activities and conditions on its property that might injure others.

The CERC Parties owned the CERC Parcels during the entire time washouts from the drainage ditch occurred and the trash and debris accumulated on the CERC Parcels. They failed to fix the berm or allow others to do so. In addition, they failed to fence the CERC Parcels, and refused for months to allow Farmland timely access to the CERC Parcels in order to construct a fence.

3. *Gore Factors Four through Six*

The fourth Gore Factor is "the degree of involvement by the parties in the generation, transportation, treatment, storage, or disposal of the hazardous waste." Farmland agreed to remediate the Site at its own expense even though it never actually owned the property or conducted any activities at the Site. Farmland's PRP status was premised on the involvement of its former subsidiary, Missouri Chemical Company, but Farmland entered a consent decree that provides expressly that it admits no liability.

In addition, there is no evidence to suggest that Missouri Chemical Company caused any of the contamination on the Site. Rather, the evidence suggests that the majority of the contamination resulted from a fire at the pesticide plant when it was still owned by Woodbury Chemical Company. Although the CERC Parties attempted to argue otherwise at trial, Farmland and the CERC Parties are in essentially the same position—buyers of already-contaminated land. If anything, the CERC Parties should be held more responsible because CERC purchased the land after it had already been placed on the NPL, whereas Farmland's subsidiary only owned the property for a short time well before the contamination was discovered.

The fifth Gore Factor is "the degree of care exercised by the parties with respect to the hazardous waste concerned." Here again, the balance favors Farmland. By all accounts, Farmland has exercised the utmost diligence with regard to cleaning up the contamination at the Site. The CERC Parties have shown little concern for anything beyond their own interests. For example, they admitted to consistently moving dirt off of their railroad tracks without regard for its effects, yet they made no credible effort to repair the breach in the berm that was causing the problems.

The sixth Gore Factor is "the degree of cooperation by the parties with the Federal, State, or local officials to prevent any harm to the public health or the environment." Once more, the CERC Parties refused to allow Farmland and the EPA access to clean up the Site until threatened by the EPA. In addition, CERC had actual knowledge that dumping of trash on the Site would interfere with the EPA-mandated cleanup. Mr. Flanders personally had knowledge of the need to fence the CERC parcels in accordance with the Site cleanup plan. Despite this knowledge, the

CERC Parties failed to install the fence as mandated by the EPA as part of the cleanup activities and engaged in various tactics that delayed the installation of the fence. CERC failed even to pay the $100,000 to the EPA as part of its consent decree.

4. *State of Mind*

Perhaps the most stark contrast between Farmland and the CERC Parties is the difference in mindset apparent during remediation. Farmland seemed eminently interested in cleaning up the Site while the CERC Parties seemed entirely engrossed with how to avoid any responsibility for the cleanup. * * * In addition, there is strong evidence to suggest that Flanders did everything he could to divert all of CERC's assets to other entities in an effort to avoid paying any remedial costs.

5. *Benefits from Cleanup*

The EPA published its notice of intent to delete the Site from the National Priorities List, and it was deleted. The parties stipulated that the value of the CERC Parcels increased by more than $600,000 as a result of the cleanup. Given that Farmland garnered no tangible benefit from the cleanup of land it no longer owns, it would be inequitable not to allocate significant additional remedial costs to the CERC Parties.

Weighing all of these factors, I hold that the CERC Parties should bear 85% of the costs associated with the ditch washouts and 90% of the costs associated with the debris cleanup. Farmland's costs associated with the ditch washouts total 51% of $715,220, or $364,762.20. Farmland's costs associated with the debris cleanup total 51% of $724,110, or $369,296.10. Therefore, the CERC Parties are jointly and severally liable for 85% of $364,762.20, or $310,047.87, and 90% of $369,296.10, or $332,366.49. Thus, the total award to Farmland is $642,414.36. Farmland is also entitled to prejudgment interest at the stipulated rate of 6.5% per annum starting from November 6, 1992, and postjudgment interest at the statutory rate of 8.5% per annum.

Accordingly, it is ORDERED that

1. The CERC Parties are jointly and severally liable to Farmland for $642,414.36, plus 6.5% prejudgment interest from November 6, 1992, and 8.5% postjudgment interest;

2. Farmland is awarded its costs.

NOTES AND QUESTIONS

1. How does the CERCLA approach to apportioning liability among responsible parties differ from the approach found in the Third Restatement and in state comparative responsibility statutes? Do you think jurors asked to apportion responsibility under state comparative responsibility statutes would benefit from an instruction that provided them with the Gore factors and other things they might consider in allocating liability?

2. Did the *Farmland* court apportion on the basis of causation? On the basis of fault? On both? What do the Gore factors call for?

3. As the *Farmland* court noted, parties subject to CERCLA liability have two statutory avenues to seek money from other parties: a cost recovery action under section 107(a) and an action for contribution under section 113(f). The majority of courts that have considered the question, including the Sixth Circuit and all other circuits, have concluded that a party which is itself partially responsible for the condition of a hazardous waste site cannot maintain a cost recovery action, under section 107(a), against another responsible party. See Centerior Serv. Co. v. Acme Scrap Iron & Metal Corp., 153 F.3d 344 (6th Cir.1998). Recall that in *Farmland*, the Tenth Circuit agreed with this position and held that the plaintiff must proceed under section 113(f). Only innocent parties may maintain a cost recovery action under section 107(a). In AlliedSignal, Inc. v. Amcast International Corp., 177 F.Supp.2d 713 (S.D.Ohio 2001) the court gave as an example of an innocent party "a person whose property is contaminated, without his permission, by the act of another." Had the defendant in *Farmland* fully cooperated with the EPA, could it have brought a section 107(a) action against the plaintiff for monies it expended for the cleanup?

4. Why do you think the defendant in *Farmland* felt so put upon by the government and the plaintiff?

5. In *AlliedSignal*, cited in note 3, the court was asked to assess contribution between two entities that put materials into a contaminated landfill. The trial court concluded that 72% of the total volume of waste in the landfill was contributed by the plaintiff and 28% by the defendant. Most significantly, however, the waste of both parties contaminated the groundwater with carcinogenic polycyclic aromatic hydrocarbons (PAH). Approximately 98% of the PAH came from the plaintiff.

The EPA required the parties to take three steps to remediate the site: a cap to be placed over the surface of the facility; the construction of a low permeability slurry wall surrounding the site and extending from the surface to bedrock; and the extraction and treatment of the groundwater both inside and outside the slurry wall until cleanup standards are achieved. With respect to this last step, the groundwater would not meet EPA standards until the level of carcinogenic PAH was no greater than 0.005 parts per billion. Because this standard was much more stringent than that for any other substance in the groundwater, cleaning up the PAH would successfully remove all other groundwater contamination.

The district court turned to the Gore factors as an aid to assess contribution. It found that the fifth and sixth factors did not apply to the facts of the case. Based on the remaining factors, the court adopted the following contribution scheme: The defendant must pay for two percent of the response costs incurred by the plaintiff, with the exception of those costs associated with the cap for the facility. With respect to the cap, the defendant is responsible for 28% of the costs incurred by the plaintiff.

How does this outcome compare to the allocation made in *Farmland*? How is it different from and similar to the allocations made by the courts in the cases discussed in Chapter 4, e.g., *Borel*, *Rutherford*, and *Sindell*?

CHAPTER **XII**

DAMAGES

■ ■ ■

A. INTRODUCTION

We now consider some special issues relating to damages in toxic and environmental tort cases. The basic principles of damages are no different here than in other areas of tort law. Damages are money awarded to someone whose interests have been violated by the tortious conduct of another. Although plaintiffs sometimes recover "nominal" damages to vindicate rights (for example, to establish boundary lines in a trespass action), most cases involve demands for compensation based on actual loss incurred. Compensatory damages in tort law "are designed to place [a plaintiff] in a position substantially equivalent in a pecuniary way to that which he would have occupied had no tort been committed." Restatement (Second) of Torts § 903 cmt. a. Depending on the circumstances, recovery might include recovery for property loss, personal injury, and in some cases, emotional harm or economic harm. Where a defendant's conduct is particularly egregious, a plaintiff can seek punitive damages, which are designed not to compensate plaintiff, but rather to punish a defendant and deter future risky conduct.

The bulk of this Chapter will address issues relating to compensatory damages that arise almost uniquely in toxic and environmental tort cases during the latency period that normally exists between exposure and disease. The Chapter's first section focuses on personal injury actions, with an emphasis on claims brought by people who have been tortiously exposed to a toxin. The second section considers issues concerning the appropriate way to compensate people who own property that has been contaminated by toxins, often due to conduct that constitutes trespass, nuisance, or abnormally dangerous activity. The third section discusses damages issues that arise in claims brought under federal statutes. Finally, the Chapter considers punitive damages, a topic of considerable contemporary debate and controversy. Throughout the Chapter, consider the unusual problems raised by the special characteristics of toxic cases, both from a substantive and procedural perspective.

B. PERSONAL INJURY

The law divides personal injury damage awards into three main components: (1) past and future medical expenses; (2) past and future lost income; and (3) pain and suffering. Compensable medical expenses must relate to defendant's tortious conduct and commonly include healthcare charges or other costs related to plaintiff's medical treatment. Lost income can consist of earnings that a plaintiff actually lost due to defendant's conduct, or diminished capacity to earn a living in the future. Pain and suffering is more difficult to describe in a general way, but can include almost any form of conscious physical or emotional suffering relating to defendant's tortious conduct. See 2 Dan B. Dobbs, Law of Remedies 381.

Toxic exposure cases pose special challenges for personal injury damage awards. As we have learned, the illnesses that form the basis for such claims are normally preceded by a lengthy latency period. This time gap between exposure and disease creates significant hurdles to tort law recovery, not the least of which are statutes of limitations and proof issues made difficult by the need for evidence that is from years past. Because of these issues, plaintiffs have increasingly sought recovery after exposure but before the manifestation of disease has taken place. These "futures" cases are among the most hotly-debated in toxic tort law. In general, one can divide futures cases into three groups: First, some jurisdictions allow claims for medical monitoring, in which plaintiffs seek recovery for the cost of surveillance to detect and prevent the onset of disease. Second, a small number of jurisdictions have permitted plaintiffs to seek recovery for enhanced risk of disease, assigning a value to the increased risk without any assurance that the disease will later manifest. Third, a number of courts allow actions for fear of disease, in which plaintiffs seek compensation for emotional distress based on exposure to a toxic substance. We will consider each of these actions in turn.

1. MEDICAL MONITORING

The roots of medical monitoring are found in cases where courts have defined the limits of damage awards for future medical expenses. Typically, such awards require a plaintiff to demonstrate some physical impact that requires medical care to treat the resulting harm. One well-known case that influenced the development of doctrine in this area is Friends for All Children, Inc. v. Lockheed Aircraft Corp., 746 F.2d 816 (D.C.Cir.1984). *Friends For All Children* involved a claim on behalf of 150 Vietnamese orphans who survived a military transport plane crash. The plaintiffs sought injunctive relief requiring that the plane's manufacturer fund a medical surveillance program to determine whether depressurization of the plane's cabin caused the children to suffer brain damage. The district court concluded that the manufacturer should compensate the children for the costs, and the appellate court agreed. The court reasoned that such compensation was no different from a damage award in an ordinary tort action. As an example, the court provided a hypothetical case involving a driver named "Smith," who knocked down a pedestrian named "Jones." In the hypothetical, Jones entered a hospital where doctors recommended that he undergo tests to determine whether he suffered internal head injuries. The tests came back negative, but Jones sued Smith for costs associated with the diagnostic exams. The court concluded:

> From our example, it is clear that even in the absence of physical injury Jones ought to be able to recover the cost for the various diagnostic examinations proximately caused by Smith's negligent action. * * * The cause of action * * * accords with commonly shared intuitions of normative justice which underlie the common law of tort. The [driver], through his negligence, caused the plaintiff, in the opinion of medical experts, to need specific medical services * * *.
>
> Similarly, in this case, the crash exposed the plaintiffs to the risk of serious brain damage * * * [and] comprehensive diagnostic examinations are needed to determine whether and to what extent treatment may be necessary.

Friends for All Children, 746 F.2d at 825.

Subsequent courts and commentators made much of this language, suggesting that it broke new ground in permitting plaintiffs to recover medical surveillance costs. But, in truth, one can easily restrict the case to its facts involving a discrete number of plaintiffs who suffered physical impact, if not physical injury. This was not surprising at the time, as little, if any, precedent existed to support medical monitoring damages absent an impact that threatened imminent harm. In 1987, however, the New Jersey Supreme Court decided Ayers v. Township of Jackson, 525 A.2d 287 (N.J.1987), opening the door to recovery in a different type of case.

In *Ayers*, residents of Jackson Township, New Jersey, brought an action against their municipality for permitting toxic pollutants from a landfill to leach into an aquifer that provided residential drinking water. The plaintiffs, none of whom sought recovery for illnesses related to toxic exposure, sought damages pursuant to the New Jersey Tort Claims Act for a variety of things, including the costs of medical monitoring. The New Jersey Supreme Court ultimately upheld a jury's decision that such costs were appropriate damages in the case.

> [W]e hold that the cost of medical surveillance is a compensable item of damages where the proofs demonstrate, through reliable expert testimony predicated upon the significance and extent of exposure to chemicals, the toxicity of the chemicals, the seriousness of the diseases for which individuals are at risk, the relative increase in the chance of onset of disease in those exposed, and the value of early diagnosis, that such surveillance to monitor the effect of exposure to toxic chemicals is reasonable and necessary.

Ayers, 525 A.2d at 312.

During the next decade, a number of courts followed the *Ayers* court's lead, permitting post-exposure, pre-symptom medical monitoring damages by evaluating factors similar to those set out above. See, e.g., In re Paoli R.R. Yard PCB Litig., 35 F.3d 717, 787 (3d Cir.1994); Redland Soccer Club, Inc. v. Dep't of Army & Dep't of Defense of the U.S., 696 A.2d 137 (Pa.1997); Potter v. Firestone Tire & Rubber Co., 863 P.2d 795, 821–25 (Cal.1993); Hansen v. Mountain Fuel Supply Co., 858 P.2d 970, 979–81 (Utah 1993); Burns v. Jaquays Mining Corp., 752 P.2d 28, 33–34 (Ariz. App.1987). In 1997, however, the U.S. Supreme Court had an opportunity to consider the issue in a case arising under the Federal Employers' Liability Act (FELA), and came to a different conclusion.

METRO–NORTH COMMUTER RAILROAD CO. v. BUCKLEY

United States Supreme Court, 1997.
521 U.S. 424, 117 S.Ct. 2113, 138 L.Ed.2d 560.

JUSTICE BREYER delivered the opinion of the Court.

The basic question in this case is whether a railroad worker negligently exposed to a carcinogen (here, asbestos) but without symptoms of any disease can recover under the Federal Employers' Liability Act (FELA or Act), 35 Stat. 65, as amended, 45 U.S.C. § 5 *et seq.*, for negligently inflicted emotional distress. We conclude that the worker before us here cannot recover unless, and until, he manifests symptoms of a disease. We also consider a related claim for medical monitoring costs, and we hold, for reasons set out below, that the respondent in this case has not shown that he is legally entitled to recover those costs.

I

Respondent, Michael Buckley, works as a pipefitter for Metro–North, a railroad. For three years (1985–1988) his job exposed him to asbestos for about one hour per working day. During that time Buckley would remove insulation from pipes, often covering himself with insulation dust that contained asbestos. * * * [H]is two expert witnesses testified that, even after taking account of his now-discarded 15–year habit of smoking up to a pack of cigarettes per day, the exposure created an *added* risk of death due to cancer, or to other asbestos-related diseases, of either 1% to 5% (in the view of one of plaintiff's experts), or 1% to 3% (in the view of another). Since 1989, Buckley has received periodic medical checkups for cancer and asbestosis. So far, those check-ups have not revealed any evidence of cancer or any other asbestos-related disease.

Buckley sued Metro–North under the FELA, a statute that permits a railroad worker to recover for an "injury ... resulting ... from" his employer's "negligence." 45 U.S.C. § 51. He sought damages * * * to cover the cost of future medical checkups. His employer conceded negligence, but * * * it argued that the FELA did not permit a worker like Buckley, who had suffered no physical harm, to recover for [medical monitoring]. After hearing Buckley's case, the District Court dismissed the action. * * *

Buckley appealed, and the Second Circuit reversed. * * * [T]he court held that Buckley could recover for the costs of medical check-ups because the FELA permits recovery of all reasonably incurred extra medical monitoring costs whenever a "reasonable physician would prescribe . . . a monitoring regime different than the one that would have been prescribed in the absence of" a particular negligently caused exposure to a toxic substance.

We granted certiorari to review the Second Circuit's holdings * * *.

* * *

III

* * *

The parties do not dispute—and we assume—that an exposed plaintiff can recover related reasonable medical monitoring costs if and when he develops symptoms. As the Second Circuit pointed out, a plaintiff injured through negligence can recover related reasonable medical expenses as an element of damages. No one has argued that any different principle would apply in the case of a plaintiff whose "injury" consists of a disease, a symptom, or those sorts of emotional distress that fall within the FELA's definition of "injury." Much of the Second Circuit's opinion suggests it intended only to apply this basic principle of the law of damages. See, *e.g.*, 79 F.3d, at 1342 ("[T]his case turns upon whether . . . emotional harm . . . is an injury compensable under FELA"); *id.*, at 1347 (monitoring costs are a "traditional element of tort damages"). * * *

Other portions of the Second Circuit's opinion, however, indicate that it may have rested this portion of its decision upon a broader ground, namely, that medical monitoring costs themselves represent a separate negligently caused economic "injury," 45 U.S.C. § 51, for which a negligently exposed FELA plaintiff (including a plaintiff without disease or symptoms) may recover to the extent that the medical monitoring costs that a reasonable physician would prescribe for the plaintiff exceed the medical monitoring costs that "would have been prescribed in the absence of [the] exposure." 79 F.3d, at 1347 (citation omitted). This portion of the opinion, when viewed in light of Buckley's straightforward claim for an "amount of money" sufficient to "compensate" him for "future medical monitoring expenses," suggests the existence of an ordinary, but separate, tort law cause of action permitting (as tort law ordinarily permits) the recovery of medical cost damages in the form of a lump sum. As so characterized, the Second Circuit's holding, in our view, went beyond the bounds of currently "evolving common law." [*Consolidated Rail Corporation v. Gottshall*, 512 U.S. 532, 558 (1994) (SOUTER, J., concurring).]

Guided by the parties' briefs, we have canvassed the state-law cases that have considered whether the negligent causation of this kind of harm (*i.e.*, causing a plaintiff, through negligent exposure to a toxic substance, to incur medical monitoring costs) by itself constitutes a sufficient basis for a tort recovery. We have found no other FELA decisions. We have put to the side several cases that involve special recovery-permitting circumstances, such as the presence of a traumatic physical impact, or the presence of a physical symptom * * *. See, *e.g., Friends for All Children, Inc. v. Lockheed Aircraft Corp.,* 746 F.2d 816, 824–825 (C.A.D.C.1984) (traumatic impact); *Hagerty v. L & L Marine Services, Inc.,* 788 F.2d 315, modified, 797 F.2d 256 (C.A.5 1986) (same); *Simmons v. Pacor, Inc.,* 543 Pa. 664, 674 A.2d 232 (1996) (physical symptom). We have noted that federal courts, interpreting state law, have come to different conclusions about the matter. Compare, *e.g., In re Paoli R. Yard PCB Litigation,* 916 F.2d 829 (C.A.3 1990) (Pennsylvania law), with *Ball v. Joy Technologies, Inc.,* 958 F.2d 36 (C.A.4 1991) (West Virginia and Virginia law). And we have ended up focusing on several important State Supreme Court cases that have permitted recovery. *Ayers v. Jackson,* 106 N.J. 557, 525 A.2d 287 (1987); *Hansen v. Mountain Fuel Supply Co.,* 858 P.2d 970 (Utah 1993); *Potter v. Firestone Tire & Rubber Co.,* 6 Cal.4th 965, 25 Cal.Rptr.2d 550, 863 P.2d 795 (1993); see also *Burns v. Jaquays Mining Corp.,* 156 Ariz. 375, 752 P.2d 28 (App.1987).

We find it sufficient to note, for present purposes, that the cases authorizing recovery for medical monitoring in the absence of physical injury do not endorse a full-blown, traditional tort law cause of action for lump-sum damages—of the sort that the Court of Appeals seems to have endorsed here. Rather, those courts, while recognizing that medical monitoring costs can amount to a harm that justifies a tort remedy, have suggested, or imposed, special limitations on that remedy. Compare *Ayers, supra,* at 608, 525 A.2d, at 314 (recommending in future cases creation of "a court-supervised fund to administer medical surveillance payments"); *Hansen, supra,* at 982 (suggesting insurance mechanism or court-supervised fund as proper remedy); *Potter, supra,* at 1010, n. 28, 25 Cal.Rptr.2d, at 580, n. 28, 863 P.2d, at 825, n. 28 (suggesting that a lump-sum damages award would be inappropriate); *Burns, supra,* at 381, 752 P.2d, at 34 (holding that lump-sum damages are not appropriate), with, *e.g., Honeycutt v. Walden,* 294 Ark. 440, 743 S.W.2d 809 (1988) (damages award for future medical expenses made necessary by physical injury are awarded as lump-sum payment); *Rice v. Hill,* 315 Pa. 166, 172 A. 289 (1934) (same); and Restatement (Second) of Torts § 920A(2) (1977) (ordinarily fact that plaintiff is insured is irrelevant to amount of tort recovery). *Cf.* [J. Weinstein, Individual Justice in Mass Tort Litigation 154 (1995)]. We believe that the note of caution, the limitations, and the expressed uneasiness with a traditional lump-sum damages remedy are important, for they suggest a judicial recognition of some of the policy concerns that have been pointed out to us here * * *.

      * * *

Moreover, tens of millions of individuals may have suffered exposure to substances that might justify some form of substance-exposure-related medical monitoring. And that fact, along with uncertainty as to the amount of liability, could threaten both a "flood" of less important cases (potentially absorbing resources better left available to those more seriously harmed), and the systemic harms that can accompany "unlimited and unpredictable liability" (for example, vast testing liability adversely affecting the allocation of scarce medical resources). * * *

Finally, a traditional, full-blown ordinary tort liability rule would ignore the presence of existing alternative sources of payment, thereby leaving a court uncertain about how much of the potentially large recoveries would pay for otherwise unavailable medical testing and how much would accrue to plaintiffs for whom employers or other sources (say, insurance now or in the future) might provide monitoring in any event. * * *

We do not deny important competing considerations—of a kind that may have led some courts to provide a form of liability. Buckley argues, for example, that it is inequitable to place the economic burden of such care on the negligently exposed plaintiff rather than on the negligent defendant. He points out that providing preventive care to individuals who would otherwise go without can help to mitigate potentially serious future health effects of diseases by detecting them in early stages; again, whether or not this is such a situation, we may assume that such situations occur. And he adds that, despite scientific uncertainties, the difficulty of separating justified from unjustified claims may be less serious than where emotional distress is the harm at issue.

We do not deny that Justice GINSBURG [in dissent] paints a sympathetic picture of Buckley and his co-workers; this picture has force because Buckley *is* sympathetic and he *has* suffered wrong at the hands of a negligent employer. But we are more troubled than is Justice GINSBURG by the potential systemic effects of creating a new, full-blown, tort law cause of action—for example, the effects upon interests of other potential plaintiffs who are not before the court and who depend on a tort system that can distinguish between reliable and serious claims on the one hand, and unreliable and relatively trivial claims on the other. The reality is that competing interests are at stake—and those interests sometimes can be reconciled in ways other than simply through the creation of a full-blown, traditional, tort law cause of action.

We have not tried to balance these, or other, competing considerations here. We point them out to help explain why we consider the limitations and cautions to be important—and integral—parts of the state-court decisions that permit asymptomatic plaintiffs a separate tort claim for medical monitoring costs. That being so, we do not find sufficient support in the common law for the unqualified rule of lump-sum damages recovery that is, at least arguably, before us here. And given the mix of competing general policy considerations, plaintiff's policy-based arguments do not convince us that the FELA contains a tort liability rule of that *unqualified* kind.

This limited conclusion disposes of the matter before us. We need not, and do not, express any view here about the extent to which the FELA might, or might not, accommodate medical cost recovery rules more finely tailored than the rule we have considered.

IV

For the reasons stated, we reverse the determination of the Second Circuit, and we remand the case for further proceedings consistent with this opinion.

It is so ordered.

JUSTICE GINSBURG, with whom JUSTICE STEVENS joins, concurring in the judgment in part and dissenting in part.

The Federal Employers' Liability Act (FELA) was enacted to facilitate recovery for railworkers who suffer injuries as a result of their employers' negligence. "Congress intended the creation of no static remedy, but one which would be developed and enlarged to meet changing conditions and changing concepts of industry's duty toward its workers." *Kernan v. American Dredging Co.*, 355 U.S. 426, 432, 78 S.Ct. 394, 398, 2 L.Ed.2d 382 (1958). * * *

* * *

Concerning medical monitoring, the Court of Appeals ruled that Buckley stated a triable claim for monitoring expenses made "necessary because of his exposure to asbestos," expenses essential "to ensure early detection and cure of any asbestos-related disease he develops." I would not disturb that ruling.

I

As a pipefitter for Metro–North, Michael Buckley repaired and maintained the labyrinth of pipes in the steam tunnels of Grand Central Terminal in New York City. The pipes were surrounded by a white insulation material that Buckley and his co-workers had to remove to perform their jobs. Without any protective gear, the pipefitters would hammer, slice, and pull the insulation material, which broke apart as it was removed, scattering dust particles into the air. Fans used to mitigate the intense heat of the steam tunnels spread further dust from insulation pieces that had accumulated on tunnel floors. The dust coated Buckley's skin and clothing; he testified that he could taste the gritty insulation material as it entered his mouth and nose. The pipefitters would emerge from their work in the tunnels covered from head to toe with white dust; for this appearance, they were dubbed "the snowmen of Grand Central."

The insulation material covering Grand Central's pipes was made of asbestos, widely recognized as a carcinogen since the mid–1970's. Metro–North did not tell the pipefitters of, or provide protection against, the danger to which the workers were exposed until 1987, two years after Buckley started working in the steam tunnels. At an asbestos awareness class on August 31, 1987, Buckley and his co-workers learned of the asbestos in the pipe insulation and of the diseases asbestos exposure could cause. Buckley was then given a respirator and some instruction on the "glove bag" method of removing asbestos. He testified that his efforts to use the respirator and glove bag method proved frustrating: the respirator fit poorly and slid down his face as he perspired in the intense heat of the steam tunnels; the plastic bags used to isolate the asbestos melted on the hot pipes, spilling out the material instead of containing it.

Buckley and as many as 140 other asbestos-exposed workers sought legal counsel after their complaints to Metro–North management went unresolved. In the FELA action now before us, Buckley is serving as test plaintiff for the claims of all the exposed employees. Metro–North stipulated in the District Court that it had "negligently exposed the plaintiff Michael Buckley to asbestos while he was working in Grand Central Terminal from June 1985 to the beginning of September 1987." "[N]o later than 1986," Metro–North also conceded, "[it] obtained actual notice of the presence of asbestos in Grand Central Terminal and notice of the hazard that working with or around asbestos posed to the health and welfare of its employees." Metro–North further acknowledged that "it exposed the plaintiff to asbestos without warning him that he was being exposed to asbestos and without training him how to safely handle and remove asbestos." *Ibid.* Prior to Metro–North's stipulation conceding negligence, the New York Attorney General's Office and the Office of the Inspector General of the Metropolitan Transportation Authority conducted a joint investigation, leading to these conclusions: Metro–North had "seriously disregarded the health and safety of its workers"; and the railroad's failings were "particularly egregious" because Metro–North was on notice of the asbestos problem as a result of complaints by its workers, a report by its own consultant, and inspections by the New York State Department of Labor.

II

Buckley asserted two claims for relief in his FELA-based complaint: first, he charged Metro–North with negligent infliction of emotional distress; second, he sought compensation for the cost of future medical monitoring. * * *

It is not apparent why (or even whether) the Court reverses the Second Circuit's determination on Buckley's second claim. The Court of Appeals held that a medical monitoring claim is solidly grounded, and this Court does not hold otherwise. Hypothesizing that Buckley demands lump-sum damages and nothing else, the Court ruminates on the appropriate remedy without answering the anterior question: Does the plaintiff have a claim for relief? Buckley has shown that Metro–North negligently exposed him to "extremely high levels of asbestos," and that this exposure warrants "medical monitoring in order to detect and treat [asbestos-related] diseases as they may arise." Buckley's expert medical witness estimated the annual costs of proper monitoring at $950. We do not know from the Court's opinion what more a plaintiff must show to qualify for relief.

A

In my view, the Second Circuit rightly held that a railworker negligently exposed to asbestos states a claim for relief under the FELA; recovery in such cases, again as the Court of Appeals held, should reflect the difference in cost between the medical tests a reasonable physician would prescribe for unexposed persons and the monitoring regime a reasonable physician would advise for persons exposed in the way Michael Buckley and his co-workers were.

Recognizing such a claim would align the FELA with the "evolving common law." *Gottshall*, 512 U.S., at 558, 114 S.Ct., at 2412 (SOUTER, J., concurring). "[A medical monitoring] action has been increasingly recognized by state courts as necessary given the latent nature of many diseases caused by exposure to hazardous materials and the traditional common law tort doctrine requirement that an injury be manifest." *Daigle v. Shell Oil Co.*, 972 F.2d 1527, 1533 (C.A.10 1992). As the Court understates, several state high courts have upheld medical monitoring cost recovery. In a pathmarking opinion, the United States Court of Appeals for the Third Circuit, interpreting Pennsylvania law, recognized a right to compensation for monitoring "necessary in order to diagnose properly the warning signs of disease." See *Paoli I*, 916 F.2d, at 851; see also *Paoli II*, 35 F.3d, at 785–788. Similarly, a number of Federal District Courts interpreting state law, and several state courts of first and second instance, have sustained medical monitoring claims. This Court, responsible for developing FELA law, finds little value in these decisions.

These courts have answered the question this Court passes by: What are the elements of a compensable medical monitoring claim? The Third Circuit, for example, has enumerated: A plaintiff can recover the costs of medical monitoring if (1) he establishes that he was significantly exposed to a proven hazardous substance through the negligent actions of the defendant; (2) as a proximate result of the exposure, the plaintiff suffers a significantly increased risk of contracting a serious latent disease; (3) by reason of the exposure a reasonable physician would prescribe a monitoring regime different from the one that would have been prescribed in the absence of the exposure; and (4) monitoring and testing procedures exist that make the early detection and treatment of the disease possible and beneficial. See *Paoli I*, 916 F.2d, at 852; *Paoli II*, 35 F.3d, at 788. Each factor must be shown by competent expert testimony. See *Paoli I*, 916 F.2d, at 852.

* * *

Traditional tort principles upon which the FELA rests warrant recognition of medical monitoring claims of the kind Buckley has asserted. As the Third Circuit explained, "[t]he policy reasons for recognizing this tort are obvious[:]"

"Medical monitoring claims acknowledge that, in a toxic age, significant harm can be done to an individual by a tortfeasor, notwithstanding latent manifestation of that harm. Moreover, . . . recognizing this tort does not require courts to speculate about the probability of future injury. It merely requires courts to ascertain the probability that the far less costly remedy of medical supervision is appropriate. Allowing plaintiffs to recover the cost of this care deters irresponsible discharge of toxic chemicals by defendants and encourages plaintiffs to detect and treat their injuries as soon as possible. These are conventional goals of the tort system. . . ." *Paoli I*, 916 F.2d, at 852.

* * *

B

The Court, as I read its opinion, leaves open the question whether Buckley may state a claim for relief under the FELA. The Court does not question the medical need for monitoring. It recognizes that cancer, one of the diseases Buckley faces an increased risk of suffering, is "unusually threatening and unusually frightening," and that detection of disease in early stages "can help to mitigate potentially serious future health effects." On the other hand, the Court notes there may be "uncertainty among medical professionals about just which tests are most usefully administered and when."

It is not uncommon, of course, that doctors will agree that medical attention is needed, yet disagree on what monitoring or treatment course is best. But uncertainty as to which tests are best or when they should be administered is not cause to deny a claim for relief. Fact triers in tort cases routinely face questions lacking indubitably clear answers: Did defendant's product cause plaintiff's disease? What will plaintiff's future disability and medical costs be? It bears repetition, moreover, that recovery on a FELA medical monitoring claim would be limited to the incremental cost of tests a reasonable physician would recommend as a result of the plaintiff's exposure.

* * *

Finally, the Court's anticipation of a " 'flood' of less important cases" and " 'unlimited and unpredictable liability' " is overblown. The employee's "injury" in the claim at stake is the economic burden additional medical surveillance entails; if an employer provides all that a reasonable physician would recommend for the exposed employee, the employee would incur no costs and hence have no claim for compensation. Nor does the FELA claim Buckley states pave the way for "tens of millions of individuals" with similar claims. It is doubtful that many legions in the universe of individuals ever exposed to toxic material could demonstrate that their employers negligently exposed them to a known hazardous substance, and thereby substantially increased the risk that they would suffer debilitating or deadly disease. Withholding relief, moreover, is dangerous, for lives will be lost when grave disease is diagnosed too late.

C

The Court emphasizes most heavily that several courts, while authorizing recovery for medical monitoring, have imposed or suggested special limitations on the tort remedy. In lieu of lump-sum damages, the Court indicates, a court-supervised fund might be the better remedy.

It is scarcely surprising that the Second Circuit did not consider relief through a court-supervised fund. So far as the record before us shows, no party argued in the District Court, the Second Circuit, or even this Court, that medical monitoring expenses may be recoverable, but not through a lump sum, only through a court fund. The question aired below was the prime one the Court obscures: Does Buckley's medical monitoring claim warrant any relief?

Buckley sought ''an 'amount of money' sufficient to 'compensate' him for 'future medical monitoring expenses.' '' He was not more precise about the form relief should take. The Court infers from Buckley's proposed charges to the jury, however, that he wanted what ''tort law ordinarily permits''—damages in a lump sum. I believe his claim qualifies for that relief. * * *

* * * If I comprehend the Court's enigmatic decision correctly, Buckley may replead a claim for relief and recover for medical monitoring, but he must receive that relief in a form other than a lump sum. Unaccountably, the Court resists the straightforward statement that would enlighten courts in this and similar cases: A claim for medical monitoring is cognizable under the FELA; it is a claim entirely in step with '' 'evolving common law.' '' I therefore dissent from the Court's judgment to the extent it relates to medical monitoring.

NOTES AND QUESTIONS

1. One issue that generated disagreement between the majority and the dissent in *Buckley* was whether a medical monitoring plaintiff should receive a lump-sum damage award, rather than reimbursement for surveillance costs from a court-supervised fund. In most tort cases, damages come in a lump sum—even for those components of an award related to future medical expenses and future lost income. Some courts, however, suggest a different approach for medical monitoring. The *Ayers* court itself addressed the issue, making the following points:

> In our view, the use of a court-supervised fund to administer medical-surveillance payments in mass exposure cases * * * offers significant advantages over a lump-sum verdict. * * *

> [A] fund would serve to limit the liability of defendants to the amount of expenses actually incurred. A lump-sum verdict attempts to estimate future expenses, but cannot predict the amounts that actually will be expended for medical purposes. Although conventional damage awards do not restrict plaintiffs in the use of money paid as compensatory damages, mass-exposure toxic-tort cases involve public interests not pres-

ent in conventional tort litigation. The public health interest is served by a fund mechanism that encourages regular medical monitoring for victims of toxic exposure.

Ayers, 525 A.2d at 314–15; see also Redland Soccer Club v. Dep't of Army, 696 A.2d 137 (Pa.1997); Hansen v. Mountain Fuel Supply Co., 858 P.2d 970 (Utah 1993). Do you agree that a court-administered fund is preferable to a lump sum award for medical monitoring? What arguments can you make in favor or against? Even if you prefer the use of a fund, should it be an absolute prerequisite to the allowance of medical monitoring recovery?

2. Is the creation of a fund a judicial function, or is this something that is best left to the legislature? Consider the following language from Henry v. Dow Chemical Co., 701 N.W.2d 684 (Mich.2005) in which the Michigan Supreme Court denied a claim for medical monitoring damages absent a present injury:

> Although we recognize that the common law is an instrument that may change as times and circumstances require, we decline plaintiffs' invitation to alter the common law of negligence liability to encompass a cause of action for medical monitoring. Recognition of a medical monitoring claim would involve extensive fact-finding and the weighing of numerous and conflicting policy concerns. We lack sufficient information to assess intelligently and fully the potential consequences of recognizing a medical monitoring claim.

> Equally important is that plaintiffs have asked this Court to effect a change in Michigan law that, in our view, ought to be made, if at all, by the Legislature. Indeed, the Legislature has already established policy in this arena by delegating the responsibility for dealing with health risks stemming from industrial pollution to the Michigan Department of Environmental Quality (MDEQ). As a matter of prudence, we defer in this case to the people's representatives in the Legislature, who are better suited to undertake the complex task of balancing the competing societal interests at stake.

Id. at 686. Do you agree with the *Henry* court's conclusion? Why or why not?

3. How important is it that medical monitoring be part of a protocol for addressing a disease that is treatable or curable? Although *Ayers* and other courts have placed importance on the value of an early diagnosis (see, e.g., In re Paoli R.R. Yard PCB Litig., 916 F.2d 829, 852 (3d Cir.1990)), at least one state supreme court has taken a different position:

> We [believe] that a plaintiff should not be required to show that a treatment currently exists for the disease that is the subject of medical monitoring. In this age of rapidly advancing medical science, we are hesitant to impose such a static requirement. In [*Bourgeois v. A.P. Green Industries, Inc.*, 716 So.2d 355, 363 (La.1998)], Chief Justice Calogero gave a poignant justification for permitting recovering even in instances where there is no proven treatment:

>> One thing that … a plaintiff might gain [even in the absence of available treatment] is certainty as to his fate, whatever it might be. If a plaintiff has been placed at an increased risk for a latent disease

through exposure to a hazardous substance, absent medical monitoring, he must live each day with the uncertainty of whether the disease is present in his body. If, however, he is able to take advantage of medical monitoring and the monitoring detects no evidence of disease, then, at least for the time being, the plaintiff can receive the comfort of peace of mind. Moreover, even if medical monitoring did detect evidence of an irreversible and untreatable disease, the plaintiff might still achieve some peace of mind through this knowledge by getting his financial affairs in order, making lifestyle changes, and, even perhaps, making peace with estranged loved ones or with his religion. Certainly, those options should be available to the innocent plaintiff who finds himself at an increased risk for a serious latent disease through no fault of his own.

716 So.2d at 363 (Calegero, C.J., concurring).

Bower v. Westinghouse Elec. Corp., 522 S.E.2d 424, 434 (W.Va.1999).

The *Bower* decision drew a sharp dissent from one justice, who stated that "the practical effect of this decision is to make almost every West Virginian a potential plaintiff in a medical monitoring cause of action." Id. at 435 (Maynard, J., dissenting). It also drew criticism from some legal commentators. See, e.g., Victor E. Schwartz, Leah Lorber, & Emily Laird, Medical Monitoring: The Right Way and the Wrong Way, 70 Mo.L.Rev. 349, 366–67 (2005) ("The court's holding in *Bower* stands in stark contrast to the medical and scientific perspective that medical monitoring programs should only be implemented for patients who have potentially treatable or curable disease. * * * Rather than being guided by principles of effective treatment or cure of disease, the court's ruling unabashedly allows for medical monitoring based on 'the subjective desires of a plaintiff for information concerning the state of his or her health.' ") What do you think? If you are inclined to agree with the *Bowers* majority, how would you describe the broader goals behind medical monitoring recovery? In other words, if medical monitoring damages are not connected to the treatment of future disease, what purposes do they serve?

4. What about the "flood of litigation" concern identified by Justice Breyer in *Buckley*? See *Buckley,* 521 U.S. at 442 ("[T]ens of millions of individuals may have suffered exposure to substances that might justify some form of substance-exposure-related medical monitoring. And that fact, along with uncertainty as to the amount of liability, could threaten both a 'flood' of less important cases * * *.") At first glance, this concern seems connected to the question of whether medical monitoring recovery should be limited to situations where a plaintiff demonstrates an existing physical injury. In other words, the "floodgates" argument would seem stronger if cases are open to the broad universe of potential plaintiffs who are exposed to toxins, but have not manifested clinical symptoms of disease connected to the exposure. See, e.g., *Henry,* 701 N.W.2d at 686. In a recent law review article, Professor Jamie A. Grodsky suggested that such thinking might be outdated. Professor Grodsky argued that courts need to re-think the concept of "physical injury" in light of developments in genetic science that make it easier to detect the consequences of toxic exposure before the manifestation of clinical symptoms of disease. These changes, she asserted, counsel for a reinvigorated use of medical monitoring as a remedy in tort law.

> [T]he primary purpose of monitoring is to detect disease in its earliest phases, allowing for timely medical intervention. Technical challenges aside, such a remedy would seem fitting as molecular biology and genomics begin to illuminate the epidemiological "black box." Whereas traditional epidemiology is limited in its ability to detect disease at a time in its natural history when intervention would be most effective, new techniques may allow for preventive intervention before disease progresses to an irreversible stage. In the future, at least for some exposures, science may provide courts with new information regarding (1) which exposed individuals have suffered genetic and/or cellular damage; and (2) which of these individuals are likely to progress to symptomatic disease.
>
>   * * *
>
> Monitoring's inherently pragmatic focus broadens its appeal relative to other nontraditional tort theories. Indeed, reconsideration of the monitoring remedy would reduce pressure on courts to respond to a potentially expanding universe of claims for mental distress or enhanced risk in the genomic age. In addition to serving fairness and deterrence rationales, medical monitoring—in the end—may serve the interests of defendants and plaintiffs alike. Discovery of disease at earlier stages may help prevent disease progression and ultimately reduce treatment costs and limit future personal injury claims.

Jamie A. Grodsky, Genomics and Toxic Torts: Dismantling the Risk–Injury Divide, 59 Stan.L.Rev. 1671, 1712–14 (2007). Is Professor Grodsky persuasive? Do the benefits she suggested outweigh concerns about the number of potential plaintiffs?

5. Developments in genetic science, however, do not necessarily portend an easier road for medical monitoring plaintiffs—especially in light of the requirement imposed by some courts that plaintiffs demonstrate a "significantly increased risk" of contracting disease as a result of an exposure. See *Redland Soccer*, 696 A.2d at 145–46; see also *Ayers*, 525 A.2d at 312 (considering "the relative increase in the chance of onset of disease in those exposed"). For example, in Sheridan v. NGK Metals Corp., 609 F.3d 239 (3d Cir.2010), the plaintiffs claimed that exposure to beryllium dust and particulates increased their risk of developing chronic beryllium disease (CBD) and sought establishment of a fund by beryllium manufacturers and suppliers to pay for the costs of medical surveillance. Applying Pennsylvania law, a district court dismissed the plaintiffs' claims, and the Third Circuit affirmed on grounds that the plaintiffs failed to provide medical tests demonstrating that they had genetic markers showing a predisposition to developing CBD after exposure to beryllium. In so ruling, the *Sheridan* court relied on a Pennsylvania appellate court decision that interpreted *Redland Soccer* in a similar fact setting. Pohl v. NGK Metals Corp., 936 A.2d 43 (Pa.Super.2007). The *Sheridan* court explained: "Because the plaintiffs in *Pohl* were not beryllium sensitized and had not otherwise made a plausible showing that they faced a 'significantly increased risk' of developing CBD, the [*Pohl* court] held that these plaintiffs failed to make a prima facie showing of their medical monitoring claim under

[*Redland Soccer*].'' The court then ruled that the same outcome applied in the case before it.

Should a plaintiff be compelled to produce genetic evidence of a predisposition to disease to obtain medical monitoring damages? What if the scientific evidence pertaining to a particular toxin is unclear or in the developing stages? Should courts ignore the data completely? If not, how should it be used in determining the availability of medical monitoring damages?

6. *Buckley* has proven to be an influential decision, and most state courts that considered medical monitoring in years subsequent to the decision came down against plaintiffs seeking the remedy. See, e.g., Henry v. Dow Chem. Co., 701 N.W.2d 684, 686 (Mich.2005); Wood v. Wyeth–Ayerst Labs., Div. of Am. Home Prods., 82 S.W.3d 849 (Ky.2002); Badillo v. Am. Brands, Inc., 16 P.3d 435 (Nev.2001); Hinton v. Monsanto Co., 813 So.2d 827 (Ala. 2001). As note 4 suggests, a recurring concern identified by courts opposed to medical monitoring is opening up such recovery to those without physical injury. But as the next case makes clear, this view has not been unanimous.

MEYER EX REL. COPLIN v. FLUOR CORP.

Missouri Supreme Court, 2007.
220 S.W.3d 712.

RICHARD B. TEITELMAN, JUDGE.

Lani Meyer, by and through her next friend, Rebecca Coplin, (''Plaintiff'') appeals from the order of the circuit court denying class certification in a tort action filed on behalf of a proposed class of children exposed to lead due to the operation of the Doe Run lead smelter in Herculaneum, Missouri. Plaintiff seeks, *inter alia*, to recover compensatory damages for the expense of prospective medical monitoring allegedly necessitated by emissions from the smelter. This Court concludes that the circuit court erred in denying class certification. The judgment is reversed, and the case is remanded.

I. FACTS

Fluor Corporation and several other entities and individuals (''Defendants'') are involved with the operation of the Doe Run lead smelter in Herculaneum. Each year, the smelter emits large quantities of lead into the local environment, allegedly resulting in higher levels of lead and other toxins than would otherwise be present in and around Herculaneum. There is no dispute that lead is toxic and that children are generally more susceptible to injury from lead poisoning than are adults. There is also no dispute that injuries from lead exposure are often latent injuries; that is, a diagnosable physical injury or illness is not immediately apparent and years may pass before symptoms are detected.

Plaintiff filed a petition asserting that she is a member of a class of children in and around Herculaneum who has been exposed to toxic emissions from the smelter. Plaintiff alleged negligence, strict liability, private nuisance, and trespass as theories of liability and sought compensatory damages to establish a medical monitoring program for class members. The purpose of the monitoring program would be to provide ongoing diagnostic testing to determine whether the exposure to lead and other toxins has caused or is in the process of causing an injury or illness. The proposed class consists of over 200 children * * *.

* * *

The circuit court held a certification hearing and found that "individual issues will necessarily predominate over common issues in this case" and that the case could not be efficiently addressed on a class-wide basis. Accordingly, the court entered an order denying Plaintiff's motion for class certification.

On appeal, Plaintiff argues that the circuit court erred because its class action analysis assumed incorrectly that a present physical injury is a necessary element of a medical monitoring claim. Plaintiff asserts that the circuit court focused on individual proof issues that are primarily relevant to a personal injury action, not a medical monitoring claim. * * *

II. STANDARD OF REVIEW

This Court reviews an order granting or denying class certification for abuse of discretion. A class certification hearing is a procedural matter in which the sole issue is whether plaintiff has met the requirements for a class action. Thus, the trial court has no authority to conduct a preliminary inquiry into whether the plaintiff has stated a cause of action or will prevail on the merits. Although the class certification decision lies in the circuit court's discretion, the courts should err in close cases in favor of certification because the class can be modified as the case progresses.

III. ANALYSIS

* * *

In toxic tort cases, there is often no immediately diagnosable physical injury or illness. Instead, the injury is latent and may not be discovered for months or even years. The widely recognized tort law concepts premised upon a present physical injury are ill-equipped to deal with cases involving latent injury. To deal with this reality, tort law has evolved over the years to allow plaintiffs compensation for medical monitoring. A medical monitoring claim seeks to recover the costs of future reasonably necessary diagnostic testing to detect latent injuries or diseases that may develop as a result of exposure to toxic substances. *Ayers v. Jackson Township*, 106 N.J. 557, 525 A.2d 287, 308 (1987). The courts that have approved medical monitoring claims recognize that "significant economic harm may be inflicted on those exposed to toxic substances, notwithstanding the fact that the physical harm resulting from such exposure is often latent." *Bower v. Westinghouse Electric Corp.*, 206 W.Va. 133, 522 S.E.2d 424, 429 (1999)(citing *In re Paoli Railroad Yard PCB Litigation*, 916 F.2d 829, 850 (3rd Cir.1990)).

This Court has not addressed whether Missouri law permits the recovery of medical monitoring damages. However, in *Elam v. Alcolac*,

Inc., 765 S.W.2d 42 (Mo.App.1988), the court analyzed the admissibility of medical testimony in a toxic tort case and, in holding that the testimony was admissible, stated that:

> The evidence of significant, albeit unquantified, risk of cancer from the exposure to the toxic [chemicals], however, was competent to prove, as a separate element of damage, the need for medical surveillance of the immune system and other organs, and hence was admissible for that purpose.

The *Elam* court recognized that among the potential damages sustained by a plaintiff who is exposed to a toxin is the need for medical monitoring for the "early detection of serious disease from the chronic exposure" to toxins. *Id.* at 209. The court further reasoned that medical monitoring costs are recoverable because "compensation for necessary medical expenses reasonably certain to be incurred in the future rests on well-accepted legal principles." *Id.* at 209. These "well-accepted" principles of Missouri law provide that a plaintiff is entitled to recover for the prospective consequences of the defendant's tortious conduct if the injury is reasonably certain to occur. Recognizing that a defendant's conduct has created the need for future medical monitoring does not create a new tort. It is simply a compensable item of damage when liability is established under traditional tort theories of recovery. Recovery for medical monitoring damages is thus consistent with a touchstone of Missouri law, the principle that a plaintiff is entitled to full compensation for past or present injuries caused by the defendant.

Defendants assert that any recovery for medical monitoring is contingent upon the existence of a present physical injury. Although some courts have so concluded, a present physical injury requirement is inconsistent with the theory of recovery. As with any claim based in tort law, the injury underlying a medical monitoring claim is the invasion of a legally protected interest. Just as an individual has a legally protected interest in avoiding physical injury, so too does an individual have an interest in avoiding expensive medical evaluations caused by the tortious conduct of others. * * * Even though a plaintiff may not have yet developed a diagnosable physical injury, it is not accurate to conclude that no compensable injury has been sustained. Thus, the theory of recovery for medical monitoring damages is that the plaintiff is entitled, upon proper proof, to obtain compensation for an injury to the legally protected interest in avoiding the cost of reasonably necessary medical monitoring occasioned by the defendant's actions. *Bower v. Westinghouse Electric Corp.*, 206 W.Va. 133, 522 S.E.2d 424, 429–430 (1999). The injury for which compensation is sought is not a present physical injury. Instead, medical monitoring damages compensate the plaintiff for the quantifiable costs of periodic medical examinations reasonably necessary for the early detection and treatment of latent injuries caused by the plaintiff's exposure to toxic substances. A physical injury requirement is inconsistent with the reality of latent injury and with the fact that the purpose of medical monitoring is to facilitate the early diagnosis and treatment of latent injuries caused by exposure to toxins. In short, a physical injury requirement essentially extinguishes the claim and bars the plaintiff from a full recovery.

These considerations have led a number of courts that have addressed this issue to conclude that recovering medical monitoring damages does not require a threshold showing of present physical injury. The general consensus that has emerged in these cases is that a plaintiff can obtain damages for medical monitoring upon a showing that "the plaintiff has a significantly increased risk of contracting a particular disease relative to what would be the case in the absence of exposure." *Bower v. Westinghouse Electric Corp.*, 206 W.Va. 133, 522 S.E.2d 424, 433 (1999). Once that has been proven, the plaintiff must then show that "medical monitoring is, to a reasonable degree of medical certainty, necessary in order to diagnose properly the warning signs of disease." *Id.* at 431. This general statement of the issues of proof provides the proper baseline for analyzing Plaintiff's argument that the circuit court erred in determining that individual issues of proof are predominant.

C. *The Circuit Court's Order*

In its order denying class certification, the circuit court identified * * * issues that the court concluded were predominant over the common issues [in part by assuming that each plaintiff would need to prove a present physical injury].

      * * *

IV. CONCLUSION

The circuit court misapplied the law by applying personal injury concepts to Plaintiff's medical monitoring claim and in holding that these individual personal injury issues were predominate over common issues. The judgment denying class certification is reversed, and case is remanded.

NOTE AND QUESTIONS

1. What is your reaction to the *Meyer* opinion? Does it set out more convincing points than do the cases that limit the application of medical monitoring? More specifically, does it adequately respond to the "flood of litigation" issue raised by Justice Breyer in *Buckley*?

2. With respect to the possibility of using collective procedural mechanisms such as class action lawsuits to handle these types of cases, see Chapter 14, where we will cover this topic in detail.

2. FEAR OF DISEASE

The debate about whether a plaintiff can receive medical monitoring damages is intertwined with another consequence that can flow from toxic exposure—emotional distress based on fear that a serious disease might later develop. See, e.g., Bourgeois v. A.P. Green Indus., Inc., 716 So.2d

355, 363 (La.1998) (Calegero, C.J., concurring) (medical monitoring might help a plaintiff "achieve some peace of mind" even where no proven treatment for a feared disease exists). In some ways, one might not view a claim based on fear of disease as a "futures" action at all—that is, the emotional distress caused by the fear is very much a present concern. Nevertheless, fear of disease claims do raise many concerns related to the other claims covered in this unit.

Tort actions for damages related to emotional distress claims are not new to the law. Courts, however, have long been reluctant to award damages for such harm when the emotional distress is unaccompanied by a physical injury. This reluctance is based, in part, on the difficulty of separating valid from trivial claims. In addition, the reluctance stems from concern about the proverbial flood of litigation. Nonetheless, courts have long encountered situations where denying emotional distress recovery would be unfair, and fear of disease based on toxic exposure is one of the areas where courts have recognized that some recovery for emotional distress might be warranted.

The challenge in fear of disease cases, as elsewhere, is determining when to open the door to litigation while balancing the concerns that counsel against recovery. Although it is difficult to definitively describe categories of approaches, it is possible to place courts that address fear of disease claims into two broad groups. First, some courts limit fear of disease recovery to situations where plaintiffs can show a physical consequence related emotional distress. As explained below, this might relate to a determination of whether defendant's conduct caused a sufficient physical impact on plaintiff. Or it might, instead, relate to physical consequences that stem from the emotional distress itself. Other courts pay less attention to the question of a physical consequence and look for different markers that might indicate whether fear of disease is "reasonable" and therefore compensable in tort law. See generally Andrew R. Klein, Fear of Disease and the Puzzle of Futures Cases in Tort, 35 U.C. Davis L.Rev. 965 (2002). This section will explore both broad approaches to the fear of disease problem.

a. Physical Consequence as a Limitation on Fear of Disease

The U.S. Supreme Court's decision in *Buckley* is an excellent example of a court using a particular physical consequence as a prerequisite to fear of disease recovery. The facts of *Buckley* are set out in the previous section on medical monitoring. The portion of the Court's opinion that addresses fear of disease is set out below.

METRO–NORTH COMMUTER RAILROAD CO. v. BUCKLEY

United States Supreme Court, 1997.
521 U.S. 424, 117 S.Ct. 2113, 138 L.Ed.2d 560.

JUSTICE BREYER delivered the opinion of the Court.

* * *

The critical question before us in respect to Buckley's "emotional distress" claim is whether the physical contact with insulation dust that accompanied his emotional distress amounts to a "physical impact" as this Court used that term in [*Consolidated Rail Corporation v. Gottshall*, 512 U.S. 532 (1994)]. In *Gottshall*, an emotional distress case, the Court interpreted the word "injury" in FELA § 1, a provision that makes "[e]very common carrier by railroad . . . liable in damages to any person suffering injury while . . . employed" by the carrier if the "injury" results from carrier "negligence." 45 U.S.C. § 51. * * *

The [*Gottshall*] Court also set forth several more specific legal propositions. It recognized that the common law of torts does not permit recovery for negligently inflicted emotional distress *unless* the distress falls within certain specific categories that amount to recovery-permitting exceptions. The law, for example, does permit recovery for emotional distress where that distress accompanies a physical injury, and it often permits recovery for distress suffered by a close relative who witnesses the physical injury of a negligence victim. The Court then held that FELA § 1, mirroring the law of many States, sometimes permitted recovery "for damages for negligent infliction of emotional distress," and, in particular, it does so where a plaintiff seeking such damages satisfies the common law's "zone of danger" test. It defined that test by stating that the law permits "recovery for emotional injury" by

> "those plaintiffs who *sustain a physical impact* as a result of a defendant's negligent conduct, or who are placed in immediate risk of physical harm by that conduct." [*Gottshall*, 512 U.S. at 547–548 (emphasis added by Court)].

The case before us * * * focuses on the italicized words "physical impact." The Second Circuit interpreted those words as including a simple physical contact with a substance that might cause a disease at a future time, so long as the contact was of a kind that would "cause fear in a reasonable person." In our view, however, the "physical impact" to which *Gottshall* referred does not include a simple physical contact with a substance that might cause a disease at a substantially later time—where that substance, or related circumstance, threatens no harm other than that disease-related risk.

First, *Gottshall* cited many state cases in support of its adoption of the "zone of danger" test quoted above. And in each case where recovery for emotional distress was permitted, the case involved a threatened physical contact that caused, or might have caused, immediate traumatic harm.

Second, *Gottshall*'s language, read in light of this precedent, seems similarly limited. [*Gottshall,* 512 U.S. at 555] ("zone of danger test . . . is consistent with FELA's central focus on physical perils").

Taken together, language and cited precedent indicate that the words "physical impact" do not encompass every form of "physical contact." And, in particular, they do not include a contact that amounts to no more than an exposure—an exposure, such as that before us, to a substance that poses some future risk of disease and which contact causes emotional distress only because the worker learns that he may become ill after a substantial period of time.

Third, common-law precedent does not favor the plaintiff. Common-law courts do permit a plaintiff who suffers from a disease to recover for related negligently caused emotional distress, and some courts permit a plaintiff who exhibits a physical symptom of exposure to recover. But with only a few exceptions, common-law courts have denied recovery to those who, like Buckley, are disease and symptom free.

Fourth, the general policy reasons to which *Gottshall* referred—in its explanation of why common-law courts have restricted recovery for emotional harm to cases falling within rather narrowly defined categories— militate against an expansive definition of "physical impact" here. Those reasons include: (a) special "difficult[y] for judges and juries" in separating valid, important claims from those that are invalid or "trivial," *Gottshall,* 512 U.S. at 557; (b) a threat of "unlimited and unpredictable liability," *ibid.*; and (c) the "potential for a flood" of comparatively unimportant, or "trivial," claims, *ibid.*

To separate meritorious and important claims from invalid or trivial claims does not seem easier here than in other cases in which a plaintiff might seek recovery for typical negligently caused emotional distress. The facts before us illustrate the problem. The District Court, when concluding that Buckley had failed to present "sufficient evidence to allow a jury to find . . . a real emotional injury," pointed out that, apart from Buckley's own testimony, there was virtually no evidence of distress. Indeed, Buckley continued to work with insulating material "even though . . . he could have transferred" elsewhere, he "continued to smoke cigarettes" despite doctors' warnings, and his doctor did not refer him "either to a psychologist or to a social worker." The Court of Appeals reversed because it found certain objective corroborating evidence, namely, "workers' complaints to supervisors and investigative bodies." Both kinds of "objective" evidence—the confirming and disconfirming evidence—seem only indirectly related to the question at issue, the existence and seriousness of Buckley's claimed emotional distress. Yet, given the difficulty of separating valid from invalid emotional injury claims, the evidence before us may typify the kind of evidence to which parties and the courts would have to look.

* * *

More important, the physical contact at issue here—a simple (though extensive) contact with a carcinogenic substance—does not seem to offer much help in separating valid from invalid emotional distress claims. That is because contacts, even extensive contacts, with serious carcinogens are common. They may occur without causing serious emotional distress, but sometimes they do cause distress, and reasonably so, for cancer is both an unusually threatening and unusually frightening disease. The relevant problem, however, remains one of evaluating a claimed emotional reaction to an *increased* risk of dying. An external circumstance—exposure—makes some emotional distress more likely. But how can one determine from the external circumstance of exposure whether, or when, a claimed strong emotional reaction to an *increased* mortality risk (say, from 23% to 28%) is reasonable and genuine, rather than overstated—particularly when the relevant statistics themselves are controversial and uncertain (as is usually the case), and particularly since neither those exposed nor judges or juries are experts in statistics? The evaluation problem seems a serious one.

The large number of those exposed and the uncertainties that may surround recovery also suggest what *Gottshall* called the problem of "unlimited and unpredictable liability." Does such liability mean, for example, that the costs associated with a rule of liability would become so great that, given the nature of the harm, it would seem unreasonable to require the public to pay the higher prices that may result? The same characteristics further suggest what *Gottshall* called the problem of a "flood" of cases that, if not "trivial," are comparatively less important. In a world of limited resources, would a rule permitting immediate large-scale recoveries for widespread emotional distress caused by fear of future disease diminish the likelihood of recovery by those who later suffer from the disease?

We do not raise these questions to answer them (for we do not have the answers), but rather to show that general policy concerns of a kind that have led common-law courts to deny recovery for certain classes of negligently caused harms are present in this case as well. That being so, we cannot find in *Gottshall*'s underlying rationale any basis for departing from *Gottshall*'s language and precedent or from the current common-law consensus. That is to say, we cannot find in *Gottshall*'s language, cited precedent, other common-law precedent, or related concerns of policy a legal basis for adopting the emotional distress recovery rule adopted by the Court of Appeals.

Buckley raises several important arguments in reply. He points out, for example, that common-law courts do permit recovery for emotional distress where a plaintiff has physical symptoms; and he argues that his evidence of exposure and enhanced mortality risk is as strong a proof as an accompanying physical symptom that his emotional distress is genuine.

This argument, however, while important, overlooks the fact that the common law in this area does not examine the genuineness of emotional harm case by case. Rather, it has developed recovery-permitting categories the contours of which more distantly reflect this, and other, abstract general policy concerns. The point of such categorization is to deny courts the authority to undertake a case-by-case examination. The common law permits emotional distress recovery for that category of plaintiffs who suffer from a disease (or exhibit a physical symptom), for example, thereby finding a special effort to evaluate emotional symptoms warranted in that category of cases—perhaps from a desire to make a physically injured victim whole or because the parties are likely to be in court in any event. In other cases, however, falling outside the special recovery-permitting categories, it has reached a different conclusion. The relevant question here concerns the validity of a rule that seeks to redefine such a category. It would not be easy to redefine "physical impact" in terms of a rule that turned on, say, the "massive, lengthy, [or] tangible" nature of a contact that amounted to an exposure, whether to contaminated water, or to germ-laden air, or to carcinogen-containing substances, such as insulation dust containing asbestos. But, in any event, for the reasons we have stated, we cannot find that the common law has done so.

* * *

JUSTICE GINSBURG, with whom JUSTICE STEVENS joins, concurring in the judgment in part and dissenting in part.

* * *

Buckley's extensive contact with asbestos particles in Grand Central's tunnels, as I comprehend his situation, constituted "physical impact" as that term was used in *Gottshall*. Nevertheless, I concur in the Court's judgment with respect to Buckley's emotional distress claim. In my view, that claim fails because Buckley did not present objective evidence of severe emotional distress. Buckley testified at trial that he was angry at Metro–North and fearful of developing an asbestos-related disease. However, he sought no professional help to ease his distress, and presented no medical testimony concerning his mental health. Under these circumstances, Buckley's emotional distress claim fails as a matter of law.

* * *

NOTES AND QUESTIONS

1. The impact rule was once widely applied as a limitation in all types of negligent infliction of emotional distress actions. Outside the toxic tort realm, most jurisdictions have expanded the rule to include not only plaintiffs who are impacted, but also those placed in the "zone of danger" by a defendant's conduct. In addition, a good number of jurisdictions allow bystanders to accidents—even if outside the zone of danger—to recover negligent infliction of emotional distress damages when the bystander witnesses an accident involving a victim with whom they have a close family relationship. See, e.g., Thing v. La Chusa, 771 P.2d 814 (Cal.1989). Fear of disease claims based on toxic exposures, however, raise special concerns. Perhaps most significant is that the number of potential plaintiffs in such cases is greater than in more isolated emotional distress claims, raising again the floodgate-of-litigation concern. On this ground, *Buckley* and *Gottshall* are not alone in applying the more restrictive impact rule to fear of disease actions. See Wood v. Wyeth–Ayerst Labs., 82 S.W.3d 849, 857–58 (Ky.2002); Temple Inland Forest Prods. Corp. v. Carter, 993 S.W.2d 88, 93 (Tex.1999). Some courts, however, have viewed the floodgates argument more skeptically. See Bass v. Nooney Co., 646 S.W.2d 765, 770 (Mo.1983) ("In answer to the argument that permitting such claims would release the floodgates of litigation, experience in jurisdictions which abrogated the impact rule proved to the contrary."). How much weight should courts place on the floodgates concern in deciding whether to entertain fear of disease claims? Does it matter whether the fear is rational? See E. Donald Elliott, The Future of Toxic Torts: Of Chemophobia, Risk as a Compensable Injury and Hybrid Compensation Systems, 25 Hous.L.Rev. 781, 785 (1988) ("Americans have a widespread, irrational fear of chemicals * * *. [W]hat science knows about chemicals in our environment suggest that they are actually a relatively minor source of risks to our health * * *.").

2. The Third Restatement of Torts addresses the zone of danger cases, permitting recovery for those in "immediate danger" of physical harm who, nevertheless, suffer only emotional harm. However, it does not include those who are exposed and fear disease, explaining:

> [T]hese cases are different from others under Subsection (a) [zone of danger], in which the risk of harm has terminated and no future event exists that might trigger bodily harm. By contrast, courts deny recovery in cancerphobia cases, at least during the latency period before the person actually suffers bodily injury. The rule stated in Subsection (a), which requires that the person be placed in "immediate" danger, does not apply to these cases. One reason for this limitation is a concern that multiple lawsuits—one when the person is exposed and another when bodily injury occurs—would be required. On the other hand, exposure to some substances, such as HIV, that create a risk of contracting a dreaded disease, might create emotional harm in a way that does not raise the issue of multiple lawsuits because the person can determine relatively quickly whether the exposure actually did cause physical injury. These cases are more akin to those in which a person is put in danger of being hit by an automobile and thereby suffers emotional harm. In both the automobile and the HIV-exposure cases, the period during which the person is subject to risk and suffers emotional harm is (unlike the cancerphobia cases) relatively confined. Thus, Subsection (a) applies to cases in which the period between exposure and determination of disease is sufficiently short.

Restatement (Third) of Torts: Liability for Physical and Emotional Harm § 46 cmt. h (Tentative Draft No. 5, 2007).

3. Since impact remains as a limitation on fear of disease claims, defining the term becomes important. The *Buckley* Court concluded that even long-term exposure to a carcinogenic substance was insufficient. But should this conclusion change if science develops ways to better understand the impact of toxic exposure on an individual's cellular or subcellular system? Little caselaw supports this position, and commentators take differing views. See Gary E. Marchant, Genetic Data in Toxic Tort Litigation, 14 J.L. & Pol'y 7, 29 (2006) ("Gene expression data can potentially help at-risk plaintiffs to demonstrate a present injury * * *."); James F. d'Entremont, Fear Factor: The Future of Cancerphobia and Fear of Future Disease Claims in the Toxicogenomic Age, 52 Loy.L.Rev. 807 (2006) (arguing that toxicogenomics will not "breathe new life into fear of future disease claims"); John C. Childs, Toxicogenomics: New Chapter in Causation and Exposure in Toxic Tort Litigation, 69 Def.Couns.J. 441, 444 (2002) ("cellular and molecular testing may cause courts to find the requisite present injury" in a fear of disease claim).

4. The issue of physical impact is different from the issue of whether a plaintiff has a physical manifestation from the emotional distress, something that courts also use to limit emotional distress actions. Physical manifestations might include things like ulcers, headaches, or hives related to plaintiff's emotional state. See, e.g., Payton v. Abbott Labs., 437 N.E.2d 171, 181 (Mass.1982) ("[P]laintiff's physical harm must either cause or be caused by the emotional distress alleged, and * * * must be manifested by objective symptomatology * * *.") What policies support the requirement of a physical manifestation before permitting a fear of disease claim—or any emotional distress claim—to go forward? Is physical manifestation any better as a marker for legitimate emotional distress than physical impact or a requirement that a plaintiff have an existing physical injury? Or does such a rule essentially base the ability to recover on the idiosyncratic reaction of each individual plaintiff?

5. The terminology in this area of the law can be confusing. Fear of disease appropriately can be viewed as a particular type of emotional distress claim. But some courts use the term "cancerphobia" to describe the same set of circumstances. See d'Entremont, supra at 811 ("[C]ancerphobia and fear of future disease are two specific types of mental anguish or emotional distress.") Although the terms are sometimes used interchangeably, it is worth noting that cancerphobia does describe a particular diagnosed condition. Id. at 811 n.18 (quoting Lawrence G. Cetrulo, 1 Toxic Torts Litigation Guides § 4:14, at 4–28–29 (2002)) (" '[C]ancerphobia' is a defined medical condition; therefore claims for 'cancerphobia' may be distinguished from those for 'fear of future disease.' An individual bringing a cancerphobia claim may be required to introduce expert medical evidence, whereas an individual bringing a fear of future disease claim generally need not introduce such evidence."). Other types of phobias also have raised issues in tort actions seeking damages for emotional distress. See, e.g., Jill Trachtenberg, Living in Fear: Recovering Negligent Infliction of Emotional Distress Based on the Fear of Contracting AIDS, 2 DePaul J. Health Care L. 529 (1999).

6. Much of the discussion in *Buckley* and this set of notes has focused on the floodgates argument. It is important to keep in mind, however, that traditional limitations on emotional distress claims are based on more than just this concern. Most significantly, courts have long placed at least equal weight on the importance of being able to separate trivial or even faked emotional distress claims from substantial and legitimate ones. On this score, one might question the value of the impact rule in fear of disease cases. In other words, is there any reason to think that the impact rule does a good job separating legitimate fear claims from trivial ones? Certainly, exposure to a substance that might lead to a disease such as cancer could generate legitimate concern, regardless of how one views the question of impact, and even if the odds of contracting disease are statistically low. See, e.g., Clark v. United States, 660 F.Supp. 1164, 1175 (W.D.Wash.1987). Given this, are you comfortable "filtering" such cases out of the tort system simply to limit the number of potential cases? Or do we need to look to different methods to decide when such claims should be considered? The next section addresses this very concern.

b. Reasonableness as a Limitation on Fear of Disease

A number of courts reject the notion that a plaintiff's ability to maintain a fear of disease action should be connected to a physical consequence—be it an impact or a physical manifestation of emotional distress. Most of these courts do not deny the importance of establishing boundaries to limit claims for fear of disease. Nevertheless, they define these limits in a very different ways. A well-known example of a broad approach is Sterling v. Velsicol, 855 F.2d 1188 (6th Cir.1988). In *Sterling,* the defendant negligently discarded hazardous substances into a landfill over a 10-year period. Citizens who lived near the landfill filed a class action, seeking damages based on exposure to the toxins. The trial court awarded damages to a representative group of plaintiffs, including recovery for emotional distress. The Sixth Circuit affirmed the emotional distress award, stating that the plaintiffs needed to demonstrate only a *reasonable connection* between the plaintiffs' distress and the possibility of future disease. The court did not base its opinion on any physical impact or manifestation. Instead, the court simply found it sufficient that the plaintiffs' fear "clearly constitute[d] a present injury * * * [and] a *reasonable fear* of contracting cancer or some other disease in the future as a result of ingesting [the defendant's] chemicals." Id. at 1206 (emphasis added).

There are a number of courts that, like *Sterling,* have used a broad reasonableness standard in establishing a standard for when to entertain fear of disease claims. See, e.g., Hagerty v. L & L Marine Servs., Inc., 788 F.2d 315, 318 (5th Cir.1986); Wetherill v. Univ. of Chicago, 565 F.Supp. 1553, 1559 (N.D.Ill.1983). However, other courts—even when rejecting the impact or physical manifestation rules—worry that a generic inquiry into reasonableness is too vague to constitute a manageable standard. Given this, some courts have tried to refine the standard for permitting fear of disease claims to limit the universe of claimants in a more precise fashion. Our next case is a well-known example.

POTTER v. FIRESTONE TIRE & RUBBER CO.

California Supreme Court, 1993.
6 Cal.4th 965, 863 P.2d 795, 25 Cal.Rptr.2d 550.

B<small>AXTER</small>, J<small>USTICE</small>.

We granted review in this case to consider * * * whether emotional distress engendered by a fear of cancer or other serious physical illness or injury following exposure to a carcinogen or other toxic substance is an injury for which damages may be recovered in a negligence action in the absence of physical injury * * *.

* * *

Our analysis of existing case law and policy considerations relevant to the availability of damages for emotional distress leads us to conclude that, generally, in the absence of a present physical injury or illness, recovery of damages for fear of cancer in a negligence action should be allowed only if the plaintiff pleads and proves that the fear stems from a knowledge, corroborated by reliable medical and scientific opinion, that it is more likely than not that the feared cancer will develop in the future due to the toxic exposure.

* * *

I.

FACTUAL AND PROCEDURAL BACKGROUND

This is a toxic exposure case brought by four landowners living adjacent to a landfill. As a result of defendant Firestone's practice of disposing of its toxic wastes at the landfill, the landowners were subjected to prolonged exposure to certain carcinogens. While none of the landowners currently suffers from any cancerous or precancerous condition, each faces an enhanced but unquantified risk of developing cancer in the future due to the exposure.

* * *

[P]laintiffs [sued] Firestone for damages and declaratory relief. Their complaints against Firestone stated [several] causes of action [including negligent infliction of emotional distress]. * * * After considering all the evidence, the court found that Firestone was negligent, * * * [and that negligent infliction of emotional distress was established]. Judgment was entered in favor of plaintiffs.

* * *

[In ruling on the negligent infliction of emotional distress claim,] the court * * * stated that * * * "plaintiffs will always fear, and reasonably so, that physical impairments they experience are the result of the well water and are the precursers [*sic*] of life threatening disease. Their fears are not merely subjective but are corroborated by substantial medical and scientific opinion." Based on these findings, plaintiffs were awarded damages totaling $800,000 for their lifelong fear of cancer and resultant emotional distress.

* * *

Firestone appealed, arguing * * * that the award for "fear of cancer" in the absence of physical injury was an unwarranted extension of liability for negligent infliction of emotional distress, that if such fear is compensable it should not be so where the plaintiff cannot establish that he or she has a "probability" of developing cancer * * *.

* * *

The Court of Appeal * * * affirmed the judgment. The court held that, given the circumstances in which plaintiffs ingested the carcinogens, it was unnecessary for them to establish a present physical injury in order to recover for their fear of cancer. It further held it was unnecessary for plaintiffs to prove they were likely to develop cancer, noting their fear was certain, definite and real, and not contingent on whether they in fact develop the disease. Plaintiffs had proven the elements of a negligence cause of action and had demonstrated, under an objective standard, that their emotional distress was serious. * * *

* * *

II.

DISCUSSION

* * *

A. *Negligence: Fear of Cancer*

"Fear of cancer" is a term generally used to describe a present anxiety over developing cancer in the future.[5] Claims for fear of cancer have been increasingly asserted in toxic tort cases as more and more substances have been linked with cancer. Typically, a person's likelihood of developing cancer as a result of a toxic exposure is difficult to predict because many forms of cancer are characterized by long latency periods (anywhere from 20 to 30 years), and presentation is dependent upon the interrelation of myriad factors.

* * *

We must now consider whether, pursuant to California precedent, emotional distress engendered by the fear of developing cancer in the

---

5. Some commentators and courts have referred to claims for "fear of cancer" as "cancerphobia" claims. Strictly speaking, however, there is a distinction between fear of cancer and cancerphobia. Cancerphobia, as a "phobic reaction," is a mental illness that is the recurrent experience of dread of a cancer in the absence of objective danger. In contrast, the fear of cancer is a claimed anxiety caused by the fear of developing cancer and is not a mental illness. This opinion is concerned only with fear of cancer as a form of emotional distress and not with cancerphobia. Furthermore, while plaintiffs identified fear of cancer as the principal basis for the emotional distress claim at issue, our discussion is equally relevant to emotional distress engendered by fear that other types of serious physical illness or injury may result from toxic exposure.

future as a result of a toxic exposure is a recoverable item of damages in a negligence action.

1. Parasitic Recovery: Immune System Impairment and/or Cellular Damage as Physical Injury

Because it initially appeared plaintiffs might have suffered damage to their immune systems, we solicited the views of the parties on whether such damage constitutes physical injury. We did so because it is settled in California that in ordinary negligence actions for physical injury, recovery for emotional distress caused by that injury is available as an item of parasitic damages. Where a plaintiff can demonstrate a physical injury caused by the defendant's negligence, anxiety specifically due to a reasonable fear of a future harm attributable to the injury may also constitute a proper element of damages.

* * *

It is not clear from the record in this case, however, that these plaintiffs' emotional distress is parasitic to this type of supposed injury. The statement of decision by the trial court does not include an express finding that plaintiffs' exposure to the contaminated well water resulted in physical injury, cellular damage or immune system impairment. The court made no mention of plaintiffs' immune system response, cellular systems or cells, and made no specific determination of damage or impairment thereto. While the trial court concluded that plaintiffs do have an enhanced "susceptibility" or "risk" for developing cancer and other maladies, it characterized this as a "presently existing physical condition," not as a physical injury. We conclude, therefore, that we lack an appropriate factual record for resolving whether impairment to the immune response system or cellular damage constitutes a physical injury for which parasitic damages for emotional distress ought to be available.

2. Nonparasitic Fear of Cancer Recovery

We next determine whether the absence of a present physical injury precludes recovery for emotional distress engendered by fear of cancer. Firestone argues that California should not recognize a duty to avoid negligently causing emotional distress to another, but, if such a duty is recognized, recovery should be permitted in the absence of physical injury only on proof that the plaintiff's emotional distress or fear is caused by knowledge that future physical injury or illness is more likely than not to occur as a direct result of the defendant's conduct. * * *

a. Independent Duty

* * *

* * * Firestone did violate a duty imposed on it by law and regulation to dispose of toxic waste only in a class I landfill and to avoid contamination of underground water. The violation led directly to plaintiffs' ingestion of various known and suspected carcinogens, and thus to their fear of suffering the very harm which the Legislature sought by statute to avoid. Their fear of cancer was proximately caused by Firestone's unlawful conduct which threatened serious physical injury.

* * *

b. *Absence of Physical Injury*

Amici curiae argue that no recovery for emotional distress arising from fear of cancer should be allowed in any case unless the plaintiff can establish a present physical injury such as a clinically verifiable cancerous or precancerous condition. Amici curiae advance several legal and policy arguments to support this position. None is persuasive.

Amici curiae first assert that, under California case law, the existence of a physical injury is a predicate to recovering damages for emotional distress in a negligence action unless the action involves "bystander" recovery or there is a "preexisting relationship" between the plaintiff and defendant which creates a duty to the plaintiff, neither of which is implicated here. This assertion is plainly without merit.

Significantly, we recently reaffirmed the principle that, in California, "damages for negligently inflicted emotional distress may be recovered in the absence of physical injury or impact. . . ." [*Burgess v. Superior Court*, 2 Cal.4th 1064, 1074, 831 P.2d 1197 (1992)]. We held that "physical injury is not a prerequisite for recovering damages for *serious* emotional distress," especially where "there exists a 'guarantee of genuineness in the circumstances of the case.'" (*Id.*, at p. 1079.)

Contrary to amici curiae's assertions, this principle has never been restricted to cases involving bystanders or preexisting relationships. Notably, amici curiae cite no authority even suggesting such a limitation. * * *

Amici curiae next contend that substantial policy reasons nevertheless support a physical injury requirement for recovery of fear of cancer damages where no preexisting relationship exists. They suggest that allowing recovery in the absence of a physical injury would create limitless liability and would result in a flood of litigation which thereby would impose onerous burdens on courts, corporations, insurers and society in general. Allowing such recovery would promote fraud and artful pleading, and would also encourage plaintiffs to seek damages based on a subjective fear of cancer. In amici curiae's view, a physical injury requirement is thus essential to provide meaningful limits on the class of potential plaintiffs and clear guidelines for resolving disputes over liability without the necessity for trial.

This argument overlooks the reasons for our decision to discard the requirement of physical injury. As we observed more than a decade ago, "[t]he primary justification for the requirement of physical injury appears to be that it serves as a screening device to minimize a presumed risk of feigned injuries and false claims." (*Molien v. Kaiser Foundation Hospitals*, 27 Cal.3d 916, 925–926, 616 P.2d 813 (1980).) Such harm was "believed to be susceptible of objective ascertainment and hence to corroborate the authenticity of the claim." (*Molien, supra,* 27 Cal.3d at p. 926.)

In *Molien,* we perceived two significant difficulties with the physical injury requirement. First, "the classification is both overinclusive and underinclusive when viewed in the light of its purported purpose of screening false claims." (27 Cal.3d at p. 928.) It is overinclusive in that it permits recovery whenever the suffering accompanies or results in physical injury, no matter how trivial (*ibid.*), yet underinclusive in that it mechanically denies court access to potentially valid claims that could be proved if the plaintiffs were permitted to go to trial (*id.,* at p. 929).

Second, we observed that the physical injury requirement "encourages extravagant pleading and distorted testimony." (*Molien, supra,* 27 Cal.3d at p. 929.) We concluded that the retention of the requirement ought to be reconsidered because of the tendency of victims to exaggerate sick headaches, nausea, insomnia and other symptoms in order to make out a technical basis of bodily injury upon which to predicate a parasitic recovery for the more grievous disturbance, consisting of the mental and emotional distress endured. (*Ibid.*)

Therefore, rather than adhere to what we perceived as an artificial and often arbitrary means of guarding against fraudulent claims, we acknowledged that "[t]he essential question is one of proof[.]" (*Molien, supra,* 27 Cal.3d at pp. 929–930.) Thus, " '[i]n cases other than where proof of mental distress is of a medically significant nature, the general standard of proof required to support a claim of mental distress is some guarantee of genuineness in the circumstances of the case.' " [*Id.* at 930].

Our reasons for discarding the physical injury requirement in [*Molien*] remain valid today and are equally applicable in a toxic exposure case. That is, the physical injury requirement is a hopelessly imprecise screening device—it would allow recovery for fear of cancer whenever such distress accompanies or results in any physical injury, no matter how trivial, yet would disallow recovery in all cases where the fear is both serious and genuine but no physical injury has yet manifested itself. While we agree with amici curiae that meaningful limits on the class of potential plaintiffs and clear guidelines for resolving disputes in advance of trial are necessary, imposing a physical injury requirement represents an inherently flawed and inferior means of attempting to achieve these goals.

c. *Likelihood of Cancer in the Future*

We next consider whether recovery of damages for emotional distress caused by fear of cancer should depend upon a showing that the plaintiff's fears stem from a knowledge that there is a probable likelihood of developing cancer in the future due to the toxic exposure. This is a matter of hot debate among the parties and amici curiae. Firestone and numerous amici curiae argue that because fear of cancer claims are linked to a future harm which may or may not materialize, such claims raise concerns about speculation and uncertainty and therefore warrant a requirement that the plaintiff show the feared cancer is more likely than not to occur. Plaintiffs and other amici curiae respond that such a requirement is inappropriate in the context of a mental distress claim, and that there are viable methods, apart from requiring quantification of the cancer risk, to screen claims and determine the reasonableness and genuineness of a plaintiff's fears.

Plaintiffs favor the approach adopted by the Court of Appeal, which requires the following showing. The toxic exposure plaintiff must first prove the elements of a negligence cause of action. The plaintiff must then establish that his or her fear of cancer is serious, and that the seriousness meets an objective standard (i.e., the distress must be reasonable under the circumstances). Although a plaintiff is not required to establish that the cancer is likely to occur, the finder of fact should consider evidence regarding the likelihood that cancer will occur (i.e., evidence that the disease is only a remote possibility could lead a trier of fact to conclude that a plaintiff's fears were unreasonable). Finally, the finder of fact should test the genuineness of the plaintiff's fear under the factors discussed in [*Molien*], including expert testimony, a juror's own experience, and the particular circumstances of the case.

In affirming the fear of cancer award, the Court of Appeal remarked that "the fact that [plaintiffs'] water supply was contaminated by carcinogens is, *by itself*, surely a circumstance which is likely to cause emotional distress in most reasonable persons." (Italics added.) In addition, although the Court of Appeal purported to call for a showing of the actual likelihood that the feared cancer will occur, the court indicated that the absence of such evidence is immaterial where, as here, the trier of fact finds a significantly increased risk of cancer.

We decline to adopt the Court of Appeal's approach. Although the court properly recognized that a toxic exposure plaintiff is required to establish the reasonableness of his or her fear of cancer, it erred in concluding that reasonableness is established by the mere fact of an exposure to, or a significant increase in, the risk of cancer.

A carcinogenic or other toxic ingestion or exposure, without more, does not provide a basis for fearing future physical injury or illness which the law is prepared to recognize as reasonable. The fact that one is aware that he or she has ingested or been otherwise exposed to a carcinogen or other toxin, without any regard to the nature, magnitude and proportion of the exposure or its likely consequences, provides no meaningful basis upon which to evaluate the reasonableness of one's fear. For example, nearly everybody is exposed to carcinogens which appear naturally in all types of foods. Yet ordinary consumption of such foods is not substantially likely to result in cancer. Nor is the knowledge of such consumption likely to result in a reasonable fear of cancer.

Moreover, permitting recovery for fear of cancer damages based solely upon a plaintiff's knowledge that his or her risk of cancer has been significantly increased by a toxic exposure, without requiring any further showing of the actual likelihood of the feared cancer due to the exposure, provides no protection against unreasonable claims based upon wholly speculative fears. For example, a plaintiff's risk of contracting cancer might be significantly increased by 100 or more percent due to a particular toxic exposure, yet the actual risk of the feared cancer might itself be insignificant and no more than a mere possibility. As even plaintiffs appear to concede, evidence of knowledge that cancer is only a remote possibility could lead a trier of fact to conclude that a claimed fear is objectively unreasonable. This concession only proves the point—the way to avoid damage awards for unreasonable fear, i.e., in those cases where the feared cancer is at best only remotely possible, is to require a showing of the actual likelihood of the feared cancer to establish its significance.

Accordingly, we reject the Court of Appeal's approach because it attaches undue significance to the mere ingestion of a carcinogen, and because it focuses on the increased risk of cancer in isolation.

We turn now to Firestone's argument that fear of cancer should be compensable only where the fear is based upon knowledge that cancer is probable, i.e., that it is more likely than not that cancer will develop. In evaluating this argument, we first consider whether it is reasonable for a person to genuinely and seriously fear a disease that is not probable, and if so, whether the emotional distress engendered by such fear warrants recognition as a compensable harm.

We cannot say that it would never be reasonable for a person who has ingested toxic substances to harbor a genuine and serious fear of cancer where reliable medical or scientific opinion indicates that such ingestion has significantly increased his or her risk of cancer, but not to a probable likelihood. Indeed, we would be very hard pressed to find that, as a matter of law, a plaintiff faced with a 20 percent or 30 percent chance of developing cancer cannot genuinely, seriously and reasonably fear the prospect of cancer. Nonetheless, we conclude, for the public policy reasons identified below, that emotional distress caused by the fear of a cancer that is not probable should generally not be compensable in a negligence action.

As a starting point in our analysis, we recognize the indisputable fact that all of us are exposed to carcinogens every day. As one commentator has observed, "[i]t is difficult to go a week without news of toxic exposure. Virtually everyone in society is conscious of the fact that the air they breathe, water, food and drugs they ingest, land on which they live, or products to which they are exposed are potential health hazards. Although few are exposed to all, few also can escape exposure to any." (Dworkin, *Fear Of Disease And Delayed Manifestation Injuries: A Solution Or A Pandora's Box?* (1984) 53 Fordham L.Rev. 527, 576, fns. omitted.)

Thus, all of us are potential fear of cancer plaintiffs, provided we are sufficiently aware of and worried about the possibility of developing cancer from exposure to or ingestion of a carcinogenic substance. The enormity of the class of potential plaintiffs cannot be overstated; indeed, a single class action may easily involve hundreds, if not thousands, of fear of cancer claims.

With this consideration in mind, we believe the tremendous societal cost of otherwise allowing emotional distress compensation to a potentially unrestricted plaintiff class demonstrates the necessity of imposing some limit on the class. Proliferation of fear of cancer claims in California in the absence of meaningful restrictions might compromise the availability and affordability of liability insurance for toxic liability risks. * * * In the end, the burden of payment of awards for fear of cancer in the absence of a more likely than not restriction will inevitably be borne by the public generally in substantially increased insurance premiums or, alternatively, in the enhanced danger that accrues from the greater number of residents and businesses that may choose to go without any insurance.

A second policy concern that weighs in favor of a more likely than not threshold is the unduly detrimental impact that unrestricted fear liability would have in the health care field. As amicus curiae California Medical Association points out, access to prescription drugs is likely to be impeded by allowing recovery of fear of cancer damages in negligence cases without the imposition of a heightened threshold. To wit, thousands of drugs having no known harmful effects are currently being prescribed and utilized. New data about potentially harmful effects may not develop for years. If and when negative data are discovered and made public, however, one can expect numerous lawsuits to be filed by patients who currently have no physical injury or illness but who nonetheless fear the risk of adverse effects from the drugs they used. Unless meaningful restrictions are placed on this potential plaintiff class, the threat of numerous large, adverse monetary awards, coupled with the added cost of insuring against such liability (assuming insurance would be available), could diminish the availability of new, beneficial prescription drugs or increase their price beyond the reach of those who need them most.

* * *

A third policy concern to consider is that allowing recovery to all victims who have a fear of cancer may work to the detriment of those who sustain actual physical injury and those who ultimately develop cancer as a result of toxic exposure. That is, to allow compensation to all plaintiffs with objectively reasonable cancer fears, even where the threatened cancer is not probable, raises the very significant concern that defendants and their insurers will be unable to ensure adequate compensation for those victims who actually develop cancer or other physical injuries. Consider, for instance, that in this case damages totaling $800,000 for fear of cancer were awarded to four plaintiffs. If the same recovery were to be allowed in large class actions, liability for this one type of injury alone would be staggering. As one commentator astutely noted: "It would be a regrettable irony if in the rush to compensate the psychically injured we make it impossible to compensate those suffering of permanent and serious physical injuries." [Willmore, *In Fear of Cancerphobia*, 3 Toxics L.Rptr. 559, 563 (Bur. Nat. Affairs Sept. 28, 1988).]

A fourth reason supporting the imposition of a more likely than not limitation is to establish a sufficiently definite and predictable threshold for recovery to permit consistent application from case to case. Indeed, without such a threshold, the likelihood of inconsistent results increases since juries may differ over the point at which a plaintiff's fear is a genuine and reasonable fear, i.e., one jury might deem knowledge of a 2 or 5 percent likelihood of future illness or injury to be sufficient, while another jury might not. A more definite threshold will avoid inconsistent results and may contribute to early resolution or settlement of claims.

Finally, while a more likely than not limitation may foreclose compensation to many persons with genuine and objectively reasonable fears, it is sometimes necessary to "limit the class of potential plaintiffs if emotional injury absent physical harm is to continue to be a recoverable item of damages in a negligence action." [*Thing v. La Chusa*, 771 P.2d 814, 828]. We have recognized, in analogous contexts, that restricting the liability of a negligent tortfeasor for emotional loss may be warranted in consideration of the following factors: the intangible nature of the loss, the inadequacy of monetary damages to make whole the loss, the difficulty of measuring the damage, and the societal cost of attempting to compensate the plaintiff. These considerations are equally relevant to fear of cancer claims in toxic exposure cases.

Plaintiffs and amici curiae advance several reasons why a more likely than not threshold for fear of cancer claims should be rejected. None is convincing.

First, plaintiffs argue that a more likely than not restriction is unworkable because the risk of contracting cancer from any one source is unquantifiable. In their view, adoption of such a rule would effectively preclude any emotional distress recovery.

We are unpersuaded by this argument because its factual premise appears highly suspect. Although the experts in this case asserted it was impossible to quantify the risk of cancer from any particular toxic exposure, experts in other cases do not share that view. * * *

Second, plaintiffs and amici curiae point out that while decisions from other jurisdictions have employed a more likely than not limitation for the so-called "increased risk" claim, they have thus far declined to do so in the context of a fear of cancer claim. Those decisions, it is asserted, allowed recovery for a plaintiff's fear of cancer in situations similar to those present here without proof that cancer was more likely than not to occur.

We remain unconvinced. Although it is true that the cited cases permitted fear of cancer recovery so long as the plaintiffs' fears were genuine and reasonable, many of them involved plaintiffs who, in addition to their emotional distress, sustained serious or permanent physical injury as a result of a particular toxic exposure. It is clear from passages in these cases that the respective courts were acutely aware of the plaintiffs' existing physical injuries and were deciding the appropriate basis for fear of cancer recovery in that context. Because these cases were decided within the context of a much narrower class of potential plaintiffs, they did not implicate or address the important public policy considerations at issue here.

* * *

Accordingly, we decline to follow the Plaintiff's rationale of the above cases, for to do so would be to ignore substantial public policy concerns. We are satisfied that the more likely than not threshold for fear of cancer claims in negligence actions strikes the appropriate balance between the interests of toxic exposure litigants and the burdens on society and judicial administration.

To summarize, we hold with respect to negligent infliction of emotional distress claims arising out of exposure to carcinogens and/or other toxic substances: Unless an express exception to this general rule is recognized, in the absence of a present physical injury or illness, damages for fear of cancer may be recovered only if the plaintiff pleads and proves that (1) as a result of the defendant's negligent breach of a duty owed to the plaintiff, the plaintiff is exposed to a toxic substance which threatens cancer; *and* (2) the plaintiff's fear stems from a knowledge, corroborated by reliable medical or scientific opinion, that it is more likely than not that the plaintiff will develop the cancer in the future due to the toxic exposure. Under this rule, a plaintiff must do more than simply establish knowledge of a toxic ingestion or exposure and a significant increased risk of cancer. The plaintiff must further show that based upon reliable medical or scientific opinion, the plaintiff harbors a serious fear that the toxic ingestion or exposure was of such magnitude and proportion as to likely result in the feared cancer.

* * *

NOTES AND QUESTIONS

1. The *Potter* court restricted fear of disease claims based on the probability that the plaintiff will develop disease in the future. Does the court's precise standard for permissible recovery—"more likely than not" that the disease will manifest—make sense? Consider that under *Potter*, a plaintiff whose risk of future disease increases from 1% to 49% would be ineligible for fear of disease recovery. But a plaintiff whose risk increases from 49% to 51% *would* be able to recover. How can this be justified? One commentator argues that it cannot, and suggests a more flexible approach:

> [T]he *Potter* court properly focused on objective probability as an appropriate gatekeeper. However, the court created a needlessly harsh "more-likely-than-not" standard that frustrates meritorious suits. * * * Hence, some middle-ground solution is warranted in cancerphobia suits. * * *

The case is thus presented for adopting a substantial probability test, rather than the more-likely-than-not, physical injury, physical manifestation, or traditional reasonability tests. * * *

* * *

[The substantial probability test] is more rigorous and difficult to recover under than the traditional reasonableness standard, but it is less arbitrary and offers a more effective screen than the physical injury/manifestation requirement that many courts apply. It is more equitable, less arbitrary, and less confusing conceptually than the more-likely-than-not rule, and still remains an effective screening mechanism.

Glen Donath, Comment, Curing Cancerphobia Phobia: Reasonableness Redefined, 62 U.Chi.L.Rev. 1113, 1133–37 (1996). Do you agree with this proposal? A "substantial probability" standard takes care of the anomalous situation described at the beginning of this note. But would it be any easier to define "substantial probability" than to ascertain general "reasonableness," as suggested by *Sterling*?

2. A dissenting justice in the *Potter* decision also criticized the "more likely than not" standard, although on different grounds than the commentator in the preceding note. Consider the following passage from his dissent:

In explaining its rationale for establishing a novel, high threshold—"more likely than not"—for recovery for emotional distress in this setting, the majority opinion suggests that, in the case of "toxic torts," a variety of "public policy" reasons support its departure from generally governing legal principles. Distilled to its essence, however, the majority's position amounts to a determination that, when a defendant's wrongful conduct has the potential to cause serious physical and emotional harm *to a large number of persons*, such conduct should be afforded a greater shield from liability than conduct possessing the potential to harm only a more limited number of persons. In my view, the controlling public policy formulated in this area—for example, the stringent legislative controls governing the discarding of toxic waste—does not support the majority's approach. Indeed, it appears distressingly ironic and inconsistent with legislatively prescribed public policy to accord the individual victim of a so-called "toxic tort" *less protection* than would be accorded the victim of a more traditional course of negligent conduct.

Potter, 863 P.2d at 832 (George, J., concurring and dissenting). What do you think of this criticism? Couldn't the same thing be said of any gatekeeping principle that limits emotional distress actions in an effort to limit the number of potential claimants?

3. What if a plaintiff engages in an activity that creates a risk for the same type of disease that is associated with the toxic exposure? For example, suppose that plaintiff was a heavy smoker during the time of exposure. Should this behavior be considered contributory negligence that might reduce or even eliminate fear of disease recovery? Or should this simply be evidence that a jury takes into account in deciding whether plaintiff's fear was reasonable? The *Potter* court considered this issue, as each of the plaintiffs involved had been long-time cigarette smokers. Ultimately, the court refused to apply comparative fault principles on the grounds that no evidence had been presented establishing a causal connection between the plaintiff's smoking and the harm claimed in the case—i.e., a fear of future disease. "[T]he critical issue," the court stated, "is not whether plaintiffs' smoking contributed to their increased risk of cancer, it is whether their smoking contributed to their emotional distress." *Potter*, 863 P.2d at 826 n.30. Does the court's conclusion potentially lead to illogical results? What if the plaintiff's smoking creates a far greater risk of disease than does the toxic exposure? Or what if the exposure only creates a "more likely than not" risk because of a synergistic effect of tobacco use?

4. The *Potter* court's provision for recovery of emotional harm if cancer is more likely than not may be a chimerical remedy. The court did not specify which cancers the plaintiffs claimed they might contract, but the lifetime probability of contracting breast (women) or prostate (men) cancer, the most prevalent of all cancers, is 12–16%. National Cancer Institute, SEER Cancer Statistics Review 1975–2006, available at http://seer.cancer.gov/csr/1975_2006/results_merged/topic_lifetime_risk.pdf. The lifetime risk of contracting lung cancer for smokers is less than 20% and considerably lower for nonsmokers, under 2%. P. J. Villeneuve & Y. Mao, Lifetime Probability of Developing Lung Cancer, by Smoking Status, 85 Can.J.Pub.Health 385 (1994). Can you imagine a circumstance in which a person exposed to an environmental carcinogen could satisfy the *Potter* court's preponderance threshold?

5. The *Potter* court also decided that the "more likely than not" standard should not apply if the nature of defendant's conduct was worse than negligent. For example, the court concluded that if defendant acted in "conscious disregard of others," the balance of policies supports broader access to a fear of disease claims.

> Under such circumstances, the potential liability of a defendant is not disproportionate to culpability. While the imposition of liability for emotional distress resulting from negligent handling of toxic substances may result in costs out of proportion to the culpability of the negligent actor, this concern is diminished or nonexistent when the conduct is despicable and undertaken in conscious disregard of the danger to the health or interests of others. The significance of the size of the potential class of plaintiffs is similarly diminished and the moral blame heightened since the defendant is aware of the danger posed by its conduct and acts in conscious disregard of the known risk. For these reasons, the more likely than not threshold should not be available as a shield when the defendant acts with a sufficient degree of moral blameworthiness.

Potter, 863 P.2d at 817. The standard also changes where a defendant intentionally or recklessly creates a fear of disease. In such situations, courts can use rules that apply in intentional infliction of emotional distress cases, rather than applying negligence principles. Such cases, of course, are difficult to establish, requiring that a plaintiff prove defendant's "outrageous" conduct caused plaintiff's "severe or extreme" emotional distress. Id. at 818–19. It also is worth noting that intentional, willful, or malicious conduct might lead to the imposition of punitive damages, a topic that is addressed later in this Chapter. What type of conduct might satisfy the higher culpability standards?

Would it make a difference if defendant was aware that it was violating state or federal law in releasing the toxins to which plaintiffs are exposed?

3. ENHANCED RISK OF DISEASE

Our final "futures" action involves claims for the value of enhanced risk of disease. In these cases, a currently healthy plaintiff seeks damages for the increased possibility of future disease caused by a toxic exposure. At first glance, one might respond to such a claim by suggesting that plaintiff should wait for the disease to manifest and file a claim then. But several legal principles make this easier said than done. First, a plaintiff who has been exposed to a toxin might face the possibility of having her claim barred by a statute of limitations before the disease manifests, particularly if the exposure has current, but less severe, consequences. Second, if plaintiff seeks relief for those less severe consequences, the rule against splitting a cause of action might preclude her from returning to court and seeking damages should the more serious disease manifest. More generally, factual evidence related to proof of causation can become more difficult for a plaintiff to obtain as time elapses.

Many jurisdictions have handled this situation, not by allowing enhanced risk claims, but instead by loosening these traditional rules—that is, extending the statute of limitations until the subsequent disease occurs, or permitting plaintiffs to split a cause of action when the possibility of a more serious disease looms. The most common fact setting raising these issues involves exposure to asbestos, where a plaintiff might currently suffer from less serious consequences (i.e., pleural plaques or asbestosis), but wants to reserve the right to seek damages for the more serious possibility of mesothelioma, a deadly form of cancer related to asbestos exposure. See James A. Henderson & Aaron D. Twerski, Asbestos Litigation Gone Mad: Exposure-Based Recovery for Increased Risk, Mental Distress, and Medical Monitoring, 53 S.C.L.Rev. 815, 820–24 (2002).

A small number of courts, however, have permitted asbestos plaintiffs to proceed with increased risk claims before the manifestation of disease. Those courts have established a two-part hurdle for plaintiffs to clear. First, the enhanced-risk plaintiff must demonstrate some present injury attributable to the exposure—even if this present injury would not be connected to the future disease. Second, the enhanced-risk plaintiff must come forward with evidence that the future disease is more likely than not to develop in the future—a limiting standard similar to what we saw in *Potter* when considering fear of disease claims. The following case provides an example of the narrow circumstances under which an increased risk claim might be permitted. As you read the opinion, consider not only the implications for the plaintiff's recovery at the time of suit, but also how the court's opinion might impact future recovery for the plaintiff later.

JACKSON v. JOHNS–MANVILLE SALES CORP.

United States Court of Appeals for the Fifth Circuit, 1986.
781 F.2d 394.

RANDALL, CIRCUIT JUDGE.

This Mississippi diversity case involves plaintiff Jackson's efforts to recover compensatory * * * damages from Johns–Manville Sales Corporation, Raybestos–Manhattan, Inc., and H.K. Porter Company, all manufacturers of asbestos products. Jackson was injured as a result of his exposure to asbestos products during the course of his employment as a shipyard worker. The district court, after a lengthy trial, entered judgment in favor of Jackson against all defendants except H.K. Porter Company * * *. On appeal, a panel of this court affirmed in part, reversed in part, and remanded for a new trial. *Jackson v. Johns–Manville Sales Corp.*, 727 F.2d 506 (5th Cir.1984) ("Jackson I"). We granted en banc rehearing, which had the effect of vacating the panel opinion. Upon rehearing en banc, we certified to the Mississippi Supreme Court three significant questions of Mississippi law. *Jackson v. Johns–Manville Sales Corp.*, 750 F.2d 1314 (5th Cir.1985) (en banc) ("Jackson II"). The Mississippi Supreme Court declined certification without discussion. *Jackson v. Johns–Manville Sales Corp.*, 469 So.2d 99 (Miss.1985). The case is consequently back before us for resolution of the issues previously certified to the Mississippi Supreme Court.

[One issue] left unresolved by this court's en banc opinion in *Jackson II* * * * follows:

> [W]hether a Plaintiff who does not presently have cancer can state a claim or recover damages in an action based upon strict liability in tort for the reasonable medical probability of contracting cancer in the future.

We [answer the] question affirmatively, and affirm the judgment of the district court.

* * *

All parties concede that Jackson does not presently have cancer. The defendants argue that if Jackson does get cancer, he will be able to sue for compensatory damages associated with cancer at that time—that is, once the disease manifests itself. Jackson maintains that recovery is appropriate now since the potential development of cancer represents a future injury based on a presently existing cause of action. Relatedly, Jackson also argues that he *must* recover for cancer now or else the claim will be barred by the statute of limitations. Jackson's position is that claim-splitting is disallowed in Mississippi and that the claim for cancer, insofar as it grows out of the same actionable tort which provides his recovery for asbestosis, must be raised now. Jackson reasons that, since the claim for cancer grows out of a single actionable tort, the statute of limitations with respect to cancer begins to run from the time the tort is actionable, that is, from the time asbestosis became manifest.

The defendants assert that claim-splitting is permitted in Mississippi when that would serve the ends of justice and fairness. In any case, the defendants insist, Mississippi would adopt the discovery rule with respect to asbestos-related injuries, with the result that the statute of limitations for cancer would not begin to run until cancer actually appears. The development of cancer would be a separate tort from the development of asbestosis. As a result, defendants conclude, recovery for cancer is neither permitted nor required at this time.

The debate between the parties pivots on a single question, namely: What is the cause of action on which Jackson seeks recovery? The defendants contend that the existing cause of action is the existence of asbestosis. Jackson's position is that his cause of action is the inhalation of asbestos fibers "and the invasion of his body by those fibers, thus causing ... physical damage." *Gideon v. Johns–Manville Sales Corp.*, 761 F.2d 1129, 1137 (5th Cir.1985). Although the statute of limitations question is concededly not dispositive of the issue of which injury provides the cause of action, the defendants' position is that if the statute of limitations would not begin to run until Jackson discovers cancer, then he should not be allowed to recover until that time: until cancer appears. Essentially, the defendants' position is that insofar as Jackson *may* bring suit for cancer at some later date, he should be required to wait until that date.

The defendants' argument must be rejected for two separate but related reasons. First, the truth of their crucial premise is not clear under Mississippi law. It is unclear whether Jackson *would* be permitted to sue to recover damages for cancer whenever cancer appears. Second, it *is* clear that under Mississippi tort law, plaintiffs may recover for probable future consequences.

* * *

* * * Jackson established that he will probably get cancer. In addition, he has already discovered, and brought suit to recover for, his asbestosis. Under these circumstances, it is clear that under Mississippi law Jackson may recover cancer damages. Further, having recovered cancer damages, he cannot later recover more if and when he develops cancer.

"The general rule is that where it is established that future consequences from an injury to a person will ensue, recovery therefor may be had, but such future consequences must be established in terms of reasonable probabilities." *Entex, Inc. v. Rasberry*, 355 So.2d 1102, 1104 (Miss.1978). Defendants respond that cancer does not develop *from* asbestosis, that it can never be a future consequence *of* asbestosis. Cancer is presumably a separate injury, and recovery must therefore await manifestation. This assertion is medically sound, but legally awry. In a sense, the injury in this case is the inhalation of asbestos fibers. It was not an *actionable* injury, however, meaning it was not legally cognizable, until at least one evil *effect* of the inhalation became manifest. There was no cause of action at all, in other words, until the asbestosis appeared. In this case, the effects of inhaling asbestos manifested themselves initially as asbestosis. In a different plaintiff, they may have manifested themselves as something as innocuous as asbestos callouses or as lethal as mesothelioma. But in any event, once the injury becomes actionable—once *some* effect appears—then the plaintiff is permitted to recover for all probable future manifestations as well.

* * *

Of course, a plaintiff who sues with nothing more than hand callouses may have a significantly lower likelihood of developing cancer than does a plaintiff who exhibits asbestosis. That would be a question for the jury, to be decided by listening to and evaluating conflicting medical testimony. This plaintiff, however, has asbestosis; and evidence adduced at trial indicates that he has a greater than fifty percent chance of getting cancer.[24] Recovery for that possibility is permissible under Mississippi law.

* * *

Following the Mississippi Supreme Court's decision to decline certification of the issues presented on this appeal, our procedure has been to apply existing Mississippi tort law to the facts of this case. Having studied Mississippi tort law, as well as decisions of other jurisdictions in cases such as this one, we conclude that * * * Jackson is entitled to * * * compensatory damages for the reasonable probability of getting cancer * * *. Accordingly, the judgment of the district court is AFFIRMED.

NOTES AND QUESTIONS

1. If an enhanced risk claim goes forward, how will a court calculate damages? *Jackson* suggested that the plaintiff will receive the same level of damages that he would have received had his cancer actually developed. This would be consistent with the traditional tort rule for future damage awards. But is it appropriate in this context? Even though the plaintiff has evidence that he is more likely than not to contract mesothelioma, there is still a chance that he will not. This means that the defendant might well pay for something that never occurs. On one level, this might not seem troubling—the defendants, after all, have acted tortiously and the plaintiff has not. However, with the possibility of multiple actions, such a rule could force defendants to internalize far more costs than they actually caused over the long haul, an unattractive outcome to those concerned with economic efficiency. Some commentators have suggested that this problem could be avoided by awarding plaintiffs damages in proportion to the level of increased risk.

---

24. There can be little doubt that the jury had ample evidence upon which it could have based its conclusion that Jackson will probably get cancer. According to Dr. James Merchant, "it's been shown conclusively that [asbestos] is a cause of cancer in human beings." Furthermore, according to Dr. Merchant, "between 40 and 60 percent of those with asbestosis who have had previous heavy exposure die from bronchogenic carcinoma [lung cancer]." Dr. Elliot McCaughey testified too that Jackson has a greater than 50 percent likelihood of developing an asbestos related cancer. * * * [Citations from trial record omitted.]

Professor Glen Robinson explains the concept as follows: "Assuming that the risk is one that would give rise to liability when the actual loss is suffered, why not adjudicate the entire case by awarding the victim the present value of the risk at the point at which the risk can be identified and given some measurable value? The value is equal to the present value of the future losses multiplied by the estimated probability of their occurrence." Glen O. Robinson, Probabilistic Causation and Compensation for Tortious Risk, 14 J. Legal Stud. 779, 786 (1985). What do you think of the proportional liability model?

2. If a court adopted the proportional liability model, should it apply even if the level of increased risk is very small? For example, what if someone is exposed to a toxin that incrementally increases the risk of cancer from an already low background rate—say from a 2 in 100,000 chance to a 3 in 100,000 chance of a serious disease. Should a plaintiff be permitted to proceed with this action, and recover damages, even though (a) the disease is very unlikely to ever manifest; and (b) even if it does, the disease would more likely than not have resulted from something *other* than the exposure? One commentator suggests that, if courts adopt proportional liability for increased risk, plaintiff should present evidence that the exposure at least doubled the risk of future disease.

> Tort law should permit enhanced risk recovery on a proportional basis, but only when a plaintiff can prove that the toxic exposure has more than doubled her risk of contracting disease in the future. Fundamentally, this standard correlates with the actual causation standard that courts apply in cases where disease is manifest. In other words, there should be no pre-manifestation recovery for possible illness that a plaintiff cannot eventually connect to a defendant's conduct using normal measures of actual causation.

> [T]his correlation would reduce the tension that enhanced risk recovery has with corrective justice theory. It would create a system that is more administratively plausible than a system of pure proportional liability. It also would still take account of the tort system's role in deterring risky conduct.

Andrew R. Klein, A Model for Enhanced Risk Recovery in Tort, 56 Wash.&Lee L.Rev. 1173, 1194–96 (1999). Do you agree that the proposal serves the purposes of tort law as the author suggests?

3. If a court permits recovery for increased risk of disease, should a plaintiff be able to return to court and seek additional damages if she does develop cancer at a later date? Why or why not?

4. The plaintiff in *Jackson* had asbestosis, and his experts, see footnote 24, testified that the plaintiff would more likely than not contract lung cancer. How can that be in light of note 4 following *Potter*, regarding lifetime risks of cancer? Note 4 is about group-based statistics, and there is wide individual variations in the prognosis for an asbestos victim. However, there is little or no ability to make individualized assessments for that prognosis. See Margaret R. Becklake, Asbestos–Related Disease of the Lung and Other Organs: Their Epidemiology and Implications for Clinical Practice, 114 Am.Rev. Respiratory Disease 187 (1976).

5. Outside the toxic tort context, the concept of proportional liability has gained traction in several other cases with regard to potential future harm. See, e.g., Dillon v. Evanston Hosp., 771 N.E.2d 357 (Ill.2002); Petriello v. Kalman, 576 A.2d 474 (Conn.1990). The *Dillon* case retained the principle that would allow a plaintiff to recover "full" damages where proof exists that medical negligence would more likely than not lead to a future consequence. But it accepted proportional liability where the level of risk is lower. The court did rule, however, that the single-action rule would apply, preventing the plaintiff from coming back to court should future disease arise and lead to a higher amount of damages. See *Dillon,* 771 N.E.2d at 370–71. Cases like *Dillon* find their mirror image in a line of decisions that have permitted malpractice plaintiffs in some states to recover limited damages when medical negligence leads to a lost chance of survival. See, e.g., Herskovits v. Group Health Coop., 664 P.2d 474 (Wash.1983); Joseph H. King, Causation, Valuation, and Chance in Personal Injury Torts Involving Preexisting Conditions and Future Consequences, 90 Yale L.J. 1353 (1981).

PROBLEMS

1. BigCo has negligently exposed 5,000 citizens in Niceville to a large quantity of "toxzene," a toxic substance. Epidemiology studies demonstrate that the level of exposure experienced by Niceville's citizens has increased the risk of liver cancer in the population from .05% to 2%. No citizen has manifested any symptom of disease that can be connected to the toxzene exposure. Nor has any citizen presented evidence of serious emotional distress after learning these facts. There are, however, medical procedures available that would permit doctors to detect and treat the early onset of liver cancer in a beneficial way. What tort law damages might be available to the citizens of Niceville at this time? See Andrew R. Klein, A Model for Enhanced Risk Recovery in Tort, 56 Wash. & Lee L.Rev. at 1202–03.

2. BigCo has negligently exposed 5,000 citizens in Niceville to a large quantify of "chemex," a toxic substance. Epidemiology studies demonstrate that the level of exposure experienced by Niceville's citizens has increased the risk of liver cancer in the population from .05% to .07%. No citizen has manifested any symptom of cancer, but a large percentage of citizens are suffering from rashes attributable to the exposure. The rashes present no long-term health risk and are treatable. In addition, some members of the group are suffering from genuine emotional distress based on a fear of contracting future disease. What tort law damages might be available to citizens of Niceville at this time? Would your answer change if Niceville's jurisdiction extended limitations periods until the time of manifestation and permitted plaintiffs to split a cause of action?

C. PROPERTY DAMAGE

In cases where a defendant's tortious behavior harms a plaintiff's property, courts often choose between two competing measures of damages. The first is a calculation of damages based on the diminution of the property's fair market value. The other is a calculation of damages based on the cost of restoring the property to its prior condition. As the following case shows, the two measures can sometimes overlap, and the choice is not always clear.

PRIMROSE OPERATING CO. v. SENN

Texas Court of Appeals, 2005.
161 S.W.3d 258.

W.G. ARNOT, III, CHIEF JUSTICE.

Wilford C. Senn and Wanda Joan Senn brought suit against various oil companies for the alleged contamination of the Senns' real property, the Covered "S" Ranch. The only defendant remaining in the suit at the time of trial was Primrose Operating Company, Inc. The jury found that Primrose had negligently caused contamination to the surface of the ranch, that the cost to clean up the contamination was $2,110,000 [and] that the diminution in fair market value of the ranch due to Primrose's contamination was $2,110,000 * * *. The trial court entered judgment on the jury's verdict, awarding the Senns $2,110,000 in actual damages * * *. We reverse and render.

    * * *

* * * Primrose challenges the $2,110,000 findings made by the jury in answer to questions regarding the cost of cleanup and the diminution in fair market value. Primrose asserts that these damage findings were based upon unscientific evidence, were excessive, and were not supported by legally or factually sufficient evidence. The Senns had the burden of proof on these questions. Therefore, in order to address Primrose's legal sufficiency/no-evidence challenges, we must consider only the evidence and inferences that tend to support the findings, disregarding any evidence or inferences to the contrary. * * *

In a case in which a surface owner asserts a claim for damage to his land caused by another's negligence, the type of compensation to be awarded depends on the nature of the injury. Where the injury is temporary and able to be remedied at reasonable expense, damages are measured by the cost of restoring the land to its condition prior to the injury. If the cost to restore the land is excessive or not economically feasible, the injury may be deemed to be permanent. In the case of permanent injuries, the appropriate measure of damages is the diminution in fair market value. The concepts of temporary and permanent injuries are mutually exclusive. Consequently, damages for both may not be recovered in the same action.

We hold as a matter of law that the cost to restore the land to its condition prior to the leaks at issue in this case is not reasonable and that the repairs are, thus, not "economically feasible." The record shows that Primrose owned an oil and gas lease covering about 3,000 acres of the Senns' 23,013–acre ranch. The Senns purchased the surface only of the ranch in June 1997 for $3,164,000. The ranch has been subject to various leases and to oil and gas production since 1939 when the discovery well was drilled. When the Senns purchased the ranch, hundreds of wells had been drilled on the leased portion of the ranch, and thousands of miles of flow lines crossed the area. According to Wilford Senn (Senn), 500–600 wells were located on his ranch, with approximately 200 of those belonging to Primrose. Primrose began its operations on the ranch in 1992 and vacated the premises in December 1999 when it sold its interest to another company. Sometime after the Senns purchased the ranch, Senn instructed his ranch foreman, Rudy Gonzalez, to photograph any leaks or spills that he observed and to report those leaks and spills to Eddie W. Seay, a regulatory environmental consultant hired by Senn. Senn also hired a chemist, Greg Bybee, to take soil samples of these sites, test for contaminants, and determine the cost of remediation. The samples taken of the 86 Primrose spill sites, which were mostly leaks from flow lines, showed high levels of petroleum hydrocarbons and/or chlorides from the oil and saltwater. According to the Senns' experts, Primrose failed to properly clean up the spill sites. The record showed that the spill sites had not adequately revegetated by the time of trial, but there was no showing that the spill sites resulted in any hazard to human or animal life or even that the sites interfered with Senns' use of the ranch. The Senns' experts testified that the soil in those spill sites, which covered a total of approximately 10 acres but were spread out across the area, needed to be remediated by digging out the contaminated dirt, hauling it to a land farm, and replacing the contaminated dirt with clean soil. Bybee testified that the cost of such remediation would be $2,110,000.

Various witnesses testified regarding the value of the Senns' ranch. When Senn purchased the ranch in June 1997 for $3,164,000, there were some old spills and some oil operation damage. At the time of purchase, the appraised value was a little over $3,100,000. In July 1998 and again in February 2000, Senn swore in his financial statements that the ranch was worth $3,600,000. In May 2000, Senn swore in another financial statement that the ranch was worth $4,200,000. Also in May 2000, Lee Sam Middleton, a real estate broker and appraiser hired by the Senns, appraised the ranch with improvements at $4,275,000. When Middleton inspected and appraised the ranch in 1997 and in 2000, he knew that there had been oil field activity on the ranch, but he appraised the ranch as if it were unaffected by environmental hazards. Middleton testified that, at the time of the appraisals, he was not aware of any environmental hazards that needed to be cleaned up. Middleton further testified that, if the Senns' ranch is contaminated and if the cost to clean up the contamination is $2,110,000, then the fair market value of the ranch would be diminished by $2,110,000—the "cost to cure." Middleton testified that the evaluation should be based upon the cost to cure.

Steven Rogers, a real estate appraiser from Amarillo, appraised the Senns' ranch in March 2001 and October 2002. Rogers testified that, if the ranch were environmentally clean, it would have been valued at $4,500,000 and $4,800,000 on those dates, respectively. Rogers testified that he reviewed the report prepared by Seay and Bybee regarding soil contamination on the ranch and that, based upon that study, Rogers believed that the market value of the ranch would be diminished by both the cost to cure, $2,110,000, and by the negative stigma attached to the contamination, $420,000. According to Rogers, stigma is "the resistance of the market place to the purchase, or under a more likely description, it is a margin that . . . any purchaser of the property would like to have above the actual cost to clean up." The stigma value is attached because the cost to cure is generally imprecise and may cost more than expected. Rogers testified that he allotted 20 percent of the cost to cure as stigma. After allowing for both the improvements made by the Senns and the deductions for the stigma and the cost to cure, Rogers valued the ranch at $2,500,000. * * *

    * * *

The only other witness to testify regarding market value was Clint Bumguardner, a real estate appraiser hired by Primrose. Bumguardner testified that he did not use the cost to cure in appraising the Senns' ranch. According to Bumguardner, the cost to cure was not appropriate in this case because the oil field activity on the Senns' ranch was typical for that area of Texas and did not impact the property and because cost to cure is only utilized when it is economically feasible. Bumguardner did not find that the market value of the Senns' ranch had diminished in value because of Primrose's activities. Bumguardner did not attach any stigma loss to the Senns' ranch because it continued to thrive and be used as a ranch, which was the highest and best use of that property. Also, according to Bumguardner, the market for similar ranches reflected that there was no stigma attached to the oil field activity. On June 15, 2001, Bumguardner appraised the ranch's fair market value considering comparable ranch sales and the oil field activity at $175 per acre for a total of $4,025,000.

We hold as a matter of law that the cost to restore the land to its condition prior to the leaks at issue in this case is not reasonable and that the repairs are, thus, not "economically feasible." Accordingly, whether injury was temporary or permanent, the proper measure of damages in this case was the diminution in fair market value. That issue was addressed during the trial and was submitted to the jury. In accord with the testimony of Senns' experts, the jury found that the diminution in fair market value was $2,110,000. However, the only evidence in support of that figure was the testimony that the market value had diminished by $2,110,000 because that was the cost to cure—the amount of money that would have to be expended to remediate Primrose's spill sites and return them to an uncontaminated condition.

First, we are barred from considering that evidence because the cost to cure is an improper measure of damages in this case. The $2,110,000 that it would cost to excavate, haul, and replace the soil on 10 acres of a ranch on which oil and gas producers have been operating for approximately 60 years is not economically feasible. Even the $420,000 stigma amount suggested by Rogers was based upon the cost to cure. Rogers estimated that amount as 20 percent of the cost to cure because the cost to cure is often imprecise.

Second, the testimony of Senns' experts regarding the diminished market value did not take into account the fact that the land was not pristine when the Senns purchased the ranch. The Senns purchased the land "as is" after observing old spills and some damage from oil and gas operations. As shown by uncontroverted testimony, some leaks and spills are inevitable. At the time of the Senns' purchase, the oil field located on their ranch was very mature. The flow lines that leaked while Primrose conducted its activities on the ranch had been on the same right-of-ways since the 1940s and 1950s. Furthermore, prior to being banned by the Railroad Commission, open saltwater disposal pits had been located on the Senns' ranch.

While we do not condone Primrose's failure to adequately clean up the sites immediately when the cost would have been much less, we hold that the Senns have failed to produce any evidence that their ranch diminished in value because of Primrose's negligence. * * *

The judgment of the trial court is reversed, and we render judgment that the Senns take nothing from Primrose.

NOTES AND QUESTIONS

1. Was the outcome of the case fair? There seems to be little dispute that Primrose negligently contaminated Senn's property and failed adequately to clean it up. Why should Senn receive no compensation?

2. As the *Primrose* case suggests, courts often use diminution in value as the measure of damages instead of repair costs if a determination is made that the harm to the land is "permanent." Permanence in this context, however, often appears to be a term of art, simply suggesting that repair cost is significantly greater than diminished value. See Dan B. Dobbs, Law of Remedies 717 (2d ed. 1993). In such cases, a determination of permanence essentially makes diminution in value a ceiling on damages, preventing costly expenditures on repairs that, ultimately, would not increase the value of the property. Is this what happened in *Primrose*? Or is the court's refusal to award repair costs based on different grounds?

3. The Restatement of Torts supports the view that diminution in value provides the appropriate measure of damage to land if "the cost of replacing the land in its original condition is disproportionate to [its] diminution in value * * *." Restatement (Second) of Torts § 929. Under the Restatement rule, however, the limitation does not apply if the land is used for a "purpose personal to the owner." Id. What might constitute such a use? The comments to the Restatement provide the following illustration: "[W]hen a garden has been maintained in a city in connection with a dwelling house, the owner is entitled to recover the expense of putting the garden in its original condition even though the market value of the premises has not been decreased by the defendant's invasion." Id. See Dobbs, Law of Remedies, supra, at 719. In such a case, the owner would be able to recover restoration costs, even though the market value of the lot has not changed. Does this rule make sense? Can you think of any problems with this approach?

4. How about a situation where a defendant's damage to a plaintiff's land also causes harm to others? For example, what if a defendant is negligently contaminating a landowner's property, and the contamination leaches into groundwater, ultimately impacting a neighbor's land, or even the public at large? In some cases, injunctive relief might solve the problem. But what about a situation where contamination continues to spread even after defendant has ceased its activity? In these situations, one can make a strong argument that diminution in value is an inadequate remedy, and that a defendant should be liable for both restoration costs and additional consequential damages. See Dobbs, Law of Remedies, supra, at 725. It also is possible that remedies might be available under statutory schemes—a topic that is the subject of the next section.

5. As you saw in Chapter 8, the Federal Comprehensive Environmental Response, Compensation, and Liability Act (CERCLA) often mandates the cleanup of contaminated properties, regardless of tort remedies. The Texas Court of Appeals did not discuss CERCLA, however—even in the full opinion. Why did CERCLA not apply in *Senn*? First, CERCLA applies to contamination of land by "hazardous substances," which the Act defines to explicitly *exclude* petroleum and crude oil. 42 U.S.C. § 9601(14). Thus, CERCLA simply did not apply to most of the contamination of the Senns' property. Second, even where CERCLA's "petroleum exclusion" might not apply, such as to hazardous additives within the petroleum, properties are not subject to CERCLA cleanup requirements until the EPA formally adds them to the National Priorities List (NPL), as Chapter 8 explained. Sites not listed on the NPL—no matter how contaminated—are outside the purview of CERCLA's cleanup requirements. Finally, as Chapter 10 discussed, CERCLA does not eliminate private tort causes of action for other kinds of damages, such as diminution in value. Thus, even if CERCLA had applied to the Senns' property, it would not have eliminated their lawsuit for damages, necessarily—although the Act might have changed how they framed their lawsuit. Can you see how? Think about this case as you read the CERCLA portion of the next section.

D. DAMAGES UNDER FEDERAL STATUTES

1. INTRODUCTION AND OVERVIEW

Remedies provided under the federal environmental laws are different from traditional tort remedies in several respects. However, as we have seen in Chapter 10, the federal environmental laws generally do not preempt ordinary tort law suits—or ordinary tort damages. Thus, an important point for discussing remedies under the federal statutes is the recognition that those remedies serve different purposes from tort damages.

First, as we saw in chapters 8 and 9, basic liability for violations of the Resource Conservation and Recovery Act (RCRA), 42 U.S.C. §§ 6901–

6992k; the Comprehensive Environmental Response, Compensation, and Liability Act (CERCLA), 42 U.S.C. §§ 9601–9675; the Federal Insecticide, Fungicide, and Rodenticide Act (FIFRA), 7 U.S.C. §§ 136–136y; the Toxic Substances Control Act (TSCA), 15 U.S.C. §§ 2601–2695d; and the Federal Food, Drug, and Cosmetic Act, 21 U.S.C. §§ 301–399, is *strict liability*, whereas most other toxic tort liability is based in negligence. Thus, simply violating the statute is enough to trigger that particular Act's remedies provisions.

Second, the main objective of these statutes, with the exception of CERCLA, is to prevent future harm. Again, this is unlike most toxic tort litigation, which seeks damages for harms already done. Enforcement of most of the environmental statutes tends to have a primary goal of bringing the violator back into compliance, and hence *injunctive relief* plays a large role in the environmental remedies. A secondary goal is to eliminate any economic advantage that the violator achieved by not "playing by the rules"—avoiding expensive upgrades to a plant or factory, avoiding having to purchase the latest technology, avoiding the costs of the permit process, and so on. Thus, *administrative penalties* and *civil penalties* are generally calculated to ensure that the violator has to pay the equivalent of any such economic advantage. If the violation causes significant damage, a third goal of the remedy will be to punish the violator for that damage, either through increased penalties or, in very serious cases, through *criminal punishment* (fines or jail or both).

Finally, those who violate environmental statutes are deemed to have harmed the public generally. (Again, remember: if the violation also causes private harm, injured private parties generally can pursue normal tort remedies, except in the specific instances where Congress has preempted tort law. Statutory remedies and tort remedies thus generally are *not* mutually exclusive.) Thus, the beneficiary of the remedy or remedies provided in environmental statutes is also the public. As a practical matter, that means that the federal governments and state governments play the primary role in enforcing the environmental statutes, and any penalties paid are paid to the U.S. Treasury. Citizens can also sue to enforce most of these statutes, but again, any penalties assessed in a citizen suit are paid to the U.S. Treasury, not the citizen plaintiff. However, citizen-suit plaintiffs can recover their attorney fees.

CERCLA, of course, is a post-damage cleanup statute, and its remedies are accordingly slightly different. Notably, however, its remedies are structurally similar to those in other federal statutes aimed at cleaning up toxic materials, such as the oil spill provisions of the Clean Water Act, 33 U.S.C. § 1321, and of the Oil Pollution Act of 1990, 33 U.S.C. §§ 2701–2762.

2. THE CLASSIC ENVIRONMENTAL REMEDIES MODEL: RCRA

RCRA, as you should recall from Chapter 8, seeks to prevent hazardous wastes from causing environmental problems by regulating all of the people who handle hazardous waste—generators, transporters, and treatment, storage, and disposal (TSD) facilities. The statute also gives the Environmental Protection Agency (EPA) and states broad enforcement authority to ensure that regulated entities comply.

Let's start with compliance orders and injunctive relief seeking to bring violators back into compliance. When the EPA Administrator learns that anyone is violating of RCRA's hazardous waste requirements, the Administrator may issue an administrative compliance order. The EPA can also require monitoring and testing at a site suspected of releasing hazardous waste. 42 U.S.C. § 6934(a). Violation of the compliance order is itself grounds for assessing civil penalties against the violator. Id. §§ 6928(c), 6991e(a)(3). The EPA describes its and states' administrative enforcement authority under RCRA in Office of Enforcement and Compliance, U.S. EPA, Civil Enforcement: RCRA Enforcement Process and Authorities, available at http://www.epa.gov/compliance/civil/rcra/rcraenf process.html.

Alternatively, the EPA or state can seek injunctive relief, temporary or permanent, in court. 42 U.S.C. § 6928(a)(1). However, if the relevant state is administering the RCRA hazardous waste program, the EPA must notify the state before filing suit. Id. § 6928(a)(2). Second, the EPA can sue a TSD facility that fails to comply with a monitoring or testing order. Id. § 6934(e). Third, if the relevant agencies learn of "an imminent and substantial endangerment to health or the environment," they may bring suit against anyone who has contributed to that problem for relief that would "restrain such person from such handling, storage, treatment, transportation, or disposal, or order such person to take such action as may be necessary, or both." Id. § 6973(a).

Private citizens can also seek injunctive relief in court—and against both the violator and the EPA—through RCRA's citizen-suit provision. This provision permits suit by a private individual against present or past generators, transporters, owners, or operators who are responsible for hazardous waste contributing to "an imminent and substantial endangerment to health or the environment." Id. § 6972(a). In such suits, the federal district court has broad authority to issue injunctive relief. Id.

Civil penalties are an important aspect of RCRA enforcement. The EPA and the states may pursue civil penalties both for violations of RCRA's solid and hazardous waste requirements and for violations of its underground storage tank requirements. Id. §§ 6928(a)(3) & 6991e(d). Citizens may also seek civil penalties in citizen suits. Id. § 6972(a).

RCRA is sparse in providing factors to consider in the civil penalty assessment, which is currently capped at $32,500 per day. It says only that "[i]n assessing such a penalty, the Administrator shall take in account the seriousness of the violation and any good faith efforts to comply with applicable requirements." Id. § 6928(a)(3).

The EPA, however, has developed comprehensive civil penalty policies. The EPA considers (1) the extent of the deviation from the requirement; (2) the probability that the violation will cause harm; (3) factors specific to the violator, including culpability, good faith in attempting to comply, ability to pay, violation history, and others; and (4) the economic gain obtained from the violation, which serves as a minimum for determining the amount of the penalty. RCRA Enforcement Division, Office of Regulatory Enforcement, Office of Enforcement and Compliance Assurance, RCRA Civil Penalty Policy 3, available at http://www.epa.gov/compliance/resources/policies/civil/rcra/rcpp2003–fnl.pdf.

Finally, RCRA provides for criminal enforcement, including criminal fines. Criminal prosecutions require that the violator knowingly violate the Act. 42 U.S.C. § 6928(d). If found guilty, the violator can be liable for criminal fines that are generally double the amounts of civil penalties, or be sentenced to two to five years in prison, or both. Id. However, if a violator also knowingly endangers another person in the course of knowingly violating RCRA, criminal fines go up to $250,000 for an individual and $1 million for organizations; individuals can also be sentenced to up to 15 years in prison. Id. § 6928(e). Thus, again, RCRA more severely punishes people who cause actual harm as a result of their violations.

3. THE CLEANUP STATUTE REMEDIES MODEL: CERCLA

CERCLA, as noted, is a cleanup statute, and its "damages" accordingly reflect its goal of removing hazardous substances from contaminated sites. Under CERCLA's basic liability provision, potentially responsible parties (PRPs) are liable for four kinds of damages:

(A) all costs of removal or remedial action incurred by the United States Government or a State or an Indian tribe not inconsistent with the national contingency plan;

(B) any other necessary costs of response incurred by any other person consistent with the national contingency plan;

(C) damages for injury to, destruction of, or loss of natural resources, including the reasonable costs of assessing such injury, destruction, or loss resulting from such a release; and

(D) the costs of any health assessment or health effects study carried out under section 9604(i) of this title.

42 U.S.C. § 9607(4).

The first thing to notice about CERCLA damages is that CERCLA distinguishes between cleanup costs incurred by a government or tribe and cleanup costs incurred by private parties: the former only have to be "not inconsistent" with the national contingency plan, while the latter have to be "consistent" with it. The national contingency plan, also known as the national hazardous substance response plan, establishes "procedures and standards for responding to releases of hazardous substances, pollutants, and contaminants * * *." 42 U.S.C. § 9605(a). While the difference in wording is slight, CERCLA creates a stronger presumption in favor of governments and tribes recovering their cleanup costs than for private parties.

Cleanup costs, in turn, cover both "removal" and "remedial" actions. Removal actions are the initial responses to a release of hazardous substances that ensure that the release is contained and that the public is kept safe. Id. § 9601(23). Remedial actions are the actions that implement the final remedy for the complete cleanup of the site. Id. § 9601(24).

Natural resource damages, in turn, compensate not for cleaning up the site *per se* but for the damage that the release of hazardous substances did to the natural resources on the site. The basic measure of natural resources damages is the costs of restoration, including restoration of ecosystem functions and ecosystem services. "Natural resources" in this context are "land, fish, wildlife, biota, air, water, ground water, drinking water supplies, and other such resources * * *." Id. § 9601(16). However, natural resources damages are assessed only for government or tribal property, including marine resources along the coast. Id.

The most comprehensive assessment of natural resources damages to date—although not under CERCLA—occurred in response to the *Exxon Valdez* oil spill off the coast of Alaska in 1989. The ship released 11 million gallons of crude oil, which eventually covered at least 10,000 square miles of coastal waters and oiled 1,000 miles of the Alaska coast. Natural resources damages assessed included the estimated costs of replacing the animals killed, which ranged from $300,000 per killer whale to $22,000 per eagle to $390 per river otter. Civil litigation over the *Exxon Valdez* spill settled, requiring Exxon to pay $900 million in damages, to be divided between the federal government and the State of Alaska. The settlement, however, also included a reopener provision, which the governments exercised in 2006, seeking additional money for damages and restoration.

Finally, under CERCLA PRPs are liable for the costs of health assessments and health effects studies carried out for the site. CERCLA created the Agency for Toxic Substances and Disease Registry (ATSDR). 42 U.S.C. § 9604(i). As one of its duties, this Agency "perform[s] a health assessment for each facility on the National Priorities List," and it may also perform health assessments at other sites "where individual persons or licensed physicians provide information that individuals have been exposed to a hazardous substance, for which the probable source of such exposure is a release." Id. § 9604(i)(6)(A), (B). A health assessment includes

> preliminary assessments of the potential risk to human health posed by individual sites and facilities, based on such factors as the nature and extent of contamination, the existence of potential pathways of human exposure (including ground or surface water contamination, air emissions, and food chain contamination), the size and potential susceptibility of the community within the likely pathways of exposure, the comparison of expected human exposure levels to the short-

term and long-term health effects associated with identified hazardous substances and any available recommended exposure or tolerance
limits for such hazardous substances, and the comparison of existing
morbidity and mortality data on diseases that may be associated with
the observed levels of exposure.

Id. § 9604(i)(6)(F).

If, on the basis of the health assessment, the ATSDR concludes that a
health effects study is appropriate, it "shall conduct a pilot study of health
effects for selected groups of exposed individuals in order to determine the
desirability of conducting full scale epidemiological or other health studies
of the entire exposed population." Id. § 9604(i)(7)(A). The Agency can
then conduct the full-scale epidemiologic and other studies for the entire
population if the pilot studies indicate that larger studies are "appropriate." Id. § 9604(i)(7)(B). In addition, the ATSDR can establish a registry
of exposed persons and engage in a full-scale health surveillance program
if the risks to human health so warrant. Id. §§ 9604(i)(8), (9). Finally,
"[i]f a health assessment or other study carried out under this section
contains a finding that the exposure concerned presents a significant risk
to human health, the President shall take such steps as may be necessary
to reduce such exposure and eliminate or substantially mitigate the
significant risk to human health." Id. § 9604(i)(11).

Health assessments and health effects studies are rarely a significant
issue in CERCLA liability litigation. However, their connection to common
law toxic torts should be obvious. First, these studies can provide additional motivation and legal authority to the EPA to act quickly to clean up a
release of hazardous substances, with the goal of preventing or minimizing
toxic tort harms from the release. Second, the studies that the ATSDR
generates can become important evidence in subsequent toxic tort litigation when a CERCLA site is alleged to be the cause of toxic tort injuries.

E. PUNITIVE DAMAGES

Punitive damages has been one of the front-line controversies in the
tort reform battles over the last 25 years. As a result, most states have
addressed the issue through legislation. In addition, the U.S. Supreme
Court has haltingly constitutionalized parts of punitive damages. The
following case touches on both of these developments and at the same
time finally brought to conclusion the decades long legal battle over the
damages caused the crash of the *Exxon Valdez*.

The *Dong Fang Ocean* (formerly the *Exxon Valdez*) in 2009. The ship has been converted into a bulk ore carrier. Source: http://www.aukevisser.nl/supertankers/bulkers/id425.htm

EXXON SHIPPING COMPANY v. BAKER

Supreme Court of the United States, 2008.
___ U.S. ___, 128 S.Ct. 2605, 171 L.Ed.2d 570.

JUSTICE SOUTER delivered the opinion of the Court.

There are three questions of maritime law before us: whether a shipowner may be liable for punitive damages without acquiescence in the actions causing harm, whether punitive damages have been barred implicitly by federal statutory law making no provision for them, and whether the award of $2.5 billion in this case is greater than maritime law should allow in the circumstances. We are equally divided on the owner's derivative liability, and hold that the federal statutory law does not bar a punitive award on top of damages for economic loss, but that the award here should be limited to an amount equal to compensatory damages.

I

On March 24, 1989, the supertanker *Exxon Valdez* grounded on Bligh Reef off the Alaskan coast, fracturing its hull and spilling millions of gallons of crude oil into Prince William Sound. The owner, petitioner Exxon Shipping Co. (now SeaRiver Maritime, Inc.), and its owner, petitioner Exxon Mobil Corp. (collectively, Exxon), have settled state and federal claims for environmental damage, with payments exceeding $1 billion, and this action by respondent Baker and others, including commercial fishermen and native Alaskans, was brought for economic losses to individuals dependent on Prince William Sound for their livelihoods.

A

The tanker was over 900 feet long and was used by Exxon to carry crude oil from the end of the Trans–Alaska Pipeline in Valdez, Alaska, to the lower 48 States. On the night of the spill it was carrying 53 million gallons of crude oil, or over a million barrels. Its captain was one Joseph Hazelwood, who had completed a 28–day alcohol treatment program while employed by Exxon, as his superiors knew, but dropped out of a prescribed follow-up program and stopped going to Alcoholics Anonymous meetings. According to the District Court, "[t]here was evidence presented to the jury that after Hazelwood was released from [residential treatment], he drank in bars, parking lots, apartments, airports, airplanes, restaurants, hotels, at various ports, and aboard Exxon tankers." *In re Exxon Valdez,* No. A89–0095–CV, Order No. 265 (D.Alaska, Jan. 27, 1995), p. 5, App. F to Pet. for Cert. 255a–256a (hereinafter Order 265). The jury also heard contested testimony that Hazelwood drank with Exxon officials and that members of the Exxon management knew of his relapse. See *ibid.* Although Exxon had a clear policy prohibiting employees from serving onboard within four hours of consuming alcohol, see *In re Exxon Valdez,* 270 F.3d 1215, 1238 (C.A.9 2001), Exxon presented no evidence that it monitored Hazelwood after his return to duty or considered giving him a shoreside assignment. Witnesses testified that before the *Valdez* left port on the night of the disaster, Hazelwood downed at least five double vodkas in the waterfront bars of Valdez, an intake of about 15 ounces of 80–proof alcohol, enough "that a non-alcoholic would have passed out." 270 F.3d, at 1236.

The ship sailed at 9:12 p.m. on March 23, 1989, guided by a state-licensed pilot for the first leg out, through the Valdez Narrows. At 11:20 p.m., Hazelwood took active control and, owing to poor conditions in the outbound shipping lane, radioed the Coast Guard for permission to move east across the inbound lane to a less icy path. Under the conditions, this was a standard move, which the last outbound tanker had also taken, and the Coast Guard cleared the *Valdez* to cross the inbound lane. The tanker accordingly steered east toward clearer waters, but the move put it in the path of an underwater reef off Bligh Island, thus requiring a turn back west into the shipping lane around Busby Light, north of the reef.

Two minutes before the required turn, however, Hazelwood left the bridge and went down to his cabin in order, he said, to do paperwork. This decision was inexplicable. There was expert testimony that, even if their presence is not strictly necessary, captains simply do not quit the bridge during maneuvers like this, and no paperwork could have justified it. And in fact the evidence was that Hazelwood's presence was required, both because there should have been two officers on the bridge at all times and his departure left only one, and because he was the only person on the entire ship licensed to navigate this part of Prince William Sound. To make matters worse, before going below Hazelwood put the tanker on autopilot, speeding it up, making the turn trickier, and any mistake harder to correct.

As Hazelwood left, he instructed the remaining officer, third mate Joseph Cousins, to move the tanker back into the shipping lane once it came abeam of Busby Light. Cousins, unlicensed to navigate in those waters, was left alone with helmsman Robert Kagan, a nonofficer. For reasons that remain a mystery, they failed to make the turn at Busby Light, and a later emergency maneuver attempted by Cousins came too late. The tanker ran aground on Bligh Reef, tearing the hull open and spilling 11 million gallons of crude oil into Prince William Sound.

After Hazelwood returned to the bridge and reported the grounding to the Coast Guard, he tried but failed to rock the *Valdez* off the reef, a maneuver which could have spilled more oil and caused the ship to founder.[1] The Coast Guard's nearly immediate response included a blood test of Hazelwood (the validity of which Exxon disputes) showing a blood-alcohol level of .061 eleven hours after the spill. Experts testified that to have this much alcohol in his bloodstream so long after the accident, Hazelwood at the time of the spill must have had a blood-alcohol level of around .241, three times the legal limit for driving in most States.

In the aftermath of the disaster, Exxon spent around $2.1 billion in cleanup efforts. The United States charged the company with criminal violations of the Clean Water Act, 33 U.S.C. §§ 1311(a) and 1319(c)(1); the Refuse Act of 1899, 33 U.S.C. §§ 407 and 411; the Migratory Bird Treaty Act, 16 U.S.C. §§ 703 and 707(a); the Ports and Waterways Safety Act, 33 U.S.C. § 1232(b)(1); and the Dangerous Cargo Act, 46 U.S.C. § 3718(b). Exxon pleaded guilty to violations of the Clean Water Act, the Refuse Act, and the Migratory Bird Treaty Act and agreed to pay a $150 million fine, later reduced to $25 million plus restitution of $100 million. A civil action by the United States and the State of Alaska for environmental harms ended with a consent decree for Exxon to pay at least $900 million toward restoring natural resources, and it paid another $303 million in voluntary settlements with fishermen, property owners, and other private parties.

B

The remaining civil cases were consolidated into this one against Exxon, Hazelwood, and others. The District Court for the District of

---

1. As it turned out, the tanker survived the accident and remained in Exxon's fleet, which it subsequently transferred to a wholly owned subsidiary, SeaRiver Maritime, Inc. The *Valdez* "was renamed several times, finally to the *SeaRiver Mediterranean*, [and] carried oil between the Persian Gulf and Japan, Singapore, and Australia for 12 years.... In 2002, the ship was pulled from service and 'laid up' off a foreign port (just where the owners won't say) and prepared for retirement, although, according to some reports, the vessel continues in service under a foreign flag." Exxon Valdez Spill Anniversary Marked, 30 Oil Spill Intelligence Report 2 (Mar. 29, 2007). [A number of sources report that at the beginning of 2010 the ship was still in use. Her Chinese owners, the Hong Kong Bloom Shipping Co., have renamed her the *Dong Fang Ocean* and converted her to an ore carrier.—Eds.]

Alaska divided the plaintiffs seeking compensatory damages into three classes: commercial fishermen, Native Alaskans, and landowners. At Exxon's behest, the court also certified a mandatory class of all plaintiffs seeking punitive damages, whose number topped 32,000. Respondents here, to whom we will refer as Baker for convenience, are members of that class.

For the purposes of the case, Exxon stipulated to its negligence in the *Valdez* disaster and its ensuing liability for compensatory damages. The court designed the trial accordingly: Phase I considered Exxon and Hazelwood's recklessness and thus their potential for punitive liability; Phase II set compensatory damages for commercial fishermen and Native Alaskans; and Phase III determined the amount of punitive damages for which Hazelwood and Exxon were each liable. * * *

In Phase I, the jury heard extensive testimony about Hazelwood's alcoholism and his conduct on the night of the spill, as well as conflicting testimony about Exxon officials' knowledge of Hazelwood's backslide. At the close of Phase I, the Court instructed the jury in part that

> [a] corporation is responsible for the reckless acts of those employees who are employed in a managerial capacity while acting in the scope of their employment. * * *

In Phase II the jury awarded $287 million in compensatory damages to the commercial fishermen. After the Court deducted released claims, settlements, and other payments, the balance outstanding was $19,590,257. Meanwhile, most of the Native Alaskan class had settled their compensatory claims for $20 million, and those who opted out of that settlement ultimately settled for a total of around $2.6 million.

In Phase III, the jury heard about Exxon's management's acts and omissions arguably relevant to the spill. At the close of evidence, the court instructed the jurors on the purposes of punitive damages, emphasizing that they were designed not to provide compensatory relief but to punish and deter the defendants. The court charged the jury to consider the reprehensibility of the defendants' conduct, their financial condition, the magnitude of the harm, and any mitigating facts. *Id.*, at 15a. The jury awarded $5,000 in punitive damages against Hazelwood and $5 billion against Exxon.

On appeal, the Court of Appeals for the Ninth Circuit upheld the Phase I jury instruction on corporate liability for acts of managerial agents under Circuit precedent. With respect to the size of the punitive damages award, however, the Circuit remanded twice for adjustments in light of this Court's due process cases before ultimately itself remitting the award to $2.5 billion.

We granted certiorari to consider whether maritime law allows corporate liability for punitive damages on the basis of the acts of managerial agents, whether the Clean Water Act (CWA), 86 Stat. 816, 33 U.S.C. § 1251 *et seq.* (2000 ed. and Supp. V), forecloses the award of punitive damages in maritime spill cases, and whether the punitive damages awarded against Exxon in this case were excessive as a matter of maritime common law. We now vacate and remand.

[Justice Alito, recently appointed to the Court, took no part in the consideration or decision of the case. As a consequence, the court was equally divided on the derivative liability question and thus left the Ninth Circuit opinion undisturbed. On the preemption question, the court held that maritime common law punitive damages were not preempted by the Clean Water Act.]

* * *

IV

Finally, Exxon raises an issue of first impression about punitive damages in maritime law, which falls within a federal court's jurisdiction to decide in the manner of a common law court, subject to the authority of Congress to legislate otherwise if it disagrees with the judicial result. In addition to its resistance to derivative liability for punitive damages and its preemption claim already disposed of, Exxon challenges the size of the remaining $2.5 billion punitive damages award. Other than its preemption argument, it does not offer a legal ground for concluding that maritime law should never award punitive damages, or that none should be awarded in this case, but it does argue that this award exceeds the bounds justified by the punitive damages goal of deterring reckless (or worse) behavior and the consequently heightened threat of harm. The claim goes to our understanding of the place of punishment in modern civil law and reasonable standards of process in administering punitive law, subjects that call for starting with a brief account of the history behind today's punitive damages.

A

The modern Anglo–American doctrine of punitive damages dates back at least to 1763, when a pair of decisions by the Court of Common Pleas recognized the availability of damages "for more than the injury received." *Wilkes v. Wood,* Lofft 1, 18, 98 Eng. Rep. 489, 498 (1763) (Lord Chief Justice Pratt). In *Wilkes v. Wood,* one of the foundations of the Fourth Amendment, exemplary damages awarded against the Secretary of State, responsible for an unlawful search of John Wilkes's papers, were a spectacular £4,000. And in *Huckle v. Money,* 2 Wils. 205, 206–207, 95 Eng. Rep. 768, 768–769 (K.B.1763), the same judge who is recorded in *Wilkes* gave an opinion upholding a jury's award of £300 (against a government officer again) although "if the jury had been confined by their oath to consider the mere personal injury only, perhaps [£20] damages would have been thought damages sufficient."

Awarding damages beyond the compensatory was not, however, a wholly novel idea even then, legal codes from ancient times through the Middle Ages having called for multiple damages for certain especially harmful acts. See, *e.g.,* Code of Hammurabi § 8 (R. Harper ed.1904) (tenfold penalty for stealing the goat of a freed man); Statute of Gloucester, 1278, 6 Edw. I, ch. 5, 1 Stat. at Large 66 (treble damages for waste). But punitive damages were a common law innovation untethered to strict numerical multipliers, and the doctrine promptly crossed the Atlantic, see, *e.g., Genay v. Norris,* 1 S.C.L. 6, 7 (1784); *Coryell v. Colbaugh,* 1 N.J.L. 77 (1791), to become widely accepted in American courts by the middle of the 19th century, see, *e.g., Day v. Woodworth,* 13 How. 363, 371, 14 L.Ed. 181 (1852).

B

Early common law cases offered various rationales for punitivedamages awards, which were then generally dubbed "exemplary," implying that these verdicts were justified as punishment for extraordinary wrongdoing, as in Wilkes's case. Sometimes, though, the extraordinary element emphasized was the damages award itself, the punishment being "for example's sake," *Tullidge v. Wade,* 3 Wils. 18, 19, 95 Eng. Rep. 909 (K.B.1769) (Lord Chief Justice Wilmot), "to deter from any such proceeding for the future," *Wilkes, supra,* at 19, 98 Eng. Rep., at 498–499.

A third historical justification, which showed up in some of the early cases, has been noted by recent commentators, and that was the need "to compensate for intangible injuries, compensation which was not otherwise available under the narrow conception of compensatory damages prevalent at the time." *Cooper Industries, Inc. v. Leatherman Tool Group, Inc.,* 532 U.S. 424, 437–438, n. 11, 121 S.Ct. 1678, 149 L.Ed.2d 674 (2001). As the century progressed, * * * American courts tended to speak of punitive damages as separate and distinct from compensatory damages. See generally 1 L. Schlueter, Punitive Damages §§ 1.3(C)–(D), 1.4(A) (5th ed.2005) (hereinafter Schlueter) (describing the "almost total eclipse of the compensatory function" in the decades following the 1830s).

Regardless of the alternative rationales over the years, the consensus today is that punitives are aimed not at compensation but principally at retribution and deterring harmful conduct. This consensus informs the doctrine in most modern American jurisdictions, where juries are customarily instructed on twin goals of punitive awards. See, *e.g.,* Cal. Jury Instr., Civil, No. 14.72.2 (2008) ("You must now determine whether you should award punitive damages against defendant[s] . . . for the sake of example and by way of punishment"). The prevailing rule in American courts also limits punitive damages to cases of what the Court in *Day, supra,* at 371, spoke of as "enormity," where a defendant's conduct is "outrageous" * * *.

Under the umbrellas of punishment and its aim of deterrence, degrees of relative blameworthiness are apparent. Reckless conduct is not intentional or malicious, nor is it necessarily callous toward the risk of harming others, as opposed to unheedful of it. See, *e.g.,* 2 Restatement § 500, Comment *a.* Action taken or omitted in order to augment profit represents an enhanced degree of punishable culpability, as of course does willful or malicious action, taken with a purpose to injure. See 4 *id.*, § 908, Comment *e.*

Regardless of culpability, however, heavier punitive awards have been thought to be justifiable when wrongdoing is hard to detect (increasing chances of getting away with it), see, *e.g., BMW of North America, Inc. v. Gore,* 517 U.S. 559, 582, 116 S.Ct. 1589, 134 L.Ed.2d 809 (1996) ("A higher ratio may also be justified in cases in which the injury is hard to detect"), or when the value of injury and the corresponding compensatory award are small (providing low incentives to sue). And, with a broadly analogous object, some regulatory schemes provide by statute for multiple recovery in order to induce private litigation to supplement official enforcement that might fall short if unaided.

C

State regulation of punitive damages varies. A few States award them rarely, or not at all. Nebraska bars punitive damages entirely, on state constitutional grounds. Four others permit punitive damages only when authorized by statute: Louisiana, Massachusetts, and Washington as a matter of common law, and New Hampshire by statute codifying common law tradition. Michigan courts recognize only exemplary damages supportable as compensatory, rather than truly punitive, while Connecticut courts have limited what they call punitive recovery to the "expenses of bringing the legal action, including attorney's fees, less taxable costs," *Larsen Chelsey Realty Co. v. Larsen,* 232 Conn. 480, 517, n. 38, 656 A.2d 1009, 1029, n. 38 (1995).

As for procedure, in most American jurisdictions the amount of the punitive award is generally determined by a jury in the first instance, and that "determination is then reviewed by trial and appellate courts to ensure that it is reasonable." *Pacific Mut. Life Ins. Co. v. Haslip,* 499 U.S. 1, 15, 111 S.Ct. 1032, 113 L.Ed.2d 1 (1991). Many States have gone further by imposing statutory limits on punitive awards, in the form of absolute monetary caps, see, *e.g.,* Va.Code Ann. § 8.01–38.1 (Lexis 2007) ($350,000 cap), a maximum ratio of punitive to compensatory damages, see, *e.g.,* Ohio Rev.Code Ann. § 2315.21(D)(2)(a) (Lexis 2001) (2:1 ratio in most tort cases), or, frequently, some combination of the two, see, *e.g.,* Alaska Stat. § 09.17.020(f) (2006) (greater of 3:1 ratio or $500,000 in most actions). The States that rely on a multiplier have adopted a variety of ratios, ranging from 5:1 to 1:1.[12]

---

12. See, *e.g.,* Mo.Rev.Stat. Ann. § 510.265(1) (Vernon Supp.2008) (greater of 5:1 or $500,000 in most cases); Ala.Code §§ 6–11–21(a), (d) (2005) (greater of 3:1 or $1.5 million in most personal injury suits, and 3:1 or $500,000 in most other actions); N.D. Cent.Code Ann. § 32–03.2–11(4) (Supp.2007) (greater of 2:1 or $250,000); Colo.Rev.Stat. Ann. § 13–21–102(1)(a) (2007) (1:1).

Oklahoma has a graduated scheme, with the limit on the punitive award turning on the nature of the defendant's conduct. See Okla. Stat., Tit. 23, § 9.1(B) (West 2001) (greater of 1:1 or $100,000 in cases involving "reckless disregard"); § 9.1(C) (greater of 2:1, $500,000, or the financial benefit derived by the defendant, in cases of intentional and malicious conduct); § 9.1(D) (no limit where the conduct is intentional, malicious, and life threatening).

Despite these limitations, punitive damages overall are higher and more frequent in the United States than they are anywhere else. See, *e.g.,* Gotanda, Punitive Damages: A Comparative Analysis, 42 Colum. J. Transnat'l L. 391, 421 (2004); 2 Schlueter § 22.0. In England and Wales, punitive, or exemplary, damages are available only for oppressive, arbitrary, or unconstitutional action by government servants; injuries designed by the defendant to yield a larger profit than the likely cost of compensatory damages; and conduct for which punitive damages are expressly authorized by statute. *Rookes v. Barnard,* [1964] 1 All E.R. 367, 410–411 (H.L.). Even in the circumstances where punitive damages are allowed, they are subject to strict, judicially imposed guidelines. The Court of Appeal in *Thompson v. Commissioner of Police of Metropolis,* [1998] Q.B. 498, 518, said that a ratio of more than three times the amount of compensatory damages will rarely be appropriate; awards of less than £5,000 are likely unnecessary; awards of £25,000 should be exceptional; and £50,000 should be considered the top.

For further contrast with American practice, Canada and Australia allow exemplary damages for outrageous conduct, but awards are considered extraordinary and rarely issue. See 2 Schlueter §§ 22.1(B), (D). Noncompensatory damages are not part of the civil-code tradition and thus unavailable in such countries as France, Germany, Austria, and Switzerland. See *id.,* §§ 22.2(A)–(C), (E). And some legal systems not only decline to recognize punitive damages themselves but refuse to enforce foreign punitive judgments as contrary to public policy. See, *e.g.,* Gotanda, Charting Developments Concerning Punitive Damages: Is the Tide Changing? 45 Colum. J. Transnat'l L. 507, 514, 518, 528 (2007) (noting refusals to enforce judgments by Japanese, Italian, and German courts, positing that such refusals may be on the decline, but concluding, "American parties should not anticipate smooth sailing when seeking to have a domestic punitive damages award recognized and enforced in other countries").

D

American punitive damages have been the target of audible criticism in recent decades, see, *e.g.,* Note, Developments, The Paths of Civil Litigation, 113 Harv. L.Rev. 1783, 1784–1788 (2000) (surveying criticism), but the most recent studies tend to undercut much of it, see *id.,* at 1787–1788. A survey of the literature reveals that discretion to award punitive damages has not mass-produced runaway awards, and although some studies show the dollar amounts of punitive-damages awards growing over time, even in real terms,[13] by most accounts the median ratio of punitive

---

13. See, *e.g.,* RAND Institute for Civil Justice, D. Hensler & E. Moller, Trends in Punitive Damages, table 2 (Mar.1995) (finding an increase in median awards between the early 1980s and the early 1990s in San Francisco and Cook Counties); Moller, Pace, & Carroll, Punitive Damages in Financial Injury Jury Verdicts, 28 J. Legal Studies 283, 307 (1999) (hereinafter Financial Injury Jury Verdicts) (studying jury verdicts in "Financial Injury" cases in six States and Cook County, Illinois, and finding a marked increase in the median award between the late 1980s and the early 1990s); M. Peterson, S. Sarma, & M. Shanley, Punitive Damages: Empirical Findings 15

to compensatory awards has remained less than 1:1.[14] Nor do the data substantiate a marked increase in the percentage of cases with punitive awards over the past several decades.[15] The figures thus show an overall restraint and suggest that in many instances a high ratio of punitive to compensatory damages is substantially greater than necessary to punish or deter.

The real problem, it seems, is the stark unpredictability of punitive awards. Courts of law are concerned with fairness as consistency, and evidence that the median ratio of punitive to compensatory awards falls within a reasonable zone, or that punitive awards are infrequent, fails to tell us whether the spread between high and low individual awards is acceptable. The available data suggest it is not. A recent comprehensive study of punitive damages awarded by juries in state civil trials found a median ratio of punitive to compensatory awards of just 0.62:1, but a mean ratio of 2.90:1 and a standard deviation of 13.81. Juries, Judges, and

(RAND Institute for Civil Justice 1987) (hereinafter Punitive Damages: Empirical Findings) (finding that the median punitive award increased nearly 4 times in San Francisco County between the early 1960s and the early 1980s, and 43 times in Cook County over the same period). But see T. Eisenberg et al., Juries, Judges, and Punitive Damages: Empirical Analyses Using the Civil Justice Survey of State Courts 1992, 1996, and 2001 Data, 3 J. of Empirical Legal Studies 263, 278 (2006) (hereinafter Juries, Judges, and Punitive Damages) (analyzing Bureau of Justice Statistics data from 1992, 1996, and 2001, and concluding that "[n]o statistically significant variation exists in the inflation-adjusted punitive award level over the three time periods"); Dept. of Justice, Bureau of Justice Statistics, T. Cohen, Punitive Damage Awards in Large Counties, 2001, p. 8 (Mar.2005) (hereinafter Cohen) (compiling data from the Nation's 75 most populous counties and finding that the median punitive damage award in civil jury trials decreased between 1992 and 2001).

14. See, *e.g.,* Juries, Judges, and Punitive Damages 269 (reporting median ratios of 0.62:1 in jury trials and 0.66:1 in bench trials using the Bureau of Justice Statistics data from 1992, 1996, and 2001); Vidmar & Rose, Punitive Damages by Juries in Florida, 38 Harv. J. Legis. 487, 492 (2001) (studying civil cases in Florida state courts between 1989 and 1998 and finding a median ratio of 0.67:1). But see Financial Injury Jury Verdicts 307 (finding a median ratio of 1.4:1 in "financial injury" cases in the late 1980s and early 1990s).

15. See, *e.g.,* Cohen 8 (compiling data from the Nation's 75 most populous counties, and finding that in jury trials where the plaintiff prevailed, the percentage of cases involving punitive awards was 6.1% in 1992 and 5.6% in 2001); Financial Injury Jury Verdicts 307 (finding a statistically significant decrease in the percentage of verdicts in "financial injury" cases that include a punitive damage award, from 15.8% in the early 1980s to 12.7% in the early 1990s). But see Punitive Damages: Empirical Findings 9 (finding an increase in the percentage of civil trials resulting in punitive damage awards in San Francisco and Cook Counties between 1960 and 1984).

One might posit that ill effects of punitive damages are clearest not in actual awards but in the shadow that the punitive regime casts on settlement negotiations and other litigation decisions. See, *e.g.,* Financial Injury Jury Verdicts 287; Polinsky, Are Punitive Damages Really Insignificant, Predictable, and Rational? 26 J. Legal Studies 663, 664–671 (1997). But here again the data have not established a clear correlation. See, *e.g.,* Eaton, Mustard, & Talarico, The Effects of Seeking Punitive Damages on the Processing of Tort Claims, 34 J. Legal Studies 343, 357, 353–354, 365 (2005) (studying data from six Georgia counties and concluding that "the decision to seek punitive damages has no statistically significant impact" on "whether a case that was disposed was done so by trial or by some other procedure, including settlement," or "whether a case that was disposed by means other than a trial was more likely to have been settled"); Kritzer & Zemans, The Shadow of Punitives, 1998 Wis. L.Rev. 157, 160 (1998) (noting the theory that punitive damages cast a large shadow over settlement negotiations, but finding that "with perhaps one exception, what little systematic evidence we could find does not support the notion" (emphasis deleted)).

Punitive Damages 269.[16] Even to those of us unsophisticated in statistics, the thrust of these figures is clear: the spread is great, and the outlier cases subject defendants to punitive damages that dwarf the corresponding compensatories. The distribution of awards is narrower, but still remarkable, among punitive damages assessed by judges: the median ratio is 0.66:1, the mean ratio is 1.60:1, and the standard deviation is 4.54. *Ibid.* Other studies of some of the same data show that fully 14% of punitive awards in 2001 were greater than four times the compensatory damages, see Cohen 5, with 18% of punitives in the 1990s more than trebling the compensatory damages, see Ostrom, Rottman, & Goerdt, A Step Above Anecdote: A Profile of the Civil Jury in the 1990s, 79 Judicature 233, 240 (1996). And a study of "financial injury" cases using a different data set found that 34% of the punitive awards were greater than three times the corresponding compensatory damages. Financial Injury Jury Verdicts 333.

Starting with the premise of a punitive-damages regime, these ranges of variation might be acceptable or even desirable if they resulted from judges' and juries' refining their judgments to reach a generally accepted optimal level of penalty and deterrence in cases involving a wide range of circumstances, while producing fairly consistent results in cases with similar facts. Cf. *TXO Production Corp. v. Alliance Resources Corp.,* 509 U.S. 443, 457–458, 113 S.Ct. 2711, 125 L.Ed.2d 366 (1993) (plurality opinion). But anecdotal evidence suggests that nothing of that sort is going on. One of our own leading cases on punitive damages, with a $4 million verdict by an Alabama jury, noted that a second Alabama case with strikingly similar facts produced "a comparable amount of compensatory damages" but "no punitive damages at all." See *Gore,* 517 U.S., at 565, n. 8, 116 S.Ct. 1589. As the Supreme Court of Alabama candidly explained, "the disparity between the two jury verdicts ... [w]as a reflection of the inherent uncertainty of the trial process." *BMW of North America, Inc. v. Gore,* 646 So.2d 619, 626 (1994) *(per curiam).* We are aware of no scholarly work pointing to consistency across punitive awards in cases involving similar claims and circumstances.[17]

E

The Court's response to outlier punitive damages awards has thus far been confined by claims at the constitutional level, and our cases have announced due process standards that every award must pass. See, *e.g.,*

---

16. This study examined "the most representative sample of state court trials in the United States," involving "tort, contract, and property cases disposed of by trial in fiscal year 1991–1992 and then calendar years 1996 and 2001. The three separate data sets cover state courts of general jurisdiction in a random sample of 46 of the 75 most populous counties in the United States." Juries, Judges, and Punitive Damages 267. The information was "gathered directly" from state-court clerks' offices and the study did "not rely on litigants or third parties to report." *Ibid.*

17. The Court is aware of a body of literature running parallel to anecdotal reports, examining the predictability of punitive awards by conducting numerous "mock juries," where different "jurors" are confronted with the same hypothetical case. See, *e.g.,* C. Sunstein, R. Hastie, J. Payne, D. Schkade, W. Viscusi, Punitive Damages: How Juries Decide (2002); Schkade, Sunstein, & Kahneman, Deliberating About Dollars: The Severity Shift, 100 Colum. L.Rev. 1139 (2000); Hastie, Schkade, & Payne, Juror Judgments in Civil Cases: Effects of Plaintiff's Requests and Plaintiff's Identity on Punitive Damage Awards, 23 Law & Hum. Behav. 445 (1999); Sunstein, Kahneman, & Schkade, Assessing Punitive Damages (with Notes on Cognition and Valuation in Law), 107 Yale L.J. 2071 (1998). Because this research was funded in part by Exxon, we decline to rely on it.

State Farm Mut. Automobile Ins. Co. v. Campbell, 538 U.S. 408, 425, 123 S.Ct. 1513, 155 L.Ed.2d 585 (2003); *Gore,* 517 U.S., at 574–575, 116 S.Ct. 1589. Although "we have consistently rejected the notion that the constitutional line is marked by a simple mathematical formula," *id.,* at 582, 116 S.Ct. 1589, we have determined that "few awards exceeding a single-digit ratio between punitive and compensatory damages, to a significant degree, will satisfy due process," *State Farm,* 538 U.S., at 425, 123 S.Ct. 1513; "[w]hen compensatory damages are substantial, then a lesser ratio, perhaps only equal to compensatory damages, can reach the outermost limit of the due process guarantee," *ibid.*

Today's enquiry differs from due process review because the case arises under federal maritime jurisdiction, and we are reviewing a jury award for conformity with maritime law, rather than the outer limit allowed by due process; we are examining the verdict in the exercise of federal maritime common law authority, which precedes and should obviate any application of the constitutional standard. Our due process cases, on the contrary, have all involved awards subject in the first instance to state law. See, *e.g., id.,* at 414, 123 S.Ct. 1513 (fraud and intentional infliction of emotional distress under Utah law); *Gore, supra,* at 563, and n. 3, 116 S.Ct. 1589 (fraud under Alabama law); *TXO, supra,* at 452, 113 S.Ct. 2711 (plurality opinion) (slander of title under West Virginia law); *Haslip,* 499 U.S., at 7, 111 S.Ct. 1032 (fraud under Alabama law). These, as state-law cases, could provide no occasion to consider a "common-law standard of excessiveness," *Browning–Ferris Industries,* 492 U.S., at 279, 109 S.Ct. 2909, and the only matter of federal law within our appellate authority was the constitutional due process issue.

Our review of punitive damages today, then, considers not their intersection with the Constitution, but the desirability of regulating them as a common law remedy for which responsibility lies with this Court as a source of judge-made law in the absence of statute. Whatever may be the constitutional significance of the unpredictability of high punitive awards, this feature of happenstance is in tension with the function of the awards as punitive, just because of the implication of unfairness that an eccentrically high punitive verdict carries in a system whose commonly held notion of law rests on a sense of fairness in dealing with one another. Thus, a penalty should be reasonably predictable in its severity, so that even Justice Holmes's "bad man" can look ahead with some ability to know what the stakes are in choosing one course of action or another. See The Path of the Law, 10 Harv. L.Rev. 457, 459 (1897). And when the bad man's counterparts turn up from time to time, the penalty scheme they face ought to threaten them with a fair probability of suffering in like degree when they wreak like damage. * * *

F

1

With that aim ourselves, we have three basic approaches to consider, one verbal and two quantitative. As mentioned before, a number of state courts have settled on criteria for judicial review of punitive-damages awards that go well beyond traditional "shock the conscience" or "passion and prejudice" tests. Maryland, for example, has set forth a nonexclusive list of nine review factors under state common law that include "degree of heinousness," "the deterrence value of [the award]," and "[w]hether [the punitive award] bears a reasonable relationship to the compensatory damages awarded." *Bowden v. Caldor, Inc.*, 350 Md. 4, 25–39, 710 A.2d 267, 277–284 (1998). Alabama has seven general criteria, such as "actual or likely harm [from the defendant's conduct]," "degree of reprehensibility," and "[i]f the wrongful conduct was profitable to the defendant." *Green Oil Co. v. Hornsby*, 539 So.2d 218, 223–224 (1989).

These judicial review criteria are brought to bear after juries render verdicts under instructions offering, at best, guidance no more specific for reaching an appropriate penalty. In Maryland, for example, which allows punitive damages for intentional torts and conduct characterized by "actual malice," *U.S. Gypsum Co. v. Mayor and City Council of Baltimore*, 336 Md. 145, 185, 647 A.2d 405, 424–425 (1994), juries may be instructed that

"An award for punitive damages should be:

"(1) In an amount that will deter the defendant and others from similar conduct.

"(2) Proportionate to the wrongfulness of the defendant's conduct and the defendant's ability to pay.

"(3) But not designed to bankrupt or financially destroy a defendant." Md. Pattern Jury Instr., Civil, No. 10:13 (4th ed.2007).

In Alabama, juries are instructed to fix an amount after considering "the character and degree of the wrong as shown by the evidence in the case, and the necessity of preventing similar wrongs." 1 Ala. Pattern Jury Instr., Civil, No. § 23.21 (Supp.2007).

These examples leave us skeptical that verbal formulations, superimposed on general jury instructions, are the best insurance against unpredictable outliers. Instructions can go just so far in promoting systemic consistency when awards are not tied to specifically proven items of damage (the cost of medical treatment, say), and although judges in the States that take this approach may well produce just results by dint of valiant effort, our experience with attempts to produce consistency in the analogous business of criminal sentencing leaves us doubtful that anything but a quantified approach will work. A glance at the experience there will explain our skepticism.

The points of similarity are obvious. "[P]unitive damages advance the interests of punishment and deterrence, which are also among the interests advanced by the criminal law." *Browning–Ferris Industries*, 492 U.S., at 275, 109 S.Ct. 2909. See also 1977 Restatement § 908, Comment *a*, at 464 (purposes of punitive damages are "the same" as "that of a fine imposed after a conviction of a crime"); 18 U.S.C. § 3553(a)(2) (requiring sentencing courts to consider, *inter alia,* "the need for the sentence imposed ... to provide just punishment for the offense" and "to afford adequate deterrence to criminal conduct"); United States Sentencing Commission, Guidelines Manual § 1A1.1, comment. (Nov.2007).

It is instructive, then, that in the last quarter century federal sentencing rejected an "indeterminate" system, with relatively unguided discretion to sentence within a wide range, under which "similarly situated offenders were sentenced [to], and did actually serve, widely disparate sentences."[19] Instead it became a system of detailed guidelines tied to exactly quantified sentencing results, under the authority of the Sentencing Reform Act of 1984, 18 U.S.C. § 3551 *et seq.* (2000 ed. and Supp. V).

The importance of this for us is that in the old federal sentencing system of general standards the cohort of even the most seasoned judicial penalty-givers defied consistency. Judges and defendants alike were "[l]eft at large, wandering in deserts of uncharted discretion," M. Frankel, Criminal Sentences: Law Without Order 7–8 (1973), which is very much the position of those imposing punitive damages today, be they judges or juries, except that they lack even a statutory maximum; their only restraint beyond a core sense of fairness is the due process limit. This federal criminal law development, with its many state parallels, strongly suggests that as long "as there are no punitive-damages guidelines, corresponding to the federal and state sentencing guidelines, it is inevitable that the specific amount of punitive damages awarded whether by a judge or by a jury will be arbitrary." *Mathias v. Accor Economy Lodging, Inc.,* 347 F.3d 672, 678 (C.A.7 2003).

2

This is why our better judgment is that eliminating unpredictable outlying punitive awards by more rigorous standards than the constitutional limit will probably have to take the form adopted in those States that have looked to the criminal-law pattern of quantified limits. One option would be to follow the States that set a hard dollar cap on punitive damages, a course that arguably would come closest to the criminal law, rather like setting a maximum term of years. The trouble is, though, that there is no "standard" tort or contract injury, making it difficult to settle upon a particular dollar figure as appropriate across the board. And of course a judicial selection of a dollar cap would carry a serious drawback; a legislature can pick a figure, index it for inflation, and revisit its provision whenever there seems to be a need for further tinkering, but a court cannot say when an issue will show up on the docket again.

The more promising alternative is to leave the effects of inflation to the jury or judge who assesses the value of actual loss, by pegging punitive to compensatory damages using a ratio or maximum multiple. As the earlier canvass of state experience showed, this is the model many States

---

19. Nagel, Structuring Sentencing Discretion: The New Federal Sentencing Guidelines, 80 J.Crim. L. & C. 883, 895–899 (1990) (citing studies and congressional hearings).

have adopted, see *supra,* at 2623, and n. 12, and Congress has passed analogous legislation from time to time, as for example in providing treble damages in antitrust, racketeering, patent, and trademark actions, see 15 U.S.C. §§ 15, 1117 (2000 ed. and Supp. V); 18 U.S.C. § 1964(c); 35 U.S.C. § 284. And of course the potential relevance of the ratio between compensatory and punitive damages is indisputable, being a central feature in our due process analysis.

Still, some will murmur that this smacks too much of policy and too little of principle. But the answer rests on the fact that we are acting here in the position of a common law court of last review, faced with a perceived defect in a common law remedy. Traditionally, courts have accepted primary responsibility for reviewing punitive damages and thus for their evolution, and if, in the absence of legislation, judicially derived standards leave the door open to outlier punitive-damages awards, it is hard to see how the judiciary can wash its hands of a problem it created, simply by calling quantified standards legislative. See *State Farm, supra,* at 438, 123 S.Ct. 1513 (GINSBURG, J., dissenting) ("In a legislative scheme or a state high court's design to cap punitive damages, the handiwork in setting single-digit and 1–to–1 benchmarks could hardly be questioned").

* * *

Although the legal landscape is well populated with examples of ratios and multipliers expressing policies of retribution and deterrence, most of them suffer from features that stand in the way of borrowing them as paradigms of reasonable limitations suited for application to this case. While a slim majority of the States with a ratio have adopted 3:1, others see fit to apply a lower one, see, *e.g.,* Colo.Rev.Stat. Ann. § 13–21–102(1)(a) (2007) (1:1); Ohio Rev.Code Ann. § 2315.21(D)(2)(a) (Lexis 2005) (2:1), and a few have gone higher, see, *e.g.,* Mo. Ann. Stat. § 510.265(1) (Supp.2008) (5:1). Judgments may differ about the weight to be given to the slight majority of 3:1 States, but one feature of the 3:1 schemes dissuades us from selecting it here. With a few statutory exceptions, generally for intentional infliction of physical injury or other harm, see, *e.g.,* Ala.Code § 6–11–21(j) (2005); Ark.Code Ann. § 16–55–208(b) (2005), the States with 3:1 ratios apply them across the board (as do other States using different fixed multipliers). That is, the upper limit is not directed to cases like this one, where the tortious action was worse than negligent but less than malicious, exposing the tortfeasor to certain regulatory sanctions and inevitable damage actions; the 3:1 ratio in these States also applies to awards in quite different cases involving some of the most egregious conduct, including malicious behavior and dangerous activity carried on for the purpose of increasing a tortfeasor's financial gain. We confront, instead, a case of reckless action, profitless to the tortfeasor, resulting in substantial recovery for substantial injury. Thus, a legislative judgment that 3:1 is a reasonable limit overall is not a judgment that 3:1 is a reasonable limit in this particular type of case.

* * *

3

There is better evidence of an accepted limit of reasonable civil penalty * * * in several studies mentioned before, showing the median ratio of punitive to compensatory verdicts, reflecting what juries and judges have considered reasonable across many hundreds of punitive awards. We think it is fair to assume that the greater share of the verdicts studied in these comprehensive collections reflect reasonable judgments about the economic penalties appropriate in their particular cases.

These studies cover cases of the most as well as the least blameworthy conduct triggering punitive liability, from malice and avarice, down to recklessness, and even gross negligence in some jurisdictions. The data put the median ratio for the entire gamut of circumstances at less than 1:1, meaning that the compensatory award exceeds the punitive award in most cases. In a well-functioning system, we would expect that awards at the median or lower would roughly express jurors' sense of reasonable penalties in cases with no earmarks of exceptional blameworthiness within the punishable spectrum (cases like this one, without intentional or malicious conduct, and without behavior driven primarily by desire for gain, for example) and cases (again like this one) without the modest economic harm or odds of detection that have opened the door to higher awards. It also seems fair to suppose that most of the unpredictable outlier cases that call the fairness of the system into question are above the median; in theory a factfinder's deliberation could go awry to produce a very low ratio, but we have no basis to assume that such a case would be more than a sport, and the cases with serious constitutional issues coming to us have naturally been on the high side, see, *e.g., State Farm,* 538 U.S., at 425, 123 S.Ct. 1513 (ratio of 145:1); *Gore,* 517 U.S., at 582, 116 S.Ct. 1589 (ratio of 500:1). On these assumptions, a median ratio of punitive to compensatory damages of about 0.65:1 probably marks the line near which cases like this one largely should be grouped. Accordingly, given the need to protect against the possibility (and the disruptive cost to the legal system) of awards that are unpredictable and unnecessary, either for deterrence or for measured retribution, we consider that a 1:1 ratio, which is above the median award, is a fair upper limit in such maritime cases.

        * * *

V

Applying this standard to the present case, we take for granted the District Court's calculation of the total relevant compensatory damages at $507.5 million. See *In re Exxon Valdez,* 236 F.Supp.2d 1043, 1063 (D.Alaska 2002). A punitive-to-compensatory ratio of 1:1 thus yields maximum punitive damages in that amount.

We therefore vacate the judgment and remand the case for the Court of Appeals to remit the punitive damages award accordingly.

It is so ordered.

JUSTICE SCALIA, with whom JUSTICE THOMAS joins, concurring.

I join the opinion of the Court, including the portions that refer to constitutional limits that prior opinions have imposed upon punitive damages. While I agree with the argumentation based upon those prior holdings, I continue to believe the holdings were in error. See *State Farm Mut. Automobile Ins. Co. v. Campbell*, 538 U.S. 408, 429, 123 S.Ct. 1513, 155 L.Ed.2d 585 (2003) (SCALIA, J., dissenting).

NOTES AND QUESTIONS

1. *Constitutional limitations on punitive damage awards.* In *Exxon Shipping*, the Supreme Court frequently referred to its constitutional law punitive damages jurisprudence. The earliest cases focused on the Eighth Amendment prohibition of "excessive fines." In Browning–Ferris Industries of Vt., Inc. v. Kelco Disposal, Inc., 492 U.S. 257 (1989), the Court rejected this argument, at least as long as none of the award went to the state. (Note that a number of states have "split-recovery" statutes under which a portion of punitive damages awards go to the state. See, e.g. Ga. Code Ann. § 51–12–5.1(e)(2) (2000); Or. Rev. Stat. § 31.735 (2003).)

Later decisions focus on the due process clause. Perhaps the three most noteworthy cases are BMW of North America, Inc. v. Gore, 517 U.S. 559 (1996); State Farm Mutual Auto Insurance Co. v. Campbell, 538 U.S. 408 (2003); and Philip Morris v. Williams, 549 U.S. 346 (2007).

a. *Gore*. In *Gore*, the plaintiff sued after discovering that his new car had been repainted to repair minor damage it had suffered during pre-sale transit. The plaintiff presented evidence that BMW had repainted nearly 1,000 automobiles and that this had diminished their value by approximately $4,000 per vehicle. He contended an appropriate punitive damage award would be $4,000,000. The jury agreed. The Supreme Court of Alabama reduced the award to $2,000,000 on the argument that the jury had improperly multiplied the plaintiff's compensatory damages by the number of similar sales across the entire country, not just in Alabama.

The Supreme Court concluded that this award was grossly excessive. Due process requires that "a person receive fair notice not only of the conduct that will subject him to punishment but also of the severity of the penalty that a State may impose." *Gore*, 517 U.S. at 559. The Court set forth three "guideposts" to be used in assessing whether defendants have sufficient notice of the likely severity of an award: (1) the degree of reprehensibility of the conduct; (2) the disparity between punitive damages and the harm or potential harm suffered by plaintiff; and (3) the difference between the punitive damages award and the civil penalties that might be imposed in similar cases.

The size of the initial punitive damages award in *Gore* presumably reflected the injury to Gore *and* to the other 900–plus unknown individuals who were also harmed by BMW. Repainting 1,000 cars is presumably more reprehensible than repainting only one car and if there were civil penalties for such conduct presumably they would impose a fine for each repainted car. A potential problem arises, however, if subsequent to the

Gore case another of the injured purchasers sues and also asks for punitive damages. How should we deal with the problem of multiple punitive damage awards for the same conduct? The Court addressed this issue in *State Farm*.

b. *Campbell*. This case involved a bad faith failure to settle within policy limits on a claim arising out of a serious car accident. The parties to the car accident litigation agreed that the plaintiff was negligent but the insurer refused to settle for the $50,000 policy limits and the jury returned a verdict for $185,000, leaving the plaintiff with a potential personal liability of $135,000. Prior to the verdict, State Farm had assured the plaintiffs that "their assets were safe, that they had no liability for the accident, that State Farm would represent their interests, and that they did not need to procure separate counsel." Although most states impose liability on the insurer for the full amount of a judgment when it unreasonably fails to accept a settlement offer within policy limits, the defendant's initial position after the verdict was to refuse to cover the excess. Its counsel apparently told the Campbells, "You may want to put for sale signs on your property to get things going." The plaintiff sued for bad faith failure to settle, fraud, and intentional infliction of emotional distress.

To bolster its case on reprehensibility, the plaintiff introduced evidence that State Farm had engaged in a decades long practice in numerous states to limit claim payouts under a so-called Performance, Planning and Review (PPR) policy designed to enhance profitability. Nearly all of this conduct involved first party claims, i.e., claims by the insured against the insurance company, not third-party claims such as those in the Campbell automobile accident litigation. Based on this evidence, the jury awarded the Campbells $2.6 million in compensatory damages and $145 million in punitive damages. The trial court reduced these awards to $1 million and $25 million respectively.

The Utah Supreme Court reinstated the $145 million punitive award. Campbell v. State Farm Mut. Auto. Ins. Co., 65 P.3d 1134 (Utah 2001). It justified its position based on the reprehensibility of the defendant's conduct, the "massive wealth" of the defendant, the low probability, which it set at one in 50,000, that State Farm would be caught and punished for this clandestine payment behavior, and the size of the award compared to potential civil and criminal penalties.

The U.S. Supreme Court reversed. The Court agreed with the defendant that the Utah courts had impermissibly considered conduct outside Utah. In a central part of the opinion, the Court found that due process precluded courts from basing punitive awards on the PPR policy:

> * * * The courts awarded punitive damages to punish and deter conduct that bore no relation to the Campbells' harm. A defendant's dissimilar acts, independent from the acts upon which liability was premised, may not serve as the basis for punitive damages. A defendant should be punished for the conduct that harmed the plaintiff, not for being an unsavory individual or business. Due process does not permit courts, in the calculation of punitive damages, to adjudi-

cate the merits of other parties' hypothetical claims against a defendant under the guise of the reprehensibility analysis, but we have no doubt the Utah Supreme Court did that here. Punishment on these bases creates the possibility of multiple punitive damages awards for the same conduct * * *.

538 U.S. at 422–423.

With respect to the second *Gore* guidepost, the relationship of the punitive damage award to the compensatory damage award, the Court refused, as it had in *Gore*, to establish a bright line. It noted, however, that few awards exceeding a single digit ratio to compensatory damages will satisfy due process. This, of course, is far less than the 145 to 1 ratio in *Campbell*. And as to the third guidepost, the Court simply noted that the civil sanction for the wrong done to the Campbells was $10,000, "an amount dwarfed by the $145 million punitive damages award."

c. *Williams*. Williams died of lung cancer allegedly caused by smoking Marlboro cigarettes. A jury found that smoking caused his death, that he smoked in significant part because he thought it was safe to do so, and that the defendant knowingly and falsely led him to this belief. For this deceit, the jury awarded $821,000 in compensatory damages and $79 million in punitive damages.

The U.S. Supreme Court vacated and remanded *Williams* and a number of other product liability cases in light of its decision in *Campbell*. However, on remand, the Oregon appellate court, citing the defendant's extraordinary reprehensibility, reinstated the punitive damage award, a decision affirmed by the Oregon Supreme Court. Williams v. Philip Morris Inc., 127 P.3d 1165 (Or.2006). The U.S. Supreme Court once again vacated. It sidestepped the excessiveness issue and ruled that the Oregon Supreme Court should have instructed the jury that in considering the defendant's reprehensibility the jury could consider its conduct with respect to other Oregonians, but the jury could not "use a punitive damages verdict to punish a defendant directly on account of harms it is alleged to have visited on nonparties." 549 U.S. at 354.

The *Williams* opinion reveals the dilemma presented by the Court's reprehensibility guideline. In *Campbell*, there was no evidence that the defendant had treated other insureds like they treated the plaintiff and it was relatively easy to say the other unrelated conduct was irrelevant. However, in *Williams* the defendant presumably deceived other smokers in exactly the same way it deceived Williams. To ask a jury to consider these other individuals in determining how reprehensibly the defendant behaved but not to consider harms done to others when determining the size of the award is, one suspects, to ask the impossible.

On remand, the Oregon Supreme Court sidestepped the remand order by ruling the defendant had failed to correctly state Oregon's law on punitive damages in its proffered jury instruction at trial. The U.S. Supreme Court granted certiorari still a third time on the limited question of whether the Oregon court had impermissibly failed to follow the Supreme Court's remand order. However, after oral argument, the Supreme Court declared that certiorari had been improvidently granted. It is worth noting that the Supreme Court had refused to grant certiorari on the question of the excessiveness of the award. The unpaid award plus interest now totaled $150 million. Under Oregon's split-recovery statute, 60% of this amount goes to the state. Does this create a conflict of interest problem of the Oregon Supreme Court?

2. *Multiple punitive damage awards.* In both *Campbell* and *Williams* the U.S. Supreme Court was searching for a way to address the problem of multiple punitive damage awards for the same wrongful act. Other than adoption of a mandatory maximum multiple of compensatory damages, as was done in *Exxon Shipping*, can you think any other ways to resolve this potential problem? See Owens–Corning Fiberglas Corp. v. Malone, 972 S.W.2d 35 (Tex.1998); Digital & Analog Design Corp. v. N. Supply Co., 540 N.E.2d 1358 (Ohio 1989); Thomas B. Colby, Beyond the Multiple Punishment Problem: Punitive Damages as Punishment for Individual Private Wrongs, 87 Minn.L.Rev. 583 (2003).

3. *State punitive damages statutes.* As the *Exxon Shipping* opinion notes, most states have passed punitive damages statutes as part of a broader set of tort reform statutes. In addition to establishing damage caps of various types, these statutes often raise the bar on the type of mental state required before punitive damages may be awarded. For example, they may require proof that defendant acted with malice or fraudulently. Additionally, they may raise the burden of persuasion to one of clear and convincing evidence and they may require a unanimous verdict. Finally, they may permit defendant to bifurcate the trial, trying the punitive damages phase only after the jury has returned a verdict for plaintiff on compensatory damages. See Vernons Tex. Code Ann. Civil Practice & Remedies Code § 41.001–41.013, for a statute that contains all of these provisions.

The statutes also frequently list factors the trier of fact shall consider in determining the amount of exemplary damages. For example, the Texas statute contains the following provision:

§ 41.011. Evidence Relating to Amount of Exemplary Damages

(a) In determining the amount of exemplary damages, the trier of fact shall consider evidence, if any, relating to:

(1) the nature of the wrong;

(2) the character of the conduct involved;

(3) the degree of culpability of the wrongdoer;

(4) the situation and sensibilities of the parties concerned;

(5) the extent to which such conduct offends a public sense of justice and propriety; and

(6) the net worth of the defendant.

Because states may differ with respect to some or all of these provisions, choice of law considerations may be particularly important in this area. See Patrick J. Borchers, Punitive Damages, Forum Shopping, and the Conflict of Laws, 70 La.L.Rev. 529 (2010).

4. *Social science research on punitive damages.* The *Exxon Shipping* opinion cites some of the voluminous punitive damages research that appeared over the last 20 years. The central findings, as reported in the opinion, are: (a) punitive damages are awarded in between 3% and 10% of cases, although there is considerable variation from jurisdiction to jurisdiction; (b) awards usually occur in cases of intentional wrongdoing or financial wrongdoing and perhaps, as a result, are relatively rare in medical malpractice and products liability cases; (c) juries do not vary greatly from judges in their propensity to give punitive damages, but their awards exhibit greater variance than do those of judges. For a discussion and critique of the Court's own review of the evidence on the unpredictability of punitive damages, see Catherine M. Sharkey, The *Exxon Valdez* Litigation Marathon: A Window On Punitive Damages, 7 Univ.St. Thomas L.J. 25 (2009).

5. In footnote 17, the Supreme Court noted but refused to rely on a body of experimental work done by a number of well-respected legal academics and social scientists, including the Nobel laureate, Daniel Kahneman, because their research was funded in part by Exxon. The note raises a number of interesting questions. First, can the court "unring the bell"? Once it became aware of the findings reported in these studies, can it easily ignore them in reaching its decision about whether to rein in punitive damages? Second, should the source of funding for a study cause us to disregard its findings or simply to keep the funding source in mind in interpreting the results? If you believe the Court was correct in stating it refused to rely at all on this research, should it also disregard the vast amount of research on the safety and effectiveness of drugs that is paid for by pharmaceutical companies? Why or why not?

6. The laboratory studies cited in footnote 17 contain some useful insights. Perhaps most relevant to the issue in *Exxon Shipping* is the finding that jurors' moral judgments about wrongfulness of conduct and its deservingness of punishment were quite consistent. This consistency breaks down when jurors are asked to translate their judgment into a dollar amount. This "horizontal inconsistency," i.e., failure to treat like cases alike in terms of dollar awards, is a problem that plagues pain and suffering awards as well. See Joseph Sanders, Why Do Proposals Designed to Control Variability in General Damages (Generally) Fall on Deaf Ears? (And Why This is Too Bad), 55 DePaul L.Rev. 489 (2006) (reviewing the empirical literature).

7. The Supreme Court noted that punitive damages are justified on several grounds. Two of the most prominent are deterrence and punishment. In what ways are these goals compatible and in what ways might they be in competition? See Dan Markel, Retributive Damages: A Theory of Punitive Damages as Intermediate Sanction, 94 Cornell L.Rev. 239 (2009).

8. *"Blockbuster" awards.* Insofar as *Exxon Shipping* was correct in arguing that the most serious problem with punitive damages is their variance, blockbuster awards may be thought to be of particular concern. One article on this topic defined a blockbuster award as an award of $100 million or more. It found that as of the end of 2008 there had been 100 such awards, the first coming in 1985. Alison F. Del Rossi & W. Kip Viscusi, The Changing Landscape of Blockbuster Punitive Damages Awards, 12 Am.L.&Econ.Rev.

116 (2010). The tobacco industry has been the target of the largest awards, but it is the defendant in only 5 of the 100 cases. More frequent defendants are the automobile industry (9 cases), the energy and chemical industry (25 cases), the finance, investment and insurance industry (23 cases), and the pharmaceutical and health care industry (16 cases). When it comes to the number of such cases in different states, California (21 cases) and Texas (20 cases) lead all others by a wide margin. Half the states have no such awards. The frequency with which such cases occur appears to be declining, presumably in response to both the Supreme Court cases and state punitive damages statutes.

The Del Rossi and Viscusi study apparently includes initial jury awards in its analysis. However, many studies have indicated that judges exercise considerable post-verdict control over the size of final awards. For example, the single largest jury award, $145 billion in a Florida tobacco case, was effectively reduced to zero by the Florida Supreme Court. Because very large awards are almost always scaled back, are blockbuster awards really much of a problem?

Chapter XIII

Insurance

■ ■ ■

A. INTRODUCTION

When we think of inventions we usually turn our minds to inventions in the physical world; the telephone, the airplane, the computer. However, some inventions are social rather than physical. Perhaps the two most significant social inventions that have radically reshaped our lives over the last few generations are the modern business corporation and insurance, the second of which is the topic of this Chapter.

Insurance is so ingrained in our lives that we often take its effects for granted, but without it many other components of our social order would be far different than they are today. Nowhere is that truer than the law of torts. Tort law and liability insurance share a symbiotic relationship. In the absence of a tort regime, there would be little need for liability insurance. However, this is a two-way street. Without insurance assets to draw upon to pay damages, the tort system itself would be a far different and much smaller creature. These assets are quite substantial. In 2008 the insurance industry wrote net premiums valued at more than $400 billion. See also Insurance Information Institute, Commercial Lines, available at http://www.iii.org/media/facts/statsbyissue/commercial/. The insurance most relevant to toxic torts is commercial property/casualty insurance. Insurance Information Institute data indicate that liability premiums in this area alone are in excess of $38 billion.[1] Not only does insurance affect the scope of tort law, the existence (or absence) of insurance also affects who is sued and the settlement practices of the parties. For two classic discussions about how insurance affects settlement practices, see H.L. Ross, Settled Out of Court: The Social Process of Claims Adjustment (1980 ed.); Tom Baker, Blood Money, New Money, and the Moral Economy of Tort Law in Action, 35 Law & Soc'y Rev. 275 (2001).

In this Chapter we limit our discussion of insurance to the toxic tort context. We focus our attention on two conflicts that arise between

---

1. See Insurance Information Institute, Commercial Lines, available at http://www.iii.org/media/facts/statsbyissue/commercial. This figure does not include premiums for commercial automobile coverage or workers compensation coverage Moreover, it does not reflect the fact that many companies are self insured or purchase policies with very large deductibles.

insureds and insurers and among insurers themselves: insurance triggers and exclusions. However, before turning to these topics, some general background is in order.

First-party and third-party insurance. There are two basic types of insurance, first-party insurance and third-party insurance. First-party insurance is an insurance policy that applies to an insured or the insured's own property, such as life insurance, health insurance, disability insurance, and fire insurance. Third-party insurance, also called liability insurance, is an agreement between an insured and an insurance company whereby the insurer agrees to cover a loss resulting from the insured's liability to a third party.

Automobile insurance is usually third-party insurance. Homeowners policies usually combine both first-party insurance, e.g., insurance against fire damage, and third-party insurance, e.g., liability for negligent injury to others while they are on the insured's property. Our focus is on third-party insurance; specifically those policies businesses carry to insure themselves against suits by their customers and others. As we shall see in the cases that follow, these policies are usually referred to as Comprehensive (or Commercial) General Liability (CGL) insurance.

The duty to defend and the duty to indemnify. Most standard liability insurance policies contain two promises by the insurer: (1) to provide a defense to the insured when the insured is sued on a claim potentially within policy coverage (the "duty to defend"); and (2) to pay—up to policy limits—the injured party (or indemnify the insured for his payments to the injured party) for any tort judgment obtained against the insured so long as the loss is within the scope of the policy's coverage (the "duty to indemnify"). Importantly, the duty to defend is not capped by the policy limits, which means an insurer is obligated to pay all legal expenses defending the insured even when those expenses exceed the policy limits.

The duty to defend is independent of and generally broader than the duty to indemnify. Insurance companies have a duty to defend whenever the underlying action alleges any facts which, if sustained, would give rise to coverage. As the court in City of Willoughby Hills v. Cincinnati Insurance Co., 459 N.E.2d 555, 558 (Ohio 1984) noted, "where the insurer's duty to defend is not apparent from the pleadings in the case against the insured, but the allegations do state a claim which is potentially or arguably within the policy coverage, or there is some doubt as to whether a theory of recovery within the policy coverage had been pleaded, the insurer must accept the defense of the claim." The Texas Supreme Court stated the point even more broadly in a coverage case involving alleged injuries from cell phone use. "An insurer's duty to defend is determined by the third-party plaintiff's pleadings, considered in light of the policy provisions, without regard to the truth or falsity of those allegations." Zurich Am. Ins. Co. v. Nokia, Inc., 268 S.W.3d 487, 491 (Tex.2008).

Occurrence vs. claims made coverage. Most liability insurance policies are "occurrence" policies. That is, they promise to pay any claims arising from injuries or harms that "occur" during the period the policy is in place. Thus, for example, if a policy is in place that promises to defend and indemnify for all injuries occurring in 1984, then the insurance company would be obligated on such a claim even though the lawsuit seeking redress for the injury did not arise until 2008. In the toxic tort arena, this might well occur because of the long latency periods between exposure to a substance and the manifestation of a disease.

Under a claims made policy an insurance company agrees to assume liability for acts or omissions of the type covered by the policy, regardless of when they occurred, if the claim arising out of the act or omission was made during the policy period. Insurers have increasingly written claims made policies as a response to the "long tails" that exist for many toxic torts.

Long and short tails. The length of a potential payout period is referred to as the "tail" of the insurance policy. Automobile accident policies usually have a relatively short tail. People know at the time of the accident whether they are hurt and statutes of limitations typically provide a two year window to bring a claim. However, in nearly all jurisdictions, the statute of limitations is tolled until the injured party discovers or reasonably should have discovered he or she has been injured. The long latency periods associated with many toxic exposures guarantee that claims may be brought years or even decades after the "occurrence" of a compensable event such as the exposure of plaintiff to asbestos. Long-tail liability lines present problems to insurance companies because they are difficult to price. Pricing is difficult for a number of reasons, including: inflation rates, evolving legal doctrine, and trends in the size of jury awards. See Harold D. Skipper & W. Jean Kwon, Risk Management and Insurance: Perspectives in a Global Economy (2007); George L. Priest, The Current Insurance Crisis and Modern Tort Law, 96 Yale L.J. 1521 (1987).

Principal/Agent issues and their control. In many affairs of life, the relationship between two individuals may be thought of as one of principal and agent. An employee is the agent of the employer. A lawyer is the agent of the client. The relationship between an insurer and insured may also be thought of in this way. A key issue in each of these areas is how to assure the principal that the agent will act in the principal's interest rather than its own interest. Professional ethics are one mechanism designed to achieve this result. Contracts may also serve this end. Finally, legal rules may be aimed at reducing principal-agent conflict, e.g., legal rules that place attorneys in a fiduciary relationship with their clients.

One of the interesting aspects of insurance contracts is that there is a sense in which both the insurer and the insured are both principal and agent. When it is handling a claim against the insured, we think of the insurance company as the insured's agent. Ideally, it would behave exactly as the insured would behave. However, one important potential conflict of interest is created by the fact that insurance contracts have policy limits. Because insurers have a duty to defend as well as a duty to indemnify, they typically take over most of the legal defense of a lawsuit, including the hiring of defense counsel. Indeed, most insurance contracts require the insured to assist the insurer in the defense of the case.

One decision insurers must make is whether to settle a case or to go to trial. If the insurance policy has a low policy limit when compared to the potential loss in a given case, an insurer might prefer to litigate the case to a conclusion rather than accept a settlement offer from the plaintiff. The potential conflict is greatest when the offer is at or near the policy limits. Absent a rule to the contrary, by going to trial the insurer would only have to pay up to policy limits no matter how large the verdict. A rational individual, confronting the entire range of outcomes, would settle because the expected cost of going to trial (i.e., the probability of losing multiplied by the expected amount one would lose if there were a plaintiff verdict) is greater than the settlement offer. In essence, the insurer can gamble on obtaining a defense verdict with its insured's money.

In order to control for this potential conflict of interest, courts have established a rule that an insurer's bad faith failure to accept a settlement offer within policy limits exposes it to liability for the entirety of a subsequent judgment. See Crisci v. Sec. Ins. Co. of New Haven, Connecticut, 426 P.2d 173 (Cal.1967); Pavia v. State Farm Mut. Auto. Ins. Co., 626 N.E.2d 24 (N.Y.1993). Both *Crisci* and *Pavia* wrestled with the question of what standard to use to judge bad faith. In *Pavia*, the court adopted a "gross disregard" standard.

> The gross disregard standard, which was utilized by the trial court here, strikes a fair balance between two extremes by requiring more than ordinary negligence and less than a showing of dishonest motives. The former would remove the latitude that insurers must be accorded in investigating and resisting unfounded claims, while the latter would be all but impossible to satisfy and would effectively insulate insurance carriers from conduct that, while not motivated by malice, has the potential to severely prejudice the rights of its insured. The intermediate standard accomplishes the two-fold goal of protecting both the insured's and the insurer's financial interests.

626 N.E.2d at 28.

Sometimes, it is useful to reverse roles and think of the insured as the agent of the insurer. How might the insured act against the interests of the insurer? One important way this may occur is if the insured misrepresents to the insurer the scope of the risk being covered. Insurers use the term "moral hazard" to describe this risk. Moral hazard exists when someone enters into a contract in bad faith. One way to control for this possibility is to exclude coverage for certain events over which the insured has considerable control. For example, insurers routinely include a suicide exclusion clause in life insurance policies. Today these clauses exclude coverage if the insured takes his own life during the first two years the policy is in place.

The moral hazard terminology is also used to refer to the danger that a party insulated from a risk may behave differently than if that party were fully exposed to the risk. See Tom Baker, On the Genealogy of Moral Hazard, 75 Tex.L.Rev. 237, 239 (1996). This concern causes insurance companies routinely to include a deductible in policies so that some of the loss associated with accidents falls on the insured. It also explains why policies insure against accidents but exclude coverage for the consequences of the intentional acts of the insured, including most intentional torts such as assault and battery. For valuable discussions of these and other ways insurers control moral hazard, see Carol Heimer, Reactive Risk and Rational Action: Managing Moral Hazard in Insurance Contracts (1985); Pat O'Malley, Risk, Uncertainty and Government (2004).

CGL policies uniformly have exclusions for intentional acts. At one time this exclusion was part of the definition of "occurrence." For example, the policy might define an occurrence as, "an accident, including a continuous or repeated exposure to conditions, which results, during the policy period, in bodily injury or property damage neither expected nor intended from the standpoint of the insured." In recent years, this exclusion is usually in a separate section that typically reads as follows: "This insurance does not apply to 'bodily injury' or 'property damage' expected or intended from the standpoint of the insured." In the context of toxic torts, insurers often exclude coverage for the intentional discharge of pollutants. See Claussen v. Aetna Cas. & Sur. Co., 380 S.E.2d 686 (Ga.1989); Morton Int'l, Inc. v. General Acc. Ins. Co. of Am., 629 A.2d 831 (N.J.1993). Not surprisingly, insureds and insurers frequently litigate the question of whether the insured's behavior was intentional within the meaning of the exclusion. See James L. Rigelhaupt, Construction and Application of Provisions of Liability Insurance Policy Expressly Excluding Injuries Intended or Expected By Insured, 31 A.L.R.4th 957; Ellen S. Pryor, The Stories We Tell: Intentional Harm and the Quest for Insurance Funding, 75 Tex.L.Rev.1721 (1997). Frequently litigated issues include: a) whether the insured's actions must be intentional or whether the harmful results of the act must be expected or intended, and b) whether the test for assessing the state of mind of the insured is objective or subjective.

The risk posed by moral hazard is that the insurer will have mispriced the insurance, charging too little given the risk. One way to deal with this problem is to group insureds into sub-groups and charge each group premiums commensurate with the risk that they will be subjected to liability. For example, workers' compensation policies are adjusted periodically to reflect not only state-wide average risk and industry-wide risk within a state, but also an individual employer's claims loss experience in previous years. See Emily A. Spieler, Perpetuating Risk? Workers'

Compensation and the Persistence of Occupational Injuries, 31 Hous. L.Rev. 119, 189–190 (1994).

Often, however, it is difficult or impossible to gather the information necessary to adjust rates in this fashion. When this occurs, insurance companies run the risk of what is called "adverse selection." If a pool of insureds varies substantially in terms of the risk that they will be sued but the insurance premium are the same for all of the insureds, those who expect or know that they will have a higher than average claims experience will see the insurance as relatively inexpensive and will, therefore, buy more coverage. On the other hand, those insureds who expect or know they will have a lower than average claims experience will choose not to buy any coverage. If this pattern persists over time, the low risk insureds will drop out leaving only the high risk insureds, and the insurance will be badly underpriced. Note that adverse selection is another aspect of the agency problem. It exists only when the insureds have information not available to the insurer and, therefore, have interests that diverge from those of the insurer. See Kenneth S. Abraham, Environmental Liability and the Limits of Insurance, 88 Colum.L.Rev. 942 (1988).

B. INSURANCE TRIGGERS

QUINCY MUTAL FIRE INSURANCE CO. v. BOROUGH OF BELLMAWR

Supreme Court of New Jersey, 2002.
172 N.J. 409, 799 A.2d 499.

STEIN, J.

This appeal raises two important issues relating to environmental pollution liability. First, we must determine under the "continuous trigger theory" of liability whether an insurance policy in effect at the time the Borough of Bellmawr (Borough) was depositing waste in a landfill provides coverage for resulting environmental pollution claims against the Borough. * * *

Second, we again must examine the appropriate allocation of coverage among the carriers whose policies have been triggered under the "continuous trigger theory." * * *

    * * *

I

The Helen Kramer Landfill (Landfill), located in West Deptford, New Jersey, operated from approximately 1963 until 1981. In April 1978, the Borough approved the Landfill as an appropriate trash disposal site, and from May 1978 until January 1981, the Borough deposited municipal waste into the Landfill. The Borough made no attempt to segregate harmful pollutants from the municipal trash that was deposited in the facility.

In 1981, after complaints were registered relating to the Landfill, the Environmental Protection Agency (EPA) revoked the Landfill's registration and a New Jersey court ordered its closure. An extensive Remedial Investigation and Feasibility Study conducted by the EPA between 1983 and 1985 revealed the presence of hazardous chemicals in the soil, surface waters and ground waters at the Landfill. On September 8, 1983, the Landfill was placed on the Superfund National Priorities List, a list of the nation's most threatening hazardous waste sites established pursuant to the Comprehensive Environmental Response Control and Liability Act (CERCLA), 42 *U.S.C.A.* § 9605(a). Two years later, in September 1985, the EPA ordered a series of remedial actions to clean up the contamination that had emanated from the Landfill.

In 1989, the EPA commenced a lawsuit against the hundreds of defendants and third party defendants, including the Borough, that allegedly had contributed to the contamination of the Kramer Landfill, to recover all response and remedial costs. In 1997, after extended negotiations, the Borough and several other defendants and third-party defendants agreed to settle with the EPA by paying $95 million over a five-year period, which would contribute to the approximately $123 million in cleanup costs incurred by the United States Government. The Borough's financial contribution to those costs under the settlement agreement totaled $449,036.39.

The Borough maintained comprehensive general liability insurance (CGL) policies with two principal insurance carriers during the time it was depositing municipal waste into the Landfill—defendant Century [Indemnity Company] and plaintiff Quincy. The Borough also maintained CGL policies with several other insurance carriers during the time the cleanup took place. The Century policy was in effect from June 18, 1977 until June 18, 1978 and the Quincy policies were in effect from June 18, 1978 until June 18, 1981.

In 1991, the Borough filed a declaratory judgment action against its insurance carriers Quincy, Century and the Harleysville Insurance Company (Harleysville). Harleysville was dismissed from the lawsuit in 1993. Thereafter, Quincy was ordered to indemnify the Borough for any liability relating to the Landfill, including litigation expenses, counsel fees and costs. Quincy and Century subsequently entered into an agreement stating that Century and Quincy would pay the Borough's defense costs but that the carriers later could pursue the allocation of indemnification costs between them.

In October 1996, Quincy filed suit seeking a declaratory judgment determining the respective liabilities pursuant to the insurance policies issued by Quincy and other insurance carriers. With the exception of Century, Quincy's claims against the other insurers were dismissed. During the ensuing non-jury trial, Dr. Ralph Lee Steiner testified for Century as an expert in landfill procedures and operations. Dr. Steiner was familiar with the Landfill because he had inspected it several times in the 1970's. Dr. Steiner testified about leachate, the liquid that passes though contaminated material. He testified that because the Kramer Landfill was unlined, it acted like a "sponge" rather than a vessel or a tank. Dr. Steiner also testified that leachate could have been discharged from the Landfill only when its waste reached "field capacity," which is the maximum amount of liquid a landfill can hold before liquid seeps through the bottom and contaminates the groundwater. Based on Dr. Steiner's calculations, including analysis of available rainfall data and the height of the landfill, it would have taken approximately 185 to 200 days from the time the Borough began dumping for the Landfill to reach field capacity. Therefore, Dr. Steiner testified that it was not possible for waste deposited on May 1, 1978, the date the Borough began depositing waste in the Landfill, to generate contamination in the groundwater before June 18, 1978. Quincy did not rebut Dr. Steiner's testimony.

The trial court resolved the coverage issue in favor of Century, finding that Quincy was not entitled to contribution for the Borough's environmental liability. Relying on *Owens–Illinois, Inc. v. United Insurance Co.,* 138 *N.J.* 437, 650 A.2d 974 (1994) and *Astro Pak Corp. v. Fireman's Fund Insurance Co.,* 284 *N.J.Super.* 491, 665 A.2d 1113 (App.Div.1995), the trial court concluded that the property damage necessary to trigger coverage under a CGL policy occurs not when waste is deposited in a landfill but when leachate escapes from it and contaminates the groundwater. Therefore, based on Dr. Steiner's undisputed testimony that the groundwater could not have been contaminated by the Borough's waste until approximately 185 to 200 days after the Borough began depositing waste in the Kramer Landfill, the court held that Quincy's policy alone was in effect when the damage occurred.

In a published opinion *Quincy* [338 *N.J.Super.* 395, 399, 769 A.2d 1053, 1055 (2001)] the Appellate Division affirmed the trial court's disposition and held that the "continuous trigger of coverage" for liability from groundwater contamination began when the leachate reached the groundwater and not when the Borough dumped its waste. It thereby absolved Century from liability because its policy was in effect only at the time of the initial dumping of municipal waste. The court also rejected Quincy's argument that if Century's policy was implicated, Century's proportionate share of liability would equal twenty-five percent of the total liability because its policy was in effect for one of the four years in question. Instead, the court found that the appropriate allocation would be based on days of coverage. Dissenting, Judge Wecker also applied the continuous trigger theory but concluded that the initial trigger of coverage was the Borough's dumping of toxic waste in the Landfill beginning in April 1978.

II

A

In general, insurance policies cover losses resulting only from "occurrences" that take place during the policy period. The Century policy that was in effect at the time the Borough began dumping defines occurrence as "an accident, including injurious exposure to conditions, which results, during the policy period, in personal injury or property damage neither expected nor intended from the standpoint of the insured." (The record does not reflect how Quincy's policy defined "occurrence"). That type of policy language frequently is used and reflects the general principle that "the insured would reasonably expect to be covered, and the insurer would reasonably expect to pay, for damage or injury occurring during the policy period, assuming all other conditions precedent to coverage have been satisfied." David J. Howard, *"Continuous Trigger" Liability: Application to Toxic Waste Cases and Impact on the Number of "Occurrences"*, 22 *Tort & Ins. L.J.* 624, 632 (1987). Therefore, when an insured has been covered by several policies over the relevant period of time, identifying the appropriate trigger of coverage, or when an occurrence took place, will be critical in determining which insurer is liable for the damages that have accrued. Litigation relating to the appropriate trigger of coverage results from the fact that insurance polices "do not refer [generally] to a 'trigger.'" *Owens–Illinois, supra,* 138 *N.J.* at 447. Instead, trigger is a shorthand term used to describe " 'the event or events that under the terms of the insurance policy determines whether a policy must respond to a claim in a given set of circumstances.' " *Ibid.* "As so conceptualized, the trigger concept is not designed to determine coverage; rather, it acts as a gatekeeper, matching particular claims with particular periods of time and hence particular insurance policies." James M. Fischer, *Insurance Coverage for Mass Exposure Tort Claims: The Debate Over the Appropriate Trigger Rule,* 45 *Drake L.Rev.* 625, 631 (1997).

In environmental contamination cases the damage that triggers liability often cannot be linked to a single event. Instead, the damage usually is attributable to events that begin, develop and intensify over a sustained period of time. Therefore, the damage has " 'occurred' or been 'triggered' along a continuous timeline during which several successive policies issued to the insured were in effect." Mary R. DeYoung & William R. Hickman, *Allocation of Environmental Cleanup Liability Between Successive Insurers,* 17 *N. Ky. L.Rev.* 291, 294 (1990).

Courts apply various theories in determining when damage has occurred so as to trigger insurance coverage under CGL policies in the context of environmental contamination and toxic tort cases. Those include the exposure, injury-in-fact, manifestation, and continuous trigger theories. Under the "exposure theory," the triggering occurrence takes place on "the date of exposure to the injury producing agent." Fischer, *supra,* 45 *Drake L.Rev.* at 643. Under the "injury in fact" theory, a policy is triggered only "if the claimant was actually injured during the policy period." *Id.* at 641. Under the "manifestation theory," the policy is triggered "when the injury became reasonably apparent or known to the claimant." *Id.* at 643. Finally, the "continuous trigger theory" provides that "all policies in effect during the aggregate trigger period, for example, during the period of exposure or injury in fact, are activated and may be called on to respond to a loss." *Id.* at 646.

In *Keene Corp. v. Insurance Co. of North America,* 667 *F.*2d 1034 (D.C. Cir.1981), the District of Columbia Circuit Court of Appeals was the first court to apply the continuous trigger theory in determining coverage for asbestos-related claims. In addition to the manifestation of asbestos-related injury, the court held that "coverage is also triggered by both inhalation exposure and exposure in residence." *Id.* at 1045. The court stated further:

> Inhalation of asbestos is an "occurrence" that causes injury for which Keene may be held liable. The possibility that the insurers may not be liable arises solely because there is a period of time between the point at which the injurious process began and the point at which injury manifests itself. In this case, during that interim period, the existence of latent injury among people who had worked with asbestos became predictable with a substantial degree of certainly. The injury and attendant liability became predictable precisely because it was discovered that past occurrences were likely to have set in motion injurious processes for which Keene could be held liable.

[*Id.* at 1046.]

Subsequent to the decision in *Keene Corp.,* many jurisdictions have applied the continuous trigger theory in both asbestos and environmental contamination cases. *See Zurich Ins. Co. v. Raymark,* 118 *Ill.*2d 23, 112 *Ill.Dec.* 684, 514 *N.E.*2d 150 (Ill.1987) (applying continuous trigger theory to personal injury asbestos claims); *Fireman's Fund Ins. Co. v. Ex–Cell–O Corp.,* 662 *F.Supp.* 71, 76 (E.D.Mich.1987)(recognizing similarity between asbestos claims and hazardous waste claims and holding that continuous trigger theory implicates "each exposure of the environment to a pollutant"); *Harleysville Mutual Ins. Co., Inc. v. Sussex County,* 831 *F.Supp.* 1111, 1124 (D. Del.1993)(finding "slow leaching of pollutants from a landfill to adjacent property" constitutes a progressive injury requiring use of continuous trigger theory); *GenCorp, Inc. v. AIU Ins. Co.,* 104 *F.Supp.*2d 740, 749 (N.D.Ohio 2000)(holding that continuous trigger will be applicable when environmental contamination claimant is able to show that damage, like asbestosis, occurred on continuing basis); *See also* Howard, *supra,* 22 *Tort & Ins. L. J.* at 632–33 ("Courts faced with coverage determinations in the toxic waste setting are likely to ... adopt the exposure, manifestation or continuous trigger theories rather than a 'single point in time' test, with those courts intent upon maximizing coverage to the greatest extent possible opting for the continuous trigger approach.").

In *Owens–Illinois,* we applied the continuous trigger theory of coverage to the asbestos-related personal injury and property damage claims at issue. Although we did not disturb the general rule that "the time of the occurrence of an accident within the meaning of an indemnity policy is not the time the wrongful act is committed but the time when the complaining party is actually damaged," *id.* at 452, we held that in asbestos-related personal injury cases the required damage occurs from the time asbestos fibers are inhaled and continues until and including the manifestation of an asbestos-related disease. We also rejected the argument advanced by the defendant insurance companies that the record did not contain sufficient medical testimony to establish that inhalation of asbestos immediately causes tissue damage, recognizing both the trial court's expertise in asbestos-induced disease cases and the " 'overwhelming weight of authority' " acknowledging that injury " 'occurs when asbestos is inhaled and retained in the lungs.' " *Id.* at 454. We contrasted that solid medical foundation to the record in *Hartford,* a case involving a drug manufacturer's liability for injuries resulting from the ingestion of one of its drugs, where the plaintiff had "failed to offer any evidence that the medication administered to the child had caused her any damage before the Hartford coverage took effect." *Id.* at 453.

Our decision in *Owens–Illinois* was compelled by important public policy considerations, including the need to adapt our tort law to the peculiarities of mass-exposure tort cases. We recognized that the Court previously had adapted the law to "the uncertainties of medical causation." *Id.* at 458 (citing *Ayers v. Township of Jackson,* 106 *N.J.* 557, 605, 525 *A.*2d 287 (1987)). For example, in *Ayers, supra,* 106 *N.J.* at 609, 525 *A.*2d 287, a case involving personal injury claims from water contamination, we had held that "mass-exposure toxic-tort cases involve public interests not present in conventional tort litigation" that "justify judicial intervention even when the risk of disease is problematic." We concluded, therefore, that the continuous trigger theory would be better suited to address the public interest in enhancing available insurance coverage for environmental damages and would give courts the opportunity to "better channel the available resources into remediation of environmental harms." *Owens–Illinois, supra,* 138 *N.J.* at 480.

Although in *Owens–Illinois* we were dealing primarily with personal injuries related to asbestos exposure, we acknowledged the applicability of the continuous trigger theory to environmental contamination cases. We noted that "[p]roperty-damage cases are analogous to the contraction of disease from exposure to toxic substances like asbestos" and that " 'while property damage is not, of course, an insidious disease, many of the same considerations apply.' " *Id.* at 455. * * * We concluded by observing that "when progressive indivisible injury or damage results from exposure to injurious conditions for which civil liability may be imposed, courts may reasonably treat the progressive injury or damage as an occurrence within each of the years of a CGL policy." *Id.* at 478, 650 *A.*2d 974.

Astro Pak, supra, a case involving environmental pollution claims resulting from landfill contamination, is factually somewhat similar to the case at hand. In that case, the Appellate Division applied *Owens–Illinois* to hold that damage resulting from landfill contamination triggered coverage under two successive CGL policies. * * *

The court applied the continuous trigger theory to determine whether Hartford and the Fireman's Fund policies were liable for the property damage resulting from the pollution of the Kin Buc Landfill. * * *

* * *

In *Carter–Wallace, Inc. v. Admiral Insurance Co.,* 154 *N.J.* 312, 712 *A.*2d 1116 (1998), this Court expressly applied the continuous trigger theory in a case involving property damage resulting from the contamination of a landfill. * * * Citing to *Astro Pak,* the Court also acknowledged that the reasoning in *Owens–Illinois* applied to "progressive environmental property damage."

In other cases involving environmental pollution and toxic-tort property damage claims, New Jersey courts consistently have applied the continuous trigger rule to determine liability coverage.

B

Despite the fact that many jurisdictions have applied the continuous trigger theory to asbestos claims and hazardous waste claims, no consensus among those jurisdictions exists regarding the scope or the commencement of the "injurious process" covered under the theory. Relevant to this appeal, courts have pinpointed different initial triggering events that set off the continuous trigger theory.

Some jurisdictions have held that the initial triggering event should be injury-in-fact. In *GenCorp, Inc. v. AIU Insurance Co.,* 104 *F.Supp.*2d 740 (N.D.Ohio 2000), the plaintiff brought a declaratory judgment action against its insurers to recover costs or indemnification for costs associated with the long-term disposal of industrial waste at several of the plaintiff's industrial facilities. While preparing for trial, the parties requested that the court provide some guidance regarding the appropriate trigger for determining coverage. The court issued an opinion that held that the continuous trigger theory would apply if the plaintiff was able to demonstrate continuous property damage, but also held that under that theory the initial trigger would be injury-in-fact as opposed to mere exposure. *Id.* at 749. * * *

> * * *

Some jurisdictions closely follow the reasoning in cases like *Keene Corporation* and have included initial exposure in the "injurious process" when applying the continuous trigger theory to environmental contamination claims. In *Chemical Leaman Tank Lines, Inc. v. Aetna Casualty and Surety Co.,* 89 *F.*3d 976 (3d Cir.1996), the Third Circuit Court of Appeals held that under New Jersey law insurance coverage under the continuous trigger theory commences at the time of the initial discharge of pollutants. The court explained that

> [u]nder the continuous trigger theory, exposure to the harm causing agent is sufficient to trigger potential coverage. Actual manifestation of the injury is not required, so long as there is a continuous, indivisible process resulting in damage. * * * [T]he district found as a factual matter that *"contaminated rinsewater from the three settling ponds started migrating through the soil to underlying groundwater almost immediately after beginning pond operation in 1960."* Accordingly, the district court correctly concluded as a matter of law that

property damage occurred upon initial exposure in 1960, and should have concluded as a matter of law that property damage occurred in each policy period from 1961–70.

[*Id.* at 995–96 (citations omitted)(emphasis added).]

The court rejected the insurers' argument that the insured had failed to demonstrate "actual injury" during the relevant policy periods and held that "[u]nder the continuous trigger theory, proof of actual injury in the sense of manifestation of injury is not required." *Ibid.*

* * *

Although factually and procedurally distinct from the instant matter, a line of cases interpreting the "owned-property" exclusion in CGL insurance policies also appears to define the "injurious process" more broadly. Many jurisdictions have held that an insured's on-site soil clean-up should not bar coverage under an "owned property" exclusion clause if the contaminants in the soil threaten to migrate to underlying groundwater or the surrounding property of others.

* * *

C

The parties to this appeal do not dispute the applicability of the continuous trigger theory of coverage to environmental contamination claims and we see no reason to depart from the sound line of cases and academic support recognizing the benefits of applying that theory to these types of claims. See *Developments in the Law–Toxic Waste Litigation,* 99 *Harv. L. Rev.* 1458, 1581 (1986) ("Because it avoids the dangers of the manifestation rule, and because it encourages all insurers to monitor risks and charge appropriate premiums, the continuous trigger rule appears to be the most efficient doctrine for toxic waste cases."). Instead, this case turns on how the theory should be applied. Indeed, the majority and dissenting appellate division opinions, although both applying the continuous trigger theory, reached different conclusions concerning Century's coverage obligation.

The majority opinion relied on *Astro Pak* for the proposition that in determining the initial trigger of the continuous trigger theory the focus should be on the discharge of contaminants from a landfill, rather than on the depositing of waste into that landfill. *Quincy Mutual, supra,* 338 *N.J.Super.* at 400. The court interpreted *Astro Pak* as holding that under the continuous trigger theory "the first pull of [the] trigger occur[s] only when there ha[s] been some 'damage,' and that waste disposal (or dumping) by itself did not cause 'damage.'" *Ibid.* Furthermore, the court rejected Quincy's comparison of the environmental contamination from the landfill in this case with the asbestos injury addressed in *Owens–Illinois,* arguing that the court in *Owens–Illinois* "took pains to discuss and ultimately approve the trial court's conclusion that 'an injury-in-fact' triggering coverage under the insurance policies occurs on the inhalation of asbestos fibers." *Quincy Mutual, supra,* 338 *N.J. Super.* at 401. The court found that Quincy had presented no evidence demonstrating the presence of injury at the time toxic waste was deposited into the Landfill that was at all comparable to the scientifically proven tissue damage associated with the initial inhalation of asbestos. Instead, damage occurred only when "the toxic leachate forming part of that waste seeped out of the landfill and reached nearby ground water." *Id.* at 402. Therefore, because Dr. Steiner's uncontroverted testimony indicated that that seepage could not have occurred until at least approximately 185 days after the Borough first deposited waste in the Landfill, a date subsequent to the termination date of Century's CGL policy, the court concluded that Quincy was solely responsible for indemnifying the Borough.

Although the court correctly relied on the underlying principles set forth in *Owens–Illinois* and subsequent New Jersey cases applying the continuous trigger theory to toxic tort and environmental contamination cases, we disagree with its analysis. Instead, we would adopt the analysis of the dissent and its conclusion that Century is partially responsible for indemnifying the Borough.

In her dissent, Judge Wecker, applying the continuous trigger theory, concluded that coverage initially was triggered when the Borough first dumped toxic waste into the Kramer Landfill while Century's policy was still in effect. Like the majority, Judge Wecker relied on Dr. Steiner's uncontroverted expert testimony, albeit a different portion, to come to that conclusion. * * *

> It is clear from Dr. Steiner's testimony that the landfill was not the equivalent of an enclosed tank or container, and that by its very nature, toxic materials deposited in the landfill would, without fail, seep into the ground and run off as leachate into the groundwater, which in turn penetrates the soil below and downstream of the landfill. The contaminated leachate therefore is not the product of some accidental leak. On the contrary, it represents the natural and unavoidable progression of the original dumping, which must be deemed the "exposure" that is the starting point of an "occurrence" that triggers coverage.

> The fact that it may have taken some 200 days for the polluting leachate to reach a particular point does not mean that damage to property did not occur earlier. The property, that is, the landfill, was contaminated as soon as the toxic material was dumped, for that is when the toxins began their damaging journey through the ground—just as the asbestos fibers in Owens–Illinois began their damaging journey through the air immediately upon installation of the insulation.

[*Id.* at 410, 769 A.2d 1053.]

* * * We believe that Dr. Steiner's testimony demonstrates the inescapable conclusion that the initial deposit of toxic wastes into the Kramer Landfill set off the injurious process resulting in groundwater contamination. As one commentator has observed, "[t]oxic waste loss will

be most analogous to asbestos loss when the leaching begins at the moment of dumping, since the resulting damage may be deemed to have resulted from one continuous, uninterrupted process or from continuous exposure to substantially the same general conditions." Howard, *supra,* 22 *Tort & Ins. L. J.* at 639.

* * *

Furthermore, we are persuaded that a bright-line rule triggering coverage when toxic waste is first deposited in a landfill is more consistent with *Owens–Illinois* and subsequent toxic tort environmental contamination cases. * * * Our goal in *Owens–Illinois, supra,* was to fashion a standard that would "narrow the range of disputes and provide procedures better to resolve the disputes that remain." 138 *N.J.* at 480. Requiring "each insurer (or a court) to calculate the date when pollutants that were dumped into a landfill most likely leached into the groundwater in order to determine the start of the continuous trigger period" complicates an already complicated area of the law. * * *

Moreover, we adopted the continuous trigger theory in *Owens–Illinois, supra,* in large part because of its ability to maximize coverage. We also recognized the ability of insurance companies to spread the costs of indemnification across the industry * * *. As Judge Pressler stated in *Winding Hills Condominium Association, Inc. v. North American Specialty Insurance Co.,* 332 *N.J. Super.* 85, 91, 752 A.2d 837 (2000), "the law's solicitousness for victims of mass toxic torts and other environmental contamination is entirely consistent with choosing that conceptually viable trigger theory affording the greatest ultimate redress."

[W]e conclude that exposure relating to the Borough's initial depositing of toxic waste into the Landfill is the first trigger of coverage under the continuous trigger theory and constitutes an "occurrence" under Century's policy. * * *

III

Based on our conclusion that Century's policy was implicated as a result of the Borough's depositing of hazardous waste into the Landfill, we now must determine the appropriate allocation of liability between the Quincy and Century policies. Again, there appears to be no dispute among the parties that the *pro rata* risk allocation rule * * * should apply. However, according to Quincy, under that rule Century should be responsible for the number of years it provided coverage during the continuous trigger period. Over the relevant time period one of Century's policies and three of Quincy's policies were triggered and each policy had a $500,000 policy limit. Therefore, Quincy contends that Century's share of the accumulative two million dollar policy limit is twenty-five percent.

Although the Appellate Division concluded that Century's policy was not implicated under the continuous trigger theory, the court addressed Quincy's contention regarding the appropriate allocation of liability. The court determined that, if both insurers' policies had been implicated, their respective liability would be allocated based on the number of days each policy provided coverage during the continuous trigger period. Therefore, the court concluded that

> Century's proportionate share of liability would only be based on one or two months exposure (between commencement of dumping in April/May 1978 and expiration of the Century policy on June 18, 1978) out of a total of some two and one-half years of dumping between May 1978 and January 1981. That would represent approximately forty-five days of a total of 880 days, or about .05 percent. That number would be little more than *de minimus*.

[*Quincy Mutual, supra*, 338 *N.J. Super.* at 403 n. 2, 769 A.2d 1053.]

* * *

* * * We now hold specifically that the *Owens–Illinois* allocation formula should reflect days rather than years on the risk when the underlying facts require that degree of precision in the allocation of liability.

[P]rinciples of "simple justice" dictate that we reject Quincy's argument that Century should be responsible for an entire year within the continuous trigger period merely because it was on the risk for a portion of that year.

IV

The judgment of the Appellate Division is reversed and the matter is remanded to the trial court for an allocation of liability between the Quincy and Century policies that is consistent with this opinion.

LaVecchia, J., concurring in part, dissenting in part.

This appeal raises the familiar question of when, in the context of a property damage claim, does an insured become legally obligated for damages to another, entitling the insured to coverage from an insurer. The question is critical to the issue here concerning which insurers should be responsible for a landfill's liability for groundwater damage. Respectfully, the majority errs when it reverses the Appellate Division. The Court's holding misapplies the notion of "continuous injury" recognized in *Owens–Illinois, Incorporated v. United Insurance Company.*

Owens–Illinois involved claims of asbestos liability. * * * The Court explained that scientific research had established that damages accrued continuously from the building inhabitants' inhalation of airborne asbestos particles, causing an injurious occurrence. Accordingly, the insurer's liability for coverage started with the moment of injury (and damages), and continued through discovery of the injury and its remediation.

In *Owens–Illinois,* and in previous decisions, this Court has reaffirmed the principle that the time of accrual of an insured's liability must be the determining factor to compel coverage when the basis of the claim is negligence. That liability occurs when damage actually is suffered.

* * *

No such evidence of injury and damage to third parties exists in this record during the period of coverage by Quincy. Quincy merely was on the risk at the time of lawful dumping of material that later seeped from the landfill after Quincy's policy period had concluded. That is not enough under our normal principles of accrual of liability to cause an insurer to be liable on a risk.

* * *

I view the majority decision of the Appellate Division as consonant with the notion that it is injury causing damage, and accrual of liability, that "triggers" coverage under an indemnity policy of insurance. The Court's notion of inevitability of injury and damage is based on a misapplication of the doctrine of "continuous injury" and leads one to wonder why coverage should start only at the time of the dumping of the material because, one could argue, it was inevitable that the discarded waste would end up at the landfill contracted to receive the waste. The open-ended approach of the majority mistakenly has severed the notion of injury and damage to a third party from the accrual-of-liability analysis.

Accordingly, I respectfully dissent from that portion of the Court's opinion that allocates any responsibility to an insurer prior to the date of damage to the groundwater. * * *

NOTES AND QUESTIONS

1. For an opinion that adopts the dissent's view on when policies are first triggered in a landfill situation, see GenCorp, Inc. v. AIU Insurance Co., 104 F. Supp.2d 740 (N.D. Ohio 2000) (applying Ohio law). Do you think the majority would have reached a different outcome if the Helen Kramer landfill had been lined?

2. Cases have adopted all four trigger theories in asbestos cases. Exposure theory: Insurance Co. of N. Am. v. Forty–Eight Insulations, Inc., 633 F.2d 1212 (6th Cir.1980). Injury-in-fact theory: American Home Prods. Corp. v. Liberty Mut. Ins. Co., 748 F.2d 760 (2d Cir.1984); Detrex Chem. Indus., Inc. v. Employers Ins. of Wausau, 746 F.Supp. 1310 (N.D.Ohio 1990). Manifestation theory: Eagle–Picher Indus., Inc. v. Liberty Mut. Ins. Co., 682 F.2d 12 (1st Cir.1982). Continuous trigger theory: Keene Corp. v. Ins. Co. of N. Am., 667 F.2d 1034 (D.C.Cir.1981).

Questions concerning triggers involve a series of questions. First, is more than one carrier liable for the injury? A single trigger solution suggests that the carrier on the risk at the time the trigger is pulled is the only carrier responsible for the harm. Second, if there are multiple triggers, when do they begin and when do they end? The *Quincy* case concerned "the first pull of the trigger."

Other cases involve whether, once pulled, the trigger stays pulled. This is an important issue in the asbestos exposure litigation. Consider the following situation: plaintiff was first exposed to asbestos manufactured by Company X in 1960 and over the next 20 years his exposure continued. However, after 1980 he was no longer exposed. In 1995 he was diagnosed with an illness that he attributes to his exposure. Several insurance companies insured Company X throughout this period. One of the insurers wrote a policy offering "occurrence" coverage against asbestos-related injury for the period from 1985 to 1990. Should that insurance company be compelled to contribute to the plaintiff's damages? Does your answer turn on the particular type of injury suffered by the plaintiff, e.g., asbestosis, pleural plaque, mesothelioma, or lung cancer? Does it depend on which kind of trigger is employed? See Keene Corp. v. Ins. Co. of North America, 667 F.2d 1034 (D.C.Cir.1981); Zurich Ins. Co. v. Raymark Indus., 514 N.E.2d 150 (Ill.1987). How would you answer the question with respect to lead paint exposure of child tenants in an apartment building? See Maryland Cas. Co. v. Hanson, 902 A.2d 152 (Md.App.2006).

3. *Allocating costs.* As can be seen in the *Quincy* case, once the court has resolved the question of which policies are implicated in an injury, it must devise a way of allocating the loss among the policies, either by way of initial allocation or by way of contribution rules in the event each of the liable insurers is jointly and severally liable for the entirety of plaintiff's injury. In Public Service Co. of Colorado v. Wallis & Cos., 986 P.2d 924 (Colo.1999), the court held that in cases of continuous, progressive, and indivisible environmental damage, where it would be unreasonable to expect juries to allocate actual damages to specific policy periods, liability must be allocated proportionally among insurance policies according both to time-on-the-risk and to the degree of risk assumed, i.e., the liability limits on each policy.

What if for part of the triggered period defendant is self-insured? How should this be factored into the allocation equation? See Michael Dore, Insurance Coverage for Toxic Tort Claims: Solving the Self–Insurance Allocation Dilemma, 28 Tort &Ins.L.J. 823 (1993).

Other articles discussing these issues include: George Robertson Murphy, Asbestosis Litigation: Prescription, Contribution, Exposure, Insurance, and the Public Interest, 54 La.L.Rev. 467 (1993); Nicholas R. Andrea, Exposure, Manifestation of Loss, Injury-in-Fact, Continuous Trigger: The Insurance Coverage Quagmire, 21 Pepp.L.Rev. 813 (1994); Jeffrey W. Stempel, Assessing the Coverage Carnage: Asbestos Liability and Insurance After Three Decades of Dispute, 12 Conn.Ins.L. J. 349 (2005–06).

4. *Owned property exclusion.* The *Quincy* court made a passing reference to the "owned property exclusion." CGL policies are third-party policies and, therefore, are not designed to cover first-party losses. The owned property exclusion typically has language stating that the insurance does not apply to damage to property owned, occupied, rented or otherwise under the control of the insured. However, insureds frequently argue that the cost of cleaning up a contaminated site should be covered because the cleanup prevents damage to the property of others or to the groundwater. Courts have sided with the insured where the contamination of other property is imminent and immediate, but not when the contamination is only speculative. See Aetna Cas. &

Sur. Co. v. Dow Chem. Co., 28 F.Supp.2d 448, 454 (E.D.Mich.1998) (Although the insured does not need to show actual damage has occurred to a third-party, the insured must first establish "the need for remediation to prevent imminent harm to a third party."); Patz v. St. Paul Fire & Marine Ins. Co., 15 F.3d 699, 705 (7th Cir.1994) (holding that coverage was triggered despite applicability of "owned property" exclusion because government had mandated remediation of the environmental contamination).

5. One complaint often advanced with respect to third party insurance is that the transaction costs are quite high. A Congressional Budget Office study estimated that victims who file claims receive and average of 46% of the direct dollars spent on the system. Of the remaining 54%, 19% went to plaintiff attorneys, 14% to defense costs, and 21% to insurance company administrative costs. Cong. Budget Office, The Economics of U.S. Tort Liability: A Primer 20 (2003). Professor Fischer, in the article cited in the *Quincy* opinion, notes that the transaction costs for asbestos and pollution insurance coverage are even greater, ranging between 75% and 88% of carrier payouts. Why do you think the transaction costs are so great in this area?

C. EXCLUSIONS

QUADRANT CORP. v. AMERICAN STATES INSURANCE CO.

Supreme Court of Washington, 2005.
154 Wash.2d 165, 110 P.3d 733.

BRIDGE, J.

A tenant in an apartment building was overcome by fumes and became ill after a restoration company applied sealant to a nearby deck. The tenant sued the restoration company and the owners of the apartment building. Both the restoration company and the building owners settled and the owners now claim that their business liability insurance should cover the loss.

The business liability policies at issue here both contain absolute pollution exclusion clauses, which the insurers now argue apply to exclude coverage for the tenant's claim. The building owners contend that after this court's decision in *Kent Farms, Inc. v. Zurich Insurance Co.,* 140 Wash.2d 396, 402, 998 P.2d 292 (2000), the pollution exclusion cannot be applied to exclude occurrences that are not "traditional environmental harms." * * *

We hold that the plain language of the absolute pollution exclusion clause encompasses the injuries at issue here and therefore the tenant's claim is excluded from coverage. We find that the *Kent Farms* case is distinguishable on its facts and instead we adopt the reasoning of *Cook v. Evanson,* 83 Wash. App. 149, 920 P.2d 1223 (1996), a case similar to this one in that it involved injuries that resulted from toxic fumes. * * *

I

Statement of Facts

The facts of this case are not in dispute. Roy Street Associates owns an apartment building located at 200 Roy Street in Seattle.[1] In 1996, the building owners hired Pacific Restoration to make repairs and improvements on the building. In the course of completing the repair work, Pacific Restoration applied waterproofing sealants to the surface of a deck. The parties agree that Pacific Restoration used PC–220 and Polyglaze AL, manufactured by Polycoat Products. Both contain various chemicals, including a toxic substance called toluene diisocyanate (TDI), whose fumes can irritate the respiratory tract and, in high concentrations, can cause central nervous system depression.

Delores Kaczor was a tenant in the apartment adjacent to the deck. Pacific failed to warn Kaczor that it would be applying the sealant and then failed to properly ventilate the area. Fumes entered her apartment as the deck dried, making her ill enough to require hospitalization. Specifically, Kaczor's estate claimed that exposure to the fumes caused "exacerbation of her preexisting chronic obstructive pulmonary disease" and led to her "debilitating and declining health." Kaczor filed a lawsuit against Pacific Restoration and the building owners claiming personal injury and property damage. Kaczor died in 1998 and her lawsuit was dismissed without prejudice. In 1999, her estate filed a second lawsuit based on Kaczor's injuries. That suit was settled for $30,000 and dismissed in July 2000.

In early 1996, Pacific Restoration held a general liability policy from American States Insurance Company. The policy provided liability coverage to Pacific Restoration and to the apartment owners as additional insureds. The American States policy was subject to the following exclusion:

This insurance does not apply to:

· · · ·

f. Pollution

(1) "Bodily injury" or "property damage" arising out of the actual, alleged or threatened discharge, dispersal, seepage, migration, release or escape of pollutants:

(a) At or from any premises, site or location which is or was at any time owned or occupied by, or rented or loaned to, any insured;

· · · ·

---

1. Quadrant Corporation and Wellsford Holly Residential Properties, Inc. were general partners of Roy Street Associates. Equity Residential Properties Trust is the successor in interest to Wellsford Holly. Collectively, the building owners are the insureds.

(d) At or from any premises, site or location on which any insured or any contractors or subcontractors working directly or indirectly on any insured's behalf are performing operations:

(i) if the pollutants are brought on or to the premises, site or location in connection with such operations by such insured, contractor or subcontractor;

. . . .

Pollutants means any solid, liquid, gaseous or thermal irritant or contaminant, including smoke, vapor, soot, fumes, acids, alkalis, chemicals and waste. Waste includes materials to be recycled, reconditioned or reclaimed.

Similarly, Roy Street Associates held a general liability insurance policy from State Farm Fire and Casualty Company, which included Quadrant and Holly Corporation as additional insureds. The policy was subject to a nearly identical exclusion. Based on the pollution exclusions, the insurers denied coverage for the Kaczor claim.

The insureds filed this action, claiming that the insurers wrongfully denied their request for defense and indemnity with respect to the Kaczor claim. * * *

The trial court granted summary judgment in favor of the insurers and denied the insureds' motion. The insureds appealed and the Court of Appeals affirmed, holding that *Kent Farms* was factually distinguishable and this case was instead comparable to *Cook,* a similar case in which toxic fumes had caused the injury. *Quadrant Corp. v. American States Ins. Co.,* 118 Wash.App. 525, 533, 76 P.3d 773 (2003). * * *

II

Analysis

We must determine whether summary judgment was properly granted in favor of the insurers. To do so, we first decide whether the absolute pollution exclusion at issue here bars coverage where the fumes of a toxic substance caused the injury. Second, we determine whether the absolute pollution exclusion is so broad that it renders the insurance contracts illusory. * * *

The criteria for interpreting insurance contracts in Washington are well settled. * * * Most importantly, if the policy language is clear and unambiguous, we must enforce it as written; we may not modify it or create ambiguity where none exists.

We will hold that a clause is ambiguous only "when, on its face, it is fairly susceptible to two different interpretations, both of which are reasonable." If a clause is ambiguous, we may rely on extrinsic evidence of the intent of the parties to resolve the ambiguity. [*Weyerhaeuser Co. V. Commerical Union Ins. Co.,* 142 Wash.2d 654, 666, 15 P.3d 115, 122.] Any ambiguity remaining after examination of the applicable extrinsic evidence is resolved against the insurer and in favor of the insured. But while exclusions should be strictly construed against the drafter, a strict application should not trump the plain, clear language of an exclusion such that a strained or forced construction results. Finally, in Washington the expectations of the insured cannot override the plain language of the contract.

Absolute Pollution Exclusion

Pollution Exclusions, Generally: Pollution exclusions originated from insurers' efforts to avoid sweeping liability for long-term release of hazardous waste. Originally, the standard pollution exclusion that was incorporated into commercial general liability policies was a " 'qualified' " exclusion that precluded coverage unless the release of pollutants was " 'sudden and accidental.' " The qualified pollution exclusion was limited to release or discharge of pollutants " 'into or upon land, the atmosphere or any water course or body of water.' "

After much litigation surrounding the meaning of "sudden and accidental," a new standard pollution exclusion was promulgated in the mid–1980s. This time, the pollution exclusion was absolute; it no longer contained the "sudden and accidental" exception. Moreover, most absolute pollution exclusions omitted the language referring to release upon the land, atmosphere, or water. The exclusions at issue in this case are absolute pollution exclusions.

The rise of absolute pollution exclusions sparked new controversy over whether the exclusion applied to incidents that did not involve so-called classic environmental pollution. Many courts have interpreted absolute pollution exclusions specifically in the context of claims for bodily injuries arising out of the release of toxic fumes. Some have concluded that the absolute pollution exclusion does not apply where personal injury has resulted from the negligent release of fumes during the ordinary course of the insured's business. *See, e.g., Nautilus Ins. Co. v. Jabar,* 188 F.3d 27, 29–31 (1st Cir.1999); *Am. States Ins. Co. v. Koloms,* 177 Ill.2d 473, 687 N.E.2d 72, 82, 227 Ill. Dec. 149 (1997) ("[T]he exclusion applies only to those injuries caused by traditional environmental pollution."). These courts have relied on several different theories. Some have concluded that the terms "discharge," "dispersal," "irritant," and "contaminant" are terms of art in environmental law, thus rendering the exclusion ambiguous. Others have concluded that because the historical purpose of the prior qualified pollution exclusion was to shield insurers from sweeping liability for environmental cleanups, the absolute pollution exclusion clause could be reasonably interpreted to apply only to traditional environmental harms. *See id.; Koloms,* 227 Ill. Dec. 149, 687 N.E.2d at 81. Finally, some courts have concluded that a "commonsense approach" is necessary and the pollution exclusion should not be read to apply to "injuries resulting from everyday activities gone slightly, but not surprisingly, awry." *Pipefitters Welfare Educ. Fund v. Westchester Fire Ins. Co.,* 976 F.2d 1037, 1043–44 (7th Cir.1992).

However, a majority of courts has concluded that absolute pollution exclusions unambiguously exclude coverage for damages caused by the release of toxic fumes. *Cincinnati Ins. Co. v. Becker Warehouse, Inc.,* 262 Neb. 746, 635 N.W.2d 112, 118 (2001) (listing cases); *Deni Assocs. of Fla., Inc. v. State Farm Fire & Cas. Ins. Co.,* 711 So.2d 1135, 1137 n. 2 (Fla.1998) (noting that insurers and amici cited to more than 100 cases from 36 other states that had applied the plain language of the exclusion clause to deny coverage). *See, e.g. Technical Coating Applicators, Inc. v. U.S. Fid. & Guar. Co.,* 157 F.3d 843, 846 (11th Cir.1998) (holding similar language unambiguously excluded coverage for bodily injuries sustained by breathing vapors emitted from roofing products); *Owners Ins. Co. v. Farmer,* 173 F.Supp.2d 1330, 1333–34 (N.D.Ga.2001) ("the unambiguous language of the policy excludes *all* pollutants and does not exclude pollutants based on their source or location").

Absolute Pollution Exclusions in Washington: The Washington Court of Appeals first interpreted an absolute pollution exclusion in 1996. *Cook,* 83 Wash.App. at 153, 920 P.2d 1223. In *Cook,* the insured contractor applied a concrete sealant to a building. The material safety data sheet described the sealant as a " '[r]espiratory irritant,' " and the product information contained warnings regarding adequate ventilation. The contractor failed to seal off an air intake vent, fumes were sucked into the building, and some of the building's occupants suffered respiratory damage. * * *

* * *

The plain language of the *Cook* policy made no distinction based on "classic environmental pollution," the exclusion specifically included injuries at the insured's work site, and a reasonable person would recognize the sealant as a pollutant. Therefore, the policy language was unambiguous and, absent ambiguity, the court could not limit the exclusion. *Id.* This court denied review.

In 1998, the Court of Appeals again interpreted an absolute pollution exclusion clause whose language was substantially similar to the clause at issue here. *City of Bremerton v. Harbor Ins. Co.,* 92 Wash. App. 17, 19, 963 P.2d 194 (1998). In *Harbor Insurance,* the city sought insurance coverage for claims based upon emission of noxious gases, odors, and fumes from the city's sewage treatment plant. The insurer denied coverage based on the absolute pollution exclusion. The *Harbor Insurance* court looked to the policy's definition of pollutant and concluded that it unambiguously included fumes and gases. Furthermore, a reasonable person reviewing the language would conclude that noxious fumes would fall within the meaning of pollutant as defined in the policy exclusion. Therefore, the pollution exclusion clause precluded coverage in that case.

Then, in 2000, this court accepted review of an absolute pollution exclusion case. *Kent Farms,* 140 Wash.2d at 397, 998 P.2d 292. In *Kent Farms,* a fuel deliveryman was injured when the farm's shutoff valve malfunctioned and diesel fuel began to spill from the farm's tank. The deliveryman attempted to reattach the hose in order to prevent the spill of thousands of gallons of fuel. *Id.* In doing so, he was doused with fuel, which went down his throat and into his lungs and stomach. The delivery-man sued Kent Farms, whose insurance company denied coverage based on a pollution exclusion that contained language identical in all relevant respects to the clause at issue in this case.

The court explained that the *Kent Farms* cause of action was "rooted in negligence, not in environmental harm caused by pollution," because the plaintiff alleged "negligence in the maintenance and design of a fuel storage facility that resulted in immediate bodily injury when a high-pressure jet of liquid struck him.", In other words, it was the defect in the shutoff valve, not the toxic character of the fuel, that was central to the injury. Thus, the court framed the issue as whether the mere fact that a pollutant "appears in the causal chain" can trigger the application of the exclusion clause.

[T]he *Kent Farms* court explained that to resolve the issue, it had to "determine the purpose and scope of the exclusion." *Id.* at 399. Relying on a case in which this court interpreted a qualified pollution exclusion, the *Kent Farms* court concluded that it was required to "view the exclusion in light of the whole policy to determine whether, in that context, the exclusion applies." *Kent Farms,* 140 Wash.2d at 400. * * *

The *Kent Farms* court explained that the qualified pollution exclusion clause, was initially adopted so that insurers could avoid the " 'yawning extent of potential liability arising from the gradual or repeated discharge of hazardous substances into the environment.' " *Id.* (quoting *Waste Mgmt. Of Carolinas, Inc. v. Peerless Ins. Co.,* 315 N.C. 688 (1986)). Later, various forms of the absolute pollution exclusion clause were incorporated into insurance policies in the wake of expanded environmental liability under federal law; thus, the absolute pollution exclusion clauses "were clearly intended to exculpate insurance companies from liability for mas-sive environmental cleanups required by CERCLA and similar legisla-tion." *Id.* at 401. Therefore, the exclusion specifically addressed "those situations in which injury was caused by *environmental damage.*" *Id.*

The *Kent Farms* court reasoned that the injured deliveryman was not "polluted" by diesel fuel and more importantly, the fuel was not "acting as a 'pollutant' when it struck him." *Id.* To hold otherwise would "broaden the application of the exclusion far beyond its intended pur-pose." *Id.* The average purchaser of a comprehensive liability policy reasonably expects broad coverage for liability arising from business operations and exclusions should be strictly construed against the insurer. Kent Farms would have reasonably believed that injuries arising from faulty equipment would be beyond the scope of the exclusion and would be covered.

The court then noted that cases from other states had similarly held that the absolute pollution exclusion did not apply "much beyond tradi-tional environmental torts." *Id.* at 402. * * * To do so would be at odds with the original purpose of the exclusion to protect insurance companies from "a potentially vast and unforeseen liability for major environmental disasters." *Id.* * * *

Finally, the *Kent Farms* court summarized:

The exclusion, when viewed in the context of its purpose, does not apply merely because a potential pollutant was involved in the causal chain. *Instead, the exclusion applies to "occurrences" involving the pollutant as a pollutant.* Our approach is consonant with the understanding of the average purchaser of insurance and consistent with the provisions of the insurance policy as a whole; that is, the pollution exclusion clause was designed to exclude coverage for traditional environmental harms. We will not expand the scope of the exclusion clause beyond its intended purpose.

Id. at 402 (emphasis added). Therefore, without mentioning *Cook,* and without explicitly determining whether the pollution exclusion was ambiguous, the *Kent Farms* court concluded that the exclusion was designed to preclude coverage in the case of traditional environmental harms or where the pollutant acted as a pollutant.

* * *

Application of the Absolute Pollution Exclusion in this Case: With this background in mind, we now turn to the case at hand. In this case, the Court of Appeals held that the underlying injury and cause of action were primarily the result of the toxic character of the pollutant and therefore the pollution exclusion would apply. *Quadrant Corp.,* 118 Wash.App. at 526 ("the underlying injury and cause of action are the result of a pollutant acting as a pollutant"). The Court of Appeals concluded *Cook* and Washington's other "fumes" cases remain good law because the facts of those cases are distinguishable from the facts of *Kent Farms. Id.* at 530–31. Unlike the diesel fuel in *Kent Farms, Cook* involved a substance whose toxicity could cause injury even when used as intended. Thus, the *Cook* reasoning and not the *Kent Farms* rule would control when fumes caused injury and where the pollutant was being used as it was intended. Because the tenant in this case was injured by fumes emanating from water proofing material that was being used as intended, the air in her apartment was "polluted." Thus, the pollution exclusion applied and the court affirmed the summary judgment dismissal of the insureds' suit. We agree.

As stated above, in Washington, if insurance policy language is clear and unambiguous, a court may not modify the contract to create an ambiguity where none exists. * * *

In this case, the policy language clearly states that the liability coverage does not apply to *bodily injury* or *property damage* arising out of the dispersal, *seepage, migration,* release, or escape of a *gaseous irritant,* including vapors, *fumes* and chemicals, at any *premises owned by the insured* or *any premises onto which a contractor* or subcontractor hired by the insured *has brought a pollutant.* The language clearly applies to bodily injury and property damage; it is not limited to actions for cleanup costs. Unlike the earlier "qualified pollution exclusion," the clause at issue here does not limit coverage to a release of pollutants upon the land, atmosphere, or water. The exclusion specifically includes injuries at any premises owned by the insured and injuries resulting from pollutants brought onto the premises by contractors working on behalf of the insured.

When considering the facts of this case, it is difficult to see how a reasonable person could interpret the policy language such that it would not encompass the claim at issue here. * * * The parties agree that the sealants at issue here, PC–220 and Polyglaze AL, contained TDI, a toxic substance which can irritate the respiratory tract and, in high concentrations, can cause central nervous system depression. The material safety data sheet for these products indicates that their ingredients are toxic and recommends precautions such as adequate ventilation, respiratory protection, protective clothing, and eye protection. Furthermore, the Federal Clean Air Act lists TDI as a hazardous air pollutant. *See* 42 U.S.C. § 7412(b)(1). The contents of the sealant unambiguously fall within the policy definition of pollutant.

The insureds argue that this court's decision in *Kent Farms requires* us to conclude that the absolute pollution exclusion can be applied only to exclude liability for "traditional environmental pollution." The *Kent Farms* court examined the history of the absolute pollution exclusion, but to do so, the court must have concluded that the exclusion was ambiguous with regard to the facts of that case. An absolute pollution exclusion clause can be ambiguous with regard to the facts of one case but not another. The *Kent Farms* facts are not present here. Where, as here, the exclusion unambiguously applies to the facts of the case at hand, the plain language must be applied without reference to extrinsic evidence regarding the intent of the parties.

The insureds also contend that the *Kent Farms* holding was so sweeping that it overruled *Cook* and *Harbor Insurance.* * * * However, it is important to note that while *Cook* was discussed in the *Kent Farms* Court of Appeals decision, this court did not mention *Cook* or *Harbor Insurance* at all in its *Kent Farms* opinion. Neither case was explicitly rejected.

Furthermore, the *Kent Farms* court did not implicitly reject the reasoning of those cases. While the *Kent Farms* case included language regarding the purpose behind the pollution exclusion, the court was careful to explain that the exclusion applies to " 'occurrences' involving the pollutant *as a pollutant.*" In other words, the *Kent Farms* court distinguished between cases in which the substance at issue was polluting at the time of the injury and cases in which the offending substance's toxic character was not central to the injury. This is emphasized by the *Kent Farms* court's careful description of the injuries at issue in that case:

> Gugenberger was not polluted by diesel fuel. It struck him; it engulfed him; it choked him. It did not pollute him. *Most importantly, the fuel*

was not acting as a "pollutant" when it struck him any more than it would have been acting as a "pollutant" if it had been in a barrel that rolled over him, or if it had been lying quietly on the steps waiting to trip him. * * *

Kent Farms, 140 Wash.2d at 401 (emphasis added).

Finally, the insureds argue that the *Kent Farms* court adopted the reasoning of *Gamble Farm,* 656 A.2d at 145 and *Continental Casualty,* 593 N.Y.S.2d 966, 609 N.E.2d at 512, both fumes cases. The insureds contend that the reasoning of those courts should now control fumes cases in Washington. However, both *Gamble Farm* and *Continental* involved policy clauses that specifically excluded personal injury or property damage arising out of the discharge of pollutants " 'into or upon land, the atmosphere or any water course or body of water.' " *Gamble Farm,* 656 A.2d at 143 (emphasis omitted) and *Continental,* 593 N.Y.S.2d 966, 609 N.E.2d at 508 (quoting relevant policy language). Both courts reasoned that the policy reference to "atmosphere" was ambiguous because it could lead a reasonable person to conclude that the exclusion referred only to traditional environmental damages. However, the policy language in *Kent Farms,* like the policy language here, did not include the dispositive reference to the atmosphere. If anything, the absence of that phrase instead indicates that the exclusionary language is not limited to traditional environmental harms.

Therefore, we conclude that the *Kent Farms* discussion of traditional environmental harms is limited by the facts of that case. Here, we adopt the reasoning of the *Cook* court; TDI meets the policy's definition of a pollutant and Kaczor's injuries fall squarely within the plain language of the pollution exclusion clause.* * *

In sum, because *Cook* follows the clear and longstanding rules for insurance contract interpretation adopted by this court, we apply the *Cook* reasoning in this case. We note that *Kent Farms* is distinguishable on its facts. * * *

       * * *

III

Conclusion

Washington law clearly requires this court to look first to the plain language of an insurance policy exclusion. If the exclusionary language is unambiguous, then the court cannot create an ambiguity where none exists. If the language is plain there is no need to consider extrinsic evidence of the parties' intent. The language of the absolute pollution exclusion is unambiguous when applied to the facts of this case. The deck sealant at issue here is clearly a pollutant as defined in the policy and Kaczor's injury falls squarely within the exclusionary language. Thus, there is no need to turn to evidence regarding the history and purpose of the standard pollution exclusion. * * * Therefore, we affirm the Court of

Appeals and uphold the trial court's dismissal on summary judgment in favor of the insurers.

CHAMBERS, J. (dissenting).

The majority embarks upon the noble quest of clarifying the law. Unfortunately, the majority confuses the "occurrence," or coverage triggering event, with the consequent damages. Specifically, the majority confuses a non polluting *event* covered by the policy with the resulting *damages,* which were caused by pollutants. Because we look at the occurrence to determine coverage, not the resulting damage, I respectfully dissent.

* * *

Consider an auto accident in which a driver was saturated in fuel, and suffered specific injuries from the irritating nature of the chemical compound and its noxious fumes. There would be coverage for this "occurrence" and the resulting damages. In this example, the occurrence is the alleged negligent act which caused the motor vehicle collision. The mere fact that a pollutant was involved in the causal chain of events does not trigger the pollution exclusion. * * * The covered peril here was the alleged negligence of the contractor and apartment owner in performing routine work necessary to maintain the apartment building.

* * *

Here, a contractor was hired by the insured to apply waterproofing to the exterior wood surface of the apartment complex. The specific allegation of negligence against the apartment owner was the failure to prevent exposure to toxic fumes and the failure to warn its tenant. Inherent in applying any water proofing material including stains and paints is the exposure of toxic fumes. But the specific contentions against the apartment owner was the failure to assure proper ventilation or to warn of the fumes.

The question before this court is whether the average purchaser of a comprehensive liability policy understands that the act or applying waterproofing to the exterior wall of an apartment building would be an act of "discharge, dispersal, seepage, migration, (or) release" of a pollutant.

This court has never held that mere injury by a pollutant triggers a pollution exclusion.* * * This court has also always viewed pollution exclusions from their traditional purpose of avoiding massive exposure for environmental damage. This history is an integral part of a proper understanding of the clauses.

* * *

Against that backdrop, it is clear that applying the clause to exclude this type of harm is appropriate only if the "occurrence" that triggers coverage is a polluting event. In my view, the average consumer of a general liability policy would not understand that applying wood preservative to the exterior of an apartment building was a polluting event. As this court has already noted, expanding the exclusion to cover any type of occurrence that involves pollution would be an "opportunistic afterthought," outside the intent of the drafters. I conclude this does violence to the meaning of the exclusion and our recent unanimous *Kent Farms* opinion. Accordingly, I respectfully dissent.

NOTES AND QUESTIONS

Near the end of its opinion, the *Quadrant* majority said that "*Kent Farms* is distinguishable on its facts." What, exactly, is the court's distinction between *Kent Farms* and *Quadrant*? Would the majority have any trouble distinguishing the *Quadrant* facts from the hypothetical automobile accident offered by the dissent? Why or why not?

Here are some more hypotheticals from South Cent. Bell Tel. Co. v. Ka–Jon Food Stores of Louisiana, Inc., 644 So.2d 357 (La.1994), judgment vacated, 644 So.2d 368 (La.1994).

If [a convenience store] customer slips on oil leaking from a quart-sized container, their ensuing claim for bodily injury would be exclude from coverage. Likewise, if a container of Drano fell from one of the convenience store's shelves onto a customer, the personal injuries resulting from the toxic chemical spill would be excluded from insurance coverage. Similarly, if, in an attempt to eradicate insect infestation, the convenience store accidentally sprayed both the insects and its customers with insecticide, or if any of the convenience store's natural gas appliances leaked gas and caused bodily injury, the "actual ... discharge, dispersal, spill, release or escape of ... fumes, acids, alkalis, toxic chemicals, ... or gases, ... or other irritants, contaminants or pollutants: (1) at or from the premises owned, rented or occupied by the named insured" would preclude insurance coverage of the incidents.

Id. at 364 n.17. How would the *Quadrant Corporation* court deal with each of these situations?

ENVIRONMENTAL LIABILITY AND THE LIMITS OF INSURANCE

Kenneth S. Abraham.
88 Colum.L.Rev. 942 (1988).

[In the following article, Professor Abraham expands on the *Quadrant* majority's insights as to why insurers moved from the qualified exclusion language of earlier policies to the absolute exclusion language litigated in *Kent Farms* and *Quadrant Corp.* In doing so, he raises important questions about the relationship between tort law and insurance.]

Environmental liability has become one of the leading legal problems of this decade. It has garnered as much publicity, energy, capital, and emotion as any other contender, and for good reason. * * *

The impact of the new environmental liability on the liability insurance market, and the role that liability insurance might play in furthering the goals of a regime of environmental liability, have generated much controversy. * * *

The problems that now trouble environmental liability insurance have their roots in the crisis that afflicted almost the entire commercial and professional liability insurance field in 1985 and 1986. * * *

     * * *

As the dust has settled, the market for most forms of liability insurance has stabilized. Although premium levels have not declined, at this point coverage generally appears to be available to most lines of business. * * * Yet unlike virtually every other line of insurance affected by the recent crisis, the problems that troubled environmental liability insurance at the height of the crisis have not ameliorated: they remain severe and fundamental. In the past two years, for example, not only has the cost of the little environmental liability insurance that is still available skyrocketed; more importantly, for most businesses in the United States insurance against environmental liability is completely unavailable.

     * * *

The thesis of this Article is that the demise of the environmental liability insurance market is a symptom of the high levels of legal uncertainty that are being created by the new environmental liability. * * *

     * * *

I.   THE INCENTIVE EFFECTS OF ENVIRONMENTAL LIABILITY INSURANCE

A. *Insurability, Information, and the Cost of Risk–Bearing*

Most types of insurance perform three related but distinct functions. First, insurance transfers risk from parties who are comparatively risk averse to enterprises more willing to bear risk. Second, insurance spreads risk by combining individual risks in a pool created by the insurer. By covering a large number of insureds against uncorrelated risks, the insurer diversifies its own risk and operates a risk-sharing arrangement. Third, insurance performs a risk-allocation function by charging premiums that reflect the level of risk posed by each individual or enterprise that is insured.

Insurance can perform these functions effectively only under very special conditions of uncertainty. At one extreme—complete ignorance about the scope of the risk to be insured—insurance would resemble a naked gamble; at the other extreme—a world in which the future were completely predictable—there would be no point in insuring. Liability insurance may operate effectively between these two extremes, but it can be undermined in several ways: by adverse selection, moral hazard, or generalized uncertainty.

     * * *

II. THE NEW ENVIRONMENTAL LIABILITY AND INSURANCE PROBLEM
* * *

The new environmental liability tests the limits of insurance in three ways. First, it has created new forms of statutory liability against which it is difficult to insure. Second, judicial strategies of interpretation have made it difficult for insurers to rely on the meaning of insurance policy language designed to avoid covering uninsurable risks. Third, the distinct threat of other, common-law expansions of liability creating additional uninsurable risks that cannot be reliably excluded by policy language renders the scope of an insurer's future obligations uncertain.

All three developments, however, have much the same result: they create forms of liability whose potential frequency and severity is extremely difficult to predict because the information upon which such calculations should be based is unavailable. The result is an increase in the level of uncertainty that environmental liability insurers would have to tolerate in order to underwrite the risk of environmental liability. * * *
* * *

A. *Developments in Statutory Liability*

The impact of environmental liability on the liability insurance market is partly the product of a series of statutory developments creating liabilities of such uncertain scope that they are inordinately difficult to insure. The two most graphic developments are the rise of retroactive strict liability and the accelerated imposition of joint and several liability.

1. *"Retroactive" Strict Liability Under Superfund.*—The Federal Superfund Act[42] imposes strict liability for the costs of cleaning up hazardous waste storage sites on the generators and transporters of the waste, and on the owners and operators of the sites. This liability attaches regardless of the time when the material was deposited and regardless of the absence of fault by the party held liable.

Liability of this sort confounds the insurance function in two ways. First, when a statute (or a common-law rule) imposing such liability is first adopted, it is largely unanticipated. Ordinary strict liability is a cost of doing business that enterprises and their insurers can anticipate and finance, even when the damages imposed are not worth avoiding. For the most part, however, retroactive strict liability—the imposition of liability for the consequences of actions that were not subject to strict liability at the time they were taken—could not have been readily anticipated or financed by the enterprises subject to this form of liability. Insurers, of course, will not have charged for any coverage that liability policies turn out to provide against this form of liability. The introduction of such an unanticipated liability necessarily undermines insurers' confidence in their ability to predict the legal future. This loss of confidence is likely

___

42. See Comprehensive Environmental Response, Compensation and Liability Act of 1980 ("CERCLA"), Pub. L. No. 96–510, 94 Stat. 2767 (codified as amended in scattered sections of 26 U.S.C., 33 U.S.C., 42 U.S.C., and 49 U.S.C.).

both to influence insurers' future willingness to market lines of insurance that seem especially susceptible to legal change and to affect the price of coverage in the lines insurers do continue to offer.

Second, retroactive strict liability, including Superfund liability, is extremely difficult to insure even if it is commonplace. By its very nature, this form of liability is unpredictable both by environmental actors and by their insurers. It is, after all, retroactive *strict* liability: liability for the failure to reduce risks that could not have been discovered through the exercise of reasonable care. In theory all strict liability is retroactive in this way; in practice, however, strict liability is often used merely to circumvent the cost and difficulty of proving negligence, or a state-of-the-art defense is made available to limit its retroactive effect.

In the case of Superfund, however, the retroactive effect of strict liability assures that the operators of waste storage sites and depositors in the sites are held liable for the cost of any cleanup that later becomes necessary, even if these parties employed state-of-the-art technology and their actions were reasonable in all other respects. Thus, under the Superfund regime, liability for the consequences of risks that were undiscovered and largely undiscoverable at the time the actions creating them were taken may be imposed twenty or more years later. Because the magnitude of such risks is inestimable—they are unknowable when insured against—it is impossible confidently to set a price for insurance against them.

It is important to recognize that this is not simply a problem for insurers under old policies that were written before the enactment of the Superfund regime. These insurers were subjected to the additional surprise of finding a new form of liability introduced after their policies were in force. But any insurer offering coverage against Superfund liability today faces the possibility that dangers neither it nor its insured can reasonably anticipate will produce an unexpected liability sometime in the future.

* * *

[T]he best insurers can do to combat the threat posed by retroactive strict liability is to avoid insuring it. * * * [M]any insurers simply have withdrawn from the environmental liability insurance market or excluded all pollution coverage from CGL policies. This withdrawal seems to have been caused at least in part by the threat that retroactive strict liability will become a prominent feature on the environmental liability landscape.

2. *Joint and Several Liability.*—Independent concurrent tortfeasors have long been held jointly and severally liable for indivisible injuries caused by their combined activities. As long as joint and several liability represents a small percentage of total liabilities insured, it need not disrupt liability insurance premium calculations unduly, because the level of uncertainty it poses is minimal. The enactment of the Superfund Act, however, has substantially expanded the threat of joint and several environmental liability, since the Act holds generators and transporters of

hazardous substances as well as owners and operators of hazardous waste storage sites jointly and severally liable for the expenses of cleaning up these sites.

The threat of joint and several liability creates special uncertainty, because the probability of liability—and of consequent loss for the insurer—is affected by the behavior of nonpolicyholders whom the insurer cannot necessarily identify in advance. When the scope of liability is potentially very large, that uncertainty is magnified. The Superfund Act creates liabilities that pose both problems of uncertainty and magnitude. A single generator of a portion of the waste deposited in a site, for example, may be held liable for all the costs of cleanup despite that generator's lack of fault, despite the presence of waste contributed by other generators, and despite the partial responsibility of the owner or operator of the sites for the release of material requiring a cleanup response; the aggregate cost can be staggering.

Although the Act as amended in 1986 details rights of contribution, and although some courts have created rights of indemnity for Superfund liabilities under special circumstances, joint and several liability has bite under the same conditions as it always has—when rights of contribution and indemnity are meaningless because other jointly liable parties are insolvent and uninsured. In order to insure against this threat, insurers would have to make nearly impossible calculations based on both the potential behavior of the other parties whose activities might combine with the insured's to cause damage, and on the probability that these parties would prove to be judgment proof. Given the uncertainties that would be associated with insuring against Superfund liability under these circumstances, it is no surprise that such coverage has virtually disappeared from the market.

B. *Developments in Insurance Law: Judge–Made Insurance*

The second area in which legal developments have reduced insurers' ability to write environmental liability insurance involves the interpretation and application of insurance policy language. Not only do new statutory obligations create uncertainties that undermine insurers' actuarial calculations; in addition, judicial interpretations of policy language that insurers had regarded as fixed, clear, and limiting have expanded the scope of coverage against both the old and new forms of environmental liability. The threat posed by the prospect that environmental liability policies increasingly will be interpreted to incorporate this "judge-made insurance" also destabilizes the insuring function.

Of course, the creation of insurance coverage through judicial interpretation is a long-standing practice. But traditionally this practice has been used as a kind of consumer protection device in cases where policy language was arguably ambiguous. Even in cases where that language was not ambiguous, the courts have tended to intervene mainly where the policyholder was an individual without ready access to legal counsel, without a strong incentive to shop for coverage, and without enormous potential liability. Judicial decisions in a number of environmental liability insurance disputes, however, have departed from these traditional constraints. They have created coverage even in the face of contrary policy language, where the policyholder was a business entity with access to counsel, and where potential liabilities were enormous. * * *

In part, the negative effects of judge-made insurance on the environmental liability insurance market are similar to those already discussed. An unexpected judicial interpretation extending coverage beyond what was intended works like a mandatory retroactive price decrease. Insurers suffer an immediate financial loss, lose a measure of confidence in the fairness of the judicial system, and come to doubt their ability to predict future judicial developments.

In addition, judge-made insurance destabilizes the market in a way that extends beyond the effects of expansions of common-law and statutory liability. Environmental liability insurers can attempt to draft around uninsurable tort or statutory liabilities by incorporating exclusions, coverage limitations, and the like in their policies. In this way, insurers can try to maintain the level of certainty necessary for effective performance of their function, and enterprises seeking insurance against conventional environmental liabilities can obtain it. By contrast, there is no completely reliable way to draft around the threat of judge-made insurance, because by definition this is coverage that ignores the apparent meaning of the policy language itself. In an atmosphere already saturated with doubt about the stability of insurer obligations, judge-made insurance pushes the environmental insurance function another large step closer to the limits of insurability. The result is that insurance against a set of liabilities that might otherwise be insurable disappears. Several examples of the interpretive process that generates this result follow.

1. *The Pollution Exclusion.*—Until recently, the standard general liability policy sold to businesses and municipal governments contained provisions designed to provide some protection against pollution liability, but also to limit that protection. Products liability policies contained similar coverage. For example, the CGL afforded protection against bodily injury or property damage caused by an "occurrence," defined as "an accident, including continuous or repeated exposure to conditions, which results in bodily injury or property damage neither expected nor intended from the standpoint of the insured." The CGL excluded coverage, however, of

> bodily injury or property damage arising out of the discharge, dispersal, release, or escape of smoke, vapors, soot, fumes, acids, alkalis, toxic chemicals, liquids, and gases, or waste materials or other irritants, contaminants or pollutants into or upon land, the atmosphere or any watercourse or body of water; but this exclusion does not apply if such discharge, dispersal, release or escape is sudden and accidental.

The combined meaning of the definition of "occurrence" and the "pollution exclusion" was that the policy afforded coverage against liability for bodily injury or property damage caused by continuous or repeated exposure to risks, unless that exposure was the result of any of the various forms of pollution detailed in the exclusion. Coverage against liability for damages caused by pollution exposures was excluded except when the exposure resulted from "sudden and accidental" pollution.

* * *

Some judicial decisions, however, have emasculated the pollution exclusion. The consequence of these decisions is that the pollution exclusion often is of no effect unless the pollution in question was intentional, or nearly so. A few of the more notable decisions are worth examining, because they suggest how dangerous it may be for insurers to rely on the language of their own policies in evaluating the insurability of the risks they cover and in setting a price for the coverage they sell.

In *Jackson Township Municipal Utilities Authority v. Hartford Accident & Indemnity Co.,*[61] the insured Municipal Utilities Authority was sued for depositing waste in a landfill that allegedly contaminated the wells of residents near the landfill. The Authority brought an action against its insurers, claiming that they had a duty to defend the suit and indemnify the Authority in the event the residents' suit was successful. The Authority's liability insurance policies contained the insuring clause and pollution exclusion quoted above. The court rejected the insurers' argument that because the pollution in question was not sudden and accidental, they had no duty to defend or indemnify. The court held that the pollution exclusion was simply a restatement of the definition of the term "occurrence" in the insuring clause, reflecting the principle that "coverage will not be provided for intended results of intentional acts but will be provided for the unintended results of intentional acts."[63] As to the meaning of the terms "sudden and accidental" in the pollution exclusion itself, the court simply read them out of existence.[64]

Similarly, in *Buckeye Union Insurance Co. v. Liberty Solvents and Chemical Co.,*[65] the insured was sued as a generator of hazardous waste for cleanup expenses under the Superfund Act. The court quoted extensively from *Jackson Township* in ruling that the pollution exclusion provided the insurer no protection.[66]

---

61. 186 N.J. Super. 156, 451 A.2d 990 (1982).

63. 186 N.J. Super. at 164, 451 A.2d at 994.

64. [T]he act or acts are sudden and accidental regardless of how many deposits or dispersals may have occurred, and although the permeation of pollution into the groundwater may have been gradual rather than sudden, the behavior of the pollutants as they seeped into the acquifer is irrelevant if the permeation was unexpected. Id. at 165, 451 A.2d at 994

65. 17 Ohio App. 3d 127, 477 N.E.2d 1227 (1984).

66. There are no allegations in the complaint that compel the conclusion that Liberty Solvents intended or expected the releases of hazardous waste substances by Chem–Dyne or the damages that such release would cause. Construing the words "sudden and accidental" most favorably to the insured . . . we conclude that the release and resultant property damages could be found to be "sudden and accidental" from the standpoint of Liberty Solvents. Id. at 134, 477 N.E.2d at 1235.

The decisions in both these cases reflect the common, though admittedly not universal, fate of the pollution exclusion. It is interpreted as a mere elaboration of the phrase "neither expected nor intended from the standpoint of the insured" in the definition of insured occurrences. So long as it is neither expected nor intended, then, damage caused by gradual pollution is covered notwithstanding the exclusion, even though the pollution in question is not sudden.

Even taken out of context, this interpretation is implausible because it makes an entire paragraph in the CGL and similar policies superfluous. * * * Taken in context, this interpretation is even more egregious, because it ignores the concern for adverse selection and moral hazard that lies behind the exclusion. If the exclusion is operative only when the pollution is expected or intended, then insurers and insureds must bear the cost of case-by-case determinations of what caused the incident and at what point the insured might have controlled it.

In some situations insurers can adjust to the importation of new meanings into old policy provisions. The two conventional adjustments to an unexpected interpretation are either to increase premiums charged for all new policies that will be subject to the unexpected interpretation or to redraft the provision in question to preclude the new judicial gloss on the provision's meaning. Unfortunately, both responses are likely to be much less effective in environmental liability insurance than in the typical setting.

Because of the long-tail on liability claims involving gradual pollution, neither increases in premiums nor changes in policy language can have much impact for years. * * *

Consequently, the occurrence insurer faced with an unexpected interpretation of its policy cannot simply take an unanticipated loss on one or two year's policies and immediately preclude further losses by redrafting the policy or increasing its price. On the contrary, losses may continue to accrue on policies that had been written over a period of many years and that are now subject to the new interpretation. Readjustment of new policies can only cut losses that would otherwise have begun to strike the insurer several years in the future.

This predicament is exacerbated by the development of new common law and statutory liabilities for environmental injuries. Not only do these new liabilities multiply insurers' losses on preexisting policies whose language expressly covers them; as new liabilities are created, courts also will tend to hold that they are covered by preexisting policies notwithstanding contrary policy language. * * *

In short, prudent insurers cannot ignore the threat that the judicial treatment of the pollution exclusion will not be an isolated phenomenon and that future courts will strive to assure that even redrafted policies cover new environmental liabilities.[73] * * *

        * * *

---

73. The property/casualty industry's action prior to the nearly complete disappearance of primary environmental liability insurance—the effort to replace the old occurrence CGL with a

CONCLUSION

Although insurance considerations have long been used to support extensions of tort and other forms of liability, where liability goes, insurance is not always sure to follow. Thoughtful courts and legislatures as well as scholars must face this fact, since the impact of the new environmental liability on insurance is extensive. Admittedly, the merits of the new environmental liability cannot be evaluated exclusively by reference to its insurability. But since the rationales for the imposition of civil liability depend so heavily on the availability and technology of insurance to achieve the goals they postulate, neither can the courts and legislatures afford any longer to ignore the limits of insurance in fashioning environmental liabilities.

NOTES AND QUESTIONS

1. Qualified pollution exclusions first appeared in the 1970s apparently in response to the sinking of the tanker the *Torrey Canyon* off the coast of Cornwall, England in 1967 and the 1969 Santa Barbara Channel oil spill. At the same time insurance companies switched over to the absolute exclusion language, many also added a specific asbestos exclusion. Given that the asbestos litigation avalanche started long before this time, why do you think they waited so long to adopt asbestos exclusions?

2. According to Professor Abraham, exclusions are a response to difficult-to-manage mass torts. Richard V. Ericson & Aaron Doyle, Uncertain Business (2004) provides empirical support for this assertion. They found that, on the whole, the greater the certainty with which the probability of a loss can be calculated, the more readily available insurance is against that loss.

3. More recently, many GCL policies added a specific lead paint exclusion. See Pope ex rel. Pope v. Economy Fire & Cas. Co., 779 N.E.2d 461 (Ill.2002). In your opinion, what underlying facts and potential changes in the law may have prompted this new exclusion? See State v. Lead Indus. Ass'n, Inc., 951 A.2d 428 (R.I.2008), p. 85 supra.

Was a specific lead paint exclusion necessary or is lead paint a pollutant covered by the absolute pollution exclusion? Compare Auto–Owners Ins. Co. v. Hanson, 588 N.W.2d 777 (Minn.App.1999) (chipping and flaking of lead paint was a "discharge, dispersal or release" within meaning of absolute pollution exclusion), with Lititz Mut. Ins. Co. v. Steely, 785 A.2d 975 (Pa.2001) (the process by which lead paint degraded and became available for ingestion and inhalation did not involve a "discharge," "dispersal," "release," or "escape" under the absolute pollution exclusion).

4. Litigation over the interpretation of "sudden and accidental" in qualified exclusions was still in full swing when Professor Abraham wrote his

---

"claims-made" form affording coverage only for claims actually made during the policy period—was a natural response to the problems posed by judge-made insurance in the environmental liability field. The effort to introduce a claims-made CGL, however, has not met with success. Some state regulators have been reluctant to approve the new policy for general use, and the consuming public has not reacted favorably to its introduction.

article. The fight often turned on the meaning given to the term "sudden." A rather obvious issue is how sudden is sudden. What of a leak over several days? See Sauer v. Home Indem. Co., 841 P.2d 176 (Alaska 1992). Another question is whether suddenness should apply to the initial release or to the entire pollution process. What of a relatively sudden release which leads to the slow contamination of groundwater over the course of several years?

Many cases, however, involved much more fundamental interpretive conflicts. Insurers argued that the term "sudden" in the phrase "sudden and accidental" was designed to permit recovery only when a release was abrupt, e.g., the bursting of a tank containing toxic chemicals, and this abrupt release was not intended, i.e., it was accidental. Even accidental pollution would not be covered if it were not sudden. Insureds argued that the term "sudden" did not have a temporal dimension. Rather, it was synonymous with accidental and thus the qualified pollution policies covered all pollution that was not intended. This interpretation leads back to the interpretation of "expected or intended." See Sharon M. Murphy, The "Sudden and Accidental" Exception to the Pollution Exclusion Clause in Comprehensive General Liability Insurance Policies: The Gordian Knot of Environmental Liability, 45 Vand.L.Rev. 161 (1992).

Although insurance companies moved away from the qualified exclusion language in the mid 1980s, the very long tail of environmental harms insured that litigation over the meaning of these policies would continue for at least a quarter of a century. See Coffeyville Res. Ref. & Mktg., LLC v. Liberty, ___ F.Supp.2d ___, 2010 WL 1740887 (D.Kan.2010).

5. *Quadrant* is a "fume" case. Most of the recent cases challenging the absolute pollution exclusion are fume cases. Are fume cases as a group different from other pollution cases? Why?

6. The litigation battles out on the frontier of the absolute pollution exclusion should not cause one to lose sight of the fact that the language in these policies succeeded in achieving the insurers' primary goal, which was to avoid liability in nearly all traditional pollution situations. See, e.g., Nat'l Union Fire Ins. Co. of Pittsburgh, Pennsylvania v. CBI Indus., Inc., 907 S.W.2d 517 (Tex.1995) (accidental release of large cloud of hydrofluoric acid from oil refinery). Nevertheless, many courts continue to express reservations about the exclusion because, as one court put it, although the language in the clause is quite specific, a literal interpretation of that language results in an application of the clause that is quite broad. Am. States Ins. Co. v. Koloms, 687 N.E.2d 72, 79 (Ill.1997).

7. At the time Professor Abraham wrote his article and for the decade following, insurance companies provided almost no pollution coverage. However, in the late 1990s some forms of pollution insurance began to reappear and this market has grown substantially in the past decade. Today, such policies go by the generic name of environmental impairment liability (EIL) insurance. Most relevant to this Chapter is a sub-species of such policies known as Pollution Legal Liability (PLL) insurance policies. Most of these policies are quite customized. Policy terms and premiums are developed on a case-by-case and sometimes a site-by-site basis. Most importantly, these policies are written on a claims-made rather than an occurrence basis. Moreover, they may have a relatively "short nose." That is, they only cover claims caused by a pollution incident that commenced on or after a specific retroactive date. For example, a policy written in 2010 might only cover claims made in 2010 concerning pollution incidents that commenced on or after 2005. Most such policies run from 1 to 10 years, often with an option for renewal. Even with these limitations, the policies generally contain multiple exclusions. In addition to the usual exclusions for intentional acts or omissions, non-compliance with legal directives, owned property, and contractual liability also typically exclude coverage for underground storage tanks (unless scheduled in the policy or unknown); injuries to employees, and damages caused by specific contaminants such as asbestos, lead paint, radioactive materials, radon, and mold. Finally, PLL policies may not offer unlimited legal defense coverage. The costs of defending the insured may be capped or they may be deducted from the overall policy limits. See Ralph A. Demeo, Carl Eldred, Leslie A. Utiger & Lynn S. Scruggs, Insuring Against Environmental Unknowns, 23 J. Land Use & Envt.L. 61 (2007); Ann M. Waeger, Current Insurance Policies for Insuring Against Environmental Risks, SP033 ALI–ABA 1209 (2008). How many different methods have insurers employed in these policies to manage their risk?

8. Much of the fight with respect to both triggers and exclusions surrounds the preliminary question of whether the language in an insurance contract is "ambiguous." In this context, ambiguous is itself an ambiguous term. Perhaps courts can do not better than the Washington Supreme Court when it said that whether language is ambiguous depends on the underlying facts in each case. If this is so, does it mean that it is impossible to draft unambiguous contracts? Is it possible to draft any unambiguous document? Literary deconstructionists would answer with a resounding no. Deconstruction ideas have slowly seeped into legal discourse. See Jack M. Balkin, Deconstruction's Legal Career, 27 Cardozo L.Rev. 719 (2005). Is the task of an insured's lawyer to play the role of a deconstructionist and attempt to render all text unclear? See Peter Nash Swisher, Judicial Interpretations of Insurance Contract Disputes: Toward a Realistic Middle Ground Approach, 57 Ohio St.L.J. 543 (1996).

Jeffrey W. Stempel, The Insurance Policy as Social Instrument and Social Institution, 51 Wm. & Mary L.Rev. 1489 (2010), argues that insurance policies are not merely contracts but also perform risk management, deterrence, and compensation functions important to the general economic and social ordering. Presumably, this means that in reading an insurance contract we should be interested in much more than the intentions of the parties to the contract. If this is correct, does it throw further into doubt the possibility of writing unambiguous contracts?

9. The retroactivity, strict liability, and joint and several liability concerns that have caused insurers to limit or eliminate pollution coverage are not a thing of the past. In the aftermath of the Deepwater Horizon fire and subsequent oil leak in the Gulf of Mexico in May of 2010, many became aware of the fact that the Oil Pollution Liability and Compensation Act of 1990, 33 U.S.C. §§ 2701–20, limits liability for pure economic loss as a result of pollution from an offshore oil facility to $75 million. The limit is waived if an entity is grossly negligent or engages in wilful misconduct. As the facts surrounding the spill emerged over the next several weeks, it seemed possible that BP's decisions leading up to the leak would be found to be grossly negligent and in any event the company promised to pay all "legitimate claims" for pure economic loss. Apparently, BP was self-insured and, therefore, none of these costs or the costs of the cleanup itself were covered by insurance policies.

Other companies involved in the spill did have some insurance. Apparently, Transocean, the owner of the rig, carried $950 million in third party liability insurance. See House Committee on Transportation and Infrastructure, Hearing on the Liability and Financial Responsibility for Oil Spills Under the Oil Pollution Act of 1990 and Related Statutes, available at http:// www.iii.org/assets/docs/pdf/OilSpillsTestimony–060910.pdf. It is unclear whether these policies addressed the question of liability for pure economic loss.

Shortly after the limitations under the Act became public, a number of United States Senators called for retroactively raising the damage cap to $10 billion, over two orders of magnitude greater. The administration expressed support for some as yet unspecified increase. See The Gulf Oil Spill: Effort to Raise BP's Liability Cap Gains Momentum, Wall St. J., May 6, 2010, at A5. As to whether raising the limit retroactively was legally possible, Senator Robert Menendez reportedly said he was confident that this was possible and cited as an example the 30–year–old Superfund law that has forced companies to pay for previously polluted hazardous waste sites. See Raise BP Liability Cap to $10 Billion?, MSNBC, available at http://www.msnbc.msn.com/id/36933743/ns/ us_news-environment/. If such legislation were to be enacted, what effect do you think it would have on the types of insurance policies available for offshore deep water drilling?

10. And what of the future? As we saw in the public nuisance discussion in Chapter 2, litigation over the environmental effect of greenhouse gases is heating up. Do global warming gases come under the absolute pollution exclusion? Why or why not? If your answer is no, should we anticipate that insurance companies will seek to amend their CGL policies to exclude liability for global warming?

CHAPTER XIV

PROCEDURAL ISSUES*

■ ■ ■

Much toxic tort litigation involves complex litigation. These case congregations may include large numbers of claimants dispersed over a large geographic area, require extensive discovery, involve multiple expert witnesses reflecting several different scientific specialties, and raise a variety of difficult factual and legal issues. When the number of claimants totals in the thousands or even in the hundreds of thousands, as occurred in asbestos, the search for mechanisms to adjudicate these claims, often with identical or similar issues, must be undertaken. We address this question in this Chapter. When there are multiple, similarly situated claimants, issue preclusion, which bars a party who has litigated and lost on an issue from relitigating that issue, might assist in providing more efficient resolution of claims for those claimants. Indeed, in the early stages of asbestos litigation, some federal judges attempted to do just that. Class actions are the ultimate aggregation device, presenting the opportunity to resolve large numbers of claims in a single suit. Yet, as we shall see, neither issue preclusion nor the class action device has been very successful in providing the kind of efficient resolution of mass personal injury claims that had been hoped for when they were first employed in toxic tort litigation.

A procedural device that does play an important role in modern complex litigation is the federal Multidistrict Litigation Act and state analogs. These enable the designation of a single judge to preside over all pretrial proceedings in the cases assigned to the judge by the MDL order, providing a significant measure of efficiency during this phase of the cases. A more comprehensive and drastic alternative is bankruptcy, which enables a company beleaguered by tort claims to attempt to resolve all of its tort obligations within bankruptcy court, but at the cost of management conceding the company's financial stress and potentially losing control of the company. Many asbestos defendants chose that course in the still-continuing asbestos litigation saga. In addition to these formal legal devices, many informal practices have developed, including group

---

* Portions of this Chapter are drawn from Fischer, Green, Powers & Sanders, Products Liability (4th ed. 2006).

settlements, that are a response to modern toxic (and other mass) tort litigation.

One widely adopted practice is the consolidation of many individual claims into the hands of lawyers who are first to develop expertise in a particular kind of case. This consolidation is achieved by marketing and through referrals from other lawyers. As the litigation progresses, plaintiffs' lawyers may exchange information or even agree to work together in pursuing their claims against a defendant or an industry. The American Association for Justice facilitates the exchange of information among plaintiffs' lawyers pursuing similar cases. Defense lawyers representing multiple defendants in complex litigation, such as asbestos, may enter into agreements to coordinate their efforts. The most formal of these efforts was the formation of the Center for Claims Resolution, a consortium of 20 asbestos manufacturers who pooled their efforts in defending asbestos cases with other members of the Center. For further elaboration of these informal efforts, see Howard Erichson, Informal Aggregation: Procedural and Ethical Implications of Coordination Among Counsel in Related Litigation, 50 Duke L.J. 381, 386–408 (2000). The seminal coordination effort among multiple counsel occurred in the MER/29 litigation, perhaps the first mass drug products liability case, in the 1960s. See Paul D. Rheingold, The MER/29 Story–An Instance of Successful Mass Disaster Litigation, 56 Cal.L.Rev. 116 (1968).

A. ISSUE PRECLUSION/COLLATERAL ESTOPPEL

As you learned in your Civil Procedure course, the doctrine of issue preclusion (also known as collateral estoppel) is designed to provide efficiency in litigation by barring a party who has litigated and lost on an issue from relitigating that issue in another action. Once having had the opportunity to present her side, it is thought to be fair to the losing party to preclude further efforts to litigate that issue. Issue preclusion can also prevent the embarrassing phenomenon of two different courts deciding the same issue inconsistently.

Issue preclusion's potential to play a significant role in complex litigation became possible with the Supreme Court's decision in Parklane Hosiery Co. v. Shore, 439 U.S. 322 (1979), which sanctioned the offensive use of nonmutual collateral estoppel. This meant that plaintiffs, who were not parties to prior litigation (hence "nonmutuality") in which the defendant litigated and lost on an issue, could bar the defendant from relitigating that issue. For collateral estoppel to be invoked, regardless of mutuality, requires that: (1) the party to be estopped previously litigated and lost on the identical issue; (2) a final judgment was entered against the party; and (3) resolution of that issue was necessary to the judgment against the party. See Restatement (Second) of Judgments § 27.

Recall the *Borel* case in Chapter 4. That was the first case in which an asbestos plaintiff succeeded in recovering damages from asbestos producers. One might think that the jury determinations made in *Borel* that were the basis for the defendants' liability would be sufficient to permit issue preclusion to be invoked against them in future asbestos litigation. Robert Parker, the federal trial judge in the next case, presided over what was at the time the largest asbestos docket in the country—one that grew to several thousand claimants. His decision to invoke issue preclusion principles to control his burgeoning docket is on appeal in the following case.

HARDY v. JOHNS–MANVILLE SALES CORP.

United States Court of Appeals, Fifth Circuit, 1982.
681 F.2d 334.

GEE, CIRCUIT JUDGE:

This appeal arises out of a diversity action brought by various plaintiffs—insulators, pipefitters, carpenters, and other factory workers—against various manufacturers, sellers, and distributors of asbestos-containing products. * * *

Defendants' interlocutory appeal under 28 U.S.C. § 1292(b) is directed instead at the district court's amended omnibus order dated March 13, 1981, which applies collateral estoppel to this mass tort. The omnibus order is, in effect, a partial summary judgment for plaintiffs based on nonmutual offensive collateral estoppel and judicial notice derived from this court's opinion in *Borel v. Fibreboard Paper Products Corp.*, 493 F.2d 1076 (5th Cir.1973), *cert. denied*, 419 U.S. 869, 95 S.Ct. 127, 42 L.Ed.2d 107 (1974) (henceforth *Borel*). *Borel* was a diversity lawsuit in which manufacturers of insulation products containing asbestos were held strictly liable to an insulation worker who developed asbestosis and mesothelioma and ultimately died. The trial court construed *Borel* as establishing as a matter of law and/or of fact that: (1) insulation products containing asbestos as a generic ingredient are "unavoidably unsafe products," (2) asbestos is a competent producing cause of mesothelioma and asbestosis, (3) no warnings were issued by any asbestos insulation manufacturers prior to 1964, and (4) the "warning standard" was not met by the *Borel* defendants in the period from 1964 through 1969. * * *

In *Flatt v. Johns–Manville Sales Corp.*, 488 F.Supp. 836 (E.D.Tex. 1980), the same court outlined the elements of proof for plaintiffs in asbestos-related cases. There the court stated that the plaintiff must prove by a preponderance of the evidence that

 1. Defendants manufactured, marketed, sold, distributed, or placed in the stream of commerce products containing asbestos.

 2. Products containing asbestos are unreasonably dangerous.

 3. Asbestos dust is a competent producing cause of mesothelioma.

 4. Decedent was exposed to defendant's products.

5. The exposure was sufficient to be a producing cause of mesothelioma.

6. Decedent contracted mesothelioma.

7. Plaintiffs suffered damages.

Id. at 838, *citing Restatement (Second) of Torts* § 402A(1) (1965). The parties agree that the effect of the trial court's collateral estoppel order in this case is to foreclose elements 2 and 3 above. Under the terms of the omnibus order, both parties are precluded from presenting evidence on the "state of the art"—evidence that, under Texas law of strict liability, is considered by a jury along with other evidence in order to determine whether as of a given time warning should have been given of the dangers associated with a product placed in the stream of commerce. Under the terms of the order, the plaintiffs need not prove that the defendants either knew or should have known of the dangerous propensities of their products and therefore should have warned consumers of these dangers, defendants being precluded from showing otherwise. On appeal, the defendants contend that the order violates their rights to due process and to trial by jury. Because we conclude that the trial court abused its discretion in applying collateral estoppel and judicial notice, we reverse.

[The court concluded that federal rather than state law governs the application of collateral estoppel in all federal court cases, even those based, as this one was, on diversity of citizenship. However, because this was a diversity case state law provides the substantive law to be applied.]

    * * *

Having determined that federal law of collateral estoppel governs, we next turn to an examination of just what that law is. In *Parklane Hosiery Co. v. Shore*, 439 U.S. 322, 99 S.Ct. 645, 58 L.Ed.2d 552 (1979), the Supreme Court was asked to determine "whether a party who has had issues of fact adjudicated adversely to it in an equitable action may be collaterally estopped from relitigating the same issues before a jury in a subsequent legal action brought against it by a new party." *Id.* at 324. The Court responded affirmatively, noting offensive collateral estoppel's "dual purpose of protecting litigants from the burden of relitigating an identical issue with the same party or his privy and of promoting judicial economy by preventing needless litigation." The Court reiterated that mutuality is not necessary to proper invocation of collateral estoppel under federal law, citing *Blonder–Tongue Laboratories, Inc. v. University of Illinois Foundation*, 402 U.S. 313, 91 S.Ct. 1434, 28 L.Ed.2d 788 (1971), and further held that the use of offensive collateral estoppel does not violate a defendant's seventh amendment right to a jury trial. To avoid problems with the use of the doctrine, the Court adopted a general rule of fairness, stating "that in cases where plaintiff could easily have joined in the earlier action or where ... for other reasons, the application of offensive collateral estoppel would be unfair to a defendant, a trial judge should not allow the use of offensive collateral estoppel." 439 U.S. at 331.

[The court concluded that due process prohibited the use of collateral estoppel against defendants who either were not parties in *Borel* or had settled before trial in *Borel* and therefore had not been subject to an adverse judgement in that case.]

* * *

THE *BOREL* DEFENDANTS

The propriety of estopping the six defendants in this case who were parties to *Borel* poses more difficult questions. In ascertaining the precise preclusive effect of a prior judgment on a particular issue, we have often referred to the requirements set out, *inter alia*, in *International Association of Machinists & Aerospace Workers v. Nix*, 512 F.2d 125, 132 (5th Cir.1975), and cases cited therein. The party asserting the estoppel must show that: (1) the issue to be concluded is identical to that involved in the prior action; (2) in the prior action the issue was "actually litigated"; and (3) the determination made of the issue in the prior action must have been necessary and essential to the resulting judgment.

> If it appears that a judgment may have been based on more than one of several distinctive matters in litigation and there is no indication which issue it was based on or which issue was fully litigated, such judgment will not preclude, under the doctrine of collateral estoppel, relitigation of any of the issues.

Federal Procedure, Lawyers Ed. § 51.218 at 151 (1981) (citations omitted).

Appellants argue that *Borel* did not necessarily decide that asbestos-containing insulation products were unreasonably dangerous because of failure to warn. According to appellants, the general *Borel* verdict, based on general instructions and special interrogatories, permitted the jury to ground strict liability on the bases of failures to test, of unsafeness for intended use, of failures to inspect, or of unsafeness of the product. Strict liability on the basis of failure to warn, although argued to the jury by trial counsel for the plaintiff in *Borel*, was, in the view of the appellants, never formally presented in the jury instructions and therefore was not essential to the *Borel* jury verdict.

Appellants' view has some plausibility. The special interrogatories answered by the *Borel* jury were general and not specifically directed to failure to warn. Indeed, as we discussed at length in our review of the *Borel* judgment, the jury was instructed in terms of "breach of warranty." Although the jury was accurately instructed as to "strict liability in tort" as defined in section 402A of the *Restatement (Second) of Torts*, that phrase was never specifically mentioned in the jury's interrogatories. It is also true that the general instructions to the *Borel* jury on the plaintiff's causes of action did not charge on failure to warn, except in connection with negligence. Yet appellants' argument in its broadest form must ultimately fail. We concluded in *Borel*:

> The jury found that the unreasonably dangerous condition of the defendants' product was the proximate cause of Borel's injury. This

necessarily included a finding that, had adequate warnings been provided, Borel would have chosen to avoid the danger.

As the appellants at times concede in their briefs, "if *Borel* stands for any rule at all, it is that defendants have a duty to warn the users of their products of the long-term dangers attendant upon its use, including the danger of an occupational disease." Indeed, the first sentence in our *Borel* opinion states that that case involved "the scope of an asbestos manufacturer's duty to warn industrial insulation workers of dangers associated with the use of asbestos." *See also* 493 F.2d at 1105 (on rehearing). Our conclusion in *Borel* was grounded in that trial court's jury instructions concerning proximate cause and defective product, which we again set forth in the margin.[10] Close reading of these instructions convinced our panel in *Borel* that a failure to warn was necessarily implicit in the jury's verdict. While the parties invite us to reconsider our holding in *Borel* that failure to warn grounded the jury's strict liability finding in that case, we cannot, even if we were so inclined, displace a prior decision of this court absent reconsideration en banc. * * * Nonetheless, we must ultimately conclude that the judgment in *Borel* cannot estop even the *Borel* defendants in this case for three interrelated reasons.

First, after review of the issues decided in *Borel*, we conclude that *Borel*, while conclusive as to the general matter of a duty to warn on the part of manufacturers of asbestos-containing insulation products, is ultimately ambiguous as to certain key issues. As the authors of the *Restatement (Second)–Judgments* § 29, comment g (1982), have noted, collateral estoppel is inappropriate where the prior judgment is ambivalent:

> The circumstances attending the determination of an issue in the first action may indicate that it could reasonably have been resolved otherwise if those circumstances were absent. Resolution of the issue in question may have entailed reference to such matters as the

---

10. The *Borel* trial court had stated in part:

Now, turning our attention to the matter of the defenses of the defendants in connection with the implied warranty or strict liability, you are charged that if there is any unreasonable risk or danger from using defendants' products containing asbestos, which risk or danger must be *the risk or danger beyond that which would be contemplated by insulation contractor or insulator with the knowledge available to them as to characteristics of the product, such unreasonable risk or danger from using defendants' product must have been reasonably foreseen by the manufacturer.* Therefore, if you find from a preponderance of the evidence that Mr. Borel came in contact with the defendants' product and developed asbestosis thereafter and at such time of contact, the product containing asbestos manufactured by the defendant and that the danger of the use of the said asbestos products by Mr. Borel could not have been reasonably foreseen by the manufacturer, then there could be no proximate cause and your verdict would be for the defendants. In other words, there would be no proximate cause of the breach of the warranty or strict liability that would justify your finding in favor of the plaintiff, but you would have to find for the defendants. Also, in connection with the implied warranty theory, you are instructed that the burden of proof is on the plaintiff in this case. Before they are entitled to recover any damages against any of the defendants to establish by a preponderance of the evidence that the product sold by the particular defendant or defendants was defective at the time it was sold. Before a product can be found to be defective it must establish that it was unreasonably dangerous to the user o(r) consumer at the time it was sold. *You are further instructed that the burden of proof is on the plaintiff to establish also by a preponderance of the evidence not only that the product was defective but also that the defect in the product was a proximate cause of the death of Clarence Borel.* * * *

intention, knowledge, or comparative responsibility of the parties in relation to each other. . . . In these and similar situations, taking the prior determination at face value for purposes of the second action would extend the effects of imperfections in the adjudicative process beyond the limits of the first adjudication, within which they are accepted only because of the practical necessity of achieving finality.

The *Borel* jury decided that Borel, an industrial insulation worker who was exposed to fibers from his employer's insulation products over a 33–year period (from 1936 to 1969), was entitled to have been given fair warning that asbestos dust may lead to asbestosis, mesothelioma, and other cancers. The jury dismissed the argument that the danger was obvious and regarded as conclusive the fact that Borel testified that he did not know that inhaling asbestos dust could cause serious injuries until his doctor so advised him in 1969. The jury necessarily found "that, had adequate warnings been provided, Borel would have chosen to avoid the danger." In *Borel*, the evidence was that the industry as a whole issued no warnings at all concerning its insulation products prior to 1964, that Johns–Manville placed a warnings label on packages of its products in 1964, and that Fibreboard and Rubberoid placed warnings on their products in 1966.

Given these facts, it is impossible to determine what the *Borel* jury decided about *when* a duty to warn attached. Did the jury find the defendants liable because their warnings after 1966, when they acknowledged that they knew the dangers of asbestosis, were insufficiently explicit as to the grave risks involved? If so, as appellants here point out, the jury may have accepted the state of the art arguments provided by the defendants in *Borel*—i.e., that the defendants were not aware of the danger of asbestosis until the 1960's. Even under this view, there is a second ambiguity: was strict liability grounded on the fact that the warnings issued, while otherwise sufficient, never reached the insulator in the field? If so, perhaps the warnings, while insufficient as to insulation workers like Borel, were sufficient to alert workers further down the production line who may have seen the warnings—such as the carpenters and pipefitters in this case. Alternatively, even if the *Borel* jury decided that failure to warn before 1966 grounded strict liability, did the duty attach in the 1930's when the "hazard of asbestosis as a pneumoconiotic dust was universally accepted," or in 1965, when documentary evidence was presented of the hazard of asbestos insulation products to the installers of these products?

As we noted in *Borel*, strict liability because of failure to warn is based on a determination of the manufacturer's reasonable knowledge:

> [I]n cases such as the instant case, the manufacturer is held to the knowledge and skill of an expert. This is relevant in determining (1) whether the manufacturer knew or should have known the danger, and (2) whether the manufacturer was negligent in failing to communicate this superior knowledge to the user or consumer of its prod-

uct.... The manufacturer's status as expert means that at a minimum he must keep abreast of scientific knowledge, discoveries, and advances and is presumed to know what is imparted thereby.

493 F.2d at 1089. Thus, the trial judge in *Borel* instructed the jury that the danger "must have been reasonably foreseen by the manufacturer." As both this instruction and the ambiguities in the *Borel* verdict demonstrate, a determination that a particular product is so unreasonably hazardous as to require a warning of its dangers is not an absolute. Such a determination is necessarily relative to the scientific knowledge generally known or available to the manufacturer at the time the product in question was sold or otherwise placed in the stream of commerce.

Not all the plaintiffs in this case were exposed to asbestos-containing insulation products over the same 30–year period as plaintiff Borel. Not all plaintiffs here are insulation workers isolated from the warnings issued by some of the defendants in 1964 and 1966. Some of the products may be different from those involved in *Borel*. Our opinion in *Borel*, "limited to determining whether there [was] a conflict in substantial evidence sufficient to create a jury question," did not resolve that as a matter of fact all manufacturers of asbestos-containing insulation products had a duty to warn as of 1936, and all failed to warn adequately after 1964. Although we determined that the jury must have found a violation of the manufacturers' duty to warn, we held only that the jury could have grounded strict liability on the absence of a warning prior to 1964 or "could have concluded that the [post–1964 and post–1966] 'cautions' were not warnings in the sense that they adequately communicated to Borel and other insulation workers knowledge of the dangers to which they were exposed so as to give them a choice of working or not working with a dangerous product." As we have already had occasion to point out in *Migues v. Fibreboard Corp.*, 662 F.2d at 1188–89, * * *:

> The *only* determination made by this court in *Borel* was that, based upon the evidence in that case, the jury's findings could not be said to be incorrect as a matter of law. But this Court certainly did not decide that every jury presented with the same facts would be compelled to reach the conclusion reached by the *Borel* jury: that asbestos was unreasonably dangerous. Such a holding would have been not only unnecessary, it would also have been unwarranted.
>
> In *Borel*, this Court said: "the jury was *entitled* to find that the danger to Borel and other insulation workers from inhaling asbestos dust was foreseeable to the defendants at the time the products causing Borel's injuries were sold." This Court did not say that, as a matter of law, the danger of asbestos inhalation was so hidden from every asbestos worker in every situation as to create a duty to warn on the part of all asbestos manufacturers. * * * This Court did not state that every jury would be required, as a matter of law, to find such warnings inadequate. * * *
>
> * * *

Id. (emphasis in original). Like *stare decisis*, collateral estoppel applies only to issues of fact or law necessarily decided by a prior court. Since we cannot say that *Borel* necessarily decided, as a matter of fact, that all manufacturers of asbestos-containing insulation products knew or should have known of the dangers of their particular products at all relevant times, we cannot justify the trial court's collaterally estopping the defendants from presenting evidence as to the state of the art.

Even if we are wrong as to the ambiguities of the *Borel* judgment, there is a second, equally important, reason to deny collateral estoppel effect to it: the presence of inconsistent verdicts. In *Parklane Hosiery v. Shore*, 439 U.S. at 330–31, the Court noted that collateral estoppel is improper and "unfair" to a defendant "if the judgment relied upon as a basis for the estoppel is itself inconsistent with one or more previous judgments in favor of the defendant." *Id.* at 330. *Accord Restatement (Second)–Judgments* § 29(4) (1982).[13] Not only does issue preclusion in such cases appear arbitrary to a defendant who has had favorable judgments on the same issue, it also undermines the premise that different juries reach equally valid verdicts. *See Restatement (Second)–Judgments* § 29, comment f (1982). One jury's determination should not, merely because it comes later in time, bind another jury's determination of an issue over which there are equally reasonable resolutions of doubt.

The trial court was aware of the problem and referred to *Flatt v. Johns–Manville Sales Corp.*, 488 F.Supp. at 841, a prior opinion by the same court. In *Flatt* the court admitted that Johns–Manville had "successfully defended several asbestos lawsuits in the recent past" but stated that "lawsuits in which Johns–Manville has prevailed have been decided on the basis that there was insufficient exposure to asbestos dust, or alternatively, the plaintiff, or decedent, did not contract asbestosis or mesothelioma." Given the information made available to us in this appeal, we must conclude that the trial court in *Flatt* and in the proceeding below was inadequately informed about the nature of former asbestos litigation. On appeal, the parties inform us that there have been approximately 70 similar asbestos cases thus far tried around the country. Approximately half of these seem to have been decided in favor of the defendants. A court able to say that the approximately 35 suits decided in favor of asbestos manufacturers were all decided on the basis of insufficient exposure on the part of the plaintiff or failure to demonstrate an asbestos-related disease would be clairvoyant. Indeed, the appellants inform us of several products liability cases in which the state of the art question was fully litigated, yet the asbestos manufacturers were found not liable. Although it is usually not possible to say with certainty what these juries based

---

13. The injustice of applying collateral estoppel in cases involving mass torts is especially obvious. Thus, in *Parklane* the Court cited Prof. Currie's "familiar example": "A railroad collision injures 50 passengers all of whom bring separate actions against the railroad. After the railroad wins the first 25 suits, a plaintiff wins in suit 26. Professor Currie argues that offensive use of collateral estoppel should not be applied so as to allow plaintiffs 27 through 50 automatically to recover." 439 U.S. at 331 n.14, 99 S.Ct. at 651 n.14, *citing* Currie, *Mutuality of Estoppel: Limits of the Bernhard Doctrine*, 9 Stan.L.Rev. 281, 304 (1957).

their verdicts on, in at least some of the cases the verdict for the defendant was not based on failure to prove exposure or failure to show an asbestos-related disease. In *Starnes v. Johns–Manville Corp.*, No. 2075–122 (E.D.Tenn.1977), one of the cases cited in *Flatt v. Johns–Manville Sales Corp.*, *supra*, the court's charge to the jury stated that it was "undisputed that as a result of inhaling materials containing asbestos, Mr. Starnes contracted the disease known as asbestosis." The verdict for the defendant in *Starnes* must mean, inter alia, that the jury found the insulation products involved in that case not unreasonably dangerous. This court takes judicial notice of these inconsistent or ambiguous verdicts pursuant to Fed.R.Evid. 201(d). We conclude that the court erred in arbitrarily choosing one of these verdicts, that in *Borel*, as the bellwether.

Finally, we conclude that even if the *Borel* verdict had been unambiguous and the sole verdict issued on point, application of collateral estoppel would still be unfair with regard to the *Borel* defendants because it is very doubtful that these defendants could have foreseen that their $68,000 liability to plaintiff Borel would foreshadow multimillion dollar asbestos liability. As noted in *Parklane*, it would be unfair to apply collateral estoppel "if a defendant in the first action is sued for small or nominal damages [since] he may have little incentive to defend vigorously, particularly if future lawsuits are not foreseeable." 439 U.S. at 330. * * * The reason the district court here applied collateral estoppel is precisely because early cases like *Borel* have opened the floodgates to an enormous, unprecedented volume of asbestos litigation. According to a recent estimate, there are over 3,000 asbestos plaintiffs in the Eastern District of Texas alone and between 7,500 and 10,000 asbestos cases pending in United States District Courts around the country. The omnibus order here involves 58 pending cases, and the many plaintiffs involved in this case are *each* seeking $2.5 million in damages. Such a staggering potential liability could not have been foreseen by the *Borel* defendants.

* * *

Like the court in *Migues*, we too sympathize with the district court's efforts to streamline the enormous asbestos caseload it faces. None of what we say here is meant to cast doubt on any possible alternative ways to avoid reinventing the asbestos liability wheel. We reiterate the *Migues* court's invitation to district courts to attempt innovative methods for trying these cases. We hold today only that courts cannot read *Borel* to stand for the proposition that, as matters of fact, asbestos products are unreasonably dangerous or that asbestos as a generic element is in all products a competent producing cause of cancer. To do otherwise would be to elevate judicial expedience over considerations of justice and fair play.

REVERSED.

NOTES AND QUESTIONS

1. The *Hardy* court provided three reasons why collateral estoppel was improperly imposed on the *Borel* defendants and an additional reason why it was improperly applied to the non-*Borel* defendants. Do you suppose the trial judge failed to appreciate the problems with his estoppel order in *Hardy*?

2. *The impact of jury compromise.* Does the $68,000 damage award in *Borel* for a worker who suffered from asbestosis before dying from mesothelioma suggest that the outcome may have been the result of a jury compromise? Does this undermine the legitimacy of employing collateral estoppel in future cases, aside from the problems noted by the *Hardy* court? See Taylor v. Hawkinson, 306 P.2d 797 (Cal.1957). Given the bar on inquiring into what went on during jury deliberations, how can courts even determine if a verdict was a compromise, much less consider whether a compromise should affect the future availability of estoppel? Cf. Mekdeci v. Merrell Nat'l Labs., 711 F.2d 1510 (11th Cir.1983). Paul Brodeur, who subsequently wrote about the asbestos industry and litigation, reports that the *Borel* verdict was the product of an effort to obtain unanimity in the face of a stubborn juror who resisted finding against the defendants. Paul Brodeur, Outrageous Misconduct 64 (1985).

3. How persuasive is the *Hardy* court's claim that the defendants in *Borel* could not have foreseen substantial future asbestos litigation? *Borel* was the second asbestos case brought. After a modest $68,000 damage award, the defendants aggressively attempted to overturn it. They appealed to the Fifth Circuit Court of Appeals, petitioned for rehearing en banc, and ultimately sought certiorari from the U.S. Supreme Court, all in a case that involved errors on state law matters, posing a very unlikely scenario for the Supreme Court to grant discretionary review. Given the timing of *Parklane Hosiery*, is there a stronger claim that the *Borel* defendants could not have anticipated that they might be collaterally estopped based on that judgment in future cases? If so, should it matter?

4. What strategical considerations are created by the fact that, if plaintiff is successful in obtaining a final judgment, the potential cost to defendant goes far beyond the actual amount of the judgment? This occurs both through the risk of future collateral estoppel as well as the likelihood that the judgment may signal to other potential claimants and their lawyers that pursuing their claims may be fruitful. How would you expect the first plaintiff and defendant to respond to these considerations? For a particularly tawdry episode, which involved a plaintiff's agreement to "tank" at trial and thereby suffer an adverse jury verdict in exchange for a side (and secret) payment by the defendant, see Potter v. Eli Lilly & Co., 926 S.W.2d 449 (Ky.1996).

5. Consider the development of scientific evidence on the question of causation in the Bendectin and breast implant litigations addressed in Chapters 3 and 5. Does that changing and apparently improving body of evidence raise concerns about employing issue preclusion on questions of causation? What about the *Hardy* trial judge's ruling that defendants could be estopped on the issue of whether asbestos was a cause of mesothelioma?

6. The difficulty in finding common issues among asbestos cases serves as a caution about commonality for other aggregative procedural devices. Keep this in mind as you proceed through the remainder of the materials in this Chapter.

7. *The role for issue preclusion in resolving mass toxic torts.* Given the decisions contrary to *Borel* referred to by the *Hardy* court, was there ever any hope for collateral estoppel to assist in resolving the glut of asbestos cases that choked the federal and some state courts? Or are other procedural and/or substantive rules required? How about a federal asbestos compensation scheme? See Roger H. Trangsrud, Joinder Alternatives in Mass Tort Litigation, 70 Cornell L.Rev. 779, 815 (1985) ("while offensive collateral estoppel may contribute to the fair and efficient adjudication of some cases, its limited utility in most mass tort cases makes it unsuitable as a primary technique for the management of mass tort litigations"); Michael D. Green, The Inability of Offensive Collateral Estoppel to Fulfill Its Promise: An Examination of Estoppel in Asbestos Litigation, 70 Iowa L.Rev. 141, 224 (1984) ("collateral estoppel has little potential to make a significant contribution in resolving the judicial administration difficulties engendered by asbestos litigation").

8. Our evaluation of the fairness of aggregative devices for resolving recurring issues in complex litigation is surely informed by our confidence that these devices provide "correct" resolutions of the disputed issues. One fascinating experiment that raises serious questions about "correct" resolutions is a trial undertaken by the same trial judge as in *Hardy.* Judge Parker consolidated five plaintiffs' cases for trial against a total of 12 defendants. Five separate juries were impaneled, one assigned to each plaintiff's case. Each jury was present in the courtroom for all proceedings. Only questions common to all cases were tried, including when the defendants should have know of the dangers of their asbestos products and whether some 100 products were defective. Each jury rendered a verdict for the case to which it was assigned. While the juries' findings were consistent on some items—ones that engendered very little dispute between the parties—some findings were stunningly varied. Answers to the question inquiring when an asbestos manufacturer should have had knowledge of the danger of asbestos exposure ranged from 1935 to 1965, with 1946 and two 1964's comprising the other three findings. Three juries decided whether nine Nicolet products were defective in design; one jury found all nine were defective in design at some time, while two juries found none of the products was defective in design. Although all of the juries found at least some products were marketed at some time without adequate warnings, there was substantial disagreement as to which products required warnings, whether a subsequently provided warning was adequate, and, most significantly, the evaluative determination of whether the failure to provide an adequate warning rendered those products defective. A summary of the juries' findings on the questions presented to them is summarized below:

Jury Interrogatories	Jury 1	Jury 2	Jury 3	Jury 4	Jury 5
1. Can occupational exposure to asbestos cause:					
(a) Asbestosis	(a) Yes	(a) Yes	(a) Yes	(a) Yes	(a) Yes
(b) Mesothelioma	(b) Yes	(b) Yes	(b) Yes	(b) Yes	(b) Yes
(c) Lung Cancer?	(c) Yes	(c) Yes	(c) Yes	(c) Yes	(c) Yes

2. Is occupational exposure to asbestos the sole cause of:					
(a) Asbestosis (b) Mesothelioma (c) Lung Cancer?	(a) Yes (b) Yes (c) Yes	(a) Yes (b) No (c) No	(a) Yes (b) Yes (c) Yes	(a) Yes (b) Yes (c) Yes	(a) Yes (b) No (c) No
3. Products unreasonably dangerous due to design.	All of the products	None of the products	No answer given	Some of the products[1]	Some of the products[1]
4. Date on which the defendant should have reasonably foreseen the dangers associated with occupational exposure to asbestos products	1946	1965	1935	1964	Jan. 1965
5. Products marketed without adequate warning.	All of the products	Some of the products	All of the products	Some of the products[2]	Some of the products[2]
6. Did failure to provide adequate warning make the product unreasonably dangerous?	All of the products	None of the products	All of the products	Some of the products[3]	Some of the products[3]
7. Was Johns–Manville grossly negligent?	N/A	No	Yes	No	Yes

1. Of the 102 products, Jury 4 and Jury 5 found consistently with regard to 38 and disagreed on the remaining 64.

2. Of the 102 products, Jury 4 and Jury 5 found consistently with regard to 13 and disagreed on the remaining 89.

3. Because of a number of "no" answers to interrogatory number 5, Jury 5 only answered this interrogatory for 12 products; Jury 4 and Jury 5 agreed on 11 of the 12 products that they both made findings on.

See Green, supra, 70 Iowa L.Rev. at 221–23; see also Byron G. Stier, Another Jackpot (In)justice: Verdict Variability and Issue Preclusion in Mass Torts, 36 Pepp.L.Rev.715 (2009) (examining verdict variability in a variety of mass litigations and the implications for issue preclusion).

B. MULTIDISTRICT LITIGATION

In the wake of complex but related antitrust litigation in the early 1960s that was filed in many different federal district courts, a committee of federal judges was formed to oversee discovery proceedings in those multiple actions. From that experience, Congress enacted the Multidistrict Litigation Act, 28 U.S.C. § 1407, which is frequently invoked when related litigation has been filed in multiple federal district courts. The multidistrict statute permits cases that have been filed in different federal district courts that have a common question to be moved to a single district and judge for pretrial proceedings. Once a multidistrict court is established, later filed cases that share the same issue can be transferred as "tag along" cases.

28 U.S.C. § 1407

§ 1407. Multidistrict litigation

(a) When civil actions involving one or more common questions of fact are pending in different districts, such actions may be transferred to any district for coordinated or consolidated pretrial proceedings. Such transfers shall be made by the judicial panel on multidistrict litigation authorized by this section upon its determination that transfers for such proceedings will be for the convenience of parties and witnesses and will promote the just and efficient conduct of such actions. Each action so transferred shall be remanded by the panel at or before the conclusion of such pretrial proceedings to the district from which it was transferred unless it shall have been previously terminated: Provided, however, That the panel may separate any claim, cross-claim, counter-claim, or third-party claim and remand any of such claims before the remainder of the action is remanded.

(b) Such coordinated or consolidated pretrial proceedings shall be conducted by a judge or judges to whom such actions are assigned by the judicial panel on multidistrict litigation. * * *

(c) Proceedings for the transfer of an action under this section may be initiated by—

(i) the judicial panel on multidistrict litigation upon its own initiative, or

(ii) motion filed with the panel by a party in any action in which transfer for coordinated or consolidated pretrial proceedings under this section may be appropriate. * * *

* * *

The multidistrict litigation statute permits resolution of all pretrial matters in the transferee court. What it does not authorize, however, is for trial to proceed in the transferee court. See Lexecon Inc. v. Milberg, Weiss, Bershad, Hynes & Lerach, 523 U.S. 26 (1998). At the conclusion of pretrial proceedings, cases are remanded to the district in which they were filed for trial, unless there is another basis (e.g., consent of the parties or forum non conveniens transfers) for retaining the case for trial in the transferee district. However, because of settlement and dispositive pretrial rulings, very few cases are in fact remanded to their home districts for trial. In addition to the federal statute, a number of states have their own provisions for centralized control of pretrial proceedings of related but dispersed cases. For example, New Jersey authorizes the designation of a group of cases to constitute a "mass tort," which then is subject to centralized oversight (including trial). New Jersey Court Rule 4:38A. See generally Mark Herrmann, Geoffrey J. Ritts & Katherine Larson, State-wide Coordinated Proceedings: State Court Analogues to the Federal MDL Process (2d ed.2004); Yvette Ostolaza & Michelle Hartmann, Overview of Multidistrict Litigation Rules at the State and Federal Level, 26 Rev.Litig. 47 (2007).

The Multidistrict Panel has virtually unlimited discretion in deciding whether to transfer actions for coordinated or consolidated pretrial proceedings and in determining where to transfer the cases and which judge should preside over them (as a matter of informal practice, the Panel secures the agreement of the district judge to whom it proposes to transfer cases before doing so). Parties may seek transfer but the statute authorizes the Panel to transfer cases on its own motion.

IN RE SILICONE GEL BREAST IMPLANTS PRODUCTS LIABILITY LITIGATION

Judicial Panel on Multidistrict Litigation, 1992.
793 F.Supp. 1098.

OPINION AND ORDER

The record before us suggests that more than a million women have received silicone gel breast implants. Since the Food and Drug Administration held highly publicized hearings a few months ago about the safety of this product, a rush to the courthouse has ensued, although some litigation concerning the product has periodically been filed in the federal courts in the last several years.

This litigation presently consists of * * * 78 actions * * * pending in 33 federal districts * * *. Before the Panel are four separate motions pursuant to 28 U.S.C. § 1407: 1) motion of plaintiffs in three Northern District of California actions to centralize all actions in the Northern District of California or any other appropriate transferee forum (these plaintiffs now favor centralization in the Southern District of Ohio); 2) motion of plaintiffs in one Northern District of California action to centralize all actions in that district; 3) motion of plaintiffs in seven actions to centralize all actions in either the Northern District of California or the District of Kansas; and 4) motion of plaintiffs in the Eastern District of Virginia action (*Schiavone*) to centralize in that district the medical monitoring claims that are presented in seven purported class actions.

The overwhelming majority of the more than 200 responses received by the Panel supports transfer. The major issue presented in the responses is selection of the transferee forum, with two large groups of parties aligned in favor of opposing views. The first large group of parties favors selection of either the Northern District of California (Judge Thelton E. Henderson or Judge Marilyn H. Patel) or the District of Kansas (Judge Patrick F. Kelly). This group includes 1) plaintiffs in at least 65 of the 78 actions before the Panel; 2) plaintiffs in at least 69 potential tag-along actions; and 3) approximately 250 attorneys who are purportedly investigating claims of more than 2,000 potential plaintiffs. The second large group of parties favors selection of the Southern District of Ohio (Judge Carl B. Rubin). This group includes 1) plaintiffs in nine of the 78 actions before the Panel; 2) plaintiffs in at least nine potential tag-along actions; 3) approximately 75 law firms that purport to represent 4,000 actual and potential plaintiffs; and 4) sixteen defendants, including major silicone gel breast implant manufacturers Dow Corning Corporation (Dow Corning), Baxter Healthcare Corporation, McGhan Medical Corporation (McGhan), Bristol–Meyers Squibb Company and Mentor Corporation (Mentor).

Miscellaneous responses received by the Panel include i) opposition of plaintiff in one Colorado action to transfer of her action (*Reid*), ii) opposition of defendant General Electric Company to transfer of the four actions in which it is a party, iii) opposition of plaintiffs in four potential tag-along actions to transfer of their actions, and iv) support of plaintiffs in one action for the motion of the *Schiavone* plaintiffs.

On the basis of the papers filed and the hearing held, the Panel finds that the actions in this litigation involve common questions of fact and that centralization under Section 1407 in the Northern District of Alabama before Chief Judge Sam C. Pointer, Jr., will best serve the convenience of the parties and witnesses and promote the just and efficient conduct of this litigation. The actions present complex common questions of fact, as nearly all responding parties have acknowledged, on the issue of liability for allegedly defective silicone gel breast implants. Centralization under Section 1407 is thus necessary in order to avoid duplication of discovery, prevent inconsistent pretrial rulings, and conserve the resources of the parties, their counsel and the judiciary.

We are not persuaded by various parties' requests for exclusion of certain actions or claims or for creation of a separate multidistrict litigation to handle medical monitoring claims. We point out that transfer under Section 1407 has the salutary effect of placing all actions in this docket before a single judge who can formulate a pretrial program that: 1) allows discovery with respect to any non-common issues to proceed concurrently with discovery on common issues, *In re Multi–Piece Rim Products Liability Litigation*, 464 F.Supp. 969, 974 (J.P.M.L. 1979); and 2) ensures that pretrial proceedings will be conducted in a manner leading to the just and expeditious resolution of all actions to the overall benefit of the parties. It may be, on further refinement of the issues and close scrutiny by the transferee judge, that some claims or actions can be remanded in advance of the other actions in the transferee district. But we are unwilling, on the basis of the record before us, to make such a determination at this time. Should the transferee judge deem remand of any claims or actions appropriate, procedures are available whereby this may be accomplished with a minimum of delay. *See* Rule 14, R.P.J.P.M.L., 120 F.R.D. 251, 259–61 (1988).

Selection of the transferee court and judge for this litigation has been a challenging task. The parties' arguments in their briefs and at the Panel hearing in this matter have focused primarily on the relative merits of the suggested California and Ohio forums. Proponents of the California forum stress that i) both Judge Henderson and Judge Patel have tried breast implant actions and are thus very familiar with the issues raised in this docket, ii) several implant manufacturers, including McGhan and Mentor, have their principal places of business in California, and iii) California is presumptively the state with the largest number of actual and potential claimants in the breast implant litigation. Meanwhile, proponents of the Ohio forum emphasize Judge Rubin's familiarity with the litigation, gained by presiding over the consolidated breast implant action (*Dante*) in his district since January 1992. During that time, Judge Rubin has conditionally certified a nationwide, opt-out class of breast implant recipients; established a document depository; appointed a Plaintiffs' Lead Counsel Committee consisting of seven members; scheduled trial on common issues for June 1993; and initiated the dissemination of notice to class members.

We observe that either the Northern District of California or the Southern District of Ohio could be an appropriate forum for this docket and certainly the judges referred to are experienced and well-qualified to handle this litigation. We are troubled, however, by the volume and tone of the negative arguments with which opposing counsel have sought to denigrate each other's forum choices, litigation strategies and underlying motives. A brief recitation of a few of these arguments sufficiently conveys their flavor. For example, various parties argue that 1) parties in the Ohio forum have engendered a flurry of pretrial activity in an effort to dictate our decision on selection of the transferee court; 2) the class in the Southern District of Ohio was certified in a precipitous fashion, without according adequate notice or opportunity to be heard to interested parties nationwide; 3) defendants oppose the California forum only because the two trials there resulted in substantial verdicts against one of them; and 4) the plaintiffs who favor the California forum are forum shopping for a judge who has tried a breast implant action in which plaintiffs prevailed.

Essentially, these arguments are fueled by an acrimonious dispute among counsel, relating to control of the litigation as well as to how it should proceed (class versus individual treatment). It is neither our function nor our inclination to take sides in this dispute. But we are indeed persuaded that the level of acrimony has caused the parties and counsel on each side to harbor a perception that they would be unfairly affected by selection of any of the suggested forums. This perception of "unfairness" is unwarranted, because this Panel believes that all of the federal judges involved in these 78 actions would conduct these proceedings in a fair and impartial manner. Nevertheless, we recognize that in a mega-tort docket of this nature, involving claimants who may be experiencing litigation for the first time, such a perception could become a dark cloud over these proceedings and threaten their just and efficient conduct.

In light of these considerations, we have determined to look beyond the preferences of the parties in our search for a transferee judge with the ability and temperament to steer this complex litigation on a steady course that will be sensitive to the concerns of all parties. Because no single location stands out as the geographic focal point for this nationwide docket, the scope of our search embraced the universe of federal district judges. By selecting Chief Judge Pointer, a former member of our Panel,

Chairman of the Board of Editors of the Manual for Complex Litigation, Chairman of the Judicial Conference's Advisory Committee on Civil Rules, and an experienced multidistrict transferee judge, we are confident that we are entrusting this important and challenging assignment to a distinguished jurist. We urge all parties and counsel to work cooperatively with one another and with Judge Pointer toward the goal of a just, efficient and expeditious resolution of the litigation.

IT IS THEREFORE ORDERED that, pursuant to 28 U.S.C. § 1407, the actions listed on the following Schedule A be, and the same hereby are, transferred to the Northern District of Alabama and, with the consent of that court, assigned to the Honorable Sam C. Pointer, Jr., for coordinated or consolidated pretrial proceedings.

NOTES AND QUESTIONS

1. By 1996, over 20,000 cases had been transferred to Judge Pointer as part of the Silicone Gel Breast Implant Multidistrict Litigation. By that time, Judge Pointer had also remanded several of the early cases to their transferor districts, including the *Hall* case which is reproduced in Chapter 5. That year is also the one in which Judge Pointer appointed several experts, designated the "National Science Panel," to evaluate the scientific evidence on whether breast implants caused connective joint disease. In re Silicone Gel Breast Implant Prods. Liab. Litig. (MDL 926), 1996 WL 34401813 (N.D.Ala.). The Panel's makeup and report are addressed in note 1 following *Hall*.

2. Why might a "bit" defendant like General Electric oppose consolidation of the four cases in which it was involved in the multidistrict proceeding?

3. If consolidated discovery is to take place, some decision will have to be made as to who, among the various plaintiffs' counsel, will conduct various aspects of discovery. Normally the transferee judge appoints a lead and liaison counsel; often a plaintiffs' steering committee is appointed as well, as the Panel mentioned had already occurred in the class action certified in the Southern District of Ohio. If the cases are then returned to the transferor districts where they began, how will lead and liaison counsel be paid for their work on consolidated discovery? See In re Phenylpropanolamine (PPA) Prods. Liab. Litig., 2009 WL 6042809 (W.D.Wash.); Federal Judicial Center, Manual for Complex Litigation § 14.215, at 202 (4th ed. 2004). Is the dispute referred to by the Panel over whether the litigation should proceed through class or individual treatment relevant to this question?

4. As the *Silicone Gel Breast Implant Litigation* reveals, the parties have a great deal at stake in where a Multidistrict Litigation proceeds and before whom. For an investigation into the factors that influence the Multidistrict Panel as to where and to whom it transfers cases, see Margaret S. Williams & Tracey E. George, Between Cases and Classes: The Decision to Consolidate Multidistrict Litigation (2009), available at SSRN:http://ssrn.com/abstract–1443377. The chief judge of the Multidistrict Panel explains the Panel's operation and approach to transfers in John G. Heyburn, A View of the Panel: Part of the Solution, 82 Tul. L.Rev. 2225 (2008).

5. Section 1407 obviously cannot provide universal pretrial procedures for all related cases because it does not include state court cases. Cases filed in state court that are not removable, either because plaintiff and the manufacturer are not diverse or, as occurs when plaintiff wants to keep the case in state court, a local person, such as a retailer or physician, is joined as a defendant, defeating diversity and thus keeping the case outside the ambit of section 1407. Nevertheless, beginning with asbestos litigation, state and federal MDL judges have developed a number of informal cooperative strategies, including sitting together to hear motions that are common to both the state and federal cases. See Barbara J. Rothstein et al., A Model Mass Tort: The PPA Experience, 54 Drake L.Rev. 621 (2006) (describing joint hearing held by federal MDL judge and several state court judges to determine the admissibility of expert testimony in cases claiming that PPA, a common ingredient in over-the-counter medication, causes strokes); Federal Judicial Center, National Center for State Courts & State Justice Institute, Manual for Cooperation Between State and Federal Courts (1997).

C. CLASS ACTIONS

An important aspect of class actions is that they provide an exception to the due process rule that requires that before individuals may be "bound" by a judgment, they must have been provided notice and an opportunity to be heard in court. Members of a class may be bound even though they are not afforded an opportunity to be heard and notice may not be provided. Being bound means that res judicata and collateral estoppel are applicable to all class members by virtue of their having adequate representation in a class action. See Hansberry v. Lee, 311 U.S. 32 (1940). Thus, if a class action is unsuccessful, the members of the class are bound by res judicata and may not sue later in individual actions.

When the modern class action rules were written in 1966, they were conceived of as a device for effectuating litigation. Small claims that were not individually viable because the costs of litigating them would not justify the small or modest stakes were the target, at least for Rule 23(b)(3) class actions. Rule 23 reveals a clear preference for individual litigation, except where there are good reasons for deviating from it. Effectuating litigation that could not proceed on an individual basis was the model. In addition to favoring individual litigation, the Advisory Committee comments in 1966 reveal that the class action device was thought unsuitable for mass torts:

> A "mass accident" resulting in injuries to numerous persons is ordinarily not appropriate for a class action because of the likelihood that significant questions, not only of damages but of liability and defenses of liability, would be present, affecting the individuals in different ways. In these circumstances an action conducted nominally as a class action would degenerate in practice into multiple lawsuits separately tried.

Fed.R.Civ.P. 23 advisory committee notes (1966).

Notwithstanding the Advisory Committee's view, the quantity of cases in a number of mass torts and the efforts of a number of plaintiffs' attorneys, beginning with the Beverly Hills Supper Club litigation, In re Beverly Hills Fire Litigation, 695 F.2d 207 (6th Cir.1982), caused courts to reconsider of the propriety of class action treatment of mass torts.

Rule 23. Class Actions

(a) Prerequisites to a Class Action. One or more members of a class may sue or be sued as representative parties on behalf of all only if

(1) the class is so numerous that joinder of all members is impracticable,

(2) there are questions of law or fact common to the class,

(3) the claims or defenses of the representative parties are typical of the claims or defenses of the class, and

(4) the representative parties will fairly and adequately protect the interests of the class.

(b) Class Actions Maintainable. An action may be maintained as a class action if the prerequisites of subdivision (a) are satisfied, and in addition:

(1) the prosecution of separate actions by or against individual members of the class would create a risk of

(A) inconsistent or varying adjudications with respect to individual members of the class which would establish incompatible standards of conduct for the party opposing the class, or

(B) adjudications with respect to individual members of the class which would as a practical matter be dispositive of the interests of the other members not parties to the adjudications or substantially impair or impede their ability to protect their interests; or

(2) the party opposing the class has acted or refused to act on grounds generally applicable to the class, thereby making appropriate final injunctive relief or corresponding declaratory relief with respect to the class as a whole; or

(3) the court finds that the questions of law or fact common to the members of the class predominate over any questions affecting only individual members, and that a class action is superior to other available methods for the fair and efficient adjudication of the controversy. The matters pertinent to the findings include: (A) the interest of members of the class in individually controlling the prosecution or defense of separate actions; (B) the extent and nature of any litigation concerning the controversy already commenced by or against members of the class; (C) the desirability or undesirability of concentrating the litigation of the claims in the particular forum; (D) the difficulties likely to be encountered in the management of a class action.

* * *

BURKHEAD v. LOUISVILLE GAS & ELECTRIC CO.

United States District Court, Western District of Kentucky, 2008.
250 F.R.D. 287.

JOHN G. HEYBURN, II, CHIEF JUDGE.

Plaintiffs are all residents of areas surrounding a power plant operated by Louisville Gas & Electric ("LG & E"), who have filed suit against Defendant seeking monetary and injunctive relief for damage allegedly resulting from fallout and noxious odors emitted by that facility. Specifically, Plaintiffs proceed under theories of nuisance, negligence and/or gross negligence, strict liability for ultrahazardous activities, and trespass.

Currently before the Court is Plaintiffs' motion for class certification, which Defendant has opposed. The parties have briefed the issue and on March 3, 2008 the Court heard oral arguments. Deciding issues of class certification in cases such as this inevitably involves the exercise of care, judgment and appropriate discretion. The Court has attempted to employ proper doses of each and, at every turn, to clearly explain its reasoning. This consideration should not be viewed as a proxy for any decision on the merits of Plaintiffs' claims.

Having considered the briefs, oral arguments, and evidentiary record, the Court finds Plaintiffs' motion to be deficient in several significant ways, and therefore, the Court will deny the motion.

I.

Named Plaintiffs, over seventy (70) residents of an area near LG & E's Louisville, Kentucky facility, have alleged that emissions from LG & E's operations in the plant have invaded their property in the form of particulate matter ("fallout") and noxious odors. The Court must take as true their testimony about the nature of the fallout on their property, but cannot give particular credence to a belief that any aspect of the fallout came from the LG & E plant. This would be for others with more specialized knowledge to suggest.

Plaintiffs characterize the fallout blanketing their property variably as [a variety of black and white contaminants]. Descriptions of the odors are similarly varied and include burnt rawhide, dirty gym socks, acid, a burning smell, sweet/foul, formaldehyde, burned electrical wire, vinegary, burning hard plastic, barnyard, fingernail polish remover, burning rubber, fish, sewer, sulfur, ammonia, chlorine, cod liver oil, horse manure, skunk, glue, mildew, mold, gas, rotten eggs, garbage, bleach, and urine.

Plaintiffs seek certification under Rules 23(b)(2) and 23(b)(3) of the Federal Rules of Civil Procedure of a class defined as follows:

> Owners or residents of single family residences within two miles of the LG & E Cane Run facility, whose property was damaged by noxious odors, fallout, pollutants and contaminants which originated from the LG & E Cane Run facility located in Louisville, Kentucky

and who have owned or resided at that single family residential home from May 9, 2003 to the present and continuing.

Plaintiffs estimate that this class may consist of as many as 14,294 people or more, and assert that for this and other reasons, the requirements of Rules 23(b)(2) and 23(b)(3) are met.

LG & E is an electric and natural gas utility. LG & E's Cane Run facility is a 510–acre coal-fired electrical generating plant. As part of its operations at the plant, LG & E burns approximately 1.3 million tons of coal annually and stores piles of coal on-site. The coal combustion process causes emissions from the plant's smokestacks which Plaintiffs allege have carried hazardous materials onto their property in the form of odors and particulate matter. LG & E has opposed class certification, arguing among other things that the proposed class definition is flawed, that the proposed class representatives do not raise claims typical of those of the class, and that individual issues will predominate over common ones, making Plaintiffs' claims unsuited for class adjudication.

II.

The Court recently had an opportunity to consider the issue of class certification in a very similar case also litigated by Plaintiffs' counsel. *Brockman v. Barton Brands, Ltd.,* 2007 WL 4162920 (W.D.Ky. Nov. 21, 2007). In that case, the Court denied certification of a proposed class defined in essentially the same manner as the one currently before the Court.

* * *

III.

A district court has broad discretion in determining whether class certification is appropriate, but in arriving at that determination the court has no authority to "conduct a preliminary inquiry into the merits of a suit." *Eisen v. Carlisle & Jacquelin,* 417 U.S. 156, 177, 94 S.Ct. 2140, 40 L.Ed.2d 732 (1974). The likelihood that these individual plaintiffs may have valid claims is not relevant to class certification. However, "sometimes it is necessary for the court to probe behind the pleadings before coming to rest on the certification question." *Gen. Tel. Co. of Sw. v. Falcon,* 457 U.S. 147, 160, 102 S.Ct. 2364, 72 L.Ed.2d 740 (1982). As such, the Court must conduct a "rigorous analysis" to determine whether the requirements of Rule 23 are met. Plaintiffs have the burden to prove the requisite elements of class certification under either or both of Rules 23(b)(2) and (b)(3).

* * *

This Court will address each Rule 23(a) requirement in turn, after considering an overriding concern particular to the type of class proposed here.

A.

"Although not specifically mentioned in [Rule 23], the definition of the class is an essential prerequisite to maintaining a class action." *Adams v. Fed. Materials Co.,* 2006 WL 3772065 at *3 (W.D.Ky.2006) (quoting *Gevedon v. Purdue Pharma,* 212 F.R.D. 333, 335 (E.D.Ky.2002)). At a minimum, the description must be "sufficiently definite that it is administratively feasible for the court to determine whether a particular individual is a member." 7A Charles Alan Wright, Arthur R. Miller, & Mary Kay Kane, *Federal Practice and Procedure,* § 1760, at 120–21 (2d ed.1986).

As this Court discussed in *Brockman,* courts have rejected proposed classes where plaintiffs failed to "identify any logical reason ... for drawing the boundaries where they did." *Daigle v. Shell Oil Co.,* 133 F.R.D. 600, 602–03 (D.Colo.1990) (holding that plaintiffs had "failed to identify a class" where the proposed boundaries did not appear to "relat[e] to the defendants' activities," but were instead "arbitrarily ... drawn lines on a map"). Usually, scientific or objective evidence closely ties the spread of the alleged pollution or contamination to the proposed class boundaries, as many mass environmental tort cases demonstrate. In weighing certification of a proposed class claiming damage from airborne radioactive materials, one court observed:

> [t]he fact that radioactive materials have escaped the confines of the plant, is, by itself, not sufficient to justify defining the class to include everyone who lives or owns property within six miles of the plant's boundaries. Although the class definition is subject to refinement ... there should be some evidence at this stage of the case that plaintiffs' definition is reasonable. *This requires an examination of the plaintiffs' evidence of the dispersion of hazardous emissions.*

Boggs v. Divested Atomic Corp., 141 F.R.D. 58, 61–62 (S.D.Ohio 1991) (emphasis added). * * *

* * *

By contrast, courts have declined to certify proposed classes where "no evidence establishes a connection between defendants' conduct and the proposed class boundaries." And courts have resisted class certification where plaintiffs fail to consider facts such as wind and water runoff in defining the class.

As noted above, Rule 23 does not explicitly command evaluation of the proposed class definition, which explains why many courts have opted not to perform such an evaluation. The Sixth Circuit has not deemed the failure to conduct such an evaluation to be an abuse of discretion. Neither has the Sixth Circuit criticized the more thorough approach. As it noted in *Brockman,* this Court believes the more thorough analysis to be the better approach.

The Court has repeatedly pressed for an evidentiary relationship between the geographic boundaries of the proposed class definition and the alleged exposure zone of pollution. Yet at bottom, Plaintiffs rest their motion upon complaints of residents in a single, geographically-confined area about various substances and odors on their property, and lengthy recitals of the emissions of the LG & E facility. Plaintiffs have presented no evidence from which the Court could infer that similar circumstances, whether ultimately attributable to LG & E or not, exist throughout the proposed two mile radius of LG & E's facility class area. Though Plaintiffs repeatedly describe the proposed class definition as "objectively reasonable," they offer no evidence whatsoever that the airborne contaminants might have spread in all directions from LG & E's facility for a distance of up to two miles.[3] Plaintiffs had an ample opportunity for class discovery, and had the benefit of this Court's feedback on at least two other similar cases. Yet Plaintiffs' request for class certification contains a startling and near-total lack of evidence linking the fallout and/or odors about which Plaintiffs complain to the substances that LG & E emits * * *.

Notably, Plaintiffs have not provided an expert report * * *. Instead, the entirety of Plaintiffs' scientific evidence appears to consist of a three-page (including cover sheet) analysis of two samples Plaintiffs assert they collected and sent to a lab. As scientific or expert evidence, the lab report is extraordinarily lacking in relevant information. Among other things, the lab analysts were not those who collected the samples, and the "Conclusions" proffered by the lab analysts apparently were primarily that the samples contained "plant matter and mold" as well as "environmental dust," none of which seems to indicate the presence of any contaminant, much less one that could be attributed to a coal-fired plant such as LG & E's. The substance discovered in the samples which Plaintiffs argue supports their theory is "organic black particulate consisting of a mixture of carbonized material, rubber dust, and *possibly* coal dust (a minor component in the mixture)." And it is from this result and the extensive documentation of LG & E's emissions that Plaintiffs ask the Court to accept that "the complaints against Defendant's odors and fallout affect citizens throughout the *Burkhead* class definition geographic area commonly and predominantly."

To be clear, the Court is not troubled by the lack of such evidence merely because the Court fears individualized or non-uniform damage calculations, but rather because without it there seems to be virtually no evidence in the record that distinguishes members of the proposed class from the general public based upon acts of LG & E. The omission of any sort of meaningful scientific evidence tying the proposed class together is particularly glaring given that Plaintiffs' counsel have at least attempted to obtain such information in other similar cases, and given how frequently such information plays a key role in class certification decisions for other courts in such cases. * * *

---

3. Though less important at the certification stage, the Court notes that Plaintiffs also do not explain how the proposed two-mile-radius class area takes into consideration many if not all of the proposed class members' proximity to other pollution-emitting facilities in the area, including Oxy Vinyl, a nearby coal-fired facility also being sued by Plaintiffs' counsel. Here again, any sort of evidentiary assurance that a particular pollutant from LG & E could have spread across the proposed class area would be helpful, but has not been provided.

Additionally, Plaintiffs' proposed class definition limits membership to those "whose property was damaged by noxious odors, fallout, pollutants and contaminants which originated from the LG & E Cane Run facility." This definition seems to make the ultimate issue in the case (property damage at the hands of LG & E) a component of the class *definition*, thereby front-loading the individualized damage determinations which ordinarily would be reserved until later in the proceedings. To properly define the class as Plaintiffs propose it, the Court would be required to determine on a person-by-person basis whether property damage had occurred and whether LG & E was responsible, which would seem to completely subsume the merits phase of the case into the class certification phase. This approach has little to recommend it, and runs contrary to the admonition that a class definition "should avoid . . . terms that depend on resolution of the merits." Manual for Complex Litigation (Fourth) § 21.222 (2004).

All of these considerations flaw Plaintiffs' proposed class definition and their case for class certification at its threshold. But as it did in *Brockman* given that proper class definition is not made an explicit stand-alone requirement by the text of Rule 23, the Court will proceed to consider the enumerated factors of Rule 23(a) and the additional requirements of Rules 23(b)(2) and (3). Throughout this analysis, the ramifications of Plaintiffs' improper class definition will be evident.

B.

A class must be "so numerous that joinder of all members is impracticable." Fed.R.Civ.P. 23(a)(1). "There is no strict numerical test for determining impracticability of joinder." *In re Am. Med. Sys., Inc.,* 75 F.3d at 1079. Nonetheless, while "the exact number of class members need not be pleaded or proved, impracticability of joinder must be positively shown, and cannot be speculative." *Golden v. City of Columbus,* 404 F.3d 950, 966 (6th Cir.2005).

As this Court has noted, "numerosity . . . is inextricably bound up in the question of class definition." Therefore, a flawed class definition can make it difficult to determine whether a class defined by geographical boundaries satisfies the numerosity requirement. Several courts faced with overbroad proposed classes have rejected plaintiffs' numerosity arguments on these grounds. * * *

Here, the proposed class would include "at least 14,294" Plaintiffs. If all 14,294 belong in the class, the Court would find that Plaintiffs have easily met the numerosity requirement, since even a much smaller class could satisfy this requirement. However, for reasons noted above it is unclear how many of these 14,294 individuals properly belong in the class. Some 72 Plaintiffs are named, and Plaintiffs indicate this total could grow to 113. A more sufficiently justified class definition properly encompassing such numbers seems quite likely to meet the numerosity requirement, and therefore the Court will not deem these deficiencies a barrier to class certification at this time.

C.

The commonality requirement of Rule 23(a) generally will be satisfied where there is a "single issue common to all members of the class." *In re Am. Med. Sys.*, 75 F.3d at 1080. The requirement seeks only identification of "a common issue the resolution of which will advance the litigation." *Sprague v. Gen. Motors Corp.*, 133 F.3d 388, 397 (6th Cir.1998). Here, Plaintiffs assert that common issues of fact include:

> (1) the cause of Defendant's emissions; (2) whether Defendant's emissions were foreseeable; (3) were there any precautions Defendant could have taken to have prevented the emissions; (4) whether Defendant exercised any available precautions to prevent the emissions; (5) the amount of Exemplary Damages the Plaintiff Class is entitled to from Defendant; and (6) the type of economic impact Defendant's emissions had upon the Plaintiff class.

According to Plaintiffs, the common questions of law include whether Defendant is liable for nuisance, negligence, gross negligence, trespass, or strict liability, whether the proposed class is entitled to exemplary damages, and whether the proposed class is entitled to injunctive relief. The Court does not necessarily accept Plaintiffs' assertion that "[t]he actions sought to be challenged by Plaintiffs are not dependent upon any case by case analysis." Nevertheless, without finding that *all* of the issues noted above would be common to all class members and given that Plaintiffs have identified several questions of law and fact that ostensibly lend themselves to adjudication on a classwide basis, the Court finds that Plaintiffs meet the requirements of Rule 23(a)(2).

D.

A plaintiff's claim may be considered typical "if it arises from the same event or practice or course of conduct that gives rise to the claims of other class members, and if his or her claims are based on the same legal theory." The representative plaintiffs' interests should be aligned with those of the proposed class, such that "as goes the claim of the named plaintiff, so go the claims of the class," and "in order to find typicality and commonality, the precise nature of the various claims must be examined.... the typicality requirement is not met if the named plaintiffs do not represent an adequate cross-section of the claims asserted by the rest of the class." *Reeb v. Ohio Dept. of Rehab. & Corr.*, 435 F.3d 639, 644–45 (6th Cir.2006).

Here, it cannot be said that the proposed representative Plaintiffs represent "an adequate cross-section" of the proposed class. This is so largely because their geographic concentration makes it unlikely in the absence of any supporting evidence that their property damage claims would be "typical" of those that might be brought by individuals elsewhere in the sizeable proposed class area. Other members of the proposed class appear to live in areas subject to completely different influences, meaning that the factual and legal issues of other proposed class members' claims, or even claims by various subgroups of class members against LG & E could [be dramatically different]. This stands in contrast to [a] situation * * * where [harm among the plaintiffs is of the same type, but different in degree].

The Court recognizes that differences in amount or apportionment of damages alone will not defeat typicality, but here the significant gaps in Plaintiffs' proffered evidentiary showing make it impossible for the Court to conclude whether the proposed representatives are "typical" of the class they purport to represent.

E.

The adequacy of representation inquiry under Rule 23(a)(4) seeks to discover conflicts of interest between named representatives and the class they seek to represent, and "a class representative must be part of the class and 'possess the same interest and suffer the same injury' as the class members." *East Tex. Motor Freight Sys., Inc. v. Rodriguez*, 431 U.S. 395, 403, 97 S.Ct. 1891, 52 L.Ed.2d 453 (1977). As the Supreme Court has noted, "[t]he adequacy-of-representation requirement 'tend[s] to merge' with the commonality and typicality criteria of Rule 23(a), which 'serve as guideposts for determining whether ... maintenance of a class action is economical and whether the named plaintiff's claim and the class claims are so interrelated that the interests of the class members will be fairly and adequately protected in their absence.' " *Amchem*, 521 U.S. at 626 n. 20, 117 S.Ct. 2231. The adequacy evaluation also takes into consideration the competency and conflicts of class counsel.

Here the adequacy determination is complicated because Plaintiffs have voluntarily foregone their original personal injury claims. Thus while Plaintiffs wish to pursue *property damage* claims on behalf of the entire proposed class, they also wish to impose upon the entire proposed class their decision to give up any personal injury claims that could be asserted against LG & E. Under Kentucky law, absent class members would be barred from later asserting such claims, which creates what some courts have identified as an inability on the part of the proposed class representatives adequately to protect the interests of absent class members.

Certain state courts have suggested "a wide array of options" to assuage concerns about the adequacy of a proposed class. These "options" include "limit[ing] the class issues to liability ... and allow[ing] each class member to use that judgment as a basis for an individual action to recover damages for the breach," as well as "divid[ing] the class into subclasses," and finally "us[ing] the class notice procedure to give those class members with [personal injuries] the opportunity to opt out of the class." However, the Court questions an argument which appears to shift the responsibility for resolving any infirmities in the proposed class definition from Plaintiffs onto the Court. The Court does not have a sufficient basis for redrawing or refining the proposed class.

Plaintiffs' own options do not satisfy the potential inadequacies of their proposed class. Their first suggestion pertains to individualized damage determinations, which are not an impediment to certification anyway. Plaintiffs' second suggestion leaves unclear how creating sub-classes would allow absent class members' foregone claims to be asserted later. And finally, in a(b)(2) class, as Plaintiffs have requested here in addition to a(b)(3) class, no opt-out rights are ordinarily available for absent class members.[7]

In short, the Court's analysis of the proposed class representatives raises questions that "the interests of the class members will be fairly and adequately protected in their absence," *Amchem,* 521 U.S. at 626 n. 20, 117 S.Ct. 2231.

IV.

In addition to meeting the four requirements of Rule 23(a), a pro-posed class must meet at least one of the requirements of Rule 23(b). Here, Plaintiffs have requested certification under Rule 23(b)(2) as well as under Rule 23(b)(3).

Certification under Rule 23(b)(2) is appropriate where "the party opposing the class has acted or refused to act on grounds generally applicable to the class, thereby making appropriate final injunctive relief or corresponding declaratory relief with respect to the class as a whole." Fed.R.Civ.P. 23(b)(2). The drafters of the Rule explained that this provision "does not extend to cases in which the appropriate final relief relates exclusively or predominantly to money damages." Fed.R.Civ.P. 23(b)(2) advisory committee's note. As the Fifth Circuit has explained, the Advisory Committee's note indicates that:

> monetary relief predominates in (b)(2) class actions unless it is incidental to requested injunctive or declaratory relief. By incidental, we mean damages that flow directly from liability to the class as a whole on the claims forming the basis of the injunctive or declaratory relief.... such damages should at least be capable of computation by means of objective standards *and not dependent in any significant way on the intangible, subjective differences of each class member's circumstances.* Liability for incidental damages should not require additional hearings to resolve the disparate merits of each individual's case; it should neither introduce new and substantial legal or factual issues, nor entail complex determinations.

Allison v. Citgo Petroleum Corp., 151 F.3d 402, 415 (5th Cir.1998) (inter-nal citations omitted) (emphasis added). * * * Thus, as a general rule, a

---

7. In support of a different aspect of their argument for certification Plaintiffs have cited a case in which a court in the Sixth Circuit exercised its discretion under Rule 23 to certify a (b)(2) class *with* opt-out rights for class members. *Fuller v. Fruehauf Trailer Corp.,* 168 F.R.D. 588, 602–05 (E.D.Mich.1996). Though this approach is not without support in other jurisdictions, *id.* at 604, it has the potential to dramatically expand the scope of Rule 23(b)(2) beyond the scope seemingly permitted and intended by the absence of notice and opt-out requirements, and therefore this Court would be extremely reluctant to adopt it here.

court should not certify a (b)(2) class where individual monetary damage issues may well predominate.

* * *

Here Plaintiffs cannot as easily avoid a searching (b)(2) analysis by claiming that "the Rule 23(a) prerequisites have been met," * * *. Plaintiffs seek various types of relief, including compensatory damages and "any and all further relief, including equitable relief," and what is clear is that the monetary damages Plaintiffs seek are more than "incidental," * * * * * *

V.

Certification under Rule 23(b)(3) is appropriate when "the questions of law or fact common to the members of the class predominate over any questions affecting only individual members, and that a class action is superior to other available methods for the fair and efficient adjudication of the controversy." Rule 23(b)(3) classes therefore must satisfy a two-part test of commonality and superiority, and should only be certified if doing so would "achieve economies of time, effort, and expense." *Sterling,* 855 F.2d at 1196. The Sixth Circuit has provided further guidance on what sorts of cases may be best suited to (b)(3) class adjudication:

> In complex, mass, toxic tort accidents, *where no one set of operative facts establishes liability,* no single proximate cause equally applies to each potential class member and each defendant, and individual issues outnumber common issues, the district court should properly question the appropriateness of a class action for resolving the controversy. However, where the defendant's liability can be determined on a class-wide basis because the cause of the disaster is a single course of conduct *which is identical for each of the plaintiffs,* a class action may be the best suited vehicle to resolve such a controversy.

Sterling, 855 F.2d at 1197 (emphasis added). In contrast to Rule 23(a)'s commonality requirement, discussed above, Rule 23(b)(3)'s "predominance criterion is far more demanding." *Amchem,* 521 U.S. at 624, 117 S.Ct. 2231.

To be sure, a need for individualized damage determinations is not fatal to (b)(3) certification. * * *

Here * * *, the question is whether common factual and legal questions predominate, that is, whether any individualized questions relate solely to the amount of damages potentially owed to each class member. Yet * * * [p]laintiffs have failed to provide evidence that "the defendant's liability can be determined on a class-wide basis." Plaintiffs have alleged that Defendant's operations result in extensive emissions, but what remains missing is any evidence that the *cause* of the entire class's damages could be determined in a single proceeding. A comparison to *Olden,* [383 F.3d 495 (6th Cir. 2004)], illustrates the problem: there the Sixth Circuit proceeded under the belief that the toxins emitted by the defendant were distinguishable from those emitted by "other industrial sources" nearby.

Olden, 383 F.3d at 508. That is, the *Olden* defendant's plant was assumed to be the sole source of any damage the class members suffered, so a causation determination as to one class member could be extrapolated to all and the defendant's tort liability could be adjudicated on a classwide basis. As noted above, similar aspects of their respective proposed class definitions distinguish *Cook,* in which a (b)(3) class defined by a "plutonium contour" was certified, and *Wehner,* in which a (b)(3) class limited to "confirmed dioxin sites" was certified.

* * *

To prove their trespass claim, for example, Plaintiffs must show "an intrusion (or encroachment) which is an unreasonable interference with a property owner's possessory *use* of his/her property." *Smith v. Carbide & Chems. Corp.,* 226 S.W.3d 52, 57 (Ky.2007). And a nuisance "arises from the unreasonable, unwarrantable, or unlawful use by a person of his own property and produces such material annoyance, inconvenience, discomfort, or hurt that the law will presume a consequent damage." *Smith v. Carbide & Chems. Corp.,* 507 F.3d 372, 379–80 (6th Cir.2007) (citing *City of Somerset v. Sears,* 313 Ky. 784, 233 S.W.2d 530, 532 (1950) (quoting 39 Am Jur. *Nuisances* § 2)). The Court has searched Defendant's extensive submissions in vain for any evidence—a report, test, or anything else— from which Plaintiffs propose to show liability on a classwide basis. Yet * * * the critical evidence of causation as to either claim, or as to the remainder of Plaintiffs' claims, is to be based upon highly individualized testimony. Thus, the Court cannot be assured that Defendant's liability to the class will be a common question or that a class action would be the superior method of adjudicating Plaintiffs' claims. As elsewhere throughout the Rule 23 analysis, the Court is again confronted with the infirmities of the class definition, and therefore the Court finds that Plaintiffs do not satisfy Rule 23(b)(3).

VI.

* * * Plaintiffs have pointed to a variety of mass environmental tort cases in which courts have certified classes, often ones alleging contamination via air pollution. Plaintiffs' Memorandum in Support of Motion for Certification of Class Action at 17. Plaintiffs correctly observe that "[t]he principles for certification ... set forth in *Sterling* have been applied consistently" in certifying such cases. However, this observation is of minimal persuasiveness, given the significant differences between the evidence supporting most of those proposed classes and that supporting the one proposed here. One could suggest in good faith, as Plaintiffs have, that this Court has the discretion to certify a class even where no evidence defines the precise nature and scope of the torts allegedly committed by Defendant. Indeed, some courts, adopting such a view, have done so based upon what this Court perceives as a less-than-rigorous analysis.

Whether certification here might fall just within the broad parameters of the Court's discretion is not precisely the question. Rather, it is whether employing the class action mechanism in this situation would achieve the "significant judicial economies" for which it is designed. Plaintiffs bear the burden of producing something more than their wholly subjective belief that their property is affected by Defendant's emissions and that all those in a two-mile radius must be similarly affected. Quite simply, Plaintiffs' strenuous arguments that mass environmental tort accidents are usually suitable for class action adjudication are beside the point until Plaintiffs demonstrate that a defined class has similarly experienced a mass environmental tort of some kind.

Upon repeated reexamination of the record, the Court finds a substantial amount of relatively uncontroverted evidence indicating that (a) Defendant, as part of its electrical generation operations, emits various pollutants into the atmosphere, and (b) Plaintiffs, a geographically concentrated group living relatively close to Defendant's plant (as well as facilities operated by other companies) have some sort of substances and noxious odors on their property. Rule 23 exists precisely to ensure that class certification is based upon something more than the generalized assumptions as to the sizeable proposed class area that this information could support. Plaintiffs have quite simply failed to carry their burden of satisfying the requirements of Rule 23 with regard to the class they have proposed, and as such the Court cannot properly conclude that certification of the proposed class is appropriate.

The Court will issue an order consistent with this Memorandum Opinion.

NOTES AND QUESTIONS

1. The court "takes as true" the allegations in the complaint about contamination of their property, but declined to treat similarly the allegations that the defendant is the source of that contamination. Why? Indeed, throughout its opinion, the court seemed troubled about the possibility that some of the contamination to which the class has been subjected was produced by others. Would the plaintiffs have had a stronger case for class certification if they sued those other potential contributors as well? How would that affect the merits of their claims?

2. *Consideration of the merits.* As the court stated, the Supreme Court, in *Eisen v. Carlisle & Jacquelin*, ruled that courts should not consider the substantive merits in deciding whether to certify a class. In *Eisen*, the district court had made a preliminary determination that the plaintiffs were likely to prevail. Because of that finding, the court allocated 90% of the costs of notice to the class to the defendants. The Supreme Court reversed, holding that the merits were irrelevant to allocating the costs of notice and that ordinarily the plaintiff must bear these costs. Yet, at the same time, the Court instructed lower courts that they must undertake a "rigorous analysis" whether the requirements of Rule 23 have been satisfied before certifying a class. What happens when the "rigorous analysis" runs into consideration of the merits of the case? Thus, did not the *Burkhead* court's effort to define the class overlap with the merits when the court observed that some members of the class may not have suffered any contamination, some of those that have may be the result of other polluters, and others may not have suffered enough contamination to constitute a trespass or nuisance?

In In re Initial Public Offerings Securities Litigation, 471 F.3d 24 (2d Cir.2006), the court confronted this apparent conflict head on. It explained that *Eisen* was concerned with consideration of the merits *independently* from the requirements of Rule 23, and thus should not impede consideration of the merits if required to analyze whether Rule 23 is satisfied. Acknowledging the risk of the class certification decision turning into a full-fledged trial of the merits, the court did grant that trial judges could exercise discretion to limit discovery and the extent of any hearing held.

Why *should* consideration of the merits be off limits? Wouldn't a preliminary determination of whether the class has a valid claim assist in deciding whether a class action is appropriate? Recall that, for preliminary injunctions, the court must make an inquiry into the likelihood that plaintiff will ultimately prevail. For commentators urging reconsideration of *Eisen*'s placing the merits off limits for certification purposes, see Robert G. Bone & David S. Evans, Class Certification and the Substantive Merits, 51 Duke L.J. 1251 (2002); Bartlett H. McGuire, The Death Knell for *Eisen*: Why the Class Action Analysis Should Include an Assessment of the Merits, 168 F.R.D. 366 (1996).

3. As the *Burkhead* opinion reveals, courts in hazardous waste and environmental pollution cases have both certified class actions and denied certification. *Sterling v. Velsicol Chemical Corp.* is one of the leading cases in which class certification was upheld. The defendant dumped its chemical waste by-products on rural land it acquired for that purpose. For nine years, "the defendant deposited a total of 300,000 55–gallon steel drums containing ultrahazardous liquid chemical waste and hundreds of fiber board cartons containing ultrahazardous dry chemical waste in the landfill." A class of residents near the waste site sued successfully for personal injury and property damage. Notably, a government report documented the migration of the defendant's chemicals from its land and their contamination of nearby residents' wells. No other source of contamination appeared to exist. Summarily, the Court of Appeals affirmed the class certification, observing that liability, causation, and exposure were common for all class members. Only the nature and amount of damages were individual. Did the *Sterling* court neglect its obligation to conduct a "rigorous analysis" of whether the requirements for a class action were established? Was the *Eisen* prohibition on consideration of the merits respected by the *Sterling* court?

4. One of the *Burkhead* court's objections to the plaintiffs' proposed class definition is that it overlaps with the merits of the case. A particular difficulty with such definitions is that they produce fail-safe classes of the sort involving "heads I win, tails you lose." Thus, if plaintiffs are successful, the entire class will be bound and recover from defendant. But if plaintiffs lose at trial, defendant will not have anyone bound because the trial finding means there is no one in the class. See Daffron v. Rousseau Assocs., Inc., 1976–2 Trade Cas. ¶ 61,219 (N.D.Ind.1976) ("The new class definition, if allowed, would result in a 'fail-safe' class, a class which would be bound only by a judgment favorable to plaintiffs but not an adverse judgment.").

5. In assessing the adequacy of representation, the court was concerned because the class representatives eschew asserting claims for personal injuries. Could that problem have been solved by modifying the class to include those who had only suffered property damage and not personal injury?

6. In addition to pollution and hazardous waste class actions, in the 1970s and 1980s, efforts were made to bring products liability class actions. Those are even more difficult to certify given their geographic dispersal and the greater heterogeneity of the class. Despite the doubts expressed by the Advisory Committee, quoted at the beginning of this section, a number of courts entertained, with open minds, the possibility of certifying such a class. One case in which a class was certified is Jenkins v. Raymark Industries, Inc., 782 F.2d 468 (5th Cir.1986), a class consisting of asbestos victims who had filed suit in the Eastern District of Texas. Note that this was not a class formed because their claims were too small to justify individual litigation. The reason for certifying the class was the backlog of asbestos cases that had clogged the docket of the district court and the concomitant delays in getting those cases to trial or settlement. Note also that all claims would be governed by Texas law. See also In re A.H. Robins Co., 880 F.2d 709, 732 (4th Cir.1989) ("Many courts are now abandoning their historical reluctance to certify mass tort class actions in light of what is often an overwhelming need to create an orderly, efficient means for adjudicating hundreds or thousands of related claims.").

7. By the 1990s, the pendulum shifted and, at least with regard to classes asserting products liability claims, courts found numerous difficulties with classes. Two cases that revealed some of the problems impeding certification of nationwide toxic substances classes were In re Rhone–Poulenc Rorer Inc., 51 F.3d 1293 (7th Cir.1995) and Castano v. American Tobacco Co., 84 F.3d 734 (5th Cir.1996), the latter a nationwide class of addicted cigarette smokers and the former a class of those with hemophilia who had become HIV infected in the early 1980s because blood derivatives they received were contaminated with the virus when infected donors' blood was used to manufacture the blood derivatives. Those cases identified several impediments to certifying the proposed classes:

    a. *Variations in state tort law.* State tort law is not uniform, and there may be so many variations that conducting a trial would be administratively difficult or impossible. Thus, some states may have one version of market share, others a different one, and some may not recognize market share, requiring proof by a preponderance about which defendant provided a class member's drug. In order to try a class action, jury instructions would have to be crafted. Differences in state law might require multiple instructions on the same issue. With multiple differences on multiple issues, managing the trial and avoiding jury confusion could be quite difficult.

    b. *Individual issues.* Issue applicable only to each class member would still remain, including affirmative defenses, specific causation, and damages that would require separate proceedings for resolution. The Seventh Amendment, which guarantees a right to jury trials, permits separate consideration by different juries of distinct issues in the same case. Thus, if on an appeal a new trial is required, the trial (before a different jury) can be limited to those issues affected by the error while retaining findings from the first trial unaffected by the error. What the Seventh Amendment does not permit is a different jury re-examining the findings of a prior jury. Consider a class action in which, during the class trial, defendant was found liable based on negligence. In the individual phase, a different jury would consider individual issues, including comparative fault. But a jury determining whether plaintiff was at fault and, if so, the comparative shares of fault for plaintiff and defendant would necessarily have to reconsider the negligence of defendant, thereby running afoul of the Seventh Amendment. See W. Russell Taber, The Reexamination Clause: Exploring Bifurcation in Mass Tort Litigation, 73 Def.Couns.J. 63 (2006).

c. *Efficiency v. claim effectuating.* The impetus for certification in *Jenkins*, finding an efficient means for addressing an overwhelming number of cases, may not be applicable to many other mass torts. For example, in *Castano*, if no class action existed it is unclear whether individual addiction claims would be brought. In *Rhone–Poulenc,* the blood factor litigation, 13 individual cases had been tried and 12 resulted in findings for the defendants. There was little enthusiasm among plaintiffs' lawyers at that point to continue trying individual cases.

d. *Settlement pressure.* Judge Posner in *Rhone–Poulenc* expressed concern about the pressure a class action would place on the defendants to settle. Calculating that certification of a class could expose the defendants to $25 billion in potential liability if they lost at trial, he observed that even with a high probability of success, few would want to go forward with a "bet your company" trial. Continuing, he opined on the unlikelihood that the plaintiffs' claims were meritorious, based on the outcome of the prior 13 litigated cases.

8. As a result of *Castano, Rhone–Poulenc,* two Supreme Court asbestos class action decisions discussed below, and other cases, the Manual for Complex Litigation reported:

> Mass tort personal injury cases are rarely appropriate for class certification for trial. In a settlement context, the proposed class must meet Rule 23 requirements, with the exception of trial manageability, and the court must carefully review the proposed settlement terms to ensure that they are fair, reasonable, and adequate. The trend appears to be that cases involving significant personal injuries should not be certified for trial, particularly on a nationwide or multistate basis, because individual issues of causation and individual damages often predominate and state law often varies.

Federal Judicial Center, Manual for Complex Litigation § 22.71(4th ed.2004).

9. *The Class Action Fairness Act.* In response to a perception that state courts had become a haven for class actions, including certification of classes that were not properly certifiable, Congress passed the *Class Action Fairness Act* ("CAFA"), Pub. L. No. 109–2, 119 Stat. 4 (2005). CAFA dramatically expands federal subject matter jurisdiction over class actions based on state law. The key provision, now contained in 28 U.S.C. § 1332(d), provides for federal jurisdiction for any putative class action with a minimum of 100 members of the class, an aggregate amount in controversy in excess of $5 million, and minimal diversity, meaning that at least one plaintiff or class member is a citizen of a different state from at least one defendant. Thus the "complete diversity" requirement for the general diversity statute is considerably relaxed, greatly expanding federal court jurisdiction over state-law class actions. Cases satisfying these requirements may be filed initially in federal court or removed from state court by a defendant. Complicated provisions declare that jurisdiction should not be exercised in cases that are essentially local, based on a large proportion of the class all being citizens of the same state in which some or all defendants are also citizens. Commentary on CAFA can be found in Symposium, Fairness to Whom? Perspectives on the Class Action Fairness Act of 2005, 156 U.Pa.L.Rev. 1439 (2008); Edward F. Sherman, Class Action Fairness Act and the Federalization of Class Actions, 238 F.R.D. 504 (2007).

10. *Settlement class actions.* In Amchem Products, Inc. v. Windsor, 521 U.S. 591 (1997), the Supreme Court confronted a Rule 23(b)(3) class action designed to settle a large swath of asbestos litigation. Twenty major asbestos defendants and experienced asbestos plaintiffs' lawyers negotiated a settlement for "future claimants." Future claimants were those exposed to asbestos but who had not yet brought suit, most of whom had yet to develop any disease. The lawyers negotiated a quasi-administrative scheme that provided payment to class members when they suffered asbestotic disease. A "settlement class action" was filed, in which the parties agreed to class status, to the negotiated compensation scheme, and to binding all class members, requiring they pursue their remedies within the compensation scheme unless they opted out of the class. The trial court, after extensive hearings, upheld the settlement as fair, reasonable, and adequate, as required by Rule 23(e) for class action settlements.

The primary issue before the Supreme Court was the effect of the settlement on the requirements of Rule 23 for certification. The Court held that the Rule 23(b)(3)(D) requirement that the class be manageable should be adjusted in light of the settlement as the difficulties encountered by a trial of the class's claim would not be encountered. However, the other requirements of Rules 23(a) and (b)(3) were not to be compromised by a settlement, even when a judge finds it meets the requirements of Rule 23(e). The Court proceeded to detail why the *Amchem* class could not satisfy those requirements—the heterogeneity of the class, in terms of the strength of their claims, their diseases, the applicable law, applicable defenses, and the different asbestos products to which they were exposed belied predominance of common questions; the interests of class representatives who had developed disease were in conflict with those who would later develop disease (and not be eligible for compensation until then) for a variety of reasons, preventing the representation from being adequate; and the impediments that existed to providing meaningful notice to persons who had been exposed to asbestos with regard to their decision to opt out.

The *Amchem* settlement was driven by the defendants' desire to obtain closure on their asbestos litigation and plaintiffs' lawyers' interest in settling the cases they had filed, which had been caught in the federal multi-district litigation and held there while the transferee judge investigated some means for a global settlement. The defendants resisted settlement of those cases without addressing future claims. In the years following the Supreme Court's decision in *Amchem* that the class was improperly certified, thereby undoing the settlement of future claims, numerous major asbestos manufacturers filed bankruptcy petitions in order to bring asbestos claims against them to a resolution.

11. *23(b)(1) classes.* A somewhat similar effort to *Amchem* reached the Supreme Court two years later in Ortiz v. Fibreboard Corp., 527 U.S. 815 (1999). Fibreboard manufactured several asbestos products, found itself caught up in a massive number of claims, and had become financially distressed as a result. Not only was it litigating against asbestos claimants, but it was also involved in a lawsuit with two of its liability insurers over their obligation to provide coverage for asbestos claims. Fibreboard had won the first round of that suit in a California state trial court but an appeal was pending and if Fibreboard lost, it would have exhausted all available insurance coverage.

Fibreboard attempted to reach a global resolution of its asbestos litigation through a Rule 23(b)(1)(B) settlement class action of "future" claimants. The advantage of a Rule 23(b)(1)(B) class by contrast with a (b)(3) class is that it is mandatory—members of the class may not opt out. Thus, settlement with a class of all future asbestos claimants would assure Fibreboard global peace. As in *Amchem*, existing asbestos suits against Fibreboard were settled simultaneously, but outside the class action structure and on more favorable terms than class members received. At the same time, Fibreboard settled its insurance coverage case, and the insurers contributed a little more than $1.5 billion that would be used to pay existing claims and members of the futures class.

The district court, after an eight–day hearing, approved the settlement, and the Fifth Circuit affirmed. The Supreme Court reversed. First, the Court addressed the theory behind Rule 23(b)(1)(B) classes: Critical requirements are a truly limited fund that is inadequate to meet all claims, exhaustion of the fund to pay those claims, and equitable treatment of the claimants. The *Fibreboard* settlement failed to meet these requirements for three reasons: (1) the amount of the "limited fund" had not properly been determined through adversarial proceedings, but instead was set privately by Fibreboard and its liability insurers in a settlement of the latters' obligation to indemnify Fibreboard for its asbestos liability; (2) claimants were not treated equitably, because those who had already filed suit settled outside the class on more favorable terms than the futures; a second problem that echoed *Amchem* was the heterogeneity of the class and the failure of the settlement to account for differences among them in setting the compensation they would receive; (3) yet another failure to meet the "limited fund" concept was that Fibreboard was only contributing $500,000 of its conservatively estimated $235 million value. Fibreboard's assets were legally available to pay claimants, so any fund isn't limited unless Fibreboard contributes its net worth. Given that creditors have priority over stockholders when a company is insolvent and goes into bankruptcy, do you appreciate the attractiveness of a 23(b)(1)(B) settlement as in *Ortiz* to a company like Fibreboard?

During the course of the *Ortiz* litigation, Owens Corning acquired Fibreboard. The year after *Ortiz,* Owens Corning, citing its asbestos liability and continuing claims, filed for bankruptcy.

D. BANKRUPTCY

Bankruptcy provides an alternative mechanism for resolution of mass tort claims when the assets available to defendant are insufficient to satisfy all of the claims against it. Detailed coverage of bankruptcy law would extend this text by hundreds of pages. Here we offer a brief description and identify some broad themes.

Jurisdiction over bankruptcy proceedings is exclusively in the federal courts. A Chapter 11 bankruptcy proceeding, which is the type most likely to be invoked because of mass tort claim, involves "reorganization" of the bankrupt company's debts. As with limited fund class actions, the idea is to have all claimants (creditors) present their claims in a single proceeding in which all of the claims can be addressed equitably while attempting to retain the value of the bankrupt as a going concern. Thus, suits by all creditors, including tort claimants, against the bankrupt are automatically stayed upon the filing of a bankruptcy petition and an injunction prevents the initiation of any other suits outside the bankruptcy proceedings. All creditors must submit their claims to the bankruptcy court. The bankruptcy court has the power to transfer all pending suits related to the bankruptcy to itself for resolution. Future claims by those exposed to the bankrupt's toxic product but who have not yet suffered disease have been included in these reorganization plans[1] even though those claims present similar problems to the ones adverted to in the discussion of *Ortiz* when the bankruptcy court makes an estimation of the value of claims against the bankrupt, as the law requires. Thus, the capacity of a bankruptcy court to aggregate all existing and future claims before it is unmatched.

However, the ability to aggregate is not equivalent to being able to resolve all of the claims—Congress has provided that personal injury claimants retain a right to jury trial for their claims. Unless an administrative scheme is established in the reorganization plan and is sufficiently attractive to claimants to divert them from litigation, bankruptcy provides little opportunity for a more efficient resolution of mass claims. Yet the universal aggregation of claimants, the provisions for equitable treatment of all classes of creditors, and the negotiation of interests in the bankrupt-

---

1. In 1994, Congress amended the Bankruptcy code to provide coverage for future asbestos claimants in bankruptcy proceedings, provided certain protections were implemented. 11 U.S.C. § 524(g) & (h). See In re Joint E. & S. Dists. Asbestos Litig., 878 F.Supp. 473, 570–72 (E. & S.D.N.Y.1995). Compare Epstein v. Official Committee of Unsecured Creditor, of the Estate of Piper Aircraft Corp., 58 F.3d 1573 (11th Cir.1995) (holding that future air crash victims who assert claims against the bankrupt, a manufacturer of general aviation airplanes, are not claimants within the meaning of the Bankruptcy code). See National Bankruptcy Review Commission, Treatment of Mass Future Claims in Bankruptcy (1997) (proposing modification of Bankruptcy code to include future tort victims as claimants in bankruptcy proceedings).

cy proceeding do frequently produce an administrative compensation scheme for tort claimants. Often the compensation scheme provides a back-end right to dissatisfied claimants to file suit in court, although this option is typically saddled with provisions making it unattractive for most.

The goal of a Chapter 11 bankruptcy is a reorganization plan that resolves the claims of all creditors and permits the bankrupt to continue operating with a discharge of all prior debts. Reorganization plans are governed by detailed substantive and procedural protections for creditors. Creditors are separated into different classes with the idea that each class will have substantially similar types of claims and therefore interests. A majority (and 2/3 of the dollar value) of each class of creditors who will receive less than 100 cents on the dollar must approve the plan, and the court must approve the plan as fair and in compliance with all requirements of the Bankruptcy Code. How do you suppose current tort claimants decide whether to vote in favor of a plan? Should that cause concern?

A process exists to approve a reorganization plan in the absence of approval by a class of creditors (known as a "cramdown"), when the court finds, in essence, that the class is either receiving full payment of its claims or no class with junior rights is receiving any payment on its claims, i.e., all remaining funds of the bankrupt are devoted to the highest priority class of creditors.

Although many creditors will have liquidated claims, tort claims are unliquidated. Before a reorganization plan can be developed and approved, estimation of the value of the unliquidated tort claims is required. An alternative to estimation is to try all of the claims to determine their value, but when there are large numbers of tort claimants, trials for each as a predicate to approval of a reorganization plan is infeasible and undesirable. For an explanation of the estimation process employed in the one mass-tort bankruptcy, see Frances E. McGovern, Resolving Mature Mass Torts, 69 B.U.L.Rev. 659 (1989).

In sum, bankruptcy seems to provide better structural protections for insuring similar (more equitable) treatment across the class of tort claimants and to make sure that tort claimants are treated fairly in relation to other creditors, a matter that mandatory class actions, such as *Ortiz*, do not address. Yet the protections for classes of creditors and the cumbersome process of developing and obtaining approval of a reorganization plan imposes substantial administrative costs. While not the final word on the bankruptcy alternative, consider the differing views from three federal judges, two of them writing in the decision that first affirmed the district court's certification of the *Ortiz* settlement class.

IN RE JOINT EASTERN & SOUTHERN DISTRICT ASBESTOS LITIGATION

United States Court of Appeals, Second Circuit, 1993.
14 F.3d 726.

WINTER, CIRCUIT JUDGE:

This is an appeal from Judge Weinstein's order issuing a preliminary injunction and certifying a mandatory limited-fund class action pursuant to Fed.R.Civ.P. 23(b)(1)(B). The underlying action's claim for relief is unique. It seeks a settlement with a mandatory class of all persons with present or future asbestos claims against Keene Corporation. Keene, however, does not claim that it has a right to such a settlement. * * *

* * *

Instead, it is clear that the complaint is an attempt to compel an adjustment of Keene's creditors' rights outside the Bankruptcy Code and is defended almost entirely by the argument that a mandatory class settlement of present or future asbestos claims would be better for all parties than a bankruptcy proceeding. Indeed, the process contemplated by Keene mirrors a bankruptcy proceeding. The finding of a limited fund corresponds to a finding of insolvency. The preliminary injunction serves much the same function as the automatic stay under Section 362(a) of the Bankruptcy Code. 11 U.S.C. § 362(a) (1988). The class representatives correspond to creditors' committees in Chapter 11 proceedings. See 11 U.S.C. § 1102 (1988). The proposed mandatory class settlement mirrors a reorganization plan and "cram-down."

Keene's argument is self-defeating, however, because it is a self-evident evasion of the exclusive legal system established by Congress for debtors to seek relief. *See In re Johns Manville*, 982 F.2d at 735. The adoption of Keene's position would surely lead to further evasion of the Bankruptcy Code as other debtors sought relief in mandatory class actions. Keene argues that such a precedent would be limited to situations, like Keene's, of mass torts in which some plaintiffs are not known at the time of the accident. We are dubious that a limit to unknown plaintiffs is feasible. Under the limited fund theory espoused here, a class representative for a large number of trade creditors might be appointed to seek a settlement on their behalf where a company was deemed to be a limited fund because of insolvency. The argument that the company and its creditors would all be better off in such an action than in bankruptcy would be as plausible in a case involving a large number of contract creditors as it is here. Breach of warranty cases involving numerous purchasers might also fall within the theory.

Moreover, even if limited to so-called mass torts with yet unknown plaintiffs, Keene's theory would cover a large number of cases. The use of aggregative techniques and inventive legal theories are causing mass torts to become rather routine. Certainly the theory pressed here would apply to many products liability cases, *see, e.g., In re Silicone Gel Breast Implants Prods. Liab. Litig.*, 793 F.Supp. 1098 (J.P.M.L.1992), environmental torts, *see, e.g., In re Love Canal Actions*, 92 A.D.2d 416, 460 N.Y.S.2d 850 (App.Div.1983), and even physical disasters.

Evasion of bankruptcy is also not without costs or other perils. The injunction in the instant matter has already prevented execution of final judgments on supersedeas bonds and funds in escrow that are not Keene's assets. Moreover, class members in cases such as this would have no say in the conduct of the court-appointed class representatives and, unlike creditors in bankruptcy, are not able to vote on a settlement. *See* 11 U.S.C. § 1126. For them, it would be "cram-down" from start to finish. Finally, unlike a lawyer for a creditors' committee, the class representatives in matters like the present one may not be compensated unless a settlement is reached, a situation fraught with danger to the rights of plaintiffs. *See In re "Agent Orange" Prod. Liab. Litig.*, 818 F.2d 216, 222 (2d Cir.) (Fee arrangement creating incentives to settle without regard to merits is void.).

Keene argues passionately that bankruptcy will be a more costly route for the defendant class than this mandatory class action. It may be that the amount distributed to the class in a Keene bankruptcy will be less than in a settlement in the instant class action. Indeed, Keene has suggested that a trial be held on that issue. However, the function of federal courts is not to conduct trials over whether a statutory scheme should be ignored because a more efficient mechanism can be fashioned by judges.

[The court held that the complaint would have to be dismissed for lack of subject matter jurisdiction because the complaint asserted no claim at all, merely a request to certify a class that would require settlement negotiations between Keene and its asbestos claimants.]

IN RE ASBESTOS LITIGATION

United States Court of Appeals, Fifth Circuit, 1996.
90 F.3d 963, vacated and remanded, 521 U.S. 1114.

[This is the Fifth Circuit's opinion from its initial consideration of the 23(b)(1) class certified in *Ortiz v. Fibreboard*, supra. Challengers (intervenors) to the class certification objected, inter alia, that the mandatory class was an improper end run around the Bankruptcy Code.

After citing other cases that had certified 23(b)(1)(B) classes based on a limited fund to demonstrate that the Bankruptcy Code was not the exclusive forum for resolving claims against insolvent or potentially insolvent entities, the court distinguished *In re Joint Eastern and Southern District Asbestos Litigation*, supra, and noted that the Second Circuit's discussion of the propriety of a 23(b)(1)(B) class action was dicta.]

[*Ortiz's*] Global Settlement Agreement was undisputedly driven by insurance coverage litigation between Fibreboard and its insurers which created a serious risk for all parties to the agreement. The Global Health Claimant Class and Fibreboard faced the real possibility that Fibreboard would be insolvent simply on the basis of claims already settled. The Insurers, on the other hand, faced the possibility of virtually unlimited liability for damage caused by Fibreboard asbestos. This pressure, felt by all parties to the global settlement, is what finally brought them together on the eve of the coverage case appeal. The unique risks posed by the coverage cases distinguish [*Ortiz*] from a blatant attempt to circumvent the Bankruptcy Code such as occurred in *Keene*.

The facts of *Keene* further distinguish it from our case. First, an already weak Keene attempted to avoid impending bankruptcy by asking the court to coerce its tort victims to settle claims in a court where no claims were filed against Keene. Second, Keene attempted to utilize the 23(b)(1)(B) injunction to halt pending actions in other courts. Third, and most importantly, Keene's complaint was dismissed on the ground that it failed to present the court with any case or controversy because it requested only that the court compel all plaintiffs in suits against Keene to appear and negotiate.

[*Ortiz*] by comparison, presents us with claims against a healthy company for personal injuries and a proposed settlement of those claims. [*Ortiz*] presents no danger that Fibreboard may simply be abusing this proceeding to delay other actions or to improve its negotiating position with present claimants because it only enjoins future proceedings, not those already pending. We agree with the *Keene* court that under the facts presented to it, a 23(b)(1)(B) action was not appropriate. We also agree that, in the vast majority of cases, the Bankruptcy Code should govern the distribution of an insolvent entity's assets. However, where concerns such as the risk of an adverse judgment in the coverage litigation support an early resolution of the claims against an entity and all parties can benefit from a settlement under Rule 23(b)(1)(B), we see no legal or policy reason to deny the parties this benefit. The essential basis of any settlement is to avoid the uncertainty, risks, and expense of ongoing litigation. In our case, the risks facing Fibreboard, the Insurers, and the health claimants as a result of the California coverage litigation were real and enormous. Holding that the bankruptcy laws require the parties to wait until catastrophe befalls one or more of them as a result of the California litigation would be a denial of justice to the parties before us and unwarranted by the law.

* * *

[*Ortiz*] presented the district court with a superior alternative to the Bankruptcy Code and did so long before any bankruptcy court would have had jurisdiction over Fibreboard's assets. Indeed, one of the most important facts of this case is that, in spite of the threat posed by future personal injury litigation, Fibreboard is currently solvent and healthy. In the short term, no trade or tort creditor has the ability or the incentive to force Fibreboard into a Chapter 11 reorganization. It is also clear that shareholders and management, who stand to lose equity and/or employment if Fibreboard enters bankruptcy proceedings, will refuse to file a voluntary petition at least until the coverage dispute is resolved against it. That, of course, would be too late for the Global Health Claimant Class.

Even in the unlikely event that Fibreboard could be persuaded to file a voluntary bankruptcy petition, the Global Health Claimant Class would be worse off than it is under the Global Settlement Agreement. Under the

Bankruptcy Code, representation for the class may not be available at all and courts that have allowed representation of future tort claimants have left them in an uncertain position that falls short of full "creditor" status. Additionally, full-blown bankruptcy proceedings would bring in all of Fibreboard's other creditors and impose large transactions costs on Fibreboard that, ultimately, would come out of any distribution. *See* Edward I. Altman, *A Further Empirical Investigation of the Bankruptcy Cost Question*, 39 J.Fin. 1067, 1077 (1984). In stark contrast to the uncertain and weak position afforded future tort claimants under the Bankruptcy Code, the plaintiff class and its representatives in [*Ortiz*] had center stage and ran no risk of encountering a cram-down reorganization approved only by trade creditors and rammed through over the objections of class representatives.

To the extent intervenors are arguing that certification is improper because Fibreboard fares better under the class action settlement than under a bankruptcy proceeding, we find their focus misplaced. The inquiry instead should be whether the class is better served by avoiding impairment of their interests. Fibreboard is clearly acting in its own interest in consummating the Global Settlement Agreement and thereby avoiding future insolvency. But the Global Settlement Agreement also serves the interests of the Global Health Claimant Class. Early settlement allows the class to recover far more as a group than it could if it was forced to wait until Fibreboard enters bankruptcy on its own and encounters the high transaction costs of insolvency. *See* Mark J. Roe, *Bankruptcy and Mass Tort*, 84 Colum.L.Rev. 846, 851–64, 905–17 (1984) (advocating early reorganizations because they avoid the waste of insolvency and distribute more to victims, but noting that no one with the ability to push the mass tortfeasor into an early reorganization has the incentive to do so). Precisely because it avoids the enormous transactions costs of litigation and insolvency, the Global Settlement Agreement can offer a deal from which all parties gain. Members of the Global Health Claimant Class receive more money in payment for their injuries and Fibreboard's shareholders keep their stake in a viable entity. The only loser under the Global Settlement Agreement is the asbestos litigation industry.

For all of these reasons, we find that the district court's decision to certify [*Ortiz*] as a 23(b)(1)(B) class action is an appropriate interpretation of Rule 23 that does not conflict with the Bankruptcy Code and upholds the principles of equity and fairness.

* * *

JERRY E. SMITH, CIRCUIT JUDGE, dissenting:

I. *Introduction.*

The district court and the majority undoubtedly are driven by a commendable desire to resolve voluminous personal injury claims against an otherwise strong American company and to ensure an orderly transfer of funds from the company's insurers to its victims. In order to accomplish this result, however, they have extinguished claims over which they have no jurisdiction and deprived thousands of asbestos victims of basic constitutional rights. The result is the first no-opt-out, mass-tort, settlement-only, futures-only class action ever attempted or approved.

Ironically, the willingness to jettison centuries-old legal precepts hurts the very victims they intend to help: The settlement forces asbestos victims to surrender their claims in exchange for a meager $10 million of Fibreboard's $225–250 million net worth. They also benefit from Fibreboard's settlement with its insurers, but Fibreboard and the insurers had powerful incentives to settle that dispute by themselves; in fact, they did so for $2 billion.

There was no need even to involve the class in those negotiations, much less to sacrifice its interests. "Thus, the class members appear to have traded Fibreboard's liability for nothing to which they did not already have a right." [John C. Coffee, Jr., *Class Wars: The Dilemma of the Mass Tort Class Action*, 95 COLUM.L.REV 1343, 1420 (1995).]

On the other hand, the district court and the majority have bailed Fibreboard's shareholders out of a mammoth liability and awarded $43.7 million to class counsel. This suit was supposedly brought on behalf of Fibreboard's victims, but of the four entities directly affected by the settlement—Fibreboard, class attorneys, courts, and asbestos victims–the victims were the only entity absent from the bargaining table. Perhaps for that reason, they also were the only losers.

How could well-intentioned judges sanction—indeed, compel—such an untoward result? Apparently this is simply a case of judges—both trial and appellate—trying too hard to solve the vexing problems posed by unending asbestos litigation. Having certified at least two other high-profile asbestos class actions, then-Chief District Judge Parker was acutely aware of the problems posed by asbestos litigation. In the end, he appears to have become too close to both the overall problem and the instant settlement to continue to act in a judicial capacity in this case.

When Fibreboard and class counsel announced at a court hearing that they had reached a settlement, Chief Judge Parker referred to "extensive negotiations between counsel that the Court has participated in." Also at that time, and long before the fairness hearing, he said, "We will trust in the scholarship, the good judgment and common sense of the . . . courts of appeal in the event this comes to their attention." In short, Chief Judge Parker tried his best to solve a perplexing problem, and it is our task to figure out whether that solution is legally sustainable.

There are two primary problems: (1) Fibreboard, class counsel, and Fibreboard's other creditors have combined to profit at the expense of absent class members; and (2) this case is an affront to the integrity of the judicial system. As we observed when reversing Chief Judge Parker's certification of another class action against Fibreboard: "The Judicial

Branch can offer the trial of lawsuits. It has no power or competence to do more." *Fibreboard*, 893 F.2d at 712.

* * *

D. *Constructive Bankruptcy.*

* * * In bankruptcy, the claims of *all* of Fibreboard's creditors, not just its "future" personal injury victims, would be crammed-down. Permitting Fibreboard to effect a reorganization bankruptcy proceeding in the guise of a futures-only class action circumvents the detailed protections of the Bankruptcy Code for the express *purpose* of imposing the entire cost of the bailout on Fibreboard's most vulnerable creditors, to the betterment of its shareholders.

* * * The amicus brief of the Trial Lawyers for Public Justice puts the point more forcefully: "[I]nstead of protecting class members from the risk that their ability to obtain relief from Fibreboard will be 'substantially impaired,' certification of the proposed settlement class here ensures that the class members' ability to obtain relief from Fibreboard will be totally *eliminated*." Amicus br. at 6.

* * *

In sum, the settlement fails either a customary legal analysis or a common-sense smell test. I respectfully but vehemently dissent from all but part III of the majority opinion.

* * *

NOTES AND QUESTIONS

1. Accepting the position of Judge Davis, representing the majority of the Fifth Circuit in *In re Asbestos Litigation*, how frequently will a 23(b)(1) class action be justified when the limited fund consists of, inter alia, the assets of the product manufacturer? How frequently should it be?

2. For thumbnail sketches of three major bankruptcy proceedings occasioned by mass product liability claims, see Marcus & Sherman, Complex Litigation 213–17 (4th ed.2004) (summarizing the Johns Manville, A.H. Robins, and Dow Corning bankruptcy proceedings); Paul D. Rheingold, Mass Tort Litigation § 18 (1996) (providing, in addition, information about over a dozen additional asbestos company bankruptcies). For detailed consideration of the Robins bankruptcy, in which the shareholders of Robins emerged with over $900 million, see Richard B. Sobol, Bending the Law (1991). For a detailed account of the trust fund established for Dalkon Shield claimants and its successful administration, see Georgene M. Vairo, The Dalkon Shield Claimants Trust: Paradigm Lost (or Found?), 61 Fordham L.Rev. 617 (1992).

3. Professor Cohen, after reviewing *Ortiz* and considering the alternative of bankruptcy, concludes that in a 23(b)(1)(B) class action all of the defendant's assets cannot be devoted to the class, otherwise trade and other nontort creditors would be worse off than in a bankruptcy proceeding. See George M. Cohen, The "Fair" Is the Enemy of the Good: *Ortiz v. Fibreboard*

Corporation and Class Action Settlements, 8 Sup.Ct.Econ.Rev. 23, 88–94 (2000). Could a class action be certified with subclasses to account for each of the different creditor classes? Does this structure, even if permissible under the Federal Rules, so resemble bankruptcy that courts should be wary of invoking it?

4. Scholarly treatment of the debate between class actions and bankruptcy includes Ralph Brubaker, Bankruptcy Injunctions and Complex Litigation: A Critical Reappraisal of Non-debtor Releases in Chapter 11 Reorganizations, 1997 U.Ill.L.Rev. 959 (1997) (describing and criticizing bankruptcy courts providing a discharge to individuals and entities related to the debtor, such as officers and insurers, as part of the reorganization plan); Cohen, supra, 8 Sup.Ct.Econ.Rev.at 88–94 ("bankruptcy may be the best alternative means for resolving mass tort litigation in this situation [yet] bankruptcy can be a very costly option for creditors as well as for the debtor"); Yair Listokin & Kenneth Ayotte, Protecting Future Claimants in Mass Tort Bankruptcies, 98 Nw.U.L.Rev. 1435 (2004) (proposing reforms to address the problem of inadequate representation of future claimants and consequent inequitable treatment in bankruptcy proceedings); Margaret I. Lyle, Mass Tort Claims and the Corporate Tortfeasor: Bankruptcy Reorganization and Legislative Compensation Versus the Common Law Tort System, 61 Tex.L.Rev. 1297 (1983); Douglas Smith, Resolution of Mass Tort Claims in the Bankruptcy System, 41 U.C. Davis L.Rev. 1613 (2008)(focusing on the bankruptcy court's authority to transfer all bankruptcy related suits to itself for resolution); Thomas Smith, A Capital Markets Approach to Mass Tort Bankruptcy, 104 Yale L.J. 367 (1994) (arguing that strong structural and psychological forces result in future claimants not being fairly treated in bankruptcy proceedings).

5. *Pre-packaged bankruptcies.* In an effort to reduce the amount of time in bankruptcy proceeding and yet take advantage of the channeling injunction and its capacity to provide resolution of all tort claims, some companies with significant asbestos exposure employed "pre-packaged bankruptcies." This practice entailed negotiations among stakeholder-creditors in advance of filing for bankruptcy and resolution of the respective rights of creditors. This negotiated plan then is presented to the bankruptcy court for approval, thereby reducing the time and expense of the bankruptcy reorganization process. See Eric D. Green et al., Prepackaged Asbestos Bankruptcies: Down but Not Out, 63 N.Y.U.Ann.Surv.Am.L. 727 (2008). For criticism of pre-packaged bankruptcies, including the presence of conflicts of interest, failure to treat claimants equally, and improper categorization of present and future claimants, see Ronald Barliant et al., From Free–Fall to Free–For–All: The Rise of Pre–Packaged Asbestos Bankruptcies, 12 Am.Bankr.Inst.L.Rev. 441 (2004).

E. OTHER PROCEDURAL DEVICES TO PROVIDE CLOSURE

After *Amchem* and *Ortiz*, class actions have been unable to provide a mechanism for resolving nationwide mass personal injury torts or provide a means for global settlement. Given the prevalence of these mass torts—

we are confident that new ones will develop after this book is published and you will find them in daily news reports—there has been a continued effort to find a means for efficient and global resolution of these case congregations. Professors Erichson and Zipursky explain the difficulty faced by defendants who seek to settle a mass tort:

> Non-class aggregate settlements have occupied the field, but this is where closure collides with consent. Outside of class actions and bankruptcy, a settlement binds only those claimants who choose to accept the deal. If too many claimants decide not to participate, the defendant faces substantial ongoing liability exposure and litigation expenses. Defendants worry that the claimants with the most serious claims may be the least inclined to settle. The last thing a defendant wants is to put serious money on the table only to find that the settlement eliminated junk claims while leaving high value plaintiffs in the litigation pipeline. Aggregate settlements can and often do resolve large bundles of mass tort claims, but when numerous law firms each represent numerous plaintiffs, true closure is hard to find. Yet closure is what defendants demand, and it is what plaintiffs need to offer if they are to maximize settlement value.

Howard M. Erichson & Benjamin C. Zipursky, Consent Versus Closure, 96 Cornell L.Rev. ___ (forthcoming 2011).

Two devices that have been employed, typically in tandem, are bell-wether trials, and non-class aggregate settlements. Professor Alexandra Lahav explains the etymology and content of bellwether trials:

> A "bellwether" is a sheep that leads a flock, around whose neck a bell is hung. In a bellwether trial procedure, a random sample of cases large enough to yield reliable results is tried to a jury. A judge, jury, or participating lawyers use the resulting verdicts as a basis for resolving the remaining cases. Judges currently use bellwether trials informally in mass tort litigation to assist in valuing cases and to encourage settlement. Instituted as a formal procedure, bellwether trials offer an innovative way to achieve collective justice in mass tort cases because they realize the democratic policies animating the jury right and the aims of the substantive law.

Alexandra Lahav, Bellwether Trials, 76 Geo.Wash.L.Rev. 576, 577–78 (2008). Professor Lahav explains that the model set out is not always the reality. Often the selection criteria for cases tried is not random, but based on timing, fortuity, or efforts by each side to put up the strongest cases on its side. The trial need not be of all issues, but may be limited to the most difficult ones requiring resolution—thus, in asbestos, where liability is often not the question, damages might be the basis for bellwether trials, as a federal court in Texas once attempted. Because of the Fifth Circuit's finding on appeal of that effort that binding other litigants violated the due process clause, the results of the bellwether trials only serve to inform the parties' negotiations about settlement.

The American Law Institute's Principles of the Law of Aggregate Litigation (2010) define an aggregate settlement in § 3.16:

§ 3.16   Definition of a Non–Class Aggregate Settlement

(a) A non-class aggregate settlement is a settlement of the claims of two or more individual claimants in which the resolution of the claims is interdependent.

(b) The resolution of claims in a non-class aggregate settlement is interdependent if:

(1) the defendant's acceptance of the settlement is contingent upon the acceptance by a number or specified percentage of the claimants or specified dollar amount of claims; or

(2) the value of each claimant's claims is not based solely on individual case-by-case facts and negotiations.

(c) In determining whether claims are interdependent, it is irrelevant whether the settlement proposal was originally made by plaintiffs or defendants.

Thus, a settlement offer by a defendant that provides a sum certain to be distributed among all plaintiffs, without specifying how individual claims will be determined and conditioned on 90 percent of those plaintiffs agreeing to the settlement is an aggregate settlement under each of Subsections (b)(1) and (b)(2). These settlements provide obvious conflicts of interest for lawyers who represent multiple plaintiffs. They also create serious hold-out problems with plaintiffs who seek special treatment in order to agree to the settlement in order to reach the threshold 90 percent. The Principles provide mechanisms for addressing these difficulties, including a controversial provision that permits plaintiffs, at the outset of the representation, to agree in the future to be bound by a majority vote of all plaintiffs with regard to any aggregate-settlement offer. Principles of the Law of Aggregate Litigation § 3.17. These provisions are designed to regulate and facilitate settlements in mass tort cases in ways that would not be acceptable in individual litigation.

The aggregate-settlement enabling provisions in the Principles may run afoul of Rule 1.8(g) of the ABA Model Rules of Professional Responsibility, which has been adopted in every state. It requires notice to and consent by each plaintiff to an aggregate settlement. Thus, the issue for the Principles of Aggregate Litigation is whether the provisions of Rule 1.8(g) can be waived in advance, as provided by section 3.17. For contrasting views on that question, compare Richard A. Nagareda, Mass Torts in a World of Settlement (2007), with Howard M. Erichson & Benjamin C. Zipursky, Consent Versus Closure, 96 Cornell L.Rev. ___ (forthcoming 2011).

We conclude this section with an explanation of the aggregate settlement in the Vioxx litigation. This occurred in a multi-district litigation after bellwether trials had been conducted both in federal court and in a several state courts.

What does the Vioxx settlement tell us about mass tort strategy, procedure, and ethics? Merck's mass aggregate settlement, which weighs in at $4.85 billion and up to 47,000 plaintiffs, matters not only to its many participants, but also to anyone interested in understanding how mass tort litigation works.

THE PARTICIPANTS. Before turning to the deal's broader implications, let's talk about its significance to the five major sets of participants—Merck, plaintiffs, plaintiffs' counsel, judges, and defense counsel. Assuming the settlement goes through (the deal is subject to several conditions, including an 85% walkaway clause), it's happy news for most of them.

- For Merck, the settlement allows the company to take its hit, slash its litigation expenses, limit its remaining exposure, and get back to business. That's why Merck's stock was up sharply yesterday despite a down day in the market. The first time I saw a stock price go up after a company announced a massive settlement, I found it odd (this is, after all, a multi-billion dollar expense); now I expect it.

- For most plaintiffs, the settlement provides compensation rather than the delay and uncertainty of litigation. Many participating plaintiffs will be disappointed with the amount of compensation they receive, but that's the nature of settlement. It's a compromise.

- For participating plaintiffs' counsel, the settlement offers a significant payday after several years of unpaid Vioxx work and significant expenditure of resources. It also offers lawyers the chance to get out of Vioxx and to move on to the next mass tort or other litigation opportunity. And for the lawyers involved in negotiating the deal, such as Russ Herman, Chris Seeger, Andy Birchfield, and Arnold Levin, yesterday's announcement represents a satisfying accomplishment and the sort of attention-generating event that cannot be bad for business.

- For the judges—particularly Judges Eldon Fallon (overseeing the MDL in E.D. La.), Carol Higbee (NJ), Victoria Chaney (CA), and Randy Wilson (TX)—the settlement clears away a huge number of docket-clogging cases. For some of the judges, the settlement also reflect a personal victory, a professional accomplishment, and, one hopes, a sense of getting justice done. Judge Fallon, in particular, had announced early on in the litigation his desire to drive the parties toward a large-scale settlement. To whatever extent he may have experienced Merck's ongoing refusal to settle as a source of frustration and embarrassment, yesterday's announcement surely brought relief, satisfaction, and some vindication of his handling of the litigation.

- Of the major participants, the only apparent losers are Merck's outside counsel, who lose an important revenue stream. But that's taking an unnecessarily grudging view of defense counsel's position. For lead counsel Theodore Mayer of Hughes Hubbard & Reed, a settlement like this caps an overall successful defense strategy, and for other lawyers involved in negotiating the deal, including Doug Marvin of Williams & Connolly, John Beisner of O'Melveny & Myers, and Adam Hoeflich of Bartlitt Beck, the deal represents a professional accomplishment and a business-generating news event. A satisfied client is always good news. Except perhaps for local defense counsel, who experience a loss in revenue from upcoming trials that won't happen, but who may get little attention or client gratitude.

STRATEGY. Nearly all the commentary on the settlement emphasizes the success of Merck's defense strategy in the Vioxx litigation, with lots of comments suggesting that future mass tort defendants should take a page from Merck's playbook. I agree that the settlement reflects the culmination of a successful strategy for Merck, but before assuming the same thing will work for other defendants, you have to look at the confluence of factors that made the strategy work in Vioxx.

Merck took an aggressive approach, fighting each case individually. This strategy had three main components: refusing to settle either wholesale or retail, opposing trial aggregation, and pouring resources into litigating each individual case on the merits. Although early on Merck suggested that it would settle cases involving over 18 months exposure, it quickly backed off and pursued a strong no-settlement strategy. On aggregation, Merck accepted and even embraced aggregated pretrial handling (MDL and statewide consolidations), but staunchly resisted class certification and any form of joint trial. And in each plaintiff's case, Merck fought hard on specific causation and every other contestable issue. Merck could have settled many of those cases more cheaply than going to trial, but by refusing to settle Merck sent a powerful message to plaintiffs' counsel: there's no easy money to be had here.

The no-settlement, individual-trial strategy worked in the Vioxx litigation because several critical factors came together:

- First, Vioxx was off the market. This is often the case, as product recalls are a common triggering event for mass tort litigation, but not always. Plenty of mass tort litigation involves products that remain available. Think Zyprexa, Oxycontin, tobacco, guns. And lots of other mass tort litigation involves products that, while no longer on the market, present an ongoing risk of exposure—lead paint, asbestos, certain medical devices. Because Vioxx was no longer available, Merck did not have to worry about a never-ending stream of potential plaintiffs, and could get some finality with a mass aggregate settlement. Also, with the product off the market, Merck could focus on litigation strategy without worrying about protecting the Vioxx brand and its ongoing prescribability by physicians, in contrast with, for example, Eli Lilly's position on Zyprexa.

• Second, Vioxx did not raise significant problems of latent disease. In some mass torts, such as asbestos and tobacco, latency creates enormous settlement difficulties. How can a defendant get peace without binding future claimants? This was the driving factor behind the Amchem and Ortiz asbestos settlement class actions, and an important cause of their failure. It was the primary reason for the multiple back-end opt-outs in the fen-phen nationwide settlement class action, which later proved so problematic. When I worked on the American College of Trial Lawyers Mass Tort Litigation Manual, asbestos and fen-phen were front and center, and we took time-dispersed disease manifestation as a defining characteristic of mass torts. So did Richard Nagareda in Mass Torts in a World of Settlement. Vioxx, by contrast, did not involve such significant latency problems. Latency was a disputed issue in the litigation, but the settlement reflects a willingness on the part of plaintiffs' counsel to let go of claims by persons who experience heart attacks or strokes long after their exposure to Vioxx. This, combined with the fact that Vioxx was off the market, and the statute of limitations, allowed Merck to seek peace in the litigation without worrying much about future claimants.

• Third, Merck had stronger individual defenses than general defenses. Like tobacco defendants, who always try to focus attention on the individual smoker, Merck focused on each individual plaintiff. In the case of tobacco, it's more about personal responsibility; with Vioxx, it's all about individual causation. Compare this with Bendectin, silicone gel breast implants, or Agent Orange, where the defendants had strong scientific defenses on general causation. In Bendectin, Merrell favored (and won) a mass aggregated trial in which it could present its scientific argument on general causation without the jury hearing from individual plaintiffs. Merck did not think it had a strong enough chance to defeat liability on a wholesale basis to be worth the risk, so it preferred to take a series of wins and losses in individual trials.

• Fourth, the issues were sufficiently individualized that Merck was able to defeat efforts at class certification and mass trials. On class certification, Vioxx is no different from most other mass tort personal injury cases (and post-CAFA, defendants have even greater confidence that mass tort class cert will usually be denied), but it differs markedly from other types of mass litigation. Aside from class cert, Merck was able to avoid large-scale joint trials. Even Judge Higbee's relatively modest effort at a ten-plaintiff consolidated trial in New Jersey fizzled. In other mass torts, even if defendants defeat class cert, they won't always have Merck's success at avoiding large multi-plaintiff trials.

● Fifth, and most important, Merck mostly won. That's because individual causation was hard for Vioxx plaintiffs to prove. Heart attacks and strokes are common. They are especially common among older people, who were Vioxx's primary consumers. So it's hard to show by a preponderance of the evidence that a particular person's heart attack or stroke was caused by Vioxx. Compare this with mesothelioma and asbestos, or PPH and fen-phen, or lung cancer and tobacco, or rhabdo and Baycol. Because of the difficulty establishing specific causation, Merck was able to win most of the individual cases that went to trial. Defense wins drive down settlement values, pure and simple. Had Merck lost several more of the individual trials, it would have cost a lot more than $4.85 billion to settle this.

Without this confluence of factors, Merck's no-settlement, no-aggregation, try-every-case strategy could easily have backfired. That's why in the future some mass tort defendants will continue to settle cases individually, others will seek early wholesale settlements whether by settlement class action or by non-class aggregate settlement, and others may even seek mass adjudication.

PROCEDURE. The Vioxx litigation shows the successful use of informal bellwether trials to drive a mass aggregate settlement. As a matter of procedural policy, the Vioxx litigation and settlement show mass tort litigation functioning reasonably well, as Byron Stier points out. There have, of course, been enormous litigation costs, unpredictable and inconsistent results along the way, and a fair amount of unseemly forum-shopping and forum-fighting, but that's par for the course in mass tort litigation. More significantly, look at what worked. The vast majority of cases were consolidated, at least for pretrial handling, in a small number of courts. Most of the cases were before Judge Higbee in New Jersey (cases were filed disproportionately in Merck's home state to make them non-removable under 28 U.S.C. 1441(b)); many others were before Judge Fallon in the multidistrict litigation, as well as in large statewide consolidations in California and Texas. Class certification was appropriately rejected; these cases are too individualized to be suitable for representative litigation that binds non-parties. Nor did courts employ formal bellwethers, in the sense of trials from which binding results could be extrapolated for other parties. Rather, Judges Fallon, Higbee and others used informal bellwether trials. That is, they scheduled cases for trial on steady basis, trying to get a range of representative cases, with the goal not only of resolving those particular actions but of providing enough data points to allow the parties to reach a widespread settlement. It worked.

ETHICS. Despite viewing the settlement mostly as good news for the participants and the litigation system, I have some concerns. Mass aggregate settlements always raise troubling ethical issues, and this one is no exception.

Here's the good news, ethically speaking. The parties seem to understand clearly that acceptance of the settlement is up to the clients, not the lawyers, and that any participating plaintiff must give informed consent after adequate disclosure. Also, the parties were wise to include a walkaway provision. The deal is conditioned upon acceptance by 85% of the plaintiffs (actually, 85% of each of a number of plaintiff groups). This provides Merck with adequate assurance of peace, while providing a safety valve so that not every plaintiff need accept the deal. As I've commented before, all-or-nothing settlements are much more troubling than those with walkaway provisions.

Now the bad news. The deal contains a term that requires each participating lawyer to recommend the settlement to 100% of the lawyer's eligible clients (paragraph 1.2.8.1 of the Settlement Agreement). That's troubling. A lawyer's duty of loyalty to each client cannot be bargained away to an adverse party. Some Vioxx plaintiffs' lawyers represent hundreds or thousands of clients, and even if the lawyer thinks the settlement's terms are generally fair, that does not necessarily mean that acceptance is the right decision for each individual client.

Worse, the deal requires that any participating lawyer withdraw from representing any client who declines the settlement (paragraph 1.2.8.2). That's really troubling. It makes it nearly impossible for a client to say no. The paragraph tries to avoid ethical impropriety by adding "to the extent permitted by the equivalents to Rules 1.16 and 5.6 of the ABA Model Rules of Professional Conduct." Withdrawing from the representation of clients under these circumstances may well violate both RPC 1.16 and RPC 5.6, but with this term in the Settlement Agreement, it is unrealistic to expect any of the plaintiffs' lawyers to continue representing Vioxx claimants.

In a mass settlement, lawyers ideally should be able to say to their clients: "Here's the settlement we negotiated with the defendant. Here are all the terms and conditions of the deal, and here's where you fit in. I think it's a good deal, and I recommend that you accept it. But you're the client, and it's your call. And if you decide not to accept the settlement, I'll be right by your side and continue to represent you."

Compromise is one thing. The lawyer-client relationship is another. The problem, of course, is that in mass aggregate settlements, the interests of the defendant, plaintiffs' counsel, and judges align, and don't necessarily correspond with the interests of individual plaintiffs. Merck, with its $4.85 billion, expects to buy not only peace from tens of thousands of plaintiffs, but also peace from the law firms that have been the biggest thorns in its side. The challenge, which the Vioxx settlement only partly surmounts, is to craft a settlement that accommodates the interests of the parties without unduly interfering with the lawyer's core duty of loyalty.

Howard M. Erichson,The Vioxx Settlement available at http://law professors.typepad.com/mass_tort_litigation/2007/11/the-vioxx-settl.html.

†